LEO BAECK INSTITUTE

YEAR BOOK

1988

November Pogrom 1938
Berlin Jews on their way to Sachenhausen concentration camp
Looted Jewish business premises

By courtesy of Antikriegsmuseum/Friedensbibliothek, Bartholomäuskirche, Berlin, GDR;
and from the Archives of the Leo Baeck Institute, New York

LEO BAECK INSTITUTE

YEAR BOOK XXXIII

1988

SECKER & WARBURG · LONDON
PUBLISHED FOR THE INSTITUTE
LONDON · JERUSALEM · NEW YORK

© Leo Baeck Institute 1988
Published by Martin Secker & Warburg Limited
54 Poland Street, London W1V 3DF
ISBN 0 436 25547 2
Photoset by Wilmaset, Birkenhead, Wirral
Printed in Great Britain by Richard Clay (The Chaucer Press), Limited,
Bungay, Suffolk

Contents

Illustrations

Preface

The November pogrom of fifty years ago, when the Nazi state irrevocably left the ranks of the civilised nations, is remembered this year by Jews and Germans alike. Today, in a different Germany, there are ceremonies of commemoration and exhibitions in cities and villages throughout the country which reflect on the shame brought upon them by their former rulers. For the German Jews the *Kristallnacht* (as it continues, controversially, to be called) was *the* point of no return. It has been exhaustively treated in historical literature and also, of course, in the Year Book of the Leo Baeck Institute. No special article is needed, but the fateful November days of 1938 cannot go unremarked in these pages.

This Year Book starts with a section on the course of emancipation spanning a century and a half, which despite many disappointments was marked by real achievements and hopeful anticipation, ever renewed. Four authors deal with patterns of perseverance, integration and acculturation. In a learned essay Ismar Schorsch shows us how the initiators of the *Culturverein* sought, by a reconnection with Jewish history, to make the Jewish past serve the needs of assimilation and modernisation. Robert Liberles demonstrates, with the inevitable Dohm as pivot point, the philosemitic demands on a "sadly deficient" Jewry for regeneration in order to qualify for civic equality, foreshadowing the dilemmas of the future. Werner Mosse, who has thoroughly investigated the German-Jewish elite, the "Jewish network", selects here a case study showing the desire for total assimilation carried to a tragic culmination. Julius Carlebach in a discerning contribution on the evolution of Jewish Orthodoxy shows how religious leaders who persevered in their ancient faith could nonetheless gradually adapt to modernity; many of them were steeped in German culture.

In the first part of the section on Jewish self-defence five historians debate amongst themselves on the political positions taken up by the *Centralverein* and the Zionists. This is not a mere rehash of ancient squabbles but a serious scholarly controversy on issues which for Jewry remain as burning and as topical as before. The Editor has refrained from participating in the dispute between Evyatar Friesel, Marjorie Lamberti, the late Abraham Margaliot, Jehuda Reinharz and Chaim Schatzker, but in the preface may be allowed a brief comment. Undoubtedly much remains to be resolved though it would seem harsh to castigate the *Centralverein* for not living up to the ideal of the brotherhood of the Jewish people, something its statutes never envisaged. However, on three outstanding features of the C.V. historians can no longer quibble. The C.V.

mounted a unique defence effort in no way matched by any other European Jewish community; its very existence brought about a revival of Jewish consciousness and self-identification; in the last years of the Weimar Republic the Jewish Defence launched a genuinely anti-fascist propaganda campaign in an attempt to preserve the values of German democracy.

The section concludes with an essay by Jürgen Matthäus who argues that the policies of the two main Jewish protagonists, the C.V. and the Zionists, were narrowly circumscribed in the conditions of the First World War, almost dictated by factors beyond their control; while Udo Beer puts forward that C.V. *Rechtsschutz* in the Weimar Republic was more effective and the protection the law accorded to the Jews more satisfactory than is generally assumed.

In our Austrian chapter the clash of Jewish opinion, "assimilationist" defence and Jewish Nationalism, recapitulates for Habsburg Vienna the Jewish divergencies of Imperial Germany. Jacob Toury concludes his persuasive, at times aptly ironic, survey of the *Österreichisch-Israelitische Union* (which he began in Year Book XXX), while Robert Wistrich makes a real contribution to our knowledge of the emergence of Zionism and Jewish Nationalism, revolving round the personality of Nathan Birnbaum. A passionate advocate of Yiddish, Birnbaum was, we must add here, undoubtedly an inspiration for his son who was eventually to become the founder of the modern academic discipline of Yiddish studies. Solomon Birnbaum, now aged 97, lives in Toronto, and still, in his turn, inspires Yiddish scholarship.

The central section of this Year Book covers a whole range of "Jewish" life in Germany, from the small band of Jewish opponents of Imperial Germany's war of 1914, to those of Jewish descent who were later prepared to throw in their lot with the Nazis. If we want to fathom the Jewish Question in Germany nothing is too peripheral. Rivka Horwitz provides a healthy antidote to the constant stressing of German-Jewish patriotism. While it would be fatuous to deny that German Jews – even if they had been so minded – had any alternative in 1914, surrounded as they were by an "imperialist" German population, but that of devoted service to the fatherland, the courage of the few who saw the hollowness of the war aims and abhorred the slaughter – and who alone were right – can now be appreciated. Francis Nicosia outlines how the German Foreign Office sought to harness Jewish aspirations in Palestine and elsewhere, to the political interests of the fledgling Weimar Republic. Doron Niederland draws a picture of the professional strata of German Jewry reluctant to emigrate in the early years of the Nazi regime, motivated largely by economic reasons. Werner Cohn, in his essay on the *Paulus-Bund* reveals how many bemused and confused Christians of Jewish origin acted and strove to protect themselves when confronted with Hitler's insane racial policies. Many would have dearly liked to jump on the Nazi bandwaggon but were frustrated and suffered a "Jewish fate".

In the last remarks on this section we revert to the previous contribution by Chaim Schatzker who concludes his study of the Jewish youth movements (begun in Year Book XXXII). He now concentrates on Zionist youth and there

November Pogrom 1938
Gutted Synagogue
Berlin Fasanenstrasse

November Pogrom 1938
Jews from Oldenburg marched to Sachsenhausen concentration camp

is no need to comment on his skilled exposition. But perhaps one point deserves emphasising: that the Leo Baeck Institute erred when it initially neglected in its research certain aspects of Jewish existence under the Nazi regime, leaving the field wide open to the distortions of a few pseudo historians, political agitators, even dramatists. Schatzker rightly refutes those who believe they can discern the impact of fascism on the Jewish youth movements. They were of course not entirely immune from strong outside influences; but this is another issue where former members of the youth movements can corroborate a younger historian's research. Many in the youth organisations received not only a Zionist or a general Jewish education, but a Socialist and anti-fascist education as well. The Jewish youth movements were an island of Liberalism and Socialism in which the spirit of independent thought and anti-totalitarianism prevailed in spite of strict surveillance and the pressures of the Nazi dictatorship.

Hebrew and Yiddish culture have not yet received the coverage they deserve in a Year Book meant to encompass every expression of Jewish life in Central Europe. Menahem Schmelzer's essay goes some way to redress this, describing the lavish printing of Hebrew works in Baroque Germany; and so enriches our perception of the pre-emancipation period. Zohar Shavit, in an essay on comparative literature, shows the dependence of Hebrew children's books on the works of the German Enlightenment. Finally, Leo and Renate Fuks take up the subject of the flourishing Yiddish publishing industry in Weimar Germany. The disdain with which German Jews for so long, and with a display of so much ignorance, dismissed both Eastern and their own Western Yiddish is only too well known. It is entirely fitting that we "atone" for this in the Year Book by printing a first, fascinating, bibliography of Yiddish publications which appeared in Germany between 1919 and 1929.

In the ultimate section Mark Gelber documents a humanist Zionism based on the writings of Max Brod; while Maurice Friedman reassesses a seminal scholarly dispute between two of the greatest philosophers of Modern German Jewry, Martin Buber and Gershom Scholem.

In Year Book XXXII we paid a tribute to the West German historical profession, despite the *Historikerstreit* which since then has by no means quietened down but has flared up even more acrimoniously. Recognition of the contribution of our close German colleagues is appropriate, as the Leo Baeck Institute has now worked amicably with many German historians for some twenty-five years; a cooperation which was underlined in November 1987 in Schloss Ringberg where forty Jewish and German scholars met at a seminar to sum up the results of post-war German-Jewish historiography.

But it must be made quite clear where we stand when it comes to the relativising or the minimising of the monstrosity of Nazism on the part of some historians. One could attempt to understand the Nazi crimes in the context of a general break-down of civilisation in Europe, but as the British historian Peter Pulzer put it in a tone of almost studied moderation, in a broadcast on BBC's

Radio 3 (printed in *The Listener* of 25th June 1987): "the Third Reich" is "the nearest that any of us have ever come to pure evil in politics", and: "To set out deliberately to annihilate an entire people solely because of who they are and to perfect a technical and logistical machine for doing so, is surely without parallel."

And lest we forget, the Holocaust of the Jews was accompanied by the Holocaust of the Gypsies and that of other groups, with further "sub-human" nations lined up for the Nazi machine of elimination. This was presented very clearly at a conference organised by the *Regione Emilia-Romagna* in 1985 on the occasion of the 40th anniversary of the liberation. Published in 1987, *Spostamenti di popolazione e deportazioni in Europa 1939–1945*, with its brilliant introductory paper by Enzo Collotti, 'Grande Germania e gerarchia di popoli nel progetto nazista di nuovo ordine europeo', should be required reading and will, we hope, be speedily translated into other languages.

It is also an Italian, the Jewish author Primo Levi, who shortly before his death had this to say, virtually anticipating the so-called "historians' debate". In the preface to *I sommersi e i salvati*, published in 1986, we read:

> ". . . fino al momento in cui scrivo, e nonostante l'orrore di Hiroshima e Nagasaki, la vergogna dei Gulag, l'inutile e sanguinosa campagna del Vietnam, l'autogenocidio cambogiano, gli scomparsi in Argentina, e le molte guerre atroci e stupide a cui abbiamo in seguito assistito, il sistema concentrazionario nazista rimane tuttavia un *unicum*, sia come mole sia come qualità. In nessun altro luogo e tempo si è assistito ad un fenomeno così imprevisto e così complesso: mai tante vite umane sono state spente in così breve tempo, e con una così lucida combinazione di ingegno tecnologico, di fanatismo e di crudeltà."*

Here every word is scrupulously weighed and balanced. What answer can there be?

The Leo Baeck Institute mourns Alexander Altmann, a member of its New York Board, who died on 6th June 1987 in his eighty-second year. Alexander Altmann, philosopher, scholar, rabbi, was one of the Jewish intellectual giants of our century and it would be presumptuous merely to enumerate his many publications in order to do justice to his scholarship and the influence he exerted on us all. Formerly a rabbi in Berlin and Manchester, he became, in 1959, Philip W. Lown Professor of Jewish Philosophy and History of Ideas at Brandeis University; a post he held until 1976. He will be remembered above all as a

---

*An English edition published by Michael Joseph Ltd. appeared only shortly before the publication of this Year Book: *The Drowned and the Saved*, London 1988. The English translation of the passage is given below.

". . . up to the moment at which I am writing, and notwithstanding the horror of Hiroshima and Nagasaki, the shame of the Gulags, the useless and bloody Vietnam war, the Cambodian self-genocide, the *desaparecidos* of Argentina, and the many atrocious and stupid wars we have seen since, the Nazi concentration camp system still remains a *unicum*, both in its extent and quality. In no other place and time has one seen a phenomenon so unexpected and so complex: never were so many human lives extinguished in so short a time, and with so lucid a combination of technological ingenuity, fanaticism and cruelty." (pp. 9–10)

Mendelssohn scholar; his *Moses Mendelssohn: A Bibliographical Study* (1973) is the standard work; and he acted until his death as Editor of *M. Mendelssohn. Gesammelte Schriften*, a work which will have to be completed without his guidance. Some years ago, in a searching two-part interview for American television he impressed a wide audience by his eloquence, tolerance and moderation. From his contributions to the Year Book we should single out his essay in 1981 where he drew a loving and scholarly picture of his father.

The early death of Abraham Margaliot on 14th May 1987, at the age of sixty-six, deprived Jewish scholarship of an historian from the younger German-Jewish generation who had made a considerable contribution to the history of the Holocaust and of German Jewry. He was a member of the Jerusalem Board of the Leo Baeck Institute. A lecturer at the Institute of Contemporary Jewry at the Hebrew University, Jerusalem, his important Ph.D. dissertation of 1971 on the political reaction of the German-Jewish organisations and institutions to Nazi persecution (in Hebrew) and his editorship of *Documents on the Holocaust* (1981) should be marked here. Only recently he wrote a frank and thoughtful essay; 'Emigration – Planung und Wirklichkeit' for *The Jews in Nazi Germany 1933–1943* (1986); and he did not live to see in print his contribution to an historians' debate which is published in this Year Book.

The present volume appears simultaneously with a seminar held by the London Leo Baeck Institute in association with the German Historical Institute, London, and the Jewish Historical Society of England, at Clare College, Cambridge, from the 14th to 19th September 1988, on 'The History of German-Speaking Jews in the United Kingdom'. It will seek to follow the Jewish emigration from Germany and other German-speaking lands to Great Britain and to evaluate its impact, from the period of the French Revolution up to our own day, thus adding another dimension to the work of the Leo Baeck Institute.

German-Jewish studies have expanded in the last decade to such a degree that the Bibliography of the Year Book has had to become increasingly selective. While we strive to accommodate most of the historiographical material, we have had to be more sparing when it comes to subjects such as participation in culture. The Institute hopes that at least from the year 1980 onwards a complete card index will eventually be available for consultation in our New York Archives. The General Index too is now not quite as exhaustive as we would wish. However, here the reader can look forward to a second comprehensive index volume, a General Index to Year Books XXI–XXXV which is already in preparation and is to be published shortly after Year Book XXXV in 1990.

The Editor wishes to extend his gratitude to his many friends and colleagues who have in various ways assisted in the preparation of this volume.

London   *Arnold Paucker*

The Course of Emancipation

Breakthrough into the Past:
The Verein für Cultur und Wissenschaft
der Juden

BY ISMAR SCHORSCH

The city of Berlin is the birthplace of modern Jewish scholarship. Towards the end of the second decade of the nineteenth century, in the shadow of its fledgling university, a gifted and alienated coterie of young Jewish intellectuals assembled to revamp Judaism for a drastically altered and still unsettled social context. The legacy of their assault was a new way of thinking about Judaism, enshrined in the name coined by them: *Wissenschaft des Judentums.*

The events of the preceding two decades had been as momentous for Jews as for Germans. Napoleon's presence on German soil had not only redrawn the chequered map of Central Europe but had also shaken Jewish life from its medieval moorings. In 1812 a vanquished but revitalised Prussia at long last extended a qualified citizenship to its approximately 32,000 Jewish inhabitants and in the ensuing three years as many as 1,300 Jews fought as volunteers in the Wars of Liberation, with seventy-two combatants earning the Iron Cross.[1] The display of patriotism notwithstanding, the fall of Napoleon unleashed a reaction that quickly imperilled Jewish advances. A renewed alliance between throne and altar and a highly charged romantic nationalism, joined to intone the Christian character of the emergent German state. In 1815 the Congress of Vienna refused to universalise emancipation throughout Germany or even to confirm those Jewish rights that derived from the French occupation, and a crescendo of antisemitic rhetoric eventually erupted in riots against Jews and their property in the late summer of 1819. Leap-frogging from town to town across Southern and Western Germany from Würzburg to Hamburg, the disorders correlated to locations where some degree of emancipation had been tendered and reflected broad resentment at the change.[2] On the Jewish side, the prospects for a

[1] Martin Philippson, 'Der Anteil der jüdischen Freiwilligen an dem Befreiungskriege 1813 und 1814', *Monatschrift für Geschichte und Wissenschaft des Judentums (MGWJ)*, L (1906), pp. 1–21, 220–247; Horst Fischer, *Judentum, Staat und Heer in Preussen im frühen 19. Jahrhundert. Zur Geschichte der staatlichen Judenpolitik*, Tübingen 1968 (Schriftenreihe wissenschaftlicher Abhandlungen des Leo Baeck Instituts 20), pp. 47–53.
[2] Jacob Katz, 'The Hep-Hep Riots in Germany of 1819. The Historical Background' (in Hebrew), in *Zion*, XXXVIII (1973), pp. 62–108; Uriel Tal, 'Young German Intellectuals on Romanticism and Judaism. Spiritual Turbulence in the Early 19th Century', in Saul Lieberman (ed.), *Salo Wittmayer Baron Jubilee Volume on the Occasion of his Eightieth Birthday*, American Academy for Jewish Research, 3 vols., Jerusalem – New York – London 1974, II, pp. 919–938.

retraction of emancipation spurred intensive political lobbying and proposals for internal reform.

Amid this foreboding atmosphere, a cluster of seven men gathered in Berlin on 7th November 1819 to found "a society for the improvement of the Jewish condition in the German states" with the hope of meeting weekly for two hours on Sunday mornings.[3] In addition to Isaak Markus Jost and Leopold Zunz, the group included Joseph Hillmar, Joel Abraham List, Isaac Levin Auerbach, Eduard Gans, and Moses Moser. Collectively they were young, with an average age of 30.7 years, only recently settled in Berlin, and barely able to eke out a living. At twenty-two Gans, the only native Berliner, was the youngest, with List at thirty-nine and Hillmar at fifty-one the only members above the age of thirty. In terms of employment, Hillmar and Moser worked as book-keepers, List and Jost conducted small private schools, and Auerbach served as a preacher in the "German synagogue" of the wealthy and naturalised (in 1809) Jacob Herz Beer, while Zunz was still completing his studies at the university and Gans was about to embark on an academic career. Though at the time Gans was the only member of the group to hold a doctorate, all except Moser, Hillmar and perhaps List had already studied at both a *Gymnasium* and a university. In short, the composition of the society was fairly homogeneous, entirely marginal, and decidedly bookish.[4]

As students they stood at the cutting edge of the emancipation experiment – immersed in the best of German culture, alienated from traditional Judaism, and vulnerable to the counter-attack of the resurgent Right. The antisemitic violence of August and September abruptly reminded them of that vulnerability, plunging them into a flurry of Jewish activity which till then they had generally avoided. Five of the founders, for example, had been among the participants of a scholarly circle of some twenty-three members, predominantly Jewish, that had met over a period of nineteen months from November 1816 to July 1817 to hear and debate presentations on thirty-one topics, only one of which related directly to a matter of Jewish substance.[5] But the intensifying assault on Jewish aspirations shattered their equanimity. According to Gans's later reconstruction:

"In many of the cities of the German fatherland those terrifying scenes had occurred which suggested to some an unforeseen return to the Middle Ages. We came together to help, wherever the need might arise, to consider the means how best to get at deeply rooted faults. Our intention was no more refined than that. At that time we stood at the very beginning of our struggle . . ."[6]

Indeed, during the next five years this disaffected band of visionaries struggled manfully to articulate and implement a programme for an emancipated

[3]Hanns Günther Reissner, *Eduard Gans. Ein Leben im Vormärz*, Tübingen 1965 (Schriftenreihe wissenschaftlicher Abhandlungen des Leo Baeck Instituts 14), p. 50.
[4]*Ibid.*, pp. 31, 50, 174–175; Jacob Jacobson, *Die Judenbürgerbücher der Stadt Berlin 1809–1851*, Berlin 1962, pp. 57, 206.
[5]Reissner, *Gans, op. cit.*, pp. 31–34; The Jewish National and University Library, Jerusalem (henceforth JNUL), 4°792/B–1.
[6]S. Rubaschoff, '"Erstlinge" (Drei Reden von Eduard Gans im Kulturverein)', *Der jüdische Wille*, I (1918–1919), p. 113.

Judaism, with little to show in the end. Their unfavourable social status, their fiercely intellectual bent, and their impervious elitism all militated against arousing the confidence of the plutocracy which governed Berlin Jewry. Their meagre institutional success is testimony of the failure to persuade the larger community that their individual dilemmas were but the harbinger of a pending collective fate.

Thus the external history of the society is filled with pathos. From the outset it was determined to form a "think-tank" which would "unite the Jewish intelligentsia" with the unsurprising result that membership grew slowly.[7] The Berlin chapter eventually reached a maximum of twenty-five members and a Hamburg chapter founded in 1821 comprised a top figure of twenty-three members. But the totals belie the diminutive proportion of active participants. The nearly weekly meetings of the chapter in Berlin, the only one that really mattered, were rarely attended by more than ten members, often in fact cancelled for lack of a quorum, and in recognition of that reality, the chapter decided on 8th September 1822 to reduce the quorum necessary for a meeting from a majority of the members living in Berlin to a figure of five.[8]

The name under which the society would eventually become known, *Der Verein für Cultur und Wissenschaft der Juden*, was not decided upon till 5th July 1821. At first, on 27th May 1821, Gans had boldly suggested "The Maccabees" as the most suitable name for the society, a choice which alluded in allegorical fashion to its goal of revitalisation. But the political and military overtones of the allusion were regarded as extraneous to the intent of the society, and Gans's second suggestion was later adopted unanimously as more clearly conveying its purpose and programme.[9] The pointed retention of the noun "Jew" in the name of the society, at a time when assimilating Jews were casting about for a less burdened nomenclature, also evinced the temerity and pride of its founders. Nevertheless, when the *Verein* soon after applied for official incorporation to secure it existence and enhance its prestige, the government, increasingly suspicious of all religious reform, misread the world "Cultur" in the name for "Cultus" and expressed its displeasure. Despite prompt clarification from Gans, who had submitted the original petition, and government approval of its instructional programme, the *Verein* was denied the advantageous privileges of an incorporated society.[10]

The publication of its statutes at long last in 1822 did little to increase the society's visibility. They did, however, serve to articulate its fervour to lead the Jewish world out of its unbearable isolation. A new age necessitated an internal transformation of Judaism to be effected by enlarging the number of Jews conversant with German culture. Higher education and economic restructuring

---

[7] Nahum N. Glatzer, *Leopold Zunz. Jude–Deutscher–Europäer*, Tübingen 1964 (Schriftenreihe wissenschaftlicher Abhandlungen des Leo Baeck Instituts 11), p. 103.

[8] Reissner, *Gans, op. cit.*, pp. 174–185; JNUL, 4°792/B–3.

[9] JNUL, 4°792/B–2. Cf. Sinai (Siegfried) Ucko, 'Geistesgeschichtliche Grundlagen der Wissenschaft des Judentums', reprinted in *Wissenschaft des Judentums im deutschen Sprachbereich. Ein Querschnitt*. Mit einer Einführung herausgegeben von Kurt Wilhelm, Tübingen 1967 (Schriftenreihe wissenschaftlicher Abhandlungen des Leo Baeck Instituts 16/I and 16/II), I, pp. 335–336.

[10] JNUL, 4°792/B–2, B–6, B–10, B–11.

were to be the bridges across which Jews would gradually integrate into German society. To husband its slim resources and to assure some results, the society announced that it would restrict its own activities to the creation of a scholarly institute, an archive on contemporary Jewry, the production of a broadly conceived intellectual journal, and a tutoring programme free of charge to facilitate the entrance of the children of the impecunious into the outside world.[11] The practical programme, in other words, carried through in the society's name: the dissemination of German culture and the cultivation of a new type of Jewish learning would help to redefine the place of the Jew in Gentile society.

On 11th March 1821, nine years to the day after Prussia's emancipation edict, Gans finally assumed the presidency and presided over a thirty-month period of frenetic activity. In truth, the precocious, self-confident, and aspiring Gans, endowed with a booming voice and more than a dash of organising talent, appears to have provided the inspiration and drive for the society from the beginning. The son of a once well-to-do Berlin banker and Court Jew who had died in 1813 impoverished and in debt, Gans was a gifted legal historian and enthusiastic Hegelian. His determination to attain an academic appointment had already begun to founder on the opposition of Hegel's academic adversary and the leading advocate of the historical approach to the study of law, Friedrich Karl von Savigny, and on the reluctance of the government to carry out its promise of equal academic opportunity for Jews.[12] In a bitter petition to the government on 3rd May 1821, Gans lamented: "I belong to that unfortunate class of people that is hated because it is uneducated and persecuted because it seeks education."[13] As his personal campaign dragged on, the cause of the *Verein* offered Gans consolation, sublimation, and an instrument of battle.

Gans's three surviving presidential addresses reflect the quickened pace. On 28th October 1821 he could report that during the previous seven-month period the society had met a total of seventeen times and the scholarly institute, comprising many of the same people, had convened twelve times.[14] During the subsequent six months the society held some twenty-five meetings, the scholarly institute an unspecified number, and twelve students had been tutored by nine different members. Plans were also afoot to offer instruction to young Polish Jews coming to Berlin, to assemble a scholarly Jewish library, and to determine on a regular basis which students might be worthy of Jewish financial assistance to study at the university.[15]

The final address of 4th May 1823, which reviewed the activities of the preceding year, reported some forty-two meetings of the society, seventeen sessions of the scholarly institute and tutorials for fourteen students. It also made mention of the appearance of the second number of the institute's scholarly

[11] *Entwurf von Statuten des Vereins für Cultur und Wissenschaft der Juden*, Berlin 1822. For a partial English translation, see Paul R. Mendes-Flohr and Jehuda Reinharz (eds.), *The Jew in the Modern World*, New York – Oxford 1980, pp. 188–189.
[12] S. S. Prawer, *Heine's Jewish Comedy*, Oxford 1983, pp. 10–43.
[13] Reissner, *Gans, op. cit.*, p. 65.
[14] Rubaschoff, *loc. cit.*, pp. 40–41.
[15] *Ibid.*, pp. 115–118.

journal, edited by Zunz, printed in quarto size, and bearing the title *Zeitschrift für die Wissenschaft des Judentums*.[16] The first number of the journal had come out in the spring of 1822 in a run of 500 copies at a cost of 124 talers and the third and final number of this first and only volume would appear in the spring of 1823.[17] Given these circumstances, the journal reached relatively few hands. As late as 1839 Zacharias Frankel was to admit to Zunz that despite strenuous effort he had never seen the journal and no one in Dresden, including his good friend Bernhard Beer who possessed a large Jewish library, owned a copy.[18] To inform the scholarly world of the new journal, Zunz sent free copies of the first number to a selection of academics and merited in return at least one noteworthy response from Silvestre de Sacy, the doyen of French orientalists. In his cordial letter of 7th October 1822 de Sacy expressed some doubts as to the feasibility of the new field. The paucity of sources – both Jewish and Gentile – for large periods of Jewish history would constitute a major difficulty and the use of the term "Judaism" suggested to him a temptation to replace facts with theoretical speculation. Prophetically, he added "that Germany was hardly the place where any one will appreciate the usefulness and difficulty of the work to which you are dedicating yourself".[19] On the other hand, Heinrich Heine, who had joined the society on 4th August 1822 and the scholarly institute a few weeks later, was appalled by the literary style and some of the contents of the journal.[20] After reading the third number, he wrote to Zunz sarcastically:

> "I have studied all kinds of German: Saxon, Swabian, Franconian – but our Journal-German I find the most difficult of all. If I did not happen to know what Ludwig Marcus and Dr. Gans want to say, I would not understand a word of what they have written."[21]

Heine did not fail to note the irony of a society dedicated to infusing Jews with culture which seemed unable to express itself with any degree of stylistic competence.[22]

Gans had concluded his first presidential address on 28th October 1821 with a rousing call to all the free and idealistic spirits of German Jewry to join the ranks of the society. "I see in the close fraternisation of such noble people the approach of the messianic era, of which the Prophets speak, and which only the common decadence of our generation has turned into a fairy-tale."[23] And indeed under Gans's leadership the society set about to enlarge its membership. Already a few

[16]*Ibid.*, pp. 199–201.
[17]JNUL, 4°792/B–13.
[18]JNUL, 4°792/G–12.
[19]Ludwig Geiger, 'Aus Leopold Zunz' Nachlass', in *Zeitschrift für die Geschichte der Juden in Deutschland* (*ZGJD*), V (1892), pp. 259–260. Apparently the letter addressed to Zunz arrived during his absence from Berlin. In a covering note to Zunz, Moser confessed that he and Gans were so eager to learn of de Sacy's reaction that they committed the indiscretion of opening the letter. "We were curious as to the man's opinion. Nevertheless, we should have expected that the Frenchman would barely be able to grasp our idea. Still, he is at least more courteous than the Germans: Eichhorn, Paulus, and Vater." [JNUL, 4°792/G–18.]
[20]Reissner, *Gans, op. cit.*, p. 94.
[21]Prawer, *op. cit.*, p. 30.
[22]*Heinrich Heine. Säkularausgabe*, 27 vols. (in progress) (Berlin and Paris 1970ff.), XX, pp. 102–103.
[23]Rubaschoff, *loc. cit.*, p. 42.

months before, at the end of August, Gans, together with Zunz and Julius Rubo, had journeyed to Hamburg, among other reasons, to assist in the formation of a small chapter there. The composition of the party evoked a memorable specimen of Zunz's flashing wit: "Three doctors tightly packed into a coach about to take a journey, each one bearing a name of four letters, without a single medical doctor among them!"[24] But the humour masked a painful premonition: that it was precisely the Jewish doctors of law and philosophy who would be most adversely affected by the incipient retreat from emancipation. During the next two years, the Berlin chapter affiliated eleven new regular members and twenty-one associated members within and outside Berlin including prominent older activists such as Joseph Perl, Israel Jacobson, Gottlob Euchel, Joseph Wolf, David Fränkel, David Friedländer, and Lazarus Bendavid.[25] But their involvement proved to be either nominal or detrimental. Heine in his aforementioned letter to Zunz astutely dismissed Bendavid's deep foray into biblical criticism in the last number of the journal as strictly vintage 1786, utterly inappropriate for the post-rationalist era.[26]

Yet despite Gans's vigour and imagination, the society was unable to break out of its isolation. The journal failed to mediate its ideology or scholarship to a large audience, expenses ran well ahead of income as the wealthy withheld their backing, and there existed almost no contact with the leadership of the Jewish community of Berlin. If anything, the dissatisfaction of the board with Zunz's performance as *Prediger*, which forced his resignation in September 1822, only deepened its suspicions.[27] As for its part, the society steadfastly refused to compromise its elitism. At a meeting on 23rd February 1823, the membership by a vote of seven to three turned aside the idea of editing a textbook on Judaism for children (a kind of catechism) in an effort to be of some use to a larger constituency, a decision with which Heine, who protested against serving up Judaism in the manner of modern Protestantism, concurred.[28] By 6th June 1823 Gans finally learned of the government's decision – some three-and-a-half years after his initial request for an appointment – to exclude all Jews from teaching and academic posts in contravention of its own edict of 1812 and, instead, to offer him a two-year stipend for retraining.[29] Although as late as 26th November 1823, the society still held its annual public celebration before an audience of invited guests at which Gans, Rubo, and Zunz read learned papers, dissolution was

[24]Central Archives for the History of the Jewish People (CAHJP), P17/127 (Letter dated 28th August 1821 from Gans to Moser).

[25]Reissner, *Gans, op. cit.*, pp. 180–184.

[26]*Heine. Säkularausgabe*, XX, p. 103. For an analysis of Bendavid's essay within the context of his work, see Jakob Guttmann, 'Lazarus Bendavid', *MGWJ*, LXI (1917), pp. 176–181. The correspondence between Bendavid and the *Verein* is in JNUL, 4°792/F–3.

[27]JNUL, 4°792/B–3. See also the letter by Zunz to Mannheimer dated 22nd August 1822 published by M. Brann and M. Rosenmann, 'Der Briefwechsel zwischen Izak Noa Mannheimer und Leopold Zunz', *MGWJ*, LXI (1917), pp. 96–97.

[28]JNUL, 4°792/B–3.

[29]Reissner, *Gans, op. cit.*, pp. 92–93. A copy of the memorandum dated 18th August 1822 from King Frederick William III to Chancellor Hardenberg in which the decision against Gans is rendered is preserved in CAHJP, P17/634.

imminent. The last meeting of the society seems to have taken place on 1st February 1824 with an attendance of five members, though without any official decision to disband.[30] On 20th April 1825, before he left Berlin in search of another career which ended with his conversion to Christianity in Paris on 12th December 1825 – some six months after Heine, Gans turned over the records of the society to Zunz with a note that implied the omission of any formal interment.

> "Since I regard the society as being dissolved de facto, I also regard my presidency as ended. If you are of another opinion, you may as the acting president [Zunz had been vice president] assume the reins at your disposal. Be well."[31]

The transfer of those precious documents to Zunz ensured their survival and enabled future historians to reconstruct the history and ideology of the *Verein*.

II

Nearly forty years after the collapse of the *Verein für Cultur und Wissenschaft der Juden*, Zunz succeeded in persuading Adolf Strodtmann, Heine's first biographer, that the history of the society deserved serious attention. Its significance was not to be measured in terms of accomplishments but rather with reference to its foresight.

> ". . . nearly every advance made by Jews in the scholarly, political, and civil arenas as well as the achievements of the reform movement in matters of school and synagogue have their roots in the activity of that society and a few of its members."[32]

That positive assessment along with the documents of the society put at his disposal by Zunz induced Strodtmann to compose a long and sympathetic chapter on the subject, which he pointedly titled "The Young Palestine". The name resonated with associations to the small and loosely-knit group of radical political writers of the 1840s known as "The Young Germany", which included Heine, and was meant to conjure up an image of comparable revolutionary idealism.[33] The truth is that the society's importance is a function of intangibles. The strident and abstruse rhetoric of its endless deliberations contained the first full-fledged articulation of the emancipation dilemma – the pursuit of individual integration without the loss of a distinct collective identity. In their search for a solution, "the Young Palestinians" fully anticipated many an idea and project to be raised independently later in the century.

What distinguished the *Verein* from the older and far more successful *Gesellschaft der Freunde* (Society of Friends) was its determination to work out a cogent intellectual justification for its two-fold programme of integration and apartness. The *Gesellschaft der Freunde*, founded in Berlin in 1792 under the leadership of Joseph Mendelssohn, the oldest son of Moses, was essentially a

---

[30]JNUL, 4°792/B–3.
[31]Reissner, *Gans, op. cit.*, p. 102.
[32]JNUL, 4°792/G–27.
[33]Adolf Strodtmann, *H. Heine's Leben und Werke*, 2 vols., Berlin 1867, I, p. 252.

fraternal organisation of dissident Jews, at first restricted to gainfully employed bachelors. Eager to soften the heavy hand of Orthodox Jewish leadership, they banded together to support each other, to advance the cause of enlightenment among other Jews, and also to procure from the community the right to request a delay in burial without penalty (which they actually won by 1794).[34] Membership soon comprised the prosperous, the assimilated, and even on occasion the converted.[35] During the first year it rose from 78 to 118 and in 1828 it stood at about 400.[36] Gans, Moser, and Zunz were admitted in January 1820 and Jost probably not long thereafter – an affiliation which endowed them with some degree of social status.[37] As late as 1836 Gans was still apparently a member in good standing.[38] Yet for all its talent, prestige, and longevity, the *Gesellschaft* never set itself the task to defend its pervasive religious laxness with any kind of ideological vindication.

The eruption of antisemitism had driven the exposed intellectuals of the *Verein* to confront their secular aspirations with their religious loyalties. Could they collectively formulate an idea of Judaism that would resolve their inner torment and keep them from spurning the claims of the past for the promise of the present? They had lost the inner repose and wholeness which came with living in seclusion on the fringes of society, precisely what Heine so admired in the impoverished and uncultured Jews of Prussian Poland he had seen in the summer of 1822, just before he joined his friend Gans in the *Verein*.

> "Despite the barbarous fur cap that covers his head and the still more barbarous ideas that fill it, I value the Polish Jew much higher than many a German Jew who wears his hat in the latest Simon-Bolivar fashion and has his head filled with quotations from Jean Paul. In rigid seclusion that Polish Jew's character became a homogeneous whole; when breathing a more tolerant air it took on the stamp of liberty. The inner man did not become a composite medley of heterogeneous emotions . . ."[39]

As host of the first meeting on 7th November 1819, Joel Abraham List opened the discussion by casting the challenge of the new era in nationalistic terms. In ages past, Jews as a nation had been held together by the force of external circumstances – exclusion from civil society, a solidarity of persecution, and a religion that stressed individual salvation in the afterlife – and not by a compelling inner idea. The force of all three was now being rapidly eroded by the combined onslaught of enlightenment and emancipation. Yet, List contended, those present were deeply conscious of the uniqueness of the Jewish nation, which was not a temporal phenomenon. The passing of outward forms must not obscure the existence of an eternal inner substance. Accordingly, the agenda of this group should be the articulation and dissemination of the character and nobility of that essence. "As Jews our national worth must be our highest good, or

[34]Ludwig Lesser, *Chronik der Gesellschaft der Freunde in Berlin*, Berlin 1842, pp. iv, 9–10, 17, 26–27.
[35]Hanns Günther Reissner, 'Correspondence', in *LBI Year Book VI* (1961), pp. 287–288.
[36]Isaak M. Jost, *Geschichte der Israeliten*, 9 vols., Berlin 1820–1828, IX, p. 94; Lesser, *op. cit.*, p. 17.
[37]Reissner, *Gans, op. cit.*, pp. 54–55; Lesser, *op. cit.*, p. 66. The admission fee to the *Gesellschaft* cost Zunz the substantial sum of 15 taler. [JNUL, 4°792/C–13, p. 34b.]
[38]Lesser, *op. cit.*, p. 81.
[39]Prawer, *op. cit.*, p. 62.

it is not worth a penny to bear the name (of Jew)." In terms reminiscent of later secular Zionism, List called on his friends to dedicate themselves to the restoration of Jewish nationhood (*Volkstümlichkeit*) in all its dignity and to the eradication of a decadent rabbinic Judaism (*Rabbinismus*).[40]

In his elaboration of the society's intellectual mission on that occasion, Moser took as his point of departure the dichotomy between European and Jewish culture. Unlike many Jews of his day, Moser rejected out of hand a reconciliation (*Aufhebung*) so complete as to entail conversion. He distinguished between the secular and religious strands of European culture and insisted that Jews had only to embrace the former. "In other words: ideal Judaism must appear to us as completely reconciled with the State, insofar as it is determined by secular culture (*bürgerliche Kultur*), but in total opposition to the dominant Church as such and in reference to its dogmas." The consciousness of a distinctive national essence prompted Moser to fight for the survival of a Judaism to be transformed through a fresh study of its sacred texts. *Wissenschaft* would mediate between the essence of Judaism and its current reality. Regarding the Bible, Moser conjectured that only four types of material would be relevant for the future – the charming historical narratives of Genesis, the sublime specimens of biblical poetry, the lofty set of religious teachings, and even some dated legal practices that are still important "for the preservation of national unity". Regarding the Talmud, Moser likewise inveighed against its destructive influence, though he stopped short of a total renunciation. And lastly, he called for a thorough study of the neglected and error-riddled history of the Jews in the Diaspora.[41]

Gans appears to have first addressed the group formally at its third meeting on 21st November 1819, a date commemorated thereafter as the official founding of the society, on the topic "How Can an Improvement of the Jews Be Conceptualised?"[42] At the outset, he drew a basic distinction between the eras of the Enlightenment and Nationalism, which bespoke an acute awareness of his own age. In the age of reason, to improve the Jews meant to raise them to a universal standard, unrelated to Christianity, that ignored their immediate surroundings and condemned only that which was deemed inferior. By contrast, the framework of the *Verein* is neither rationalism nor ethics but history and therefore quite particularistic. In consequence, its mission is not to improve the Jews but to change them, to bring them into harmony with the values and ideas of the nation in which they live, even to the point of discarding what might be virtuous. Each Jewish community in the Diaspora must be infused with the national sentiments of its neighbours. But Gans immediately added that "out of higher considerations" this did not include their religion. What this conceptualisation did imply was a programme to transform the Jewish state of mind which viewed everything non-Jewish with alarming suspicion. A product of Jewish political and religious history, that state of mind could be altered only by a radical change in the factors

---

[40]Ucko, *loc. cit.*, pp. 324–326 (quotation p. 326). Ucko's splendid essay, written in the early 1930s, treats the *Verein* as a secular expression of ethical nationalism.
[41]*Ibid.*, pp. 328–332 (quotation pp. 328, 331). The original text is in JNUL, 4°792/B–10.
[42]JNUL, 4°792/B–11.

that gave it rise. With the process of political amelioration well under way, Jews must be diverted from trade and directed into wholesome pursuits. Equally urgent was "the demolition of Rabbinism and the return to pure Mosaism, which, properly understood, does not stand in the way of merging (*Verschmelzung*) with the inhabitants of the country".[43]

Exactly one year later, on the occasion of its first anniversary, Gans gave unabashed expression to the society's sense of elitism and mission.

> "Representatives of Israel, not elected by the non-saying voices of the people, but summoned here by virtue of greater intelligence and a deeply felt need and out of an authority that is legitimately yours, fulfil the task you have set for yourselves . . . No revolution is more difficult than the overturning and recasting of a state of mind. Here no force or movement from outside is effective; a psychic malady requires a psychic remedy. You will bring it about."[44]

The presumption that fuels this rhetorical flourish is a measure of personal desperation. In seeking to remake German Jewry, the members of the society were struggling to fortify their own attenuated and strained links to Judaism.

It is abundantly clear from these early statements that their affirmation of Judaism entailed a large amount of rejection. There could be no continuity without discontinuity. Born in a flurry of anti-clericalism, the society envisioned itself as the rallying point for all the laymen, teachers, and preachers across Germany already on the battlefield. When the government misread "Cultus" for "Cultur" in the name of the *Verein*, it committed no error. The society rested on the conviction that social and cultural assimilation dictated religious reform, and some of its members fought simultaneously on both fronts. Zunz was as wedded to the creation of a Western mode of Jewish worship as to a Western mode of Jewish scholarship, and his early career is marked by denunciations of contemporary Rabbinism. In a key note towards the end of his essay in 1818 on rabbinic literature, to which we shall soon come, he called for an end to the reign of what he termed "vulgar Rabbinism" and especially its sophistic method of studying Talmud.[45]

Coincidental with the founding of the society a year later, he published two impassioned attacks on Rabbinism. The first was an anonymous review in a Berlin paper, pulsating with anger and sarcasm, of the set of *responsa* against the "German synagogue" (*Eileh Divrei ha-Brit*) collected by the Hamburg rabbinate. The review attracted wide attention, even catching the eye of Hardenberg, the liberal chancellor of Prussia, and ran to a second printing. In addition to some choice examples of the rabbis' alleged benightedness, Zunz declared his intention to publish a work on the "spirit of the rabbis" in which he would demonstrate "that Rabbinism as presently constituted is a decadent institution of ignorance, arrogance and fanaticism, diametrically opposed to the better efforts of some Jews and the humanitarian measures of the government". But at the same time, Zunz insisted on a distinction he would make for a lifetime: that

---

[43]JNUL, 4°792/B–10.
[44]JNUL, 4°792/B–11.
[45]Leopold Zunz, 'Etwas über die rabbinische Literatur', in *Gesammelte Schriften*, 3 vols., Berlin 1875–1876, I, p. 29 note 1.

contemporary Rabbinism was not to be confused with its talmudic and medieval namesake, but rather should be seen as the nadir of a long decline beginning with the period of the Reformation.[46]

The second attack was published under the name of Levi Lazarus Hellwitz, a teacher in Westphalia, but drafted entirely by Zunz.[47] Far more substantial, systematic, and restrained, it offered a reasoned programme for the religious restructuring of German Jewry. The basic argument for dismantling the cumbersome and separatistic structure of much of rabbinic Judaism was the lateness of its origins. In its present form it consisted of the accumulated deposits of countless generations. To avert anarchy but ensure progress, Zunz proposed replicating the process of religious and communal reorganisation in France. The Prussian government should convene an assembly (Sanhedrin) of learned and enlightened Jews to undertake a revision of the entire corpus of Jewish law still in effect, which would eventually yield a religious code suitable for an emancipated Jewry. Every post-biblical institution of Jewish life would be subject to the assembly's examination, and the sum total of its work would someday be administered by a new type of religious leadership unrelated to the traditional judicial role.

> "The rabbi must be a morally good and enlightened man, equipped with courage, determination, and solid learning. He must be entirely familiar with the state of his diocese (Sprengels), enjoy the confidence of his community, and be able to deliver a useful, comprehensible, and stirring public address."[48]

Despite such strong views on Judaism, the society never threw itself openly into the campaign for religious reform. To be sure, its deliberations periodically focused on proposals of a religious nature – to organise the *Prediger* of the various "German synagogues" into a special group, to select a *Prediger* for the "German synagogue" which annually graced the Leipzig fair, or to undertake a new German translation of the Hebrew Bible – but each time the society shied away. One of the consequences of the attempt to incorporate had apparently been a specific warning from the government not to meddle in religious affairs, and the society was not eager to incur any official displeasure. Under these circumstances, the members also refused, in their meeting of 22nd December 1821, to introduce the teaching of Judaism from the perspective of religion into their educational programme for adolescents. Still, the discussion is worth examining for the additional light that it throws on their personal views of Judaism.

The proposal itself came from Auerbach, who pleaded that the society must also do its part to stem the widespread defection from Judaism through conversion. The root of the problem, he felt, lay in an abysmal ignorance of Judaism and hence the society should offer its students some "congenial instruction in the Mosaic religion". Immanuel Wohlwill (Wolf), one of the three

[46]*Allgemeine Zeitung des Judentums (AZJ)*, 1916, pp. 413–414.
[47]Moritz Steinschneider, *Die Schriften des Dr. L. Zunz*, Berlin 1857, p. 11, note 23.
[48]Levi Lazar Hellwitz, *Die Organisation der Israeliten in Deutschland*, Magdeburg 1819, p. 29. See also Zunz's letter to Ehrenberg, dated 5th January 1821, in Glatzer, *op. cit.*, p. 117. ["Meine Wirksamkeit gehet jetzt grossenteils dahin, den ganzen Rabbinismus zu stürzen."]

Hegelians in the group (Gans and Moser being the others), did not think the suggestion contradicted the original commitment of the society to "teach a pure, national Judaism". The hitch was that there was simply no consensus about how best to teach religion. If, indeed, Judaism is a revealed religion which ought to be preserved, then it must be taught and the society could actually assume a pioneering pedagogic role. However, Gans objected strongly. The larger purpose of the *Verein* was to curb the all-inclusiveness of religion in traditional Judaism and to create an independent realm for reason. In this regard, the society was actually "anti-religious". Then too, a special course devoted just to religion was a blatant imitation of Christianity, unknown among the peoples of antiquity. On the basis of the wisdom dispensed by philosophy on such problems as God and immortality, each person should formulate his own subjective religious position.[49]

Zunz spoke twice on the subject and sided with Gans for reasons that had nothing to do with the latter's secularised conception of Judaism. On the contrary, Zunz held the teaching of religion to be so fundamental to the character and life of the child that it transcended the competence of the society. With a perspicacity born of want, Zunz understood the primacy of affective education: the imbuing of a child with love for Judaism can be achieved only at home. At best the society could dispense instruction aimed at the child's intellect, an explanation of the ritual exterior of Judaism. Nearly two years before, Zunz had had occasion to elaborate his thinking when he applied to the Jewish community of Königsberg for a post as its teacher of religion. Zunz argued that at present the teaching of Judaism suffered from the superstitions of the pietists and the sophistry of the sceptics.

> "Pure religious instruction does not subject children to dry history, silly fairytales or hatred of Christianity . . . It does not consist of a dreadful memorising of passages or a hollow defence of mystical superstitions. Rather it seeks to enthuse the spirit of the child for religion with words of inspiration and by even more inspiring example, to give children a staff for the storms of life, to implant in their hearts the gentle virtues of love and thus to endow them with the happiness which the believer in divine providence enjoys."[50]

As the child matures, fortified by such emotional attachment, he can gradually be exposed to the systematic, cognitive study of Judaism – its laws, beliefs, and history. In sum, the essential task of the religious teacher is not to fill the child's head but his heart; not to offer a few weekly hours of religious instruction, but to ensure a lifetime of religious practice.[51] Zunz's vision of Jewish education throbbed with all the passion of a genuine calling, though he failed to receive the position in Königsberg.[52]

The most complete articulation of the society's ideology belongs to Gans. His

---

[49]Ucko, *loc. cit.*, pp. 333–335; JNUL, 4°792/B–2.

[50]Hermann Vogelstein, 'Beiträge zur Geschichte des Unterrichtswesens in der jüdischen Gemeinde zu Königsberg i. Pr.', *Sechs und dreissigster Bericht über den Religions-Unterricht . . . zu Königsberg . . .* Königsberg i. Pr. 1903, pp. 12–13.

[51]*Ibid.*, p. 15.

[52]*Ibid.*, pp. 16–17. Zunz could hardly expect to attack Rabbinism with impunity. When the leadership of Königsberg inquired of Simon Weyl, the traditionalist rabbi of Berlin, about Zunz, it apparently received an unfavourable opinion, which seems to have put an end to his candidacy.

three aforementioned presidential addresses cohere as a single sustained effort at clarifying its purpose. Redolent with Hegelianism, they define the challenge of the age for Judaism, prescribe a suitable Jewish response, and unveil the means by which to effect it. Gans spoke in a mood of excitement at the momentous change in the status of Prussian Jewry, as a citizen of the Prussian state and a proud and grateful member of the body politic. For Jews a thousand-year period of insecurity and humiliation, of admission through backdoors and confinement to cellars, had been mercifully brought to an end, and the progress of history was irreversible, not subject to the protests and outbursts of Christian adversaries still rooted in the medieval world. Jews did not need to approach their new freedom with all the wariness and trepidation of a long incarcerated prisoner. Citizenship did not require a surrender of deep-seated religious loyalties. Every member of the *Verein* was connected to the Jewish community by ties of birth, family, friendship, education, and, above all, childhood memories. To rupture those ties was not merely an act of ingratitude but of betrayal. The goal of the society had to be to hold aloft the ideal of reconciliation, to think through the relationship of a double set of loyalties.[53]

Towards that end, Gans devoted his second address to an analysis of the present. In the spirit of Hegel, he posits a historical development guided by reason and free of the fortuitous that has at last arrived at an all-encompassing union of many diverse parts, past and present. Historically speaking, the union is a composite of the monotheism of the Orient, the ideals of beauty and freedom of Greece, the Roman concept of statehood, the Christian notion of humanity, medieval feudalism, and modern philosophy, all preserved therein long after their moment of exclusive domination has passed. In terms of the present, each diverse part is complete in itself, but derives significance alone from its integration into the whole. "That is the good fortune and meaning of European man, that within the manifold estates (*Stände*) of civil society he may freely choose his own and that in that choice he can feel all the other estates of society."[54] The strength and power of contemporary Europe is to be found "in the richness and abundant variety of countless particularities and formations (*Besonderheiten und Gestaltungen*), which nevertheless find their unity in the harmony of the whole".[55]

If it is hard to recognise the reality of Restoration Europe in Gans's glowing abstractions, it is possible to catch a glimpse of a social vision both integrationist and pluralistic. The emphasis may have been on unity and conformity, but there is a notion of the right to be different. Without it, Gans and his friends would have converted immediately. When that vision did founder in the face of government retraction and Jewish resistance, Gans was prepared to concede that the vision itself was flawed.[56] In the meantime, he laboured to formulate the legitimate parameters of Jewish existence after emancipation.

What the present offered Jewry, according to Gans, was a chance to leave their

[53]Rubaschoff, *loc. cit.*, pp. 37–39.
[54]*Ibid.*, p. 111.
[55]*Ibid.*, p. 112.
[56]*Ibid.*, p. 41.

state of quarantine and to re-enter the civilised world. But at a price: "Where the organism (i.e. the whole) demands a wavy line, there a straight line is an abomination."[57] Concretely that meant the discarding of all otherness and particularity. The protective walls of separation must come down. Only that which is universal in Judaism and serves the whole may retain its distinctive identity, though without any claim to exclusive truth.[58] Nothing impairs the harmony of the social order more than intolerance. The particular must become subordinate to the whole without necessarily disappearing. "Thus neither will the Jews vanish nor Judaism disintegrate, but rather appear submerged in the great movement of the whole while still surviving, as the current survives in the ocean."[59] The mandate of the age was absorption without dissolution.

Gans's third address rightly takes up the instrument by which this transformation of Jewish life is to be wrought. Gans invokes the supreme achievement of his day, the category of consciousness, the embodiment of reason as self-reflection. "The Jewish world must be conceptualised."[60] It must become the object of systematic, critical, and comprehensive reflection. Whatever can no longer be understood, justified, and related to an immutable and unifying core has lost not only the right but also the ability to exist. Continued existence becomes a function of rationality, and in the form of *Wissenschaft*, its purest expression, consciousness must assess the rational content of every aspect of Judaism. With history as the key to meaning, nothing could be more practical than the scholarly enterprise, though for Judaism it did not exist as yet. That was the mission of the society: to create a scholarship free of the limited horizons and prejudgments of traditional Rabbinism or Christian humanism, a scholarship grounded in respect for the uniqueness and independence of the phenomenon.[61]

The salient point of these discourses, as Gans reiterates in his peroration, is that the society represents a return to Judaism. It is not to be confused with the enlightened disciples of Mendelssohn who never transcended their unrelieved negativism. As traditional Judaism lost its moorings and inner directedness, they fled headlong into the outside world to pursue their own interests. They died metaphorically like old bachelors, unmourned because unconnected. In contrast, Gans and his circle personify a state of genuine freedom, in which one voluntarily reconnects with his origins. Their goal is to discover a new form of cohesion to replace the spiritual and communal ties of their ancestors.[62]

But not everyone in the *Verein* was brought to his feet cheering by Gans's high-flown rhetoric. No one had deeper reservations about this evaporation of an unbroken historical reality into a Hegelian idea than Heine, whose letters in the weeks before and after Gans's third address on 4th May 1823 simply bristle with sardonic contempt. Not that Heine was then any more religious than Gans. A day before the address, he described his own attachment to Judaism as

[57]*Ibid.*, p. 112.
[58]*Ibid.*, p. 112.
[59]*Ibid.*, p. 113.
[60]*Ibid.*, p. 196.
[61]*Ibid.*, pp. 114, 195–196.
[62]*Ibid.*, pp. 197–198.

consisting primarily in a profound antipathy for Christianity. His animus for all positive religions notwithstanding, he respected "the crassest Rabbinism" as an effective polar opposite. Unlike the prevailing sentiment in the society, he valued its tenacity and resilience, its fighting spirit, irrespective of content.[63] In that vein, he had exploded a month earlier in a letter to Wohlwill over the constant blood-letting of Judaism by rationalists "eager to pour that world-wide ocean into a pretty basin of *papier-mâché*". "We no longer have the strength to wear a beard, to fast, to hate, and to endure out of hate. That is the motive of our Reformation."[64]

Since Heine left Berlin for Lüneburg only a few days after 4th May, it is most likely that he was in attendance when Gans spoke. And his letter of 23rd May 1823 to his dear friend Moser, whom he affectionately regarded as "the epilogue of Nathan the Wise", has all the earmarks of a violent reaction.[65] As so often, Heine ingeniously cast his criticism in the form of an outlandish dream. Taunted by a mob of children, Heine ran fuming into Moser's open arms, only to be greeted with the reassurance that he was merely an idea. Jeers could not harm him. To convince him, Moser seized a volume of Hegel's logic and pointed out a totally confusing passage, while Gans knocked on the window. But Heine became enraged instead and ran around the room screaming, "I am not an idea, and know nothing about any idea, and never even had an idea." Gans kept raising his voice and the diminutive Marcus sitting on his shoulders belted out a chorus of quotations.[66]

It is in this state of revulsion that Heine resolved to write an essay for the society's journal on the tragedy of Jewish history (*der grosse Judenschmerz*), a resolve which would eventually yield, piecemeal and truncated, his justly famous *The Rabbi of Bacherach*. In his next letter to Moser, dated 18th June 1823, he made mention of his plan in conjunction with another witty diatribe against the emasculating philosophic Idealism of Gans that turns deadly earnest. "For heaven's sake, don't tell me again that I am only an idea. It makes me raving mad. As far as I am concerned, you can all become ideas; just leave me my beard. Because you and the old Friedländer and Gans have become ideas, you want to seduce me and make me over into an idea."[67]

For all his religious impiety and Judaic ignorance, Heine felt unerringly the travesty of dismantling a venerable and proven religion down to a set of theological maxims. Emancipation on such terms was merely another form of servitude. Gans had fatally chosen to minimise the illiberalism of the Prussian state. Intuitively, Heine had grasped hold of the same weapon for battle in the cause of Judaism – the study of history. In a setting of partial emancipation and progressive Westernisation, the study of Jewish history could serve to pare down or shore up, to vindicate radical reform or plead for preservation. The inchoate skirmish between Gans and Heine was a harbinger of confrontations to come.

[63] *Heine. Säkularausgabe*, XX, p. 122.
[64] *Ibid*., p. 72.
[65] *Ibid*., p. 133.
[66] *Ibid*., p. 86.
[67] *Ibid*., p. 97.

III

There was nothing "academic" about the centrality of *Wissenschaft* in the programme of the society. Its ideology accorded the study of the past a normative role formerly reserved to Jewish law alone. The historian was to replace the rabbi as the expert on Judaism, as the mantle of religious authority passed to the master of a new universe of discourse. And yet for all the urgency and presumption of the impetus, the few lasting scholarly achievements of the society managed to unveil the enormous potential of the discipline.

By the spring of 1820 the society had begun to consider the organisational form of its academic activity, and a year later its scholarly seminar bearing the official name of the *Institut für die Wissenschaft des Judentums* and led by Zunz was fully operative. Membership was by invitation and predicated on participation, with the result that it never rose above fourteen. Only a handful of the members of the society actually belonged to the seminar also, but those few were thus committed to at least one society function a week. In conception the seminar was a collective effort at "doing" Jewish scholarship, obliging each member to offer periodically a paper for discussion. According to the minutes of the seminar preserved by Zunz, some twenty-five papers were presented during the course of the seminar's existence, including six each by Gans and Zunz, five by Moser, three by Marcus, and two by Rubo. A goodly number ended up in the society's journal, for which the seminar was responsible and served as a splendid laboratory. At the last meeting of the seminar on 7th January 1824 with an attendance of three, Zunz read a revised version of his essay on Rashi that had appeared a year before in the journal. Many years later (1846), Zunz added the following poignant codicil to the minutes of the seminar:

> "After forty-five meetings the seminar was buried by its three founders, its last gasp being Rashi. Since then Gans and Moser have also died. The individuals and their forms disappear, the idea lives on."[68]

The decision to place a new type of Jewish scholarship at the heart of the society's agenda had been made possible by the publication of a revolutionary tract just a year before its founding. Zunz's *Etwas über die rabbinische Literatur* has long been justifiably revered as the cornerstone of the *Wissenschaft* edifice. Without it the *Verein* would have been just another Jewish fraternal or cultural organisation; with it the *Verein* became the testing ground for the viability and application of rethinking Judaism historically. In a single majestic sweep, a twenty-three-year-old university student had succeeded in transferring the canons of Western scholarship to the study of Judaism and conceptualising it afresh.[69] Yet it was not the cognitive anomalies of an outmoded paradigm that

---

[68]JNUL, 4°792/B–7, p. 15. In his first paper to the seminar, Moser urged that it be conceived "als einen Verein zum gemeinsamen *Studium* der Judenthumswissenschaft". [CAHJP, P47.]

[69]Zunz, *Gesammelte Schriften*, I, pp. 1–31. Zunz reached twenty-four only on 10th August 1818 and the essay had been completed the previous December. [See *Das Buch Zunz*, ed. by Fritz Bamberger (n.p. n.d.) p. 20.]

brought Zunz to formulate his vision of a new Jewish learning, but rather the challenge of academic antisemitism.

We know from Zunz's cryptic diary that in his first semester at the University of Berlin in the winter of 1815–1816, he dropped a course in ancient history by Friedrich Rühs because "he writes against the Jews".[70] The reference is to Rühs's assault on the basic liberal argument on behalf of Jewish emancipation entitled *Ueber die Ansprüche der Juden an das deutsche Bürgerrecht* (On the Claims of the Jews for German Citizenship), which went through two quick editions in 1815 and 1816. The prestige of a revitalised professoriate lent credence to an inherently important contention: that current Jewish depravity, which no one denied, was the product not of endless Christian abuse but of Judaism itself. Rühs assembled a welter of historical data from pre-Christian times through the Iberian experience down to his own day to demonstrate the unbroken uniformity of Jewish traits. Diverse historical settings failed to alter the basic identity of Second Commonwealth, Spanish, Polish, and recently emancipated Jews. Rühs posited three decidedly internal factors that accounted for a national character impervious to outside influence: the supremacy of the rabbinic aristocracy which killed any prospect for religious development; a sense of chosenness that inculcated unbridled national arrogance; and a theologically rooted abhorrence of physical labour that gave rise to a parasitic economic profile. The conclusion followed incontrovertably that as long as Jews adhered to Judaism they could not conceivably qualify for German citizenship. Their obnoxious religion, and not their allegedly dolorous history, condemned them to be an economic blight and an alien national body.[71] Whatever else this attack may have signified, it served to rivet attention once again on the need to study Judaism.

An unpublished manuscript among Zunz's papers confirms the young student's agitation over Rühs's entry into the emancipation debate. Dated 31st March 1816 and signed "Maskil", the eight-page manuscript is written in Zunz's tell-tale miniscule script and bears the title 'To the Wise Counsellor of the Wise Directors of Germany' along with the bracketed subtitle 'Against Rühs'. The essay addresses Rühs directly and throughout in the familiar style and abounds with apparent praise and admiration for his singular achievement in having brought the classical period of the eighteenth century to an end.

> "Where can I find the words to portray properly my rapture over your refutation of Jewish claims? Only some future age, at a more advanced stage of enlightenment than we obtuse contemporaries, will immortalise you in its chronicles in recognition of your services. It is a pity that Lessing and Mendelssohn did not live to witness their defeat."[72]

These opening lines are sufficient to convey the real intent: to disarm through irony. To the very end Zunz sustains the pose of a fulsome, if clever, expositor eager to amplify and confirm the vilifications of his chosen text. Adroitly he interlaced his own flowing discourse with countless quotations from Rühs,

---

[70] *Das Buch Zunz*, p. 9.
[71] Friedrich Rühs, *Ueber die Ansprüche der Juden an das deutsche Bürgerrecht*, Berlin 1816. See also Jacob Katz, *From Prejudice to Destruction. Anti-Semitism, 1700–1933*, Cambridge, Mass. 1980, pp. 76–82.
[72] JNUL, 4°792/D–1, p. 1.

always taking the trouble to underline the words and note the page references in the margin. The resulting mosaic pulsates with wit and consternation.

Yet Zunz withheld his outburst from publication for good reason, and not merely because he was a vulnerable university student. The essay was susceptible to easy misinterpretation. Irony did not always disguise an underlying sympathy for much of Rühs's criticism of Judaism and the distance between agreement and disagreement often seemed to blur into consent. Zunz yearned "to become an instrument to arouse the lost tribe of Israel", as he swore to Rühs.[73] But confused and disgruntled, he had not yet found his true voice. Dissembling was an ineffectual retort, perhaps no more than a desperate substitute for the inability to articulate a conception of Judaism distinct from those espoused by archaic rabbinists, Jewish deists, and the new romantic German nationalists.

It was in this agitated state of mind that Zunz composed his famous essay on rabbinic literature. Completed in December of 1817, it was not an expression of cognitive dissonance brought on by the first flush of enthusiasm for university studies but an inspired response to Rühs. Zunz had seized the weapon of *Wissenschaft* and turned it on his academic adversary. If the heart of the emancipation matter was the nature of Judaism, then the key to its proper evaluation lay in subjecting it to the same critical scholarship being applied in the university to other bodies of knowledge. Though Rühs had raised the right issue, he had simply recycled old stereotypes. Enlightened political action could flow only from informed understanding. Hasty and ill-conceived legislation merely entrenched archaic practices and institutions.

> "Thus to be able to recognise and separate what is old and useful, what is outmoded and detrimental, what is new and desirable, we must sensibly approach the study of a people and its history, both political and spiritual. But this is precisely what creates the greatest obstacle, that the matter of the Jews is handled like its literature. People tackle both with biased passion, assessing them either too low or too high."[74]

Zunz lamented the fact that in an age when scholarship deemed no language or culture unworthy of serious study, the content of rabbinic literature remained singularly ignored. Thus by continuing to brood on the import of Rühs's challenge, Zunz eventually forged a weapon whose immense range and utility transcended and concealed the circumstances of its birth.[75]

The emancipation debate similarly determined the parameters of the discipline as set down by Zunz in 1818. What was conspicuously omitted was any discussion of biblical literature, although in his initial response to Rühs he had seen fit to touch upon this realm of Jewish creativity as well. But Zunz knew that

---

[73]The passage is worth quoting in full. "Und heute, an diesem doppelt gefeierten Sonntage, auf dem Tage, der Paris gedemüthigt (1813 [sic], 31. März) und eine halbe Million ungläubiger Juden dem Elende preisgegeben (1492, 31. März, Ferdinands Edict) sah, schwöre ich in deinen Händen, du grösserer denn *Talavera* [sic], auch *ein Werkzeug zu werden, um den verlorenen Stamm Israels zu erwecken.*" [P. 6.]

[74]Zunz, 'Etwas über die rabbinische Literatur', *loc. cit.*, p. 5.

[75]There is but a single, brief reference to Rühs in the entire essay, and this at the very end in a note in which Zunz delivers a mild reproof of his harsh assessment of rabbinic literature in a historical handbook. ['Etwas über die rabbinische Literatur', *loc. cit.*, p. 31, note 1.]

Judaism had been decisively reshaped by its long rabbinic phase and that much of the opposition to the admission of its adherents into civil society stemmed from its rabbinic character. Moreover, the non-Jewish world was far more in the dark about rabbinic literature than its biblical foundation. Hence the practical urgency for a "scientific" study, reinforced by internal Jewish developments. Zunz was convinced at the time that integration spelled the end of Judaism's rabbinic phase. Traditional institutions of higher Jewish learning were fast disappearing from the landscape of Central Europe, German Jews were appropriating the language and culture of their society, and Hebrew as a literary idiom was about to vanish. Passing from the scene, rabbinic culture in all its amplitude deserved to be given a scholarly assessment, a process that had to begin as long as its literary products and aficionados were still accessible.[76]

The enduring value of Zunz's departure was his dramatic enlargement of what comprised the field of rabbinic literature and how it ought to be studied. Properly understood, it was not restricted to works by rabbis or on rabbinics. Zunz bristled at the theological overtones of the very term "rabbinic literature", coined and defined by seventeenth-century Christian savants of Judaism, and much preferred the more neutral and comprehensive rubric "neo-Hebraic" or "Jewish literature".[77] Beyond nomenclature, Zunz exhibited with stunning detail a vast expanse of literature written in Hebrew by literate laymen as well as practising rabbis that matched all the literary genres of a living people. And in accord with the study of classical literature, philology alone, in this case a grammatical and historical command of Hebrew and its cognates, had the power "to divest the past of its veil".[78] No less important than analytic dissection was an eye for synthesis, a sense for how the minutiae of any given text might relate to all of Jewish literature and, indeed, to the common spiritual legacy of all mankind. Above the numerous workshops of the scholarly craft, Zunz assigned, in the spirit of German Idealism, pride of place to philosophy – "the most exalted guide . . . in recognising and disseminating the intellectual greatness of a people. In this spirit, every historical fact becomes . . . a contribution to the understanding of man, the noblest purpose of all research".[79]

In the span of a single essay of unbelievable richness, compression, and fervour, Zunz had enlisted scholarship in the service of progress. A new conception of Judaism as a religious civilisation would lead to religious reform within and political rehabilitation without. As the revival of classical learning in the Renaissance had paved the way for the Reformation, so a new mode of Jewish scholarship would secure emancipation for a transformed Judaism.[80] Towards that end, Zunz invited others to join him in the publication of critical editions of

[76]*Ibid.*, p. 4.
[77]Ismar Schorsch, 'The Emergence of Historical Consciousness in Modern Judaism', in *LBI Year Book XXVIII* (1983), p. 418.
[78]Zunz, 'Etwas über die rabbinische Literatur', *loc. cit.*, p. 17.
[79]*Ibid.*, p. 27. See Fritz Bamberger, 'Zunz's Conception of History', *Proceedings of the American Academy for Jewish Research*, XI (1941), p. 4, note 14 for possible influence of August Boeckh.
[80]Zunz, 'Etwas über die rabbinische Literatur', *loc. cit.*, p. 4.

worthy specimens of rabbinic culture. His own choice of a Spanish philosophic text from the end of the thirteenth century conveyed unmistakably the impression that such were not be found in the world of medieval Ashkenaz. More broadly still, Zunz's essay implied a direct threat to the rabbinic leadership of his own age. Knowledge was power and henceforth the most reliable spokesman for Judaism was no longer the traditional rabbi, who at best presided over a single literary expression of rabbinic culture, but the modern scholar with his encompassing knowledge and critical method. By mediating the past, he offered a new source of direction for the present.[81]

If then the genesis of Zunz's essay may be attributed to Rühs, its transcendence comes from his teacher Friedrich A. Wolf, of Homeric fame. At the university Zunz attended four of his courses on the legacy of Greece and Rome and confided to his diary that "Wolf attracts me". In fact, Zunz seems to have composed his rebuttal during the very semester he heard Wolf discourse on the *Encyclopaedia der Altertumswissenschaft*.[82] A decade earlier, after a teaching career of nearly a quarter of a century, Wolf had attempted in a single essay to provide a conceptual and methodological overview of classical studies, which provided Zunz with a model for the definition of an untidy academic discipline. For all their specific differences, Wolf's 'Description of the Academic Study of Antiquity' (*Darstellung der Altertumswissenschaft*) and Zunz's 'On Rabbinic Literature' faced the same problem – to reconceptualise a well-mined field from a fresh vantage point. Nothing signifies discontinuity more vividly than a new nomenclature, and Wolf insisted on replacing the sundry names in use for the field of classical studies with the term "Altertumswissenschaft", with "antiquity" in his judgment reserved exclusively for the Greeks and Romans, who alone of all ancient peoples had risen to the level of culture.[83] While Zunz only half-heartedly proposed a name change for "rabbinic literature" in 1817, a few years later in the context of the *Verein* he unfurled his chosen terminology of *Wissenschaft des Judentums* in the name of the scholarly institute and its journal. In both substance and structure, the term is analogous to Wolf's own designation, whose genitive form was occasionally reversed into "Wissenschaft des Altertums".[84] Similarly in the deliberations of the institute, one did not hesitate to speak of "Judentumswissenschaft".[85]

The dimensions of the now full-blown field of Jewish studies were depicted for the first time by Immanuel Wohlwill (Wolf) in his seminal introductory essay to the journal. Wohlwill had joined the *Verein* in June 1820 while an impoverished student at the university, where Hegel agreed to admit him to his lectures without the requisite fees provided he pay him or his heirs within five years. The gesture of respect for his talents furnished the society with another convinced

[81]*Ibid.*, pp. 26–27.
[82]*Das Buch Zunz*, pp. 19–21. Cf. Bamberger, *loc. cit.*, p. 4.
[83]F. A. Wolf, 'Darstellung der Altertums-Wissenschaft', in *Museum der Altertums-Wissenschaft*, I (1807), pp. 15–19, 30.
[84]*Ibid.*, p. 6.
[85]See above, note 68.

Hegelian, at least until January 1823 when he moved on to Hamburg to begin a long teaching career at its Jewish Free School.[86]

Wohlwill's essay is a two-tiered statement comprising an *a priori* theory of Jewish history and a programme of empirical Jewish studies. On the level of speculation, he employs German Idealism to posit an essence of Judaism, a religious idea that powers and unites Jewish civilisation through the millenniums. The idea, which is a gift of revelation, is the recognition of a single, unifying divine presence amid the diversity of existence and is best expressed in the four-lettered Hebrew name of God. The first benefit yielded by this essence is that it grounds the sense of continuity in Jewish history in an identifiable, ever-present core idea. The second is that everything else in Judaism is of limited duration, at best a temporary measure necessitated by historical circumstances. The third benefit is the grant of universal significance to Judaism, even after Christianity has become a vehicle for the dissemination of the unity idea. In embryonic form, Wohlwill had combined here for the first time the main ingredients of what would soon coalesce into a full-fledged reform theory of Jewish history. Diaspora-orientated, Wohlwill identified with the Jews who refused to return to Palestine after Cyrus, transvalued Jewish statehood and talmudic law into prophylactic institutions, reduced medieval Messianism to a function of persecution, embraced the idea of a Jewish mission, and held up Spinoza as a supreme expositor of Judaism.

The theory, of course, was an affront to the research imperative. Scholarship had not yet begun to generate the empirical evidence to support such meta-historical claims, if it ever could. The urgency of the moment had prompted Wohlwill and his comrades to put the proverbial cart before the horse, to venture in miniature a phenomenology of the Jewish spirit prematurely. Nevertheless, the horse itself was a healthy animal. Remarkably, Wohlwill formulated a balanced and coherent research programme far more comprehensive than what Zunz had proposed earlier. While the object remained Judaism as a religious civilisation, its study was to reach back to the biblical period and forward to the present. A philological analysis of the literary texts of each period, now demarcated by the changes in the form of Judaism's central idea, would yield the evidence for a broad external (relating to the religious, political, and literary) and internal (relating to the unfolding of its inner idea) history of Judaism. Despite a nod to the non-partisanship of modern scholarship, Wohlwill intoned the relevance of *Wissenschaft des Judentums*, to the state as well as to contemporary Judaism, and closed with a special plea to Jews to enter its ranks.[87]

The tension between method and relevance is thus a consequence of the on-going character of Judaism. Moreover, as conceived by the society, Jewish

[86]Reissner, *Gans, op. cit.*, p. 174; Albert Friedlander, 'The Wohlwill–Moser Correspondence', in *LBI Year Book XI* (1966), p. 280.

[87]Immanuel Wolf, 'Ueber den Begriff einer Wissenschaft des Judenthums', in *Zeitschrift für die Wissenschaft des Judentums (ZWJ)*, I (1822–1823), pp. 1–24. For an English translation, see *LBI Year Book II* (1957), pp. 194–204. On the sources of Wolf's thinking, see Luitpold Wallach, 'The Beginnings of the Science of Judaism in the Nineteenth Century', in *Historia Judaica*, VIII (1946), pp. 39–43.

scholarship was not to ignore the present state of the Jews. According to Wohlwill, the study of contemporary Jewry in the various lands of its dispersion was fully as important as the study of Jewish history. It was precisely this interconnectedness between past and present which informed Zunz's own methodological contribution to the journal. As the last substantive essay therein, his 'Grundlinien zu einer künftigen Statistik der Juden' (Guidelines to a Future Statistical Study of the Jews) bequeathed a conception of the discipline so all-encompassing that it was not even approximated until the twentieth century.[88]

The term "statistics" derived from the eighteenth-century German version of political science and connoted an all-inclusive description of a country in its present state. Applied to the past by the Göttingen universal historian August Ludwig von Schlözer, it meant halting the historical continuum at a given point to depict a single cross-section. If history was the study of man along a dynamic vertical axis, then "statistics" (in a sociological sense) was the horizontal study of a society at a static moment.[89] In the words of Zunz, who proposed to transfer the distinction to Jewish studies: "A statistical study of a human group deals with its existence in a single moment, an existence which is the consequence of a preceding history . . . and conversely history is the result of an unending series of statistics".[90] Zunz suggested treating Judaism as a construct equivalent to the State and subjecting it to a series of exhaustive sociological studies along the course of its historical trek. Each "statistical" exposure was to be built stereoscopically from both Jewish and non-Jewish sources and include some fourteen different foci. The cumulative result would be a profound understanding of contemporary Jewry "which should be the culmination of this immense statistical edifice".[91] In short, not sterile antiquarian interests but deep engagement in the present motivated the projection of this awesome vision of what today we would call "total history".

An earlier essay by Zunz in the journal acquires added significance when read from the perspective of this "statistical" programme. His effort to collect and identify Iberian place-names mentioned in some twenty-five medieval Hebrew sources corresponded to one of the topics to be covered by any static depiction of a specific Jewish community. Zunz recognised that Judaism exhibited distinctive features in every regional setting and that initially any sociological sounding should be restricted to a single regional community. One of the first steps towards such a study was to assemble the names of all localities in which Jews had resided.[92] From Wolf, Zunz had learned that geography is an indispensable part of history.

"Nothing is more necessary than first to familiarise yourself with the area in which the known peoples of antiquity lived and traded, in order to appreciate the variety of conditions over time

[88]*ZWJ*, pp. 523–532.
[89]Luitpold Wallach, 'Ueber Leopold Zunz als Historiker', in *ZGJD*, V (1935), pp. 251–252.
[90]*ZWJ*, p. 523.
[91]*Ibid.*, p. 532.
[92]Leopold Zunz, 'Ueber die in den hebräisch-jüdischen Schriften vorkommenden hispanischen Ortsnamen', in *ZWJ*, pp. 114–176.

which marked their places of settlement. Much that is distinctive to the nature of man in antiquity becomes explicable thereby."[93]

The attention to geographical detail by Zunz epitomised the centrality of context for the proper understanding of historical phenomenon.[94]

But traces of present-mindedness seeped even into a subject as concrete as Spanish toponyms in Hebrew literature. Cognisant of his pioneering effort, Zunz affixed a theoretical introduction to his essay. He lists therein the larger geographical blocs in which Jews were to be found, including America and Australia, classifies the types of Jewish sources that might contain geographical information, and reflects on the methods of extracting it. He also issues a sterling declaration on the extraordinary combination of attributes necessary for Jewish scholarship. Its practitioner must embody

> "not only objectivity and a disregard for acquired and fashionable prejudices, not only a majestic view capable of obliterating the solitary, incidental, and momentary [phenomenon], not only a favourable disposition toward that which has proven itself true by surviving all the arenas of world history, but also that many-sided knowledge that attunes the eye to the developmental path of Judaism – namely, a command of detail and a firm grasp of the whole along with great erudition in Jewish literature".[95]

Yet the ethos patently does not extend to a study of his own immediate cultural legacy. Quite oblivious to his own standards, Zunz soon slips into a jarring invocation of the Spanish bias. He has chosen to begin his excavations on Spanish soil, because its literary treasures are unpublished and unknown in the Ashkenazic world. While "every piece of trash from the Polish period is printed . . . good Spanish works gather mould in libraries, without anyone interested in redeeming them".[96] For all its dry technicality, Zunz's essay shares the prevailing zeal to expose Ashkenazic Jewry to a nobler brand of Judaism.

In this regard, Zunz's celebrated biography of Rashi, the acme of early medieval Ashkenazic Judaism, bespoke an honest awareness of precisely this shortcoming.[97] By abandoning the tactic of whipping contemporary rabbinism with the rod of Spanish rationalism, Zunz achieved a triumph of the scholarly ethos. The essay marks the first time since the *Haskalah* began to cultivate the genre of didactic biography that an Ashkenazic Jew, other than Mendelssohn, was deemed fit for biographical treatment.[98] As Zunz was later to explain, what prompted his choice was the realisation that the aversion of the *Maskilim* simply confirmed the prejudice of Christian scholars. If the written record of mankind all too often bore the scars of human passion, then modern scholarship entailed an act of self-transcendence. But the *Maskilim* were ensnared by the vices of the Enlightenment; they had little stomach for a Jewish culture totally dominated by

---

[93]Wolf, *Museum der Altertums-Wissenschaft*, p. 50.
[94]*ZWJ*, pp. 118–119.
[95]*Ibid.*, p. 117.
[96]*Ibid.*, p. 129.
[97]Leopold Zunz, 'Salomon ben Isaac, genannt Raschi', in *ZWJ*, pp. 277–384.
[98]Ismar Schorsch, 'From Wolfenbüttel to Wissenschaft. The Divergent Paths of Isaak Markus Jost and Leopold Zunz', in *LBI Year Book XXII* (1977), pp. 124–125.

religion. To the extent that Jews had been excluded from Christian society, Judaism came to embrace all forms of Jewish self-expression. The greater openness of Moslem Spain allowed for the common cultivation of a religiously neutral cultural legacy.[99] In protesting the Sephardic bias, Zunz mustered the courage to face the centrality of religion in the Jewish historical experience and the empathy to treat it fairly.

To focus on Rashi permitted Zunz also to demonstrate the difference between fact and fiction. As the exegete par excellence, Rashi was not exactly a peripheral figure to Jewish consciousness. But indifference to historical thinking had obscured him behind a veil of legend. According to Zunz, the last two hundred years in particular had created a bogus Rashi, bereft of spirit and laden with nonsense. Even such elementary facts as the date and place of his birth or his actual name had been subject to corruption. To assault that citadel of ignorance, Zunz drew all his information about Rashi's life, intellectual world, linguistic competence, religious views, and literary works only from sources written by Rashi himself. He showed that Rashi was wholly a product of the rabbinic culture of his time, that he was part of a living exegetical tradition, that in both sets of commentaries (biblical and talmudic) he aspired to elucidate the plain meaning of the text, "to serve as Aaron for a mute Moses", and that he often revised his work.[100] And not to lose sight of the larger scholarly landscape, Zunz presciently pointed out the inestimable value of Rashi's commentaries for a host of other worthy topics. The practical import of Zunz's painstaking research echoed audibly throughout: contemporary rabbinism had betrayed its own noble heritage.[101] Scholarly integrity had induced him to switch tactics, but the adversary remained the same.

No less significant for the introduction of historical thinking into Judaism were the three major contributions by Gans to the journal.[102] His role in the *Verein* was by no means restricted to the heady realm of ideology. If Zunz unearthed the wealth and diversity of Hebrew sources available for the recovery of the Jewish past, Gans revealed just how vital was the consultation of non-Jewish sources, and in tandem the two of them imbued the journal with a solid balance of alternative modes of Jewish scholarship. Incomparably less learned in Jewish sources than Zunz, though not Hebraically incompetent, Gans was far more attracted by the intersection of Jewish and general history.[103] The history of Judaism could no longer be studied apart from its Gentile environment or in ignorance of its legal status. Thus he opened his first essay, in consonance with the emancipation struggle of his own age, with a brilliant proposal of staggering

[99]*Ibid.*, p. 125.
[100]*ZWJ*, p. 325.
[101]*Ibid.*, pp. 377 ("Das Erschweren [in *Halakhah*] nimmt zu mit der Ignoranz."), p. 380.
[102]Eduard Gans, 'Gesetzgebung über Juden in Rom, nach den Quellen des Römischen Rechts', pp. 25–67; 'Vorlesungen über die Geschichte der Juden im Norden von Europa und in den slavischen Ländern', pp. 95–113; 'Die Grundzüge des mosaisch-talmudischen Erbrechts', pp. 419–471.
[103]Cf. Reissner, *Gans, op. cit.*, p. 105. There is no mention whatsoever in Gans's essay on Jewish inheritance law that he received help from Zunz. My impression from internal evidence is that Gans certainly read Hebrew and probably could handle the Jewish legal sources in the original.

proportions – to collect systematically all laws and regulations pertaining to Jews ever issued in Europe.[104]

By way of illustration, the essay itself deals with the legal status of Jewry in the Roman Empire and makes a crucial distinction between the pagan and Christian periods in reference to their treatment of Jews. The novelty of his method did not signify a break with the deep-seated medieval Jewish perception of Diaspora history as saturated with suffering and persecution. Gans too regarded the precariousness of Jewish existence in both periods as a constant. What he did argue for was the recognition that the source of the danger changed. In pagan Rome, persecution derived from social tensions and not legal discrimination. The widespread anti-Jewish sentiment was rather a consequence of friction engendered by Jewish allegiance to Jerusalem, pagan ignorance of Judaism, and a tendency to view the early Christians as Jews. In contrast, the triumph of Christianity with its conviction of a single truth turned law into an instrument of religious coercion. Only Christian reverence for the Hebrew Bible and the expectation of an ultimate conversion stayed the wrath of the Church. This indictment of the Church as the direct cause for the steady deterioration of Jewish status in the empire after the conversion of Constantine was to become a staple of *Wissenschaft* scholarship.[105] A peroration by Gans at the end of this section of the essay, censored in some copies of the journal, underscores the connection between past perception and present reality.

> "How long will that pernicious half-heartedness go on? Has history not sufficiently taught that one can only choose between two paths: Either to take as your point of departure the principle of the only saving Church and then in a completely logical manner (and thereby at least praiseworthy) wipe the Jews off the planet and fill the resulting gap with their interred bodies, or to forget in all matters of law that there may be Jews and thus fill the gap with their resurrected spirits. Only that which lies in the middle is evil."[106]

Apart from the ideological thrust, this essay is a grand example of integrative scholarship. Gans measures the impact of Christianity on Jewish status in terms of the office and authority exercised by Jewish communal leaders in the Roman Empire and in conjunction with that study tries to match up titles of leadership mentioned in the Hebrew sources with what appear to be their equivalents in the Roman legal codes.[107]

But the integration of disparate sources was not only of utility for communal or political history. In another major essay, Gans unfurled the benefits to be gained from studying the institutions of Jewish law comparatively and within the context of the Roman legal system. His pioneering study of 'Die Grundzüge des mosaisch-talmudischen Erbrechts' (The Fundamentals of the Mosaic-talmudic Law of Inheritance) was part of his majestic four-volume history of inheritance

---

[104]*ZWJ*, p. 25.
[105]*ZWJ*, pp. 27–51. For a recent challenge of this "reading", see Jeremy Cohen, 'Roman Imperial Policy Toward the Jews from Constantine until the End of the Palestinian Patriarchate (ca. 429)', in *Byzantine Studies*, III (1976), pp. 1–29.
[106]*Ibid.*, pp. 50–51.
[107]*Ibid.*, pp. 51–67. Unfortunately, the essay was never completed.

law world-wide and thus published twice in quick succession.[108] The larger
project was conceived as a historical illustration of Hegel's philosophy of law,
with the chronological order and cultural development of the specific legal
institution of inheritance accounted for by rational necessity rather than
historical accident. In accord with Hegelian periodisation, biblical law is placed
squarely within the oriental stage of the human spirit, though to be sure its
highest form of expression.[109] But more important for Gans is to demonstrate the
process of Westernisation that biblical institutions underwent by virtue of
talmudic exposition. Studied from the perspective of Greco-Roman law, talmudic legal practice can be shown to exhibit development, outside influence, and a
decided resemblance to the West. Gans identified examples of substantive and
linguistic affinities which bespoke cultural interaction and credited the rabbis
with transforming the fragmentary injunctions of biblical law on inheritance into
a coherent and advanced legal system.[110] Ironically, the rehabilitation of
talmudic law had been launched by one of its "cultured despisers". The
intellectual counterpart of political emancipation, integrative scholarship, illu-
mined a landscape of new meaning.

The contribution which Gans might have made to the course of Jewish
scholarship is amply adumbrated in these forgotten essays. Conversion terminated his engagement as it would that of others whose career aspirations
foundered on the religious intransigence of the German university. *Wissenschaft
des Judentums* constituted the society's most important legacy, a new weapon
forged in a two-front war – for emancipation and against Rabbinism, but with
limitless utility for future crises. Its eventual perfection would be effected largely
through the defiant and selfless dedication of Zunz. Despite bouts of abject
despair, he emerged from the fiasco of the *Verein* with the resolve to pursue that
vision as a vocation. In a searing flashback on the society thirty years after its
demise, Heine bedecked Zunz with an unexaggerated accolade for his solitary
perseverence.

> "This excellent, eminent man, who stood firm, constantly and unshakeably, in a period of
> transition, hesitation, and vacillation; and who, despite the sharpness of his intellect, his
> scepticism, and his learning, remained faithful to the promise he had made himself, to the
> generous caprice of his soul. A man of words *and* a man of action, he worked unceasingly, he
> did what needed doing, at a time when others lost themselves in dreams and sank to the
> ground, bereft of courage."[111]

[108]Eduard Gans, *Das Erbrecht in weltgeschichtlicher Entwicklung*, 4 vols., Berlin 1824–1835.
[109]*ZWJ*, pp. 420, 428, 430–431.
[110]Some of Gans's etymological derivations for rabbinic terms such as *parna* (*ZWJ*, p. 437) and
   diyyatiki (*ZWJ*, pp. 465–466) were accepted by later rabbinic lexicography. (Jacob Levy,
   Neuhebräisches und chaldäisches Wörterbuch, 4 vols., Leipzig 1876–1889, pp. I, p. 404, IV, p. 119.)
[111]Prawer, *op. cit.*, p. 470. See also Michael A. Meyer, *The Origins of the Modern Jew*, Detroit 1967, pp.
   180–181.

Dohm's Treatise on the Jews
A Defence of the Enlightenment

BY ROBERT LIBERLES

In 1780 Christian Wilhelm von Dohm, a ranking Prussian civil servant, collaborated with Moses Mendelssohn on a memorandum submitted on behalf of the Jews of Alsace to the French Council of State. A year later Dohm issued a treatise on the civil improvement of the Jews, which contained a comprehensive programme for increasing the utility of the Jewish population to society as a whole. Although discussions on the Jews were already intensifying by the late 1770s, that treatise served as the basis for extensive debate on the question of the Jews during the years to come.

No discussion of the attitudes towards the Jews during the latter part of the eighteenth century – during the heyday of the Enlightenment and the beginnings of the debate on emancipation – can ignore Dohm. Yet Dohm, as revealed in these discussions of his involvement in the issue of the Jews, appears as a mere appendage to the dominant personality of Moses Mendelssohn. Dohm may not have been a particularly forceful figure, but in the context of his time the role he played was important within the circles of Enlightenment in Germany, as was, for that matter, the question of the Jews. In defending his position on the Jews, Dohm found himself defending his understanding of Enlightenment principles – to both its opponents and adherents. Thus, the controversy on the Jews should be understood as reflecting some of the broader currents within the intellectual stirrings of the day.

I. DOHM'S EARLY CAREER

Christian Wilhelm von Dohm was born in 1751 in Lemgo in the county of Lippe, an independent city in Westphalia. His father was a preacher, but Dohm was an orphan by the time he was eight.[1] In 1770, Dohm at the age of nineteen turned to

[1]There are two full-length biographies of Dohm. The first was written shortly after Dohm's death in 1820: W. Gronau, *Christian Wilhelm von Dohm nach seinem Wollen und Handeln. Ein biographischer Versuch*, Lemgo 1824. A newer biography does more to place Dohm within his historical context and to synthesise his thinking: Ilsegret Dambacher, *Christian Wilhelm von Dohm*, Frankfurt a. Main 1974. More specifically, on Dohm's Jewish involvement, see Horst Möller, 'Aufklärung, Judenemanzipation und Staat. Ursprung und Wirkung von Dohms Schrift "Über die bürgerliche Verbesserung der Juden" ', in *Deutsche Aufklärung und Judenemanzipation*, edited by Walter Grab, Tel-Aviv 1980, pp. 119–149.

Dohm has been discussed frequently and with insight in the various volumes of the Year Book. See especially, H. D. Schmidt, 'The Terms of Emancipation', in *LBI Year Book I* (1956), pp. 28–33; and Julius Carlebach, 'The Forgotten Connection. Women and Jews in the Conflict between Enlightenment and Romanticism', in *LBI Year Book XXIV* (1979), pp. 118–123 and *passim*. The following summary of Dohm's early career is based on Gronau, *Dohm, op. cit.*, pp. 1–133, and Dambacher, *Dohm, op. cit.*, pp. 1–31.

the philosopher Johann Bernhard Basedow asking him to become his teacher and mentor. Dohm joined Basedow in some of his work on educational textbooks, but primarily assisted him in his correspondence. During his brief stay with Basedow, Dohm became acquainted with the Swiss theologian, Johann Caspar Lavater. Later, Dohm continued working on Lavater's translation of Charles de Bonnet's *Essai de Psychologie, ou Considérations sur les Opérations de l'Âme*.

While still a student at the *Gymnasium*, Dohm established a long-lasting friendship with a poet and church official in Halberstadt named Johann Gleim.[2] In the early 1770s, Gleim hoped to attract Dohm and several other friends to Halberstadt to form a society with the objective of publishing cultural works for a wide audience. However, Dohm decided to undertake studies at Leipzig, where he concentrated on jurisprudence, philosophy, and economics. There he came under the influence of the philosopher Christian Garve, who strengthened Dohm's inclinations towards the influence of British writers as well as Dohm's wish to become involved in practical affairs of politics and economics. Garve was especially close to the thinking of Adam Smith, and Dohm shared Garve's enthusiasm.[3] Shortly thereafter Dohm decided to spend some time in Berlin and found employment as a tutor at the court of Prince Ferdinand.

Dohm arrived in Berlin in 1773 with the hope that through the prince he would meet the most worthy men of Berlin. It was part of his nature to conceive of ambitious projects and upon moving to Berlin, he wrote to Gleim of his plan to write a textbook of Prussian history, geography, and statistics. With reference to Gleim's plans for the group in Halberstadt, Dohm wrote that "this would be an appropriate project for our society. Perhaps it would also serve me as preparation for more important historical works, in which we Germans lag so far behind the French, Italians, and British".[4] In 1774, Dohm decided to continue his studies, this time at Göttingen.

In 1775, Dohm was involved in the establishment of a new political and economic journal, the *Deutsches Museum*, which he co-edited with Heinrich Christian Boie. In a letter to Gleim that accompanied a copy of the first issue, Dohm summed up their objectives:

> "The *Deutsches Museum* has taken as its main objective making the Germans better acquainted with themselves and more aware of their own national affairs. Until now . . . attention has been given primarily to foreign statistics in order to increase the political spirit of the nation. Nevertheless, it is to be hoped that many patriots will endeavour to broaden and increase their knowledge of the constitutions of German lands (these being so useful but so little studied)!"[5]

---

[2]Dohm's letters to Gleim, quoted extensively in Dambacher's biography, add considerably to our knowledge and understanding of his career. On Gleim (1719–1803) see *Allgemeine Deutsche Biographie*, IX, pp. 228–233.

[3]Dambacher, *Dohm, op. cit.*, pp. 5, 99.

[4]*Ibid.*, pp. 6–7.

[5]*Deutsches Museum* (1777), p. 4. A year earlier, with the appearance of the first issue, Dohm had written to his friend Gleim: "Our main objective is to make Germany better acquainted with herself and more aware of her various constitutions and her internal and external affairs; to arouse in us a sense of 'public spirit' [English in original]; and to offer political and statistical data and inquiries." Quoted in Gronau, *Dohm, op. cit.*, pp. 39–40.

This increased knowledge was to bring the various German states closer to each other, and even more fundamentally, the journal sought to awaken public spirit in Germany, in emulation of the active role played by the citizens of England. Dohm made frequent reference to the high "public spirit" of the British, while complaining that the German intelligentsia were only interested in literary affairs. The *Deutsches Museum* was intended to serve Germany's interests in practical matters.

In Dohm's view, statistics had an important part to play in the campaign to increase the role of public information. The absolutist governments were attempting to run their affairs under utmost secrecy, and Dohm saw statistics as a means of spreading knowledge and sharing information.[6] During the first year of publication, Dohm regularly contributed a column entitled 'Miscellania of Statistical and Historical Content'. His other articles in the early volumes of the *Museum* included a short history of European exploration of America; a proposal for expanding mortality tables; a study of coffee laws in the German states (in which he argued for liberalising the restrictions on its import); a study of factories and manufacturing in Kurpfalz; and an article on the status of guilds in France.[7]

Several people had influenced Dohm towards statistical research, among them his teacher at Göttingen, August Ludwig von Schlözer, successor to the founder of statistical studies in Germany, Gottfried Achenwall.[8] Achenwall had employed statistics as a means towards the critical study of political systems. For Achenwall, who apparently had originated the use of the term, statistics referred to "the knowledge that a statesman should possess". It was Schlözer who extended the scope of statistical studies to include historical material as well.[9]

In 1777, Dohm established a new journal, the *Materialien für die Statistik und neuere Staatengeschichte*. Soon thereafter, Dohm stepped down as co-editor of the *Deutsches Museum* apparently in order to focus his attention more exclusively on political and statistical material. While the *Museum* was intended to serve the broad public, the *Materialien* sought to collect pure statistical materials primarily for the benefit of scholars.[10] The *Materialien* joined several other statistical journals, including that of Schlözer, as well as one edited by Anton Friedrich Büsching, whose approach to statistics differed somewhat from the line taken by Achenwall and Schlözer. Among the essential differences were Büsching's interest in comparative studies as well as his primary emphasis on social

[6]Dambacher, *Dohm, op. cit.*, pp. 38–40.

[7]*Deutsches Museum* (1776), pp. 49–62, 372–381; (1777), pp. 215–221; (1777), pp. 123–145; (1778), pp. 97–125; (1778), pp. 413–429.

[8]Dambacher, *Dohm, op. cit.*, pp. 32–33.

[9]On the contribution of Achenwall and Schlözer to the study of statistics, see V. John, *Geschichte der Statistik*, Stuttgart 1884, pp. 74–114. Helen Walker wrote of Achenwall's understanding of statistics that he and his followers "did not devote themselves so much to enumeration and computation as to verbal descriptions of the political situation and of all facts of interest in their countries, and they looked with considerable unfriendliness and displeasure upon the 'Table-statisticians' ". *Studies in the History of Statistical Method*, Baltimore 1929, p. 32. Schlözer's extension of the field of statistical study is discussed in *Handwörterbuch der Sozial-Wissenschaften*, X (1959), p. 31.

[10]Dambacher, *Dohm, op. cit.*, p. 52.

statistics concerning population and the economy rather than an exclusive focus on the political state.[11]

While Dohm was strongly influenced by both men, Büsching's impact would seem to have been the greater. Thus, Dohm revealed a strong preference for comparative studies, and his methods of analysis were frequently inclined towards comparisons between different German states and between different countries. This was true even when, as in the case of his treatise on the Jews, he employed very few statistics, but made a number of comparisons between different sectors of the German population and between Jews of different countries. Dohm's relations with Schlözer were also strained by a literary dispute between them. In 1776 Dohm had published an essay in which he argued the significance for England of its trade with its American colonies. The following year Schlözer published a refutation of Dohm's claims by the Dutch Jewish philosopher and economist Isaac de Pinto (1717–1787), and a series of polemical essays between Dohm and Schlözer followed. Pointed evidence of Dohm's partiality towards Büsching is that Dohm employed comparative statistics published by Büsching to refute the position maintained by Schlözer.[12]

Dohm's early writings frequently dealt with distant lands. He conceived the idea of writing on the history, literature, religion, philosophy, and laws of India, and he issued translations of two travel books, one concerned with India and Persia, the other with the Levant. He subsequently prepared an annotated edition of Engelbert Kämpfer's travel book on Japan.[13] It was due to Büsching that Dohm was led to publish his travel books on the East.[14]

Two factors drew Dohm to this part of the world, and both were rooted in Europe. First, Dohm joined those who hoped to demonstrate that the true cradle of world civilisation lay not in Egypt or within Judaism or Christianity, but in the remote, small, humble countries of the Far East. Travel literature was popular within enlightenment circles precisely because it broadened the perspectives of Christian Europe.

> "The old medieval conception of a world bounded by the frontiers of Christendom crumbled before the awe-inspiring spectacle of an infinitely varied and vaster world, peopled by races and civilisations which had no common ethnical [sic!] or cultural origins and certainly owed nothing to the tradition of Judaism or Christianity, hitherto conceived to be universal."[15]

Thus, Dohm turned to the East in order to support his deistic philosophy. Observing that the different religious systems are similar in their essentials, he concluded that they must, therefore, be mutually tolerant of each other.[16]

Dohm's concern with travel books also derived from the amount of statistical material they provided. His interest in the application of statistical methods for

---

[11]On Büsching and the differences in approach, see John, *Statistik, op. cit.*, pp. 90–95.
[12]On the dispute, see especially *Deutsches Museum* (1776), pp. 835–851 and (1777), pp. 159–173 and the references there to Schlözer's publications. The reference to Büsching is in (1776), p. 845. The disagreement with Schlözer is discussed in Dambacher, *Dohm, op. cit.*, pp. 41–43.
[13]*Ibid.*, pp. 30–33 (E. Kämpfer, *History of Japan and Siam*, 2 vols., 1727, German 1777).
[14]*Ibid.*, pp. 34–35.
[15]Walter Dorn, *Competition for Empire*, New York 1940, p. 192.
[16]Dambacher, *Dohm, op. cit.*, pp. 67–70.

increased political and economic understanding required more material than was then available in Germany. To counteract this need, Dohm collected material from whatever countries and sources he could find.[17]

As by the mid-seventies Dohm began to think of his career plans, we find that he had become quite attached to Prussia. He wrote to his friend Gleim in 1775 that he loved the land of Prussia and would gladly dedicate himself to it if he could attain a state position in statistics. The following year he wrote to Gleim that he was seeking an active position and not one in academic life:

> "I wish only to lead an active life, for the academic way pleases me less and less because of its monotony, intrigues, and the like. I believe I have now accumulated sufficient theory."[18]

Nevertheless, in 1776 Dohm accepted a professorship in finance and statistics at Cassel.[19]

In 1779, Dohm entered the Prussian civil service under the sponsorship of the foreign minister, Ewald Friedrich von Hertzberg, whom he had previously met in Berlin. Dohm was engaged in a dual capacity as a registrar of the archives and as a counsellor in the department of foreign affairs. His archival responsibilities placed him in charge of the Silesian, West-Prussian, and Ostfriesland files. Dohm was apparently well-integrated into the enlightenment circles of Berlin, and he was a member of several closed societies in which enlightenment personalities gathered regularly. Thus, Dohm frequented the *Montags-Club* and in 1783 participated in the founding of the better-known and exclusive Society of Friends of the Enlightenment, which conducted its meetings in secret and devoted its discussions to matters of enlightenment and "human welfare". Members of the Society of Friends included the publisher Friedrich Nicolai, the theologians Johann Joachim Spalding, Johann Samuel Diterich, Wilhelm Teller, and Johann Friedrich Zöllner, the jurist Karl Suarez, Johann Möhsen, physician to the king, and the economist Karl August von Struensee.[20] A few months after his return to Berlin, Dohm was approached by Moses Mendelssohn to write a memoir on behalf of the Jews of Alsace.[21]

II. DOHM'S TREATISE ON THE JEWS

In 1780, the Alsatian Jewish leader Herz Cerfberr turned to Moses Mendelssohn with a request for assistance in combatting a wave of popular antisemitism and repressive state measures that were seriously damaging Jewish finances and threatening Jewish safety. In 1777 and especially in 1778, Alsatian peasants who had taken loans from Jewish moneylenders began to submit falsified receipts indicating partial or even full repayment of the loans. The receipts were made

[17]*Ibid.*, p. 52.
[18]*Ibid.*, p. 12.
[19]Two years later Dohm was given an opportunity to join the Austrian civil service on the condition that he convert to Catholicism. According to Gronau, *Dohm, op. cit.*, pp. 59–60, because of the tensions at that time between Prussia and Austria, Dohm rejected the offer.
[20]Dambacher, *Dohm, op. cit.*, pp. 26–28, and Alexander Altmann, *Moses Mendelssohn, A Biographical Study*, London 1973, pp. 653–656.
[21]*Ibid.*, pp. 449–461.

out in Hebrew characters, giving an appearance of authenticity. The phenomenon of submitting forged receipts was not new, but previously had generally involved only isolated incidents. In Alsace, the deceit turned into a wide-spread social movement.[22]

The number of receipts involved indicated that not individuals but a group was responsible, and the preparation of Hebrew receipts precluded the possibility of disorganised imitations. Investigations indicated that among those involved were a few converts from Judaism who had rendered their services and that the conspiracy against the Jews was directed by François Hell, the bailiff of Landser in Upper Alsace. Hell was arrested in February 1780 for his involvement in the receipt affair and for his antisemitic pamphlet which had appeared anonymously in 1779. In that work, Hell characterised the Jews not only as the killers of Christ, but also, at least throughout the previous century, as the murderers of children as well. Hell admitted that the forgery of receipts was morally wrong, but was justified as benefiting the Christian peasants against the Jews.[23]

Even with the exposure of the affair and Hell's arrest, Alsatian Jewry still faced considerable difficulties and threats. Court cases to adjudicate the validity of the receipts resulted in new expenses and although these decisions were often in favour of the Jewish creditors, conditions for repayment of the original debts were relaxed and payment spread over long-term periods. Relationships between Jews and peasants obviously suffered as a result of the entire episode, and it was within this tense atmosphere that Cerfberr turned to Mendelssohn for his assistance.

In 1780, Dohm collaborated with Moses Mendelssohn in preparing the memoir on behalf of the Jews of Alsace that had been requested by Cerfberr. The following year Dohm issued a longer treatise, *Über die bürgerliche Verbesserung der Juden*, which included a more comprehensive programme on how best to make the Jews useful members of society. In that work, Dohm described the Jews of his time as corrupt, and Judaism as encouraging separation between Jews and others, but he explained that these adverse characteristics were the responsibility of Christians, who for centuries had persecuted and restricted the Jews, and of the states, which had failed to rescue the Jews from these oppressions. The Jews themselves were no different from any other people, and any group of people would have been affected the same way by the policies that were employed against the Jews.

> "Everything the Jews are blamed for is caused by the political conditions under which they now live, and any other group of men, under such conditions, would be guilty of identical errors."[24]

[22]Zosa Szajkowski, *The Economic Status of the Jews in Alsace, Metz, and Lorraine*, New York 1954, pp. 123–140.
[23]Hell's pamphlet is discussed briefly in Arthur Hertzberg, *The French Enlightenment and the Jews*, New York 1968, pp. 287–288.
[24]The work has been reissued in German combined with Dohm's second part discussed below: *Über die bürgerliche Verbesserung der Juden*, Hildesheim 1973. References to the initial treatise are from the English translation: Christian Dohm, *Concerning the Amelioration of the Civil Status of the Jews*, translated by Helen Lederer, Cincinnati 1957, p. 19.

The idea that the Jews were victims of historical circumstances was certainly not new. Dohm's contribution to the discussion lay primarily with the role he entrusted to the State in the improvement of the Jewish condition. First, the State was responsible for the wrongs of the past. The continued tension between Christians and Jews "is the fault of the governments which were unable to reduce the friction between the religious principles separating them and could not incite in the hearts of Jews and Christians alike a patriotic feeling which should long ago have abolished the prejudices of both groups".[25] It was now the task of the State to rectify the situation.

> "The great and noble business of the government is to mitigate the mutually exclusive principles of all these varied groups so that they will not harm the greater union which comprises all of them . . ."[26]

Dohm's programme was based on the premise that by increasing the liberties allowed the Jew, the Jew himself would respond and shed the barriers of separation.

> "More than anything else a life of normal civil happiness in a well ordered State, enjoying the long-withheld freedom, would tend to do away with clannish religious opinions. The Jew is even more man than Jew, and how would it be possible for him not to love a State in which he could freely enjoy it."[27]

Dohm presented his programme in nine points which emphasised equal opportunities in pursuing a livelihood and in attaining education. Maintaining that it had been the exclusive dependence on trade that had adversely affected the Jewish character, Dohm reasoned that without occupational restrictions Jews would freely diversify themselves, thus breaking their concentration in the commercial sector. The State should undertake to ensure that Jews received appropriate instruction in moral education. This might be done in Jewish or in Christian schools. Dohm presented the educational process as two-directional, as Christians would also have to be educated to overcome the common prejudices that are so strongly maintained. Jews should be guaranteed freedom of religion, including the right to build synagogues. Dohm also called for the continued judicial autonomy of the Jewish community in cases between Jews and the right of the community as an ecclesiastical society to issue bans. Among other matters Moses Mendelssohn strongly objected to the right of excommunication. With Dohm's agreement, Mendelssohn expressed his point of view in the introduction to a German translation of Menasseh Ben Israel's *Vindication of the Jews*, which was issued in 1782.

Altogether Dohm wrote three essays on the Jews during this period: the *mémoire* on Alsatian Jewry, his 1781 essay on the improvement of the Jews, and a second edition which appeared in 1783 and included a selection of critiques of the treatise together with Dohm's responses. Dohm wrote on the subject of the Jews because he had been requested to do so by Moses Mendelssohn, yet his interest

[25] *Ibid.*, p. 20.
[26] *Ibid.*, p. 12.
[27] *Ibid.*, p. 14.

in the subject went well beyond that relationship. In the introduction to the 1781 treatise, Dohm indicated that he had long planned to write a history of the Jews. Furthermore, while Mendelssohn requested Dohm's participation in writing the *mémoire* on behalf of Alsatian Jewry, Mendelssohn's role in the 1781 treatise on the Jews is less clear. Also, Dohm maintained his involvement still further with the additional and enlarged second edition in 1783.[28]

What were the reasons for Dohm's interest in the Jews? Dohm revealed no philo-Judaism of the kind that occasionally surfaced in England and influenced some to work on behalf of Jewish rights. Indeed, his attitude towards contemporary Jews was contemptuous.[29] Yet the Jews were a fitting subject for his pen. They provided an excellent subject for the comparative historical analysis to which Dohm was inclined. Furthermore, the issue of the Jews had emerged in German society even prior to Dohm's works, and by joining that debate,[30] Dohm offered his prescription of how to improve – not just the Jews – but German society in general.

In Dohm's earlier plan to write a history of the Jews he had intended to study the moral and political conditions of the Jews and the reciprocal influences in the various periods and countries in which they had dwelt; the results of the various constitutions of these nations; the effects on their character which derived from the economic restrictions; their influence upon the industry, trade, and mores of their environments; and the influences that changed their original mentality.[31] The Jews, with their long history of global dispersal, had lived under a wide range of political systems. By comparing the effects of these systems on the Jews and their religion, one had an example to hand by which to judge the efficacy of diverse political structures. Whether Dohm had reached this conception years before or only after Mendelssohn had requested his participation in preparing the Alsatian memoir, he has clarified for us part of his own scholarly interest in the Jewish discussion.

There were also professional reasons for Dohm to pursue the topic of the Jews. When Mendelssohn requested Dohm's assistance in preparing the French *mémoire*, Dohm was a young civil servant, still under thirty years of age who had just recently returned to Berlin. Dohm enjoyed no professional advancement from that undertaking. The *mémoire* was not publicly circulated, and in any case was prepared anonymously. He did receive financial compensation from Cerfberr, and this we know from his letters to Nicolai was of considerable importance to him.

The new treatise offered additional inducements. Here was an opportunity to

---

[28]The relationship between Mendelssohn and Dohm is best described by Altmann, *Mendelssohn, op. cit.*, pp. 49–61 and in 'Letters from Dohm to Mendelssohn', in *Salo Wittmayer Baron Jubilee Volume*, Jerusalem 1974, vol. I, pp. 39–62. Altmann maintains that Mendelssohn also urged Dohm to write the full treatise. Although this certainly seems plausible, I have not seen any direct evidence of this. On Nicolai's encouragement to Dohm, see Ludwig Geiger, 'Aus Briefen Dohms an Nicolai', *Zeitschrift für die Geschichte der Juden in Deutschland*, V (1890), p. 76.

[29]See, for example, Dohm, *Amelioration, op. cit.*, p. 18 and *Verbesserung, op. cit.*, II, pp. 152–153.

[30]On some of the main contributions to that debate, see Volkmar Eichstädt, *Bibliographie zur Geschichte der Judenfrage*, Hamburg 1938, vol. I, pp. 6–7.

[31]Dohm, *Verbesserung, op. cit.*, I, pp. 1–2.

publish a work of his own, with Cerfberr again providing financial arrangements and Nicolai interested in publishing the work. True, as we have seen, Dohm was no novice to enlightenment circles, but the letters from Dohm to both Mendelssohn and Nicolai demonstrate Dohm's preoccupation with the details and adventure of publication. The letters are full of financial agreements and technical arrangements. Dohm was preoccupied with becoming an author, far more than he was with the Jews. The Jewish issue was being written about and debated, and Dohm joined that debate in part in order to express his own ideas on how both the State and the Jews should be reformed.

III. AN ENLIGHTENMENT APOLOGIA

Christian Dohm's treatise on the Jews does not fit the more common explanations that have been given for the gradual change in attitudes towards the Jews in the seventeenth and eighteenth centuries. What historical forces played a role or are manifested in Dohm's work? Much of Dohm's programme is concerned with the potential impact of economic opportunities on the Jewish character. Several years before, Dohm had attacked the physiocratic school of economic thinking, and so one might well have expected from Dohm a mercantilist defence of Jewish utility quite similar to the arguments put forth in England earlier in the century. But Dohm's treatise maintains, if anything, an anti-mercantilist perspective, as it absolutely discourages Jewish commercial activity.

Dohm's attitude towards contemporary Jewry revealed scorn and distance. True, Dohm distanced himself even further in subsequent exchanges after his book appeared, but even in the original treatise there are several derogatory references of moral suspicion. Dohm argued that moral behaviour derived in part from one's economic endeavours: "Every kind of occupation and trade has some special effects on the way of thinking and on moral character." Excessive love of profits and unfair business practices were pronounced in the Jewish character because of their exclusive concentration in commerce. Dohm explained these defects as the combined result of historical oppression and of Jewish economic concentration within the commercial realm.

> "But, as I remarked already, all these crimes do not stem from the national character of the Jews, but from the oppressed state in which they live, and are in part consequences of the profession to which they have been exclusively restricted."[32]

Dohm, therefore, was hardly sympathetic to the idea of Jewish usefulness in commerce. In fact, within the presentation of his programme for improving the Jews, Dohm urged that ways be found to limit Jewish commercial involvement.

> "It might even be useful, in order to achieve this great purpose, if the government would first try to dissuade the Jews from commercial occupation, and endeavour to weaken its influence by encouraging them to prefer such kinds of earning a living as are most apt to create a diametrically opposed spirit and character – I mean artisan occupations."[33]

[32]Dohm, *Amelioration, op. cit.*, pp. 51–52.
[33]*Ibid.*, pp. 61–64. The quotation is from p. 61 (English here slightly amended).

Dohm's preference for the artisan occupations was expressed in profound admiration: "In fact, the life of a skilled craftsman is perhaps the purest happiness to be found in our civil society."[34] Dohm was, however, less conclusive about the moral advantages of agriculture for the character of the peasant.

> "The occupation of the peasant is very different from that of the artisan in that it does not offer the same certain and always equal compensation for industry . . . Most peasant families remain loyal to the soil, they tend to cling to old customs, a simple way of life, and remain in happy ignorance of the many new things the city dwellers think necessary. A laudable aversion to new customs and new luxuries (which a wise government should not try to change) often helps to maintain the peasant in the same happy condition which his ancestors have taught him to enjoy. The majority of peasants are therefore less corrupt, more good-natured, and, if the political conditions are not too oppressive, more noble in their thinking and more hospitable than the artisans, especially than those living in large cities."[35]

So far Dohm certainly sounds surprisingly sympathetic for an opponent of physiocratic thinking, and this conclusion is only partially marred by what follows:

> "However, the political conditions in most European states are such that they leave the peasant, after he has paid his taxes to the state and his landlord, hardly more than is needed for his daily necessities, and he differs from the artisan only in this – and to his disadvantage – that his occupation seldom allows him to rise to better financial status."

Interestingly, the analysis presented in Dohm's treatise does not prescribe artisanship as representing the most useful economic contribution to the state, but rather as the most effective occupational force for achieving moral reform of the Jewish character. Although Dohm emphasised the notion of increasing Jewish usefulness, he did not measure that utility in terms of economic value, but rather endeavoured to bring about moral change. Of course, that moral improvement was Dohm's primary objective underscores the *double entendre* contained within his title on the "improvement of the Jews". That he chose artisanship as the best means towards that objective reflects Dohm's particular economic outlook which rejected both the extreme position of Physiocracy, that only *Landwirtschaft* represented economic productivity, and that of Mercantilism, with its corresponding emphasis on the primary importance of trade.[36]

To explain Dohm's position exclusively in terms of his economic position is, therefore, unsatisfying. Such an explanation would also be thoroughly incomplete. Dohm's primary position on how to reform the Jew was steeped in his political outlook. Despite his rather significant hesitations regarding equal opportunities for Jews in public service, it would be remiss to ignore that Dohm repeatedly emphasised the primary role of political improvement in changing the Jewish condition.

Thus, it was representative of Dohm's thinking that the first element in his nine-point programme stated that it is necessary "to give them equal rights with

---

[34] *Ibid.*, p. 53.
[35] *Ibid.*, pp. 55–56. (English slightly amended).
[36] On Dohm's economic thinking, see Mordechai W. Rapaport, *Christian W. Dohm: der Gegner der Physiokratie und seine Thesen*, Berlin 1908, *passim* and Dambacher, *Dohm, op. cit.*, for example, pp. 99–106 and 133.

all other subjects". Here Dohm differed radically from Joseph II's *Toleranzedikt*, where expanded political rights were explicitly denied to the Jew.

The treatise on the Jews was not the analytical history Dohm had once conceived of writing; rather, it was primarily a prescriptive work on how best to deal with a problem in German society.[37] Yet not so far removed from Dohm's original plan of a comparative history, he still sought to demonstrate that the Enlightenment provided the best tools for alleviating the Jewish situation. Thus, he used his essays on the Jews to provide a concrete example of the efficacy of enlightened government. Indeed, Dohm was emphatic in the second edition that his purpose had not been to represent the Jew of his day or to have written an *apologia* on their behalf:

> "This was not so much to take up the cause of the oppressed Hebrews, but of humanity and of governments. I did not wish to stir pity for the former, nor to solicit a better treatment for them; but to demonstrate that common sense and common humanity as much as the interests of civil society demand this better treatment."[38]

What were those principles of the Enlightenment that according to Dohm guaranteed the eventual successful integration of the Jew into European society? The axiom of Dohm's programme was that Jews were human beings like all others and, thus, subject to the same laws of human behaviour as any other being. In the treatise, Dohm has posed the question whether once the Jew was treated like all citizens, he would under such different circumstances still be the object of hatred. When one of his critics answered this rhetorical question: "Ja, weil der Jude Jude sey . . .", Dohm responded in Part Two:

> "Everything, therefore, which education, enlightenment, and external circumstances have the power to make otherwise is for him in vain. I confess that I cannot comprehend the idea of an absolutely *unimprovable human race* . . . That seems to me a contradiction, counter to all of psychology, history, and human experience."[39]

In discussing his opponents' position that even were Dohm's proposals to be adopted, the Jew would remain as he had always been, Dohm explained that once the causes were removed, the effects would disappear. This was "in accordance with all the laws of psychology".[40] Dohm persisted in his claim that the historical treatment of the Jew had shaped his personality and even elements of his religion. While his opponents claimed that the Jews could not be improved,

---

[37]Those familiar with the treatise will realise that it does contain elements that echo Dohm's earlier formulation for a history of the Jews, such as the long legal discourses and the comparison of various Jewish communities of the period.

[38]Dohm, *Verbesserung, op. cit.*, II, pp. 151–152. "Diese war nicht sowohl die Sache der unterdrückten Hebräer, sondern der Menschheit und der Staaten zu führen. Ich wollte nicht Mitleid für jene erregen, nicht von diesen eine bessere Behandlung derselben erbitten, sondern zeigen, dass gesunde Vernunft und allgemeine Menschlichkeit, so wie das Interesse der bürgerlichen Gesellschaft, diese bessere Behandlung fordern.

[39]*Ibid.*, II, pp. 23–24. "Alles also, was Erziehung, Aufklärung, äussere Lage sonst vermögen, ist bey ihm umsonst. Ich gestehe, dass ich mir von einer durchaus unverbesserlichen Menschen-Rasse keinen Begriff machen kann; sie scheint mir ein Widerspruch wider alle Psychologie, wider alle Geschichte und Erfahrung."

[40]*Ibid.*, p. 153.

Dohm argued repeatedly: there are no exceptions to our principles.[41] Education and open employment opportunities would overcome the negative traits of the Jewish character. This was Dohm's way of demonstrating the efficacy of enlightenment principles. Even the Jew can be made useful and integrated into society. Toleration would succeed where oppression had failed.

IV. LATER PERSPECTIVES

Dohm's essay remained the focus of debate on the Jews for well past a decade.[42] This was true even while Jews and state officials alike were engaged during the years 1787–1792 in preparing memoranda with specific proposals for implementation. Dohm himself explained in the second edition that the wide-spread response to his essay was precipitated by the virtually simultaneous issuing of the *Toleranzedikt* by Joseph II. I think Dohm is partly correct, for Joseph, far more than Dohm, could raise the status of the issue from scepticism to legal reality. Mendelssohn's participation in the debate may also have contributed to the increased interest, both because of his own stature and because the participation of a Jew in the political discourse had its own way of indicating that Jews were indeed ready for increased responsibilities and rights.

Dohm soon disappeared from direct discussions of the Jewish issue. Thus, while under the leadership of David Friedländer, Prussian Jewry initiated several petitions and commissions during the late 1780s, Dohm's name never appears as one of the regime's representatives.[43] However, Dohm did continue to maintain the view that citizenship was not dependent on religious beliefs, and he proposed clauses to that effect in his draft of a constitution for Cologne in 1787.[44]

It was only forty years after the writing of his treatise on the Jews – near the end of his life – that Dohm returned to the Jewish issue in two different contexts. In his autobiographical reflections that Dohm issued during the years 1814–1819, he discussed the Jewish Question in his treatments of both Frederick II and Joseph II. In Dohm's view, Joseph's initiatives should have served as a model for the proper treatment of the Jews, yet Frederick had failed to confront the Jewish problem adequately, although he had extended toleration to a number of other minority groups.[45] In both discussions, Dohm reiterated his view that full opportunities would eventually have the desired effect on the Jews. Dohm also echoed his earlier position that immediate and full emancipation would prove too fast an undertaking. In Dohm's words, civil improvement

---

[41]*Ibid.*, and p. 10.

[42]See the list in Eichstädt, *Bibliographie, op. cit.*, pp. 8–15, and the comment in Dohm, *Denkwürdigkeiten meiner Zeit*, Lemgo 1814–1819, vol. II, p. 284n.

[43]On the efforts during this period, see Ismar Freund, *Die Emanzipation der Juden in Preussen*, 2 vols., Berlin 1912, vol. I, esp. pp. 35–63. Dohm had, however, left Berlin by this time, which may explain his absence from these bodies.

[44]Franz Reuss, *Christian Wilhelm Dohm's Schrift "Über die bürgerliche Verbesserung der Juden" und deren Einwirkung auf die gebildeten Stände Deutschlands*, Kaiserslautern 1891, pp. 11–12.

[45]Compare Dohm, *Denkwürdigkeiten, op. cit.*, vol. II, pp. 283–288 and vol. IV, pp. 480–488.

provided the slowest, but surest way to make the Jews a useful component of society.

It was on these grounds that Dohm had been criticised by Wilhelm von Humboldt in an essay of 1809. Humboldt argued that the peculiar situation of the Jews would best be solved by immediately eliminating all legal distinctions and compelling the Jews to conform with the demands of the State or to leave it. He attacked the very conception of law on which Dohm's entire programme was based:

> "The whole basis of the system of gradual emancipation is, in my opinion, grounded upon a theory of legislation which, though at one time accepted, has long since been properly abandoned. It is in fact one which regards legislation as a method of educating the citizen . . ."[46]

Dohm defended his position in a short memorandum he prepared for the discussions taking place at the Congress of Aix-la-Chapelle in 1818. He reviewed the opinions that he had set forth in his treatise of 1781, adding that these had now been "confirmed by forty years of experience". Summarising his position, that only an end to the adverse conditions under which Jews lived could lead to their rehabilitation, Dohm added:

> ". . . the amelioration of the Jews will necessarily follow such manner of treatment, but this change can only be brought about slowly; the effect of centuries cannot be destroyed in a few years."[47]

But it was to this gradual emancipation that Humboldt had strongly objected: "A gradual emancipation merely emphasises the segregation which it desires to abolish."[48]

Humboldt's view seems to reflect the influence of the intervening events in France, where the National Assembly had decided upon complete and immediate emancipation. In comparison, Dohm's treatise was in some ways a faint-hearted attempt to alleviate the Jewish condition. That is a harsh judgment, but considering that Dohm was in other matters an outspoken opponent of physiocratic thinking, with regard to the Jews he did not dispute the values of his opponents. His programme sought to make the Jews what they were not, while supplying no measure of appreciation for who they were or what they had contributed. Dohm the economist had prescribed diversification for the German economy, but his treatise directed the Jew to reconstitute himself into spheres of activity that German society did not need and certainly did not want the Jew to enter. Humboldt was correct: Dohm's moralising efforts only underscored Jewish deficiencies.

Yet Dohm marked a significant transition in the discussion on the status of the Jews. From the time of Simone Luzzatto's seventeenth-century apologetic treatise on behalf of the Jews of Venice up to Joseph II's Edict in Austria, the discussion had revolved around the issue of toleration. Most of Dohm's

---

[46]The important 1809 memo by Humboldt was published by Max J. Kohler in *Publications of the American Jewish Historical Society*, vol. XXVI (1918), pp. 103–115. Quotation is from pp. 104–105.
[47]*Ibid.*, pp. 87–88.
[48]*Ibid.*, p. 104.

precursors in Germany had dealt with economic rights. It was Dohm who moved the discussion forward to political rights as well, and it was in Dohm's formulation that the French Enlightenment adopted the question and, in less than a decade, passed the first acts of Jewish emancipation in the National Assembly. Ironically enough, if Germany had followed the French example, Dohm – with his commitment to gradual amelioration – would not have approved, but Germany did not adopt the French conception as reflected in Humboldt's critique. Dohm's treatise was a product of his times and of his place.

Problems and Limits of Assimilation
Hermann and Paul Wallich 1833–1938

BY WERNER E. MOSSE

Jews of the post-emancipation Diaspora find themselves placed between the twin poles of on the one hand the preservation of a form of Jewish identity, on the other the constant attraction of assimilation to a Gentile environment. Jewish families and individuals are subject to the rival gravitational pulls of forms of Jewish identification and the allurements of non-Jewish society. Inevitably, tensions occur for the individual who must establish an identity and, at the same time, achieve a degree of integration in the surrounding society. Both "self-determination" and the search for integration create problems – problems that are inter-related. Various factors are involved: influences of family and processes of socialisation, of sociability and informal networks, social control and pressures for conformity, religious belief, ethnic solidarity, marriage strategies and personal aspirations. From a balance of conflicting pressures and tensions there emerges both the individual's evolving concept of "identity" and his (or her) integration in society at large.

How, in these circumstances, does the individual face and resolve his or her problems of identity and integration? How does the interaction of a variety of factors shape the eventual outcome? How far is that outcome influenced by fortuitous circumstances, how far by individual choice? Which among many factors involved are the decisive ones? To understand the situation of the post-emancipation Jew in the Diaspora, it is necessary to analyse both the major influences tending to the preservation of Jewishness and those promoting its dilution.

With regard to the twin issues of "identity" and "integration" the German-Jewish economic elite could be seen as exemplary. Its members, thanks to their wealth, "respectability" and social prestige, were, for the Gentile middle and upper classes, at least potentially, the socially most acceptable (or least unacceptable) part of German Jewry. Accordingly, the "temptation" to abandon Jewish identity for the sake of a (perceived) closer integration in Gentile society was higher amongst them than amongst other segments (except for intellectuals) of the Jewish community. They enjoyed amongst Jews the widest choice with regard to sociability, occupation, "life style" and, if within fairly narrow limits, marriage options. More particularly was this the case with the generation of the "heirs" to economic achievement (and corresponding wealth), those born with

43

"silver spoons in their mouths". The "gilded youth" could, in fact, range from aspiring men of affairs seeking to follow in the parental footsteps (probably a majority) through others "distracted" by the lure of intellectual or artistic pursuits (a small but significant minority) to the playboys, wastrels and café-society types interested in fast cars, women and race-horses (another and somewhat larger minority). Before each lay diverse marriage options, the choice of Jewish, half-Jewish, baptised or, more rarely, Gentile partners. The choices made in various respects throw light on different attitudes towards issues of identity and integration.

Where individual histories can be studied in some detail, these reveal, on the one hand the forces making for the preservation of Jewish identity, on the other those pulling in the opposite direction. Subjectively, some autobiographical writings reveal the problems confronting the individual placed between the rival "pulls". In some instances, it is possible to study problems connected with the preservation of traditional Jewish observances, in others those arising from determined efforts at assimilation. In either case, due to external conditions, there were limits to what was possible. It is more particularly with the problems and limits of consistent assimilation that the present paper is concerned.[1]

The bankers Hermann and Paul Wallich, spanning between them more than a century (1833–1938), are remarkable not so much for the systematic "assimilationist" strivings shared with others than for the historical sense which led both to write memoirs[2] that are a boon to the historian. Hermann Wallich produced his autobiographical fragment in the nineties for the benefit of his children following his retirement from the directorate of the *Deutsche Bank* in the early development of which he had taken a leading part. His son Paul composed his frank autobiographical sketch, probably not intended to see the light of day, in 1916 at the age of only 34. Paul Wallich's widow Hildegard (née Rehrmann) in her turn published a volume of memoirs,[3] whilst his older son, Henry C. Wallich, added the story of the later lives of his father and grandfather. What emerges from these writings is a unique picture of the evolution of a German-Jewish family from the Orthodox household of a modest Jewish skin-merchant in Bonn to the tragic end by suicide of his banker grandson in Cologne.

Whilst the memoirs of Hermann Wallich touch on Jewish matters only incidentally, problems of assimilation play a large part in those of his son. The baptised son, in fact, was more conscious of the problem of his "Jewishness" than the unbaptised father had been. It was the son rather than the father, who was

---

[1]The present essay is, in fact, part of a trilogy to appear in the Year Book, illustrating divergent patterns of assimilation and integration.
[2]Hermann Wallich, *Aus meinem Leben*; Paul Wallich, *Lehr- und Wanderjahre eines Bankiers*; in *Zwei Generationen im deutschen Bankwesen 1833–1914*, Schriftenreihe des Instituts für bankhistorische Forschung e.V. Band 2, Frankfurt a. Main 1978. Paul Wallich's son Henry C. Wallich of the Federal Reserve Bank of the United States deserves the gratitude of historians for having sponsored the publication of these invaluable memoirs. Footnote numbers shown in italics following quotations refer to the page numbers of *Zwei Generationen, op. cit.*
[3]Hildegard Wallich, *Erinnerungen aus meinem Leben*, Altenkirchen 1970.

confronted to the full with the problems and limits of assimilation in Imperial Germany. It was the son also who came to face the issue with the greater honesty.

Between them the writings of the two Wallichs, covering the movement from traditional Jewish culture to extreme assimilation, throw light on factors favouring the preservation of Jewish identity as well as on others tending to dilute it. In so doing, they illustrate on the one hand the mechanics of the process of assimilation, on the other its problems and its limits.

I

Hermann Wallich was born on 28th December 1833 in Bonn. Both parents, in his own words, were descendants of "respectable" Jewish families. The paternal one had resided on the Rhine for centuries and produced some distinguished doctors. The mother's family, recent immigrants from Alsace, enjoyed lesser local prestige. Wallich's father conducted, together with some relatives, a once flourishing trade in skins. However, he had neither energy nor skill to develop the business with the times. It was in slow but relentless decline. Never energetic, the father's will had been further sapped by several legacies that had freed him from immediate want. Wallich describes his outlook:

> "Meine Familie väterlicherseits begnügte sich mit der patriarchalischen Existenz des orthodoxen Judentums. Ihre Ansprüche an das Leben waren gering und im hergebrachten Schlendrian wurde das zum Leben nötige leicht verdient . . ." (*32*)

More important than material success, however, was strict religious observance:

> "Die strenge Befolgung der durch den Ritus befohlenen Religionsübungen war die wesentliche Beschäftigung und füllte fast das Leben der damaligen Familienmitglieder aus." (*32*)

The decline of his business was borne by Wallich's father with a resignation facilitated by his religious feelings. Inclined to melancholy by the prospect of gradual impoverishment and increasing ill-health he was always cheered by his religion, the bright spot in his life. As his son would later recall:

> "Wenn er am Vorabend des Sabbats sein Gebet verrichtete und bei der Abendtafel, die bei Festtagen reichlich mit Silber (alte Erbstücke der Familie) geschmückt war, im Kreise der Seinen den Segen austeilte, tauschte er mit keinem Fürsten und fühlte sich über die Massen glücklich in der Ausübung seiner Religionspflichten." (*32*)

"Ich habe ihn", his son would write many years later, "später oft um diese Glaubenszuversicht beneidet und um die Leichtigkeit, mit der er alle Schwierigkeiten des Lebens durch den Trost der Religion überwand!" (*32*)

Thus lived Hermann Wallich's father in the strict observance of the Jewish tradition. Very different, however, was Wallich's mother, the immigrant from Alsace.

> "Aufgeweckt, heiter veranlagt, beliebt bei allen Freunden und Bekannten, erkannte sie sofort die Bedeutung der deutschen Erziehung, so dass ihr Einfluss uns Kinder alsbald von jüdisch-

orthodox erzogenen Kindern der Nachbarschaft trennte. Der mir nach der Geburt erteilte Name war das Symbol der neuen Zukunft, zu welcher sie uns erziehen wollte. (*32f.*)

It was the mother who thus laid the foundations for future assimilation. It was not, in fact, unusual for "assimilationist" impulses to originate primarily from women.

Wallich's mother, whose character had not been understood by her husband, died early after which Wallich senior contracted two further marriages. Her influence, however, persisted in the form of her brothers who took partial charge of the neglected half-orphans. Two of the uncles were already prosperous bankers abroad. First Wallich's older brother left home "to receive a better education than was appropriate to the family's situation". Then, in 1846 came the turn of the twelve-year-old Hermann. The uncles considered it desirable that his education at a private school should be continued at a secondary institute. They chose an institution in Bonn at which Wallich became a day-boarder. The syllabus was "simple and solid". Besides "Gottesfurcht" (it was a strictly Protestant establishment), pupils were taught love for the fatherland and its rulers. A further step in an "assimilationist" direction had been taken.

Wallich became a staunch Conservative. Though still an "immature boy", he yet recognised the seriousness of the events of the year of revolutions. His monarchical sense, he writes, was already sufficiently developed to disapprove of revolutionary excesses. 1848, the mature Wallich later observes, was the time also of the emancipation of the Jews. Though unexceptionable (nicht zu missbilligen) in principle, it would yet, in practice, also produce negative results. An interesting reflection follows:

> "In unserem kleinen bescheidenen Kreis hatten wir von einer Bedrückung der Juden nichts gespürt, die Familie meines Vaters erfreute sich eines Ansehens, das nur ein langer Aufenthalt im Lande einflössen kann; unser Ehrgeiz ging nicht weiter, als ungestört in der Ausübung unseres religiösen Kultes zu bleiben. Der Ehrgeiz, eine öffentliche Rolle im politischen Leben zu spielen, lag uns fern." (*35f.*)

Regrettably, Wallich observes, such sentiments were not generally shared. From this time, he claims, dates the change which enabled Jews to embark upon careers hitherto closed to them. A new generation grew up which, less modest than its fathers, regarded the concessions made to them as a right. An excess of freedom led them into transgressions which, unforeseen by them, would bring grave troubles on their co-religionists. Wallich's reflections are interesting in a number of ways. In the first place, there is the somewhat idealised description of a modest Jewish family in the *Vormärz* period and its integration in surrounding society – admittedly in the relatively tolerant Rhineland. Orthodox Jews then made no demands for equal rights and careers open to the talents. There follows the "Umbruch" of 1848 provoking in Wallich (retrospectively) ambivalent feelings. Interestingly, he blames certain abuses, by some Jews, of the newly gained freedom for the later wave of antisemitism. It is an attitude perhaps not wholly exceptional among those who grew up during *Vormärz*. What Wallich in fact appears to commend, in theory and retrospectively, is Jewish integration without assimilation. Whether this was indeed a viable model is, of course, an open question.

II

In 1849 Wallich's father died. The following year, one of the uncles living in Cologne apprenticed him to the modest banking firm of Cassel and Kirchberg whose senior partner, Jacob Cassel, had been a friend of Wallich's mother. Wallich describes his departure from Bonn:

> "... still weinend über meine Verlassenheit drückte ich mein Antlitz in die Kissen des Eisenbahnwagens, der mich an meinen Bestimmungsort trug. Mein ganzes Hab und Gut war neben einer dürftigen Ausstattung in einem kleinen Handkoffer, der auch meine Schulbücher barg, enthalten." *(37)*

It was the first step on the road to a prestigious directorship of the *Deutsche Bank* and a fortune of many millions.

It was Wallich's relative poverty which influenced his motivation in a direction very different from that which had inspired his pious father. He writes:

> "Ich wusste, dass ich nichts besass, und dass von meinem Fleiss meine ganze Zukunft abhing. Dementsprechend fasste ich den festen Entschluss, vorwärts zu kommen und mir meine Unabhängigkeit zu erringen. Dieser Entschluss war richtig, und ich habe ihn mit eiserner Willenskraft ausgeführt." *(37)*

An economic motivation had thus replaced a religious one.

The price to be paid for material success was a high one – paid to a greater or lesser extent by many upwardly mobile (in economic terms) young Jews.

The resolve to succeed, Wallich writes:

> "... beherrschte zu sehr mein ganzes inneres Leben. Das Gefühl der langen Dauer bis zu seiner Verwirklichung vergiftete oder verbitterte mir meine schönsten Jugendjahre. Streng an den engen Familienkreis [of the Cassels – Wallich was "living-in"] angeschlossen, kannte ich nur meine Berufspflichten, in denen ich vollständig aufging. Kein Austausch mit den Ideen gleichaltriger Jugendgenossen, die ich entbehren musste, erhellte mein einförmiges Leben." *(37)*

Social graces also had to be sacrificed on the altar of business success:

> "Ich entbehrte die Freuden meines Alters, und der fortwährende Gedanke an meine materielle Zukunft machte mich melancholisch und wenig für frohe Geselligkeit geeignet. Die Folge davon war ein Mangel an gesellschaftlichen Formen, der zu einer gewissen Befangenheit Damen gegenüber ausartete und mich auch später nicht mehr verliess, obwohl ich eigentlich keine Abneigung gegen das schöne Geschlecht empfand." *(37)*

The reward for Wallich's sacrifices was a thorough and invaluable training in banking techniques. Soon, not yet eighteen, he had come to occupy the first position in the office. Old Jacob Cassel was displeased when at the end of his three-year apprenticeship, Wallich informed him that he intended to continue his training in the banking house of his uncle Cahen d'Anvers (originally plain Cahen, he had started his business in Antwerp) in Paris. In 1854, aged twenty-one, Hermann Wallich moved to the Paris of Napoleon III.

In fact, Wallich had paid a further hidden price for his successful apprenticeship in Cologne, that of religious conviction:

> "Meine Absicht Christ zu werden (Wallich does not state the reasons) konnte ich leider in meinem neuen Milieu nicht ausführen. Mein Prinzipal gehörte jener Richtung von Reformjuden an, die jeder Religion entbehrten, und so verfiel auch ich mangels anderweitiger

Anregung dem Rationalismus mit seinen üblen Folgen. Ich sollte es später bereuen, dass es so kam." (*37*)

Thus the later Wallich ascribes the withering away of his religiosity primarily to the influence of the Cassel household, where he took all his meals. "Meine Mahlzeiten nahm ich in der Familie, in der mich alle sehr liebten. Die übrige Zeit verbrachte ich in den Kontorräumen." (*38*) In fact, the influence of mother, uncles and school had cut Wallich off from his observant Jewish roots, as did that of the Cassel household. The latter, at the same time, had barred his way to conversion. Religious sentiment, in the circumstances – whether Jewish or Christian – could find little place in Wallich's life, despite what appears to have been a life-long craving. Later, when he could have converted – for reasons which will emerge – he had lost the wish to do so.

What kept Wallich within the Jewish fold was thus, essentially, his membership of a Jewish network; his apprenticeship, arranged by one of his uncles, in the Jewish banking house of Jacob Cassel, the owner of which, moreover, had been a "Jugendfreund" of Wallich's mother and his close association with the Cassel household which had frustrated his wish to become a Christian. In essence therefore, social connections had tied Wallich, even against his inclinations, to his Jewish identity.

III

After seven years in Paris followed by work for a Paris bank on the islands of Réunion and Mauritius and in China, Wallich, shortly before the outbreak of the Franco-Prussian war,[4] accepted an invitation from his old patron from his Paris days, Ludwig Bamberger, to assume the direction of a German overseas bank, presently to be part of the *Deutsche Bank*.

Wallich moved to Berlin, thus realising one of his childhood ambitions.[5] It would take the born Rhinelander (deficient in social graces) years to settle down in his new environment.[6] Already over forty, the *bon vivant* bachelor decided to start a family. At a dinner with an almost unknown acquaintance,[7] Wallich was placed next to the host's niece, "ein liebliches Mädchen mit angenehmen Gesichtszügen und sehr unterhaltend" (*129*) and twenty years his junior. In

---

[4]The war and its outcome Wallich, in spite of divided sympathies, greeted with delight: "Welch welterschütterndes Ereignis! Der Traum meiner Jugend erfüllt. Deutschland durch Preussen geeint." (*110*)

[5]"Als richtiger Provinzler war von Kindheit an Berlin mehr noch als Paris das Ziel meiner Wünsche gewesen . . ." (*115*)

[6]"Die Menschen waren nicht übertrieben liebenswürdig, meistens frostig kalt und zugeknöpft, wenig gastfrei. Es war die erste Stadt, in die ich ohne vorherige Bekanntschaften kam, und ich blieb ihr lange fremd." (*115*)

[7]The meeting between Wallich and his future wife shows an interesting conjunction of the operation of a Jewish network, pure chance and, perhaps, an element of contrived opportunity. Wallich had secured a job at a subsidiary bank for which he was responsible for Ernst Jacoby, son of an acquaintance from his club. Jacoby, to show his gratitude, felt obliged to ask Wallich to dinner. "Ich hatte mich lange gegen diese Einladung gesträubt, denn Herr Ernst Jacoby war berüchtigt wegen seiner schlechten Weine, und ich, als alter Junggeselle, war in diesem Punkt sehr empfindlich." (*129*) However, Wallich accepted in the end and was placed, at table, next to his future wife.

addition, Anna Jacoby had the inestimable merit of being the only child of and
heiress to a wealthy Jewish rentier. The courtship was brief; on 16th February
1875, the marriage was celebrated in a small circle of relatives and friends. It
does not appear to have been what one would describe as a love match.[8]

Anna, thanks partly to her musical talents, helped to enlarge Hermann
Wallich's social circle. Among the Wallichs' closest friends were Max Steinthal,
fellow director of the *Deutsche Bank*, and his wife. In the bank, Wallich rapidly
gained a prominent position, and could soon be described as its "second-in-
command". In 1878, Anna's father died, leaving to his heirs "a not inconsiderable fortune".[9] Hermann Wallich had become a wealthy man: his youthful
dream of economic independence had been realised.[10]

One shadow in the happy picture, besides Anna's weak health, was the
absence of children during the first five years of marriage. In 1882 however there
appeared, after a daughter, the long-awaited son and heir. He was given the
name of Paul, more than once chosen by Jewish parents for its programmatic
significance (Saint Paul). Together with his older sister, he was baptised into the
evangelical faith.

Eighteen years later, in the memoirs intended for his children, Wallich seeks to
explain (and justify) the step. In the process, he makes clear also his own attitude
towards the Judaism of his parents. His explanations, somewhat muddled and
more interesting than convincing, probably also contain the true reasons for his
decision, one not uncommon among Jewish parents. In fact, Wallich offers a
multiple explanation that ill-conceals his embarrassment.

The first strand in Wallich's explanation might be described as "historical".
He had early understood, he writes, "dass der jüdischen Überheblichkeit, die
sich überall breit machte, eine fürchterliche Reaktion folgen musste". (*132*) His
fears were only too soon to be realised. He had just begun to found a family when
the first signs of the antisemitic movement made their appearance. Even if he
had expected this, he was still surprised by the actual event and determined not
to become its victim. Although the movement could not touch him personally,[11]
he was resolved to avoid even the remotest possibility. Having spent most of his
youth abroad where friends had never enquired about his confession, he decided
to emigrate in face of the rising intolerance. His wife was unwilling to leave
Germany.[12] As Wallich felt obliged to respect her reasons, he agreed to drop his

[8]". . . aber heute nach 25jähriger Dauer können wir beide mit der Ehe zufrieden sein." (*129*)
[9]He brought his heirs "in den Besitz eines nicht unansehnlichen Vermögens." (*130*) A consequence of
this "unexpected wealth" at a relatively young age was that, at least for a time, the professional
assiduity of the "workaholic" Wallich slackened. "Von dieser notwendigen Sparsucht befreit, ward
ich bequemer in meiner Lebenshaltung, weniger eifrig in meinen geschäftlichen Pflichten." (*130*)
[10]In 1894, Wallich would retire from the directorship of the *Deutsche Bank* and, whilst continuing as a
member of its board, would henceforth live the life of a wealthy rentier.
[11]"Obwohl ich teils durch meine Stellung an der Spitze eines grossen Bankinstituts [Wallich was, as
indicated, in fact the second man after Georg (von) Siemens], teils durch meine persönlichen
Beziehungen, von jedem nachteiligen Einfluss des Antisemitismus bewahrt blieb, wollte ich auch
jeder Möglichkeit aus dem Wege gehen, jemals davon berührt zu werden." (*133*)
[12]"In Berlin geboren und erzogen, weigerte sie sich entschieden, ihr Vaterland zu verlassen und ihre
Zukunft in der Fremde, vielleicht bei reichen, hochmütigen Verwandten [in view of Wallich's
wealth hardly a valid argument] . . . zu suchen." (*133*)

plan. However, he consented to remain in Germany – the connection is somewhat obscure – only on condition that should their marriage be blessed with children, these would be baptised and brought up in the evangelical faith. That, as an historical "explanation", even if not entirely convincing, would have sufficed.

However, Wallich felt impelled to add a religious justification. Even though he could not himself, out of respect for the memory of his ancestors, think of changing his religion, he had no right to put into the world children without a faith. Instead of "bad Jews", he wished to make them into good Christians.[13] Judaism, in his view had become archaic, materialism had long since undermined religious ideas and it would therefore be foolish to become a martyr to a cause which no longer commanded one's full allegiance.[14] The religious explanation was, of course, weak. If Wallich did indeed – though he probably did not – consider Christianity to be the superior religion, why did he not convert himself? As to the charge that Judaism had been undermined by materialism was this not true also, to a large extent, of Christianity?

Perhaps aware of the weakness of the religious argument, Wallich also resorted to a parallel civic explanation – the true "assimilationist" argument. Following the ritual disclaimer of considerations of material advantage, he defended the step on the grounds of conformity with the beliefs of the majority:

> "Nicht äusserer Vorteil hat mich zu diesem Schritt geleitet, sondern der Gedanke, meinen Kindern eine wirkliche Religion zu geben, sie von der Ausnahmestellung zu befreien und sie aufgehen zu lassen in der Allgemeinheit des Landes, in dem sie geboren waren." (*134*)

In seeking to reinforce the "civic" argument, Wallich again enmeshed himself in contradictions:

> "Es blieb nur der Wunsch beider Eltern, die Kinder gut zu erziehen, um sie zu brauchbaren und nützlichen Mitgliedern der Gesellschaft zu machen [which evidently *as Jews* they could not be – and how did matters stand with the parents?]. Durchdrungen von diesem Gefühl, liessen wir unsere Kinder taufen und in der christlichen Religion erziehen, und es wird hoffentlich der Erfolg zeigen, dass wir das Richtige getroffen haben." (*132*)

In fact, the multiplicity of Wallich's arguments employed as justification *vis à vis* his teen-age children betrays his embarrassment. As a rationalist, he could not logically use the argument of religious conviction (or "truth") and had he done so, he would have been unable to defend his (and his wife's) decision to remain a Jew. The "assimilationist" argument again he could hardly use convincingly without becoming a Christian himself. What kept Wallich within the Jewish fold was familial piety for the memory of his ancestors as well as the rationalism imbibed in the house of the Cassels which made conversion to

---

[13]"Wenn ich auch persönlich, aus Achtung vor dem Andenken meiner Vorfahren, an einen Glaubenswechsel nicht denken konnte, so hatte ich doch kein Recht, Kinder ohne Glauben in die Welt zu setzen. Statt schlechte Gläubige des Judentums wollte ich aus meinen Kindern gute Christen machen." (*133*)

[14]"Ich war zu der Erkenntnis gekommen, dass das Judentum sich überlebt, dass die Sucht nach materiellen Gütern längst die religiösen Ideen untergraben, dass es demnach töricht wäre, Märtyrer einer Sache zu sein, für die man nicht mehr das volle Gefühl hatte." (*133*)

Christianity (except from motives of pure opportunism which Wallich was neither capable of nor needed) impossible.

Did the Wallichs believe that, in baptising their children, they had broken the "Jewish connection", freed them from the position of "outsiders"? Would, in particular, the new Paulus become absorbed in the mass of the German people, a good Christian and a useful citizen?

IV

If Hermann Wallich's motivation had been primarily economic, that of his son lay in the social sphere. Paul Wallich, son of wealthy parents – though he would, throughout his life, work as a "practising" banker – had neither the need nor an overwhelming desire to increase the family fortune.

Instead, Wallich's overriding object was to raise his family's social standing ("Hebung des sozialen Standards der Familie"). To achieve this, he had set himself three objectives: membership of a student corps, the patent of an officer of the reserve and marriage to a wife "of family" ("von Familie") (*167*). It was to these tasks that he would single-mindedly devote his youth.

Such social goals – in effect nothing less than entry into the German "upper-class" – raised in a new form (as it did for some others like him) the twin questions of identity and integration. On the one hand, there was the question of the extent to which Wallich would be able to "shed" his Jewish background. He was indeed formally a Christian and had been brought up as such. His socialisation had been completed in the Christian-aristocratic boarding school of Pforta, the nearest German approach to an English public school. Parental wealth, moreover, and the prestige and connections of Hermann Wallich as a director of the *Deutsche Bank* (on occasion confused by the more innocent with the *Reichsbank*) could not but facilitate the attainment of his objectives.

On the other hand, however, Paul Wallich, if against his wish, remained part of a Jewish network. Moreover, he could conceal from himself as little as from the outside world the fact that he was the son of a Jewish bank director. This, in the eyes of many, brought with it the double stigma of Jewish origin and relatively recent wealth. Wealth, in any case, when derived from banking rather than manufacture, was held (at any rate in theory) in relatively low esteem by many members of the German upper class wedded to pre-industrial values. The reception the wealthy Jewish banker's son with his snobbishness and unbridled social ambitions would meet at the hands of the Gentile "upper class" was, to say the least, uncertain. Wallich's essentially Jewish "psyche", to which he himself alludes, would add yet a further complication.

Objectively, Wallich's experiences in his quest for social integration into the German upper class reveal the extent to which Wilhelminian society was prepared to accept into its midst fully assimilated and acculturated men of Jewish origin (the position with regard to women was somewhat different). They would throw light on the limits of possible assimilation.

V

Reading of German literature – typically – had made the young Wallich an enthusiastic idealist and led him to the decision to study philosophy. (His father at the same stage of his career had entered on the drudgery of his apprenticeship with Jacob Cassel.) His first university was to be either Heidelberg or Freiburg. In the former university a Gentile school-friend was a member of the corps *Westphalia* and Wallich hoped that through his good offices he might also be admitted.

> "In Heidelberg war damals Friedel Böttinger, der alte Mitsextaner und zuletzt auch Freund aus Pforta, bei dem Westphalen-Korps aktiv. Hätte er angeboten, einen dort unterzubringen, man wäre . . . nach Heidelberg gegangen. Friedel tat das, obwohl es ihm vielleicht sogar nahe gelegt wurde, nicht und kühlte damit die herzlichen Beziehungen nicht unerheblich ab." (*160*)

Since he did not want to walk "in mufti" at the side of his "green-capped" friend[15] Wallich gave his preference to Freiburg.

When Wallich went to Freiburg in 1901, he records, he was more of an antisemite than at any time afterwards.[16] At the university, he met a whole circle of old Berlin acquaintances of Jewish extraction, whom he sought "ostentativer als geschickt" to avoid.[17] Even here, however, he still made no fewer than three exceptions. By contrast he attempted – with minimal success – to establish relations with "aryan" and, above all, aristocratic fellow-students.[18] Three social circles – Wallich offers an interesting sociological analysis of his fellow-students – remained unattainable: the most desirable ones. Two others he disdained, including "die jüdische Gesellschaft, wahrscheinlich die geistvollste und gemüt-lichste". (*163*) An introduction from one of his father's colleagues to an agreeable family was ignored because the people were Jewish.[19] The overall result of Wallich's "social policy" was that, one or two older "Fachkollegen" – again of Jewish origin – apart, he had hardly any social contacts.

> "Dass ich das Schwergewicht meines Verkehrs in eine rein arische Richtung zu legen suchte, hat mir den ganzen Freiburger Aufenthalt verdorben. Ich habe dadurch eben gar keinen Verkehr gehabt." (*162*)

Wallich, in fact, stood socially between two worlds, one to which he would not and another to which he could not belong.

Membership of a "reputable" student corps was not to be thought of, as one timid effort revealed:

> "Hätte ich etwa verraten sollen, dass ich mich in einer unbedachten Stunde durch einen ganz fremden Herrn, der nur die Farbe meines Geldes aber nicht die meiner Haare kannte, den

---

[15]"Da man nicht ohne Mütze neben dem Grünbemützten . . . so nebenher laufen wollte, also nach Freiburg." (*160*)
[16]". . . war ich Antisemit mehr als ich es je wieder gewesen". (*161*) Wallich, of course, uses the term purely in a social sense, i.e. in terms of his social ambitions.
[17]It took him five years, Wallich adds, to remove the enmities he thus aroused.
[18]The details of Wallich's relations with "aryan" and aristocratic fellow-students, though interesting, cannot be considered here.
[19]"Eine Empfehlung von Mankiewitz an ein sehr nettes Haus – Sport und junge Mädchen – liess ich ostentativ unbenutzt, weil die Leute Juden waren." (*164*)

Hermann Wallich
(1833–1928)

Paul Wallich
(1882–1938)

Freiburger Rhenanen als Fuchs vorschlagen liess – unter der Hand, Gott sei Dank – und dass mir nach eingezogener Erkundigung abgewinkt wurde?" (*160*)

Freiburg, in short, proved a disappointment and following two further terms in Berlin, Wallich lost interest not only in his metaphysical studies but in abstract study in general. At the suggestion of his parents, he decided to do his military service. The patent of a reserve officer beckoned. "Reserveoffizier werden. Das stand als Leitstern über diesem ganzen Jahr [1902/1903] und den beiden folgenden." (*167*)

VI

Wallich's description of his military experiences is fascinating, but only some high-lights can be considered here. One day a Lieutenant Schramm, a well-disposed superior, took Wallich aside after duty and, after a few introductory remarks, asked him point-blank whether he was a Jew or baptised. When the situation had been explained to him, he remarked:

"Da Sie nicht mehr Jude sind, ist noch nicht alles verloren. Ich selbst kenne keine antisemitischen Vorurteile, aber Sie wissen, dass Sie hier im Regiment eine starke Strömung gegen sich haben, die wir bekämpfen müssen. Dazu werde ich sehen, Leutnant v. Sichart . . . für Sie zu interessieren; er hat Einfluss im Offizierskorps. Vielleicht . . . machen Sie trotz alledem bei uns gutes Geschäft." (*173*)[20]

And Wallich felt greatly encouraged.

Another officer of the squadron (Wallich was serving in an "inferior" cavalry regiment) at first viewed the Jewish banker's son with distrust. He was a racialist antisemite, but relented on receiving an assurance that Wallich intended to do his best to shed his race (which was hardly possible) and his "Asiatic culture".[21] Of the various officers and officer-cadets Wallich describes, whilst some were incorrigibly hostile, two at least became lasting personal friends. In the end, a majority of officers of the recently formed *Kombiniertes Jägerregiment zu Pferde* based in the city of Poznań overcame their scruples and voted to accept him as a "brother-officer". Wallich was delighted at his somewhat modest triumph.[22]

This "triumph" the later Wallich, in a mood of self-analysis, ascribes in the first place to his father's wealth, that is to say to the social prestige attaching to it.

---

[20]". . . diese Worte sind mir das ganze Jahr als Hoffnungsstern vor den Augen gewesen, und darum sind sie mir noch heute im Gedächtnis, als hätte ich sie gestern gehört." (*173*) Schramm's irony, like the sarcasm of some others, was directed not at the Jew but, by the impecunious officer, at the wealthy bank-director's son.

[21]". . . bis es denn einmal im Manöver zur Aussprache zwischen uns kam und er hörte, dass ich mich durch den Genuss der Taufe keineswegs als in einen Vollblutarier umgewandelt ansähe. Feiner kultiviert und mehr Rassenpsychologe als Schramm, sah er den Antisemitismus nicht mehr als Religionsfrage an – ein Standpunkt, den man übrigens heute selbst in der Armee nur noch selten findet – sondern war erst befriedigt, als er bei mir die löbliche Absicht zur Aufgabe auch meiner Rasse und asiatischen Kultur wahrnahm." (*175*)

[22]"Dadurch, dass ich dem zuerst doch ziemlich fernen Ziele allmählich immer näher kam und schliesslich mein Ziel erreichte, gehört das Jahr wohl zu meinen schönsten." (*168*)

Besides this, however, he was helped by his "Jewish psychology".[23] Wallich, at any rate when he wrote his memoirs, had come to terms with his "Jewishness" which he, like several of his fellow-officers, clearly considered a "racial" and not a religious matter. His interesting account of his social life during his year in Poznań, reminiscent of his Freiburg experiences, cannot be considered here.[24]

The delight at being able to put the "Leutnant der Reserve" on his visiting card, however, was of relatively short duration. It involved the increasingly irksome duty of participating in extended annual exercises in Poznań in uncongenial company. In relation to one of these, extending over eight weeks, Wallich recalls his discomfort at the lack of real contact with his "brother-officers".[25] An exercise in the autumn of 1910 proved particularly disagreeable.[26] From the two following ones Wallich asked to be excused. Then, in the autumn of 1912 he received a visit from the regimental adjutant who advised him to apply for transfer to the *Landwehr* (i.e. withdrawal from "active" service) as this would otherwise be initiated by the regiment. This he did – but just late enough to still have the right to use the precious designation *Leutnant der Reserve* for the announcement of his engagement.[27] Notwithstanding some satisfaction to his *ego*, the coveted title had yielded little of substance.[28]

Ironically, the major credit entry on Wallich's Poznań balance sheet appeared on the "Jewish" side of the ledger. It was the acquaintance with Joseph Jalowicz, a Jewish book dealer, the "awakener" of his life-long bibliophile interest:

> "Da erregte Joseph Jalowicz, der alte Antiquar am Markt in der Innenstadt, zuerst in mir das Interesse an ersten Ausgaben durch ein paar Bände von Kotzebue und Jean Paul. Der liebenswürdige und kenntnisreiche Mann, den die Rücksicht auf den eigenen Vorteil niemals hinderte, dem jungen Kunden und Schüler ehrlichen Rat zu geben, ist mir mit der Zeit ein lieber alter Freund geworden." (*185*)

Nor was book collecting under the guidance of Jalowicz Wallich's only intellectual interest. Besides publishing (privately) a volume of (apparently "risqué") verse, he also produced a family history ("eine Art von moralischer Familiengeschichte") based on some detailed research:

> "Die 'Rückblicke' . . . waren die Frucht der Familienforschung, die ich zusammen mit meinem Freund Hans Schultze seit dem Sommer 1902 getrieben. Damals waren wir zusammen den Rhein hinauf gezogen, zu Fuss, zu Schiff, per Bahn, von Köln über Bonn und

[23]"Es gehörte das zu den kleinen Triumphen meiner jüdischen Psychologie, über die ich nachher noch sprechen werde." (*169*) "Ich darf nicht leugnen, dass ich einen wesentlichen Teil meiner militärischen Erfolge meinen Künsten danke, durch die ich in meinem Dienstjahr oft ein anderer geschienen habe als ich war." (*182*)

[24]"Ich brachte ein halb Dutzend merkwürdig zusammengewürfelte Empfehlungen an Leute mit, die mich zu einem Teil ebenso brüskierten, wie ich den anderen Teil brüskierte." (*182*)

[25]". . . der unbehaglichen Stimmung, in die mich auch damals wieder die geringe innere Fühlung mit dem Regiment versetzte . . ." (*274*)

[26]"Von der stets empfundenen Unbehaglichkeit des kameradschaftlichen Lebens abgesehen, hatte ich diesmal noch dienstliche Schwierigkeiten." (*342*)

[27]" . . . es klappte noch gerade, dass ich mich in meiner Verlobungsanzeige als Leutnant der Reserve aufführen lassen konnte". (*343*) The official notification of the transfer stated, despite Wallich's application, that it was at the request of the regiment.

[28]"Damit hörten meine Beziehungen zu den Offizieren des Jägerregiments so gut wie ganz auf; wer konnte, bezahlte seine Schulden, und wer es nicht konnte, liess wenigstens nichts mehr von sich hören." (*343*)

Koblenz bis Mainz und Frankfurt, hatten Archive, Bibliotheken, Rabbiner und Kirchhöfe besucht. In den darauffolgenden Semestern hatten wir unsere Funde in der Berliner Bibliothek ergänzt, gesichtet und durch eine Reihe glücklicher Käufe von Manuskripten und Drucken, die Bezug auf die alte Ärztefamilie Wallich hatten, in der Tat ein recht reichhaltiges Material als Grundlage für eine Familiengeschichte zusammenbekommen." (*234*)[29]

It was for the social "antisemite", Paul Wallich, a curious "return to the roots" as well as an expression of the historical sense seemingly an heirloom of the Wallich family. Book-collecting, the composition of cynical verse and researches into (Jewish) family history, moreover, were hardly the pursuits of a typical officer of the *Kombiniertes Jägerregiment zu Pferde*. Wallich, by his own choice, was a man of two worlds and none, at the same time social snob and Jewish intellectual. By the next stage of his career at the latest, he had become conscious of the dichotomy.

VII

In the autumn of 1903, having achieved the qualifications of an officer of the reserve (formal election by the officers of the regiment was to follow later), Wallich returned to Berlin. He now turned to the question of a career designed, characteristically, to "underpin" his newly acquired status. For this, the professional pursuit of philosophy did not appear entirely appropriate.[30] On the other hand, much of his military "success" he attributed to his father's prestige as a bank-director.[31] Wallich's youthful idealism had, by this time, almost completely evaporated and he was ready to follow the advice of his ambitious mother to become a banker in his turn.[32] A combination of maternal prompting, his father's position and connections and the desperate quest for social status thus produced a decision neither wholly in accord with Wallich's temperament and inclinations nor with his membership of the generation of "heirs" with their often non-economic aspirations. Whilst Hermann Wallich disliked his son's lack of perseverance in his chosen course, two former colleagues and family friends considered the decision a downright mistake.[33] The immediate consequence was that Wallich decided to study economics (*Nationalökonomie*).

[29]Whilst Wallich knew no Hebrew, his friend Schultze was a Hebraist. It was under Schultze's name that the study appeared in the *Braun'sche Zeitschrift für die Geschichte des Judentums*. Ten copies were printed of a specially designed edition, presents for family members for the Christmas of 1905. One copy was reserved for Schultze.

[30]"Mir schien es, als nehme man sich nicht ganz satisfaktionsfähig neben einem Leutnant der Jäger zu Pferde aus, wenn man als Philosoph nicht mindestens einen der beiden ordentlichen Lehrstühle der Universität Berlins innehatte." (*186*)

[31]"Dem Philosophen in mir hatte manches Scherzwort beim Regiment gegolten, während die Basis meiner Erfolge der einstige Bankdirektorenstand meines Vaters gewesen war." (*186*)

[32]"Da sprach meine Mutter davon, wie in einer anderen Karriere als der wissenschaftlichen, namentlich in der Bankkarriere, die zahlreichen Beziehungen meines Vaters mir wesentlich und nützlich sein könnten. Und wie eine Erleuchtung ging mir der Gedanke von der Ökonomie, der Verwertung von Erfahrungen und Errungenschaften einer Generation für die folgende ein. . . . schien solche Ökonomie die nötige künftige soziale Stellung zu garantieren. – Als wir in der Bellevuestrasse ausstiegen, war ich entschlossen, Bankdirektor zu werden." (*186*f.)

[33]"Herr Max Steinthal wie Roland – Lücke führten, beide in richtiger Abschätzung der Verhältnisse . . . die Schwenkung auf äussere Motive, vor allem auf die Überredung der als klug und energisch bekannten Mutter zurück. Beide warnten vor dem Schritt, zu dem sie den wissenschaftlich und träumerisch veranlagten Jungen für nicht geeignet hielten." (*187*)

The second part of Wallich's student career, mainly in Munich under the aegis of the celebrated Lujo Brentano, cannot be considered here in detail. The old social problem persisted, as did the fatal Freiburg tactics. In Munich, Wallich shared a flat with Friedel Koch, son of an antisemitic director of the *Deutsche Bank*. Socially, he was torn between senior members – Jewish or of Jewish origin – of the seminar conducted by Brentano (a notorious philosemite) and former fellow-pupils of Koch from the aristocratic boarding school of Rossleben. With the Jewish scholars of the seminar Wallich shared first and foremost their intellectual interests – whilst disdaining their company on social grounds:

> "Dass die Leute uns nicht in das Haus kamen, dafür sorgte schon Koch, und mir schien ein gleichzeitiger Verkehr mit der schwarzhaarigen Intelligenz des Seminars und der blonden Crème der Gesellschaft unvereinbar." (*200*)

However, much as Wallich felt attracted to the "blonde crème", he could not but note their entire lack of intellect.

> "Diese Crème bestand in einer Reihe ehemaliger Schulkameraden von Koch, durchwegs junge Leute von stattlichem Äusseren, guten Manieren und gewandtem Auftreten . . . Vergebens aber bemühe ich mich, mehr als die blossen Namen der jungen Leute zu berichten. Wie fast immer, lag auch hier das Charakteristikum der Gentlemen in ihrem Mangel an Originalität." (*200*)

Wallich did not, in fact, share a single one of their characteristics. Again, as before, he found himself torn between two worlds without belonging to either.

After completing his studies, Wallich spent a year (1905/1906) in Hamburg as "Volontär" (trainee) in the trading firm of *Oetling Gebrüder*. Two Jewish banking houses, *E. J. Meyer & Co.* in Berlin and *M. M. Warburg & Co.* in Hamburg, had, in the friendliest of terms, refused Hermann Wallich's request to accept his son; on account, Wallich believes, of the fear that information he gained might later benefit the *Deutsche Bank*. Wallich senior had then applied to an old business associate, a Gentile, who, however reluctantly, had finally agreed:

> "Ich habe später erfahren, dass Adolf Oetling meinem Vater sein Jawort nicht gern gegeben hat. 'Ich habe nie einen Juden in mein Haus aufgenommen', soll er gesagt haben, 'aber einem so alten Kollegen kann ich es nicht abschlagen.'" (*215*)[34]

What is, perhaps, worth noting is that, in this instance, Wallich's baptism did not make the slightest difference. For Adolf Oetling (and others) though a Christian, he still remained a Jew.

Paul Wallich lovingly describes his undiminished social snobbery, limited successes and gradual disillusionment experienced during his Hamburg apprenticeship.[35] With curious detachment, he sums up his social existence:

> "Mein Leben in Hamburg war der typische Werdegang des langsam reüssierenden Strebers mit allen Sorgen und Besorgnissen, mit gelegentlichen Niederlagen, die man einstecken muss,

---

[34]Wallich speaks of the "natürliche Liebenswürdigkeit des alten Adolf Oetling, der meinem Vater trotz des Rassenunterschiedes, den er offenbar nicht vergass, persönlich befreundet war . . ." (*227*) Was Wallich, perhaps, over-sensitive in the matter of "Rassenunterschiede"? In any case, his own awareness is significant.

[35]"In der Tat habe ich kaum je – mit Ausnahme einiger militärischer Übungen – eine unerfreulichere Zeit als die Hamburger durchgemacht . . ." (*218*)

und schliesslich ein paar kleinen Erfolgen, die nach all den Mühen und Unannehmlichkeiten nicht mehr die Freude machen, die man sich erst von ihnen versprochen hat." (*218*)

Two aspects of Wallich's detailed account deserve mention. The first is his description of three Hamburg clubs. The most prestigious, the *Union Club*, was reserved for old gentlemen. The *Sportklub*, on the other hand, "das Rendezvous der jüngeren Lebewelt" (*224*) was, especially after the races, a hive of lively activity. As a gambling club, however, and on account of some Jewish members, it did not attract young men "of family".

> "Aber gerade wegen seines Rufes als Jeu-Klub und wegen der Rolle, die einige jüngsthin oder noch gar nicht getaufte Sportleute dort spielten, war von Hermann Münchmeyer, damals dem Doyen der Hamburger jungen Leute von Familie, Parole gegen den Sportklub ausgegeben. Dort sammelte sich der vergnügte und wahrscheinlich sehr amüsante Kreis der Morpurgo, Beit, Wächter, Behrens und Emden, die ausser für ihre sportlichen Passionen vielbeneideten Ruf wegen ihrer eleganten Mätressen und der von diesen veranstalteten Festlichkeiten genossen." (*224*)

From such partly "Jewish" pleasures, Wallich was self-excluded. Instead, Adolf Oetling Jr. introduced him in the *Harmonie* where foregathered "die solide Hamburger Jugend, die Söhne der Senatorengesellschaft". When Oetling junior had first announced "dass er einen jüdischen Volontär aus Berlin in der Harmonie werde einführen müssen" (*225*), there had been opposition. In the end, however, Wallich had been accepted, if unenthusiastically, at the table of "those from elsewhere" (*Tisch der Auswärtigen*). The few "Jewish" members, however, were hardly made welcome. The *Harmonie*, Wallich writes,

> ". . . war nicht so exklusiv, dass nicht einige Unerwünschte hätten Eingang finden können. Aber das Zusammenhalten der tonangebenden Elemente unter Hermann Münchmeyers Führung war stramm genug, ihnen den Aufenthalt im Klub zu verleiden, so dass man dort ausser der stattlichen Zahl der Zugehörigen von den andern nur ganz wenige der Allerzudringlichsten traf." (*224f*).

The second notable feature of Wallich's Hamburg sojourn, its only bright spot (*Lichtblick*), was his friendship with Julius vom Rath. Vom Rath, member of a patrician Cologne family of sugar manufacturers, was a fellow-trainee in the Oetling business. The two young men became fast friends,[36] with vom Rath helping materially to smoothe Wallich's social path.

At his friend's invitation, Wallich visited the house of his widowed mother in Cologne where he was received with open arms:

> "Der Gefährte des Sohnes, der den jungen Phlegmatiker nicht alleine zum Eifer im Geschäft, sondern auch zu allerhand gesunden Sports, wie Reiten und Schwimmen anhielt, wurde freundlich empfangen . . ." (*220*)

During a two-day stay, predisposed by her brother's descriptions, Wallich "fell in love" with vom Rath's younger sister.[37] It was from subsequent military

---

[36]"Meine Zähigkeit, die er Energie nannte, und mein Intellekt, den er gleichfalls übertrieben einschätzte, imponierten ihm, der nur an das kavaliermässige "laissez aller" und die mässige Intelligenz mehr oder weniger degenerierter Patriziersöhne gewöhnt war." (*220*)

[37]". . . eine gut entwickelte 19-jährige Blondine, die mit den Vorzügen der Herkunft und Erziehung die eines freundlichen molligen Äusseren und eines vergnügten rheinischen Temperaments verband". (*221*)

exercise in Poznań, that he sent Julius vom Rath some verses with barely concealed allusions to his hopes. And it appears that this excellent friend overcame his patrician prejudices to the point of asking for his sister's hand on Wallich's behalf.

A second visit to Cologne, from which vom Rath had tried by every means to dissuade him, seemed to confirm the surmise. This time, all was different. Frau vom Rath hardly spoke.

> ". . . Fräulein Maria lächelte mir nicht mehr beim Tee-Einschenken freundlich im Spiegel zu – ich sah von ihr kaum mehr als den Rücken, wie sie bei meinem Eintritt das Zimmer verliess." (*221*)

It was not wholly his fault, Wallich observes stoically in retrospect, that he only understood somewhat late in the day where the line was to be drawn. "Ich habe", he concludes, "das Haus der Frau vom Rath nicht wieder betreten." (*221*)

To his experiences in Hamburg with their minor social "successes" attributable largely to vom Rath, Wallich ascribes his gradual "sobering-up".

> "Aber ganz abgesehen von der ehrlichen Absicht, in der er mich gesellschaftlich zu lancieren gesucht hat, bin ich ihm dankbar, weil meine Hamburger Erfahrungen den Grundstein für eine allmähliche Ernüchterung gebildet haben." (*219*)[38]

VIII

The "sobering up" of the young Wallich remained however, a slow and somewhat incomplete process. This is shown by his circumstantial and entertaining account of his prolonged "Brautschau", not to say "Brautjagd", his desperate search for a wife "of family". Wallich, not without some justification, considered himself a "good catch": "Ich begann damals, für die besseren Bürgerklassen Berlins [significantly, the aristocracy was beyond reach; there is no evidence to suggest that an aristocratic alliance was even desired] eine gute Partie zu werden. Eigentlich mein einziger Nachteil in den Augen der Betrachter [clearly only Gentiles "need apply"] war meine jüdische Herkunft." (*242*)

However, Wallich considered, his assets outweighed the blemish.

> "Dem standen entgegen: das ansehnliche Vermögen meines Vaters . . . , die – wie allgemein bekannt – ehrenhafte, von allen spekulativen Mitteln ferne Weise, wie dies Vermögen erworben, und damit zusammenhängend die angesehene Stellung, die mein Vater über geschäftliche Kreise hinaus in Berlin einnahm . . ." (*242*)

In addition to a wealthy and respected father, Wallich could also offer some modest personal qualifications:

> ". . . mein Titel als Dr. der Staatswissenschaft und Leutnant der Reserve-Kavallerie, schliesslich der Ruf als solider, gescheiter und fleissiger junger Mann, der voraussichtlich einmal eine leitende Stellung im deutschen Bankwesen einnehmen würde". (*242*)

---

[38]"Bei näherer Betrachtung scheint mir . . . als sei die selbstbescheidene Ruhe, die jenen Sturm so früh abgelöst hat, eher eine zur Geltung kommende, schon früher vorhandene Anlage, als ein wirklicher oder posierter Zusammenbruch." (*160*)

In a self-critical assessment, Wallich finally discusses his personal qualities: "Ein nicht imponierendes, aber im Grunde indifferentes Äusseres [i.e. Wallich did not conform to a Jewish stereotype] und eine geschickt-ironische Weise, mit jungen Mädchen umzugehen [was this a "Jewish" characteristic?] machten mich bei diesen im allgemeinen zwar nicht beliebt, taten mir aber bei den von ernsteren Gesichtspunkten geleiteten Eltern keinen Abbruch." (*242*)

It was a daunting prospectus. Not only must the desired wife be a Gentile but she must also belong to a family combining high social status with wealth roughly comparable to that of the Wallichs. In other words, Wallich – undeterred by his experience with the vom Raths – meant to find a wife in the Gentile *haute bourgeoisie*. That this was a virtual impossibility – the Gentile *haute bourgeoisie* (with minute exceptions) simply did not contract marriage alliances with its Jewish counterpart – he would learn only by bitter experience. A large (perhaps the major) part of the wealthy Berlin families were Jewish or of Jewish origin – as indeed was the more intimate circle of the Wallich household (including the majority of Paul Wallich's childhood friends). Hermann Wallich's business contacts (and resulting loose social ties) with "suitable" families formed, as Wallich would learn, a wholly inadequate basis for possible connubium. The "solution" adopted occasionally by young men in his position – marriage to an "eligible" non-German – was hardly open to Wallich with his social deficiencies, the "Germanism" of his background, and the somewhat confined bourgeois life-style of his parents. Among all the young women "considered" by him there was only one "foreigner", an Anglo-Saxon who, in any case, hardly met the remaining "specifications".

It is against this discouraging background that Wallich passes in review all even remotely "eligible" young women of his acquaintance. The great majority – given both the composition of the Berlin *haute bourgeoisie* and Wallich's "natural" social circle – were Jewish or of Jewish origin and hence "ineligible".

What is of interest and deserves some consideration are Wallich's forays into the Gentile world. Thus among his early "flirts" had been a girl hardly conforming to his ambitious requirements. She was

"... die Tochter eines Mannes, der als Major a.D. und Handelsrichter eine Mittelstellung zwischen dem Nähr-und Wehrstand einnahm. Sie hiess Else Boentsen, war schlank, brünett und eher pikant als hübsch, sehr lustig, ein wenig auffallend und nicht mehr in den Kinderjahren." (*242*)

The harmless "flirtation" "nahm ein überaus schnelles Ende, als ihr Vater – ohne Hinterlassung jedes Vermögens – starb." (*343*) "Gentility" alone was not enough.

When, in the autumn of 1911, Wallich took a six weeks' holiday he made a determined attempt ("nahm ich einen kräftigen Anlauf" (*349*)) to find a wife. His father had more than once told him of the family of Schütte in Bremen, the father a former representative of Standard Oil and according to Wallich "einer der reichsten und angesehendsten Leute seiner Stadt". (*343*) The two young daughters, "blond und hübsch", appeared desirable. However, the younger, whom Wallich would have preferred, was only fifteen – so it had to be her older sister. The experience proved discouraging:

"... mit dieser älteren wollte sich keinerlei Berührungspunkt finden lassen. Himmel und Erde, Kunst und Gesellschaft und was mir sonst einfiel, entlockte ihr nur ein wohlerzogenes Wort der Zustimmung und höchstens einen höflich leisen Ausruf der Verwunderung. Auch wenn ich auf meine geringe Gabe als Causeur einen guten Teil der Schuld nahm, so darf ich doch nachträglich schliessen, dass sie ein Gänschen war." *(349)*

More significant was a second experience which followed almost immediately. The Staudts were "eine sehr wohlhabende Kaufmannsfamilie, deren finanzielle Basis ihr eine bessere gesellschaftliche Stellung gab als ihr noch junges Patriziertum". *(350)* Here, though the situation appeared a little more promising than with the Schüttes, the problems were similar:

"Gleichfalls hübsche blonde Töchter, mit denen mir jedes gemeinsame Unterhaltungsthema fehlte. Aber wenigstens bestand hier in der jahrelangen intimen Freundschaft der Familie eine Art von Grundlage für Heiratspläne . . ." *(350)*

Wallich's choice fell on the middle daughter, Mercedes (aged twenty or twenty-one), a childhood acquaintance. Again, conversation proved a problem, as the girl's interests appeared confined to horses:

"Nicht dass ich mich mit ihr je besser als mit ihren Schwestern hätte unterhalten können. Auch ihr Gesichtskreis . . . schien ganz in den Rahmen des Pferdesports gebannt. Reiten, Fahren und was damit zusammenhing – darüber hätte ich mit ihr stundenlang conversieren können – wenn ich eben davon etwas verstanden hätte." *(350)*

Nevertheless, Wallich persuaded himself that Mercedes Staudt would be his future wife. From small signs, he had gained the delusion that the lady would welcome a proposal. Accordingly, late in January 1912, Wallich asked the widowed mother's permission to pay court to her daughter. Frau Staudt, amiable as always, could not conceal her surprise. Had Wallich, she asked, any reason to believe that his affections were returned – to which he could only reply in the negative (the indication he thought he had detected being wholly imaginary). With this, the conversation ended. Some weeks later Wallich received the official notification of Mercedes Staudt's engagement to a wealthy Ruhr industrialist.

Eventually, in near-desperation, Wallich had recourse – under an assumed name – to a "high-class" marriage-broker. The result described in some detail, was pure farce. Wallich was put in touch with a Herr von Katzler (did he lend his name to one of Theodor Fontane's characters?), a former cavalry officer, invalid of the Franco-Prussian war and "Lotteriekollekteur" by occupation. Katzler in fact, was seeking to marry off two nieces, strictly Catholic and wholly without means, to more or less socially acceptable ("standesgemäss") husbands. In conversation, Wallich discovered that the position of a bank-director, on which he based his pretensions, was not highly regarded by Katzler: ". . . ein Schönheitsfehler", sagte er (der Lotterie-Einnehmer!), "der sich bei ihrer Wohlhabenheit aber gelegentlich durch einen Gutskauf reparieren lässt!" *(356)* Katzler, convinced that Wallich must jump at the opportunity of marrying one of the nieces, presented a bad photo which conveyed only a blurred impression of the object-to-be of Wallich's affections. When challenged on the point, Katzler replied with a superior smile:

"Allerdings denke ich mir, dass für einen Herrn Ihrer Kreise die Verbindung mit dem unseren einen ganz besonderen und vieles andere aufwiegenden Wert haben muss!" *(356)*

An appointment to meet the nieces "casually" in a restaurant Wallich failed to keep.

A more serious candidate for Wallich's affection was Marion Brennan, an American actress living in London and his good friend of several years' standing. Close on thirty, and with limited resources, she was separated from her husband and eking out a precarious living by minor literary labours (mainly translations). Wallich was attracted by both her personality and her person. But objections to marrying her were strong. Among them were her Anglo-Saxon origin and the stern opposition of Wallich's mother. "Auch hierüber", he writes "wie über einige mich stark störende Angewohnheiten wäre ich hinweggekommen, so ihren übermässigen Zigarettenkonsum und gewisse Bohème-Allüren in Haltung und Kleidung, die ihr fahrendes Leben mit sich brachten." (*359*) What, however, Wallich could not overcome were his doubts about the unknown:

> "Wer, ausser ihrem Mann, hatte Marion besessen? Hatte eine hübsche, liebenswürdige und lebenslustige Frau, eine Frau, die in Künstler- und Bohème-Kreisen zu Hause war, die mehr als einmal in materieller Not gewesen sein mochte – hatte eine solche Frau ihre Unbescholtenheit im strengen bürgerlichen Sinne wahren können?" (*359*)

Paul Wallich decided against proposing to Marion Brennan.

Wallich was approaching the age of thirty when, at long last, he found himself a wife. "Was ich auf künstlich verschlungenen Pfaden vergeblich gesucht hatte", so ends his account of his matrimonial quest, "fand ich ein paar Monate später, als ich auf weit natürlicherem Wege meine Frau kennenlernte." (362) The rest is silence. Had Paul Wallich, finally, found his "Gattin 'von Familie'"?

IX

Hildegard Wallich (née Rehrmann), in the family tradition, also wrote her memoirs. She came from an "aryan" middle-class family of "Bildungsbürgertum". Her father was an (academic) instructor at a military training establishment, whilst of her brothers one was a tenant-farmer (*Gutspächter*), another a painter. The acquaintance between Paul Wallich and his future wife, however, had arisen in the following manner. Shortly after Christmas 1912 Wallich had gone to have tea with a Frau Mulert, the wife of a Protestant clergyman.[39] Among the guests was Hildegard Rehrmann, who had become the friend of a Mulert daughter after a joint stay in Paris. Another visitor was the historian Hans Rothfels. Hildegard left early to make another call. Wallich and Rothfels left with her. At a corner Rothfels discreetly disappeared. Hildegard Rehrmann wanted to take a tram, Wallich – whose name she learnt only later – suggested a walk. He had, writes Hildegard,

> ". . . bereits beschlossen, dass er mich heiraten wollte und schlug vor, noch ein bischen zu gehen, dann würde er mich per Taxi dahin bringen, da er auch in der Richtung fahren müsste, was natürlich erfunden war".[40]

---

[39] As Wallich's sister Ilse married a husband of the same name, this was probably his brother-in-law's family.

[40] Hildegard Wallich, *Erinnerungen*, *op. cit.*, pp.106f.

They talked about many things, among others of Romain Rolland, whose lectures Hildegard had enjoyed at the Sorbonne. She liked, above all, Wallich's quiet humour. At parting, he expressed a hope that they would meet again but "das nahm ich nicht so ernsthaft". How old Frau Mulert and Rolland's *Jean-Christophe* became marriage-brokers – the marriage took place in February 1913 – need not be developed here.

What is significant, however, is Hildegard Wallich's reaction to the new world which now opened before her, "Berlin W.":

> "Es war eine andere Welt, in die ich nun kam, und eigentlich gerade die, vor der ich immer Scheu gehabt hatte, weil es ein Teil von "Berlin W." war. Aber zu meinem Erstaunen war nur der äussere Rahmen so prächtig. Die Menschen darin waren klug und gütig, hatten vielerlei Interessen und waren unendlich arbeitsam, wohltätig und sehr liebenswert."[41]

On the occasion of the formal engagement, the old Wallichs gave a party:

> Zum Empfang der Gäste standen wir in dem sogenannten grossen Salon vor dem Kamin und alle kamen vorbeidefiliert und gratulierten uns. Es war eine Art Spiessrutenlaufen vor dem kritischen Berlin W. – aber auch hier wieder erwies es sich, dass sie nicht so schlimm waren, wie ich gedacht hatte. Jedenfalls waren sie sehr freundlich zu uns."[42]

Thus ended Paul Wallich's quest for a wife "of family". That Hildegard Rehrmann wholly met his original aspirations would be difficult to maintain. However, vom Raths, Schüttes and Staudts had proved unattainable – and Hildegard Wallich with her background in the "Bildungsbürgertum" had the advantage of an education and intellectual interests. She had the indispensable quality – in Wallich's eyes – of being a Gentile. The Jewish girls of his acquaintance who possessed both wealthy parents and intellectual interests had been "ruled out" by their "Jewishness". Nor did they belong to the "élite" of Jewish and baptised families, to which Wallich had no access. He therefore "settled" (or had to "settle") for a middle-class Gentile marriage. Lesser wealth and a somewhat lesser social status of the Gentile wife were the price which, typically, had to be paid to compensate for the husband's "Jewishness".

X

Paul Wallich's subsequent career cannot be considered here. His marriage, it would appear, was a happy one. Before he took his life on 11th November 1938 – by an odd coincidence it was in Cologne, close to Bonn where the family originated – he wrote a farewell letter to his wife:

> "Mein Liebling – ich wollte es erst morgen tun, aber will es nun doch heute machen, weil ich keine Gefahr laufen will. Sei mir nicht böse – aber Du weisst ja: ich habe nie am Leben gehangen – und nun, wo alles dafür spricht, dass Nicht-Sein besser ist als Sein – kann ich es mir nicht versagen. Ich bin so müde und weiss, dass ich Dir und den Kindern nichts Gutes tue, wenn ich anders handele."[43]

[41] *Ibid.*, p. 109.
[42] *Ibid.*, p. 113.
[43] *Zwei Generationen, op. cit.*, p. 27.

He no longer felt able to face the worry and stress of a new beginning and even lacked the nerve to cross the frontier with or without a passport. He continues:

"Grüsse alle Freunde, danke Dir für alles Gute, was ich von Dir empfangen habe. Grüss die Kinder und schenke ihnen etwas von mir. Ich habe viel Gutes im Leben genossen und darum scheide ich ohne Groll."[44]

And then Wallich adds a wholly unexpected passage – possibly intended to protect his family from persecution by the Nazi authorities. There was no longer a reason, he writes, against hoisting the swastika flag on their old family home:

"Die Macht, der ich unterlegen bin,[45] ist eine Weltmacht. Du brauchst Dich meines Endes nicht zu schämen, musst aber den Sieger anerkennen, ebenso wie ich es selbst tue."[46]

And then follows Paul Wallich's final farewell: "Ich werde an Dich denken, mein liebstes Gutes, im letzten Augenblick. – Alles Gute Dir und den Kindern. Dein Mann."[47]

XI

Thus ended Paul Wallich's "selbstbescheidene Ruhe" which, already in Hamburg had so early begun to replace "jenen Sturm", the frenetic quest for social assimilation. That quest, in fact, had met with indifferent success, indeed might be considered largely to have failed. Wallich had been unable to secure election to a student corps. His status as a reserve officer had proved a doubtful pleasure. The wife "von Familie" had largely eluded him as had aristocratic society. Already in 1916 when composing his memoirs, he had written off his more extreme aspirations. With critical irony he looks back on his youthful snobbery. In fact, Wallich had reached and experienced the limits of what was socially attainable for even a baptised Jew. He had learnt to accept his social situation, to content himself with limited achievement.

The baptism arranged by the parents had proved a doubtful blessing. There is nothing to suggest that, in accordance with his father's wishes, Paul Wallich had become a "good" or sincere Christian. Baptism had barely sufficed to secure his election as reserve officer in a very modest regiment. It is clear that in the eyes of the world at large (as indeed in his own consciousness) Wallich had remained a Jewish banker's son (later himself a moderately successful Jewish banker).

The fact that he remained, at the same time, a sensitive Jewish intellectual, a bibliophile, versifier and joint author of a valuable historical study,[48] did little to promote his assimilation. Neither aristocrat nor the average "Grossbürger" was

[44] *Ibid.*
[45] To one of his sons, Wallich wrote in a somewhat different spirit: "Die Dinge sind in Deutschland für mich nicht mehr erträglich. In's Ausland zu gehen habe ich nicht mehr die Energie . . . Du brauchst Dich Deines Vaters und seines Endes nicht zu schämen. Niemand kann mir vorwerfen, dass ich mich nicht bis zum Letzten gewehrt habe . . ." (*ib.*) The keynote, here, was resistance.
[46] *Ibid.*
[47] *Ibid.*
[48] Paul Wallich, Hugo Rachel, Johann Papritz, *Berliner Grosskaufleute und Kapitalisten*, vol. 1, Berlin 1934, vols. 2 and 3, printed ms. 1938. New edition in 3 vols. Berlin 1967.

likely to view such activities with sympathy. It was a fate which Paul Wallich shared with Walther Rathenau and others. It was difficult – perhaps indeed impossible – to shed the Jewish intellectual tradition.

Wallich's attitude to his Jewishness was deeply ambivalent. Originally, he had been filled with profound Jewish "self-hatred." Tenaciously – if unsuccessfully – he had endeavoured to avoid all social intercourse with people of Jewish origin. This, however, was an impossibility alike for the Jewish banker's son and for the intellectual, especially in Berlin. Moreover, with all his craving for "blondness", Wallich felt constantly drawn to Jewish intellectuality and the Jewish psyche which was, indeed, his own. Repeatedly he remarks that he felt (or would have felt) most at home in the company of Jewish intellectuals. Yet he was determined not to "belong", to keep his distance.

However, hand in hand with his longing for Jewish intellectuality went the craving – his unrequited love – for blond – and preferably aristocratic – Gentiles. And yet, such contacts as could be achieved, revealed a striking lack of common interest whether with the gentlemanly "Rossleber" or with "Gänschen" and horsewomen from the upper middle class. Despite friendships like those with Johannes Schultze, Friedel Koch, Julius vom Rath, perhaps Harald von Sichart, the gap between Jew and Gentile was difficult to bridge. And, at the end, a Jewish husband and wife would perhaps have struggled on or would have ended their lives together.

Paul Wallich, like others in a similar position, was in fact a man of two worlds fully at home in neither. To no small extent this was the result of his upbringing. It was the aristocratic boarding-school of Pforta which determined the direction of his youthful aspirations. The choice of the school, almost certainly, was due to Wallich's ambitious and determined mother who also influenced her son's choice of a future career. Like Hermann Wallich's mother before her, Anna Jacoby, through the processes of socialisation first promoted the son's "assimilationist" propensities.

XII

Much in the evolution of the Wallichs – from the Orthodox skin-merchant in Bonn through the bank-director rising into "Berlin W." to the grandson with his largely unsatisfied social ambitions – is typical of one form of "assimilation" (there were others) to be found in the German-Jewish *haute bourgeoisie*. The possibilities of upward mobility in the economic sphere were great, those in the social sphere modest. Objectively, ethnically- and culturally-conditioned "psychic" differences persisted, informal networks remained largely distinct. Subjectively, Gentile receptivity to Jews in the social sphere at the level of the Wallichs was severely circumscribed. Shared Christianity had become meaningless as a factor of integration into society, constituting on the Jewish side at best an act of social conformity, perhaps solidarity. In mixed marriages, the Jewishness of the husband had, nearly always, to be compensated by the lower social status of the Gentile wife.

Complete assimilation, as the experience of Paul Wallich shows was – at least for Jewish men – virtually impossible. There always remained a Jewish residue "painful to bear". The Jewish roots, often expressed at least for *cognoscenti* even in the very name, were not to be denied. Gentile comrades as well as complete outsiders were as aware of these roots as were the "victims" themselves. So, of course, as a rule were "fellow-Jews". Facts, in the end, would have to be faced. Paul Wallich did so relatively early, with ironic resignation and a certain good humour and with a degree of detachment and "fair-mindedness".

The story of the Wallichs illustrates alike major factors promoting assimilation and others retarding it. In the first category what is conspicuous is the influence of education (socialisation) and the role of the mother in determining its direction. Again, it is the wife who appears to exercise a major influence on the husband's decision.[49] The occupation of banking on the other hand, does not appear as noticeably promoting assimilation. Neither is wealth a decisive factor. The major retarding element is the persistence and tenacity of informal Jewish networks which it seems all but impossible to escape. These are, moreover, perpetuated and, indeed, reinforced, by antisemitism in the outside world and by if not outright unwillingness at least reluctance – as in the student corps, the Hamburg *Harmonie* or Paul Wallich's regimental mess – to admit people of Jewish origin into high-status institutions of formal sociability. It was the invisible social barriers erected against them that, above all, constantly reminded Jews of their Jewishness. The strength of informal Jewish networks, moreover, tended to favour endogamy, as shown in the case of Hermann Wallich. Connubium with Gentiles at the social level of the Wallichs required, as the case of Paul Wallich shows, a single-minded determination. The "obvious" marriage partners in terms of status, wealth and, not least, compatibility would still be, in the main, Jewish or of Jewish origin. The evidence, in fact, suggests that in the economic élite, the natural forces promoting the preservation of a form of Jewish identity still balanced those making for its abandonment. The attempt at total assimilation, as the experience of Paul Wallich shows, was in any case a problematical undertaking. Even among men who, like Wallich, deliberately chose this path, those who finally reached their goal – at any rate in Imperial Germany – were few and far between.

[49]Whether this applies also in the case of Paul and Hildegard Wallich is impossible to determine for lack of evidence.

The Foundations of German-Jewish Orthodoxy

An Interpretation

BY JULIUS CARLEBACH

It could be argued that German-Jewish Orthodoxy, that is to say, a strict adherence to Jewish law (*Halakhah*) and unswerving commitment to German national culture, in the nineteenth century, came closer to creating a viable synthesis between these two systems than in comparable groups in other countries. This was due in no small measure to the willingness of a few leading rabbis to confront the issues of their times head on and to explicate political principles which moulded the processes of change. The advent of emancipation was the most fundamental change the Jews had to face in a millennium, and many of its advocates and opponents recognised the destructive potential of political freedom for the survival of the Jews as autonomous groups. In this paper I would like to revisit a small number of well-known personalities and conflicts, to show that through the medium of conflict and confrontation a consistent and coherent determination of religious orientations was forged, which, in many ways created models of adaptation for Jewish communities in many lands.

Contrary to some widely held views, I do not consider the rabbis to be discussed here as "conservative" or "traditionalist",[1] defending the past against any encroachment by the present, but as men who had the sagacity (if not always the temperament) to identify central issues and to respond to the challenges of their time, not merely by trying to stem the tides of inevitable progress, but in order to shape and influence the outcome. It is by now well established that the supposed political incompetence of the Jews was a myth.[2] In fact, the accepted political role of the rabbi, which was consolidated during the Middle Ages,[3] continued openly and deliberately and plays an important part in the analysis which is presented here. Emancipation meant not only the abolition of civil disabilities, it also called for a transition of allegiances – even obedience, from communal leaders to the head of state or the State as such. For as long as the Jewish communities in Europe formed "a state within a state", their political

[1]Jacob Katz, *Out of the Ghetto. The Social Background of Jewish Emancipation 1770–1870*, Cambridge, Mass. 1973, esp. Chap. 9.
[2]Ismar Schorsch, *On the History of the Political Judgment of the Jew*, Leo Baeck Memorial Lecture No. 20, New York 1977.
[3]Byron L. Sherwin, *Mystical Theology and Social Dissent. The Life and Works of Judah Loew of Prague*, London-Toronto 1982.

relationship to the rulers of host countries was minimal and mediated through Jewish communal leadership. We are not surprised then if, for example, for Rabbi Jehuda ben Bezalel Löw of Prague (1520–1609) (The *Maharal*) "the relationship of the rabbi to the community ought to be like that of a king to his subjects . . . As a king rules his subjects, so should the rabbi be the ruler of his constituency."[4] In that role the rabbi would have the task of interpreting imperial or royal decrees for his flock in much the same way that he would interpret *halakhic* rules to his people. In their different ways, the four rabbis to be discussed here acted in the spirit of such a conception. They worked on the assumption that Jews, dissenters by choice in the political arena of the *Galut*, would be subject to constant pressure by the State to move from dissent to conformity and that it was their task to mediate between the demands of the State and loyalty to Torah.

Our four rabbis in particular can be shown to have been lastingly influential in identifying central issues in the quest for modernity and in formulating appropriate models for participation in civil society without sacrificing an overriding loyalty to Jewish religious life. There was Rabbi Ezekiel Landau of Prague (1713–1793) who sought to ward off secular influences by exercising control over social institutions, and Rabbi Moses Sofer (1762–1839) who insisted on an explicit separatism, Rabbi Samson Raphael Hirsch (1808–1888) who used emancipation to realise Torah, and Rabbi Esriel Hildesheimer (1820–1899) who used Torah to extend the benefits of emancipation. Landau and Sofer both relied on the political concept of toleration, which, for them, meant loyalty to the ruler of the time. They saw this not merely as politically expedient, but as a positive religious requirement. By focusing the loyalty of the people on the ruler, the rabbis also hoped to deflect attention and interest from lesser and more seductive elements in the host culture. They understood correctly that the dangers in the emancipation process came not from those who decreed and legislated it, so much as from the ever increasing contacts between ordinary Jews and ordinary Gentile fellow citizens. The Jew who is not externally defined as such is liable to forget his identity.

Landau was persuaded by his own skills in manipulating his personal relationship with Joseph II that he could retain control over the processes of change (which is why he strongly resented outside interference). Thus, for example, he was quite willing to allow children in his community to learn German and other secular subjects, provided that secular teachers did not use that opportunity to undermine religious attitudes. He warned both teachers and pupils that he would not hesitate to use state sanctions to intervene in the classroom.[5] Moses Sofer, on the other hand, witnessed the steadily decreasing adherence of Jews to their ancestral faith after Landau's death and tried to

---

[4]*Ibid.*, p. 165.
[5]See below note 30. A good example of Landau's subtle and sophisticated relationship with Joseph II can be gleaned from a report of a visit by Landau to the imperial palace shortly after the promulgation of the Edict of Tolerance. At the end of his visit Landau was asked to write in the visitors' book. He chose a characteristically ambiguous quotation from *Genesis* (XLII:8): "And Joseph recognised his brothers, but they did not recognise him." Cf. *Mofeth Ha'Dor* by Y. Kamelhar, Pietrokov [2]1934, p. 80n.

persuade state authorities to maintain a system of toleration rather than emancipation, by emphasising the *halakhic* basis of loyalty to the State. At the same time, as we shall see, Sofer redefined the classic rabbinic concept of *Derech Eretz*, so that it would no longer include that secularity which Jews could share with Gentiles, on the contrary, he gave it a content which would disqualify Jews from sharing it, again, on a principle derived from a strict interpretation of *Halakhah*. Samuel Raphael Hirsch clearly recognised the Sofer model as untenable in its pristine severity in the social climate of mid-nineteenth century Germany, where the political arena was steadily opened to participation by an expanding bourgeoisie. The challenge of emancipation, as Hirsch saw it, was to find that element in civil society which had the greatest affinity with Jewish religiosity, and that, he thought, was to be found not in a vaguely conceptualised *Bürgertum*, but quite specifically in the then dominant notions of *Sittlichkeit*, which he incorporated brilliantly in a famous, if ill-defined, rabbinic principle of *Torah im Derech Eretz*.[6] Here, too, however, social change overtook the new mode of adaptation. A liberal *Bürgertum*, enchanted by its own preoccupation with *Sittlichkeit*, gave way to a harder, harsher and divisive nationalism, which was inimical to Jewish religious autonomy. It was left to Esriel Hildesheimer to try to maintain the primacy of Judaism for Jews by extending and universalising the Hirschian conception.[7]

For all the differences in prevailing conditions and styles of adaptation, all four rabbis adhered to the same fundamental approaches to deal with their respective problems. They all relied on the State to strengthen and protect their religious position; they varied, but did not change their attempts to find a *modus vivendi* with the secular world and Reform Judaism, but above all, they insisted, in one way or another, on a form of separatism and differed on this only in the identification of which out-group had to be avoided most of all. An element of separatism was regarded as essential for the maintenance of a Jewish-*halakhic* existence. Yet, separatism did not necessarily mean isolation and certainly excluded any form of discrimination; it was seen as a basic Torah concept, which had its origin in the dawn of Jewish history, when it was proclaimed with apodictic simplicity in *Leviticus* XX:26 (". . . I will separate you from the peoples, that ye should be mine"), and acknowledged in the name of the Gentile world in *Numbers* XXIII:9 (". . . behold, the people shall dwell alone, and shall not reckon itself among the nations"). As a concept, separatism assumes that, to survive, cultures must have clearly delineated boundaries, and that the greatest challenge to the organisation of social life is the creation of balanced relation-

[6]For broad and detailed discussions of *Sittlichkeit* see Maria Ossowska, *Bourgeois Morality*, London–New York 1986; and Peter Gay, *The Bourgeois Experience – Victoria to Freud*, vol. I, *Education of the Senses*, Oxford 1984, pp. 18 ff. As a special issue in Germany see George L. Mosse, 'Jewish Emancipation: Between Bildung and Respectability', in Jehuda Reinharz and Walter Schatzberg (eds.), *The Jewish Response to German Culture. From the Englightenment to the Second World War*, Hanover–London 1985.

[7]Jakob Rosenheim for example has suggested that Hirsch did not attempt to train rabbis because he would have had to allow them to go too far (in his view) into German culture (specifically biblical criticism). It was Hildesheimer who took on that task. See *Samson Raphael Hirsch's Cultural Ideal and Our Times*, London 1951, p. 28.

ships for all on the boundaries of cultural interaction. It is a challenge which, since the advent of emancipation, Jewish Orthodoxy has been trying to meet and which was, and remains, under constant threat from alternate ideologies.

Historically, as has been indicated, Jewish attitudes to the different, hostile, friendly or coldly tolerant societies which they had to come to terms with, were expressed and negotiated through the concept of *Derech Eretz*. This concept has its roots in the *Pentateuch* where alien customs and cultures are given a degree of recognition which might be seen as an inverse facet of toleration. Thus, Jacob cannot marry his beloved because "it is not the custom in our place to give the younger [sister] before the elder" (*Genesis* XXIX:26). Joseph does not seat Egyptians and Hebrews at the same table, because Egyptians would not eat with them (*Genesis* XLIII:32) and Moses refused to let Israelites worship in Egypt – "it would be wrong to do so because Egyptians are repelled by Jewish sacrifices" (*Exodus* VIII:22). From such beginnings the concept of *Derech Eretz* was developed. In rabbinic Judaism it acquires elaborate dimensions which are broadly concerned with the formalisation of normative conduct within Jewish communities, patterns of responses to the natural, material world and a delineation of rules of conduct towards the Gentile world. The more a Gentile environment impinged on Jewish life, the more extensively were questions of education and secular knowledge, employment and ethics incorporated in the application of *Derech Eretz*. External hostility on the other hand produced intensely inner-directed discussions of ethical standards and internal social etiquette.[8]

It has not been possible here to deal with important questions like the demographic distribution of Orthodox Jewry, its organisation, institutions, literature and (perhaps the most neglected topic) its lay leadership. Nor has it been possible to do justice to the large number of rabbis who guided the spiritual life of their respective communities.[9] Instead, I have concentrated my attention on the four rabbis whose ideas and activities dominated Orthodox Jewry in Germany throughout the emancipation period.

I

The Tolerance Edict of 13th October 1781 was a royal decree very much in the spirit of its time. While it provided for new opportunities in education and

[8]Cf. Leopold Zunz, *Zur Geschichte und Literatur*, Berlin 1845, p. 159. Our main concern here is, of course, the evolution of the concept *Derech Eretz* during the period of emancipation, but we might note that similar developments can be seen in the work of Saadia Gaon (*Sefer Ha'Emunoth Veha'Deoth*, esp. the last section on 'The Conduct of Man' – see also the English version *The Book of Beliefs and Opinions*, translated by Samuel Rosenblatt, New Haven 1948, esp. Treatise X) and Moses Maimonides's *Book of Knowledge* (*Sefer HaMada*). We might note that for an (to me) unknown reason, both Saadia and Maimonides avoided the term *Derech Eretz* though their subject matter is on the same lines.

[9]Since this paper was written, Mordechai Breuer has published his massive and impressive *Jüdische Orthodoxie im Deutschen Reich 1871–1918. Die Sozialgeschichte einer religiösen Minderheit*, Frankfurt a. Main 1986, Veröffentlichung des Leo Baeck Instituts, which deals at length with the topics I have mentioned. Important material may also be found in Robert Liberles, *Religious Conflict in Social Context. The Resurgence of Orthodox Judaism in Frankfurt am Main 1838–1877*, London 1985.

employment for Jewish subjects of Joseph II,[10] and while it was hailed, in its time, as an act of enlightenment, it owed little to lofty motives, but a great deal to a much wider process of imperial reorganisation to meet external threats and internal discontent.[11] Nevertheless, for many disenfranchised Jews it appeared as the dawn of a brighter future and earlier Jewish historians were enraptured by it.[12] Not surprisingly, the *Maskilim*, a small group of educated and enlightened Jews around Moses Mendelssohn in Berlin, saw the decree as the herald of a new era. One of them, Naphtali Herz Weisel (1725–1805) (Hartwig Wessely),[13] was inspired to produce a letter, *Divrei Shalom Ve'Emeth* (Words of Peace and Truth),[14] in which he called on the Jewish subjects of Joseph II to take the fullest advantage of the opportunities offered to them by their Emperor.[15] This missive drew considerable hostility from leading Orthodox rabbis, variously described as *Finsterlinge*,[16] "Zealots",[17] "Fanatics"[18] and "Obscurantists",[19] though their position has gradually gained increasing respect.[20] The most distinguished, and, in our context, the most important opponent of Weisel was Rabbi Ezekiel Landau (1713–1793), the Chief Rabbi of Prague at that time.[21] The intensity of the conflict which arose over Weisel's book makes it apparent that what was at stake here were not disagreements over preferred strategies of educational

[10]Though excluding, until 7th May 1789, the Jews of Galicia.

[11]See the searching critique by Josef Karniel, 'Die Toleranzpolitik Kaiser Josephs II.', in Walter Grab (ed.), *Deutsche Aufklärung und Judenemanzipation*, Tel-Aviv 1980, pp. 155–177.

[12]See, for example, Isaak Marcus Jost, *Geschichte des Judenthums und seiner Sekten*, vol. 3, Leipzig 1859, p. 312; Markus Brann, *Geschichte der Juden und ihrer Literatur*, Breslau 1895, p. 395, who refers to Joseph II "Hoch und herrlich und von reinem Edelmut eingegeben . . ." though all historians, with the benefit of hindsight, also expressed reservations.

[13]He wrote his name in Hebrew as Weisel though Hartwig Wessely was used, certainly by his own family, in German, cf. *Allgemeine Zeitung des Judenthums*, II, 31, pp. 121–122.

[14]Both title and format are taken from *Esther*, IX:30.

[15]On Weisel see Wolf A. Meisel, *Leben und Wirken Naphtali Hartwig Wesselys*, Breslau 1841; Charles L. Ozer, 'Jewish Education in the Transition from Ghetto to Emancipation', in *Historia Judaica*, 9, 1 and 2 (1947), pp. 75–94 and 137–158; Simcha Assaf, *Mekoroth Le'Toldot Ha'Chinuch Be'Yisrael* (Sources for a History of Jewish Education), vol. 1, Tel-Aviv 1954; Mordechai Eliav, *Hachinuch Hayehudt Be'Germania Bimei Ha'Haskalu Ve'Ha'Emanzipatia* (Jewish Education in Germany in the Period of Enlightenment and Emancipation), Jerusalem 1960; Ruth Kestenberg-Gladstein, *Neuere Geschichte der Juden in den böhmischen Ländern*, Tübingen 1969 (Schriftenreihe wissenschaftlicher Abhandlungen des Leo Baeck Instituts 18); Alexander Altmann, *Moses Mendelssohn. A Biographical Study*, London 1973; Hillel J. Kieval, 'Caution's Progress. The Modernisation of Jewish Life in Prague 1780–1830', in Jacob Katz (ed.), *Toward Modernity. The European Jewish Model*, New Brunswick, N. J. 1987, publication of the Leo Baeck Institute. Since Wessely was primarily a literary figure, this issue was also discussed at length by literary historians, cf. Meyer Waxmann, *A History of Jewish Literature*, New York–London 1936 (1960), and Israel Zinsberg, *A History of Jewish Literature*, vol. VIII, New York 1976.

[16]Jost, *op. cit.*, p. 312.

[17]Heinrich Graetz, *History of the Jews*, vol. V, Philadelphia 1967, p. 370.

[18]Brann, *op. cit.*, p. 400.

[19]Simon Dubnow, *History of the Jews*, vol. IV, New York–London 1971, p. 346.

[20]See esp. Ruth Kestenberg, *op. cit.*; and Hillel Kieval, *op. cit.*

[21]Also known as the *Noda Be'Yehuda* after his best known volumes of Responsa. Additional material on Landau, apart from the sources quoted above is in Kamelhar, *Mofeth Ha'Dor* (Model of a Generation), *op. cit.*, first published in 1903, I have used a third Israeli edition of 1968; Gutmann Klemperer, 'The Rabbis of Prague: Ezechiel Landau', in *Historia Judaica*, 13, 1951, pp. 55–82; Solomon Wind, 'Ezekiel Landau' in Leo Jung (ed.), *Jewish Leaders, 1750–1940*, Jerusalem 1964 (orig. 1953); Chimen Abramsky, 'The Crisis of Authority within European Jewry in the Eighteenth

reforms, or subtleties of political adjustment, but fundamental conceptual problems in the delineation of a Torah-true Judaism, which are bound to arise when political and educational forces intervene to change an existing *status quo*.

To some extent the Jews of pre-emancipation Europe elevated their isolated position into a virtue and paid scant attention to the nature of their relationship with the Gentile world,[22] or to the possible consequences of speculative writing in the interpretation of holy texts. Thus, for example, in 1775, Weisel published a long, wordy commentary on *Pirkei Avoth* under the title *Yein Levanon*,[23] in which he anticipated many of the arguments which were later incorporated in his *Divrei Shalom Ve'Emeth*. In *Avoth* 6:7[24] there is a list of 48 qualities which an aspiring scholar should cultivate to "acquire Torah", including "sedateness, knowledge of scripture and Mishnah". Weisel linked this with another talmudic text, "He who is conversant with Scripture, Mishnah and correct conduct (*Derech Eretz*) will not speedily sin",[25] and argued that the word "sedateness" means settled, i.e. having an established place in the world. This, he continued, presupposes correct behaviour, which, in turn, assumes a thorough grounding in etiquette, the natural sciences and all other studies necessary for a scholar and essential in a truly God-fearing person. He went on to elaborate his discussion to show that ultimately correct conduct (*Derech Eretz*) and secular knowledge are so essential, that a person with only that knowledge would be preferable to one versed solely in Scripture. Such a daring claim was further supported by two references from the *Midrash*, the first of which suggests that a scholar without worldly knowledge is "less than a carcass",[26] while the second one acknowledges that there must have been twenty-six generations of human beings from Adam to Moses, who understood and practised correct conduct before the revelation of Sinai.[27] The propositions that secular and social knowledge were essential and should precede religious knowledge were controversial but not really original. Similar ideas had been put forward by Rabbi Jehuda Löw of Prague, who may well have been Weisel's inspiration.[28] Weisel's book in which these ideas were developed was warmly endorsed by Landau and other leading rabbis.[29]

Century', in Siegfried Stein and Raphael Loewe (eds.), *Studies in Jewish Religious and Intellectual History*, Alabama 1979. More detailed studies are Leon Gellman, *Ha'Noda Be'Yehuda Umishnato*, Jerusalem 1960 (dealing mainly with his *halakhic* role) and Solomon Wind, *R. Yecheskel Landau, Toldot Chayav U'Pe'ulotav*, Jerusalem 1961 (a biographical study).

[22] A point made at length by Weisel in Chapter 2 of his *Divrei Shalom Ve'Emeth*. He pointed out that as a result of Gentile hostility, Jews took the view that Gentile values had no relevance for the Jews; cf. also Assaf, *op. cit.*, pp. 125–126.

[23] *Yein Levanon* (Wine of Lebanon), first published in Berlin 1775. I have used a later edition, Warsaw 1908.

[24] In some editions it is given as 6:6.

[25] (Mishnah) *Kiddushin* 1:10.

[26] *Levit Rabbah* 1:15.

[27] *Ibid.*, 9:3, cf. *Yein Levanon, op. cit.*, p. 362.

[28] See the discussion of *Avoth*, 2:2 in *Derech Hachaim*, Jerusalem 1971 and the chapter on *Derech Eretz* in *Netivot Olam*, vol. 2, Jerusalem 1971.

[29] Moshe Pelli has argued correctly and at length that Weisel was and remained, a traditionalist. See his 'Naphtali Herz Wessely. Moderation in Transition', in *Hebrew Studies*, 19 (1978), pp. 43–45, but in a later paper, Pelli quotes Weisel's opponents out of context, thus giving a misleading impression of them and of Weisel. Cf. 'The Attitude of the First Maskilim in Germany towards the Talmud', in *LBI Year Book XXVII* (1982), pp. 243–260, esp. note 1 and p. 243.

Weisel's *Divrei Shalom Ve'Emeth* repeated many of the arguments which he had rehearsed in his earlier commentary, *Yein Levanon*, but there were a number of subtle differences which turned his seemingly innocuous piece into a serious challenge to traditionalists, and Landau was quick to perceive this. The changes which led him to challenge Weisel[30] were firstly that, whereas in the earlier book Weisel had followed the common pattern of discussing the need for *Derech Eretz* and secular knowledge for scholars well versed in Scripture and *Mishnah*, he now related the question exclusively to the education of children. Secondly, to aggravate matters, he reinterpreted the *Midrash* from an historical observation to a developmental rule. Where the *Midrash* had referred to the historical fact that the Torah records acceptable levels of moral behaviour of people prior to the standards laid down in the Torah, Weisel argued that such standards of a general morality should be imparted to children before they were taught the rules and beliefs of Judaism.[31] Thirdly, Weisel had usurped the biblical concept of *Torath Ha'Adam* (the Torah *for* man),[32] by contrasting a *Torath Elokim* (the teachings of God) with a *Torath Adam* (the teachings *of* man). This threatened to blur the distinction between the two sources of knowledge by stipulating a Torah of man instead of an exclusive Torah for man.[33]

The bitter disputes which followed the publication of Weisel's *Divrei Shalom*

[30]Landau's opposition to Weisel's pamphlet has been widely discussed and sometimes exaggerated, yet it manifested itself in no more than two responses. The first was a brief reference to Weisel's publication in a sermon before Passover. Landau protested against this unnecessary intervention from an outsider, especially his offensive, if unintended, implication that rabbis without secular learning were unacceptable. (Weisel had used exactly the same argument in his earlier book, *Yein Levanon*, so there is little likelihood that he intended to offend either Rabbi Landau or Rabbi David Tevele, but both assumed that he did and responded accordingly, though they may also have reacted because they had approved the earlier book, and, certainly in the case of Landau, without actually reading it.) The main thrust of Landau's sermon was in the closing remarks in which he warned teachers of the *Normalschulen*, to which Jewish children were now compelled to go by the Edict of 1781, that, while they were authorised to teach secular subjects, they would be acting against the Imperial Decree, if they used that opportunity to persuade children away from their religious convictions. Cf. *Drushei Hazlach*, Jerusalem 1964, pp. 105–107. The second response came considerably later. Weisel decided to take issue with his opponents, especially the fierce attack of Rabbi Tevele of Lissa, by publishing three epistles to deal with rabbinic objections. The dispute began to attract the attention of governmental officials (Zinsberg, *op. cit.*, pp. 73–74) and Landau was concerned about possible consequences for Tevele. He therefore wrote a strongly worded letter (Assaf, *op. cit.*, pp. 239–240) to the lay leaders of the Berlin community and asked them to reprimand Weisel severely because he was interfering in matters which did not concern him. Weisel was also presumptuous in acting as a rabbi when he was a mere layman. (Eliav, *op. cit.*, pp. 46–47.) For a detailed analysis of Tevele's response see especially Abramsky, *loc. cit.*, pp. 19–21. The full text of Tevele's sermon is available in L. Lewin, 'Aus dem jüdischen Kulturkampfe' in *Jahrbuch der Jüdisch-Literarischen Gesellschaft*, 12 (1918), pp. 165–197. See also *Jeschurun*, VI, 1 and 2 (1919), pp. 112–113.

[31]Although the primacy of *Derech Eretz* was fiercely contested by traditionalist rabbis, it had been, in fact, advocated much earlier by the *Maharal* of Prague, in his comment on *Avoth*, 2:2. He explained that each person has a body and a soul. The Torah fills the need of the soul and *Derech Eretz* the needs of the body, i.e. a livelihood and similar things. Satisfying one's needs will help to prevent a person from falling into evil ways. *Derech Chaim*, Jerusalem 1971, pp. 70–71.

[32]*2 Samuel*, VII:19.

[33]Here again, the *Maharal* had anticipated the division into two types of knowledge, but he used the word *Chochmah* (Wisdom) and contrasted *Chochmah Ha'Elyonah* (the higher wisdom) with *Chochmah Shel Adam* (the wisdom of man). *Netivot Olam*, vol. 2, Jerusalem 1971, p. 247.

Ve'Emeth, though occasionally expressed in personal terms, were not concerned with persons. They owed their origins and their occasional ferocity to the accurate perceptions of most participants[34] that they were dealing with one of the most fundamental challenges the Jews of Europe had had to face. The book focused attention on the question of the relationships between Jews and Gentiles, that in the transition from passivity in domination to participation in liberalism, a social ethic – a *Derech Eretz* was needed, to guide and pattern Jewish communities. As yet, no appropriate model was available, no suitable solution was at hand.

It was only natural that if changing conditions called for new and extended guidance on social behaviour, Jewish thinking should turn to the concept of *Derech Eretz*. For all the various interpretations which had been linked with it, it was broadly the equivalent of a social ethic and there was much in the literature dealing with *Derech Eretz*, which addressed itself quite specifically to questions concerning proper and correct attitudes to the world of Gentiles and the laws of host societies.[35] The dispute between Naphtali Herz Weisel and his rabbinical critics was so influential because it raised central questions of the what and when of *Derech Eretz*. That is to say, what is the proper meaning of the concept, what part should it play in the life of the Jew and when should it be imparted to the people. The *Maharal*, as we have seen, tried to encompass all the different characteristics associated with *Derech Eretz* by defining it as the principle which concerned itself with all things related to the body, while Torah was concerned with the needs of the soul. Since the needs of the body are continuously manifest and precede the capacity to acquire Torah, it follows that *Derech Eretz* must come first.[36] Weisel's formulation was very similar.[37] He did not regard secular learning and social behaviour as purely instrumental activities, but elevated them to a plane where, especially to a child, they would appear as moral values of an importance equal to any religious code he might later study. It was this which created the strong opposition to Weisel.

The core of the dispute remained unresolved, but the inexorable changes which swept over Europe carried the Jews with them. The Tolerance Edict was extended eastward in 1789, secular schools for Jewish children were established and Jews were recruited into the Austrian army.[38] The French Revolution led to

[34]With the likely exception of Weisel himself, who seems to have been a naive and insensitive catalyst in events which he does not appear to have understood.

[35]For an extended discussion, see Jacob Katz, *Exclusiveness and Tolerance*, Oxford 1961.

[36]The text is quite unequivocal, 'Kodem Derech Eretz ve'acher Kach Ha'Torah' (First comes Derech Eretz and after that the Torah), *Derech Chaim, op. cit.*, p. 70, but he elaborates this later by arguing that man has been given two evil inclinations. Those who are occupied with *Derech Eretz* (the body) are liable to succumb to temptations of immorality, while those who are occupied with Torah (soul/mind) are liable to succumb to temptations of alien ideologies, *ibid.*, p. 72.

[37]Cf. Assaf, *op. cit.*, p. 225, 'Torath Ha'Adam Kodemeth bi'sman Le'Chukei Ho'Elokim' (Human knowledge precedes in time the laws of God.)

[38]Rabbi Ezekiel Landau, the vigorous opponent of Weisel, was nevertheless deeply involved in the changes which were taking place. In 1782 (only a few weeks after delivering the sermon we have discussed – note 20 –), he opened a school for girls and in 1789 he addressed Jewish soldiers recruited into the Austrian army. See Ruth Kestenberg-Gladstein, *op. cit.*, pp. 70–72, where Landau's address is reported.

the full emancipation of the Jews of France and the Stein-Hardenberg administration was preparing the way for an eventual emancipation of the Jews of Prussia. The steadily growing level of state intervention in Jewish communal affairs led to a continuous decline in communal influence and control although this was more evident in larger communities in the cities of Europe than in the small rural settlements, where people, in the spirit of their environment, tended to preserve a more conservative response to change. The fact that neither Jew nor Gentile had a clear conception of what emancipation could or should mean to and for those who aspired to obtain it, led to division and ambivalence. By the end of the eighteenth century, some Jews had responded to the uncertainty of their position by rejecting Judaism outright through conversion to Christianity, others sought to "reform" what they considered to be archaic elements in Judaism and to meet the Gentile population by adopting their mores and social expectations. There were also those who pretended that nothing was changing and that any alteration of traditional practice was neither necessary nor desirable. But most Jews, though bemused and bewildered, regarded such trends as altogether too extreme. They wanted guidance on how to combine the best of both the worlds clamouring for their loyalty.

II

In 1811, Moses Sofer also known as the *Chatham* Sofer, originally from Frankfurt a. Main, at the time Chief Rabbi of Pressburg (Hungary) and the most widely known and respected rabbi of his day,[39] addressed himself once more to the problem of *Derech Eretz*, its meaning, its timing and its relationship to Torah. Sofer developed his theme in the context of a sermon addressed to a group of fathers concerned about the education of their children. His text was *Exodus* XIII:17, the opening sentence of "the portion of the week" (*Beshallach*).[40] He reminded his audience that there had long been established principles in traditional Jewish attitudes to secular knowledge, dating back to the Talmud and supported and reiterated by such eminent authorities as "the father of philosophers", Maimonides, and Rabbi Moses Isserles.[41]

[39]Cf. *Der dreifache Faden*, vol. I; *Rabbi Moses Sofer*, by Solomon Schreiber, Basel 1952; S. Ehrmann, 'Moses Sofer', in Leo Jung (ed.), *Jewish Leaders, op. cit.*, pp. 115–138; Mordechai Breuer, 'Emancipation and the Rabbi', in *Niv Hamidrashia*, Jerusalem 1978–1979, pp. 26–51.
[40]The Torah is recited weekly in fixed portions, named after a key word in the first sentence, in this case, *Beshallach*. I have not been able to discover why Sofer should have turned again to the theme of the Weisel dispute twenty-nine years after it took place and six years after the death of Weisel.
[41]Moses Isserles (R'MOH) (1530–1572) was a leading Polish rabbi. His gloss on the *Shulchan Aruch* (the main Code of Law for observant Jews) is accepted as binding to this day. Secular studies are referred to in the Talmud as "a walk in the garden". The Talmud (*B Chagigah* 14b) relates the story of four great rabbis who undertook such a "walk". One died, one became demented, one apostatised and one came through unharmed. Maimonides, commenting on this (*Hilchoth Yesodei Torah*, 4:13), argued that the rabbis were strong to undertake this walk, because "it is not proper to dally in the garden till one has first filled oneself with bread and meat", i.e. mastered the Torah in full. Isserles took the view that once a person has mastered all (Jewish) Law, it is permissible to study "other wisdom", although such study will bring no reward. (Comment on *Shulchan Aruch-Yore De'a*, 246:4.)

In any event, said Sofer, basic sciences were part and parcel of essential Jewish knowledge, because they were necessary for understanding laws concerning permitted and forbidden foods, the construction of boundaries for Sabbath observance, the construction of huts for Tabernacles and many other laws. That left the more speculative sciences,[42] and these, as had been decreed, could be studied by those well versed in Jewish law, but not, acccording to the best authorities, until a person had reached the age of twenty-five. Sofer then pointed out that the Israelites, whilst in Egypt, had neither wisdom nor knowledge. According to the Talmud, they did not possess the most elementary rules of social behaviour (*Derech Eretz*) until Moses came and taught them.[43] It might have been supposed that, as a first stage in their liberation, the Israelites would spend some time during their wanderings in the desert learning some basic rules of social intercourse and the benefits of a formal etiquette, but they were destined to carry out a sacred mission, and so they were led straight to Sinai to receive the Torah. Only later did they learn the rudiments of *Derech Eretz*. To Sofer, this sequence was clear evidence that the study of Torah must be the prior task, and that all other kinds of knowledge were to be secondary. He continued his sermon by offering an interpretation of *Exodus* XIII:17 which was to have far-reaching consequences for religious Jewry in Germany. The biblical sentence states that, when Israel came out of Egypt, "God did not lead them by way of the land of the Philistines (in Hebrew: *Derech Eretz P'lishtim*), although that was near; for God said 'Lest peradventure the people repent when they see war, and they return to Egypt.'" Sofer read this as: "God did not lead them to the way of life of the Philistines" because it was too much like the way of life of the Egyptians, so that, if the Israelites were faced with conflicts over "their appetites and their evil inclinations" they would revert to the customs and norms of slavery they had learned in Egypt.[44] Sofer thus offered a new interpretation of *Derech Eretz*. It was no longer a collective concept for a variety of social needs. It now described the way of life, the life-style, the culture of a given people. Accordingly, education for *Derech Eretz* went far beyond the social adaptation discussed by Weisel and the *Maskilim* of his time. It would now become a question of acculturation and assimilation, processes which Sofer regarded as inimical to Jewish survival. He rejected emancipation altogether, relying instead on a doctrine of complete loyalty to the secular rulers of his time. In the letters he contributed to the *Tempelstreit* in Hamburg in 1818 he repeatedly insisted on the absolute obligation of the Jew to observe Jewish tradition unchanged and to be a loyal subject to his rulers.[45] Sofer saw no conflict between the Jews' messianic expectation and loyalty to the king. Even in the Hasmonean period Jews prayed for the restoration of the house of David.[46] So strong is the demand for loyalty to the king that "Every person is obliged to love his king as himself and hate his enemies".

[42] Referred to in the *Talmud* as "Creation and *Merkava*" (*B Chagigah* 14b).

[43] *B Yoma*, 75b.

[44] *Sefer Torath Moshe* (The Chatham Sofer on the Torah), vol. 2, New York 1960, pp. 20–22, quote on p. 216.

[45] *Eile Divrei Habrith*, Altona 1819.

[46] First letter, *ibid*., pp. 6–11.

This applies to fellow Jews loyal to another king. In the event of conflict the duty to remain loyal is paramount. Reasons for such unswerving loyalty given by Sofer are: firstly that the king has power of life and death and secondly that "We believe that kings are divinely appointed", hence it is forbidden to criticise the king. For all that, Jews should keep aloof from the people in the kingdom. The expulsion of the Jews from Spain was due to their closeness to the *Umoth*, in other words emancipation was too dangerous. A system of toleration would help Jews to remain true to "the sages of Israel and their leaders".[47]

The determination to soften the impact of emancipation by retaining complete control over the institutional means for change could only survive as long as Landau's powerful personality exerted influence over current events and it collapsed with his death. Sofer's exclusiveness was seen as a hindrance by Jews and non-Jews alike. Whilst their basic attitudes did not entirely disappear, they certainly lay dormant in the restless and exciting years of the Napoleonic era. Long before Jews achieved full and formal emancipation, many of them enjoyed the advantages of higher education, were able to move into the ranks of merchants, bankers and professionals and, above all, were able to leave the confining atmosphere of small town communities and move to the big cities, into Gentile neighbourhoods and metropolitan worlds of culture and entertainment.[48] As a result of these freedoms, the drift from the ancestral faith among the Jews became a flood and neither governmental constraints nor the appearance of a Reform Movement which tried to stem the flood by legitimating the rejection of religious practices,[49] could prevent the widespread disarray of the Jews or quieten the discontent of their young. If the great rabbinical leaders were temporarily forgotten or ignored, Naphtali Weisel was much remembered and his reputation does not appear to have suffered greatly as a result of the fierce dispute over his *Divrei Shalom Ve'Emeth*. On 13th March 1838, the *Allgemeine Zeitung des Judenthums* carried an appeal from the descendants and relatives of Weisel for funds to publish his literary *Nachlass*, in particular *Olelot Naftali*, a commentary on the book of *Genesis*. The appeal was supported in glowing terms

---

[47]Second letter, *ibid.*, pp. 30–45, quote on p. 41.

[48]Kurt Wilhelm quoted some startling figures for Jewish populations:

	1850	1871	1925
Berlin	9,595	36,015	171,912
Frankfurt	5,200	7,620	29,658
Leipzig	320	2,903	10,068

'Kleinstadt- und Grosstadtgemeinden', in *Bulletin des Leo Baeck Instituts*, Nr. 5 (1958), p. 22. Similar figures are given by Alfred Jospe in 'A Profession in Transition. The German Rabbinate, 1910–1939', in *LBI Year Book XIX* (1974), p. 51.

[49]For all the new freedoms enjoyed by Jews, governmental control of Jewish populations and activities remained strong throughout the century. To give but one example, the notorious *Matrikelgesetz*, which ordained that only the oldest son in a family had the right to marry was in force in Bavaria until the mid-nineteenth century. In 1850, the Bavarian Government embarked on a searching inquiry into the activities of its Jewish population. Cf. David Alexander Winter, 'Geistige Kämpfe um Lebensfragen und Weltanschauung des Judentums . . .', in *Jeschurun*, XVI, 3/4 (1929), pp. 144–166. It is not possible to do justice here to this important topic or to the Reform Movement. For a standard history, see David Philipson, *The Reform Movement in Judaism* (new rev. edn.) New York 1967.

by *Chacham* Isaak Bernays (1792–1849)[50] and was followed by a short article on Weisel by the editor of the *Allgemeine Zeitung des Judenthums*, Ludwig Philippson. He described Weisel as a purely literary man, wholly committed and loyal to Jewish tradition. Unlike Moses Mendelssohn, who sought to combine Judaism with European culture, Weisel's purpose had been to "develop Judaism within itself" (*in sich selbst zu bilden*). Weisel wanted only to restore timeless Jewish treasures of old to their former glory. There is no mention of *Divrei Shalom Ve'Emeth*. The project was supported by men like Michael Creizenach of Frankfurt a. Main and Abraham Geiger of Wiesbaden.[51] Weisel was greatly admired by the fiery champion of Orthodoxy, Salomon Plessner, and, according to Meisel, Weisel was offered the position of *Chacham* by the Sephardic community in London around 1800.[52] It is possible, even likely, that Weisel influenced a youthful Samson Raphael Hirsch, the man destined to resolve the bitter conflict over the way in which Jewish children should be taught in conditions of freedom.[53]

III

In the 1830s, a young rabbi, Samson Raphael Hirsch (1808–1888), a pupil of Isaak Bernays and Jakob Ettlinger (1798–1871),[54] addressed himself to the central question of his time: is a Judaism loyal to the Torah possible for Jews living in civilised societies and about to have the benefits and freedoms of emancipation. Hirsch, a modern traditionalist, a conservative innovator, examined the problem in his *Neunzehn Briefe über Judentum*, which was published in

---

[50]Written in the traditional form of a rabbinic approbation it opens thus: "Who is there among us from all the remnant of Israel who has drawn from the well of living waters giving forth Torah and wisdom which the singer, crammed with name and glory, his honour, our teacher, the Rabbi Naftali Herz Weisel dug for us etc. etc.", *Allgemeine Zeitung des Judenthums*, II, 31 (1838), p. 122.
In the event the appeal in the *Allgemeine Zeitung des Judenthums* was unsuccessful. After some attempts by Weisel's son to get the manuscript printed it was eventually published by the *Mekizei Nirdamim* in stages between 1868 and 1871. The manuscript was edited by Elieser Lipmann Silbermann of Lyck who chose an unoriginal title, *Imrei Shefer*, for the commentary.
[51]*Allgemeine Zeitung des Judenthums*, ibid., pp. 121–123.
[52]Meisel, *op. cit.*, p. 169.
[53]There are a number of reasons why it seems likely that Weisel influenced Samson Raphael Hirsch.
   1. S. R. Hirsch was a student of *Chacham* Bernays who, as we have seen, strongly supported Weisel's work.
   2. Meisel dedicated his biography of Weisel to Gabriel Riesser and Z. H. May, the Registrator of the Jewish community in Hamburg and a great friend of Hirsch. (See Hirsch's letter to Z. H. May in Isidor Grunfeld's translation of *Horeb. A Philosophy of Jewish Laws and Observances*, 2 vols., London 1962, vol. I, pp. 141–145.)
   3. Like Weisel, S. R. Hirsch showed a strong interest in linguistic analysis (cf. Hirsch's commentary on the *Pentateuch*).
   4. While Weisel wanted to present Judaism "in sich selbst", S. R. Hirsch sought to explain it "aus sich selbst".
[54]Pinchas E. Rosenblüth, 'Samson Raphael Hirsch. Sein Denken und Wirken', in *Das Judentum in der Deutschen Umwelt 1800–1850, Studien zur Frühgeschichte der Emanzipation*, herausgegeben von Hans Liebeschütz und Arnold Paucker, Tübingen 1977 (Schriftenreihe wissenschaftlicher Abhandlungen des Leo Baeck Instituts 35), esp. pp. 297–302.

1836[55] under the pseudonym Ben Usiel. The first letter, from "Benjamin" to a young rabbi, offers a remarkably concise, astute and comprehensive review of the attitudes and discontents which reflected the disenchantment and alienation of the young with their ancestral traditions and explained the reasons for the widespread desertions from the ranks of the faithful. Hirsch argued that young people learned about Judaism first from their parents, then from mainly Polish teachers who had neither the language nor the comprehension to make their lessons meaningful, also through the destructive influence of Christian writers, and advocates of Reform in Judaism, and, finally, through the pressure of constant conflict between religious and social demands on the one hand and personal convenience on the other. The purpose of religion should surely be happiness and fulfilment, but what happiness was there for Jews, unknown or despised by those who were constantly achieving new heights in culture, well-being and happiness, while Jews remained impoverished in all that which elevated and ennobled? What fulfilment had there been for Jews in science, art, culture, discovery; in fact, what greatness had Jews achieved compared with other nations?[56] Jews were denied national status, but were still regarded as a nation, and it was Jewish teaching that was responsible for this. It insisted on Jews being separate, which gave rise to ill-feeling and mistrust. Its counsel of suffering in silence led to contempt. It disavowed creative arts, speculative thinking. It concentrated on petty and trivial rules – how could that be combined with, or compared to the study of Virgil and Shakespeare, Leibniz and Kant? The Jew was told to fear God, to pray, to fast and to read meaningless

[55]Hirsch published this originally under the name *Ben Usiel* in Altona 1836. I have used the 3rd edition, Frankfurt a. Main 1901. An English version was published in New York in 1969. There is a very large, though widely scattered, literature on and by Hirsch. Among the more important items I have been able to consult are the paper by Rosenblüth already referred to above, and his earlier paper, 'Die geistigen und religiösen Strömungen in der deutschen Judenheit', in *Juden im Wilhelminischen Deutschland 1890–1914*. Ein Sammelband herausgegeben von Werner E. Mosse unter Mitwirkung von Arnold Paucker, Tübingen 1976 (Schriftenreihe wissenschaftlicher Abhandlungen des Leo Baeck Instituts 33). There is valuable information also in Mordechai Breuer's 'Emancipation and the Rabbis', in *Niv Ha' Midrashia*, 13/14, Tel-Aviv 1978–1979, pp. 26–51. Isaac Breuer has a chapter on Hirsch in Leo Jung, *Jewish Leaders*, *op. cit.*, which in its adulation comes near to being idolatry. He also has a paper, 'S. R. Hirsch as a Guide to Jewish History', in Jacob Breuer (ed.), *Fundamentals of Judaism*, New York 1969, which includes some of Hirsch's writings. Isidor Grunfeld has a long and profound introductory chapter on Hirsch in his translation of *Horeb*, *op. cit.*, and a shorter equally profound introduction to the two volume edition of *Judaism Eternal. Selected Essays*, *S. R. Hirsch*, London 1967. He had earlier published a small volume, *Three Generations – The Influence of S. R. Hirsch on Jewish Life and Thought*, London 1958. See also Hermann Schwab, *The History of Orthodox Jewry in Germany*, London n.d. [1950], Jakob Rosenheim, *Hirsch's Cultural Ideal . . . op. cit.*, and *Erinnerungen 1870–1920*, Frankfurt a. Main 1970. Noah Rosenbloom, *Tradition in an Age of Reform*, Philadelphia 1976; Friedrich Thieberger, 'Samson Raphael Hirsch', in *Der Jude*, IV, 12 (1920), pp. 556–566; Yechiel Weinberg, 'Mishnato shel R. S. R. Hirsch', in *Seride Esh*, Pt.4, Jerusalem 1977; Isaac Heinemann, 'S. R. Hirsch. The Formative Years of the Leader of Modern Orthodoxy', in *Historia Judaica*, 13 (1951), pp. 29–54; J. Wohlgemuth, 'S. R. Hirsch und das gesetzestreue Judentum', in *Jeschurun*, XIV, 1/2 (1927), pp. 1–24. Of course Breuers' *Jüdische Orthodoxie im Deutschen Reich*, already referred to supersedes much of the above and also the more recent study by Liberles, *Religious Conflict in Social Context*, *op. cit.*

[56]This line of argument was also a dominant theme among the young Hegelians. Bruno Bauer made this criticism strongly in his critique of Jewish Emancipation and Karl Marx repeated it in his contribution to the debate. See my *Karl Marx and the Radical Critique of Judaism*, London 1978.

Scriptures. He faced great difficulties when he tried to earn a living, establish social relations with Gentiles; even when he travelled. Reform Judaism was no solution because that would mean moving out of Judaism, while traditional rabbis were no help because they held too widely divergent views. "Benjamin" posed one more question. He was about to get married – was there any point in transmitting this discredited Judaism to his children?

In his reply to this imaginary but widely-held criticism of Judaism, Hirsch, who was then twenty-eight years old, set out his conception of the place of Judaism in *Bürger* society, which is sharply delineated, systematic and programmatic. It summarises everything he was to achieve, create and write in a long life of dedicated service, of spiritual, communal and educational leadership. Hirsch was a reformer, a moderniser, who justified his innovations (L19)[57] by exploring and explaining Judaism "from within itself" (*aus sich selbst heraus*). (L2) He postulated four pillars of his system – the *Mensch* who becomes Jew (Yisroel) through his faith in and fear of God, whom he serves by a complete acceptance of his Torah. (L2) This "Mensch-Yisroel" is chosen, not in the sense that "other peoples cannot belong to God, but in that no other God belongs to Yisroel". (L14) The worth of a Jew is measured not by the extent of his service but in its proportion. The Jew has a calling (*Beruf*),[58] a lifelong obligation to study and practice. (L13) He obeys the Torah as an objective reality, because, like nature, the Torah is a fact. Like nature it has immutable laws, and just as we cannot defy the laws of nature without violating ourselves and our environment, so we cannot defy the laws of Torah without doing violence to our spiritual selves and our spiritual environment. Judaism is oppressive for those for whom freedom only means indulgence. (L14) This message is forced home again and again. Ownership (*Besitz*) and personal indulgence (*Genuss*) are acceptable only as a means to an end (*Mittel*), never as an end in itself (*Zweck*). In this sense, Hirsch welcomes emancipation as an opportunity for the Jew to live as "Mensch unter Menschen" (L16), but, he continues, although emancipation is to be welcomed, "it does not make us bigger or smaller". (L17) It brings demands for reforms of empty, mechanical practice, of distorted religious rituals, of magic and superstition (*Amulettenkram*) to ward off physical evils.[59] Not, however, by levelling Judaism down to its environment, as the Reform Movement tried to do, but by raising the environment to the level of the Torah, for only Torah makes true reform possible. (L17) Hirsch is critical of Maimonides and of Mendelssohn; the former because he tried to harmonise Judaism with the philosophy of his time, and the latter because he thought that it was possible to be an observant Jew and yet be a German Plato. It was the "and yet" which showed up Mendelssohn's

---

[57]References to the *Neunzehn Briefe* will be given here in parenthesis e.g. (L5) = The Fifth Letter.

[58]In the sense that Max Weber has developed the concept in *The Protestant Ethic and the Spirit of Capitalism* (originally published 1923), transl. by T. Parsons, London 1962.

[59]In a letter to Z. H. May written in April 1835, in which Hirsch explained his reasons for writing *Horeb*, he complained that "Judaism has become an inherited mummy", venerated but, "a veneration without spirit". In Grunfeld, *Horeb, op. cit.* vol. 1, pp. cxlii–cxliii (see below). We should note here that *Horeb* was completed before the *Neunzehn Briefe*, which were published as a sort of prospectus for *Horeb*.

error. (L18) The real challenge was to be accepted *as* a Jew, not *in spite* of being Jewish. (L15) Education was the key to achieving a sound Judaism with emancipation, and Hirsch gave notice, fifteen years before putting his plan into practice, that the establishment of Jewish schools was his aim. (L18) Nationhood and independent statehood were brushed aside as potentially desirable but unimportant, not least because Yisroel had achieved more in the *Galut* than in its days of glory. (L9)

A year after the publication of the *Neunzehn Briefe*, which were tremendously successful, Hirsch published *Horeb*, a compact code of Jewish law, addressed, in the first instance, to Yisroel's thinking young men and women.[60] Both these books were written while Hirsch was in Oldenburg, when he wanted to capture the attention of the young. "I see a younger generation" he wrote to Zwi Hirsch May, "aglow with noble enthusiasm for Judaism – or rather for Jews. These young men do not know authentic Judaism . . ."[61] He was appointed Rabbi of the *Israelitische Religionsgesellschaft* in Frankfurt a. Main in 1851, where his prodigious literary output was less generalised and gave much attention to practical issues. He espoused an increasingly separatist approach to the wider Jewish community and formally ratified this position when he was able to persuade the Prussian Government to recognise his community as a separate organisation, legally differentiated from the more broadly based *Gemeinde* (1876). The greatest disappointment of his life was the refusal of all but a handful of his followers to accept his lead and to dissociate themselves from the *Gemeinde*.[62]

Hirsch's literary output included a long commentary on the *Pentateuch*,[63] a study of Jewish symbolism,[64] and short, but incisive and important essays on Jewish education.[65] For all that, it was not the voluminous literary activity, the successful schools he established in Frankfurt a. Main, or the single-minded intensity with which he insisted on an uncompromising observance of every detail of Jewish law, which made the deepest impression on his contemporaries

---

[60]*Versuche über Jisroels Pflichten in der Zerstreuung zunächst für Jisroels denkende Jünglinge und Jungfrauen*, Altona 1837. I have used the 3rd edition Frankfurt a. Main 1899. In the translation by Grunfeld, *Horeb, op. cit.*, the change in sub-title is characteristic of the change in audience since the Second World War, which is now predominantly intellectual rather than the intelligent lay public Hirsch addressed himself to. Grunfeld, in his seminal Introduction to *Horeb* writes on "A Jewish theory of knowledge, of moral law and symbolism in Jewish Law". In the wake of the powerful Breuer family and men like Jakob Rosenheim, Grunfeld has contributed much to the representation of Hirsch and his work in the English-speaking world of Jewish studies.

[61]See note 59, *op. cit.*, p. cxliii.

[62]Rosenheim (*Erinnerungen, op. cit.*, p. 33) has stated that only seventy persons joined the *Austrittsgemeinde*, including all teachers and employees of the *Religionsgesellschaft*, and he records a moving sermon delivered by Hirsch in his final years in which he gave vent to his bitterness. Rosenheim has also suggested that it led Hirsch to give up the Directorship of his School (1877) in favour of his son, Mendel, *ibid.*, pp. 36 and 37.

[63]The first volume was published in 1867 and the fifth in 1878. They were published in Frankfurt a. Main.

[64]A new, English version, *Jewish Symbolism*, has recently been published as vol. 3 of *S. R. Hirsch. The Collected Writings* by the Joseph Breuer Foundation with the S. R. Hirsch Publication Society, New York 1984.

[65]These are in the six volume *Gesammelte Schriften*, Frankfurt a. Main 1906. Some of them are available in English in I. Grunfeld (ed.), *Judaism Eternal*, vol. 1, London 1956.

and on his later admirers. Hirsch was identified in the first instance by a motto he used to popularise the challenge facing emancipated Jewry – *Torah im Derech Eretz*. Significantly, for all the popularity and pervasiveness of the motto, for all that it was destined to become the hallmark of Orthodox German Jews, Hirsch, the prolific writer, the indefatigable exegete, did not offer a basic discussion or theoretical explanation of this motto. Not surprisingly, it came to mean many things to many people and this indeterminacy was probably deliberate, part of its charm and part of its utility. Nevertheless, S. R. Hirsch did go some way towards an elaboration of his ideas in his commentary on *Genesis* III:24 (published in 1867) where *Derech Eretz* is described "als der Weg der Kultur", the road to social wisdom, morality and order. In this respect he agreed with the view of Moses Sofer. He explained *Midrash Leviticus Rabbah* (9:3) did indeed imply that *Derech Eretz* precedes Torah, as Weisel had interpreted it to his cost, but that this applied only to Gentiles, to those who used culture "im Dienste der Sittlichkeit", which would eventually lead them to God. He thus also accepted Landau's critique of Weisel, because; "Für uns Juden fällt Derech Eretz und Torah zusammen." This is how the bitter conflicts of the past were resolved and the acceptance of emancipation was made possible. *Sittlichkeit* was that element of a host culture which indicated that its adherents were realising their way to God, and "darum soll auch der Jude allem Wahren und Guten der Kultur hold sein". Where culture becomes an aim in itself and does not lead to Torah, it can only lead to degeneration (*Entartung*). Schiller embodies the perfect spirit of true culture. His poetry speaks above all "of the moral elevation of man" (*sittliche Erhebung*); Jewish sages would have celebrated him as "a sage of the nations", because his work is "consciously or unconsciously" saturated with Jewish ideas and Jewish attitudes.[66]

It is not at all clear when Hirsch began to make use of the motto. Some basic views on education are discussed in the *Neunzehn Briefe* (L12 and L18) and in *Horeb* (Chapter 84), but without the use of the motto, or the concept *Derech Eretz*. Yet the image of the "Mensch-Yisroel" is very close to the model suggested by Naphtali Herz Weisel whose concept of a *Torath Adam* (science of man) is also used by Hirsch in the same way.[67] As Mordechai Breuer has pointed out, Hirsch's conception of Torah and nature as sources of divine revelation made the study of nature as obligatory and as proper as was the study of the Torah,[68] and Isaac Breuer has stressed that Hirsch wanted to reject the approach of the "rabbis of the old days" who "clung defiantly to the wreckage of the old circumstances" with the "tragic tenacity of desperation".[69] Hirsch himself, in the letter to May we have already mentioned, refers to people who "are out of date and relics of the last decades of the previous century". We have also noted that Hirsch's teacher, Isaak Bernays, took a very favourable view of Weisel and as we have seen, commended a posthumous work by him in 1838. All this suggests that Hirsch approved of Weisel's educational proposal, albeit with some reservations,

---

[66]On Schiller see Hirsch's address to the *Schillerfeier* of 1859 in *Gesammelte Schriften*, vol. 6, esp. p. 311.
[67]*Judaism Eternal, op. cit.*, vol. I, p. 163.
[68]Cf. 'Emancipation and the Rabbis', *loc. cit.*, esp. p. 45.
[69]*Fundamentals of Judaism, op. cit.*, pp. 244–245.

and resolved the partial opposition of Ezekiel Landau and the total opposition of Moses Sofer. However, when *Horeb* and *Neunzehn Briefe* were written, Moses Sofer was still very much alive. Hirsch was then young and extremely conscious of his lack of stature. In any event, he had also declared unequivocally, "I never attack real or imaginary persons",[70] but we may be justified in assuming that Hirsch developed his educational ideas and the use of the motto *Torah im Derech Eretz* from Weisel's *Divrei Shalom Ve'Emeth*. The objections he would have raised would have been to Weisel's parallelism, of seeing secular and Torah studies pursued side by side. Hirsch's unique contribution was the notion of demanding that secular studies themselves be infused with the spirit of Torah, and that the learning process be dedicated to the service of God quite as much as any Torah studies.

It has been suggested that the motto was not used by Hirsch until the establishment of his *Realschule* in Frankfurt a. Main in 1853.[71] As a slogan for creating a new approach to education it was spectacularly successful and spread quickly beyond the confines of the school. When the school was opened, Hirsch set out its aim as follows: "dass sie religiöses Wissen und religiöses Streben mit echter, wahrhaft sozialer Bildung im innigen Zusammenhang bringe, das religiöse Ewige mit dem menschlich Zeitlichen, das speziell Jüdische mit dem allgemein Menschlichen als einheitliches Bildungselement pflege . . ."[72] Hirsch defined the purpose of the school in very similar terms in a famous article:

> "Die innige Vermählung des religiösen Wissens und des religiösen Lebens mit echter, wahrhaft sozialer Bildung; das ist die innige aufrichtige Vermählung der Torah im Derech Eretz."[73]

Hirsch and his disciples insisted that the concept, *Torah im Derech Eretz*, was not new, that it had its source well-established by Saadia Gaon (tenth century) and after him Bachya ibn Pakuda in 'The Second Gate' of his *Chovoth Halevavoth*.[74] The motto, nevertheless, came to be perceived as "gesellschaftlich verflacht" by an observer who was a product of Hirsch's School, who subsequently became Chairman of its Board of Management and who was one of Hirsch's most ardent admirers, disciples and publicists.[75] There are a number of reasons for this. Hirsch's mission was primarily intended for and addressed to an educated lay audience.[76] He did not address himself to intellectuals, who, although full of admiration for his dedicated service to the cause of Jewish integrity, felt free to

[70]In the letter to Z. H. May reproduced by Grunfeld in *Horeb, op. cit.*
[71]Pinchas Rosenblüth in his essay on Hirsch (*loc. cit.*, p. 317), but according to Hirsch this slogan was adapted as "leitende Devise" when the *Religionsgesellschaft* in Frankfurt a. Main was founded in 1851. Cf. S. R. Hirsch *Gesammelte Schriften*, vol. 4, p. 338.
[72]*Festschrift zum 75 jährigen Bestehen der Realschule mit Lyzeum der Isr. Religionsgesellschaft Frankfurt am Main* (hereafter *Festschrift*), Frankfurt a. Main 1928, p. 1.
[73]'Jüdisches Schulwesen', *Gesammelte Schriften*, vol. 1, p. 262.
[74]Cf. Rosenheim, *Hirsch's Cultural Ideal . . . , op. cit.*, p. 38.
[75]Rosenheim, *Erinnerungen, op. cit.*, p. 41. There is a marked difference between this little volume, which was published posthumously and the essay by Rosenheim quoted earlier (note 74). The *Erinnerungen* are strikingly frank and offer a critical view of Hirsch and his work which is refreshing and ultimately leads to a better understanding of the man. The other essay reads in many respects like an apology for the strictures in the *Erinnerungen*.
[76]Wohlgemuth, 'S. R. Hirsch und das gesetzestreue Judentum', *loc. cit.*, p. 21.

interpret his message to suit their own ideas and evaluations, or refrained from criticising aspects of his system in loyalty to its greater objective.[77] Linked to this was the reservation that the Hirsch system was not only closed but too inner-directed,[78] so that it failed to lead its followers from Hirsch's school to the *Yeshivah* and, in the hands of the less able disciples, the system was in danger of replacing *Judentum* with "Hirschtum".[79]

The concept of *Torah im Derech Eretz* conjured up an image of a devoutly observant German Jew, loyal to Torah, steeped in German culture, a model citizen, outgoing, socially aware and conscientious. Yet the originator of the motto and the ideal withdrew steadily from the demands he had himself imposed and appeared to prefer an isolation which contrasted sharply with the bold programme of his youth. To some extent, this was due to the growing imbalances in Jewish community structures. Governmental legislation, notably the Prussian Act of 1847, shifted the power towards a lay leadership which was predominantly Reform-orientated, with the effect that religious provisions were neglected or ignored. As we have seen, this was eventually to lead to the formation of separatist communities and their formal recognition in the Act of 1876. Germany, too, was changing. In the second half of the nineteenth century, as we have suggested, the humanistic *Bürgertum* gave precedence to nationalist aspirations. For the Jews, this led to, what Moritz Lazarus called, "national-deutsche Bürger jüdischer Religion". Yet, Hirsch's system was precisely tailored to the civil society of earlier years and he appeared to be unwilling to change it. In his last major work, a translation and the commentary on the Prayerbook,[80] which includes the *Pirkei Avoth*,[81] the source and inspiration of the motto, *Torah im Derech Eretz*, Hirsch offers an explanation of *Derech Eretz* which, characteristically, does not deviate from, or elaborate, earlier deliberations.[82] *Derech Eretz* is explained as that "which embraces everything conditioned by the fact that man has to cope with his existence upon earth, his destiny and his common life with others".[83] This includes adequate preparation for involvement in "bürgerliche Ordnung" and social responsibility concerning "Sitten und Rücksichten der Höflichkeit und des Anstandes" and everything concerned with "allgemeine menschliche und bürgerliche Bildung". Civic responsibility is the recurring theme but the level of involvement is couched in terms of restraint. In the school, "the aim was not to teach Jewish and secular subjects separately, but to show

---

[77]Rosenheim, *Hirsch's Cultural Ideal* . . . , *op. cit.*, p. 54.

[78]Rosenheim, *Erinnerungen, op. cit.*, p. 18. Hirsch's son, Mendel, is reported to have taught *Pentateuch* exclusively with his father's commentary.

[79]*Erinnerungen, op. cit.*, p. 24, where Rosenheim admits that there was some truth in the accusation, though it should be noted that in the later essay, he rejects it altogether, *Hirsch's Cultural Ideal* . . . , *op. cit.*, p. 56.

[80]*Israels Gebete*, Frankfurt a. Main 1895. It was published posthumously by his son, Mendel Hirsch.

[81]This was published separately in English, cf. *Chapters of the Fathers*, Jerusalem-New York 1972.

[82]The concept, *Derech Eretz*, occurs four times in *Pirkei Avoth*, each time having a different meaning in line with the loose way in which this concept is used in rabbinic literature, but Hirsch's translation is significant. Thus for *Avoth* 2:2 he has "bürgerliche Geschäftstätigkeit"; 3:6 "bürgerliches Leben"; 3:21 "bürgerliche Lebensgemeinschaft", 6:6 "bürgerliche Angelegenheiten". The prefix "bürgerlich" emphasises Hirsch's thought and gives the concept a sustained unity.

[83]*Israels Gebete, op. cit.*, p. 436.

their interrelationship. Thus the teacher tried to foster in his pupils a fine Jewish outlook based on a profound grasp of Judaism."[84] For all that Isaac Breuer insisted that Hirsch was opposed to any synthesis of Torah and secular knowledge,[85] the theme of a synthesis was advocated by the School itself[86] but rejected by Hirsch's immediate successor, Salomon Breuer, who defined the relationship between Torah and *Derech Eretz* as "the point at which two lines going in opposite directions meet."[87] The faithful Rosenheim described it as "Torah and culture" and as a "synthesis of West European culture with ancient Torah wisdom".[88] Joseph Wohlgemuth was even more expansive (and, we might note, patriotically German), when he described an "Einswerden der beiden Kulturen",[89] while Friedrich Thieberger, put out by Hirsch's rejection of Jewish Nationalism, caustically referred to two axes "konzentrisch ineinandergeschoben".[90]

IV

If those who followed S. R. Hirsch felt free to interpret the motto he had suggested, this was due to the wider, greater and more universal application of it by one man, a contemporary, an admirer and an antithesis of Hirsch, Esriel Hildesheimer (1820–1899), Rabbi of Eisenstadt (1851–1869), Rabbi of a separatist community in Berlin, founder and director of the *Rabbinerseminar* in Berlin and in the field of Jewish social welfare unmatched by any apart from Moses Montefiore.[91] Esriel Hildesheimer was born in Halberstadt in 1820 and

[84]Zvi E. Kurzweil in *Tradition*, 1, 2 (1960), p. 299.
[85]Cf. Isaac Breuer, 'Samson Raphael Hirsch as a Guide . . .', *loc. cit.*, p. 245.
[86]E.g. *Festschrift, op. cit.*, p. 42.
[87]At the 50th anniversary celebration of the Hirsch School, Salomon Breuer, recently appointed to follow S. R. Hirsch, preached a sermon in which he elaborated on Psalm 118, "The stone which the builders rejected has become the cornerstone." This cornerstone was *Torah im Derech Eretz* in the School, but defined as quoted in the text. See *Festschrift, op. cit.*, p. 5.
[88]*Erinnerungen, op. cit.*, pp. 40 and 69.
[89]Wohlgemuth, 'S. R. Hirsch und das gesetzestreue Judentum', *loc. cit.*, p. 24.
[90]Thieberger, 'Samson Raphael Hirsch', *loc. cit.*, p. 560.
[91]As in the case of S. R. Hirsch, there is, as yet, no definitive biography of Esriel Hildesheimer. A useful collection of essays is the 'Hildesheimer–Gedenkheft', a special issue of *Jeschurun*, VII, 5/6 (1920) (hereafter *Gedenkheft*). Mordechai Eliav has edited *Rabbiner Esriel Hildesheimer Briefe* with very valuable notes, Jerusalem 1965, Isaac Unna has a chapter on Esriel Hildesheimer in Jung, *Jewish Leaders, op. cit.*, there is useful information in Isi Jacob Eisner's 'Reminiscences of the Berlin Rabbinical Seminary', in *LBI Year Book XII* (1967), pp. 32–52. The essays by Rosenblüth mentioned earlier also deal with Esriel Hildesheimer. Hermann Schwab has a chapter on him in *The History of Orthodox Jewry in Germany*, London n.d. [1950]. Generally speaking devotees of S. R. Hirsch often ignore Hildesheimer which is puzzling, but reflects Hirsch's ambivalence towards Hildesheimer and particularly to the Rabbinical Seminary. Grunfeld in his *Three Generations. op. cit.*, makes no mention of Hildesheimer but reports at length on the last two directors of the Rabbinical Seminary who showed an interest in Hirsch's work (pp. 74–79). On Hildesheimer's own work very little is readily available. Apart from the Letters, there is a useful collection, *Gesammelte Aufsätze*, edited by his son, Meir Hildesheimer, Frankfurt a. Main 1923, which contains an especially interesting long paper, 'Die Palästinafrage und ihre Geschichte', pp. 180–217; and a volume of Responsa, *She'eloth u'Tshuvoth Rabbi Esriel*, was published in Tel-Aviv as recently as 1969. Hildesheimer might well be regarded as one of the most neglected major figures in recent Jewish history.

studied, like Hirsch, under Jakob Ettlinger in Altona and Isaak Bernays in Hamburg. He also studied semitics, philosophy and mathematics at the University of Berlin, and received his doctorate in semitics from the University of Halle. Through his marriage to Henrietta Hirsch of Halberstadt he was financially independent and, after a short spell of communal work in his home town, was appointed rabbi of the community of Eisenstadt (Hungary) in 1851. There he established in the same year a *Yeshivah* which was revolutionary because it included in the curriculum German, Greek, Latin and mathematics, all of which Esriel Hildesheimer taught himself, in addition to Talmud and Bible. For eighteen years, Esriel Hildesheimer remained in Eisenstadt, and gathered around him a large group of able and devoted young men, but he also attracted an increasingly fierce hostility from *hasidic* and ultra-Orthodox elements who were strongly opposed to the introduction of secular subjects in his *Yeshivah*. The conflict came to a head at a rabbinical congress in 1868–1869 when Esriel Hildesheimer and a few of his supporters formed themselves into an independent group which was determined to adhere to a dual commitment to Orthodoxy and secular interests, and was dubbed "Kulturorthodoxie".[92] Faced with unrelenting opposition from ultra-Orthodox and Reform advocates, Esriel Hildesheimer decided to accept a call from a small group of Orthodox Jews who felt unable to accept the growing lack of religious practice in the Berlin community. Esriel Hildesheimer began his new ministry by opening a *Religionsschule*. In 1873, in the face of fierce opposition from Reform and Conservative groups, Hildesheimer opened a Rabbinical Seminary and brought some well-known scholars to Berlin to teach there.[93] Following the Act of 1876, Esriel Hildesheimer, like S. R. Hirsch, left the *Gemeinde* and set up an independent *Kehillah*. As in Frankfurt, this drastic step led to an improvement in the attitudes of the *Gemeinde* authorities towards the needs and demands of Orthodox members, which in turn led to a ruling by the famous Talmudist and Rabbi of Würzburg, Seligmann Baer Bamberger (1807–1878), that there was no objection to full membership of a community which included members of the Reform Movement, under certain specified conditions. Esriel Hildesheimer had held that view in the context of his welfare work for a long time and carefully avoided any involvement in the bitter dispute which this issue sparked off between S. R. Hirsch and Bamberger.[94]

Esriel Hildesheimer wrote as he spoke as he thought and might put together "a mathematical principle, a biblical verse, a quotation from Shakespeare, a talmudic ruling and a Latin phrase", in a single sentence.[95] He was dedicated to study ("Belief is Knowledge") but the right route was from belief to knowledge.

[92] *Encyclopaedia Judaica*, vol. 8, Berlin 1931, cols. 34–37.
[93] I.e. David Hoffmann (1843–1921), a former student from Eisenstadt and later director of the Seminary, Abraham Berliner (1833–1915) and Jakob Barth (1851–1914), later also Hildesheimer's son-in-law.
[94] *Hildesheimer Briefe, op. cit.*, pp. 117–119.
[95] *Gedenkheft, op. cit.*, p. 10. He is also said to have had a strong sense of humour. In a review of Geiger on reform of the services he divided his analysis into four parts: "Sinn, Unsinn, Leichtsinn, Wahnsinn". *Ibid.*

The reverse order would destroy belief. Hence he went to a *Yeshivah* first, then to university.[96] Although a separatist in his religious life, Esriel Hildesheimer was quite exceptional in his charitable and humanitarian activities. He was the first European Jew to draw attention to the plight of the "Falashas", Ethiopian Jews who were under considerable pressure at the time from Christian missionaries (1864). He had a lifelong commitment to the education, training and support of the Jews of Palestine, but failed to enlist S. R. Hirsch's backing for the extensive activities which were connected with this. While his broad sympathies led him to be hailed as a saviour by the *Chovevei Zion*,[97] he was placed under a ban by the ultra-Orthodox for introducing secular studies in Palestinian schools. He appealed to the Austrian government to make kosher food and other religious facilities available to Jewish soldiers, organised care for all wounded soldiers in the Franco-Prussian war, helped cholera-stricken Jews in Baghdad, procured assistance for Jews in Russia and for Jewish refugees from Russia, supported the Jewish poor of Romania and East Prussia and was always willing to help, from the personal level of a penniless student to the international level of the plight of the Jews of Russia. It was done in the name of "Jewish Solidarity" in the spirit of *Torah im Derech Eretz*.[98] He was the only person of his time to suggest Palestine as a haven for refugees from Russia.[99]

Esriel Hildesheimer brought his best students to teach in Berlin's schools and did so himself up until his old age.[100] The immense range of his activities did not prevent him from taking a personal, indeed fatherly, interest in his students, whom he taught systematically through lectures and seminars, but most of all, through his example.[101] Known affectionately as "the Rebbe" by all, he inspired the students and in the course of time these students spread the principle of *Torah im Derech Eretz*, which they had observed and absorbed in the Seminary, across the length and breadth of Germany and beyond.[102] Many carried with them a love and devotion for German culture as strong and as all-embracing as their love for Judaism and Torah. One of them, Nehemia Nobel (1871–1922) wrote: "Ich kann nicht ohne nationales Judentum leben, aber auch nicht ohne Goethe . . ."[103] When another graduate, Salomon Carlebach (1845–1919) published a popular guide to "Moral Purity", sources from Bible and Talmud and sections from S. R. Hirsch's *Horeb* alternated effortlessly with quotations from Friedrich Hebbel and Franz Grillparzer.[104] Esriel Hildesheimer came to be

[96]It will be recalled that this was also the substance of the dispute between Weisel and Rabbi Landau who thus held the same view as Esriel Hildesheimer (see above).
[97]A mainly Russian-based movement for agricultural settlement in Palestine before Zionism.
[98]There is a reference in *Gedenkheft*, *op. cit.*, p. 325, to a book, *Jewish Solidarity*, by Esriel Hildesheimer, Berlin 1880.
[99]Cf. I. Unna, in Jung, *op. cit.*, p. 229.
[100]*Hildesheimer Briefe*, *op. cit.*, p. 279.
[101]*Gedenkheft*, *op. cit.*, p. 57 (Hebrew section, S. Greenberg in a dramatic phrase wrote that "there the shepherds of the children of Israel imbibed a holy spirit".)
[102]I. J. Eisner, *loc. cit.*, has discussed some of the famous graduates of the Seminary.
[103]Quoted by Rosenblüth in *Juden im Wilhelminischen Deutschland*, *op. cit.*, p. 597.
[104]Salomon Carlebach, *Sittenreinheit*, Berlin 1919, 2nd edn., e.g. pp. 34 and 39.

described as the "religious conscience of his time".[105] He had an abiding admiration and regard for S. R. Hirsch[106], but differed quite fundamentally from the older sage; especially on the question of association with "heretics", those who denied the religious position of the Orthodox. Esriel Hildesheimer declared himself firmly in favour of cooperating with all, if it were in the interest of the general welfare.[107] This attitude profoundly influenced the students of the Seminary and through them the role of Orthodoxy in the wider community. By the end of the nineteenth century, S. R. Hirsch and Esriel Hildesheimer had passed away. A new generation of spiritual leaders had taken over, most of them graduates of the Berlin Seminary. The ideas on *Torah im Derech Eretz* which Hirsch had initiated and Esriel Hildesheimer had disseminated were to be tested in the new century by very different tasks and challenges.

V

The innovatory principle of *Torah im Derech Eretz* as conceptualised by S. R. Hirsch and put into operation by Esriel Hildesheimer, is often subsumed under a heading of "New- or Neo-Orthodoxy". There are interesting divides in the use of that term, which deserve to be explored. Originally, the word carried a somewhat pejorative connotation, matching the purposely contemptuous use of "Neologie" to describe Reform Judaism.[108] David Philipson wrote of the "romanticism . . . of Neo-Orthodoxy that delights in the dim half-light of medievalism . . .".[109] This pejorative intent as well as strong conceptual objections, led S. R. Hirsch's immediate heirs and successors to oppose vigorously the use of that term. Joseph Wohlgemuth commented caustically that Hirsch "did not invent Orthodoxy, nor did he create Neo-Orthodoxy as has been suggested by uninformed writers and superficial historians".[110] Salomon Hugo Lieben felt compelled to "reject the accusation that today's Orthodoxy was a new creation of a kind that had never existed previously".[111] Raphael Breuer was even more emphatic. "Rabbi Hirsch lives on in the memory of many as the creator of a new, modern Orthodoxy . . . Nothing could be further from the truth." (*Nichts ist falscher als das*).[112] Such protests notwithstanding, modern

---

[105]*Gedenkheft, op. cit.*, p. 312.

[106]He described Hirsch as "the regenerator of modern Orthodoxy", "the foremost fighter for Orthodox Judaism", *Hildesheimer Briefe*, pp. 119–120.

[107]Cf. *ibid.*, p. 242.

[108]S. R. Hirsch frequently used this term in contrast with "Orthodoxy".

[109]David Philipson, *The Reform Movement in Judaism*, Ktav, 1967 (orig. 1907), p. 395. This is, of course, the Reform position on all Orthodoxy, e.g. David Goldberg defined Orthodoxy as "an attempt to preserve unchanged, and to reassert, medieval Judaism in the modern world", in *The Jewish Chronicle*, 10th March 1973.

[110]*Jeschurun*, IV, 3/4 (1917), p. 135.

[111]*Jeschurun*, IV, 6 (1917), p. 306.

[112]*Nachlat Zvi*, I, 3 (1931), p. 88. We may note here that the *Encyclopaedia Judaica*, Berlin 1931, in an article on S. R. Hirsch makes no mention of neo-Orthodoxy, while the *Encyclopedia Judaica*, Jerusalem 1971 (vol. 12), has a full entry on neo-Orthodoxy. It should also be noted that according to Jacob Toury (*Soziale und politische Geschichte der Juden in Deutschland 1847–1871*, Düsseldorf 1977, pp. 146–147) the term "neo-Orthodoxy" was first used for what we would now call "conservative" Judaism in the American sense, i.e. the Judaism of men like Michael Sachs and Zacharias Frankel.

scholarship appears to be determined to establish "Neo-Orthodoxy" as a legitimate intellectual concept. Beginning perhaps with Max Wiener, who wanted to differentiate an older, total acceptance of adherence to Torah, from a later, "modern" Orthodoxy,[113] the term appears to commend itself to most recent scholars as a specific, analytic tool. Paul Mendes-Flohr and Jehuda Reinharz refer to Samson Raphael Hirsch as "the founder of the movement of Neo-Orthodoxy";[114] Robert Liberles described neo-Orthodoxy as "the confrontation between tradition and modernity",[115] while Mordechai Breuer devotes a whole section to it. Like Wiener, Breuer saw in nineteenth-century Orthodoxy a new type of building, a construction put together from the ruins of the past.[116] Orthodoxy after emancipation differed from its earlier form of "Ghetto Judaism" by its education, *Bildung* and language, by the way Jews dressed, wore beards and limited the use of head-coverings, and in the aesthetics (decorum) in the synagogue. It defined itself not in relation to its older version but in the tension between emancipation and Reform Judaism. Many neo-Orthodox innovations were introduced to keep pace with Reform, so that it was also referred to as "Gegenreform". Neo-Orthodoxy was "modern" in its adaptation to urbanisation,[117] to *Bildung*, the use of mass media and in its willingness to participate in the emancipation process. Its political activities in relation to communal affairs and governmental agencies was "something completely new" (*etwas völlig Neues*).[118] Neo-Orthodoxy stressed different aspects of *Halakhah* than its older form in, for example, its great stress on *Kashruth* and the lesser stress on the separation of the sexes, to emphasise that it was not merely intensified traditionalism but a modernised Orthodoxy. Breuer concluded his argument: "For Hirsch, European culture had a substantive, not merely an instrumental value. His attitude enables us to speak of a Neo-Orthodoxy."[119]

In the light of the material I have presented in this paper, it would seem justified to question the current trend of using the term neo-Orthodoxy and to elevate it to an academic respectability which should be challenged. There are a number of reasons why this term should be rejected. Firstly it had, and has retained, its pejorative inuendo. To accept neo-Orthodoxy means accepting the Reform-based notion of Orthodox medievalism, a polemical, not an academically valid, point. Secondly, the term was clearly in use during S. R. Hirsch's own life-time, though he never employed it, preferring instead to adhere to the usual

---

[113]Max Wiener, *Jüdische Religion im Zeitalter der Emanzipation*, Berlin 1933, pp. 78–81. Wiener was quite emphatic that "die religiös-geistige Geschichte des Judentums ist faktisch ein völliger Neubau . . .", p. 24.

[114]P. R. Mendes-Flohr and J. Reinharz, *The Jew in the Modern World*, New York–Oxford 1980, p. 144.

[115]Liberles, *Religious Conflict in Social Context*, *op. cit.*, p. 228. Kurzweil, in a recent book, has made "neo-orthodoxy" the central concept of his argument, but he is incorrect in crediting Wiener with having coined the expression, cf. Zvi Kurzweil, *The Modern Impulse in Traditional Judaism*, Hoboken 1985, esp. p. XI.

[116]Mordechai Breuer, *Jüdische Orthodoxie* . . . , *op. cit.*, p. 28. For my summary of his argument see the section on 'Neo-Orthodoxy', pp. 27–34.

[117]It is difficult to see what form of adaptation is meant here. The most critical factor for all Orthodox terms was residential segregation, which most of them, by and large, adhered to voluntarily.

[118]*Breuer, op. cit.*, p. 32.

[119]*Ibid.*, p. 33.

"Orthodox". If the "founder" of "neo-Orthodoxy" had no time for the expression, why should we now impose it on him? Thirdly, on a purely linguistic level, the term makes no sense. Orthodoxy means traditional. To have a new traditionalism would seem to be a contradiction in terms. Fourthly, the very existence of the term leads to increasingly far-fetched definitions. We have already referred to the rather loose definition offered by Liberles. More far-fetched is a recent comment by Zvi Kurzweil that "neo-Orthodoxy may be . . . characterised by a fundamentally positive attitude to Zionism . . ."[120] Finally and most importantly, the concept denies the context and historicity of the period in which it was coined. As we have tried to demonstrate throughout this essay, Orthodoxy is based on two fundamental principles. The absolute supremacy of Torah as expressed in *Halakhah* and the inevitability of a degree of separation (*Trennungsprinzip*) at social and communal levels. In their respective ways, the four rabbis we have discussed, in the course of a full century, made a concrete realisation of these two principles, their primary concern. If we take Breuer's chief characteristics of the "neo-Orthodoxy" period, we would have to note that, as far as urbanisation is concerned, all four rabbis functioned in an urban context, though Landau and Sofer had less difficulty with separatism because this, in their time, was for the most part externally imposed. Mass media were not a widespread mode of communication for the earlier period, but in conditions of residential concentration in Prague and Pressburg the use of sermons and rabbinic Responsa may be regarded as appropriate equivalents.[121] While it is true that *Bildung* was not a feature in the lives of Landau and Sofer, it would not be correct to say that they did not participate in the emancipation process because, on the contrary, they were wholly involved in it. If they were less enthusiastic than Hirsch and Hildesheimer, then their attitudes owed as much to the sociopolitical climate of their time, which they understood only too well, as it did to their religious traditionalism. The least convincing and most surprising characteristic identified by Breuer is the participation in political activities. If pre-Hirschian Orthodoxy is represented by Landau and Sofer, then it would be difficult to think of anyone more actively and directly involved in political processes. Both Landau and Sofer had to protect their respective flocks in periods of war and governmental hostility and, in the case of Landau particularly, the Jews of Prague benefited greatly from the high standing he enjoyed at the courts of Maria Theresa and Joseph II. If anything, Hirsch and Hildesheimer are remarkable in that they were able to use their political skills and sophistication so effectively, at a time when the political role of the rabbi was being steadily eroded.

Landau and Sofer belonged to the era of transition from toleration via civil

---

[120]Zvi Kurzweil, 'Meaning and Message of Neo-Orthodoxy', in *The Jewish Chronicle*, 27th March 1987.

[121]Not least because to this day they are primary sources for attitudes and values of that period. In the manner of their time, both were effective publicists. We need only think of the effectiveness of Landau's attack on Weisel and Sofer's intervention in the Hamburg *Tempelstreit*. Cf. *Eile Divrei Habrith, op. cit.*

improvement to equality and emancipation,[122] periods when Jewish responses to the external world were, in the main, passive and reactive. Hirsch and Hildesheimer, on the other hand, were products of and participants in the explosive decade 1835–1845, the period of social unrest, of the decline of absolutism, the period of the "Jewish Question". Germany was dominated by idealist philosophy, by a vigorous Liberalism and by a newly emergent materialism.[123] If S. R. Hirsch's new conceptualisation of Judaism appeared at this time, then it was because it was in the spirit of the day. It was not only Hirsch who set out to bring order into a disorientated traditionalism. This was also the time when Reform representatives like Salomon Steinheim, Salomon Formstecher and Samuel Hirsch tried to bring intellectual coherence to the experimental confusion of early nineteenth-century attempts at reforming Judaism;[124] the time when the critique of Orthodox Judaism in the Reform camp was taken over by elements hostile to the struggle for Jewish emancipation,[125] a time when the existence of a "petrified" Orthodoxy was condemned as a "medieval luxury".[126]

The *Halakhah* of Orthodox Judaism was never static and its separatism was not, in itself, a barrier to intellectual, cultural and political interaction.[127] If the perpetuation of these two factors remains a part of a critique of Orthodoxy, then this is due in no small measure to the retention of outdated views on a supposed Orthodox medievalism, which is part of its nineteenth-century negative image, which was projected to bolster the legitimacy of its opponents. We can see now why the followers after Hirsch objected to the use of the term "neo-Orthodoxy", and how its more recent drift into academic usage is persuading even Orthodox scholars to perpetuate it.[128]

[122]This classification of periods was suggested by Volkmar Eichstädt in his *Bibliographie zur Geschichte der Judenfrage 1750–1848*, Hamburg 1938, p. V.

[123]See for a general background Theobald Ziegler, *Die geistigen und sozialen Strömungen des neunzehnten Jahrhunderts*, Berlin 1899, and specifically Albert Lewkowitz, *Das Judentum und die geistigen Strömungen des 19. Jahrhunderts*, Breslau 1935.

[124]Michael A. Meyer, 'Reform Jewish Thinkers and their German Intellectual Context', in Reinharz and Schatzberg, *The Jewish Response to German Culture, op. cit.* It is of interest that some of the changes of the experimental period were subsequently adopted by Orthodox Judaism, e.g. the pulpit, canonical dress etc., cf. Michael A. Meyer, 'Christian Influence on Early German Reform Judaism', in Charles Berlin (ed.), *Studies in Jewish Bibliography. History and Literature in Honour of I. E. Kiev*, New York 1971.

[125]The Reform movement also adopted much of Christian criticism of Judaism. For a full discussion see Carlebach, *Karl Marx and the Radical Critique of Judaism, op. cit.*

[126]Bruno Bauer, *Die Judenfrage*, Braunschweig 1843, p. 115.

[127]Even the bitter dispute between S. R. Hirsch and Rabbi Seligmann Bamberger about the "Austritt" demonstrates its dynamism. See S. R. Hirsch, *Gesammelte Schriften, op. cit.*, vol. 4. A brief but brilliant recent paper by Jonathan Sachs ably illustrates the point. Cf. 'Three Approaches to Halachah', mimeographed 1987.

[128]E.g. Avraham Shalev, 'Torah im Derech Eretz. Germany and Beyond', in *L'Eylah*, 21 (1986).

Jewish Self-Defence

PREAMBLE

At the Leo Baeck Institute Conference on 'The Jews in Nazi Germany' held in October 1985 in Berlin the Editor felt justified in observing that when it came to the *Centralverein deutscher Staatsbürger jüdischen Glaubens* a remarkable consensus amongst Jewish and non-Jewish historians had by now been achieved. Having had to correct myself there on several points I now stand further corrected. Controversy is alive and stirring as the following two debates and their five protagonists amply demonstrate.

The first of the two debates consists of an elaboration of ideas expressed during a public lecture in 1986 in Jerusalem, organised by the Zalman Shazar Centre of the Israel Historical Society and the Frank Green Program for the Research of Modern Jewish History in Europe. Evyatar Friesel, from the Hebrew University of Jerusalem, delivered a lecture on the *Centralverein* which was largely culled from his essay published in LBI Year Book XXXI (1986). Chaim Schatzker, from Haifa University, and the late Abraham Margaliot, from the Hebrew University, commented on the arguments presented and on the policies and structure of the *Centralverein* in general. Friesel responded to their observations and criticism. The three participants of this debate previously worked together on historical questions relating to German Jewry and they were obviously familiar with each other's respective viewpoints. The discussion as it developed also touched on some fundamental questions and the Editor agreed with the three Israeli historians that this debate deserves a place in the Year Book. The reader will, naturally, have to consult Evyatar Friesel's essay in Year Book XXXI first.

Marjorie Lamberti and Jehuda Reinharz belong to the small group of historians whose work on the *Centralverein* can be called seminal. They have shaped and influenced our perception of this, the main defence organisation of European Jewry. They are, however, particularly where the relationship between the *Centralverein* and the German Zionists is concerned, quite often in vociferous and profound disagreement. Marjorie Lamberti's contribution to LBI Year Book XXVII provoked much controversy in general and Jehuda Reinharz felt impelled to present a detailed refutation of some of her arguments. Naturally Marjorie Lamberti has exercised her right to answer. Again the reader will first have to consult the Lamberti article in Year Book XXVII.

Some of the disputants have urged me to participate in this debate, as it is recognised that to a certain degree I have myself been an initiator of the post-war historiography of Jewish Defence. My own stand is well-known and some comment may be called for in the Preface to Year Book XXXIII; but interference by the Editor in the debates themselves is not warranted. The Year Book of the Leo Baeck Institute is a free forum for German-Jewish historiography and the historians must be allowed to present, unhindered, the results of their research, and to voice their disagreement.

A.P.

Comments on Evyatar Friesel's Essay in Year Book XXXI

BY CHAIM SCHATZKER

The article of my friend and colleague, Evyatar Friesel, is undoubtedly an important contribution to the history of the *Centralverein deutscher Staatsbürger jüdischen Glaubens* (C.V.). Even if disagreeing with part of his interpretation, I recognise the objectivity of his approach and the richness of the historical material he offers in his research.

Friesel states that, historically seen, the *Centralverein* was an organisation that fought for the civil rights of German Jews. From that point of view, we are told, the C.V. was similar to the *Alliance Israélite Universelle* in France, or to other associations in England, Austria and elsewhere.

But the French *Alliance* should not be considered as an organisation whose primary task was to act for civil rights. The *Alliance* aimed to raise the education level of Jews in less developed countries, in order to improve their situation, and in that way to add to the good name of Jewry in general. As an indirect consequence of that educational enhancement, it was hoped that the obstacles to the attainment of civil rights would be removed. Therefore, it seems to me that the German-Jewish organisation equivalent of the *Alliance* was not the *Centralverein*, but rather the *Hilfsverein der deutschen Juden* (in Hebrew, "*Ezra*").

But the main difference of opinion between Friesel and myself is about the evaluation of the work of the *Centralverein*. Friesel gives three reasons that justify his objective approach, which avoids any critical dimension while analysing the C.V.'s activities. First, he considers that as an historian it is not his task to pass judgement. Second, he considers the members of the *Centralverein* as bound by the time in which they lived, who have to be comprehended as such. And third, the C.V. leadership acted according to their best understanding and as circumstances seemed to indicate. In Friesel's own words, in the conclusions to his article: ". . . one should not judge or sermonise on the attitudes adopted or the measures taken by the C.V. and its leadership. The *Centralverein* activists were children of their time, rooted in its concepts and hopes. In a complex Jewish situation, they did their best to provide answers for the problems and the challenges of their era. They went as far as reality, as understood by them, made it possible. About their future, they were no better prophets than we are about ours."

I would disagree with all three components of Friesel's conclusions. My own

97

approach, which I shall present further on, is also defined as historical. I too subscribe to the principle of objectivity. And my opinions about the *Centralverein* are far from any lack of sympathy or, so I hope, lack of understanding about the activities of the C.V., or the difficulties under which it laboured.

During the last few years we have witnessed the emergence of a trend in the historical research dealing with the *Centralverein* which is in part apologetic, and which tries to rehabilitate and to legitimise the assimilationist approach in modern Jewry. We hear arguments like: "Why should we start again debates of half a century ago?" Or: "Let bygones be bygone"; "let the dead rest in peace", "even if they were wrong, they did as well as they could"; and so on. Such arguments and such an approach tend to relate to those past disputes in an almost metaphysical way, and to make them seem more and more remote, less and less significant. But the acceptance of that position endangers the very basis of historical research. How could we evaluate historical events even further away in the past, like the Thirty Years' War? Or the internal struggles between the different sects at the time of the Second Temple, which are so important for the understanding of the circumstances that brought about the destruction of the Jerusalem sanctuary? The question, therefore, is not what position we take about the C.V., be it apologetic or critical. It concerns the essence of historical research and its justification.

It is true that the members of the *Centralverein* were children of their time, but people in their own time make mistakes too. Indeed, they were not prophets, and could not have foreseen their future. But they did not see – they did not want to see – their present either. They organised themselves as German citizens of the Jewish faith at a time when German organisations were not ready to accept them as Jews, be it as individuals or as the largest Jewish association of the time. Consequently they were forced, they and other Jewish assimilation-minded groups, to organise in a Jewish frame. Deluded by their innermost wishes they refused to recognise the realities of their time. Stating that conclusion, I have no intention of pretending to be wiser about events that happened in the past. What I am referring to is historical fact that no researcher can fail to accept.

One may well wonder if the *Centralverein* leadership acted as reality dictated. The differences of opinion, during the Weimar years, between the younger activists and the older generation of leaders show that even inside the *Centralverein* there were many doubts about the direction of the organisation. If so, the historian is entitled to an even larger measure of doubt. One may also wonder if the *Centralverein* really developed political action in a larger mass-orientated frame, as Friesel stated in his article. It is to be doubted if the C.V. leadership really understood what the political characteristics of their times were, or the make-up and ways of action of the new political mass parties. In addition, one should ask if the preference for social class interests over existentialist considerations, which expressed itself in the political behaviour of the C.V. until close to 1933, was not a grievous mistake.

True, as Arnold Paucker emphasises in his work on the *Centralverein*, it is easy to criticise the C.V. with hindsight, knowing as we do what happened in Germany. On the other hand, we should not fall into the pit of an historical approach that accepts every event of the past as dictated by "reality" and consequently unavoidable.

Last but not least, Friesel stated that the main task of the *Centralverein* was the struggle for the civil equality of German Jewry and against German antisemitism, while it left other issues to other Jewish organisations.

I wonder. The very name, "Centralverein deutscher Staatsbürger jüdischen Glaubens", indicated a self-definition and a set of goals which the C.V. leadership pursued tirelessly. They were ready to struggle against everybody, outside as well as inside German Jewry, who dared to question these goals. Sometimes it seems that the fight of the *Centralverein* against the Zionists, who obviously had a different conception of the definition of German Jewry, was no less sharp – and perhaps even more so – than the fight against antisemitism. There was not one Jewish organisation in Germany, whether a youth movement, a grouping of adults, or a teachers' association, or a community circle, which was spared the wrath of the *Centralverein*, if they showed the slightest sign of being tainted by Zionist ideas.

Here too there were differences during the Weimar years between the attitude of the older generation of the *Centralverein* and its younger activists. The latter were ready for greater flexibility in their position respecting Zionism, and for a broader definition of their responsibilities in issues which belonged to the "*Klal-Israel*" category. For instance, they viewed positively the participation in matters such as the *Keren Hayesod* campaign, aiming to help in the development of the Jewish National Home in Palestine, or the support for the establishment of a chair in Botany at the Hebrew University of Jerusalem. The older generation obstinately refused any concessions to that party in German Jewry which seemed to question their own Jewish self-definition. As Abraham Margaliot rightly points out, they held to their beliefs even when these were in clear contradiction to the concept of "*Klal-Israel*ness".

The assimilationists fought the Zionists with all the means in their possession. The divergences between both camps were fundamental, dealt with matters of principle, and had fateful consequences. The task of the researcher and of the historian is to define these differences, and not to blur them.

It may well be, as Friedrich Brodnitz writes in the book dedicated to Ludwig Tietz, that among those who opposed Zionism fiercely there were "many too with honest and dearly-won convictions, but who just were out of step with the course of history".[1] Nevertheless, the course of history is not a small matter, which we can afford to ignore in our evaluation.

---

[1]Friedrich Brodnitz, 'Kampf um die Jewish Agency', in Gustav Horn (Hrsg.), *Jüdische Jugend im Übergang; Ludwig Tietz 1897–1933, sein Leben und seine Zeit*, Tel-Aviv 1980, p. 187. (The original: "Es stand dort auch sehr viel ehrlich erkämpfte Überzeugung, Meinung von Männern, die nur den Lauf der Geschichte gegen sich gehabt haben.")

Remarks on the Political and Ideological Development of the Centralverein before 1914

BY ABRAHAM MARGALIOT

Evyatar Friesel includes the *Centralverein deutscher Staatsbürger jüdischen Glaubens* (C.V.) of Wilhelminian Germany in the same category as the *Alliance Israélite Universelle*, the Anglo-Jewish Association, the American Jewish Committee and other Jewish civil rights organisations. I would argue that, in fact, the policies of the C.V. were different in principle from those practised by the latter organisations, despite the fact that all were engaged in defence activity.*

The purpose of the organisations based in France, England and the United States, as stated in their programmes (with slight variations in wording), was to prevent the violation of the civil and religious rights of Jews "in any part of the world".[1] Taking as their guide such traditional bywords as: "All Israel is responsible one for another" and: "All Israel are brethren," they undertook "to work everywhere for the emancipation of the Jews and to offer assistance to Jews suffering from antisemitism".[2] In contrast, the C.V. deliberately limited the scope of its legal and political activities to Germany alone. This self-limitation was not a question of geography, but one of ideology, and it expressed the guiding principles of its leadership in the matters of German-Jewish identity and of German Jewry's relations with Jews beyond the German frontier.

In applying the dictum, "All Israel is responsible one for another," the *Alliance* and the other Western Jewish organisations appealed to their governments to intervene on behalf of their co-religionists in Russia, the Balkans and the Ottoman Empire. They took steps to secure the protection of Jewish life and property by the Persian Shah and the Sultan of Morocco, and turned to the Vatican for help when blood libels proliferated in Romania and Russia. In addition to their diplomatic efforts in the international arena, they regularly published surveys of World Jewish conditions, detailing the plight of the various communities abroad. Claude G. Montefiore, head of the Anglo-Jewish Association (A.J.A.), defined the nature of this activity as holding "a sort of watching brief for the interests of Jews throughout the world".[3] Moreover, these organisa-

---

*I would like to thank my friend and colleague Jacob Toury who kindly read a draft of this article and gave me the benefit of his views on it.
[1]Aims of the Anglo-Jewish Association, as quoted in *Encyclopedia Judaica*, vol. 2, Jerusalem 1971, p. 997.
[2]Aims of the *Alliance Israélite Universelle*, as quoted in *Encyclopedia Judaica*, vol. 2, p. 650.
[3]Annual Report of the Anglo-Jewish Association, London 1900, p. 41.

tions set up emergency funds to aid the victims of antisemitic violence in Eastern Europe. The C.V., as already noted, refrained from participation in any of these international efforts undertaken in the name of World Jewish solidarity.

From the day of its establishment in 1893, the C.V. dissociated itself from any political form of cooperation with Jewish communities outside Germany. It operated in accordance with the provision included in its first charter in September 1893:

> "We stand firmly on the ground of German nationality. We have no other common interests with the Jews of other lands, except in the sense that Catholics and Protestants have with Catholics and Protestants of other countries."[4]

Its leaders were wont to stress their utmost devotion to their German homeland and to declare that their political consciousness and loyalties were thoroughly and immutably German.[5] The leaders of the C.V. saw their struggle against antisemitism in Germany as their "patriotic duty",[6] in the sense that anti-Jewish manifestations in German society harmed Germany's good name and its integrity as a *Rechtsstaat*.

One may gain an inkling of what the attitude of the C.V. was towards Germany on the one hand, and towards foreign Jews on the other from the words of Eugen Fuchs:

> "I am deeply convinced that were I banished with other people to a desert, I would first try to establish contact with a German, be he Jew or Christian, and that I would not be drawn first to someone who is not German, but a Jew."[7]

Even when the heads of the C.V. demonstrated an interest in the fate of Jews in other lands, as members of the same faith, they did not translate that interest into political acts of international solidarity. It is true that there were some members who were dissatisfied with this position, and who asked: "Where was the C.V. when we heard the shocking reports of the . . . pogroms?"[8] But this did not alter the basic attitude of the C.V. leadership towards other Jewish communities. This attitude of estrangement also explains the reluctance of the C.V. to turn for help to Western Jewry when German Jewry itself was threatened by the rise of National Socialism at the conclusion of the Weimar period.

So much for the C.V. and the question of Jewish solidarity, as distinguished from the policies of Jewish defence organisations in other countries.

I should like to question, as well, the author's contention that in the middle of

---

[4]This paragraph originated in the pamphlet published in 1893 by Raphael Löwenfeld, *Schutzjuden oder Staatsbürger? Von einem jüdischen Staatsbürger*, Berlin 1893.

[5]*Im deutschen Reich*, No. 4 (April 1900), p. 183 ("Kerndeutsch unsere politische Gesinnung und Empfindung").

[6]Paul Rieger, *Ein Vierteljahrhundert im Kampf um das Recht und die Zukunft der deutschen Juden*, Berlin 1918, p. 52 ("eine vaterländische Pflicht").

[7]*Im deutschen Reich*, No. 5/6 (May–June 1913), pp. 224–225. English translation from Jehuda Reinharz, *Fatherland or Promised Land. The Dilemma of the German Jew, 1893–1914*, Ann Arbor 1975, pp. 77–78.

[8]"Wo war der C.V., als die erschütternde Kunde von den . . . Pogromen zu uns kam?" *Mitteilungen des Syndikus des Centralvereins deutscher Staatsbürger jüdischen Glaubens*, No. 1 (8th February 1919), p. 5, Wiener Library, Tel-Aviv.

the first decade of our century the C.V. was transformed in accordance with democratic principles and on the basis of a mass membership, and that this transformation was of fundamental importance in the subsequent development of the organisation. He bases his argument on the fact that the original centralised structure was exchanged for one consisting of a *Hauptvorstand*, a *Hauptversammlung*, provincial associations and local chapters. This change in structure was accompanied by a new system of representatives which, he contends, resulted in the active involvement of the mass membership in defence work. This thesis is supported by reference to Ludwig Holländer's article, 'The Democratic Foundations of the C.V.',[9] which singled out the local chapters as the "carriers of the democratic organisation",[10] and that championed the idea of mass political mobilisation in the Jewish community in order to engage in wide-ranging defence work. Holländer viewed this as a salutary shift away from the patronising politics of notables towards a popular struggle focused on the issues that truly concerned the majority of the Jewish public.

Friesel sees the injection of such concepts as "democratic policies" and "the Jewish masses" as evidence "that this organisational development . . . implied an ideological dimension".[11] It must be asked, whether a) the work of Jewish defence was indeed carried out at the mass-base level, and b) the local chapters really played the central role in the C.V.'s organisational activity in general and in defence work in particular?

In brief, while it is true that the C.V. fostered a sense of Jewish self-confidence and pride in its members, it is nonetheless also true that the bulk of defence activity was carried out not by the rank and file, but by the central board, in the first instance, with the assistance of two committees: the "publications-apologetics committee" and the *Rechtsschutzkommission* and their professional staffs. Holländer's demand for the mobilisation of the Jewish "masses" at the grass-roots level to influence the attitude of the entire German population[12] remained an unfulfilled dream, as did Eugen Fuchs's call for "all Jews to enter the struggle".[13] The rank and file of the C.V. though it identified with the leadership's efforts, had but a limited capability for taking an active part in them. Moreover, it was not the mass membership that set policy objectives or methods of operation.

It was well worth noting at this point that the use of such terms as "the masses" with regard to the C.V. membership is somewhat misleading. The term was fashionable in Liberal circles, and was a concept used by Friedrich Naumann, for example, in connection with the process of industrialisation and the burgeoning industrial working class. In the context of the C.V. however, it is ill-suited not only in terms of size, but also in terms of the social composition and the tenor of political response of the organisation. The mentality and forms of

[9]Ludwig Holländer, in *Im deutschen Reich*, No. 1 (January 1912), pp. 1–10.
[10]*Ibid.*, p. 6.
[11]Evyatar Friesel, 'The Political and Ideological Development of the Centralverein before 1914', in *LBI Year Book XXXI* (1986), p. 141.
[12]Holländer, *loc. cit.*, p. 1: "auf die Masse unserer Gesamtbevölkerung kann nur gewirkt werden durch die Masse der Juden".
[13]The quotation is from Rieger, *op. cit.*, p. 24.

activity in the C.V. remained those of a *Bürgerverein*, and never became those of a *Volksbewegung*[14], or mass organisation.

As to the provincial associations and local chapters, they undoubtedly served an important purpose in monitoring antisemitic manifestations in the local press and state offices as well as in facilitating a swift reaction to local incidents. This is especially true of the work of the Syndici. The latter tended to relieve the central board of the burden of dealing with comparatively minor affairs. All this, however, still does not justify the description of the local chapters as the "carriers of the democratic organisation" and as an active political force exercising initiative on the Jewish defence struggle nationwide. We learn from the reports published in *Im deutschen Reich* that the chapter meetings seldom dealt with any truly important political questions, such as: should the C.V. maintain close ties with the Progressive Parties; should the apologetic-patriotic line of argumentation in educational-political campaigns be continued; should legal defence be preferred to political measures; or ought the institutions of the Jewish community also to be mobilised for resisting discrimination and defamation? These and other such issues were resolved from above, by the central board, without the benefit of membership discussion in the local chapters. Indeed, meetings of the chapters were infrequent and did not serve as a sounding board for the wider membership:

It is not surprising then, that the local chapters failed to attract the participation of the lower socio-economic strata. Very few artisans or shop-assistants played an active role in them. This much is implied by the oft-repeated laments about the apathy among these strata voiced by those leaders of the C.V. who were unhappy with this situation. They demanded a true democratisation of the local chapters so that others besides the professional classes might be heard in chapter affairs.[15]

A further point to consider is the fact that despite the steps towards decentralisation, the centre of gravity of the C.V. remained very much in Berlin.[16] Almost half the members of the central board came from there, although Berlin accounted for far less than half of the membership at large. This regional imbalance was correctly cited as an impediment to true democratic procedures. The same can be said of the system used for elections to C.V. bodies. According to available evidence it would appear that secret ballots were not constitutionally required;[17] rather, votes in the general assembly were made publicly and *en bloc* for factional lists of central board candidates.[18] We cannot tell from the evidence we have whether this system was also followed in the

[14]Terminology, "*Bürgerverein*", "*Volksbewegung*", taken from Friedrich Brodnitz, *Leistung und Kritik. Eine Untersuchung über den C.V. und seine Arbeit*, Berlin 1931, p. 30.

[15]*Mitteilungen des Syndikus, op. cit.*, p. 6; Brodnitz, *op. cit.*, p. 30. See also *Im deutschen Reich*, No. 5/6 (May–June 1913), p. 252; and Holländer, *loc. cit.*, p. 3.

[16]"Satzungsänderung des C.V.", par. 18, *Im deutschen Reich*, No. 3/4 (March–April 1909), p. 235. See also Ludwig Foerder, *Die Stellung des Centralvereins zu den innerjüdischen Fragen in den Jahren 1919–1926. Eine Denkschrift für die Vereinsmitglieder*, Breslau 1927, p. 29.

[17]Minutes of the "Ordentliche Delegiertenversammlung des C.V.", 26th February 1909, *Im deutschen Reich*, No. 3/4 (March–April 1909), p. 263.

[18]*Ibid.*

chapters. In any event, the 1918 list[19] of those elected to the central board, the provincial boards and those at the chapter level shows an over-preponderance of professionals – especially lawyers, doctors and rabbis – and members of the upper middle class.[20] In contrast, there were very few shop assistants, artisans, labourers or sales representatives. In this context, we might mention two proposals for broadening the socio-economic base of the leadership and of the active membership. In 1911 it was suggested that a number of "tätige Kaufleute" be co-opted to the general assembly.[21] On another occasion it was proposed that travel expenses be paid to those with small means, in order to facilitate their participation in the provincial assemblies.[22] This last proposal, intended to open the assemblies to the greatest range of social classes within the community, was apparently rejected because of budgetary considerations, *Im deutschen Reich* reported.[23] Whether the proposal to co-opt a number of "tätige Kaufleute" was put into effect is impossible to judge from the sources at our disposal.

From yet another viewpoint one may seriously question the degree to which the C.V. adhered to democratic principles. About twelve percent of the Jewish population in Germany in 1910 were foreign nationals,[24] and, as such, were ineligible for membership in the C.V.[25] Moreover, the C.V. did not deal with the vexed problem of the special social and legal rights of this considerable portion of the Jewish population, including the securing of permanent residence authorisation, work permits, licences for changing residence from city to city, and naturalisation. It would appear, then, that the C.V. aspired to a relationship of equals with other, non-Jewish German citizens, but was less disposed to seek a relationship of equals with fellow Jews in Germany who were not citizens.

Here we may point to the mounting controversy in the 1912–1914 period over the right of Jewish immigrants from Eastern Europe to vote in elections in Jewish communal institutions.[26] Although the C.V. as an organisation took no stand on

[19]Rieger, *op. cit.*, pp. 73–81.

[20]*Ibid.* See also Reinharz, *op. cit.*, pp. 54 ff.; Arnold Paucker, 'Zur Problematik einer jüdischen Abwehrstrategie in der deutschen Gesellschaft', in *Juden im Wilhelminischen Deutschland 1890–1914. Ein Sammelband herausgegeben von Werner E. Mosse unter Mitwirkung von Arnold Paucker*, Tübingen 1976 (Schriftenreihe wissenschaftlicher Abhandlungen des Leo Baeck Instituts 33), pp. 489–493, notes 40–42; Reiner Bernstein, *Zwischen Emanzipation und Antisemitismus. Die Publizistik der deutschen Juden am Beispiel der "C.V.-Zeitung". Organ des Centralvereins deutscher Staatsbürger jüdischen Glaubens 1924–1933*, Phil. Diss., Berlin 1969, pp. 66 ff.

[21]Minutes of the "Hauptversammlung des C.V.", 26th February 1911, *Im deutschen Reich*, No. 4 (April 1911), p. 188.

[22]Minutes of the "Hauptversammlung des C.V.", March 1913, *Im deutschen Reich*, No. 5/6 (May–June 1913), pp. 253–254.

[23]*Ibid.*

[24]S. Adler-Rudel, *Ostjuden in Deutschland, 1880–1940. Zugleich eine Geschichte der Organisationen, die sie betreuten*, Tübingen 1959 (Schriftenreihe wissenschaftlicher Abhandlungen des Leo Baeck Instituts 1), p. 164.

[25]Ismar Schorsch, *Jewish Reactions to German Antisemitism, 1870–1914*, New York–London 1972, p. 243, note 11.

[26]See Naomi Katzenberger, 'Dokumente zur Frage des Wahlrechts ausländischer Juden in den preussischen Synagogengemeinden', in *Michael*, 2 (1973), pp. 191–203. See also Jack Wertheimer, 'The Duisburg Affair. A Test Case in the Struggle for "Conquest of the Communities"', in *Association for Jewish Studies Review*, 6 (1981), pp. 186f; Shmuel Maayan, *The Election in the Jewish Community of Cologne (Köln) in the Years 1900–1921*, (in Hebrew), Givat Haviva 1979, pp. 23–25;

the internal activity of the communities, Liberals – most of whom were members of the C.V. and included prominent and influential C.V. leaders – often took the position at the time that non-citizens were not to receive the franchise in Jewish communal elections. They made this the rule in Duisburg, Bochum, Chemnitz, Leipzig and Hamm. In the legal debate over the question of the status of foreign nationals in Prussian Jewish communal life, the head of the anti-enfranchisement camp was the lawyer Dr. Michaelis of Hamm,[27] leader of the local Liberals and head of the C.V. there. The Liberals also took a negative position on the question of abolishing the three-class electoral system in Köln and other communities, and thus perpetuated a long-standing, anti-democratic procedure.[28]

In conclusion, I would not assert that the C.V. was lacking in democratic tendencies. On the contrary, its representative system certainly imposed limitations upon the notables' style of politics, without, however, doing away with it entirely. The C.V. leaders did try to arouse the Jewish public at large to defend its civic rights, and in consequence heightened Jewish awareness of discriminatory practices. When seen against the political norms of Wilhelminian Germany, no one can belittle the importance of the "partial democracy"[29] practised by the C.V.

At the same time, I cannot accept Friesel's view that the C.V. instituted a mass-democratic system of defence work, and that one may therefore sum up the development of the C.V. in that period under the heading "organisation as ideology".[30] The C.V. was not only a civil rights organisation; it was just as much an ideological organisation that attracted a large following. Studies of the C.V. ought to reflect the entire range of its ideological components, and devote commensurate attention to them. The German-Jewish ideology that the C.V. espoused, from the day of its creation until its demise, was central to its existence, and was unaffected by the structural changes in the organisation. Thousands of people supported the C.V. because it championed the integration of the Jew as individual in German society and because it fostered a German consciousness of a patriotic tenor. At the same time some Jews, who were themselves far-removed from Judaism or from the Jewish national idea, saw in the C.V. the proper way to maintain at least some link with the Jewish community. But what the C.V. leadership really did in order to give content and meaning to the Jewishness of its membership is a topic that falls outside the limits of my discussion of Evyatar Friesel's thought-provoking essay.

Ludger Heid, 'Harry Epstein – Ein Anwalt der Ostjuden in der Zeit der Weimarer Republik', in Walter Grab und Julius Schoeps (Hrsg.), *Juden in der Weimarer Republik*, Studien zur Geistesgeschichte 6, Stuttgart-Bonn 1986, pp. 279–283.
[27]Katzenberger, *loc. cit.*, p. 191.
[28]Maayan, *op. cit.*, pp. 17–18, 72 ff.
[29]Paucker, *loc. cit.*, p. 493.
[30]Friesel, *loc. cit.*, pp. 140f.

A Response to the Observations of
Chaim Schatzker and Abraham Margaliot

BY EVYATAR FRIESEL

The lecture alluded to in the foregoing papers, which was based on my essay on the *Centralverein deutscher Staatsbürger jüdischen Glaubens* (C.V.) in Year Book XXXI, had, indeed, a surprising effect as one would think that the C.V. has been so deeply researched and so widely analysed that little new remained to be said on that organisation. And suddenly a whole range of differences came up, of approach and of interpretation, between the lecturer and the commentators, between them and the audience. One of the reasons (another one will be mentioned at the end) for that excitement comes out quite clearly from the present comments of my colleagues and myself. It is not only the *Centralverein* with which we are dealing. It is the *Centralverein* as a key to some of the major historical questions of Jewish life in Europe during the first part of the twentieth century. There seem to be few organisations in modern Jewish history that are as significant as the C.V. for the understanding of the larger trends in modern Jewish life. For myself, one of the conclusions about the present debate is that far from being over, the analysis of the *Centralverein*, its role, its meaning, will continue for a long time yet.

I have to ask my friends Chaim Schatzker and Abraham Margaliot to forgive me for treating only part of their learned and significant comments. It is their merit – but my problem – that they created a situation of intellectual *embarras de richesse*. In the present frame it is simply impossible to give to all their observations the attention they certainly deserve. This applies, unfortunately, to Margaliot's comments on the distinction between *"Bürgerverein"* and *"Volksbewegung"*, as well as to his observations of the organisational developments inside the *Centralverein*. Worse, we shall have to postpone the matter of the typological analysis of the C.V. compared to other organisations, their differences and similarities – an issue, on which both Schatzker and Margaliot dwelt extensively and which interests me very much. This is a theme that has been dealt with less and it deserves extensive consideration, and I hope we shall find opportunity to do so.

The central question I posed in my article on the *Centralverein* was, whether that organisation had contributed to the strengthening of Jewish life in Germany, or the weakening of it. If, in terms of German-Jewish history, or even in the broader terms of the history of the Jews in Europe, the activities of the

107

Centralverein had added to a more positive Jewish consciousness, or if the contrary had happened? The answer I suggested was that the *Centralverein* had been a very positive factor in the life of modern German Jewry.

At the same time, I called attention to one of the contradictions in the development of the C.V. After all, its declared aim had been to strive for the better social, cultural and national integration of the Jews in their general environment, for their better "Deutschtum". What had occurred had been the opposite: the *Centralverein* ended acting as an agency leading towards a stronger Jewish consciousness among German Jews. Having opposed confessional politics as a question of deep-rooted principle, the *Centralverein* came as close to confessional politics as it could. I should add that such a result had not been within the stated aims of the C.V., but happened because reality has its own way of dealing with human intentions.[1]

My colleagues accepted at least some of my conclusions. I myself certainly subscribe to many of their observations. I was especially struck by the comments of Schatzker and Margaliot about the lack of "*Klal-Israel*ness", the sense of unity of the Jewish people everywhere (and not only in Germany) that was characteristic of the *Centralverein*, and also of other sectors of German Jewry. Indeed, there was something quite haughty (to say the least) in German Jewry's attitude towards other Jewish communities, or towards non-German Jews living in Germany.

We also agree, I believe, on other basic questions. For instance, we all tend to the "idea-based" approach when dealing with the history of German Jewry. We all relate to Jewish life in Germany as an historical phenomenon of specific character, although German Jews were integrated, up to a point, in the general history of German society. We differ in this from the approach I call "assimilationist", (to be found not only in the Diaspora but, strangely enough, also in Israel) whose tendency is to minimise, in this or that way and degree, Jewish specificity in Germany.

Regarding the questions on which, it seems, our ways part, I shall concentrate on two issues: one, the matter of prognosis in historical evaluation; the other, the *Centralverein* in relation to German Zionism.

When working on German-Jewish history, one of the methodological problems we constantly engage in is the urge to explain what people actually should have done. Considering the type of history we are concerned with, that tendency may be understandable, or even unavoidable. But as a basis for historical analysis such "prognosis-in-reverse" cannot be accepted. Prognosis, in the sense of the evaluation of the future based on our knowledge of the present, is centred on our present experience, which incorporates lessons from the past, but is not built on the past as such. From our present experience (in its larger sense),

---

[1]A similar trend of thought is to be found in a recent and very interesting article by Shulamit Volkov, 'The Dynamics of Dissimilation. Ostjuden and German Jews', in Jehuda Reinharz and Walter Schatzberg (eds.), *The Jewish Response to German Culture. From the Enlightenment to the Second World War*, Hanover, N.H. – London 1985, pp. 195–211.

we try to develop some view about the future. On a personal level, if there is one lesson to be learnt from the succession of "present times" one lives through – their surprises, their bewildering patterns, our own clumsiness when we attempt to predict what will happen next – that lesson is: to be very humble when judging people who in the past tried to evaluate their own tomorrow. To indulge in "reversed-prognosis", to judge a past generation for not having predicted rightly its own future is, surely, an exercise in futility.

The best we can do is to understand the past on its own terms: its sources, its components, its views, its development. Unavoidably, much of this "understanding", this "historical interpretation" – will be influenced by our own (present) subjective values and evaluations. But there should be some check on our subjectiveness. I suggest that the limit for it should be the point where hindsight becomes confused with wisdom.

If we consider the issue at hand, the *Centralverein*, we may find that a sound methodological approach also brings about a deeper understanding of the historical situation. For example, if we concentrate mainly on the so-called failure of its leaders to grasp the inherent weakness of German Jewry in general German society, than as a matter of intellectual consistency we should regard in the same way also other organisations, who in their time committed the same so-called mistake. And they are legion: the *Centralverein* was only one among a whole list of Jewish civil organisations that were established in different countries in Europe and America, and they all considered the situation of European Jewry along similar lines. Furthermore, the same happened also to Jewish organisations not of the "civil-rights" category: *viz* the Jewish Socialist organisations, of which the *Bund* was the outstanding representative; the religious movements (be they the Liberals in Germany, the German neo-Orthodox, or the different Orthodox or ultra-Orthodox groups and movements in Eastern Europe, acting alone or in the frame of *Agudath Isroel*). Thus we would be pushed into a negative attitude *vis-à-vis* a broad spectrum of Jewish associations, that together represented the backbone of organised Jewish life from the late nineteenth century to the Second World War – a frame of mind that hardly enhances a full understanding of Jewish organisational life in modern times.

German Zionism *versus* the *Centralverein* loomed large, as a topic, during the oral debate we had. In the present written comments the issue is raised only briefly in Schatzker's observations. But it seems obvious that the question influences implicitly the approach of both my colleagues. For Schatzker, it is quite axiomatic that German Zionism offered German Jewry an alternate – and better – Jewish way. This is a position I am increasingly uncomfortable with. Being a Zionist myself, I believe that Zionism brought out a new conception about Jewish life in modern times. But what exactly the German Zionists did with it, is another matter.

The Zionist idea was a complex concoction. Its ultimate aims were relatively clear, but regarding its means there were many contradictions. As a result, the Zionists' attitude towards Jewish realities in the different countries was sometimes quite bewildering: the Zionists sought the "normalisation" of the Jewish people – in order to preserve its specificity; they proclaimed the dissolution of the Diaspora, but worked for its strengthening; they preached *Aliyah*, and remained in *Galut*.[2] Full, constructive Zionism involved a profound personal and social revolution of which, as it turned out, only a minority of young pioneers and intellectuals were capable. Among the members of the German-Jewish middle class that adopted Zionism, it is the contradictions that demand our attention. I cannot find it in myself to say that their views about the future of German Jewry were clearer, or more lucid, or more realistic than the views of the *Centralverein* spokesmen. On the contrary: confused between dream and reality; undecided between one world they were supposed to leave but felt very comfortable in, and another one they were supposed to reach but knew too little about; complacent about the growing dangers to Jewish existence in Germany, the German Zionists were at least as astonished as the C.V. activists by the developments in Germany in 1933 and after.

To state that German Zionism presented German Jewry with an alternate Jewish way seems increasingly to me to be a continuation of that same "prognosis-in-reverse" I rejected regarding the *Centralverein*. Even if Zionism armed its German adherents with a new overall approach to Jewish life, these were matters that remained in the lofty realm of social and ideological speculation. When it came to more immediate matters connected with their present German-Jewish situation, then it was a different story. As long as it was possible no sizeable German Zionist contingent left Germany. When they were forced to do so in the thirties, it happened very much in the same way as the *Centralverein* members left.

All of which does not mean that German Zionism was not a most important ideological factor in German-Jewish life during the years considered, and influenced deeply, according to its concepts, Jewish self-definition in Germany. But I wonder if even on that level there were not many similarities between the German Zionists and the C.V. activists, in spite of their obvious differences. It is generally accepted that until 1912 the Zionists and the *Centralverein* managed to co-exist and even to co-operate in different German-Jewish issues. It has been stated that the radicalisation of the German Zionists under the influence of Kurt Blumenfeld was a central factor in the deepening ideological conflict between them and the *Centralverein*, from 1912 on. Nevertheless, a more detached look shows us that this process did not happen only among the Zionists. The *Centralverein* too underwent a process of radicalisation in its Jewish aims and perceptions, which happened at about the same time, roughly, between 1907 and 1912 (the period also that I dealt with in my article). Historically seen, these two dominant movements in German Jewry were moving in a direction that had some remarkable similarities, since it meant a fuller and deeper definition of their aims as Jewish organisations. But their ideological premises were different, and consequently the radicalisation of both movements brought about an

---

[2]A more systematic analysis of the composition of the Zionist idea is to be found in my article, 'The Ideological Components of Zionism and their Historical Development', to be published in *Studies in Zionism*, during 1987.

increased tension between them.[3] Schatzker stated that during the twenties the *Centralverein* acted as if the main problem of German Jewry were the Zionists. Jehuda Reinharz, in a most interesting article recently published, broadly agrees with that opinion, but also shows that a similar attitude was to be found among many of the German Zionist leaders in their attitude towards the *Centralverein*.[4] For different reasons, the two most important organisations of German Jewry never managed to build bridges between them and to create ways of collaboration, as happened, at least in particular hours of crisis, in American Jewry.

Finally, there seems to be a more general reason why the controversy on the C.V. continues, with a broad spectrum of conflicting opinion, into the present day. That this is not always the outcome, is shown by what happens in recent Jewish historiography dealing with another major Jewish organisation that was active in Europe at almost the same time as the C.V.: the *Bund*. Scholars have been writing about the ideology of the *Bund*, its organisational development, its achievements. Almost no-one lapses into "prognosis-in-hindsight", although the *Bund* offers a most tempting target for such an intellectual indulgence. Why did the same not happen with regard to the *Centralverein*? Apparently, because the Jewish ideological position of which the *Centralverein* was so outstanding a representative in its time is alive and active in our own day too. The *Bund*, that magnificent creation of East European Jewry, disappeared in the upheavals of the first part of our century. There is no equivalent body in contemporary Jewry preaching a similar Jewish prognosis. Not so with the *Centralverein*. The organisation is gone but its message remains alive, carried on today by other groups and tendencies in Diaspora Jewry. But this too is another discussion.

[3]In the same vein Marjorie Lamberti has shown in a recent article, that the real issues of the first great confrontation between the *Centralverein* and the Zionists were not matters of ideological self-definition, but the clash between two expanding movements over their influence on German-Jewish youth. See Marjorie Lamberti, 'From Coexistence to Conflict. Zionism and the Jewish Community in Germany, 1897–1914', in *LBI Year Book XXVII* (1982), pp. 53–86.*
*See now the following debate between Jehuda Reinharz and Marjorie Lamberti in this volume of the Year Book – (Ed.).
[4]Jehuda Reinharz, 'The Zionist Response to Antisemitism in Germany', in *LBI Year Book XXX* (1985), pp. 105–140.

Advocacy and History:
The Case of the Centralverein and the Zionists

BY JEHUDA REINHARZ

Over its long history, the *Centralverein deutscher Staatsbürger jüdischen Glaubens* (C.V.) has had many distinguished advocates who have forcefully espoused its cause. There have also been a number of historians who have studied the C.V. and analysed the conflict between this and other contemporary German-Jewish organisations.[1] Marjorie Lamberti is unique in her attempt to play both roles simultaneously.[2] The picture that emerges from this effort is of a completely powerless and indecisive C.V. leadership who suffered the onslaught of the Zionists with patience, a view from which other historians seem to differ.[3]

Lamberti's advocacy is amply demonstrated by her open hostility to Kurt Blumenfeld and his group of radical Zionists who, she apparently feels, did not behave properly.[4] Thus, Berthold Feiwel "sneered".[5] The *Vereine Jüdischer Studenten* (V.J.St.) were "hives of radical Zionist activism".[6] Hans Gideon Heymann turned against the C.V. with "virulent hostility".[7] Blumenfeld, it is implied, used "coercive indoctrination". He also "beat his opponents through

---

[1]See Ismar Schorsch, *Jewish Reactions to German Anti-Semitism, 1870–1914*, New York 1972, pp. 186–209, and Jehuda Reinharz, *Fatherland or Promised Land. The Dilemma of the German Jew, 1893–1914*, Ann Arbor 1975, pp. 171–224. See also Arnold Paucker, 'Zur Problematik einer jüdischen Abwehrstrategie in der deutschen Gesellschaft', in *Juden im Wilhelminischen Deutschland 1890–1914*. Ein Sammelband herausgegeben von Werner E. Mosse unter Mitwirkung von Arnold Paucker, Tübingen 1976 (Schriftenreihe wissenschaftlicher Abhandlungen des Leo Baeck Instituts 33), pp. 479–548. For a full listing of C.V. historiography in English and German see Arnold Paucker, 'Die Abwehr des Antisemitismus in den Jahren 1893–1933', in Herbert A. Strauss and Norbert Kampe (eds.), *Antisemitismus. Von der Judenfeindschaft zum Holocaust*, Schriftenreihe der Bundeszentrale für politische Bildung, Bonn 1985, pp. 143–171.

[2]See Marjorie Lamberti, 'From Coexistence to Conflict. Zionism and the Jewish Community in Germany, 1897–1914', in *LBI Year Book* XXVII (1982), pp. 53–86. See also her declaration about the role the C.V. had in Germany for non-Jews. Lamberti, *Jewish Activism in Imperial Germany. The Struggle for Civil Equality*, New Haven 1978, p. 15. I doubt whether the C.V. leaders would have made such claims for themselves.

[3]See, for example, Reinharz, *Fatherland or Promised Land, op. cit.*, pp. 193, 198, 203.

[4]Lamberti, 'From Coexistence to Conflict', *loc. cit.*, p. 68. This attitude by Lamberti is extended to all Zionists who, unlike Max Bodenheimer and his group, were not distinguished by "dignified conduct [aiming at] winning the respect of the leaders of other Jewish organisations". Thus, a leader of a Zionist group, who in 1904 wished to challenge the leadership of the German branch of the *Alliance*, is called by Lamberti "the ringleader of this venture". *Ibid.*, pp. 57–58. A few sentences later she refers to "Zionist agitators". *Ibid.*, p. 58.   [5]*Ibid.*, p. 61.

[6]*Ibid.*, p. 62.   [7]*Ibid.*, p. 62.

adroit tactics and tough infighting".[8] "In the *Vereine Jüdischer Studenten* partisan activism blended with self-righteous idealism",[9] the new leaders of the V.J.St. "boasted", "competed aggressively" and recruited with "zealous energy". Blumenfeld, like his friend Richard Lichtheim, was "rigidly set in [his] convictions" and seems to have been disposed to turn ideological differences . . . into "a relationship of competitive enmity".[10] The Zionists "begrudged" and "suspected" the C.V. and these were, of course, "exaggerated suspicions".[11]

Blumenfeld is portrayed as "an idol of Zionist youth" who led "an assault on Apfel". Moreover, "fanatical Zionists" were under orders from "the youth propaganda commission of the Zionist Organisation",[12] an office which seems to have been invented by the *Allgemeine Zeitung des Judentums*, and given confirmation by Lamberti. The radical Jewish nationalists "gibed about Trotzjudentum".[13] And whenever members of the *Vereine Jüdischer Studenten* went to hear Sombart, they "trooped to the lectures"[14] while elsewhere they not only "trooped", but also "invaded", "agitated" and "caused commotions" when they came to *Centralverein* meetings.[15] Blumenfeld and Hantke are said to have "aroused and manipulated" other Zionists[16] and thus "provided [themselves] with the solid support of the radical youth".[17] But the real villain in the Lamberti story is Blumenfeld. After all, Arthur Hantke simply "fell under the influence of young radicals . . . who brought to the [*Zionistische Vereinigung für Deutschland* (ZVfD)] leadership an attitude . . . that was aggressively defensive and competitive . . ."[18]

By contrast, Lamberti describes the speech of Rabbi Benno Jacob at a C.V. *Hauptversammlung* in 1909 as a "moving appeal".[19] By the end of 1912 the C.V. members were simply "perturbed".[20] Moreover, the C.V. resolution of 30th March 1913 "was essentially an attempt to restore the coexistence between the *Centralverein* and the Zionist Organisation".[21] Was it not instead meant to place a wedge between the "good" Zionists and the radicals? Did Fuchs and Holländer really believe that Bodenheimer, Friedemann, Moses and others would flock to the C.V. and leave the radical Zionists? After all, by the time the conflict occurred these radicals were no longer so tiny a "minority" as Lamberti maintains, but had won the leadership of the ZVfD, through democratic elections at a *Delegiertentag*. No doubt this was due to "manipulation" and "coercive indoctrination", but a fact nonetheless.

In the advocate role, Lamberti suggests that when Maximilian Horwitz, Paul Nathan and other leaders of the C.V. signed the anti-Zionist resolution of 5th February 1914, they were simply "hoping that this stern rebuke would embolden responsible and mature men in the Zionist Organisation to speak out against the young radicals and to take the reins of leadership firmly in their hands".[22] If they wanted to make sure of destroying any hope for rapprochement with "mature men in the Zionist organisation", signing the declaration was the best way to do

---

[8]*Ibid.*, pp. 62–63.   [9]*Ibid.*, p. 63.   [10]*Ibid.*, p. 64.   [11]*Ibid.*, p. 67.   [12]*Ibid.*, p. 68.
[13]*Ibid.*, p. 69.   [14]*Ibid.*, p. 72.   [15]*Ibid.*, p. 76.   [16]*Ibid.*, p. 81.
[17]*Ibid.*, p. 82.   [18]*Ibid.*, p. 85.   [19]*Ibid.*, p. 65.   [20]*Ibid.*, p. 78.
[21]*Ibid.*, p. 79. Lamberti implies that as late as 1913, the C.V. was not anti-Zionist. *Ibid.*, p. 69.
[22]*Ibid.*, p. 83. But a few pages earlier she writes that "[Fuchs] and Horwitz had made a clear pledge to the Zionist delegation . . ." not to join the Anti-Zionist Committee. See Lamberti, *loc. cit.*, p. 78.

so. In any case, this was an academic question since, as has been pointed out, the "immature" radicals – the "chauvinists"[23] – were in control of the ZVfD. In my view, by 1913 the C.V. had turned against the ZVfD for other reasons.

Since it is quite possible that not all readers of the Year Book of the Leo Baeck Institute have recently familiarised themselves with the historiography of the conflict between the C.V. and the ZVfD, it may be worthwhile to review a few issues. In the following paragraphs I attempt to recap these, pointing out places where additional detail may be found.

To begin, there were generational differences between the founders and the second, more radical, generation of the ZVfD.[24] The young generation was influenced not only by events in Germany, but by an evolutionary process which took place within the World Zionist Organisation (WZO) after – at the latest – the Fifth Congress in 1901.[25] The fact that during the period under discussion the headquarters of the WZO and of the ZVfD were in the same building in Berlin and that their staffs often overlapped, simply quickened the process by which these events influenced the ZVfD leadership. The ZVfD could also count on the moral and even financial backing of the world movement.

Under these circumstances Kurt Blumenfeld took up his duties as the secretary of the ZVfD in 1909 and systematically sought to break with both the German-Jewish liberal establishment and the older generation of German Zionists. His strategy was deliberate, calculated, functional and eminently successful. First he planned control over the ZVfD. To achieve this he passed a resolution at the Frankfurt *Delegiertentag* and mobilised support among the student organisations. The culmination of this strategy came at the Poznań *Delegiertentag* in 1912 and the Leipzig *Delegiertentag* in 1914. It should be added here, that it was not Blumenfeld – who seems to be Lamberti's *bête noire* – who introduced the famous (or infamous?) resolution at Poznań, but Theodor Zlocisti and Leo Estermann. Nor did that resolution flatly call for emigration. Rather it left room for other ways of incorporating Palestine into one's life-programme.[26]

Apart from the storms aroused by the *Protestrabbiner* and the Emil Cohn affair, there are no indications of any significant conflict between the ZVfD leadership and the Jewish liberal establishment until 1912, although there were occasional disputes between local Zionist chapters and the communities, especially on the question of communal elections. Occasionally the *Jüdische Rundschau* printed articles calling for "the conquest of the communities" (*Eroberung der Gemeinden*), but in practice little was done to accomplish this goal. The ZVfD maintained peaceful contacts with the major German-Jewish organisations such as the

[23]*Ibid.*, p. 79.
[24]See e.g. Reinharz, *Fatherland or Promised Land*, chapters three and four; *idem*, 'Consensus and Conflict between Zionists and Liberals in Germany before World War I', in *Texts and Studies. Essays in Honor of Nahum N. Glatzer*, 1975, pp. 226–238; *idem*, 'Three Generations of German Zionism', in *The Jerusalem Quarterly*, No. 9 (1978), pp. 95–110; *idem*, 'Ideology and Structure in German Zionism 1882–1933', in *Jewish Social Studies*, XLII, No. 2 (Spring 1980), pp. 119–146; and 'Martin Buber's Impact on German Zionism before World War I', in *Studies in Zionism*, No. 6 (1982), pp. 171–183.
[25]On this see also Jehuda Reinharz, *Chaim Weizmann, the Making of a Zionist Leader*, New York 1985, pp. 65 ff.
[26]Lamberti errs on both points. See 'From Coexistence to Conflict', *loc. cit.*, p. 71.

Deutsch-Israelitischer Gemeindebund and the *Verband der Deutschen Juden*, as well as the *Hilfsverein der deutschen Juden*. These organisations took a neutral position towards Zionism, and in return the Zionists did not interfere in their internal affairs and refrained from antagonising them.[27]

The ZVfD permitted and even encouraged the participation of Zionists in other organisations. In 1906 the Central Committee of the ZVfD issued guidelines "to regulate the relations of German Zionists with other Jewish organisations":

> "No Zionist may be a member of an organisation which espouses anti-Jewish national ideas. For the rest we recommend that Zionists join organisations which are indifferent to Zionism. Zionists, however, who occupy leadership positions within the ZVfD, should always be careful not to assume leading positions in other organisations which might interfere with their work for the ZVfD . . . In all cases where a doubt exists whether or not an organisation is in fact anti-Zionist or whether the assumption of a position in another organisation would interfere with the goals of Zionism, one should consult the president of the ZVfD."[28]

The ZVfD recommended Zionist participation in the *Hilfsverein der deutschen Juden*, *Verband der Deutschen Juden*, *B'nai B'rith*, *Esra*, C.V., and the *Jüdische Turnvereine*; in fact, in all the major Jewish liberal organisations in Germany. The ZVfD expressed doubt only about participation in the German branch of the *Alliance Israélite Universelle* (*Deutsche Konferenzgemeinschaft der Alliance*), but it explained in the same memorandum that the two organisations might soon come to an understanding.[29]

During the first decade of the century the relations between the ZVfD and the *Hilfsverein der deutschen Juden* were particularly good. The first encounter between the *Hilfsverein* and the Zionists was in a meeting called by the *Hilfsverein* and the *B'nai B'rith* in Frankfurt a. Main in 1904, in regard to the Eastern European Jewish Question. The *Hilfsverein* was the first large Jewish organisation to agree to cooperate with the Zionists and this at a time when Herzl's death in 1904 had left the Zionists confused and disorganised. This made a great impression on the Zionists, especially since Max Bodenheimer, the president of the ZVfD, was accorded the honour of chairing the meetings in Frankfurt. In a report to the Seventh Zionist Congress, Alexander Marmorek wrote that this was the first time that Zionists and non-Zionists had cooperated and that in return the Zionists would support the *Hilfsverein*.[30]

In 1905, when David Wolffsohn issued a call to all German-Jewish organisations to help in the work on behalf of the *Ostjuden*, only the *Hilfsverein*, represented by Paul Nathan, responded favourably. Relations between the *Hilfsverein* and the ZVfD became increasingly close, especially since they were working together in Palestine on matters not touching upon the internal affairs of the German-Jewish

[27]Reinharz, *Fatherland or Promised Land, op. cit.*, p. 179. See also the introduction and relevant documents in Jehuda Reinharz, *Dokumente zur Geschichte des deutschen Zionismus, 1882–1933*, Tübingen 1981. (Schriftenreihe wissenschaftlicher Abhandlungen des Leo Baeck Instituts 37).

[28]Reinharz, *Fatherland or Promised Land, op. cit.* p. 179.*

*In order to standardise the authors' English and American publications on this subject all quotations from American publications have been brought in line with the house style of the Year Book – (Ed.).

[29]*Ibid.*, pp. 179–180.

[30]*Ibid.*, p. 180.

community. The Zionists appreciated the fact that a large German-Jewish organisation, of some twenty thousand members, was willing to establish schools in Palestine where Hebrew was an important part of the curriculum. The *Hilfsverein* was continually praised by the *Jüdische Rundschau* as a constructive and efficient organisation.[31]

The attitude of the C.V. towards the ZVfD should be examined against this background. The C.V., whose membership comprised mainly Jewish liberals, was of course affected by the attitudes of the other liberal organisations. Since the liberals and the Zionists found it possible to coexist peacefully, the C.V. adopted the same position. In addition, it should be kept in mind that the original intent and purpose of the C.V. was to be exclusively a defence organisation (*Abwehrverein*).[32] Thus, the C.V. was free to adopt a neutral course in all extra-defence matters that could be dealt with by other organisations. The C.V. leaders did not attack Zionism or the Zionists in Germany unless they felt a strong directive by the general community to do so, or unless their own ideology and purpose seemed to be endangered.[33]

Even though there were no major conflicts until 1912, neither organisation compromised its ideology or principles. The basic position of the C.V. was a total rejection of Zionist ideology. As early as 6th October 1895, Eugen Fuchs stated:

"We are not Zionists! As important as pride and self-confidence, which are symbolised by the Zionists, might be; we think that the basic ideology of the Zionists is mistaken. It has in common with the antisemites the fact that it tries to denationalise [from German nationality] the Jews, and this is the greatest danger to Judaism. We are Germans and want to remain Germans."

The *National-jüdische Vereinigung* responded to the C.V. statement in kind:

"The *Centralverein deutscher Staatsbürger jüdischen Glaubens* says we stand firmly on the basis of German nationality, we are not Zionists. This party has in common with the antisemites the fact that it tries to denationalise the Jews [from Jewish nationality] and this is the greatest danger to Judaism."[34]

Herzl's *Judenstaat* had been received by the C.V. organ *Im deutschen Reich* with a mixture of mockery and condescension. *Im deutschen Reich* had dismissed the pamphlet as the work of an Austrian so overcome by feelings of outrage against antisemitism that he was willing to forsake the fatherland. "The feelings of the German citizens of the Jewish faith, however, are very different from those of their Austrian brethren . . . we say 'no' to his proposals." When shortly afterwards the pamphlet by Max Jaffe, *Die Nationale Wiedergeburt der Juden*, appeared, the C.V. denounced both him and Herzl as "utopian and dangerous dreamers who want to forsake the hard-won emancipation of the Jews and force them back into the ghetto. They deserve thanks and recognition only from the antisemites."[35]

Eugen Fuchs was responsible for presenting the C.V.'s ideological position and

[31] *Ibid.*, p. 180.
[32] In my book I have shown in some detail how the C.V. evolved before the First World War into a *Gesinnungsverein* as well. *Ibid.*, pp. 70–89.
[33] *Ibid.*, pp. 180–181.
[34] *Ibid.*, p. 181.
[35] *Ibid.*, pp. 181–182.

its stance towards Zionism. His policy statement, made shortly after the Zionist Congress met in Basel in 1897, remained in force for sixteen years:

> "1. The C.V. has no objections to the colonisation of Palestine by people who have not found a haven in their countries of origin. Palestine, however, is not to be preferred over other countries where colonisation is also feasible; the only criterion for choosing land for Jews should be its suitability for farming.
> 2. The C.V. objects to the formation of an international Jewish organisation.
> 3. There is no possibility of strengthening Jewish national feelings, since the Jews are no longer a nation; they constitute merely a community of faith.
> 4. According to our nationality, which comprises language, education, thinking and feeling, we are Germans. We are Jews by virtue of our faith alone.
> 5. The Zionist movement is only a temporary phase in the development of Judaism and affects it as little as does antisemitism. Zionism represents an excess of devotion to Judaism [*Glaubenstreue*]; antisemitism is an expression of an excess of nationalistic feelings. Both have the virtue of shocking Judaism out of its indifference and of making Jews self-aware and proud of their Judaism. Both phenomena, however, will be overcome. Zionism and antisemitism are committing the same mistakes by not drawing a precise line between nationalism and religion. They do not realise that the modern concepts of statehood and devotion to the fatherland have as little to do with religion as with scholarly, ethical or aesthetic convictions."[36]

This statement by the foremost ideologue of the C.V. was very mild in comparison with the reactions of the rest of the German-Jewish liberal establishment. In essence the C.V. looked on Zionism with some derision as a temporary reaction to antisemitism; as such it did not deserve much attention. Yet Fuchs described Zionism as an "excess of *Glaubenstreue*", which, even if it was mistaken in direction, was a positive and valid reaction. The C.V. always acknowledged that Zionism had some positive effect since it restored Jewish pride.[37]

Even though it had no intention of opposing Zionism publicly, as an integral part of the liberal establishment the C.V. made its opposition to the principles of Zionism known. In their eyes the Zionist ideology clearly contradicted everything that liberal German Jews respected and valued. Long before the rest of the liberal establishment, the C.V. concluded that the best way to overcome Zionism was to ignore it completely. The C.V.'s reaction to the Zionist proposal to meet in Munich was typical of its policy until 1912. It merely printed the protest of the *Allgemeiner Deutscher Rabbinerverband* in its "correspondence" section without comment. In the same vein, the C.V.'s report on the Congress in Basle was objective and factual. The reporter even complimented the young movement on "the enthusiam and energy it had generated among Jews". Nevertheless, the C.V. considered Zionism a mistaken response:

> "The only way to solve the Jewish Question is for the Jews to assimilate as a national entity into the nations in whose midst they reside. It is merely the influence of antisemitism that makes serious men chase after the Zionist phantom. In Germany the Zionist goals have found no response or sympathy, and we are certain that this will continue to be the case in the future as well."[38]

[36]*Ibid.*, p. 182.
[37]*Ibid.*, p. 183.
[38]*Ibid.*, p. 183.

The C.V.'s lack of concern was not only the result of its evaluation of Zionism as a passing phenomenon. Added to this was the fact that in its early years the C.V. was seriously trying to be a neutral organisation whose platform could include all members of the German-Jewish community. The C.V., having been established for defence (*Abwehr*) and not for a particular ideology, was unlike such organisations as the ZVfD and later the *Verband nationaldeutscher Juden*. The basic demand of the C.V. was that its members should have "German feelings" (*deutsche Gesinnung*) and could welcome into its membership orthodox, liberal and non-religious Zionists. As a consequence, paragraph one of the statutes had said:

> "The C.V. intends to represent German citizens of the Jewish faith without regard to their religious and political orientation, in order to protect their civil and social equality and to cultivate them in their German *Gesinnung*."[39]

The consensus among the C.V. leadership was that as a neutral organisation, they were not required to decide whether or not Zionism had a right to exist. ("Die Frage, ob der Zionismus berechtigt sei oder nicht, geht den C.V. eigentlich nichts an.") It was left to each member to examine the Zionist ideology and to take a stand consistent with his individual convictions. The C.V. leadership would take no stand against the Zionists provided the Zionists took no stand against the C.V.[40]

The C.V.'s policy of not interfering with its membership's religious and political views so long as they did not violate their loyalty to Germany, and the Zionists' same ideals of *Deutschtum*, made for peaceful and even friendly relations. For their part, the Zionists also maintained their basic positions and stressed the primacy of *Judentum* over *Deutschtum*. In practice, however, these ideological positions led to no difficulties. Until 1912, *Im deutschen Reich* mentioned German Zionism and its ideology only in passing, or when reporting Zionist meetings or *Delegiertentage*: for the most part these notices remained simply factual.[41]

Relations between the C.V. and the ZVfD were indeed so cordial that at the tenth anniversary celebration of the C.V. in 1903, Alfred Klee, a member of both organisations, arrived at the head of a Zionist delegation and said:

> "The Zionist movement feels close to the C.V., because it too fights indifference among Jews . . . The ZVfD wants to stand shoulder to shoulder with the C.V. in its fight for the rights and honour of the German citizens of the Jewish faith."[42]

At the eleventh *Delegiertentag* in 1908, the ZVfD broadened its basic for cooperation with the C.V. and other organisations: "The eleventh *Delegiertentag* welcomes the work of the other large Jewish organisations who try to strengthen Jewish self-esteem."[43] And the C.V. reciprocated these friendly sentiments:

> "The Zionist movement had done its share to fight indifference among Jews. Even though there is a wide abyss between the basic *Weltanschauungen* of the C.V. and the ZVfD, we must concede that the ZVfD, like the C.V., tries to promote pride, self-confidence and loyalty to

[39]*Ibid.*, pp. 183–184.
[40]*Ibid.*, p. 184.
[41]*Ibid.*, p. 184.
[42]*Ibid.*, pp. 184–185.
[43]*Ibid.*, p. 185.

Judaism among the German Jews; the ZVfD tries to banish the spirit of assimilation from their ranks."[44]

In view of the C.V.'s attitude, the ZVfD leadership thought that in time the Zionist members of the C.V. might swing the C.V. towards Jewish values and perhaps even to support of Zionist work in Germany.[45]

Due to internal changes within the ZVfD a new and radical group rose to leadership in 1910. The various conflicts that erupted in Germany were used by the radical Zionists to good advantage: the Sombart affair, the debate over the *Kunstwart* article of Moritz Goldstein,[46] as well as the Zionists' attempts to gain a position of power and influence through community elections and infiltration into the *Jugendverband*.[47] Throughout this period – all through 1912 – the C.V. tried to stay out of the conflict between the Zionists and the anti-Zionists, though it disapproved of the Zionists' actions and positions on all the issues described above.[48] The Zionists, on the other hand, eagerly sought a confrontation with the liberals.[49] When it no longer had a choice, the C.V. published a "mild resolution"[50] on the subject of Zionism, rejecting a more radical amendment,[51] while the Zionists seized the opportunity to declare this resolution a *casus belli* and to attack the C.V. as an anti-Zionist organisation, no different from the rest of the anti-Zionists.[52] Once the C.V. entered the fray,[53] it became, due to its size and importance in the community, "the most representative body of the liberal establishment in its struggle against the Zionists". Thus, whatever its intentions, the C.V. resolution provided the Zionists with the pretext they needed to polarise the community and to distinguish effectively between them and the C.V. Their attack on the C.V. only served to stiffen that body's opposition to Zionism and assign it a central role in the struggle that ensued.

In sum, as had been pointed out some seven years prior to the publication of Lamberti's essay, the harmonious coexistence between Zionists and liberals was

[44]*Ibid.*, p. 185.
[45]*Ibid.*, p. 185. This was not such a far-fetched idea. See e.g. the article by Alphonse Levy, 'Der C.V.', *Im deutschen Reich*, (January 1898), p. 12. On the increasingly positive Jewish affirmation of the C.V. before 1914 see Jehuda Reinharz, 'Deutschtum and Judentum in the Ideology of the Centralverein deutscher Staatsbürger jüdischen Glaubens 1893–1914', in *Jewish Social Studies*, XXXVI, No. 1 (January 1974), pp. 19–39.
[46]Reinharz, *Fatherland or Promised Land, op. cit.*, pp. 190–199.
[47]*Ibid.*, pp. 188–203.
[48]See e.g. *Ibid.*, pp. 193–195. I quote at length Fuchs's speech in February 1912: "I do not want Sombart to sow the seeds of controversy among us. We are at one with the Zionists in fostering pride and self-consciousness among the German Jews and in trying to ban the spirit of assimilation which has become so dangerous to Judaism. We are also united with them in the efforts for peaceful cooperation which ultimately aim to improve the cultural and social position of the Jews." Describing the differences between the C.V. and the Zionists, Fuchs then continued: "But these differences of opinion are trivial in view of our common and basic goals and in view of the long road on which we must travel together towards a renaissance of the Jewish spirit . . .", Reinharz, *Fatherland or Promised Land, op. cit.*, p. 195.
[49]*Ibid.*, pp. 199, 204.
[50]*Ibid.*, p. 213.
[51]*Ibid.*, pp. 210–214.
[52]*Ibid.*, pp. 214–218.
[53]In fact, the C.V. began to respond in kind to the Zionists towards the end of 1912, Reinharz, *Fatherland or Promised Land, op. cit.*, p. 205.

shattered between 1910 and 1914 by the radicalisation of the second generation of German Zionists. Kurt Blumenfeld, Richard Lichtheim, Felix Rosenblüth and many others were influenced by the general trend within the WZO towards practical and cultural work in Palestine and the Diaspora, by the ideas of the Democratic Faction within Zionism and its spiritual founder Ahad Ha'Am,[54] and by the general *völkisch* ideology current in Germany. Their ideological orientation became a composite whose main features were influenced by Herzl's negation of the *Galut* and Martin Buber's admonition to search for their own roots in *Judentum*.[55] The result was that, whereas the first generation of German Zionists had believed that they were rooted (*verwurzelt*) in Germany and had therefore the right and even the obligation to participate fully in Germany's culture and politics, these young Zionists adhered to Blumenfeld's "uprooting" theory (*Entwurzelung*), which negated the Diaspora and concentrated all Zionist efforts on Palestine.[56]

Blumenfeld's conflict with the liberal Jewish middle class began with a rebellion against the ideology of the older generation of German Zionists. The young Zionists very often came from the same assimilated background as their elders, but their differences of *Weltanschauung* stemmed from differences in their generational experiences with antisemitism, from dissatisfaction with what the older generation had failed to accomplish, and from ideological, practical and political transformations that had taken place during the first decade of the twentieth century within the ZVfD and the WZO. Buber's exhortations, coupled with the lessons they extracted for their Jewish purposes from the German *völkisch* movement, made the young Zionists reject all that interfered with their Zionist convictions. Whereas the first generation of German Zionists had been content to wait in Germany for a charter for the *Ostjuden*, the young Zionists declared, that all who did not incorporate Palestine into their life's programme were not true Zionists.[57]

Thus the radical Zionists could not accept compromise, either with early Zionism or with the liberal establishment; they viewed *Deutschtum* and *Judentum* as incompatible, rejecting Eugen Fuchs's theory of synthesis, and tried to achieve a modicum of consistency by seeking to put their theories into practice. Their practical achievements before 1914 were threefold: (a) the formulation of a theory to express their existential needs; (2) the break with the liberals; (3) the systematic ideological indoctrination of their members and of the newly created *Turnvereine* and assorted Zionist *Wandervögel* and clubs to the end that they should maintain a "distance" between themselves and German nationalism.[58]

[54]Jehuda Reinharz, 'Achad Haam und der deutsche Zionismus', in *Bulletin des Leo Baeck Instituts*, No. 61 (1982), pp. 3–27.
[55]Jehuda Reinharz, 'Ahad Ha'Am, Martin Buber and German Zionism', in *At the Crossroads. Essays on Ahad Ha'Am*, edited by Jacques Kornberg, Albany 1983, pp. 142–155. The roots of their hostility to the C.V. were not simply a generational conflict, nor solely due to Herzl's "rallying cry" (*sic*) that "Zionism is a return to Jewishness [not "Judaism" as Lamberti has it], even before the return to the Jewish homeland." Lamberti, *loc. cit.*, p. 70.
[56]Reinharz, *Fatherland or Promised Land*, *op. cit.*, p. 230.
[57]*Ibid.*, pp. 230–231.
[58]*Ibid.*, p. 231.

They struggled with the conflict imposed by the propagation of Zionism within the German cultural sphere. Instead of rationalising or compartmentalising their loyalties, the members of the Blumenfeld faction within the ZVfD decided to abandon the fervour of their elders for German nationalism in favour of a total commitment to *Judentum*. To achieve the same commitment from the entire ZVfD membership, a conflict was necessary with those who refused to abandon their double loyalties to *Deutschtum* and *Judentum*. In other words, one might argue that the radicalism of Blumenfeld's faction at the Poznań and Leipzig *Delegiertentage* was not only the result of sincere convictions and deeply-felt ideology, it was also a political move to dislodge the older generation from the leadership of the ZVfD.[59]

As a tiny minority within a hostile Jewish community, the young Zionists could succeed only through the process of radicalisation. Their conflict with the older generation of German Zionists, the C.V. and the rest of the liberal establishment was functional for the achievement of their goals. Once the conflict crystallised and the young Zionists seized positions of power within the ZVfD, the older Zionists receded into the background, and the heightened commitment of the young leadership was adopted by those members who decided to stay with the movement. This reorientation had a homogenising effect on the eight to ten thousand Zionist members, while it made it difficult for non-radicals to join the ZVfD. The goals of the Blumenfeld group were not realised in respect to emigration to Palestine. Even though the Poznań Resolution demanded either emigration or some other personal commitment to Palestine, it was not until the Leipzig *Delegiertentag* of 1914 that the resolution was absorbed by members of the ZVfD in such a way that they might feel a conflict in not fulfilling it. The outbreak of the First World War, however, suspended for a while[60] all questions of personal commitment to Palestine. Between 1912 and 1914 the radical theories of the ZVfD served to "purify" the organisation of all other positions. Those who remained within the movement were totally committed to the Zionist organisation and ideology; external opposition served only to heighten their sense of internal unity.[61]

The foregoing does not imply that this is the final word on the subject. It is simply a response to an invitation by the Editor to discuss whether my original analysis more than fifteen years ago requires modification in light of Marjorie Lamberti's more recent work.

---

[59]*Ibid.*, p. 231.
[60]On the war period see: David Engel, 'Relations between Liberals and Zionists in Germany during World War I' (in Hebrew), in *Zion*, 4 (1982), pp. 435–461. See also Jürgen Matthäus, *Das Verhältnis zwischen dem "Centralverein deutscher Staatsbürger jüdischen Glaubens" (C.V.) und der "Zionistischen Vereinigung für Deutschland" (ZVfD) im Ersten Weltkrieg*, M.A. thesis, University of Bochum, 1986.*
*See also the essay by Jürgen Matthäus, 'Deutschtum and Judentum under Fire. The Impact of the First World War on the Strategies of the Centralverein and the Zionistische Vereinigung', which follows this debate in the current volume of the Year Book, and the essay by David Engel, 'Patriotism as a Shield. The Liberal Jewish Defence against Antisemitism in Germany during the First World War', in *LBI Year Book XXXI* (1986), pp. 147–171 – (Ed.).
[61]Matthäus, *Das Verhältnis* . . . , *op. cit.*, pp. 231–232.

The Centralverein and the Anti-Zionists
Setting the Historical Record Straight

BY MARJORIE LAMBERTI

Jehuda Reinharz's book *Fatherland or Promised Land*[1] and my article 'From Coexistence to Conflict',[2] published six years ago in the Year Book of the Leo Baeck Institute discuss the circumstances that divided the German Jews into two hostile ideological camps in the years before the First World War. The clash between the Zionists and their opponents that culminated in the organisation of the Anti-Zionist Committee in Berlin in 1913 made Imperial Germany the birthplace of anti-Zionism. Although the foremost leaders of the *Centralverein deutscher Staatsbürger jüdischen Glaubens* were not among the initial organisers of this committee,[3] the dispute between them and the Zionist Organisation of Germany is frequently identified with the anti-Zionist campaign of a militant faction of liberal Jews.

In our conceptualisation and interpretation of the history of the *Centralverein* Reinharz and I stand poles apart[4], and accordingly we arrived at different answers to the questions of what were the relations between the *Centralverein* and the Zionists from 1897 to 1914 and why did a conflict break out in 1913. At the time I wrote my article, I did not comment in detail on his work. His interpretation following closely the version of the conflict popularised by the *Jüdische Rundschau*, the official organ of the Zionist Organisation, was mentioned in a footnote.[5] I presented an analysis of the strains and stresses in the relations between the *Centralverein* and the Zionists based on the evidence that I had found in the Central Zionist Archives, and left it to the readers to make their own comparisons and evaluations. It was my hope that readers would see that I had successfully challenged the accuracy of the reports in the *Jüdische Rundschau* and had set the record straight.

When the Editor of the Year Book invited me to write a reply to Reinharz's

---

[1] *The Dilemma of the German Jew, 1893–1914*, Ann Arbor 1975.
[2] 'Zionism and the Jewish Community in Germany, 1897–1914', in *LBI Year Book XXVII* (1982), pp. 53–86.
[3] *Ibid.*, p. 78.
[4] See my comments on Reinharz's interpretation in my book, *Jewish Activism in Imperial Germany. The Struggle for Civil Equality*, New Haven 1978, p. 176. See also my reflections on the interpretation of the history of the *Centralverein* in post-Second-World-War scholarship in 'Liberals, Socialists and the Defence against Antisemitism in the Wilhelminian Period', in *LBI Year Book XXV* (1980), pp. 147–162.
[5] Lamberti, 'From Coexistence to Conflict', *loc. cit.*, p. 54, note 4.

critique of my article, I was disappointed in not finding any substantive discussion of my research and analysis. In the opening paragraph "the picture" of my interpretation of the conflict that he presents oversimplifies and tends to misrepresent what I actually wrote. In the following paragraphs he quotes words and phrases out of context to prove his contention that my account was coloured by "advocacy" or sympathy for the *Centralverein* and by "open hostility to Kurt Blumenfeld and his group of radical Zionists". The rephrasing of my statements easily lends itself to distortion, as a few examples illustrate:

My text: "To understand how these tensions led to open conflict in 1913, the historian must examine how a generation of Zionists, younger than Bodenheimer and Heymann, sharpened the distinction between the Zionist movement and the non-Zionist Jews and turned against the *Centralverein* with virulent hostility."[6]

His rendition: "Hans Gideon Heymann turned against the C.V. with 'virulent hostility'."

My text: "From the beginning the radical Zionists begrudged the foothold that the *Centralverein* had acquired in the Jewish youth movement and suspected its motives. The exaggerated suspicions prevailing in the Berlin office were conveyed to the local leaders in a confidential letter that Badrian sent out in July 1909.[7]

His rendition: "The Zionists 'begrudged' and 'suspected' the C.V. and these were, of course, 'exaggerated suspicions'."

My text: "Non-Zionists resigned when they saw [the Berlin *Jugendverein*] becoming 'a centre of fanatical Zionist agitation' and discovered that the chairman was acting under orders from the youth propaganda commission of the Zionist Organisation."[8]

His rendition: "Moreover, 'fanatical Zionists' were under orders from 'the youth propaganda commission of the Zionist Organisation', an office which seems to have been invented by the *Allgemeine Zeitung des Judentums*, and given confirmation by Lamberti."

In my sentence, immediately above, the words in quotes are taken from a newspaper article and are not my own, as Reinharz seems to indicate. Furthermore, the youth propaganda commission is not quite the fantasy he implies. In the Central Zionist Archives is a letter of the *Jugendpropaganda-Kommission*, marked "*streng vertraulich*", dated 1st December 1911, and signed by Felix Rosenblüth for the commission and Arthur Hantke for the Central Committee. The task of the commission, set up earlier, was "to suggest Zionist work in the neutral *Jugendvereine* and to provide uniform guidelines for Zionist *Jugendvereinspolitik*".[9]

The other alleged errors that Reinharz finds in my article should come under the heading of being pernickety rather than of revealing mistakes. To cite one example, I did not attribute the Palestine Resolution to Blumenfeld alone, as he states. I wrote that "Blumenfeld and his political friends introduced" it at the

---

[6]*Ibid.*, p. 62.   [7]*Ibid.*, p. 67.   [8]*Ibid.*, pp. 67–68.
[9]Central Zionist Archives, Files of Max Bodenheimer, A15/VII/24.

Poznań *Delegiertentag* in 1912. This statement is not very far from what he wrote in his book: "The first [resolution] was proposed by Zlocisti and Estermann and was based on the ideological changes suggested by Blumenfeld."[10]

With such remarks as "Blumenfeld seems to be Lamberti's bête noire" and "is the real villain in the Lamberti story", my detailed analysis is obscured and the research findings that document my conclusions ignored. Instead of refuting his arguments[11] point by point, however, I think that it would be more illuminating to discuss how and why he and I arrived at different interpretations.

In his analysis Reinharz distinguished two periods: 1897 to 1912 "when the two organisations coexisted in an atmosphere of relative harmony", and 1912 to 1914 when "the C.V. became the most representative body of the liberal establishment in its struggle against the Zionists".[12] He observed that "no conflict occurred during the pre-1912 period" and that the two organisations "maintained peaceful and even friendly relations".[13] Referring to the guidelines on the relations of the German Zionists to other Jewish organisations issued by the Central Committee in 1906, he gave a questionable interpretation to this document when he wrote that "the ZVfD [*Zionistische Vereinigung für Deutschland*] recommended Zionist participation in . . . the C.V.".[14] In his explanation for the absence of conflict during these years, he contended that even the rabbis who protested against Zionism in 1897 came to see that "the C.V.'s policy of *Totschweigen* might be a much more powerful weapon against the Zionists and that constant protest would only serve to put the Zionists in the public limelight".[15]

In my article I related how the *Centralverein*, under the leadership of Eugen Fuchs and Maximilian Horwitz, stated its differences with the Zionists without taking an adversary position and adopted a policy of neutrality in the interests of uniting Jews of all religious and political orientations in the defence of their honour and rights. This decision was not a conspiracy of silence to deny Zionism publicity. Since the Zionists under the leadership of Max Bodenheimer followed a policy of toning down Jewish Nationalism in official propaganda and were restrained in their agitation tactics, both organisations achieved a *modus vivendi*.[16] However, even in the years before 1912, indeed as early as 1906 and 1908, some Zionists expressed disapproval of the strategy of "quiet infiltration" of the *Centralverein* and wanted to prohibit Zionist participation in it. When the Central Committee adopted a set of rules on Zionist membership in other Jewish organisations on 27th August 1906, it left open the question of the *Centralverein*. The Zionist Organisation had no clear-cut official policy on the *Centralverein*.[17]

At the *Delegiertentag* in Breslau in 1908 and afterwards in the *Jüdische Rundschau* the Zionists disputed about their relations with the *Centralverein*. A restless younger generation demanded a sharp separation from the *Centralverein*, con-

---

[10]Jehuda Reinharz, *Fatherland or Promised Land. The Dilemma of the German Jew, 1893–1914*, Ann Arbor 1975, p. 160.
[11]For instance the point he makes in his note 55.
[12]*Ibid.*, p. 171.   [13]*Ibid.*, pp. 137, 229.   [14]*Ibid.*, p. 179.   [15]*Ibid.*, p. 137.
[16]Lamberti, 'From Coexistence to Conflict', *loc. cit.*, pp. 56–57.
[17]*Ibid.*, p. 59.

tending that the differences between the Zionists and "assimilationist" Jewry should not be blurred and warning that a policy of cooperation would compromise the principles of Zionism. The arguments raised by the young radicals reveal that the question of Zionist policy towards the *Centralverein* was entangled with a host of burning issues that the Zionists were debating at a crossroad in 1908.[18] Reinharz apparently did not grasp the significance of this debate and wrote that "at the 11th *Delegiertentag* in 1908, the ZVfD broadened its basis for cooperation with the C.V. and other organisations".[19]

Neither did Reinharz discern the prime source of tension in the relations between the *Centralverein* and the Zionists before 1912 – the agitation of the Zionist student associations in the *Bund der jüdischen Corporationen* and the change in strategy introduced by members of the *Bund* who rose to leadership positions in the Zionist Organisation from 1910 on. The mentality of this young leadership was different from the outlook of Bodenheimer and his generation, and soon an aggressively defensive posture towards non-Zionist Jewry replaced the policy of moderate agitation and peaceful coexistence of the Bodenheimer era.[20] The young Zionists assigned top priority to youth propaganda and recruitment and sought to capture leadership of the Jewish youth movement from mid-1909 on. Here the Zionist Organisation came into conflict with the *Centralverein*, whose promotion of a neutral Jewish youth movement thwarted the ambitions of Blumenfeld and his radical friends.[21]

Reinharz's account of Blumenfeld's activities during these years is incomplete. He erred when he stated that "the Zionists focused their attention for the first time on propaganda among German-Jewish youth" in 1912. I would submit that the historically significant discussion on Zionist youth activity at the Central Committee's meeting on 4th February 1912 really requires a far more perceptive reading than is evident in Reinharz's general remark about Blumenfeld's proposal of a strategy for drawing the youth to Zionism.[22] Sources in the Central Zionist Archives, *Der Jüdische Student*, and the *Mitteilungen des Verbandes der jüdischen Jugendvereine Deutschlands*, reveal that from 1909 to 1911 the young Zionists worked with the utmost energy to penetrate the neutral Jewish youth movement and to propagate Zionism. By the end of 1911 the radical Zionists were aware of their failure to infiltrate it. This setback was discussed by the Central Committee on 4th February.[23]

Blumenfeld was a far more controversial figure than the portrait that emerges from Reinharz's viewpoint. He claimed that Blumenfeld "was an immediate success in winning the Zionist youth movements, such as the *Verein Jüdischer Studenten* and the *Bund Jüdischer Corporationen*, to his ideas".[24] In fact, from 1907 to 1910, Blumenfeld and Rosenblüth fought a long battle to win over the *Bund* for a

---

[18]*Ibid.*, pp. 59–62.
[19]Reinharz, *op. cit.*, p. 185.
[20]Lamberti, 'From Coexistence to Conflict', *loc. cit.*, pp. 62–65.
[21]*Ibid.*, pp. 65–69.
[22]Reinharz, *op. cit.*, pp. 200–201.
[23]Lamberti, 'From Coexistence to Conflict', *loc. cit.*, pp. 67–68.
[24]Reinharz, *op. cit.*, p. 152.

Zionist educational programme.[25] More provocative was Blumenfeld's attempt to challenge the leadership of Alfred Apfel in the *Jugendverband* and to overturn its policy of neutrality. This story is omitted from his book. Within the Zionist Organisation Blumenfeld's agitation tactics and radical ideology aroused much criticism, as the private correspondence in the Central Zionist Archives discloses.[26] Among the individuals whom Reinharz interviewed in Israel in 1970, Gershom Scholem was particularly critical of Blumenfeld. Scholem's views were, however, tucked away in a footnote.[27]

In his analysis of the deterioration of the relationship of the *Centralverein* and the Zionist Organisation, Reinharz attributed the origins of the conflict to the "attacks" of the *Centralverein* and the decision of its leadership at the end of 1912 "to give up neutrality and officially denounce Zionism".[28] He explained that "it was under pressure from the liberal community that the C.V. had abandoned its neutral position and taken the lead in the anti-Zionist campaign".[29] By what kind of historical analysis and with what evidence did he arrive at this conclusion? Statements scattered throughout the book show the chain of reasoning that guided his research and ultimately his understanding of the behaviour of the *Centralverein*'s leadership. He wrote that "within the framework of the C.V. positions, it was logical for it to attack the ideology of the Zionists".[30] Continuing to emphasise the deep differences in ideology, he contended that the Zionists "challenged the very foundations of the C.V." and that "a clash was inevitable".[31] In his view, what determined the decisions of the *Centralverein*'s executive board in respect to the Zionists was "the Jewish liberal establishment":

> "This view is important, because the C.V. was so integral a part of the German-Jewish liberal establishment that developments within the liberal group at large had an impact on the C.V. Despite the fact that the impact was not always direct and immediate, there was a cumulative effect that was finally expressed in the C.V. resolution of 1913."[32]

> "The C.V., whose membership comprised mainly Jewish liberals, was of course affected by the attitudes of the liberal organisations . . . The C.V. leaders did not attack Zionism or the Zionists unless they felt a strong directive by the general community to do so . . ."[33]

The outcome of this chain of reasoning is an analysis that for me is neither probing enough nor sufficiently documented. Reinharz mentioned the *Centralverein*'s "assaults" and "attacks" against the Zionists without stating how and where they occurred and without identifying the assailants. Apart from the assertions of the radical Zionists who misconstrued polemical articles in the monthly journal of the *Centralverein* against Moritz Goldstein and Werner Sombart – neither one was a member of the Zionist Organisation – as "anti-Zionist attacks," he provided no concrete evidence.[34] He used the terms "the liberal establishment" and "liberal Jewish organisations" indiscriminately, without making any distinction between the non-Zionist liberals in the *Centralverein* and the anti-Zionist

[25]Lamberti, 'From Coexistence to Conflict', *loc. cit.*, pp. 62–63.   [26]*Ibid.*, pp. 73, 81, 83.
[27]See footnote 118 in Reinharz, *op. cit.*, p. 277.
[28]*Ibid.*, p. 210.   [29]*Ibid.*, p. 212.   [30]*Ibid.*, p. 88.
[31]*Ibid.*, p. 89.   [32]*Ibid.*, p. 172; see also p. 183.   [33]*Ibid.*, pp. 180–181.
[34]*Ibid.*, pp. 199, 205–206; see also p. 88.

liberals in the *Vereinigung für das liberale Judentum*, who took the initiative in forming a committee to combat the spread of Zionism. Eventually he implied that the Anti-Zionist Committee was speaking for the *Centralverein*:

> "The programme also indicates that the most notable German-Jewish liberal leaders and organisations felt free to try to thwart Zionism . . . The *Antizionistisches Komitee* claimed to speak on behalf of the entire German-Jewish liberal establishment. In an early leaflet the *Komitee* praised the *Verband der Deutschen Juden*, the C.V., and the *Deutsch-Israelitischer Gemeindebund* . . ."[35]

There are inconsistencies and omissions in Reinharz's account of how the general assembly of the *Centralverein* passed the resolution of 30th March 1913 and how the Zionist Organisation responded with a protest declaration on 1st April. He conceded that the resolution's language was "mild" and that "its intent was to clarify publicly the C.V.'s position towards *Deutschtum* and *Judentum* without jeopardising the cooperation of the majority of German Zionists". Then why did the Zionist leadership regard so moderate a resolution as "a direct attack on Zionism in general and the ZVfD in particular"? The answer in his book is that "the resolution infuriated the ZVfD", and its leadership "saw in the C.V. resolution a declaration of war on Zionism by the liberal establishment".[36] This answer is modified slightly in his updated version. Sources in the Central Zionist Archives provide a more complicated answer.[37] The members of the Central Committee were divided in their reaction to the resolution. Dissenting opinions were expressed when Hantke hastily issued the protest declaration of 1st April. The dissenters aired their disagreement once again during the closed-door session at the special meeting of the Zionist *Vertrauensmänner*, convened to discuss this matter, on 1st May.

Reproaching Blumenfeld and Hantke in a letter to Bodenheimer on 3rd April 1913, Julius Moses declared, "I must put part of the blame for the entire course of events on our leadership and especially on the harmful influence of Blumenfeld."[38] The conflict in 1913 was the outcome of the new strategy advocated by Blumenfeld – a change in tactics from infiltration to confrontation. The protocols of the Central Committee's meetings in 1912 disclose the differences of opinion within the Zionist leadership over the agitation tactics of the young radicals as well as the objectives that Blumenfeld and Hantke hoped to achieve through a strategy of confrontation and a sharpening of the ideological divisions within the Jewish community. They expected radical Zionist agitation to provoke the *Centralverein* into a fight against Zionism – a fight that they believed would be advantageous to the Zionist Organisation.[39]

---

[35]*Ibid.*, pp. 206–207.*

*In order to standardise the authors' English and American publications on this subject all quotations from American publications have been brought in line with the house style of the Year Book – (Ed.).

[36]*Ibid.*, pp. 213–214, 217.

[37]Lamberti, 'From Coexistence to Conflict', *loc. cit.*, pp. 78–82.

[38]Quoted *ibid.*, p. 81.

[39]*Ibid.*, pp. 69, 71, 74–75. As far as I know, Ismar Schorsch was the first scholar to point out the significance of the discussions of the Central Committee's meetings in 1912 to an examination of the conflict between the *Centralverein* and the Zionist Organisation. See Ismar Schorsch, *Jewish Reactions to German Anti-Semitism, 1870–1914*, New York 1972, pp. 188–189, 198.

Deutschtum and Judentum under Fire

The Impact of the First World War on the Strategies of the Centralverein and the Zionistische Vereinigung

Historians prefer clear-cut demarcations in time and space in order to come to definite conclusions.* Separating the periods of the *Kaiserreich* and the Weimar Republic, the four years of the First World War have obviously been regarded by historical research on German-Jewish history as an interlude of minor importance. While the significance of these years seems so obvious for the rise and mass-mobilising effect of German antisemitism, their impact on the *Centralverein deutscher Staatsbürger jüdischen Glaubens* (C.V.) and the *Zionistische Vereinigung für Deutschland* (ZVfD) is still open to speculation.[1] It is to the merit of David J. Engel that in his thesis he has corrected the former rather uncritical assumption of a generally unspoilt *Burgfrieden* between the C.V. and the ZVfD during the First World War.[2] In a more recent attempt to synthesise the two dominating trends in post-1945 historiography in the assessment of the German-Jewish defence organisations – the "conventional wisdom" displayed by an older school, typified by the evaluations of a Hannah Arendt, with its condemnation of the majority's passivity on the one hand, and newer studies stressing the positive and active elements in the traditional defence work on the other – Engel has pointed out that especially during the First World War "the liberal defence establishment's approach to its task was often determined not entirely by an objective and

---

*This article summarises the argument of my M.A. thesis submitted to the Fakultät für Geschichtswissenschaft of the Ruhr-Universität Bochum in February 1985. My thanks are due to Dagmar Koch for her assistance with the translation.
[1]See the brief references to the First World War in Jehuda Reinharz, *Fatherland or Promised Land. The Dilemma of the German Jew, 1893–1914*, Ann Arbor 1975, pp. 224, 233–234; Arnold Paucker, 'Zur Problematik einer jüdischen Abwehrstrategie in der deutschen Gesellschaft', in *Juden im Wilhelminischen Deutschland 1890–1914*. Ein Sammelband herausgegeben von Werner E. Mosse unter Mitwirkung von Arnold Paucker, Tübingen 1976 (Schriftenreihe wissenschaftlicher Abhandlungen des Leo Baeck Instituts 33), p. 525.
[2]David J. Engel, *Organized Jewish Responses to German Antisemitism during the First World War*, Diss. University of California, Los Angeles 1979. See also Reinharz's observations in 'The Zionist Response to Antisemitism in Germany', in *LBI Year Book XXX* (1985), pp. 108–109.

calculated examination of the nature and import of anti-Jewish feelings and of the possible results of various alternative strategies but to a significant extent by the exigencies of politics within the German-Jewish community itself".[3]

The present article follows a different line of argument in dealing with the First World War and organised German Jewry. Its purpose is to show that both the short-term and the long-term war aims of the C.V. and the ZVfD, as well as their expressions of consensus and dissension on war-time problems, were strongly influenced by apparent or anticipated reactions of the German outer world. The years between 1914 and 1918 clearly indicate that in times of crisis the traditional sensitivity of German Jewry to the Gentile environment dominated over considerations of inner-Jewish tactics or influence wielded within the Jewish community. Pressure from outside did not only cause conflicts between the divergent factions, but at times led to a postponement of hostilities and even to a rapprochement between the C.V. and the ZVfD.

II

With the outbreak of war the C.V. and the ZVfD had to adjust their strategies to the new domestic and international situation. The process of reorientation was just as much influenced by pre-war developments within organised German Jewry as by expectations and exigencies resulting from the war itself. With regard to the *Centralverein*, the *Kaiser*'s proclamation of a nation-wide *Burgfrieden* caused two important changes. Firstly, the C.V.-leadership around Maximilian Horwitz and Eugen Fuchs was able to put a stop to the conflict with the ZVfD over the question of how to define and delimit *Deutschtum* and *Judentum*. This debate, which had been forced on a reluctant leadership in 1913 by an aggressive ZVfD-propaganda on the one hand, and by a belligerent C.V.-rank and file on the other, had by then completely lost its positive effect, i.e. that of consolidating their own organisation and demonstrating its aim to the German public.* It had only resulted in blocking the constant efforts of Horwitz and Fuchs towards an organisational unification of German Jewry and in fostering the influence of the more radically German-Nationalistic wing within the *Centralverein*. Thus, at the outbreak of war *Im deutschen Reich*, the monthly organ of the C.V., eagerly included the German Zionists in its affirmation of total loyalty to the nation-wide "party truce".[4]

[3]David Engel, 'Patriotism as a Shield. The Liberal Jewish Defence against Antisemitism in Germany during the First World War', in *LBI Year Book XXXI* (1986), p. 149.

*For both the *Centralverein* in Wilhelminian Germany and Zionist policies before 1914 see the debates by five contributors which precede this essay in the Year Book – (Ed.).

[4]On the pre-war controversy between the *Centralverein* and the ZVfD see Reinharz, *Fatherland, op. cit.*, pp. 171–221; Paucker, 'Zur Problematik', *loc. cit.*, pp. 520–525; Ismar Schorsch, *Jewish Reactions to German Anti-Semitism, 1870–1914*, New York 1972, pp. 179–202; Stephen M. Poppel, *Zionism in Germany 1897–1933. The Shaping of a Jewish Identity*, Philadelphia 1976, pp. 45–67; Richard Lichtheim, *Die Geschichte des deutschen Zionismus*, Jerusalem 1954, pp. 147–148, 164–174; Marjorie Lamberti, 'From Coexistence to Conflict. Zionism and the Jewish Community in Germany, 1897–1914', in *LBI Year Book XXVII* (1982), pp. 53–86. For the C.V.'s desire for a permanent peace between all German-Jewish factions see *Im deutschen Reich*, XXI (January 1915), p. 15.

Secondly, this party truce led to a decisive, though not surprising, shift in the C.V.'s activities. From its foundation in 1893, the C.V.'s aim had been a double one: ". . . to gather together the German citizens of Jewish faith regardless of religious and political orientation in order to encourage them in the energetic preservation of their civic and social equality as well as in the cultivation of a German sentiment (Pflege deutscher Gesinnung)".[5] As an "Abwehr- und Gesinnungsverein" the C.V. now adjusted its defence work to the exigencies of the domestic *Burgfrieden*. Before the war the declared, though not always implemented, aim of the *Centralverein* had been to fight all the manifestations of antisemitism in Germany "out in the open"; at the first war-time C.V.-assembly in November 1914 Ludwig Holländer, the organisation's director, departed significantly from this practice by proclaiming a new motto:

> ". . . Im stillen Kämmerlein werden diese Dinge abgemacht, zumal sie viel zu winzig sind gegenüber dem Ernste und der Heiligkeit dieser Stunde . . ."[6]

Despite early signs of pessimism in regard to the eradication of German antisemitism because of the war, *Im deutschen Reich* warned its readers in the very first war issue "not to give vent to any oversensitivity which could easily blur the fact that in times of danger for the Fatherland what counts for us is only that which must unite *all* Germans".[7] The magic phrase *Burgfrieden* with its implicit promise of an unprejudiced treatment of all former social outsiders seemed to confirm the C.V.'s fundamental philosophy that in the end the legal emancipation of German Jewry would be followed by an egalitarian treatment in all spheres of social life. Thus the C.V.-leaders became willing prisoners of outside pressure; from now on they tried to transform a momentary phenomenon of German unity into a permanent social state. It was in this sense that for Eugen Fuchs the war meant "internal peace, the strongest force towards unification",[8] while Ludwig Holländer demanded, in the name of his organisation, far more than a party truce; a sort of divine peace for all eternity, with the Jewish citizen a loyal and true component of the German nation:

> ". . . wir wollten einen Gottesfrieden für die Ewigkeit; wir wollten durch unser Auftreten, durch die ganze Wucht unserer Organisation dafür eintreten, daß alle Bürger unseres Landes erkennen sollten, einen wie treuen und echten Bestandteil des gesamten deutschen Volkes die jüdische Bevölkerung bildet. So wollten und wollen wir alles zurückstellen, was da trennt, und nur das eine Ziel im Auge behalten, den endlichen Sieg der grossen Sache, des guten, deutschen, ehrlichen Namens."[9]

Reducing its defence work to the countering of extreme cases only, the C.V.'s inherent inclination towards creating the image of total allegiance to Germany

---

[5]This *Centralverein* slogan headed every issue of *Im deutschen Reich*.

[6]*Im deutschen Reich*, XXI (January 1915), p. 22. For pre-war statements on the C.V. function see Eugen Fuchs, *Um Deutschtum und Judentum. Gesammelte Reden und Aufsätze (1894–1919)*, ed. by Leo Hirschfeld, Frankfurt a. Main 1919, pp. 51–65, 84–99.

[7]*Im deutschen Reich*, XX (September 1914), p. 354. As to early signs of scepticism of *Centralverein* functionaries concerning a waning of antisemitism see *ibid.*, pp. 343, 370–373; *ibid.*, XXI (1915), pp. 20–21.

[8]*Ibid.*, XXI (January 1915), p. 5.

[9]*Ibid.*, p. 19.

became the dominant feature of its war-time strategy. Having since its foundation "quietly practised an inner mission which notwithstanding some minor exceptions has shown pleasing successes", the C.V. saw its main task from August 1914 as that of preventing its members from any manifestations of a sectional Jewish interest which might cast doubts upon their loyalty:

> "Wir müssen beweisen, daß unser Streben dahin geht, mit dazu beizutragen, daß der große Moment ein großes und würdiges Geschlecht finde . . .
> Wir sind uns dessen bewußt, daß die Juden wie alle Menschen ihre Fehler haben, aber als Minderheit doppelt verpflichtet sind, an ihr Verhalten, an ihr ganzes Auftreten den strengsten Maßstab zu legen."[10]

The C.V.'s reorientation in the early weeks of the war must be regarded as a logical consequence of its traditional function as both a defence and an ideological organisation. Without wishing to diminish its defence work it has to be said that the attraction of the C.V. for the majority of German Jews in the *Kaiserreich* did not arise primarily from its efforts towards defending and fostering the legal and social status of its followers, but from the fact that membership in the C.V. offered to many Jews a way of articulating a specific German-Jewish identity. As the appeal to *Deutschtum*, however it be defined, became, with the outbreak of war, the dominant justification for policy-making in Imperial Germany, an important section of the Jewish minority in Germany, with the C.V. out in front, adhered once again to the basic developments within German society as a whole.[11]

Unlike the C.V., whose leaders saw at least some of their long-cherished wishes come true, the ZVfD was badly shaken by the immediate consequences of the war. As its president, Arthur Hantke, stated more than a year after the outbreak of hostilities, the contact between the leadership and the rank and file had vanished, and the activities of the local branches ground to a halt as Zionist

---

[10]*Ibid.*, XX (September 1914), pp. 358–359.

[11]For the divergent assessments of the *Centralverein*'s fight against antisemitism cf. Reinharz, *Fatherland, op. cit.*, p. 227; Schorsch, *Jewish Reactions, op. cit.*, pp. 204–209; Paucker, 'Zur Problematik', *loc. cit.*, pp. 541–545; Marjorie Lamberti, *Jewish Activism in Imperial Germany. The Struggle for Civil Equality*, New Haven 1978, pp. X, 188; for the Weimar period the standard work is: Arnold Paucker, *Der jüdische Abwehrkampf gegen Antisemitismus und Nationalsozialismus in den letzten Jahren der Weimarer Republik*, Hamburg 1968. Paucker has followed up his positive assessment of the C.V. in many articles, the last of which is 'Jewish Self-Defence', in *Die Juden im Nationalsozialistischen Deutschland/The Jews in Nazi Germany 1933–1943*, herausgegeben von Arnold Paucker mit Sylvia Gilchrist und Barbara Suchy, Tübingen 1986 (Schriftenreihe wissenschaftlicher Abhandlungen des Leo Baeck Instituts 45), pp. 55–65. His positive evaluation is shared by most historians of Weimar Germany but for a contrary opinion see Sidney M. Bolkosky, *The Distorted Image. German Jewish Perception of Germans and Germany, 1918–1935*, New York 1975, pp. 14–15, 107. The ideological function of the C.V. is often described as a "surrogate Judaism", see Reinharz, *Fatherland, op. cit.*, p. 61; Schorsch, *Jewish Reactions, op. cit.*, p. 207; Lamberti, *Jewish Activism, op. cit.*, p. 110; Paucker, 'Zur Problematik', *loc. cit.*, p. 518. Engel, 'Patriotism', *loc. cit.*, p. 155, interprets the war-time changes in C.V.-strategy as "something of a retreat" from its pre-war course against antisemitism. In my opinion, this assessment stems from a neglect of the C.V.'s dual purpose and tends to overemphasise its task of combatting German antisemitism prior to the war which was more a broad-based application of legal means than a "policy of aggressive confrontation" (*ibid.*, p. 157). How far the reorientation of the C.V. strategy was carried out at all levels can only be decided after extensive research in regional C.V. history.

youth rushed to the German colours.[12] Encouraged by the seeming confirmation of their interpretation of Zionism, the moderate faction within the ZVfD, around Max Bodenheimer, Adolf Friedemann, and Franz Oppenheimer, re-emerged on the scene which had been dominated for years by the radical wing. With the radicals' silence the task of articulating a German Zionists' assessment of the war was eagerly taken up by the moderates. While Adolf Friedemann confided in his private diaries his belief in a future "destruction of the Asians",[13] Heinrich Loewe confronted German Zionists through the most important medium of the ZVfD during the First World War, the *Jüdische Rundschau*, with the enemies that surrounded them:

> "Uns gegenüber stehen härteste Tyrannei, blutigste Grausamkeit und finsterste Reaktion . . . Unsere Waffen erkämpfen nicht bloß den Schutz unserer Frauen und Kinder gegenüber den Feinden des Landes, sie schützen nicht bloß Haus und Herd unserer eigenen Familien, sie sind zugleich die einzige Hoffnung von Millionen und Abermillionen von Unterdrückten im russischen Reiche . . .
> Als Juden haben wir mit den Barbaren des Ostens noch eine besondere Rechnung zu begleichen."[14]

The battle cry "revenge for Kishinew" must be regarded as both the expression of a deeply-felt disgust against the tsarist warmongers and Jew-haters and as a justification of the evident shift in Zionist soldiers' solidarities.* Moritz Goldstein, the initiator of the famous *Kunstwart-Debatte* of 1912 and a German soldier during the war, wrote in 1916 that in order to fight one had to forget that Israel was a people:

> ". . . um zu kämpfen, müssen wir vergessen, daß Israel ein Volk ist – oder wenn es uns gegenwärtiges Erlebnis wäre, so müßte es uns unmöglich sein, einen Schuß abzugeben".[15]

Like Goldstein, many Zionists wanted to feel "that this fight may be in some sense my fight",[16] thus proving that the insistence of the ZVfD-radicals prior to the war on differentiating between the land where they dwelled and the land of their longing, *Wohnland* and *Vaterland*, had been a totally unrealistic abstraction. With the "new situation"[17] Nationalism underwent a re-interpretation in the columns of the *Jüdische Rundschau*, confronting the private cultural concern of one group with the duty owed to the State:

> "Nationalismus ist die kulturelle Angelegenheit einer Bevölkerungsgruppe, die, ähnlich wie Religionsgemeinschaft oder Familie, Angehörige verschiedener Staaten umfassen kann . . . Nie können die Pflichten, die sie auferlegt, mit den staatlichen in Konflikt kommen, wenn sie

---

[12]Cf. *Jüdische Rundschau*, XX (1915), p. 361; *ibid.*, XXI (1916), p. 431. Just like the C.V., at the outbreak of war the ZVfD issued a call to German Jews to do their utmost in supporting Germany during the war; see *Jüdische Rundschau*, XIX (1914), p. 343; *Im deutschen Reich*, XX (1914), p. 339.
[13]Cf. Poppel, *Zionism, op. cit.*, p. 81.
[14]*Jüdische Rundschau*, XIX (7th August 1914), p. 343.
*For the very small minority of German Jews, Zionists or non-Zionists, who did not share in the general war enthusiasm see the essay by Rivka Horwitz, 'Voices of Opposition to the First World War among Jewish Thinkers', in this volume of the Year Book – (Ed.).
[15]Moritz Goldstein, *Westöstliche Konfessionen*, unpublished manuscript dated 1916, Institut für Zeitungsforschung Dortmund, Nachlaß Goldstein, p. 31.
[16]*Ibid.*, p. 32. For similar statements see *Jüdische Rundschau*, XIX (1914), pp. 388, 295; *Der Jude*, I, Heft 1 (1916/1917), pp. 54–56.
[17]Title of the *Jüdische Rundschau*-leader, XIX (11th September 1914), p. 361.

nur als die rein kulturelle Bindung angesehen wird, die sie ist. Dem Staat gegenüber ist sie Privatsache, und man verläßt ihren Dienst wie allen privaten Dienst, um den Staat zu verteidigen."[18]

While the moderate Zionists, a minority within the ZVfD at any rate since the "decisive battle"[19] of the *Delegiertentag* at Leipzig six weeks before the war began, used the official mouthpiece of the ZVfD to express their views, the elected leadership remained silent. Arthur Hantke's intention immediately after the outbreak of war to go on "as if nothing had happened"[20] clearly indicates the insecurity which distinguished the radicals. To continue with their pre-war strategy of attacking the non-Zionist establishment for their policy of assimilation, in a time of apparently nation-wide unity, would have caused an immediate loss of sympathy from the German outside world as well as considerable discontent within Zionist ranks. Robbed of their main task which had materially fostered the increase of Zionist membership and had endowed its protagonists with a sense of self-realisation, the longer the war lasted the more urgent seemed the need for a workable alternative.[21]

For a short time it looked as if Max Bodenheimer, and with him moderate Zionism, would dominate the future strategy of the ZVfD. His plan of creating a multinational state in Eastern Europe under the aegis of Germany with the twin political goals of freeing Imperial Germany "from the permanent threat of a Russian attack" while at the same time securing "a tremendous national upswing" for the Polish Jews, which could also facilitate the creation of a Jewish state in Palestine",[22] coincided with Germany's early war aim of provoking insurrectionary movements in the Russian Empire. In autumn 1914, in order to keep a hand on the major developments determining the fate of their Eastern brethren, leading Zionists as well as their non-Zionist opponents joined Bodenheimer's "Committee for the Liberation of the Russian Jews", later to become the *Komitee für den Osten* (KfdO).[23] Although holding different views on

---

[18]*Ibid.*, XIX (16th October 1914), p. 387.

[19]Kurt Blumenfeld, *Erlebte Judenfrage. Ein Vierteljahrhundert deutscher Zionismus*, Stuttgart 1962, Veröffentlichung des Leo Baeck Instituts, pp. 69, 113. On the *Delegiertentag* in Leipzig and its repercussions see *Jüdische Rundschau*, XIX (1914), pp. 263–273, 277–278, 289–290, 311–312, 323–325, 333–336.

[20]Blumenfeld, *Erlebte Judenfrage, op. cit.*, p. 116.

[21]On radical Zionism and its origins see Reinharz, *Fatherland, op. cit.*, pp. 144–170; Schorsch, *Jewish Reactions, op. cit.*, pp. 182–195; Poppel, *Zionism, op. cit.*, pp. 85–101; Sanford Ragins, *Jewish Responses to Antisemitism in Germany, 1870–1914*, Diss. Brandeis University 1972, pp. 226–252 (published as *Jewish Responses to Anti-Semitism in Germany 1870–1914. A Study in the History of Ideas*, Hebrew Union College Cincinnati 1980). There is some confusion in the literature concerning the ZVfD's membership figures; cf. Poppel, *Zionism, op. cit.*, p. 176 Table 3; Lichtheim, *Geschichte, op. cit.*, p. 178; Jehuda Eloni, 'Die umkämpfte nationaljüdische Idee', in *Juden im Wilhelminischen Deutschland, op. cit.*, p. 662.

[22]Cf. Max Bodenheimer, *So wurde Israel*, ed. by Henriette H. Bodenheimer, Mannheim 1958, p. 184. For a discussion of Bodenheimer's plans see Egmont Zechlin (unter Mitarbeit von Hans Joachim Bieber), *Die deutsche Politik und die Juden im Ersten Weltkrieg*, Göttingen 1969, pp. 118–128.

[23]Apart from the moderate Zionists, Oppenheimer and Friedemann, some members of the ZVfD's *Geschäftsführender Ausschuß*, including Arthur Hantke, joined the Commitee. While the membership of Eugen Fuchs seems certain, secondary literature allows speculation as to the membership of Maximilian Horwitz and Kurt Blumenfeld (cf. Bodenheimer, *So wurde Israel, op. cit.*, p. 189; Zechlin, *Deutsche Politik, op. cit.*, pp. 133, 171–172, note 87).

the question as to how that future should look, and although other German-Jewish organisations preferred going their own way in dealing with the Eastern Jews to collaboration with the Zionists, the contacts between ZVfD and C.V. officials via the KfdO at the end of 1914 could have led to a gradual emergence of mutual confidence. Instead, the further progress of the war created a new period of polarisation between the two factions within German Jewry.

While the ZVfD was still in search of an adequate substitute for its out-dated pre-war strategy, growing scepticism in regard to Bodenheimer's methods and his apparent loss of political prestige induced German Zionist officials to withdraw from the KfdO at the beginning of winter 1914.[24] In this situation the entry of the Ottoman Empire into the war on the side of the Central Powers brought "a decision"[25] for the ZVfD's future war strategy. Richard Lichtheim, the Zionist representative in Constantinople, saw the best chances for securing and extending the influence of his organisation in Palestine lay in tying Zionism to the political-military aims of Germany and its allies. Supported by the unquestionable fact of the sovereignty of Turkey over Palestine, as well as by expectations, widely held among German Jews, of a German victory, Lichtheim succeeded in convincing the ZVfD-leadership of the urgent necessity for improving the rather cool relationship with German political and diplomatic circles. With the decision of one Zionist faction "to operate in the German-Turkish camp, as Palestine was to be found in this camp"[26] and the opposing strategy of the other, those Western Zionists who clustered around Chaim Weizmann, the race between these two factions within the World Zionist Organisation (WZO) for political support for their aims from one of the warring power blocs could begin.[27]

From the beginning of 1915 the strategy of the ZVfD was two-pronged. Firstly, political attempts were made to induce German and Turkish officials to lend their protection to the existing Jewish settlements in Palestine as well as to propel them towards the acceptance of German Zionist aims in general.* Secondly, the ZVfD started a campaign to attract the attention of the German public towards its aims by stressing how German, Turkish, and Zionist interests converged.

[24]See Lichtheim, *Geschichte, op. cit.*, pp. 212–213; Monika Richarz (ed.), *Jüdisches Leben in Deutschland*, Band 2: *Selbstzeugnisse zur Sozialgeschichte im Kaiserreich*, Stuttgart 1979, Veröffentlichung des Leo Baeck Instituts, p. 411.
[25]Title of the *Jüdische Rundschau*-leader, XIX (6th November 1914), p. 411.
[26]Richard Lichtheim, *Rückkehr. Lebenserinnerungen aus der Frühzeit des deutschen Zionismus*, Stuttgart 1970, Veröffentlichung des Leo Baeck Instituts, p. 259.
[27]On the Copenhagen-decisions of the WZO's *Großes Aktionskomitee* in December 1914 allowing the divergent political courses of German and Western Zionists see *ibid.*, pp. 255–256; *idem, Geschichte, op. cit.*, pp. 207–208; Zechlin, *Deutsche Politik, op. cit.*, pp. 312–314; Isaiah Friedman, *Germany, Turkey, and Zionism 1897–1918*, Oxford 1977, pp. 236–238. For an assessment of the WZO's postulate of neutrality cf. *ibid.*, pp. 228–230; Zechlin, *Deutsche Politik, op. cit.*, pp. 313, 334, 446; Engel, *Jewish Responses, op. cit.*, p. 434, note 68. On the attempts of Western Zionists see Leonard Stein, *The Balfour Declaration*, London 1961.
*On the *Komitee für den Osten* and later German Zionist war-time policies for Palestine see also the first part of the essay by Francis R. Nicosia, 'Jewish Affairs and German Foreign Policy during the Weimar Republic. Moritz Sobernheim and the Referat für jüdische Angelegenheiten', in this volume of the Year Book – (Ed.).

While the first component of this strategy is only of minor importance in this connection, [28] the revival of the ZVfD's propaganda potential caused the short-lived *Burgfrieden* within German Jewry to collapse. In order to explain the aggressiveness of the Zionist's campaign early in 1915, three factors have to be taken into account. First, radical German Zionism had neither politically experienced leaders nor influential advocates at its disposal. To make itself and its aims known, the ZVfD had to draw the attention of the German public towards the differences between the Zionist and the non-Zionist organisations within German Jewry. Second, Zionist propagandists saw their best chance for achieving their aims in addressing Conservative-Nationalistic circles of German political life. Among these influential groups the ZVfD had to neutralise the "counter-actions"[29] of Paul Nathan and his *Hilfsverein der deutschen Juden* as well as refute the prevailing view that Zionism was supranational-orientated and thus detrimental to German interests. Third, there was the reappearance of Kurt Blumenfeld, the most vigorous critic of non-Zionist ideology, on the propaganda scene, after having recovered from the initial shock of war. In dealing with his "till now rather strange"[30] political task, Blumenfeld provided devastating appraisals on the effects of Jewish attempts towards integration or assimilation. "Morally disadvantageous" as those attempts seemed to him, he characterised their logical outcome as an "unrestrained striving after superficial aspirations" and "an antisocial, decadent philosophy of life", so that in the end "purely material interests and shallow rationalism" would supersede idealistic goals.[31] In July 1915 Blumenfeld's attack reached its peak with an article in the *Jüdische Rundschau* headed 'Antisemitism' but predominantly dealing with the established defence organisations' inability to recognise the real nature of antisemitism and their futile fight against it:

> "Die jüdischen Kreise, die sich vornehmlich mit der Bekämpfung des Antisemitismus beschäftigen, haben niemals den ernsthaften Versuch gemacht, die inneren Gründe des Antisemitismus zu begreifen. Den Mut zu der Erkenntnis, daß Antisemitismus nicht nur ein Mißverständnis, nicht nur eine zufällige, zeitliche Strömung ist, kann auch niemand aufbringen, dem der Mut zu seinen Judentum fehlt . . . Nie ist ein Kampf mit schlechteren

---

[28]For Zionist diplomacy see Lichtheim, *Rückkehr, op. cit.*, pp. 263–382; *idem, Geschichte, op. cit.*, pp. 207–214; Friedman, *Germany, op. cit.*, pp. 191–429; Zechlin, *Deutsche Politik, op. cit.*, pp. 310–448; Stein, *Balfour Declaration, op. cit.*, pp. 206–217, 533–542. By this time the ZVfD had broken off all official contacts with the KfdO (see Zechlin, *Deutsche Politik, op. cit.*, p. 138).

[29]*Ibid.*, p. 341. See also Lichtheim, *Geschichte, op. cit.*, p. 211; Kurt Blumenfeld, *Im Kampf um den Zionismus. Briefe aus fünf Jahrzehnten*, ed. by Miriam Sambursky and Jochanan Ginat, Stuttgart 1976, Veröffentlichung des Leo Baeck Instituts, pp. 44–47. On the so-called pre-war "Sprachenstreit" between the ZVfD and the *Hilfsverein* in Palestine see *inter alia* Friedman, *Germany, op. cit.*, pp. 167–185; Lichtheim, *Geschichte, op. cit.*, pp. 171–174; Zechlin, *Deutsche Politik, op. cit.*, pp. 303–307. As a result of this struggle, the relationship between the ZVfD and *Hilfsverein* as well as the German Foreign Office was rather strained.

[30]Blumenfeld, *Im Kampf, op. cit.*, p. 48.

[31]*Jüdische Rundschau*, XX (5th March 1915), p. 79. This article in the *Jüdische Rundschau* was a reprint of Blumenfeld's earlier essay issued in *Das größere Deutschland*, a paper closely associated with the so-called "liberal imperialists" in Germany. For Blumenfeld's better-known article 'Der Zionismus. Eine Frage der deutschen Orientpolitik', in *Preussische Jahrbücher*, 161 (1915) see citation in Zechlin, *Deutsche Politik, op. cit.*, p. 330; Engel, *Jewish Responses, op. cit.*, pp. 307–319.

Mitteln geführt worden als der sogenannte Kampf gegen den Antisemitismus. Er ist in Wahrheit nichts anderes als ein Kampf gegen den Semitismus, gegen die jüdische Eigenart der Juden selbst . . . Durch dauernde Kapitulation vor dem Antisemitismus sucht man ihn zu besiegen. Feige Mimikry war die erprobteste Waffe in diesem Kampf."[32]

After this slap in the face for the Jewish defence organisations, Blumenfeld's appeal for a "concentration of all Jewish endeavours on the great feat of the new Jewish life in Palestine"[33] could have had only rhetorical meaning. There can be little doubt that in 1915 the non-Zionist organisations felt their position sufficiently consolidated to refrain from any public rejoinder to the Zionist attack which ceased after Blumenfeld was called up for military service. The C.V.'s mere ignoring of these attacks derived from its war-time strategy of concentrating on the maintenance of the *Burgfrieden* within as well as outside German Jewry.[34]

When in 1915 the ZVfD had overcome its crisis and commenced its policy of winning the support of the Central Powers, the two basic strategies dominating the conduct of the C.V. and the ZVfD during the remaining war years were shaped. Both organisations set out to achieve their aims without the help of the opposing faction; in the first place neither was orientated towards winning greater inner-Jewish strength but towards the implementation of fundamental political aims with the assistance of some influential German groups or with German society as a whole. If either the C.V. or the ZVfD was to be successful in achieving its respective objectives by adapting them to alleged, or apparent, war aims of Imperial Germany, a securing of their position within German Jewry would have been the almost automatic by-product. Although no inevitable contradiction existed between both these war aims, the next years were to show which faction would gain more support from the surrounding German world and as a result could strengthen its place within organised German Jewry.

III

In fact, neither the C.V. nor the ZVfD achieved its aims. From mid-1915 both organisations were confronted with mighty counterforces which sprang from the war's progress. Whilst the greatest external problem facing the C.V. – the rise of German antisemitism – can hardly be overlooked,[35] it is more difficult to discern

---

[32] *Jüdische Rundschau*, XX (23rd July 1915), pp. 239–240.

[33] *Ibid.*, p. 240.

[34] Engel, *Jewish Responses, op. cit.*, pp. 306–329, gives quite a different interpretation of the ZVfD's change of strategy as well as of the reaction of the C.V. Equating the efforts of Bodenheimer for the Eastern Jews with the later ZVfD-policy towards Palestine, he dates the beginning of the German Zionists' propaganda campaign immediately after the outbreak of war. In order to prove his argument that the C.V. "even at this relatively early date in the war . . . allowed its internal struggle against Zionism to interfere with its principal function of combatting antisemitism", he interprets an article by Felix Goldmann 'Deutschland und die Ostjudenfrage', in *Im deutschen Reich*, XXI (October-November 1915), pp. 195–213) as an instrument of the C.V.'s "counter-attack" (*ibid.*, p. 323).

[35] On the rise of German antisemitism during the First World War see Werner Jochmann, 'Die Ausbreitung des Antisemitismus', in *Deutsches Judentum in Krieg und Revolution 1916–1923*. Ein Sammelband herausgegeben von Werner E. Mosse unter Mitwirkung von Arnold Paucker,

the growing obstacles against the ZVfD-war aims, as they rarely found space in the newspapers: after a promising start the German Zionist arguments demanding a German declaration in favour of a Jewish Palestine soon fell on deaf ears.[36] Furthermore, German Jewry grew more and more sceptical towards the *Kaiserreich*'s dealing with the Jews in occupied Poland. Neither Zionist nor non-Zionist plans for the future of their co-religionists met the expectations of German political-military leaders in their attempts to set up a Polish vassal-state.[37]

In so far as the sources allow any statement on the decision-making process and the formation of factions within the German-Jewish organisations during the First World War,[38] there is evidence for the assumption that the debate amongst the German public on the so-called *Ostjudenfrage* caused tensions inside the C.V. The extreme German-Nationalistic members, who would seem to be identical with the upholders of anti-Zionism within the organisation and the post-war followers of such new Right-wing groups as the *Verband nationaldeutscher Juden*, tried to push the C.V. leadership towards a more restrictive policy against the *Ostjuden* in order to prevent an alleged mass-immigration into Germany. On this question the leaders of the C.V. saw more bonds with the ZVfD and its unanimous rejection of the *Grenzsperre*, i.e. the closing of the German borders demanded by Nationalistic circles ever since the German occupation of wide areas of Russian Poland. After an exchange of arguments in *Im deutschen Reich* – an unusual event indicating the depth of the division in the C.V. on this crucial issue – the dissenters were appeased.[39] Nevertheless, doubt prevailed over the question of how far the subordination of Jewish to German interests should go.

The ZVfD could react to the threat of a *Grenzsperre* with one voice because there existed no internal opposition demanding such a measure. What troubled the ZVfD-leaders was the threat to their position of strength within the WZO which could arise from a success of their Western colleagues at a time when their own endeavours had reached a dead-end. Fully aware of the Turkish junta's distrust of national or religious minorities within their borders, German Zionism had to rely on the help of German officials, who themselves aimed more and

Tübingen 1971 (Schriftenreihe wissenschaftlicher Abhandlungen des Leo Baeck Instituts 25), pp. 409–510; Engel, *Jewish Responses, op. cit.*, pp. 15–133.

[36]The instruction of the German Embassy in Constantinople of 22nd November 1915, reprinted by Friedman, *Germany, op. cit.*, pp. 422–423, brought no breakthrough towards a binding German declaration in favour of Zionist aims in Palestine. On the political value of this declaration cf. Lichtheim, *Rückkehr, op. cit.*, pp. 322–323; Friedman, *Germany, op. cit.*, pp. 266–267; Zechlin, *Deutsche Politik, op. cit.*, p. 339.

[37]For the C.V.'s and the ZVfD's expectations from German policy-making in occupied Poland see *Im deutschen Reich*, XX (1914), pp. 381–382; XXI (1915), pp. 101–108; *Jüdische Rundschau*, XX (1915), pp. 63–64, 77–78, 104, 121–122. On the German plans for a Polish vassal-state see Fritz Fischer, *Griff nach der Weltmacht. Die Kriegszielpolitik des kaiserlichen Deutschland 1914–1918*, Düsseldorf 1961; Imanuel Geiss, *Der polnische Grenzstreifen 1914–1918. Ein Beitrag zur deutschen Kriegszielpolitik im Ersten Weltkrieg* (Historische Studien Band 378), Lübeck 1960.

[38]On the lack of sources see Engel, 'Patriotism', *loc. cit.*, p. 160, note 62.

[39]See Goldmann, *loc. cit.*, *Im deutschen Reich*, XXI (October–November 1915); Kurt Alexander, 'Deutschland und die Ostjudenfrage. Eine Erwiderung', *ibid.*, XXII (January–February 1916), pp. 20–26, for a rejoinder to Goldmann.

more at keeping Turkey as an ally instead of fostering ambitious Zionist plans.[40] Moreover, the world-wide rumours about Jewish congress movements, although greeted by the *Jüdische Rundschau* as signs of a Jewish awakening, for the first time gave the ZVfD-officials the feeling of lagging behind instead of leading new developments within the Zionist movement.[41]

While the C.V. as well as the ZVfD had had, since 1915, to cope with serious troubles facing their war strategies, the blow which hit the C.V. in the shape of the so-called *Judenzählung* in October 1916 had been the most severe up till then. One of the most puzzling questions about the decree of the Prussian War Ministry concerns the obvious discrepancy between the disillusioning effect of the *Judenzählung* within German Jewry on the one hand and the passivity of the Jewish defence organisations on the other.[42] Refraining from any initiative of their own to achieve a revocation of the decree, the C.V. leaders backed the "appeasement-tactics"[43] of Oskar Cassel from the *Verband der Deutschen Juden* at the C.V. assembly of February 1917. Three factors came together here which made the majority of the delegates agree with the argument that any discussion about the decree should be postponed till the end of war. First, in view of the C.V.'s bad experiences with the Prussian War Ministry when engaged in its pre-war efforts to facilitate Jewish access to the reserve-officer corps, a revocation seemed highly improbable anyway.[44] Second, following Chancellor Bethmann Hollweg's promise of "Freie Bahn für alle Tüchtigen" given in September 1916, the hopes of liberal Jews centred around a "new orientation" of German policy and thus enabled many, for instance Eugen Fuchs, to suppress the highly negative effect of the *Judenzählung*.[45] Third, even the dissenters inside the C.V., who criticised the passivity of the leadership,[46] showed no signs of lasting consternation, mainly because of the apparent necessity for recognising the even more threatening signs of the future. The times which *Im deutschen Reich* expected

[40]In Palestine the Zionists had constant difficulties with the Turkish junta member and commander-in-chief Djemal Pasha; at the end of March 1917 with the evacuation of Jaffa the "beginning of a persecution of the Jews on the Armenian model" (Lichtheim, *Rückkehr, op. cit.*, p. 365) seemed imminent.

[41]On the various congress-movements of this time see *Jüdische Rundschau*, XX (1915), pp. 213–215; XXI (1916), pp. 108–109, 200, 260, 281–282, 321, 342–343; XXII (1917), pp. 60, 190–193, 237, 238, 396; XXIII (1918), pp. 36–37, 58–59, 67–68.

[42]For a detailed analysis of the *Judenzählung* and the reaction of the Jewish defence organisations see Werner T. Angress, 'Das deutsche Militär und die Juden im Ersten Weltkrieg', in *Militärgeschichtliche Mitteilungen*, 19/1 (1976), pp. 77–146; *idem*, 'The German Army's "Judenzählung" of 1916. Genesis-Consequences-Significance', in *LBI Year Book XXIII* (1978), pp. 117–135.

[43]Angress, 'Das deutsche Militär', *loc. cit.*, p. 87.

[44]See *idem*, 'Prussia's Army and the Jewish Reserve Officer Controversy before World War I', in *LBI Year Book XVII* (1972), pp. 19–42.

[45]For the Jewish hopes connected with such a "new orientation", which in reality was an ideological sham just like the phrase *Burgfrieden*, see *Im deutschen Reich*, XXII (1916), pp. 194–195, 198–199; XXIII (1917), pp. 106–117, 158–161. Fuchs's opinion that "the government has become progressively freer from prejudice" (ibid., XXIII, 1917, pp. 57, 350, XXIV, 1918, p. 125), is indeed a "curious statement in view of the War Ministry's recent census order" (Engel, 'Patriotism', *loc. cit.*, p. 157).

[46]See *Jüdische Rundschau*, XXII (1917), p. 53; Angress, 'Das deutsche Militär', *loc. cit.*, p. 144, note 345.

to follow the war would be no less menacing than the present and would allow no looking back. A belligerent antisemitism was to be anticipated:

> "Lange, allzulange haben wir ihren [der Antisemiten] eifrigen Rüstungen zugesehen, haben wir ihre Mobilisierung beobachtet. Nun wir sie bereit sehen, die Giftwolken ihrer Verleumdungsgase auf uns abzublasen, sowie der rechte Windhauch ihrem tückischen Plane sich günstig zeigt, ist es an der Zeit, daß wir unsere Abwehrtruppen sammeln und die Verteidigung organisieren."[47]

At the beginning of 1917 with the knowledge of growing antisemitism, which now gradually gained space in the pages of *Im deutschen Reich*,[48] the C.V. began to shape its post-war strategy. Having no opportunity whatsoever for a more active stand against antisemitism until the war ended, its preparations for the future were confined for the time being to the taking up of new means of inner-organisational stabilisation and the strengthening of inner-Jewish unity.[49] Thus at the end of the C.V. assembly of 1917 Maximilian Horwitz expressed his hope that between his organisation and the Zionists, who during the war "had not only stood the test of time as national Jews, but had also loyally fulfilled their duty towards their Fatherland", a positive post-war "cooperation" would be possible.[50] It must be regarded as a pointer to its own crisis that the ZVfD missed the chance of striking at the C.V.'s weakest spot: its passivity and clumsiness in dealing with the *Judenzählung*. Having no alternative to offer to the C.V.'s effete way of countering the *Judenzählung* in particular and to its defence work in general, at the end of 1916 German Zionism wanted no revival of the former war between brothers.[51] In its comment on the ZVfD's first war-time *Delegiertentag* in December 1916, the *Jüdische Rundschau* echoed the wish of leading Zionists to overcome differences instead of continuing a meaningless fight; after the C.V. assembly of February 1917 the Zionist paper assessed Horwitz's friendly gesture not as mere rhetoric, but as a "vague indication of a certain reorientation inside the C.V." according to which "the old blind opposition" seemed to give way to "a certain understanding" of Zionist aims.[52]

From the beginning of 1917 both the C.V. and the ZVfD had realised that in face of a more and more hostile German world the likelihood of implementing

[47]*Im deutschen Reich*, XXIII (February 1917), p. 49.
[48]See *Im deutschen Reich*, XXIII (1917), pp. 97–100, 149–156, 201–206; Engel, *Jewish Responses, op. cit.*, pp. 221–238.
[49]It seems highly questionable whether "a policy of aggressive public confrontation with official bodies over their failure to live up to the promises of the *Burgfrieden*", suggested by Engel, 'Patriotism', *loc. cit.*, p. 157, would have been possible during the First World War. In the face of the constraints of the state of siege and press-censorship as well as the socio-ideological orientation of German Jewry the expectation of such an alternative course would appear to be unrealistic. The same goes for Engel's earlier statement that the C.V. should have attached its cause "to the overall political platform of the German Left, their natural allies in the fight against antisemitism" (*idem*, *Jewish Responses, op. cit.*, p. 269, and a similar statement, pp. 377–378). Such ideas entertained by some post-Holocaust historians are best characterised as belated wishful thinking taking the actual historical situation in the *Kaiserreich* insufficiently into account (on the impossibility of such a step see Paucker, 'Zur Problematik', *loc. cit.*, p. 504).
[50]*Jüdische Rundschau*, XXII (9th February 1917), p. 49.
[51]For the ZVfD's view on German antisemitism during the *Kaiserreich* see Reinharz, 'The Zionist Response', *loc. cit.*, pp. 105–110.
[52]*Jüdische Rundschau*, XXII (9th February 1917), p. 49; *ibid.*, XXI (29th December 1916), p. 431.

their respective aims had become increasingly doubtful. As a result they began to look for allies within the Jewish camp. With the time of direct confrontation not long past and the continuing ideological, political, and personal animosities, it is not surprising that the C.V. as well as the ZVfD saw both negative and positive aspects in a rapprochement, irrespective of its practical aims and contents. It took time and a further deterioration of their prospects to make both organisations put aside their mutual reservations and scepticism. Its traditional greater flexibility and the more urgent pressure of the political situation induced the ZVfD to take the first step in putting its offer in more concrete terms. The German Zionists' earnest desire to initiate a new phase in the relationship with the non-Zionist organisations was indicated by the fact that it was Kurt Blumenfeld, the leading ideologist inside the ZVfD, who answered the question whether a rapprochement between both factions was possible. It was not feasible in fundamental matters but desirable for specific aims:

> "Zwischen den Lebensanschauungen des zionistischen und des anderen Lagers kann es eine Verständigung der Natur nach nicht geben.
> Es ist jedoch durchaus möglich, daß die zionistische *Organisation* sich mit anderen jüdischen *Organisationen* zu bestimmten Zwecken verbündet. Solche allen erwünschte Ziele gibt es. Wer es für wertvoll hält, sie mit uns im Bunde zu erreichen, kann unserer Bündnistreue gewiß sein."[53]

When in the course of 1917 German antisemitism rose to formerly unknown proportions,[54] Blumenfeld's proposal was taken up by the Vice-President and – after Maximilian Horwitz's death in October 1917 – the unchallenged political and ideological leader of the C.V., Eugen Fuchs. Although Fuchs's article dealt at length with the fundamental differences separating Zionists from the German-Jewish majority, its essential purpose was not the prolongation of the debate over *Deutschtum* and *Judentum*.[55] During the debate between the leading thinkers within liberal and Zionist German Jewry, Hermann Cohen and Martin Buber, which had lifted the topic to new abstract levels, the C.V. and the ZVfD had stood aside listening to the arguments of the opponents with interest, though not with burning enthusiasm.[56] The real concern of the leaders of both organisations was with the practical problems resulting from the progress of the war in general and the establishment of a "methodical, organised cooperation"[57] between the two bodies in particular. By presenting areas of common interest, Fuchs developed Blumenfeld's proposal further towards its implementation. These areas were, according to Fuchs, the fight against "antisemites and renegades" at

---

[53]*Der Jude*, I, Heft 11 (1916/1917), p. 717. The title of this article – 'Innere Politik. Zur jüdischen Entwicklung in Deutschland' – indicates that Blumenfeld's predominant object was to address inner-German groups; cf. his later interpretation in Blumenfeld, *Erlebte Judenfrage, op. cit.*, pp. 21, 119; *idem, Briefe, op. cit.*, p. 16.

[54]See Engel, *Jewish Responses, op. cit.*, pp. 221–238.

[55]In January Fuchs wrote on the aim of his article: "After having sharply singled out the contrasting nature of *Weltanschauung* . . . , we can meet the Zionists where these differences are not relevant" (Eugen Fuchs, *Glaube und Heimat*, Berlin 1928, p. III). For a different interpretation of Fuchs's article cf. Engel, *Jewish Responses, op. cit.*, pp. 351–353.

[56]On the Cohen-Buber-debate see *ibid.*, pp. 329–340.

[57]*Im deutschen Reich*, XXIII (September 1917), p. 350.

home, under the leadership of the C.V. and the *Verband der Deutschen Juden*, and the fight for "a homeland, human rights, and freedom" for the *Ostjuden*. Fuchs stressed that the C.V. as well as the *Verband* was open to "the activity of Zionists towards a revival of Jewry for the time being within the German Fatherland".[58]

IV

As in the case of the changes in the relationship between the C.V. and the ZVfD which followed the re-orientation of strategies after the outbreak of war, the new phase of mutual longing for cooperation was forced on organised German Jewry by external developments. Political-military events were pushing them towards a rapprochement.

When at the end of 1917 a peace-settlement at Germany's Eastern frontier seemed imminent, German Jewry was startled. Since the industrious efforts of all factions to influence German policy in favour of the *Ostjuden* had mostly been in vain, the dawning of peace with a victorious Germany determining the outcome made the divergent parties within German Jewry look for ways of gaining the attention of German officials in order to improve the future life of their Eastern brethren. Knowing that there was no time to lose in exerting at least some influence on the peace-negotiations, what before had seemed impossible now came true with almost breath-taking speed. In November 1917 the top-officials of the C.V. and the ZVfD met to discuss the creation of an assembly which should represent all Jews living in the lands of the Central Powers; at the end of the month officials of all major factions of German Jewry came together at the invitation of the heads of the *Hilfsverein der deutschen Juden* to elaborate an internal peace-settlement.[59] The imminent Russo-German peace was not the only reason for such unusual haste; the shift in prestige which accrued to Zionism in the wake of the Balfour Declaration in November 1917 turned out to be no less important. In the long run it secured the "victory of the Zionist cause";[60] its immediate consequence was to turn Zionism into a "political factor" involved in the struggle of the warring camps.[61] Showing sympathy towards Zionist aims in Palestine was now no longer primarily a matter of ideological commitment, but had become a necessity for every true patriot, as it could perhaps contribute to the final victory of the Fatherland. Despite scepticism about the seriousness of the British declaration, Eugen Fuchs now urged the Central Powers to make a similarly positive gesture for a Jewish Palestine in order to take "the Jewish wind

[58]*Ibid.*, pp. 350–351.

[59]See *ibid.*, XXIV (February 1918), pp. 53–55; *Neue Jüdische Monatshefte*, 1917/1918, pp. 244–246; Jacob Toury, 'Organizational Problems of German Jewry. Steps towards the Establishment of a Central Organisation (1893–1920)', in *LBI Year Book XIII* (1968), pp. 80–84.

[60]Blumenfeld, *Erlebte Judenfrage, op. cit.*, p. 121; Lichtheim, *Rückkehr, op. cit.*, p. 373.

[61]This development was not always viewed as positive. Martin Buber, especially, feared that Jewry would be embroiled in the "chaos of exploitation and attrition of this degenerate war" (*Der Jude*, II, Heft 5/6, 1917/1918), p. 290; likewise *ibid.*, Heft 10/11, pp. 711–712. Zionist officials caring little about these warnings came close to Fuchs's assessment (see *Im deutschen Reich*, XIX (1913), p. 221; *Neue Jüdische Monatshefte*, 1918/1919, p. 140).

out of the sails" of the *Entente*. As German interests were at stake, the C.V.-leadership could easily silence internal voices calling for a rejection of Zionism in general; refusing to give in to these "rabble-rousers", Fuchs deemed their proposal "from the patriotic view point, too, as a mistake".[62]

Unless the strategies of the C.V. and the ZVfD and their adaptation to the progress of the war are taken into account it is difficult to understand why Fuchs reacted to the Balfour Declaration by supporting Zionist aims in Palestine and why the ZVfD showed no signs of jubilation over the victory Chaim Weizmann had achieved. As a result of its opposing political strategy during the war, the ZVfD's assessment of the Balfour Declaration was distinguished by mixed feelings. On the one hand, an old dream of Zionism had come true; on the other, German Zionist officials were troubled with the unpleasant feeling that during the whole war they had backed the wrong horse. Thus, the ZVfD's former unquestioned leading role within the WZO suffered a decisive blow while Zionism as a whole developed from being a utopian dream to becoming an important factor in international policy-making. As they had to stick to their basic war strategy if they did not wish to risk compromising themselves, the ZVfD-leaders reacted to the British declaration by asserting that it remained, just as before, the task of Zionist policy "to get the agreement of Turkey and the Central Powers to the implementation of Zionism"; an agreement of all major powers would prevent one camp from making demands on Zionism and thus would add to the hoped-for multi-national declaration.[63] Nevertheless, the comment of the *Jüdische Rundschau* on the Balfour Declaration did not solely appeal to German officials to recognise the signs of the time but to their co-religionists:

> "Für die Zentralmächte ist jetzt die Zeit des offenen Wortes und der Tat gekommen. Die Juden Deutschlands und seiner Verbündeten sollten das Gebot der Stunde erkennen und ihren Regierungen dieses Wort und diese Tat erleichtern."[64]

German Jewry indeed tried its best. After the Turkish junta had reluctantly promised to allow "free immigration and settlement within the limits of the country's capacities",[65] the united efforts of the ZVfD and the KfdO brought about an almost identical declaration from the German Foreign Office.[66] Although practically worthless because of its non-committal character and on account of the changing military situation in the Middle East, this declaration removed the remaining obstacles against a Jewish united front in Germany. While the *Jüdische Rundschau* greeted the cooperation with the KfdO as a

---

[62]*Im deutschen Reich*, XXIV (February 1918), p. 54.
[63]*Jüdische Rundschau*, XXII (23rd November 1917), p. 377. This new argument foreshadowed the ZVfD's retreat from its war-time strategy the more a final victory of the Allies seemed imminent. Although "Zionist patriotism had from the onset been rooted largely in considerations of *Realpolitik*" (Engel, *Jewish Responses, op. cit.*, p. 358), there can be no doubt that, apart from tactical considerations, social precedence as well as political sympathy influenced the factions within the WZO during the war (see Zechlin, *Deutsche Politik, op. cit.*, p. 422).
[64]*Jüdische Rundschau*, XXII (23rd November 1917), p. 377.
[65]*Ibid.*, XXIII (4th January 1918), pp. 1–2.
[66]See *Ibid.*, 11th January 1918, p. 9; *Im deutschen Reich*, XXIV (February 1918), p. 55.

promising sign that "amongst the overwhelming majority of the Jews certain basic ideas of Zionism had gradually awoken" and that "a general consensus" was underway,[67] the C.V. could now, with the backing of the German declaration, easily reject the suspicion of German-Nationalists within its own ranks that collaboration with the Zionists was a crime against the Fatherland.

Thus, in January 1918 the *Vereinigung jüdischer Organisationen Deutschlands zur Wahrung der Rechte der Juden des Ostens* (VIOD), could be officially established. In order to achieve its aim – "to represent jointly the attitude of German Jewry on all Jewish problems in the East and the Orient *vis-à-vis* the relevant authorities for the duration of the war as well as afterwards at the peace negotiations"[68] – the new organisation drew up special 'Guidelines' to be accepted by German politicians:

> "1. Rechtliche und tatsächliche Gleichberechtigung mit allen Rechten und Pflichten als Staatsbürger
> 2. Freiheit der Religionsübung
> 3. Recht auf Pflege selbständiger jüdischer Kultur
> 4. Recht auf freie Einwanderung und wirtschaftliche Betätigung in allen Teilen des osmanischen Reiches
> 5. Recht auf freie Niederlassung und Pflege selbständiger jüdischer Kultur in Palästina."[69]

As these objectives clearly demonstrate, predominantly political considerations based on the expectation of a German victory, or, at least, of far-reaching German influence in the East and Middle East induced German Jewry to give up its traditional internal sectarianism at the beginning of 1918. Compared with the prospect of losing all initiative in dealing with vital questions of future Jewish life by leaving it in the hands of Christian-dominated authorities, the German-Jewish organisations regarded a temporary rapprochement at any rate as a lesser evil. None of the participants in the VIOD had conceded any major part of their traditional ideological commitment to another faction, nor was there unanimity concerning the assessment of the VIOD's significance.

The early commentaries of the C.V. and the ZVfD on the creation of the VIOD give only vague hints of both organisations' real aims and hopes as regards this "united front". Forced to explain to its Zionist adherents its tactical *volte-face* from active confrontation to cooperation with the non-Zionist organisations, the *Jüdische Rundschau* pointed to the VIOD's value for establishing Zionism inside German Jewry:

> "Die deutschen Zionisten fühlen sich heute stark genug, um es ungescheut vor der breiten Öffentlichkeit aussprechen zu können, daß sie es begrüßen, durch ihre Zustimmung zur Einladung der Teilnahme an der VIOD aus der splendid isolation herausgekommen zu sein und sich zu einer führenden Rolle bei der Vertretung des deutschen Judentums durchgesetzt zu haben. Sie können dieses Eingeständnis der Genugtuung wagen, weil es mit der Feststellung verbunden ist, daß das gesamte deutsche Judentum – ohne Ausnahme – sich

---

[67] *Jüdische Rundschau*, XXIII (11th January 1918), p. 9.
[68] *Ibid.*, 15th February 1918, p. 50.
[69] *Ibid.*, see also Friedman, *Germany, op. cit.*, p. 394. Because it was shortlived the VIOD is at the most mentioned in passing by historians dealing with the history of German Jewry (see e.g. Toury, 'Organizational Problems', *loc. cit.*, p. 83).

den zionistischen Forderungen soweit angepaßt hat, daß die Aufstellung eines gemeinsamen Programms ohne Opferung zionistischer Grundsätze möglich geworden ist."[70]

The C.V., although not directly affected by the creation of a German-Jewish "foreign ministry",[71] pointed to other repercussions the VIOD might have for future Jewish life in Germany:

"Wenn erst einmal die Führer der verschiedenen Organisationen gemeinsam in einer alle berührenden Frage der auswärtigen Politik Hand in Hand arbeiten, so wird auch in den Fragen der inneren Politik, in denen eine verschiedene Weltauffassung besteht, verhütet werden, daß die sachliche Gegnerschaft zur persönlichen Feindschaft führt, daß dem Gegner guter Glaube und ehrliche Überzeugung abgesprochen wird, und es werden die notwendigen Auseinandersetzungen lediglich sachlich mit den Waffen des Geistes geführt werden. Nur wenn wir einig sein werden, werden wir stark sein."[72]

Apart from the tactical value of these statements – i.e. calming sceptical voices within their own organisations by pointing to positive effects the cooperation might have for the respective organisational aims[73] – it is obvious that the C.V. and the ZVfD had very divergent opinions as to the VIOD's basic function. While the ZVfD regarded the VIOD as the ultimate chance for implementing its political aims, the C.V. envisaged "resistance, united resistance"[74] of all German-Jewish organisations against German antisemitism after the war. Thus, for its idealistic leader Eugen Fuchs the VIOD was the first step towards a domestic united front of German Jewry based on compromise between its most important organisations. C.V. and ZVfD aims seemed, at least on their periphery, compatible to Fuchs:

"Warum sollen die Zionisten nicht gemeinsam mit uns hier die Abwehrkämpfe gegen Antisemiten und Renegaten führen, mit uns an der innerlichen Wiederbelebung des Judentums auf deutschem Boden mitarbeiten; warum sollen wir ihre humanitären, kulturellen, kolonisatorischen Bestrebungen für die östlichen Juden nicht stützen, das Los der Ostjuden nicht zu lindern versuchen?"[75]

In fact, what Fuchs envisaged remained wishful thinking. The negative answer the future gave to his questions was neither evidence for the C.V. leader's

[70]*Jüdische Rundschau*, XXIII (15th February 1918), p. 50.
[71]*Im deutschen Reich*, XXIV (February 1918), p. 56.
[72]*Neue Jüdische Monatshefte*, 1917/1918, p. 246; cf. *Im deutschen Reich*, XXIV (February 1918), p. 56.
[73]The ZVfD especially had to cope with internal voices criticising the VIOD as an artificial construction as well as with criticism from foreign Zionists (see *Der Jude*, II, 1917/1918), p. 736; *Jüdische Rundschau*, XXIII, 1918, p. 118).
[74]*Im deutschen Reich*, XXIV (January 1918), p. 21.
[75]Fuchs, *Deutschtum, op. cit.*, p. 330. For the important role Fuchs played during the negotiations preceding the VIOD see Friedman, *Germany, op. cit.*, p. 394; Eva G. Reichmann, 'Der Bewußtseinswandel der deutschen Juden', in *Deutsches Judentum, op. cit.*, p. 563. At the beginning of 1918 Fuchs interpreted the fact that the C.V. by then represented 200,000 German Jews as a vindication of the C.V.'s strategy (*ibid.*, pp. 321, 342). Nevertheless, this upward trend in membership figures indicates as little about the quality of the C.V. strategy as the opposite trend in the years 1915/1916. Such fluctuations can be regarded as a gauge of German Jewry's hope for integration after the outbreak of war, which made membership in the C.V. seem superfluous, followed by increased disillusionment during the course of the war when more Jews again turned to the C.V. as the sure haven it had previously been. The answer to the question whether there exists a correlation between the short-term decreases in C.V. membership and an increase in adherence to the ZVfD during the war as is suggested by Engel, 'Patriotism', *loc. cit.*, p. 165; *idem, Jewish Responses, op. cit.*, p. 329, can only be established by further research (see above, note 21).

tendency to build castles in the air nor a proof of the ZVfD's general unwillingness to become involved in such a deal; what destroyed the hopes of both organisations for a future collaboration was the total rejection of any of the VIOD's proposals by the governments of Turkey and the Central Powers. Coming too late to influence in any way the peace-talks of Brest-Litovsk, the VIOD not only failed to enforce even minimal guarantees for the Romanian Jews in the peace-treaty of Bucharest signed in May 1918,[76] but it had no success either in moving Turkish officials towards a more positive stand on Zionist wishes until the military breakdown of Turkey, in summer 1918, made any agreement superfluous.[77] The final blow to Jewish hopes in connection with the VIOD came with the decision of the Prussian government in April 1918 to impose a *Grenzsperre* against Polish Jews, a measure which ignored the remonstrations of organised German Jewry as a whole.[78]

As soon as it became apparent that the VIOD was based on an illusion – i.e. the willingness of the Central Powers to pay attention to fundamental Jewish demands –, the "united front" disintegrated. Its last action seems to have taken place in November 1918;[79] already from the summer of 1918 the C.V. and the ZVfD had gone different ways towards different aims. The imminent collapse of Germany's Western front made the ZVfD retreat from its war-time strategy complete to the point of claiming that Zionism had "nothing to do with this war",[80] while the C.V. felt itself more than ever bound to the Fatherland eagerly avoiding any indication of weakening patriotism.[81] At the end of 1918, after the short interlude of the VIOD, animosity between the C.V. and the ZVfD reached almost pre-war proportions. The German Zionists' efforts to set up a congress movement,[82] fostered by the German November Revolution, not only threatened to overthrow the organisational structure of German Jewry but posed the much greater danger for the non-Zionist organisations of marring their efforts to demonstrate, even in times of national disaster, a totally loyal Jewish minority to the German public. Although in the end nothing came out of the German-Jewish congress, its implicit threat moved the C.V. and its traditional allies to issue a

[76]On the Jewish question in Romania see *Im deutschen Reich*, XXIV (1918), pp. 111, 136, 157–158, 210–212; *Jüdische Rundschau*, XXIII (1918), pp. 82, 117, 149; Zechlin, *Deutsche Politik, op. cit.*, pp. 238–250.

[77]For the negotiations between the VIOD and Turkey in summer 1918 see *Jüdische Rundschau*, XXIII (1918), p. 253; Friedman, *Germany, op. cit.*, pp. 404–413; Zechlin, *Deutsche Politik, op. cit.*, pp. 437–441. After the Balfour Declaration the ZVfD had revived its efforts towards creating a favourable image in the German public mind which had come to a standstill after Blumenfeld's call-up in 1915; for the results see *Jüdische Rundschau*, XXIII (1918), pp. 17–18, 34–36, 57–58, 66–67, 133–134, 150; Friedman, *Germany, op. cit.*, pp. 393, 398–401, 406; Zechlin, *Deutsche Politik, op. cit.*, pp. 437–441.

[78]The *Grenzsperre* became first known in summer 1918; see *Jüdische Rundschau*, XXIII (1918), pp. 229, 261. The C.V. reported on the *Grenzsperre* in the column 'Miscellaneous', *Im deutschen Reich*, XXIV (1918), p. 360.

[79]See *Jüdische Rundschau*, XXIII (1918), p. 349.

[80]*Der Jude*, III, Heft 5 (1918/1919), p. 197.

[81]It found its most telling expression at the C.V. assembly of November 1918; see *Im deutschen Reich*, XXIV (1918), pp. 427–438.

[82]See *Jüdische Rundschau*, XXIII (1918), pp. 363, 379, 389, 403–404, 417, 422, 425–426, 431–432, 450–451; Toury, 'Organizational Problems', *loc. cit.*, pp. 84–88.

public declaration stating that in contrast to the small Zionist minority the majority of German Jews felt themselves to be an "indissoluble part of the German people, that we constitute a community of faith and not a Jewish people in Germany, and that we are opposed to any national segregation".[83]

V

Thus, at the end of 1918 it seemed as if nothing had changed in the relationship between the C.V. and the ZVfD compared with 1913, the year of mutual resolutions expressing unbridgeable differences of opinion.[84] We have here tried to show that the First World War brought important changes for both the C.V. and the ZVfD: their strategies underwent significant reorientation, their views of each other altered from latent hostility in 1914/1915 to hesitant recognition of common aims from the end of 1916 and returned to mutual antagonism at the end of the war. These changes had been caused by outside pressures arising from the war which – like antisemitism in its new form of a political mass movement or the orientation of German policy-making towards aggressive expansion – determined the fate of German Jewry until its destruction. As a minority in a non-pluralistic society, German Jewry could never act according to Jewish interests alone. As organisations representing large sections of this minority, the *Centralverein* as well as the ZVfD was always compelled to take into account the effects of their actions on the Gentile world which surrounded them. Thus, the study of the history of German Jewry has to be embedded in the context of the social and political history of Germany as a whole. Any attempt to explain German Jewry's fragmentation and inability to react unanimously to threats from outside by looking only at inner-Jewish ideological and organisational divergencies may give rise to a distortion of historical responsibility: the creation of the false impression that the victims-to-be might, in any way whatsoever, have contributed to their own eventual destruction.

[83]*Neue Jüdische Monatshefte*, 1918/1919, p. 111.
[84]See *Im deutschen Reich*, XIX (1913), pp. 194–247, 296–304; *Jüdische Rundschau*, XVIII (1913), pp. 135–136, 147–149, 159–160, 162, 177–178, 187–190, 251–254.

The Protection of Jewish Civil Rights in the Weimar Republic

Jewish Self-Defence through Legal Action

History – according to Egon Friedell – is an open-ended epic, a story spun out by the collective consciousness of mankind, each generation adding its specific contribution.[1] The picture of the past is continually illuminated by the spotlight of the present. Yet today's light still falls on yesterday's thought constructs.

In regard to the Weimar Republic in particular, many of yesterday's thoughts, stereotyped concepts, have come to be uncritically accepted as received wisdom. Some of these stereotypes add up to the picture of an anti-Jewish judiciary and administration faced by societies of ineffective Jewish worthies who made only feeble efforts to combat antisemitism. Propositions to that effect were hardly ever formulated in such extreme terms; nevertheless, they have largely determined the historical picture. There is only one way to get our thinking out of these ruts, and that is through a study of the contemporary sources.[*]

The charges laid against the Jewish organisations on the grounds of the alleged inadequacy of their self-defence measures were refuted by Arnold Paucker as long ago as 1968 and even earlier in 1965,[2] but so far there has been no detailed investigation of the role played in particular by legal action in the Jewish self-defence effort. Whereas Doskow and Jacoby, writing in 1940, took a poor view of the legal defence effort, Donald Niewyk, thirty-five years later, arrived at a decidedly more favourable conclusion.[3] Arnold Paucker, too, who in his earlier book treated the subject only cursorily, now takes a more positive

---

[1] Egon Friedell, *Kulturgeschichte Ägyptens und des alten Orients*, reprint of the special edition 1963 (the first edition was *Kulturgeschichte des Altertums. Ägypten und Vorderasien*, London 1936), p. 30.
[*] This essay was translated from the original German and edited by Dr. Lux Furtmüller, Reading, to whom both the Editor and the author would like to express their gratitude here.
[2] Arnold Paucker, *Der jüdische Abwehrkampf gegen Antisemitismus und Nationalsozialismus in den letzten Jahren der Weimarer Republik*, Hamburg 1968 (Hamburger Beiträge zur Zeitgeschichte Band IV). Previously in 'Der jüdische Abwehrkampf', in *Entscheidungsjahr 1932. Zur Judenfrage in der Endphase der Weimarer Republik*. Ein Sammelband herausgegeben von Werner E. Mosse unter Mitwirkung von Arnold Paucker, Tübingen 1965, ²1966 (Schriftenreihe wissenschaftlicher Abhandlungen des Leo Baeck Instituts 13). See also note 203.
[3] Ambrose Doskow and Sidney B. Jacoby, 'Antisemitism and the Law in Pre-Nazi Germany', *Contemporary Jewish Record*, 1940, pp. 498ff.; Donald Niewyk, 'Jews and the Courts in Weimar Germany', *Jewish Social Studies*, vol. XXXVII, No. 2 (1975), pp. 99ff.

view.[4] In these circumstances the author was prompted to undertake in his doctoral thesis a thorough study, based on original source material, of the role of legal action in Jewish self-defence in the Weimar Republic.[5] This study also deals with the general debate on the "crisis of confidence in the administration of justice".

While little material is available in the archives, there is no lack of printed sources, which allow us to retrace today the events of that period. The picture that emerges is one of a Jewish minority in the Weimar Republic that was on the point of disintegration when the process was reversed and Jewry was welded together again by the onslaught of antisemitism. This coalescence included even the Zionist group, which in its advocacy of emigration as a solution to the "Jewish Question" seemed in this respect at any rate to be of one mind with the antisemites. Yet the German Jews could not imagine a Germany without Jews. What they wanted was to work alongside Christian Germans in order to put Germany back on her feet after the lost war, and until the unthinkable became reality under Hitler, they were able to take comfort in the thought that Germany, as a civilised nation, surely would not settle a minority problem by brute force.[6]

At least until the end of the 1920s many politically experienced Jews looked with equanimity upon the antisemitic attacks, which after all were by no means the first anti-Jewish occurrences in their lifetime, and expected temporarily excited passions to calm down after a while. In furtherance of that process they engaged on a large scale in actions, including legal actions, of self-defence.

The term "self-defence through legal action" or briefly "legal self-defence" is used here in the broad sense of the activity that is necessary in order to defend or amend a legal state of affairs; this is done in the first place by direct approaches to the central state authorities. In the narrow sense, legal action for self-defence is defined as the activity that is necessary in order to deal with individual instances in which the law is violated. Such action ranges from legal advice to the bringing of court actions in test cases, but can extend also to non-litigious actions accompanied by press publicity. Furthermore there is preventive legal action for self-defence comprising publication and dissemination of authoritative legal opinions and other explanatory literature.

Legal self-defence in this broad sense was practised by nearly all Jewish organisations. Some of them, notably sports and youth organisations, confined such activities to matters affecting their standing in society, others operated at the level of governmental institutions. Leaving out of account organisations whose efforts were shortlived or directed only to their own narrow parochial concerns, the *Centralverein deutscher Staatsbürger jüdischen Glaubens* (C.V.) emerges as the most important exponent of the legal defence efforts. In particular it undertook to extend legal assistance to individual Jews, a task for which it was

[4]Arnold Paucker, 'Jewish Self-Defence', in *Die Juden im Nationalsozialistischen Deutschland/The Jews in Nazi Germany 1933–1943*, herausgegeben von Arnold Paucker, mit Sylvia Gilchrist und Barbara Suchy, Tübingen 1986 (Schriftenreihe wissenschaftlicher Abhandlungen des Leo Baeck Instituts 45), pp. 55ff., this reference p. 63.
[5]Udo Beer, *Die Juden, das Recht und die Republik*, Frankfurt a. Main–Bern–New York 1986.
[6]Ernst Berg, *Wohin treibt Juda?*, Leipzig 1926, p. 63.

well equipped, professionally as well as financially. (East European Jews, on the other hand, were excluded from this scheme. Their problems have been dealt with at length by Leon Sklarz and Schalom Adler-Rudel.[7])

Although the C.V. was clearly the most important organisation in its field, its position was not unchallenged. In fact, the relations between the various organisations concerned with legal self-defence were subject to marked fluctuations. An element of discord was introduced throughout the period, most stridently up to the end of the nineteen twenties, by the *Verband nationaldeutscher Juden*. Another unhelpful factor was the ambition of the C.V. to keep the conduct of the self-defence struggle strictly in its own hands. Competition was tolerated only grudgingly. Collaboration functioned smoothly with the *Reichsbund jüdischer Frontsoldaten*, where there was an obvious division of labour, and with such bodies as the *Kartell-Convent der Verbindungen deutscher Studenten jüdischen Glaubens* (K.C.) and the *B'nai B'rith*, which accepted the leadership of the C.V. So long as the Zionists did likewise or showed no interest in Jewish self-defence in Germany, relations with them were similarly trouble-free. However, when the Zionists attempted to gain influence by working through the synagogue congregations, the differences came to a head. The C.V. was able to draw on the support of the Jewish Liberals in general – hardly surprising as the leading figures in both the *Centralverein* and religious Liberalism were often identical – and in this way managed to secure the political neutrality of the congregations. Whether the endeavours of the C.V. to monopolise the political leadership were sensible in the circumstances is open to doubt, since large segments of the Jewish population in Germany – Zionists, East European and Orthodox Jews – were left to fend for themselves. Had there been a political federation embracing all German Jews at regional or *Reich* level, the chorus of German Jewry would surely have struck a more harmonious note for the public ear.

There were also non-Jewish organisations whose activities included legal defence in the broad sense, most prominent among them the *Verein zur Abwehr des Antisemitismus, (Abwehrverein)*, founded in 1890. Yet the virulence of the controversies during the final years of the Weimar Republic was more than the *Abwehrverein* could cope with, so that its activities in the fields of publicity and legal defence declined continually.[8]

It is difficult to appraise retrospectively the extent to which the *Reich* and the individual German *Länder* took action in defence of Jewish rights. On this point neither official nor Jewish sources are extant. Furthermore it must be borne in mind that the state dealt with Jewish issues in a broader context. In many cases specific Jewish problems were inextricably bound up with wider questions of Republican or democratic import. It was impossible, for instance, to separate the

[7]Leon Sklarz, *Geschichte und Organisation der Ostjudenhilfe in Deutschland seit dem Jahre 1914*, Dissertation, Rostock 1930; S[chalom] Adler-Rudel, *Ostjuden in Deutschland 1880–1940. Zugleich eine Geschichte der Organisationen, die sie betreuten*, Tübingen 1959 (Schriftenreihe wissenschaftlicher Abhandlungen des Leo Baeck Instituts 1); now also Trude Maurer, *Ostjuden in Deutschland 1918–1933*, Hamburg 1986 (Hamburger Beiträge zur Geschichte der deutschen Juden Band XII).
[8]Barbara Suchy, 'Der Verein zur Abwehr des Antisemitismus (II). From the First World War to its Dissolution in 1933', in *LBI Year Book XXX* (1985), pp. 67ff., this reference p. 98.

Jews' basic right to freedom of worship from the same right of other religious communities. Similarly the defence of Jewish legal rights was inseparable from the general constitutional guarantee of civic legal rights. To cultivate and extend the rule of law in the State was one of the aims of the Weimar Republic. The State was well placed to intervene in order to safeguard civic legal rights, and it did so occasionally by decree, statutory instrument or executive action.

A key role in the prosecution of antisemitic offences fell to the public prosecutors. This responsibility was recognised. As early as 29th November 1919 the Senior Public Prosecutor at the Berlin Regional Court issued a questionnaire on antisemitic activities to all Prussian police directorates.[9] During the first antisemitic wave the Prussian Minister of Justice on 23rd September 1922 issued an instruction to all Public Prosecutors General to the effect that public interest in a prosecution must invariably be presumed to exist whenever an insult was inspired and engendered by an antisemitic ideology.[10] The same Order instructed the Public Prosecutors to get in touch with Jewish organisations whenever there was some doubt about Jewish customs. This Order shows that the Prussian authorities were co-operating with the Jewish organisations and were helpful in emphasising the public interest in the prosecution of antisemitic offences.

The way in which the principle of public interest or public concern was applied by the Prussian Minister of Justice in the light of political considerations is illustrated by the case of the National Socialist Thuringian Minister Wilhelm Frick, who had laid charges against newspaper editors on several occasions for alleged violation of the Law for the Protection of the Republic. The Prussian Public Prosecutors' Offices, however, ruled that the use of insulting language against a member of a State Government was not in itself indictable under the Act, unless it was combined with disparagement of the Republican form of government. On the other hand, purely personal abuse directed against a Minister was not a matter of public concern, and therefore did not warrant prosecution.[11] The Prussian Minister of Justice issued a statement making it clear that he did not disapprove of the decision of the Public Prosecutors' Office.[12] The differentiated interpretation of the concept of public concern attracted attention also in less conspicuous cases. P. Bloch, a lawyer, contrasted two cases: on the one hand the defamation of Ernst Lissauer by Friedrich Carl Holtz, the editor of *Fridericus*, in his journal,[13] on the other articles in the Left-wing press which described Baron Eberhard von Senden after his acquittal by a court of law as a "Vehm assassin". In the former case the Public Prosecutor had

[9]'Die Staatsanwaltschaft gegen Antisemitismus', *Mitteilungen aus dem Verein zur Abwehr des Antisemitismus*, 1919, p. 198, reproduced by Beer, *op. cit.*, p. 122.
[10]For the full text see Ludwig Foerder, *Antisemitismus und Justiz*, Berlin 1924, Appendix II, p. 27, and Beer, *op. cit.*, p. 123. An original specimen is extant in the Landesarchiv Bremen, Nachrichtenstelle der Polizeidirektion, 4, 65–1125.
[11]'Sind Nationalsozialisten ohne Rechtsschutz?', *Hamburger Nachrichten*, 1st November 1930; 'Frick erhebt vergebliche Klage', *Kölnische Zeitung*, 5th September 1930 (both articles at Landesarchiv Schleswig, Akten des Regierungspräsidenten, Abt. 309, No. 22592).
[12]*Amtlicher Preußischer Pressedienst*, 1st November 1930 (Landesarchiv Schleswig, *loc. cit.*).
[13]'Liebesgesang auf England', *Fridericus*, First Supplement to No. 41/1925.

agreed that it was a matter of public concern, in the latter he decided that it was not. Bloch concluded his article in a Berlin evening paper with the provocative question: "Why is it that Lissauer arouses public concern and Senden does not?".[14] For the reader the answer was clear: because Lissauer was a Jew. This instance points to the drawback of the discriminatory practice adopted by the Minister of Justice and the Public Prosecutors: the Jews came to be seen as a privileged caste, as a new version of the old-style *Schutzjuden* ("Protected Jews"). Ludwig Münchmeyer, the National Socialist orator, repeatedly inveighed against the instruction of the Minister of Justice.[15]

The Prussian Ministries were in a position to prune rank growth in their departments when necessary. Thus, when in the notorious Magdeburg scandal an innocent Jew was tried for murder as a result of the antisemitic attitude of both police and judiciary, the authorities – the Prussian Minister of the Interior, Carl Severing; the Magdeburg *Oberpräsident* Otto Hörsing; and the *Regierungs-direktor* Bernhard Weiss – promptly intervened and the true culprit was soon identified.[16] The affair had a disciplinary sequel, which led to the transfer of two senior judges of the Regional Court, Johannes Kölling and Richard Hoffmann.[17] In another instance of disciplinary action Gellin, a senior judge at the Breslau Regional Court, was actually dismissed because, when drunk, he had in public insulted the Diet Deputy Hermann and called him a Jew. This case is not devoid of irony, for as it happened Gellin himself was of Jewish extraction, while Hermann was not.[18]

Numerous orders banning the wearing of swastika badges were issued by Ministries and other authorities. This applied in particular to the *Reichswehr*, the postal services, hospitals and schools.[19] Altogether it can be said that the State of Weimar endeavoured to live up to its role as guarantor of domestic peace.

Following the enactment of a so-called "Lex Holländer" on 21st November 1921, Ludwig Holländer was at the head of the C.V. as Director and Central Executive member in charge of day-to-day management.[20] He turned the C.V.

[14]P. Bloch, 'Der Staatsanwalt und Herr Ernst Lissauer: öffentliches Interesse', *Berliner Nachtausgabe*, 16th June 1926 (Landesarchiv Berlin, Akten der Generalstaatsanwaltschaft, Rep. 58, Acc. 399, No. 249).
[15]Ludwig Münchmeyer, *Das Sturmjahr 1925/26*, Borkum 1926, p. 81; 'Münchmeyers Erzählungen', *C.V.-Zeitung*, VI (1927), p. 272.
[16]'Magdeburg', *Abwehr-Blätter*, 1926, pp. 85f.; cf. Birger Schulz, *Der Republikanische Richterbund (1921–1933)*, Frankfurt a. Main–Bern 1982, and Robert Kuhn, *Die Vertrauenskrise der Justiz (1926–1928)*, Cologne 1983. – The C.V. enjoyed very cordial relations with Otto Hörsing, the leader of the *Reichsbanner Schwarz-Rot-Gold*. Cf. Paucker, *Der jüdische Abwehrkampf, op. cit.*, p. 98. With Bernhard Weiss likewise, later Vice-President of the Berlin Police, the C.V. had always closely collaborated. See *ibid.*, pp. 82, 105, 107.
[17]'Gerichtete Richter: Der Fall Kölling-Hoffmann', *Abwehr-Blätter*, 1929, p. 28.
[18]'Gerichtete Richter: Der Fall Gellin', *ibid.*, p. 29.
[19]Foerder, *op. cit.*, pp. 28ff.; 'Hakenkreuzerlasse', *Im deutschen Reich,* November 1920, p. 358.
[20]On the "Lex Holländer" which made Ludwig Holländer Director and Executive Council member of the C.V. and its significance for Jewish organisational life in Germany see Alfred Hirschberg, 'Ludwig Hollaender, Director of the C.V.', in *LBI Year Book VII* (1962), pp. 39ff., in particular pp. 52–53. Hirschberg, an active functionary of the C.V. served later as its *Syndikus* and as editor of the *C.V.-Zeitung*.

into an effective legal defence organisation. In this he was ably assisted by Alfred Wiener, the Legal Secretary (*Syndikus*) of the C.V. and his Deputies, Artur Schweriner (Berlin), Martin Marx (Frankfurt) and Hans Reichmann (Berlin). At the Central Office of the organisation there were, in addition, specialists for specific legal problems. The lawyer, Hans Lazarus, for instance, dealt chiefly with the boycott of Jewish businesses.[21]

Apart from the Central Office, the 21 regional organisations[22] likewise engaged in legal defence activities. Nearly all of them were able to call on qualified jurists. To keep the regional organisations and local branches informed, the Central Office sent out duplicated copies of relevant documents from its archives, drawing attention in particular to their potential usefulness in court cases.[23] To save time, regional organisations occasionally exchanged information directly, bypassing the Central Office, especially when productions of the press had been seized by the authorities.[24]

An important part in the legal defence activities of the C.V. was played by the training of the legal staffs. The *C.V.-Zeitung* gradually developed into the authoritative journal specialising in all legal problems affecting the Jewish population. It featured a large number of court decisions which were not commented on in any other law journal.

In June 1927 the C.V. organised a two-day Jurists' Congress in Berlin, which was attended by over four hundred jurists.[25] The proceedings were published in book form.[26] Welcoming the participants, on Saturday, 18th June, the C.V. Chairman Julius Brodnitz said:

> "Our Jurists' Congress is not meant to add one more to the number of manifestations that have been mounted in response to the catchword of the crisis of confidence besetting justice. Instead, it will be incumbent on us to discuss the question as to whether in a situation of general legal distress – a situation in which ordinary people are deprived of the effective protection of the law – we are entitled to speak specifically of a state of Jewish legal distress."[27]

Papers were then read by Jacques Stern on 'Völkisch Philosophy of Law and Government' and by Siegfried Löwenstein on 'A Draft of a General Criminal Code'. The Congress continued with contributions by Erich Eyck on 'The Stance of the Administration of Justice *vis-à-vis* Jews and Judaism',[28] and by Bruno Weil on 'Political Trials'. Summing up the results of the Congress, Alfred Wiener wrote:

[21]Beer, *op. cit.*, p. 258.
[22]*Ibid.*, pp. 180ff; *C.V.-Tätigkeitsbericht 1926–1927*, pp. 19–27.
[23]One such document, Beleg-No. 3154, is preserved in the Bundesarchiv Koblenz, Nachlaß Julius Streicher, Akte No. 6.
[24]Letter of C.V. Central Office to Nuremberg Untersyndikat, dated 20th December 1932, *ibid.*
[25]'Juristentagung des C.V. am 18. und 19. Juni 1927', *C.V.-Zeitung*, VI (1927), p. 327; 'Juristentagung des Centralvereins deutscher Staatsbürger jüdischen Glaubens e.V.', *Der Schild*, 1927, p. 192.
[26]*Deutsches Judentum und Rechtskrise*, published by the Centralverein deutscher Staatsbürger jüdischen Glaubens, Berlin 1927.
[27]Julius Brodnitz, 'Unserer Juristentagung zum Gruß!' *C.V.-Zeitung*, VI (1927), p. 337.
[28]Erich Eyck, 'Die Stellung der Rechtspflege zu Juden und Judentum', in *Deutsches Judentum und Rechtskrise, op. cit.*, pp. 31ff.

"Whether or not we wish to speak of a specific Jewish legal distress, it is clear that the protection extended by the law to Jews, Jewry and Judaism has been inadequate, if not totally worthless."[29]

This criticism referred in substance to the protection extended by criminal law. No further major congress of this kind was held; one, planned for 1928 at Essen, did not materialise,[30] but smaller gatherings of jurists under C.V. auspices did take place.

C.V. guidelines for the work on legal defence are not extant, but the instructions on boycott cases issued by the Bavarian regional organisation give an idea of the methods used. The following procedures were prescribed:
1. Informing the regional headquarters;
2. Supplying reliable evidence;
3. Obtaining power of attorney enabling legal action to be brought;
4. Co-operation of the lawyer handling the case with the regional organisation, or else entrusting the case to the Legal Secretary of the regional organisation;
5. A final warning against taking any unauthorised action, costs of which would not be met by the regional organisation.[31]

The importance attached by the C.V. in general to the last point concerning the handling of court cases was highlighted by Bruno Weil on the occasion of a discussion by a group of jurists:

"Political trials and law-suits agitate and influence the public; their effect on public opinion should not be underrated . . . We must train political defending counsel, especially in the provinces. The possible consequences of inept defence in a political trial have been well illustrated by the Erzberger-Helfferich trial, which is still fresh in our memory. We need a new generation of defending counsel who have grasped the essential nature of political trials and appreciate their long-range effect . . . The trial in itself is nothing, the repercussions are everything . . ."[32]

The C.V. also operated an information service for barristers, supplying ample material that could be useful in court cases. Another aid for barristers was a card index of National Socialist lawyers kept at the Central Office. This was started only during the closing years of the Weimar period and did not include known supporters of the nationalist *Deutschnationale Volkspartei*. The list was drawn up after an unfortunate experience when a Jewish barrister representing a Jewish client had unknowingly called on the services of a National Socialist colleague to assist him.[33] A "positive" list was established much earlier by the *Kartell-Convent*, so very closely allied with the C.V. This list contained the names of all lawyers among its members (*Alte Herren* retained, as a matter of course, membership in the Jewish students' association), which presumably meant the vast majority of

[29]Alfred Wiener, 'Die Juristentagung des C.V.', *C.V.-Zeitung*, VI (1927), p. 355.
[30]Leo Baeck Institute Archive, New York, Hirschberg Collection, AR A 1074–3698, No. 1, p. 2.
[31]Rundschreiben No. 18 des C.V.-Landesverbandes Bayern an seine Ortsgruppen und Vertrauensleute vom Oktober 1931, Bundesarchiv Koblenz, Nachlaß Julius Streicher, Akte No. 6; reprinted in Beer, *op. cit.*, pp. 186f.
[32]Bruno Weil, in C.V. (eds.), *Gegen die Rechtsnot der deutschen Juden*, Berlin 1927, pp. 8f.
[33]'Korrespondenzanwälte', *Führerbriefe*, II, No. 1 (14th November 1930), pp. 10f.

the lawyers sympathetic to the C.V.[34] In addition there was a list of Zionist lawyers.[35]

How personally committed and dedicated the Jewish lawyers were in the pursuit of legal defence we cannot know in general, but, as an example, the case of Julius Charig, an Emden lawyer, is one that can easily be retraced today.[36] It concerns conditions on the holiday island of Borkum, going back to pre-Weimar Imperial Germany. Antisemitic visitors were in the habit of singing an antisemitic song, the so-called *Borkum-Lied*, which made it unpleasant for Jews to stay on the island. The driving spirit behind this campaign was the local Lutheran Pastor Wilhelm Münchmeyer. The state authorities had tried in vain to curb these activities. The situation changed, however, when the *völkisch* agitators became aggressive towards Catholic visitors as well.[37] There was alarm among the hoteliers,[38] when numbers of Catholics cancelled their bookings,[39] and Münchmeyer promptly lost the support of part of his congregation. The opposition demanded the opening of disciplinary proceedings against Münchmeyer by the Regional Church administration. Some members of the congregation went so far as to leave the Church altogether, stating that they would rejoin if another parish priest were appointed.[40] Disciplinary proceedings were instituted but failed to produce the desired result.[41] Many court cases in which Münchmeyer confronted local citizens were equally inconclusive.[42] The opposition found a spokesman in one of the holiday visitors, one Albrecht Völklein, who wrote a pamphlet against Münchmeyer,[43] entitled *The False Priest, or the Cannibal Chieftain of the North Sea Islanders*.[44] The C.V. arranged for its printing and distribution. Charig had the pamphlet distributed for the first time at a public meeting of the *Deutsche Demokratische Partei* (DDP) at Emden on 24th November 1925.[45] After that the police did not grant permission for the further distribution of the pamphlet.[46] Charig's intention may well have been to provoke Münchmeyer to sue him for defamation, enabling him to prove the truth of the damaging allegations in open court. But it was the Evangelical Regional Church administration, which was also insulted, which sued Charig and Völklein and

[34]'K.C.-Anwaltsverzeichnis 1927 neu herausgegeben', *K.C.-Mitteilungen*, No. 7/8 (31st August 1929).
[35]Bernhard Breslauer, 'Der jüdische Anwalt', *C.V.-Zeitung*, II (1923), p. 277.
[36]Cf. Udo Beer, '"Der falsche Priester". Eine Borkumer Kampfschrift aus der Zeit der Weimarer Republik', in *Jahrbuch der Gesellschaft für bildende Kunst und vaterländische Altertümer zu Emden ("Emder Jahrbuch")*, 66 (1986), pp. 152–163; and Beer, *op. cit.*, pp. 191ff.
[37]Staatsarchiv Aurich, Akten des Regierungspräsidenten, Rep. 21a, No. 5061, Bl. 284.
[38]*Ibid.*, No. 5027, Bl. 284.
[39]Alfred Hirschberg, 'Münchmeyer-Prozeß auf Borkum', *C.V.-Zeitung*, V (1926), p. 271.
[40]Otto Dubro, 'Borkum im Kampf mit seinem völkischen "Diktator". Der Krieg des Pfarrers Münchmeyer', *Deutscher Herold*, 20 (August 1925); 'Disziplinarverfahren gegen Pastor Münchmeyer?', *Rhein-Ems-Zeitung*, 31st October 1925 (both at Staatsarchiv Aurich, Rep. 21a, No. 5061).
[41]Münchmeyer, *Warum ich mein Amt niederlegte*, Borkum 1926, pp. 43ff.; Staatsarchiv Aurich, Akten der Staatsanwaltschaft, Rep. 109C, vol. I, Bl. 135ff.
[42]Hirschberg, 'Münchmeyer-Prozeß . . .', *loc. cit.*
[43]Münchmeyer, *Warum . . .*, *op. cit.*, p. 3.
[44]*Der Falsche Priester oder der Kannibalenhäuptling der Nordseeinsulaner*; two copies are preserved in the Staatsarchiv Aurich, Rep. 21a, No. 4988, Bl. 58ff. and Rep. 109C, No. 39, vol. I, Bl. 222ff.
[45]*Ibid.*, Bl. 28.
[46]Staatsarchiv Aurich, Rep. 21a, No. 5610, Bl. 55ff.

induced Münchmeyer to come forward as joint plaintiff.[47] During the proceedings the defendants and the C.V. barrister Bruno Weil (later Assistant Chairman of the *Centralverein*), who had come from Berlin, succeeded in proving the truth of the allegations against Münchmeyer,[48] and for a while a settlement seemed to be within reach,[49] but the Church administration refused. The proceedings continued and ended with the defendants being heavily fined for formal insults directed at the Church administration.[50] The Court of Appeal reduced the fines to 500 Marks for Völklein and 1,000 Marks for Charig.[51]

The case was reported at length in the local press,[52] and it came to be known not by the names of the defendants, but as the "Münchmeyer case". This example bears out the thesis put forward by Bruno Weil on the significance of political trials. The C.V. made sure that the proceedings became known throughout the *Reich*.[53] Münchmeyer had lost face and resigned his office when the Church administration intimated renewed disciplinary proceedings.[54] He remained on the island for another two years and continued to present his "German Evenings", but eventually he left Borkum, travelling widely as a popular orator. (In September 1930 he was elected to the *Reichstag* as an NSDAP Deputy.) Conditions on the island had improved, yet this result was achieved at a heavy price exacted above all from Dr. Charig. He lost many clients; in the end he had to give up his chambers in Emden and move to Berlin.[55] He did not survive the Holocaust.[56]

What influence were Jews in a position to bring to bear within the sphere of justice? There were many Jews among the scholars in the fields of jurisprudence and political science. A list of Jewish authors who had contributed to juridical literature contained some 900 names,[57] names of German jurists who had done their part in establishing the world-wide reputation of German jurisprudence. At the end of the Weimar period – on 7th April 1933, to be precise – there were 4,500 Jewish barristers in the *Reich* out of a total of 19,200, according to National Socialist sources.[58] This high proportion gave rise to antisemitic outbursts. In the early years of the Republic Jewish barristers were confident of their ability to

[47]As note 45, Bl. 32f.
[48]Hirschberg, 'Münchmeyer-Prozeß . . .', *loc. cit.*; Bruno Weil, 'Borkum', *C.V.-Zeitung*, V (1926), p. 298.
[49]Hirschberg, 'Münchmeyer-Prozeß . . .', *loc. cit.*; Borkumer Beobachter (eds.) *Veröffentlichungen zum Münchmeyer-Prozeß*, Borkum 1926, p. 9.
[50]As note 45, Bl. 224.
[51]'In der Strafsache Völklein/Charig/Pels', *Borkumer Zeitung*, 7th July 1927 (Staatsarchiv Aurich, Rep. 21a, No. 4988, Bl. 205); 'Laßt euch nicht beschimpfen!', *C.V.-Zeitung*, VI (1927), p. 341.
[52]Cf. Staatsarchiv Aurich, Rep. 21a, No. 4988.
[53]Weil, *Gegen die Rechtsnot . . ., op. cit.*; Hirschberg, 'Münchmeyer-Prozeß . . .', *loc. cit.*; 'Laßt euch nicht beschimpfen!', *loc. cit.*
[54]Münchmeyer, *Meine Antwort an den C.V.*, Düsseldorf 1930, p. 25; 'Münchmeyer erledigt', *Abwehr-Blätter*, 20th May 1925, p. 56; Staatsarchiv Aurich, Rep. 21a, No. 4988, Bl. 91.
[55]As note 45, vol. II, Bl. 8f.
[56]According to an official statement, dated 7th June 1950, Charig died on 29th March 1943.
[57]Erwin Albert, *Verzeichnis jüdischer Verfasser juristischer Schriften*, Stuttgart [2]1937.
[58]Erwin Noack, 'Die Entjudung der deutschen Anwaltschaft', *Juristische Wochenschrift*, 1938, p. 2796; Helmut Weniger, 'Die zahlenmäßige Entwicklung der Anwaltschaft seit 1933', *ibid.*, 1937, p. 1391.

counter antisemitic tendencies within the ranks of the profession by resolute action.[59] They also noted with some pride that even antisemitic clients often preferred to entrust their cases to Jewish lawyers.[60] In the latter years of the Republic, however, the aggressiveness of the National Socialist lawyers changed the tone of the controversy. Even so, Jewish colleagues were highly esteemed. Out of the twenty-five members of the Executive Committee of the German Bar Association (*Deutscher Anwaltsverein*) eleven were Jews,[61] among them Eugen Fuchs and Max Hachenburg.[62] The latter was invited by Alfred Kurlbaum, the retiring President of the Association to take over as his successor, but thought it prudent as a Jew to decline that honour.[63]

When Wilhelm Kube, the leader of the National Socialist group in the Prussian Diet, used grossly insulting language against the German barristers and the Jews among them in particular, the President of the Bar Association, Rudolf Dix, protested in an open letter, in which he said:

> "No matter what a man's views are on the ideological, political and racial aspects of the Jewish Question, one is bound to deplore the appalling lack of culture, both human and political, revealed by such antisemitic tirades against my Jewish colleagues. As a German and representative of a profession that forms part of the German people I am obliged once again to note with a sense of shame the abysmal depth of the political and cultural level inherent in such remarks . . .".[64]

The National Socialists, of course, were not moved by this rebuke. When the letter was read out in the Prussian Diet, another National Socialist lawyer, the subsequently notorious Roland Freisler, responded by repeating the insults in an even more virulent manner. When the Prussian Minister of Justice wanted to reply he was shouted down.

There were also substantial numbers of Jewish judges and public prosecutors.[65] On 7th April 1933, the 6,560 established higher-grade civil servants of the Prussian Administration of Justice included some 500 Jews.[66] For the *Reich* as a whole a National Socialist source put the total number of Jewish judges and public prosecutors at 612 in 1919 and 782 in 1933.[67] It is interesting to note in this context that four *Reich* Ministers of Justice were of Jewish extraction: they were Otto Landsberg (February to June 1919); Eugen Schiffer (October 1919 to April 1920 and May to October 1921); Erich Koch-Weser (June 1928 to April 1929); and Curt W. Joël (October 1931 to May 1932).[68] Joël in addition held the

---

[59]Bernhard Breslauer, 'Der jüdische Anwalt', *loc. cit.*

[60]*Ibid.*; reader's letter, in *C.V.-Zeitung*, II (1923), p. 213.

[61]Fritz Ostler, *Die deutschen Rechtsanwälte 1871–1971*, Essen 1971, p. 229.

[62]Max Hachenburg, *Lebenserinnerungen eines Rechtsanwalts und Briefe aus der Emigration*, Stuttgart–Berlin–Köln–Mainz 1978, p. 75.

[63]*Ibid.*, p. 94.

[64]Rudolf Dix, 'Menschliche und politische Kulturlosigkeit', *C.V.-Zeitung*, XI (1932), p. 299.

[65]Felix Naumann, 'Der Richter', *C.V.-Zeitung*, VI (1927), p. 369.

[66]Sievert Lorenzen, *Die Juden und die Justiz*, Berlin–Hamburg 1942, p. 180.

[67]*Idem*, 'Das Eindringen der Juden in die Justiz vor 1933', *Deutsche Justiz*, 1939, pp. 956ff., in particular p. 964.

[68]Cf. Werner T. Angress, 'Juden im politischen Leben der Revolutionszeit', in *Deutsches Judentum in Krieg und Revolution 1916–1923*. Ein Sammelband herausgegeben von Werner E. Mosse unter Mitwirkung von Arnold Paucker, Tübingen 1971 (Schriftenreihe wissenschaftlicher Abhandlungen des Leo Baeck Instituts 25), pp. 137–315, in particular pp. 312–315.

post of Under-Secretary of State in the *Reich* Justice Department from 1920 to 1931. (He, incidentally, went out of his way to conceal his Jewish descent.)

Personnel policy was dominated by Joël, whose conservative views were reflected in the choice of persons he proposed – as a rule successfully – for positions in the *Reich* Court of Justice and the *Reich* Prosecuting Authority. Until 1929/1930 he succeeded in preventing members of the Republican Judges' League (*Republikanischer Richterbund*) from being appointed *Reich* Judges or *Reich* Prosecutors. The Republican Judges' League had a high proportion of Jewish members; generally, the idea of the Republican state was more deeply rooted among German Jews than amongst the population at large.[69] The part played by Jewish jurists within the Republican Judges' League is well illustrated by the list of contributors to the journal *Die Justiz*. Out of some 160 named authors, who contributed articles to the periodical during its first eight years, over twenty per cent bore Jewish names, and six of the ten most prolific writers were Jews.[70] The Jewish contributors included the C.V. barristers Erich Eyck and Ludwig Foerder. Foerder was the author of the only article referring to antisemitic tendencies; it was headed 'Judicial Practice in the "Jews' Republic" '.[71] Even this article treated the subject exclusively from the angle of the general defence of the Republic. Specific Jewish problems were not broached in this jurists' journal, which tended to be a voice of protest. Topics of specific Jewish concern were similarly ignored, even by Jewish contributors, in the largest law journal *Juristische Wochenschrift*, whose editorial board included Eugen Fuchs and Max Hachenburg.[72] It was much the same with the *Deutsche Juristenzeitung*.[73] Summing up, it can be said that the part played by Jews in the legal profession was far in excess of their proportion of the total population. On the other hand, the Jewish lawyers focused their attention on general legal problems; specifically Jewish issues were discussed rarely if at all, and in their judicial decisions Jewish jurists remained strictly loyal to the professional principle of impartiality.

It is of some interest that the National Socialist Erwin Albert in his list of Jewish authors who had written on legal subjects[74] omitted nearly all C.V. jurists who should have been included, notably Kurt Alexander, Erich Eyck, Ludwig Foerder, Alfred Hirschberg, Hans Lazarus, Wilhelm Levinger, Jakob Marx, Hans Reichmann, Artur Schweriner, Bruno Weil and Alfred Wiener. Included were only Ludwig Holländer, Eugen Fuchs, Jacques Stern and Kurt Zielenziger. The selective approach seems arbitrary, but it indicates that those C.V. lawyers who had written articles and books on legal subjects were little known and could safely be ignored by the National Socialists.[75]

---

[69]Schulz, *op. cit.*, pp. 158f.; Klaus-Detlev Godau-Schüttke, *Rechtsverwalter des Reiches, Staatssekretär Dr. Curt Joël*, Frankfurt a. Main–Bern–Cirencester 1981, pp. 172ff.

[70]Theo Rasehorn, 'Carl Schmitt siegt über Hans Kelsen', *Aus Politik und Zeitgeschichte*, 48 (1985), pp. 3ff., in particular pp. 12f.

[71]Ludwig Foerder, 'Judenrepublik in der Rechtsprechung', *Die Justiz*, vol. I (1925/1926), pp. 519ff.

[72]Hachenburg, *op. cit.*, p. 137.

[73]Cf. Beer, *op. cit.*, p. 208.

[74]Albert, *op. cit.*

[75]As regards the exceptions, cf. Beer, *op. cit.*, pp. 209ff.

As regards the judiciary, Kurt Alexander, contributing to the discussion on the crisis of justice, insisted that Jewish complaints were justified only in exceptional cases. Glib generalisations were out of place, as the Jews themselves often had occasion to point out. Judges, he went on, were only human and individual lapses were understandable. Alexander drew a distinction between criminal and civil justice. Talk about a lack of confidence in the administration of justice referred almost exclusively to cases of criminal law.[76] Even during the last days of the Weimar Republic, Martin Wassermann (Hamburg) stated that the Jewish scholars in the field of jurisprudence were in honour bound to affirm that there was hardly any ground for complaints against official judicial practices. Even though there were some men with antisemitic proclivities among the members of civil courts, there was no evidence that such secret inclinations had affected judicial decisions.[77] Even in the realm of criminal law the situation, according to Hans Lazarus, was more favourable than was generally believed.[78]

Whereas from 1926 to the end of the Weimar period it was the judges who attracted most of the controversy, in the early years of the Republic discussion centred on the attitude of public prosecutors. Jews complained about discrimination. There were public prosecutors who invoked public concern and instituted prosecutions in the most trifling cases of violence against *völkisch* agitators, while Jews, even when badly beaten up by antisemites, were told to take private legal action.[79] In the event of complaints, however, the higher prosecuting authorities as a rule set aside a negative decision taken at lower level and acknowledged public concern.[80] The C.V. put the matter to the Prussian Minister of Justice,[81] who thereupon issued the aforementioned Order of 23rd September 1922, which put an end to such difficulties caused by the behaviour of some public prosecutors.[82] Even so, there remained room for complaints against antisemitic prosecutors who were said to show little zeal in pressing on with their prosecutions. In one case cited by the *C.V.-Zeitung* the Public Prosecutor Speer in Breslau acted in court more like a defending counsel than an accuser, and in the end demanded a fine of no more than fifty *Goldmark* for a very grave insult. The court, however, imposed a fine of eight times that amount. Following a complaint, Speer was severely reprimanded by the Central Prosecuting Authority.[83]

Such cases, however, were rare and not typical of the practice of criminal justice in cases in which Jews were involved. All in all, it can be said that while the fierce political controversies that divided the country gave rise to some contradictions in the sphere of justice too, it was nevertheless possible as a rule to resolve them within a reasonable time-span. In particular the instructions issued

[76]Kurt Alexander, 'Wir und die Justiz', *C.V.-Zeitung*, V (1926), pp. 557f.
[77]Martin Wassermann, 'Die Bekämpfung des Boykotts', *C.V.-Zeitung*, XI (1932), p. 516.
[78]Hans Lazarus, 'Antisemitismus und Justiz', *C.V.-Zeitung*, III (1924), p. 678.
[79]Foerder, *op. cit.*, pp. 16f.; *idem*, 'Antisemitismus und Justiz', *C.V.-Zeitung*, I (1922), p. 39.
[80]For individual cases cf. Beer, *op. cit.*, p. 224.
[81]Foerder, 'Antisemitismus und Justiz', *loc. cit.*, p. 39.
[82]Weil, in *Gegen die Rechtsnot . . .* , *op. cit.*, p. 6.
[83]'Ein antisemitischer Staatsanwalt', *C.V.-Zeitung*, III (1924), p. 494.

by the Minister of Justice had a moderating effect. By and large the relations between Jews and the administration of justice can be described as good.[84]

Which were the questions of law that actually affected Jewish interests? Critical attention was focused in the first place on the practice of criminal justice. Criminal proceedings were effective in bringing influence to bear on the enemy; it was important for antisemites to know that any attack could end in court. The C.V. was known as a keen observer and feared for its resolute actions. Thus, Gregor Strasser advised his party friends to moderate their tone, since otherwise the National Socialist newspapers would be ruined financially by criminal proceedings.[85]

Such statements encouraged the C.V. leaders to continue their activities. Yet, in spite of many successes, it was clear that there were some norms of the existing criminal law that failed to accord adequate protection to Jews. Defamation of individuals, apart from very few exceptions, was always punished.[86] Collective insults were a different matter. When, at *deutschvölkisch* public meetings or in the press, accusations were levelled at the Jews as a whole, the question arose as to whether the insult was an indictable offence. Jewry as a collective entity was not entitled to initiate criminal proceedings. Some hope of a change hung on the prospect of a future all-embracing Jewish organisation.[87] In the meantime submissions demanding criminal prosecutions could only be made by individuals and possibly by the Executive Committees of synagogue congregations. According to a ruling handed down by the *Reich* Court of Justice as far back as 6th October 1881, charges for defamation of a collective body will be laid only if it can be proved that the accused party had intended to insult particular individuals.[88] One instance of a collective insult clearly aimed at every one of the Jews living in a particular locality ended with a successful prosecution.[89] The *Reich* Court's ruling of 1881, which referred to an insult against the Jews as a whole, was thenceforth accepted by the German courts as an authoritative precedent. Yet by and by other collective bodies were deemed to be entitled to take action against collective insults. Even before the 1881 ruling the *Reich* Court had ruled on 29th January 1880 that defamation of the Prussian judiciary was possible,[90] and up till 1929 the *Reich* Court, adjudicating in a number of individual cases, had accepted collective insults as indictable for various

[84]For individual problems, cf. Beer, *op. cit.*, pp. 209ff.
[85]Kurt Alexander, Circular dated 3rd February 1931, p. 8, Bundesarchiv Koblenz, Nachlaß Julius Streicher, Akte No. 6. Reproduced by Arnold Paucker, 'Documents on the Fight of Jewish Organizations against Right-Wing Extremism', *Michael*, II (1973), The Diaspora Research Institute, Tel-Aviv University, pp. 216–246, in particular p. 235; Hans Reichmann, 'Erzwungene Höflichkeit!', *C.V.-Zeitung*, VIII (1929), p. 119.
[86]Cf. Beer, *op. cit.*, p. 230.
[87]Foerder, *op. cit.*, p. 12; *idem*, 'Zweierlei Maß in der Justiz?', *Israelitisches Familienblatt*, XXXIV (31st March 1932), p. 9.
[88]*Rechtsprechung des Deutschen Reichsgerichts in Strafsachen* (=*RGSt*), vol. 3, p. 606.
[89]A. Kuntzemüller, 'Um die Frage der Kollektivbeleidigung', *C.V.-Zeitung*, V (1926), p. 88; Erich Eyck, 'Um die Frage der Kollektivbeleidigung', *ibid.*, p. 101.
[90]*RGSt*, 1, p. 292.

162 *Udo Beer*

collective bodies. According to the authoritative commentary on the *Reich* Criminal Code, the Jews were the only group explicitly excluded from this right.[91]

Ludwig Foerder had an explanation for the inconsistent record of court decisions in cases of insults directed against collective bodies:

"When the Christian clergy or the German officers are the victims of abuse, the idea of acquitting the accused is emotionally repugnant to the judge. Swayed by his innermost feelings he will sentence the accused. A rationalisation of his decision comes later, retrospectively. Processes of this kind happen to most people, and as a rule the tendency remains subconscious. And so it is with judges, who are only human after all. When Jewry is defamed, on the other hand, there is no such emotional resistance against an acquittal of the accused who uttered the insult."[92]

Neither did the said inner resistance arise, when insults were aimed at the Jewish lawyers, although all other groups participating in the administration of justice were protected.[93] To remedy this parlous situation, the jurists of the C.V. felt that in the absence of a short-term solution all they could do was to argue the matter out in the juridical literature, which in the long run should lead to a change.[94] The C.V. accordingly published in its *Philo-Verlag* a closely argued legal opinion by Alfred Hirschberg on the subject of the defamation of collective bodies.[95] However, the courts did not accept his interpretation.

Defendants accused of defamation often pleaded in their defence that they had acted to protect legitimate interests of their own, which in view of section 193 of the Criminal Code would lead to a verdict of not guilty. Some courts went to such lengths in interpreting this defensive gambit when Jews were the injured party that the protection against defamation had virtually ceased to exist.[96] This practice, however, was rejected by the superior courts and the juridical literature. Defamatory allegations – the authoritative commentary said – were only admissible when the person uttering them was in a state of acute distress, and when in the collision of interests the interests pursued by the defendant were to be rated more highly than the honour of the injured party.[97] Impartially applied, the balancing of interests suggested here should have led nearly always to a decision in favour of the aggrieved Jew.

Under section 130 of the Criminal Code the incitement of some classes of the population against others is classified as a criminal offence, a penal norm that seemed to be made-to-measure for the Weimar Republic. Yet, although the population at that time was disunited to an extent rarely paralleled in German history, the courts seldom passed sentence on these grounds. No more than 402 defendants were convicted of this offence throughout the *Reich* during the period 1918 to 1932.[98] The number of prosecutions rose during the turbulent years of

[91] *Leipziger Kommentar, Reichs-Strafgesetzbuch*, Berlin-Leipzig [4]1929, section 185, note 6.
[92] Foerder, 'Zweierlei Maß . . .', *loc. cit.*
[93] *Idem*, 'Der jüdische Anwalt', *C.V.-Zeitung*, II (1923), pp. 28f.
[94] *Idem*, 'Zweierlei Maß . . .', *loc. cit.*
[95] Hirschberg, *Kollektiv-Ehre und Kollektiv-Beleidigung*, Berlin 1929.
[96] For a relevant case, cf. Foerder, *op. cit.*, p. 14; also Beer, *op. cit.*, pp. 235f.
[97] *Leipziger Kommentar . . .*, *op. cit.*, section 193, note 7.
[98] Cf. Beer, *op. cit.*, p. 237.

the inflationary period. Then, from 1925, things calmed down. Surprisingly, the National Socialist campaigns in the following years did not give rise to a substantial increase in the number of prosecutions on the strength of section 130. Reports in the *C.V.-Zeitung*, however, presented a different picture. The paper reported acquittals and convictions in such cases more than ever during the closing years of the Republic.[99]

The wording of section 130 contained one ambiguity which was promptly spotted by the defence counsel. They pleaded in court that the Jews did not constitute a "class" within the meaning of the law, but a race. A number of jurists accepted this interpretation, although as long ago as 31st May 1901 the *Reich* Court of Justice had ruled that the Jews formed an integral part of the population and were entitled as such to benefit from the domestic peace guaranteed by section 130 of the Code.[100] In the same decision the *Reich* Court had pronounced on the effects of incitement: even if the incitement did not lead to actual violence, the class that was the butt of the incitement could feel alarmed; whether in any particular case there was reasonable ground for such alarm was a question of fact.[101] This unambiguous interpretation of section 130, which clearly favoured the Jews, was subsequently confirmed and further extended by the *Reich* Court,[102] notably in its decision of 6th February 1928,[103] which closed the loophole to covert antisemitic threats, and thus made a significant contribution to the certainty of law.[104]

Prosecutions for defamation of religious bodies under section 166 of the Criminal Code similarly played a subordinate role in the judicial practice of the Weimar Republic, in much the same way as incitement against a class. The number of convictions throughout the *Reich* ranged from twenty in 1925 to 206 in 1927.[105] Here, the defence resorted to some sophisticated arguments. As in cases of incitement against a class, it was argued that the hostile remarks had been aimed not at the Jews as a religious body, but at the Jewish race.[106] Alternatively the defence pleaded that the butt of the insult was the doctrine of Judaism rather than the actual institutions of the Jewish religious faith.[107] Even in respect of the first sentence of section 166, which declares blasphemy a criminal offence, defence counsel construed a subtle distinction: abuse of the "God of the Jews" had been punished by the *Reich* Court as early as 1882;[108] now some defendants, in particular Fritsch, pleaded that his strictures had been directed against the "former Israelite God" rather than against the current Jewish concept of God.

---

[99]For examples, cf. *ibid.*, p. 238.
[100]*RGSt*, 34, pp. 268ff., in particular p. 270.
[101]*Ibid.*, p. 271.
[102]Gustav Radbruch, 'Anmerkung zum RG-Urteil vom 6.2.1928 – 2 D 927/27', *Juristische Wochenschrift*, 1928, p. 2218.
[103]*Ibid.*
[104]'Antisemitismus und Justiz', *Abwehr-Blätter*, 1929, pp. 13ff., in particular p. 14.
[105]Cf. Beer, *op. cit.*, p. 240.
[106]Erich Eyck, 'Die Stellung der Rechtspflege . . .', *loc. cit.*, p. 37.
[107]*Gegen die Rechtsnot . . .* , *op. cit.*, p. 4.
[108]*RGSt*, 6, p. 77.

Several courts accepted this distinction.[109] The *Reich* Court made short shrift of such spurious logic when on 20th June 1921 it gave its authoritative definition of the concept of God, and thus made sure that the culprits were punished.[110]

A special class of cases under section 166 was presented by attacks on the Talmud. Here, again, the National Socialists argued that the attacks had been targeted not at the Jewish religious institutions but at the doctrine of Judaism; moreover, the inclusion of baptised Jews in the strictures made it clear beyond doubt that it was the Jewish race that was being attacked.[111] This argument was rejected by the *Reich* Court in its ruling of 5th July 1932.[112] An additional problem arising in the Talmud trials was the question of expert witnesses. Most judges had no knowledge of Jewish religion. Hebrew sources were closed to them. The pool of expert witnesses was not extensive, and some courts held them to be biased. Windfuhr, the Hamburg Professor of Rabbinical Hebrew, for instance, was turned down by the Court in a trial of Julius Streicher and Karl Holz before a Nuremberg jury on the ground of his being paid for articles contributed to the *C.V.-Zeitung* and lecturing on the Talmud to C.V. audiences. Professor Michael Guttmann of the Breslau Rabbinical Seminary was not admitted as expert witness simply because he was a C.V. member.[113] Since *völkisch* experts were in most cases readily allowed to address the court, the outcome of a case often hinged on the court's decision concerning the defending counsels' demand for the exclusion of Jewish experts. Only in rare cases were defendants convicted in spite of the exclusion of the experts.[114] The *Reich* Court of Justice on the other hand did protect the Jewish religion. It never overturned a sentence passed by a lower court for violation of section 166. None the less, a well-meaning *Reich* Court judge advised Ludwig Holländer and Rabbi Felix Goldmann in private to refrain from laying such charges, which in the end could only be harmful to German Jewry.[115] Even before 1929 the C.V. acted with the greatest caution and initiated proceedings only when conviction seemed certain. Towards the end of 1930 the local branches were warned not to initiate court proceedings without prior consultation of the Central Office. Talmud court cases likely to attract publicity were to be avoided altogether.

In his article on judicial practice in relation to Jews and Judaism, Erich Eyck deplored the discrepancy between the penalties imposed and the value of the injured's legal rights. Thus Julius Streicher, who had accused a Jewish judge of having perverted the course of justice by favouring a co-religionist, was only fined 200 Marks, although one would have expected that an *esprit de corps* among the judiciary would have led to a different sentence. The Hamburg Criminal

[109]Foerder, *op. cit.*, p. 9; 'Das Obergutachten im Gotteslästerungsprozeß Fritsch', *Mitteilungen aus dem Verein zur Abwehr des Antisemitismus*, 1919, p. 78.
[110]*RGSt*, 56, pp. 128ff., in particular p. 129.
[111]For details cf. Beer, *op. cit.*, p. 242.
[112]'Reichsgericht hebt Talmudurteil auf', *C.V.-Zeitung*, XI (1932), p. 290.
[113]Hirschberg, 'Der Nürnberger Talmudprozeß', *C.V.-Zeitung*, VIII (1929), p. 587.
[114]For a case in point cf. Hirschberg, *ibid.*, pp. 600f.
[115]Paucker, *Der jüdische Abwehrkampf . . .*, *op. cit.*, p. 83; see also 'Aus der Arbeit des C.V.', *C.V.-Zeitung*, VI (1927), p. 683.

Tribunal allowed Theodor Fritsch to get off lightly, arguing that however heavy a penalty might have been imposed it would not have stopped the accused from sticking to his convictions and expressing them freely.[116] Donald Niewyk in his evaluation of press reports on criminal trials found that severe penalties were imposed by the courts in 87 out of a total of 321 court cases, a proportion of 27 per cent. In Hamburg – a target of Eyck's special censure – the proportion was as high as 67 per cent.[117] In the light of the motto "The trial is nothing, the repercussions are everything", the C.V. ensured the widest possible publicity for court decisions in Jewish affairs. Accordingly it may be presumed that all cases of any importance were covered. Confidential reports, too, confined themselves on the whole to discussing cases already known through the press.[118] According to Niewyk, the average fine imposed in cases reported by the press was higher than the average fine in all cases;[119] accordingly, the fines imposed in cases that escaped press notice must have been below average, which is not surprising since the unpublished cases were in general of a comparatively trivial nature.

During the Weimar period, Jewish organisations – notably the C.V. and, until its demise in 1922, the *Verband der Deutschen Juden* – made significant contributions to the debate on the reform of the Criminal Code. Initiated as long ago as the 1880s, this debate was in full swing during the early years of the twentieth century, when a special commission was set up under the auspices of the *Reich* Justice Department and the Prussian Ministry of Justice. Tentative drafts were published every few years. While the predominant motive behind the reform movement was the wish to replace or supplement the purely punitive function of criminal law by a sociological approach, the contributions of the Jewish organisations were focused in the main on problems affecting the Jewish population in particular. The *Verband der Deutschen Juden*[120] and the C.V.[121] made relevant submissions to the Prussian Ministry of Justice and the *Reich* Justice Department.[122]

The draft submitted by the C.V. in 1925 suggested the retention of the penal norm laid down by section 130 of the Criminal Code, but recommended in the light of recent experiences that the protection of religious teaching under section 166 be extended by ensuring that utterances intended to hold a religion up to contempt should be punished with the same severity as defamatory remarks, and by raising the maximum custodial sentence from two to three years. The draft furthermore proposed a tightening of provisions concerning disturbance of religious services under section 167 and disturbance of funerals by making such acts punishable if deliberate, though not necessarily premeditated as stipulated by the existing law. Here, too, it is suggested that the maximum custodial sentence be raised to three years. Provisions penalising disturbance of the

---

[116]Erich Eyck, 'Die Stellung der Rechtspflege . . .', *loc. cit.*, p. 63.

[117]Niewyk, *loc. cit.*, p. 109.

[118]*C.V.-Tätigkeitsberichte*; *Gegen die Rechtsnot . . .* , *op. cit.*

[119]Niewyk, *loc. cit.*, pp. 107f.

[120]Geheimes Staatsarchiv, Akten des preußischen Justizministeriums, Rep. 84a, No. 8419, Bl. 354–357.

[121]*Ibid.*, No. 8420, Bl. 500–608.

[122]Cf. Beer, *op. cit.*, pp. 248ff., and for a synopsis of the drafts pp. 307ff.

peaceful rest of the dead under section 170 were to be amplified by including unlawful refusal to hand over the remains of a deceased person. No reason was given for this new draft provision. What incidents or considerations prompted this suggestion remains an open question.

Section 238 of the C.V. draft was altogether new. It provided explicitly that acts of surgery, including in particular the ritual circumcision of boys, were distinct from acts inflicting bodily harm. As regards sanctions against defamation, the draft clarified the concept of defamation of collective bodies and the admissibility of the defence of "safeguarding legitimate interests". Under section 290 of the draft the right to initiate proceedings in cases of the defamation of collective bodies was to be extended to the organisations recognised as representing collective entities. The C.V. draft (like that of the *Verband der Deutschen Juden*) made sure that the ritual slaughter prescribed by the Jewish religion should not contravene provisions for the protection of animals. The protection of the dress and badges worn by members of certain vocational groups should be extended to servants at places of religious worship. In the provision penalising the performance of acts of indecency in the vicinity of churches the word "churches" should be replaced by "houses of God".

The draft submitted by the C.V. was comprehensive and carefully formulated, yet the Bill presented to the *Reichstag* in 1927 included only one of the numerous suggestions made by the C.V. Section 392 of the parliamentary Bill penalised the unauthorised assumption of designations, titles or dignities of religious bodies, or the wearing of the dress or badges prescribed for their representatives. Most likely this change had also been supported by other religious communities. In addition a purely stylistic amendment in section 180/I of the *Reichstag* Bill showed some resemblance to a C.V. suggestion. The C.V. annual report for 1926–1927 warned its readers that, although the suggestions contained in the C.V. draft were not promoting solely Jewish interests, it would be unwise to expect too much as regards their acceptance by the relevant committee. The Left-wing parties had misgivings about such demands, fearful of opening the door to one-sided legal action against their supporters, while the Right-wing parties were not prepared to scrutinise suggestions that happened to come from Jewish quarters on their own merits.[123]

In a survey looking ahead to 1929, Bruno Weil foresaw more difficulties, which promptly materialised.[124] The Social Democrat members of the Criminal Law Committee wanted to abolish the section penalising blasphemy.[125] Then the parliamentary deliberations were interrupted by another *Reichstag* election. In the meantime the Criminal Law Committee, sitting under the chairmanship of the octogenarian Wilhelm Kahl, one of the country's most eminent jurists, had amended the 1927 draft, and the new Bill, named after Kahl, was laid before the House on 3rd December 1930.[126] It was opposed from the outset by the

[123]*C.V.-Tätigkeitsbericht 1926–1927*, p. 95.
[124]Weil, 'Die Politik in den Vordergrund', *C.V.-Zeitung*, VII (1928), p. 510.
[125]Otto Landsberg, 'Gegen Gotteslästerungsparagraphen', *Vorwärts*, 9th February 1928.
[126]*Reichstagsdrucksache*, V. Wahlperiode, No. 395, *Anlage zu Verhandlungen des Reichstags, Stenographische Berichte*, vol. 448.

Communists and National Socialists.[127] One modification of the 1927 draft adopted by the *Reichstag* Criminal Law Committee during the preceding electoral period was the addition of a paragraph to section 412 stating that Jewish ritual slaughter was not covered by the regulations for the prevention of cruelty to animals. This provision was inserted to invalidate regulations prohibiting ritual slaughter which had been passed in some German *Länder*. The Kahl draft still failed to specify what actions would constitute the offence of defaming a collective body. In the end the draft was dropped altogether; faced with a strained political situation, Parliament and Government did not have the strength to introduce a comprehensive reform of the Criminal Code.

A malfunctioning of civil justice would have been most harmful to the Jewish community on economic grounds. Generally, many Jewish rights could be safeguarded more effectively by civil law-suits rather than by the laying of criminal charges. The foremost problem in the field of civil justice was that of the boycott.

The boycott as a political weapon appeared in the Weimar Republic towards the end of the first antisemitic wave. Early in February 1924, the Pomeranian regional organisation of the *Deutschnationale Volkspartei* (DNVP) campaigned for the boycott of "alien racial elements". The C.V. dismissed this as a "rusty weapon" of the past.[128] Apparently it took some time for the rust to be removed. The next case was reported by the *C.V.-Zeitung* in November of the same year. After that boycott reports increased in number from year to year. By mid-November 1931 the number had risen to some fifty cases. By the end of the Republic the C.V. files contained over two hundred such reports.[129]

The slogan "Don't buy from the Jew!" had a long history, going back to Imperial Germany, when boycott leaflets were distributed, especially during the weeks before Christmas. There was a lull during the early post-war years and the inflation due to the shortage of goods,[130] a fact of which the C.V. was well aware. Accordingly it responded without delay when the first boycott reports came in from Pomerania, and lost no time in commissioning an expert opinion on the subject from the eminent academic jurist Paul Oertmann.[131] This document became a valuable weapon in the hands of the C.V., with the help of which it later on won in the majority of cases.[132]

Another method for the enforcement of Jewish interests was the application to a civil court for an injunction temporarily restraining the defendant from specified actions.[133] This method was increasingly applied after an important decision by the *Reich* Court of Justice on 15th February 1927,[134] which marked a

[127]Eberhard Schmidt, *Strafrechtsreform und Kulturkampf*, Tübingen 1931, p. 16.
[128]'Boykott!', *C.V.-Zeitung*, III (1924), p. 71.
[129]Many instances quoted by Beer, *op. cit.*, pp. 257f.
[130]Georg Baum, 'Der völkische Boykott und seine Rechtsfolgen', *C.V.-Zeitung*, IV (1925), p. 221.
[131]*C.V.-Tätigkeitsbericht 1924–1925*, p. 38; Paul Oertmann, *Der politische Boykott*, Berlin 1925.
[132]Doskow and Jacoby, *loc. cit.*, p. 508.
[133]Rudolf Wertheimer, 'Der politische Boykott und seine Abwehr', *Der Schild*, 1931, pp. 91ff., in particular p. 92.
[134]*Rechtsprechung des Deutschen Reichsgerichts in Zivilsachen (=RGZ)*, 116, p. 151.

decisive change. Until then, the *Reich* Court had ruled that such preventive suits could not be brought if the action to be forbidden was punishable under public law.[135] This restriction was now abolished, and as a result the C.V. was in a position to curb certain actions of its opponents sooner by resorting to civil law rather than criminal proceedings.[136]

The National Socialists, however, intensified their boycott campaign and set up a separate centre charged with organising the boycott movement.[137] In these circumstances the C.V. had good reason to welcome a number of Presidential Emergency Decrees (*Notverordnungen*), which invested the police with far-reaching new powers to prevent disturbances of the domestic peace.[138] Under Article 10 of the Decree of 28th March 1931,[139] as restated in the Decree of 7th October 1931,[140] and under Article 2 of the Decree of 17th July 1931[141] the police were authorised to ban, seize and sequester printed publications, posters or leaflets whose contents endangered public security or public order. Under Article 11 of the last named Decree it was an offence to affix, exhibit or disseminate political posters or pamphlets without prior permission of the competent authorities. Moreover, the Decrees of 24th April[142] and 18th July 1931[143] empowered the President of the Berlin Police Directorate to take requisite measures valid throughout Prussia, thus supplementing the actions of the local police. This provision was particularly helpful to the Jewish organisations; it presented the C.V. with a central point of reference, a partner with whom good relations had been established.

In addition to the instruments of civil law and police intervention, the Jews had yet another weapon at their disposal: they, too, were able to resort to boycotts. A purely defensive counter-boycott was neither unlawful nor contrary to public policy, hence legitimate.[144] A successful counter-boycott is recorded in C.V. annual reports: in East Prussia a Nationalist Shoe Traders' Association (*Völkischer Schuhhändlerverband*) had been formed in order to eliminate the Jewish traders. Having been attacked, the Jewish traders responded by appealing to the wholesale trade to cut supplies to the antisemitic Association.[145] The appeal achieved its aim: the Nationalist Association was dissolved.[146] Jewish boycotts, however, were not always purely defensive. One regional organisation was rebuked by the C.V. Central Office for proclaiming a boycott against *völkisch* shopkeepers.[147] During the early years of the Weimar Republic the defensive

[135]*RGZ*, 91, p. 265.
[136]*C.V.-Tätigkeitsbericht 1926–1927*, p. 91.
[137]H(ans) L(azarus), 'Nationalsozialistische Boykottzentrale', *C.V.-Zeitung*, X (1931), p. 502.
[138]*Idem*, 'Boykott', *ibid.*
[139]*Reichsgesetzblatt*, 1931, I, p. 79.
[140]*Ibid.*, p. 568.
[141]*Ibid.*, p. 371.
[142]*Preußische Gesetzsammlung*, 1931, p. 63.
[143]*Ibid.*, p. 133.
[144]Oertmann, *op. cit.*, p. 57.
[145]*C.V.-Tätigkeitsbericht 1924–1925*, pp. 41f.
[146]*C.V.-Tätigkeitsbericht 1926–1927*, p. 68.
[147]As note 45.

counter-boycott directed against antisemites, many of whom were themselves actively engaged in business or agriculture, may have been reasonably effective, but later on, in the face of the National Socialist boycott campaigns, Jewish counter-boycotts were of no avail. This may well be why no further defensive counter-boycotts are on record.

Another facet of the boycott problem concerned the labour market. During the latter years of the Republic Jewish employees found it increasingly difficult to get jobs, as many employers did not want Jews. The problem was discussed by the annual general meeting of the C.V. in 1928,[148] but there was little that could be done by resorting to the law, as an employer was free to choose his employees. This being the case, the C.V. therefore addressed itself to Jewish employers who, prompted by considerations of convenience or utility, refrained from giving jobs to their co-religionists.[149] Thus one means to counter the anti-Jewish boycott in the field of employment was the intensified employment of Jews by Jews. An alternative means consisted in bringing economic pressure to bear on antisemitic employers. This was the approach recommended by Ludwig Holländer.[150]

Summing up, it can be said that the C.V. achieved some success through strenuous effort. It left nothing untried, it exhausted all the possibilities that were open in order to counter antisemitic actions by invoking the civil law. In curbing the boycott campaign the C.V. acted promptly at the very beginning, so that subsequently, thanks to the clarification of the law by Oertmann's expert opinion, it was in a position to apply successfully for injunctions and sue for damages. Yet, in the long run the processes of civil law cannot operate successfully unless the poison is taken out of political life, and that did not happen. The ever increasing calls for antisemitic boycotts burdened the C.V. in its legal defence activities with a Sisyphean labour: no sooner was one case decided than several others had cropped up in the meantime. Even so it would be wrong to assert that, seen from the angle of the law, the struggle against the boycott campaigns was fought in vain.

In the field of public law two issues preoccupied the Jewish organisations: first, the application of the principle of civic equality, secondly the safeguarding of the freedom of religious worship. In respect of both issues a large number of individual problems called for a solution. Apart from those two issues there were not many unsolved problems concerning the relations between Jewry and the State.

Under Article 135 of the Weimar Constitution all inhabitants of the *Reich* were granted full freedom of faith and conscience. The undisturbed practice of religious worship was guaranteed in the Constitution. Nevertheless, the Christian Churches were granted a privileged position. Article 137 did not provide for any established church, but Article 139 protected Sunday observance, whereas no similar provision was made to protect the Sabbath. This confronted Jewry with special problems.

---

[148]'Der Weg des C.V.', *C.V.-Zeitung*, VII (1928), p. 93.
[149]Moritz A. Loeb, 'Freie Bahn dem Schaffenden', *ibid.*, pp. 365ff., in particular p. 366.
[150]'Boykott jüdischer Angestellter', *Führerbriefe*, I, No. 1 (15th September 1929), p. 10.

Another constitutional issue affecting Jewry concerned the status of ritual slaughter. This method, prescribed by Jewish religious laws, was condemned by the antisemites, who wanted it abolished, ostensibly in order to improve the regulations for the prevention of cruelty to animals. A prominent part in the legal defence efforts against prohibitions of ritual slaughter was played by Rabbi Esra Munk on behalf of the *Halberstädter Bund* and the *Freie Vereinigung für die Interessen des Orthodoxen Judentums*. Munk also headed the Office for Matters Concerning Ritual Slaughter in Berlin,[151] which co-operated with the C.V.,[152] who had seconded two members of its staff on a permanent basis to the Ritual Slaughter Office.[153] In the various German *Länder* these efforts were conducted by the appropriate Regional Federations of Jewish Communities; until its dissolution in 1922 the *Verband der Deutschen Juden* also played a part.[154] The Jewish organisations had previously published expert opinions on the issue of ritual slaughter in 1894, 1902 and 1908. These publications featured 837 statements in favour of ritual slaughter,[155] but that did not put an end to the public debate on this issue, which continued throughout the Weimar period and occupied the governing bodies at all levels: *Reich*, *Länder* and communes. Above all, the *Otto-Hartmann-Bund*, a Federation of Animal Protection Societies, campaigned systematically from 1927 on to get ritual slaughter banned.[156]

Towns and communes considered the possibility of banning the practice at municipal abattoirs. Munich was the first to act in 1925.[157] Bans were rejected by Barmen,[158] Berlin,[159] Quakenbrück, Leipzig, Königsberg, Cologne, Mülhausen (Thuringia), Soest, Ratibor, Schweidnitz, Rostock, Ulm, Mannheim and Bremen, but were imposed by Gotha, Zwickau, Hirschberg and Bielefeld.[160] During the first half of 1932, motions seeking to ban ritual slaughter locally were tabled in some thirty municipalities.[161] The legal argument behind such municipal bans was based on the concept of domiciliary prerogative (*Hausrecht*), which authorised a householder to forbid in his premises actions which otherwise were not unlawful.[162] In 1901[163] and 1904[164] the Prussian Senior Administrative Court had upheld municipal bans on ritual slaughter, thus setting precedents,[165] which induced Gustav Radbruch in his expert opinion of 1925 to agree that such

[151]'Um die Schächtfreiheit', *C.V.-Zeitung*, X (1931), p. 50.
[152]*Ibid.*; also A(lfred) H(irschberg), 'Um die Schächtfreiheit', *C.V.-Zeitung*, XI (1932), p. 264; 'Gegen das Schächten', *ibid.*, p. 68.
[153]*C.V.-Tätigkeitsbericht 1926–1927*, p. 60.
[154]'Die Auflösung des Verbandes der deutschen Juden', *Jüdische Rundschau*, XXVII (1922), p. 280.
[155]*Zur Schächtfrage*, published by the Verband Bayerischer Israelitischer Gemeinden und Bayerische Rabbinerkonferenz, Munich 1926, pp. 12f.
[156]Korn, *Kommentar zum Reichs-Tierschutzgesetz vom 24. November 1933*, Meißen 1934, p. 7.
[157]'Neue Vorstöße gegen das Schächten', *C.V.-Zeitung*, IV (1925), p. 487.
[158]'Ein abgeschlagener Angriff', *C.V.-Zeitung*, V (1926), p. 682.
[159]'Ein nationalsozialistischer Antrag', *C.V.-Zeitung*, IX (1930), p. 303.
[160]'Tierschutzvereine und Schächtfrage', *C.V.-Zeitung*, X (1931), p. 197.
[161]A.H., 'Um die Schächtfreiheit', *loc. cit.*
[162]Otto Mayer, *Deutsches Verwaltungsrecht*, II, Munich-Leipzig [3]1924, p. 286.
[163]*Entscheidungen des Preussischen Oberverwaltungsgerichts* (=*OVGE*), 38, pp. 58ff.
[164]*OVGE*, 44, pp. 68ff.
[165]Grünpeter, 'Sind die Schächtverbote rechtsgültig?', *C.V.-Zeitung*, X (1931), pp. 251f.

bans were legal.[166] Yet, this interpretation ignored the changes that had occurred since the Court's ruling of 1904. For one thing, the Federal Council, representing the German States within the *Reich*, had explicitly sanctioned ritual slaughter in its Decree of 2nd June 1917;[167] for another, the domiciliary prerogative was overridden by a public law provision on the compulsory use of municipal abattoirs, which rested in the main on Article 135 of the Weimar Constitution.[168] Accordingly, statements issued by the Prussian Ministry of the Interior in mid-April and by the *Reich* Ministry of the Interior on 21st July 1932 declared municipal bans on ritual slaughter to be unconstitutional.[169] These decisions put an end to the controversy over the bans at local government level.

Attempts to have ritual slaughter banned were also made at *Länder* level. In Bavaria it was the Munich Society for the Protection of Animals which pressed for legislation on the subject. In a petition the Society called on the Bavarian Diet "to prescribe by law the compulsory stunning of all animals before slaughter, and thus to ban in Bavaria Jewish ritual slaughter which omits the stunning of animals".[170] The Federation of Bavarian Israelite Communities and the Bavarian Rabbinical Conference countered this move with a petition of their own,[171] which, however, did not prevent the Diet from adopting a motion calling on the Bavarian Government to issue an order banning slaughter without prior stunning of the animals. The motion was carried with the votes of the DNVP, the National Socialists, the *Bayernbund*, the Social Democrats and the Communists.[172] After a delay of five years the Bavarian Government obliged and laid the requisite legislation before the Diet in mid-January 1930.[173] This was the first ban at *Länder* level. Brunswick and Anhalt followed suit.

How did the Jewish organisations respond to the campaigns for bans on ritual slaughter at state level? On 21st July 1926 Rabbi Munk put the Jewish case in person to *Reich* Chancellor Marx, and on 8th August of the same year he presented his arguments in a letter[174] in which he begged the Chancellor to examine whether the *Länder* were entitled under the Constitution to legislate on these issues, since ritual slaughter had been sanctioned by an Order of the Federal Council. He added that the imposition by law of such a ban would cause misgivings abroad.[175] On 22nd August the *Reich* Chancellory forwarded copies of Munk's petition to the *Reich* Ministers of the Interior and Justice with the request to take appropriate action. On 27th August Munk called again on the

---

[166]Gustav Radbruch, *Der amtliche Entwurf eines Allgemeinen Deutschen Strafgesetzbuches und das Schächten nach jüdischem Ritus*, Consultant's Report, Geheimes Staatsarchiv, Akten des preußischen Justizministeriums, Rep. 84a, No. 8420, Bl. 400ff., in particular Bl. 406.

[167]*Reichs-Gesetzblatt*, 1917, p. 471.

[168]Grünpeter, *loc. cit.*; S. Lichtenstaedter, 'Sind die Schächtverbote rechtsgültig?', *C.V.-Zeitung*, X (1931), p. 414.

[169]'Kommunale Schächtverbote verfassungswidrig', *C.V.-Zeitung*, XI (1932), p. 238; A.H., 'Um die Schächtfreiheit', *loc. cit.*

[170]'Auch gegen das Schächten', *C.V.-Zeitung*, V (1926), p. 350.

[171]*Zur Schächtfrage, op. cit.*

[172]A(lfred) H(irschberg), 'Schächtverbot in Bayern?', *C.V.-Zeitung*, V (1926), p. 383.

[173]W(ilhelm) L(evinger), 'Schächtverbot in Bayern', *C.V.-Zeitung*, IX (1930), p. 50.

[174]Bundesarchiv Koblenz, Akten der Reichskanzlei, R 431/2192, L 381851f.

[175]*Ibid.*, L381852, L381854.

Chancellor, urging him to issue a statement expressing his personal view. This Marx was not prepared to do; however, he instructed the *Reich* Chancellory "to get in touch with the two Ministries in line with the suggestions of the applicant". In the meantime Munk had had a personal interview with *Reich* Minister of Justice Johannes Bell.[176] We do not know what measures the two Ministries took, but the delaying tactics adopted by the Bavarian Government appear to indicate that the *Reich* Government did exert some influence. Covert suggestions in the *C.V.-Zeitung*, to the effect that the C.V. was preparing measures (whose nature could not be revealed) to counter a prospective ban on ritual slaughter in Bavaria, point in the same direction.[177] The C.V. seems to have been hoping that after the passage of the Act the *Reich* Government would appeal to the State Court[178] since an examination of the Bavarian Law in respect of its compatibility with the Constitution seemed promising for the Jewish cause. The *Reich* did not appeal to the State Court; instead it introduced the aforementioned section 412 of the abortive Kahl Draft of a reformed Criminal Code.

When State offices or courts of law fixed appointments or hearings for the Sabbath or Jewish holidays, Jews, especially the Orthodox, were faced with a conflict of conscience, as they were called upon to violate the peace prescribed by Jewish law for those days. To deal with this situation, the Prussian Minister of Justice, acting presumably on a suggestion by Ludwig Foerder, on 27th January 1927 issued an Order instructing the authorities concerned to take account of the religious scruples of members of the public summoned to appear in person.[179] Another favourable ruling was obtained by the *Deutsch-Israelitischer Gemeindebund*, which succeeded in getting Jewish civil servants exempted from working on the three main Jewish holidays.[180]

Serious difficulties arose at the Thuringian schools, when the Right-wing parties in this *Land* agreed on 13th January 1930 to put Wilhelm Frick in charge of a Ministry, the first National Socialist Minister in any German *Land*. On 24th January he was confirmed by the Diet as Minister of the Interior and Education.[181] On 16th April of the same year he gave instructions for any one of five prayers, of which he submitted the texts, to be said at the beginning and end of every week in every school.[182] None of the prayers referred explicitly to the Jews, but Numbers 2, 3 and 4 offended the feelings of persons holding different views. It was not only Jews who felt personally insulted by passages such as "Therefore deliver us from deceit and treason", "I believe Thou punishest the betrayal of our land", or "I know that godlessness and treason disrupted and annihilated our people". The outrage was felt far and wide.[183] *Reich* Minister of

[176]*Ibid.*, L381889–91.
[177]'Kommt ein Schächtverbot in Bayern?', *C.V.-Zeitung*, V (1926), p. 663.
[178]W.L., *loc. cit.*; 'Das Schächtverbot in Bayern', *Jüdische Rundschau*, XXXV (1930), p. 57.
[179]*Justizministerialblatt*, 1928, p. 68.
[180]Bundesarchiv Koblenz, Akten der Reichskanzlei, R 431/2192, L 381928f., L 381936.
[181]Richard Freyh, 'Stärken und Schwächen der Weimarer Republik', in *Die Weimarer Republik*, edited by Walter Tormin, Hanover [20]1981, pp. 137ff., here p. 178.
[182]*Amtsblatt des Thüringischen Ministeriums für Volksbildung*, 1930, No. 52, pp. 39f.
[183]W. Nithack-Stahn, 'Haßgebete', *C.V.-Zeitung*, IX (1930), p. 273; 'Protest der thüringischen Lehrer', *ibid.*, pp. 273f.

the Interior Joseph Wirth acted swiftly. In a letter of 12th May 1930 addressed to the Chairman of the Thuringian State Ministry he conveyed his misgivings on the grounds of constitutional law. He considered it particularly odious that Frick had stated in the Budget Committee of the Thuringian Diet that the prayers were directed against the Jews.[184] On 24th May the Chairman of the Thuringian State Ministry announced the Ministry's decision to uphold the Order of 16th April.[185] In doing so, the Thuringian authorities laid themselves open to further action by the *Reich* Minister of the Interior. Under Article 143/I of the Weimar Constitution, the *Reich* and the individual *Länder* had to act jointly in setting up institutions for the education of the young. Article 148/II made it incumbent on the parties concerned to respect the feelings of persons holding different views. That injunction was violated by the school prayers, which accordingly were contrary to *Reich* Law. The *Reich* Minister of the Interior, acting in accordance with Article 15/III, Paragraph 1, had asked for this deficiency to be rectified. Since the repeal of the Order had been refused, the *Reich* was enabled under Article 15/III, Paragraph 2 to appeal to the State Court.[186] This step was taken by *Reich* Minister of the Interior Wirth on 26th May.[187]

In this particular case the *Reich* Government had acted so promptly that the C.V. for once was hard put to it to match that speed with its own counter-measures. It distributed in Thuringia tens of thousands of copies of a special issue of the *C.V.-Zeitung*.[188] On 15th June 1930 the C.V. held a protest rally at Eisenach, and on the 17th three public meetings in Berlin.[189] On the same day there was a debate in the *Reichstag* on the issue, in the course of which Wirth attacked Frick in a hard-hitting speech.[190] Only a few weeks later, on 11th July 1930 the State Court handed down its ruling that prayers Numbers 2, 3 and 4 were contrary to Article 148/II of the Weimar Constitution.[191] Thus the issue was settled in favour of the *Reich* Government.

More difficult to tackle was another source of discrimination against Jews, which arose when civil servants exercised their discretion in a racially biased manner. The C.V. complained especially about unjust treatment by the financial administration.[192] It suggested therefore that in order to eliminate extraneous influences for the process of decision-making the official questionnaires should no longer ask for a person's religious affiliation.[193]

Much resentment was caused by meetings in public buildings which banned

[184]'Der Reichsinnenminister Wirth gegen Fricks Haßgebete', *ibid.*, p. 273; Holländer, 'Herrn Minister Frick!', *ibid.*, p. 257.
[185]*RGZ*, 129, Appendix pp. 9*ff., in particular p. 13*.
[186]*Ibid.*, p. 18*; 'Die thüringischen Haßgebete vor dem Staatsgerichtshof', *C.V.-Zeitung*, IX (1930), p. 285.
[187]'Der Reichsinnenminister antwortet dem C.V.', *ibid.*, p. 365.
[188]'Was tut der Centralverein?', *ibid.*, p. 298.
[189]'Bedeutsame Protestkundgebung in Eisenach', *ibid.*, p. 330; Julius Brodnitz, 'Unsere Antwort an Dr. Frick', *ibid.*, p. 325.
[190]*Verhandlungen des Reichstags. Stenographische Berichte*, vol. 428, pp. 5518ff., in particular p. 5520; 'Abrechnung der deutschen Volksvertretung mit Frick', *C.V.-Zeitung*, IX (1930), p. 329.
[191]*RGZ*, 129, Appendix, pp. 9*ff.
[192]*Gegen die Rechtsnot . . .*, *op. cit.*, p. 10.
[193]'Gewerbesteuer und Religion', *Führerbriefe*, I, No. 5 (30th April 1931), pp. 67f.

Jews from attending. In particular when meetings were held in school premises, the heads concerned often turned a blind eye to the illegality of such exclusions. In such cases the C.V. appealed successfully to the provincial education authorities. In the case of municipal premises, on the other hand, the Government was reluctant to interfere and advised the C.V. to approach the elected local government body concerned. On the grounds of tactical considerations the C.V. decided not to make the fight against exclusion from public meetings an issue of principle, which it could have done, for instance, by campaigning for an amendment to the law on public meetings.[194]

There was little the Jewish organisations could do to challenge unfavourable decisions by the administrators of municipally owned property. Thus the National Socialist municipal government of Koburg terminated an arrangement that had been in force for over fifty years, whereby the Jews had been allowed to use, free of charge, a former Evangelical chapel as a prayer room. An appeal to the municipal council would have been hopeless. Even the motion by the DNVP which sought to extend the period of notice was voted down by the National Socialist majority.[195]

In the light of the reports here presented it can be said that the belief of the Jews in the possibility of defensive action against excesses was not altogether groundless. The various Jewish organisations were successful in bringing about peaceful solutions to nearly all problems that were arising. Shortcomings in the field of law were redressed in most cases by Ordinances of the highest *Reich* or *Länder* authorities or through decisions by courts of the highest instance. The few open questions in this field, notably the defamation of collective bodies, eluded a solution on the basis of the existing law. Here the successful assertion of Jewish interests was frustrated by the polarisation of the political forces during the final years of the Weimar Republic. In other issues, for instance that of a new law regulating the official status of the Jewish religious community, disunity within the Jewish camp helped to obstruct a satisfactory solution.[196]

In spite of the skilled and successful work for legal self-defence, some warning voices were raised at an early stage, arguing that extensive resort to the courts might turn out to be counter-productive. *Reich* Chancellor Hermann Müller, for instance, concluded after a while that Münchmeyer should not be taken seriously, and refrained from initiating any further proceedings against him.[197] Indeed, each new defamation trial was greeted by the *Völkische* and National Socialists as welcome publicity; each instance of defamation was hailed with jubilation as an effective thrust against the hated "November Republic".[198] The

[194]*C.V.-Tätigkeitsbericht 1924–1925*, pp. 36ff.
[195]'Den Koburger Juden wird der Betsaal gekündigt . . .', *C.V.-Zeitung*, XI (1932), p. 425.
[196]On this question see in great detail Max P. Birnbaum, *Staat und Synagoge 1918–1938. Eine Geschichte des Preussischen Landesverbandes jüdischer Gemeinden (1918–1938)*, Tübingen 1981 (Schriftenreihe wissenschaftlicher Abhandlungen des Leo Baeck Instituts 38), in particular pp. 274–278.
[197]Bundesarchiv Koblenz, Akten der Reichskanzlei, R 431/2192, L 382279.
[198]Walter Oehme and Kurt Caro, *Kommt "Das Dritte Reich"?*, Berlin 1930, p. 109.

more vigorously the Jews championed the cause of democracy and the Republic, the more clearly was the State revealed in the eyes of its enemies as the *Judenrepublik*.[199] On the other hand a Nuremberg jury accepted in a case of defamation of a religious body that the C.V. had effectively demolished the defence plea that the accused had acted in good faith.[200] Such instances show that the legal defence efforts of the C.V. were certainly not futile.

Yet, when all is said and done, the fact remains that emotionally motivated mass movements cannot be stemmed by courts of law. This was understood at the time, in the 1920s,[201] and it was confirmed by the first study of the legal defence efforts of the C.V. published after the Third *Reich* had placed the Jews outside the pale.[202] Furthermore, it must not be forgotten that legal action was not the only means adopted by the Jewish organisations to counter the onslaught of the antisemites. Arnold Paucker has provided a telling picture of the multifarious Jewish efforts in this field.[203] During the final years of the Weimar Republic especially the Jewish organisations resorted increasingly to covert actions and clearly focused propaganda measures so as to encourage moderate elements to come out in support of the Jews. These activities were paralleled by the anti-fascist efforts for the protection of the Republic on the part of other democratic organisations.

Whether the Jews in the Weimar Republic were disadvantaged in legal terms to the extent of being in a state of distress is more than dubious in the light of the present study. Ernest Hearst rests his damning judgement of Weimar justice on only twenty articles in the *C.V.-Zeitung*,[204] indicating that Jews had been treated unjustly by the German courts.[205] The far more thorough study by Donald Niewyk presents a very different picture.[206] Those in charge of the C.V. Legal Defence Department, too, declared themselves satisfied by the judicial decisions of the German courts.[207] It is not surprising that judicial practice should have been felt to be most satisfying in civil cases, since that was the field in which

[199]Robert Weltsch, 'Entscheidungsjahr 1932', in *Entscheidungsjahr 1932, op. cit.*, pp. 535–562, here p. 558.

[200]Hirschberg, 'Das Urteil von Nürnberg', *C.V.-Zeitung*, VIII (1929), p. 601.

[201]Walter Sulzbach, 'Die Juden und die Deutschen', *Der Jude*, Sonderheft 3, *Judentum und Deutschtum* (1926), pp. 1ff., in particular p. 6.

[202]Doskow and Jacoby, *loc. cit.*, p. 498.

[203]Paucker, *Der jüdische Abwehrkampf . . .* , *op. cit.*; also *idem*, 'Der jüdische Abwehrkampf' in *Entscheidungsjahr 1932, op. cit.*, pp. 405–499. See also his later essays in which he counters criticism of the defence efforts of the *Centralverein*, e.g. 'Jewish Defence against Nazism in the Weimar Republic', *The Wiener Library Bulletin*, XXVI, Nos. 1/2 (1972), pp. 21–31; 'Die Abwehr des Antisemitismus in den Jahren 1893–1933', in Herbert A. Strauss/Norbert Kampe (Hrsg.), *Antisemitismus. Von der Judenfeindschaft zum Holocaust*, Bonn 1984, pp. 143–171; 'Jewish Self-Defence', *loc. cit.* (see note 4), pp. 55–65; 'The Jewish Defense against Antisemitism in Germany, 1893–1933', in Jehuda Reinharz (ed.), *Living with Antisemitism. The Jewish Response in the Modern Period*, Hanover, New Hampshire 1987, pp. 104–132.

[204]Ernest Hearst, 'When Justice was not done. Judges in the Weimar Republic', *The Wiener Library Bulletin*, XIV, No. 1 (1960), pp. 10ff.

[205]*Ibid.*, p. 11.

[206]Niewyk, *loc. cit.*, p. 113.

[207]See above, pp. 160f.

German judges had been trained in the first place; in order to settle civic disputes.[208]

It appears that the question of a specific Jewish state of distress in respect of law and justice arose in connection with the wider debate on the "crisis of confidence besetting justice", initiated among others by Erich Eyck.[209] His talk on the crisis of German judicial practice, given before the Berlin *Juristische Gesellschaft* on 9th January 1926 and subsequently published in book form,[210] sparked off a debate which was promoted in the main by the *Republikanischer Richterbund*[211] and lasted from autumn 1926 to the autumn of 1927.[212] At the meeting of the *Reichsbund jüdischer Frontsoldaten* in 1927 Hermann Großmann, a senior judge at the Berlin *Kammergericht* and Vice President of the *Republikanischer Richterbund*,[213] talked on "The state of distress in German law and justice". He was followed at the same meeting by Alfred Klee who spoke on "Jewish distress in respect of German law and justice".[214] On behalf of the C.V. Ludwig Foerder had expressed similar views as early as 1924 in his book, *Antisemitism and Justice*.[215] At the Jurists' Congress of the C.V. on 18th and 19th June 1927 it was again Erich Eyck who delivered the most telling contribution on the "Crisis of confidence besetting justice".[216]

Such pessimistic views of the state of justice in general and of its treatment of Jews in particular were by no means widely shared among the legal profession. Conservative Jewish jurists, too, dismissed the "chatter" of a "crisis of justice" as grossly exaggerated.[217] Thus, the attitude of Jewish jurists to the debate on the "crisis of justice" bears out the results of the investigation of Jewish contributions to the law journals: "united in discord", the vast majority of Jewish jurists in Germany were German jurists in the first place.

In the light of the relevant facts, then, it is plain that at least in the field of legal defence the Jews were far more widely recognised as equal citizens with equal rights than has so far been accepted. Indeed, during the life of the Weimar Republic the collective and individual rights of the Jews were effectively protected and enforced by the State and the Jewish organisations.

[208]Hans Hattenhauer, 'Zur Lage der Justiz in der Weimarer Republik', in Dietrich Erdmann and Hagen Schulze, *Weimar*, Düsseldorf 1980, pp. 169ff., in particular p. 174.
[209]Kuhn, *op. cit.*, p. 48.
[210]Eyck, *Die Krise der deutschen Rechtspflege*, Berlin 1926.
[211]Hans Hattenhauer, *Geschichte des Beamtentums*, Cologne etc. 1980, p. 336; Schulz, *op. cit.*, pp. 95ff.
[212]Kuhn, *op. cit.*, p. 275.
[213]Cf. Schulz, *op. cit.*, p. 208.
[214]'Die Rechtsnot der Juden in Deutschland', *Jüdische Rundschau*, XXXII (1927), p. 105.
[215]Foerder, *op. cit.*
[216]Eyck, 'Die Stellung der Rechtspflege . . .', *loc. cit.*
[217]For a nearly identical formulation, see Hachenburg, *op. cit.*, p. 85; similarly Hans Lazarus, 'Antisemitismus und Justiz', *C.V.-Zeitung*, III (1924), p. 678; Kurt Alexander, 'Wir und die Justiz', *C.V.-Zeitung*, VII (1928), p. 557; Martin Wassermann, 'Die Bekämpfung des Boykotts', *C.V.-Zeitung*, XI (1932), p. 516.

Fin de Siècle Austria

Years of Strife

The Contest of the Österreichisch-Israelitische Union for the Leadership of Austrian Jewry

BY JACOB TOURY

I. FIRST STEPS IN THE JEWISH COMMUNITY OF VIENNA

In an earlier paper[1] I traced the slow emergence of the *Österreichisch-Israelitische Union* (ÖIU) up to its official constitution (26th April 1886). Although inaugurated on the strength of a fulminant political and cultural programme, first outlined by Joseph Samuel Bloch in his weekly *Österreichische Wochenschrift*, the new organisation was hampered from the outset by frequent vacillations as to the aims and methods of its activities. At first the minimalists, having the upper hand, tended to content themselves with the strengthening of Jewish cultural ties in an atmosphere of social middle-class togetherness. And indeed, most of the members, who were comparative newcomers to the Austrian capital, felt the lack of roots keenly and were even, at first, interested in sponsoring mutual aid among themselves and lending a helping hand in cases of economic difficulties.

But this was already too much for a majority of members, who strictly adhered to the minimalistic statutes, as confirmed by the government and approved by the general assembly. Yet, there was another group among the founding-members, especially younger lawyers and university lecturers, whose attitude had been influenced by Bloch's original concept of a citizens' union and of a valiant struggle against the rising antisemitic tide in Vienna. They also upheld Bloch's initial fighting stance *vis à vis* the oligarchic board of the Jewish community of Vienna, the *Israelitische Kultus-Gemeinde* (IKG), and some of them even hankered after turning the new ÖIU into a kind of political lobby, influencing the choice of candidates in general elections and furthering anti-antisemitic measures behind the scenes, or even in public.

At first, this group of activists stole a march on the more staid elements of the board, although with dire results to themselves. When in May 1886, shortly after the *Union*'s constituting assembly of 24th April, an antisemitic mass-rally was called, featuring as main speakers the Hungarian rabble-rouser Sigmond Simonyi and the then most famous German antisemite, Court-Preacher Adolf

---

[1] Jacob Toury, 'Troubled Beginnings: The Emergence of the Österreichisch-Israelitische Union', in *LBI Year Book XXX* (1985), pp. 457–475.

Stoecker, the activist members on the board of the *Union* persuaded the majority to petition the Prime Minister, Count Taaffe, and the Chief of the Metropolitan Police for a prohibition of the antisemitic meeting. But, before taking such a vigorous political step, some cautious members of the board saw fit to enquire at Count Taaffe's office, whether the Premier would condescend to receive a delegation of the *Union*. The answer was swift – and utterly negative. Consequently, the board abstained also from petitioning the Chief of Police. Moreover, it immediately resolved that the ÖIU had no further business meddling in politics ("dass die 'Union' keine Politik zu treiben habe").[2] This put an untimely stop to the activists' zeal. For seven years and more their aspirations at combatting antisemitism in public, by turning the new association into an instrument for general political activities, were hamstrung by the minimalistic over-cautiousness of the majority. In short, the *Union* "was afraid of its own political character".[3]

In retrospect, the débâcle of the *Union*'s first public action is not at all surprising, when one considers that in the first years of its existence the number of paying members barely reached two hundred and fifty.[4] The more surprising therefore was the vigour of the activist wing which even threatened to stage a secession.[5] In the end, they were kept in the fold, when the board initiated a new direction of activity: the *Union* started a vigorous attack on the leadership of the IKG, first and foremost criticising the haphazard form of religious instruction for youngsters and the lack of facilities for studying the Hebrew language;[6] and – from the particular to the general – soon the whole *in camera*-autocracy of a small circle on the board of the IKG came in for sharp censure. In this situation, one of the notables on the board, Emanuel Baumgarten, a sworn enemy of J. S. Bloch and all he stood for, even exacerbated the conflict by publicly calling the *Union* a mere "debating forum" (*Sprechsaal*),[7] which carried no specific weight in the community.

Thus, the ÖIU was eager to show its mettle at the elections to the IKG in 1888. A coincidence furnished them with an outstanding and rather popular candidate. Dr. Alfred Stern, one of the Liberal town-councillors of Vienna,[8] suddenly appeared at a voters' meeting of the IKG (18th November 1888) and castigated the passivity of the board in combatting antisemitism and its laxity in upholding the interests of "Jewry as a whole" ("Gesamtjudentum"). He himself did not propose his candidacy, but the *Union* did, and so did the *Israelitischer*

---

[2] *Monatsschrift der Österreichisch-Israelitischen Union* (henceforth *Monatsschrift*) XXII, No. 4 (April 1910), "erscheint als Festschrift zur Feier des 25. Jubiläums der ÖIU". This is the one and only source of this episode.

[3] Quotations from *ibid.*, p. 9.

[4] *Dr. Blochs Österreichische Wochenschrift*, 1887, pp. 218–221. Report on the first regular general assembly.

[5] *Ibid.*, p. 220, reported by one of the co-founders of the ÖIU, advocate Dr. Zins, on whom see below.

[6] *Ibid.*, pp. 303, 316–319.

[7] *Monatsschrift*, No. 4 (1910), p. 10.

[8] For his biography, including the episode preceding this election, cf. Joseph S. Bloch, *Erinnerungen aus meinem Leben*, vol. III, Wien 1933, pp. 257–264 and especially p. 258.

Wählerverein[9] and the *minyanim* in the outlying districts, who felt alienated by the notables on the board and tended to sympathise with the ÖIU. The outcome was that Dr. Stern found himself on the board of the IKG, and the *Union* tasted its first, although indirect, success in Jewish public affairs.

The activists in the ÖIU immediately wanted to re-establish their influence in the exhilaration of victory, but again saw themselves blocked by the minimalists. Consequently, some thirty members once more[10] established an autonomous circle, naming it "Equality of Rights" (*Gleichberechtigung*). They stated as their aims "fighting antisemitism and its deleterious influences" and "the defence against any encroachment on and infringement of constitutional rights and liberties".[11]

Another aim, embodied in the name of the group, seems to have been a demand for their equitable representation on the board of the ÖIU. In any case, after some discussions and negotiations the secessionists returned to the fold after having been accorded substantial influence on the board,[12] although without a corresponding increase in the fighting spirit of the *Union* as a whole – notwithstanding the growing danger of virulent antisemitism in Vienna.

Thus, the only tangible and immediate result of this manœuvre was a personal change in the presidency of the *Union*. The first president, Heinrich Berger, vacated his chair, and the lawyer Dr. S. Zins, one of the co-founders of the *Union*, who had acted as the spokesman of the minimalists, felt compelled to relinquish his position on the board as well. For years to come Berger and Zins abstained from actual involvement in the activities of the ÖIU, though without giving up their membership.

II. THE GRÜNFELD ERA

The new president was a university lecturer, Dr. med. Josef Grünfeld, who had been active in the ÖIU since its inception. He first came to the fore as one of the leaders of the earliest secessionists in 1886. His long term as president, starting from January 1889 and continuing until April 1897, brought about certain positive developments in the character of the *Union*. The board received and acted upon several proposals aimed at strengthening the social and personal ties between the members. The frequency of meetings was stepped up,[13] and some

---

[9]On the *Israelitischer Wählerverein* headed by Dr. M. Spitzer, cf. Toury, *loc. cit.* (as in note 1), pp. 466 ff. The *Handwerkerverein* also endorsed A. Stern. The board was mainly upheld by the voters of the I precinct, and to some extent also by parts of the *Leopoldstadt* electorate (II precinct). For the Jewish population in the various Viennese districts, cf. Ivar Oxaal and Walter R. Weitzmann, 'The Jews in Pre-1914 Vienna. An Exploration of Basic Sociological Dimensions', in *LBI Year Book XXX* (1985), pp. 395 ff.

[10]The first time even before the official constitution of the *Union* (1885/1886, cf. Toury, *loc. cit.*, as in note 1, p. 467); the second time they tried to convene a separate meeting in 1887, but finally relented, as shortly mentioned above, and cf. note 5.

[11]*Monatsschrift*, XXII, No. 4 (1910), pp. 10 f.

[12]*Ibid.*, p. 11.

[13]*Österreichische Wochenschrift*, 1889, p. 234.

active spirits again advocated the intensification of the fight against antisemitism.[14] At this juncture a proposal for the organisation of a "Legal Defence Bureau" (*Rechtsbüro*) was first proffered,[15] and though it took at least six years, was finally realised in 1895/1897.

The one immediate outcome of the renewed vigour within the ÖIU was the publication of a manifesto 'An unsere Glaubensgenossen!', calling for enrolment of new members. Its relative success in filling the *Union*'s ranks "for a common defence of our equality"[16] soon became evident: more than 700 new members joined the *Union* during 1889 alone. Yet, it is perhaps significant of the still rather parochial character of the Grünfeld era that the total membership during this period[17] never exceeded 1,200. Women were not yet eligible, but they were now invited to participate in the lectures and in social gatherings.

In order to ensure a functioning organisation, a permanent office was established and an honorary secretary appointed – Josef Fuchs.[18] He also took over the publication of a monthly bulletin: *Mitteilungen der Österreichisch-Israelitischen Union* (October 1889–1900, continued as: *Monatsschrift* 1901–1914).[19] The bulletin was intended to strengthen the bonds between the members and to inform them about the activities of the board and its secretary.[20] In order to lend significance to the rather scanty first information sheets of four pages, or even less, the *Mitteilungen* soon began to report – *verbatim* or in a shortened version – the content of the lectures, now given almost monthly by members or by invited speakers. The subjects included Jewish and general topics – the latter generally enhanced by a Jewish slant.[21] Occasionally, antisemitism was discussed, though more as a historical, than an actual, issue of the day – the exception being the acclamation of Bloch's sporadic but thunderous speeches in the *Reichsrat*.

But more than the questions of general or Jewish culture and the problem of antisemitic successes in Vienna and the whole of the Empire, the *Union* under Grünfeld again chose to attack the field of its first victory – the IKG. In November 1889 seven members of the community board were to be re-elected or replaced. There seemed to be a good chance that – after having gained a tenuous foothold on the board through the election of Dr. Alfred Stern – the *Union* might now be able to win a leading position on the board of the IKG. The coincidence, if such it was, of the first publication of the *Mitteilungen der Österreichisch-*

[14]*Monatsschrift*, XXII, No. 4 (1910), p. 11.

[15]The proposal of 1889 is documented *ibid.*, p. 12.

[16]Quoted in *Österreichische Wochenschrift*, 1889, p. 234, the date of the manifesto is the 9th March.

[17]For the membership: *Mitteilungen der Österreichisch-Israelitischen Union*, No. 12 (1890), p. 3 and No. 72 (1895), p. 5. *Monatsschrift*, No. 4 (1910), p. 23 mentions even less for 1897: "wenig über 1 100".

[18]*Ibid.*, p. 12.

[19]For particulars cf. Jacob Toury, *Die Jüdische Presse im Österreichischen Kaiserreich 1902–1918. Ein Beitrag zur Problematik der Akkulturation*, Tübingen 1983 (Schriftenreihe wissenschaftlicher Abhandlungen des Leo Baeck Instituts 41), pp. 82–84.

[20]*Mitteilungen*, No. 1 (October 1889), pp. 2 f.

[21]E.g. 'On Usury' (Dr. J. S. Bloch, March 1889), 'On Polar Explorations' (Dr. Sigismund Fessler, September 1889), where Jewish members of Polar expeditions were named.

Israelitischen Union (October–November 1889) may serve as an indicator of the *Union*'s electoral ambitions and the scope of its exertions.

Spice was added to the campaign by an open insult flung at the *Union* by one of the heads of the IKG – probably once more Emanuel Baumgarten – who shortly before the election refused permission to one of the teachers at the *Beth-Hamidrash* to lecture, at the *Union*'s invitation, at one of its meetings.[22] In a spontaneous reaction to this affront, the meeting without a lecturer constituted itself as an election-committee and invited "the heads of the *minyanim* and other influential personalities from the precincts" to join the common front against the oligarchic remnants on the board of the IKG.[23] As of old, the *Israelitischer Wählerverein* and the *Handwerkerverein* again joined forces with the *Union*. This sudden zeal in the generally rather indifferent attitude towards community elections led to an unexpected success: all the seven candidates nominated by the self-appointed election-committee of the *Union* and its allies were elected and a substantial majority on the board was secured. This victory elevated the *Union* for years to come, and without further struggle, to a leading position in the affairs of the IKG, while Emanuel Baumgarten, the most influential of the old board, and also Angelo Ritter von Kuh, another of the old notables, lost their seats.[24] Alfred Stern was elected president of the IKG and – most gratifying for the *Union* – its chairman, Josef Grünfeld, gained a seat on the board in November 1889.[25] From now on the heads of the IKG were frequent guests at the meetings of the *Union* and – in the words of J. S. Bloch – "peace reigned"[26] between the two leading Jewish organisations of Vienna.

Nevertheless, the *Union* did not by any means lose its middle-class character. If the occupations of the fifteen members mentioned[27] as election-committee and elected candidates are in any way representative for the whole, the social picture in 1889 was not overly different from that of the first founders of the *Union*, which means that the upper strata of Viennese Jewry were still holding back:

5 represented major commercial firms and minor banking houses
2 represented the retail trade
2 were senior citizens of independent means
3 were mastercraftsmen and/or "industrialists"
3 represented the liberal professions, i.e. two lawyers and one university lecturer (medicine) – the latter being the incumbent president of the *Union*, Dr. med. Josef Grünfeld.

---

[22] *Mitteilungen*, No. 2 (November 1889), pp. 2 f.
[23] *Ibid*.
[24] *Österreichische Wochenschrift*, 1889, pp. 830, 842. Baumgarten's downfall was especially mentioned in Bloch's paper, as Bloch held him responsible, probably not without justification, for his dismissal from his post as rabbi of the district (*Distriktrabbiner*) of Floridsdorf. Cf. Bloch, *Erinnerungen, op. cit.*, vol. I, 1922, *passim* and esp. p. 168.
[25] *Ibid.*, and *Mitteilungen*, No. 5 (1890), p. 2.
[26] *Ibid*.
[27] *Österreichische Wochenschrift*, 1889, as in note 24. Eight serving on the committee and seven others being elected to the board.

Yet, the promising beginnings of the Grünfeld era did not lead to a logical sequel in the field of direst need – the fight against antisemitism. On the contrary, the *Union* seems to have lost all its fighting spirit after its victorious entry into the IKG. It rested content to feature – albeit rather prominently – the rise of antisemitism in its lectures,[28] but in practice the open day-to-day struggle against the racist-German and Christian-Social Jew-baiters fell to Bloch's *Österreichische Wochenschrift* and to his rather frequent attacks on antisemitism in the *Reichsrat*, where he remained a member until 1895. Bloch's forced abdication was not unconnected with his vitriolic attacks on the then foremost clerical antisemite, the parson of Weinhaus, Dr. Josef Deckert, and on an influential antisemitic Austrian nobleman in the *Reichsrat*, Prince Alois Liechtenstein, whose weight with the members of the "Polish Club" finally tipped the scales against Bloch,[29] when his mandate was impeached and annulled.

Bloch, the spiritual originator of the ÖIU, was almost the only political figure of Jewish origin to take a lively interest in its development and in strengthening its anti-antisemitic activities. Almost none of his Jewish colleagues in the *Reichsrat* – save Dr. A. Zucker[30] – and almost none of the Jewish municipal councillors of Vienna[31] had so far acknowledged the existence of the *Union*.

A gradual change was wrought by Karl Lueger's spectacular ascent in Austrian political life. While shortly before the municipal elections of 1890 one member of the *Union* was still forecasting the downfall of that candidate and the "return of peace and quiet" to the town-hall, and while his listeners in a meeting of the ÖIU reaffirmed "the holy duty . . . of each and everyone of the Israelites . . . to vote for the Progressive candidates"[32] – the "progressives" being the staid German Liberals – the results of the election came as a shock: Lueger was victorious and established himself as a force to be reckoned with; the Liberals lost i.a. the IX precinct, where Jews of the upper-middle class had begun to take up residence, and this was partly due to the abstention from the polls "of many Israelites".[33] Small as the first tremor was, it boded the beginning of a deep crisis in Viennese Jewry. The Jews finally started to question in earnest the unbroken adherence of their older generation to the German Liberals – an adherence

[28]E.g., in January 1890, the newly elected *Kultus-Vorsteher*, Dr. Maximilian Steiner on 'Auto-Antisemitism' (*Über inneren Antisemitismus*); in April 1890, the lawyer Dr. Moritz Frankl on 'Causes and Effects of Antisemitism and the Means to its Obliteration'; in October 1890, MdR Dr. J. S. Bloch, 'On Antisemitism'.

[29]Cf. Bloch, *Erinnerungen, op. cit.*, vol. II, 1922, *passim*. Almost the whole volume deals with Deckert, while Liechtenstein was contemporaneously attacked in *Österreichische Wochenschrift*, 1893–1895.

[30]*Mitteilungen*, No. 7 (1890) contained a supplement with the full text of an anti-antisemitic speech in the *Reichsrat* by Professor Alois Zucker from Prague besides one of J. S. Bloch's before the same forum.

[31]One possible exception may have been Sigmund Mayer (of whom more later), who seems to have participated in the preparations for the election in the IKG in November 1889. Cf. *Mitteilungen*, No. 3 (1889) p. 4.

[32]*Ibid.*, No. 9 (1890), pp. 3 f. (meeting of 8th March 1890).

[33]*Ibid.*, No. 10 (1890), pp. 15 f. During the first two years of the appearance of this bulletin, the numeration of the issues was changed and rechanged. At last, from October 1891 (No. 29) and until the end of the year 1900, a retroactive numbering system was used, starting from No. 1 in October 1889.

which had withstood even occasional anti-Jewish slights meted out by that party; for – and that was the core of the crisis – there was no real alternative power to the once mighty Liberal Party in the political arena. Certain splinter candidates of democratic or social-reformist hue might appeal to the progressive conscience of Jewish voters, but they could not provide them with a reasonably effective political defence position. Consequently, some Jewish outsiders, even as early as 1890, started hinting at the possibility of a Jewish defence by "retreating in a social direction"[34] – meaning an orientation towards the newly emerging Social Democratic Party; but such an alignment was still unacceptable to Jewish middle-class voters, albeit to a lesser degree than, for comparison's sake, in Imperial Germany of that period.

Yet, just at this juncture, certain prominent non-Jewish Liberals responded valiantly to the upsurge of antisemitism and the opening of a perceptible rift between the Liberal Parties and their erstwhile Jewish adherents. They founded the *Verein zur Abwehr des Antisemitismus* (VAA), first in Berlin,[35] and soon afterwards in Vienna, both in the spring of 1891.[36] The meritorious activities of these organisations cannot here be properly appreciated; but the difference between Berlin and Vienna has to be stressed: While the non-sectarian *Abwehrverein* of Berlin produced a definite stir within the Jewish community and led, among other factors, to the founding of the central Jewish defence organisation, the *Centralverein deutscher Staatsbürger jüdischen Glaubens*, the effect of the VAA in Vienna, at least on the *Österreichisch-Israelitische Union*, was somewhat negligible: No concerted defence-action was planned or initiated and it has to be deduced that the *Union*'s preoccupation with candidates, elections and certain attempts at political lobbying was still regarded as an appropriate and sufficient answer to antisemitism in all its manifestations.

In any case, the question of a political alternative to the German-Liberal Party came under continuous review in the assemblies of the ÖIU. In the several elections during the years 1891/1892 a spate of candidates – Liberals, Democrats and Social Reformers – paraded before the packed meetings of the *Union*, openly asking for endorsement by this newly emerging Jewish body. All of them solemnly promised to take up an intrepid stand against antisemitism. Thus, the veteran Jewish Liberal MP, Dr. Heinrich Jacques[37] seeking re-election was followed by his Democratic adversary Professor Benedict;[38] after them, even a municipal politician of a rather rightist hue caused surprise by seeking the endorsement of the ÖIU. This was none other than Professor Heinrich Friedjung,[39] the erstwhile German-National follower of Georg von Schönerer,

[34] *Ibid.*, words of Jacob Jaiteles.
[35] On the founding of the German *Abwehrverein* cf. the excellent essay of Barbara Suchy, 'The Verein zur Abwehr des Antisemitismus (I) – From its Beginnings to the First World War', in *LBI Year Book XXVIII* (1983), pp. 205 f; now concluded: 'From the First World War to its Dissolution in 1933', *LBI Year Book XXX* (1985), pp. 67 f.
[36] On the founding of the Austrian VAA, cf. lengthy reports in *Die Neuzeit*, 1891, pp. 111, 202 f.
[37] *Mitteilungen*, No. 10, 1891, cf. note 33 above. Jacques died barely a year after the meeting.
[38] *Ibid.*, No. 11.
[39] *Ibid.*, No. 12, pp. 2 ff.

and now an adherent of the veteran German National-Liberal party-leader, Ernst von Plener. Plener steadfastly pursued his arduous quest for an understanding with the Right-wing Germans, until he succeeded two years later in returning to power in a coalition government of rather conservative leanings under Count Windischgraetz in 1893/1895. Friedjung, who countenanced Plener's manoeuvres, had always been a controversial personality and it should not surprise anyone that the appearance in the meetings of the *Union* of this "vigorous intellectual force" – as he was introduced by the chairman – led to a rather turbulent scene. Although he promised the assembled members (for the first time in his career) "proudly to uphold the glorious history of Judaism", his old and relentless foe, Joseph Bloch,[40] not only castigated those empty phrases, but also tersely stated that any Jew purporting to be "German-National" of Plener's hue was already a partisan of antisemitism. The outcome was a premature closing of the meeting amidst "general commotion".[41]

This was not the only meeting which ended in a political fracas.[42] After all, no less than six board-members of the *Union* were also active in diverse parties and belonged to opposing election committees,[43] from Plener's National Liberals to the Leftist Democrats, now being led by the senescent, but in Jewish circles quite popular, Ferdinand Kronawetter. Some interested themselves in the newly emerging Social Reform Movement, of which more must be said later.

Except for the successful candidacy of the veteran Democrat Kronawetter[44] in the elections to the *Reichsrat* in the autumn of 1892, no political unanimity could be reached in the *Union* and altercations were frequent. Thus, even the favourable reception accorded to a modest literary venture of the *Union*, the *Kalender für Israeliten* in the autumn of 1892, appearing regularly until 1914, did not obscure the fact that the association had entered a new period of crisis and agitation.

In particular the general, and often vociferous, debates at the end of each meeting exacerbated political and social friction between the various factions and professions. Whether an address-book of Jewish artisans and craftsmen was proposed, or the establishment of a legal aid committee was again suggested, whether the founding of youth groups was ventilated or a political candidacy discussed – each and every item aroused heated arguments *pro* and *contra*, without, however, leading to tangible results. At last it was decided to disallow spontaneous proposals of any kind from the floor. Only motions tendered in writing to the presidium before the meeting were to be put to the vote.[45]

This was a useful technique which helped to restore external order; but what was lacking was a renewal of the spirit prevailing at the onset of the Grünfeld era.

---

[40]Cf. Bloch, *Erinnerungen, op. cit.*, vol. I, *passim*, and Jacob Toury, 'J. S. Bloch und die jüdische Identität im Österreichischen Kaiserreich', in *Beiheft 6 des Instituts für Deutsche Geschichte*, Universität Tel-Aviv 1984, *passim*.
[41]*Mitteilungen*, No. 12 (1891), pp. 4 f.
[42]E.g. also the assembly of 9th December 1893, cf. *Mitteilungen*, No. 57 (1894), p. 3.
[43]*Ibid.*, No. 15 (1891), p. 3.
[44]He had been unanimously endorsed as candidate by the ÖIU, *Mitteilungen*, No. 43 (1892), p. 4.
[45]*Ibid.*, No. 58 (February 1894), p. 15.

The president himself seems to have arrived at an impasse and did not reveal imagination or inspiring initiative, except in one instance to be mentioned further on. The honorary secretary, Josef Fuchs, was a useful and painstaking organiser, but no leader.

In contradistinction to them, the antisemites were served by unscrupulous rabble-rousers, such as Ernst Schneider in the Lower Austrian Diet; Deckert in the pulpit of Weinhaus; and above them all towered the debonair idol of Vienna's lower middle classes, the Christian-Social leader Karl Lueger. He had already started his all-out onslaught on the Town Hall of the Imperial City and the Jewish public grew progressively more apprehensive of this new menace. Thus, many of them began looking for a man, who might point the way out of their predicament. Consequently, in the ÖIU itself the scene was set for the emergence of a new leading personality. The one who offered himself was the "Viennese Merchant" Sigmund Mayer.[46]

III. SIGMUND MAYER'S FIRST STEPS IN JEWISH POLITICS

Mayer himself gives a rather dramatic account of his *quasi* spontaneous and unpremeditated political debut in the *Union*. This retrospective narrative has only one disadvantage – it does not entirely fit the otherwise established facts. He relates that "in the spring of 1894" he had suddenly been invited "to a conference" by the *Union*, "which was quite unknown to me, apart from the fact that it had been founded in 1885 by Dr. Joseph Bloch". And there and then, when he sharply criticised a rather vague political exposé, outlined by the main speaker at the meeting, he was immediately asked to develop new guide lines for the political activities of the *Union*. He spontaneously responded to the bid and compiled "within a few days, a memorandum several sheets long".[47]

As ample proof exists of Mayer's participation in several earlier meetings of the *Union* (since 1889!),[48] his own account ought to be corrected in accordance with the version contained in the jubilee issue of the *Monatsschrift* (April 1910):

"Sigmund Mayer . . . the town-councillor of the district of Leopoldstadt . . . alienated from the Liberals by their ambiguity with regard to the Jewish Question, relinquished his municipal office in order to join the fight as a common soldier in the ranks of Viennese Jewry . . . He was at the *Union*'s disposition as a voluntary adviser. His first deed in this capacity was the formation of a political committee as part of the board, and soon after came his proposal to convene a consultation of all the Liberal mandatories of Vienna with the heads of the *Union*."

[46]Thus reads the title of one of his autobiographical volumes: Sigmund Mayer, *Ein jüdischer Kaufmann, 1831–1911*, Leipzig 1911.
[47]*Ibid.*, pp. 308 f.
[48]E.g. in November 1889, *Mitteilungen*, No. 3 (1889), p. 4, February 1891, *Mitteilungen*, No. 10 (1891), pp. 10–11 and almost regularly after that date. Cf. also *Mitteilungen*, No. 48 (February 1893), p. 13, where Mayer is quoted extensively. Later he himself added a rider to his naive narrative, which is apt to verify the construction of events in our text, cf. S. Mayer, *op. cit.*, as in note 46, pp. 312 f.

The above versions agree in two points – sufficient for our purpose. A political meeting took place on 25th June 1894, strongly criticising the utter complacency of the Liberals in the Plener-Windischgraetz government (since November 1893), who did nothing at all to stem the ruthless antisemitic onslaught against Viennese Jewry in the Town Hall and in the streets. The meeting ended without tangible concessions from the Liberal politicians to the *Union*'s demand for definite steps against antisemitism. One logical outcome of the Liberal failure to heed Jewish appeals for help was the eventual establishment in March 1895 of a "Defence Committee" (later: "Defence Bureau") which was to assume responsibility for all non-political, i.e. essentially legal and judicial, issues of the fight against antisemitism.[49]

The second point of agreement between Mayer's report and the account in the jubilee issue of 1910 involves a new approach to party-politics. This approach, as indeed propounded in Mayer's first memorandum, rested on his bitter admission that most non-Jewish members of the Liberal Party had come "to think they don't need us any longer".[50]

But what was the alternative now offered by Mayer as a political defence against antisemitism? In the premises of his analysis he adopted one of the basic tenets of J. S. Bloch's and Bernhard Münz's articles of 1885 (in the then newly-founded *Österreichische Wochenschrift*),[51] which were inspired by the federalist theories of Adolf Fischhof (1816–1893): progressive liberalism and exclusive nationalism are mutually incompatible. But while the alternative proposed by Bloch in 1885 was the creation of a Jewish pressure group with federalist-autonomous leanings, Mayer's proposal of 1894 lacked – not by accident[52] – any trace of an actively Jewish concept. In the face of the widening rift between a Jewish-Progressive outlook and the Austro-German National-Liberal[53] tendencies towards repressive Right-wing policies and convenient electioneering agreements with the forces of antisemitism, Mayer's programme was purely defensive in character. It envisaged three stages in the behaviour of the Jewish electorate: in the first place, Mayer proposed an attempt at "combining some small parties in an alignment". Its centre of power would be in "the I, the II, and the IX districts, whose incumbents we would have to oust, in order to elect "the men of our choice".[54] Mayer unequivocally advocated endorsement of the new

---

[49]The activities of the *Union*'s Defence-Committee and Bureau before the First World War have been treated extensively in my essay 'Defense Activities of the 'Austro-Israelite Union'' before 1914', in Jehuda Reinharz (ed.), *Jewish Reactions to Antisemitism*, Brandeis University 1987, and may be omitted here.

[50]Quoted as a saying of Mayer, *Mitteilungen*, No. 68 (February 1895), p. 11.

[51]Cf. the first part of this essay, in *LBI Year Book XXX* (1985), pp. 461–464; and also my paper on Bloch as in note 40 above.

[52]Mayer tried to vindicate his strict negation of Jewish nationalism and of any form of group-reaction, except on a strictly denominational basis. Cf., for instance, his second autobiographical volume: S. Mayer, *Die Wiener Juden 1700–1900*, Wien-Berlin 1917, pp. 467–497: 'Die jüdisch-nationale Partei und die Wiener Judenschaft'. And see also in the text below.

[53]Mayer in 1896, as quoted in *Monatsschrift*, No. 4 (1910), p. 17: "Keine spezifisch 'nationale' Partei kann gerecht sein oder bleiben . . ."

[54]Quoted according to the summary of Mayer's memorandum, reprinted in his *Ein jüdischer Kaufmann*, *op. cit.*, (as in Note 46), pp. 309 ff.

splinter group of "Sozialpolitiker", whose candidates "as our elected representatives" would be compelled to "take on our case".[55]

If this stage miscarried, whatever the causes, there still remained two possibilities for a Jewish counteraction, the first being: total abstention from political activity.[56] And indeed, there were several members of the *Union*, who had tended, since 1891 when antisemitism began its political ascent, to advocate a general Jewish boycott of the polls.[57] Yet although Mayer mentioned such an alternative, he nevertheless found its "implementation quite impossible".[58] He probably was aware that a not inconsiderable number of his co-religionists were actively engaged in party-politics and would in no way respond to a suggestion of forsaking their political loyalties.[59]

Consequently, he tentatively examined a third form of Jewish political reaction: the "tactics . . . of assisting with all our strength the Social Democratic Party in its fight against the Christian Socials", even if, in final analysis, it meant Jewish support for the implementation of universal suffrage in Austria – a course not overly popular with the majority of Jewish middle-of-the-road Liberals. Mayer himself seems to have made an early peace with the various measures gradually being carried out in Austria for the enlargement of the franchise towards universal male suffrage, which finally became law in 1907. In consequence of such an orientation he predicted, as early as 1894, that "the Social Democrats are . . . the one and only *Kampfpartei* . . . able to . . . prepare the breaking-up of the Christian Socials and to absorb their followers from among the 'little people' ".[60]

In retrospect, Mayer's analysis of 1894 should have led him to a quick and clear-cut decision in favour of the Social Democratic Party. But the existing socio-historic conditions of Austrian Jews did not at all predispose them to countenancing such a decisive severing of their religious or secular, cultural or

[55]*Ibid.*, p. 310. The Fabian-inspired *Sozialpolitischer Verein* had existed since 1893 in the I. District. Out of it grew the *Sozialpolitische Partei*, whose candidates first tried to win seats in the Lower Austrian Diet in 1896. Three of their leading men were indeed elected: E. von Philippovich, Ferdinand Kronawetter (the first "official" candidate of the ÖIU since 1892) and the lawyer Julius Ofner, later repeatedly endorsed by the ÖIU. For a short résumé, cf. Ingrid Belke, *Die sozialreformerischen Ideen von Josef Popper-Lynkeus*, Tübingen 1978, especially pp. 14–15: the following doctoral thesis of the University of Vienna contains ample material and biographical sketches of the leading personalities: Eva Holleis, *Die Sozialpolitische Partei*, Vienna 1977, typescript.
[56]*Mitteilungen*, No. 71 (1895), p. 12; No. 73 (1895), p. 3 *et al.*, where "a large part of Viennese Jews" abstaining from the polls are mentioned.
[57]For 1891: *Mitteilungen*, No. 13 (April 1891): About 500 Jews abstained from voting in the II. District. Similar figures are mentioned for another election in the IX. District.
[58]Mayer, *Ein jüdischer Kaufmann, op. cit.*, p. 311.
[59]The growing tendency towards political abstention was one of the causes why the *Israelitischer Wählerverein*, a concomitant of the *Union* (cf. text and notes above) in 1895 "decided to renew its activities that for years had been suspended in favour of another . . . Jewish-political association" (i.e. the ÖIU).Quoted in *Österreichische Wochenschrift*, 1895, p. 327. Another factor speeding up the renewal of the *Wählerverein*, now under the name of *Politischer Volksverein* – and under the chairmanship of Dr. Hermann Fialla – was the election of a Lueger-majority in the Vienna Municipality. Although Fialla was not a member of the ÖIU, several others on the board of the *Volksverein* (e.g. S. Brod) belonged to the ÖIU too, and the cooperation between the two associations continued in an amicable spirit.
[60]Mayer, *Ein jüdischer Kaufmann, op. cit.*, p. 311.

economic ties with middle-class orientations, as entailed by a shift to political Socialism. In fact, neither Austrian nor German Jewry in its majority did overcome, until it was too late, its ingrained Liberal-bourgeois heritage in order to adapt itself to the Social Democratic alternative.

Thus, one cannot rightly blame Mayer and his contemporaries of the ÖIU, when they finally chose the first way – that of the splinter group of *Sozialreformer* – and stubbornly stuck to them, even when they immediately proved to be of no avail in the acute crisis that shook Vienna during the years 1895–1897.

One of the focal points of the political turmoil was the municipality of Vienna. The elections of September 1895 endowed Lueger's Christian Social Party with an absolute majority (92 out of 138 seats), and only the Emperor and his Premier, Count Kasimir Badeni (September 1895–November 1897) stood between Lueger and the Mayoralty. It took four consecutive polls in the town and several vote-takings in the council to have Lueger elected again and again, until the Emperor confirmed him, first (1896) as Deputy Mayor[61] and ultimately as Lord Mayor (1897). But as early as 1895 it had become evident that in the fracas the German-Liberal Party had lost its hold on the Inner Town, and especially on the *Leopoldstadt* (II district), with a Jewish electorate of about 30% of the total population.

It was only small comfort that a part of the Liberal votes went to the "Social Reformers". For it was brought home to the Jews by the elections to the Diet of Lower Austria – when Karl Lueger himself won a seat in the *Leopoldstadt* and his party an absolute majority in the Diet – that the split of votes between the German Liberals and the Social Reformers (3:3 in the I and II districts) had fatally weakened both of them.

Even Sigmund Mayer, who had endorsed the latter candidates in the name of the *Union*, soon expressed his deep disappointment with these "brave, yet anything but practical politicians", whose sorry lot in the Diet was "derision and ridicule . . . and early oblivion".[62]

Thus, when the year 1895 neared its end, a feeling of utter despondency made itself felt in many Jewish circles of Vienna. The board of the *Union* seems to have been deeply shocked, at least for a short while, by the adverse events. As a sign of near panic, a "concept" for a "strictly confidential" circular letter 'To our Jewish fellow-citizens' was drawn up.[63] For its finalisation, the board of the *Union* convoked a gremium of specially chosen "Vertrauensmänner" for the 5th November 1895, in order to test their reaction to such a desperate step. The proofsheets of the circular were probably sent to trusted community leaders for endorsement.

The bitter tenor of the circular is contained in the one sentence: "Vienna has

---

[61]Cf. the short but well-informed reports from Vienna in *Im deutschen Reich*, May and November 1896, the earlier on Lueger's so-called "Dermalium" (his temporary renouncement of the mayoralty), the latter on the elections to the Lower Austrian Diet.

[62]Mayer, *Ein jüdischer Kaufmann, op. cit.*, p. 322.

[63]Central Archives for the History of the Jewish People (CAHJP), Jerusalem, AW/315. 'Entwurf – Streng Vertraulich'.

an antisemitic municipality and an antisemitic mayor,[64] but where is the alleged
Jewish power and the much-reviled so-called Jewish influence?" The circular
gave expression to deep feelings that pre-empted the tenor of things to come one
generation later:

> "We are an insignificant minority, we cannot give battle, but at least let us be united in
> bearing with dignity our unfortunate lot."

There followed practical directions for such dignified behaviour, which are
significant of the traditional exhortations in the face of inimical public attitudes
towards the Jews: quit organisations that do not conform to the "tenets of justice
and equality", avoid ostentatious behaviour in public, cultivate humility in every
respect, as befitting mourners, refrain from attending Christian functions,
continue economic ties with former suppliers, but avoid those who

> "stand as agitators in the foreground of that hateful movement . . . and last not least, let us
> help those thousands of poor Jews, who under the present regime are even more vulnerable
> than before in their economic circumstances".

The circular letter remained a concept and was never made public in any
form. It was the outcome of sudden shock, after which most of the Viennese Jews,
and with them the leaders of the *Union*, seem to have returned to that kind of
lackadaisical Austrian attitude, which expects nothing ever to turn out as badly
as it might have done.

In short, Mayer and his newly-established political committee, as well as the
whole of the *Union*'s board, returned to the business in hand by slowly setting up
another committee, the *Abwehr-Comité*, for combatting antisemitism,[65] without,
however, curbing Mayer's avowed preoccupation with electioneering. Mayer
soon got over his first disappointment with the *Sozialpolitiker* and continued
sponsoring their cause within the ÖIU. Yet certain incidents during the elections
to the Lower Austrian Diet should have given him sufficient cause for renewed
deliberation on his political credo. For he could not but recoil from the fact that
in certain boroughs, when no candidate reached the required majority and a
second ballot became necessary, the organised *Sozialpolitiker* tended to prefer
Social Democrats over Liberal candidates – a practice which was, in his opinion,
"apt to further antisemitism". Mayer's dictum was echoed by Bloch, who at this
juncture denounced "the Viennese Social Democrats" as bearers of the "infection
with the antisemitic plague".[66]

This short-sighted misrepresentation almost led to a still graver decision. In
Mayer's memorandum of 1894 an ultimate alternative to the *Sozialpolitiker* and
the Social Democrats had been briefly touched upon: total political abstention.
Now, current political developments in Moravia and the dilemma of the Jewish
voters there between Czech and German antisemitic tendencies seemed to
further and promote the Jewish trend towards a boycott of general political

---

[64]*Ibid.*, in heavy type. Lueger's election was at that juncture not yet confirmed.
[65]Late in 1895. Cf. note 49 above.
[66]Both utterances in *Mitteilungen*, No. 79 (March 1896), in a report on the meeting of the *Union*, 8th
February 1896. Bloch, more than Mayer, had from his earliest political steps shown a certain
affinity to the labour movement. Cf. Toury, 'J. S. Bloch . . .', *loc. cit.*

events. Since 1895 the German-Liberal Party in Moravia had imitated its
Austrian sister-party and sought contact with the German antisemites (the
capital, Brno, excepted), notwithstanding the fact that the success of German
Liberal candidates, at least in seven Moravian constituencies, decisively
depended upon the Jewish vote. Moravian Jews, who took pride in a certain
tradition of self-reliance and quasi-autonomous political rights, categorically
demanded of the German Liberals a clear-cut front against any form of
antisemitic activity,[67] otherwise the Jewish voters in the seven constituencies
would boycott the elections to the Diet, with dire consequences for the German
candidates. Yet, as Mayer tersely puts it, "the ultimatum was duly despatched;
as foreseen, no success was achieved, and abstentions from voting did not take
place".[68]

In this context, Mayer again averred that collective abstention from voting
was not feasible. Moreover, he consoled himself and others by retrospectively
pointing to the fact that in years to come the ascent of the Social Democratic
Party was to free Moravian Jews from their dilemma.[69] Yet he never conceded
that for Jews in Austria proper the Social Democrats might have been a viable
political alternative. Instead, he continued to put his hopes on a turning of the
antisemitic tide with the eventual enactment of the general, equal and direct
male vote in Cisleithania. And, in fact, when this finally happened in 1907, the
sharp increase in Social Democratic voters put a temporary check to the
antisemitic Christian Social preponderancy.

In other words, Mayer, the ÖIU and Austrian Jewry as a whole, benefited
from the general political trend, without actively trying to influence it. For, in
effect, the *Union*'s campaigning for the election of some well-meaning but
powerless Social Reformers, like Julius Ofner, proved almost as futile as a total
abstention from voting.

IV. WAS THERE A VIABLE ALTERNATIVE?

It is perhaps of no mean significance that neither Mayer's memoranda to the
ÖIU, nor his own reminiscences, took into account the residual traces of Jewish
autonomous townships in Moravia,[70] or the beginnings of a new kind of Jewish
political autonomism, which was in 1895/1896 already on the ascent in Galicia,
in Bukovina, in Moravia and in Vienna itself. Jacob Kohn – himself a member of
the board of ÖIU (until his death in 1901) – had repeatedly agitated for the

---

[67]First reports: *Die Neuzeit*, 1895, pp. 226 ff. After that – continuously throughout 1896. Also
Österreichische Wochenschrift, Nos. 36, 37 *et al.* (1896). For background cf. J. Toury, 'Jewish Townships
in the German-Speaking Parts of the Austrian Empire. Before and after the Revolution of 1848/
1849', in *LBI Year Book XXVI* (1981), pp. 55 ff. and especially pp. 65–72.
[68]Mayer, *Ein jüdischer Kaufmann, op. cit.*, p. 320.
[69]*Ibid.*, p. 321.
[70]Toury, 'Jewish Townships . . .', *loc. cit.*

strengthening of autonomous Jewish participation in Austrian politics.[71] In 1896 he actually founded in Vienna a new *Jüdischer Volksverein*[72] with autonomistic tendencies (later also with its own weekly: *Jüdisches Volksblatt*). But above all, just at that point, notice had to be taken of the first public emergence of Dr. Theodor Herzl as a new Jewish leader, and – curiously enough – his debut before the Jewish public in Vienna was made possible by the invitation of Dr. Josef Grünfeld, the ÖIU's president who had repeatedly urged Herzl to appear as a guest-speaker at the *Union*, until he finally agreed to address the assembly of 7th November 1896, on 'Judentum'.[73]

Notwithstanding his central conception of a "Jewish State", Herzl in 1896 had not yet quite abandoned – as he was to do later – the possibility of "forming a Jewish Party" in Austria, "with the help of the government" (then under Count Badeni). The political dilemma of the *Union* is abundantly evident from the fact that Grünfeld, besides inviting Herzl to speak before the ÖIU, also tried to further his plans for founding a "Liberal-Conservative and anti-antisemitic daily" that would serve at the same time as an organ for government-policies and for national-Jewish interests – a curious plan indeed![74]

Thus a confusing situation developed at the meeting of the ÖIU in November 1896. Herzl – although speaking without a manuscript and alluding to his idea of a "Jewish State" only in passing – was accorded a standing ovation,[75] as if the majority of the attending public was ready to embrace at least his, and President Grünfeld's, hankering after a Jewish-political engagement of some kind or other.

Yet, in reality, the outcome of Herzl's speech before the *Union* proved to be nil. Typical was the reaction of Sigmund Mayer. He did not waste one word on the possibility of a political alternative with a Jewish-autonomous, not to speak of a Jewish-national component, and no other member of the ÖIU dared to express a deviating opinion. In short, Herzl's address fell on deaf ears and remained an insignificant episode in the history of the *Union*.

Mayer, too, did not achieve tangible results with his organisational innovations in the ÖIU – apart, perhaps, from the slow evolution of the Defence Committee towards a fully-fledged Defence Bureau.[76] But he seems to have bolstered morale to such an extent that even a prominent (and party-liberal) member of the *Union*, *Landesschulinspektor* Dr. Gustav Kohn, apostrophised him as "valued friend and leader (*Führer!*)", whose conceptions "came nearest to Fischhof's political programme."[77]

---

[71]Cf. Toury, *Die jüdische Presse, op. cit.*, pp. 96 f., and *idem*, 'Herzl's Newspaper. The Creation of "Die Welt" ', in *Zionism*, No. 2 (Autumn 1980), Tel-Aviv University, pp. 165 ff.

[72]Not to be confused with the *Israelitischer Wählerverein* of 1882 which called itself from 1895: *Politischer Volksverein*.

[73]*Mitteilungen*, No. 88 (November 1896), carried a full report.

[74]Toury, 'Herzl's Newspapers . . .', *loc. cit.*, based upon entries in Herzl's diary, dated 24th September, 22nd October, 24th October, 4th November, 10th November 1896.

[75]*Mitteilungen*, No. 88 (November 1896), and cf. Alex Bein, *Theodor Herzl*, Wien 1934, pp. 318 ff.

[76]Cf. Toury, 'Defense Activities . . .', *loc. cit.* The "Committee" was not established by Mayer's initiative. Only its development into a "Bureau" was his work.

[77]G. Kohn, referring to one of Mayer's programmatic speeches on 26th September 1896. *Mitteilungen*, No. 92 (March 1897), p. 3.

With this blandishment Gustav Kohn endorsed the latest formulation of Mayer's political directions to be implemented with regard to Social Reformers, Liberals and Democrats alike, "to treat the question of candidates no longer as a question of party-nuances but as a question of *personalities*" (September 1896).[78]

But just then a new problem arose: in the newly-established electoral class (*Fünfte Curie* = lowest tax bracket) the Liberal candidates had no chance at all, but the Social Democrats were expected to perform successfully against antisemitic candidates. How did the *Union* advise Jewish voters of this class? They were told by Kohn, with Mayer's consent, neither to oppose the new party nor to abstain from voting, as this might adversely affect the chances of the Left-wing parties. But they were not expressly directed to vote for the SD-candidates![79] Such pusillanimity was not at all appreciated by the Social Democrats.

Moreover, although the members of the *Union* could agree on such an ambiguous platform, they did not refrain from scrutinising before each new election the merits and personal politics of various Progressive candidates. This led to long and fruitless debates, often ending in a lame compromise. Nevertheless, the outer unity of the organisation was saved and Mayer's tactics even seemed to enhance the *Union*'s weight as a Liberal pressure group, that made – if at all – only slight concessions to the Social Democratic Party.

Whether such electioneering tactics did indeed further the Liberal cause or strengthen the Jewish defence-position against antisemitism, remains a moot point. In any case, they strengthened Mayer's own position within the *Union*, and Grünfeld had to pay the price of the changes wrought by time and circumstances, as well as by his own vacillations between the "national purposes of today's youth" and his Liberal and "cosmopolitan" inclinations.[80] Finally, on 29th April 1897, he formally resigned the presidency of the *Union*, "aware of the fact that I have not achieved all that was necessary (dissent was expressed)".[81]

The termination of Grünfeld's presidency may well give rise to the question whether there really existed an alternative course for him and his organisation in their Jewish-political affiliation. Was it within the scope of the ÖIU to choose a path towards Jewish Nationalism, either of a Zionist or an autonomist hue,* or were the members of the *Union* in any form predisposed to countenance a Jewish swing towards Social Democracy? True, there prevailed a general feeling of uneasiness with the political developments in Cisleithania, and especially with the Jewish position between the devil of antisemitism and the deep, deep aversion of almost all the other parties to take on the task of a *Judenschutztruppe*;

---

[78] *Ibid.*, p. 4. Italics are mine, J. T.

[79] *Ibid.*, pp. 5–6. Mayer's attitude is recapitulated here in the words of Dr. Gustav Kohn, who as a government-official was not then in the running for a political candidacy or a place on the board of the ÖIU.

[80] *Mitteilungen*, No. 90 (January 1897), p. 8. Grünfeld's own words.

[81] *Mitteilungen*, No. 96 (May 1897), on the general meeting of 29th April 1897, p. 11.

*On the emergence of Jewish Nationalism see the following essay by Robert S. Wistrich, 'The Clash of Ideologies in Jewish Vienna (1880–1918). The Strange Odyssey of Nathan Birnbaum', in the current volume of the Year Book – (Ed.).

there were even individual members who personally chose this or that departure from the directives laid down by Sigmund Mayer and were either embracing Jewish-National or Socialist creeds, or practising demonstrative political abstention; but a representative organisation which even kept its hand at the helm of the *Kultusgemeinde*, simply could not advocate a course that might be interpreted as anti-loyalist, unpatriotic, or even revolutionary – a course that was spurned by the vast majority as unworthy of an orderly Jewish *Bürger* who had attained a standard of living a notch above the *petit-bourgeois* level of barely making both ends meet. These elements endorsed Sigmund Mayer's concept of an *ad hoc* connection with convenient candidates of the *Sozialpolitiker* as the only acceptable way out of their political quandary. Whether this acceptance was a wise choice is easy to deny after what happened later; but neither Mayer, nor most of his contemporaries, was clairvoyant and ought not to be judged by mere hindsight.

V. SIEGFRIED FLEISCHER, THE NEW SECRETARY GENERAL, AND HIS PRESIDENTS

Yet Mayer did not officially appear as Grünfeld's successor in the chair of the *Union*. For the time being he had to content himself with the vice-presidency – as had the exponent of autonomism on the board, Jacob Kohn. The presidency went – for the first time in the history of the *Union* – to a scion of the upper (though not yet the uppermost) echelons of Viennese Jewry: to *Kaiserlicher Rat* Wilhelm Anninger (1897–1900).[82]

Anninger did not enjoy the best of health; Kohn now concentrated his activities on the "*Jüdischer Volksverein*"[83] and so the main task of organising the *Union*'s activities devolved, naturally enough, on Sigmund Mayer. But just then, when the establishment of the Defence Bureau on 15th December 1897 opened up new channels of activity, his initiative seems to have been exhausted. His intellect was no longer open to new political concepts and the real leadership of the *Union* gradually passed into the hands of the Secretary General, Siegfried Fleischer. A journalist by profession, Fleischer had been the acting director of the Defence Bureau since 1898, and he soon supplanted the former secretary of the *Union*, Josef Fuchs, in all the other functions of general administration – Fuchs being "promoted" to the Secretariat of the Theological Seminary and appointed *Beirat* in the *Union*.[84]

Even Fuchs's last remaining activity in the ÖIU, the editorship of the

---

[82]*Ibid.*, pp. 12 f.

[83]Cf. above text and note 72.

[84]*Mitteilungen*, No. 114 (November 1899). This "Beirat" quickly turned into a place of honourable retirement for worthy dignitaries, like the founding members S. Zins, Dr. J. S. Bloch and Dr. Josef Grünfeld. One might call it a council of discarded alternatives: Zins's culturally-orientated minimalism; Bloch's one-man counter-attack against antisemitism in the law-courts, in his *Wochenschrift* and in the *Reichsrat*; and Grünfeld's conciliatory manoeuvring between different Jewish political approaches, including Zionism, which was ultimately superseded by Mayer's and Fleischer's alliances with Social Reformers of scant Jewish leanings.

Mitteilungen, was finally taken over by Siegfried Fleischer on the 1st of January. Under his aegis the bulletin turned into a substantial and quite regular monthly: *Monatsschrift der Österreichisch-Israelitischen Union* (1901–1917).

These and similar innovations were the outcome of a new spirit, furthered by the second *Kaiserlicher Rat* in the chair of the ÖIU, Adolf Ruzička, who had been acclaimed president on 28th April 1900 on the insistence of his ailing predecessor, Wilhelm Anninger. Sigmund Mayer – purportedly declining the offer of becoming president[85] – continued to act as vice-chairman, in close co-operation with Fleischer, the Secretary General.

During Ruzička's short term of office (April 1900–October 1901) a significant change occurred in the character of the ÖIU and it is a moot point who initiated it: the new president or the now well-established secretary, Fleischer. The official chronicle of the *Union* has it that "President Ruzička pointed out" the necessary steps in the development of the ÖIU "from a local Viennese club to a *Reichsverein*", at least in the "whole of Cisleithania". One of his reasons was the fact that the *Union*'s Defence Bureau was being used by an ever-growing number of individuals and communities throughout Cisleithania and the expenses for legal aid to be defrayed by the ÖIU increased commensurably. Therefore, it became an obvious necessity to organise "the Jewish middle classes" everywhere, because – as Fleischer put it – the upper echelons "were found wanting".[86]

Possibly it was, indeed, Ruzička's reasoning that stood behind the new venture of propagandising the *Union* outside the capital and of organising local sympathisers and local wardens (*Vertrauensmänner*) throughout Austria, Bohemia and Moravia; but no proper autonomous chapters were founded in the provinces. It may be argued that an earlier failure of Mayer to unite Galician Jewry (1898) in a common umbrella-organisation[87] had given rise to that slacker form of contact with provincial communities, which was now being established by Ruzička, Mayer and Fleischer. In any case, the day-to-day labours of travelling, speech-making and attending conferences were all Fleischer's task. Between 1900 and 1910 he appeared and lectured in more than 500 places and organised circles and wardens in more than 400 communities, bringing the total membership of the *Union* up to 7,000 and more.[88] During this period, the Defence Bureau, which was also under Fleischer's personal supervision, handled more than 5,000 cases – although not always with resounding results.

Although the membership of the *Union* did not compare favourably with the development of the *Centralverein deutscher Staatsbürger jüdischen Glaubens* in Germany, its Defence Bureau scored some important successes,[89] possibly even more than the *Centralverein*. In any case, the ÖIU became Austria's largest and foremost Jewish organsiation – at least until 1907, when the upsurge of Jewish

---

[85]Mayer, *Ein jüdischer Kaufmann, op. cit.*, p. 339.

[86]*Monatsschrift*, No. 4 (1910), pp. 22 f.

[87]Cf. Mayer, *Ein jüdischer Kaufmann, op. cit.*, pp. 326 ff., where he also gives details of his activities as chairman of the "Industrial Committee" for Galicia, whose achievements were slight.

[88]*Monatsschrift*, No. 4 (1910), p. 23.

[89]Cf. Toury, 'Defense Activities . . .', *loc. cit.*

Nationalism in Vienna and Galicia* consecutively weakened the *Union*'s claim to the role of being the sole representative of Cisleithanian Jewry.

Indeed, the question of Jewish Nationalism did much to hamper the growth of the ÖIU, for Fleischer belonged to the Liberal camp and was openly antagonistic to Zionism and autonomism. Mayer shared the same views and firmly stood behind Fleischer's policies. In his position as vice-chairman he played an important part in shaping the *Union*'s progressively anti-Zionist course. Consequently, the first spectacular success of the Jewish-National forces in the elections of 1907, when four National-Jewish members were returned to the *Reichsrat*, simultaneously implied a serious setback to the ÖIU and its leading ideologies.

Yet even Jewish Nationalists had to acknowledge the work of the Defence Bureau, which successfully tackled a number of cases involving the infringement of Jewish rights in Galicia. In short, the party-politics of the *Union* did nothing to enhance its standing within the Jewish and the general political scene, whereas its Defence Bureau was everywhere regarded as, at the least, serviceable and useful.

However, immediately after the retirement of Ružička and after Maximilian Paul-Schiff was unanimously declared his successor to the presidency in October 1901, there began a period of three years when a reconciliation between the contending Jewish camps might still have been possible. Paul-Schiff, a well-to-do gentleman of leisure and cultural leanings, was the first of the *Union*'s presidents who represented the uppermost Jewish circles of Vienna. He seems to have been brought into the ÖIU through personal contacts with Mayer, both of them having sponsored the *Hilfsverein für die notleidende jüdische Bevölkerung Galiziens.*[90] Paul-Schiff apparently acted from the highest of motives and was intent upon broadening and deepening the scope of the *Union*'s activities. His attitude to Jewish concerns might best be described in a term borrowed from later times: "*gesamtjüdisch*". He himself had first outlined this orientation when he accepted the presidency of the Union, on the 5th October 1901:

> "I have accepted your call, because I see the *Union* . . . as the first and sole representative of the political rights of the Jews in Austria . . . Also the Zionists, and even the most rabid ones, have a place in our midst, as well as all the other Jews . . . Every political or religious conviction . . . has to find its place in our corporation."[91]

This declaration may be interpreted as a return to Bloch's erstwhile conception of a Jewish civic pressure lobby, engaging primarily in anti-antisemitic, group-conscious and public-spirited actions. All the known activities of Paul-Schiff as head of the ÖIU point in this direction. As an illustration one might mention his connection with a man of similar convictions, the banker Heinrich Meyer-Cohn from Berlin, whom he invited to address one of the *Union*'s meetings in 1902. Meyer-Cohn was a philanthropist, one of the early sponsors of Herzl, but no party-Zionist. In his lecture on the 'Rights and Duties of the Austrian

---

*See the essay by Robert S. Wistrich referred to in the previous editorial note – (Ed.).
[90]Mayer, *Ein jüdischer Kaufmann, op. it.*, p. 341, and *Monatsschrift*, No. 4 (1910), pp. 25 f.
[91]Reported verbatim in *Monatsschrift*, No. 4 (1910), p. 25.

Jacob Toury

Jews' he pointed out that a Jewish-orientated electioneering-organisation
("*Jüdische Wahlorganisation*") ought to take active steps in order to ensure the
candidacy of fitting personalities in precincts with a predominantly Jewish
electorate[92] – a thesis that every one of the members could accept, as long as no
actual candidates presented themselves for endorsement, thus arousing personal
and ideological controversies.

In any case, it has to be stressed that the centre of Paul-Schiff's interests was
less in party-politics than in a Jewish policy of legal defence, of *Rechtsschutz*. In
this spirit, the statutes of the ÖIU were revised in 1902 and the main aim of the
Union was defined as . . . "protecting the general and political rights of the Jews
and aiding those who belong to Judaism in utilising those rights".[93]

Notwithstanding Paul-Schiff's intentions, the spirit of general Jewish reconciliation did not prevail in the *Union* and the squabble between general-political
and Jewish-political factions continued unabated. The polarisation between
anti-Zionists and Zionists, between autonomists and Austro-Germans, grew in
bitterness and was one factor which also severely impeded the numerical growth
of the *Union*. The ensuing chronic inadequacy of the ÖIU's coffers, which always
lacked funds for large-scale actions,[94] seriously interfered even with day-to-day
defence work.

One reason for this was given by Paul-Schiff himself, when he submitted that

> "the rich Jews regarded the activity and the necessity of our organisation as superfluous, and
> this is the more regrettable because of the fact that it is the poorer Jews who have to bear the
> brunt of antisemitism, which has mainly been occasioned by their well-to-do co-religio-
> nists".[95]

Thus, in spite of his dedicated work, Paul-Schiff's presidency does not seem to
have been a period of outstanding success for the *Union*. Nevertheless, even
Sigmund Mayer, who possibly felt himself overshadowed, credited Paul-Schiff
with three important achievements:[96] he reopened public discussions of the
Hilsner Affair, fearlessly branding it as "Justizmord"[97] and sponsoring the
publication of a scientific edition of all the materials pertaining to the trial;[98] he
consistently fought against every form of discrimination, even in the armed
services (non-promotion of Jewish army-physicians); and he finally led a
successful campaign against the Galician financial authorities, who had tried to
expropriate small Jewish salt-retailers in favour of larger Christian co-opera-

[92]*Ibid.*, No. 4 (1902), p. 11.
[93]*Ibid.*, No. 4 (1910), p. 8.
[94]According to *Monatsschrift*, No. 4 (1911), p. 12, the *Union*'s budget for the 25th year (1910) balanced
at less than 40,000 *Kronen*, which were about 34,000 *Mark*, or about £1,700, not including a reserve
of about 7,000 *Kronen* for specific, but unspecified, defence activities. Currency values kindly
supplied by my colleague and friend Professor N. T. Gross of the Hebrew University, Jerusalem.
For comparison's sake one may take a random budget of the *Centralverein* in Berlin, which already in
its fifth year (1897) had topped the figures given for the ÖIU, with a balance of more than 40,000
Mark and a reserve fund of 21,000 *Mark* (*Im deutschen Reich*, January 1896, p. 54).
[95]Reported in *Monatsschrift*, No. 4 (1910), p. 26.
[96]Mayer, *Ein jüdischer Kaufmann, op. cit.*, p. 341.
[97]This expression is reported in *Monatsschrift*, No. 4 (1910), p. 26.
[98]Under the editorship of Arthur Nussbaum, *Der Polnaer Ritualmordprozess*, Berlin 1906.

tives. "And then" writes Mayer in his next sentence,[99] slurring over the reasons for Paul-Schiff's sudden step, "in 1904 he tendered his resignation". And thus, Sigmund Mayer himself was finally elected first chairman.

Paul-Schiff's capitulation seems to have expressed a loss of confidence in his programme, or at least in the possibility of its realisation within the *Union*. Now the way was finally cleared for the presidency of the 73 year-old Sigmund Mayer, whose firmness behind the scenes had in fact led the *Union* for the last five to six years – with the able assistance of S. Fleischer, the Secretary General. But now, in the president's chair, his firmness tended to turn to stubbornness, and Fleischer, his main executive, had always lacked intellectual flexibility. The *Union*'s last opportunity of becoming a broad-based, or even common, denominator for Austrian Jewry had been lost. From now on, the ÖIU as a leading elite organisation in the Jewish community of Vienna, proudly rested on the laurels of having arrived at the inner core of the Austro-German Jewish-Liberal establishment.

Although the Defence Bureau continued its activities with some positive results, as well as with several rebuffs,[100] neither Fleischer nor Mayer himself could marshal many positive deeds with which to enhance the period of Mayer's presidency.[101] This became evident at the 25th anniversary of the *Union* in 1910, which was duly extolled by Fleischer, without overmuch self-criticism.[102] Nothing changed from there on to the outbreak of the First World War: stagnation was the enduring lot of the *Union*.

This holds true also for the fifteen years of the ill-fated First Austrian Republic. Still more questionable was the *Union*'s behaviour in the era of the *Ständestaat* (1934–1938) and up to Hitler's annexation of Austria in March 1938. But that belongs, as the saying goes, to a separate chapter.

---

[99]Mayer, *Ein jüdischer Kaufmann*, *op. cit.*, p. 341.

[100]Toury, 'Defense Activities . . .', *loc. cit.*

[101]Fleischer in his review '25 Jahre ÖIU' in *Monatsschrift*, No. 4 (1910), pp. 3–31, and Mayer himself in his reminiscences *Die Wiener Juden, 1700–1900*, Berlin 1917, pp. 473 f. And cf. also Mayer's earlier account in *Ein jüdischer Kaufmann*, *op. cit.*, pp. 341 f.

[102]Fleischer, '25 Jahre ÖIU', *loc. cit.* Even in 1919 Fleischer was still regarded as the leading personality in Jewish Vienna. Politisches Archiv des Auswärtigen Amtes, Bonn (Kent II, p. 77), Pol. III, Nachlass Sobernheim, Jüdische Angelegenheiten 1918/1919.

The Clash of Ideologies in Jewish Vienna (1880–1918)
The Strange Odyssey of Nathan Birnbaum

BY ROBERT S. WISTRICH

Nathan Birnbaum (1864–1937), the founder of Austrian Zionism, was born in Vienna to parents who came from a West Galician and Hungarian religious background. His father, the son of Polish *Hasidim*, had arrived in Vienna from Cracow with the first wave of Galician immigration. On his mother's side, Nathan Birnbaum was descended from an old and distinguished North Hungarian rabbinical family whose roots can be traced back to the medieval scholar Rashi.[1] Educated in Viennese elementary and secondary schools, Birnbaum soon became estranged from his moderately Orthodox family background though he did not take the assimilationist path typical of most of his adolescent contemporaries.[2] Already at secondary school, in spite of the tremendous influence of German culture, Birnbaum shocked his peers by expressing the conviction that Austrian Jews were not German but belonged to a distinct nation whose destiny must lead it to regain the land of Palestine.[3] Building on the early training in Jewish studies he had received at home, Birnbaum steeped himself in Hebrew journals, especially Perez Smolenskin's *Hashahar* and avidly devoured literature about the Jewish national movement in Eastern Europe.[4] The firm belief that the Jews were an ethnic entity with a unique history and culture tied to *Erez Israel* prompted the eighteen-year-old law

[1] Nathan Birnbaum, *The Bridge. Selected Essays*, London 1956, p. 11.
[2] Nathan Birnbaum, 'Gegen die Selbstverständlichkeit', in Ludwig Rosenhek (ed.), *Festschrift zur Feier des 100. Semesters der akademischen Verbindung Kadimah*, Mödling 1933, p. 29 and 'Iberblik iber Mayn Lebn', *Yubileum-Bukh*, Warsaw 1925 (in Yiddish), p. 10. Also Julius H. Schoeps, 'Modern Heirs of the Maccabees. The Beginnings of the Vienna Kadimah, 1882–1897', in *LBI Year Book XXVII* (1982), pp. 155–170.
[3] 'Gegen die Selbstverständlichkeit', *loc. cit.* Writing on 19th April 1932, Birnbaum recalled that in his school days in Vienna it was unthinkable for any young Jew "sich nicht der deutschen Nation zuzuzählen". According to this autobiographical account his Jewish Nationalist revelation came in 1879/1880 (in the fifth or sixth form). In a conversation with a friend he insisted that Jews should declare themselves as members of the Jewish nation with their own unique past and look to Palestine for their future.
[4] Joseph Klausner, *Historiya shel hasifrut haivrit hahadasha*, Tel-Aviv 1955, 5, pp. 14–231; E. Silberschlag, *From Renaissance to Renaissance*, New York 1973, pp. 145 ff. Emmanuel S. Goldsmith, 'Nathan Birnbaum', in *Architects of Yiddishism at the Beginning of the Twentieth Century. A Study in Jewish Cultural History*, London–New York 1976, p. 100, suggests that "the various phases of Birnbaum's ideological odyssey, including his Diaspora Nationalism, may be traced to aspects of Smolenskin's

201

student, then in his first year at the University of Vienna, to found *Kadimah*, together with Reuben Bierer from East Galicia and Moritz Schnirer who came from Bucharest.[5]

In 1884, the twenty-year-old Birnbaum issued his first publication, a pamphlet provocatively entitled *Die Assimilationssucht. Ein Wort an die sogenannten Deutschen, Slaven, Magyaren etc. mosaischer Confession. Von einem Studenten jüdischer Nationalität*. It was the beginning of what was to be a remarkably volatile career as a publicist, editor and agitator which in its metamorphoses spanned all the major ideological trends in *fin-de-siècle* Central-European Jewish life. For nearly fifteen years Birnbaum was the leading Zionist ideologue in Austria-Hungary, the founder and editor of the first Jewish Nationalist journal in the German language, *Selbst-Emancipation!*, where he coined the term "Zionism".[6] After disagreements with Herzl which caused him to leave the newly-created Zionist organisation, he became for a while a protagonist of "cultural" as against "political" Zionism, turning increasingly after 1900 to an autonomist philosophy of "Diaspora Nationalism". His advocacy of the national autonomy principle duly led him to develop a full-blown ideology of Yiddishism and in 1908 he was the initiator and architect of the first Yiddish Language Conference at Czernowitz (Bukovina), where he lived for the next three years.[7] Finally, in the closing years before the First World War, Birnbaum moved closer to Jewish religious tradition, eventually becoming a practising Orthodox Jew and in 1919, the first General Secretary of the *Agudat Israel* World Organisation.[8]

writings". Goldsmith plausibly claims that Birnbaum was also influenced by Hebrew Radical-Socialist writers of the 1870s like Aron Lieberman (his periodical *Ha-emet* was published in Vienna in 1877), Morris Winchevsky and Moses Leib Lilienblum, as well as Smolenskin and Pinsker.

[5]'Gegen die Selbstverständlichkeit', *loc. cit.*, p. 30. Birnbaum recalled how difficult it was in the early 1880s to win over the "Westerners" in Vienna to *Kadimah* since "they had no living *Volksjudentum*" to serve as their inspiration. The "Easterners", on the other hand, came "aus einem lebendigen jüdischen Volksmilieu . . . , wo es auch schon eine Bewegung der Selbstemanzipation oder der nationalen Wiedergeburt gab . . ."

[6]G. Kressel, 'Selbst-Emancipation', *Shivat Zion*, IV (1956), pp. 58–62. The first issue of *Selbst-Emancipation!* appeared on the day Perez Smolenskin died, 1st February 1885, with an appeal to brother Jews (*Stammesgenossen*) that began: "Die Lebenskraft, die im Körper des jüdischen Volkes wohnt, ist unvergänglich, unzerstörbar! Weder das hasserfüllte Walten des wildesten Rassenhasses, der von aussen an unserem Untergange arbeitet, noch der innen fressende Wurm des nationalen Lebensüberdrusses werden je im Stande sein, die zähe Natur unseres ewigen Volkes zu erschüttern!" The second issue on 16th February 1885 carried a glowing tribute to Smolenskin which *inter alia* deplored the fact that "In Wien selbst, wo der grosse Todte lebte und seine Zeitschrift herausgab, da war er freilich verhältnismässig wenig bekannt . . ."

[7]See 'Eröffnungsrede auf der jüdischen Sprachkonferenz in Czernowitz', gehalten am 30. August 1908 (retranslated by Birnbaum himself from the original Yiddish version) in Dr. Nathan Birnbaum, *Ausgewählte Schriften zur Jüdischen Frage*, vol. II, Czernowitz 1910, pp. 41–45. See also in the same collection 'Der "Jargon"', *ibid.*, pp. 46–51 and 'Zum Sprachenstreit. Entgegnung an Achad Ha'am', *ibid.*, pp. 52–74.

[8]*Vom Sinn des Judentums. Ein Sammelbuch zu Ehren Nathan Birnbaums*, A. E. Kaplan und Max Landau (hrsg.), Frankfurt a. Main 1924, documents this final metamorphosis or "return" to Judaism. See especially Samuel Rappaport, 'Der Gottsucher', *ibid.*, pp. 34–43 and Joseph Carlebach, 'Stil und Persönlichkeit', pp. 70 f. The latter regards Birnbaum as the embodiment of "einen grandiosen Kampf gegen den neujüdischen Intellektualismus, gegen die jüdische 'Aufklärungsperiode' . . .", p. 70. Max Landau, 'Nathan Birnbaum und das Jüdische Volk', *ibid.*, p. 83 also transforms the later Birnbaum into a crusader against "die maskilische Mentalität im jüdischen Volke" and its scornful arrogance towards the true spiritual values of Judaism.

This extraordinary personal odyssey, bewildering in its sharp intellectual turns, marked off Birnbaum from most of his Austrian-Jewish contemporaries. Like another prominent ideological nomad of his day, the Russian-Jewish revolutionary Chaim Zhitlovsky, Birnbaum seemed almost predestined by such inconsistency to become a forgotten figure.[9] Yet his sudden shifts, doubts, hesitations and contradictions were in many ways a faithful mirror of the cultural dilemmas confronting Austrian Jewry. His individualism, his originality and breadth of intellectual interests, the prophetic strain in his writings and the intensity of his commitment to Jewish life gave him a special position in the eyes of contemporaries which even his difficult temperament and relative lack of political *savoir-faire* could not entirely erase. Birnbaum remains therefore, in some respects, a particularly sensitive barometer for the era of transition in which he lived, crystallising in his various mutations many of the central problems of the Jewish National renaissance in Central and Eastern Europe.

On one issue at least Birnbaum did remain reasonably consistent to the concepts he first enunciated in 1884 as a twenty-year-old student. From the outset of his career as a young Zionist until its close as a *Ba'al tschuva* he remained adamantly opposed to the assimilation of Jews into the surrounding society and their adaptation to the practices of peoples whom he considered culturally inferior.[10] In *Die Assimilationssucht*, Birnbaum had denounced in ringing tones the "suicidal" policy of Jewish Germanisation, Magyarisation and Slavicisation which was based in his view on self-deception, self-abnegation and an unnatural desire for self-dissolution.[11] This "mania for amalgamation" with surrounding peoples deliberately sought to ignore the national character and special features of a 4000-year-old Jewish history;[12] it was a modern form of "Hellenisation" in which the servile imitation of alien cultures had come to assume pathological proportions and had directly provoked the rise of political antisemitism in Central Europe.[13] According to Birnbaum, antisemites justifiably saw in this Jewish "mimicry" and self-dissolution a clear sign of moral inferiority and the admission of weakness rather than an expression of equality.

The only antidote for post-emancipation Jewry against the antisemitic virus, so Birnbaum argued, (following Leon Pinsker and Isaak Rülf) lay in the reawakening of national consciousness and in encouraging Zionist colonisation in *Erez Israel*. Jews must seek national equality as a group in order to regain their

[9]On Chaim Zhitlovsky, see Jonathan Frankel, *Prophecy and Politics. Russian Jews, Nationalism and Socialism 1881–1917*, Cambridge 1982, pp. 258–287. Like Zhitlovsky, Birnbaum could be described as a creature of transient mood who remained loyal to certain key concepts (anti-assimilationism, belief in the eternal and indestructible character of the Jewish spirit, in the uniqueness of the Jewish nation etc.), but applied them to reality in sharply different ways at different periods. Birnbaum was however at no time a revolutionary Socialist in spite of his early sympathy for aspects of Socialist teaching.
[10]David Vital, *The Origins of Zionism*, Oxford 1975, p. 223.
[11]Nathan Birnbaum, *Die Assimilationssucht . . ., op. cit.*, Wien 1882 or 1883, pp. 8–9. In his obituary for Perez Smolenskin, *Selbst-Emancipation!*, I, Nr. 2 (16th February 1885), p. 1, Birnbaum again attacked "die ganze Erbärmlichkeit der assimilatorischen Selbstmordtheorie", a formulation to which he was to return through countless variations.
[12]*Die Assimilationssucht . . . , op. cit.*, p. 6.
[13]*Ibid.*, pp. 9–11.

inner balance and the respect of other nations.[14] Even beyond the issue of self-humiliation, implicit in a policy of assimilation within nations that rejected them, Jews should recognise that they had never been merely a "religious community" or an "amorphous mass of individuals", but that they were historically a nation with a heroic past and the most sublime intellectual creations to its name. They had the closest physical and spiritual ties with *Erez Israel*, the return to which had been, for 1,800 years, the focus of their prayers and longings. The love of the Holy Land must now assume a more activist and consciously national character for it represented their only salvation as "a place of refuge for those weary of exile and a pillar in the moral and material sense for those who will remain in exile".[15]

Once the Jews had regained their fatherland "contemporary Jew-hatred in its specific form would disappear from the earth and the whole of Jewry breathe again after a long and fearful millennial nightmare".[16] To strengthen this rather optimistic youthful scenario, Birnbaum pointed in particular to the establishment of new Jewish settlements in Palestine, the growing number of Jewish national associations, clubs and periodicals in the Diaspora and the revival of the Hebrew language in Eastern Europe.[17] What was lacking was, above all, a common national will to promote large-scale action on behalf of Jewish territorial concentration and agricultural settlement in the Holy Land.

Birnbaum was to devote the next decade and a half of his doctrinal and propagandist activity in Central and Eastern Europe to the promotion of this Palestinocentric credo. Only a territorial centre in *Erez Israel*, he continued to argue, would cure Jewry of the sickness of exile and dispersion, provide a secure home for the "superfluous" Jews of Europe and bring to an end the plague of antisemitism. This territorial centre would not run counter to the social, economic and political interests of Diaspora Jewry, but, on the contrary, would increase the loyalty of those who remained behind to their countries of domicile, by reinforcing their self-confidence.

In an address delivered at a discussion evening sponsored by the *Admath Yeshurun* Association in Vienna on 23rd January 1892, Birnbaum, expounding on "The Principles of Zionism", explained:

> "We are a people without a land and a nation without soil, and that is our misfortune. Our best friends cannot help us when we are thrashed somewhere, for there is no interfering in the internal affairs of another state. We ourselves are even more impotent and the most that we can do is to stand at the border of the state in question and await our persecuted and expelled brethren with old and new clothes, with soup, coffee and boat tickets to America. This cannot suffice forever. A territory must be found which is truly ours, even if it is under the most modest title of international law. This land must become the focal point of our people which is

---

[14]*Ibid.*, p. 14.

[15]*Ibid.*, also N. Birnbaum, 'Die Ziele der jüdisch-nationalen Bestrebungen', Pt. II, *Selbst-Emancipation!*, III, Nr. 4, (16th May 1890), pp. 1–2.

[16]*Die Assimilationssucht* . . . , *op. cit.*, p. 15.

[17]*Ibid.*, Birnbaum already considered in 1884 that the diffusion of Hebrew was such in Eastern Europe "dass ihr zu einer vollständigen Nationalsprache sehr wenig fehlt und dies Wenige würde und müsste eine territoriale Concentration alsbald nachholen. Ein von Hebräern bevölkertes Judäa schüfe auch ein von Juden gesprochenes Hebräisch".

scattered all over the earth – a focal point and support. All of our fellow Jews (*Stammesgenossen*), whether they go to that country or not, should enjoy its protection; some will benefit from the material gain of a home for themselves, others from the moral gain of a homeland (*Heimat*) for the people as a whole. With a Jewish fatherland the position of Israel among the nations would at once become a normal and respected one, based on the principle of mutuality."[18]

Significantly, in his concluding remarks, refuting certain charges constantly levelled by Jewish critics at Zionism, Birnbaum emphasised that the new movement was not "unpatriotic" any more than it was "reactionary", "anti-religious", "dangerous" or "impracticable". On the contrary, Zionism would reinforce feelings of local patriotism which Jews already felt for their adoptive fatherlands.

"A person who sincerely loves his people has truer patriotic feelings (*Vaterlandsgefühl*) than an opportunist. He who can abandon his people lightheartedly is not reliable. The Zionist seeks a fatherland for the whole Israelite people (*das ganze israelitische Volk*) because the facts demand it: but he also loves the fatherland in which he was born, because he lives in it and is more or less protected. The interests of his particular fatherland and of the longed-for fatherland of the Jewish nation do not collide in any way."[19]

Birnbaum's Zionism in these early years found its expression mainly through the Jewish Nationalist student fraternity, *Kadimah*, and above all in his editorship of *Selbst-Emancipation!*, the first Zionist journal in any West European language, dedicated to "the national, social and political interests of the Jewish people".[20] Always lacking money and hampered by a small circulation, the journal stopped publication after fifteen months; renewed in 1890, it continued for four more years in Vienna, then moved to Berlin for publication purposes under a new name (*Jüdische Volkszeitung*), though still edited by Birnbaum, who remained in the Austrian capital. *Selbst-Emancipation!* took up most of Birnbaum's energy at this time since he served not only as editor but also as publisher, chief contributor, bookkeeper, typist, and office boy. During the first years it was published at his own expense and at one point his mother even sold her kitchen-ware shop to help cover the costs. Several times Birnbaum was on the point of bankruptcy and fellow-students would bring him bread to keep him from starving.[21]

Poverty would continue to be the base of his existence. Though he had qualified as a lawyer from the University of Vienna in 1885, Birnbaum never succeeded in law practice, partly because his pronounced "Semitic" features discouraged clients in the increasingly virulently anti-Jewish atmosphere of the Habsburg metropolis. Abandoning a legal career, Birnbaum decided in the early 1890s to devote himself wholly to journalism and Zionist affairs, adopting the pen name Mathias Acher, to symbolise his radical break with religious tradition

[18]'Die Prinzipien des Zionismus', *Selbst-Emancipation!*, V, Nr. 5 (4th March 1892), p. 53. Birnbaum's important lecture was published in three issues on 1st February, 4th March and 7th April 1892.

[19]*Ibid.*, p. 58.

[20]Kressel, *loc. cit.*, pp. 79–89 for the history of the journal and its difficulties.

[21]Josef Fraenkel, 'Halifat Hamikhtavim Beyn Nathan Birnbaum leveyn Siegmund Werner', *Shivat Zion*, 2–3, Jerusalem 1953, p. 275 (in Hebrew). Also by the same author, 'Mathias Acher's Fight for the Crown of Zion', *Jewish Social Studies*, April 1954, pp. 115–134.

and the espousal of a new synthesis between European modernism, Jewish Nationalism and a moderate Socialism.[22]

Selbst-Emancipation! throughout its chequered existence had been devoted to the didactic propagation of the idea of Jewish national renaissance. In the early issues the focus had been on the challenge of antisemitism and on a war against all forms of assimilationism within the Jewish camp.[23] Birnbaum consistently contended that the efforts of Liberalism to neutralise the "Jewish Question" and to dilute the "national, social and religious opposition between the Jews and Europeans" were futile.[24] Not only a millennial Jewish history but also the natural sciences and political economy, in his opinion, supported the hypothesis of deeply-rooted racial differences.[25] Birnbaum certainly believed in a Jewish race – indeed race was to him in these early years perhaps the central concept of human existence, responsible for creating the *Volksgeist* (folk-spirit) with all its national peculiarities. For example, just as the "Aryan" race-spirit created the *Nibelungenlied*, so in Birnbaum's view has the ancient Jewish *Volksgeist* brought forth the Bible.[26]

This Zionist race-thinking was clearly founded on the biological concepts that had become fashionable in an age of positivism, which naturally favoured ideologies based on the natural sciences. It sought to ground Jewish identity in secular and "scientific" concepts which were based neither on the religious heritage nor on the liberal abstract Judaism of the post-emancipation era.

The fact that modern antisemites increasingly exploited racial arguments did not deter Zionist ideologues like Birnbaum from using similar notions to refute their claims even though they were accused by Liberal Jews of thereby encouraging antisemitism. Birnbaum, however, argued that it was the Jewish assimilationist refusal to recognise a primordial national individuality which had incited and intensified *völkisch* antisemitism.[27] The undignified effort to deju-

---

[22]Mathias Acher was the pseudonym taken by Birnbaum in 1891 at a Seder evening of the *Kadimah* students' fraternity in Vienna where he made a speech denouncing the *Yavneh* tradition. If the name Mathias re-called the Hasmonean uprising against Hellenism, Acher was the Hebrew name meaning "a stranger" given by the rabbis to an admired sage and heretic in the Jewish tradition, Elisha ben Avuya, a second-century scholar who became an adherent of the gnostic dualism derived from Greek philosophy and who later renounced Judaism. This combination of zealotry, idealism and heresy revealed in the choice of pen-name seems to capture appropriately the psychological ambivalence behind many of Birnbaum's ideological positions.

[23]See 'Antisemiten, Assimilanten, Nationaljuden', *Selbst-Emancipation!*, I, Nr. 5, (3rd April 1885), pp. 2–3, with its sharp attack on the Schönerer movement ". . . jene unsaubere, fanatisch blinde Partei", for distorting the inextinguishable "racial differences between Jews and the Aryan peoples" in such a way as to defame an entire nation.

[24]'Ist Wahrhaftigkeit Zugeständnis?', *ibid.*, II, Nr. 5 (2nd March 1886), pp. 1–2. See also other early articles by Birnbaum which relate to this theme: 'Verjudung-Entjudung', *ibid.*, I, Nr. 7 (1st May 1885); 'Der Judenhass', II. Nr. 1 (1st January 1886); 'Antisemitismus und Nationaljudenthum', III, Nr. 2 (16th April 1890).

[25]'Nationalität und Sprache', *ibid.*, II, Nr. 4 (16th February 1886). In this article Birnbaum claimed: "Vermöge des Rassengegensatzes denkt und fühlt auch der Deutsche oder Slave anders als der Jude."

[26]'Volkstum und Weltbürgertum', *ibid.*, III, Nr. 2 (16th April 1890), p. 1, where Birnbaum postulates an unbridgeable chasm between the Jewish and German *Volksgeist*.

[27]'Ist Wahrhaftigkeit Zugeständnis?', *loc. cit.*, pp. 1–2.

daise Jewry in order to achieve social acceptance at all costs had merely exacerbated an irresolvable national antipathy.[28] The vain attempt to suppress Jewish national and messianic hopes, to stifle Jewish self-criticism and reject antisemitism *tout court*, without considering that it might reflect (though in vulgar, distorted form) certain realities of Jewish life in Europe, was in his opinion harmful.[29] Recalling in 1902 his earlier feelings about antisemitism, Birnbaum made the following rather revealing confession:

> "There was a time when I regarded Jew-hatred with a certain benevolence. I observed its activity with a kind of pleasure, I was almost happy with its successes and progress. If I did not always express these feelings freely, this was only out of a kind of tactical discretion which I had to impose upon myself so as not to offend too much those whom I wished to win over to Jewish national aspirations. How gladly I would have rather vexed them with the whole truth by calling out: the wicked antisemitic rascals are completely right, their insults you might prefer not to listen to and they are certainly inappropriate in their absolute form, yet they are but the stammering expressions of a very correct feeling that an unbridgeable gulf yawns between Jews and non-Jews – that both have antithetical ideals of beauty and morality. They are right and we are right and it is good that they storm so. At least we now know where we are."[30]

As this and other passages in his early writings make clear, Birnbaum did see a certain justification in Central European antisemitism, looked at from a Zionist standpoint. Precisely because classical Zionism aimed at the physical and moral regeneration of the *Golusjude*, it contained from the beginning a powerful element of self-criticism. This sometimes gave Zionist polemics a certain affinity to antisemitic argumentation, even beyond the self-confessed attraction of some Jewish Nationalist intellectuals to race-thinking. The dislike of Jewish "Mammonism", of *parvenu* characteristics, *schnorrer*ing and vulgar mannerisms provided some common ground with the antisemites, as did the critique of assimilation in general. The Zionists, however, were primarily concerned with changing these negative characteristics through the creation of a new, more harmonious environment in which Jews would become productivised and recover both their moral and physical balance. Unlike the antisemites, Birnbaum and other early Zionist thinkers in Central Europe certainly did not believe in the "eternity" of racial characteristics, or in a hierarchy of higher and lower races, let alone in the permanent degeneration of the Jews. On the contrary, they assumed that Zionism as a doctrine of national self-help must lead to a dramatic transformation in the way of life and thought prevalent among Diaspora Jews and thereby provide a radical therapy for the sickness of *Galut*.

Nevertheless, Nathan Birnbaum was convinced that until this national redemption came about, antisemitism would remain an ineradicable historical phenomenon which neither revolution, reform nor enlightenment could

---

[28]'Erlöschung-Erlösung', *Selbst-Emancipation!*, I, Nr. 1 (1st February 1885), p. 2. "Dieser instinctive Ekel vor der moralischen Unselbständigkeit eines Stammes, der von dem merkwürdigen Wahne befallen ist, sich selbst vernichten zu wollen, ist der Keim des modernen Antisemitismus."
[29]'Unsere Mängel', *ibid.*, pp. 2–3.
[30]Nathan Birnbaum in *Ost und West*, II, Nr. 8 (August 1902), pp. 517–518. Reproduced as 'Einige Gedanken über den Antisemitismus', in *Ausgewählte Schriften zur Jüdischen Frage, op. cit.*, vol. I, p. 154.

uproot.[31] In spite of its obvious socio-economic components, Birnbaum emphasised that "Jew-hatred is not primarily an economic but a national phenomenon". It was essentially a form of national friction and even of "pure racial
antipathy", exacerbated by the dispersion of the Jews and their fundamental
powerlessness.[32] Hence the absurdity of efforts at *Abwehr* engaged in by Jewish
communal leaders ("social conservatives" as Birnbaum liked to call them) in
Vienna and elsewhere, who vainly tried to change the emotional bias of the
masses through rational argument and to counter by enlightened propaganda
their congenital "need to hate".* Jewish self-defence was basically a stillborn
idea:

> "*Abwehr* could only emerge in rationalist minds, among men who want to explain history
> armed solely with logic, and who overlook the strength of influences from the life of the
> instincts and emotions . . . A movement which is based on such pre-instinctual philosophical
> foundations cannot succeed and therefore it is understandable that *Abwehr* has suffered
> setback after setback . . ."[33]

Birnbaum's disparagement and open ridicule of Jewish defence against
antisemitism was characteristic of early Zionist thinkers immersed in the issues
of national revival, emigration and territorial concentration. Already in February 1885 Leo Pinsker, in a letter, had advised Birnbaum to deal less with the
antisemites and to focus more on the moral values, the productivisation and the
national health of the Jewish people.[34] Significantly, after the third issue, *Selbst-
Emancipation!* did include a section on *Erez Israel*, its climate, conditions and the
development of agricultural settlements during the First *Aliyah*.[35] The journal
began to place greater emphasis on the virtues of manual labour, the need to
regenerate the Jewish masses and on the return to the soil as key concepts of
Zionism. In his 1892 lecture to the *Admath Yeshurun* association, Birnbaum
explained:

> "Land is the magic charm that arouses in nations a feeling of proud strength, guards them
> against unnaturalness and utter demoralisation, and gives them physical and moral strength.
> Israel will have to cultivate its soil again; it will develop a peasantry that will enjoy its work
> and its life. The marrow of this class will rejuvenate the entire body of the Jewish people; the
> nervousness and distraction that are so frequently found in educated Jews will decrease and
> the idolatry of money will become less intense."[36]

---

[31]See the remarks of Sanford Ragins, *Jewish Responses to Anti-Semitism in Germany 1870–1914*, Cincinnati
1980, pp. 125 ff.

[32]Nathan Birnbaum, *Die Nationale Wiedergeburt des jüdischen Volkes in seinem Lande*, Wien 1893, reprinted
in *Ausgewählte Schriften, op. cit.*, vol. I, p. 41.

*For the question of Jewish *Abwehr* (self-defence) in Austria the reader is referred to the preceding
essay by Jacob Toury, 'Years of Strife. The Contest of the Österreichisch-Israelitische Union for the
Leadership of Austrian Jewry', which is the second of his two contributions to the Year Book on this
topic (for the first see *LBI Year Book XXX* [1985]) – (Ed.).

[33]*Ibid.*, p. 26. From Birnbaum's lecture entitled *Die Jüdische Moderne*, Wien 1896, delivered before the
academic society *Kadimah* in 1896.

[34]Kressel, 'Selbstemanzipation', *loc. cit.*, pp. 64–65.

[35]See Nathan Birnbaum, 'Die Colonisation Palästinas', *Selbst-Emancipation!*, II, Nr. 4 (16th February
1886); 'Colonisationspläne', *ibid.*, VI, Nr. 10 (15th May 1892); 'Organisation der Colonisationstä-
tigkeit', VI, Nr. 6 (18th May 1893).

[36]Nathan Birnbaum, 'Die Prinzipien des Zionismus', *ibid.*, V, Nr. 5 (4th March 1892), p. 53.

Both *Selbst-Emancipation!* and its successor, the *Jüdische Volkszeitung*, stressed the need for Zionists to encourage more actively the settlement of Palestine, praised the fertility of its soil and provided detailed information on the progress of its Jewish colonies.[37] Birnbaum himself set off in May 1892 for a lecture tour of Galicia and Bukovina, designed to promote a more energetic settlement programme.[38] As part of this campaign, *Selbst-Emancipation!* also fought vigorously against the alternative colonisation plans developed by Baron Hirsch in Argentina and by other philanthropists for Jewish settlement in the United States.[39]

In this propaganda for Zionism as a programme of national redemption, Nathan Birnbaum underlined that "the emotions of a whole people are a force", which should be used to mobilise the Jewish masses.

> "The cry 'Zion' arouses a world of such emotions in the hearts of our fellow Jews and brings out hosts of enthusiastic fighters, whereas the cry of 'America' (if, for instance, one wished to found the new home for Israel there), leaves the Jewish national soul (*die jüdische Volksseele*) cold . . . It is also not easy to make a people of farmers (*ein Ackerbauvolk*). Only enthusiasm can overcome this Herculean task; it cannot be undertaken with business-like sobriety. The Jewish farmer will derive this enthusiasm from the soil of his ancestors, whereas the smallest failure will drive him from a foreign soil which means nothing to him."[40]

To this quasi-mystical view of the link between land and people, tinged with an agrarian romanticism, Birnbaum added another consideration – namely that Palestine was a "Semitic country" located in the Orient.

> "The Jews are an oriental people. This is where they will feel at home and be able to undertake a cultural mission which, in line with the entire course of their history, belongs to them and to them alone . . . they are qualified to rouse the Orient from its lethargy, restore it to history, and do great work in the service of mankind."[41]

Birnbaum was convinced that only when the Jewish nation was reconnected to its "natural" surroundings in the Orient would its creative energies be fully released and radiate outwards throughout "Semitic" Asia, helping to bring its backward peoples into the orbit of Europe. The "civilising mission" of the Jews was not, however, merely to be an agent of Europeanism but rather to be a true mediator between East and West.[42] Though a sharp critic of the materialistic culture of Europe which he believed was contrary to the idealism of the "Jewish spirit", Birnbaum nonetheless prophesied its future regeneration by Jews returning to Palestine. They would become the *avant-garde* of this civilisation in its most modern form. Zionism would provide the desired East-West synthesis, as a result of the exodus of idealistic Jews from Europe who would revive and

[37]'Osten oder Westen', *ibid.*, III, Nr. 14 (17th October 1890), pp. 1–3.
[38]'Colonisationspläne', *loc. cit.* (15th May 1892). Also Kressel, *loc. cit.*, p. 91.
[39]'Die wichtigste Frage', *Jüdische Volkszeitung*, VII, Nr. 5 (30th January 1894), pp. 34–35. See also 'So lange es Zeit ist!', *ibid.*, VII, Nr. 14 (3rd April 1894), p. 2.
[40]Nathan Birnbaum, 'Die Prinzipien des Zionismus', *loc. cit.* (7th April 1892).
[41]*Ibid.* Birnbaum also saw an advantage in the fact that Palestine was "easily and quickly accessible from the major countries of the Jewish Diaspora" and that the Turkish government and people "are very favourably disposed to the Jews".
[42]Shmuel Almog, *Zionut ve-historia*, Jerusalem 1982 (in Hebrew), pp. 1–5, 109.

purify the best of modern culture through their renewed encounter with the "Semitic" Orient.[43]

In order to achieve this visionary goal, Birnbaum recognised that the Zionist movement would have to win the confidence of the Turkish government which in the 1890s still showed no signs of accepting a large-scale Jewish settlement, let alone political independence in Palestine-Syria. The Turks must be persuaded that there would be cultural, material and political benefits for the Ottoman Empire in encouraging Jewish colonisation in this sensitive region. Birnbaum consequently argued that not only would incoming Jewish settlers bring the positive benefits of industry, prosperity and education to the Orient, they would help it resist the constant humiliations incurred at the hands of the Western powers.[44] Turkey would thereby obtain a zealous defender of its leadership in the Orient as well as the bulwark against recurring European violations of its sovereignty.[45] The European Powers, for their part, would find the Jews to be ideal middlemen between themselves and the Orient.[46]

Birnbaum's nationalist philosophy, developed in Vienna in the early 1890s, clearly anticipated many features of Herzl's Zionist programme as announced in *Der Judenstaat* only a few years later. Like Herzl he held that a gradual process of Jewish emigration from Europe would end the pressure of antisemitism on the remaining Jews and moderate the relentless economic struggle for existence.[47] In addition to the demographic factor, the establishment of a Jewish *Heimat* in Palestine would "ennoble and civilise, strengthen and harden the Jews of the Diaspora", normalising their position and in the long run making possible far more effective protests on behalf of persecuted Jewry.[48] Once the Jews had their own national centre, it would automatically become their advocate and defender in international affairs. Jews would no longer be despised outlaws or free game (*vogelfrei*), whose powerlessness virtually invited antisemitic persecution.[49]

---

[43]'Die Heilung des jüdischen Volkes', Vortrag von N. Birnbaum in Lemberg, *Selbst-Emancipation!*, V, Nr. 21 (15th November 1892), p. 202.

[44]Nathan Birnbaum, 'Die Türkei und die Palästina-Colonisation', *Selbst-Emancipation!*, VI, Nr. 17 (1891), reprinted in annexe to *Die Nationale Wiedergeburt des jüdischen Volkes*, in *Ausgewählte Schriften, op. cit.*, vol. I, pp. 38–40.

[45]*Ibid.*, p. 40, Birnbaum suggested that the instinct of self-preservation would oblige the Jews "ein übrigens friedliches und im versöhnenden Geiste wirkendes Gegengewicht gegen das Araberthum abzugeben und für den osmanischen Staatsgedanken immer und überall einzutreten".

[46]*Ausgewählte Schriften, op. cit.*, vol. I, p. 18. Birnbaum, like Moses Hess before him, liked to quote from the futurist vision of the French Gentile Zionist, Ernst Laharanne, whose *La nouvelle Question d'Orient. Reconstitution de la Nation Juive*, Paris 1860, spoke of the great calling of the Jews "to be a living channel of communication between three continents"; Birnbaum's notion of Jewry as mediators between Europe and the Orient probably owed something both to Laharanne's cultural imperialism and Hess's secular Jewish messianism.

[47]*Die Nationale Wiedergeburt* (1893), in *Ausgewählte Schriften, op. cit.*, vol. I, p. 9, where Birnbaum writes that once the percentage of Jews falls below the saturation point at which intolerance becomes manifest "das würde natürlich eben so sehr ein beträchtliches Nachlassen der antisemitischen Spannung als eine Milderung des Daseinskampfes der jüdischen – und übrigens auch der nichtjüdischen – Volksmassen bedeuten".

[48]*Ibid.*

[49]*Ibid.*, p. 10. "Ein Volk ohne völkerrechtliche Geltung ist vogelfrei. Je rascher und gründlicher die zivilisierte Welt diese Vogelfreiheit bezüglich der Juden aufheben will, desto früher und radikaler wird sie von dem Judenhasse . . . befreit werden."

Like Herzl after him, Birnbaum also insisted that Zionism was consonant with the universalist traditions of the Enlightenment; that the purity of its national idea would enable Jews to make a much fuller contribution to human civilisation, once they were freed from the bitter yoke imposed by antisemitism.[50] Jewish Nationalism did not contradict the idea of humanity (*Menschheit*). It was devoid of the aggressive spirit of earlier European epochs and in essential harmony with the most advanced processes of social development.[51] In an independent Jewish homeland, the Jews would finally be able to develop their distinctive social and ethical genius for the greater welfare and redemption of mankind.[52]

In contrast to Herzl and most of the leading German Zionists, Birnbaum had been markedly influenced in his youth by Socialist teachings and devoted considerable attention to the challenge of Social Democracy which he saw as a serious rival for the hearts and minds of Jewish youth.[53] Already in his seminal lecture on the 'Principles of Zionism' on 23rd January 1892, Birnbaum had polemicised with those Social Democrats who attacked Zionism as a narrow-minded, reactionary form of Nationalism:

> "The Zionists are Nationalists in that they want to help their people to engage in cultural competition with other nations on an equal footing. Nationalistic in this non-aggressive sense, a Zionist may even espouse Socialistic principles in the realm of economics, but he will never be able to accommodate himself to official Socialism which decrees that existing national differences and the consequent differences in morality and temperament should be disregarded and the social question should therefore be solved in a stereotyped way. This error of official Socialism becomes especially glaring with regard to the Jewish Question, which is supposed to be solved automatically along with the social question."[54]

Birnbaum firmly rejected the optimistic belief of the German Social Democratic leader August Bebel that the victory of Socialism was imminent. Nor was there in his opinion any basis to the Marxist dogma that antisemitism was merely a function of the crisis in the capitalist system and that under Socialism it would simply evaporate.

> "It is not true because the peculiarities, weaknesses, whims, sympathies and antipathies of the nations will naturally persist even in a Socialist society, and thus Jew-hatred will not be buried either, for it is deeply ingrained in the psyche of the peoples. In fact, the Jews will be even worse off in a Socialist society unless their specific Jewish Question is solved first. Only the national rebirth of the Jewish people can prevent antisemitism from being dragged into the

---

[50]*Ibid.*, p. 15.

[51]*Ibid.*, pp. 18–20.

[52]Birnbaum struck a secular messianic note with his prophecy: "Im eigenen Heim wird die jüdische Nation wieder ihre gewaltigen sittlichen, d. i. sozialen Anlagen entfalten und kraft derselben die endliche soziale Erlösung des Menschengeschlechtes herbeiführen helfen; der seiner Ketten ledige jüdische Genius wird den Weg zum allgemeinen Menschheitsglücke verkürzen." *Ibid.*, p. 20.

[53]Letter of Dr. Solomon Birnbaum (son of Nathan Birnbaum) to the author of 24th February 1980. Dr. Birnbaum writes that "during his Zionist phase he (N.B.) was influenced by Socialism", but "never belonged to a Socialist Party". Solomon Birnbaum also reminded me that his father was highly critical of the Austrian Social Democrats for expelling the newly-founded Jewish Social Democratic Workers' Party of Galicia from its ranks in 1905. For this episode, which occurred during Birnbaum's Diaspora Nationalist phase, see Robert S. Wistrich, 'Austrian Social Democracy and the Problems of Galician Jewry 1890–1914', in *LBI Year Book XXVI* (1981), pp. 89–124.

[54]'Die Principien des Zionismus', *Selbst-Emancipation!*, V, Nr. 5, (4th March 1892), p. 54.

Socialist era, where it would be even more dangerous because of the omnipotence of the people's will as represented by public officials."[55]

In his lecture, *Die Jüdische Moderne*, delivered on the 7th of May 1896 to the students of *Kadimah* in Vienna, Birnbaum elaborated at greater length on this theme. While acknowledging the importance of Karl Marx's historical materialism for the understanding of society, economics and human evolution in general, Birnbaum argued that it ignored "the history of man as a racial being".[56] Nationality and race were no less potent historical factors than social and class conflicts. Indeed, Birnbaum insisted that "the firm foundation of nationality is always and everywhere race, whether a pure or mixed race (*einheitliche oder Mischrasse*)".[57] In the course of development, races became "ennobled" and attained the level of a "nationality", which had "nothing to do with the state or language".[58] Therefore there was no basis for the Socialist denial of Jewish nationality on the grounds that the Jews lacked a state, territory or a unified national language. For the proof of its existence and reality was rooted precisely in its "racial quality".[59] Indeed, Birnbaum even claimed that the Jews had "the strongest national feeling of all peoples, which is natural enough from the materialistic standpoint, since it is racially the most strongly distinct nationality".[60] Basing himself on these *völkisch* premises, Birnbaum maintained that antisemitism would not disappear even in a new Socialist order any more than would its underlying roots, which lay in national tensions, racial antipathies and in the dispersion of the Jews. Social Democracy could offer no practical solution to the "Jewish Question" except to wait for the promised revolution whereas the Jews manifestly required an immediate remedy for their plight.

Nevertheless in the 1890s Birnbaum still regarded himself as a quasi-Socialist within the Zionist movement, deeply concerned with the economic and social regeneration of the Jewish people. He strongly identified with the hostility of most Socialists in Central Europe towards feudal values, clericalism, Manchester Liberalism and the materialist ethos of bourgeois society. Moreover, for Birnbaum it was self-evident that there could be no room for stock-exchange Jews, private enterprise or "profiteering" in the settlement of *Erez Israel*.[61] In the

[55]*Ibid.* For a similarly prophetic formulation, see *Ausgewählte Schriften zur Jüdischen Frage, op. cit.*, vol. I, p. 21. "Greift der Zionismus nicht durch, so wird nach einem allfälligen, scheinbar völligen Siege der Gleichheitsidee die Judenfrage als ungelöstes Residium, der Judenhass als ein verhängnisvoller Keil im Fleische der neuen Gesellschaft zurückbleiben."
[56]*Die Jüdische Moderne*. Vortrag gehalten im Akademischen Vereine *Kadimah* in Wien von Mathias Acher, Leipzig 1896, p. 10. "Die landläufige materialistische Geschichtsauffassung vernachlässigt die Geschichte des Menschen als Rassewesen und berücksichtigt ausschliesslich die Geschichte des Menschen als Gattungswesen."
[57]*Ibid.*, p. 13.
[58]*Ibid.*
[59]*Ibid.*, pp. 13–14. "Gehören nun aber Staat und Sprache nicht zum eisernen Bestande der Nationalität, dann gibt es keinen Zweifel an der gegenwärtigen Existenz der jüdischen Nationalität. Denn ihre Rassenqualität kann ihr niemand bestreiten."
[60]*Ibid.*, p. 24.
[61]Birnbaum's anti-capitalist vision led to differences of opinion with the Galician Zionist Abraham Salz who did not share his emotional affinities with Socialist thought. See A. Salz, 'Sozialismus oder Colonisation Palästinas', *Selbst-Emancipation!*, IV, Nr. 9 (1891), p. 2.

spirit of agrarocentric, anti-industrial nineteenth-century theorists like Charles Fourier, Louis Blanc, Henry George and the German *"Kathedersozialisten"* he looked to Palestine not simply as a refuge from antisemitism but as the only possible centre for building up a class of free and independent Jewish farmers. The creation of a healthy peasant stock was held by Birnbaum and most early Zionists to be the *sine qua non* for a solid and organic national development which would free Jewry from the curse of "Mammonism" and the commercial, speculative spirit.[62]

Birnbaum's moralistic critique of the assimilationist Jewish upper classes in Vienna for their vulgar materialism and *parvenu* lack of tact, clearly owed something to the powerful anti-capitalist and anti-urban values of the intelligentsia in Central Europe.[63] But there was still a considerable gap between this populist anti-Mammonism tinged with "Socialism" and the doctrines of class-war advocated by the Marxist labour movement.[64] Even greater was the gulf between Social Democratic internationalism and Birnbaum's unshakeable conviction that ethnic differences were primordial. His "Socialism" was firmly predicated on the primacy of national liberation, which led him to regard Social Democracy as a particularly dangerous rival ideology for the Zionist movement. Aware of the charismatic appeal which revolutionary radicalism exercised on Jewish youth in Eastern Europe Birnbaum sought to incorporate into Jewish Nationalism some of its more rational elements, such as the need for social reform and greater economic equality, while rejecting its "cosmopolitanism" and call for a violent overthrow of the capitalist system.[65] The *Zukunftsmusik* of the Social Democrats, their promise of universalist redemption awakened a palpable echo in Jewish hearts – attuned by centuries of suffering to messianic chords. Precisely for this reason, Birnbaum feared that the Socialist mirage might prove even more destructive than the Liberal dream of assimilation.[66]

The inroads of Social Democratic propaganda among impoverished Jewish workers in Galicia made concrete the "assimilationist" danger to the young Zionist movement stemming from this source. The Polish Socialists led by

---

[62]N. B., 'Die Ziele der jüdisch-nationalen Bestrebungen', Pt. II, *loc. cit.*, p. 2. For Birnbaum, the epitome of this capitalist profiteering spirit was the United States. His opposition to Jewish settlement in America derived as much from "social" as it did from national considerations.

[63]'Die Ziele der jüdisch-nationalen Bestrebungen', Pt. III, Ethischer Teil, *ibid.*, III, Nr. 5 (2nd June 1890).

[64]There was a certain parallel between Nathan Birnbaum's view of Socialism and that of Theodor Hertzka, editor of the *Wiener Allgemeine Zeitung*. See Birnbaum's long report on a lecture that Hertzka delivered before the *Österreichisch-Israelitische Union* on 14th January 1893, published in *Selbst-Emancipation!*, VI, Nr. 3 (28th February 1893), pp. 2–4, under the title 'Arischer und semitischer Geist'. Birnbaum remarked that "Dr. Hertzka sprach als Socialist – ein Wort, das man nicht mit der Parteibezeichnung Socialdemokrat verwechseln darf – und als Jude. Er ist ein Mann, der die Eigenart des jüdischen Wesens erkannt hat und diese Eigenart vollständig mit Bewusstsein in sich verkörpert."

[65]'Die Socialdemokratie und die Juden', *ibid.*, III. Nr. 6 (16th June 1890), pp. 1–2.

[66]*Ibid.*, p. 1. See also the report on 'Der internationale Arbeitercongress in Brüssel', *ibid.*, IV, Nr. 17 (2nd September 1891), p. 3, which pointed to the ambivalence of the Socialist International on the "Jewish Question" and criticised the extreme assimilationist position adopted by the Austrian Socialist leader, Victor Adler.

Ignacy Daszyński, sought to encourage class-consciousness among the Galician Jewish proletariat as a step towards their eventual absorption into the Polish nation. Both Birnbaum and the Cracow-born Socialist Zionist, Saul Raphael Landau (1869–1946), opposed this campaign as detrimental to the national interests of Galician Jewry.[67] Jews had bled long enough in the social and national liberation struggles of other peoples. It was an illusion to believe that such participation would lead to the elimination of antisemitism or end the isolation of the Jews among the nations of Eastern Europe; equally naive was the assumption that the abolition of states, nations or religious communities would end social inequalities, economic exploitation and mass poverty.[68]

Zionism, on the other hand, aspired to a synthesis of Jewish patriotic and religious traditions with progressive, democratic ideals which would overcome "the materialistic and egoistic mode of thinking of European society".[69] It sought the national redemption of all classes of Jewry in an independent homeland, an ideal for which contemporary internationalist Social Democrats displayed little sympathy. Indeed, in impoverished regions like Galicia the ideologies of proletarian and Jewish solidarity still stood in glaring antithesis to one another in the early 1890s.[70] The strike of the *tallith* weavers in Galicia during the summer of 1892 was a case in point. The cause of the strikers, who worked fifteen hours a day in appalling conditions for wages of one to three gulden a week, was eagerly taken up by Austrian and Polish Socialists who organised collections on their behalf.[71] *Selbst-Emancipation!* acknowledged their efforts to better the conditions of the Galician proletariat but pointed to the danger that Social Democracy could gain a firmer foothold among their co-religionists, unless Zionists devoted more concern to the solution of the social problem.[72] At the same time, it warned its readers against the chimera of class-struggle and emphasised that as long as Jews remained in *Galut* (exile) they would continue to be "a dependent and unprotected minority".[73]

Birnbaum was also sceptical at this time of efforts by Jewish Nationalists to organise Jews as an independent political factor in Galicia.[74] As a Zionist he still believed that only an independent territorial centre for the Jewish people as a whole could provide a long-term solution to the problem of Jewish poverty. However, local Jewish political activity in a national framework might be a

[67]Saul Raphael Landau, 'Der Socialismus und die Juden in Galizien', *ibid.*, V, Nrs. 6/7 (7th April 1892), pp. 55–56.
[68]Nathan Birnbaum, 'Zum ersten Mai', *ibid.*, V, Nr. 9 (1st May 1892), pp. 79–81.
[69]*Ibid.*, p. 80.
[70]Nathan Birnbaum, 'Die Tallisweber von Kolomea', *ibid.*, V, Nrs. 16/17 (29th August 1892), pp. 166–167.
[71]'Der jüdische Weberstreik', *Arbeiter-Zeitung*, 5th August 1892. Also 'Zum Kolomaer Weberstreik', *ibid.*, 16th September 1892, and Max Zetterbaum, 'Klassengegensätze bei den Juden', *Die Neue Zeit*, II (1892–1893), p. 39.
[72]'Die Tallisweber . . .', *loc. cit.*, p. 167. "Der Strike [sic] der Tallisweber von Kolomea kann der Socialdemokratie die schönste Gelegenheit geben, sich unter der galizischen Judenheit einzunisten."
[73]*Ibid.*, ". . . auch im sozialistischen Zukunftsstaate wird die Judenhetze nicht aufhören, wenn die Juden wie heute und damals allerwärts die abhängige und schutzlose Minorität sein werden".
[74]See Nathan Gelber, *Toldot Ha-Tenu'ah ha-Ziyyonit be-Galitsiah*, Tel-Aviv 1956, vol. 1, p. 15.

necessary and useful adjunct to colonisation in Palestine.[75] The growth of the Zionist idea in Galicia and the claim of its leaders that the Viennese-based movement had no understanding of local conditions in the Polish province, inevitably led to a modification of this standpoint. The Lemberg Zionists had already developed a detailed programme in 1891 and began publishing their own Zionist newspaper *Przyszłość* (*Future*) in Polish, which had a considerable impact on Jewish public opinion in Galicia. Birnbaum who in the summer of 1892 had travelled through many cities in Galicia and Bukovina, founding new Zionist clubs and promoting the idea of unifying *Hovevei-Zion* groups in one national organisation, was eager to avoid further tension with the Galicians.[76]

Together with Abraham Salz, the chairman of the executive committee of the Galician Zionists, Birnbaum convened a conference for this purpose in Cracow on 1st November 1893.[77] The conference clarified the principles, the means of information and methods of propaganda to be adopted by the "Organisation of Austrian Zionists".[78] The Austrian Zionist Party declared as its first basic principle, the striving "for the resurrection (*Wiedergeburt*) of the Jewish nation and ultimately the reconstruction of Jewish communal life (*Wiederherstellung des jüdischen Gemeinwesens*) in Palestine". At the same time it also recognised the "duty of guarding the political, social and economic interests of Jews in Austria". In addition, resolutions were adopted calling for the "abolition of the present guild system in Austria", proclaiming opposition to the *numerus clausus* and demanding the abolition of Sunday as an obligatory day of rest for Jews. The conference also called for participation by Zionists in elections, the publication (in Yiddish) of a pamphlet to enlighten the masses about electoral reforms, and for the submission of a petition to the authorities for the recognition as literate (*Alphabeten*) of "those individuals who read and write Hebrew".[79]

Birnbaum at this stage in his career as a Jewish Nationalist had already crystallised a programme of political Zionism which sought to combine legal guarantees for a Jewish home in Palestine with participation in Austrian politics in order to strengthen the Zionist movement.[80] The Zionist cause had to be put

---

[75]N. B. 'Parteiprogramme', *Selbst-Emancipation!*, V, Nr. 12 (21st June 1892), p. 116. Also 'Die zionistische Partei', V, Nr. 4 (23rd February 1892), p. 41.

[76]The first conference of Jewish Nationalists had been convened on 23rd to 25th April 1893 and was attended by representatives from all the existing Zionist societies in Galicia. Nathan Birnbaum, who represented the Austrian Zionists, was elected honorary chairman of the conference.

[77]See *Selbst-Emancipation!*, VI, Nr. 18 (15th November 1893), pp. 3–5.

[78]'Corporationen und Versammlungen', *ibid.*, VI, Nr. 20 (15th December 1893), p. 7, for the change in the name of the organisation to "The Austrian Jewish National Party", which was proposed by Birnbaum.

[79]*Selbst-Emancipation!*, VI, Nr. 18 (15th November 1893), pp. 3–5. Also Kressel, *loc. cit.*, p. 90. At this stage in his career, Birnbaum (possibly influenced by the Hebrew writer Reuben Brainin [1862–1939], who had recently settled in Vienna), attached great importance to the role of the Hebrew language for Western Jews, in promoting the national renaissance. Yiddish, on the other hand, he still regarded as the language of the ghetto and *Galut*, unfit for a civilised nation seeking its auto-emancipation.

[80]N.B., 'Politischer Zionismus', *Selbst-Emancipation!*, V, Nr. 23 (19th December 1892); 'Jüdische Politik', *ibid.*, VI, Nr. 8 (15th June 1893); 'Die Wahlreform und die Zionisten', *ibid.*, VI, Nr. 16 (15th October 1893), Nr. 17 (1st November 1893). Also *Die Nationale Wiedergeburt des jüdischen Volkes*, *op. cit.*

on the international agenda in order to overcome obstacles placed by the Turkish government in the way of Jewish settlement in Palestine. No less importantly, Zionism had to propagandise and organise itself among the Jewish masses as a political movement; it had to become more involved in Austrian electoral activity without losing sight of the "final goal".

The fight of Austrian Jews for their national rights and their liberation from the illusion that antisemitism could be definitively eradicated were objectives considered attainable by political agitation.[81] So, too, was the aim of cultivating the Hebrew language and knowledge of Jewish history, and encouraging the settlement of Palestine. The immediate goal of a centralised Zionist party organisation was intended to achieve not so much external diplomatic successes as self-education and enlightenment. In the pursuit of this purpose, Birnbaum regarded Vienna as an ideal centre for the Zionist movement:

> "Vienna lies on the frontier between East and West in Europe. It lies in the midst of a Jewish population numbering millions; it is the point where German and Russo-Polish, Ashkenazi and Sephardi Jewry meet and can best be united in common work; it is as if born to be the centre of Jewish national agitation – which for a long time will have to be the chief preoccupation of our movement. Vienna is moreover a German city, which is of the greatest significance for the winning over of the very important German-Jewish element in Austria and Germany. Finally, Vienna is the capital of a nationalities' state, and hence incomparably more suitable for our movement than, for example, Berlin."[82]

Vienna was also far better placed than London or New York to be the bridge between Russian and Western Jewry, since its geo-political position gave it close proximity to the heartland of the Jewish masses. It was irrelevant, Birnbaum insisted, that the bulk of Viennese Jewry did not support the movement. Zionism could in any case expect no sympathy from the millionaire stock-exchange Jews, the liberal rabbis (*Seelsorger*), or journalists of the *Neue Freie Presse*, who "hate every national movement of an oppressed people and grudgingly surrender only in the face of success".[83] Nor did it matter that Vienna was not exactly the centre of world politics and lacked a tradition of supporting movements for national self-determination such as had long existed in London or Paris; for Zionism at this early stage in its development had to concentrate on education, internal consolidation and the centralisation of its meagre resources.[84]

Birnbaum pointed out that the assimilationist leaders of Viennese Jewry and the so-called *Judenpresse* undoubtedly feared Zionism as a "danger" to their position which they even placed on a par with Socialism and anarchism. Thus, though the Zionists in Vienna were still only a *Privatpartei*, limited to a relatively narrow circle, the Jewish leadership fulminated against them as unwelcome disturbers of the "sweet tranquillity and comfortable prosperity of Viennese

[81] N.B., 'Der neue Cours (Ein Wort an alle Zionisten)', *Selbst-Emancipation!*, IV, Nr. 21 (2nd November 1891), pp. 1–2.

[82] 'Die zionistische Partei', *loc. cit.*, p. 40.

[83] *Ibid.*, p. 41. Birnbaum contrasted here the bitter opposition of the *Neue Freie Presse* to the Slav and Irish national movements and the paper's reluctant capitulation before Hungarian demands.

[84] *Ibid.*, ". . . die Politik, die wir wünschen, soll eben mehr eine innere als eine äussere, mehr Selbsterziehung als Diplomatik sein."

Jewry",[85] they were seen as rebellious trouble-makers whose aims, argumentation and methods seemed to reinforce those of the antisemites and threatened to undermine the hard-earned status of the "Mosaic Germans".[86] Against this challenge the Jewish notables and press barons would surely seek to employ the time-honoured Viennese tactic of *totschweigen* – attempting to kill the movement by silence.

Nonetheless Birnbaum remained confident that in the long run this strategy would not succeed. In the Austrian provinces, above all in Galicia, the movement had already encountered a more fertile soil and receptive public opinion which augured well for the future.[87] However, Vienna remained "the key to the Jewry of Austria", for even in far-off Galicia, the magic of the name exercised a remarkable spell over provincial Jews. Hence the crucial importance for the Zionist movement of increasing its strength in the Habsburg capital.[88] The Viennese Zionists would have to extend their appeal beyond student circles and reach out to all classes of Austrian Jewry. They would have to counteract "the lack of idealism among Austrian Jews" and the indifference of the assimilationists to Jewish history and literature by energetically promoting associations whose goal was the cultivation of "Jewish science and consciousness".[89] Along with the creation of *Colonisations-Vereine* that encouraged the settlement of Palestine, such Jewish cultural associations were potentially a most important avenue for the percolating of Jewish national feeling into wider strata of the population. So, too, were the religious organisations of the Jewish community. Zionists could not remain indifferent as a "national-social Party" within Jewry, to key insitutions such as the Viennese *Cultusgemeinde*, which, though they might be based on "the fairy-tale of a de-nationalised 'Mosaic confession' ", still provided the nucleus for preserving the national character and residues of the traditional solidarity within Jewry. Hence, the task of Zionism, Birnbaum contended, was to transform these "confessional communities" into autonomous foci of Jewish national life, culture and science, into working centres for "the future of our people".[90]

At the more general Austrian level, the intensification of national conflicts, the proposals for electoral reform and the crisis of the parliamentary system in the Monarchy had forced the Zionists to relate more seriously to questions of

[85]'Der gegenwärtige Stand unserer Sache in Österreich', *ibid.*, V, Nr. 21 (15th November 1892), pp. 1–2.

[86]*Ibid.*

[87]*Ibid.*, p. 1. Birnbaum acknowledged that outside Galicia, the situation was much less promising for Zionism. He blamed this primarily on the entanglement of Jews in the struggle between Germans and Slavs, which had led to "such a high level of estrangement from their own nationality".

[88]*Ibid.* "Das Wort Wien hat einen guten Klang bei den österreichischen Juden, man muss ihn daher den Leuten vorspielen können."

[89]'Pflege der geistigen Güter unseres Volkes', *ibid.*, VI, Nr. 7 (1st June 1893), pp. 1–2, for Birnbaum's critique of "die materialistische Trockenheit des österreichischen Judenthums", which he compared unfavourably with the achievements of German Jewry in the domain of Jewish *Wissenschaft*.

[90]'Das neue Statut der Wiener jüdischen Gemeinde', *ibid.*, VI, Nr. 17 (1st November 1893), pp. 1–2. Birnbaum was especially critical of the inadequacy of Hebrew language instruction in the educational programme of the Viennese *Cultusgemeinde*.

everyday politics.[91] Thus Birnbaum argued in Feburary 1891 that both as patriotic Austrian citizens and as Jews, Zionists could not remain indifferent to the outcome of *Reichsrat* elections. Though the final goals of their movement were unrelated to the fate of the Empire, the Zionists as Austrian citizens must place the interests of the Habsburg State before those of "blind party fanaticism".[92] As Jews they would therefore support political parties which defended the cause of freedom and equality and rejected antisemitism. Thus in Viennese districts the Zionists were in favour of Liberal against antisemitic candidates and as a principle sought to favour the "democratic" camp rather than their rivals, who had to be opposed on account of their crude racism. In mixed nationality areas, Jews would have to decide in terms of their own national interests whether to back Germans or Czechs, Poles or Ukrainians, Italians or Slavs.

Birnbaum recognised that the Zionists themselves were still far too disorganised and ill-prepared to engage on their own account in Austrian electoral politics, though a few deputies in the *Reichsrat* might eventually provide a useful platform for the cause. Moreover, he constantly emphasised that electoral politics could provide no panacea for the ills of the Diaspora, which could only be cured by territorial concentration in a Jewish homeland.[93] At the most, electoral participation could be considered a palliative to ease the sufferings of the *Galut* and to raise the national consciousness of the Jewish masses.[94] Birnbaum remained, however, adamantly opposed to the growing tendency (even among Liberal Jews) towards "Jewish politics" based on self-defence against antisemitism. The representatives of this new trend had in his view been forced by the logic of Austrian political conditions to recognise the bankruptcy of their exclusive reliance on German Liberalism. But they remained as inimical as ever to the collective aspirations of the Jewish nation as a whole.[95]

By the mid-1890s Birnbaum had built up a small circle of disciples in Vienna, Berlin and Galicia as well as established contacts with leaders of *Hovevei Zion* in many European countries. A brilliant speaker and a tireless worker for the Zionist cause with heart and pen for nearly fifteen years, he had clearly become the most distinguished intellectual among Jewish Nationalists in Austria and Germany. His Vienna lecture on *Die Jüdische Moderne* was widely considered to be an outstanding exposition of the Zionist cause. Elaboration on the common German distinction between the particularism of *Kultur* and the universal features of civilisation, he argued that emancipation had not brought in its wake a genuine Jewish assimilation to the specific national cultures in Europe.

[91]Almog, *Zionut ve-historia, op. cit.*, p. 133.
[92]'Zu den Reichsrathswahlen', *Selbst-Emancipation!*, IV (16th February 1891), pp. 2–3.
[93]*Ibid.*, p. 2. "Nur die Schaffung eines Heims für unser Volk kann dessen Unglück beheben; alle andern Versuche sind Flickwerk." See also *Die Jüdische Moderne, op. cit.*, p. 26.
[94]See 'Die Wahlreform und die Zionisten', *Selbst-Emancipation!*, VI, Nr. 16 (15th October 1893), p. 5, where Birnbaum remarked that ". . . die zu erwartenden Wahlen müssen wenigstens benutzt werden, um der Todtschweigerei, welche von der deutsch geschriebenen Tagespresse gegenüber unseren Bestrebungen betrieben wird und unsere Fortschritte bedeutend verlangsamt, entgegenzuwirken".
[95]Nathan Birnbaum, 'Jüdische Politik', *ibid.*, VI, Nr. 8 (15th June 1893), pp. 1–2.

"When we compare the so-called assimilated Jews with their surroundings, we find a similarity between them only in that circle of ideas and emotions common to all civilised European peoples (*Culturvölker*) – but this similarity is almost completely absent when it comes to the national peculiarities of individual nations. The assimilated Jew has more or less the same extensive needs, social conscience, political maturity, bold scientific outlook, refined epicureanism and purified artistic taste . . . of the cultured European. But he does not possess, or at least only to a very small degree, the robust defiance and formal pedantry of the German, the élan and frivolity of the Frenchman, the elemental simplicity and melancholy of the Slav."[96]

For Birnbaum, the universalistic Europeanisation of the Jews had not led to genuine "national assimilation", but had merely increased antisemitism and Jewish insecurity. Only through Zionism, he told his student audience, could the Jews become integral and authentic *Culturmenschen*.

Birnbaum had become increasingly preoccupied in the mid-1890s with the cultural and spiritual dimensions of the Jewish problem at the expense of Palestinian colonisation programmes and party-political Zionism.[97] Nevertheless, he initially welcomed the publication of Theodor Herzl's *Der Judenstaat*, sympathising with its clarion call for Jewish sovereignty and the bold outline of the organisational means to achieve this goal. In particular, he identified with its vision of the international dimensions of the "Jewish Question" and the need for a comprehensive legal-political solution that would finally end their pariah status and normalise the position of the Jews.[98] Herzl's watchword of economic and political independence for the Jews in their own sovereign State seemed to complement and confirm what Birnbaum had been saying for over a decade.

At first, the two men co-operated and Birnbaum was invited by Herzl to deliver an address on 'Zionism as a Cultural Movement' at the First Zionist Congress in Basle (1897) which continued the critique of "abstract Europeanism" he had earlier expressed in *Die Jüdische Moderne*.[99] Here he envisaged Zionism as a synthetic movement of national renaissance which would breathe the spirit of Western progress into the ghetto Jewry of Eastern Europe and renewed life into the "dead Europeanism" of Western Jewry".[100] Only through possession of their own land would the "Europeanism" of Western Jews become fruitful and the national culture of the *Ostjuden* emerge from its stagnation;[101] only in *Erez Israel* would Western Jews be liberated from the curse of "ruthless Mammonism" and the *Ostjuden* from the blight of endemic pauperism. The

[96]Mathias Acher, *Die Jüdische Moderne, op. cit.*, p. 3.
[97]*Ibid.*, p. 31 for Birnbaum's rejection of political "Partei-Zionismus" as a pure abstraction and the inadequacy of small-scale colonisation in Palestine in the face of Turkish resistance.
[98]See his review of Herzl's *Der Judenstaat* in Hermann Bahr's periodical, *Die Zeit*, Wien, VI, Nr. 873 (22nd February 1896). Also *Die Jüdische Moderne, op. cit.*, pp. 31–38.
[99]Mathias Acher, *Zwei Vorträge über Zionismus*, Berlin 1898, pp. 1–12. 'Der Zionismus als Culturbewegung', Referat, gehalten auf dem Zionisten-Congress in Basel am 29. August 1897, in *Ausgewählte Schriften, op. cit.*, I.
[100]*Ibid.*, p. 5. Birnbaum stressed in this speech the indissoluble bond between Zionism, the future of the Jewish people and European civilisation. Zionism could not have blossomed in the "ghetto": "Erst als durch den Massenaufstieg zum Europäismus im Westen wie im Osten eine Generation erstand, die von der abendländischen Civilisation mit ihren grossen thatkräftigen Nationen das Wollen erlernt hatte, war die Bahn für den Zionismus geebnet." *Ibid.*, pp. 5–6.
[101]*Ibid.*, p. 6.

ghetto culture of the East would be transformed with the help of Western Jews into a progressive national culture that integrated the highest political, technical and aesthetic achievements of Europe with the prophetic teachings of social justice that were the historic legacy of Israel.[102] No other people were better suited than the Jews, with their inherited oriental character and European education, to act as mediators between East and West; no land was more predestined for this role than Palestine, at the confluence of three continents and a nodal point in modern communications, in closest proximity to the Suez Canal.[103]

At the First Zionist Congress Birnbaum was elected Secretary-General of the Zionist Organisation, yet within a year he had left the movement, after Herzl opposed his re-election. The frictions between the two men which made their further co-operation impossible were as much personal as political, rooted in their different social backgrounds, material circumstances, temperament and outlook.[104] Birnbaum undoubtedly felt betrayed when members of *Kadimah* and other Zionist groups in Vienna pledged unconditional loyalty to Herzl, a complete newcomer to the cause and in many ways a stranger to Jewish life. He rapidly came to see in Herzl a power-hungry tyrant and usurper who sought the "crown of Zion" while propagating ideas which Birnbaum himself had been preaching for years.[105]

Birnbaum clearly had no desire to play the role of a lieutenant rather than a general in the movement he had done so much to initiate. No less touchy and sensitive than Herzl in matters of personal prestige, his envy was aroused by the lightning speed with which his new rival succeeded in firing the enthusiasm of the Jewish masses and Zionist youth in Central and Eastern Europe, whom Birnbaum had painstakingly educated for over a decade in the cause of Jewish Nationalism.[106] Too impulsive, inconsistent and critically-minded to play the role of a *Führerpersönlichkeit*, Birnbaum found himself thrust unceremoniously into the background by Herzl's meteoric rise. Too much a wanderer in the realm of ideas to feel at home even in his own mental constructions, he gradually turned his back on Zionism, the movement which in Austria at least, had been virtually his personal creation.

An interesting insight into the growing animosity between Birnbaum and Herzl before their final rupture is provided by the former's correspondence with Siegmund Werner (1867–1928), the first *Kadimahner* to have fought a duel and paradoxically enough, the founder in 1894 of the Jewish Socialist non-duelling fraternity, *Gamalah*. Birnbaum hoped to win over Werner and some other *Kadimahner* in Vienna and Galicia, who still regarded him as their intellectual leader, to a more radical "Leftist" Zionism than that advocated by Herzl. But virtually all the Jewish national fraternities, beginning with *Kadimah*, *Ivria*, *Gamalah*, *Libanonia*, fascinated as they were by Herzl's personality and the idea of

[102]*Ibid.*, p. 9.
[103]*Ibid.*, pp. 10–11.
[104]Alex Bein, *Die Judenfrage. Biographie eines Weltproblems*, Bd. II, Stuttgart 1980, p. 280.
[105]Josef Fraenkel, *Mathias Achers Kampf um die "Zionskrone"*, Basel 1959, p. 10.
[106]*Ibid.*, pp. 12–13.

a Jewish State, had quickly declared their support for the new Herzlian orientation in Austrian Zionism. On 21st July 1897 Birnbaum acknowledged in a letter to Werner that it was impossible to counter Herzl's influence by "open resistance" and that calm, patient work would be necessary to gain more support for the Leftist trend.[107] At the same time, he declared his support for the calling of the First Zionist Congress as a major step in transforming the Jewish community into a national entity with an organised will of its own.[108] Moreover, during the preparations for the Basle Congress Birnbaum found himself opposing fellow-Zionists in Berlin like Hirsch Hildesheimer and Willy Bambus who favoured "practical work" in Palestine. He identified himself openly with the Herzlian rejection of such methods of gradual "infiltration".

Nevertheless Birnbaum still hoped for a common Leftist front against Herzl at the First Congress. On 28th July 1897, Werner writing from Vienna to Birnbaum (who had moved for financial reasons to Berlin) informed him that the *Kadimahner* were solidly behind Herzl and there was no support among the Viennese Zionists for more Leftist positions, with the single exception of Saul Raphael Landau – the first Editor-in-Chief of *Die Welt*.[109] However, in another letter from Vienna on 5th August 1897, Werner explicitly mentioned Landau's plans to create a "Social-Zionist group" within the movement which would be centred around Birnbaum and the Swiss Socialist Zionist David Farbstein.[110] Landau, he observed, also hoped to win backing for his radical views from the Galician Zionists.[111]

Birnbaum's hopes that Werner would line up Leftist support in Austria for his brand of "Social Zionism" were, however, quickly to be dispelled as the latter came more and more under Herzl's influence.[112] Replying to Werner on 15th August 1897 Birnbaum now described Herzl as "a real bourgeois and an opportunist despite his radical tendencies", who would soon turn to the Right.

> "This would drive us Leftists into open opposition and we would stand no chance for the time being. We can only make headway if people regard us as the closest allies of Herzl."[113]

In the same letter, Birnbaum declared that Zionism really had nothing to do with internal politics "but Zionists, who after all are also human beings and Jews, should participate in political life – if possible, within a Social Jewish *Volkspartei* . . ."[114] Birnbaum like Landau clearly recognised the importance for Zionism of the "social question" and the need to free the Jewish proletariat from the terrible conditions imposed on it by the *Galut*. He was, moreover, convinced,

---

[107]*Ibid.*, p. 22. "Wir können uns gegen den Wagen nicht stemmen. Es heisst allenfalls in der Partei Platz und Einfluss gewinnen. Dann wird sich alles geben."

[108]See *Zion*, 31st May 1897, p. 382. This Zionist monthly, founded in Berlin in 1895, was edited by Birnbaum with the help of collaborators like Oskar Kokesch, Hirsch Hildesheimer, Heinrich Loewe and some other leading Berlin Zionists. Birnbaum, whose financial situation was desperate, had left Vienna for Berlin to assume the editorship in 1896.

[109]Frankel, *Prophecy and Politics*, *op. cit.*, pp. 31–36.

[110]*Ibid.*, pp. 41–42.

[111]*Ibid.*, p. 46.

[112]See Werner's letter of 13th August 1897 to Birnbaum, pp. 49 ff.

[113]*Ibid.*, p. 55.

[114]*Ibid.*, p. 56.

as he had already explained in *Die Jüdische Moderne*, that if Socialism triumphed, it would also be adopted in the Jewish state. But Birnbaum was manifestly not prepared to lead a social-political fraction at the First Congress in open opposition to Herzl. The same reluctance was exhibited by Saul Raphael Landau, Isidor Schalit, David Farbstein and Nachman Syrkin, all of whom opposed "bourgeois Zionism" but whose allegiance to the movement as a whole proved greater than to any single faction within it.

Birnbaum's wretched material circumstances acted as a further brake on his initial hopes of challenging Herzl's leadership of the movement. Unlike Herzl, who was able to finance the organisation of the Zionist Congress, of *Die Welt*, and the wages of his collaborators and most of his political work largely from his own pocket, Birnbaum was frequently unable even to buy food and medicine for his children.[115] This discrepancy in material position despite his fourteen years of service to Zionism evidently intensified Birnbaum's resentment of Herzl. He complained bitterly to Werner:

> "If Dr. Herzl – who with his strong character and capacity for enthusiasm possesses a very hard, un-Jewish heart – had to spend only one day as I have been living in the past years . . . I feel sure that he would sing a different tune. But then, he would not have become so famous . . ."[116]

Birnbaum now seemed to be blaming his own dire straits on Herzl and "die Herren in Wien", even speculating that his own plight might never have arisen if he had not devoted his abilities ("which are certainly not inferior to Herzl's") to Zionism.[117] The only solution that he saw for straightening out his financial affairs was a decently paid position within the movement and he privately appealed to Werner and to his Galician colleagues to intercede at the Basle Congress out of "humanity, party feeling and perhaps also to compensate me for a longstanding injustice".[118]

Still only thirty-three years old and already a "veteran" of the Jewish national cause, Birnbaum did not disguise his desire to be General Secretary of the Zionist movement and eventually even to dictate its policy. In a letter from Vienna on 23rd August 1897 Werner sought to lower his expectations and dissuade Birnbaum from placing his hopes of a secured financial existence on becoming a paid official of the Zionist organisation.[119] He strongly advised Birnbaum to secure the graces and good-will of influential individuals in the movement (by flattery, if necessary) and not to rely on the Viennese leadership which had no resources to spare and was preoccupied with more important matters. Werner, as a close collaborator of Herzl, was doubtless well aware of the latter's deep

---

[115]*Ibid.*, pp. 60–61. See also Birnbaum's letter of 19th August 1897 to Werner, pp. 66–67. "Ich lebe seit Jahren in den furchtbarsten Verhältnissen. Deshalb ging ich auch aus Wien weg. In Berlin ging's noch ärger."

[116]*Ibid.*, p. 67. Birnbaum went on to describe the desperate situation of his family, with a chronically sick wife and his young children suffering from bronchitis: "five persons in one room, and my wife, with her lung trouble, doing the washing without any help . . .", *ibid.*, p. 69.

[117]*Ibid.*, pp. 69–70.

[118]*Ibid.*, p. 70.

[119]*Ibid.*, pp. 75–78.

distrust of Birnbaum's political motives and of his growing irritation. Herzl's diaries record the mutual sense of antagonism and dislike. As early as 1st March 1896, Herzl noted:

"Birnbaum is unmistakably jealous of me. What the baser sort of Jews put into vulgar or sneering language, namely that I am out for personal advantage, is what I catch in the intimations of this cultivated gentleman . . . I judge Birnbaum to be an envious, vain and obstinate man. I hear that he had already turned away from Zionism and gone over to Socialism, when my appearance led him back again to Zion."[120]

Three days later Herzl observed in even harsher terms:

"Dr. Birnbaum wrote me today a letter bemoaning his financial straits. I gave him twenty florins, which I herewith duly record, because I am certain he is inimical to me and will grow more so.

In conversation he spoke slightingly to me about Landau. During the evening, at the meeting convened by Landau, he made a Socialistic speech; and from Landau's report I gather that it contained an argument against a discussion of my pamphlet, which was on the agenda. These are discouraging signs. Landau further writes that Birnbaum wants to become the Socialist leader in Palestine. We haven't got the country, and they already want to tear it apart."[121]

At the First Zionist Congress in Basle matters came to a head, with a motion proposed by Isidor Schalit that the Secretary-General (Birnbaum) be elected by the Congress and have a vote and seat on the *Aktionskommittee*.[122] The motion which implied that the Secretary-General, as trustee for the Congress, would in Herzl's words "counter-balance the other twenty-two members of the Executive Committee", was voted down.[123] Birnbaum was indeed elected to the top leadership, the Viennese *Aktionskommittee* (along with Herzl, Moritz Tobias Schnirer, Oskar (Oser) Kokesch and Johann Kremenetzky) but could not retain this position under Congress rules and at the same time remain Secretary-General. Birnbaum's inevitable resignation from the *Aktionskommittee* provoked however a demonstration by his friends, one of whom, Malz, publicly declared:

"Dr. Birnbaum must have the mandate. We should not accept his resignation. Without Birnbaum there would be no Herzl, no Zionist movement in Austria."[124]

Malz's clumsy protest that Birnbaum had no means of support because of his sacrifices for the Zionist cause aroused some stormy, tumultuous reactions which obliged him to leave the platform. Herzl himself believed that Birnbaum had orchestrated the whole scene and contemptuously noted in his diary on 3rd September 1897:

"Another critical moment – when the Birnbaum business occurred. This Birnbaum, who had dropped Zionism for Socialism three years before I appeared on the scene, poses himself and imposes himself as my 'predecessor'. In shameless begging-letters, written to me and others,

---

[120]*The Diaries of Theodor Herzl*, op. cit., p. 102.
[121]*Ibid.*, p. 103.
[122]Frankel, *Prophecy and Politics*, op. cit., p. 83. Schalit argued: "Bei den Sozialdemokraten ist es auch so. Wir sind keine Bourgeois-Partei", a phrase repeated by a number of delegates which particularly irritated Herzl.
[123]*The Diaries of Theodor Herzl*, op. cit., pp. 226–227 described the motion as "the only discordant note at the Congress; and instigated by Schalit, a young man whom I had overwhelmed by kindness".
[124]Frankel, *Prophecy and Politics*, op. cit., pp. 83–84.

he represents himself as the discoverer and founder of Zionism, because he had written a pamphlet like many another since Pinsker (of whom, too, I had of course been unaware.) He now induced a few young people to put forward a motion that the Secretary-General of the Executive Committee be directly appointed and paid by the Congress. And this fellow, who at the First National Assembly of the Jewish people has no other thought but to get himself voted a stipend, dares to draw comparisons between himself and me. Here too, as in his begging-letters, he adds audacity to his mendicancy."[125]

Clearly, given this degree of antagonism Herzl could not work for long with such a rival as his General Secretary. Within a year Birnbaum had left the movement, no longer attended Zionist Congresses or contributed again under his own name to *Die Welt*, the new Zionist newspaper founded in Vienna by Herzl. Nevertheless, Birnbaum still saw himself as a Jewish Nationalist and like Ahad Ha'am, the leading ideologue of Russian Zionism and opponent of Herzl, at first focused his criticisms on Herzlian "Charter Diplomacy" as a dead end for the movement. Like Ahad Ha'am, he also began to emphasise that the purpose of the Jewish national renaissance was to provide a solution for the "problem of Judaism" rather than the "problem of Jewry".[126] But unlike the Russian thinker, Birnbaum now took fundamental issue with the Zionist "negation of the Diaspora", proclaiming instead that *Israel geht vor Zion* (Israel comes before Zion) – the needs of the Jewish people must have precedence over the creation of a national centre in Palestine. The *Galut* could no longer be downgraded "simply as valuable cultural manure for just one potential culture in a soil which is not yet ours".[127] Jewish Nationalism had to become more concerned with the here-and-now, with an understanding and appreciation of the central core of the Diaspora experience – namely the lives of the compact masses of East European Jewry.

At the First Zionist Congress in 1897, Birnbaum had indeed acknowledged the "national individuality" and "unique culture of this Eastern Jewry (three-fourths of the world Jewish population), "expressed in costumes and language, literature and art, customs and traditions, in religious, social and legal life . . ."[128] But in his Zionist phase he was still highly critical of the self-enclosed culture of the ghetto and pessimistic about its future. Having left the Zionist movement he changed his mind about the *Ostjuden* and began moving towards the ideology of *Golus* Nationalism based on the centrality of their language, culture and history.

"When I found them to be a people with all the signs of a live, separate nation, it became more and more clear to me that a nation that already exists does not have to be created again *de novo*, and that what is of principal importance is preserving its life. Thus I developed my *Golus* Nationalism. In Western Europe I stood up for Eastern European Jews, pointing out their lively folk-existence and I requested of the latter that they guard what they possess and especially that they should not destroy it for the sake of dreams of the future."[129]

Birnbaum called his theory of non-Zionist Nationalism, worked out between 1902 and 1905, *Alljudentum* (Pan-Judaism), since it sought to embrace Jewish national and cultural life throughout the Diaspora and secure the recognition of

[125]*The Diaries of Theodor Herzl, op. cit.*, p. 226.
[126]Goldsmith, *loc. cit.*, p. 105.
[127]*Ibid.*, p. 106.
[128]'Der Zionismus als Culturbewegung', *loc. cit.*, p. 70.
[129]*Yubileum-Bukh, op. cit.*, p. 13. Goldsmith, *loc. cit.*, p. 107.

World Jewry as a nationality by the great Powers. He now reversed his earlier views concerning the inevitability of assimilation outside Palestine, arguing that the demographic, socio-economic, cultural and political factors which had led to the disintegration of Jewish identity in the West did not apply to the *Ostjuden*. They still lived in dense concentrations, were imbued with a strong national consciousness and Jewish folk tradition and their culture was undergoing a powerful literary renaissance.[130]

Moreover, the prospects of Jewish survival as a national group with rights of cultural autonomy despite their non-territorial and minority status had increased as a result of the political crisis then overtaking the multi-national empires (Austria-Hungary, Russia) in Europe. After 1900 these empires seemed to be in the process of losing their legitimacy as centralised states, with federalism becoming increasingly discussed as an optimal solution to their intractable nationality problems. Birnbaum's turn to Diaspora Nationalism and then to autonomism as a realistic political programme for Austrian and East European Jewry was thus part of a wider trend in both the Jewish and non-Jewish worlds. It was no accident that the first decade of the twentieth century saw the blossoming of theories of national autonomy developed by thinkers as diverse as the Austro-Marxists Karl Renner and Otto Bauer, the Russian-Jewish historian Simon Dubnow or the populist revolutionary Chaim Zhitlovsky. No less significant was their adoption as concrete electoral programmes by Jewish political parties and other national minorities in both Russia and Austria-Hungary.[131]

Nathan Birnbaum was perfectly aware of the more favourable climate of opinion towards autonomism in Austrian politics which happened to coincide with the national renaissance of East European Jewry. National autonomy, he asserted in an editorial in the *Neue Zeitung* on 9th August 1907, was an idea whose time had come; it had supporters in all Austrian political camps, among old and young, conservatives and revolutionaries, bourgeois and workers, Germans and Slavs.[132] The old dualistic system in Austria-Hungary and the centralist constitution were bankrupt. The Habsburg Monarchy could only survive if it abandoned anachronistic national and confessional structures in favour of socially progressive, democratic and autonomist principles, thereby transforming itself into a federation of nations bound together by common economic and

---

[130]'Ostjüdische Aufgaben', Vortrag, gehalten am 8. Juli 1905 in der Akademischen Verbindung "Zephirah" in Czernowitz, *Ausgewählte Schriften, op. cit.*, I, pp. 260–275. Also 'Etwas über Ost- und Westjuden', *ibid.*, pp. 276–282, first published in *Jüdischer Volkskalender für das Jahr 5665*, (1904–1905).

[131]On the theory and practice of autonomism, see Simon Dubnow, *Nationalism and History. Essays on Old and New Judaism*, ed. and introd. K. S. Pinson, Philadelphia 1958; Oscar Janowsky, *Jews and Minority Rights (1898–1919)*, New York 1933; Kurt Schillswieg, 'Nationalism and Autonomy among East European Jewry. Origin and Historical Development up to 1939', *Jewish Social Studies*, April 1944, pp. 27–68. Robert S. Wistrich, *Socialism and the Jews, op. cit.*, pp. 209–348 and Frankel, *Prophecy and the Jews, op. cit.*, pp. 162–167, 217–224.

[132]'Nationale Autonomie', *Neue Zeitung*, II, Nr. 9 (9th August 1907), p. 1. Birnbaum had founded this weekly in 1906 to further his autonomist political objectives.

cultural interests.[133] This reconstituting of the Monarchy on the basis of cultural-national autonomy must include official recognition of the Jews as a nationality and, as a preliminary step towards this goal, a reorientation of Austrian-Jewish politics, to seek alliances with other ethnic groups prepared to support Jewish aspirations.[134]

In 1906, as the electoral struggle hotted up throughout the Austrian Empire, this strategy was by no means unrealistic. For example, the Ukrainian leader, Romanczuk, in order to divert Jewish support away from the Poles in Galicia, had proposed to the Austrian Parliament the recognition of the Jews as a nationality with a parliamentary representation of their own.[135] Birnbaum, like other Jewish national leaders, strongly advocated an alliance with the Ukrainians against the Polish *Schlachta* (landowners) whom he regarded as the oppressors of both the Ukrainian and Jewish national minorities.[136] In the general elections of 1907, the first to be contested in Austria under conditions of universal suffrage, the three successful Jewish national candidates in Galicia were elected partly thanks to an electoral agreement with the Ukrainians.[137] Birnbaum himself was unsuccessful in his attempt to become a member of the *Reichsrat* as a representative from East Galicia, in spite of Ukrainian support.[138] In Bukovina, too, where Benno Straucher was elected as representative of the Jewish National Party in Czernowitz, autonomism had taken root among the Jewish population living in a multi-national environment, who demanded their full linguistic rights and political representation as a distinct ethnic entity.[139]

Birnbaum already recognised at this time the centrality of the Yiddish vernacular to the life of East European Jewry and began to propagandise actively on behalf of Yiddish language, literature and drama. He organised "Yiddish evenings" in Vienna, established *Yidishe Kultur* (a student organisation for the promotion of Yiddish culture) and translated the works of outstanding Yiddish

[133]Hermann Kadisch, 'Rück- und Ausblicke', *ibid.*, I, Nr. 11 (16th November 1906), p. 1. "Jede Nation und jede Religion hat wohl das unveräusserliche Recht auf Autonomie, keine aber kann das Recht auf Herrschaft über alle anderen beanspruchen . . ."

[134]*Ibid.* "Eine Einigung aller auf national-sozialem Boden fussenden österreichischen Juden und weiter eine Verständigung mit den nationalen Autonomisten der übrigen Völker, welche die Juden als gleichberechtigte Nation anerkennen, ist unbedingt notwendig."

[135]Goldsmith, *loc. cit.*, p. 108.

[136]'Jüdische Polen', *Neue Zeitung*, I, Nr. 7 (19th October 1906), pp. 2–3; 'Juden und Ruthenen', *ibid.*, I, Nr. 4 (28th September 1906), p. 2. Also, 'Unser Hass gegen das Polentum', *ibid.*, II, Nr. 2 (28th June 1907), p. 1.

[137]'Galizische Wahlen', *Arbeiterzeitung*, 11th June 1907, pp. 1–3; Janowsky, *op. cit.*, pp. 136–140.

[138]See 'Wie eine strahlende Welt', (first published in *Die Welt*, XI, Nr. 23 on 7th June 1907) in *Ausgewählte Schriften*, II, pp. 3–5; Birnbaum's personal account of his electoral experience is full of lyrical enthusiasm for the courage and self-sacrifice of the Galician *Ostjuden*. On the electoral chicanery, see *idem*, 'Die galizischen Raubwahlen', *Neue Zeitung*, II, Nr. 1 (12th June 1907), pp. 1–2. Goldsmith, *loc. cit.* p. 109, claims however that "many Jews declined to vote for him because they were afraid that if he were elected, his Jewish physiognomy would set off a new wave of anti-Semitic ridicule and slander".

[139]'Die Sprachenfrage in der Bukowina und die Juden', *Neue Zeitung*, II, Nr. 7 (26th July 1907), pp. 1–2. On the Jewish national movement in Bukovina, see now Gerald Stourzh, 'Galten die Juden als Nationalität Altösterreichs?', *Studia Judaica Austriaca*, X. *Prag-Czernowitz-Jerusalem*, Eisenstadt 1984, pp. 73–98. On Birnbaum's role in this movement, *ibid.*, p. 80.

writers such as Sholem Aleichem, Shalom Asch and Y. L. Peretz into German.[140] Not only did he conduct an unremitting crusade to raise its prestige among Jews and non-Jews alike, but he worked hard to master the language himself so as to be a more effective propagandist of the new cause. Yiddish became indeed the vehicle of his *Golus* Nationalism, the symbol of the pan-Judaist consciousness which he sought to instill in the Jewish masses throughout the Diaspora.

Rejecting the typical prejudices of assimilated German Jews against the bastardised, mongrel "Jargon" and Zionist aspersions against the servile language of the *Galut*, Birnbaum glowingly portrayed Yiddish as the mirror of a proud, creative tradition. Moreover, as the language of nine million Jews dispersed throughout the world, it had to be considered a major factor of national cohesion. Without Yiddish as a living *Umgangssprache*, the Jews of Eastern Europe would, according to Birnbaum, sink to the level of Western Jewry and the organic unity of Jewish *Volkstum* would rapidly disintegrate.[141] During his Czernowitz period (1908–1911) Birnbaum even developed a complete theory of Yiddishism designed to demonstrate its indispensability to Jewish national life and consciousness. Yiddish, he now argued, was the vehicle of uniquely Jewish cultural values; its intimacy, elasticity and hybrid character a testament to the genius of adaptation combined with tenacious resistance to assimilation, displayed by Diaspora Jewry throughout its long exile. Those Jewish intellectuals who denounced it as a semi-barbaric "Jargon", whether they were *Maskilim*, assimilationists or Zionists, merely demonstrated how totally estranged they were from Jewish life and the soul of the Jewish people.

Birnbaum's radical break with Enlightenment stereotypes of Yiddish was part of his broader revision of standard Western myths concerning the *Ostjuden*. The East European Jews had become for him the cultural yardstick of Jewish integrity which now had to be defended at all costs from the incursions of the West. By 1909 he was openly calling for the emancipation of the *Ostjuden* from the yoke of Western Jewry, even at the price of shattering what he considered to be a largely fictitious unity of the Jewish people.[142] The call for separation was motivated less by hatred of the West than by the feeling that only the insulation of the *Ostjuden* could preserve their organic culture and folk life from the threat of decomposition.[143]

In the Austrian-Jewish context, Birnbaum's defence of autonomism, Yiddishism and the *Ostjuden* had placed him in open opposition to the two central warring blocks – the assimilationists and the Zionists. Nevertheless, as Austrian Zionism itself began to adopt the autonomist programme after 1905 and engage more intensively in domestic politics (*Landespolitik*), the differences were some-

[140]See 'Für die jüdische Sprache', 29th November 1907, and 'Der "Jargon"', in *Ausgewählte Schriften*, *op. cit.*, II, pp. 34–40, 46–51. Also Goldsmith, *loc. cit.* pp. 109–118.

[141]'Zum Sprachenstreit. Eine Entgegnung an Achad Ha'am', *Ausgewählte Schriften*, II, p. 71.

[142]'Die Emanzipation des Ostjudentums vom Westjudentum' (Herbst 1909), *ibid.*, pp. 13–33.

[143]*Ibid.*, p. 30. ". . . nicht Sympathien und Antipathien, nicht vorgefasste Meinungen über 'faulen Westen' und 'gesunden Osten' liegen dem Wunsche und der Hoffnung zugrunde, dass sich das Ostjudentum gegenüber dem Westjudentum durchsetze, sondern die Einsicht in die Todesgefahr des ganzen jüdischen Volkstums, wenn dies nicht geschieht".

what blurred. The right of the Jewish masses to develop their own autonomous institutions and adapt the religious communities to modern needs, to develop an independent national life and *Sozialpolitik* in the Diaspora, to use their own language freely, and to seek official recognition as a nationality (*Volksstamm*) became a key basis of co-operation between Zionists and Diaspora Nationalists.[144] In particular, the struggle for the acceptance of Yiddish as a minority language that could be used in schools, offices and public life, a demand opposed by Habsburg officialdom, by dominant nationalities like the Germans and Poles and by the assimilated *Westjuden*, provided a common front. The pursuit of Jewish national politics, especially in Galicia, which aroused the vehement opposition of the ruling Polish aristocracy and its assimilationist *Hausjuden* reinforced the links within the Jewish national camp.[145]

Nevertheless, autonomism clearly differed from Zionism in that the national struggle which it waged was centred exclusively in the Diaspora. By viewing nationality independently of statehood, in terms of a common language and culture and by defining national affiliation in personal rather than territorial terms, autonomism sought to provide a definitive answer to the problem of the dispersed Jewish population in the multi-national Monarchy.[146] Cultural-national autonomy, as enunciated by Birnbaum and other like-minded Jewish intellectuals, intended to integrate the Jews into the state organism as a national unit, along with other minorities. In contrast to liberal assimilationism and Zionism, this view held that national autonomy would bring about a definitive equalisation of the Jewish status and thereby effectively dissolve the problem of antisemitism. Relations between Jews and non-Jews would be normalised, so Nathan Birnbaum had argued in 1905, once Jewry no longer served as cannon-fodder for the bourgeois parties of other nations or for the Austrian Social Democrats but voted in separate electoral *curias* for their own lists.[147]

Birnbaum, it must be said, regarded national autonomy as providing the best hope of a more secure present and a richer, more creative cultural life not only for Austrian Jewry in Galicia and Bukovina but for all of the eight million Jews in Eastern Europe.[148] In 1907 he believed that genuine national equality without assimilation and the full development of the cultural individuality of the Jewish people was a real possibility within a democratised, federal Austrian nationalities' state which would emerge in the wake of universal suffrage. Such a solution

---

[144]See Schillsweig, 'Nationalism and Autonomy . . .', *loc. cit.*, pp. 30 ff. Also Max Rosenfeld, 'Die jüdischen Gemeinden in Österreich', *Der Jude*, II, Heft 3 (June 1917), pp. 152–162 for the Zionist view.

[145]Leila P. Everett, 'The Rise of Jewish National Politics in Galicia 1905–1907', in Andrei S. Markovits and Frank E. Sysyn (eds.), *Nationbuilding and the Politics of Nationalism. Essays on Austrian Galicia*, Harvard 1982, pp.149–177.

[146]Nathan Birnbaum, 'Die nationale Autonomie der Juden', *Der Weg*, I, Nr. 14 (30th December 1905), in J. Fraenkel (ed.), *The Jews of Austria. Essays on their Life, History and Destruction*, London 1967, p. 134.

[147]*Ibid.*, p. 135. In this article Birnbaum polemicised against assimilationist critics who suggested that the recognition of the Jewish nationality meant a return to the ghetto and the acceptance of antisemitic theories. Against this claim he retorted: "kein Ghetto kann geschlossener sein als diese Atmosphäre von Zwielicht und Zweideutigkeit . . ." – produced by the failure of assimilation.

[148]'Jüdische Autonomie', *Ost und West*, VI, No. 1 (January 1906); *ibid.*, p. 146.

Nathan Birnbaum
(1864–1937)
Vienna 1929

Nathan Birnbaum with his son, the philologist Solomon Birnbaum, and grandson Jacob
Hamburg 1931

would help resolve the deepest problem which faced contemporary Jewry – one to which neither emancipation nor political Zionism had provided a satisfactory answer – namely the renewal of Jewish national creativity. National autonomy within Austria based on the cultivation of Yiddish and the further development of the existing organisational and cultural frameworks of the *Ostjuden* would offer the optimal framework for the creation of a new more rooted Jew and a genuine Jewish renaissance.[149]

Nathan Birnbaum's progression through *Golus* Nationalism and autonomism to Yiddishism and the glorification of East European Jewish folk culture was in many respects a smooth and logical transition. His adoption of an Orthodox religious position in the First World War was to be the final and most unexpected stage in his long quest for an authentic Jewish identity. Birnbaum had long since rejected the Zionist attempt to forge a new East-West synthesis in Palestine by secular political means; he had turned his back on the dream of building a modern Zionist culture of the future by negating the vibrant national life of the present; from his Diaspora Nationalist phase he had been persuaded that the real *Kulturjuden* were to be found in the ghettoes of Eastern Europe but he was soon to be assailed by doubts as to whether this world of secular *Yiddishkeit* could survive the intrusions of Western modernity. Even national autonomy, which had seemed so promising an option during the high point of autonomist agitation in 1907, began to pale as a realistic Jewish political option, with the continued decay of the Habsburg State and its eventual disintegration during the First World War. Thus Birnbaum's re-affirmation of East European *Golus* was being gradually stripped of its credibility unless it could somehow be anchored to the oldest of Jewish sacred missions – that of preserving the monotheistic faith of Israel.[150]

The path for secular Zionism through Pan-Judaism and Yiddish culture to Torah Judaism was to be the last metamorphosis – the return of the *Ba'al-tschuva* to the religious roots of Jewish being.[151] All his life, Birnbaum had been preoccupied by the "essence of Judaism" and remained consistent in this stubborn search in spite of all apparent contradictions and incoherences. Repelled in his youth by the liberal, assimilated milieu and hedonistic materialism of Viennese Jewry, his prophetic passions had first been inflamed by the Jewish national idea whose torch he carried in Central Europe for more than twenty years. The youthful apostle of Austrian Zionism, he had sought to be the cultural mediator between East and West in the movement until Herzl's dramatic appearance on the stage drove him to the periphery and eventually led him to rediscover the national life and unique culture of the *Ostjuden* at first hand.

Birnbaum was in fact the first German-speaking intellectual to transform the image of the despised *Schacherjuden* and *Schnorrer* into a counter-myth of vibrant folk creativity. Like Martin Buber, a Viennese intellectual with Galician roots,

---

[149]'Die Autonomiebestrebungen der Juden in Österreich', *ibid.*, p. 143. "Die nationale Autonomie wird uns den neuen Juden schaffen helfen, nach dem unsere Seelen so lechzen."
[150]See Nathan Birnbaum, *Gottes Volk*, Wien–Berlin 1918.
[151]*Vom Sinn des Judentums, op. cit.*, p. 9.

Birnbaum came to see in the *Ostjuden* the best hope for the regeneration of the Jewish nation. In his writings they became the incarnation of true *Geist* and *Kultur* and their maligned Yiddish language the embodiment of vital Jewish traditions and spiritual values. Birnbaum's rediscovery of the grandeur of the Jewish Diaspora, of its martyrdom and creativity, had brought him to a deeper sense of the mystery of Jewish survival. The search of the alienated intellectual for the roots of his own people and its specific genius led him to a new appreciation of the peculiar spiritual uniqueness of the Jews. Abandoning the pagan idols of land and *Volk*, the resurgent temptations of modern secular Nationalism, he returned finally to the religious sources of the Jewish experience – to the Sinaitic revelation, the God of Israel and the "inner faith" of the eternal people.[152]

Birnbaum had experienced, with a rare intensity, the dilemmas and tensions of all the central ideologies which helped shape modern Jewish history in Central and Eastern Europe – Zionism, Socialism, autonomism, Yiddishism – before finding peace from his restless search in the pre-modern refuge of Orthodox faith. This strange odyssey with its often mystifying twists and turns reflected not only a profound personal quest but also many of the underlying social, cultural and psychological realities behind the first stirrings of the Jewish national renaissance in Austria-Hungary. Carl Schorske has written in another context of ideological collages "made of fragments of modernity, glimpses of futurity and resurrected remnants of a half-forgotten past" – which characterised the aesthetic politics of such Austrian masters of the "new key" as Schönerer, Lueger and Herzl.[153] Nathan Birnbaum was in some ways a similar kind of Viennese artist, though one who played on the keys of the "Jewish spirit" and sought the secret of its being in the soul of the *Volk*. Pioneer of Zionism, agitator, publicist, educator and inspirer of *fin-de-siècle* Jewish youth in the Habsburg lands, Birnbaum remained an eternally dissatisfied spiritual rebel. In Franz Rosenzweig's words, he was a "living exponent of Jewish intellectual history".[154]

[152]*Ibid.*, pp. 41 ff.
[153]Carl E. Schorske, *Fin-de-Siècle Vienna. Politics and Culture*, New York 1980, p. 120.
[154]Letter of Rosenzweig to Maximilian Landau, February 1924, quoted in Steven E. Aschheim, *Brothers and Strangers. The East European Jew in German and German Jewish Consciousness, 1800–1923*, Madison, Wisconsin 1982, p. 114.

From the First World War to Nazi Rule

Voices of Opposition to the First World War among Jewish Thinkers

BY RIVKA HORWITZ

With the outbreak of the First World War a new epoch in world history commenced. Whilst before the war bourgeois existence was tranquil and unruffled in Central Europe, the very fact that this war was unleashed shattered faith in a life of stability, in the march of progress and in the hope that universal security was within reach of mankind. Before the war the world looked to many as though it were fast improving; that reason could solve man's problems; and that the world was moving towards an almost messianic era. Now, suddenly, Germany too awoke from a dream, the world of yesterday was destroyed; German men had to fight at the front, live the wretched life of a soldier, defend the political interests of their country and in the end accept defeat. There was an essential difference in the spiritual atmosphere between the serene pre-war times and the destruction and despair of the post-war era. Moreover, this war was different from all earlier wars, because it gradually involved the "whole world". Furthermore due to the rapid advances in technology, the suffering of the civilian population and the sheer cruelty of warfare assumed much larger dimensions than hitherto. All this made justification of the war all the more questionable.

Unlike the Second World War, where crucial moral issues were at stake, the First World War did not pose such clear-cut ethical questions on which to base a decision as to which side to support. Also from a general Jewish point of view there was certainly no decisive issue, moral or political, that unambiguously required the support of one side against the other. Therefore the World Zionist Organisation, for example, was neutral;* from a Zionist point of view the Jews could support either side.[1] British Jews could therefore support England and write in favour of British war aims whilst German Jews could support Imperial German politics. It was axiomatic and accepted as inevitable that Jew would fight Jew. One could say that this war was more like a *milhemet reshut* than a *milhemet hova*. To German Jewry, which had been extremely patriotic for many decades, the war opened up new possibilities of serving their country and of

*On the Zionist policies during the war years see the essay by Jürgen Matthäus 'Deutschtum and Judentum under Fire. The Impact of the First World War on the Strategies of the Centralverein and the Zionistische Vereinigung', in this volume of the Year Book – (Ed.).
[1]Kurt Blumenfeld, *Erlebte Judenfrage. Ein Vierteljahrhundert deutscher Zionismus*, Stuttgart 1962, Veröffentlichung des Leo Baeck Instituts, p. 116.

demonstrating to their compatriots their love of the fatherland. Despite enormous efforts to achieve equal rights, German Jews had continued to suffer disabilities and were frustrated by the ambivalence of German society. In the aftermath of the First World War the Jewish experience was to show how superfluous all their strivings had been, and seen in hindsight the extreme patriotism of the German Jews must seem to us altogether misplaced. Therefore viewed in perspective the few dissident Jewish voices are heroic and meaningful.

German-Jewish thinkers were not granted the gift of prophecy and it was natural for them to express a total identity with Germany. For them the fact of conscription was a natural by-product of their emancipation and an important milestone on the road to complete social equality. They were committed optimists in their beliefs; and they considered ethics, justice and God to be on the side of their country. The Emperor becomes, in the writings of Joseph Wohlgemuth, the editor of *Jeschurun* and a teacher in the Orthodox Rabbinical Seminary, a symbol of morality, and German political aims appear as pious and good; the Emperor's piety is considered to have a good effect on the Jews as it actually teaches them to be God-fearing. Hardly any grain of scepticism, humour or doubt is to be found in the writings of the Jews around 1914. Wohlgemuth regards the Germans as the people of God and the Russians as his enemies; God is come, as he puts it, to judge the world.[2] He, as many others, painted the war in messianic colours. One feels in many writings of that period an intoxicated devotion and an overwhelming desire of the Jews to sacrifice themselves for their fatherland. When we study this chapter of Jewish history nowadays, we sense the deep German roots of German-Jewish existence and how their *Weltanschauung* was adapted to these German values. (How far all this is, for example, from the notions of a Rav Kook who saw the First World War from Switzerland or London in the light of Jewish apocalyptic tradition, is only too apparent.)[3]

Russia and its backward social order thus appear as a target of attack in many Jewish writings. Joseph Carlebach, the well-known educator and rabbi, quotes[4] for example, in an article on ethics and the war, Jeremiah: XXXIV as a text which met the hour; Jeremiah was demanding the freeing of the slaves and the proclamation of their liberty as a pre-condition of a political victory. Carlebach interpreted this passage as an allusion to the Russian tyranny likely to lose the war because of its despotic regime. Germany, on the other hand, appeared to him as the land where politics and morality coincided, hence worthy of victory. Wohlgemuth also emphasised Russia's crimes:[5] It had annexed the lands of

[2]Joseph Wohlgemuth, *Der Weltkrieg im Lichte des Judentums*, a collection of his war essays from *Jeschurun*, Berlin 1915.

[3]Rav Kook, *Orot*, Jerusalem 1963, pp. 13 ff. (in Hebrew); and Zvi Yaron, *The Philosophy of Rabbi Kook*, Jerusalem 1974, p. 311 (in Hebrew).

[4]'Moral und Politik', *Jeschurun*, I (1914), pp. 410–413 (see also 'Die grosse Zeit', *ibid.*, p. 334). Later in the *Festschrift für Jacob Rosenheim*, pp. 82–107, he wrote 'Moral und Politik', an article in favour of Pacifism. See also Haim H. Cohn, 'Joseph Carlebach', in *LBI Year Book V* (1960), p. 72. Nahum Goldmann, the prominent Zionist leader was also a war enthusiast during the First World War, something he also was later to regret. See Nahum Goldmann, *Von der weltkulturellen Bedeutung und Aufgabe des Judentums*, München 1916 and then *Mein Leben als deutscher Jude*, München-Wien 1980, p. 101.

[5]'Der Weltkrieg', *Jeschurun*, I (1914), pp. 255–274.

other people, destroyed their inhabitants and despised the religion of its minorities. The Emperor's war appears to him just, Germany was fighting for its very existence. "*Dulce et decorum est pro patria mori.*" Two years later the great liberal philosopher Hermann Cohen in his pamphlet *Deutschtum und Judentum* identifies the spirit of Germany with that of the Jews.[6] Many German Jews agreed with Cohen, even Isaac Breuer then wrote an article in this vein; the Jewish cause was identified with the German cause, without any genuinely broader perspective either as regards world politics or World Jewry.

As constantly reiterated in the Jewish press, the fight was particularly justified when it came to Russia and the Tsar, whereas the war against the democracies, France and England, appeared to them a less convincing cause. Russia was also the country in which the Jews had suffered most; hence one reads in the Jewish papers of the hardships of Russian Jewry and there are reminders of the Beilis Blood Libel (1911–1913) which had been engineered by the Russian Minister of Justice Shcheglovitov and which was still fresh in the memory of the reader. This evil accusation was symbolic of the contest between Liberals and reactionaries and German Jews could argue a real commitment; they could see a point in fighting this tyranny. Yet to fight for the sake of the *Ostjuden* – how sincere was that really?

The idea of volunteering, of expressing a desire to sacrifice oneself for the fatherland is a novel *halakhic* issue. It appears in Samson Raphael Hirsch's *Horeb* of the middle of the nineteenth century. In 1914 Rabbi Joseph Carlebach wrote in the same spirit "with all thy heart and all thy soul and with all thy might, this is the demand of the day".

Rabbis, if they were to judge solely on *halakhic* grounds, might perhaps have stressed Jewish identity more and have suggested that serious Talmud students should go to study in Hungary for instance and thus avoid war service. Instead they voiced the general political aspirations of German Jewry and did not question joining the army. Being well versed in *Halakhah* they might also have alluded to some *halakhic* difficulties when it came to joining the army in Germany, and so strengthen Jewish consciousness. In 1870 Rabbi Esriel Hildesheimer[7] still furnished in the *Jüdische Presse* some *halakhic* instructions to the Jewish soldier. But in 1914 nothing of that kind was published in the Jewish press. Mordechai Breuer[8] in his important recent study on German Orthodoxy demonstrates convincingly how during the First World War Orthodox Jews joined the army and expressed themselves as war enthusiasts in a manner no different from that of Liberals or Zionists, and that one cannot distinguish any difference in tone between the various Jewish strands. Hildesheimer still exhorts the Jewish soldier to keep the Jewish law in war-time conditions within the army as much as he can; he instructs the young Jew that in the event of his being near a dying fellow Jew he should leave everything behind and stay with his suffering co-religionist; Hildesheimer also demands that in accordance with the spirit of

[6]Hermann Cohen, *Jüdische Schriften*, II, Berlin 1924, pp. 237–302.
[7]*Die Jüdische Presse*, I (1870), p. 54.
[8]Mordechai Breuer, *Jüdische Orthodoxie im Deutschen Reich 1871–1918. Die Sozialgeschichte einer religiösen Minderheit*, Frankfurt a. Main 1986, Veröffentlichung des Leo Baeck Instituts, p. 342.

Halakhah one should also help one's fellow Jew in emergencies, even if it means transgressing the law.

We have a particularly significant observation by Rabbi David Zvi Hoffmann who, in the pre-war period, was asked by a Jew[9] whether he should obey the command of the government and fulfil his army duty which might extend to two or three years and cause him to break Jewish laws or whether he should refrain from such a duty. Hoffmann replied to him that avoiding army duty would be a *Hillul Hashem*, the government would discover the culprit and Jew-haters would raise their voices and claim that the Jews do not obey the laws of the land. It would seem that what he depicts is a fair estimate of the state of affairs.

Jewish law demands that one should be faithful to the land in which one resides providing that the law of that land is based on ethical grounds. It does not, however, demand that one volunteer for the army nor that one display such war enthusiasm as the German Jews demonstrated in 1914. Instead one finds numerous war volunteers in Germany – equally numerous among the Orthodox Jews as well[10] – and no rabbinical warnings against this wave of nationalism. This was the Jewish fight for recognition. The majority enrolled patriotically and voluntarily, the rest joined up to fulfil their duty and there were hardly any Jews who avoided conscription or deserted.

Jewish rejection of the war was extremely rare; some of the dissident voices came from Jews who had not been mobilised; others are the voices of Jews who served in the army and yet found ways to express their opposition to the war. Some voiced dissent because they believed in the universal emancipation of mankind and abhorred any narrow nationalism; they believed in reason and thought that Socialism or universalism would persuade man to stop this general madness. War appeared to them as a sinister peculiarity of the human species which demands that hordes of people should pursue other hordes of people for the sole purpose of destroying them. They were Pacifists and sought a quick end to the war. Was not the First World War to cost Europe the lives of ten million people? Was it not to bring famine and disease in its wake, to swallow the wealth of Europe, impoverish the people and shake the foundation of moral and social order? Only very few Jews joined with non-Jews, and also non-Germans, as Pacifists, Social Anarchists and Internationalists rejecting the war, favouring the unity of Europe and opposing extreme nationalism.[11] There was, however, also a uniquely Jewish rejection of the war. This is a matter which is much less known. There were those who on account of their deeply Jewish orientation argued against fighting a war "which is not ours".

[9]*Sefer Melamed Lehoil. The Responsa of David Zvi Hoffmann*, I, New York 1954, p. 42.
[10]Breuer, *Jüdische Orthodoxie, op. cit.*, pp. 342–350.
[11]These other Jewish objectors to the war aims of Imperial Germany or the Habsburg monarchy are not within the scope of this essay, though some of them are also mentioned below. Quite often they were already estranged from the Jewish community, even converts. Naturally these staunch opponents of the war also deserve much commendation. Kurt Tucholsky later proudly proclaimed his shirking of German military service in many of his writings of Weimar Germany. The philosopher Sir Karl Popper, for instance, claimed to have been a Pacifist and an objector in 1914 (cf. the report in *The Times* of 11th April 1987 on a speech Popper delivered in Austria early in April.) These are but some examples.

Albert Einstein, Gustav Landauer and the young Gershom Scholem were among those few who voiced dissent and criticised the attitudes of Imperial Germany or of German Jewry. But much attention will here also be given to Isaac Breuer who served in the army, but left behind a highly revealing document which constitutes a rare attack on the war, a deep Jewish outcry against it.

THE CASE OF ALBERT EINSTEIN

Einstein's involvement in the war came by chance. In his youth he had left Germany and relinquished his German citizenship. In the years preceding the First World War he lived in Switzerland, working at the Zürich Institute of Technology. In 1914, having achieved world fame through his discoveries in mathematics and physics, he was offered a professorship at the University of Berlin and a position as the director of the physics institute founded by the *Kaiser-Wilhelm-Gesellschaft zur Förderung der Wissenschaften* in Berlin. This position was actually created for him; Einstein was to receive a liberal salary and would have no teaching obligations. Though disliking Germany, he accepted the offer. The fact that he had some close members of his family living in Berlin may have helped him to reach a positive decision just a few months before the outbreak of the war. Had he waited another few months he would probably never have returned to Germany.

In the case of Einstein one should take into consideration his unique personality and the unusually high position he had attained at the age of thirty-five. Einstein was a very gentle man who needed peaceful and harmonious surroundings in order to proceed at his own pace and develop his bold scientific discoveries. He abhorred authoritarianism and militarism. He was also a Jew who had obtained Swiss citizenship. Nobody in Germany dared to touch him. In his eyes the war of 1914 had no moral justification; it shocked him deeply. It was a war that created suffering and destruction on a large scale and the sudden closing of borders had turned former friends into enemies overnight. The Pacifism of Einstein was not a form of "naive" and total opposition to all wars. Naturally, if we want to make this comparison, his reaction to the Second World War, for which he saw a moral justification, was bound to be utterly different. He was actively involved in it, he firmly demanded of others that they be too; it was a just war against Hitler and fascism.

In 1914, at the very start of hostilities, when opposition to the war was still extremely limited, only a small splinter group among the Social Democrats, composed of people such as Karl Liebknecht, Hugo Haase and Rosa Luxemburg, actively opposed the war.[12] Einstein rejected it on his own terms. He did

[12]Jews on the Socialist Left in opposition to Imperial Germany's war have more than once been written about in the publications of the Leo Baeck Institute. Consult, for example, Werner T. Angress, 'Juden im politischen Leben der Revolutionszeit', in *Deutsches Judentum in Krieg und Revolution 1916–1923*. Ein Sammelband herausgegeben von Werner E. Mosse unter Mitwirkung von Arnold Paucker, Tübingen 1971 (Schriftenreihe wissenschaftlicher Abhandlungen des Leo Baeck Instituts 25), pp. 137–315.

not belong to Socialist circles, but throughout his life he cared for the individual and for individual liberty; he acted according to his own convictions as an internationalist and with his opposition to that war he became a confirmed Pacifist. He wrote in a letter to Paul Ehrenfest on 19th August 1914:[13]

"Europe, in her insanity, has started something unbelievable. In such times one realizes to what a sad species of animal one belongs."

And in December 1914 he wrote in another letter:[14]

"The international catastrophe has imposed a heavy burden upon me as an internationalist. In living through this great epoch, it is difficult to reconcile oneself to the fact that one belongs to that idiotic rotten species which boasts of its freedom of will. How I wish that somewhere there existed an island for those who are wise and of good will!"

Einstein opposed Germany's violation of Belgium's neutrality, he was among the very few who refused to sign the notorious "Manifesto To The Civilised World" issued in October 1914 which justified the invasion of Belgium and launched a declaration in which Germany adopted the epithet *Kulturwelt* for itself and attempted to deny its guilt for initiating the war. Ninety-three important scientists, artists, historians and philosophers were among the signatories of this disgraceful document, and one could single out from its prominent subscribers Max Planck, Fritz Haber, Ernst Haeckel and the Jewish painter Max Liebermann. Its object was to influence public opinion abroad and it put forward that opposition to the war was opposition to "German culture": it made the claim that German militarism was coming to the rescue of Goethe, Beethoven and Kant, whose values were endangered, and whose legacy was no less sacred to the Germans than hearth and home. Those who had drafted the Manifesto hoped that it would help show the world that the war was not Germany's fault. It had, however, the opposite effect, as it rather demonstrated the chauvinism of Germany and revealed that even its scientists acted as mere government stooges.

The Pacifist Georg Friedrich Nicolai, a cardiologist of the University of Berlin, tried to counter this act with an opposing declaration, a "Manifesto To Europeans", but only three men agreed to sign it; one of whom was Albert Einstein. They were not even in a position to print such a manifesto, let alone reach a wider public to obtain signatures. This "Manifesto To Europeans" demanded cultural unity of Europe and surrender of war gains, expressed opposition to extreme nationalism and asked that men of education throughout Europe should exert influence for an immediate peace treaty. Nicolai and Einstein believed that such peace and unity would lead to a scientific and technological development of Europe.

Although Einstein opposed the war, he remained in Berlin and was prepared to continue receiving his salary from the German government. He also remained friends with Fritz Haber, the inventor of poison gas and with Max Planck who was involved in the development of the U-boat. There is even some indication

[13]*Einstein on Peace*, ed. by Otto Nathan and Heinz Norden, preface by Bertrand Russell, New York 1960, p. 2.
[14]*Ibid.*

that he offered a certain patent to the German Air Force. Nevertheless, the war had made him a Pacifist. In 1914 he was exceptional in his stand against the war and his recognition of the destruction which followed in its wake; and he did not believe that "the new order" to ensue was preferable to the old.

In September 1915 Einstein met the famous writer and Pacifist Romain Rolland at Vevey in Switzerland and they became friends. Rolland recorded the meeting with Einstein in his diary.[15] He had been impressed that Einstein was so very outspoken about Germany. No other German he had met acted and expressed himself with a similar freedom. He wrote

> "I know more than one man in the French camp who could match his partiality for the other side. (It is noteworthy that Einstein is Jewish which explains the internationalism of his position and the caustic character of his criticism.)"

During the war years Einstein found it possible to write important scientific works. He said to Rolland that he did not reveal his ideas about the war and Germany to his German friends but that he limited himself to putting questions to them in a Socratic manner in order to challenge their complacency.

Einstein judged the German situation in September 1915 as less favourable than previously. The victories over Russia had made the Germans arrogant. They admired force and were greedy in their desire to annex territory. It appeared to him that the German people were worse than their government; the latter was weak, especially the *Kaiser*. Einstein particularly blamed the school system; the education in Germany, he thought, was poor, cultivating pride and blind obedience to the State. He thought that conditions in Germany were bad and they might become worse if the war continued for a longer period. He also thought that Germany would lose the war. Though the war appeared to him to be a fight between two monsters, he preferred a victory of the Allies which would destroy the power of Prussia. The victory of England, he thought, would let the rest of the world breathe more easily.

Einstein knew of the relatively small independent element of Pacifist Social Democrats gathered around Eduard Bernstein, but he never joined them.[16] On 13th November 1917, Einstein wrote a letter which could be taken to refer to this small and upright band:

> "I am convinced that we are dealing with a kind of epidemic of the mind. I cannot otherwise comprehend how men who are thoroughly decent in their personal conduct can adopt such utterly antithetical views on general affairs . . . Only men of extraordinary independence of character seem able to resist pressure of prevailing opinion. There does not seem to be one single man of that calibre in the Academy."[17]

And a few months earlier, on 3rd June 1917, he indicated his preference for Germany's defeat; saying that instead of the spirit of Schiller and Goethe, the spirit of Treitschke had become dominant. Einstein complained that the Germans lack a sense of equality towards non-Germans, he even proposed the

[15]*Ibid.*, p. 14, and see also pp. 17–18.
[16]On Einstein's Pacifism see also Banesh Hoffmann, 'Albert Einstein', in *LBI Year Book XXI* (1976), pp. 286 f.
[17]*Einstein on Peace, op. cit.*, p. 18.

division of Germany so that this country could bring no further sorrow to the world in the future.

He was confident in his judgement, he rejected the Prussian mentality and as it turned out he was right. Germany lost the war, much of what he said came true. Later, after the war, many looked at him and his political understanding with different eyes.

THE CASE OF THE EUROPEANISM OF GUSTAV LANDAUER

Views similar to Einstein's in a quest for Europeanism and Pacifism are to be found in the writings of the Socialist Gustav Landauer (1870–1919). He too thought that there was no ethical justification for the war. He also took a public stand against it.

Gustav Landauer, born in Karlsruhe in Baden in 1870, was one of the few spirits in Germany who saw danger in the political manoeuvres of the Imperial government in the years preceding the war. Landauer strongly rejected the war and he even severed relations with those of his friends who had become war enthusiasts, as for example Florens Christian Rang or Erich Gutkind.[18] The critical attitude of Gustav Landauer to the war enthusiasm of Martin Buber, for instance, has been depicted in great detail by Paul Mendes-Flohr.[19] Buber, whose initial war enthusiasm is of course well known, appears as an aesthetic, mystical war enthusiast who in his thinking connects the war of the Maccabees and the war of Germany, Zionism and Germanism.[20] He spoke in Nietzschean language maintaining that the war would give birth to a new type of Jew, or would awaken Europe from the slumber of bourgeois life and create a new communal spirit. Landauer utterly rejected such ideas; he did not believe that anything positive could result from the war and he had many bitter debates with Buber. In the beginning he refused to collaborate in Buber's new journal, *Der Jude*.[21]

Landauer favoured Europeanism. But it was not his way to advocate the erasing of differences between groups, or to overlook the character of the small units for the sake of universalism, rather he was very interested in the self-expression of minorities; he sympathised with national aspirations and rejected their suppression by the big powers. Nations, or cultural units were very important in his romantic political philosophy which was based on Herder.

[18]Eugen Lunn, *Prophet of Community. The Romantic Socialism of Gustav Landauer*, Berkeley-Los Angeles 1973, p. 245.
[19]Paul R. Mendes-Flohr, *Von der Mystik zum Dialog*, Frankfurt a. Main 1978, pp. 131 ff; also *idem*, 'Buber – Between Nationalism and Mysticism', in *Iyyun*, 29 (1980), pp. 69–92 (in Hebrew). On Buber and the First World War see also Steven S. Schwarzschild, 'A Critique of Martin Buber's Political Philosophy. An Affectionate Reappraisal', in *LBI Year Book XXXI* (1986), pp. 367 ff.
[20]Martin Buber, 'Die Tempelweihe' (Reprint of a talk given at the *Makkabäerfeier der Berliner Zionistischen Vereinigung*, 19th December 1914), in *Die Jüdische Bewegung. Gesammelte Aufsätze und Ansprachen 1900–1915*, Berlin 1916, vol. I, p. 232; and Mendes-Flohr, *Von der Mystik, op. cit.*, p. 134.
[21]*Ibid.*, p. 139.

During the war years Landauer published[22] in his journal, *Der Sozialist*, quotations from Herder, Fichte, Novalis and Schlegel to express his national philosophy. Landauer insisted on the important difference between chauvinistic nationalism and a just nationalism. Germany or Austria were, according to him, following a false trail. It was a mistake for Germany to make a treaty with Austria, a state which lorded over so many national minorities. He thought that Germany's foreign policy had been at fault when it allowed England, France and Russia to build an alliance against her. In the war Germany conquered small nations around the Baltic Sea in the East, but did not allow them national freedom. Landauer also took the view that it was Germany which had started the war, a course which in his eyes constituted a crime; in this sense he was "anti-German" and he spurned the German war propaganda which claimed that this was a fight for German culture or against a Russian invasion. How could that be true, he argued, when Germany's major front was in the West and when it fought against democratic countries. In 1917 Landauer sent a letter to President Wilson[23] of the United States on whom he rested hopes that he could be instrumental in bringing about the future unity of Europe.

Landauer considered the State as the source of evil; the State, rather than developing and supporting cultures, suffocated national groups and killed their culture. Landauer was truly a key figure in the German opposition to the war. He publicly joined the anti-war groups, and it is likely that he had some contact with Einstein. Gershom Scholem approvingly recalls Landauer's anti-war speeches in the German Zionist organisation.[24] Gustav Landauer survived the end of the war by only a few months. He was murdered in May 1919 in the aftermath of the Bavarian *Räterepublik*.[25]

ISAAC BREUER

A resemblance may be discerned between Landauer's anti-war stance and that of Isaac Breuer; both attacked the injustice of the State on which they laid the blame for the terrible wars, both favoured a cosmopolitan spirit over that narrow nationalism which had taken hold of the nations and both hoped that the creation of a united *Völkerbund* would help the ailing world. Yet Breuer, in contrast to Landauer and Einstein, did not reject a Germany at war; he was on the German side and regarded the other countries as worse. He was close to Hermann Cohen and judged Cohen's *Germanism and Judaism* favourably. In his review of this pamphlet,[26] he wrote that there were evil tongues who were saying

[22]Lunn, *Prophet of Community*, *op. cit.*, pp. 243–244; 258–262.
[23]*Ibid.*, pp. 253–254.
[24]See Gershom Scholem, *From Berlin to Jerusalem* (in Hebrew), enlarged version, Tel-Aviv 1982, p. 58. In the English version, New York 1980, pp. 52–53. (See there also Scholem's reaction to Landauer's Socialism.)
[25]Landauer's role in the Bavarian *Räterepublik* has often been described. See a. o. Angress, 'Juden im politischen Leben . . .', *loc. cit.*, pp. 253–267 (his murder, pp. 264–265).
[26]*Jüdische Monatshefte*, II (October 1915), pp. 341–352.

that the Jews were "strangers" in Germany, but the present moment would give the Jews an opportunity to defend German culture. Cohen was – as Breuer explained – a German philosopher and a Jew who philosophically developed a new synthesis of Germanism and Judaism. Breuer did not agree with everything Cohen stood for, but accepted that one had to admit that Cohen was an expert in both areas and that he stood head and shoulders above other thinkers. Breuer rated Cohen above Mendelssohn and accepted the existence of a profound analogy between Germanism and Judaism, in their *Volksgeist*, their religion, philosophy and national character. Breuer, to strengthen his point, reminded the reader that his grandfather Samson Raphael Hirsch also had noted such an affinity between Judaism and Schiller, and considered that there was nothing incompatible between Judaism and German culture.[27] Though born in Hungary, and a student in Strasbourg, engaged to a Belgian, Jenny Eisenmann, from Antwerp – the enemy territory – Breuer was at that time a fervent German patriot. For Breuer, unlike Landauer, the war was a sudden shock; and perhaps on this account, he expressed his thoughts on it in an unusually strong manner.

Pacifism, humanism and Liberalism had a special place in Jewish intellectual life; moreover, humanism and Liberalism were also essential to the Jewish struggle for equal rights. Hence, despite the strong German-Jewish patriotism, one may yet say that Liberalism and enlightened internationalism are perhaps more typical of the Jewish outlook. Jews, in comparison to other people, are less bound by the limits of their country; they wander more freely from one country to the other. They often have family ties abroad, know many languages, or study beyond the confines of their own country; hence they feel themselves more to be citizens of the world.

Isaac Breuer (1883–1946), lawyer, philosopher, and leader of *Agudath Israel* who, after a life-long commitment to *Eretz Israel*, was to settle in Palestine in 1936, began his war diary on the 28th October 1915 and continued it until 1918.[28] It is a manuscript of some 300 typed pages, called *Ich und der Krieg*, a uniquely interesting document, an accusation of humanity against war which turns man into an animal. It reveals at times such profound insights that it makes one wonder that such a cry of anguish by a Jew against the misery and insanity of war should have arisen during the First World War rather than amid the Holocaust.

Breuer who in all his other writings, whether published or not, expressed his Jewish involvement – his religious, philosophic, political or national convictions – speaks here like a German humanist. His Jewish nationalism or his strict *halakhic* obedience is almost absent here, although it can be found in his earlier writings: this omission of his otherwise major point of departure could have been the reason he never published the manuscript. The tone is that of an intellectual of his time. Earlier in a short essay published at the outset of the war[29] he had

---

[27] *Ibid.*, p. 350.
[28] The author is greatly indebted to Professor Mordechai Breuer for having drawn her attention to this manuscript.
[29] *Jüdische Monatshefte*, 'Der Friedrichskrieg', I (1914), p. 345.

seen Mars, the idol of war, ruling supreme and wisdom becoming mute. The war appears to him as a breakdown of culture. He yearns for Pacifism, which belongs to an ideal world, and looks to ethical reason (which has its source in Kant and Goethe, Moses and Isaiah) and whose rule should say: there should be no war.[30]

In July 1914, with no expectance of the coming war, he travelled around Switzerland, in a mood of elation because he had just become engaged, by way of an exchange of letters. Switzerland appeared to him a heavenly paradise, a place where tolerance and universal values prevailed. On 26th July, only one week after his engagement, he read in the papers that Austria and Russia were mobilising their armies; nevertheless he did not believe that war would break out.[31] Yet in his hotel everybody spoke of war, various views and different reactions were expressed. Little by little it dawned on him that an enormous change had taken place; he went to the museum, sat in front of his favourite statue and wept.[32]

He started his diary in 1915, sixteen months after the outbreak of hostilities, when he felt bitterly frustrated by the war and when he had become aware of what a State can do to an individual. Breuer, having occupied himself intensely with the problems of war, felt violently opposed to the politicians, the official writers of "history", the war propagandists and the government officials. "Let my grandchildren learn the truth from me", he wrote, with fingers frozen stiff by the bitter cold of the nights while he was on guard duty. At night, after having returned from his duty, he put down a record of his experiences and his thoughts so that it might one day help his grandchildren to discern the truth behind the veil of deception which was furnished by the official spokesmen: it was an era in which truth was in hiding.

Surprisingly, the diary, which is the work of a young man, is addressed to his grandchildren.[33] He wishes to relate the truth to his grandchildren, so that at some distant date they would not believe the lies which are spread amongst the multitudes by the newspapers, centres of the swindling notion[34] of "the great epoch" – this almost messianic term, which one finds so frequently in the literature of that time. Breuer expresses in his diary, far more than in his printed writings, his bitter opposition to the war which appeared to him as an absolute evil. In his manuscript, in which he continuously attacks the war machine, he implies quite clearly that it is not just the enemy who is at fault: it is no less Germany as well, something he certainly did not declare openly in his published writings. In the manuscript[35] he stated, for example, that this war which started as a war of the nations had become a war of the states and of the rulers.

Switzerland seemed to him a haven; it was "God's land". It showed a possibility of various nationalities living together; in a land where there were no

[30]*Ibid.*, p. 346. There were other rabbis who sympathised with Pacifism, as for example Isaak Unna. Cf. Breuer, *Jüdische Orthodoxie, op. cit.*, p. 343.

[31]*Ich und der Krieg* (manuscript), Frankfurt a. Main 1914–1918, vol. I, p. 41.

[32]*Ibid.*, I, p. 44.

[33]*Ibid.*, I, p. 11; and Breuer, *Jüdische Orthodoxie, op. cit.*, p. 341.

[34]*Ich und der Krieg*, I, p. 5.

[35]*Ibid.*, I, p. 131; and 'Die Wurzel des Krieges', *Jüdische Monatshefte*, III (1916) p. 224.

Englishmen, no Germans, only human beings.[36] Though he had been, as we have seen, opposed to the war when it started, he had been carried away by the war enthusiasm and pleaded: "my grandchildren, do not blame me for that".[37] "My poor Germany is in trouble and it craves the help of its sons."

> "Willst du, kannst du wollen, dass der Russenzar mit seinen Kosaken in jene geweihte Stadt einreite, in der jeder Stein die Spuren deines Kant trägt? Kannst du ruhig dabeistehen, wenn das Volk Goethes und das Volk Schillers den bitteren Kampf ums Leben kämpft?"

For Breuer the Germany which he defended meant German culture; he did not perceive at this point its selfish nationalism.

Nevertheless he did not volunteer for the army, because, as he explains, he was a follower of Kant who considered the fulfilment of one's duty superior to the fulfilling of one's desires; furthermore, he was not assigned to the front for reasons of health and last but not least, he had no particular desire to satisfy the insatiable appetite of the cannons. In the second year of the war he had begun to realise that the war was a catastrophe. Breuer, though he himself tended towards Socialism had, as his diary shows, during this period no real sympathy with the Pacifists or the Social Democrats who to him were fanatics and who only wanted to be heard abroad.[38] They could have stopped the war, but they had been too weak, mere speechifiers.

There is an interesting description in Breuer's diary of how man becomes diminished by the advent of war. Suddenly[39] trains could only rarely be used by civilians, frontiers were closed, telegrams could no longer be sent abroad, telephone conversations were listened to, foreign languages appeared suspicious, a paranoid fear of spies developed everywhere. If a woman was elegant, if she had a strange name or an exotic hairstyle, or if a man wore a trimmed pointed beard, they were suspected of being French or Russian. Spies were spotted everywhere and if anyone did not speak enthusiastically about the war, he or she was suspected of being an alien. Hotels which sported French or British names were looted. The crowd had a good time and life and property became cheap. A new spirit was abroad, the voices of revenge or war spoke – raucous songs were heard in the middle of the night on the streets; bars remained open to the small hours and couples were not ashamed of making love in public. Everything was permitted in the name of the "great historic times"; people drank to and toasted these "great times". Breuer abhorred the rule of the masses. Man lost his dignity, he became transformed into an animal. Thus he wrote:[40] "If someone had told me sixteen months ago that I would be happy if I would not be treated like an animal or like a cockroach, which one seeks to destroy by poisonous chemicals, I would not have believed it." Disgust with the war penetrated his being. Breuer saw in Germany, or rather in states in general, the rule of hell.

He relates that before the war, when he was classified by the German army as

---

[36] *Ich und der Krieg*, I, p. 32.
[37] *Ibid.*, I, p. 75.
[38] *Ibid.*, I, pp. 7 and 130.
[39] *Ibid.*, I, p. 80.
[40] *Ibid.*, I, p. 10.

Isaac Breuer
(1883–1946)

Die blauweisse Brille
A journal edited by Gershom Scholem and Erich Brauer in the First World War

a *Landsturmmann* it appeared to him simply ridiculous. He did not take it seriously. He did not believe that one day the State might make use of this. Would they need him to watch for the enemy at the gates of Frankfurt? He considered himself absolved from any duty because the possibility of his being needed at all appeared to him most remote. Therefore Breuer was shocked when immediately at the beginning of the war he, too, was mobilised. The Emperor had apparently no time to lose. It was proclaimed on the bulletin boards that he was needed at once.

Through his war-time occupation he learned to know his comrades with whom he had sympathy; ordinary men for whom there is no room at the conference tables of the falsifiers of world history; people who did not see in the war any advancement of their ambitions, increased zest for life, or fulfilment in their profession.[41] These simple folk only wished to live, they did not wax enthusiastic over the war; they had relatives at the front and prayed for their health and hoped for their well-being. Their homes became empty as the State sent those whom they loved to the front. Breuer's comrades in the *Landsturm* did not want war. One of them told him:[42] "Isn't this war crazy, that forces me to shoot at somebody whom I do not know and who has not done me any harm?" Breuer sometimes confesses himself sorry that God had given man intelligence, for otherwise there would have been no wars.[43]

In his despair he was able to find consolation in the presence of his future wife, whom he married in 1916, and who personified for him all the good there was. It was to her that he escaped from the nightmares of war, from the blood, guilt and darkness. He dreamed that a flood covered the whole face of the earth and he and his wife hovered far away, alone in a boat. Yet he still heard in his ears the sobbing and the crying of the suffering and he still saw before him the innumerable corpses. Still they sailed on in the lonely boat on a voyage that had no hope.

A number of times Breuer tried to analyse the sudden change that had occurred at the outbreak of the war. Whereas in July he had been living in a civilised Europe and war was an empty phrase; in August, the soul of the people sickened, aged, and within a few hours the State had succeeded in sweeping justice and right from the surface of Europe, and nationalism held the centre of the stage. One was aware only of Germans, Englishmen, Frenchmen and Russians, but not of human beings. Man became an alien in Europe; Breuer was bitter and said that the war recognised no values, no logic, no ethics, no justice, no beauty, it knew only destruction. He wrote that one should put the war in chains. At the beginning of the war, Breuer observed, man was still normal, but slowly the war robbed him of his peace and developed in him the idea of having to hate England and France. The war taught him hatred of peace; it took away from him his cultural consciousness.

Breuer mocked at the philosophers who pretended to solve the problem of the

[41]*Ibid.*, I, pp. 6–7.
[42]*Ibid.*, I, p. 54.
[43]*Ibid.*, I, p. 56.

State, They did not know what to tell suffering mankind. The priest, who out of faith in God whispered words of consolation to the sick or dying, was better than those philosophers who spoke of the "necessity" of war, or of the noble "ideas" which the war brought forth. Breuer warned the philosophers against usage of such flowery language because "war is not an object of philosophy", nor an answer to economic problems. "Far away at the front people are suffering." Their suffering is not grandiose heroism; it is not heroism at all; it is mere slaughter. Breuer who lived in that very same Frankfurt where his learned grandfather S. R. Hirsch was a rabbi, was far removed from the latter's optimism.

Breuer in all his bitterness felt that one thing could not be taken away from him: his right to complain and to expose the suffering and the great crisis of European culture. He tended to see matters in dualistic frames of reference, distinguished between the sovereign State which personified cruelty, selfishness, and brutality, and the *Kulturmensch*.[44] States should be changed and made to represent the ethical, righteous man; and this could, according to his thinking, only be done when the States were submitted to the control of an international body administering just laws. But what he saw in reality was the brutal State which was not restricted by international law. It took advantage of those who lived beyond its borders. The sovereign State acted as though no ethics bound it when it came to those who live outside its boundaries.

"Evil" sent its messenger to us, it took the form of the State, which changed the face of man by secret incomprehensible forces. Diplomats[45] appeared to Breuer to be the messengers of the powers of evil. They were not human beings, but only assumed their shape. In reality they had nothing in common with mankind. Their language was not ours, they used their tongues to express secret meanings. They understood us, but we did not understand them. They demanded obedience and spoke of the "necessity" of the war, which had to be pursued.[46]

His thought reached metaphysical heights when the issue became one of religious sincerity. Breuer, out of the great crisis which the war brought on him, attained a gnostic mode of thinking: considering that this war was the war of the Powers of Darkness, the war of Evil (as it is called in his published essays), of the Non-God (as it is called in the manuscript) or of the *Sitra Ahra* as it would have been called in kabbalistic writings. He was outraged that the State used God in its war propaganda as if it were a holy war; this appeared to him as sheer blasphemy. He related that at the beginning of the war, along with their orders for general mobilisation, the Germans were told to "praise God".[47] The Emperor even wanted to mobilise God on his side. That seemed to Breuer rank treason, the ruler was using God for his own advantage. Breuer asked how it was possible

[44]'Die Wurzel des Krieges', *loc. cit.*, pp. 215–228.
[45]*Ich und der Krieg*, I, p. 71; see also *Weltwende*, Jerusalem 1979, pp. 2–15, also p. 123; in his book *Moriah* (Hebrew, Jerusalem 1982), pp. 72–73, Breuer formulates the dichotomy between the diplomats as the emissaries of evil and the heavenly reign of God over Israel in the messianic era. I have referred to it in 'Galut u-geulah be-mishnath Yizhak Breuer', *Eshel Be'er Sheva*, III (1986), p. 301.
[46]*Ich und der Krieg*, I, p. 72.
[47]*Ibid.*, I, p. 71.

that they used the language of providence, of human happiness to commit all those crimes. In his article against Wohlgemuth who mobilised Judaism on the side of Germany and who was proposing that England be destroyed, Breuer also saw an unacceptable mixture of politics and religion.[48]

Breuer compared his own times with those of the Black Death. In the Middle Ages when the Black Death raged, when the people perished, no-one spoke of the "great times", of historic epochs, of the "spirit" of the Black Death; instead people mourned, they put on sackcloth and ashes and sought out the carriers of infection. They did not believe that God had sent them the plague. Yet Breuer determined that the plague was an act of God; this war, however, was not. This war was a revolt against God. It was the revolt of the evil-doer against God. Man was more cruel than God. Breuer asked why did God create such evil-doers? We should mourn. But why was God silent? Breuer was unable to find a rational solution for that horrible evil, hence he turned to *Kabbalah*.

Kabbalah helped him, as we shall see, in developing further the dualism between the cultural individual, who wanted peace, and the selfish nationalism which turned human life into hell and destroyed human beings. Man was sent to war for the advantage of the State. Breuer was certain that the State duped man, who then suffered the torments of hell, shaken out of his equilibrium, expelled from his cultural life, told to stand on his head, the world upside down. The war propaganda disordered man's mind, and so he ended up believing the propaganda that the war was his only refuge. And then the State told him: "Now you all have to praise God!"

One day he wrote into his diary:[49] "A few days ago I was standing as a *Landsturmmann* on guard by a bridge. At very short intervals train after train passed by, all filled with soldiers to nourish the hell in the East and in the West with fresh cannon fodder. The frightening whistling of the wind, which was heard through the telegraph wires, sounded as if the souls of those killed in battle rushed on the wings of the wind to heaven. And above there was a starry heaven clear and beautiful, remote beyond any conception."

And Breuer asks: "Where is God in this war?" The grandson of Samson Raphael Hirsch appears here more as a freethinker or as an anarchist, but hardly as an obedient scion of the great and learned German-Jewish rabbinical family.

For an answer Breuer turned to *Kabbalah*. This certainly needs some explanation, especially since Gershom Scholem, the great historian of *Kabbalah*, thought that no *Kabbalah* remained in Germany by that time.[50] It appears however that in Bavaria, where Scholem found its last traces, there had survived a small kabbalistic tradition which had escaped his eye. Rabbi Dr. Pinchas Kohn (1867–1941) was a key figure in the preservation of *Kabbalah* in Germany into the twentieth century. Having studied at the Orthodox Rabbinical Seminary in Berlin and having received a doctorate from the University of Berlin, he had then

[48]'Der Weltkrieg im Lichte des Judentums', *Jüdische Monatshefte*, III (1916), p. 104.
[49]*Ich und der Krieg*, I, p. 133.
[50]Gershom Scholem, 'Die letzten Kabbalisten in Deutschland', in *Judaica*, III, *Studien zur jüdischen Mystik*, Frankfurt a. Main 1973, p. 228.

pursued the study of Sanskrit at the University of Vienna. Kohn was a close friend of Breuer, a leader of *Agudath Israel*, and co-editor of the *Jüdische Monatshefte* together with Rabbi Dr. Salomon Breuer. In 1914 he published an article, 'Das Verhältnis der Orthodoxie zur Kabbalah', which shows much erudition in the subject[51] and in which he wanted to demonstrate that the Talmud did not contradict the foundation of *Kabbalah*, in fact it expressed similar ideas.[52] Kohn was the link between Breuer and the *Kabbalah*; through him Breuer was initiated into the secret teaching. Breuer in fact mentions in his diary having returned to Frankfurt from Switzerland via Ansbach where Pinchas Kohn was then rabbi.[53] Kabbalistic theories helped Breuer to form his opposition to the war and later also to develop his own philosophy.

In relation to his understanding of the First World War *Kabbalah* helped him in refuting the prevailing thought that the war was the will of God. Breuer rejected that way of pacifying the conscience, he wished to unmask those supporters of lies who sought the support of God in the sea of tears and blood; he claimed the war was a revolt against God. It was the war of the Non-God. Breuer indeed developed an almost dualistic system by considering the powers of the opposite direction more or less as independent forces. Yet he avoided a complete dualism by applying the system of *Zimzum*, of contraction: the war was possible because God contracted Himself and made room for the Non-God, the *Sitra Ahra*. In that way the powers of evil grew in the world and war came into existence. Breuer was convinced that the good, the beautiful, truth, light and peace were direct emanations of God, they came from God, they were divine as they were in God. Likewise nature as a whole (or "Switzerland") could be conceived as divine; but the *Sitra Ahra* did not come from God, it was not divine emanation, but merely a "creation". God had no part in it. The *Sitra Ahra* was a new creation and this war was the war of the *Sitra Ahra*. It was false to assume that God was everywhere. Developing a dualistic form of thought, he said that only on account of darkness could we see light, and only on account of evil could we see the good.[54] The war was evil and the Non-God dominated man at war and converted him into a beast.

The refuge of the powers of evil was the State. That was the hiding place where all the powers of evil were concentrated, and whence all the satanic powers act. Breuer considered the State as an absolute evil. He refuted those who blamed other forces as causing the war; the State alone was guilty of it. The State decided that man should have no other value than itself. The State exemplified the national selfishness in its extremity. Breuer perceived then that which others recognised only later: the danger of the selfishness of a totalitarian State. He

[51]*Jüdische Monatshefte*, I (1914), pp. 125–132, 180–186, 217–221, 242–245.
[52]This was an attack on S. R. Hirsch who in *Neunzehn Briefe über Judentum*, Altona 1836, rejected *Kabbalah*.*
  *In addition to the excellent study on Jewish Orthodoxy by Mordechai Breuer, quoted by the author, the reader is also referred to the essay by Julius Carlebach, 'The Foundations of German-Jewish Orthodoxy. An Interpretation', in this volume of the Year Book – (Ed.).
[53]*Ich und der Krieg*, I, p. 61.
[54]*Ibid.*, I, p. 134.

thought that the danger was connected with the State being overly organised and too impersonal. He saw much that others were only to realise during the time of the Holocaust.

Breuer noted that individuals who in their private life were unable to kill even a fly were able to shoot other human beings in times of war. The government which demanded law and order within its own realm committed the most notorious crimes when its forces were unleashed outside its own confines. Breuer saw in the development of the First World War the rule of demonic powers. That war was a revolt against God, it showed how weak the rule of God was on earth. He believed that this Evil had abysmal dimensions and had no source in the divine.

"THIS IS NOT OUR WAR"

Another form of opposition to the First World War was to be found amongst those Jews who had a stronger Jewish identity, who voiced privately or in momentary public outbursts their misgivings and asked the question why "we Jews" were fighting that war. Here we should single out in particular Franz Rosenzweig, Rabbi Joseph Carlebach, and Gershom Scholem. The first two did their duty during the war like their German fellow citizens. They were German patriots but nevertheless they also expressed what could be termed "non-German" feelings; Rosenzweig did so in his correspondence and Rabbi Carlebach once in a public speech. It was only Gershom Scholem who found himself in complete opposition to Germany, which meant, as must be apparent from what we indicated at the beginning, that he was also at odds with the official policy of the Zionist movement in Germany.[55]

FRANZ ROSENZWEIG

The Jewish philosopher Franz Rosenzweig (1886–1929) was, unlike Martin Buber, no war enthusiast, and neither did he believe that war was a time when hidden constructive powers came to the fore. He was a German Jew and believed in the future of German Jewry. Yet he refused to teach German philosophy at a German university because he wished to devote his life to his co-religionists, to the cause of Jewish education. In the war he fulfilled his duty, but he shared no illusions when it came to the horrors of bloodshedding or the virtues of warfare.

It is more significant in our context that Rosenzweig wholly disagreed with Hermann Cohen's *Deutschtum und Judentum*.[56] He embarked on a very critical review entitled 'Judentum und Deutschtum' which was, however, never com-

[55]See above, p. 239.
[56]A fragment is published in Franz Rosenzweig, *Kleinere Schriften*, Berlin 1937 ('Das jüdische Volkstum', pp. 26–28.) See also Rivka Horwitz, 'Hermann Cohen and Franz Rosenzweig', in *Jerusalem Studies in Jewish Thought*, vol. 4 (1986), p. 312.

pleted. His thoughts on Cohen's work are best expressed in a letter to his parents of 20th September 1917.[57] Rosenzweig felt that the "and" of Cohen's "Germanism and Judaism" became a problem only when the two terms were taken in their strict sense. Cohen when he wanted to feel German, like others, looked towards the small group of Germans who approved of him.

> "In Cohen's case all this becomes heightened because it is purely intellectual. He allows nothing as German, save his own philosophy and whatever he can muster in support of it. Under these circumstances it is easy for him to consider himself a better German than the 'real ones'. Of course he is a better Cohenite! . . . To be a German means to be *fully* responsible for one's nation, to harmonise not only with Goethe, Schiller, and Kant, but also with the others, and especially the trashy and mediocre ones, the assessor, the fraternity student, the petty clerk, the pig-headed peasant, the stiff school teacher; the true German must either take all these to his heart or else suffer from them . . . Cohen, however, has only Europeanism; there is no genuine Germanism for it to combine with, and Judaism, of which he has plenty, is notoriously incapable of crossbreeding. So in the man everything remains merely juxtaposed, while in his writing we find the mad acrobatics of 'Deutschtum und Judentum', in which Cohen, after speculating upon the Christian element in the German, proceeds to pronounce this element Jewish."

Rosenzweig, unlike Cohen, was not an advocate of internationalism or "Europeanism" as were many Jewish cosmopolitans.

In August 1914 Rosenzweig volunteered for the Red Cross and was stationed from September 1914 until January 1915 in Belgium whence he came back to Berlin, before he was called up. He had studied Arabic and had hoped to go to Turkey and learn to know the Orient, probably with the idea of getting to know Palestine, but nothing came of it. When he was called up for army duty he did his bit. In his philosophy he expresses a pessimistic outlook both on war and on world history; he thought like Hobbes that man is like a wolf; in almost every generation wars occur, the State will never be able to lay down its sword which causes death and bloodshed. He also accepted the pessimistic philosophy of Schopenhauer and after the war he appreciated Oswald Spengler's *Decline of the West*.

In November 1912 when he was doing reserve training, he wrote to Hans Ehrenberg,[58] "We are standing before a new epoch of wars", adding, "the little I have seen of the army does not inspire confidence in me". In October 1916 he wrote to Ehrenberg: "The war itself does not signify an epoch in my life, I experienced so much in 1913 (meaning his personal crisis of reversing his decision to be baptised and his remaining a Jew), that in 1914 there would have had to be a cataclysm to make any impression on me . . . I have experienced nothing of the war, I know nothing of it, I expect nothing from it, I carry my life through it, as Cervantes did his poem." In complete contrast to Breuer's diary which shows so much involvement in the political events of his time, Rosen-

---

[57]Quoted from the English translation in *Franz Rosenzweig. His Life and Thought*, presented by Nahum N. Glatzer, Philadelphia–New York 5713/1953, pp. 59–60.

[58]All the other letters of Rosenzweig from which we quoted here are translated from Franz Rosenzweig, *Briefe und Tagebücher*, edited by Rahel Rosenzweig and Edith Rosenzweig-Scheinmann in collaboration with Bernhard Casper, Den Haag 1979, p. 123.

zweig's letters and diary express an aloofness from politics. He lived inwardly a very rich intellectual life and maintained an enormously wide correspondence in which he rarely discussed his thoughts on politics or described the front in the Balkans, where he was stationed on Mount Dub in an anti-aircraft unit. He preferred being at that observation post though it was more dangerous, but there he had less contact with the army and more time to himself to read, write and think. Unlike Breuer, he developed his philosophy as a soldier serving at the front. He read on subjects related to Judaism and Christianity and also on current Jewish events. From the front in 1916 he conducted a lively debate with Eugen Rosenstock on Judaism and Christianity.[59] In 1917 he wrote a pro-gramme 'Zeit ist's', an open letter to Hermann Cohen to revive Jewish learning in Germany.[60] At the end of the war, at the time of the retreat, from an army hospital in Belgrade, he wrote the first draft of his *opus magnum*, *The Star of Redemption*. It was written on war-time postcards which he directed to his home address in Cassel. In those months he was wholly detached from the political events.

In a letter to his parents of 9th September 1914[61] he wrote: "I was never aware before the outbreak of war, how completely I do not feel at all like a German." He even thought that were he not physically dependent on a German victory, he would have no reason to prefer a victory of Germany, Austria and Turkey over that of France, Russia and Japan; and he added:

> "Wie widerwärtig die ganze Menschenschlächterei überhaupt ist, kann ich gar nicht sagen. Hoffentlich ist es bald zu Ende. Freilich wird der Frieden nach einem deutschen Sieg wahrscheinlich so widerwärtig werden, daß man sich vielleicht die Zustände dieser Kriegsmonate wieder zurückwünschen wird."

In a letter of 29th December 1916[62] he wrote: "My hopes are today as lively for England and Russia as for Germany", "I am a Jew, and in Germany only a resident (*Staatsangehöriger*)!" And on 23rd July 1917:[63] "I have no interest in this war waged because of Brieg and Belgium . . . I do not know this Germany. I was born in it, but I am not responsible for that." When the notorious *Judenzählung* occurred, he wrote on 16th February 1917[64] to his mother: "We are Germans, this you can safely say about our political affiliation, as long as this State which 'counts' so wonderfully still recognises us among its citizens . . . the people, however, (in contrast to the State) do not count us among themselves." Paradoxically the war afforded him a respite and a chance to consider new directions without having to make any decisive commitment. As an antithesis to

---

[59]English translation published by Eugen Rosenstock-Huessy, *Judaism Despite Christianity. The Letters on Christianity between Eugen Rosenstock-Huessy and Franz Rosenzweig*, Alabama 1968. The original German version is in *Briefe und Tagebücher, op. cit.*, pp. 174ff.
[60]English translation, by N. N. Glatzer, 'It's Time', in *On Jewish Learning. Franz Rosenzweig*, New York 1955, pp. 22–54. Original German text is in *Kleinere Schriften, op. cit.*, pp. 56–78.
[61]*Briefe und Tagebücher, op. cit.*, p. 174.
[62]*Ibid.*, p. 326.
[63]*Ibid.*, p. 424.
[64]*Ibid.*, p. 349.

Germany he considered the Jewish people a unique nation: "it knows nothing of war".[65]

As a son of well-to-do parents, a member of a close-knit group of friends, a man of great intellectual stature and a strong Jewish identity, a life at the front with simple soldiers was probably not easy. We find in his writings no idealisation of Germany. He was also aware of antisemitism, though it does not play an important role in his letters. In a letter of 20th September 1917, he related that an officer asked him how he, as a Jew, could expect to be an officer and added: "I accept everything as a dumb dog and read." In another letter he explained how he taught himself to keep aloof from current events and that he followed this consistently. This is certainly related to his inward-looking inclination which also played an important role in his philosophy – in which Judaism is described as a religion turned in on itself and Christianity as a missionary religion looking outward towards the world. The life of the Jew in the Diaspora appeared to him as a life turned inward, the Jew as basically a Pacifist.[66]

The war gave Rosenzweig opportunities to visit Jewish communities outside Germany. The German government tried to meet the religious needs of the Jewish soldiers by making arrangements to enable them to spend the major holidays in Jewish surroundings. Rosenzweig's "fanaticism", his heartfelt enthusiasm for the mass of the Jewish people, for both the Sephardic community in Üsküb (Scopia) on Passover 1917 and later the Ashkenazic community in Warsaw (May 1918), should be mentioned as they complete the picture. They demonstrate another aspect of his alienation from Germany and his strictures on German Jewry which he pilloried as "philistine and bourgeois".

A conversation with a ten-year-old boy, Immanuel Noah Navarro, in Üsküb may serve as an example of such a dialogue between East and West. In a letter of 13th April 1917[67] Rosenzweig relates how the boy asked him why he, as a scholar, did not devote himself entirely to the Jews, adding, "To this I did not know what to answer", and continuing, "the boy looked at me so pointedly, as though the people itself were interrogating me. I tried to explain to him as well as I could that one had to study everything in order to understand one thing, but my answer did not completely satisfy him." While they were walking along the Wardar river, suddenly the boy inquired why he had joined the German army at all, why had not his father bought him out of army service, as was customary in Yugoslavia especially in a case like Rosenzweig's, he being an only child. Rosenzweig tried to explain his dual obligation and that his fatherland was in danger, but the boy did not understand this. He said, "God guard you that no evil should befall you". Rosenzweig wrote: "I almost started to cry . . . and had we not been in the street, I would have kissed this little 'representative of the people'!" And it is on this note, a moving almost haunting encounter between East and West, that we leave Rosenzweig in time of war. His later letters from

[65]Glatzer, *op. cit.*, p. 337. (For a complete translation of *Der Stern der Erlösung*, see *Star of Redemption*, translated by W. Hallo, New York 1971.)

[66]Cf. *Der Stern der Erlösung*, *op. cit.*, p. 368 ("Der Jude ist der einzige Mensch in der christlichen Welt, der den Krieg nicht ernst nehmen kann, und so ist er der einzige echte 'Pazifist'.")

[67]*Briefe und Tagebücher*, *op. cit.*, pp. 393 f.

Warsaw display a similar enthusiasm for Eastern Jewry and a growing criticism of German-Jewish attitudes. Many other German Jews discovered Eastern Jewry during those years. While it did not detach most German Jews from their patriotism there can also be no doubt whatsoever of the connection between this encountering of other Jewries in alien and occupied lands and the disenchantment with Germany and its war aims experienced by the small band of Jews from Germany who increasingly felt that this war was indeed not "their" war.

RABBI JOSEPH ZVI CARLEBACH

A brave act of opposition to the war is recorded of Joseph Carlebach who, in 1917 in German-occupied Eastern Europe, was driven on the spur of the moment to express publicly his Jewish identity and to disregard all German military rules and regulations. This momentary opposition to Germany's war is the more remarkable as at the beginning of hostilities he had published a number of pro-war articles. It does leave us with the question though, why is there no record of it in his writings? His daughter, Miriam Gillis,[68] interviewed an eyewitness, Joseph Ahai, many years later in Israel and wrote down what he told her of the event.

The fact that any opposition to Imperial Germany and its war by Jewish thinkers and rabbis (such as Carlebach's) went unrecorded would indicate how much it was a mere undercurrent. It went, of course, totally against the official policy of German Jewry and it constituted treason against Germany. Breuer and Rosenzweig did not voice their dissenting opinions in public but confided them to diaries or to private correspondence. In fact, Rosenzweig's rejection of Germany still remained partially unpublished even in the first edition of the letters which appeared in 1935[69] and was added after the Second World War only in the second edition of 1979. The published writings of Breuer refer to war as being most terrible; it is only in his private diary that his uncensored thoughts are really and truly expressed and reveal a deeper truth. For him, as we have seen, the war was a crisis and from that time he grew pessimistic about political events. It could also be argued that a Jew never felt completely secure in Germany. He spoke differently when he was under public scrutiny than when amongst his own people. The voice of dissent could not utter.

Rabbi Joseph Carlebach (1883–1942) was among those Jewish representatives who were sent by the German authorities to the occupied parts of Eastern Europe to undertake official duties in Jewish education there. Joseph Carlebach had spent some time in Palestine after completing his studies in Germany. In 1914 he was stationed in Poland, and in 1915 he came as an officer of the German army to organise a German *Gymnasium* in Kovno, then German-occupied territory. On the Saturday night before Rosh Hashanah 1917, when he preached

---

[68]Miriam Gillis, *Chinuch ve'Emunah* (*Education and Faith. Principles and Practice in the Pedagogies of Joseph Zvi Carlebach*), Tel-Aviv 1979 (in Hebrew), pp. 146–158.

[69]*Briefe und Tagebücher, op. cit.*, p. XXV.

in the synagogue in place of his brother-in-law Rabbi Rosenack, he spoke out against Germany. He blamed his country for putting the German Jew into the position of an enemy of the East European Jew. This speech took place in the great synagogue *Ohel Yaakov* where Dr. Rosenack used to organise the prayers for the German-Jewish soldiers. As the services were held in the special conditions of war it was customary to place the Jewish soldiers serving in the German army on one side of the synagogue whilst the Russian-Jewish war prisoners sat on the other side, and all communication between the two groups was prohibited. The local Jewish community sat in the middle between the two camps. On that Saturday night, in the crowded synagogue, Rabbi Carlebach rose and commenced his sermon with the words:[70] "Wir haben diesen Krieg nicht gewollt!" Now the expression "We did not want this war" was not meant here in the sense it was so often applied in the German writings of that time, that we, the German people, did not want this war, but the wicked allies forced it on us. Rather it signified here that we Jews did not want the war, but fate had brought it about and now Jews from the West were forced to encounter Jews from the East as enemies. Carlebach also emphasised that it was wrong for German Jewry to assume that it had nothing to learn from the *Ostjuden*. Only in the East was the Torah really preserved. He noted that some German-Jewish soldiers were learning Torah from their Eastern brothers. Carlebach, who had spent some time in the East, favoured the opportunity given then to German Jews to learn *Gemoroh* in depth from Lithuanian Jews who were known for their erudition. However, Carlebach went beyond the importance of Jewish learning; that night he also preached on the unity of the Jewish people. He expounded in his sermon how symptomatic it was that on both sides of this *shul* two separate groups of Jews sat and it was only because of a German ruling that they were unable to mingle freely.

The congregation hardly believed their ears. Carlebach barely mentioned the Germans in this sermon and when he did, they were mentioned as those who had brought the war on "them". His speech no doubt displayed considerable personal bravery. However, not all the German-Jewish soldiers agreed with what he had said. He was reported to the authorities and punished by being sent to the front for one month; the intervention of friends helped to prevent a harsher punishment.

We have singled out this act of courage; and we should also remember the outstanding behaviour of Carlebach when the hour of trial came for German Jewry. He was not amongst those Jewish leaders who left Germany in time, but with Leo Baeck and others stayed behind with his suffering community. Leo Baeck, however, miraculously survived whilst Carlebach was sent with his Hamburg community, his wife and three of his children to Riga where on the 26th March 1942[71] he met his death.

[70]Gillis, *op. cit.*, p. 151.

[71]On Joseph Carlebach's last days see Julius Carlebach, 'Orthodox Jewry in Germany. The Final Stages', in *Die Juden im Nationalsozialistischen Deutschland/The Jews in Nazi Germany 1933–1945*, herausgegeben von Arnold Paucker mit Sylvia Gilchrist und Barbara Suchy, Tübingen 1986 (Schriftenreihe wissenschaftlicher Abhandlungen des Leo Baeck Instituts 45), pp. 92–93.

GERSHOM SCHOLEM

A public and forthright rejection of Germany, motivated by Jewish Nationalism, and persevered with to the point of courting great personal risk, was Gershom Scholem's stance.

[Gerhard] Gershom Scholem (1897–1982) certainly showed a great deal of resolute courage in his opposition to Imperial Germany, and it would be utterly false to explain away his stand as merely the spirited act of a very young man. His dissent must be accounted for by his strong Zionist conviction, his unyielding personality, his disdain of the German state, his strong disapproval of its official policies which obstructed freedom, and by the influence of his older brother, Werner, who was a Socialist and who, by his uncompromising antagonism to the German establishment, introduced a rebellious atmosphere into the parental home. There was much friction between the authoritarian father and his two sons, and the extent to which this went was exceptional and a rare phenomenon in a German-Jewish family. Gershom Scholem's violent opposition to Germany, his strong anti-authoritarian attitude, his bitter arguments with his father were uncharacteristic for his surroundings. Gerhard no doubt admired the courageous resistance of his older brother Werner, who was at that time a Social Democrat.[72] He also drew strength from his unusually close ties with East European Jews who resided in Berlin.

Even before the beginning of the First World War Scholem had become a Zionist. As we have seen, the Zionists went as readily as other Jews to the war and fought faithfully at the front for Germany; some tried to justify their acts even in the name of Zionism, claiming that they were fighting to help Germany's ally Turkey; to back Palestinian Jews; that they fought against the Tsar. Many may have felt apprehensive that Jew would fight Jew, but all this caused no real dissent; furthermore, German Zionism was rather a movement that intended to send the poor Jews of Eastern Europe to Palestine than one whose adherents were going to settle there themselves. Opposition to Germany and its war aims from a Zionist point of view, such as that of Scholem who led a splinter group of the *Jung Juda*, was a rarity indeed.

While still attending the *Gymnasium*, Scholem had already decided to reject the war. His opposition was not that of a Pacifist or a Liberal fighting for the ideal of Europeanism, but that of a Jew who was convinced that there is a true contradiction between the Jewish interest and that of military service on behalf of Germany.

What had led to his awareness of the problem, and to his leanings towards Zionism, had come about much earlier. When he was only fourteen years old, he had started to read the works of Zionist thinkers and ideologists[73] – Moses Hess,

---

[72]Werner Scholem (1895–1940) became, after the November Revolution, Communist Deputy in the Prussian Diet and the *Reichstag*, and an editor of the Communist party organ, *Die Rote Fahne*. Like other Jewish Communists he was not renominated by the party after 1928 (cf. Ernest Hamburger, 'One Hundred Years of Emancipation', in *LBI Year Book XIV* [1969], p. 50); Scholem was arrested by the Nazis in 1933 and murdered in Buchenwald concentration camp in 1940.

[73]*From Berlin to Jerusalem* (Hebrew version), *op. cit.*, p. 43.

Leo Pinsker, Max Nordau, Theodor Herzl, Nathan Birnbaum and Richard Lichtheim. They made a deep impression on him and caused him to develop a very critical attitude to German Jewry. He became convinced that they lived in a world of self-deception, that they saw only what they wished to see and not what was actually happening around them. The young Scholem also became absorbed in antisemitic literature (where, in the writings of the famous and, of course, also notorious economist Werner Sombart, he discovered statements such as: one should not take away from Jews their rights,[74] no, but rather they should be asked to give them up of their own free will). Furthermore, he was also very much disturbed by the Beilis Blood Accusation.[75] Scholem thought that the Jewish leaders in Germany such as Hermann Cohen, Fritz Mauthner, Constantin Brunner or Ludwig Geiger lacked proper judgement.[76] He felt that there was a kind of self-exercised censorship practised by German Jews that made them sometimes afraid even to touch on the sore subject of antisemitism. Reading antisemitic literature made him aware of the enormous dimensions of the hatred to which the German Jews were subjected. As he was to testify later,[77] he even then gleaned from *Der Hammer*, published by the industrious antisemitic agitator Theodor Fritsch, many forebodings of the outrages which the Nazis were later to perpetrate. His keen sensitivity caused him to preoccupy himself with anti-semitic literature throughout his life. For him Zionism was not just an abstract *Weltanschauung*, but a call for action and for personal fulfilment (*Verwirklichung*), a term which Martin Buber had coined. Very early in his life, he had already decided to leave Germany, something which he actually did once he had completed his education in 1923. He saw in *Eretz Israel* the possibility of a spiritual revival. In this land, he thought, the Jew would encounter "himself, his people and his roots".[78] He was always close to the ways of thinking of Ahad Ha'am and Buber; whilst preferring the former, he yet struggled for a way of his own.

In the year 1915, the *Jüdische Rundschau*, the organ of the German Zionist movement, published an article by an admirer of Buber, Heinrich Margulies, who spoke out firmly in favour of the war saying that "we went to the war – not despite our being Jews, but because of our being Zionists".[79] This statement in particular roused Scholem's ire. He had heard Buber speaking that year at *Hanukkah* at a Zionist meeting, comparing the German war with that of the Maccabees. It had "scandalised" him.[80] It was here that Scholem's critical attitude to Buber began.* He and some friends sent a letter to the editor of the *Jüdische Rundschau* putting forward the view that the war was solely that of

---

[74]*Ibid.*, p. 31.
[75]*Ibid.*, p. 49.
[76]*Ibid.*, p. 31.
[77]*Ibid.*, pp. 49–50.
[78]*Ibid.*, p. 59.
[79]*Jüdischer Rundschau*, XX (January 1915).
[80]Letter of Gershom Scholem to David Biale of 31st March 1978, quoted in David Biale, *Gershom Scholem. Kabbalah and Counter-History*, Cambridge, Mass. 1979, pp. 215–216.
*In another context see also Maurice Friedman, 'Interpreting Hasidism: The Buber-Scholem Controversy', the final essay in the current volume of the Year Book – (Ed.).

Germany and none of their business (as Jews); they also insisted that the editor refrain in future from publishing articles of this kind in a Zionist journal. Their vociferous demand was refused and the letter was not published.[81] As a consequence, Scholem was invited by the Zionist leader Arthur Hantke who asked him not to cause any trouble for the Zionist organisation,* though in his heart he had some sympathy for their line of thought. Scholem disregarded these warnings and instead attempted to bolster Jewish dissent to the war by trying to gather more signatories to this letter; but one day it was snatched from his satchel in the *Gymnasium*. The letter was handed to the headmaster, and as a consequence Scholem was expelled from school.

To express his Zionist ideas, he and Erich Brauer, acting as editors, printed a paper, *Die Blauweisse Brille*, in Scholem's father's printing works and without his knowledge. In it they expressed their view on Zionism and their anti-militarism. They criticised the official policy of the Zionist movement, Buber, *Jung Juda et al.* Three issues of the youthful publishing venture appeared altogether, besides a special Purim issue. The first number dates "Ab 5675" (August 1915); in it the *Blauweisse Brille* demanded: "Juden sollt Ihr sein", "aktivistisch sollt Ihr sein". They voiced three major demands: a rejection of the war, Jewish self-reliance, and an insistence on the deepening of Jewish learning and Jewish culture. As they put it: "Zionism is not German, nor French, nor Brazilian, it is Jewish." In his own article in the first issue Scholem wrote that a "Jewish movement without youth, Jewish youth without a movement, a youth movement without Judaism", are impossible. He demanded more Jewish culture and more activism, something he then also repeated in his article 'Jüdische Jugendbewegung' published 1917 in *Der Jude*.[82] In this later, printed, article his anti-war feelings were less outspoken. In connection with his strong anti-war stance Scholem also published a poem in the first issue of the *Blauweisse Brille*,[83] in which he called the war an "Irrlicht", a light that leads to destruction, while God above is laughing.

On the front cover of the first issue they featured an anti-war picture of men with their weapons of war, showing how they[84] smash and butcher others and how they are turned into cannon-fodder. This telling illustration could well have landed them in difficulties with the government, but it would seem that they were in no way concerned about this, as they printed Brauer's address on the back page, asking for a response.[85]

In 1916, after a violent scene between Gerhard Scholem and his father – during which Gerhard defended his brother Werner's participation, in full uniform, in an anti-war demonstration, as a result of which he was court-marshalled – Gerhard was asked by his father to leave home. He moved to the "Pension Struck" in West Berlin and there became even closer to East European

---

[81]This letter was preserved by Scholem.
*On Zionist war policies see again the essay by Jürgen Matthäus in this Year Book quoted above – (Ed.).
[82]Gerhard Scholem, 'Jüdische Jugendbewegung', in *Der Jude*, I, Heft 12 (März 1917), pp. 822–825.
[83]David Biale has translated this poem in full (see Biale *op. cit.*, pp. 62–63).
[84]See the illustration opp. p. 257.
[85]One of the replies came from Martin Buber whom Scholem met in consequence.

Jewish students and especially with Zalman Rubashov (later Zalman Shazar, the third President of Israel).

In May 1917 Scholem was called up. Rubashov accompanied him to the barracks, providing him with a book of Psalms for company. In the army camp Scholem, however, refused to obey orders and pretended to be deranged. Rubashov who visited him in hospital when he was under psychiatric observation, could not make out what had happened.[86] Scholem screamed constantly and refused to look anybody in the eye, lest it might interrupt him.[87] He was guided, as he later related, by intuition, as he had not read any books on mental illness. In January 1918, he was declared unfit and released from the army as incurable. The army called on his father to receive him, but the son preferred to move to Jena and to study there.

Politically, Scholem was not on the side of Germany in the war; he thought that a British victory would be the more advantageous to the Jewish cause. In many of his future writings he expressed his strong anti-German feelings and castigated the injustice which Germany had done to its Jews (and such statements should also be seen against the background of his record during the war). He wrote[88] for instance: "To be sure, the Jews attempted a dialogue with the Germans, starting from all possible points of view and situations", yet it was a hopeless cry into the void. The Jews put all their talents at the disposal of Germany to the point of complete self-abnegation, but the Germans never responded. The Germans were willing to accept the Jews only as individuals or at best as an historical phenomenon. Scholem totally rejected the great slogan of the emancipation, first uttered in France during the Revolution: "For the Jews as individuals, everything; for the Jews as a people (that is to say as Jews), nothing." That was precisely it; the Jew was just fooling himself, he did not really engage in a dialogue with the German but in one with his fellow Jew. David Biale is quite correct in writing[89] that Scholem's uncompromising Zionism is strangely reminiscent of that of Vladimir Jabotinsky's "monism".

Scholem always maintained that there had never been a true dialogue between Germans and Jews. The Germans wanted to convert the Jew and to assimilate him into Germany. Yet unlike Einstein, who after leaving Germany would never agree to set his foot on German soil again, Scholem did not refrain from frequent visits to Germany after the Second World War. He did this despite his deep anti-German feelings; he met his German colleagues, lectured in public and published books on *Kabbalah* in Germany. All this would seem quite inconsistent with his theories. But in his anti-German stance in the First World War he was absolutely consistent. It was the logical outcome of his Zionist and Jewish orientation.

[86]The story was related to me in detail by Zalman Shazar in Ithaca, N.Y., in Summer 1962.
[87]Gershom Scholem, *Devarim Bego. Explications and Implications. Writings on Jewish Heritage and Renaissance*, Tel-Aviv 1976 (in Hebrew), p. 24.
[88]Gershom Scholem, 'Against the Myth of the German-Jewish Dialogue', in Werner J. Dannhauser (ed.), *On Jews and Judaism in Crisis*, New York 1976, pp. 61–64.
[89]Biale, *op. cit.*, p. 66.

In conclusion one could say that almost all German Jews fully identified with Germany and German Nationalism, which seemed to them the most reasonable way to social equality and to the achievement of complete emancipation; they did not probe too deeply into the question of the justification of the war. Most of them had little doubt that their country was waging a just war. Yet some non-conformist and introspective spirits, some of the greatest talents German Jewry has produced, dared to oppose the approved tenets, by using their own judgement, considering the war unjust and immoral. Some were also quite disturbed by outbreaks of antisemitism in the war years, whilst they questioned the general trend, either publicly or privately, or reached for Zionism or were impelled by their innermost feelings. It is also significant that much of this brief survey is based on writings which remained unpublished for a long time; Breuer's work still only exists in manuscript form. Other manifestations of dissent were published much later on when it no longer mattered whether one had opposed the war aims of Imperial Germany or had been anti-German. Finally, this study also shows that the rejection of Germany's war was not, as some historians say, primarily the act of certain Social Democrats (in our case Jewish Socialists). It came as we have seen, from diverse directions and had more than one cause.[90] All such dissent was courageous. It may have been subjected to execration and vilification at the time, yet seen from a distant perspective it becomes a beacon of light.

[90]Further examples of Jewish Pacifism could be adduced. The noted sociologist and historian, Eva G. Reichmann, was, as a student, engaged in anti-war propaganda late in 1917 and was nearly arrested in connection with the dissemination of a memorandum by Fürst Karl Max Lichnowsky, the last German Ambassador in London before the outbreak of the First World War – for which he blamed his own country. (Information from Dr. Arnold Paucker, London, obtained in an interview with Dr. Eva G. Reichmann, London, in July 1987.)

Jewish Affairs and German Foreign Policy during the Weimar Republic

Moritz Sobernheim and the Referat für jüdische Angelegenheiten

BY FRANCIS R. NICOSIA

I. ORIGINS, ESTABLISHMENT AND SURVIVAL

The creation of a special department for Jewish affairs in the German Foreign Office in November 1918 was at once a reaffirmation of the continuing importance of Germany's historic relationship with the masses of Jews in Eastern Europe, a recognition of missed opportunities in a lost war, and a part of the broader revolution in German political life at the end of that war. It marked the beginning of what would become an important element in German foreign policy during the Weimar Republic, namely the recognition of World Jewry as an important protagonist in international relations and, as such, a desirable and valuable ally in the pursuit of German foreign policy aims. The *Referat für jüdische Angelegenheiten* became the principal link between Germany and the Jews of the world, with the primary task of cultivating the sympathy and support of Jews in Europe, America and around the world for the new German Republic.[*]

The Jewish Affairs section grew out of the war-time *Komitee für den Osten*, an unofficial organisation of mostly Zionist German Jews formed shortly after the outbreak of war in 1914 ". . . in der Absicht, sich durch seine Kenntnisse und Beziehungen unter den Juden des Ostens und der neutralen Länder den Interessen der Zentralmächte dienlich zu erweisen".[1] According to Moritz

---

[*]A concise version of this essay appeared previously as 'Moritz Sobernheim and the Jewish Affairs Section of the German Foreign Office, 1918–1933', in Karl Odwarka (ed.), *Proceedings of the Eleventh European Studies Conference*, 1986 European Studies Conference, University of Nebraska at Omaha, European Studies Journal, University of Northern Iowa, Cedar Falls, pp. 185–193.

[1]Leo Baeck Institute (hereafter LBI)/New York: Merkblatt des Komitees für den Osten, November 1915. For a detailed account of the origins, composition, activities and Zionist character of the *Komitee für den Osten*, see Zosa Szajkowski, 'The Komitee für den Osten and Zionism', *Herzl Yearbook*, VII (1971), pp. 199–240. And see furthermore by the same author, 'Jewish Relief in Eastern Europe 1914–1917', in *LBI Year Book X* (1965), pp. 24–56. The *Komitee für den Osten* is treated here in great detail, as it is in *idem*, 'The Struggle for Yiddish during World War I. The Attitude of German Jewry', in *LBI Year Book IX* (1964), pp. 131–158. See also Max Bodenheimer, *So wurde Israel. Aus der*

Sobernheim, one of its original members, the Committee endeavoured to win the sympathy of Jews in Eastern Europe for Germany, and to facilitate the relationship between German occupation forces and the Jewish communities of Poland and Lithuania.[2] It also worked to protect the rights of the East European Jews under German occupation.[3] It worked very closely with German authorities throughout the war, particularly with the General Staff, the Foreign Office and the Interior Ministry, ending its work shortly before the signing of the Versailles Treaty. The link between the Committee and the post-war *Referat für jüdische Angelegenheiten* can actually be traced to the creation of two small *Referate* for Jewish Affairs in the *Generalgouvernement Warschau* and *Oberost* by the German government during the war, at the request of the *Komitee für den Osten*. Sobernheim commented on the effectiveness of these *Referate* in a memorandum of the 4th September 1919 in the following manner:

> "... und hatten sich an beiden Stellen als praktisch erwiesen, da die einschlägigen Angelegenheiten schnell und sachgemäss erledigt wurden, während vorher dauernd Beschwerden an die Reichsämter und Ministerien gelangten. In Litauen gestaltete sich das Verhältnis der Judenschaft zur deutschen Verwaltung seit Ernennung des Referenten, Herrn Struck, bedeutend besser. Noch heute kommt die Wirkung seiner Tätigkeit zum Ausdruck."[4]

The Balfour Declaration of 2nd November 1917, promising the creation of a National Home for the Jewish people in Palestine as part of any post-war settlement, had a profound effect on the Imperial German government during the last year of the war, particularly as to the manner in which it sought to cultivate Jewish opinion in Central and Eastern Europe.[5] It prompted the German declaration of sympathy for Zionist aims in Palestine,* the rough equivalent of Britain's Balfour Declaration, which was formally presented to a

---

Geschichte der zionistischen Bewegung, Frankfurt a. Main 1958, pp. 200–217; Isaiah Friedman, *Germany, Turkey and Zionism, 1897–1918*, Oxford 1977, pp. 233–236; Richard Lichtheim, *Rückkehr. Lebenserinnerungen aus der Frühzeit des deutschen Zionismus*, Stuttgart 1970, Veröffentlichung des Leo Baeck Instituts, p. 260; Jehuda Reinharz (Hrsg.), *Dokumente zur Geschichte des deutschen Zionismus 1882–1933*, Tübingen 1981 (Schriftenreihe wissenschaftlicher Abhandlungen des Leo Baeck Instituts 37), p. 148n, and Document Nr. 85, pp. 176–179; Egmont Zechlin, *Die deutsche Politik und die Juden im Ersten Weltkrieg*, Göttingen 1969, pp. 144 ff. As of 17th November 1914, the *Komitee* was made up of the following fifteen members: Paul Ahrens, Max Bodenheimer, Martin Buber, Oskar Cohn, Dr. Feitelberg, Adolf Friedemann, Eugen Fuchs, Sammy Gronemann, Alfred Klee, Julius Magnus, Eugen Mittwoch, Franz Oppenheimer, Professor Moritz Sobernheim, Hermann Struck and Berthold Timendorfer. See Zechlin, *op. cit.*, p. 133, note 18.

[2]See Politisches Archiv des Auswärtigen Amts (hereafter cited as PA)/Bonn: Nachlass Sobernheim, Allgemeines, Bd. 1, Aufzeichnung Sobernheims, 1. April 1921.

[3]Szajkowski, 'The Komitee für den Osten', *loc. cit.*, p. 206.

[4]PA/Bonn: Personalakten-Professor Sobernheim, 'Aufzeichnung über das Jüdische Referat im Auswärtigen Amt', 4. September 1919.

[5]See Lichtheim, *op. cit.*, p. 377.

*On German Jews and Eastern Jews in the occupied territories, and on Zionist war-time policies consult also the following two essays in this volume of the Year Book: Rivka Horwitz, 'Voices of Opposition to the First World War among Jewish Thinkers'; and Jürgen Matthäus, 'Deutschtum and Judentum under Fire. The Impact of the First World War on the strategies of the Centralverein and the Zionistische Vereinigung' – (Ed.).

group of five German Zionists and Zionist sympathisers on 5th January 1918.[6] Yet the sudden and obvious renewal of active German interest in and support for the aims of Zionism in Palestine was but one of several important shifts generated by the Balfour Declaration in the policies of the German government towards the Jews of Central and Eastern Europe.

Berlin assessed the impact of the Balfour Declaration on German interests in decidedly negative terms, specifically connecting the Declaration to what it perceived as a significant shift of Jewish sympathy and support in Eastern Europe away from the Central Powers towards the Allies. It appears that this conclusion was the result in large measure of the reports and advice of the *Komitee für den Osten* to the German government during the final year of the war. On 13th May 1918, Adolf Friedemann of the *Komitee für den Osten* sent a long report to Under State Secretary von Radowitz in the *Reich* Chancellory reviewing the reasons for the decline in German influence and prestige among Jews in the East.[7] Friedemann emphasised the popularity of the Balfour Declaration among East European Jews, and of Great Britain for its public support for Zionism. He urged the German government to press its Ottoman ally to allow the Zionists a free hand in Palestine as a way of off-setting the Balfour Declaration and the propaganda coup achieved by Britain and the Allies among the Jewish masses in the East. Yet Friedemann's report went beyond the Balfour Declaration in its assessment of Germany's declining prestige among East European Jews. He noted the paucity of German leaders and diplomatic representatives abroad, particularly in Eastern Europe, who were Jewish, and contrasted this with the relatively large number of Jews amongst Allied leaders and diplomatic personnel. Moreover he observed that the British Foreign Office had set up its own Jewish Affairs department, under Zionist leadership, which enabled Britain to effectively cultivate Jewish opinion around the world. If Friedemann was trying here to plant the idea that German foreign policy might also benefit from such a department in the German Foreign Office, he seems to have been successful as von Radowitz noted in the margin of Friedemann's letter: "möchte Friedemann auch bestimmt haben".

A more detailed and more ominous report on declining German fortunes

[6]The five included Moritz Sobernheim, Franz Oppenheimer and Adolf Friedemann of the *Komitee für den Osten*, as well as Otto Warburg and Arthur Hantke of the *Zionistische Vereinigung für Deutschland*. See Zechlin, *op. cit.*, pp. 426–427.

The German government had actually prevailed upon its Ottoman ally in December of 1918 to end publicly its long-standing opposition to official Zionist settlement in Palestine. The German declaration of 5th January 1918 stated:

"Hinsichtlich der von der Judenheit, insbesondere von den Zionisten, verfolgten Bestrebungen in Palästina begrüssen wir die Erklärungen, die der Grosswesir Talaat Pascha kürzlich abgegeben hat, insbesondere die Absicht der kaiserlich-osmanischen Regierung, gemäss ihrer den Juden stets bewiesenen freundlichen Haltung, die aufblühende jüdische Siedlung in Palästina durch Gewährung von freier Einwanderung und Niederlassung in den Grenzen der Aufnahmefähigkeit des Landes, von örtlicher Selbstverwaltung, entsprechend den Landesgesetzen, und von freier Entwicklung ihrer kulturellen Eigenart zu fördern."

See Reinharz, *op. cit.*, pp. 212–213n.
[7]PA/Bonn: Nachlass Sobernheim, Comitee f.d. Osten, Bd. 1, Friedemann an von Radowitz, 13. Mai 1918.

among Jews in the East was submitted to State Secretary von Hintze in the German Foreign Office by Dr. Franz Oppenheimer, the chairman of the Committee, on 24th September.[8] Oppenheimer warned von Hintze that the mood of Jews in the East was increasingly anti-German and pro-Allied. The reasons cited for the anti-German mood included the *Judenzählung* of 1916,[9] the prohibition against the naturalisation of foreigners, the closing of Germany's borders to East European Jewish immigration, and Germany's general Jewish policy in the East European lands under German occupation; those cited for the rise in Allied prestige included the Balfour Declaration and Allied support for Zionism and the Jewish National Home, as well as the appointment of Jews to high positions in Allied governments and diplomatic posts. After reviewing the past efforts of the *Komitee für den Osten* to maintain and promote German influence among Jews in the East, Oppenheimer made several specific policy recommendations designed to halt the decline in German influence in the East, the most important of which was the need to fight actively against antisemitism in Germany, as well as to appoint Jews to important positions in the German government:

> "Denn natürlich kann das deutsche Judentum nur dann auf die ausländischen Juden einwirken, wenn es selbst die Stellung von Vollbürgern im eigenen Lande einnimmt. Endlich ist es notwendig, dass die Regierung durch positive Massnahmen ein wirkliches Interesse an der Judenfrage bekundet."

Further emphasising the dangers of antisemitism at home, and the absolute need for the German government to be seen actively opposing it, Oppenheimer called for the clearest public declarations from the highest offices of the government that the Jews of Germany had done their patriotic duty during the war, both at home and at the front. He also called for active government measures against the increasingly vitriolic antisemitic campaign in Germany, for the immediate naturalisation of those foreign Jews whose sons had served voluntarily in the German army, for the lifting of the *Grenzsperre* against immigration, for German support for the national and cultural rights of the Jewish masses in Eastern Europe, and for the ". . . Ernennung von Juden mit Einfluss auf das Judentum in propagandistisch wichtige Stellungen an den Gesandtschaften und den Berliner Zentralbehörden".

[8]PA/Bonn: Nachlass Sobernheim, Comitee f.d. Osten, Bd. 1, Oppenheimer an von Hintze, 24. September 1918.

[9]The *Judenzählung* of 1916 was an attempt by antisemites in the *Reichstag* and in the army to undertake a census of the number of Jews serving at different levels of the military, as well as those actively involved in and allegedly benefiting from the war economy. See Saul Friedländer, 'Die politischen Veränderungen der Kriegszeit und ihre Auswirkungen auf die Judenfrage', in *Deutsches Judentum in Krieg und Revolution 1916–1923*. Ein Sammelband herausgegeben von Werner E. Mosse unter Mitwirkung von Arnold Paucker, Tübingen 1971 (Schriftenreihe wissenschaftlicher Abhandlungen des Leo Baeck Instituts 25), pp. 36–39. On the *Judenzählung* see in particular and in great detail two important contributions by Werner T. Angress. His essay 'The German Army's "Judenzählung" of 1916. Genesis – Consequences – Significance', in *LBI Year Book XXIII* (1978), pp. 117–137; and his comprehensive documentation with a historical introduction, 'Das deutsche Militär und die Juden im Ersten Weltkrieg. Dokumentation', in *Militärgeschichtliche Mitteilungen*. Hrsg. vom Militär-geschichtlichen Forschungsamt durch Friedrich Forstmeier und Manfred Messerschmidt u.a., Jg. 19, Nr. 1, Freiburg i. Br. 1976, pp. 77–146.

By the end of November 1918, the *Komitee für den Osten* was satisfied that the recent establishment of a Jewish Affairs section in the German Foreign Office was without question the result of its own influence and pressure on the German government during the previous year. A memorandum of the 25th November 1918 from the Committee *Vorstand* to fellow-members interpreted the appointment of Professor Moritz Sobernheim, one of its members, as *Referent für jüdische Angelegenheiten* in the Foreign Office as a reflection of the strong influence exercised by the Committee on the course of German policy.[10] The memorandum noted: "Wir erblicken in dieser Ernennung ein erneutes Zeichen des Vertrauens und der Anerkennung, die die Regierung den Arbeiten des Komitees entgegenbringt." It also observed that the Committee would remain in existence, in spite of the fact that the creation of the Jewish Affairs section in the Foreign Office had made it redundant, until the uncertainty in post-war Germany and the conditions of the forthcoming peace settlement with its former enemies could be resolved, and presumably until the new Jewish Affairs section could be considered a permanent part of the Foreign Office apparatus. In the meantime, the Committee continued its war-time task of seeking to promote German influence and prestige amongst the Jews of Europe and America by pressing Sobernheim to secure the appointment to German diplomatic posts of well-known German Jews familiar with the problems of the *Ostjuden*, with German-Jewish relations in general and with the aims of the Zionist movement. In a letter to Sobernheim of 28th November 1918, the Committee chairman Franz Oppenheimer reiterated the value to the Allies of this kind of policy during the war, suggested the immediate appointment of German Jews to diplomatic posts in the German embassies in Washington, London, Constantinople, Bern and Den Haag, and concluded: "Dies ist notwendig mit Rücksicht auf die Politik des Reiches, damit nicht unwiederbringlich der Einfluss auf das Judentum der neutralen und feindlichen Länder verloren geht . . ."[11]

Thus the new *Referat für jüdische Angelegenheiten* began its existence more or less as an official German government version of the *Komitee für den Osten*, with aims and tasks that were generally similar if somewhat broader in scope.[12] It was to be the central bureau for the collection of information about Jewish affairs

[10]PA/Bonn: Nachlass Sobernheim, Comitee f.d. Osten, Bd. 1, 'An die Herren Mitglieder des Geschäftsführenden Ausschusses und Vorsitzenden der Ortsgruppen des Komitees für den Osten', G/E. 619, 25. November 1918.

[11]PA/Bonn: Nachlass Sobernheim, Comitee f.d. Osten, Bd. 1, Oppenheimer an Sobernheim, E.630, 28. November 1918. One of the founders and leading members of the *Komitee für den Osten*, Dr. Adolf Friedemann, was appointed German Consul in Amsterdam early in 1919, an appointment which the Committee viewed as an important step in breaking the long-standing antisemitism in the German Foreign Office which excluded German Jews from important diplomatic posts abroad. See PA/Bonn: Nachlass Sobernheim, Comitee f.d. Osten, Bd. 1, 'Komitee für den Osten an die Ortsgruppen und Vertrauensleute des Komitees für den Osten', Fr./N.36, 14. Februar 1919.

[12]The *Referat für jüdische Angelegenheiten* was formally established in the German Foreign Office on 26th November 1918. It was made part of *Politische Abteilung III*, which was responsible for Austria, the Balkans and Turkey. In April 1919, it was made a separate Referat, A6, within Abteilung III. See *Akten zur Deutschen Auswärtigen Politik 1918–1945* (hereafter cited as ADAP), Serie A (1918–1925), Bde.I–III, Geschäftsverteilungspläne des Auswärtigen Amts.

everywhere for the German Foreign Office, as well as an instrument for the active promotion of German interests and prestige among the Jews of the world. Like its war-time predecessor, the *Referat* started from the premise that the Jewish and the Eastern Questions were closely linked, and that the pursuit of policies sympathetic towards and supportive of Jewish interests in the former was the best guarantee for success of German interests and aims in the latter.[13]

In his 'Aufzeichnung über das Jüdische Referat im Auswärtigen Amt' of 4th September 1919, Moritz Sobernheim made the strongest possible case for the retention of his *Referat* in the forthcoming reorganisation of the German Foreign Office, and outlined the three areas in which it would be active.[14] Its first task was to provide various departments in the Foreign Office with information ". . . über alle politisch wichtigen Vorgänge des Gesamtjudentums, seine religiösen, kulturellen und sozialen Strömungen". Sobernheim alluded specifically to information about the relationship of Jews in Eastern Europe with their governments and with their fellow-citizens, about the progress of the Zionist movement and the building of the National Home in Palestine, the work in Paris of the Jewish delegation for the protection of minorities, and the efforts of World Jewry to convene a World Jewish congress. The primary instrument for the dissemination of this information would be an in-house publication which the *Referat* would publish on a weekly basis. According to Sobernheim, the *Referat* had at its disposal many reliable sources of information, including the excellent Jewish news bureaux in Copenhagen, Stockholm and Zürich, as well as the many important Jewish political personalities passing through Germany, the German Zionist Organisation (*Zionistische Vereinigung für Deutschland*), and the officer in charge of the Jewish press in the German Consulate in Amsterdam. Sobernheim also mentioned as sources the Jewish press in Hebrew, Polish and Yiddish, which were edited and translated for the *Referat* by Professor Pick.

The second task of Sobernheim's office was to work closely and constantly with the various departments in the German Foreign Office, and with the *Referenten* in those departments responsible for specific countries, on special issues and problems in Jewish affairs from around the world. Thirdly, it was to ensure that ". . . die auf jüdische Angelegenheiten bezüglichen politischen Massnahmen geeignet sind, die Sympathien der anderen Länder, vor allem aber der internationalen Judenheit zu erwerben". In this instance, Sobernheim used Palestine and the Jewish National Home as an example of the kind of strategy his department should pursue. He argued that since the Jews were now to become the most significant political and economic factor in Palestine, German interests and aims in the Middle East would best be served by cultivating close, friendly relations with the Zionist Organisation. He observed that Zionism and the growing Jewish presence in Palestine were the best possible vehicles for the promotion of German interests in Palestine and the Middle East because of the traditional East European Jewish affinity to Germany, its language and culture.

[13]See PA/Bonn: Personalakten-Professor Sobernheim, 'Aufzeichnung über das Jüdische Referat im Auswärtigen Amt', 4. September 1919, p. 3.
[14]*Ibid.*

He also pointed to the American-Jewish community, with its deep historical roots in Germany, as a vehicle for the promotion of German interests in and better relations with the United States. Finally, he argued that the Jewish communities in neighbouring countries would be most helpful in seeking the protection of the rights of German minorities.

In arguing for the retention and expansion of the Jewish Affairs section in September 1919, Sobernheim was fearful that the war-time and immediate post-war perception of the value of Jewish affairs in the pursuit of German foreign policy and of the consequent need for a special department within the Foreign Office might be lost in any Foreign Office reorganisation under the new Weimar system. This is evident in the concluding paragraph of his memorandum of the 4th September, in which he argued:

> "Aus allen diesen Gründen erlaubt sich der unterzeichnete Referent der Anschauung gehorsamst Ausdruck zu verleihen, dass das jüdische Referat bei einer Neuorganisierung im Auswärtigen Amt erhalten bleiben und weiter ausgestaltet werden sollte."

Moreover, at least one German newspaper questioned the wisdom of maintaining and expanding the Jewish Affairs section in 1919. In its evening edition of 11th September 1919, the *Deutsche Tageszeitung* criticised the section for engaging primarily in combating antisemitic propaganda in Germany.[15] Although Sobernheim's memorandum of the 4th September did not specifically include the struggle against antisemitism in Germany as one of its tasks, the antisemitic wave sweeping Germany in the immediate post-war period did have obvious foreign policy implications for Germany, with the potential for neutralising the aims of the Jewish Affairs section. The *Deutsche Tageszeitung* argued that any involvement in German domestic politics was wrong, and that the German taxpayer should not be expected to pay for it.

Sobernheim's *Referat* did survive the process of change in the German Foreign Office which took place between 1918 and 1920.[16] Among the aims of the reorganisation, great emphasis was placed on opening up the diplomatic service to individuals outside the traditional aristocratic mould, and on areas such as political economy and foreign trade. Within the general context of enlisting economists and individuals with business expertise and experience, and of promoting German exports and economic interests as primary aims of German foreign policy, opportunities for Jews in the Foreign Office, and for Jewish affairs in German foreign policy were greatly enhanced. The Jewish Affairs section eventually became part of a new *Politische Abteilung III–2 (Orient)* which was

---

[15] *Deutsche Tageszeitung*, 11th September 1919.
[16] The conservative character and structure of the German Foreign Office had become the target of considerable criticism and calls for reform even before the war. These efforts intensified during the war, and resulted in the first changes during the last months of the war. The establishment of the *Referat für jüdische Angelegenheiten* shortly after the armistice in November 1918, was certainly part of this process which picked up momentum throughout 1919, after the revolutionary upheavals had subsided. For the only complete account of the transition of the German Foreign Office from the Second Empire to the Weimar Republic, see Kurt Doss, *Das deutsche Auswärtige Amt im Übergang vom Kaiserreich zur Weimarer Republik*, Düsseldorf 1977.

responsible for the Middle East and South Asia, including Turkey, the Arab
countries, Persia/Afghanistan/India, and Jewish-Political Affairs.[17]

II. THE OSTJUDEN, GERMANY AND EASTERN EUROPE

The work of the Jewish Affairs section from the end of the First World War until
its dissolution in 1933 reflected Sobernheim's own personal identity, loyalties
and consequent priorities as a German Jew, as well as the interests and priorities
that had been defined by the Imperial German government and the *Komitee für
den Osten* during the First World War. It manifested itself primarily in two
specific areas, namely the relationship of both the East European Jewish masses
as well as of Zionism and the Palestine question to the interests and aims of
German foreign policy. Sobernheim alluded to these two questions as they
affected him personally in a letter to Otto Warburg of the *Zionistische Vereinigung
für Deutschland*, dated 4th December 1918.[18] He explained to Warburg that while
he considered himself German in the *völkisch* sense, he also possessed a deep
attachment to Palestine and a recognition of the *Ostjuden* as a distinct *Kulturge-
meinschaft* with perhaps the right to some form of political autonomy.[19] In effect,
he recognised the intimate link between the two questions, something not
uncommon among assimilated German Jews; he considered Zionism and
Palestine as intended primarily for East European rather than German Jews,
and as such, an important part of the solution to the Jewish Question in Eastern
Europe. This view is certainly evident in his reaction to the criticism of the work
of his *Referat* by the assimilationist, ultra German-nationalist, intensely anti-
Ostjuden and anti-Zionist *Verband nationaldeutscher Juden* throughout the 1920s.[20]
The task of his office was to promote German foreign policy interests in both
areas, while at the same time his own view of the solution of the Jewish Question
in Eastern Europe would be realised.

During the immediate post-war years, the Jewish Affairs section devoted its
energies primarily to the acute and many-faceted crisis of the Jewish population
in Eastern Europe. The First World War ended with the collapse of the three
eastern empires, the consequent re-drawing of the map of Central and Eastern

[17]The new *Politische Abteilung III* was divided into three sections. Section I was responsible for Great
Britain and America, Section II for the Middle East, South Asia and Jewish Political Affairs, as
described above, and Section III for Colonial Affairs. See ADAP, Serie B (1925–1933), Bd. I/1,
Geschäftsverteilungsplan des Auswärtigen Amts, Stand vom November 1925.

[18]PA/Bonn: Nachlass Sobernheim, Handakten Ausgänge, Bd. 1, Sobernheim an Warburg, 4.
Dezember 1918.

[19]Sobernheim was born on 13th August 1872, in Berlin. He was a well-known scholar and orientalist
before the First World War, particularly in semitic epigraphy. He was a member of the Prussian
government-sponsored Baalbek Expedition, made many trips to Palestine and Syria for the *Institut
Français d'Archéologie Orientale*, and published books on the peoples of Tripolitania, Baalbek,
Palmyra and Samaria. He was also the stepson of Dr. Eugen Landau, the famous industrialist and a
leading member of the *Hilfsverein der deutschen Juden*.

[20]See PA/Bonn: Pol. Abt. III, Jüd. Politische Angelegenheiten-Allgemeines, Bd.6, Verband
nationaldeutscher Juden e.V. an das Auswärtige Amt, Nr. III 0 757, 25. Mai 1925, and
Aufzeichnung Sobernheims, zu III 0 1191, 3. Juni 1925.

Europe, and the unleashing of nationalist passions and hysteria as the various nationalities of Eastern Europe achieved independent statehood. The Jews in the East, the inevitable targets of hatred and violent persecution in these upheavals, became the focus of concern and action for Sobernheim's *Referat*. His memorandum of the 4th September 1919 identified, as we have said, the fate of the Jews in Eastern Europe, their relationship with the governments and non-Jewish majorities in their respective states, as well as with Zionism and the building of the Jewish National Home in Palestine as the first area of responsibility for his *Referat*.[21] However, the energies of the Jewish Affairs section during those years were devoted increasingly to one of the chief consequences of the war-time and post-war plight of the Jews of Eastern Europe, namely their immigration into Germany, their impact on Germany's volatile domestic political situation, which in turn had potentially negative consequences for German foreign policy.

Sobernheim rather naively considered the immigration of East European Jews during and after the war to be the primary cause of post-war antisemitism in Germany, and as such undesirable. In a letter of the 5th July 1920, the recipient of which is not known, Sobernheim observed that German antisemitism ". . . richtet sich hauptsächlich gegen die Einwanderung der Ostjuden, die sicherlich im Interesse unseres Reiches nicht wünschenswert ist."[22] Between 1919 and 1923, the Jewish Affairs section devoted considerable energy towards countering the practical application of that antisemitism and the potentially harmful consequences for German foreign policy, namely the expulsion of Eastern European, mainly Polish, Jews from various parts of Germany.

Sobernheim's office was actively working to stop expulsions of *Ostjuden* from

[21]Sobernheim and the Jewish Affairs section followed the antisemitic excesses in post-war Eastern Europe, especially in Poland, very closely. In the early 1920s, Sobernheim wrote several lengthy essays for use within the Foreign Office on antisemitism and the situation for Jews in Poland. Among these were the following undated examples: 'Die jüdischen Parteien und ihre Forderungen', 'Zur polnischen Judenfrage', and 'Der Antisemitismus der Polen'. See PA/Bonn: Nachlass Sobernheim, Antisemitismus, Bd. 1.
[22]PA/Bonn: Nachlass Sobernheim, Allgemeines, Bd. 1, Sobernheim letter, 5. Juli 1920. Sobernheim also noted that his *Referat* had been trying to explain this phenomenon as one of the tragic results of the lost war, and that he favoured a more effective sealing of the German border against such immigration, as well as pressure from the great powers on Poland to remove the causes of Jewish emigration from that country. In a memorandum of the 12th of July to the Prussian Interior Ministry, the Jewish Affairs section set the number of *Ostjuden* in Germany at upwards of 70,000, raised from the estimated 45,000 to 50,000 in Germany at the outbreak of war in 1914. In that memorandum, Sobernheim pointed out the extreme difficulty of moving East European Jews from Germany to North and South America, and argued that the sealing of Germany's borders had effectively halted the immigration of Jews from Eastern Europe, thus precluding the need for special measures to remove those still in Germany. See PA/Bonn: Nachlass Sobernheim, Ausweisung von Ostjuden, Bd. 1, Sobernheim an Preussisches Ministerium des Innern, Nr. III Jüd. 20, 12. Juli 1921. However, the estimates of the number of *Ostjuden* in Germany were revised upwards almost a year later. In March 1922, the Jewish Affairs section put the total East European Jewish immigration into Germany during and after the war at between 100,000 and 105,000, with some 47,000 subsequently emigrating from Germany in the post-war period. Keeping in mind the 45,000 to 50,000 *Ostjuden* in Germany before the war, this would still leave over 100,000 in Germany in 1922, about 55,000 of whom had entered Germany after the war. See PA/Bonn: Nachlass Sobernheim, Ausweisung von Ostjuden, Bd. 1, 'Denkschrift über die Ein- und Auswanderung nach bzw. aus Deutschland in den Jahren 1910 bis 1920', Nr. 8, 30. März 1922.

Upper Silesia and from Berlin as early as February 1919.[23] It appealed to the German and Prussian Interior Ministries to consider the negative repercussions that the expulsions would have on Allied and Jewish public opinion, and thus on German foreign policy interests, particularly in the light of the peace conference in Paris and the terms of an eventual peace settlement. In March, Sobernheim brought the attention of the *Reich* Interior Ministry to the expulsion of East European Jews from the *Regierungsbezirk* of Oppeln in Upper Silesia. He argued that it was ridiculous for Germany to claim Upper Silesia, partly on the basis of Jewish fears of Polish antisemitism, and at the same time to expel Jews from the area.[24] On 2nd April, Sobernheim sent a lengthy memorandum to Foreign Minister Graf Brockdorff-Rantzau expressing his alarm at the spread of expulsions of *Ostjuden* from Germany, particularly from Berlin.[25] He complained that Polish Jews were being expelled with no formal charges against them, while Polish Christians were allowed to remain in Germany. He warned that the expulsions were generating concern in Jewish circles in Germany, and expressed the fear that the expulsions could soon appear in the foreign press, in spite of the patriotic efforts of German Jews to prevent this from occurring. He urged the Foreign Minister to consider Germany's hopes of keeping the eastern provinces in the forthcoming peace settlement, and the negative effect that the expulsions could have on those hopes. He also reminded Brockdorff-Rantzau of the delegation of German Christians and Jews from Upper Silesia visiting Scandinavia, Holland and Switzerland, seeking support for Germany's efforts to retain the province; one of their arguments was that the Jewish community in Upper Silesia feared for its safety and future should the province revert to Poland. Sobernheim noted: "Es wäre den Herren unmöglich, weiter dafür einzutreten, wenn sie Kenntnis von diesen Ausweisungen erhielten."

It was not until a year later that interested ministries from the *Reich* and Prussian governments met to consider jointly the continuing question of the expulsion of *Ostjuden* from Germany. On 10th April 1920, representatives from the Foreign Office, including Sobernheim; the *Reich* and Prussian Interior Ministries; the Ministry of Agriculture; the *Reich* Ministry of Culture; the *Reich* Ministry for Demobilisation; the Police Presidium and the Workers' Welfare Office of the Jewish Organisations of Germany met in the Foreign Office in an attempt to resolve the issue.[26] After the Foreign Office representatives stressed the need to be mindful of the negative impact of the expulsions on foreign public opinion, especially on American and American-Jewish opinion, and the need to cultivate American sympathy for Germany, Sobernheim presented a list of four guidelines to be adopted in the matter of the *Ostjuden*, and all other foreigners, in

[23]PA/Bonn: Nachlass Sobernheim, Handakten Ausgänge, Bd. 1, Aufzeichnung Sobernheims, April 1919.

[24]PA/Bonn: Nachlass Sobernheim, Allgemeines, Bd. 1, Sobernheim an Reichsministerium des Innern, März 1919.

[25]PA/Bonn: Nachlass Sobernheim, Handakten Ausgänge, Bd. 1, Sobernheim an Brockdorff-Rantzau, 2. April 1919.

[26]PA/Bonn: Nachlass Sobernheim, Ausweisung von Ostjuden, Bd. 1, 'Protokoll der Sitzung über die jüdischen Ausweisungen im Auswärtigen Amt am 10. April'.

Germany. First, he suggested that all foreigners resident in Germany before the war, or brought to Germany as workers during the war, with the exception of those who had broken the law or had been involved in "bolshevik" activities, be allowed to stay. Secondly, Sobernheim pleaded that those who had entered Germany between the armistice in November 1918, and 1st April 1919, and who were willing to work or had already found work, should not be expelled. Thirdly, he favoured the immediate expulsion of all foreigners who had entered Germany without permission after 1st April 1919. Fourthly, he suggested that those foreigners who had come to Germany before 1st April 1919, but were unwilling or unable to work, and thus were to be expelled, should not be placed under arrest by the police, but instead, until their departure, be placed in camps run by the Employment Office of the Jewish Organisations of Germany. At the end of the meeting, Sobernheim also requested the Prussian Ministry of the Interior to make the expulsions that had to take place easier, kinder, more humane than had previously been the case. Finally, Sobernheim sought to break the link in the minds of many between Bolshevism and the Jews. He recognised that much of the public support for the expulsion of East European Jews from Germany in those crisis-filled post-war years stemmed from the fear of a bolshevik threat from the East, and the perception that Bolshevism attracted the overwhelming support and enthusiasm of the bulk of East European Jewry. He therefore made the following statement to the assembled representatives: "Kein Jude, der mit dem Judentum, sei es durch den Glauben oder durch das Nationalgefühl, noch irgend einen Zusammenhang hat, ist Bolschewist. Ein grosser Teil Bolschewisten sind aus dem Judentum ausgetreten."

In order to help alleviate the crisis, the Jewish Affairs section became increasingly involved in the difficult process of facilitating the emigration of those East European Jews who were not considered eligible to remain in Germany. Sobernheim was very active in the functioning of the *Arbeiterfürsorgeamt der jüdischen Organisationen Deutschlands* (the Workers' Welfare Office of the Jewish Organisations of Germany). Founded through the initiative of the *Komitee für den Osten* and other Jewish organisations in January 1918, at a time when many Jewish workers in Germany from Poland and Lithuania were being ill-treated by German factory officials, the *Arbeiterfürsorgeamt* sought to promote, in an orderly manner, the emigration of East European Jewish workers from Germany to desirable destinations.[27] Working closely with the Berlin police presidium, and with the *Reich* Interior Ministry and the *Reichsamt für Arbeitsvermittlung*, it also acted as an employment agency finding temporary work for Jewish workers while they were in Germany awaiting the opportunity to reach the countries of their final destination. It strongly counselled East European Jewish workers in Germany that Germany was not a desirable immigration

---

[27]See PA/Bonn: Nachlass Sobernheim, Antisemitismus, Bd. 1, Aufzeichnung Sobernheims, 17. Mai 1920. Other German-Jewish organisations that participated in some way in the creation of the *Arbeiterfürsorgeamt* were the *Zionistische Vereinigung für Deutschland*, the *Hilfsverein der deutschen Juden*, the *Jüdische Grossloge*, the *Jüdischer Volks-Verein*, and the *Vertretungen der ostjüdischen Arbeiter*. At the end of 1918, the *Jüdische Gemeinde* of Berlin became involved, and in 1920, the *Centralverein deutscher Staatsbürger jüdischen Glaubens* also began to lend its support.

country, and devoted most of its energies to facilitating the movement of *Ostjuden* out of Germany to other destinations. Sobernheim was a member of its *Vorstand* from the beginning, and remained so with the blessing of the German Foreign Ministry from the establishment of his *Referat*.[28]

Sobernheim and his *Referat* were also involved in trying to resolve the problem of the *Ostjuden* in Germany in a number of other ways during the early 1920s. Early in 1921, he established a working relationship with representatives of the American Jewish Joint Distribution Committee in Germany in order to ease the *Durchwanderung* of East European Jews from and through Germany to the United States.[29] He also visited the United States in 1921 to explore the possibilities for increased East European Jewish immigration there. He travelled to twelve American cities in the East and the Mid-West, and met with important Jewish and non-Jewish officials, including Louis Brandeis and President Harding.[30] The Jewish Affairs section was also supportive of the re-establishment of the *Centralbüro für jüdische Auswanderungsangelegenheiten* in 1921. It had originally been founded in 1904 within the *Hilfsverein der deutschen Juden* by major German and foreign Jewish organisations to help the emigration of *Ostjuden* from Germany. Finally, the Jewish Affairs section began to lend its support to the German section of *ORT-Gesellschaft zur Förderung des Handwerks und der Landwirtschaft unter den Juden* in 1923.[31] ORT had originally been designed to promote and support agriculture and *Handwerk* among the Jews of Tsarist Russia. Sobernheim and the German Foreign Office considered it worthwhile to do their utmost to improve the condition of Jews in Eastern Europe in order to dampen their enthusiasm for emigration to Germany. In Sobernheim's view, ORT was ". . . eine reine Wohlfahrtsgesellschaft und verhilft den Juden, die aus diesen Ländern nicht auszuwandern wünschen, zur Sesshaftigkeit. Das Auswärtige Amt steht daher der Wirksamkeit dieser Gesellschaft mit Sympathie gegenüber."

All these efforts by Sobernheim and his *Referat* to neutralise in various ways the domestic political conflict over East European Jews in Germany, and its

---

[28]Representatives from the *Arbeiterfürsorgeamt* attended meetings at the Foreign Ministry, the *Reich* and Prussian Interior Ministries, and the *Reichsamt für Arbeitsvermittlung*. Its presidium was composed of three representatives from "*bürgerlich*" organisations and one from the East European Jewish workers, while its *Ausschuss* was composed of nine representatives from "*bürgerlich*" organisations and three East European Jewish workers. Besides helping with the search for employment, the *Arbeiterfürsorgeamt* provided East European Jewish refugees with clothing and tools. It also received a monthly subsidy of RM 500,000 from the American Jewish Joint Distribution Committee in New York. Sobernheim asserted that its representatives ". . . sind ausgesprochene Gegner des Bolschewismus". See PA/Bonn: Pol. Abt. III, Jüd. Politische Angelegenheiten, Allgemeines, Bd. 1, Aufzeichnung Sobernheims, zu III Jüd. 248, 14. Oktober 1920.

[29]See PA/Bonn: Pol. Abt. III, Jüd. Politische Angelegenheiten, Allgemeines, Bd. 2, Aufzeichnungen Sobernheims, 3. Januar & 12. Januar 1921. Specifically, Sobernheim helped representatives of the Joint Distribution Committee to establish contacts with the German embassies in Poland and Lithuania. Sobernheim emphasised the need to promote ". . . die starke Auswanderung von Polen nach Amerika über deutsche Häfen".

[30]PA/Bonn: Pol. Abt. III, Jüd. Politische Angelegenheiten, Allgemeines, Bd. 2, Abschrift (no name, no date). It is not known what if anything came out of this trip.

[31]PA/Bonn: Pol. Abt. III, Jüd. Politische Angelegenheiten, Allgemeines, Bd. 5, Sobernheim an ORT/Berlin, III Jüd. 77, 24. April 1923.

perceived negative effects on Germany's image and policies abroad, appear to have achieved little success by 1923. Casting its shadow over the question of the *Ostjuden* was a continuous debate within the German government between Sobernheim in the Foreign Office and the *Reich* and Prussian Interior Ministries over the scope and severity of the problem. While recognising the dangers and negative consequences of the problem of the *Ostjuden* in Germany, Sobernheim's strategy was quietly to direct the energies of his office to halting Jewish immigration into Germany, to promoting the emigration of as many East European Jewish refugees from Germany as possible, and to the effective integration of those who were to remain in Germany into the Jewish community and the larger German society. The interior ministries, on the other hand, certainly much more directly affected by the vitriolic political campaigns of the antisemitic Right in post-war Germany, tended to see the problem in much larger terms, and as such, perhaps in need of more drastic measures to effect its resolution. This is evident in the disagreement, which continued into 1923, over the exact number of East European Jews in Germany. At a meeting on 10th January 1923, attended by representatives of the Foreign Office (including Sobernheim), the Prussian Interior Ministry and the League of Nations, Sobernheim strenuously countered Interior Ministry claims that there were 200,000 *Ostjuden* in Berlin alone with the assertion that 56,000 was a more realistic figure, and that many of the refugees from the East living in Berlin were Russian refugees, Jewish and non-Jewish, from the Bolshevik Revolution.[32]

Several months later, the Prussian Interior Ministry was still viewing the problem in crisis terms in a memorandum to the *Reich* Interior Ministry, complaining of the continuing "unerwünschter Zustrom von Ausländern" into Germany since the end of the war.[33] Nevertheless, the two ministries agreed to pursue a policy that Sobernheim might have been able to accept, at least in part. Those who could prove continuous residence in Prussia for at least four years, who had a secure economic existence and who had never disturbed the public order, would not be expelled, even if they had entered Germany without permission or had stayed on in Germany after their visas had expired. The policy also stipulated that there would be no punishment for those expelled, beyond that of their expulsion.

As the problem of the *Ostjuden* was finally achieving some modicum of agreement and stability in Prussia by the middle of 1923, it was entering a more critical and controversial phase in Bavaria. Of course the vast majority of Jewish refugees from the East had always flocked to Prussia, especially to Berlin, either to find refuge there or on their way to North and South America via North German ports. Yet the virulent antisemitic reaction to any East European Jewish presence in Germany was probably much greater in the South where the new radical, antisemitic Right in post-war Germany was far stronger and more firmly

[32] PA/Bonn: Nachlass Sobernheim, Ausweisung von Ostjuden, Bd. 1, Besprechung vom 10. Januar 1923.
[33] PA/Bonn: Nachlass Sobernheim, Ausweisung von Ostjuden, Bd. 1, Preussisches Ministerium des Innern an das Reichsministerium des Innern, IVb 5434, 18. Mai 1923.

rooted. In the autumn of 1923, the Bavarian government began expelling East European (Polish) Jewish families from Munich, creating a crisis of varying degrees between the *Reich* and Bavarian governments, the German and Polish governments, and for the problem of Germany's image in the West.[34] Sobernheim immediately reported to his superiors in the Foreign Office that forty Jewish families had been expelled, with more expulsions expected, and that the *Völkischer Beobachter* and the entire antisemitic Right were responsible for the prevailing anti-Jewish hysteria in Munich.[35] Sobernheim and the Jewish Affairs section were also deluged with questions and concern from abroad, sent via German diplomatic missions, about the expulsions, and about Hitler, the National Socialist movement and the swelling antisemitic tide. On top of this, the Polish government protested about the expulsions and threatened retaliation against German farmers in former Prussian territory which had reverted to Poland at the end of the war.[36] The Foreign Office in Berlin advised the Bavarian government of the negative consequences of the expulsions on Germany's image and policies abroad, especially in England and the United States, but refrained from involving itself in what it considered an internal police matter for the Bavarian government.[37] The problem was dissipated after the crisis of November 1923, the failure of the National Socialist *Putsch* in Munich and the subsequent restrictions placed by the Bavarian government on Hitler and the National Socialist movement.

The political turmoil in Bavaria generated by the National Socialists in 1923, including the virulent antisemitic campaign and the crisis surrounding the expulsion of Polish Jews from Munich, involved the Jewish Affairs section in a vigorous effort to neutralise the effect it would have on Germany's image abroad. Sobernheim appears to have been quite effective in guiding the German Foreign Office into the position of publicly opposing the activities of the antisemitic Right in Bavaria and throughout Germany. He arranged an interview for the editor of the Jewish Correspondence Bureau in Berlin with the German Foreign Minister, Frédéric Hans von Rosenberg, on 9th April 1923.[38] In preparing for the interview, Sobernheim persuaded the Foreign Minister to take the following positions on the four questions that were to be posed by the interviewer. First,

---

[34]The only full account of the expulsion of Polish Jews from Bavaria in 1923 can be found in Reiner Pommerin, 'Die Ausweisung von "Ostjuden" aus Bayern 1923. Ein Beitrag zum Krisenjahr der Weimarer Republik', *Vierteljahrshefte für Zeitgeschichte*, 34, No. 3 (July 1986), pp. 311–340.

[35]PA/Bonn: Pol. Abt. III, Jüd. Politische Angelegenheiten, Allgemeines, Bd. 5, Aufzeichnung Sobernheims, III Jüd. 166, 29. Oktober 1923.

[36]See PA/Bonn: Pol. Abt. III, Jüd. Politische Angelegenheiten, Allgemeines, Bd. 5, Aufzeichnung Sobernheims, III Jüd. 170, 6. November 1923, Deutsche Gesandtschaft/Warschau an das Auswärtige Amt, Telegramm, 9. November 1923, Auswärtiges Amt an die Deutsche Gesandtschaft/Warschau, Telegramm, 10. November 1923, and Aufzeichnung IVa Pol6292, 10. November 1923.

[37]See PA/Bonn: Pol. Abt. III, Jüd. Politische Angelegenheiten, Allgemeines, Bd. 5, Auswärtiges Amt (von Schubert) an die Vertreter der Reichsregierung in München, Nr. III Jüd. 166, 30. Oktober 1923.

[38]PA/Bonn: Pol. Abt. III, Jüd. Politische Angelegenheiten, Allgemeines, Bd. 5, 'Entwurf zu einem Interview des Herrn Reichsaussenminister mit dem Vertreter des Jewish Correspondence Bureau in Berlin, zu Jüd. 54', 9. April 1923.

von Rosenberg asserted that the *Reich* government always held to the principle that all Jews in Germany should receive the same treatment as non-Jews, that all occupations and professions should be open to Jews, and that foreigners should be treated without concern for their religion in an equal and friendly manner, but ". . . dass sich zur Zeit die Regierung eine grosse Zurückhaltung in dieser Beziehung auferlegen muss, ist ohne weiteres aus der Notlage des Reiches erklärlich". Secondly, the Foreign Minister noted that the *Reich* and state governments believed in the necessity of an *Einheitsfront* of all German citizens, regardless of religion, and thirdly, that the antisemitic propaganda campaign had been actively opposed by the *Reich*, Prussian and Bavarian governments because it was damaging to German interests. Finally, von Rosenberg reaffirmed the German government's complete support for the Jewish National Home in Palestine.

III. ZIONISM AND THE JEWISH NATIONAL HOME IN PALESTINE

In 1924, the Weimar Republic finally began to achieve a level of domestic political and economic stability similar to that of the pre-war years. That stability also brought with it a considerable, if temporary, decline in the strength and activities of the radical Right and its vitriolic antisemitic campaign inside Germany. At the same time, changed attitudes in Berlin, London, Paris and other European capitals resulted in the beginning of a new era in Germany's post-war relations with its former enemies. The international cooperation in the German economic recovery and the easing of German reparation payments, embodied in the Dawes Plan of 1924, the Locarno Agreement of 1925 and the spirit of cooperation it engendered, according to which Germany, France and Belgium recognised and guaranteed their common borders, and Germany's entry into the League of Nations as a permanent member of the League Council in 1926, brought Germany out of the isolation that had been imposed on it after the war. As a recognised great power and an active participant in the mainstream of international politics, Weimar Germany began to pursue a foreign policy designed to restore the substance of great power status; this meant, of course, the peaceful revision of many of the provisions of the hated Versailles Treaty as they related to Germany, within the context of friendly relations with the Western powers and unwavering German recognition and support for the broader post-war settlement which secured for Britain and France their pre-eminent positions throughout the world.

If the fate of the Jews in Eastern Europe and the question of the *Ostjuden* and antisemitism in Germany had preoccupied Sobernheim's Jewish Affairs section during the difficult years before 1924, Germany's relative domestic tranquillity and new position in world affairs after 1924 tended to make Zionism and the Jewish National Home in Palestine the new focus of its activities. In fact, as early as the spring of 1920, the German Foreign Office had already established the outlines of a Palestine policy which provided full German support for the British Mandate and for Zionist efforts to establish a Jewish National Home in

Palestine, one which would be adhered to by all subsequent Weimar governments.[39] In May 1920, Foreign Minister Adolf Köster made the following public
declaration of German support for the Zionist cause:

> "Das neue Deutschland, das wiederholt in unzweideutiger Weise seine Entschlossenheit
> kundgetan hat, an einer gerechten, den Interessen der Menschheit dienenden Weltpolitik
> mitzuwirken, wird auch den Aufbau und die Entwicklung des jüdischen Palästinas mit
> warmer Sympathie verfolgen."[40]

The following September, Karl von Schubert, State Secretary from 1924 to 1930
and an active supporter of Zionism and the National Home, identified the
economic and political benefits for Germany in Palestine and throughout the
Middle East of a policy that lent full support to the Mandate and the Jewish
National Home.[41] Moreover, a Foreign Office circular of 8th May 1922 to all
German diplomatic missions abroad identified the important advantages of such
a policy, among them the economic benefits of increased German exports to an
expanding Palestine market, the sympathy of Jews throughout the world for
Germany, and the rebuilding of Germany's general political, economic and
cultural position in Palestine.[42]

In a variety of ways, Sobernheim's office was at the forefront in executing this
policy for the German Foreign Office even before 1924/1925. In Germany itself,
the Jewish Affairs section lent the support of the entire Foreign Office to the
Zionistische Vereinigung für Deutschland in the process of expediting visa appli-
cations and securing living quarters for foreign Zionists visiting and working in
Germany.[43] In every instance, Sobernheim reasoned that complete support for
and cooperation with the German Zionist organisation was in the national
interest as it would enhance the position and influence of German Zionism in the
World Zionist Organisation, and thereby the image and foreign policy objectives
of Germany. In this context, Sobernheim was also responsible for organising and
smoothing the way for the visits of Chaim Weizmann, President of the World
Zionist Organisation, to Germany in 1921 and 1925, and of Nahum Sokolow,

---

[39]For an account of the Palestine policy of the Weimar Republic, see Francis R. J. Nicosia, 'Weimar
Germany and the Palestine Question', in *LBI Year Book XXIV* (1979), pp. 321–345.

[40]See PA/Bonn: Nachlass Sobernheim, Allgemeines, Bd. 1, Zionistische Vereinigung für Deutschland an den Herrn Reichsaussenminister, 10. Mai 1920, and Aufzeichnung des Reichsaussenmini-
sters, Mai 1920.

[41]Nicosia, 'Weimar Germany', *loc. cit.*, p. 325.

[42]PA/Bonn: Gesandtschaft Bern, Palästina 1922–1937, Aufzeichnung des Auswärtigen Amts über
die Lage in Palästina, Nr. IIb 245, 8. Mai 1922, as cited in Nicosia, 'Weimar Germany', *loc. cit.*, p.
325.

[43]See PA/Bonn: Nachlass Sobernheim, Handakten Ausgänge, Bd. 1, entire file. This file contains
much information on Sobernheim's efforts to help obtain visas for visiting Zionists from Poland.
Sobernheim's office provided a great deal of assistance to Zionist publishers and publications in
Germany by facilitating the granting of entry visas and by finding apartments for foreign Zionists
working for those publications. In 1920, for example, he played an important role in securing entry
into Germany and living quarters in Berlin for some prominent Czech Zionists, among them
Robert Weltsch, for their work at the Zionist publishing house, the *Jüdischer Verlag*, and the Zionist
newspaper, the *Jüdische Rundschau*. See PA/Bonn: Pol. Abt. III, Jüd. Politische Angelegenheiten,
Allgemeines, Bd. 1, Sobernheim an den Wohnungsverband für Gross-Berlin, 12. Mai 1920;
Nachlass Sobernheim, Allgemeines, Bd. 1, Auswärtiges Amt an das Wohnungsamt/Berlin-
Wilmersdorf, III. Jüd. 169, 17. Juli 1920, and Sobernheim an den Wohnungsverband für Gross-
Berlin, Dezember 1920.

Moritz Sobernheim
(1872–1933)
Photo taken on joining
the German Foreign Office in 1918

another high-ranking official in the WZO, in 1926.[44] During these visits, Weizmann was received by the German Chancellors and Presidents as if he were a head of government. Sobernheim undertook a mission to London with decidedly diplomatic undertones in the summer of 1924.[45] Ostensibly there to visit the Palestine pavilion at the London Exhibition, he met with Chaim Weizmann, who in turn arranged a meeting for Sobernheim with Sir Herbert Samuel, the British High Commissioner for Palestine. After pressing Samuel on the need for a German diplomatic mission in Palestine, Sobernheim met the editors of the *Jewish Chronicle* and the *Jüdische Telegrafen-Agentur* in London, as well as the Jewish politician Lucien Wolf and Colonel Josiah Clement Wedgwood in an effort to reaffirm Germany's support for the British Mandate in Palestine and the Jewish National Home, and thereby to rebuild Germany's image and influence in Palestine and the Middle East.

Sobernheim also made it his business to attend the bi-annual congresses of the World Zionist Organisation in order to assess the role and influence of the German Zionist movement in the world organisation, as well as to report to the German Foreign Office on the development of the Jewish National Home in Palestine. After the 12th Congress at Karlsbad in September 1921, Sobernheim noted that the influence of the German Zionists had grown immensely within the World Organisation, something that was very much in the German interest.[46] After returning from the 13th Congress, which also took place in Karlsbad in August 1923, Sobernheim happily reported that the German Zionists had exercised a very strong influence on the congress, and ". . . dass die Stimmung des gesamten Kongresses ausgesprochen pro-deutsch war".[47] He further noted that there was overwhelming support for Germany and hostility towards France in the crisis over the Franco-Belgian occupation of the Ruhr, and that all the delegates expressed their enthusiasm for the continuing increase in trade between Germany and Palestine.

Sobernheim also became involved in Foreign Office attempts to counter Vatican antagonism towards the Jewish National Home in Palestine as early as 1921. In June 1921, he wrote to Leo Motzkin of the *Comité des Délégations Juives* in Paris expressing his alarm over the recent public accusations levelled by Pope Benedict against Zionism and the National Home.[48] According to Sobernheim,

[44]See PA/Bonn: Jüd. Politische Angelegenheiten, Allgemeines, Bd. 3, Sobernheim an den Herrn Reichskanzler, 15. Dezember 1921; Nachlass Sobernheim, Allgemeines, Bd. 1, Aufzeichnungen Sobernheims, 29. Dezember 1924, 13. Januar 1925. See also Nicosia, 'Weimar Germany', *loc. cit.*, p. 335.

[45]PA/Bonn: Pol. Abt. III, Jüd. Politische Angelegenheiten, Allgemeines, Bd. 5, 'Bericht über meine Reise nach London im Monat Juli 1924', e.o. III E 1671 (no date).

[46]PA/Bonn: Pol. Abt. III, Jüd. Politische Angelegenheiten, Allgemeines, Bd. 2, Aufzeichnung Sobernheims, 4. Oktober 1921.

[47]PA/Bonn: Pol. Abt. III, Jüd. Politische Angelegenheiten, Allgemeines, Bd. 5, 'Bericht über den Zionistenkongress in Karlsbad', III Jüd. 130, 25. August 1923.

[48]PA/Bonn: Pol. Abt. III, Jüd. Politische Angelegenheiten, Allgemeines, Bd. 2, Sobernheim an Herrn Leo Motzkin/Paris, III Jüd. 228, 24. Juni 1921. Sobernheim believed that Vatican hostility towards the British Mandate and the Jewish National Home was generated by fears of Protestant gains in the Holy Land, with Jewish support, at the expense of Catholicism. See PA/Bonn: Nachlass Sobernheim, Allgemeines, Bd. 1, Aufzeichnung Sobernheims, 9. Januar 1925.

"Der Papst beschuldigt die Juden, Stätten der Wollust in Jerusalem gegründet und dem Luxus und der Schwelgerei Einlass verschafft zu haben." He expressed his concern over the effect that such Vatican accusations might have on the Polish masses, and the obviously bad consequences for Polish Jewry. By the following year, the Foreign Office was receiving reports from the German embassies in Rome and the Vatican about both Italian and Vatican antipathy towards the Palestine Mandate and the Jewish National Home; moreover, it had begun to instruct the German Embassy in the Vatican to do everything possible to bring about an understanding between the Vatican and the Zionist movement as this was in the German interest.[49]

Finally, Sobernheim was personally involved in the National Home in Palestine itself during the early 1920s. In 1919 and 1920, he was active in planning the proposed University Library, to be built in Jerusalem in the coming years. He appears to have been instrumental in the appointment of Heinrich Loewe as Director of the proposed library, characterising the appointment as a positive step for Germany for the following reason: "Es ist im deutsch-politischen Interesse zu begrüssen, dass dieser wichtige Posten, dessen Inhaber auf das geistige Leben in Palästina Einfluss auszuüben in der Lage ist, von einem Deutschen besetzt wird." In 1924, Sobernheim was one of three German Jews, along with Martin Buber and Leo Baeck, appointed to the board of trustees of the *Judaistisches Institut* of the Hebrew University. In a report on a meeting of the central committee of the Institute, of which he was also a member, in London in 1925, he observed with satisfaction that the strong representation of German scholars in the Institute would enhance overall German prestige and influence in Palestine.[50]

By the time Sobernheim went to Palestine in March 1925, to participate in the opening of the Hebrew University in Jerusalem, Germany already had been pursuing a Palestine policy based upon full acceptance of the post-war *status quo*, namely the British Mandate and the Jewish National Home.[51] The Jewish Affairs section had played an important role in the promotion of this policy, with

[49]See Nicosia, 'Weimar Germany', *loc. cit.*, p. 326. See also PA/Bonn: Pol. Abt. III, Jüd. Politische Angelegenheiten, Allgemeines, Bd. 4, Deutsche Botschaft/Rom an Auswärtiges Amt, Nr. I 2976, 30. Juni 1922, and Deutsche Botschaft beim Heiligen Stuhl an Auswärtiges Amt., Nr. 105, 26. Juli 1922.

[50]PA/Bonn: Pol. Abt. III, Jüd. Politische Angelegenheiten, Allgemeines, Bd. 7, 'Bericht über eine in London stattgehabte Sitzung des Zentralkomitees für das Judaistische Institut an der Universität Jerusalem', zu III 0 1585, 1. Juli 1925.

[51]Sobernheim was sent by the German Foreign Office to participate in the opening ceremonies as a representative of German ". . . wissenschaftliche Kreise und Gesellschaften". The German Consul-General in Jerusalem, Kapp, was the official representative of the German government. Sobernheim had long been a member of the *Vorstand* of the *Gesellschaft zur Förderung der Wissenschaft des Judentums*, founded in 1903 in Berlin and devoted to the promotion of Jewish scholarship in Germany through scholarly publication, the awarding of annual stipends for Jewish academics, and the establishment of the support for endowed chairs for Jewish scholars. In 1926, Sobernheim became chairman of the society. See PA/Bonn: Pol. Abt. III, Jüd. Politische Angelegenheiten, Allgemeines, Bd. 6, (entire file), and Nachlass Sobernheim, Gesellschaft zur Förderung der Wissenschaft des Judentums, Bd. 1, 'Sitzungen des Vereins Gesellschaft zur Förderung der Wissenschaft des Judentums e.V.'.

its emphatically pro-Zionist orientation, among Jews in Germany and abroad, and Sobernheim's lengthy stay in Palestine in 1925 only reinforced his commitment to that policy in the developing Palestine question. When he returned to Berlin in April, he filed a comprehensive report on his trip in which he outlined his views on the Palestine question, with its triangular conflict between the Arabs, the Jews and the British, and on Germany's national interests in the question.[52]

Sobernheim rejected the Arab cause at the outset. He reasoned that they had done nothing to develop Palestine, while the Jews had done everything to that end. It was, therefore, in Germany's interest to support the National Home because it was providing a rapidly growing market for German exports. The natural trade connections between Jewish businesses in Germany and Palestine, as well as the strong cultural and spiritual bond between Germany and the masses of East European Jews who had settled and were expected to settle in Palestine would, in Sobernheim's view, guarantee Germany a strong position and a high degree of influence in that important region. Finally, Sobernheim emphasised that Great Britain remained the most important element in German foreign policy, not only in the Middle East, but more importantly in Europe. He argued that friendship and cooperation with England were essential to achieve Germany's relatively limited aims in the Middle East, as well as the more important ambition of revising greatly the settlement for Europe laid down in Versailles.

While membership in the League of Nations formally committed Germany to backing the British Mandate and the Jewish National Home, the Jewish Affairs section, in order to provide support for this position, once again focused its attention and energies on the domestic political arena, specifically that of the predominantly non-Zionist/anti-Zionist German-Jewish community.[53] The task of promoting the government's pro-Mandate, pro-Zionist policies encountered its strongest opposition from the majority liberal/"assimilationist" Jewish organisations in Germany which had been engaged in an often bitter ideological conflict and propaganda war with the German Zionist organisation since the late nineteenth century.[54] The increasing virulence and public tolerance of antisemi-

---

[52]PA/Bonn: Botschaft Ankara, Pol.3-Palästina, 1924–1938, 'Bericht über meine Reise nach Palästina im März und April 1925', III 0 1269.

[53]Upon entry into the League of Nations, Germany became treaty-bound to the Mandate system as contained in Article 22 of the League Covenant, and specifically to the British Mandate over Palestine as adopted by the League on 24th July 1922. The Jewish National Home, as envisioned by the Balfour Declaration of 1917, was incorporated into the Preamble of the Palestine Mandate and into Articles 2, 4, 6, 11, 22 and 23. For the complete text of the Palestine Mandate and of Article 22 of the League of Nations Covenant, see J. C. Hurewitz, *Diplomacy in the Near and Middle East. A Documentary Record, 1914–1956*, New York 1956, pp. 61–62, 106–111.

[54]See Arnold Paucker, 'Zur Problematik einer jüdischen Abwehrstrategie in der deutschen Gesellschaft', in *Juden im Wilhelminischen Deutschland 1890–1914*. Eine Sammelband herausgegeben von Werner E. Mosse unter Mitwirkung von Arnold Paucker, Tübingen 1976 (Schriftenreihe wissenschaftlicher Abhandlungen des Leo Baeck Instituts 33), pp. 591 ff; Jehuda Reinharz, *Fatherland or Promised Land. The Dilemma of the German Jew, 1893–1914*, Ann Arbor 1975, chapter V; Ismar Schorsch, *Jewish Reactions to German Anti-Semitism, 1870–1914*, New York–London–Philadelphia 1972, pp. 179 ff, 195 ff.

tism during the Weimar years, with its direct attack on the identity of Jews as Germans and their position in Germany, only intensified these divisions, making many German Jews more militant either in their Zionism or in their opposition to it.[55] In order to facilitate their task, the German Foreign Office and the *Zionistische Vereinigung für Deutschland* combined to secure the re-establishment of the war-time *Pro-Palästina Komitee* (PPK) in December 1926, with Sobernheim playing a direct role in its organisation and activities.[56]

Like its short-lived war-time predecessor, the reconstituted *Pro-Palästina Komitee* was composed of prominent Jews (Zionists and non-Zionists) and Gentiles mainly from the Liberal centre of the German political spectrum.[57] It adhered to the same basic programme and goals, which included support for the Zionist effort to build the National Home in Palestine primarily by educating German public opinion about that effort. In its official programme, the PPK stressed ". . . dass das jüdische Aufbauwerk in Palästina ein hervorragendes Mittel für die wirtschaftliche und kulturelle Entwicklung des Orients, für die Ausbreitung deutscher Wirtschaftsbeziehungen und für die Versöhnung der Völker ist".[58] According to its first chairman, Count Johann-Heinrich von Bernstorff, the PPK enjoyed the complete support of the German government, including the active involvement of the German Foreign Office, in collaboration with the *Zionistische Vereinigung für Deutschland*.[59]

In its efforts to influence German opinion, particularly German-Jewish opinion, the PPK always emphasised German national interest as the primary reason for supporting German policy. It repeatedly cited the political, economic and cultural advantages for Germany in supporting the Mandate and the National Home in Palestine, as well as the obligations Germany had undertaken when it entered the League of Nations in 1926. With the only serious opposition to government policy and to the establishment of the *Pro-Palästina Komitee* coming from within the German-Jewish community itself, Sobernheim, a member of the PPK presidium, undertook the responsibility of defending the PPK against its non-Zionist and anti-Zionist critics in the Jewish community. He reasoned that the PPK had been established first and foremost in the German interest, that it was not a tool in the hands of the international Zionist movement, and that the support of German Jews for Zionist efforts in Palestine in no way compromised

[55]See Nicosia, 'Weimar Germany', *loc. cit.*, pp. 328–329.

[56]In May 1918, the Imperial German government had been directly involved in the creation of the *Deutsches Komitee zur Förderung der jüdischen Palästinasiedlung* in Berlin. It had been part of the German government's belated attempts to offset the perceived advantages won by England with its Balfour Declaration in November 1917. It was composed of prominent Jewish and non-Jewish Germans from across the political spectrum, brought together by the common conviction that Germany's war-time interests were best served by promoting the Zionist cause in Palestine. See Nicosia, 'Weimar Germany', *loc. cit.*, pp. 329–334; and Joseph Walk, 'Das Deutsche Komitee Pro-Palästina, 1926–1933', in *Bulletin des Leo Baeck Instituts*, XV, Nr. 52 (1976), pp. 162–193.

[57]See Nicosia, 'Weimar Germany', *loc. cit.*, pp. 330–331; Walk, 'Pro-Palästina' *loc. cit.*, pp. 168–178.

[58]PA/Bonn: Nachlass Sobernheim, Jüdische Angelegenheiten, Deutsches Komitee Pro-Palästina, Bd. 1.

[59]See J. H. Graf von Bernstorff, *Memoirs of Count Bernstorff*, New York 1936, pp. 331–333. Bernstorff had been the German Ambassador to the United States and to the Ottoman Empire during the war.

their national and cultural identity as Germans or their loyalty to Germany.[60] Sobernheim spoke with the conviction of a non-Zionist German Jew who sympathised with Zionism and the Jewish National Home in Palestine, but who considered himself a German by nationality, and Zionism a worthy ally in the pursuit of German foreign policy interests and aims, and the best solution to the Jewish Question in Eastern Europe.

IV. CONCLUSIONS

In 1931 and 1932, Sobernheim and the Jewish Affairs section had to deal with the mounting concern from abroad over the electoral successes of the National Socialist Party, the accompanying antisemitic pressures and excesses in German political life and the likelihood of a National Socialist government in Germany.[61] As was the case during the early post-war years, the German Foreign Office was concerned about the harmful consequences of these events on Germany's prestige, interests and general foreign policy objectives throughout the world; as before, it was the responsibility of the Jewish Affairs section to deflect and otherwise neutralise that concern in order to avoid any damage to German interests. By the middle of 1932, the *Reich* Chancellory was urging Sobernheim to do everything necessary to calm fears of an imminent National Socialist takeover, and more importantly, to assert that the German government would continue to do everything necessary to protect the rights of all Jews in Germany.[62] The German government was particularly concerned about the threats from abroad of an economic boycott of German goods in the event of a Hitler government, threats which the export-dependent, depression-plagued German economy could ill afford.[63]

The files of the Jewish Affairs section and those in Sobernheim's own *Nachlass* do not, however, betray the same high level of activity between 1930 and 1932 on behalf of Germany's image and interests abroad, as had been evident during the early post-war years in the matter of stilling foreign fears about the power and excesses of the Radical Right. Clearly the political realities in Germany in the early 1930s were substantially different from those of the immediate post-war years. Germany was no longer the recently-defeated, occupied and friendless outcast of Europe, confronting all the harshness of the Versailles settlement and in the process of a radical political transformation from the conservative order of the Second *Reich* to the new left of centre, Liberal/Social Democratic order of the

[60]Nicosia, 'Weimar Germany', *loc. cit.*, p. 334.

[61]See for example the following regarding concern in the United States: PA/Bonn: Nachlass Sobernheim, Ausland, Bd. 1, Deutsche Botschaft/Washington an das Auswärtige Amt, Nr. 1450, 18. September 1931, and Auswärtiges Amt an Deutsche Botschaft/Washington, zu III 0 3367, Oktober 1931.

[62]PA/Bonn: Nachlass Sobernheim, Aktuelles, Bd. 1, Der Staatssekretär in der Reichskanzlei (Planck) an Sobernheim, Nr. 5346, 10. Juni 1932.

[63]See for example PA/Bonn: Nachlass Sobernheim, Ausland, Bd. 1, Deutsche Gesandtschaft/ Bulkeley (Ägypten) an Auswärtiges Amt, Nr. 417, 14. Juli 1932, and Deutsche Botschaft/Paris an Auswärtiges Amt, W.2505, 3. August 1932.

Weimar Republic. By 1930, however, Germany had regained its status as a great power, had successfully won the revision of many of the most damaging provisions of the Treaty of Versailles, and had been welcomed back into the international community of nations. At the same time, the economic disintegration brought on by the depression destroyed the left of centre, Liberal/Social Democratic coalition that had dominated the Weimar Republic since the end of the war, and generated a shift to the new, albeit more unstable, coalitions of the parties on the Right. Thus, there does not appear to have been, on the part of the German government, the same sense of necessity and urgency based on philosophical or practical considerations, to identify and then avert any harmful effects that Germany's domestic political condition might have on its foreign policy interests.[64]

Sobernheim's *Referat für jüdische Angelegenheiten* was able to exercise some influence on German foreign and domestic policies as long as the governments of the Weimar Republic identified World Jewry as an important and positive actor in the international political arena, and World Jewish opinion as an invaluable ally in the pursuit of German foreign policy interests and objectives. This had

---

[64]On the *Auswärtiges Amt* and the activities of Moritz Sobernheim in the last phase of the Weimar Republic see now Donald M. McKale, 'From Weimar to Nazism: Abteilung III of the German Foreign Office and the Support of Antisemitism, 1931–1935', in *LBI Year Book XXXII* (1987), pp. 297–307. However I would maintain that the essay is not entirely satisfactory in its account of the attitudes and policy of the German Foreign Ministry, particularly of *Abteilung III*, regarding the antisemitic outrages and the threat of the Nazi movement during the last eighteen months of the Republic.

Almost half of the essay is devoted to the period between 1931 and the *Machtübernahme*, and the author puts forward (*ibid.*, p. 297) that *Abteilung III* ". . . involved itself in defending Nazi antisemitism against foreign criticism at least a year and a half before Hitler's appointment". He then asserts, again on the first page, that this "pro-Nazi" attitude simply continued, indeed reached its fulfilment, after January 1933, as ". . . the zealous nature of the *Abteilung*'s support of Nazi attitudes after Hitler took office, not only permitted but encouraged by Bülow and the German Foreign Minister, Constantin von Neurath, suggest[s] that the conservative and elitist bureaucracy of the AA agreed more with Nazi policy towards the Jews than was previously thought".

McKale, I feel, does not sufficiently substantiate his charge that *Abteilung III* was sympathetic to Nazism and its excesses against the Jews before 1933. He rightly outlines the manner in which it sought to deflect foreign concern about the situation in Germany, particularly to avert an anti-German economic boycott. Yet there is a considerable difference between defending Nazi actions and seeking to downplay their significance, so as to influence foreign public opinion in Germany's favour. Although one might be justly disappointed that the AA would go no further than this, it was neither unnatural for the German Foreign Office to seek to blunt foreign criticism of and concern over events in Germany, and thus some of the negative repercussions that consequently could arise, nor does it necessarily prove that what the Nazis were doing in the streets of Berlin and elsewhere was supported by *Abteilung III* or any other department in the German Foreign Office. Seeking to neutralise foreign opinion is not the same thing as approving of and supporting Nazi activities.

Few would deny the lingering traditions of antisemitism among the old Conservative elite in the German Foreign Office during the Weimar Republic. Yet the anti-Communism of a Prüfer or Dieckhoff and even the opposition of Conservatives to the political philosophy of the Weimar Republic, did not automatically mean that they supported or sympathised with the virulent antisemitism of the Nazis, any more than support for the Left or for the political institutions of the Weimar Republic would necessarily preclude antisemitism.

While I cannot disagree with McKale's evidence, far more is required to substantiate his thesis that *Abteilung III* and the German Foreign Office defended and supported Nazi antisemitism between 1931 and 1933.

been done belatedly by the government of Imperial Germany during the last year of the war, and by the governments of the Weimar Republic during the 1920s, in particular through Germany's re-emergence as an active and accepted great power in 1925 and 1926, and the revision of much of the Versailles Treaty by 1929. To achieve these ends, Weimar Germany considered it essential to cultivate Jewish opinion and support as a way of positively influencing the attitudes of Germany's former enemies. The efforts of Sobernheim and the Jewish Affairs section in dealing with the critical situation of the Jewish masses in Eastern Europe, with the sensitive and volatile question of the *Ostjuden* in Germany after the war, and with the role of Zionism and the Jewish National Home in Palestine in German foreign policy, reflected an approach which soon evaporated in the changing domestic political circumstances and foreign policy priorities after 1930.[65]

[65]There has been a tendency in the recent literature to interpret the activities of the largely Conservative elite in the German Foreign Office as inherently and philosophically supportive of the antisemitism and anti-Jewish policies of the Hitler regime after 1933. See for example Hans-Jürgen Döscher, *Das Auswärtige Amt im Dritten Reich. Diplomatie im Schatten der Endlösung*, Berlin 1987. Implicit in this argument is the view that this elite had really been hostile towards the generally friendly and supportive policies of the governments of the Weimar Republic in all facets of Jewish affairs, domestic and foreign. This implication, however, is difficult to accept. Notwithstanding the attitudes of Foreign Office officials after 1933, upon which Döscher concentrates in his book, the records for the period between 1919 and 1929 do not reflect any serious dissatisfaction. At least during the Stresemann period, Weimar Germany considered World Jewish opinion an ally in the pursuit of German foreign policy aims; as a result, the Foreign Office was generally responsive to the suggestions of the Jewish Affairs section, and supportive of issues and policies that were in keeping with the wishes of the German-Jewish community.

The Emigration of Jewish Academics and Professionals from Germany in the First Years of Nazi Rule

BY DORON NIEDERLAND

The rise of the Nazis to power on the 30th of January 1933 brought in its wake substantial Jewish emigration from Germany.* However these emigrants did not leave *en masse*, simultaneously. What then, were the factors which determined who would emigrate, why, when and where to? This question has not been systematically considered in the historiography of the period. The usual explanations for the emigration of German Jews in the 1930s focus on the psychological shock caused by the Nazi rise to power; the loss of equal civil rights previously enjoyed by German Jews; their unwillingness to live under totalitarian rule; the racist legislation; political and physical persecution etc. German Jews were depicted as refugees who were under compulsion to leave the land of their birth, but were prevented by difficulties arising from both Nazi policy, and the immigration policy of the Western states and the Jewish organisations dealing with immigration. In contrast to this view,[1] which stresses the political

---

*This article is part of a wider research project (Ph.D. dissertation) entitled *Emigration Patterns of German Jews 1918–1938*, which attempts to determine a typology of the emigrant at the group and individual level. Motives for emigration or remaining in Germany will also be traced in order to reach conclusions about the decision to emigrate, its timing and the choice of host country.

[1] The basic post-war research on the problem of German-Jewish emigration is Werner Rosenstock, 'Exodus 1933–1939. A Survey of Jewish Emigration from Germany', in *LBI Year Book I* (1956), pp. 373–390. This pioneering research presents a quantitative analysis of the scope of emigration, its chronological course and direction. Along with Rosenstock's analysis, there are works on emigration from the political and organisational point of view. Two representative works are: Shalom Adler-Rudel, *Jüdische Selbsthilfe unter dem Naziregime 1933–1939. Im Spiegel der Berichte der Reichsvertretung der Juden in Deutschland*, Tübingen 1974 (Schriftenreihe wissenschaftlicher Abhandlungen des Leo Baeck Instituts 29), pp. 72–120; Abraham Margaliot, 'The Problem of the Rescue of German Jewry during the Years 1933–1939. The Reasons for the Delay in their Emigration from the Third Reich', in Yisrael Gutman and Efraim Zwolff (eds.), *Rescue Attempts During the Holocaust*, Jerusalem 1977, pp. 247–266. Both authors deal with the activity of the Jewish Organisation in Germany and abroad in regard to the Jewish emigration from Germany, and the Nazi attitude and policy towards it. The most comprehensive and updated contributions to this subject are Herbert A. Strauss's two detailed articles: 'Jewish Emigration from Germany. Nazi Policies and Jewish Responses', Part I, in *LBI Year Book XXV* (1980), pp. 313–363; Part II, in *LBI Year Book XXVI* (1981), pp. 343–411. This large-scale synthesis covers the spectrum of all organisational and political aspects of the problem. Although Strauss touches also on the economic factors in the first part of his article (pp. 338–346), it cannot serve as a systematic analysis, and this paper answers the call for such an analysis. This research is novel also in the choice of sources. In contrast to the previous works, depending on Jewish source material, the present author uses in this paper also German and other, non-Jewish sources.

and organisational aspects of the emigration of German Jews, and their status as refugees rather than emigrants, this paper will discuss some economic motives and considerations, at the level of the group and of the individual. It will be argued that, at least until the autumn of 1935 (the Nuremberg Laws) and perhaps even up till the pogrom in November 1938, the *Kristallnacht*, most German Jews could still weigh up the decision whether to stay or go, despite the new and difficult conditions created for them by Hitler's rise to power. The importance of tracing their economic considerations is therefore obvious. An examination of the factors leading to emigration, its timing and destination will therefore play a central role in the discussion and will be conducted by outlining the emigration patterns of Jews belonging to that occupational sector known as "academic and professional".

This group in particular was chosen as the subject of discussion since it formed a dominant element of the total number of Jewish emigrants, especially in the first year after Hitler's rise to power. This can be proved by comparing the relative proportion of Jewish professionals among all Jewish bread-winners in Germany to their relative proportion in the Jewish emigration of 1933. Less than 13% of all Jewish bread-winners in Germany (before 1933) belonged to the professions, whereas their relative proportion among the emigrant Jewish bread-winners of 1933 was about 20%.[2] Furthermore, as will be seen below, the emigration of Jewish academics and members of the professions was particularly striking during the first half of 1933. It was therefore considered at the time one of the important and pressing problems connected with Jewish emigration from Germany.

The central significance of the emigration of Jewish academics and other professionals from Germany in 1933 is also evidenced by the intensive organisational activity on the international and national level during this period, which aimed at finding a professional place for these emigrants in their host countries. The reports of James McDonald, the League of Nations High Commissioner for Refugees Coming from Germany, show that this international body, which was designed to co-ordinate relief efforts on behalf of Jewish refugees from Germany, devoted much of its time and effort to dealing with the academics and

---

[2]Data on the occupational distribution of the Jewish bread-winners in Germany can be found in the tables appearing in Esra Bennathan, 'Die demographische und wirtschaftliche Struktur der Juden', in *Entscheidungsjahr 1932. Zur Judenfrage in der Endphase der Weimarer Republik*. Ein Sammelband herausgegeben von Werner E. Mosse unter Mitwirkung von Arnold Paucker, Tübingen [2]1966 (Schriftenreihe wissenschaftlicher Abhandlungen des Leo Baeck Instituts 13), pp. 105–106.

It should be noted that among the 13% given by Bennathan are included "those engaged in public and private services". Most, but not all of these are included in the category "academics and professionals". This means that the proportion of the latter was almost certainly even lower.

The data on the relative proportion of academics and professionals among all Jewish emigrant bread-winners from Germany in 1933 are found in 'Statement of J. G. McDonald, High Commissioner for Refugees Coming from Germany, made at the Opening Session of the Governing Body', Lausanne (5th December 1933), p. 4, Leo Baeck Institute Archives, New York (LBA, N.Y.), AR–7162.

An identical figure (20%) also appears in the anonymous report 'The Effects of the German National Socialist Policy', p. 1, YIVO Archives, New York, RG 348, Box 6, File 130.

professionals amongst them. McDonald justified this not only because "these groups contitute an important part of the total emigration." He also claimed that they represented the intellectual elite of the emigrants and as such created special problems, which differed from those of other emigrants.[3] Furthermore, he believed:

> "Less than for any other group is a general solution possible for these categories. If their contribution to learning and science is to be preserved, they have to be slowly and individually absorbed in new places of work on lines of their training."[4]

In order to cope successfully with the special problems connected with the organisation of the emigration of academics and other professional Jews from Germany and their absorption in other potential host countries, many Jewish organisations dealing specifically with this problem were founded, especially in the West. These organisations generally specialised in one of the three sub-groups included in this wider definition of academics and professional people, i.e. academics (professors, lecturers etc.), those in the liberal professions (doctors, lawyers, teachers, artists, writers, etc.) and students.[5] Among these were the Academic Assistance Council (A.A.C.) in London, and the Emergency Council for Displaced German Scholars, New York, which led the way in organising the emigration of holders of university positions, mainly to Britain and the U.S; the International Student Service, Geneva, which carried out most of the organisation of the emigration and absorption of students, and the *Comité de Placement pour les Refugiés Intellectuels*, which specialised in the emigration of members of the professions, first and foremost to France, which in 1933 was the main destination of Jews leaving Germany.[6]

After discussing the quantitative and qualitative importance of the emigration of Jewish academics and professional people from Germany, and the organisational activity connected with it, we will consider the question of the periodisation of this emigration. and the character of the emigrants in each period.

During the first two months after Hitler came to power (February/March 1933) the tendency to emigrate obviously increased among the Jews of Germany. However, at this period there was not yet a phenomenon of mass emigration. The reports of both the Jewish and the German emigration bureaux show that most of the applicants in those months requested information on the possibilities of

---

[3]See, for example, High Commissioner for Refugees Coming from Germany: 'Report of the Representative of the High Commissioner, on Activities during the Period May to July 1934' (4th to 5th July 1934), p. 1, LBA, N.Y., AR–7162, Box 7; 'Report on Activities of the Organizations Dealing with Academic, Professional and Student Emigrants' (April 1934), p. 1, LBA, N.Y., AR–7162, Box 6. *Ibid.*, pp. 1–2.

[4]High Commission for Refugees Coming from Germany, 'Report on the Present Position of the Refugees' (not dated), p. 11, LBA, N.Y., AR–7162, Box 8.

[5]The detailed lists of all Jewish organisations active outside Germany on behalf of academic, professional and student emigrants can be found in High Commissioner for Refugees Coming from Germany, 'Report of the Representative . . . (4th to 5th July 1934)', *loc. cit.*, p. 1–8.

[6]*Ibid.* The censuses and reports produced by these organisations provide much data, both quantitative and qualitative, on the migration patterns of emigrants according to their occupations. These data will be presented and analysed below.

emigration to various countries, but had not yet commenced the emigration process.[7]

Parallel to the rise in the number of "inquiries" and "requests" for information in February/March, a particular kind of actual emigrant can be noted during these months, mostly academic or professional. These were the Jewish intellectuals (writers, artists, journalists etc.), who had previously been active in the two main Left-wing parties, e.g. the *Sozialdemokratische Partei Deutschlands* (SPD) and the *Kommunistische Partei Deutschlands* (KPD), and who had become, as a result of their activity or of Pacifist principles, enemies of the new regime. These people, who were in fact political refugees, were threatened at this period (especially after the *Reichstag* fire at the end of February) with death or imprisonment in a concentration camp. They therefore escaped secretly across the border to Western European countries close to Germany (France, Holland, Belgium, Denmark, Switzerland, etc.), leaving behind them their jobs, their property and generally their families as well.[8]

This flight by Jews, endangered, like Gentile political refugees, by their political affiliation, was completely different from the Jewish emigration of April onwards. An anonymous report on emigration from Germany to Belgium in 1933–1938 illustrates the significant differences between them. It states that:

"At the outset most of them were political refugees opposed to the Nazi regime and trying to escape the measures taken against them. [Their] number was rather small . . . But after the antisemitic trend of the German government, a new afflux arrived at the Belgian frontier. Now whole families arrived and not only men."[9]

Indeed, April 1933 brought about a major turning point in the extent of Jewish emigration from Germany and in its character, as reported in both German and Jewish sources. An anonymous report on the activities of the *Hilfsverein der deutschen Juden* in Berlin during 1933 states that

"Der erste grosse Andrang war am 29. März. Täglich kamen dreihundert und manchmal mehr Petenten zu uns. Schon in den ersten Apriltagen zeigte es sich, dass wir mit unserem ständigen Beamtenapparat (11 Personen) die ständig wachsende Arbeit nicht zu bewältigen in der Lage sein würden."[10]

The Jewish press in Germany also reports mass emigration during the last few days of March and the first few days in April. On 7th April 1933 the *Jüdische Rundschau* reported that during the previous week about two thousand Jews from

[7]On the phenomenon of people "making inquiries" during the first months of Nazi rule, see report of the *Hilfsverein der deutschen Juden* (untitled), p. 1, YIVO Archives, New York, RG 116, Folder 4; Die Reichsstelle für das Auswanderungswesen, München, Vierteljahresbericht, Januar-März 1933, p. 2, Bayerisches Hauptstaatsarchiv, Ministerium des Innern (BAYHSTA, MInn) 74182; Die Reichsstelle für das Auswanderungswesen, Berlin – Stand der Auswanderungsbewegung im 1. Kalendervierteljahr 1933, p. 2, BAYHSTA, MInn 74165.

[8]For two typical examples of such political refugees see: A letter from William Pickens to Dr. Hyman concerning Dr. Arnold Kalisch (30th April 1935), Joint-German Case Files, AR–7196, Box 10, Folder 7, LBA, N.Y., and the memoirs of Rudolph Sachs, 'A German-Jewish Refugee', LBA, N.Y., Memoirs Collection, p. 11.

[9]A report (untitled and undated) concerning the immigration to Belgium 1933–1939, YIVO Archives, New York, RG 116, Folder 5, p. 1.

[10]Report of the *Hilfsverein der deutschen Juden* from 1933 (see note 7), p. 1.

Germany had arrived in Holland, half of them in Amsterdam. On 13th April 1933, the same newspaper reported an announcement from the management of HICEM in Paris that hundreds of German Jews had approached their office in the past few days. Lawyers, doctors, engineers and architects were especially prominent among them.[11]

Die Reichsstelle für das Auswanderungswesen, which handled emigration on behalf of the German authorities, described a similar situation. A report from the central office of the Bureau in Berlin states:[12]

> "Der Auswanderungsdrang der Juden setzte schlagartig im April ein und hat im Mai und Juni an Stärke noch zugenommen."

The writers of the report continued to illustrate the turning-point of April by comparing the number of people expressing interest in emigration to Palestine in the first quarter of 1933 with the number in the second.

> "Ihre Zahl hatte im 1. Kalendervierteljahr 417 betragen, sie stieg im April auf 830, und im Mai und Juni auf 1074 bzw. 1062, so dass in der Berichtszeit insgesamt 2926 Auskünfte über Palästina erteilt [wurden] . . ."[13]

The report gave the following details of the occupation and the last place of residence of Jewish emigrants.

> "Ganz besonders stark trat die Judenauswanderung in Berlin, Frankfurt a.M., Breslau und Köln in Erscheinung . . .[14] Unter den jüdischen Rechtsanwälten, Ärzten, Beamten und Gelehrten, die bisher keine grossen Existenzsorgen hatten, herrscht grosse Rat-und Ziellosigkeit."[15]

The report added that the emigration of Jewish professionals and doctors drastically increased the representation of this occupational sector among the emigrants.[16] Another report by the district bureau for emigration affairs in Cologne provides more specific information on the link between the type of emigrant and the exact timing of emigration. According to the report, the first to emigrate were Zionist Jews who wanted to go to Palestine. Afterwards came lawyers, doctors, officials, whereas now (the report was apparently written in July/August) business people were coming. The writers of the report add that in May there was a particularly strong impetus towards emigration among Jewish lawyers, doctors and medical students.[17] In view of the data presented up to that point, it may be asked why Jewish academics and professionals chose to emigrate *en masse* during the spring months of 1933, and especially during May. The answer to this question may be found in the national day of boycott held on 1st April, and in the antisemitic legislation of the same month, directed against Jews

[11] *Jüdische Rundschau*, Nos. 28/29 (7th April 1933), *Jüdische Rundschau*, Nos. 30/31 (13th April 1933).
[12] Die Reichsstelle für das Auswanderungswesen, Berlin – Stand der Auswanderung im 2. Kalendervierteljahr 1933, BAYHSTA, MInn 74165, p. 1.
[13] *Ibid.*
[14] *Ibid.*, p. 3.
[15] *Ibid.*, p. 2.
[16] *Ibid.*, p. 7.
[17] Tätigkeitsbericht für April, Mai, Juni 1933 der öffentlichen Auswandererberatungsstelle, Köln, Hauptstaatsarchiv Düsseldorf, Reg. Aachen, 18467, pp. 7–8.

in the academic and other professions, and especially those of them working in the public sector. In the instructions of the Nazi Party (printed in the Nazi Party organ, on 29th March 1933) for the organisation of the 1st of April boycott it was stated[18] that action committees were to be set up immediately in order to plan and carry out the boycott of Jewish-owned shops, Jewish doctors and lawyers. Similarly, the committees were ordered to demand quotas in the employment of Jews in all the professions, according to their relative numerical strength in the population. In order to increase the force of the campaign, it was stated that the demand should be limited temporarily to three fields: attendance at secondary schools and higher education institutions; the medical profession; the legal profession.

These instructions illustrate the central importance placed on the attack on academics and professional people in the framework of the 1st of April boycott. The members of the SA who carried it out fulfilled their instructions, displaying signs with the slogan "Meidet jüdische Ärzte und Rechtsanwälte".[19] The economic and psychological effects of the boycott on Jewish academics and professionals were aggravated during April and the following months by a series of antisemitic laws and regulations which expressed the Nazi desire to reduce Jewish employment in these occupations, especially in the public sector, and led to the dismissal of thousands of Jews.

The *Gesetz zur Wiederherstellung des Berufsbeamtentums* (law for the restoration of the professional civil service) of 7th April 1933 (paragraph 3) declared that:

> "Government officials who are non-Aryans will be retired. Officials who already held their positions on 1st August 1914, or who fought at the front for the German *Reich* during the Great War or whose fathers and sons fell in the war are exempt from this provision."[20]

Similar regulations, containing the same exemptions were published on 22nd April 1933 and on 2nd June 1933 relating to doctors and dentists working in public hospitals and for sickness benefit schemes.[21]

In order to strike at Jews hoping to engage in these professions in the future, a *numerus clausus* law was passed on 25th April 1933 limiting the numbers of new non-Aryan pupils and students permitted to study in schools and universities according to the relative proportion of non-Aryans in the population (1.5%).[22]

All these laws and regulations undermined the livelihood of thousands of Jews and served as a major factor encouraging and hastening their emigration. According to one contemporary observer, the fact that they were generally not property owners also influenced the tendency of Jewish academics and professional people adversely affected by the antisemitic legislation to emigrate, sometimes at extremely short notice. He claimed that the professional person is

---

[18] *Völkischer Beobachter* (Süddeutsche Ausgabe), Nr. 88 (29th March 1933).

[19] Martin Broszat, Hans-Adolf Jacobsen, Helmut Krausnick, *Anatomie des S.S.-Staates*, Band II, Freiburg 1965, p. 313.

[20] *Reichsgesetzblatt*, I, 1933, p. 175. A translation from the Hebrew version appearing in Yitzhak Arad, Yisrael Gutman, Abraham Margaliot (eds.), *Ha'Shoah Be'Teud*, Jerusalem 1979, p. 44.

[21] *Reichsgesetzblatt*, I, pp. 222, 350.

[22] *Reichsgesetzblatt*, I., p. 225. The summary of the law is taken from Joseph Walk (Hrsg.), *Das Sonderrecht für die Juden im NS-Staat*, Heidelberg–Karlsruhe 1981, pp. 17–18.

generally mobile, needing to take with him or her only the knowledge and skills he or she has acquired. On the other hand, the trader or craftsman had to sell shops, stock and tools, generally at a loss, before emigration.[23] However, it emerges that the effects of the legislation were not uniform. A differential examination of some of the occupations included in the definition "academic and other professionals" shows that emigration patterns varied from occupation to occupation.

The data given in the reports of the League of Nations High Commissioner for Refugees Coming from Germany[24] shows that the Nazi legislation of spring 1933 brought about the dismissal of about 1,200 Jews holding academic posts in German universities. Of these, about 550, i.e. about 45%, left Germany during 1933; the other 650 remained in Germany. The relatively high percentage of emigrants (nearly 50%) among dismissed academics can be explained by the absence of real possibilities of alternative employment: a Jewish professor or lecturer dismissed from the university, who wanted to stay in Germany, had to undergo some form of retraining, which inevitably led to a major drop in status, social standing and wages. In most cases, he was unable to continue working in his profession in the private sector or among Jews, as could some of his professional colleagues, for example. As a result, he preferred to emigrate. A further major factor, which made it very easy for Jewish academics to decide on emigration, and which has been referred to earlier, was the intensive organisational activity around their settlement in Western countries. The reports collected by the A.A.C., which dealt with the activities of all organisations engaged in settling Jewish academics from Germany, show[25] that about 380 of these – about 70% of all Jewish academics leaving Germany – found permanent or temporary posts abroad (between April 1933–April 1934). The A.A.C. alone helped directly or indirectly to settle 173 Jewish academics and place them in posts in Britain. As to finances, the organisations succeeded in raising $1,232,000 for the settlement of academics up to the beginning of 1935.[26] The successful organisational activity on behalf of the émigré academics arose also, of course, from the fact that among them were many famous scientists, even several Nobel Prize winners. The Western states, headed by Britain and the U.S.A., viewed this addition of scientific manpower favourably, and it is therefore not surprising that, unlike other professional people, who were scattered among many countries, including developing countries, academics tended to emigrate to developed Western countries, especially Britain and the U.S.A.

A similar pattern to that of the dismissed academics is found among Jewish chemists and engineers. At the beginning of 1933 there were about 1,000–1,200 Jewish chemists and engineers in Germany, to whom about 200 "non-Aryan"

[23]Georg Flatow, 'Zur Lage der Juden in den Kleinstädten', *Jüdische Wohlfahrtspflege und Sozialpolitik*, 4 (1933/1934), pp. 237–245.
[24]'Report of the Representative of the High Commissioner', *loc. cit.* (July 1934), p. 3; Report on Activities of the Organisations . . . , *loc. cit.* (April 1934), pp. 1, 3.
[25]*Ibid.*, p. 3.
[26]High Commissioner for Refugees Coming from Germany: Report on Present Position of the Refugees (undated, *circa* 1935/1936) LBA, N.Y., AR–7162, Box 8, p. 12.

chemists and engineers should be added. About 400–500 of them, i.e. about 40%, emigrated during 1933 and the first half of 1934. The explanation for the high percentage of emigrants among chemists and engineers is apparently to be found in the great demand for these professions in the host countries. In this respect the chemical and engineering professions were in sharp contrast to the other professions for which there was only a limited demand in countries of refuge. The Jewish chemists and engineers dismissed from their jobs in Germany could easily find a new job abroad, and this fact made the decision to emigrate easier.[27]

At the opposite end of the continuum with regard to emigration patterns was the teaching profession.[28] At the time of Hitler's rise to power, there were about 1,200 Jewish teachers in Germany, some 600 of them in Jewish schools. The Nazi legislation of Spring 1933 thus affected only half of the Jewish teachers, i.e. those who worked in the general schools. Furthermore, one of the typical reactions of the German Jews, after the Nazis came to power and the first anti-Jewish legislation was enacted, was to extend the economic, cultural and educational activity within the Jewish community.[29] As part of this process, the network of Jewish schools was expanded and absorbed within a short time 300 teachers expelled from the general school system. The dismissed Jewish teachers thus found an acceptable employment alternative, with no fall in status and social standing, within the expanding internal Jewish educational system. As a result, most of them tended to stay in Germany and the percentage of emigrants among them was low, almost negligible.[30] On the other hand, the situation of the 500 Christian "non-Aryan" teachers who had lost their source of income was extremely difficult. Unlike their Jewish colleagues, they could not be absorbed in the Jewish educational system, and it is not surprising that some 40% of them (200 out of 500) were forced to emigrate.[31]

Between the two extreme patterns described above can be found the rest of the professions. Members of these professions (e.g. doctors, dentists, lawyers, artists, writers, journalists) had, at least in part, possibilities of satisfactory alternative employment in the private and/or Jewish sectors. At the same time, their settlement in the countries of refuge was certainly not as sure. These two factors operated together in the direction of a limited tendency to emigrate, expressed numerically at about 20–30% of all those engaged in these professions and affected by the Nazi legislation.[32]

Two professions, medicine and law, will be discussed individually in view of the special problems arising from their importance. The relative proportion of Jews among German medical doctors and lawyers was far higher than their

[27]'Report of the Representative . . . (4th to 5th July 1934)', *loc. cit.*, p. 7.

[28]*Ibid.*, p. 6.

[29]On this matter see Abraham Margaliot, 'Megamot veDrachim Be'Ma'avaka HaKalkali Shel Yahadut Germania be'tekufat Ha'Redifot Ha'Naziot', *Uma Ve'Toldoteha*, Part 2, The Modern Period, Shmuel Ettinger, (ed.), Jerusalem 1985, pp. 339–357.

[30]'Report of the Representative . . .', *loc. cit.* (July 1934), pp. 6–7.

[31]*Ibid.*

[32]*Ibid.*, pp. 5–7.

proportion in the German population as a whole. Jewish doctors and lawyers formed a very high proportion of all Jewish professionals.

At the beginning of 1933 some 5,000 Jewish and "non-Aryan" lawyers and notaries were active in Germany.[33] About a third of them (1,650) were dismissed as a result of the antisemitic legislation of April 1933. Among the latter about 300 (a little less than 20%) left Germany during 1933 and the first half of 1934. However, the position of those who were not dismissed was also extremely difficult: about 55% of them (1,850 out of 3,350) earned less than the minimum required to support their families. This situation arose out of the drop in the number of both criminal and civil cases during 1933, by about 60% in comparison to 1932, as a result of the rise in power of the totalitarian Nazi regime. In addition, about 50% of the remaining cases were included in the category of cases where the state paid the lawyer's fees. Naturally Jewish lawyers were excluded from dealing with these cases. If these two figures are added it will be seen that, in comparison to 1932, only about 20% of the legal cases in Germany were open to Jewish lawyers. Moreover, as a result of the Nazi rise to power, Jewish lawyers also lost private clients (companies, corporations and private individuals) who preferred, for obvious reasons, "Aryan" lawyers. The employment situation of Jewish lawyers was thus very hard, and it is easy to understand why the ranks of the 300 lawyers who emigrated on being dimissed were swelled by another 300 who also decided to leave Germany. In all, about 600 Jewish lawyers emigrated during the period between April 1933 and June 1934. However, it should be emphasised that despite the severity of employment conditions for the Jewish lawyers in Germany, the number emigrating was not high. The explanation may be found in the difficulty of settling in the host countries. Unlike the doctor, the lawyer needed not only a perfect grasp of the language but also of the local legal system, which could not be quickly acquired. As a result many lawyers were forced to change their profession in the countries where they settled, a factor which deterred them from emigration on a large scale.[34]

An important sub-group among the Jewish lawyers, which was even more severely affected than were the lawyers as a whole, was that of the notaries, who were closely linked to the public legal system. As a result they were doubly affected by the *Gesetz zur Wiederherstellung des Berufsbeamtentums* of 7th April 1933. It might be expected that this fact would increase the notaries' tendency to emigrate, in comparison to other lawyers. In fact, the quantitative data available confirm this assumption:[35] during one year from 7th April 1933 to 1st April 1934

[33] *Ibid.*, p. 5. This report gives the data on lawyers brought below.

[34] Tätigkeitsbericht für April, Mai, Juni 1933 . . . *loc. cit.*, p. 7; Reichsstelle für das Auswanderungswesen, Berlin, *loc. cit.*, p. 2.

[35] *Israelitisches Familienblatt*, No. 17 (26th April 1934), p. 3. It should be emphasised that the drop in the number of lawyers and notaries in Prussia does not necessarily coincide with the number of emigrants, since it includes emigration plus internal migration plus those undergoing professional retraining and remaining in Germany. However, this does not detract from the importance of these data, since they are presented here only for purposes of comparison of the decrease in the number of notaries to that of lawyers, and not as absolute numbers.

the number of "non-Aryan" lawyers in Prussia fell by 39%, whereas the number of "non-Aryan" notaries there fell by 56%. In Berlin alone their number fell by 56.5% and in Kassel it reached its lowest point of 73%, a phenomenon not found among lawyers anywhere else.

Two sets of data are available with regard to the total number of Jewish medical doctors in Germany on the eve of Hitler's rise to power, the number of them affected by the Nazi legislation and the number of doctors who emigrated. According to the "maximalistic" numbers given in McDonald's reports,[36] in January 1933 there were in Germany some 9,000 Jewish and "non-Aryan" doctors. About 4,000 of them were affected by the Nazi legislation: 3,000 were expelled from the *Krankenkassen* (sickness benefit schemes) and another 1,000 were dismissed from the public hospitals. About 1,100 of those losing their jobs (about 27%) left Germany during the April 1933–June 1934 period.

Other, more "minimalistic" figures appear in the German doctors' journal, *Das deutsche Ärzteblatt*. They were based on a census held among doctors in Germany and were quoted in the general German and the German-Jewish press.[37] According to these figures, on the eve of the "Nazi Revolution" there were 6,488 Jewish doctors in Germany. Their relative proportion among the total population of doctors in Germany (50,000) reached about 13%. As a result of the April 1933 legislation 1,667 "non-Aryan" doctors were dismissed from the *Krankenkassen* and of these about 500 (30%) emigrated during that year.

Despite the difference in absolute numbers between the two sources, it may be noted that the percentage of those emigrating among the dismissed doctors is almost identical in both of them, 27% and 30% respectively. The second, German, source provides further information on the effect of the antisemitic legislation on the emigration of Jewish doctors. According to this source, a total of 578 Jewish doctors emigrated in 1933. Five hundred of them were, as stated above, doctors who emigrated as a result of their dismissal from the *Krankenkassen*. The emigration of these doctors was especially noticeable in the large cities, in which the relative proportion of "non-Aryan" doctors was much higher than the national average, which was 26% of all the *Krankenkasse* doctors in the *Reich*. For example, in Berlin the percentage of "non-Aryan" *Krankenkasse* doctors on the eve of the Nazi legislation was 43%, in Breslau 39.8%, and in Frankfurt a. Main 38.7%. It will be remembered that these three cities were the "main suppliers" of Jewish emigrants in the April–June 1933 quarter.[38]

A more exact figure on the relatively high proportion of doctors from the large cities among the total number of doctors emigrating may be found in another German source – the Berlin doctors' journal.[39] According to this journal 86% of

[36]High Commissioner for Refugees Coming from Germany, 'Report of the Representative . . . (4th to 5th July 1934)', *loc. cit.*, pp. 5–6.

[37]The data given below, quoted from *Das deutsche Ärzteblatt* are found in *Israelitisches Familienblatt*, No. 2 (10th January 1935); *Jüdische Rundschau*, No. 2 (4th January 1935); *Berliner Tageblatt*, No. 614 (31st December 1934).

[38]Reichsstelle für das Auswanderungswesen, Berlin, *loc. cit.*, p. 3.

[39]The data quoted from the Berlin journal for doctors are found in *Der Innsbrucker*, No. 26 (31st January 1934), BAYHSTA, Praslg 3924. It should be noted that according to this source 412 Jewish doctors emigrated from Germany in 1933 as against the 500 given in *Das deutsche Ärzteblatt*.

all doctors emigrating were residents of the large cities in Germany. About 70% of all doctors emigrating came from Berlin alone, where 40% of all the Jewish doctors in Germany lived.[40]

These quantitative figures thus indicate that the vast majority of doctors emigrating came from those dismissed from the *Krankenkassen*, mainly in the large cities: from Berlin, Breslau and Frankfurt a. Main. This shows the link between the Nazi legislation against the Jews and their decision to emigrate. However it should be noted that only 30% of the doctors dismissed actually did emigrate. An important explanation for this is found, as in the case of the other professions discussed above, in the ability of those dismissed from the *Krankenkassen* to continue to support themselves by relying on the demand of the private sector. For the Jewish doctor affected by the Nazi legislation the move from the public to the private sector was relatively easy, especially in Germany. The public medical system there was based on the traditional pattern of private medicine; the German-Jewish doctor working for a *Krankenkasse* was not a salaried employee. He received patients, both private and *Krankenkasse* members, in his private surgery, and the insurance funds did not dictate his work conditions. The *Krankenkassen* in Germany did not maintain independent medical institutions. They merely served as agents for health insurance, covering the costs of treatment, medicines and hospitalisation provided by private institutions and doctors with whom they had signed contracts.[41]

McDonald's report quoted above[42] also shows the importance of private practice as a factor encouraging Jewish doctors to remain in Germany. In the section dealing with the medical profession, the High Commissioner states that the employment situation of the dismissed doctors was not so serious, able as they were to engage in private practice, enabling them to maintain themselves economically.

The same conclusion is reached from the study of an autobiographical source,[43] using a specific case to demonstrate some of the wider emigration patterns. The writer, a lawyer, describes how in 1930 he joined the firm of a relative who had been active in the *Unabhängige Sozialdemokratische Partei Deutschlands* (USPD) in the early years of the Weimar Republic. At the end of February 1933, only one night after the *Reichstag* fire, his partner fled to Paris, because he was now considered an "enemy of the German people". The writer himself, who was not yet either physically or economically threatened, continued to work in the office for several months. He left Germany only in June 1933, as a direct result of his disbarment. His brother, a doctor by profession, remained in Germany even longer. Most of his patients continued to attend his private surgery and he had an income sufficient even to support his elderly mother.

Differential examination of the various academics and the professions as we have shown thus proves that among those injured by the Nazi legislation the

[40]*Statistik des Deutschen Reichs*, Band 451, Heft 5 – Die Glaubensjuden im Deutschen Reich (Volkszählung, 16.6.33), Berlin 1936, p. 98.
[41]Ludwig Preller, *Sozialpolitik in der Weimarer Republik*, Düsseldorf 1978, pp. 284, 329.
[42]High Commissioner for Refugees . . . *loc. cit.* (July 1934), pp. 5–6.
[43]Sachs, 'A German-Jewish Refugee', *loc. cit.*, pp. 2, 11–16.

tendency to emigrate or to remain in Germany depended largely on two factors: the existence of realistic possibilities of alternative employment in the Jewish/private sector which did not involve a drop in status, social standing and income (Jewish teachers, doctors, journalists, artists) or the absence of such an alternative (university professors and lecturers, notaries, Christian "non-Aryan" teachers); good chances of economic absorption in another country (engineers and chemists, university professors and lecturers) or prospective difficulty in economic absorption in those countries (lawyers).

To these should be added another important factor affecting all academics and professional people – the degree of vulnerability to the Nazi legislation of members of different age groups among Jews belonging to these professions. As stated, the dismissal of civil servants, lawyers, doctors and dentists did not apply to Jews who had held their posts since before the First World War, who had fought at the front in that war or whose relatives had been killed in it. Thus the younger age groups (20–35) were more exposed to Nazi legislation than the older age groups. It would therefore be expected that a greater incidence of emigration would be found among the young than among their older colleagues. In fact, the sources do suggest such a trend; for example, in an article in a German-Jewish newspaper on emigration from East Prussia[44] it is stated that young academics affected by the Nazi legislation are the leading group among the emigrants. A similar picture is obtained from the memoirs of contemporaries. Liselotte Kahn, the wife of a Nuremberg Jewish doctor, writes that her husband was able to continue to work since he had served as a doctor in the First World War and had been wounded. [45] However a young doctor whom she met in the street told her that he was forced to emigrate since he had lost his job; he was too young to have served in the war. The writer goes on to make a generalisation that the Jewish doctors who were too young to have seen war service were the first to be affected by the Nazi legislation. To conclude her discussion of this issue, Liselotte Kahn quotes another young doctor who told her that "It is probably better to be forced out of the country than to be able to continue working like Ernst and having the torture of making the decision to leave on your own."

A survey of the "German case files" of the Joint[46] also confirms this impression. The younger doctors had found it difficult to build up an extensive private practice within the relatively short time since they had completed their studies. Thus they did not have alternative employment in the private sector which would support them decently. Quantitative confirmation of the over-representation of the younger age groups among the emigrants in the academic and professional category can be found, at least in part, in the data referring to emigration of Jewish doctors in the first two years of Hitler's regime:[47] 66% (860

---

[44]*Israelitisches Familienblatt*, No. 3 (18th January 1934), p. 10.

[45]Liselotte Kahn's Memoirs, LBA, N.Y., Memoirs Coll., pp. 15–16.

[46]A letter by Frida Mansbacher concerning her son (23rd December 1936), Joint–German Case Files, AR–7196, LBA, N.Y., Box 15, Folder 5; A letter by Otto Rubens and John Lanzkron (17th November 1933), Joint–German Case Files, AR–7196, Box 12, Folder 5.

[47]*Jüdische Rundschau*, No. 44 (31st May 1935), p. 2. The data are quoted from *Das deutsche Ärzteblatt*.

out of 1307) of all doctors emigrating in those years were aged 30–45, and a further 10% were still younger.

Up till now the emigration of academics and professionals has been examined mainly at the sectoral level. However, in order to trace the decision to leave or to stay, the choice of timing and destination, examination must be made at the level of the individual. The main sources for this are the "German case files" of the Joint and the memoirs of emigrants of the period.

An important factor, already mentioned in the discussion at the sectoral level, was dismissal or disbarment. Expulsion from their workplace, which generally struck Jewish academics and professionals as a bolt from the blue, is frequently mentioned in the "case files" of the Joint as an immediate cause of emigration. Furthermore, the proximity in time between the date of job loss and the decision to emigrate is often striking.[48]

Another important factor, which also affected those not dismissed, and was therefore influential after 1933 as well, was a fall in income. This affected mainly doctors and dentists who could continue to practise in the private sector, but who felt, subjectively, that their income was no longer sufficient, to provide a decent living.[49]

Jewish students who had just completed, or were about to complete, their course of study, especially in medicine or law, were affected by another economic aspect. They assumed that as a result of the antisemitic legislation of April 1933, they had almost no chance of finding a livelihood in Germany in their field of study in the future. As a result, they were inclined to emigrate in order to finish the remaining years of study, or to begin their specialisation, in another country where they could continue working in that field.[50]

It is known that 44% (3,500 out of 8,000) of the Jewish students expelled from German universities in 1933 as a result of the law against "overcrowding of German schools and institutions of higher learning" emigrated.[51] The relatively large extent of emigration among the students is similar to that of the university lecturers and of the engineers and chemists. The main explanations for this were the relatively promising economic prospects in the host countries set against the inability of finding future employment in Germany; the youth of the students,

[48]Joint–German Case Files, AR–7196, LBA, N.Y.; 1. A letter by the lawyer E. Löwenthal (July 1933), Box 14, Folder 6; 2. A letter concerning Dr. Zeuner, palaeontologist (6th November 1933), Box 5. Folder 1. 3. A letter by Otto Rubens and John Lanzkron (17th November 1933), Physicians, Box 12, Folder 5; 4. A letter concerning Willy Israel, engaged in the film industry (13th June 1933), Box 9, Folder 3; 5. A letter concerning the lawyer Dr. Hirschfeld who left Germany just two days after he lost the right to practise law (7th February 1936), Box 8, Folder 5.
[49]Joint–German Case Files, AR–7196, LBA, N.Y.; 1. A letter by Richard Lefkowitz, a dentist (29th January 1934), Box 13, Folder 1; 2. A letter concerning Mrs. Freund's daughter, a paediatrician (13th January 1936), Box 4, Folder 3. 3. A letter by Frida Mansbacher concerning her son, a paediatrician (23rd December 1936), Box 15, Folder 5.
[50]High Commissioner for Refugees from Germany, Memorandum on Refugees Employment (undated), pp. 1–2, LBA, N.Y., AR 7162, Box 6; Joint–German Case Files, LBA, N.Y., AR–7196; 1. A letter concerning the student Jacques Malkiel (12th September 1933), Box 15, Folder 5; 2. A letter by Heinz David (6th November 1933), Box 1, Folder 3; 3. A letter by Hans Krefeld (6th November 1933), Box 13, Folder 4.
[51]According to a report of the International Student Service (May 1933–August 1937), pp.6–7. *Central Zionist Archives*, Section A–255, File 860.

which made professional retraining easy if it became necessary; the fact that many of them held leftist views, i.e. they were political refugees; the students' unwillingness to become a burden on their parents.[52]

Until now mainly "push" factors have been discussed. We will now discuss "pull" factors attracting people to the countries of refuge, which had a decisive effect on the direction of emigration and its timing.

The prospects for economic integration and obtaining employment in the host countries have already been mentioned as an important catalyst for emigration in the case of academics, engineers and chemists. However, it was also important for members of other professions. One of the earliest examples was connected with emigration attempts by doctors and lawyers to go to Egypt, which met with no success: at the beginning of May 1933 the English newspaper *The Daily Telegraph* followed by the German-Jewish press[53] reported that the Egyptian government had decided to grant rights of settlement and employment to about 200 lawyers and doctors from Germany, victims of the Nazi legislation. As a result of the publication of this information the number of Jewish lawyers and doctors who sought to emigrate to Egypt rose considerably during May.[54] However, about a week later it turned out that the rumour was incorrect.[55] The Egyptian government denied it completely, and the Jewish doctors and lawyers who had hoped to settle in Egypt were disappointed.

This unsuccessful attempt illustrates the importance that information on employment opportunities in the host countries, or, on the other hand, on limitations of employment, held for the decision to emigrate to those countries and for the timing. A similar case with regard to the link between a government measure concerning the employment of emigrants and the timing of their arrival occurred in connection with the emigration of doctors to Palestine some two-and-a-half years later, in the summer and autumn of 1935. On 25th July 1935 the Mandatory Government of Palestine published a draft law limiting the number of work permits to be given to doctors reaching Palestine after 1st December 1935, by setting annual quotas. As a direct result of the publication of the proposed law, in the summer and autumn of 1935, mainly during October/November, about 400 doctors, mostly of German origin, arrived in Palestine in order to obtain a work permit before the quota law came into force.[56]

The reports of the *Reichsstelle für das Auswanderungswesen*[57] show that those doctors who were already preparing their emigration brought their plans forward and carried them out during the summer and autumn of 1935, in order

[52] *Ibid.*
[53] *Israelitisches Familienblatt*, No. 19 (11th May 1933), p. 2.
[54] Die Reichsstelle für das Auswanderungswesen, Berlin, *loc. cit.* (April–Juni 1933), p. 5.
[55] *Israelitisches Familienblatt*, No. 20 (18th May 1933).
[56] A letter from Moshe Brachmann to Fritz Noak (Chairman of the Health Committee of the Vaad Leumi) (16th December 1935), Central Zionist Archives JI/2456; S. Kanowitz, 'Ein verfehltes Gesetz', *Mitteilungsblatt der Hitachdut Olej Germania* (1st January 1936), pp. 10–12.
[57] Die Reichsstelle für das Auswanderungswesen, München, Vierteljahresbericht Juli–September 1935, p. 9, BAYHSTA, MInn 74182; Tätigkeitsbericht der öffentlichen Auswandererberatungsstelle, Köln für Juli–September 1935, p. 2. Hauptstaatsarchiv Düsseldorf, Reg. Aachen, 18957.

to anticipate the target date. These reports show that in the first quarter of 1936 there was a drastic fall in the number of German-Jewish doctors requesting to emigrate to Palestine. The reason is clear: the promulgation of the quota law considerably reduced employment prospects for doctors in Palestine from the beginning of 1936 and made Palestine, from that time on, an unattractive destination for them.[58]

Another important factor deciding the destination and timing of emigration was the emigrant's ability to transfer property, capital and pension rights to a particular country.[59] A clear example of the dependence between the possibility of transferring pension rights and the destination and timing of emigration was the attempt of the Central Bureau for the Resettlement of German Jews in Palestine to effect the emigration of Jewish civil servants in Palestine.[60] As cited above, as a result of the *Gesetz zur Wiederherstellung des Berufsbeamtentums* (paragraph 3) thousands of Jewish civil servants were retired. About 100 of them expressed to the Bureau representatives their willingness to emigrate to Palestine. However they would actually emigrate only if their pension rights from the Ministries which had employed them (the Ministries of Justice, Interior, Culture) were transferred to them in Palestine.

The economic prospects for finding employment in a particular host country were not linked only to special laws and regulations published on this or that date by the local government. One particular country would sometimes have a consistently favourable reputation as to its ability to provide employment for members of a specific profession. It may be assumed that this was based on the experience of previous emigrants. Thus for example Italy was considered to be a country where historians, dealers and students of art had a good chance of finding employment in their field. Indeed, emigrants of this type formed a prominent group among the total number of emigrants to Italy during 1933–1934.[61]

A similar image was created for Britain as a country suitable for the settlement of doctors. Jewish doctors emigrating to Britain could obtain a doctor's licence after supplementary studies and examinations. This opened up to them the possibility of continuing to work in their profession not only in Britain itself but also in all the countries of the British Empire. Furthermore, as bi-lateral agreements had been signed between Britain, Italy and Japan, doctors with a British diploma could find work in these countries too. It is, therefore, not surprising that Jewish doctors tended to emigrate to a country which opened up for them such a variety of employment opportunities.

---

[58]Tätigkeitsbericht für Januar–März 1936, *ibid.*, pp. 3, 15.

[59]The question of transfer of property and capital as a deciding factor for the timing and destination of emigration is worthy of separate systematic discussion elsewhere. One example from the academic and professional sector will be presented.

[60]A letter from the Central Bureau for the Resettlement of German Jews to Foley, the British Passports Office in Berlin (28th June 1933), Central Zionist Archives S7/64.

[61]Reichsstelle für das Auswanderungswesen, Berlin–Stand der Auswanderung im 3. Kalendervierteljahr 1934, p. 14, BAYHSTA, MInn 74165; die Reichsstelle für das Auswanderungswesen, München, Vierteljahresbericht für Juli–September 1934, p. 6, BAYHSTA, MInn 74182.
The reports emphasise that the emigration to Italy of art historians, students and dealers was striking in previous periods as well.

Nevertheless, the attraction of Britain for Jewish academics, professionals and students pertained only during 1933 and the beginning of 1934.[62] The reason for this was the new regulations (from spring 1934) which limited the export of capital from Germany. As a result of the *Haavara* Transfer Agreement these regulations did not apply to emigrants to Palestine. Academics and professional people therefore preferred Palestine to Britain from the second half of 1934 onwards.[63] In this case it can be seen that the consideration of ability to transfer capital and property outweighed the consideration of varying employment possibilities.

For the members of certain professions such as the performing arts, writing and journalism, the German language was an important condition for professional success. It may be assumed that such people hoped wherever possible to emigrate to countries such as Austria, Czechoslovakia or Switzerland, where they could continue to work in a German-speaking environment. A general census held among academic and professional emigrants registered with relief organisations in Europe[64] shows that such a tendency did exist: of 117 emigrants listed in Austria 72 (61 performing artists and 11 writers and journalists), i.e. over 60%, clearly belonged to professions based on the use of the German language. Furthermore, the number of performing artists enumerated for Austria (61) was even greater than the number for France (55), then the most popular destination for the German Jews. A similar trend is found when examining the destinations of writers and journalists. Apart from France (where 64 members of these professions had settled) all the other important countries of refuge for writers and journalists could offer a German-speaking audience. Thus for example, a small country like Switzerland received 43 writers and journalists (2/3 of the number received by France), Czechoslovakia 20, Austria and the Saar region 11 each. Altogether German-speaking countries received over 50% (85 out of 167) of all the writers and journalists enumerated in the census in Europe.

Discussion of the emigration of Jewish academics and professional people, at both the sectoral and individual level, reveals the importance of economic motives and considerations. These factors worked in both directions, from the country of origin on the one hand, and from the host countries on the other. They largely determined the tendency to emigrate or to stay, the timing and the choice of destination.

[62]Tätigkeitsbericht der öffentlichen Auswandererberatungsstelle, Köln, für Januar–März 1934, p. 6, Hauptstaatsarchiv Düsseldorf, Reg. Aachen, 18467.
[63]*Ibid.* (April–Juni 1935), p. 2.
[64]Partial results of this census, held in 1934, were published in High Commission for Refugees Coming from Germany, Central File of Professional Refugees, London (4th–5th July 1934), LBA, N.Y., AR–7162, Box 7, p. 2.
It should be emphasised that this census was problematic for two reasons: a) Britain, Holland and Belgium had not completed it by the date for returning results. The findings for these countries are therefore partial only. b) It included only people registered with the national and international relief and welfare associations, and not all academics and professional immigrants from Germany living in Europe.
As a result it will be used only to suggest trends, ignoring the absolute numbers which are, as stated, fragmentary only.

The Jewish Youth Movement in Germany in the Holocaust Period (II)

The Relations between the Youth Movement and Hechaluz

BY CHAIM SCHATZKER

Hechaluz was founded in Russia following the First World War, and established branches in Germany in 1923. However, only a small number of individual *stam chaluzim* joined it in Germany for either ideological or economic reasons, and the organisation therefore had no choice but to concentrate its activity on the youth movements that had anticipated it, such as the *Praktikanten-Bund* of the *Blau-Weiss*, even in the matter of *hachscharah* and emigration to Palestine.*

An organisation that was formed along the lines of *Hechaluz* was *Brith Hachaluzim Hadathiim (Bachad)*.[1] Moreover, most of the institutions that were common to the *Hechaluz* organisation and the *chaluz*-orientated youth movements followed a similar operational pattern. So, for example, the institutions of *hachscharah*, the *hachscharah* kibbutz, the *garin*, counselling and management at the branches of *Hechaluz*, liaison with the Labour Movement and with various groups in the Kibbutz Movement, had all been fully formed before the Nazis came to power. Indeed the successful work of the *chaluz* youth movements in absorbing so many young men and women[2] after the *Machtübernahme* in 1933, and

---

*This is the second part of an essay published in the Year Book of the Leo Baeck Institute. For Pt. I see Chaim Schatzker, 'The Jewish Youth Movement in Germany in the Holocaust Period (I). Youth in Confrontation with a New Reality', in *LBI Year Book XXXII* (1987), pp. 157–182 – (Ed.).

[1]On the history of the *Bachad*, see Joseph Walk, 'The Torah va-Avodah Movement in Germany', in *LBI Year Book VI* (1961), pp. 236–256; see also the oral testimonies of Joseph Walk, Ezra Bromberger, Rudi Herz, David Ben-Arieh, and Eliezer Seligmann, in the *Makhon le-yahadut zmanenu, Hamahlaka le-tiud be-al-pe* (Centre for Contemporary Jewry, Department of Oral Documentation), The Hebrew University in Jerusalem.

[2]We have no exact membership figures for the *chaluz* youth movements. Whatever figures are available are confined to particular periods, so that they cannot be used to arrive at an estimate of the total number of members for the entire period of the movement's existence. It was in the nature of the youth movement that each generation of its members succeeded the other every few years, and that these generations had no knowledge of one another. Moreover, its voluntary nature and the irregularity with which its institutions were maintained tended to create a situation of constant flux. Finally, its branches were widely dispersed throughout Germany. All of these factors make it difficult to arrive at a reliable membership figure. Nevertheless, it can be stated with certainty that

in preparing them for settlement in Palestine, would have been unthinkable were it not for the fact that the instruments for doing so had already been created and refined beforehand.

In setting out to examine the collaboration between the *chaluz* youth movements and the *Hechaluz* organisation, we have no intention of retelling the story of the German-Jewish community at that time, nor of any individual youth movement or *hachscharah* kibbutz. Nor do we intend to survey, evaluate and judge the actions or errors of the leaders of the youth movement and the activists in *Hechaluz*. These young people had taken on one of the most formidable tasks, both organisationally and humanly, ever to have been assumed by any youth movement, or for that matter by any organisation of young people anywhere. Our only purpose is to attempt to understand, from a comparative structural point of view, the essential nature and distinct contributions of both of these partners in their common enterprise, and the specific way in which each had exerted an influence upon it.

There were fundamental differences between the *Hechaluz* organisation and the youth movements during the entire period of their close collaboration.[3] The source of these differences did not merely consist in what a superficial observer might have discerned to be the obstinate insistence of the youth movement to preserve its autonomy, or the result of an esoteric outlook which was a vestige of the bourgeois origins of most of the members of the youth movement.

The most profound differences between these two groups were intellectual, and resided in their distinct perceptions of both Zionism and Socialism; in their differing perceptions of the essential nature of youth and its social function; in their wholly antithetical attitudes towards the significance of the idea of "vocation"; and, finally, in the value they attached to the half-playful symbolism of the various "scouting" methods. These last were regarded by the *Hechaluz*, in the light of the gravity of the times, to be an infantile and bourgeois survival that had seen its day; whereas for the youth movement they constituted an essential educational focus whose loss would have struck at the very core of the movement's existence and survival.

Although there were disagreements within each of the youth movements concerning all of these issues, and the division between the movement as a whole and *Hechaluz* was far from being absolute, an underlying principle which was shared by all the youth movements may be distinguished and differentiated them from other types of organisations – namely the unmistakable tendency of a substantial number of them to dismiss the value of the rational, scientific and sociological factor, and to keep its influence upon them at bay.

The long and continuous polemic between the youth movements and the Zionist movement and the Socialist parties was not based on an ideological

the membership of all of the youth movements, taken together, never included more than a small part of young Jews in Germany, and the total number of members at no point exceeded several thousand, and certainly less than ten thousand.

[3]See Chaim Schatzker, 'Tnuat ha-noar ha-yehudit be-Germania ve-yaheseha im tnuat Hechaluz' ('The Jewish Youth Movement in Germany and Its Relations with the Hechaluz Movement'), in *Asufot*, 3, 16 (October 1972); and 4, 17 (July 1973) (in Hebrew).

disagreement between Zionists and non-Zionists or Socialists and non-Socialists. It was rather in the nature of a psycho-educational controversy over the problem of "what determines human choice most, and how this choice should be influenced in the most effective, most moral, and best way".[4]

> "We do not arrive at a choice after making a profound study of the state of mankind in our times; but the choices we make day by day, hour by hour, moment by moment, are determined by our feeling, which binds the relation of facts to us and our relations to the facts. However since what determines, as we know, is not the facts but the way in which we perceive them, every choice made – even every political choice – will be a human choice, a choice made by our nature."[5]

This is also the pattern of thought adopted by the youth movement towards Socialism. In contrast to the school of Socialist thinking, which sought to effect a change in human consciousness by altering man's economic conditions, the youth movements were primarily concerned with changing consciousness in the belief that this would ultimately bring about a change in reality as well. This was in line with Gustav Landauer's insistence that "Socialism means a revolution of the spirit".[6] And it was in much the same spirit that Mordechai Orenstein wrote in the *Blätter des Haschomer Hazair*:

> "There is no full realisation of Zionism and Socialism if it does not arise out of an inner [mental] bearing [*Lebenshaltung*], out of a Zionist and Socialist substantiality that is deeply rooted in the soul of the individual; there is no realisation without human beings that do the realising ... The revolution in the individual's heart is the necessary fundamental assumption of the revolution in life; the revolution in the individual's heart is the supreme fundamental law of the Jewish youth movement – this is the revolution in the Diaspora . . ."[7]

This Socialism, which was called "ethical" or "religious" Socialism, was influenced by a number of schools of thought that were then current in Germany, among which were those of Gustav Landauer,[8] Paul Tillich,[9] and Franz Oppenheimer.[10] The youth movement not only doubted that a Socialist revolution could be achieved without a human renewal, but had reservations concerning the outcome of such a revolution. "Socialism – and in this I am not in agreement with Hermann[11] – is not a matter of politics, and the victory of the working class does not of itself necessitate the emergence of a just social order, much less a society replete with meaning. It will not arise so long as people are not ripe for it."[12] And in the same vein, we read in the *Blätter des Haschomer Hazair*:

---

[4]For example, at the conference held jointly by the National Administration of the German Zionist Organisation and the Administration of Zionist Youth Organisations, held in 1926; see *Bundesleitung des Jung-Jüdischen Wanderbundes (JJWB), Choser Jod Daleth*, März 1926, pp. 3–4.

[5]Siegfried Moos, *JJWB, Choser Jod Daleth*, Mai 1927, pp. 16–17.

[6]*Jungjüdischer Wanderer*, 2. Jahrg., Heft 2/3 (Juni 1922), pp. 8–11; and Sergey Racusin, 'Stellung zum Sozialismus', in *Kameraden*, 11. Bundesblatt, Dezember 1929, pp. 6–7.

[7]Mordechai Orenstein, 'Die Jugendbewegung und die Erziehungsidee', in *Blätter des Haschomer Hazair*, Heft 2 (Januar 1931), pp. 13–16.

[8]*JJWB, Choser Waw*, Juni 1926, p. 5.

[9]*Kameraden*, 10, Mittleren-Rundbrief, Dezember 1931, pp. 14–15.

[10]*Führerschaftsblätter des Esra*, Jahrg. 3, Heft 3 (1926), p. 27.

[11]The reference is to Hermann [Menachem] Gerson, leader of the movement.

[12]Max Otto, *Kameraden*, 15/16, Bundesblatt, April/Mai 1930, p. 16.

"The Socialist revolution and the dictatorship of the proletariat will not establish the new social order of labour based upon the will of the individual and his independent and free choice. It is within the power of the Communist revolution to destroy only the objective possibilities for exploitation and bondage, but it cannot establish a Communist reality if this is not already potentially in existence beforehand among the people as a social value. Otherwise there can be no revolution, only a prologue to a new system of coercion, enslavement, and the submission of society to the will of the few . . ."[13]

The Zionism and Socialism of the youth movement were of an essentially unpolitical character and fundamentally opposed political parties. The idea of the *Bund* was conceived of as being synonymous with individual liberty, the absence of constraints, transcendence of the mundane, with truth, sincerity and nobility. The idea of party, on the other hand, was associated with the restriction of freedom, subjugation, immersion in quotidian reality, with politics, diplomacy and unrestrained conflict. *Bund* meant morality, party meant materialism.[14]

"Thus the seriousness of the error inherent in this is patent in the attempt to gauge the *Kibbutz Haarzi* by the standards of party. While parties conduct the political struggle by means of people who are united purely on the basis of a political platform, the *Kibbutz Haarzi* is an expression of the totality of the interests of society, and bases itself not upon the affiliation of isolated individuals, but upon a merging of fraternity-life and autonomous ideas. Hence the perspectives of these two organisations differ. The party seeks to achieve a majority, to take over political power; whereas the *Kibbutz Haarzi*, although it tries to influence the working class in keeping with its ideology, is expressing in its political activity the view of its members and, being based on kibbutzim, is absolutely incapable of seeking power and of achieving power in order to carry out the aim of a party to organise the masses . . . In this *Hashomer Hazair* is, both in the Diaspora and in Palestine, a new social manifestation which cannot be gauged by the ordinary standards of party."[15]

Thus politics was identified with the struggle for the political and economic advantage of organised interest groups, which sought to exert their influence upon the greatest possible number of people, without, however, being in the least concerned with the intellectual outlook of their following.[16]

Facing the non-political youth movement were the Left-wing Zionist political parties, whose

"unequivocal, natural position was that every party had, of course, the right and duty of spreading its ideas among the ranks of *Hechaluz*, thereby preparing its members to take a position on the issues and problems they would encounter in Palestine. Only a certain degree of loyalty can be demanded from them [the Left-wing parties], so that they should not undermine the structure of the organisation in the course of their work."[17]

Hechaluz leadership argued that

"the camp of Labour and its organisations are Socialist. Therefore if *Hechaluz* regards itself to be on the Labour wing, it could no longer allow itself to remain politically neutral as it was in the past. This fact it must take into account in regard to the education of its membership, to bring them closer to the idea of Socialism, to instil in them a consciousness of the issues of the

[13]See note 7.
[14]Siegfried Moos, 'Bund, Partei, Politik', in *JJWB, Choser Jod Daleth*, 16. Mai 1927, p. 17.
[15]Arthur Israelowitz, 'Zum Weg des Haschomer Hazair', in *Informationsblatt Hechaluz*, hrsg. vom Hechaluz, Deutscher Landesverband, Jahrg. 4, Nr. 37 (September 1931), p. 15.
[16]Sergey Racusin, *Kameraden*, 11, Bundesblatt, Dezember 1929, p. 3; and see note 15.
[17]Moshe Schapira, 'Über das Wesen der Chaluzbewegung', in *Hechaluz, Monatsschrift des 'Hechaluz'*, *Deutscher Landesverband*, Konferenz-Jahrg. 2, Heft 2 (Februar 1925), p. 127.

international Labour Movement, so that after they have made the transition to Palestine they will be able to make an independent choice of which Socialist party they will support."[18]

As the *Hechaluz* sought increasingly to unify the political opinions of its membership around a single "general line" (*Generallinie*) which would be in keeping with that of *Mapai* and the *Kibbutz Hameuhad*, it encountered growing opposition from the youth movement as well as from the "youth-movement" faction in *Habonim* that had originated in *Kadimah*. The latter were completely out of sympathy not only with the general line of *Hechaluz*, but with what they regarded to be the anti-democratic efforts of the centre of the organisation to impose such a policy upon them.

In the view of the youth movement, *Hechaluz* was making absurd the very idea of "independent choice", which the organisation claimed it was allowing its members to exercise. This was something to which no authentic youth movement, so long as it retained that character, would be able to agree.[19]

Another difference was one of intellectual traditions, and had to do with the conception the youth movements had of themselves in regard to their role in society. The thinking of the youth movement was rooted on the one hand in the Kantian tradition, in which man was regarded as an end in himself, and on the other hand in the tradition of educational reform in Germany represented by Gustav Wyneken, according to which youth was an end in its own right. This outlook was now being challenged by a functional sociological outlook that was characteristic of the sort of Marxist dialectic being practised in Eastern Europe.

To these differing conceptions of the nature of youth were added differing attitudes towards the nature of the youth movement. The youth movement saw itself as a force inspired by youthful enthusiasm and dedicated to influencing inner convictions; action was something to be postponed to the end of this process, and was placed beyond the domain of the movement itself. On the other hand, the organisation of *Hechaluz* asserted the need for action, and action was its principal content and end. "*Hechaluz* . . . is not built upon conviction [*Gesinnung*] but upon performance and achievement [*Leistung*]."[20] By contrast, in the case of a movement like *Hashomer Hazair*,

> "the basic tendency of its nature has always been the education of the individual, the development of his manifest and latent qualities of mind, the actualisation of personality, these being the very things that enable him, in full consciousness, to fulfil his national and social purpose".[21]

These differences of outlook between *Hechaluz* and the youth movement were of significance to the very task which was the object of the activities of *Hechaluz*, and for whose purpose the partnership between it and the youth movements had been established – which is to say, vocational training and *hachscharah*.

The Jewish youth movement in Germany was committed to the principle of

[18]Sch. [Shalom Adler] Rudel, 'Zwei Jahre Hechaluz in Deutschland', *ibid*, p. 135.
[19]See, for example, Adolf Schiff, 'Generallinie oder Autonomie', in *Informationsblatt*, hrsg. vom Hechaluz, Deutscher Landesverband, Berlin, Jahrg. 6, Nr. 51/52 (Januar/Februar 1933), pp. 20–26.
[20]Elieser Ascher, *Hechaluz*, Konferenznummer, Jahrg. 2 (Februar 1925), p. 136.
[21]See note 15.

personal choice in its admission of members, and thought of itself as an élite body. And it was this attitude which, in great measure, determined the character of its disagreement with *Hechaluz* over the organisation's nature, purpose and orientation. The position taken by *Mapai* and *Hakibbutz Hameuhad*, whose line of thinking dominated within the organisation, was that *Hechaluz* was a mass organisation incorporating a variety of elements because of its responsibility to its public as a whole, and operating on a pattern similar to that of the *Histadruth*. However, *Hashomer Hazair* adhered to the idea of a vanguard which must eschew accommodating itself to the preferences of the masses, and try instead to put itself forward as an educational principle in order to raise the masses up to the level of the task that had to be accomplished.[22] The youth movement required its members to undergo extensive and thorough vocational training that fitted in with their personal inclinations and talents, whether these were for farming and horticulture or for the technical fields. This had to be done moreover within the context of the tradition and opportunities of vocational training available in Germany. But *Hechaluz*, in its capacity as a mass organisation of the proletariat, set itself the aim of turning members of the middle class into labourers, rather than merely transferring them from one profession to another.

> "The work of *hachscharah* in *Hechaluz* is suited to large groups whose members receive elementary training intended simply for work; the training of specialists must not be thought of as a principal goal of *Hechaluz*."[23]

The youth movement also believed that the individual should be allowed to choose his profession freely and following his own natural bent:

> ". . . in this way the individual is given the opportunity, sometimes his only opportunity, to mould his life himself in accordance with inner truth and by his own responsibility",[24]

as was inherent in the "Meissner" formula on the choice of vocation and an integral mode of existence.[25]

> ". . . our point of departure is that a vocation also means a calling [*Beruf – Berufung*] and that the strict vocational training of our members is a major principle of nation-building. It is from this position that we arrive at a special conception of the *chaluz* principle which differs from that of other *Bünde*. To us it is no ideal to have no vocation, and to work one day here and one day there, without any inner relation to the work in itself."[26]

[22]See the discussion on this issue between Eliyahu Dobkin and Meir Yaari at the 4th Congress of the Histadruth: *Informationsblatt*, hrsg. vom Hechaluz, Deutscher Landesverband, Berlin, Jahrg. 6, Nr. 53/54 (März/April 1933), pp. 4–16; and Jona Ringel, 'Zu unserem Weg im "Hechaluz"', in *Haschomer Hazair* (bulletin for *bogrim*) Oktober 1935, pp. 13–17.
[23]*Ibid.*, p. 138.
[24]Lucie Zobel, Berufswahl, *Hechawer* (*Bundesleitung des JJWB*) 6/7. Nummer, 1. Jahrg., Berlin (Oktober/November 1928), pp. 98–99.
[25]In 1933, at a country-wide meeting of the *Freideutsche Jugend* held on the Hohe Meissner, at which representatives of most of the youth movements in Germany participated, a declaration of intent was drafted which was to serve as a beacon to all youth movements and would be known as the "Hohe Meissner Formula". The gist of its wording – there is no complete record of the Hohe Meissner speeches – is as follows: "The *Freideutsche Jugend* is resolved to fashion its existence according to its own lights, on its own responsibility and in the spirit of inner truth. It will stand up for this inner freedom in solid unity under any circumstance."
[26]Hardy Swarsensky, *Unser Weg zum Volk. Ein Beitrag zur Ideologie des Makkabi Hazair*, hrsg. von der Bundesleitung des jüdischen Pfadfinderbundes "Makkabi Hazair", Berlin 1936, p. 21.

For *Hechaluz*, however, this view represented a survival of bourgeois distinctions that had to be rooted out completely, since it suited neither *chaluz* Socialism nor the needs of Palestine.

> "Our starting point is the movement and its needs. Palestine needs workers prepared for any job, capable of taking over any position likely to meet the requirements of collective living. What is most essential is not learning a trade, [but] becoming accustomed to work as such, no matter how uninteresting. Indeed it is this very sort of education for menial and ungratifying labour – out of which a readiness to do similar work in Palestine will emerge – which is the basis and principle of education for work."[27]

It was precisely this view of work that the youth movement found totally unacceptable.

> "The vocational bond is the only defence against changing one's occupation. The false conception *chaluzim* have of being 'without vocation' does not instil the attitude to work which will ensure that people will remain in their occupation."[28]

With this, *Makkabi Hazair* breathed new life into a controversy that had taken place before 1933 between *Kadimah* and Enzo Sereni, the representative of *Hechaluz*.[29] The *Werkleute*, on the other hand, reversed its stand after 1933, and abandoned its position on the importance of vocation to join *Hechaluz* on this issue.[30]

These, then, were the circumstances that clouded relations between *Hechaluz* and the youth movements. Most of the youth movements opposed "mixed" *hachscharah* that would include *stam chaluzim* who had not been movement members, and regarded such integration as a threat to their autonomy and particular approach to education. *Hechaluz*, for its part, would not allow the matter of the preparation of *chaluzim* for settlement in Palestine to be determined independently by the youth movements. For if they were to allow this, *Hechaluz* would become a mere federation of independent *Bünde*, which would demonstrate the impossibility of any compromise being reached between the partisan aims of *Hechaluz* and those of general Zionist education.[31]

This approach entailed a conception in which *Hechaluz* represented a more advanced stage of the development of the youth movement, while the youth movements would exist as organisational frameworks with few functions and the primary purpose of serving as a manpower reserve for *Hechaluz*. *Hechaluz* therefore strongly opposed any effort of the youth movement to maintain itself in Palestine following arrival, whether under the guise of *Bund* settlements or as settlements based on country of origin. However, the youth movements took a different view:

> "We regard *Hashomer Hazair* not as a passing episode in our lives, but as the very essence of our lives. Our values, which were formed within the youth movement in the Diaspora, are

[27]Georg Pape, 'Die permanente Synthese', in *Haboneh. Älterenblatt der jüdischen Jugendgemeinschaft Habonim. Noar Chaluzi*, Juli 1933, p. 20.
[28]See note 26.
[29]'Kadimah, Bund jüdischer Jugend', in *Haboneh. Älterenblatt*, Nr. 2, November 1932, pp. 5–7.
[30]Hermann Gerson, *Werkleute. Ein Weg jüdischer Jugend*, Berlin 1935, p. 70.
[31]See note 19.

evolving in Palestine into original kibbutz features that are becoming manifest in building the kibbutz, in its essential nature, its existence, and in its ideological community."[32]

And in the view of *Makkabi Hazair*:

"Since our people have fulfilled the demands of life in Palestine, of *chaluz* existence and the collective, it is necessary that the *Bund* as such should offer a goal for its people, a goal that should be achieved if the *Bund* does not regard its work as being ended and complete because its people have gone to Palestine . . . The *Bund*, as a community of life, must also point out the direction of its existence in Palestine."[33]

This was quite unacceptable to the leaders of *Hechaluz*:

"The error of German *chaluzim* is that they look at affairs in Palestine from the perspective of *chaluzim* living in Germany – they forget that their role in settlement and building up the country is very small indeed, so they have no right to demand that their problems should determine the ways in which the country should be built, these being in any case very complicated. Greater modesty must be demanded of the German *Hechaluz*. It must accommodate itself to conditions in Palestine, and not the other way around."[34]

This situation can be regarded as still another blow to the Jewish youth movement in Germany. For the position of *Hechaluz* not only remained unchanged in the face of the events which were overtaking German Jewry, but became even more extreme, persisting as the dominant attitude in *Hechaluz* circles and among the settlement movements in Palestine up to the very time of the destruction of the Jews of Germany.

The conclusions that followed from this position were stated in unmistakable terms, as follows:

"*Hechaluz* itself sets no additional demands before its members who are emigrating to Palestine. Here its functions end. The youth movement, too, will have to acknowledge that once emigration to Palestine takes place, a considerable part of the purposes of its education is at an end. It must give its people the fullest measure of liberty, and allow them to choose the extent to which anyone belonging to the workers' organisations can continue to maintain his relations and connections with his past."[35]

This was how the situation was in fact understood by those who had passed through the youth movement – or at least so their conduct indicated. Most of those who joined *Hechaluz* were products of the youth movement who, on graduating from their movements, severed their connections with them both organisationally and psychologically. As a result, they were lost to the youth movement as a guiding force. Moreover, the ideological activities and interests that demanded their attention during their period of *hachscharah*, emigration to Israel, and eventual absorption in the kibbutz, so preoccupied them that, apart from correspondence and occasional meetings with movement members in Palestine, their connection with the youth movement ceased entirely. And although the process was less evident in movements like the *Werkleute* and *Makkabi Hazair*, in which the "youth movement" orientation was stronger, it

[32]See note 15.
[33]See note 26.
[34]See Sch. Rudel, 'Zwei Jahre Hechaluz in Deutschland', *loc. cit.*
[35]*Ibid.*

On Hachscharah, Mögeldorf near Nuremberg 1936

Führertagung of Hechaluz Habonim
With Yitzhák Ben Aharon, 1935

By courtesy of Beit Lohamei Haghetaot, Israel

Alija-Schule, at the end of 1940

By courtesy of Beit Lohamei Haghetaot, Israel

The last meeting of Hechaluz in Berlin, August 1941 (Lotte Kaiser, Arthur
Posnanski, Hans Wolfgang Cohn, Sonja Selbiger, Lucho Kuttner, Kurt
Silberpfennig, Herbert Grobwohl, Jizchak Schwersenz)

Kibbutz Hachscharah in Jessen, July 1941
(with Chana Ben Joseph)

By courtesy of Beit Lohamei Haghetaot, Israel

Auf Vorschlag des Rosch Chewra beschliesst die Chewra mit
grosser Freude Schawuot 1943 die Schaffung eines קרן חי"ם
und verpflichtet sich, trotz der finanziellen Notlage, Geld
aufzubringen, um es durch die Ueberlebenden dem Land zu brin-
gen zur Pflanzung von Bäumen zum Gedenken der Gefallenen unserer Bewegung. Ein kleiner Teil soll zur Finanzierung unser
Arbeit dienen.   Eine Büchse wird geschaffen.

CHUG CHALUZI / M.H.
Brith Hazofim

Bild, durch den Chug-
Chaluzi zum Geburtstag
für jeden Chawer ange-
fertigt.
Geschaffen und erdacht:
13.2.43 = Geburtstag
Ewo's.

Pages from an album of the Chug Chaluzi, Berlin, February 1943

By courtesy of Beit Lohamei Haghetaot, Israel

could nevertheless be found among these movements as well,[36] and particularly in the case of *Habonim*.

Not even the rise to power of the National Socialists in 1933, nor the persecutions of German Jews in the years that followed, were apparently sufficient to draw the attentions of *Hechaluz* away from its preoccupation with kibbutz management and ideological controversy, so that it might consider the plight of youth movement members in Germany. Bitter testimony of this is furnished by the leader of *Habonim*, Georg Pape, and a variety of more or less similar complaints was voiced among the other youth movements.

Georg Pape spoke of the dangers of what he called *mishkism*,* which he characterised in the following terms:

> "Everyone lives within his own group, is concerned with issues bearing on his own milieu, and regards the *meshek* to be the primary goal. They therefore forget that the group on its present scale, the *meshek*, and the rest of the things created by Jews in Palestine assume significance only as means in the service of the loftier end of Zionism. The burden of the considerable problems of the *meshek* are felt so keenly that it all seems impossible from the very outset. And afterwards, as inexplicable and pointless to disengage oneself and turn one's attention to anything beyond it. What is sought is not to make the *meshek* suit the needs of settlement, but to make settlement suit the needs of the *meshek*. This "mishkistic" attitude may make one a good Palestinian but not a good Zionist, for the Zionist position gives first place to unceasing concern for the fate of the Jewish masses . . ."[37]

In accounting for the difficulties experienced by *Habonim* in ideologically resolving the issue of joining the kibbutz movement, Pape considers some of the reasons for the uncertainty and indecision in this matter:

> ". . . the *Bund* received inadequate and, at times, no support at all from its members in Palestine. For the time being, these members were entirely absorbed by kibbutz affairs and their occupations; kibbutz society so preoccupied them that, as regards this ideological disagreement, they were far from prepared to come to the aid of the movement from which they had originated. Moreover, a disastrous mistake had been made: the liaison office of the *Bund* in the kibbutz was dissolved or, more accurately, was turned into a general department of German immigration in the kibbutz . . ."[38]

The attitude of the Kibbutz Hameuhad on this issue has to be understood in the light of its general policy. That organisation's rejection of settlement on the basis of country of origin (*Landsmannschaften*), and its reluctance to allow the youth movements to interfere in the decisions of its major institutions about the distribution of new *chaluzim* from Germany, derived from economic reasons and its evaluation of the requirements of settlement and immigrant absorption. In 1937 similar difficulties arose between the *Hever Hakvutzot* and *Makkabi Hazair*. Thus a demand of the leadership of *Habonim* to establish a section of its own alongside the department of German emigration, or at least to include within it a

---

[36]See for example *Der Makkabi, Jüdische Turn-und Sportzeitung*, 34. Jahrg., Nr. 5 (Juli 1933), Berlin, p. 3.

Meshek = a collective or private agricultural settlement as an economic unit, including its property, finances and division of labour. "Mishkism" would mean, accordingly, focusing the main interest on these aspects rather than on ideological ones.

[37]Georg Pape, 'Unser Weg im Hechaluz', in *Wege der Verwirklichung. Zu palästinensischen Gegenwartsfragen. Sammelschrift des Habonim Noar Chaluzi*, Berlin 1935, p. 101.

[38]Georg Pape, 'Brith Haolim 1930 bis Habonim 1934', in *Haboneh. Sammelschrift des Habonim*, Juli 1938, p. 56.

member of *Habonim* who would maintain contact with the movement in Germany
and look after the absorption of its members in Palestine, was rejected even as
late as 1938.[39]

Quite apart from disagreements between *Hechaluz* and the youth movements
on organisational matters, there were also differences between them over
education and the best way of exerting an influence on the young. There was
considerable impatience in *Hechaluz* with the scout rituals in use among youth
movements which seemed to them mere games, their symbolic and educational
significance misunderstood:

> "It seems to me that this whole preoccupation of the *bogrim* with pedagogic questions has
> become a pedagogic phenomenon. Instead of dealing with really important things, they keep
> threshing over this chaff; and what's more the subject is not in the least so rich in significance
> as to deserve monotonous and trite repetition. The scout or *Wandervogel* approach, the way of
> handing out badges, the system of platoons or of separate groups – you can talk about all of
> these things once, but no more. This should be left to youngsters; and though they couldn't
> come up with anything new, they could at least work up their enthusiasm."[40]

Adults, on the other hand, had no need of enthusiasm:

> "Bonds are tightened in a completely different way; the idea, the intellectual content, the
> pursuit of a common goal, these are the things that unify, whereas emotional relationships will
> substantially wane and be reduced to near insignificance."[41]

The criticism of "game-playing" and "scout" methods became even more
severe when *Bund* members arrived in Palestine and experienced the harsh
realities of the country at first hand. One such member wrote back from
Palestine:

> "We do not escape into the world of fancy. We are building for ourselves a real world of our
> own. We do not play games. We are educating for a reality which is serious. Yes, that is our
> romanticism. This is why we have no need of game-playing methods. In teaching our young
> people especially, we shall not forget that our reality, the reality in Palestine, the reality of the
> kibbutz, is romanticism in its highest sense."[42]

Not everyone agreed with this view, even in *Habonim*, and certainly not in the
Werkleute or *Makkabi Hazair*. The "scout" conception and the spirit of youth
animated by its enthusiasm was to remain in force in the youth movement, where
the transition from scouting ideology to *chaluz* ideology would be regarded as
being retrograde rather than an advance.[43]

As prohibitions were increasingly imposed in Germany on the youth movement's outdoor activities and appearances in public, the movement was
constrained to focus its attention on intellectual activities in the form of lectures
and discussions. It nevertheless went on with its hikes and walking tours, which
it secretly maintained at considerable risk even during the war, until the

[39]See 'Be-mesila', in *Habonim Noar Chaluzi*, für die Bogrim des Bundes, Nr. 7 (Juli 1938), pp. 2–25.
Concerning the conflicts between *Chever Hakibbuzim* and *Makkabi Hazair*, see *Makkabi Hazair*,
Mittlerenblatt, Oktober 1937, pp. 16–19.
[40]Karl Stein, *Jung-Jüdischer Wanderbund*, Bundestag 1927, p. 261.
[41]*Ibid.*, p. 262.
[42]*Habonim Noar Chaluzi*, *Bundesschreiben*, Nr. 29, Berlin (Januar 1936), p. 39.
[43]*Ibid.*, Nr. 28 (September 1935), p. 24; and 'Grundlagen unserer Erziehung', *Ha-makabi ha-tsair be-
hagshama*, 1939, pp. 4–5.

campaign of liquidation was actually instituted. This close adherence to youth movement patterns, in circumstances in which one might have thought that such "childish games" could well be dispensed with, can be accounted for only by the efficaciousness of the movement's system of "comprehensive education" and the transformative influence it exerted upon the mental attitudes of youth movement members.[44]

The differences of approach within the movement, and between it and other Jewish youth movements, depended upon the stage of development each of the movements had reached at a given time, and primarily upon the make-up and origin of its membership. This circumstance accounts for one of the major distinctive features of the Jewish youth movement in Germany.

The members of the youth movement who were of Eastern European origin when joining had already reached a point at which their Western European comrades hoped to arrive when leaving it. The sense of Jewish identity and social and national affiliation with which, by means of a comprehensive and drawn-out process, the movement sought to imbue its troubled and irresolute members, was something that was taken for granted and a primary state of mind among the Eastern Europeans in the movement. It was for this reason that the latter regarded the youth movement's modes and methods as infantile, with no significance beyond the movement itself, and as an altogether wasteful activity that only distracted one from achieving the main goal, which consisted in fulfilling the Zionist ideal by living as a *chaluz*. However, before 1933 and even afterwards, young Western European Jews for the most part had neither the psychological nor the economic motivation to commit themselves to act as *chaluzim*. Such action seemed to them remote and had no real significance for them. It was therefore the function of the Jewish youth movement in Germany to arouse the sort of motivation that was required. And to the degree that the *Jung-Jüdischer Wanderbund* and, later on, the *Habonim* neglected the factor of psychological motivation because of the influence of their Eastern European contingent, they also lost their hold over young Jews in Germany. And notwithstanding the very aura surrounding the actions and image of the *chaluz* as an educational ideal – however justifiably – it was the narrow political scope of this ideal, and the reduction of political goals exclusively to settlement in kibbutzim, which put off thousands of young Jews in Germany, and at a time when they were most in need of it.

> "One reason for the cessation of reserves was that the JJWB could no longer offer satisfaction in human terms. We keep forgetting that a not inconsiderable part of the *Bund* are not *chaluzim* and for all sorts of reasons never will be. No efforts of any kind are being made to integrate these people in any way into the *Bund* and you can be sure that there are very valuable people among them, who will eventually be lost to the *Bund* because it offers them nothing, and concerns itself one-sidedly only with the Palestinians-to-be . . . If these, too, are lost then the *Bund* will cease to exist at which point it will be incapable of absorbing reserves into its ranks. Not only will it have weakened itself in this way, but it will have to bear the responsibility for having ruined [the lives of] some of its members."[45]

[44]See Schatzker, 'The Jewish Youth Movement in Germany in the Holocaust Period, I', *loc. cit.*
[45]Ernst Loebenstein, *JJWB, Choser Jod-Gimmel*, April 1927, pp. 17–18.

Retrospectively, Georg Pape seems to have had second thoughts as well about whether it has been to his movement's advantage to make settlement in the kibbutz its sole educational aim:

> "For the German *Bund* did not go so far as those of its members who were working in Palestine, whose pragmatic demand was simultaneously the demand of their everyday lives. It is perhaps for this reason that the pressure brought to bear on the *Bund* by these comrades was treated with undue respect, because of a purely Palestinian perspective, and [was] therefore somewhat hasty."[46]

The historian of the youth movement is surprised to discover that it was the very school of thought anchored in reality that wanted to educate its members in keeping with its needs which would ultimately be responsible for depriving its teaching of the power to attract and influence the young, and so be the cause of its own demise. By contrast, the largest ideological camp within the youth movement, one whose pre-occupation with symbolic transformative games seemed entirely unrealistic, was to show itself capable of recovering its powers to influence the young. The movement of *Habonim* in 1930–1931,[47] and in the period following 1933, is a case in point which we shall now consider in detail.

The new reality created in the aftermath of the National Socialist take-over in 1933 had, among its other far-reaching consequences, a profoundly unsettling effect on the inwardly orientated intellectual and educational world of the Jewish youth movement, which suddenly found itself confronted by organisational, social and human challenges that were without precedent in the history of youth movements.

The first of these resulted from the rush of young people to *Hechaluz*, which many had sought out in order to solve their private difficulties rather than out of any real Zionist conviction.

> "Hundreds of frightened, hopeful and sad eyes are turned on us – the Zionist *chaluz* movement – seeking an answer, and only the future will tell if we can provide one."[48]

It was then that *Habonim* stepped in:

> "The members of *Habonim* were the first to take upon themselves the entire job of *Hechaluz*. They took over the work of the Centre, they established and ran most of the branches, they began the colossal enterprise of German *Hechaluz*; it was they who strengthened German *Hechaluz*'s new [undertaking], which stood on weak foundations, and kept it going until the arrival of the first representatives from Palestine. It was clear that the fact of the *Bund*'s having taken over the work of *Hechaluz* had necessarily left its stamp and impress upon *Habonim* and its work. The whole of the *Bund*, all of its activity, were now brought into line with *Hechaluz* and the completion of the urgent tasks in this area. Here was the objective, here the mustering point of true *chaluz* responsibility."[49]

---

[46]See note 38. *Ibid.*, p. 42.

[47]See *Gemeinschaftsarbeit der Jüdischen Jugend*, Berlin 1937, Verlag Zentralwohlfahrtsstelle der Juden in Deutschland, hrsg. von Dr. Friedrich Brodnitz, pp. 50–51.

[48]Leo St., 'Vor grossen Aufgaben', in *Haboneh, Älterenblatt der jüdischen Jugendgemeinschaft Habonim. Noar Chaluzi*, Juli 1933, p. 5.

[49]'Zwei Jahre Habonim. Die Bundesleitung, Atte, Jaakov, Seev', in *Binjan, Sammelschrift des Habonim*, Berlin, März 1935, hrsg. von der Bundesleitung . . . , Verlag Hechaluz, verantwortlich Dr. Georg Josephthal.

The upshot of this identification with *Hechaluz* was total politicisation in the spirit of *Mapai* and the *Kibbutz Hameuhad*. But in a short time it became apparent that the consequence of *Habonim*'s throwing itself so fully into outside work was its neglect of internal activities, of its educational work within its own ranks. One of the questions raised in discussions in the leadership council was: "Do we have a right to give up the unity and integrity of our education for the attraction of a greater force?" It was decided that now more than ever the integrative scope of the members of *Habonim* had to be enlarged, that the movement had to concentrate upon itself, deepen its educational influence, and lay greater stress on group work and the *Bund* spirit. But the dangers of isolation were spoken of as well; and it was thought that the unity of the *Bund* should not be treated as a value for its own sake, but should serve as a means for preparing movement members to undertake the historic mission that had been put before them by the times.[50] There were those who warned against becoming an attenuated mass-movement.[51] Others demanded "to learn once more to touch the private, profound and critical domain of the soul".[52] Some complained of the absence of a *Bund* atmosphere, which was a significant educational factor without which *Habonim* would be unable even to meet the demands being made on it by the outside world.[53] And, finally, a number of members took issue with those who regarded the formal features of the youth movement to be nothing more than "games".[54]

The final outcome of these debates within *Habonim* was a compromise policy formulated by Georg Pape and called the "Permanent Synthesis".[55] This was a synthesis between the principles of the youth movement and *Hechaluz*, whose opposite attractions had been experienced by *Habonim* – and would eventually be experienced by all of the Zionist youth movements with increasing degrees of intensity. It was a synthesis that merged the sociological view of the youth movement respecting its social and national role, with the conception which attached an autonomous value to the movement as a self-enclosed *chavrutha* (*Gemeinschaft*) that was its own end and purpose. It was also a synthesis that sought a middle course between "external work" in society – especially as regards the daunting educational and organisational responsibilities taken on by *Habonim* when the National Socialists assumed power – and the "internal work" of education among and between the movement's members: this was to be a balance struck between the principles of open eclecticism and closed selectivity; between a mass movement and a society of the elect. It was a combination, as well, of the idea of vocation and vocational training as *hachscharah*, in the way it was conceived of by the *Hechaluz*, and the youth movement's conception of vocation as "calling"; a resolution of the principles of common need and personal

[50] *Jüdische Jugendgemeinschaft – Habonim, Noar Chaluzi, Bundesschreiben* Nr. 3, Berlin, 6. Juni 1933, p. 1.
[51] See note 48, *ibid.*, pp. 12–13.
[52] Arje L., 'Zur Lage im Bund', in *Haboneh. Sammelschrift des Habonim, anlässlich seines fünfjährigen Bestehens*, Juli 1938, p. 63.
[53] *Jüdische Jugendgemeinschaft-Habonim, Noar Chaluzi, Rundschreiben* Nr. 13, 29. September 1933, p. 1.
[54] *Ibid.*, Anlage, pp. 1–5.
[55] Georg Pape, 'Die permanente Synthese', *loc. cit.*, pp. 11–25.

fulfilment. And, finally, it was a synthesis that attempted to bridge the difference between the *chaluzim*'s emphasis on political actualisation and the spiritual inner-orientation of the youth movement; between the pursuit of goals that were societal and political, and the quest for the comprehensive and deep psychological integrity of the individual.

The times conspired to prevent *Habonim* and the other Jewish youth movements from quietly working towards an amalgam of this kind. But it is also doubtful that Pape's synthesis represented anything more than a verbal resolution of differences that were actually not amenable to being resolved in such a way.

No similar identification with *Hechaluz* developed among the other Jewish youth movements – neither among the *Werkleute* and *Hashomer Hazair*, nor in *Makkabi Hazair*. And for its part, *Hechaluz* was not always well disposed to the emergence of *chaluz* movements that were likely to offer an alternative to *Habonim* and the policy line of the *Kibbutz Hameuhad*. Thus *Hechaluz* initially opposed the establishment of *Hashomer Hazair* cells in Germany.[56] These movements repeatedly asserted that they would neither join nor merge with *Hechaluz*.[57] Nevertheless, external circumstances, as well as the transition of the movements to the stage of operationally implementing their purpose, led to their increasing collaboration with *Hechaluz*, most particularly in the fields of *hachscharah*, emigration, and joining kibbutz movements in Palestine.[58]

Hashomer Hazair had been a movement of *chaluzim* from the very moment it was established in Germany, and had the advantage of being able to rely on the cumulative experience of its world movement and the *Kibbutz Haarzi*. Other movements, such as the *Werkleute* and *Makkabi Hazair*, became *chaluz* movements in response to events in Germany, on the one hand, and as a result of their desire to realise the ideal of *chavrutha* through the establishment of an existential community. Both of these groups increasingly took part in the activities of

[56]Moshe Schapira, 'Der Hechaluz und die Jugendbewegung', in *Informationsblatt 'Hechaluz'*, Deutscher Landesverband, Jahrg. 3, Nr. 25 (April 1930), p. 54. See now also the recently published and most substantial publications of Jehuda Reinharz on *Hashomer Hazair* which throw new light on the political background of the movement in Germany. Reinharz's work may be regarded also as the most important contribution to our understanding of the political aspects of *Hashomer Hazair* in Germany. Cf. Jehuda Reinharz, 'Hashomer Hazair in Germany (I) 1928–1933', in *LBI Year Book XXXI* (1986), pp. 173–208; *idem*, 'Hashomer Hazair in Germany (II). Under the Shadow of the Swastika, 1933–1938', in *LBI Year Book XXXII* (1987), pp. 183–229; *idem*, 'Hashomer Hazair in Nazi Germany', in *Die Juden im Nationalsozialistischen Deutschland/The Jews in Nazi Germany 1933–1943*, herausgegeben von Arnold Paucker mit Sylvia Gilchrist und Barbara Suchy, Tübingen 1986 (Schriftenreihe wissenschaftlicher Abhandlungen des Leo Baeck Instituts 45), pp. 317–350.

[57]See *Der Makkabi, Jüdische Turn- und Sportzeitung*, 34. Jahrg., Nr. 5 (Juli 1933), Berlin, p. 5; and *Choser IPD – Makkabi Hazair*, 1935, p. 24; also 'Mi-tik ha-mikhtavim,' a letter from the *Hechaluz* Centre in Denmark to the *Mahleka*, 31. Juni 1927.

[58]The *Werkleute* in 1933, in the course of their "re-orientation" – this with reservations and without giving up youth movement ideas. See the article of Leni Westphal (Jechiel), 'Neuorientierung', in *Werkleute, Bund deutsch-jüdischer Jugend, Bundesblatt*, Juni 1933, p. 3. Similarly, also *Makkabi Hazair* in 1935, with the reservation that a fully autonomous organisation should be preserved; see 'Die Idee des Makkabi', in *Handbuch des Makkabi Hazair*, 1935, p. 32. Only in 1936 does the movement's newspaper report that its members "joyfully and without hesitation joined the German *Hechaluz*"; see *Makkabi Hazair, Mittlerenblatt*, Berlin, Oktober 1936.

Hechaluz and its councils, established *chaluz* hostels and vocational farms, organised *hachscharah* programmes both for their graduates and on an intermediate level, and saw to the vocational training of its members either in groups or individually. Thus Gustav Horn, who was a member of the *Werkleute*, became Secretary of *Hechaluz*, and the same movement established Kibbutz Hazorea, which eventually joined *Hashomer Hazair* and the *Kibbutz Haarzi*.[59] *Makkabi Hazair* together with *Makkabi* founded the *Mahleket Chaluzim*, which established a complex network of *hachscharah* outside Palestine for *bogrim* of the movement, as well as for the intermediate level. And in collaboration with *Makkabi Hazair* in Czechoslovakia and other countries, it founded a number of *kvutzot* in Palestine, and in 1937 decided to co-operate with the *Hever Hakvutzot*.

As the members of these were integrated in the kibbutz movements in Palestine, and struggled to cope with the realities and conditions of the country, it was inevitable that they should find themselves relinquishing a degree of commitment to the highly spiritualised ideal of the youth movement in Germany, such as the principle of the actualisation of *chavrutha* (*Gemeinschaft*), that of independent and personal choice based on inner truth, of complete autonomy, and so on. Moreover, the efforts of these *chaluzim* to adjust to the new conditions of their existence so greatly absorbed their attention that they forgot about the problems faced by the comrades they had left behind, and there were complaints from both sides about the alienation that was developing between them.

The rush of young men and women to *Hechaluz* raised the immediate problem of selecting candidates from among them for certificates to Palestine. On this point, *Habonim* adopted the principle that

> "selection and preferential treatment should be bestowed on those who are going to Palestine firmly resolved not to be swept along on the waves of circumstance, but to follow the path that is necessary in Palestine from the Zionist point of view. This was also our demand at the *Palästina-Amt*."[60]

What this "necessary path in Palestine" should be was laid down in nearly axiomatic fashion by *Hechaluz* as consisting exclusively of joining the Labour camp in Palestine within the context of the Kibbutz Movement. The principal activity of *Hechaluz* was therefore to prepare young people at *hachscharah* kibbutzim or training farms, as well as sending them to work on farms owned by peasants.

> "On *hachscharah* kibbutzim the *chaluz* learns contempt for the idle life and the pursuit of wealth. He is trained for a life of work and to understand his duties as a *chaluz* in Palestine. He remains at his place of *hachscharah* until he leaves for Palestine, and does not return to his home town

[59]See [Hermann] Menachem Gerson, 'Darka shel tnuah ha-"Werkleute" la-Kibuts ha-Artsi' ('The Road of the "Werkleute" movement to the Kibbutz Haarzi'), in *Sefer Hashomer Hatzair*, Sifriyat Poalim, Merhavia 1956, pp. 417–425 (in Hebrew).

[60]*Jüdische Jugendgemeinschaft-Habonim, Noar Chaluzi*, Rundschreiben Nr. 11, 8. September 1933, Berlin, p. 1.

and its corrupt way of life because he has broken with it forever. *Hachscharah* was and always will be for us the principle by which the privilege of settling as *chaluzim* is earned."[61]

That privilege was withheld from middle-class heads of families who were not members of the *Histadruth* and the Workers' Party.

"Is it conceivable that this sort of human material could ever manage to get along in Palestine and carry out the duties of a *chaluz* there? Would it occur to anyone to conscript the old, the ill and people who wear glasses in wartime? Their problem is really tragic, but their place is not within the borders of Palestine, and not because someone doesn't want it but because no objective possibility for this exists."[62]

Meir Yaari of *Hashomer Hazair* went further, arguing: "The bridge between the terrible needs of Jewish troubles and our capabilities has not yet been spanned", and those who build foundations have to make certain about the material that goes into them.[63] This attitude was maintained even in the face of the unremitting enactments of anti-Jewish decrees (which were quite well known in Palestine) and did not change up to the beginning of the Second World War. A letter from the German *Aliyah* Section at Ein Harod, dated 8th October 1937, included a number of "unpleasant observations": (1) It being difficult to accommodate families with children at the kibbutz because of insufficient space in the children's quarters, their numbers should be kept down to a minimum. (2) Some people are arriving with bone fractures and other conditions requiring surgery. They are accepted by the *Kupat Cholim* on the basis of limited eligibility only. Particular care should therefore be taken that surgery is performed prior to emigration. (3) It is impossible to absorb older people who have undergone only short-term *hachscharah*, which comes out in their attitude towards kibbutz life.

"There exists only one way: in distributing certificates, a careful check must be made on those to whom certificates can be given. Always depend more on good sense than on good intentions and kindness and other points of view (mistakes like those we made in the past in accepting people to *Hechaluz*), and do not try, by means of handing out certificates, to solve problems which cannot be solved by being transported geographically."[64]

The Zionist youth movements acquiesced in the demands of *Hechaluz* – expecially while they were still in their pre-operational phase of development – both in the matters of their joining the Labour wing in Palestine and of their choice of a kibbutz mode of existence, which they in any case regarded as representing a fulfilment of their ideal of *chavrutha* (*Gemeinschaft*). At the same time they disliked most of the political factions in the Labour wing and the Kibbutz Movement. Nor did they have any sympathy for the concept of the "Great Kibbutz", which was totally out of keeping with their idea of *chavrutha*. And they were most particularly put off by the demand of *Hechaluz* and the Kibbutz Movement that they surrender their autonomy on arrival in Palestine,

[61]'Aus dem Referat von Dobkin auf der 4. Weida der Histadruth', *Informationsblatt*, hrsg. vom Hechaluz, Deutscher Landesverband, Jahrg. 6, Nr. 53/54 (März/April 1933), p. 9.
[62]*Ibid.*, p. 5.
[63]*Ibid.*, p. 15.
[64]See 'Mi-tik ha-mikhtavim' of the State of our Movement in Germany (in Hebrew), No. 7, Ein Harod, November 1937, pp. 2–3.

and that they should merge with kibbutz society by severing all their connections with the youth movement *Bund* both organisationally and intellectually.

At a conference of *Habonim* which met from the 2nd to the 5th of July 1937, directives were put to the vote that called for obedience to kibbutz institutions, and for the representation in *Habonim* of only those views on kibbutz forms of existence that were in keeping with an affiliation with the *Kibbutz Hameuhad*. The results of the vote show very clearly the split within the movement; with those of its members who were primarily active within *Habonim* opposing the directives, and those who were especially active in *Hechaluz* voting in favour, and in sufficient numbers even to win by a small majority.[65] Similar tendencies were revealed in *Makkabi Hazair* in regard to the *Hever Hakvutzot*.[66] And *Hashomer Hazair* sought as well to influence the Agricultural Centre in Palestine to distribute German *Hechaluz* members among all of the collective settlements, including those of *Hashomer Hazair* in Palestine and also to avoid having *Hechaluz* members formed into specific associations of a kibbutz nature when they were still in Germany. *Hashomer Hazair*'s position in this regard was not entirely based on its attitude towards the issue of autonomy of the youth movements, but derived from economic considerations as well, since kibbutzim in Palestine also depended financially on immigration from Germany.[67]

Disagreements between *Hechaluz* and the *Jugendbünde* persisted on a variety of issues: the autonomy of the *Bünde* within *Hechaluz*; relinquishment of graduates needed by the movement and *madrichim* to *Hechaluz*; participation in "mixed *hachscharah*", together with persons who were not members of the youth movements, a situation which the latter regarded as being dangerous to their educational purpose.

The youth movements complained that the *shlichim* being sent from Palestine had been chosen more out of party considerations than because of their experience in education. They complained of the tendency of these representatives to give precedence to party politics over educational matters, and of their unsympathetic view of the right of free choice of the preferred form of kibbutz in Palestine.[68] The youth movement, adhering to its sacrosanct principle of "truly inner and independently responsible choice", was unable to come to terms with being dictated to from Palestine about requirements that ran counter to its own. "It seems to me that there is on the part of the Kibbutz a lack of understanding

[65]The position of the youth movement was represented by Georg Pape, and that of party ideology by Arje L. and A. T. (Avraham Tarshish). The directives were passed by a majority of 11 to 8. See 'Mi-tik ha-mikhtavim', letter from the leadership of *Habonim* to the *Mahleka* of 7th July 1937, p. 4.
[66]See, for example, Hardy Swarsensky, 'Die Aufgabe des Bundes', in *Makkabi Hazair, Mittlerenblatt*, Berlin, Oktober 1937, pp. 9–10; also Hans Sternberg, *Primum vivere, Deindere Philosophari*, hrsg. von der Bundesleitung des jüdischen Pfadfinderbundes Makkabi Hazair (Brith Hazofim), Berlin, August 1936, p. 16.
[67]See 'Mi-tik ha-mikhtavim', letter of Berlin *Hechaluz* of 21st June 1937 to the *Mahleka*. Funds provided by the Council for German Jewry made it possible to pay a substantial sum of money for each German immigrant to Palestine (£60 in 1937), the amount being paid to the *Kvutza* or kibbutz which the immigrant joined; see *Makkabi Hazair, Mittlerenblatt* (note 66), p. 17.
[68]See, for example, Adolf Schiff, 'Generallinie oder Autonomie?', *loc. cit.* (see note 19).

for our position", wrote a member of *Habonim* and *Hechaluz* in Berlin to the Secretariat of the *Kibbutz Hameuhad* in August of 1938:

> "Out of all those members of *Habonim* who had chosen to educate their comrades in the movement to join the *Kibbutz Hameuhad*, indeed obliged them to do so, not a single one of them is living here among us. They are all in Palestine. Whereas we, as a youth movement, regard ourselves as under an obligation to re-examine each time what we demand of ourselves and of those whom we are educating. Today, more than ever, we regard it as important to maintain this principle everywhere, and to act against [the situation] in which our members accept choices and views without thinking them through by themselves. In accordance with this principle, it has been felt for some time now that the issue of unconditional integration with the *Kibbutz Hameuhad* has to be re-opened for discussion . . ."[69]

The response of Jisrael Idelson, writing in the name of the Secretariat, reveals the full extent of the difference of outlook:

> "Everyone who knows and understands will regard *Erez-Israel* not as a refuge for unfortunate emigrants, but as the field for the creation of the enterprise of a people, [one which is] homogeneous despite all the social and other differentiations within it, and has a homogeneous culture (in the broadest sense of that word) . . . We see the grounds of our unrelenting struggle *solely* in a number of questions . . . Anyone who sees before him a grand idea, and sees himself as part of the army dedicated to its fulfilment, cannot be 'soft and flexible'. He is obstinate in fulfilling the idea, and he is severely exacting, but only in regard to *himself* and to those who, by their own good will, are ready to join this army . . . You write: 'I think nevertheless that there is a lack of understanding for our situation and our needs on the part of the Kibbutz.' And the question is, why must there be understanding for *your* situation and for *your* needs, as though you are an end in your own right, or for the situation of our enterprise and the needs of the enterprise – and what must you and we do in this regard? . . ."[70]

Even as late as 1939, when reports from Germany were appearing in the *Mi-tik ha-mikhtavim* about subjects like the "liquidation of German Jews", *Hechaluz* was primarily concerned about the issue of the "criteria" for distributing certificates and the fact that "very soon there will be almost no one left here who embodies our concepts in regard to Jews . . ."[71] And the report of the German Department turns on only one issue:

> "We do not have to agree to this sort of make-up for the *aliyah* of the last transport. We know that the whole organisation of the business is in the hands of our members. It is impossible that they should not be engaged in educational work."

Or, again, with the question of "to what extent will they [the new stratum that does not know the content of the movement] be members of our movement, and shall we succeed in building anything with them . . ."[72]

This, then, is the background against which we shall examine the collaboration between the Jewish youth movement and *Hechaluz* in Germany.

"The concept of *hachscharah*, which was until now significant only for the *chaluz* youth movement, has today become the common problem of the Jews of

[69]'Mi-tik ha-mikhtavim', from the *Hechaluz* Centre in Berlin to the Secretariat, October 1938.
[70]'Mi-tik ha-mikhtavim', letter from *Hechaluz* in Berlin to Ludwig Stern, Berlin, 25th October 1938, pp. 12–13.
[71]'Mi-tik ha-mikhtavim', Brief vom M.Z. an die Maskiruth Hakibbuz vom 10. Februar 1939, p. 8.
[72]'Mi-tik ha-mikhtavim', meeting of the German Section in Ein Harod, 26th April 1939.

Germany."[73] Centres for vocational training were established in Germany between 1933 and 1939 by various Zionist groups, such as *Hechaluz* and *Bachad*, as well as a minority of non-Zionist groups. To these were added the *hachscharah* kibbutzim of the *Youth Aliyah* project, the "intermediate *hachscharah*" of the youth movements. In time the distinction between these became blurred. Technical and organisational problems, matters of *hachscharah* locations, questionnaires, financial assistance, and so on, were worked out with the appropriate institutions of the *Reichsvertretung der deutschen Juden*, and later with the *Reichsvereinigung der Juden in Deutschland* and community representatives.[74] All problems concerning vocational training were put into the hands of the *Palästina-Amt* of the *Reichsvereinigung*, which also included members of *Hechaluz*. In addition, a *chaluz* section was added to the "Department of Vocational Training" in which members of *Hechaluz* participated as well.[75]

Ora Borinski and Jizchak Schwersenz, as well as others, have described the strong dependency of *hachscharah* kibbutzim on the *Reichsvereinigung* during the final years of German Jewry.[76] All *hachscharah* members who were unable to meet the cost of their training received a sum of 45 marks contributed by Jewish institutions. The *chaluz* section of the *Bünde* received financial support from the *Reichsvertretung*. Most of the money for *hachscharah* came from Jewish sources abroad.[77] The *Reichsvertretung* also paid a "leadership allowance" to teachers who had resigned from their teaching posts in order to work as *madrichim* among youngsters participating in "intermediate *hachscharah*" programmes; nevertheless there were growing complaints about the insufficiency of these allowances.[78] Beginning in 1938, the *Reichsvertretung* had difficulty in finding money with which to subsidise those involved in *hachscharah*, which made the work all the more difficult and forced *Hechaluz* to place members in "external *hachscharah*" programmes. *Hechaluz*'s contact with the authorities was maintained through the *Reichsvereinigung*, which appointed a liaison officer to the *Gestapo* to deal with the affairs of *hachscharah* centres.[79]

For their part, German authorities initially had no objections to the idea of vocational training for Jews in agriculture, so long as this was done in organised groups and for the purpose of preparing the members of such groups for emigration from Germany. What was more, every member of a *hachscharah* group paid a monthly sum of 30–60 marks to the farmer for whom he worked, and reports from everywhere in Germany indicate that the work of these young people was highly regarded.[80] The farmers' attitudes towards *chaluzim* varied considerably. Some were sorry to see the *chaluzim* leave when their turn to

[73]*Der Makkabi, Jüdische Turn- und Sportzeitung*, 34, Nr. 4, Berlin (Juni 1933), p. 3.
[74]'Mesila', *Habonim*, Mittleren Choser Nr. 6, 1937, p. 44.
[75]'Mi-tik ha-mikhtavim', letter from KG to the Secretariat of the kibbutz, 5th December 1938, p. 6.
[76]Anneliese-Ora Borinski, *Erinnerungen 1940–1943*, Germany 1970, pp. 8, 17–18; and Jizchak Schwersenz, *Mahteret halutsim be-Germania ha natsit (The Chaluz Underground in Nazi Germany)*, Kibbutz Hameuhad 1969 (in Hebrew), pp. 34–36.
[77]See *Makkabi Hazair, Mitteilungsblatt*, August 1938, p. 13.
[78]*Chajenu, Bundesblatt des Brith Hanoar und Bachad in Deutschland*, Nr. 23 (Januar 1938), p. 18.
[79]Schwersenz, *Mahteret halutsim be-Germania ha-natsit, op. cit.*, p. 12.
[80]See for example, Reichsführer SS, Chef des Sicherheitsamtes, Lagebericht Mai/Juni 1934, p. 52.

emigrate came and would even advise them "to convert to Christianity and stay".[81] Elsewhere we read of farmers objecting to the presence of *chaluzim* in their villages.[82] Still another report expresses concern over the possibility that large concentrations of young Jews might offend the sensibilities of the local population to the extent of jeopardising public order. In the meantime, as the number of *hachscharah* members grew, the period of time they were forced to remain at their places of training stretched into several years. Moreover the number of suitable *hachscharah* locations in Germany was insufficient to absorb all the applicants, particularly following the *Kristallnacht*, the pogrom in November 1938, when affiliation with a *hachscharah* protected young Jews from arrest or could obtain their release. In these circumstances *Hechaluz* found itself constrained to send candidates to the *hachscharah* network that was maintained abroad, especially in the countries bordering Germany.[83]

When we consider the overall position of German Jews, the shrinking scope of the means at their disposal to cope with their situation, the very small number of representatives from Palestine permitted to enter the country in order to work at *Hechaluz*, and the average age of the members of the Zionist youth movements, there can be no doubt that we are dealing with one of the most extraordinary and responsible enterprises ever undertaken by a youth movement. Even when the goals of *hachscharah* and settlement in Palestine were already beyond reach, the *hachscharah* centres continued to serve as sanctuaries of companionship, collective fraternity, and human dignity in a sea of hate – the fruit of an effort "to build a constructive zone amid the general ruin of German Jewry".[84] The dry, businesslike reports written by *Hechaluz* and the youth movement members to Palestine reveal admirable courage on the part of activists and *madrichim* who gave up their turn for *aliyah* out of a sense of responsiblity to their movement and the *hachscharah* programme,[85] although they were fully aware that in doing so they were sealing their fate.

"Who will believe that at this time, 1939, when the world is facing extraordinary political events, in the Passover and Easter season, a circle of totally responsible comrades remained at *hachscharah* kibbutzim, there to organise seminars on Zionist ideology, give parties, and play football. You could say – this is madness. And I am not at all sure which attitude is more correct . . . Then there is still another point of view: why we should be busying ourselves in recent weeks, of all times, with 'internal work'. It's psychological . . . All of us here in Berlin are looking for an inner justification for our work, one which we would not be able to find in office work unless we exerted ourselves for other people. We are putting all our strength into this work in order to forget about everyday existence, and so that we don't have to think about our personal situation."

The work now took on a more "soulful" character than it had had in 1937–1938:

"The work anaesthetises us, we draw our vitality from it, even though we complain about it every day – and if there is ever a quiet moment, such a mood immediately descends that it's hard to recover from it. *Was wird im Ernstfall?* [What will happen when matters come to a

[81]*Werkleute, Bund jüdischer Jugend, Verbindungsbrief Nr. 2*, Berlin, September 1933, p. 14.
[82]Lagebericht, Köln, den 4. März 1935, p. 23.
[83]Perez Leshem, *Strasse zur Rettung, 1933–1939*, Verband der Freunde der Histadruth, Tel-Aviv 1973.
[84]'Mi-tik ha-mikhtavim', Brief von Habonim Noar Chaluzi London an die "Mahleka", 1939.
[85]See for example, *Makkabi Hazair, Mittlerenblatt*, Berlin, Juli 1937, p. 27.

head?] is the question one wishes to put off, and which remains and troubles one at all times."[86]

"Intermediate *hachscharah*" (*Mittleren Hachscharah – Miha*) occupied a special place in the *hachscharah* complex. Beginning in 1934, fresh difficulties arose in coping with the demand for vocational training among Jewish teenagers. Earlier, Jewish young people were able to continue their studies until the age of eighteen and complete their grammar school education. Now they were being forced to leave school at fourteen or fifteen,[87] and the issue of their further schooling became an acute cultural as well as an educational problem.[88] It was this problem to which *Mittleren Hachscharah* addressed itself. The programme was maintained by the two *chaluz* organisations *Hechaluz* and *Bachad*, and by *Aliyat Hanoar* and the youth movements.[89] In 1937 there were about 800 young people enrolled in *Mittleren Hachscharah*, which had adopted the principles of education that had been developed at the time by *Aliyat Hanoar*. The intention of the programme was to combine vocational training, preparation for a life dedicated to the ideal of work, and "intellectual *hachscharah*". Additionally, the programme was also designed to offer supplementary general education and Hebrew studies to young men and women whose educational level had fallen because of the structural changes that had taken place in that period in the institutions and educational practices of the German-Jewish community. Again, on this issue too, the factions of the youth movement were divided, with one group supporting the idea of a programme offering a thorough grounding in a vocation (which was what the parents wanted as well), and *Hechaluz* insisting that those enrolled should be trained for a life devoted to labour without the option of it being tied to a particular trade of their choice.[90]

Notwithstanding the structural differences between the youth movement and *Hechaluz*, the two groups collaborated very closely, and to a degree that met the urgent needs of the time. And it was because of their partnership that thousands of young German Jews received *hachscharah*, survived, and were able to realise the *chaluz* ideal.[91] Moreover, all of their differences apart, the two movements

[86]'Mi-tik ha-mikhtavim', Brief von Kurt G. an die "Mahleka", 1939.

[87]*Der Makkabi, Jüdische Turn- und Sportzeitung*, 37, Nr. 2 (April 1936), p. 7.

[88]In 1935, about 1,200–1,500 boys were in this way deprived of the opportunity to choose their vocation. In this regard, see Georg Josephthal, 'Die Berufsfrage der jüdischen Jugend', in *Gemeinschaftsarbeit der jüdischen Jugend, op. cit.*, pp. 40–48.

[89]Josephthal claims that the idea of *Mittleren Hachscharah* was accepted very reluctantly, because it was felt that the enrolment of this intermediate level in a non-*Bund* context was likely to have an undermining effect on the programme (see *ibid.*, p. 47). On the other hand, the sources from the youth movements indicate that the youth movements were wholeheartedly enthusiastic about the programme, which they believed would be more effective in instilling a youth movement spirit among its trainees than would regular *hachscharah*. On this, see 'Rechenschaftsberichte des Makkabi in Deutschland', in *Berichtsperiode*, Oktober 1936–Oktober 1938, pp. 20–21; *Binjan, Sammelschrift des Habonim*, Berlin, März 1935, pp. 7–9.

[90]See for example, *Makkabi Hazair, Mittlerenblatt*, Berlin, Dezember 1937, pp. 1–7.

[91]There is no doubt that in this they were following a principle of biological and ideological selection, and that the idea of *aliyah* being a rescue operation was remote to them. On the moral issue, see Jon and David Kimche, *The Secret Roads. The "Illegal" Migration of a People, 1938–1948*, London 1954; and Hannah Arendt, *Eichmann in Jerusalem. A Report on the Banality of Evil*, London 1963. Also, Hermann

complemented one another in essential ways. The youth movement provided *Hechaluz* with a steady supply of new recruits imbued with an ideal and ready to serve. It was these young men and women who carried the brunt of the work of *Hechaluz* in the organisation's branches in Germany after 1933. And *Hechaluz*, for its part, functioned as a nation-wide Jewish democratic corrective to the youth movement, which, by virtue of its character and intellectual traditions, was highly vulnerable to the influences of the world that surrounded it – which in this instance was one of the collapse of the Weimar Republic and the rise of the National-Socialist Third *Reich*. The youth movement's connection with *Hechaluz* inclined it in the direction of goals that were concrete and down-to-earth, and in this way prevented it from turning inwards upon itself, from becoming immersed in fantasies, as had happened in the case of the *Blau-Weiss* towards its end, and of the *Schwarzes Fähnlein* and the *Deutscher Vortrupp*.

In recent years criticism has been repeatedly levelled at the Zionist youth movement as a whole, and at *Hechaluz* and the Jewish youth movements, that they had all in one way or another been influenced by the ideologies of Fascism and National Socialism. In addition, they have been charged with having adopted an unsavoury Social Darwinist line.[92]

In the foregoing, our concern has been solely with the Jewish youth movements themselves. As regards the external influences upon them, three sources of such influence must be distinguished and, correspondingly, three utterly different kinds of experience that are associated with these influences. The first and major source of influence is the world of the German youth movement out of which the Jewish youth movement arose and to which it responded. We have considered the characteristic features of the youth movement elsewhere. The fact is that most of the characteristics that critics of the youth movement regard as being the products of "fascist" influence were an integral part of the youth movement before the concepts of "Fascism", "Social Darwinism" and "National Socialism" had been made known to it. Ideas such as that of the "total" *Bund* which encompasses and binds the individual entirely and for life, down to his very choice of profession; or the rejection of the fragmented, mechanistic and atomised state of society, with its division into parties and system of classes, and the yearning for *chavrutha* (*Gemeinschaft*) in its stead, for an organically integrated and corporate order – all of these were inherent in the Jewish youth movement at its very source and origin.

Meier-Cronemeyer, *Deutschlands jüdische Jugendbewegung. Versuch eines Fazits* (forthcoming), *passim*. The author of the present study has no clear answers to offer. What is certain, however, is that in a situation in which only a limited number of certificates was available, and the number of people requesting them was constantly on the increase, some system of selection had to be applied as a matter of course. So those who were responsible for distributing the certificates were faced by a very real moral dilemma. As for the decision concerning the criteria for selection, this was an ideological matter, and depended on a deep commitment to the *chaluz* ideal. It should be added, moreover, that the criticism of this procedure also depends on ideological motives, albeit of a different kind.

[92]See especially Hermann Meier-Cronemeyer, 'Jüdische Jugendbewegung', in *Germania Judaica*, VIII, Nos. 1/2, 3/4 (1969), II, pp. 104–105; and also his *Deutschlands jüdische Jugendbewegung. Versuch eines Fazits, op. cit.*

At some stage in the development of each of the Jewish youth movements, and well before 1933, anti-democratic and authoritarian attitudes could be discerned, with an attendant insistence on the leadership principle coupled with demands that "voices should be weighed not counted", that "the people have to be pulled along without their advice being sought", that the authority of one among us should be acknowledged as self-evident without putting the matter to a vote,[93] and so on. But none of these views took hold for any length of time, and in no case did they prevail over the democratic principles that were maintained by the Zionist movement at large, by the Zionist organisation in Germany, and by *Hechaluz* or any of its institutions.

Heinz Kellermann was right when he observed in 1935:

> "Whoever reads the writings of the young generation of Germans without prejudice and compares them with those of young German Jews will sometimes find striking similarities. The reason is clear, and not even officially denied, and is that German youth, like German-Jewish youth, springs from the same common youth movement which had called for the Meissner Formula."[94]

The second source of influence was that of the surrounding world, that of the manipulative propaganda techniques of the Nazi Party coming to power, to which young German Jews were no less susceptible than were young German Gentiles. The effect of this influence was for the most part external, and reflected in the imitation of military ceremony and ritual in uniforms, flags, and dress parades. These were maintained, so long as they were allowed, by the non-Zionist Jewish youth movements and some of the Zionist ones, such as *Betar* and *Makkabi Hazair*. Apart from being the result of the very natural inclination to imitation, these practices may have also originated in the need felt by Jewish young people to compensate within their own circles for what was being denied them by society at large.

But even if the Jewish youth movement seems to fit in with the spirit of the *Aufbruch der Nation* ("Resurgence of the Nation") and its exhibitionism and ceremonies, and regarded these as representing the triumph of the *chavrutha* over individual will and aspiration, which had until then determined the shape of the world,[95] the conclusions drawn by recent critics of the movement are not

---

[93]For examples of this sort of attitude, see: Fritz Lichtenstein, 'Demokratie und Führerschaft', *JJWB Führerblatt*, Nr. 2 (März 1924), pp. 6–10; or by way of comparing the situation of the *Bund* with that of the Weimar Republic, Ernst Loewenthal, 'Von Jugend und Staat', in *Kameraden, Bundesblatt*, Neue Folge, 1. Hefte (Juni 1924), pp. 4–6; and *ibid.*, Friedrich Carl Hellwig, 'Jugend und Staat', pp. 19–20; and an article written for the *Esra* movement in which Mussolini's Italian Fascism is compared to a complex youth movement, Kurt Salomon, 'Das moderne Führerauswahlproblem', in *Führerschaftsblätter des Esra*, Jahrg. 3, Heft 4/5 (1927), pp. 39–41; also, *Jüdische Jugendgemeinschaft – Habonim Noar Chaluzi, Rundschreiben Nr. 22*, Berlin, 31. Mai 1934, pp. 1–3; and finally, *Chajenu, Bundesblatt des Brith Hanoar und Bachad in Deutschland*, Nr. 23, Berlin, Januar 1938, p. 8.

[94]Heinz Kellermann, 'Der "Bund"', in *Deutschjüdischer Weg. Eine Schriftenreihe*, Nr. 2, Wille und Weg des deutschen Judentums, Vortrupp Verlag, Berlin 1935, pp. 44–43.

[95]See Leo St., 'Vor grossen Aufgaben', *loc. cit.*, pp. 3–4. The content calls to mind the sort of sentiments inspired by Nazi ideology, such as: "Einst schien das Ich der Angelpunkt der Welt / und alles drehte sich um sein Leiden. / Doch allmählich kam erkennendes Bescheiden / und hat den Blick aufs Ganze umgestellt. / Nun fügt das Ich dem grossen Wir sich ein / und wird zum kleinen Rad in der Maschine . . ." (Heinrich Anacker, *SA-Gedichte, Die Trommel*, Munich 1931; *Die Fanfare*,

altogether warranted. What was taking place was the same as what had occurred in the early months of the First World War. At that time, when the whole of Germany was bent on the war effort, and the German military machine was in full swing, there were many young Jews – among them Martin Buber, Hugo Bergmann and Ernst Simon – who found themselves thinking about the atomised and fragmented state of Jewish existence, and who yearned for Jewish *chavrutha*.[96]

A different situation is presented by the case of the third source of influence, which consisted in ideas and principles whose point of origin was fascist ideology, and whose effects were not merely external. For these did take root among a few of the Jewish youth movements, and their residues could be found among the non-Zionist youth movements and, on occasion, among the Zionist movements as well. Even so, concepts like those of *Mensch und Scholle* and *Blut und Boden*, or sentiments on the order of "Liberalism, meaning the extinction of responsibilities, which thereby drives men into the crisis of having nothing to sustain them",[97] or a partiality for thinking in terms of "human material", although discernibly present, never took hold of the youth movement to the extent of determining its essential nature. Here again Kellermann is correct in accounting for the noticeable similarities of state of mind in the Jewish and Gentile youth movements by pointing to their shared past, time of life, landscape, language, and history.[98]

Indeed, we should not be greatly surprised to discover that eighteen-year-old youths who left Germany in 1939, after having lived for over six years under a fascist regime, should have absorbed some of the Nazi racist vocabulary. Nor should such reported instances serve as an occasion for round moral condemnation of the sort indulged in by Hermann Meier-Cronemeyer, who seizes upon such a case in order to support his own particular thesis.[99]

What is astonishing, however, is the capacity of the Jewish youth movement to sustain itself as a bastion – possibly the last – of the ideas and traditions of the youth movement as it was originally, and at a time when no trace of these survived within the ambience of the Third *Reich*.

> "Makkabism means faith in the might of moral power. We therefore stand for that part of mankind which does not believe in the enduring success of brute force and sophistry. We believe that these dark forces are laying siege to human progress, which increasingly ennobles and is guided by the laws of true community, democracy and humanity."[100]

1933.) However, no Jewish-Zionist youth movement would ever agree with the concluding line of this poem: "Nicht ob es lebe – ob es willig diene / bestimmt den Wert von seinem eigenen Sein."

[96]See Chaim Schatzker, 'Emdato ha-yehudit-germanit shel tnuat ha-noar ha-yehudi be-Germania be-et milhemet ha-olam ha-rishona, ve-hashpaato shel ha-milhama al emda zu' ('The Jewish-German Position of the Jewish Youth Movement in Germany during the First World War, and the Influence of the War on that Position'), in *Mehkarim be-toldot am ysrael ve-Erets-Yisrael*, vol. II, Haifa 1972, p. 192 (in Hebrew).

[97]See *Hasolel. Blatt der Mittleren der jüdischen Jugendgemeinschaft Habonim Noar Chaluzi*, September 1933, pp. 12–13.

[98]See note 94.

[99]Meier-Cronemeyer, *Deutschlands jüdische Jugendbewegung*, *op. cit.*, p. 369, note 31.

[100]'Die Idee des Makabi', in *Handbuch des Macabi Hacair*, Czechoslovakia, Bratislava 1935.

In Germany itself words like these could no longer be said openly, but even there the written statements of the Jewish youth movement warn against the threat of "cultural fascism".[101]

Thus *Habonim* declared of itself: "We have always striven in our education to reject those authoritarian ways of thinking, as they are called, which are current in the world today." But, more than this, it was in its very mode of existence that the Jewish youth movement in Germany showed its rejection of the evils of such authoritarianism.

---

[101] *Jüdischer Pfadfinderbund Makkabi Hazair*, Hachschara Arzith, *Mitteilungsblatt*, April 1936.

Bearers of a Common Fate? The "Non-Aryan" Christian "Fate-Comrades" of the Paulus-Bund, 1933–1939

BY WERNER COHN

In Hitler's Germany, as everywhere in the Jewish Diaspora, there were Jews, there were non-Jews, and there those who partook a little of each and whom I shall call the partial Jews.[1] This latter group was as numerous as the Jews themselves. Since they combined what Nazi theory held to be incombinable – the "Aryan" and the Jewish – the partial Jews were something of an embarrassment in the Nazi state. And, from what I have learned from interviewing some partial Jews who survived the Nazi era, it would appear that most of them tried to hide their status, to keep it, if not secret, at least as inconspicuous as possible.[2] But some among them, for a variety of reasons, saw fit to organise as a special interest group.

Six months after Hitler's rise to power, on 20th July 1933 to be exact, the otherwise unknown Gustav Friedrich of Berlin organised the *Reichsverband christlich-deutscher Staatsbürger nichtarischer oder nicht rein arischer Abstammung e.V.* The group changed names several times during its six-year existence:[3] to *Reichsverband der nichtarischen Christen e.V.* in December 1934; to *Paulus-Bund, Vereinigung nichtarischer Christen e.V* in September 1936; and finally, after membership became

---

[1] I have been able to put together an almost complete set of copies of the original documents of the *Paulus-Bund* through the extraordinary kindness of a number of individuals and institutions, to all of whom I owe gratitude. The two largest sets of documents came from 1) Archiv, Institut für Zeitgeschichte, Munich, Sammlung ED 198 (Rudolf Schiff), Miss Karin Popp, Archivist; and 2) a collection of documents in the private possession of Professor Klaus Herrmann, Concordia University, Montreal. Smaller sets came from Yad Vashem in Jerusalem, Miss Ora Alcalay, Head Librarian; Professor Werner Jochmann, Hamburg; The Reverend Ernest Gordon, Bungay, England; Mr. Werner Goldberg, Berlin; and Mrs. Christiane Ilisch, Berlin. I have also received memoirs and other information from Dr. Lutz-Eugen Reutter of Düsseldorf, Mrs. Ursula Gaupp of Havertown, Penna., Mrs. Claire Gysin-Morgenstern of Riehen (Switzerland), Mrs. Lulu Gembicki of Frankfurt, Mrs. Ingeborg Hecht-Studniczka of Freiburg, Mr. Werner A. Zehden of Berlin, Mr. Gerhard Wundermacher of Hamburg, Mr. Rudolf Schiff of Bremerhaven, and others too numerous to mention. Additional archival collections where some of this material may be found are reported in Lutz-Eugen Reutter, *Katholische Kirche als Fluchthelfer im Dritten Reich. Die Betreuung von Auswanderern durch den St. Raphaels-Verein*, Hamburg 1971, pp. 212f. and 227.
[2] Cf. Appendix II, Document M.
[3] The name changes seem to have been effected under pressure from the government. See Reutter, *op. cit.*, pp. 212–213.

327

restricted on "racial" grounds, to *Vereinigung 1937 vorläufiger Reichsbürger nicht volldeutschblütiger Abstammung e.V.* in July 1937. The organisation was finally dissolved by governmental decree on 10th August 1939. Following the informal custom of some of its former members I shall here use the term *Paulus-Bund*, as a matter of convenience, to refer to the organisation in all its stages.[4]

From the beginning, the group actively sought to recruit as members all those Christian Germans who had some discernible Jewish ancestry. It saw its primary purpose as representing the interests of its members *vis-à-vis* the authorities. Together with this practical aim, and undoubtedly as part of it, the organisation propounded a point of view concerning the status of its constituency. This point of view can be summarised as follows: 1) We are German and our loyalty is exclusively German; the fact that we had Jewish ancestors, which we do not deny, in no way detracts from this. 2) We are sincere Christians,[5] whether Catholic or Protestant. The Christian baptism has permanently cut all ties not only to Judaism but to the Jewish people.[6] 3) We are absolutely loyal to the National Socialist government.

There is one term that appears and reappears from the beginning to the end in the voluminous printed and mimeographed material issued by this organisation: *Schicksalsgenosse*, "fate-comrade". In time this term became emblematic of the *Paulus-Bund* and its literature; it characterised and identified the organisation and was in many ways comparable to the term *Genosse* ("comrade") in the Left-wing press of the Weimar Republic and the characteristic *Parteigenosse* and *Volksgenosse*[7] in that of the Nazis.

The German *Schicksalsgenosse*, a compound noun that combines the notion of

[4]The documentation relating to the group consists mainly of its monthly "newsletter", actually more of a monthly journal of opinion and contemplation as well as news, which was originally known as *Mitteilungsblatt des Reichsverbandes christlich-deutscher Staatsbürger nichtarischer oder nicht rein arischer Abstammung e.V.* Each issue prominently displayed the warning "For Members Only". The complete name of this publication changed a number of times to indicate the changing names of the organisation. However the first term, *Mitteilungsblatt*, remained throughout. I have been able to examine all the monthly issues, from October 1933 to June 1939, with the following exceptions: issues 10 and 11 of 1937, and issues 5 and 9 of 1938. Henceforth, I shall cite this publication simply as *M*, followed by date of publication. The journal appeared in mimeographed form until December 1934 and was printed beginning with the issue of January 1935. When I cite from this publication, or from any of the other documents, it is in my translation from originally German texts.
[5]"We are not just holders of a baptismal certificate (Wir sind keine Taufscheinchristen) . . . but believing Christians, deeply rooted in Christian education and *Weltanschauung*." Richard Wolff, *M*, 20th July 1934, p. 1. The term *Taufscheinchristen* – literally "baptismal-certificate-Christians" – became one of the *Shibboleths* of the organisation.
[6]"For all of us, the religious and ethnic (volksmässig) ties to Judaism have been broken precisely by this baptism . . . we state with emphasis that we, baptised non-Aryans, whether of mixed or unmixed blood, continue to feel ourselves as Germans." Pastor Paul Leo, *M*, October 1935, p. 55. This is one of several such pronouncements. The view is contrary to the "racial" antisemitism that the Nazis took over from nineteenth-century thinkers, according to which no baptism can diminish the Jewish qualities of the new Christian. See Adolf Hitler, *Mein Kampf* (English translation), Sentry Edition, Boston 1962, pp. 120, 311, 307, and *passim*. Cf. also Jacob Katz, *From Prejudice to Destruction. Anti-Semitism 1700–1933*, Cambridge, Mass. 1980, pp. 207 and *passim*.
[7]On *Volksgenosse*, see Appendix II, note to Document A. On *Genosse* and its compounds, see also Herbert Bartholmes, *Bruder, Bürger, Freund, Genosse*, Göteborg 1970, pp. 175ff.

"fate", *Schicksal*, with that of *Genosse*, "comrade", can more generally be translated as "fellow sufferer". It was used by the organisation to designate its individual members as well as all those whom it wished to recruit to membership. Until February 1937 at least, these included all Christians who had identifiable Jewish ancestors. The term was never used to include Jews; one passage describes Jews as helping "their own fate-comrades" (see Document B in Appendix II).

A word needs to be said about the potential constituency of the group. Since the days of Moses Mendelssohn, a hundred and fifty years previously, substantial numbers of Jews had married non-Jews and had become Christian in the process; others had converted to Christianity without benefit of intermarriage. Insofar as the Jewish origins were known, there was always a tendency to regard all such "new Christians"[8] as in some way partially Jewish.

In defiance of this social reality, formal rules did not (and do not!) recognise "partially Jewish"; neither the traditional German civil law, nor the Jewish *Halakhah*, nor Christian religious legislation: a person is formally either Jewish or not. In the autumn of 1935, as we shall see, the Nuremberg Laws sought to divide the whole world of the partially Jewish artificially by counting the number of Jewish grandparents. But since the degree of "racial mixture" could not always be determined with any reliability, and since, moreover, various degrees of such "mixture" could typically be found in the same family (the child of a "half-Jew" would be a "quarter-Jew", for instance), the world of the partially Jewish continued to form, in fact if not in law, a richly variegated but nevertheless seamless whole.

It was to this world that the new organisation sought to appeal. The founding leadership referred to this population as the "non-Aryan Christians", reflecting the Nazi tendency in the pre-Nuremberg days to lump together all those who were less than "purely Aryan". Some Christian charitable activities aside,[9] the *Paulus-Bund* was alone, in the whole Hitler period, in taking upon itself the task of providing some institutional shelter for the partially Jewish population.

We shall never be able to ascertain precisely the size of this population of potential members of the *Paulus-Bund*. The very boundaries of the category, no matter what scheme of classification one uses, are necessarily imprecise. First, the amount of "Jewish blood" considered for defining Aryan purity varied, not only informally, in the public mind, but even in the formal rules of the government and Party. For example, a "quarter Jew" (or "*Mischling* Second Degree") was to be considered the equal of a "German-blooded" under the Nuremberg Laws;[10] but there were all kinds of exceptions: he could not enter the

---

[8]Yosef Hayim Yerushalmi has shown similarities to the situation in the Portugal and Spain of the fifteenth and sixteenth centuries: *Assimilation and Racial Anti-Semitism. The Iberian and the German Models*, Leo Baeck Memorial Lecture 26, New York 1982.

[9]Regarding the Catholic church, see Reutter, *op. cit.* For the Protestant efforts, see the memoirs of the man who directed them: Propst Heinrich Grüber, *Erinnerungen aus sieben Jahrzehnten*, Köln 1968.

[10]See Bernhard Lösener and Friedrich A. Knost, *Die Nürnberger Gesetze*, Berlin 1942; Joseph Walk (ed.), *Das Sonderrecht für die Juden im NS-Staat*, Heidelberg 1981, p. 404.

Party, and according to the law of 29th September 1933, nobody whose family contained even a single Jewish ancestor at any time after January 1800 could be a "farmer" (*Bauer*).[11] Second, the amount of genealogical information that was available to the authorities, or even to the individuals affected, naturally varied with circumstances. Third, neither the administrative policies of the government, nor the willingness of its constituent agencies to enforce them, were uniform or even predictable.[12]

With these limitations in mind, I have nevertheless arrived at an estimate of approximately half a million partial Jews, about the same number as religiously affiliated Jews, in the Germany of 1933. The grounds for this estimate are given in Appendix I.

Of this half million eligible members, what proportion ever joined the *Paulus-Bund*? I have nowhere found an accounting of national membership figures, but each issue of the monthly newsletter published the number of copies that had been printed. This number was 3,400 in January 1935, then climbed to 5,000 in 1936 (reaching a height of 6,000 for the single issue of July–August 1936), then went down to 3,500 after the split of mid-1937, and finally stabilised at 3,300 until it ceased publication in 1939.[13] The publication was sent to family units, so we can multiply these figures by three or four to get an idea of how many individuals were reached by it. It would seem that the very maximum that could have been reached is less than twenty thousand, or four percent of the partially Jewish population. Comparable figures for the Jewish press in Germany at the time show a total circulation of more than a million copies of Jewish periodicals; as the *Philo-Lexikon* points out, every Jewish adult and child read an average of two Jewish periodicals per month.[14] These circulation figures point to a state of affairs, borne out by conversations I have had with numerous Jewish and partially Jewish survivors of the Nazi era in Germany, in which the Jewish organisations encompassed their total potential constituency, while most of the partial Jews – *Mischlinge*, Christian "full Jews", or whatever mixture – had never as much as heard of the *Paulus-Bund*.[15]

[11] *Ibid.*, p. 53. The law concerning farming remained in force even after the Nuremberg Laws despite the fact that it seemed to contradict the principles enunciated at Nuremberg.

[12] Uwe Dietrich Adam, *Judenpolitik im Dritten Reich*, Düsseldorf 1972, pp. 330–333.

[13] The issues in 1933 and 1934 were mimeographed and did not carry this information.

[14] *Philo-Lexikon*, Berlin 1935, p. 558.

[15] At least two recent books of memoirs by *Mischling* survivors of the Third *Reich* do mention the *Paulus-Bund*: Ingeborg Hecht, *Invisible Walls. A German Family under the Nuremberg Laws*, New York 1985, p. 24; and Elsbeth von Ameln, *Köln, Appellhofplatz. Rückblick auf ein bewegtes Leben*, Köln 1985, pp. 81–85. But on the other hand, one key document concerning the fate of Christians of Jewish origin (Arthur Goldschmidt, *Geschichte der evangelischen Gemeinde Theresienstadt, 1942–1945*, Tübingen 1948) makes no such mention. Another way of looking at this question is to inquire how many of the known "non-Aryan" Protestant clergymen belonged to the group. Eight such names are mentioned by Richard Gutteridge, *Open Thy Mouth for the Dumb! The German Evangelical Church and the Jews, 1879–1950*, Oxford 1976, pp. 122–124. Of these, it would appear that only one had any connection with the *Paulus-Bund*, judging by Heinrich Spiero's listing of clergymen who were members of the organisation (I obtained this list through the kindness of his daughter, Mrs. Christiane Ilisch – see below for further information on this material). Spiero gives sixteen names, and there are an additional four, who were from time to time mentioned in the *Paulus-Bund* literature.

Before recounting the story of the *Paulus-Bund* and the stages it traversed in its six-year history, I must sketch, as background, the evolution in status of the partial Jews in Nazi Germany.

The doctrinaire Nazis, and other "racist" antisemites before them, refused to see any difference whatever between a Jew and a Christian who was "tainted" by partial or wholly Jewish origin. This doctrine, at least in its strict interpretation by official Nazi party sources, lumped together all those who had any Jewish ancestors whatever; in the Nazis' specialised vocabulary of racism, the fight was to be conducted equally against *"Juden und Judenstämmlinge"*.[16]

While the partially Jewish never received as much emphasis as full Jews, some unfavourable attention was paid to them from the beginnings of "racist" antisemitism in the late nineteenth century. Before the *Machtergreifung* and after, during the years of Nazi rule, antisemitic agitators would castigate Christians who had Jews among their ancestors: "It is impossible to count as Jew only one who has a Jewish father or a Jewish mother, i.e. fifty percent Jewish blood. Experience shows that Jewish blood is frequently stronger than Aryan blood, not only in grandchildren, but also in great-grandchildren and even further on down the line."[17] Hitler thought that offspring of intermarriage would always take on the characteristics of Jews.[18]

As far as "baptised Jews" – former Jews who had converted to Christianity – were concerned, the Nazis' hatred and contempt knew few bounds. Hitler criticised the religious antisemitism of the Austrian Christian Social Party of his youth because it failed to regard such people as Jews.[19] The Nazis' specialised vocabulary had a term for such converts: *Taufjude*.[20]

It was under the influence of such doctrines that the first laws and regulations concerning the partial Jews were promulgated by the new Nazi government in 1933. In April there was a new civil service law that contained the first "Aryan paragraph", a requirement that civil servants from then on were to have no Jewish ancestors.[21] Such "Aryan paragraphs" were then introduced into many new laws and regulations; a great many non-governmental and voluntary organisations followed suit.[22] While some discriminatory regulations were specifically directed against "Jews", as many were written against "non-Aryans"

[16]Cf. Christoph Cobet, *Der Wortschatz des Antisemitismus in der Bismarckzeit*, München 1973, p. 229.
[17]Graf E. Reventlow, *Judas Kampf und Niederlage in Deutschland. 150 Jahre Judenfrage*, Berlin 1937, p. 69. See also F. Roderich-Stoltheim [Theodor Fritsch], *Das Rätsel des jüdischen Erfolges*, Leipzig 1919, pp. 238–239.
[18]Hitler, *op. cit.*, pp. 315–316.
[19]Hitler, *op. cit.*, p. 120.
[20]Julius Streicher's publishing house, for example, published a lengthy fulmination against Jews in which a special section is devoted to the writings of *Taufjuden*. The chapter ends with an exclamation: "Baptismal water indeed does not possess too much power. Yid simply remains yid [Jud bleibt eben doch Jud]!" Richard Wilhelm Stock, *Die Judenfrage durch fünf Jahrhunderte*, Nürnberg 1939, pp. 263–299.
[21]Exceptions were provided for combat veterans and for those who had already been in office on 1st August 1914. The law of 7th April was amplified by regulations on 14th April. The latter specified that all grandparents must be "Aryan". See Walk, *op. cit.*, pp. 12–13.
[22]Walk, *op. cit.*, Part I, pp. 1–128, gives a comprehensive account of this body of law and regulation.

and therefore included all the "non-Aryan" Christians of whatever degree of Jewish ancestry. The result is that the "fate-comrades" found that their legal status, if perhaps not their actual treatment by the authorities, approximated that of Jews.[23]

For roughly two and a half years this radical approach to racial purity was essentially the law of the land. Apparently it was found sufficiently unwieldy or inconvenient or embarrassing[24] to be profoundly modified by the Nuremberg Laws of September 1935 and subsequent administrative regulations. These laws gave considerable relief to many partial Jews by distinguishing sharply among four classes: 1) three or four Jewish grandparents made one a "Jew", regardless of one's own religion; 2) two Jewish grandparents resulted in a *Mischling* First Grade; 3) a single Jewish grandparent defined the *Mischling* Second Class; 4) an individual with no Jewish grandparent was to be considered "German-blooded". This four-fold classification was to replace the old dichotomous scheme of "Aryan" versus "non-Aryan".[25]

It has been claimed that this distinction between "full Jews" and the two classes of *Mischlinge* represented a victory of non-Nazi officialdom over the zealots of the Party.[26] But be that as it may, and despite the difficulties and ambiguities of the scheme, to which we shall return, there is no doubt that it resulted in a substantial and unexpected improvement in the legal position of many of the partial Jews.

If there was a pendular swing in Nazi policy towards partial Jews, from a doctrinaire racism in the early days to concessions to *Mischlinge* by the Nuremberg Laws, it seems that towards the end of the war there was some movement back towards greater persecution of *Mischlinge*. After the invasion of Russia in June 1941, the Nazi apparatus began to plan for the Holocaust, and it seems that at least some of the planners wished to include the partial Jews. In the

---

[23]Regarding this first period, see Adam, *op. cit.*, pp. 69ff.; Lösener and Knost, *op. cit.*, pp. 26ff., and Bernhard Lösener, 'Als Rassereferent im Reichsministerium des Innern', *Vierteljahrshefte für Zeitgeschichte*, IX (July 1961), pp. 264–313.

[24]Since it would appear that almost one percent of the population had ascertainable Jewish ancestors (see Appendix I), it is not surprising therefore to find some partial Jews also among the Nazi elite. Cf. H. G. Adler, *Der verwaltete Mensch. Studien zur Deportation der Juden aus Deutschland*, Tübingen 1974, pp. 302, 335; Raul Hilberg, *The Destruction of the European Jews*, rev. edn., New York 1985, p. 79.

[25]See Lösener and Knost, *op. cit.*, pp. 32–34. This publication by Nazi officials is the most thorough, detailed, and precise legal commentary on the Nuremberg Laws, with special attention to the problems of partial Jews.

[26]The remarkable story of how this legislation was drafted was first told, undoubtedly with some self-exculpatory motive, by Lösener, 'Als Rassereferent', *loc. cit.*, one of the key legal experts involved. Lösener professes to have had great concern for the welfare of the partial Jews, and there is no compelling reason to doubt him. But we now have a more complete and more balanced account: Jeremy Noakes, 'Wohin gehören die "Judenmischlinge"? Die Entstehung der ersten Durchführungsverordnungen zu den Nürnberger Gesetzen', in Ursula Büttner (ed.), *Das Unrechtsregime. Internationale Forschung über den Nationalsozialismus. Festschrift für Werner Jochmann zum 65. Geburtstag*, Band 2, Verfolgung – Exil – Belasteter Neubeginn, Hamburg 1986, pp. 69–89. Noakes shows how the final draft, under Hitler's personal guidance, was influenced both by Party ideologues and by the more pragmatic bureaucrats of the government ministries.

end most of the "non-Aryan Christians" were not killed like Jews, but their position deteriorated substantially.[27] But these developments lie outside the period of the *Paulus-Bund*.

The *Paulus-Bund* was formed immediately after the first "Aryan paragraphs" were set out; it existed throughout the preparation for, and then the amplification of the Nuremberg legislation. These developments must obviously be kept in mind when looking at the stages which the organisation itself traversed. I suggest that there were three such stages in the history of the *Paulus-Bund*.

In the first stage – to September 1935 – the organisation was as young as the Nazi regime itself, and there was room to experiment with various themes and emphases. On the whole, the period was one of stressing the theme of German Nationalism. The second stage – to February 1937 – took place after the regime had consolidated itself, and, most important for the *Paulus-Bund*, had enacted the Nuremberg Laws. Outwardly the main theme became one of adaptation to the new legislation. But since this legislation was directed at introducing "racial" division among "non-Aryan Christians", events were building up to the crisis of February 1937 when the group split.

These first two stages flow into one another and are marked more by a change in emphasis than by any apparent radical reorientation. They represent the rising action in the drama of the *Paulus-Bund*. After the crisis came a third period and the action fell.

One way of labelling the stages is by reference to the men who served as leaders of the group. The leadership as a whole was unstable. For example, of the eight men[28] who are shown as Council members in November 1933,[29] only three had appeared on a similar list the previous August.[30] By the following March, only six of the eight are still on the Council.[31] The two chairmen of the future – Spiero and Lesser – do not make their appearance in any of these early lists.[32]

The founding chairman of the group was Gustav Friedrich, who died on 31st October 1933.[33] The Berlin lawyer Günter Alexander-Katz became a temporary chairman while a search was instituted for someone who would be known "as

[27]See Adam, *op. cit.*, pp. 316–333, and Walk, *op. cit.* During the very last days of the Nazi regime, and apparently against all dictates of rational self-interest, the Nazis instituted a frenzied "cleansing" of remaining partial Jews in government ministries. The story is told by Uwe Dietrich Adam, 'Persecution of the Jews, Bureaucracy and Authority in the Totalitarian State', in *LBI Year Book XXIII* (1978), pp. 139–148. Finally, we have a general discussion of the place accorded to the *Mischlinge* in the planning of the Holocaust: John A. S. Grenville, 'Die "Endlösung" und die "Judenmischlinge" im Dritten Reich', in Büttner (ed.), *Das Unrechtsregime, op. cit.*, pp. 91–121.
[28]The leadership was overwhelmingly male. My materials show only one woman Council member, Alice Salomon, and that apparently for only a short time. Her name appears in a 1935 document. See Appendix II, Document H; we know that she emigrated from Germany in 1937.
[29]*M*, 10th November 1933, p. 1.
[30]First circular letter, signed by Gustav Friedrich, dated August 1933.
[31]*M*, 20th March 1934, p. 2.
[32]Lesser is listed, in what appears to have been a supplement to *M*, 9th February 1934, as one of the many lawyers who belonged to the organisation.
[33]*M*, 10th November 1933, p. 1.

widely as possible among the German people".[34] By March 1934, Richard Wolff, already on the Council since at least the previous November, was elected the new chairman. In September 1935 Heinrich Spiero replaced him, only to be himself replaced by Karl Friedrich Lesser in February 1937.

This coming and going of leaders was certainly not in the spirit of the "*Führerprinzip*" that the group professed to practise, and about which more later. We can only speculate why there was so much turnover. Friedrich died in office, and Spiero was replaced in time because he had too many Jewish grandparents. But why Spiero took over from Wolff and why the Council's membership experienced the instability it did must remain matters of conjecture. None of the remaining former members of the group whom I questioned could give an explanation; they had been too young at the time and too far from the leadership to have gained insight into this question. Three possible reasons suggest themselves, and in the absence of more information it seems safest to assume that all three played a role: 1) some of the leaders no doubt had personal reasons to drop out, for example emigration; 2) there are muted hints in the documents of occasional internal conflict in the group, and this may have resulted in some rotation of leadership; 3) the government's secret services may well have insisted on some of the changes.

I. JULY 1933 TO SEPTEMBER 1935: FRIEDRICH AND WOLFF

Neither Friedrich nor Wolff were people in any way known to the public. As far as Friedrich is concerned, even the organisation's literature gives no clue about his background or occupation. His successor Wolff pays him homage after his death: "A courageous, imaginative man, scarcely known in broader circles, Gustav Friedrich founded the organisation in stormy times. Today we thank him for this courageous deed . . ."[35]

On Wolff there is a little more information. He is listed in the 9th edition (published in 1928) of *Wer ist's?* (the German *Who's Who*), as a doctor of philosophy and lecturer in Leipzig. On the occasion of his fiftieth birthday, 9th March 1935, the newsletter published a biographical sketch of 500 words.[36] From this we learn that his ancestors can be documented as resident in Germany since the sixteenth century; that his father had been an architect; that he himself had been baptised Protestant; that he had been a business man, historian, and finally an editor in the service of the Weimar government; and finally that he was married and had four children. Wolff survived the Nazi regime and the war. In 1958 he wrote an article on the *Reichstag* fire; a brief biographical note states that

[34]*Ibid.*
[35]*M*, 20th July 1934, p. 1.
[36]*M*, March 1935, p. 10.

he emigrated from Germany in 1938 and, at the time the article was published, was living in Nairobi as a British citizen.[37]

The first six documents in Appendix II stem from the summer and autumn of 1933. The first, labelled A, is a mimeographed circular letter from Gustav Friedrich, from which I present translated excerpts. Next, B, are excerpts from a speech by another leader of the group, Dr. Günter Alexander-Katz, to a press reception in November. Item C is the translation of a printed sheet of general information. The original bears a logo of the Iron Cross superimposed by the Christian cross (this logo never again appeared in the literature of the organisation). The other material consists of D, an appeal to join, directed to "Christian-German non-Aryans"; E, a page containing a "profession of faith"; and F, the twenty-three paragraphs of the organisation's statutes with a blank "declaration of membership" form. I translate all of items C, D, and E, and excerpts from F.

Some of the themes revealed in these materials were to feature in the organisation's literature throughout its existence, others are specific to this period.[38]

The first and most persisting theme, to remain until the very end, is adaptation. It is repeatedly pointed out that the organisation exists because it has been sanctioned by the government and that absolute loyalty and obedience is owed to that government. Dr. Günter Alexander-Katz, member of the Council, boasts that the group submits its membership records to the Gestapo "for verification" (Document B). The message from the leadership is that the government's policies on "non-Aryan" Christians are to be regretted, but that no power on heaven or earth can change them; that not only must "fate-comrades" accept their fate with dignity but, above all else, that they must indeed accept it.

In adapting to what they considered the organisational principles that modern times required – the *Führerprinzip* of the Nazis (see Document A) – the *Paulus-Bund* organisers were even more in vogue than they perhaps realised. It is true that *Führerprinzip* was a Nazi slogan; but it is also true that the German Communist Party, partly under the influence of the Nazis and partly under that of the Stalin leadership cult, applied it no less vigorously by about 1929.[39] In any case, the *Führer* "business" seems to have been troublesome to the new organisation. In August 1933, two different circular letters from Friedrich list him on the printed letterhead as "*Führer*" of the organisation, but by October the

---

[37]Richard Wolff, 'Der Reichstagsbrand 1933. Ein Forschungsbericht', *Aus Politik und Zeitgeschichte*, (Beilage zu *Das Parlament*), 18th January 1956, pp. 25–52.

[38]Any discussion of materials published in Germany during the Nazi period necessarily raises the question of the extent to which the government had a direct influence on what was published. There is no question that on certain issues there was direct pressure, but we must assume, both from the internal evidence and from what we know about the Jewish press in the same period, that the *Mitteilungsblätter*, too, "by and large . . . functioned independently". Cf. Jacob Boas, 'German-Jewish Internal Politics under Hitler, 1933–1939', in *LBI Year Book XXIX* (1984), pp. 6–7.

[39]Since at least the twelfth party congress of the *Kommunistische Partei Deutschlands* (KPD) in June 1929 – the last of the legal pre-war congresses – the KPD celebrated Ernst Thälmann as the *Führer* of the German proletariat. See Ossip K. Flechtheim, *Die KPD in der Weimarer Republik*, Frankfurt a. Main 1976, p. 256; also Bartholmes, *op. cit.*, pp. 151–154.

word is pasted over and replaced by *Vorsitzender*. The title *"Führer"* is never again assumed by any member of the organisation. No doubt it appeared unseemly and *lèse-majesté* at the time; but we do not know whether it was dropped voluntarily or under pressure from the government.

Secondly, there is the persistent theme of distress. Much of the writing, some in the form of poetry, expresses a sense of unexpected, sudden, undeserved misfortune. The monthly *Mitteilungsblatt* was to become an organ of addressing and consoling the "fate-comrades", of describing their great distress and expressing their modest aspirations. Throughout the history of the organisation the publication mirrors the drastic economic downward mobility of much of the membership. When members with administrative or academic credentials are mentioned, almost invariably their titles are followed by the tell-tale *"i.R."* (*im Ruhestand*) or *"a.D."* (*ausser Dienst*).[40] The newsletter also frequently featured advice on occupational training for the young (become manual workers!), on re-training for adults (ditto), and on emigration (don't expect too much; learn foreign languages). The publication does not often give precise figures, but one report from Frankfurt in March 1935 tells us that a third of the membership is unemployed.[41]

The distress about which we learn in *Paulus-Bund* publications, perhaps very naturally, is exclusively that of "fate-comrades"; Jewish distress, while sometimes alluded to, never provokes the regret, let alone the sympathy of the organisation's writers. This theme and this way of treating it mark the entire history of the organisation.

The subject of mutual aid also makes its appearance at the very beginning and was to become more and more prominent as time went on. The group always seemed to have seen that one of its most important reasons for existence lay in the social services that it could provide to "fate-comrades". The files of the monthly journal give evidence of a vigorous promotion of lectures, musical and theatrical performances, exhibitions of paintings, etc., all of which are described as giving opportunities to "fate-comrade" artists and performers as well as giving edification to the audiences. Much space is taken up by detailing the organisation's employment agency, its counselling facilities, its many courses for adults and children, its youth groups, its dances and social get-togethers. While the scale of all this could of course never equal that of the Jewish *Kulturbund* in the early years of the regime, the spirit is altogether comparable.

These were the items that were to become permanent features of the group, more or less with constancy of emphasis. Other themes proved to be more problematic and variable.

The very early material shows an attenuated but unmistakable antisemitism.

---

[40]This is not true of the Protestant or Catholic clergy who seemed to have continued by and large in service in some capacity. The teaching profession seems to have been particularly hard hit; one symptom is the profusion of "i.R."s and "a.D."s in the announcement for the lecture series. See, for example, the Berlin supplement to *M*, April 1936.

[41]*M*, March 1935.

Both the original circular letter by Gustav Friedrich (Document A) and the speech by Alexander-Katz (Document B) contain the kind of antisemitic references that were common among the "German-Nationalists" (i.e. the circles of the Right-wing non-Nazis) at the time.[42] The leaders of the *Paulus-Bund* always maintained that they were not, and would never be, antisemitic. But they apparently could not resist the fashionable Right-wing formulations of the time; they found a Jewish spirit linked to all that is "un-Germanly" liberal, Pacifist, Left-wing, democratic.

This antisemitism obviously had to be ambivalent: these men, after all, had Jewish ancestors and were considered partially Jewish themselves. Furthermore, unlike so many of their "fate-comrades" who chose to stay out of the organisation, these men would not deny their Jewish ancestors; in fact they often had occasion to polemicise against attempts at hiding one's background. So being partly or fully of the "Jewish race" themselves, the Jewishness they attacked was that of the spirit – the "Talmud spirit", or "Bolshevism", as the occasion demanded – rather than that of "blood". They turned against what they conceived as a voluntary Jewishness which they personally had "overcome".

After 1933, there was no further open expression of antisemitism. We know that the matter was a problem for the "fate-comrades" because the monthly journal would from time to time report that antisemitism, unfortunately, persisted in "our circles". But by the time the group issued its only printed pamphlet in November 1934, explicit antisemitism, racial or otherwise, was

[42]Cf. George L. Mosse, 'Die deutsche Rechte und die Juden', in *Entscheidungsjahr 1932. Zur Judenfrage in der Endphase der Weimarer Republik*. Ein Sammelband herausgegeben von Werner E. Mosse unter Mitwirkung von Arnold Paucker, Tübingen 1965 (Schriftenreihe wissenschaftlicher Abhandlungen des Leo Baeck Instituts 13), pp. 183–248. One of the most striking exemplars of the pervasive antisemitism of the non-Nazi Right wing is a man whose record is nowadays often whitewashed. Pastor Martin Niemöller, later himself to be persecuted by the Nazis, never made a secret of his strong, racial antisemitism. In his *Sätze zur Arierfrage in der Kirche* of November 1933, he opposed the introduction of the "Aryan paragraph" in the Protestant Church on doctrinal grounds, but takes care, nevertheless, to opine that Jews had done great harm to Germany; he also indicates that baptised Christians of Jewish origins are personally distasteful to him (text in Günther van Norden, *Der deutsche Protestantismus im Jahr der nationalsozialistischen Machtergreifung*, Gütersloh 1979, pp. 361–363). As late as 1935, Niemöller goes out of his way to preach hatred against the Jews: "What is the reason for [their] obvious punishment, which has lasted for thousands of years? Dear brethren, the reason is easily given: the Jews brought the Christ of God to the cross!" The text of this sermon, in English, is found in Martin Niemöller, *First Commandment*, London 1937, pp. 243–250. Pastor Paul Leo, a member of the *Paulus-Bund* and, like Niemöller, engaged with the *Bekennende Kirche* in the fight against the "Aryan Paragraph", also expresses antisemitic sentiments in his 1933 memorandum on 'Church and Judaism'. Like Niemöller's *Sätze*, Leo's memorandum maintains that Germany had suffered from the Jews. The memorandum is reported (and described as "a remarkably original, thoughtful and objective composition") by Gutteridge, *op. cit.*, pp. 118–119. Pastor Leo, born in 1893 in Göttingen and related to Moses Mendelssohn through Wilhelm Hensel, emigrated from Germany in 1939 and taught at the Lutheran Seminary in Dubuque, Iowa, where he died in 1958. According to his widow, he and his family had been Christian for several generations but had been designated more than 75% Jewish under the Nazis' race laws. (Interview on 26th July 1986). See also Rudolf Elvers and Hans-Günter Klein (eds.), *Die Mendelssohns in Berlin*, Berlin 1983, p. 55. On the attitude of the *Bekennende Kirche* to the Jews see also the revealing essay by Uriel Tal, 'On Modern Lutheranism and the Jews', in *LBI Year Book XXX* (1985), pp. 203–213.

advisedly rejected.[43] This did not deter writers of the group's publications, however, from continuing to rejoice that they had "overcome" Jewishness.[44]

In any case, this was not a period for generosity of spirit or humane enlightenment. At the end of 1933, made uneasy by rumours of further racist legislation, the group made representations to the authorities: "Speaking on behalf of our membership, we have *protested most sharply* against being compared to Negroes" (emphasis in original).[45]

A theme that was in those days related to antisemitism, German Nationalism, saw some variation in emphasis over time. Stridently political in the first period, it was to become more muted, and more "cultural" rather than political, as time went by.

In the first period of its history, the group's position was similar to that of what was left of the non-Nazi German-Nationalist movement which supported the Nazis from a conservative perspective:[46] without declaring themselves as National Socialists, they went out of their way to show support to the new government and its *Führer*.

There was, of course, always one very important point on which the *Paulus-Bund* leaders differed from the "Aryan" politicians of the Right wing. Where the latter usually tended towards some form of racist interpretation of German nationhood, a matter of "blood" rather than culture, the *Paulus-Bund* leaders insisted that German character was determined by German culture – the German language, German education, participation in Germany's wars. It was those who held to the Jewish religion, according to the leaders of the group, unlike they themselves who had embraced Christianity as part of their attachment to German culture, who were un-German.

Of course the *Paulus-Bund* people were far from disinterested participants in this kind of discussion; their personal status, welfare, and ultimately their safety was involved.

Some of the organisation's pronouncements in this period can only be described as obsequious, not to say sycophantic. The November 1933 newsletter notes with great pride that its press reception had been attended not only by representatives of the domestic and foreign press, but also by dignitaries of the

---

[43]Richard Wolff, *Wir nichtarische Christen*, Frankfurt a.d. Oder 1934. Like the newsletter, this publication is marked "not intended for the general public". Copies of this booklet are now found in the collections of several of the world's larger libraries. This is, unfortunately, not true either of the files of the *Mitteilungsblatt* nor of the ephemera that were produced by the central office in Berlin and the branches in other cities.

[44]These views were frequently expressed by Protestant clergymen who were members of the group, or as religious devotions written by apparent laymen. One such essay, signed by Ernst Cahn and entitled 'Paulus', celebrates St. Paul, the eponym of the organisation, as "the actual vanquisher [*Überwinder*] of the Judaism of his time, which in its religious form is basically still the Judaism of our time". *M*, February 1937, p. 11.

[45]*M*, 23rd December 1933, p. 24.

[46]The most important of these groups had been the *Deutschnationale Volkspartei* (DNVP), see John A. Leopold, *Alfred Hugenberg, The Radical Nationalist Campaign against the Weimar Republic*, New Haven 1977. As we shall see, many if not most of the *Paulus-Bund* leaders had either been members of the DNVP or had belonged to the right-of-centre DVP.

government and the Party.[47] The same issue calls upon the "fate-comrades" to vote *Ja* in the plebiscite of November 12th that was to approve Hitler's withdrawal from the League of Nations. "Non-Aryans", even Jews, still had the right to vote.

This style persisted for more than another year.

When Hindenburg died on 13th August 1934, the chairman of the *Paulus-Bund* solemnly declared that "it is the obvious duty of each German, upon meeting with those of like mind in an organisation for the first time after 2nd August 1934, to commemorate the painful event . . ."[48]

The newsletter's issue of January 1935 carried a front-page editorial by then-chairman Richard Wolff, declaring 1) that "fate-comrades" are in every way loyal Germans, "neither émigrés nor spiritually emigrated" (but he himself did emigrate in 1938, see above); 2) that fellow Germans in the Saar will soon have the opportunity of "returning home to the *Reich*"; and 3) that the "fate-comrades", similarly, hope for this chance.[49] Two months later, the returns from the Saar plebiscite now in, the "fate-comrades" expressed their satisfaction.[50]

On 16th March 1935 Hitler breached the Versailles prohibition against universal military conscription. Richard Wolff welcomed the step: "Once again the people's best – fathers, sons and brothers – are called on to work for the protection of the country's honour and the maintenance of peace." At the same time he wrote to the Minister reponsible for the Army to urge that "fate-comrades", too, be eligible for conscription.[51] (Eventually certain ones were.)

While the *Paulus-Bund* in this period shows outspoken political support for the Nazi government, it also assumes a surprisingly frank and implicitly anti-Nazi tone when it takes sides in the Protestants' "church struggle" at this time. This conflict inside the Protestant churches, it will be remembered, had as its fulcrum a question of great interest to the "fate-comrades", *viz.* whether the "Aryan paragraph" should be applied to the Protestant clergy.[52]

The organisation goes on record, without mincing any words whatever, for the full spiritual equality in the Protestant Church for Christians of Jewish ancestry. The relevant statements – translated as Documents E and F in Appendix II – are both found in ephemera rather than in the newsletter. Such outright defence of the "non-Aryans" interests was never again to appear in the literature of the organisation. Document F, the original of which exists in mimeographed form, is

[47]*M*, 10th November 1933, p. 2.
[48]*M*, 1st September 1934, p. 1.
[49]*M*, January 1935, p. 1.
[50]*M*, March 1935, p. 12.
[51]*M*, April 1935, p. 15. It is of some interest here to note that in welcoming Hitler's withdrawal from the League of Nations in 1934 and his introduction of conscription in 1935, the *Paulus-Bund* was in full accord with leaders of the non-Nazi *Bekennende Kirche*. Pastor Martin Niemöller, for example, gave enthusiastic support to Hitler on both of these issues. See Jürgen Schmidt, *Martin Niemöller im Kirchenkampf*, Hamburg 1971, pp. 40ff., 277–278, 317f., and *passim*; also James Bentley, *Martin Niemöller*, Oxford 1984, pp. 78–79 and *passim*.
[52]The two standard works on the "church struggle" are by German scholars, one from the German Democratic Republic, the other from the Federal Republic: 1) Kurt Meier (G.D.R.), *Der Evangelische Kirchenkampf*, 3 vols., Göttingen 1976, 1984; 2) Klaus Scholder, *Die Kirchen und das Dritte Reich*, 2 vols., Berlin 1977, 1984.

particularly noteworthy since it completely omits the customary show of deference to the Nazi government. I have seen no record of how the supervising authorities reacted. We do know that all *Paulus-Bund* activities were watched by the secret services of the regime (more on this below), and it may well be that the publication of this particular circular was eventually punished in some way.[53]

II. SEPTEMBER 1935 TO FEBRUARY 1937: SPIERO

The succession from Richard Wolff to Heinrich Spiero occurred on 16th September 1935. The October newsletter announced in a framed panel on the front page that Wolff had requested a leave of absence until the following January because he had undertaken "a great scholarly task". Heinrich Spiero, "famed historian of German literature", was named acting chairman. In the January issue a similar panel announced the election of Spiero as permanent chairman. Wolff, it was said, would devote himself to scholarly work on a permanent basis. He was thanked, perfunctorily, for "what he had done for the construction of the organisation". The available materials give no satisfactory explanation for the causes of this change in leadership.

But a great deal is known of the life and work of Heinrich Spiero.[54] Where the other leaders of the *Paulus-Bund* had been almost totally obscure, Spiero, if not exactly famous, had gained a reputation in pre-Hitler Germany as a critic and historian of German literature.

Born on 24th March 1876 to a Jewish family in Königsberg (then East Prussia, now Soviet Union), he had been baptised a Protestant at the age of eighteen by a well-known preacher of the day, Alfred Thaer. He studied both literature and law, worked in his father's business and as a university lecturer, and wrote more than thirty books in the course of his life. Most of his publications deal with nineteenth-century German writers. In 1929 he published an autobiographical work, *Schicksal und Anteil*, in which he recounts his personal acquaintance with many of the literary figures of his time.[55]

There are several indications in these materials that Spiero's relationship to his Jewish background was disturbed. His autobiography does not mention his origins. When relating encounters with Jews he talks like a curious outsider. He mentions his friendship with the preacher Alfred Thaer without disclosing that

---

[53]The copy I have comes from Professor Herrmann's collection of *Paulus-Bund* materials. In its appearance it conforms to that of the other ephemera issued at the time. It would seem to have been circulated to the whole of the Protestant membership but there is no absolute guarantee that it actually was.

[54]One of Spiero's daughters, Mrs. Christiane Ilisch of Berlin, has kindly furnished me with information about her father; she has also sent me some recently published and unpublished commemorative materials; in addition, she has provided me with unpublished autobiographical notes which her father compiled after the war.

[55]Radio programme devoted to Spiero by *Sender Freies Berlin*, 20th October 1961, script by Gert Dimmer, p. 2. In 1958, the West Berlin government named a small street after him: *Spieroweg*, in a new section of Spandau.

this man had converted him to the Christian faith. There are other oddities of this kind in the book.

Spiero became best known for his work on the nineteenth-century German novelist Wilhelm Raabe (1831–1910). Spiero devoted several books to Raabe and is sometimes credited with having brought Raabe to the attention of the German reading public. In 1931, as part of its celebration of Raabe's 100th birthday, the University of Göttingen awarded Spiero an honorary doctorate in recognition of his Raabe studies.

Whatever Raabe's place in the history of literature, he and Gustav Freytag, with whom his name is usually linked in this context, merit at least a mention in the history of German antisemitism. Both Raabe and Freytag are considered Liberals but their hostile portrayal of Jews is often cited as one of the contributing factors in the "racial" antisemitism of the late nineteenth century.[56] In Raabe's novel *Hungerpastor* (1862), which is the one most often mentioned in this connection, the thoroughly repulsive villain is not only a Jew but a Jew who converts to Christianity. One need not have recourse to a psychoanalytic interpretation to suspect that this novel had a personal meaning for Spiero.

George Mosse finds that Raabe's antisemitic bias is shown in his portrayal of Heinrich Heine.[57] Perhaps to counter criticism of this kind, Spiero reports having seen Raabe nine days before the latter's death in 1910. Spiero tells him that the Hamburg Senate has just approved a memorial statue for Heine, and Raabe is delighted: "He pounded the table, in the old-fashioned manner of swinging the right arm wide: 'that really is splendid!' "[58]

Spiero's own writings show considerable open-mindedness. The negative comments concerning Jews that mark the writings of many other "non-Aryan Christians" seem to be completely absent in Spiero's. In *Schicksal und Anteil* he reports friendships and positive judgements for various political personalities, including some on the Left. But there is no doubt that his own commitments were on the Right, and in the context of the times this was bound to have some antisemitic implication. He carried his monarchist sympathies into the Weimar Republic: "The monarchy cannot be restored, but the monarchic principle will become extinguished for the author only with the end of his life."[59] More relevant is his membership[60] on executive committees of the antisemitic *Deutschnationale*

[56]See Katz, *From Prejudice to Destruction, op. cit.*, pp. 203–209; and George L. Mosse, *Germans and Jews. The Right, the Left, and the Search for a "Third Force", in Pre-Nazi Germany*, New York 1970, London 1971, pp. 34–60. The Nazi propaganda volume by Theodor Fritsch, *Handbuch der Judenfrage*, 21st edition, Leipzig 1937, lists Spiero as a "Jew" but gives him credit for his work on Raabe (*ibid.*, p. 379). Raabe and Freytag, in turn, are praised for their "serious" contributions to antisemitism (*ibid.*, p. 522).

[57]Mosse, *op. cit.*, pp. 51–52.

[58]Heinrich Spiero, *Schicksal und Anteil*, Berlin 1929, p. 164.

[59]From Heinrich Spiero, *Deutschlands Schicksal und Schuld*, published in 1920, cited in an unpublished biographical study by Dr. Sabine Gova, Toulouse, a daughter of Spiero's.

[60]After the war, Spiero compiled a number of lists to cover various aspects of his past activities. One such list is headed 'Meine ehrenamtliche Tätigkeit', and shows membership on two different executive committees of the DNVP.

Volkspartei (DNVP), Hitler's allies in 1933.[61] His relationship to Jews and Jewishness was not simple.

Other leaders of the *Paulus-Bund* had similar Right-wing backgrounds. When Spiero entered the Council in September 1935, he found there, among others, three former board members of the DNVP and one former board member of the *Deutsche Volkspartei* (DVP).[62] The latter party, smaller than the DNVP, had also been on the Right and had also had antisemitic tendencies, but in both respects had been more moderate than the DNVP.

The only other leading member of the *Paulus-Bund* about whom we have party-political information is Rudolf Schiff who was chairman for Leipzig in the final period of the *Paulus-Bund*. Before 1933 he had been a member of the student group of the DVP.[63]

Of course these political proclivities were the leadership's and not necessarily those of the rank and file. I have corresponded about this question with some former members of the group. One such correspondent has pointed out that he himself had had Socialist sympathies during those years. He and his friends, all young members of the rank and file, simply found the organisation useful because it provided social fellowship among the afflicted partial Jews and practical help in dealing with the authorities. The politics of the Council and the newsletter, in his opinion, represented the views of the formal leadership and perhaps its older members, but they meant very little to the young people; the Right-wing pronouncements, did, however, provide a convenient cover *vis-à-vis* the government.

In the period of Spiero's leadership we can discern two major themes in the literature and activities of the *Paulus-Bund*. One is manifest and explicit: adaptation to the Nuremberg Laws. The other is not explicitly expressed, but it is foreshadowed in the group's insistence on adapting to Nuremberg; this is the theme of the coming split of the organisation along "racial" lines.

Spiero took office at the very start of what we may call the Nuremberg system of classificatory persecution. We have already sketched the basic four-fold taxonomy of this method: 1. Jews defined "racially"; 2. non-Jews; 3. and 4., two in-between groups. The system was initiated on 15th September 1935 with the enactment of a new citizenship law and another one "to protect German blood and German honour". It would appear that the system was difficult to institute in one fell swoop; in any case it evolved over time to the accompaniment of a flood of additional regulations,[64] and for almost a year and a half the *Paulus-Bund* continued to join together that which Nuremberg would put asunder: "racial" (but baptised) "full" Jews on the one hand, *Mischlinge* on the other.

---

[61]Concerning the antisemitic nature of this party, see George L. Mosse, 'Die Deutsche Rechte und die Juden', *loc. cit.*
[62]Heinrich Spiero, unpublished notes on the *Paulus-Bund*, post-war.
[63]Information sheet to accompany the Rudolf Schiff collection, Institut für Zeitgeschichte, Munich. After the war, Schiff lived in the German Democratic Republic where he was a member of the *Sozialdemokratische Partei Deutschlands* and then of the *Sozialistische Einheitspartei Deutschlands*. Later he moved to Bremerhaven in West Germany, where he lives today.
[64]Walk, *Das Sonderrecht*, *op. cit.*, Part II, lists the regulations. See also Lösener and Knost, *op. cit.*

Adapting to the Nuremberg system, for the *Paulus-Bund*, meant first of all understanding it, and much of the newsletter in this period was devoted to reporting on the newest developments in the evolving system. The language was often technical. As the writers saw it, the main areas of concern were *suffragium*,[65] by which was meant the question of who was a citizen and to what extent; *connubium*,[66] who could marry whom; and *occupation*,[67] restrictions on opportunities for earning a living. It must have become very clear to the reader of this material – and there was no need to read between the lines – that those who were still ritually referred to as "fate-comrades" in fact were treated very differently in all these areas.

Under the Nuremberg Laws a novel distinction was created between *Staatsangehörige* (subjects) and *Reichsbürger* (citizens). Everyone was a "subject" but only those considered racially qualified could become "citizens".[68] It was decided that "Jews" (those with three or more Jewish[69] grandparents) could not be "citizens", but that both kinds of *Mischlinge* could. While this rule appears simple enough on paper, in practice there were countless complications. The greatest difficulty lay in establishing the "race" of the grandparent. Document I in Appendix II gives something of the flavour of the hair-splitting that the Nuremberg system required.

The Nuremberg regulations concerning *connubium* of partial Jews were as follows: 1. "Jews" (as legally defined) may marry only "Jews"; 2. *Mischlinge* of the "first degree" may marry only others of the same status; 3. *Mischlinge* of the "second degree' ("quarter Jews") are treated as "German-blooded" for this purpose. The regulations also provided that certain other marriages could be authorised under special circumstances, for instance that of a "first-degree" with a "second-degree" *Mischling*, but such special permission was apparently almost never granted. There were, of course, difficulties in applying this law with any great consistency or logic, again mainly because of the practical problems in defining a "Jewish" grandparent. The *Paulus-Bund* newsletter faithfully reported on how such complications were treated by the authorities as they arose.

The regulations must have been particularly difficult for "*Mischlinge* First

---

[65] *M*, December 1935, and many other issues of the publication.
[66] *M*, February 1936.
[67] This matter is discussed in just about every issue. *M*, December 1937, gives a good recapitulation of the occupational disabilities of *Mischlinge* at that time.
[68] There was the additional complication that the Nuremberg Laws conferred no more than a provisional citizenship on anyone; we need not concern ourselves with this matter here.
[69] Since the Nuremberg system required information about the religion of a grandparent, it is sometimes said that the Nazis here deliberately violated their oft-repeated principle that "race" rather than religion defines a "Jew". But both the letter and the administration of the law make it clear that a grandparent's religion was looked upon only as a manifestation of his "race". It was thought possible to ascertain religion, and this was thought to be a good though not perfect indicator of race. But what is true without a doubt is that the use of this indicator involved the Nazi authorities in many incongruities. (Cf. Appendix II, Document I). On the other hand, since the categories of the "race" theory are probably, by their very nature, not determinable with any precision, it is hard to see how the framers of the Nuremberg system could have devised a more perfect procedure.

Degree" of marriageable age since the pool of possible partners could not have been very large. Each issue of the *Paulus-Bund* newsletter carried numerous advertisements in the personal columns in which such people looked for partners. I have also been told by a survivor of the *Paulus-Bund* that it was the social aspect – the many dances, hikes, and other get-togethers – which he remembers most about the group. Obviously such activities were more urgent for the "half Jews" than for the "quarter Jews". After the organisation was forbidden in 1939, some of the members, according to a number of my informants, continued to see one another in informal *Mischling* clubs.[70]

Throughout the Spiero period it was the professed position of the leadership, evinced in numerous speeches and articles in the newsletter, that all "non-Aryan Christians" are "fate-comrades" regardless of "blood", that no distinction among them is conceivable within the organisation. The group was still explicitly Christian in religion, and the position was similar to that of the *Bekennende Kirche* (Confessional Church) which rejected any "Aryan paragraph" within the community of Christian faith. But adjustment to the Nuremberg system of classification was at least as high a priority for the *Paulus-Bund*, and, at least in hindsight, a separation on "racial" grounds was always in the wings.

The dilemma created by this interplay between professed "fate-comradeship" and the desire to adjust to Nuremberg is illustrated in the school issue.

In September 1935 the government announced that Jewish children would no longer be able to go to state schools, and it appeared to an (anonymous) *Paulus-Bund* writer that all "non-Aryans", i.e. "*Mischlinge*" included, might be consigned to *Judenschulen*. This was seen as a terrible threat: "The education of our Christian non-Aryan children in Jewish schools must provoke the most serious objections on both religious and racial grounds . . . We see a solution in separate classes and schools for Christian non-Aryan children." The article certainly had antisemitic overtones but did not explicitly violate the principle of the faith-comradeship of all "non-Aryan Christians". But it was immediately followed by a news item, presented without further comment, according to which the Berlin school authorities had tentatively agreed to a private school which would be open only to those with at least two non-Jewish grandparents.[71]

December 1935 brings the cheerful news that the organisation itself has decided to establish a school, and that all non-Aryan Christian children would be able to attend the junior classes; only in the senior classes would there be restrictions in accordance with the number of Jewish grandparents.[72] Two months later there is still talk of preparations for this school, but we also learn that new government regulations allow not only "25% non-Aryans" but also

[70]Some of my informants from Berlin have told me that it was the custom to refer to one another, informally and ironically, as *Mampes*. Apparently there is a Berlin-made "half and half" alcoholic beverage that consists of a mixture of two different alcoholic ingredients. Other informants have not encountered this term.
[71]*M*, October 1935.
[72]*M*, December 1935.

"50% non-Aryans" to attend state schools.[73] Three months after that we are told that any school for "full non-Aryans" – by now these are the only "fate-comrade" children who would require one – is being postponed.[74]

There is no more mention of organisation-sponsored schooling after this, but there is an epilogue: more than a year later, the *Paulus-Bund* – having rid itself of the "full non-Aryans" in the meantime – is able to publish the good news that the *Reich* Minister for Education has definitively established that *Mischlinge* of both grades are to be treated just like the "German-blooded" throughout the entire school system. It is also specified that *Mischlinge* of the "first grade" can attend Jewish schools instead, but that those exercising this option would lose German citizenship.[75]

III. FEBRUARY 1937 TO AUGUST 1939: LESSER

To greet the New Year in 1937, Spiero writes a front-page editorial of good wishes to the membership; he also reveals that there had been some dissension on the Council which has now been resolved by agreement on the tasks ahead: "We seek, on the basis of our German fatherland, in Christian dedication, to obtain for ourselves and our families whatever it is possible to obtain within the framework of the laws of the *Reich*." Finally, chairman Spiero announces that the Council has regretfully accepted the resignation of vice-chairman Dr. med. Wilhelm Caro and has unanimously voted to make the Cavalry Captain (Retired), Attorney-at-Law Karl Friedrich Lesser the new vice-chairman of the organisation. "All of us are convinced that he will be the right man in the right place."[76]

The next thing we know, through a prominently displayed panel on the front page of the newsletter, is that a lecture which Spiero was to have delivered on 26th January 1937 is abruptly cancelled. No reasons are given.[77]

Now follows a month in which nothing happens, as far as the reader of the newsletter can tell. But then, in April, there is a front-page announcement entitled "Change of Statutes", in which it is explained that, in accordance with the letter and spirit of the Nuremberg Laws, the organisation has just expelled all those who are of "more than 50% Jewish descent". New statutes have been adopted. It should now be possible to attract personalities who have previously stayed away in view of the Jewish connection of the former organisation. Because

[73]*M*, February 1936. In view of the fact that *Mischlinge* from this time on – the Nuremberg system having evolved for their benefit – apparently could attend state schools, one wonders about the report by Selma Schiratzki, 'The Rykestrasse School in Berlin. A Jewish Elementary School during the Hitler Period', in *LBI Year Book V* (1960), pp. 299–307, according to which both *Mischlinge* and "fully Jewish" Christian children were found as late as 1939 in the Jewish school that she describes. But her report is valuable in any case for the light it throws on the antisemitic attitudes of these children from "non-Aryan Christian" homes.
[74]*M*, May 1936.
[75]*M*, July 1937.
[76]*M*, January 1937.
[77]*M*, February 1937.

of all the new organisational work, it is earnestly requested that all members remit an emergency donation of at least three marks. The change in statutes has necessitated a change in leadership, and Dr. Spiero has dropped out; in his place there is now the Attorney-at-Law at the Court of Appeal, Friedrich Karl Lesser. All those leaving, especially those who have been in leading positions, are heartily thanked for what they have done for the organisation in its previous form.[78]

The re-organised leadership of the group went to some lengths to disclaim responsibility for the expulsion of their "fully non-Aryan" "fate-comrades": "Already at the beginning of October 1935, that is to say little more than two weeks after the proclamation of the Nuremberg Laws . . . the government demanded that the organisation conform to the new law . . . [Only] in March of 1937 did this reorganisation occur . . . Now I ask you . . . who has the right to claim that one group forced out the other so that it would itself 'fare better'?"[79] Two months later the newsletter publishes a curious correction. It is now said that the date of October 1935 for the first demands by the government is in error and that these demands were in fact first voiced in May of 1936.[80] Looking at the record from this distance, it seems strange that the first assertion could have been made with such confidence and accompanied by such convincing supporting detail.

Reutter has examined documents of the Ministry of the Interior, and there is no doubt now that the government made a definitive demand for the change in February of 1937.[81] Whether or not previous demands had been made and resisted, as the Lesser leadership claimed, we do not know. After the war, Spiero writes about the incident as follows:

"The Nuremberg Laws put an end to my work [in the organisation] after a year and a half. Following the tenor of these laws, which distinguished between *Mischlinge* and full Jews, some of the *Mischlinge* were in a great hurry to rid the organisation of the so-called full Jews. In this they were successful with the aid of the government. But I must add for the sake of justice that when first faced with the government's demand for a split, Herr Mendelsohn [of the *Paulus-Bund* leadership – W.C.] had a long conversation with Hinkel [of the *Reich* Ministry for People's Enlightenment and Propaganda – W.C.] in order to obtain permission to keep the group undivided, and at that time he was still successful. [But] in January 1937 the government ordered the split."[82]

---

[78]*M*, April 1937.
[79]Bernhard Bennedik, 'You Yourselves Bear the Responsibility', *M*, July 1937. See also Appendix II, Documents M and O, for explanations along the same vein.
[80]*M*, September 1937.
[81]Reutter, *op. cit.*, pp. 212–213.
[82]Unpublished manuscript in the possession of Mrs. Christiane Ilisch. An additional insight into the incident is afforded by von Ameln, *op. cit.*, pp. 83–84. The author, a "half-Jew", had been a member of the local group in Köln and was asked to represent her group at a national meeting in Berlin in March of 1937. The new statutes were explained to this gathering; the "full Jews" had already been excluded. The author states that she declared her inability to belong to any organisation to which her father could not belong, and she therefore announced her resignation. She also reports that a Herr Mendelssohn, a "quarter-Jew", rose to associate himself with her remarks and similarly left the organisation.

Spiero thereupon started a "Bureau" (*Büro Dr. Heinrich Spiero*) through which he sought to continue some counselling and charitable work with those who had been excluded from the *Paulus-Bund*. In 1939 he closed this work and, according to his post-war memoirs, transmitted his records to Propst Grüber.[83]

The old organisation, meanwhile, was able to maintain itself with a fairly stable membership of over 3,000, now all *Mischlinge*. This last period of its life – the Lesser period – began with a fair number of lengthy articles and features in the newsletter which sought to lay down the new orientation. Documents K through O should convey the general tenor. It was said that the group now existed on a racial and no longer on a religious basis, in conformity with the Nuremberg system of racial taxonomy. Religion from now on would be each member's private business. The group would represent the interests of the *Mischlinge*, and would try to see to it that every *Mischling* was aware of whatever rights and privileges the law provided for him.

One very striking feature of the early months in the Lesser period is the heavy moralism. To stay out of the organisation would be egotistical. Each must help the community of "fate-comrades". "*Gemeinnutz geht vor Eigennutz*", "the common good comes before the welfare of the individual".[84] (This phrase is also the last sentence of the twenty-fourth point in the programme of the Nazi Party). But by then, these words coming so soon after the jettison of the Christian "full Jews", it must have been clear to the remaining "fate-comrades" that "the common good" was somewhat narrowly conceived.

In reviewing the newsletter after 1937, the reader is struck by a new mood of even greater sombreness. In the earlier years, especially under Spiero, the literary and intellectual level of the paper had been high. Spiero had contributed several essays – in the style of his books on literary history – recalling the life and work of famous Christian Germans who had been converts from Judaism. The legal essays concerning the Nuremberg Laws were closely-reasoned analyses and very well-written. But early in 1938 the newsletter contained an announcement, signed by Lesser, according to which there would be no further long articles. The step was taken not only for reasons of economy but also "in order to follow the suggestions of many members".[85] The remaining issues were almost completely taken up by two types of items: news about the ever-developing legal status of *Mischlinge*, and the very vigorous classified advertisement section (employment offered and wanted, search for marriage partners).

The lead item in almost every issue was now entitled 'Neues aus Gesetzgebung und Verwaltung', 'News About Legislation and Administration'. And almost always there was both good news and bad news. The good news would consist of

---

[83]I have been able to collect the following mimeographed and typed circular letters that were issued by *Büro Spiero*: the founding announcement, dated 12th March 1937, one page; a follow-up to this, dated 7th April 1937, one page; a three-page report to supporters, dated 3rd October 1937; a four-page report, dated April 1938. All these are very modest productions compared to the *Paulus-Bund* literature. Propst Heinrich Grüber, *op. cit.*, who was in charge of the Protestant charitable work with "non-Aryan Christians", does not mention Spiero.

[84]*M*, July 1937.

[85]*M*, March 1938.

a decision by some administrative board that *Mischlinge*, not being Jews in the sense of the Nuremberg Laws, were eligible for some right or privilege. The bad news typically was that a particular function could not be occupied by a *Mischling* because it was administered by an affiliate of the Party, and the Party had, after all, been specifically empowered in Paragraph 6 of the First Administrative Regulation of the *Reich* Citizenship Law to demand a greater "purity of blood" than non-Party agencies. One issue carried a communication from the Berlin Real Estate Board to the effect that, yes, *Mischlinge* are not Jews in the eyes of the law and can therefore practise the profession of estate agent, Heil Hitler! The column facing had a letter from the *Reich* Stenographers' Guild saying no, the Stenographer's Guild is part of the National Socialist Teachers' Guild and therefore is in no position to accept *Mischlinge* as members, Heil Hitler![86]

Only now and then was there some explicit reference to the difference in legal status between "half Jews" and "quarter Jews". It was an issue that spelled potential trouble, for the leadership had not quite stated the facts when it had claimed, immediately after the split, that the organisation now conformed to the Nuremberg taxonomy. The language continued to be one of "fate-comradeship" of all those eligible to membership. But in fact the difference in legal status between the two types of *Mischlinge* was substantial, especially with regard to *connubium*: "quarter-Jews" could marry non-Jews (with minor exceptions) while "half-Jews" could generally only marry one another. So here there was a contradiction between what was said in the official pronouncements of the organisation and what must have been painfully obvious to the membership.

When the end came for the organisation on 10th August 1939 there was neither bang nor whimper. The government order was issued without any apparent forewarning, just two weeks before the Stalin–Hitler pact, three weeks before the beginning of the Second World War. The travail of the *Paulus-Bund*, in its various guises and stages, was at an end; but that of the Christian "Jews" and "*Mischlinge*" was entering its war-time period of still greater danger and suffering.

There were up to half a million people in Hitler's Germany, who had not thought of themselves as Jews, who certainly did not want to be regarded as Jews, but who found themselves, much to their discomfort, stigmatised as partially Jewish. The overwhelming majority had no desire to contribute to this stigma by joining an organisation of "non-Aryan Christians". But there was a small minority, perhaps four per cent, who did just that.

Just how those who joined differed from the majority we do not know. There is some evidence that the group consisted predominantly of middle-class and professional people,[87] but that may have been just as true for those who did not join. There is one characteristic of the membership, however, that emerges from a study of the printed materials: there seems to have been a determination on the

---

[86]*M*, April 1938.
[87]See Appendix II, Documents J and O. Some additional evidence on this point may be found in the personal columns of the newsletter; for Berlin, the addresses given by the advertisers are almost always in the middle-class sections of West Berlin.

part of these people to face their status as partial Jews with openness; there was a constant polemic, sometimes explicit, sometimes merely implicit, against those who would hide their status or deny their ancestors.

The picture of the group and its leaders which these materials provide is certainly not one that would now, fully fifty years later, inspire great admiration. Aside from the fleeting support given to the *Bekennende Kirche* in 1933, there is little here that shows any independence from Nazi thinking, much that shows enthusiastic assent.[88] Moreover the main task which the group apparently set itself – to save what could be saved on behalf of its constituency – may in retrospect be thought to have been chimerical. But this judgement could not very well have been made at the time. The student of the *Paulus-Bund* record, especially if he does not expect heroism from very ordinary people, may well conclude that the group's enterprise was a reasonable response to a very frightening situation.

[88]There is ample evidence, on the other hand, that the group was thoroughly supervised by the Nazi authorities; the newsletter makes no secret of that. Moreover, it was no doubt also spied upon by the Gestapo. Von Ameln, *op. cit.*, p. 84, tells how she discovered one incident of such espionage; and the Reverend Ernest Gordon, a veteran of the group, recalls in correspondence with me (17th March 1986) the appearance of two mysterious strangers when he led a study group on the Ten Commandments.

The Size of the Partially Jewish Population

The number of partially Jewish people in Germany during the Hitler period continues to be a matter of controversy and speculation.[1] I intend to discuss here three ways of estimating their number: 1) an estimate based on known intermarriage rates since the emancipation; 2) the official government census of 1939; and 3) an estimate based on certain corrections to this census. The official census yields an estimate of one partial Jew for every two "full Jews", or about 228,000 in 1933; the other methods yield a substantially higher number, viz. about 500,000 in 1933. I consider the latter figure more precise.

a) Estimate based on intermarriage rates.[2]

One can make an estimate of people of "mixed blood" based on what is known about the following three parameters: a) the proportion of Jews in the whole population at some beginning point of a period of intermarriage; b) the proportion of Jews who marry non-Jews during this period; and c) the length of time of such period, expressed in number of generations.

Let us now say, simply for purposes of illustrating this approach, that at some early stage of Jewish assimilation in Germany everyone was either "purely" Jewish or "purely" non-Jewish; that the Jews constituted 1% of the population; and that one percent of the Jews married non-Jews. At the end of the first generation, then, making certain simplifying assumptions about equality of fertility, etc., we could say the new "purely" Jewish population would no longer be 1% of the total population because one percent of it had been lost to become "*Mischlinge*". It would, in fact, now only constitute 99% of 1%. Similarly, the non-Jewish population (to a much smaller degree) would also have lost a certain proportion to the "*Mischlinge*". It can be shown, under these assumptions, that the "*Mischlinge*" would then amount to .02 of one percent of the total population. (For details of such calculations, see note 6, below).

For Berlin, for the period of Jewish assimilation – roughly the period between 1750 and 1933 – we have substantially higher reported values both for Jewish percentage in the population and outmarriage rates.[3] The proportion of Jews went up and down during this period, but averaged approximately 3.5% of the population; the outmarriage rate averaged approximately 13% of all marrying Jews. Applying these parameters to the procedure outlined in the previous paragraph, we find that just under 5% of the Berlin population of 1933 was of

[1]Various authors and institutions have offered diverse estimates, usually in accordance with the particular axe they had to grind. Joseph Walk, 'Jüdische Schüler an deutschen Schulen in Nazideutschland', in *Bulletin des Leo Baeck Instituts*, 19, No. 56–57 (1980), pp. 101–109, gives a useful compilation of these various estimates. They differ wildly among themselves.
[2]I wish to thank Dr. Malcolm Greig of the Computing Centre, University of British Columbia, for help with these computations.
[3]Esra Bennathan, 'Die demographische und wirtschaftliche Struktur der Juden', in *Entscheidungsjahr 1932, op. cit.*; Arthur Ruppin, *The Jews in the Modern World*, London 1934, p. 319; *Encyclopædia Judaica*, Jerusalem 1971, vol. 4, pp. 639 ff.

Jewish-Christian mixed origins. Since the official census of that year[4] shows that the 160,500 Berlin Jews made up just under 4% of the population, we can estimate the number of partial Jews as roughly 200,500.[5,6]

The situation in the rest of Germany was somewhat different. The proportion of Jews in the population was much lower, and this would depress the proportion of partial Jews in the population. Moreover, there are fewer available out-marriage estimates. But while probably somewhat lower, the overall proportion of partial Jews to "full Jews" can be assumed to be similar to that of Berlin; so it would seem reasonable to assume that there were perhaps as many partial Jews of various types – baptised "full Jews" and "*Mischlinge*" of varying degrees – as there were full Jews. In sum, using this method of estimation, we come to the conclusion that in 1933 the number of partial Jews in Germany roughly equalled or slightly exceeded that of the half-million registered members of the Jewish communities.

b) The 1939 census.

The only official census which yielded figures of partial Jews was done in 1939, after the Nuremberg Laws defined Jews "racially" (i.e. included the converts to Christianity) and also defined two degrees of "*Mischlinge*". The new census tabulated separately the categories of "Jew" (three or four Jewish grandparents), "*Mischling* First Degree" (two Jewish grandparents), and "*Mischling* Second Degree" (one Jewish grandparent), and for each showed the number of *Glaubensjuden*, i.e. members of Jewish communities (*Gemeinden*). (The 1939 census uses this term for what had traditionally been known as "Mosaic" persons, i.e. believers in the Jewish religion. I use the two terms here interchangeably). The total number of "non-Aryan Christians" reported by the 1939 census, for the enlarged *Reich* of that date, was 138,500.

By 1939 German Jewry had already lost fifty-six percent of its members to

---

[4]There were two censuses during the Nazi years, one in 1933 and the other in 1939. I use the official figures here of the *Statistisches Reichsamt: Statistisches Jahrbuch für das Deutsche Reich*, vol. 53 (1934) and vol. 59 (1942) respectively. For a discussion of the Nazi censuses as they relate to Jews and *Mischlinge*, see Götz Aly and Karl Heinz Roth, *Die restlose Erfassung. Volkszählen, Identifizieren, Aussondern im Nationalsozialismus*, Berlin 1984.

[5]I have done a more detailed calculation, using the various reported Jewish population and outmarriage rates for Berlin (see previous note) for all the sub-periods from 1670 to 1933. This resulted in an estimate for the year 1933 as follows: Jews in population: 3.8%; partial Jews: 4.8%; non-Jews: 91.4%. (See the next note for the mechanics of the calculation). These estimates must obviously be looked upon with considerable caution. Figures for "partial Jews" here are estimates of people of "mixed blood" and leave out the baptised "full Jews." On the other hand, they count people whose Jewish ancestors are so far in the past that there may be no trace of them left in the consciousness or in the records of anyone in the twentieth century. I assume here that these two factors roughly cancel one another.

[6]Technical note: to calculate the proportion of people of "mixed blood" in the population at any one time, given information on intermarriage rates and proportion of Jews in the population, I have used the following:

(1) $M_{n+1} = 1 - J_n(1 - j_n)^{t\{n\}} - C_n(1 - c_n)^{t\{n\}}$

(2) $C_{n+1} = 1 - J_{n+1} - M_{n+1}$

Let T_n be the nth focal year for which we have data, with T_0 the initial year considered. For my Berlin calculation, this was 1670. Then J_n is the proportion of full Jews in the population at T_n, and C_n the proportion of non-Jews at that time. j_n is the proportion of marrying Jews who marry non-Jews for the period beginning with T_n. Similarly, c_n is the proportion of non-Jews who marry other than full non-Jews in that period; it is here assumed to be $j_n J_n / C_n$. $t\{n\}$ is the time period between focal years, measured in generations, with a generation assumed to be 29 years. If we assume $M_0 = 0$ (and thus $C_0 = 1 - J_0$), we may recursively calculate the M's and C's by formulas (1) and (2) above.

emigration,[7] and we must assume that the partial Jews as well had emigrated to a substantial extent. In my analysis of the census, I have focused my interest on the numerical relationship between those registered as Jews in a religious sense, and all others whom the government regarded as fully or partially Jewish in the "racial" sense.

TABLE I

	Some Analyses of 1939 Census: *The Five Largest Jewish Centres*		
	(1)	*(2)*	*(3)*
	% *Mosaic**	Mischling *II/Full***	*Jewish Population****
Vienna	72.4	0.06	91,530
Berlin	71.0	0.11	82,457
Frankfurt a. Main	81.5	0.06	14,191
Breslau	79.8	0.07	10,848
Hamburg	48.4	0.31	9,943
German *Reich*	68.7	0.13	330,539

* Percentage of members of Jewish communities among all "Jews" and *Mischlinge*. The official 1939 term for these "Mosaic" believers was *Glaubensjuden*.
** Proportion of "*Mischlinge*, Second degree" (i.e. "one-quarter Jews") to "full Jews" (using a "racial" criterion).
*** Population of "full Jews", using a "racial" criterion.

Source: all figures computed from official census statistics in *Statistisches Reichsamt: Statistisches Jahrbuch für das Deutsche Reich*, vol. 59 (1942), p. 27.

In all interpretations of this 1939 census, it must be kept in mind that while there were penalties for misreporting one's status, there were also very obvious and powerful incentives for failing to report oneself as partially "non-Aryan" if it appeared likely that the truth could not easily be determined from official records. Moreover, in the absence of such complete records, many individuals might simply not have known about a Jewish ancestor. So any errors in self-reporting of "non-Aryan Christians", clerical mistakes aside, must be assumed to tend towards under- rather than over-reporting.

According to the official figures, there were almost 70 *Glaubensjuden* for every 30 "non-Aryan Christians" (Table I, column 1) which, taken at face value, would lead us to the conclusion that the number of "full Jews" was substantially higher than that of partial Jews. However, it is obvious that it was far more difficult to hide the fact that one was a *Glaubensjude* from the census taker, since *Glaubensjuden* were officially registered as such; no comparably thorough and reliable registers ever existed for "non-Aryans" of Christian religion. While it can be taken as

[7]This figure is the result of some calculation because both the definition of "Jew" and the territory of the German *Reich* had changed between the two censuses. The number of Jews in 1933 was 499,682. For 1939, I have here counted only the *Glaubensjuden* (see above) from among both "racial Jews" and *Mischlinge*, and I have excluded the new territories of the Saar, Austria, and the Sudetenland. This total came to 219,050.

virtually certain that the census counting of *Glaubensjuden* was well-nigh complete, there is considerable doubt about the other "non-Aryan" categories.

Table I shows the five cities with the highest Jewish populations. We note that, except for Hamburg, the proportion of "Mosaic" Jews is higher in these cities – about 75% on average – than in the country as a whole, where it is under 70%. In other words, there are fewer reported "non-Aryan Christians" per Jew in the smaller than in the larger centres. It seems a reasonable surmise that there may have been as many such people in the larger cities and that, due to the anonymity of large city life, the "non-Aryan Christians" were more often able to escape detection.

The great exception for the country as a whole, and especially for the larger cities, was Hamburg. The "non-Aryan Christians" here actually outnumbered the "Mosaic" Jews (see Table I, column 1); moreover, the proportionate number of "*Mischlinge*, Second Degree" (i.e. the "quarter Jews" who would be particularly difficult to trace in official records) was more than twice as high in Hamburg as in the rest of the country, three times as high as in Berlin, and almost five times as high as in Vienna, Frankfurt a. Main, and Breslau. (See column 2, same table). While Hamburg may indeed have had a larger proportionate number of such partial Jews, it seems more likely that the reporting for the old Hanseatic cities was more complete:

> "Perfekt war das Meldewesen in Bremen entwickelt; vor allem aber in Hamburg, das es schon 1891 'in zweckmäßiger Weise gesetzlich geregelt' und 1929 das letzte Mal verschärft hatte . . . Die Hamburger Verhältnisse wurden Vorbild für das ganze Reich."[8]

According to the work of Aly and Roth, then, it was in Bremen[9] and especially in Hamburg, unlike the rest of Germany, that records of civil status had been reliably kept since the nineteenth century. It may well be that the Hamburg statistics for partial Jews, far from pointing to an atypical population there, should actually be used as an indicator for the true numbers in all of Germany. If we were to make such an extrapolation from the Hamburg results to the rest of Germany, we would arrive at an estimate of "non-Aryan Christians" very similar to that of our estimate based on intermarriage rates: a number roughly equal to the number of religious-registered Jews, or about 305,000 in 1939.

In conclusion, we are led to regard the officially-reported number of "non-Aryan Christians" of 1939 (i.e. 138,500) as the lower limit for reasonable estimates, and 300,000 as a more realistic figure. Extrapolating from the proportions on which these estimates are based to the 1933 census, before the "racial" definition of Jews and also before the large-scale emigration movement, we would estimate the number of "non-Aryan Christians" in the smaller territory of the then-Germany to have numbered at the very least 228,000, and much more likely about 500,000.

[8]Aly and Roth, *op. cit.*, p. 41.
[9]The Bremen results, not given in the table because of the small size of the Jewish community (722), were even more extreme than those of Hamburg: 46.9% "Mosaic", a ratio of "*Mischlinge*" II to "Full Jews" of 0.38.

Documents in Translation

Note: Emphases and parentheses are as in original. Material in brackets and in footnotes is supplied here; it consists of either items from the original German text which are shown to clarify the translation, or some other explanation.

A

Circular letter (excerpts), August 1933, from Gustav Friedrich, Reich *League of Christian-German State Citizens of non-Aryan or not Completely Aryan Origins, Inc.*

[Letterhead of the organisation; Gustav Friedrich: 'Führer" of the group]

You have undoubtedly been informed by items in the German newspapers about the formation of the *Reich* League of Christian-German State Citizens of non-Aryan or not Completely Aryan Origins, Inc. The main purpose of this organisation arises out of the pressing necessity to bind together, *without exception*, all fate-comrades [*Schicksalsgenossen*] into one benevolent community.

It is for patriotic motives that I requested permission from the relevant governmental agencies to found the *Reich* League of Christian-German State Citizens of non-Aryan or not Completely Aryan Origins. I was able to obtain this permission after much effort.

The reason for this step lay in the fact that as a result of the so-called Aryan paragraphs many valuable Germans are excluded from participating in the construction of the new state. This exclusion affects the non-Aryans and the not fully-Aryans with particular painfulness because they feel themselves German and Christian and stand, by inner conviction, with today's government . . .

The *Reich* League has been recognised for its positive disposition towards the new Germany, as well as for its *Führerprinzip*. We have freed ourselves in every way from the old, never-to-live-again democratic parliamentarianism . . .

Let admission to our ranks be barred to all wreckers [*Umstürzler*] whether of the Left or the Right. Whoever wishes to come to us must seek, to the best of his abilities, to contribute to the well-being of today's Germany. Our distress in hard times can only be overcome by deeds, not with phrases or ideologies . . .

Let us show our Aryan Volksgenossen (ethnic comrades),[1] *to whom we are bound inextricably by culture and nature [Art],* how we act; they will then recognise that we, like they, fulfil loyally our holiest duty to the rebirth of the German people and to the construction of the new German *Reich* . . .

Whoever believes that modifications can be made in the *strong foundations* of the

---

[1]In the context of the times, *Volksgenosse* is a Nazi antisemitic term that suggests that while Jews may be citizens of the state, they cannot be German "ethnic comrades". For a discussion of the term, see Christoph Cobet, *Der Wortschatz des Antisemitismus in der Bismarckzeit*, München 1973, pp. 155–156. Friedrich does use the term "Volksgenossen" to refer to Jews a few paragraphs further on, but that would seem to be a piece of elegant irony.

new *Reich*, or even that the well-established present form of government can in any way be changed in the foreseeable future, is stupid and foolish . . .

The [Weimar Republic's] Marxist government has given ample cause for strong measures [by the new government]. *Let us not be surprised that the injustices that were done to today's leading Volksgenossen* have caused resentment and justified anger to play a dominant role in the regulations that so harshly affect us German Christians of non-Aryan or not purely Aryan origin. We, above all the particularly hard-hit Nationalist German Christians, must stand firm and, truly German, must continue, undeterred, to do our duty, despite spiritual and economic distress . . .

The affected ethnic comrades of Jewish religion and race issued an SOS when they felt themselves harmed, and the Jews of the whole world immediately came to their aid. *We German Christians cannot and do not wish to do anything like that* . . .

That our *Reich* League will never serve general antisemitic purposes, as long as I have the honour to be its leader, that I wish to profess here openly; equally openly I declare myself as the strongest opponent of the Jewish, wrecking, dissension- and poison-sowing elements and pledge to fight them with all means at our disposal.

With respectfully loyal German greeting [Mit verehrungsvollem treu deutschen Gruss]

B

Speech by Dr. Günter Alexander-Katz at press reception of new organisation, Summer 1933 (excerpts); source: mimeographed version.

. . . The government, ladies and gentlemen, needs the League, so that those non-Aryans who always were Germans, who have always proved themselves German and who wish to remain so, can have the opportunity again to proclaim their German nature . . .

The authorities realise that we recognise the Nationalist government as such without reservation. For there is nobody among us who would not welcome this government's struggle against the over-refined intellectualism, Pacifism, Communism, and so forth, that has gathered together in Germany in previous years . . .

A person is not accepted as a member just because he is non-Aryan. Only those can come to us who are German, who wish to be German, and who find themselves obligated, under all circumstances, to hold to that. I can also reveal to you that nobody is admitted to our ranks about whose political activities and convictions there could be even the slightest doubt. A further guarantee for the soundness of our membership lies in the fact that membership lists are being submitted to the *Gestapo* for verification . . .

Ladies and Gentlemen, as you know yourselves, the Jews, both in Germany and abroad, have numerous facilities which help their own fate-comrades with great energy and substantial funds. But who helps the Christian non-Aryan, whose mother or grandmother was a Jewess and whose father or grandfather had already become a Christian? . . .

We do not wish to contradict anyone concerning the matter of race, but we maintain, with deepest conviction, that in addition to the communion of blood there is also another German national communion, which consists of common fate, common experience, common feeling: of German fate, German experience, German feeling. I can express this even more clearly. Un-German is he who, from childhood, has accepted the Talmud as a guide to his action and thinking; German is he who has been told German fairy tales as a child, who, in school, has imbibed the spirit of Schiller and Bismarck and Frederick the Great, who, as an adult, has experienced the works of the great Germans, Goethe, Dürer, Beethoven, or Richard Wagner . . .

C

Information sheet, Autumn 1933

[heading: logo, name and address of organisation]

Founded: 20th July 1933
Registered: 13th October 1933, Register of Societies Berlin, registration No. 7278
Orientation: German Nationalist and patriotic. [*Deutschbewusst und heimattreu*]. Standing firm in German and Christian belief and culture.
Organisation: Constructed according to the principle of individual leadership [*Führergrundsatz*] in harmony with the regulations of the government (see statutes). Division into district and local groups. Full responsibility to the chairman, who is advised by a council.
Purpose: Organisation of all Christian-German state citizens of non-Aryan or not purely Aryan origin, and their Aryan family members. Representation of their common interests, such as: a) legal advice; b) help in obtaining employment, insofar as permitted by law; c) educational counselling; d) solution to problems of youth; e) concern for new occupational opportunities for our members and their children; f) welfare assistance in collaboration with existing agencies; g) contact with existing sports organisations. Organisation of the members for social purposes through lectures, theatrical presentations and similar events; mutual exchange of views, and thereby spiritual support. Maintenance of the German-thinking, German-feeling Christian non-Aryans in the community of German *Volksgenossen*.[2]

D

Appeal to join, Autumn 1933

Christian-German Non-Aryans! Do not allow current difficulties to discourage you! Do not forget that you were German, are German, and remain German! Reflect upon yourselves! Consider that nobody can rob you of your German nature, your German feeling, your German sensitivities; you have inherited all this from your fathers and have cultivated it since childhood! Organise yourselves in the organisation that has been designed for you and is authorised by the government, the *Reichsverband christlich-deutscher Staatsbürger nichtarischer oder nicht rein arischer Abstammung e.V.* Beware of all splintering and close ranks! Donate beyond the small membership payments as much as you can! (Postal cheque account 4025 Berlin). Enlist friends and family members. The individual is

[2]Re: *Volksgenosse*, see the note above.

nothing, in closed ranks we are strong. All together we are a communion of millions!

E

Profession of Faith, Autumn 1933 (printed sheet)

We believe:
We are Germans.
Therefore we love Germany as our only home.
Therefore we profess our faith, like all Germans, in that government that the German people have created for themselves. But we also know that Germany's future demands the willing respect and utilisation of personalities and values that have contributed to a unified German fatherland and to Germany's greatness in war and peace.
Therefore, for us, our German nature derives from a common, spiritual, historical process and thus is a matter of inner attitude, loyalty and the heart.
We are Christians.
Therefore we are, with all our hearts, "subject to the government that has power over us."[3]
Therefore we must, in matters of faith, "be more obedient to God than to man."
Therefore we must, like all those of true Christian faith, reject all falsifications of the true teaching of Christ and His apostles.
We are of completely or partially non-Aryan origins.
Therefore we are proudly conscious that Jesus belonged to the Jewish people and proclaimed the Gospel first to the Jews.
Therefore we know that our families consciously accepted the Christian teachings in depth.
Therefore we feel pride that our steadfast engagement for nation and fatherland shows our true German and Christian nature.

F

Statutes (excerpts), August 1933; source: printed sheet

. . . §5. Membership may be requested by all those over 18 years of age who are male or female German subjects of non-Aryan or not purely Aryan descent and who belong to a Christian religious community and who profess adherence to National Germany [. . . *auf dem Boden des nationalen Deutschland stehen* . . .] . . .
   §8. The chairman is elected by the Council for the period of one year . . .
   §11. In addition to the chairman and his deputy, there will be a Council consisting of at least four and at the most twelve members of the organisation. The members of the Council are named by the chairman.
   §12. Any member of the Council may be dismissed by the chairman, but only with the consent of the majority of Council members, with the affected member not voting . . .

---

[3]The reference is to Romans XIII:1 in Luther's translation; the endorsement of the powers that be is even stronger here than in the Authorised Version.

§15. The Council has the right to dismiss the chairman by a three-quarter vote of all Council members . . .

§18. The chairman calls the general meeting of members by announcing its date and the agenda, which he determines, at least two weeks in advance . . .

§19. Decisions of the general meeting are to be written up and must be signed by the chairman and one member of the Council . . .

§21. A member may be expelled from the organisation by the chairman with the agreement of the majority of the Council; a) if he acts contrary to the interests or aspirations of the organisation; b) if he has been convicted of a crime by a German court; c) if he has made false statements upon joining; d) if his payments due are more than three months in arrears . . .

§22. The statutes may be changed by the general meeting or by the chairman in agreement with the majority of the Council.

§23. In case of dissolution, remaining funds after payment of debts are to be given to the German Red Cross.

Berlin, 23rd August 1933

G

Circular to Protestant members, 1st December 1933; source: mimeographed version.

To our Evangelical Members!
A struggle has erupted in the German Evangelical Church in which the overwhelming number of "evangelical Christians", joined also by a part of the "German Christians", regard the introduction of any racial distinction in the church as incompatible with the teachings of Christ and the principles of the Gospel. More and more the thought is established that evangelical Christianity is incompatible with *völkische Weltanschauung*. This holds for the congregation as well as for the teaching office. In the view of the current overwhelming majority of the Evangelical Church, neither the formation of "Jewish Christian" congregations nor the application of the Aryan paragraph to the clergy is scriptural.

It goes without saying that the *Reich* League, encompassing as it does the non-Aryan Christians, is thoroughly and completely of the same opinion; and this out of the deepest religious conviction of its members. In our membership, some of whom have professed Christianity for generations, there is not and never will be a thought other than that the holy baptism has dissolved any worldly racial distinctions in the new communion of Christian faith. (Cf. Galatians III: 28: "There is neither Jew nor Greek, there is neither bond nor free, there is neither male nor female: for ye are all one in Christ Jesus.")[4] This alone is Christian according to our deepest conviction, and this alone will persist as Christian doctrine. In this battle of faith we are of good cheer. We know, on the basis of several conversations we have had, that we are at one with influential men in the Evangelical Church, and we have not hesitated to communicate our Christian convictions firmly to the leadership of the Evangelical Church.

Let our Evangelical members, on their part, participate in this battle of faith and be of good courage.

[4] I am using the King James translation here. The original German is close to but not quite that of Luther. I have corrected the obvious mistake in the original which makes reference to Gal. *II*:28.

H

'Our Tasks and Aims', by Dr. jur. Johannes Fuchs, lecture to District Leipzig of the Reichsverband der nichtarischen Christen e.V., 1st June 1935, published as a printed supplement to circular letter number 3 of the Leipzig branch, dated 10th June 1935 (excerpts)

The Leipzig branch was founded in September 1934 . . .

In general, the difficulties that faced us were similar to those of other branches. But perhaps the territory of the Leipzig district, which includes Halle, was actually more difficult. Relatively few non-Aryans and non-Aryan Christians live in the areas that belong to the Leipzig district, such as, for instance, the former Free State of Anhalt and parts of Thuringia. Added to that was the aversion [*Scheu*] many non-Aryans in our district felt to declaring themselves as such. Objections, based on principle or imaginary, were voiced. We non-Aryan Christians and our *Reich* League were suspect: to some as antisemites, to others as a club of "baptised Jews". Some demanded a close relationship to Jewish organisations, others a conspicuous distance from them. Some demanded a profession of Judaism, others a clear profession of the opposite . . . But if one looked behind what was said, one discovered very soon that these were rationalisations for a refusal to come to us. Actually it was occupational consideration and social motives that accounted for it. We have understanding for the occupational considerations, but not for the behaviour of those non-Aryans who simply do not wish to recognise their own origins and who will do everything to avoid recognising us and our fate-comrades in public [. . . *alles daran setzen, uns und unsere Schicksalsgenossen nicht, wie man zu sagen pflegt, "unter den Linden grüssen" zu müssen*] . . .

The membership has doubled since the founding of the organisation, and today consists of approximately 150 people. It would be better to speak of member-families here since in general a family of several people is represented by only one person.

We can say thankfully that in addition to the membership there are persons of note who, with a laudable sense of solidarity, stand with us spiritually and give us valuable help with both advice and deeds . . .

As is well known, our members come predominantly from intellectual circles and the business class. Members of the intellectual professions are, after all, hardest hit. But in no way does this mean that we value only members of such professions or of the professional or social "elite". On the contrary, we see it as an important task to include non-Aryan Christians from among the so-called simple people; we know that in those circles, too, there are numerous non-Aryans. Such people are already members of the *Reich* League and our branch. We are particularly happy to have them. In get-togethers with us, they surely will not feel disadvantaged, let alone lonely. *We are all fate-comrades and know no differences among us. We only know the common aim, to be helpful to one another and to give one another spiritual strength* . . .

It goes without saying that conditions are more difficult for our group than for the Jewish organisations. The Jewish non-Aryans are easily reached; the religious congregations themselves provide contact. The characteristic trait, yes, the typical trait of non-Aryan Christians is that they cannot be easily reached and – as already described above – that they do not like to be reached . . . The non-Aryan Christian is being excluded from a communion to which he has heretofore belonged. It must and will appear to Jews as more natural to be designated as such than to non-Aryan Christians who, as is predominantly the case in our membership, have been without social or spiritual contact with

Judaism for two to three generations. Many – and unfortunately this is often sarcastically questioned – many did not know about their origins until they constructed their family trees and examined the documents. So we realise very well that we shall never equal the Jewish organisations in strength, but strength alone does not guarantee impact and success . . . We are particularly happy to report that, especially in this last period, more and more well-known personalities have come to us; heretofore a certain hesitation kept them away. No less than Alice Salomon and Herr *Senatspräsident* Caspary, Berlin, have joined our Council. The famous educator, Susanne Engelmann, has also joined our *Reich* League . . .[5]

The question of our military service has now been essentially clarified.[6] I use this opportunity to stress that we non-Aryan Christians, in our unshakably proud commitment to Germany and Christianity, and despite bitter disappointments, wish to, and indeed will, meet our finest obligation, that of serving Germany weapon in hand . . .

I

'Question and Answer' (excerpts); source: Mitteilungsblatt des Reichsverbandes der nichtarischen Christen e.V., vol. 3, No. 3 (March 1936), pp. 21–22.

. . . Question: What can be said about the marriage of a half-Aryan with a girl who also has one Aryan parent, but whose Aryan mother converted to Judaism so that the girl was also raised as a Jew? What can be said, further, about the children of this marriage?

Answer: The girl, actually half-Aryan, is not a *Mischling* but is without any doubt regarded as Jewish in the sense of the law because she belonged to the Jewish religious community on the deadline date, i.e. 15th September 1935; belated conversion does not alter this status in any way. The husband – a *Mischling* First Degree – is likewise regarded as a Jew since he married a statutory Jew.

The children of this marriage are in any case regarded as Jews since they have three Jewish grandparents (two by race, one by religion). This would not have been different if the mother had left the Jewish community before the deadline. She herself would then have been a *Mischling*, but the children would still have had three Jewish grandparents. In other words, it is quite possible that children who are regarded as Jews may result from a marriage in which both partners are half-Aryan.

Question: A man has two Jewish grandparents, one Aryan grandmother and a half-Aryan grandfather; the latter was born Jewish and became Christian only later. Is this 62% Jewish person a *Mischling* or a Jew?

Answer: The man is a Jew according to the Nuremberg Laws because of the

[5]The *Encyclopædia Judaica* lists the two women. Alice Salomon, 1872–1948, converted to Protestantism during the First World War. She was known as a social worker and feminist and emigrated from Germany in 1937. Susanne Engelmann, born in 1886 and known as an educationalist, emigrated to the United States in 1940. Wilhelm Caspary died on 1st November 1936; a brief obituary is devoted to him in *M*, December 1936, p. 101.
[6]Army service became obligatory for *Mischlinge* after the Nuremberg Laws, but they could not become either commissioned or non-commissioned officers. At the time the present speech was given, the matter had not, as a matter of fact, been clarified.

one grandparent who was of the Jewish religion; this grandparent is assumed to have been a full Jew and this assumption cannot be contested. So this 62% Jew has three full Jewish grandparents. On the other hand, if the half-Aryan grandfather had been Christian by birth, he would not then have been a full Jew and would not have counted at all for this calculation; his grandson would have been a *Mischling* First Degree . . .

Question: A young, half-Aryan girl, half-orphan, was raised by her Jewish father in the Jewish faith. Her frequently voiced desire to convert to the Protestant religion was decisively rejected by the father. The girl could realise her desire for conversion only upon maturity, i.e. on her twenty-first birthday, i.e. on 1st December 1935, and she was therefore still Jewish on 15th September. Would an application by her to be nevertheless regarded as a *Mischling* be granted, and to whom should it be directed?

Answer: The application would have to be directed to the *Reich* Chancellor, but there is hardly a chance of success. Lösener's Commentary states explicitly: "The decision of parents to introduce their child to this (i.e. Jewish) religious community must be regarded as decisive also for the racial status of the child." (page 22). By the way, it is not true that a change of religion without the parents' permission can only be effected after the twenty-first birthday. Paragraph 5 of the Law of Religious Instruction for Children, dated 15th July 1921, provides expressly that, *upon completion of the fourteenth year of life*, the decision concerning religious faith belongs to the child . . .

J

'Work of the organisation around the country. District East Prussia.' By Professor Dr. Paul Stettiner (retired). (Excerpts).
Source: as for H, vol. 3, No. 9 (September 1936), pp. 72–73.

Dr. Wolff founded the East Prussia branch in Königsberg in September 1934 by speaking and writing and contacting those circles among our fellow citizens whom it concerned. The formal organisation of the branch followed in November. It would seem that Königsberg should have provided particularly fertile soil for this purpose.

While all of Prussia saw 1,800 conversions from 1812 to the beginning of the thirties of the nineteenth century, 160 of these came from Königsberg. The reasons why so many Jewish parents had their children baptised are explained by Frau Julie von Adelson in a letter that was reprinted in *Historische Zeitschrift* in 1930 . . .

. . . a great number of families took this decisive step . . . often they were severely reproached by their relatives. One need only mention the names Oppenheim, Friedländer, Friedberg, Simson, Hirschfeld, Borchard, Lewald, and Lehrs . . .

[But] within the Christian non-Aryan circles here there are very striking differences regarding the acceptance of religious, moral, and social standards. The wish and the hope which we voiced in our first appeal in October 1934 were not fulfilled. Let no-one, we said then, use the excuse that a legal loophole protects him or that he himself is not affected. If someone believes himself free of worry in this regard, he has an even greater moral obligation to support, through his membership, those in dire need . . .

We tried in our appeal to reach 200 Christian non-Aryans in East Prussia.

About 35 already belonged to the organisation. In the course of the years this figure rose to about 80, so that we have responsibility for about 200 *Weggenossen*, including family members. Of these there are 58 male and 23 female members. 40 are *Mischlinge*, 5 are pure Aryans who are tied to us by marriage; most of the rest are tied to us [*Mischlinge*] mostly through marriage to Aryans or through children who are *Mischlinge*. By profession, we are 3 university professors in retirement, 6 physicians, 5 lawyers, 1 apothecary, 12 independent business men, 10 employed persons. Only one adult (academic) is unemployed . . .

All our *Mischlinge* have become members of the *Arbeitsfront*.[7] . . . On our advice, all our younger people have registered for the year of military service before this became obligatory; they have in fact been called up. The work of the district consists mainly of counselling . . .

There are English and French lessons, taught by an English and a French woman . . . An excellent gymnastics teacher gives lessons for the ladies without fee . . . Every month until the end of May, musical evenings provided proven means for bringing our circle together. Musicians and amateurs of more than average talent performed in song, string music and piano; the works were mostly classical, by Beethoven, Brahms, Bach, Händel, Mozart, and Wagner . . .

K

Statutes, March 1937 (excerpts); shown here are the changes from the 1933 Document F. Source: printed sheet.

§1. The organisation bears the name "Vereinigung 1937" . . .

§5. All those may become members who are over 16 years of age, of either sex, of German nationality [*Deutsche Staatsangehörige*], who, as *Mischlinge*, fulfil the blood requirements [*blutmässige Voraussetzungen*] for provisional *Reich* citizenship[8] and who profess adherence to Nationalist Germany; also their next of kin who are of German or related blood.[9]

Children under 16 years of age who fulfil the other requirements may have membership acquired on their behalf by next of kin of German or related blood.

The chairman makes decisions on admissions to membership.

§5a. The chairman is empowered to effect, on his own, any further changes of the statutes that may be required by the authorities . . .

§21. In case of dissolution, two thirds of remaining funds after payment of debts go to the Brandenburg Provincial League for Home Missions in Berlin–Lichterfelde,[10] one third to the *Caritas* organisation.[11]

Signed: Friedrich Karl Lesser

[7]*Arbeitsfront*: the Nazi obligatory labour organisation, closed to Jews but open to *Mischlinge* after the Nuremberg Laws.

[8]The Nuremberg Laws provided for provisional *Reich* citizenship for both non-Jews and *Mischlinge*. It seems that that "provisional" nature was emphasised only among the fate-comrades.

[9]This formula replaced the notion of "Aryan" after the Nuremberg Laws. The paragraph of the statutes here allows for membership of the non-Jewish but not the Jewish close relative of the *Mischlinge*.

[10]A Protestant Church agency.

[11]The Catholic relief agency.

L

'A Hopeful Beginning', report of speech by Friedrich Karl Lesser delivered 3rd June 1937. Source: Mitteilungsblatt für den Paulus-Bund, vol. 4, No. 6 (June 1937), pp. 56–58.

. . . Our organisation has now become strictly an interest group. Whereas the members of the old *Paulus-Bund* were held together by ties of religion and the religious factor was therefore by far the most important, the present members of the organisation are bound to one another because they have achieved a *special status* through the Nuremberg Laws. A special status not only *vis-à-vis* the purely German-blooded German nationals, but above all also *vis-à-vis* those who, though Christian through baptism, have been characterised as racial Jews by the legislation. It is obvious that because of this reorganisation the religious emphasis of our group must recede. If members no longer come to us only because of religious ties, but because of other reasons, well, then the consideration of these other reasons must take precedence. The religion of each member is his personal business. The religious need of the members is primarily the responsibility of the churches while our work concerns more their political and economic needs.

From this it obviously does not follow that we would in any way utilise the law to play politics. That would be completely outside the task that has been assigned to us or that we could allow ourselves. We have to keep strictly to the laws of the German *Reich*, and if I have used the word "politics" I wish to say only that we must seek to see to it that the racial legislation of the *Reich*, insofar as it is favourable to us, becomes generally recognised and applied, and that we are everywhere accorded the place to which we have a right under the Nuremberg Laws and the various regulations; and I can say to my great joy that this is happening more and more . . .

It must surely be clear to everyone that an organisation which includes only a fraction of those who, according to its statutes, should belong, characterises itself by that fact as weak . . . Therefore it is the duty of each member to recruit on behalf of the organisation, above all those who still keep away for reasons that I deliberately do not mention here, but that you well understand . . .

M

'Conversation with a Mother' (excerpts); source: as for Document L, pp. 59–60.

Editor: So, dear Madam, you do not wish to join our organisation?

M.: No, I see no possibility of joining with you. As you know, my husband is a Jew according to the Nuremberg Laws, and I myself am a pure Aryan – so a *Mischling* organisation surely has nothing for us.

Ed.: You should enrol in our organisation as a proxy for your two children . . .

M.: I don't know why I, an Aryan, would want to be in a Jewish organisation.

Ed.: Nor do I. But the competent authorities have made it very clear that we are not a Jewish organisation . . .

M.: But one does not wish to stand out, especially in our case . . .

Ed.: You would be justified in your worry about self-exposure if I were to ask you from now on to wear a brooch with an emblem of the organisation. But surely you are not going to hang the membership card on your wall?

N

'Fall In!' *[Einordnung!] by Bernhard Bennedik (excerpts); source:* Mitteilungsblatt der Vereinigung 1937 e.V., *vol. 4, No. 9 (September 1937), pp. 85–86.*

The Nuremberg Laws have designated the *Mischlinge* as a special group among German nationals. It has been often and sufficiently clearly explained that they constitute a special group and that they must learn to adjust to the status to which they have been assigned. But this does not yet suffice. We still must learn more. The continuing work of our organisation brings us into contact with the most varied set of individual and character types from among the circles that belong to us. Many still like to misunderstand the basic facts. Reference here is made to those who believe that they can occupy a special status for themselves alone and who therefore decline to join us as members. The number of people who think this is larger than one would assume, given the clarity of the situation. But if one seeks the cause of this type of thinking and the rejection which results from it, it is always the same: an egotistical way of thinking which either cannot or will not look further than the tip of its own nose.

The truth is that nobody can deny the fact that we are now all in the same boat. We did not place ourselves there, we were placed. The authority of the State is in the nature of all government-regulated life; nothing can alter that. Nothing can alter the necessity for accepting the discipline of obeying the laws that have been promulgated by the authority of the State. In the same way, nothing can alter the necessity of having every one of us recognise that he has been put together with us. Yes, to be consistent one must go even further and say that it would actually be a sign of faulty state-political discipline if one of us were to attempt to assume a special status on his own, or if he tried in any way to keep himself aloof from the status which the State has assigned to him together with all the rest of us. How can one overlook the fact that this discipline is the first and one of the most important signs of a positive disposition to any ordered, government-regulated life? It is therefore amazing almost to the point of disbelief that it is precisely those who pretend to a particularly positive disposition towards the State who desire a special status for themselves and who thereby violate the discipline of a State citizen.

They practise exactly the opposite of what should be the first consequence of this professed positive disposition. The first such consequence, naturally, should be a declaration on their part that they will proceed to where the law of the State places them, and right now that is with us . . .

As soon as the most elementary duty of a citizen has led the individual to proceed to that place to which he has been assigned, he must realise that he is not alone there. Even beyond the enforced nature of the communion in this assigned status, a closer unity is necessary. But there is no such realisation if the individual concerns himself only with himself instead of seeing himself as part of the community to which in fact he does belong . . . The State itself, which has established this community in its present form, is interested in seeing that this community receives that to which it is entitled, and the State itself therefore provides the opportunity to create [our] organisation, one of whose tasks, and not the least, is the preservation of [our] rights.

The person who is doing well thinks otherwise. He feels himself in possession of his rights, but he does not see the necessity to join an organisation that would preserve these rights. But here he thinks egotistically. And that is wrong for two reasons . . . In fact nobody stands by himself . . . The optimism which leads him to stand aloof from us is, so to speak, directed backwards. It is based on too few bad experiences, it is grounded in the past, it overlooks the possibilities of the future in which decisions can be made about him, any day, not as an individual but as part of our community.

O

'Report of the Meeting of District Group Rhein-Ruhr of the Vereinigung 1937 e.V., *held 13th November 1937 in Köln/Rhein', by Klaus Stern-Eilers (excerpts); source: as for Document N above, vol. 4, No. 12 (December 1937), pp. 102–103.*

District leader of Rhein-Ruhr, Herr Bernhard Bennedik,[12] had invited the members and friends of the organisation for Saturday, 13th November . . .

We have often had the pleasure of hearing our district leader in larger or smaller groups. This time we were offered a lecture that was, both oratorically and from the point of view of contents, unexcelled . . .

First we were given a purely statistical overview of our organisation in the whole *Reich* since the reorganisation that took place in March. Here we mention only figures for Rhein-Ruhr.

On 1st March 1937, i.e. before reorganisation, 390 members. On 15th March 1937, i.e. after reorganisation, 160 members. On 30th September 1937, 329 members. This means a gain, which one should not underestimate, of 169 members, i.e. a strengthening of 117 percent . . .

The district leader then spoke about our relationship to Judaism, and pointed to the difficulties of this problem. He summarised his comments in two main points:

1) Those who lean in their nature to Judaism move away from the German nature [*Deutschtum*].

2) Those who tend towards German nature move away from Judaism.

After a loyal profession to the German ethnic community, Herr Bennedik said . . . [that] the most difficult problem perhaps is that of mixed marriages in which there are children under-age, in which the German-blooded parent is to exercise a proxy [i.e. join the organisation in his name on behalf of his minor *Mischling* child – W.C.]. This proxy is then easily interpreted – understandably but wrongly – to the effect that the marriage partner [i.c. the Jewish partner – W.C.] is somehow deserted. . . . But one can only speak of desertion if because of one's action or failure to act the other side is directly or indirectly harmed. But this is not at all the case in taking out membership in our organisation . . . The position of those who are Jews in the eyes of the law is clear and unequivocal. Nothing is altered in this status, from the point of view of the State, if the father or the mother joins us. The position of the child, however, is not so clear. We hope and we wish that it will be possible to influence the child's opportunities in a positive direction. It is our organisation, alone and exclusively, that is in a position to do this . . . You can see from all this how important it is for us to make our relationship to Judaism very clear, and that this clarity can only be achieved by a clear-cut distinction between family and State. When a mother joins our organisation, she makes a declaration of what she wishes and aspires for her child in the framework of the State, and her relationship within the family has nothing whatever to do with this . . .

[12]Herr Bennedik can be identified by a small display advertisement which he frequently placed in the newsletter: "3B – Bernhard Bennedik Bürobedarf, Köln, Moltkestrasse 57"; i.e. he seems to have owned a stationery business. See, for example, *M*, June 1938.

P

'News Concerning Legislation and Administration!' source: as for Document N above, vol. 6, No. 3 (March 1939), p. 9.

. . . Concerning the marriage of *Mischlinge* Second Grade with civil servants, the *Reich* Minister of the Interior has issued the following regulation by means of a Bulletin dated 8th December 1938 – Pol O-Kdo P I (1a) Nr. 268/38:

"(1) According to §25, Part 2 of the German Civil Service Law of 26th January 1937 (RGBl. I Page 39), marriage of *Mischlinge* Second Grade with civil servants may be authorised. However, the required authorisation procedure by three Higher *Reich* Authorities – §25 Part 3 – indicates that such cases would have to be very exceptional. (2) Because of the special position of the police in the civil service, especially in consideration of the close connection between police and SS, I decline to grant such authorisation, even in exceptional cases, to police officers."

Q

Circular letter from Friedrich Karl Lesser, 11th August 1939; source: printed sheet.

[Letterhead of Vereinigung 1937 i.L *(League 1937, in Liquidation)]*

In accordance with an edict of the supervising authority dated 10th August 1939, the *Vereinigung 1937* has been dissolved and thereby placed in a state of liquidation. The former chairman is the liquidator of the organisation and therefore must transact all business related to the liquidation.

The organisation is no longer in a position to exercise any counselling or charitable function for its members. It is therefore requested that inquiries of whatever nature, except those directly related to the liquidation, be avoided. Other inquiries should from now on be directly addressed to the competent agencies, i.e. to a German lawyer or legal counselling agency, to the authorities or other groups (German Labour Front, National Socialist People's Welfare, Employment Office, etc.).

In order to effect the liquidation as smoothly as possible, it is urgent and essential that members remit any dues that may be in arrears for the period inclusive of August. The dues obligation ceases beginning September.

I thank all members for the confidence they have shown me as chairman and for their loyalty to the organisation. I wish them all the best for the future.

Friedrich Karl Lesser
Attorney-at-Law, Court of Appeal [*Kammergericht*]
Captain of Cavalry, (ret'd.) [*Rittmeister a.D.*]
Chairman as Liquidator

Hebrew and Yiddish in Germany

Hebrew Printing and Publishing in Germany, 1650–1750

On Jewish Book Culture and the Emergence of Modern Jewry

BY MENAHEM SCHMELZER

There was a century in early modern Jewish cultural and religious history in Europe that perhaps could best be characterised as an orphan. The approximately one hundred years that fall between the Chmielnicki massacres and the events surrounding the appearance of the pseudo-messiah Sabbatai Zvi at one end, and the emergence of *Hasidism* and Enlightenment at the other end, i.e. the second half of the seventeenth and the first half of the eighteenth century, are usually accorded scant treatment and are denied the kind of scholarly attention given to other, more spectacular periods in European Jewish cultural and religious history.* In contrast to the times that begin with Mendelssohn, the century preceding him is relegated into a kind of twilight zone that is regarded as the end of the vanishing Jewish Middle Ages. On the other hand, the years between 1650 and 1713 were recently characterised as a time when Jews, in the realm of economic and political activity, exerted "the most profound and pervasive impact on the West which they were ever to exert, whilst still retaining a large measure of social and cultural cohesion".[1] Culturally and religiously, however, the period still remains to be looked upon as inward-directed, self-contained, stagnating and rigid. It seems that a systematic and extensive study of the intellectual life of the German-Jewish community in the century preceding

*This paper is based on lectures delivered in 1986 at the Leo Baeck Institute, New York and at Yeshiva University, in conjunction with the latter's exhibition, *Ashkenaz: the German Jewish Heritage*. I wish to express my deep gratitude to Mr. and Mrs. Ludwig Jesselson for encouraging me to explore this subject during a sabbatical year that I spent at Yeshiva University in 1985–1986. I would also like to thank Yehudah Mirsky for his helpful comments on a draft of this paper.
[1]Jonathan I. Israel, *European Jewry in the Age of Mercantilism, 1550–1750*, Oxford 1985, p. [1]. Israel explicitly states that he has "not attempted to say anything new, or impart any substantially new emphases, on the religious history of the period". Surprisingly, Israel does not even mention in his bibliography any of Jacob Katz's books that are relevant to the period. Attention should be called here to Azriel Shohet's *Im hillufei tekufoth* (*Beginnings of the Haskalah among German Jewry*), Jerusalem 1960 (in Hebrew) that deals with the first half of the eighteenth century, mainly from the point of view of the social background. See Jacob Katz's discussion of Shohet's book in *Out of the Ghetto*, Cambridge, Mass. 1973, pp. 34ff.

the entry of Jews into modern society could lead to substantive change in this perception. By choosing to explore, albeit tentatively, some aspects of Hebrew printing and publishing in Germany during this period, we hope to gain new insights into the cultural, intellectual and religious conditions of the Jews. This activity, although it may look peripheral now, occupied central stage then, and therefore it may serve as a good instrument to be used for drawing a cultural profile of pre-emancipation German Jewry. After the Thirty Years' War, in the middle of the seventeenth century, the rulers of the numerous small sovereignties on German territory were eager to reconstruct the land and to develop strong, independent principalities. Jews were welcomed to settle in areas from which they had been excluded previously. Large numbers of Jews from Polish and Russian localities devastated by Chmielnicki, others who were expelled from Vienna in 1670, as well as co-religionists who fled the turmoil in Buda that resulted from the recapture of the city from the Turks in 1686, gravitated towards the German lands, where prosperity and relative protection awaited them. In the wake of this movement Hebrew printing in Germany rapidly expanded and by the end of the seventeenth century a steady and ever increasing flow of Hebrew and Yiddish books left the recently established printing presses.[2] In order to demonstrate the multifaceted nature of this activity, a few personalities and trends have been selected for describing the phenomenal expansion of Hebrew printing in a relatively short period of time. Through these selections we hope to illustrate the interplay of many factors which were responsible for this development.

Our first example is Shabbetai Bass,[3] printer, bibliographer and rabbinic scholar. Bass was a native of Kalisz, Poland, where his parents were killed in a pogrom in 1655. He and his brother survived and fled to Prague. There he became an assistant to the cantor of the *Altneuschul*. After a while he moved to Amsterdam. The Amsterdam Sefardi community made a tremendous impression on Bass to which he gave expression in the introduction to his book, *Siftei yeshenim*.[4] In a glowing portrayal of the advanced, progressive ways of the Sefardim, Bass described the organised, graduated, communally financed educational system of the Sefardi Jews of Amsterdam and contrasted them with what he considered to be the backwardness of the Eastern European Jews. *Siftei yeshenim* is the first Hebrew bibliography compiled by a Jewish author and in it Bass provided not only lists and classifications of books, but also a programme for the establishment of a Jewish educational system which could properly serve

---

[2]See Moritz Steinschneider and David Cassel, *Jüdische Typographie und jüdischer Buchhandel*, originally published in Ersch und Gruber, *Encyclopädie der Wissenschaften und Künste*, Teil 28, Leipzig 1851, reprinted in Jerusalem 1938, pp. 57–70. This is still the most comprehensive survey on the subject. See also *Encyclopaedia Judaica* (German), vol. 6, cols. 66–70: *Druckwesen* and *The Hebrew book; an Historical Survey*, ed. by Raphael Posner and Israel Ta-Shema, Jerusalem 1975, pp. 106–111.

[3]On the life and personality of Bass see the bibliography in Herbert C. Zafren, 'Dyhernfurth and Shabtai Bass: a Typographic Profile', in *Studies in Jewish Bibliography, History and Literature in Honour of I. Edward Kiev*, New York 1971, pp. 546–547.

[4]Amsterdam 1680, f. 8a-b.

the cultural and religious needs of all elements of Jewish society: the learned, the simple, the child, those who were familiar with Hebrew as well as those who only knew Yiddish. In this book, Bass demonstrated openness towards secular subjects, such as mathematics and medicine, and he even included a list of rabbinic works which were available in Latin translations.

The various interests of Bass and his concern for the raising of the educational level of the Jews, prompted him to acquire the technical knowledge required for the establishment of a Hebrew printing press. In 1689 Bass took up residence in a small Silesian town, Dyhernfurth. The town was founded just shortly before this time and the authorities, in order to promote the development of the new locality, granted Bass and a number of Jewish assistants the right to settle in the town and to start operating a Hebrew printing house.[5]

He and his assistants, mainly Jewish craftsmen from Prague and Cracow, constituted the foundation of the Jewish community in the new town. In the foreword to the first book that Bass published in Dyhernfurth he thanked God for making the heart of the local prince favourably inclined towards him by granting him the privilege to settle there and to establish a Hebrew printing press.[6] Bass eagerly availed himself of the new opportunity. His first publication, *Beith Shemuel*, a commentary on *Even haezer*, a section of Joseph Caro's *Shulhan Arukh*, composed by Samuel ben Uri Shraga, was ready even before the agreed deadline.[7] Samuel himself was of Polish origin, he studied in Cracow and served as rabbi in Szydlowiecz. He came to Dyhernfurth in 1689 in order to supervise the printing of his book. Soon afterwards he was invited to become rabbi and head of the famous *yeshiva* in one of the most important Jewish communities in Germany, in Fürth. It was there that Samuel published a second edition of his work,[8] incorporating into it comments and suggestions that emerged as a result of his learning together with his pupils in the Fürth *yeshiva*. Subsequently Samuel returned to Poland permanently.[9] These brief sketches of the lives of Bass and Samuel may serve as typical illustrations to the steady flow of two-way traffic between East and West[10] and to the mutual enrichment derived from this mobility. The basic commodity of the Jews was easy to transport: it consisted of knowledge, or as Bass formulated it: "wherever Samuel went, his house [the House of Torah] went with him".[11] Bass's first effort was followed by many more and during the existence of the press, operated by him and by his descendants until 1762, hundreds of Hebrew and Yiddish books were published. The output included Bibles, Talmuds, codes, responsa, prayerbooks, sermons, ethical and

[5]See Markus Brann, 'Geschichte und Annalen der Dyhernfurther Druckerei', in: *Monatsschrift für Geschichte und Wissenschaft des Judentums* (*MGWJ*), vol. 40 (1896), pp. 474–477.
[6]*Beith Shemuel*, Dyhernfurth 1689, afterword by Bass, f. 106b.
[7]*Ibid.*
[8]Fürth 1694.
[9]See *Encyclopaedia Judaica*, vol. 14, cols. 814–815.
[10]See Moses A. Shulvass, *From East to West. The Westward Migration of Jews from Eastern Europe during the Seventeenth and Eighteenth Centuries*, Detroit 1971.
[11]See note 6.

kabbalistic works, but also books of popular entertainment in Yiddish as well as a book on arithmetic.[12]

Let us now turn to another Hebrew publishing and printing venture. In Anhalt-Dessau we find the Court Jew, Moses Benjamin Wulff,[13] in the service of King Leopold I. The King was one of the pioneers of modernisation and Wulff was perhaps the most capable, dynamic, influential and wealthy Jew of his time. Wulff was deeply interested in Jewish matters. He established a *Klaus*, but also a Hebrew printing press in Dessau, in 1694. The privilege granted to him by the Duchess Henrietta Katherina included most liberal conditions: the new firm was to enjoy complete tax and duty freedom and these freedoms were to be extended to the staff, too.[14] More than 30 books were published between 1696 and 1704.[15] Wulff himself, because of his entanglements in stormy financial and legal affairs relinquished his role as the principal of the firm and transferred his press, equipment and stock to one of his relatives.[16] The press continued to operate in the neighbouring cities of Halle, Jessnitz and Köthen.[17] The highlight of this press was its Jessnitz period. Not only standard biblical, rabbinic and liturgical works were published in large numbers, but important books in other areas of learning as well. Mention should be made of a few: a new, etymological dictionary of the Hebrew language by an Ashkenazi author, Yehudah Aryeh Loeb, who settled in Provence, included an introduction that dealt with the history of languages in general and in which the author had also announced his plan to compose a book on French glosses found in Rashi's commentary on the Pentateuch.[18] Another interesting book printed in Jessnitz was the second edition of the medical and scientific encyclopaedia, *Maaseh Tuviah*, by Tobias Cohen. The work of this famous physician contained the latest information on medicine and on the natural sciences.[19] *The Guide for the Perplexed* by Maimonides was published in Jessnitz in 1742, for the first time after two hundred years, the previous editions having been published in the middle of the sixteenth century in Italy.[20] The astronomical work, *Nehmad ve-naim*, by David Gans, remained in manuscript for one hundred and thirty years until the Jessnitz printers issued it for the first time in 1743.[21] In the field of rabbinical studies an outstanding

---

[12]See the list in Moses Marx's 'A Bibliography of Hebrew Printing in Dyhernfurth, 1689–1718', in *Studies in Jewish Bibliography, etc.* (cited above in note 3), pp. 221–234, esp. numbers 45, 82, 94 and 108.

[13]See Max Freudenthal, *Aus der Heimat Mendelssohns*, Berlin 1900. A large part of Freudenthal's book deals with Wulff and his family. See also Selma Stern, *The Court Jew. A Contribution to the History of Absolutism in Central Europe*, Philadelphia 1950, index; and Alexander Altmann, *Moses Mendelssohn. A Biographical Study*, Philadelphia 1973, pp. 5–8.

[14]Freudenthal, *op. cit.*, pp. 157–160.

[15]*Ibid.*, pp. 163–173 and pp. 235–246.

[16]*Ibid.*, p. 174 and p. 181.

[17]For a list of books printed in Halle, see Freudenthal *op. cit.*, pp. 246–249, for Jessnitz, *ibid.*, pp. 251–270 and for Köthen, *ibid.*, pp. 249–251.

[18]*Oholei Yehudah*, Jessnitz 1719, f. [4b].

[19]Printed in 1721.

[20]Freudenthal, *op. cit.*, pp. 219–221 and p. 259, No. 82. See also Altmann, *op. cit.*, pp. 10–11.

[21]Freudenthal, *op. cit.* pp. 222–223 and p. 264, No. 87. See also, André Néher, *Jewish Thought and the Scientific Revolution of the Sixteenth Century. David Gans (1541–1613) and his Times*, Oxford 1986, pp. 67–71.

Title-page of 'Yefeh Anaf' by Samuel Jaffe, Frankfurt a.d. Oder 1696
Printed by J.Ch. Beckmann. The decorations depict Moses and Aaron and biblical scenes

Title-page of 'Bigdei Aharon' by Aharon Teomim, Frankfurt a. Main [1710]
Printed by Johann Koelner. The woodcut frame displays mythological figures

achievement was a new edition of the Maimonidean code, *Mishneh Torah*, which included the text of commentaries unpublished previously as well as geometrical figures specially etched for the new edition, all arranged in a pleasing typographical harmony.[22]

Back in Dessau, the son of Moses Wulff, Elijah, re-opened the printing house for a short time in 1742.[23] Among the most important publications leaving the renewed Dessau press was a commentary on the Talmud of Jerusalem by David Fränkel,[24] the teacher of Moses Mendelssohn. The interest in the Jerusalem Talmud, usually neglected by traditional students of rabbinics, is another indication of the widening horizons characterising the period. The importance of the intellectual atmosphere that prevailed in Dessau for the shaping of Mendelssohn's personality and the role of Hebrew printing in that city and vicinity in creating that atmosphere was fully recognised by Max Freudenthal who devoted more than half of his book, *Aus der Heimat Mendelssohns*, to the printing history of the Dessau, Halle, Jessnitz and Köthen presses.[25]

Hebrew printing presses in many other places were opened up one after the other. Some were established because of scholarly interests, others owed their existence to commercial ambitions. In Sulzbach, Northern Bavaria, Prince Christian August allowed the printer Moses Bloch to settle there and to open a Hebrew printing press.[26] The Prince was strongly drawn to mysticism and deeply interested in *Kabbalah*. He invited the Christian theologian and poet, Baron Knorr von Rosenroth, to join his court and encouraged him to publish his *Kabbala Denudata*, a study of the theosophical teachings of the Jews which contained many passages from the *Zohar* in Latin translation. The publication of *Kabbala Denudata* was completed in 1684 and in the same year Moses Bloch printed a magnificent, folio edition of the *Zohar* in the original, accompanied by a Latin dedication to Christian August composed by Baron Knorr von Rosenroth. There can be no doubt that Christian August's motives in granting Bloch the privilege to print Hebrew books were intellectual: namely, his desire to become familiar with Jewish mystical teachings.[27] Bloch took advantage of the grant and launched Sulzbach as one of the most prolific of Hebrew presses in Europe. From 1684 until 1851, Bloch, his successors, as well as other printers produced well over seven hundred Hebrew and Yiddish titles bearing the imprint Sulzbach, thereby making the name of this small Bavarian city well known in every Jewish community.[28]

[22]Freudenthal, *op. cit.*, pp. 214–219 and pp. 261–263, No. 85.
[23]*Ibid.*, p. 219.
[24]Printed in 1743, see Freudenthal, *op. cit.*, pp. 229–230 and pp. 240–241, No. 19; see also Altmann, *op. cit.*, pp. 13–14.
[25]Freudenthal, *op. cit.*, pp. 155–276 and 291–304.
[26]See Magnus Weinberg, 'Die hebräischen Druckereien in Sulzbach', in *Jahrbuch der jüdisch-literarischen Gesellschaft*, vol. I (1903), pp. 32–34 (and about previous attempts to print Hebrew books in Sulzbach, *ibid.*, pp. 25–32).
[27]On *Kabbala Denudata* and its influence see *Mishnath ha-Zohar*, by I. Tishby, vol. 1, Jerusalem 1971, p. 48 and pp. 113–114.
[28]See Weinberg, *loc. cit.*, vol. 1 (1903), pp. 19–202, vol. 15 (1923), pp. 125–155 and vol. 21 (1930), pp. 319–370.

In contrast to Sulzbach, the Wilhermsdorf Hebrew press was founded as a result of economic interests. Wolfgang Julius, Count of Hohenlohe, granted the privilege to establish a Hebrew press to Isaac Cohen, for the purpose of supporting the production of the local paper mills. The first Hebrew book left the Wilhermsdorf press in 1670 and in subsequent years many important, elegant and large format books were produced by the Hebrew printers of the city.[29] The convergence of various factors, chief among them the involvement of wealthy Court Jews who were ready to supply the initial financing, and the interest of local rulers in the large and active Jewish book market, encouraged the flourishing of more than twenty independent Hebrew presses in Germany in the period under consideration. The consumers were members of the German-Jewish communities and to a smaller extent German Christian Hebraists, but to a large measure it was the Eastern European community that had the capacity of absorbing a considerable portion of the production. Russia and Poland had no printing presses in the second half of the seventeenth century, with the exception of the fledgling Zolkiew press that was established in 1692.[30] Accordingly, the needs of Russian and Polish Jews had to be supplied from abroad and the German Hebrew presses were eager to do so.

As an excellent illustration of this state of affairs mention should be made of the 1697–1699 Frankfurt an der Oder edition of the Babylonian Talmud.[31] This major publication effort was the result of a combination of forces that joined together to produce the first complete Talmud in Germany. Behrend Lehmann,[32] the famous and influential Court Jew, who was Polish Resident to the Court of Brandenburg, underwrote the expenses of this major undertaking. According to some sources Lehmann spent 50,000 talers to produce the work. He was also instrumental, through his excellent connections, in obtaining the required permission for the Talmud. Indeed, such permissions were granted by Frederick III of Brandenburg and by King Leopold I. The application for the privilege was drafted by a Christian scholar, perhaps Johann Christoph Beckmann, professor at the University of Frankfurt an der Oder and business associate of the Gentile bookdealer, Michael Gottschalck. The latter operated a Hebrew printing press and had sufficient technical means and adequate staff to carry out such a major undertaking as the printing of the Talmud. Gottschalck also used the services of M. Berninger, a Christian engraver, who was the artist

[29]See Aron Freimann, 'Annalen der hebräischen Druckerei in Wilhermsdorf', in *Festschrift zum siebzigsten Geburtstage A. Berliner's*, Frankfurt a. Main 1903, pp. 100–115.

[30]See Hayyim Dov (Bernhard) Friedberg, *History of Hebrew Typography in Poland*, Tel-Aviv 1950 (in Hebrew), p. 41 and esp. note 2 there; pp. 59–60, 62–63 and esp. note 4 on p. 63. See also I. Heilprin, 'The Council of Four Lands and the Hebrew Book', in *Kirjath Sepher*, vol. 9 (1932–1933), pp. 373–374 (in Hebrew).

[31]See Max Freudenthal, 'Zum Jubiläum des ersten Talmuddrucks in Deutschland', in *MGWJ*, vol. 42 (1898), pp. 80–89, 134–143, 180–185, 229–236 and 278–285 and Raphael Nathan Rabinowitz, *Maamar al hadfasath ha-Talmud*, ed. by Abraham Meir Habermann, Jerusalem 1952, pp. 96–100. See also Manfred R. Lehmann, 'A Jewish Financier's Lasting Investment', in *Tradition*, vol. 19 (1981), pp. 340–347; Stern, *op. cit.*, p. 225 and see also Hans Joachim Schoeps, *Philosemitismus im Barock*, Tübingen 1952, pp. 188–189 with quotations from an eyewitness' report describing the scene in the printing house during the printing of the Talmud.

[32]See Stern, *op. cit.*, pp. 73–85 and *passim*.

in charge of the figures that were incorporated into the edition. The background of this venture was described by Rabbi David Oppenheim in his approbation.[33] Oppenheim referred to the burnings of the Talmud and other Hebrew books in the wake of the Chmielnicki massacres, to the frequent fires that destroyed Jewish books and the resulting dire need for Talmud volumes so that the study of Talmud in the *yeshivoth* could be continued. According to Oppenheim, the entire Jewish educational system was endangered because of the lack of sufficient copies of the Talmud. Needless to say, Oppenheim heaped praise on Lehmann for his generosity and mentioned that Lehmann distributed half of the edition to needy scholars, free of charge. As a result of the involvement of Christian scholars and businessmen in this venture, the text of the Talmud itself was cleansed from some of the corruptions that had previously disfigured it as an outcome of the intervention of Church censorship. Although the title-pages of this edition bear a statement that the volumes were printed in accordance with the regulations of the Council of Trent and that they followed the censored Basel Talmud (1578–1581), in actual fact many passages and the entire Tractate *Avodah Zarah* (on idolatry), which had been omitted in Basle, were restored in Frankfurt.[34] The publication of the Frankfurt Talmud was rightly considered an event of major importance for the Jewish community and apparently the edition was rather rapidly sold out. Soon, other complete editions of the Talmud were printed, in Frankfurt a. Main, in Berlin and Sulzbach, and the resulting fierce competition and occasional infringements of prior privileges and copyrights kept many secular and rabbinic courts busy.[35] In any case, the first complete edition of the Talmud ever printed in Germany demonstrates the cooperation of Jewish and Gentile, scholarly and financial, as well as Eastern and Western European Jewish forces.

More limited in nature, serving narrower interests and smaller geographic areas, were the printing presses established by a Christian and a rabbinic scholar, respectively. Heinrich Jacob Bashuysen, a Calvinist theologian and accomplished Hebraist, in addition to his translations of rabbinic works into Latin, had also operated a Hebrew printing press in his native Hanau, beginning in 1708.[36] It is worthwhile to call attention to the fact that Bashuysen printed not only such standard commentaries to the Bible as that of Don Isaac Abarbanel, but also difficult and very technical books on Talmud. In 1712 Bashuysen

[33]His approbation on the verso of the title-page of Tractate *Berakhoth*.

[34]See Rabinowitz, *op. cit.*, p. 100.

[35]On the various editions of the Talmud printed in German cities see Rabinowitz, *op. cit.*, p. 101, pp. 108–112, 115–117, 120–124, on legal controversies see *ibid.*, pp. 106–107, 111, 121 and 123–124; see also Nahum Rakover, *Ha-haskamoth li-sefarim ki-yesod li-zekhuth ha-yotzrim*, Jerusalem 1970, pp. 25–39.

[36]Ernst J. Zimmermann's 'Die Hanauer hebräischen Drucke (1610–1744)', in *Hanauisches Magazin* (Supplement to *Han. Anzeiger*), Jg. 3, Nr. 7 (1. Juni 1924) lists 52 entries according to Shlomo Shunami's bibliography (cited in note 42), number 2880. Unfortunately, Zimmermann's work was not available to me. On an earlier period in Hebrew printing in Hanau see Herbert C. Zafren, 'A Probe into Hebrew Printing in Hanau in the 17th Century or How Quantifiable is Hebrew Typography', in *Studies in Judaica, Karaitica and Islamica presented to Leon Nemoy*, Ramat Gan 1982, pp. 273–285.

published the pilpulistic *novellæ* on various tractates of the Talmud written by
Rabbi Yona Teomim (*Kikayon de-Yona*) and in 1714 he issued a book called
Sugyoth ha-Talmud by Moses of Rohatyn, in the original Hebrew, with a Latin
translation, under the title, *Clavis Talmudica*. This work was an important
methodological introduction to the pilpulistic way of Talmud study as it was
practised in many Polish and German *yeshivoth*.[37] Apparently, Bashuysen
believed that without an understanding of the rules governing the specific
method of *pilpul*, one could not understand the mentality of the contemporary
rabbis. Such deep familiarity with rabbinic writings must have developed
through personal contacts, and the interaction between scholars of different
faiths and scholarly backgrounds must have exerted an influence on both sides.
The large number of Latin dissertations produced in German universities on
Jewish topics by non-Jews show one side of the coin.[38] It is less obvious to
observe the other side, namely the influence of Christian scholars on the rabbis.
One may speculate that the exposure of rabbinic scholars to Christian orientalists may have led some of the former to become more inclined towards an
historical, methodological and more critical approach to their own heritage. A
thorough re-examination of rabbinic literature produced during this period may
detect such influences even in the traditional fields of learning and may point to
the existence of a subtle, perhaps hardly discernible phenomenon which could be
regarded as some kind of precursor of nineteenth-century *Jüdische Wissenschaft*.[39]

Let us now turn to another scholarly press, the one which was established by
the famous Rabbi Jakob Emden in Altona.[40] In 1743 Emden received a royal
privilege from Christian VII of Denmark that allowed him to print Hebrew
books. The privilege contained two restrictive conditions: Emden must refrain
from printing books in German and in Latin and he must submit all books
printed by him for approval to the local rabbinic and lay authorities. The first
condition, apparently imposed on Emden at the insistence of a Christian
publisher who feared that the new press would compete with his, was fulfilled.
We have no knowledge of any non-Hebrew book ever printed by Emden. On the
other hand, the second condition was flouted by the controversial rabbi. Emden
published a stream of polemical pamphlets against his great foe, Rabbi Jonathan
Eibeschütz, without proper approbation. Emden realised the power of the press
as a political tool and used it with great enthusiasm. Many of his tracts were
published without a prepared manuscript, improvising while setting the type
and camouflaging the fact that they were produced in Altona.[41] The fact that a

[37]On the nature of *pilpul* in Germany around this time see Hayyim Zalman Dimitrovsky, 'Al derekh
ha-pilpul', in *Salo W. Baron Jubilee Volume*, Hebrew section, Jerusalem 1974, pp. 128–130; see also
his 'Leket Yosef and Suqyot ha-Talmud', in *Alei Sefer*, vol. 4 (1977), pp. 90–98.

[38]See the extensive literature and list in Raphael Loewe's article in *Encyclopaedia Judaica*, vol. 8, cols.
9–71 ('Hebraists, Christian').

[39]Compare Altmann's remarks on David Fränkel's commentary on the Palestinian Talmud in his
work cited above (note 13), top of p. 14.

[40]On Emden's activities as printer of Hebrew books see Bernhard Brilling, 'Die Privilegien der
hebräischen Buchdruckereien in Altona (1726–1836)', in *Studies in Bibliography and Booklore*, vol. 9
(1969–1971), pp. 155–156 and vol. 11 (1976), pp. 41–56.

[41]*Ibid.*, vol. 9, p. 156 and p. 165, note 16.

scholar of Emden's stature invested his time and effort in learning the printing craft himself and the trouble he took to acquire the equipment and the type, as well as his skilful use of the press in his polemics against his adversary, indicate that Emden had recognised the potential of the printing press as an effective and quick instrument in furthering his cause. In this respect, Emden may be compared to other eighteenth-century public figures in Europe and in the American colonies who made similar use of the press. In addition to the Hebrew printing presses mentioned above there existed many others, some major and some minor. The very prolific Fürth press should be singled out, but others, in Berlin, Hamburg, Leipzig, Wandsbek, Homburg vor der Höhe, Karlsruhe, Neuwied, Offenbach, Rödelheim and elsewhere deserve to be remembered, too.[42] Despite some recent, important scholarship on the subject,[43] much more remains to be done and it is to be hoped that the history of Hebrew printing in Germany in the period will soon attract the kind of scholarly attention that it deserves.

Beyond the study of the history of the various printing presses, there are other areas that could offer insights into the life of the Jewish community, especially in the cultural and religious realm. In the following we shall briefly refer to some such aspects. The existence of well-run printing establishments served as a stimulus to many authors to publish their works and to migrate to places where such presses operated. On the title-page of a book on talmudic *aggadoth*, *Zinzeneth Menahem*, by Menahem Mendel ben Zevi Hirsch, we find the text of a letter issued by the Council of the Four Lands in Yaroslav in 1691. The signatories recommend the publication of the book and urge that the printer who will undertake the printing of the book, should proceed efficiently and quickly, in order to enable the author to return to his home without delay, otherwise the students in his *yeshiva* would be forced to be idle in their Talmud study. For some reason, the admonition of the Council was not heeded and the book remained unpublished until 1719 when printers in Berlin completed its 100 folios in four months. Rabbi Menahem Mendel enjoyed the hospitality of the son-in-law and

[42]See the literature cited above in note 2. See also Aron Freimann, *A Gazetteer of Hebrew Printing*, New York 1946 (reprinted in *Hebrew Printing and Bibliography*, ed. by Charles Berlin, New York 1976, pp. 255–340); see also Sh. Shunami, *Bibliography of Jewish Bibliographies*, 2nd edn. Jerusalem 1965, pp. 510–514: and also H. B. Friedberg, *History of Hebrew Typography of the Following Cities in Central Europe: Altona, etc.*, Antwerp 1935 (in Hebrew).
[43]See especially Bernhard Brilling's articles in *Studies in Bibliography and Booklore*, *Kirjath Sepher* and elsewhere. Mosche N. Rosenfeld of London has published a number of articles on Hebrew printing in Fürth in the bulletin of the *Israelitische Kultusgemeinde Fürth*. I understand that he is also planning to publish a comprehensive work on the history of Hebrew printing in Fürth. His paper on centres of Hebrew printing in the seventeenth and eighteenth centuries is scheduled to appear in a book to be published by the New York Public Library in 1988, under the title: *A Sign and a Witness. The Hebrew Book from Antiquity to Our Time*. On Yiddish books printed in the period much important material is found in the works of Chone Shmeruk and his school at the Hebrew University in Jerusalem. See his *Yiddish Literature. Aspects of its History*, Tel-Aviv 1978; and his *The Illustrations in Yiddish Books of the Sixteenth and Seventeenth Centuries*, Jerusalem 1986; and Sarah Zfatman, *Yiddish Narrative Prose*, Jerusalem 1985; as well as Chavah Turniansky, 'The "Bentsherel" and the Sabbath-Hymns', in *Alei Sefer*, vol. 10 (1982), pp. 51–92 (all in Hebrew).

daughter of the influential Court Jew, Joseph van Geldern, during the time that he was engaged in the supervision of the printing in Berlin.[44]

Rabbi Yair Haim Bacharach also dealt with the significance of the availability of efficient printing facilities for Hebrew works. He described the devastation of his city, Worms, in 1689, and his decision to settle in Frankfurt a. Main, among whose attractions he singled out the existence of a good, well-organised printing press. Once in Frankfurt, Bacharach began the publication of his book which was due to the favourable circumstances in the new domicile.[45] In a similar vein, Rabbi Ezekiel Katzenellenbogen, of Altona, Hamburg and Wandsbek, in the introduction to his collection of responsa, counted among his blessings the establishment of a printing press for Hebrew books in Altona which provided him with the opportunity to publish his work.[46]

An important aspect of the history of Hebrew publishing was the issue of freedom of the press, or rather the lack of it, namely censorship.[47] Control over publishing rested not only with the civil authorities but also with the rabbinate and with internal Jewish communal leadership. These authorities had the right to regulate the flow and contents of Hebrew and Yiddish books. The privileges extended to Jewish printers included, as a matter of course, the requirement that expressions that might be construed as offensive to Christianity be excluded from the text of the works to be produced. The enforcement of this provision, however, was not as strict as it had been when it was in the hands of centralised Church censorship which originated in sixteenth-century Italy. As an example of less stringent attitudes, reference should again be made to the Frankfurt 1697–1699 Talmud edition as well as to subsequent editions of the Talmud produced in various German cities.[48] Despite the more liberal times accusations against Hebrew books continued to be levelled and confiscation of Hebrew books took place in Fürth in 1702[49] and Shabbetai Bass was forced to face trials in Dyhernfurth in 1694 and again in 1712, having been accused by Jesuits for not excising from the Hebrew books published by him passages that allegedly contained anti-Christian statements.[50] Internal Jewish control was exercised through the instrument of rabbinic approbations, the *haskamoth*.[51] These served multiple purposes: they provided copyright protection, contained praise and recommendation for the author and attested to the reliability of the work from the point of view of religious beliefs and laws. The granting of *haskamoth* was one

[44]Verso of title-page of *Zinzeneth Menahem*, Berlin 1719.

[45]*Havvoth Yair*, Frankfurt a. Main 1699, f. [2a].

[46]*Keneseth Yehezkeel*, Altona 1732, f. [2a].

[47]On censorship of Hebrew books in general see William Popper, *The Censorship of Hebrew Books*, New York 1899, reprinted, with an introduction by Moshe Carmilly-Weinberger, New York 1969. Also Carmilly-Weinberger, *Censorship and Freedom of Expression in Jewish History*, New York 1977.

[48]See above note 35.

[49]See Leopold Löwenstein, 'Zur Geschichte der Juden in Fürth', in *Jahrbuch der jüdisch-literarischen Gesellschaft*, vol. 10 (1912), p. 51.

[50]See Brann's article cited above in note 5, pp. 560–562, 572–573.

[51]See Rakover's book cited above in note 35 and, on an earlier period in Italy but containing much important general material as well, M. Benayahu's *Copyright, Authorization and Imprimatour for Hebrew Books Printed in Venice*, Jerusalem 1971 (in Hebrew).

of the functions of the local rabbinate, but was also entrusted to the Council of Four Lands;[52] accordingly, in many Hebrew works printed in Germany, the *haskamoth* were divided into two groups, one by German rabbis and the other by their Polish and Russian colleagues. *Haskamoth* occasionally were issued with reservations. Rabbi Ezekiel Katzenellenbogen of Altona granted an approbation to Rabbi Efraim Heckscher's *halakhic* work, but took exception to one of his particular rulings, depriving it of its validity.[53] There are Hebrew and Yiddish books that lack *haskamoth* completely. Usually, their absence is a clear indication of either a copyright violation or questionable contents.[54] The latter applies especially to the area of popular literature, mainly works of belletristics that were issued in Hebrew characters, many originally composed in High German.[55] Despite the fact that in such works, containing popular German novels, the explicitly Christian expressions were neutralised (instead of cathedrals, fortresses, instead of Christian pilgrims, merchants were substituted, etc.), the lack of rabbinic approbations betray the displeasure of the rabbis with the dissemination of secular literature.[56]

The proliferation of Hebrew and Yiddish books provides an opportunity for research in various related areas, such as the reading and study habits of the Jewish population, the practices of the booktrade, the status of books in Jewish society, the book as a commodity, the book as an artifact etc. Since, to the best of this writer's knowledge, no systematic study has ever been conducted concerning these and related subjects,[57] the observations that follow must remain at this time of very tentative nature. First of all, on the basis of available lists of Hebrew printed books produced in various localities, one may venture to suggest that during the approximately one hundred years under discussion at least 2,500 separate editions of Hebrew and Yiddish books appeared[58] and if we assume that the average size of each edition was 1,000 we arrive at a total of two and a half

[52]See Yisrael Heilprin, 'The Council of Four Lands and the Hebrew Book', in *Kirjath Sepher*, vol. 9 (1932–1933), pp. 367–378; and his 'Approbations of the Council of Four Lands in Poland', *ibid.*, vol. 11 (1934–1935), pp. 105–110, 252–264; and also *ibid.*, vol. 12 (1935–1936), pp. 250–253. It would be useful to investigate the differences between the Polish and German *haskamoth*, although it seems that they were basically similar and concerned with more or less the same issues.

[53]*Adnei Paz*, Altona 1743, verso of title-page.

[54]See s.v. 'Approbation', *Jewish Encyclopedia*, vol. 2, esp. p. 28.

[55]See Arnold Paucker, 'Yiddish Versions of Early German Prose Novels', in *The Journal of Jewish Studies*, vol. 10 (1959), pp. 151–167, and his 'The Yiddish Versions of the Schildbürgerbuch', in *Yivo Bleter*, vol. 44 (1973), pp. 59–77; and his other articles cited there in notes 18–19. See also Zfatman's book cited above in note 43.

[56]Approbations are lacking in most of the books containing narratives that are listed in Zfatman's work.

[57]See, however, Zafren's various articles on the typographical aspects of Hebrew printing and esp. his statement in his paper cited above in note 3, pp. 543–544.

[58]We arrived at this figure by using the number of books listed in some of the bibliographies, e.g. Sulzbach (*Jahrbuch der jüdisch-literarischen Gesellschaft*, vol. 21 [1930], p. 348) has 701 items, Fürth (*ibid.*, vol. 10 [1912], p. 167) lists 533 entries, for Dyhernfurth (see Marx as cited in note 12, p. 234) we have 132 books, for Wilhermsdorf (Freimann, *op. cit.*, see above note 29, p. 113) 150, for Dessau, Jessnitz, etc. (Freudenthal, *op. cit.*, above note 13, p. 270) 104 books are listed. Using these figures and extrapolating the rest, it seems, that 2,500 for more than twenty presses is a rather conservative estimate.

million copies of books printed in Hebrew characters. Moritz Steinschneider and David Cassel estimated that about one third of all Hebrew books printed up to the beginning of modern times came from German-Jewish presses.[59] The average size of each edition, of course, is only an estimate, although we do have information on the size of some specific editions, e.g. Behrend Lehmann's 1697–1699 Talmud was published in 5,000 sets,[60] the Yiddish *Maasse-bukh* was issued in 3,500 copies in 1708–1709, while at the same time the bulky *Yalkut Shimoni* was printed, by the same publisher who issued the popular *Maasse-bukh*, in 1,600 copies.[61]

As to the subjects on which Hebrew and Yiddish books were published, one immediately observes that the largest proportion of them were of a liturgical nature. Prayerbooks of all kinds, *siddurim*, *mahzorim*, *Haggadoth*, *selihoth*, *tehinnoth*, etc., amount to at least half of all books published.[62] The standard editions of the Pentateuch, with Rashi's commentary, Targum Onkelos, *Haftaroth* and the Five Scrolls were also issued frequently and often they included the Sabbath prayers as well. Very popular were books on *mussar*, such classics of ethics as *Hovoth ha-levavoth*, *Menorath ha-maor*, and later works such as *Simhath ha-nefesh*, *Kav ha-yashar* and *Lev tov* saw dozens of editions.[63] Rabbinic works, besides the Talmud itself, i.e. codes, responsa, *novellæ*, etc. occupy a significant portion of this production. Popular entertainment, in the form of stories as well as transcriptions of German novels into Yiddish, also appeared in large numbers.[64] Philosophy, mysticism, medicine and astronomy were also represented, but in smaller numbers than the above mentioned categories. It would be rewarding to examine this area carefully and at the same time to pay attention to the relation between the number of original works by contemporary authors and between that of the re-issues of older works. One can judge the taste of the public also by the frequency of the editions of particular works. Books that had a practical bearing on *halakhic* matters, especially commentaries on those parts of the *Shulhan Arukh* that deal with the dietary laws were re-published over and over again. Still, works on *Midrash* and *aggadah* were also in demand as may be seen from the fact that the *Midrash rabba* and the *aggadic Yalkut Shimoni* and *Ein Yaakov* appeared fre-quently.[65] *Aggadic* works were considered potentially more profitable because of the wider readership and authors preferred to publish their *aggadic* books first in order to obtain the funds needed for subsequent publication of more technical

[59]*Op. cit.* (above note 2), p. 57.

[60]Rabinowitz, *op. cit.* (above note 31), p. 98, end of note 1; but see Freudenthal, *MGWJ*, vol. 42 (1898), p. 84, note 3.

[61]See Bernhard Brilling, 'Letters of a Jewish Publisher in Frankfurt on the Oder, 1708–1709', in *Studies in Jewish Bibliography and Booklore*, vol. 8 (1966–1968), p. 25.

[62]See e.g. the index (compiled by Joseph Prys) of books printed in Sulzbach, in *Jahrbuch der jüdisch-literarischen Gesellschaft*, vol. 21 (1930), pp. 368–370 and see also, *ibid.*, pp. 366–367.

[63]On *Hovoth ha-levavoth* see the bibliography by A. M. Habermann in *Sinai*, vol. 28 (1950–1951), pp. 320–329; the editions of *Menorath ha-maor* are listed in Naftali Ben-Menahem's introduction to the Jerusalem 1952 edition of the work and Jacob Shatzky listed the editions of *Simhath ha-nefesh* in his New York 1926 facsimile reprint of the work, pp. 23–29.

[64]See the literature cited in note 55.

[65]See their respective entries in H. D. Friedberg's *Bet Eked Sepharim*, Tel-Aviv 1951–1956.

halakhic or rabbinic works. As one rabbi puts it succinctly: *aggadah* is more appealing and therefore more people buy it![66]

It is generally assumed that a certain type of book, especially the very popular *Zena Ur'ena*, was directed towards the female reading public. Women were avid readers and also patronesses of publishing ventures, workers in the printing trade and accomplished scholars. Behrend Lehmann's wife, Haenele, urged her husband to lend hundreds of talers to the Jessnitz printers in 1721 to cover the cost of the printing of Rabbi Moses Alsheik's commentary on various biblical books.[67] Alsheik's works were very rare in Central Europe, because they had not been published for over a hundred years, since their first edition in Venice at the beginning of the seventeenth century. Among women who were accomplished scholars mention should be made of the grandmother of Yair Haim Bacharach,[68] and the wife of Joseph Steinhardt (who was Isaiah Pick Berlin's sister).[69] Women printers are mentioned from time to time, among them a nine-year-old girl who worked as a typesetter in Dessau at the end of the seventeenth century.[70]

Another aspect of the role that books played in this era is the question of book prices. It would be interesting to compare the prices of books to that of other commodities. In the meantime, it suffices to record some prices that are known: e.g. the scholarly *Beith Shemuel*, consisting of 160 folios was sold for 1 taler and 10 groschen, while four copies of the liturgical book, *Shaarei Zion*, which contained 48 quarto leaves were priced at ten groschen.[71] The main channels of book distribution were the fairs. Jewish merchants from East and West used to meet at the fairs of Königsberg, Leipzig, Breslau and Frankfurt an der Oder, and large quantities of books changed hands there.[72] Of course, there were also local booksellers and various other methods of promotion and sale.

The rabbinate in Poznań, in 1733, imposed upon the Jews of the district the compulsory acquisition of copies of *Even ha-shoham*, by the local rabbi, Eliakum Goetz ben Meir.[73] In a different vein, the Gentile printer, Johann Koelner of Frankfurt a. Main, planned to finance his edition of Alfasi's *Halakhoth* by selling lottery tickets that entitled the purchaser to a set as well as to a prize.[74] For some unknown reason Koelner's edition of this work never appeared. It is to be assumed, on the basis of general impressions and especially because of the large quantities of Hebrew books available, that the Hebrew book occupied a central

---

[66]In Zevi Hirsch Bialeh's (Hirsch Harif's) approbation to Jehiel Michael Glogau's *Nezer ha-kodesh*, Jessnitz 1719, f. 2a.

[67]See *Rommemuth el*, Jessnitz 1721, verso of title-page.

[68]See the introduction to his *Havvoth Yair*. Frankfurt a. Main 1699, f. [3a–b].

[69]See *Zikhron Yoseph*, Fürth 1773, f. [3a].

[70]See Abraham Yaari, *Studies in Hebrew Booklore*, Jerusalem 1955, pp. 256–302 (in Hebrew). On the nine-year-old girl see *ibid.*, p. 262 and also Freudenthal, *op. cit.* (above note 13), p. 271 and Alexander Marx, *Bibliographical Studies and Notes on Rare Books and Manuscripts in the Library of the Jewish Theological Seminary of America*, New York 1977, p. 326.

[71]See M. Marx, *loc. cit.*, (cited above in note 12), p. 221, Nos. 1 and 5.

[72]See esp. in Brilling's article, *loc. cit.*, note 61, p. 25 and see *Encyclopaedia Judaica*, s. v. 'Market Days and Fairs', vol. 11, cols. 1000–1005.

[73]See Heilprin, *loc. cit.*, *Kirjath Sepher*, vol. 9, p. 377.

[74]See Steinschneider and Cassel, *op. cit.*, cited above p. 59, note 2.

place in the average Jewish household. Again, the data are very scarce and not
collected, but some limited observations may be appropriate. It was pointed out
in a recent study that in the estate of normal, seventeenth-century Gentile
German citizens book collections did not constitute, either relatively or absolutely, a quantifiable portion; books are rarely mentioned in estate inventories and
if they are included their value is usually less than 1% of the total estate.[75] This
state of affairs could be compared to what is known to us about the estates of
Viennese Jews in the seventeenth and eighteenth centuries, where books are
regularly included.[76] Although the following is a far from typical example, it is
significant to single out the estate of Samson Wertheimer in whose household
articles were valued at 6,000 florins at the same time that the value of his book
collections, kept in his houses of study in Nikolsburg and Frankfurt, was
estimated at 13,000 florins.[77]

The proliferation of Hebrew and Yiddish books carried with it negative
phenomena as well. Criticism was levelled against some rabbis who published
their work, of limited scholarly or educational value, mainly for reasons of self-
aggrandisement and financial benefit. Rabbi Joseph Samuel of Cracow, who was
active in Frankfurt a. Main, advocated the prevention of the publication of books
of homilies and *novellæ* on codes, at least for a period of ten years, because the
quality of the books in those areas had declined and their authors were only
interested in promoting themselves. Rabbi Joseph Samuel was quite blunt:
"there are sufficient books in existence and we do not need any more".[78] Rabbi
Hirsch Charif of Halberstadt was perhaps even more outspoken about the work
of some of his contemporaries: "the publication of books of inferior quality is
actually harmful, they cause students to neglect the study of Talmud and their
publication should be prevented".[79]

It was not only the contents of the books that was found wanting but also their
external appearance. The Council of Four Lands thundered against those
printers who produced shabbily printed, inaccurately proof-read books, on
cheap paper. The poor readability and the corrupt text were considered to be
detrimental, especially in teaching children proper reading and understanding of
the basic Jewish texts.[80]

Perhaps as a reaction to the deterioration of mass-printed books, especially in
the area of liturgical books, some of the affluent Court Jews began to commission

[75]See *Stadt im Wandel. Kunst und Kultur des Bürgertums in Norddeutschland, 1150–1650*, hrsg. von Cord
Meckseper. Ausstellungskatalog, Band 3, Stuttgart–Bad Cannstatt 1985, pp. 653–659, esp. p. 655:
". . . die privaten Büchersammlungen weder absolut noch relativ einen besonderen Anteil an den
bürgerlichen Vermögen des 17. Jahrhunderts hatten".
[76]Israel Taglicht, *Nachlässe der Wiener Juden im 17. und 18. Jahrhundert*, Wien–Leipzig 1917, p. 44.
[77]*Ibid.*, p. 45, end of note 1.
[78]In his approbation to Hayyim Krochmal's *Mekor hayyim*, Fürth 1697, f. [3a].
[79]In his approbation to *Nezer ha-kodesh* (see above note 66) and elsewhere. See Benjamin Hirsch
Auerbach, *Geschichte der israelitischen Gemeinde in Halberstadt*, Halberstadt 1866, p. 66. In general, see
also Heilprin, *loc. cit.*, *Kirjath Sepher*, vol. 11 (1934–1935), pp. 105–110 and Rakover (note 35),
index, s. v. *nimmukim neged mattan haskamah*.
[80]See Heilprin, *loc. cit.*, *Kirjath Sepher*, vol. 9, p. 373.

beautifully written and decorated calligraphic manuscripts and expensively printed books produced on vellum or on blue paper.[81]

One more aspect of the period's great interest in publishing was the discovery and utilisation of Hebrew manuscripts for the editing of texts which had been unpublished previously. The most significant personality in this respect was David Oppenheim. His great collection of manuscripts served not only anti-quarian interests, but also furthered the publication, for the first time, of important works. It was Oppenheim who published the first edition of Samuel ben Meir's commentary on the Pentateuch and we have evidence that he made available his manuscript collection to contemporary scholars.[82] Many manu-scripts were utilised for the various Talmud editions and in general, old Hebrew manuscripts were used for critical text studies and for the establishment of an apparatus of variant readings.[83] This trend culminated in the activities of Rabbi Isaiah Pick Berlin in the second half of the eighteenth century.[84]

The interaction of many social, economic and political forces, the prominence of Court Jews in the community and outside of it, the contacts between Jews and Gentiles, in the commercial as well as in the scholarly realm, the mobility of Jewish scholars and the migration from East to West and back, the growth of *yeshivoth* and the establishment of the *Klaus* in many communities where rabbis had the opportunity of undisturbed study, made the period outstandingly productive in many areas of Jewish learning. The phenomenal development of Hebrew printing in a relatively short period of time in so many German cities is a testimony to this vitality. Accordingly, the second part of the seventeenth and the first part of the eighteenth century were not only crucial economically and socially but also culturally and religiously. Further competent and detailed research in the diverse aspects of the history of the Jewish book in Germany in the period before the emancipation may reward us with many new insights and with a reappraised image of the intellectual profile of pre-modern German Jewry.

---

[81]On eighteenth-century manuscript illumination, a very popular topic lately, still the best survey is Ernest Naményi, 'La miniature juive au XVIIe et au XVIIIe siècle', in *Revue des études juives*, vol. 116 (1957), pp. 27–71 and its English version in *Jewish Art* ed. by Cecil Roth, rev. edn., Jerusalem 1971, pp. 149–162. See also Chaya Benjamin, Introduction to the facsimile edition of the Copenhagen Haggadah, 1986 and my list, 'Decorated Hebrew Manuscripts of the 18th Century in the Library of the Jewish Theological Seminary of America', in *The Alexander Scheiber Memorial Volume* (in press). On books printed on vellum and on coloured paper in this period, esp. those commissioned by David Oppenheim, see Alexander Marx, *Studies in Jewish History and Booklore*, New York 1944 (reprint: 1969), pp. 217–218.

[82]See Yitzchok Dov Feld in his introduction to Oppenheim's *Nishal David*, vol. 2, Jerusalem 5736 [1976], pp. 36–39.

[83]See Rabinowitz, *op. cit.*, pp. 103–105, note 1, quoting at length from the introduction to the Frankfurt a. Main 1720–1722 edition of the Talmud.

[84]See Abraham Berliner, *Rabbi Jesaja Berlin; eine biographische Skizze*, Berlin 1879.

From Friedländer's Lesebuch to the
Jewish Campe
The Beginning of Hebrew Children's
Literature in Germany

BY ZOHAR SHAVIT

INTRODUCTION

Hebrew children's literature began to develop in Germany in the framework of the Jewish Enlightenment movement (*Haskalah*) in the last decade of the eighteenth century, and the first decades of the nineteenth and was the outcome of complex societal and cultural factors. This is why its pattern of development and the structure of its inventory should be examined in the light of a complex net of relationships: its relations with German children's literature, its function in the Jewish Enlightenment movement and in particular in modern Jewish education, its need to overcome children's reading of Yiddish and later its need to combat the preference for German culture in general and German children's books in particular.

The study of this forgotten chapter in the history of Hebrew culture is still in its initiative steps, and it will take years to accomplish. The study faces many difficulties because of its need to reconstruct an inventory the remnants of which had been destroyed during the Holocaust, but even long before that had ceased to exist as a living inventory. Moreover, except for the books themselves (of which a great part is lost for ever), very little evidence with regard to the circumstances of their creation is available. Many of the questions concerning the scope and dimensions of this fine chapter of Hebrew culture seem to be left open.*

Another difficulty results from the complicated, even paradoxical, course of

von Humboldt-Stiftung which enabled me to work under ideal conditions in the Arbeitsstelle für Kinder- und Jugendliteraturforschung in Köln University. I am most grateful to the people connected with this unique project, especially to its director, Professor Brüggemann, who was very helpful in every possible way, and to Dr. Hruby and Mrs. Michels who were always very willing to assist. I am also grateful to the Basic Research Foundation of the Israeli Academy of Sciences and Humanities for its support.

development: It seems to me, at this stage of my research,[1] that in less than two generations, Hebrew children's literature had totally changed its direction; from being an exclusive product of the Enlightenment movement, it was more and more written and absorbed by its opponents, namely the religious circles of the New Orthodoxy. At first it was aimed at the offspring of the Enlightenment circles who composed an economic and cultural élite. However, since most of those children were enrolled in German schools and became culturally assimilated, they could not fulfil for Hebrew books the function of a readership. As far as the newly written Hebrew books for children were concerned this had an immediate impact. The books could not reach their intended audience, who preferred to read books in German, a language that became either their mother tongue or their second language. On the other hand, the new network of schools of the Enlightenment movement was often populated by children of other strata than the élite: those whose parents sent them to study in these schools not because they identified with the ideology of the Enlightenment movement, but because the schools were free. These children never became a real reader potential for the new books in Hebrew.

Since Hebrew children's literature in Germany had based the demand for its books for children on ideological premises, this situation created an unbearable state of affairs for its existence. The lack of a real source of readers could have meant its destruction before it even began to develop. This would most likely have been the case, had it not been for a new audience that began to emerge. While Hebrew children's literature was losing its intended audience in less than two generations, a new audience grew out of an unexpected source: the circles of the New Orthodoxy.

The Enlightenment movement did not leave the Orthodox circles indifferent to the new developments in the field of education. They reacted to the upheaval in Jewish history by establishing their own schools where subjects other than Talmud were taught. For the children of these religious circles new books were required. They created once more a demand for books for children which had a religious teaching but nevertheless would be written according to a different model from that of traditional religious books for children.

Hence, a paradoxical process took place: after the Hebrew language had been neglected by the second generation of the Enlightenment movement, it was taken over by Orthodox Jews who were opposed to the Enlightenment but continued the course of development initiated by it. This resulted in a demand for Hebrew books for children and preserved writing in Hebrew for them even after the centre of Hebrew culture had been transferred to Eastern Europe.

A full survey of the development of Hebrew children's literature in Germany cannot ignore these two contradictory trends of development. However, my current discussion will be limited to the description of the development of

---

[1]At the current stage of research I deal only with the children's books of the Enlightenment movement. Even this study is still in its initial phase. Hence many of the hypotheses, and especially those concerning the relations with the Yiddish system, are, as is indicated later on, for the time being only working hypotheses.

Hebrew children's literature within the Enlightenment movement. That is to say, until the transfer of the cultural centre to Eastern Europe in the middle of the nineteenth century.

While the inquiry into the history of Hebrew children's literature is still in its early stages and many of the hypotheses to be advanced here are only working hypotheses, the background for this study, namely the history of Jewish education in Germany, and to a larger extent, the history of the Jewish Enlightenment movement, has been thoroughly researched. The excellent studies by Katz,[2] Liberles,[3] Eliav and Elboim,[4] Kober,[5] Levin,[6] Stern-Taeubler,[7] Reinharz and Schatzberg,[8] serve as a reliable foundation for this study which otherwise stands on such shaky soil. This article will be based on the above-mentioned works and will focus mainly on the motivations and legitimisations of Hebrew children's literature at its inception. It will present here its main characteristics and patterns of development and then describe some specific cases in more detail.

CIRCUMSTANCES OF EMERGENCE

The history of Hebrew children's literature is a history of delayed development, regressions and "ab-normal" processes, as shown in the works of Even-Zohar[9] and Ofek.[10] Hebrew children's literature took its first steps when European children's literature was in a rather advanced stage and was rapidly approaching its so-called "Golden Age". At that time (the end of the eighteenth century, the beginning of the nineteenth) European children's literature in general, and German children's literature in particular, had already been recognised as a cultural institution with a hundred years of history; the systems of various

[2]Jacob Katz, *Die Entstehung der Judenassimilation in Deutschland und deren Ideologie*, Inaugural-Dissertation, Frankfurt a. Main 1935; *idem, Out of the Ghetto. The Social Background of Jewish Emancipation 1770–1870*, Cambridge, Mass. 1973 (enlarged Hebrew version: Tel-Aviv 1986).
[3]Robert Liberles, 'Was There a Jewish Movement for Emancipation in Germany?', and 'Emancipation and the Structure of the Jewish Community in the Nineteenth Century', both in *LBI Year Book XXXI* (1986), pp. 35–67.
[4]Mordechai Eliav, *Jewish Education in Germany in the Period of Enlightenment and Emancipation*, Jerusalem 1960 (in Hebrew); Rachel Elboim-Dror, *Hebrew Education in Eretz Israel*, vol. I: 1854–1914, Jerusalem 1986 (in Hebrew).
[5]Adolf Kober, 'Emancipation's Impact on the Education and Vocational Training of German Jewry', *Jewish Social Studies*, vol. 16 (1954), pp. 3–33.
[6]Mordechai Levin, *Social and Economic Values. The Idea of Professional Modernisation in the Ideology of the Haskalah Movement*, Jerusalem 1975 (in Hebrew).
[7]Selma Stern-Taeubler, 'The Jew in the Transition from Ghetto to Emancipation', *Historia Judaica*, vol. 2;2 (1940) pp. 102–119; *idem*, 'Der literarische Kampf um die Emanzipation in den Jahren 1816–1820 und seine ideologischen und soziologischen Voraussetzungen', *Hebrew Union College Annual*, vol. xxiii, Part ii (1950–1951), pp. 171–196.
[8]Jehuda Reinharz, Walter Schatzberg (eds.), *The Jewish Response to German Culture. From the Enlightenment to the Second World War*, Hanover–London 1985.
[9]Itamar Even-Zohar, *Papers on Historical Poetics*, Tel-Aviv 1978, especially: 'Interference in Dependent Literary Polysystems', pp. 54–62; 'Israeli Hebrew Literature. A Historical Model', pp. 75–94.
[10]Uriel Ofek, *Hebrew Children's Literature. The Beginnings*, Tel-Aviv 1979 (in Hebrew).

European children's literatures became both heterogeneous and stratified. (For the history of German children's literature, one has to consult especially Brüggemann,[11] Grenz,[12] Ewers,[13] Hurrelmann,[14] Baumgärtner,[15] Dyrenfurth,[16] Wegehaupt,[17] Scheunemann[18] and Schmidt[19]).

Hebrew children's literature, on the other hand, began to develop only from that point. This delay was rooted in the peculiar circumstances of the development of Hebrew literature which involved the special status of Hebrew language as the language of high culture and the multi-territorial existence of Hebrew literature; a situation which came to an end only when the centre of Hebrew literature was transferred to Palestine in the late twenties of the twentieth century.

Furthermore, the Hebrew texts were written for children whose mother tongue was not Hebrew. The intended audience for those books were children who came to study in the new network of schools the Enlightenment movement had established in Germany between the years 1780–1850 (several schools continued to exist even later, some remained active until the Second World War). The number of Jewish pupils in those years never exceeded, during the entire period, a couple of thousand. According to Eliav,[20] the average number of pupils in the Berlin school between the years 1800–1813 did not go beyond 55. The school in Breslau, which was opened in 1791, had in its first year 120 pupils, but their number declined to 90 in the second year and never went up again. The entire number of pupils in Jewish schools in 1807 (including girls) was around 440, and in 1812 about 900 children studied in the schools of the Enlightenment movement. My purpose in mentioning all these data is only to point to the incredible discrepancy between the number of books and the number of their readers. This ratio is more than puzzling. In spite of the fact that a reconstruction of an entire inventory seems to be an impossible task, one can still trace a couple of hundred books. The ratio implies that there were almost as many books as children who could read them. It makes it quite clear why it is impossible to account for the development of Hebrew children's literature in terms of a real demand under normal market conditions (which was partially the case with

[11]Theodor Brüggemann, in Zusammenarbeit mit Hans-Heino Ewers, *Handbuch zur Kinder- und Jugendliteratur. Von 1750 bis 1800*, Stuttgart 1982.

[12]Dagmar Grenz, *Mädchenliteratur. Von den moralisch-belehrenden Schriften im 18. Jahrhundert bis zur Herausbildung der Backfischliteratur im 19. Jahrhundert*, Stuttgart 1981.

[13]Hans-Heino Ewers (Hrsg.), *Kinder- und Jugendliteratur der Aufklärung*, Stuttgart 1980.

[14]Bettina Hurrelmann, *Jugendliteratur und Bürgerlichkeit*, Paderborn 1974.

[15]Alfred Clemens Baumgärtner, *Das nützliche Vergnügen. Goethe, Campe und die Anfänge der Kinderliteratur in Deutschland*, Würzburg 1977.

[16]Irene Dyrenfurth, *Geschichte des deutschen Jugendbuches*, Zürich–Freiburg [3]1976.

[17]Heinz Wegehaupt, *Vorstufen und Vorläufer der deutschen Kinder- und Jugendliteratur bis zur Mitte des 18. Jahrhunderts*, Berlin 1977.

[18]Beate Scheunemann, *Erziehungsmittel Kinderbuch. Zur Geschichte der Ideologievermittlung in der Kinder- und Jugendliteratur*, Berlin 1978.

[19]Egon Schmidt, *Die deutsche Kinder- und Jugendliteratur von der Mitte des 18. Jahrhunderts bis zum Anfang des 19. Jahrhunderts*, Berlin (East), 1974.

[20]Eliav, *op. cit.*, p. 163.

European children's literature, as I have shown elsewhere[21]). On the other hand, it only puts more weight on the role of ideology in this development.

IDEOLOGY AS A SOLE BASIS

The basis for the development of Hebrew children's literature in Germany was the ideology of the Enlightenment movement which created a demand for books for children. As is well known, the Enlightenment movement firmly believed in the importance of "secular" culture and philosophy, whose acquisition could be achieved by rational education. Hence the adherents of the movement turned to a change in the curriculum, regarded as the main means for shaping a new mode of Jewish life. This change was put into practice in the new network of schools, where a demand for new and different books was created.

This demand was a totally new phenomenon in the history of the Jews in Germany and later on in Eastern Europe (though it is true that similar developments took place among Sephardi communities in Amsterdam, Bordeaux and Hamburg even earlier (as has been demonstrated by Machmann-Melkmann[22]). Until then children were taught Hebrew in order to enable them to read the holy books and the Talmud. The deliberate production of Hebrew texts for a non-religious use as children's reading was an entirely new idea and consequently a totally new cultural institution. Furthermore, this was an artificial creation because it was not based on the usual premise of demand and supply, and fulfilled the demand of writing much more than the demand of reading.

It was, then, ideology that served as the main motivating force in the creation of Hebrew children's literature over more than a century and determined its distinguishing features, including of course the selection of certain texts as well as the prohibition of others.

The choice of Hebrew as the language of the books was also a result of ideological decision. This decision was neither automatic nor self-evident. It is true that Moses Mendelssohn had considered the Hebrew language a national treasure, but already in his time his devoted pupil and adherent, David Friedländer, had a different view and regarded German as the preferable language. Hence, it was from the very beginning that the production of books for Jewish children involved two opposing trends: the "Hebrew" and the "German". The latter was unequivocally demonstrated in the very first Jewish book for children, David Friedländer's *Lesebuch für jüdische Kinder*.[23] This book was written in German, and except for a copper plate engraving which presented the Hebrew

---

[21] Zohar Shavit, *Poetics of Children's Literature*, Athens–London 1986. Especially chapter six: 'The Model of Development of Canonized Children's System', pp. 133–157.

[22] Yoseph Machmann-Melkmann, 'First Fruit of Education', *Leshonenu La-Am*, vol. 18 (1967), pp. 84–88 (in Hebrew).

[23] David Friedländer, *Ein Lesebuch für jüdische Kinder*, Berlin 1779. For a description of this book see: Moritz Stern, *Lesebuch für jüdische Kinder, mit Einleitung*, Berlin 1927; Zohar Shavit, *The Lost Search for the Jewish-German Enlightenment Jew: David Friedländer's Lesebuch für jüdische Kinder* (in preparation).

letters, Hebrew was not used. Friedländer's attempt was characterised by its effort to find Jewish equivalents for German elements, in other words, to choose from the available Jewish heritage only those elements that could carry functions which were carried by similar elements in German children's literature.

During the first period Friedländer's attempt was an exception rather than the rule. It was defeated by the other tendency, namely that of "Hebrew". The Hebrew tendency, which prevailed during the first generation of writers for children, endeavoured either to translate German texts into Hebrew, or to follow German models in the writing of Hebrew texts. However, in spite of the fact that the Hebrew tendency succeeded at first, it declined when the entire Hebrew centre declined, and gave way to the German tendency some decades later. It is true that school books in Hebrew continued to be written for those children who studied in the Jewish schools, but they were no longer part of an effort to create Hebrew culture in Germany. Once the Enlightenment movement declined, Hebrew children's literature as well as the Hebrew literature itself, did not any longer have a cultural justification in Germany. It continued to develop first at the periphery of Germany and later on in Eastern Europe, where the Hebrew cultural centre had been transferred.

In Germany, the process of abandoning Hebrew in favour of German already began with the second generation of writers and dominated the third and the fourth generations of the Jewish Enlightenment movement. Jewish writers in Germany gave up Hebrew and began to write books in German for Jewish children. This process reached its peak when Jewish writers, who regarded themselves as Germans, wrote books for children in the German language, without differentiating between Jewish and non-Jewish children.

However, at first the ideological trend which promoted the "Hebrew" tendency did prevail and was responsible for the production of books for children. Its decline later on was not a result of market constraints, but simply the victory of another trend of ideology. Ideology was then the governing factor in the development of Hebrew children's literature and its sole basis. As a matter of fact, Hebrew children's literature managed to liberate itself from the exclusive hegemony of ideology only very late, in Palestine, where the commercial factor began to play a role in publishing for children.

Before that time, publishing for children was rarely profitable and was motivated by the wish to use the books as a vehicle for expressing certain values. This hegemony of ideology resulted in the Hebrew children's literature system being for a long time a "defective" system lacking some components which existed in other European children's literature at the time (as has been shown by Even-Zohar[24]). What strikes one in particular is the lack of popular texts whose existence as literature for amusement was inconceivable in terms of Hebrew literature.

The prevailing notion of literature at the time of the Enlightenment resulted in a kind of taboo on certain texts. This was accompanied by a desperate effort to combat Yiddish reading. On the other hand this notion evolved a demand for

[24]Itamar Even-Zohar, 'Polysystem Theory', *Poetics Today*, vol. 1 (1979), pp. 287–310.

didactic texts for children. I would not argue that ideological considerations implied only "destructive" or "negative" consequences for the development of Hebrew children's literature. Quite the contrary, those were factors that actually enabled the very beginning of Hebrew children's literature and supported it for a long time.

The complete reliance of Hebrew children's literature on ideology was responsible for two decisive phenomena in its development:

(a) The prevalence of a concept of children's literature as a main vehicle for distributing ideas (first of the Enlightenment movement, later on of the Renaissance movement).

(b) Hebrew interference with the German texts.

(c) A fight against Yiddish.

Being one of the main products of the Enlightenment movement, it is not surprising that Hebrew children's literature was, in its German period, entirely dependent on German children's literature and had developed in a continuous mode of interference with the German originals. On the other hand, the function of Yiddish literature in this development is indeed surprising. In spite of its enormous hostility towards Yiddish culture and Yiddish literature, the Enlightenment movement could not afford to ignore it, because it had to face children's preference for the reading of popular Yiddish texts over Hebrew texts. These texts attracted children firstly because they were written (at least in some cases) in the children's mother tongue. And secondly, as was the case of the European chapbooks, because they were textually much more attractive. For a rather long time the reading of Yiddish predominated over the reading of Hebrew among children, though this was at no time officially recognised. Afterwards, when children mastered German, the German children's literature predominated over the Hebrew.

However, unlike the case of Yiddish, this move to German literature was officially approved, but it also meant the end of Hebrew children's literature in Germany. It is interesting though to note that even when the cultural centre was transferred to the East, Hebrew children's literature continued to be dependent on German children's literature for quite a long time.

THE ENLIGHTENMENT MOVEMENT AND WRITERS FOR CHILDREN

While the history of European children's literature teaches us that not before the emergence and crystallisation of the concept of childhood could books which were deliberately orientated towards children be written,[25] Hebrew children's literature was in need of something different before it could begin to develop. It had to wait for a considerable change in the concepts of Jewish society, especially those

[25]Cf. Philippe Ariés, *Centuries of Childhood*, London 1962; John Rowe Townsend, *Written for Children*, London 1977.

concerning education and the attitude towards the outside world, in order to permit a system of children's books to begin to develop. Only when such a change took place was there room for Hebrew books for children. This is the reason for the relatively late development of Hebrew children's literature. It ensued when European books designed for children had already been in existence for a whole century as an institutionalised phenomenon. It began to develop when German children's literature was on the eve of the Romantic period, leaving behind it the Enlightenment period, which nonetheless, despite this, became godfather to Hebrew children's literature.

Thus, the creation of Hebrew children's literature became possible due to internal societal developments. The Jewish Enlightenment movement was active mainly in the cultural field, and in particular in that of education. The first Hebrew books for children developed out of these activities, and were meant to serve their goals. Due to the strong link between the Jewish and the German Enlightenment movements, German children's books of the German Enlightenment movement had a far-reaching function in the development of the Hebrew genre.

The relations between the two movements have been described and analysed in well-documented and exhaustive studies. It is not our intention here to add anything to this topic, but only to refer to the well-known fact that the connections between the two Enlightenments were especially strong in the field of education. For example: Moses Mendelssohn and Johann Bernhard Basedow used to correspond, and it was Mendelssohn who recommended that the Jews support Basedow in his *Elementarwerk*.[26] Furthermore, the protagonists of the Enlightenment were greatly influenced by ideas of philanthropism in their educational views.[27] Adopting the German Enlightenment movement's attitude towards it, education was regarded as the most important means for speeding up assimilation processes. For the purveyors of the Enlightenment, the *Maskilim*, education was the best venue for achieving the desired synthesis between the Jewish culture and that of the surrounding world.

The protagonists of the Jewish Enlightenment movement occupied themselves continuously with pedagogic issues. *Hame'asef* and *Shulamit* regularly published articles concerning problems of pedagogy, which often cited Locke, Rousseau, Basedow, Campe and to a lesser extent Pestalozzi. Quite a few schools which

[26]As is well known Basedow and Mendelssohn had been corresponding on philosophical issues. Mendelssohn had sent Basedow his essay, 'Das Daseyn Gottes a priori erwiesen' (Alexander Altmann, *Moses Mendelssohn. A Biographical Study*, London 1973, p. 323) and rejected Basedow's notion of a "duty to believe". Their relations stretched also beyond intellectual exchange. Basedow asked Mendelssohn to help him to obtain financial support for his *Philanthropin* in Dessau (and indeed the Jews of Berlin donated 518 Talers to his school). Karl Adolf Schmid (Hrsg.), *Geschichte der Erziehung vom Anfang bis auf unsere Zeit*, Stuttgart 1898. Vierter Bd.: 2, pp. 110–112. In his *Elementarwerk* Basedow devoted almost an entire *Tafel* (80) to Jewish matters. Of the four pictures one is a portrait of Mendelssohn by Chodowiecki (the only portrait to be included in the book), and two pictures that depict the persecution of Jews.
[27]See the excellent article by Ernst Simon on the connections in the field of education, 'Philanthropism and Jewish Education', *Mordecai M. Kaplan Jubilee Book*, New York 1953, pp. 149–187 (in Hebrew).

were established as an alternative to the traditional system of education, endeavoured to follow in practice the philanthropist model. The schools were established in the cities of the biggest Jewish communities in Germany: Berlin, Frankfurt a. Main, Breslau and Hamburg, but also in small communities such as Wolfenbüttel and Seesen where they were established mainly for children from outside and were initially built as an *Internat*.

Under the influence of the *Philanthropin* they started to preach in favour of returning to nature, to proclaim human happiness as an educational ideal and to emphasise the concepts of beauty, love and physical labour. Special attention was given to the natural sciences, justifying it by religious, moral and aesthetic claims. The influence of the *Philanthropin* system was so strong, that Eliav[28] goes even so far as to claim that the Jews were the first to apply the ideas of the *Philanthropin* to the letter in their schools, even before they were applied in the German schools.

However, as already mentioned, the Enlightenment movement faced many difficulties in attracting pupils to the new network of schools. This fact had a far-reaching effect on the character of the books and determined to a large extent the options for the development of Hebrew children's literature in Germany: more limitations were on the books, and less and less themes and writers were accepted. This is one of the explanations for the rather monolithic character of the books for children and the very limited number of titles chosen for translation. It also explains why the same titles were repeated over and over again. Hebrew writers adopted from the very beginning a limited number of texts and hardly deviated from this fixed repertoire during the entire period. In this sense Hebrew children's literature was very different in its course of development from European children's literature, where a process of intensive stratification took place.

Hebrew writers for children could not afford, for ideological reasons, to adopt later developments in German children's literature and had to remain within the boundaries of the German Enlightenment books for children. Those first writers for children were adherents of the Jewish Enlightenment movement (for instance, Yehuda Ben-Sew, Aharon Wolfsohn, Schalom Ha-Cohen, Yizhak Satanow, Marcus Boss, Baruch Schönfeld, Yehuda Yeiteles, Moritz Steinschneider, Schmuel Fin, Naphtali Wessely and Herz Homberg. They had been active in every field of Hebrew culture and most of them had published their works in the various organs of the Enlightenment movement, such as *Hame'asef* (1784–1797, 1809–1811) and *Bikure Ha-Itim* (1820–1831).[29] As stated already, they hardly ever gained any financial benefit from their writing and more often than not they had to defray the publishing costs. The lack of any financial compensation in writing for children did not prevent them, however, from continuing to produce children's literature which was used to express their ideas and disseminate them by means of these texts. If one looks at the question from the writer's point of view, writers must have been labouring under the strong

---

[28]Eliav, *op. cit.*, p. 4.
[29]Cf. Menucha Gilboa, *Hebrew Periodicals in the 19th Century*, Tel-Aviv University, 1986.

influence of ideology and one is tempted to describe them as zealots, as they continued to write books for children in such conditions.

Their views were implicitly expressed in the books themselves, but they were also given explicit expression in the introductions to the books. Here writers' motivations for translating or writing a book were presented. The types of motivation repeat themselves in various books, and are characterised by three formulas. The first two refer to the book's possible contribution to the child's knowledge, while the third one speaks about the writer's experience with the book, which he now wishes to offer to all the Jewish children:

1. As the study of both Hebrew and German was one of the main goals of the Enlightenment education, writers set about emphasising the text's contribution to the learning of the language. Even when a book was written in a different genre from that of a reader (and many of them were indeed meant as readers), a writer would call attention to the linguistic contribution of the book. For instance, in his introduction to *Robinson der Yingere*,[30] Samostz says:

> ". . . and when my dearest boy is grown, I shall order him to find the time to learn this book by heart in both Hebrew and Ashkenaz [German]. And I shall hope that after he has done so, never again will he be ignorant. The book will help him in learning good manners and other Jewish children will see and follow it also."[31]

2. Mastering good manners and learning good morals was another prime aim of the Enlightenment movement, and writers used to stress the likely contribution of the book in this direction as well. Thus for instance, Schalom Ha-Cohen promises in his introduction to *Mishle Agur*,[32] that the book will teach children morals and good manners:

> "And in my love for eloquence and lucidity, and in my care for the children of Israel, in order that they hear morality and learning in an easy and eloquent style, and will learn good manners, I have composed this book and have given it the name *Mishle Agur*. And for those who do not read Hebrew, I have translated it into Ashkenaz, so that they might also read it."[33]

3. The writer has read the book in his youth. The book had greatly impressed him. He wants to translate it into Hebrew, so that those of his readers who are not proficient in German will be able to enjoy it. Thus for instance David Samostz says in his introduction to the translation of *Robinson der Yingere*:

> "As in my youth I have read this book and learned so much of worth from it . . . I have decided to translate it into Hebrew, so that our people in other countries who cannot read Ashkenaz will see that it is indeed not good to prevent their children from reading in this language".[34]

THE READERSHIP

In their *ars poetica* all writers, without exception, speak on behalf of their readers. It was always the welfare of the child which served as their strongest motivation

---

[30]Breslau 1824.
[31]Introduction to *Robinson der Yingere* (Yiddish title), unpaginated, my translation.
[32]Berlin 1799.
[33]Introduction to *Mishle Agur*, unpaginated, my translation.
[34]Introduction to *Robinson der Yingere*, unpaginated, my translation.

in producing the book. But what was indeed the impact of these children's books on their readership? How did they manage to reach a Jewish child during the late eighteenth century and the early nineteenth century? In what ways did they really shape his character and determine his future functioning in society and culture? What sort of relations developed between the writers and their intended readers?

The range and the character of the actual readership of the Hebrew books for children is unknown to us and will probably always remain so. Unfortunately I was unable to trace any references to the reading of these books in memoirs or autobiographies. What is left as testimony are some histories of the Jewish schools.[35] According to these sources it is possible to characterise the nature of the readership as follows:

1. The books addressed children whose native language was not Hebrew. This of course greatly reduced their potential appeal. If we add to the linguistic difficulty the nature of the books, their strong moralistic tenor and their tendency to serve solely educational goals, we can assume that these books were hardly ever read voluntarily outside school.

2. The books addressed primarily children who studied in the schools of the Enlightenment movement. As already mentioned, their numbers were relatively small. According to Eliav,[36] less than 20% of Jewish children attended these schools.

3. When analysed from a class point of view, it can be maintained that Hebrew books of the Enlightenment were actually read by children of the lower strata. The Enlightenment ideology which aimed at democratisation of education, and the attempt to increase the appeal of the schools by making them accessible without fees, resulted, ironically, in populating the schools with pupils who came from the lower classes. This state of affairs implied that books, though often written by the élite, did not create an élite group of readers. It meant not only an immediate decrease in the number of potential readers of Hebrew books, but also, and of more importance, the loss of a second generation which is always *sine qua non* for any developing literature. On the other hand, the actual composition of the readership imposed an even stronger need to fight the reading of Yiddish and the predilection for Yiddish chapbooks, which were so very popular among the lower strata.

The wide social gap between writers and their actual readership, between what the authors expected from the readers and its realisation, and above all, the

---

[35]For instance: Moses Büdinger, *Die israelitische Schule*, Kassel 1831; Karl Ochsenmann, 'Chronik. Schulgeschichte der letzten 25 Jahre', in *Festschrift zum 75jährigen Bestehen der Realschule mit Lyzeum der isr. Religionsgesellschaft Frankfurt am Main*, Frankfurt a. Main 1928, pp. 1–33; Salomon Adler, 'Die Entwicklung des Schulwesens der Juden zu Frankfurt am Main bis zur Emanzipation' (Schluss), in *Jahrbuch der jüdisch-literarischen Gesellschaft*, vol. 19 (1928), Frankfurt a. Main, pp. 237–260; Moritz Stern, 'Jugendunterricht in der Berliner jüdischen Gemeinde während des 18. Jahrhunderts', in *Jahrbuch der jüdisch-literarischen Gesellschaft*, vol. 19 (1928), pp. 39–68; Joseph Gutmann (Hrsg.), *Festschrift zur Feier des Hundertjährigen Bestehens der Knabenschule der jüdischen Gemeinde in Berlin*, Berlin 1926; Beruh Wechsler, *Über jüdische Schul- und Lehrerverhältnisse*, Oldenburg 1846.
[36]Eliav, *op. cit.*, p. 174.

inability to create succeeding generations of readers, determined more than anything else the artificial character of Hebrew children's literature in Germany.

This brief survey of the circumstances of the development of this literature suggests that conditions were very unfavourable to the prevailing "rules of the game". This raises, of course, the question of how it was eventually possible for a Hebrew children's literature to develop in Germany notwithstanding all the obstacles. What patterns of development were chosen that enabled Hebrew children's literature in Germany to grow in size in spite of all, and to produce a relatively large number of books?

PATTERN OF DEVELOPMENT

The need to institute the children's system from the very beginning, the lack of "normal" market conditions and the close relations between the Hebrew and the German Enlightenment movement, made German children's literature an ideal model for imitation. The fact that Hebrew children's literature began to develop in Germany made German a most natural frame of reference. German children's literature had enjoyed such a high status that Hebrew children's literature endeavoured to follow in its footsteps in every possible way. Yet, it should be emphasised immediately that the wish to imitate the German case was conditioned by the Enlightenment's interpretation and understanding of German children's literature and its development. This process, which involved a translation of concepts and ideas, did not always accord with the "real" situation in German children's literature. Furthermore, once Hebrew children's literature created a certain image of the German genre, it adhered to this image for a long time, without paying attention to changes and developments in the German literature itself.

It is probably due to the need for Hebrew children's literature to repeat its first stages of development several times on the one hand, and the lack of factors that are normally responsible for the dynamics of literary systems on the other, that a fixed and almost static image of German children's literature continued to function for the Hebrew literature as a model for imitation. It was as if a certain circle was drawn at a specific point of time around various texts and various processes of development of German children's literature; this circle later became the signal frame of reference of Hebrew children's literature for almost a century.

The dominant patterns of historical processes, which resulted from this image, can be schematically described as the following:

1. The historical development of German children's literature during the eighteenth-century Enlightenment served as a model for the development of Hebrew children's literature. This was the case even when Romanticism prevailed in German children's literature.

2. Most texts for children were either translations of German Enlightenment texts or adaptions based on the German originals.

3. The German children's literature of the Enlightenment served as an

intermediary between the Hebrew and other systems. Texts translated from other systems, like the French or the English, were usually translated via the German.

4. The few original texts were based in most cases on German textual models, whether informative texts, poems and fables, or plays. The dominance of German model over Hebrew original texts is made clear by the fact that it is frequently hard to distinguish between original and translated texts.

MODEL OF DEVELOPMENT

At the beginning of the nineteenth century German children's literature was in a process of liberating itself from the hegemony of the Enlightenment didactic notion of children's literature. This did not mean that didactic books orientated towards philanthropist theories were no longer written. It means only that new books of a different nature were then produced and started to gain recognition in the system. In other words: the German system became more stratified and generically more heterogeneous.[37]

However, Hebrew children's literature, which began to evolve towards the end of the eighteenth century, did not adjust itself to later developments of German children's literature, as might have been expected. Rather, it went back to the first decades of the eighteenth century and thence drew its model of development; The nature of the texts, the process of their insertion into the system, as well as its pace, followed the German pattern. Like German books of the beginning of the eighteenth century, the first Hebrew texts for children at the end of the eighteenth century and throughout the first half of the nineteenth century, were alphabet books and readers, which were succeeded by moral tales, fables and some plays.

Why was it necessary to go back several decades? Why did the eighteenth century continue to be of such importance for the Hebrew children's literature of the nineteenth century? The reason was the similarity between cultural conditions and cultural components and institutions which were involved in the creation of books for children. From the functional point of view, Hebrew children's literature had no choice but to return to this earlier state in order to respond to expectations desired from it and to legitimisations given to it. Both expectations and legitimisations concerned the welfare of the child in regard to his education. The governing assumption concerning children's books was the didactic task attributed to them. Consequently it became totally impossible to think of producing books for other than didactic reasons, as for example, books for amusement and entertainment. It was also impossible to change this assumption later, as was the case with European children's literature when other educational views as well as commercial factors entered on the scene.

As a result of this state of affairs, Hebrew children's literature in Germany

---

[37]For a similar process in English children's literature cf. Shavit, *Poetics, op. cit.*, 'Stratification of a System', pp. 158–176.

never went beyond what might be described as the "didactic age" of children's literature. Rather was it forced, as we have said, to adhere to models which were rooted in certain educational views, mainly of the *Philanthropin*. This becomes clear when the first Hebrew books for children, namely, readers, are analysed. Hebrew readers used as their source for imitation various German readers, which were based on philanthropist views. They imitated them in their pedagogic aspirations as well as in their structure and the character of the texts. Hebrew writers were probably well acquainted with the following German readers: Felix Christian Weisse's *Neues ABC-Buch*,[38] Joachim Campe's *Neue Methode, Kinder auf eine leichte und angenehme Weise Lesen zu lehren*, as well as *Abece-und Lesebuch*,[39] Basedow's *Kleines Buch für Kinder aller Stände*,[40] and Rochow's *Der Kinderfreund*.[41] However, it seems to me that of greatest importance was Sulzer's *Vorübung zur Erweckung der Aufmerksamkeit und des Nachdenkens*.[42] This was probably the case because Sulzer's reader served as the main source for Friedländer's *Lesebuch*.[43] It is also referred to directly by another member of the *Me'asfim* circle. Ben Sew, whose own reader became very popular. Entitled *Bet Ha-Sefer* (Ben Sew, 1802–1806), it was not only published in more than ten editions, but was also translated into Italian, German and Russian.[44] In any case, it should be emphasised that Hebrew readers were usually based on more than one German text and by way of manipulating several German texts they actually created a new model, probably without intending to do so. Furthermore, there was not one case that I know of where a German reader was translated into Hebrew in its entirety; rather, German readers provided the pattern for the Hebrew readers.

Let us take a look at a typical example: Ben Sew's *Bet Ha-Sefer*. An exhaustive study of this reader would call for a separate article. I would like only to make some remarks in regard to it, in order to point to some of its characteristics and their link with the German. The most striking fact about this reader is its reliance

[38]Felix Christian Weisse, *Neues ABC-Buch*, Frankfurt–Leipzig 1773.

[39]Joachim Heinrich Campe, *Neue Methode, Kinder auf eine leichte und angenehme Weise Lesen zu lehren*, Altona 1778; *idem, Abece- und Lesebuch*.

[40]Johann Bernhard Basedow, *Kleines Buch für Kinder aller Stände. Zur elementarischen Bibliothek gehörig*, Stück 1. Mit drei Kupfertafeln, Leipzig 1771.

[41]Friedrich Eberhard Rochow, *Der Kinderfreund. Ein Lesebuch*, Brandenburg–Leipzig 1776.

[42]Johann Georg Sulzer, *Vorübung zur Erweckung der Aufmerksamkeit und des Nachdenkens* (Neubearb. von Heinrich Ludwig Meierotto), Berlin [1771], 1780–1782.

[43]In Friedländer's *Lesebuch, op. cit.*, the last part of the seventh chapter 'Beispiele von Tugenden und Lastern, guten und schlechten Gesinnungen' is taken from Sulzer's *Vorübungen zur Erweckung der Aufmerksamkeit und des Nachdenkens, op. cit.* It is the only part of the book which was taken directly from a German reader. This was done primarily in order to enable Friedländer to present texts which originate from different cultural sources, but nevertheless convey similar ideas, and grow out of the same humanistic tradition. Another reason for the choice of Sulzer's reader was probably the acquaintance between Mendelssohn and Sulzer. It was Sulzer, who in the year 1771 had moved the resolution of the Royal Academy in Berlin that the vacant place of a "membre ordinaire de la classe de philosophie spéculative" be filled by the appointment of "le juif Moses", a resolution vetoed by Frederick the Great (Altmann, *Moses Mendelssohn, op. cit.*, p. 264).

[44]In Vienna itself the book had been published in several editions: 1802, 1806, 1816, 1820, 1837, 1842, 1849. There were numerous adaptations of the book. Italian version: L. Romani, Wien 1825; German version: J. Kneipelmacher, Wien 1866; Russian version: A. J. Papirna, Warschau 1871, [2]1873.

on Weisse and especially on Sulzer. In spite of the fact that Ben Sew's reader was written more than twenty years after Friedländer's *Lesebuch*, and regardless of the many new texts and even models of German readers, Ben Sew uses the models which were already transplanted into the Jewish world of the Enlightenment. Like Sulzer's or Weisse's readers, the book opens with the teaching of the alphabet, starting with simple constructions of consonants and vowels and moving gradually to more difficult ones. Compare for instance these lines of Ben Sew with those of Weisse:

> "Mo-de Ani Lefane-cha Me-lech Chai Veka-yama Sh-he-che-zarta Vi Et Nish-ma-ti Bechem-la Ra-ba Emu-na-te-cha" (Ben Sew[45]).

> "Thu-e nichts Bö-ses, so wi-der-fährt dir nichts Bö-ses" (Weisse[46]).

In passing it is interesting to note that Ben Sew borrowed from Weisse the principle of the teaching of reading (to which he paid great importance, as shown in his introduction[47]). Unlike Weisse who uses reading exercises for teaching short moral lessons, Ben Sew uses these exercises for introducing several Jewish prayers such as *Mode Ani* and *Shma Israel*. In his insertion of Jewish prayers and his moderate and even favourable attitude towards Jewish religion and the Talmud, one can find an explanation for Ben Sew's success.

This however did not imply that Ben Sew gave up the teaching of Enlightenment values. Rather the contrary: the reader does systematically purvey Enlightenment values in every possible way. It follows the above mentioned German readers in that it contains morals, poems and fables as well as various texts about nature, geography and man and society. It endeavoured to fulfil two goals at the same time: To teach the child knowledge about the world; and to inculcate into him the values of the Enlightenment movement. For instance, the following paragraph, which describes the structure of society, draws an ideal picture of society as seen in the eyes of the Enlightenment:

> "And the other people in the state of the kingdom: officers, noblemen, aristocrats, wise men, writers, teachers and priests . . . Sages write books of science and knowledge. Teachers teach the sciences to their students in the academies. Priests preach the Torah and morality and guide the people in religion and divine service in the house of prayer . . . Happy is the boy who in his youth industriously studies a science or craft and when he grows up this ensures that he will not be hungry or suffer any lack. But the lazy boy who in his youth does not study anything, will grow up with nothing with which to earn a living and will remain poor and wretched for the rest of his life." (Ben Sew[48].)

Such texts were either explicitly subjected to Enlightenment ideas or were chosen because they could be accommodated to them. The selection of texts was always guided by the question of their adjustment to the Enlightenment values. For instance, the entire chapter of the second part of Ben Sew's reader, entitled 'Moral Lessons', is composed of aphorisms (more than fifty). They all deal with

---

[45]Yehuda Leyb Ben Sew, *Bet Ha-Sefer*. i: *Mesilat Limud*; ii: *Limude Ha-Mesharim*, Wien [1802], [6]1820, p. 24.

[46]Weisse, *op. cit.*, p. 13.

[47]Ben Sew speaks in his introduction to *Bet Ha-Sefer* of the importance of gradual studies for children, *op. cit.*, 'Introduction', unpaginated.

[48]*Ibid.*, p. 57.

the question of Wisdom, which, as is well known, occupied primary status in Enlightenment thought. Moreover, in order to express these ideas unequivocally, Ben Sew was even willing to change traditional and well-known texts so that they adjusted better to Enlightenment views. This is illustrated for instance by Ben Sew's handling of proverbs and aphorisms in the second part of his reader (*Limude Ha-Mesharim*).

Like Sulzer and Weisse, Ben Sew dedicated one chapter of his reader to 'Divre Chachamim' ('Words of the Learned'). In this chapter Ben Sew, who was most probably following Sulzer, introduced Greek proverbs. However, unlike Sulzer, he included some talmudic sayings as well. The inclusion of talmudic sayings in the reader served several goals, apart from Ben Sew's distinct tendency to produce a rather "moderate" reader (that is from the Enlightenment point of view), and hence to increase its possible attraction to Orthodox Jews. By placing talmudic sayings with Greek proverbs under the category of the sayings of "Wise Men", Ben Sew presented them as part of a general humanistic heritage, hence promoting the idea of a merging with Western culture. Yet, by granting Greek sayings thirty pages, whereas only a page and a half is allotted to talmudic sayings he expressed implicitly what was in his view the adequate proportion between Jewish heritage and European heritage. In such a way he succeeded in presenting the idea of a merging with German culture (where Greek culture was also accorded more and more appreciation). This tendency found, of course, more explicit expression in the texts themselves, as is evident from the following example:

> "So said the sages: A man should always be in empathy with his friends, should not laugh among the weeping, nor weep among the merry, nor be awake among the sleeping nor sleep among the wakers, nor stand among the seated nor sit among the standing, nor change his friends' manners." (Ben Sew[49].)

Of course Ben Sew included in his reader only those sayings which suited the societal ideas of the Enlightenment and as has already been mentioned, he was even willing to change traditional and well-known texts so that they served better. In at least one case Ben Sew altered a well-known saying of the Talmud in order to express the ideal of merging with one's environment. The famous saying of "In three ways a man is distinguished: his pocket, his cellar and his anger" was altered to: "In four ways the sages are distinguished: their pocket, their cellar, their anger and their dress." (Ben Sew[50].)

There is one chapter in Ben Sew's reader where the link to German readers is most obvious. This is the case of Bible teaching. Here too, in spite of a long and rich Jewish tradition, both legitimisations and practice were taken from the German models without any consideration for the Jewish ones. The positive attitude of the Jewish Enlightenment movement towards the Bible was not just the natural outcome of Mendelssohn's translation and the newly created opposition which ensued between Bible and Talmud. It can be traced to the

[49]*Ibid.*, p. 219.
[50]*Ibid.*, p. 219.

great deference and respect displayed towards the Bible and its language by the German Gentile scholars.

While the teaching of the Bible was not part of Jewish education, where children learned only some parts of the Pentateuch and immediately afterwards began to study the Talmud, the men of the Enlightenment adopted the German model and made it a subject of study at their schools where books other than the Pentateuch were taught. Furthermore, the translation of biblical paragraphs was regarded as a means of teaching both German and Hebrew. In any case, quite soon, the teaching of the Bible was abandoned altogether in favour of teaching *biblische Geschichte*, the common way of teaching not the Bible itself but the history of the Bible. Ben Sew also includes in his reader a 'Short History from the Creation of the World to the Destruction of the Second Temple'. This chapter replaced a previous chapter which was dedicated to the principles of religion that Ben Sew preferred to include later in his moral book, *Yesode Ha-Dat* (1811). In these texts an attempt to imitate the biblical style was made, as well as an effort to relate the text to the Chronicles. It is interesting to note that the text covers not only the biblical period but the period of the Second Temple and its aftermath as well.

The preference for the German model in the case of Bible teaching even by such a moderate writer as Ben Sew shows the extent to which Hebrew children's literature became deliberately enslaved to the German model. In spite of the attraction that Bible teaching in the traditional way must have held for Jewish parents, Ben Sew, who was moderate enough to use Jewish prayers as well as Jewish teaching, preferred to follow the German example in cases where the German model varied from the traditional Jewish model.

Or perhaps the explanation for the preference of the German model in the case of the Bible teaching is different. It may have been necessary precisely because it was important for the Enlightenment movement to distinguish between traditional methods of teaching the Bible and the method favoured by the Enlightenment movement. This suggested a possibility of being an enlightened Jew in Germany merging into German culture without giving up one's Jewish heritage.

The desire to stress the link to German culture is evident also in a simpler and technical aspect – the format of some books. The question of the format was not just a technical matter but it was employed to stress the writer's intention to his addressee and his implicit attitude towards German culture. The Jewish children who studied at the schools of the Enlightenment movement were supposed to learn both German and Hebrew. In order to achieve this most of the first texts were written in both Hebrew and German (or at least a German translation was given to several texts or words). There were three formats for printing Hebrew and German: Hebrew opposite German in Latin letters, Hebrew opposite German in Hebrew letters and Hebrew with German in Hebrew letters below. The first format was to emphasise the strong connection to German. The last one was written in the traditional Yiddish-Hebrew form with, possibly, the intention of misleading Orthodox Jews who were used to reading texts written in Hebrew and Yiddish in this form.

To sum up: Hebrew children's literature followed the German model of development in two ways: in its stages of development and its textual models. This was the case because of the similar legitimisation given to both at their respective formative stages and because of the great dependence on ideology which made the German children's literature of the Enlightenment the natural frame of reference. The reliance on the German literature signified certain stages of development, a certain selection of texts, and determined the nature of the texts themselves, whether original works or translations.

TRANSLATIONS AND ADAPTATIONS

Translations dominated Hebrew children's literature of the Enlightenment movement and enjoyed the same status as or even higher than the original texts. The production of translations was regarded as creative textual work, which was somehow linked to the source text; hence the source text was very rarely referred to.[51] This status of translated texts had of course textual implications concerning the norms of translation.[52] A discussion of the translational norms of the Enlightenment period calls for a separate study. Here I limit myself to the examination of some principles of translation at the time of the Enlightenment.

As far as children's books were concerned, the governing principles directing the selection process of the books were similar. They were strongly rooted in ideological claims; it was their adjustment to ideology that decided for or against their translation into Hebrew. Such a need can, for instance, be discerned when the question of generic selection is reviewed. Texts were chosen for translation primarily on the basis of their generic affiliation. Only those genres which were understood to be approved by the German Enlightenment (through the filter of the Jewish Enlightenment movement) would have been translated.

These principles of selection resulted in an abundance of moralistic poems and fables, and the total neglect of fictional narratives such as short stories and novels, even in the middle of the nineteenth century. Furthermore, translated texts had to be definite products of the German Enlightenment movement: either they were written by Enlightenment writers, as was the case with all poets translated by Ben Sew, or they expressed unequivocally Enlightenment values, as was for instance the case with a poem by Schiller, which was included in Samostz's Reader, *Esh-Dat*.[53] Thus, Schiller's poem was chosen for translation because of the importance it attaches to learning and to wisdom:

Das Glück und die Weisheit

> "Entzweit mit einem Favoriten
> Flog einst Fortun' der Weisheit zu:
> 'Ich will dir meine Schätze bieten,
> Sei meine Freundin du!

[51]Ben Sew's reader is in this sense an exception because he does supply a full list of his sources.
[52]Gideon Toury, *In Search of a Theory of Translation*, Tel-Aviv 1980, especially chapters 2, 3, & 8.
[53]David Samostz, *Esh Dat*, Breslau 1834.

Mit meinen reichsten, schönsten Gaben
Beschenkt ich ihn so mütterlich,
Und sieh, er will noch immer haben
Und nennt noch geizig mich.

Komm, Schwester, lass uns Freundschaft schliessen,
Du marterst dich an deinem Pflug;
In deinen Schoss will ich sie giessen,
Hier ist für dich und mich genug.'

Sophia lächelt diesen Worten
Und wischt den Schweiss vom Angesicht!
'Dort eilt dein Freund, sich zu ermorden,
Versöhnet euch! – Ich brauch dich nicht.' "[54]

Success and Wisdom (translation of the Hebrew version)

"Successful man Success deserted,
She gave her hand to Wisdom of her own free will
To you I'll give all that I possess
From now on, be my love!

The honour of my wealth and treasure I gave to him,
None is as great as he in the wide world,
But his all-devouring thirst I have not yet quenched
I was called mean and miserly.

Come my sister we will make an eternal covenant
During the season of ploughing there will be no strewing of fennel
In your bosom I'll set the glory of my greatness,
My fertile lands will bear enough for both.

Wisdom laughed to hear her words
And wiped the sweat from off her face.
'Your lover's gone to take his life,
Forgive his crimes. I can live quietly without you.' "[55]

The high status of translation as an activity becomes more clear when the question of fables is examined. In spite of the relative abundance of Hebrew fables, and their availability in Hebrew, translation predominated even in the case of fables. Here again the wish to use German literature as the preferable source for translations is evident. The German system functioned as a source system for original German texts or as a mediating system (especially for the translation of Aesop). This tendency is particularly notable because original fables did exist in the Hebrew inventory and could easily have been used. David Friedländer, for instance, included Hebrew fables in German translation in his *Lesebuch*.[56] This option was hardly ever used by Hebrew writers.

Of the 38 fables and poems which Ben Sew included in the second part of his

[54]Friedrich Schiller [1812–1815], *Sämtliche Werke*, 1924, vol. 19, p. 79.

[55]Samostz, *Esh Dat, op. cit.*, p. 30.

[56]In spite of the good relations with Lessing, Friedländer did not include any of Lessing's fables in the *Lesebuch*, as could have been expected. Instead he was looking for a possible Hebrew text which could serve as an equivalent for the German fables. He found it in Mendelssohn's translation to *Berachia Hanakdan*. This enabled Friedländer to kill two birds with one stone: To include in his *Lesebuch* a text which agreed with modern concepts of education and to introduce a clear instance of a Jewish equivalent to German elements. The fables which were included in the *Lesebuch* were first translated by Moses Mendelssohn from the Hebrew edition of 1756 (Berlin edition) and published in the *Briefe, die neueste Literatur betreffend* of 1759.

reader, 26 pieces were translations of German Enlightenment texts. The texts were either translations of German writers such as Magnus Gottfried Lichtwer, Christian Gellert, Albrecht von Haller and Friedrich von Hagedorn, or of ancient writers like Aesop who, since his rediscovery by the German Enlightenment, enjoyed immense popularity. Aesop's fables were published in many miscellanies of fables, among them Lessing's *Fabeln*;[57] later, Lessing's fables were included by Sulzer and Meierotto[58] and Campe[59] in their books, and most probably came to be translated into Hebrew via these works.

Only thirteen fables in Ben Sew's reader were original Hebrew fables, some of which had already been published for adults in *Hame'asef*, the periodical of the Jewish Enlightenment movement. This preference for translated fables is to be discerned in almost any reader or miscellany for children. Most popular of all were several fables by Aesop. Since they were included in the first Hebrew reader for children, *Avtalion*,[60] and the first Hebrew book of fables for children, *Mishle Agur*,[61] they were consequently included by other writers. The fables 'Von einem Löwen und einer Maus', 'Von dem Löwen und Fuchsen', 'Von dem mit einer Löwenhaut bedeckten Esel', which were very popular also in German miscellanies,[62] were furthermore included in many Hebrew books for children, even in a miscellany which was prepared by Moritz Steinschneider for "Jewish Youth in the Eastern Countries".[63] They preserved their popularity also after the cultural centre had been transferred to Eastern Europe. Here they were continuously included in books for children, which were either reprints of books published first in German-speaking countries (for instance, *Ktav Yosher*[64]) or in new books.

Translations of German texts dominated not only in the case of readers and miscellanies, but also, and perhaps mainly, in the case of translations of entire books. I do not know of any book for children, published at the time of the Jewish Enlightenment in Germany, which was not a translation or a pseudo-translation. (The question of pseudo-translation will be discussed later on.) There were two criteria for selection of books for translation: that of theme and that of author.

The criterion of theme was not a very common one and was mainly effective in cases where the theme related to Jewish matters. Hence, for instance, two books by Samostz, one of the most prominent Jewish writers for children, were selected for translation because they were biblical stories. *Rohot Midyan o Yaldut Moshe*,[65]

---

[57]Gotthold Ephraim Lessing, *Fabeln*, Berlin 1759.
[58]Meierotto went back to Lessing's recommendations concerning the use of fables for child education. See Sulzer, *Vorübungen zur Erweckung der Aufmerksamkeit und des Nachdenkens, op. cit.*, vol. 4, pp. 29, 46.
[59]Joachim Heinrich Campe, *Kleine Kinderbibliothek*, Hamburg 1785, vol. 12, pp. 127, 132, 156–158.
[60]Aharon Wolfsohn, *Avtalion*. Wien [1790] 1814.
[61]Shalom Ha-Cohen, b.r.y.k. from Mezrich, *Sefer Mishle Agur*, Berlin 1799.
[62]For instance it was included in one of the most popular German fable books for children: *Esopi Leben und auserlesene Fabeln mit deutlichen Erklärungen und nützlichen Tugend-Lehren,* Nürnberg [1723] 1760.
[63]Moritz Steinschneider, *Mashal U-Melitsa* (A collection of fables and parables for the use of Jewish youth in the Eastern countries), Berlin 1860.
[64]Shalom Ha-Cohen, *Ketav Yosher Chadash*, Warschau [1820] 1869. This fable book retained its popularity and was published in several editions until the end of the nineteenth century. Its 14th edition was published in Wilna in 1896.
[65]David Samostz, *Rohot Midyan o Yaldut Moshe. Die Hirtinnen von Midjan oder Moses Jugend*, von Frau von Genlis. Ins Hebräische übersetzt, Breslau 1843.

Lesebuch

für

Jüdische Kinder.

[hier David Friedländer]

Zum Besten der jüdischen Freyschule.

Berlin
in Commißion bey Christian Friedrich Voß und Sohn
1779.

David Friedländer's 'Lesebuch'. Title-page of the first Jewish modern reader for children

The Hebrew copperplate of Friedländer's 'Lesebuch'

8

Römische Zahlen.
I, II, III, IV, V, VI, VII, VIII, IX, X, XI, bis
XX, XXX, XL, L, LX, bis C, D, M, XM, CM.

§. 8.

Gebräuchliches jüdisches Alphabet im Schreiben.
Siehe die Kupfertafel.

Leßübungen.

Der Mit-lei-di-ge, der dem E-len-den nicht zu na-he kom-men will, weil er E-kel fürch-tet, ver-räth Weich-lich-keit, und Här-te zu-gleich.

Was du thust, thu-e recht; sprichst du mit je-man-den, so den-ke auf das, was du hö-rest, lie-sest du, so prü-fe was du lie-sest.

Gehe nie-mals mü-ßig, so hast du nie-mals lan-ge-wei-le, und lan-ge-wei-le macht Ver-druß.

Sprich und thu-e nichts, wo-von du nicht willst, daß es die gan-ze Welt se-hen und hö-ren kön-ne.

Grund-

מציאת הארץ החדשה

כולל כל הגבורות והמעשים אשר
נעשו לעת מצוא הארץ הזאת, לכל
אנפיה ומבינותיה, ומשפטיה, ואנשיה,
ללשונתם ומשפחותם.

נאסף ונעתק ונכלל מספרי העמים ללשון עברי,
בשפה ברורה וקלה, ללמד נערי בני ישראל יופי
הלשון הזה, ולהודיעם גבורות ה' ונפלאותיו אשר
יעשה בכל הארץ.

מאת הצעיר לימים
משה בן א"א ומורי התורני ורהרבני
המפורסם מהור"ר מענדל פ"פ.

כי הנני בורא שמים חדשים וארץ חדשה (ישעי' ס"ה)

ספר ראשון
בהוצאת המחבר

נדפס באלטונא תקס"ז

על ידי ... המשותפים כמר שמואל וכמר יהודה
בן ס"ל ...

מבוא

טרם אחלהו לספר את כל אשר קרה להגבורים
אנשי שם, אחלה פניך הקורא וה.ק כרת
לי, ואודיעך מאת אשר קראו: אורך ורוחב
התבל, למען תרע הדרך אשר עברו בה.
שים נא עיניך וראה את אשר חקקתי על לוח
צד אחרת מכדור הארץ, כאשר השכילו וסרו
האחרונים בטוב טעם ודעת אשר אין להשיב.
הן המה העמידו ליסור מוסר שתי נקודות זאת
מול זאת (ב—1) על קצוי הארץ, וקראו להן
צירי הארץ.
את שם הראחת—נגד כיכב צפוני—ציר
צפוני; ושם השנית נגד כוכב דרומי—ציר
דרומי.
עתה שית לבך להעגולה הזאת אשר כבר עשוהו
במחשבהם בין חצי הארץ נגד הצירים, ויקראו לה
קו המשוה (א—ב) באשר הוא שם משוה, יום
ולילה על פני כל התבל (מלבד על פני הקוטבים)
כורח השמש נגד הקו הזה.
עוד חלקו הארץ מציר צפוני לציר דרומי
באופנים רבים וקראו להם קשתות צהרים:

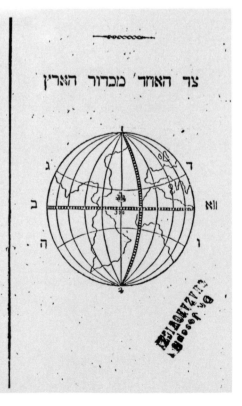

צד האחד' מכדור הארץ

אֵשׁ דָּת
צום
אונטעררִיכט אים לעזען
אונר
אנפאנגסגרינדע דער רעליגיאן
נעבסט איבונגסשטיקקע
צום איבערזעטצען אוים דעם העברעאישען אינס רייטשע
פיר
דיא איזראעליטישע יוגענד
פאן
דוד זאמאָשטש
ערשטער טהייל

ברעסלויא
געדרוקקט בייא יעבעל זולצבאך אונר יאהן
בשנה בית יעקב לפ׳׳ק

Title-page of 'Esh Dat'
by David Samostz

— (57) —
28.

פֿאָרטוועטצונג דעם פֿאָריגען

וְשָׁאַר אַנְשֵׁי הַחֶבְרָה אֲשֶׁר בִּמְדִינַת מַמְלָכָה • קְצִינִים • חוֹרִים • אַצִּילִים • חֲכָמִים • סוֹפְרִים • מוֹרִים וְכֹהֲנִים: הַחֲכָמִים כּוֹתְבִים סְפָרִים בְּכָל חָכְמָה וּמַדָּע • הַמּוֹרִים מְלַמְּדִים הַמַּדָּעִים לְתַלְמִידֵיהֶם בְּבָתֵּי הַמִּדְרָשׁ: הַכֹּהֲנִים דּוֹרְשִׁים הַתּוֹרָה וְהַמּוּסָר וּמַדְרִיכִים אֶת הָאֲנָשִׁים בְּדַת וּבַעֲבוֹדַת אֱלֹהִים בְּבֵית הַתְּפִלָּה • וְאַחֲרֵיהֶם הַסּוֹחֲרִים וְהָרוֹכְלִים מוֹכְרִים כָּל סְחוֹרָה וּמִכְרָם וְרִכְבָּה: וְאַחֲרֵיהֶם הֶחָרָשִׁים וְאָמָּנִים וְעוֹבְדֵי אֲדָמָה • יֵשׁ שֶׁהֵם עֲשִׁירִים לָהֶם הוֹן וָעֹשֶׁר וּנְכָסִים • יוֹשְׁבִים בְּבָתִּים גְּדוֹלִים וַחֲדָרִים מְרֻוָּחִים וְלוֹבְשִׁים בִּגְדֵי חֹפֶשׁ לִכְבוֹד וּלְתִפְאָרֶת • וְיֵשׁ מֵהֶם רָשִׁים עֲנִיִּים דַּלִּים וְאֶבְיוֹנִים • בְּמַסְכֵּנוּת יִחְיוּ וּבַשֵּׁפֶל יֵשְׁבוּ רָעֵבִים וּצְמֵאִים וּבְגָדֵיהֶם קְרָעִים בְּלוֹא סְחָבוֹת כִּי אֵין לָהֶם כָּל מְאוּמָה: וְהֵם שׁוֹאֲלִים עַל הַפְּתָחִים לָתֵת לָהֶם צְדָקָה וּמְסַת עֶרְכָּה אֲגוֹרַת כֶּסֶף אוֹ פַת לֶחֶם: אַשְׁרֵי הַנַּעַר אֲשֶׁר הוּא חָרוּץ בִּנְעוּרָיו לִלְמֹד הַחָכְמָה אוֹ מְלָאכָה • וְכַאֲשֶׁר יִגְדַּל יִבְטַח כִּי לֹא יֵרַע וְלֹא יֶחְסַר לַחְמוֹ: וְאִי לוֹ לַנַּעַר אֲשֶׁר הוּא מִתְעַצֵּל בִּנְעוּרָיו • וְלֹא לָמַד מְאוּמָה • וְכִי יִגְדַּל וּבְיָדוֹ אֵין כָּל בַּמֶּה לִמְצוֹא מִחְיָתוֹ וְהוּא דַל וְאֶבְיוֹן כָּל יָמָיו:

חֶבְרָה	געזעלשאפֿט	תַּלְמִיד	שׁילער
קָצִין	הערר • פֿאָרנעהמער	בֵּית מִדְרָשׁ	האַזע שולע
חוֹר	פֿרייהערר	תּוֹרָה	לעהרע
אַצִּיל	עדעלמאן	מוּסָר	ערמאַן
סוֹפֵר	געלעהרטער • שריפֿטשטעללער	עֲבוֹדַת אֱלֹהִים	גאטטעסדיענסט
מוֹרֶה	לעהרער	בֵּית תְּפִלָּה	בעטהויז
כֹּהֵן	פריסטער	סוֹחֵר	האַנדעלסמאן
יַדָּע	וויסענשאפֿט	רוֹכֵל	קרעמער
		סְחוֹרָה	וואַרע

Ben Sew's 'Bet Ha-Sefer'
This paragraph deals with a description of an
ideal society

— 13 —
ז׳ אַיָל וּכְלָבִים

הַמִּתְגָּאֶה כְּרֹב חֵילוֹ • יִפּוֹל וְאֵין עֹזֵר לוֹ.

הָאַיָּל עַל אֲפִיקֵי מַיִם כְּבוֹאוֹ • רָצָה לִשְׁבּוֹר אֶת צְמָאוֹ • וַיֵּחַן אֶת עֵינָיו בַּמָּיִם • וַיֵּרַא בְּצֵלוֹ כִּי הוּא כְּעַל קַרְנַיִם • וַיֹּאמֶר עֲשָׂרְתַּנִי מִצָּאתָאי אוֹן לִי • מִי יַעֲרָךְ אֵלַי לְהִתְהַלֵּל כְּמָהֲלָלִי • קַרְנַי לֹא כְקַרְנֵי הַשּׁוֹר • אַךְ נְטוּעִים בְּמִצְחִי כַּמִּשּׂוֹר • וְסְדוּרִים בָּרוּם הַמַּעֲלוֹת • וּבְכֵן וַיֹּפִי שְׁנֵיהֶם כְּלוּלוֹת • וּמִי הוּא אֲשֶׁר לְפָנַי יִתְיַצֵּב • מִשְׁפַּט מָוֶת לוֹ חָרוּץ וְנֶחֱצָב • לַאֲשֶׁר לִי עָלַי תְּלוּנָה • אֲנִי נָאֶה יָפֶה וְתָפוּנָה • וְכַאֲשֶׁר רַגְלָיו הַמַּיִם נָרִים • הִנֵּה כְלָבִים הוֹלְכִים צְמָדִים • וּסְבִיבוֹתָיו מְסִיחִים בּוֹ • וַיְהַל לָנוּס בְּחָפְזָה • אָמַר בְּלִבּוֹ • וַיָּנָס וְלֹא פָנָה אוֹ דֶרֶךְ וְאֶל הַמִּשְׁעוֹלִים • אַךְ אֶל עֲבִי הַיַּעַר וְאֶל סְבָךְ הַחֲרוּלִים • וּמַכְשְׁילֵהוּ צַצְחָו • וַיַּעַגְּשׁוּ בְּנַאֲוָתוֹ • כִּי כְשֶׁיחוּ אֶל הַסְּבָכִים עֵינָיו • וְהִנֵּה נֶאֱחָז בְּסַבַּךְ בְּקַרְנָיו • וְשָׁם הַכְּלָבִים הַרְבִּיקוּתוֹ • וְהָעֲיֵפִים נְחָתוּהוּ • וַיַּעַגְשׁוּ בְּקַרְנָיו אֲשֶׁר הָיוּ לוֹ לְאוֹן • לִפְנֵי שֶׁבֶר גָּאוֹן.

ח׳ הַחֲמוֹר

עוֹר אַרְיֵה עָטָה הַחֲמוֹר לוֹ כְבוֹדֶךְ
כִּי אָמַר • אַפְלִיטָה מֵעֲבוֹדָה פֶּרֶךְ •
וַיְהִי כָל רֹאֵה וְנָם סְנָדֶךְ •
וַיֵּרָא וַיֹּאמֶר • אַרִי כְּדַרְכֶּךְ •
אוּלָם בְּקוֹל אָזְנוֹ — תָּם כִּי אַרְכּוּ •

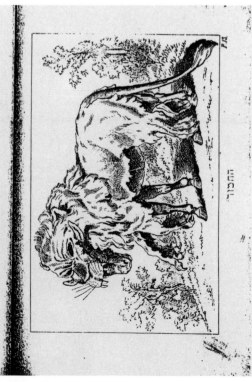

Steinschneider's 'Mashal U-Melitsa'
An illustrated fable

Title-page of 'Die Hirtinen von Midjan'
translated by David Samostz

Hübner's 'Biblische Geschichte' in Hebrew translation

by Stéphanie-Félicité Genlis, which describes the childhood of Moses, was translated from the French most probably via the German.[66] Also Hübner's *Biblische Historien*[67] was translated for the same reason. Samostz was indeed careful to omit the last chapters of the first part of Hübner's work, which related stories from the Apocrypha (Judith and Tobias), though they were translated into Hebrew by Ben Sew in 1819. Samostz was also careful to omit the entire second part of the book which related stories from the New Testament, as well as illustrations and Latin rhymes (some German editions did not include the Latin rhymes either).

In spite of that, Samostz's choice of Hübner is, to say the very least, suprising, especially if we take into account Hübner's status as the most popular Christian writer for children in the eighteenth century, a popularity which continued in the nineteenth century.[68] It is true that Samostz included in *Nahar Mahadan* only biblical stories such as the creation of the world, the story of Babel, Exodus etc., but he still presented them according to the Lutheran tradition and did not hesitate to include passages of the "pose a question, point a moral" type whose function was to instruct the child in Christian religious teachings. His choice of Hübner can be accounted for only on the basis of allegedly thematic adjustment. Indeed, in his introduction to the book Samostz explains his motivation for translating the stories of the Bible for Jewish children. Here he claims that Jewish children were otherwise deprived of biblical stories:

> "Da der grösste Theil der israelitischen Jugend mit dem Studium der schönen Wissenschaften beschäftigt ist und leider die Bibel aus dem Urtexte zu studieren vernachlässigt, so dass viele die wichtigsten Ereignisse nicht einmal dem Namen nach kennen, so habe ich für zweckmässig gefunden, dieses allgemein beliebte Werk, nämlich die Hauptbegebenheiten aus dem alten Testament ins Hebräische zu übertragen."[69]

The criterion of theme, which became later very decisive in the sphere of translation,[70] did not however play such a major role in the production of books for children at the time of the Enlightenment. Much more important was the author's name. Once certain writers were marked as writers of the Enlightenment, they became an object for translation into Hebrew. The writer most

---

[66]Stéphanie-Félicité Genlis, *Kleine Romane und Erzählungen*, übers. von Th. Hell., in 16 vols., vol. 14: *Die Hirtinnen von Midien*, Leipzig 1807.

[67]Johann Hübner, *Zweymahl zwey und fünffzig auserlesene biblische Historien aus dem Alten und Neuen Testamente*, Leipzig 1731, David Samostz, *Nahar Mahadan, oder Biblische Geschichte nach Hübner*, Breslau 1831.

[68]Hübner's book was one of the most popular Christian books of Bible stories for children in the eighteenth century. Since it first appeared in 1713 it was pubished in numerous editions (though Samostz had probably used the Leipzig edition of 1731 (Auflage letzter Hand). On Hübner's function in German children's literature, see Christine Reents, 'Johann Hübners biblische Historien nach ihrem erziehungs- und theologiegeschichtlichen Hintergrund, ihrem Autor und ihren theologischen Grundlinien', in Johann Hübner, *Zweymahl zwey und fünffzig auserlesene biblische Historien* [1713], Hildesheim 1986, pp. 1 22. Hübner's popularity in Germany can be seen from the fact that in 1859 the 107th (!) German edition appeared. Cf. Theodor Brüggemann, *Kinder- und Jugendliteratur, 1498–1950. Kommentierter Katalog*, Osnabrück 1986, p. 119; Adalbert Brauer, 'Schulbücher im 17. und 18. Jahrhundert', *Blickpunkt Schulbuch*, Heft 2 (Oktober 1967), pp. 13–15.

[69]Samostz, *Nahar Mahadan, op. cit.*, 'Introduction' [German in Hebrew letters], unpaginated.

[70]Toury, *In Search, op. cit.*, especially chapters 3, 4, 7.

translated into Hebrew at the time was Heinrich Joachim Campe, who was regarded by Jewish writers as the most important German writer for children of the Enlightenment.

As far as Hebrew was concerned, Campe was the paramount representative of German children's literature. Not only were his books translated into Hebrew, but late into the nineteenth century they served as a model for the imitation for quite a few original texts. Campe continued to be translated into Hebrew and to serve too as a model for original texts even after the cultural centre had moved East and even in the late nineteenth century in Palestine. For instance, one of the books of the series *Bet-Ha-Sefer* composed by Yehuda Garzovski with Zifrin and Yudileviz,[71] was dedicated to moral teaching and was based on *Theophron*.

The popularity of Campe and his great importance for Hebrew children's literature was first and foremost connected with Mendelssohn's acquaintance with him. As formulated so aptly by Simon, it was Mendelssohn who "served both as a bridge as well as a dam. In other words: values which he adopted for himself, he then transferred to Eastern Europe as well. Values that he had put aside and never touched hardly ever entered the consciousness of the typical enlightened East European Jew, at any rate not until the middle of the nineteenth century."[72]

Mendelssohn had formed a very close relationship with Campe, which became known through their correspondence and Mendelssohn's letter to Campe, where he had analysed the status of the Jews in Germany.[73] An indication of the closeness between Campe and Mendelssohn is also to be found in Campe's report on a Sabbath eve which he spent in Mendelssohn's house:

> "Es war an einem Freitag Nachmittage, als wir, meine Frau und ich, mit Berliner Gelehrten bei Mendelssohn zum Besuche waren und mit Kaffee bewirthet wurden. Mendelssohn, immer der freundlichste Gesellschafter, stand etwa eine Stunde vor Sonnenuntergang von seinem Sitze auf, trat auf uns zu mit den Worten: 'Meine Damen und Herren! Ich gehe nur in das Nebenzimmer, um meinen Sabbat zu empfangen und bin dann gleich wieder in Ihrer Mitte; unterdess wird meine Frau Ihre Gegenwart um so mehr geniessen'."[74]

Campe's function in the development of Hebrew literature stretched far beyond his acquaintance with Mendelssohn and other members of his circle, and even far beyond mere translation. His function can be analysed from at least four perspectives:

1. Campe's status among the adherents of the Enlightenment movement (especially among those who were interested in educational problems).

2. The preservation of his status in the Jewish Enlightenment movement in Russia.

3. Campe's books which served as a model for original Hebrew texts.

4. Mass translation of Campe's books into Hebrew.

[71] Jerusalem 1891–1892.
[72] Simon, *loc. cit.*, p. 179, my translation.
[73] Moses Mendelssohn, *Gesammelte Schriften. Jubiläumsausgabe, Briefwechsel*, ii,2. Bearbeitet von Alexander Altmann, Stuttgart–Bad Cannstatt 1976, p. 443.
[74] Moritz Meier Kayserling, *Moses Mendelssohn. Sein Leben und Wirken*, Leipzig [2]1888, pp. 422–423.

Here I shall limit myself almost entirely to the last aspect and I will only touch briefly on the third one.

Of the numerous books Campe wrote (more than two dozen) only five books were translated into Hebrew (the reason for this selection will be dealt with below). However, those books that had been rendered into Hebrew were all translated more than once. The following titles of Campe were translated: 1. *Robinson der Jüngere*. 2. *Die Entdeckung von Amerika*. 3. *Theophron, oder der erfahrne Rathgeber für die unerfahrne Jugend*. 4. *Merkwürdige Reisebeschreibungen*. 5. *Sittenbüchlein für Kinder aus gesitteten Ständen*.

The first of Campe's books to be translated into Hebrew was *Die Entdeckung von Amerika*. The translator, Moshe Mendelssohn-Frankfurt, published it in 1807,[75] after corresponding with Campe. I have not been able to trace this exchange of letters, but Mendelssohn-Frankfurt himself sums it up in his introduction to the book. According to him, Campe emphasised in his letter his great pleasure in hearing about the future translation of his book into Hebrew. Mendelssohn-Frankfurt also mentions Campe's expression of sympathy for the fate of the Jewish people.[76] Encouraged by Campe, Mendelssohn-Frankfurt published the first part of the book and hoped to be able to publish the two other parts once the first one sold. This was probably not the case, because, as far as can be ascertained, the two other parts were never published.

The translational process of *Die Entdeckung von Amerika* was guided by several principles, which were also typical of later translations of Campe. They can be described as follows:

1. As was always the case during the Enlightenment period, the translation was to be understood as an independent transformation of the original text; the translator was responsible for what he regarded as the main idea of the book, and it was only this idea that had to be transformed by the translation. An indication of this attitude towards the original text can be found already on the front page of the book: Campe's name appears neither on the cover nor on the front page. The original title is not mentioned either. The Hebrew title reads instead: *Meziat Eretz Chadasha* (The Discovery of New Land), and hints at the transformation of the book into a geography book. This neglect in mentioning either the writer's name or the original title was in no way due to lack of respect for the original author. Mendelssohn-Frankfurt had a great respect for Campe, as is evident from the introduction to the book. The omission was simply a result of the governing translational norms at that time.

2. Due to the uncertain status of Hebrew books for children, whose existence had just begun to gain recognition, writers preferred to address themselves to a larger audience than that of children. In the case of Mendelssohn-Frankfurt he chose to address the book to adolescents. Indeed the book was received as a book for adults and children. This is evident also from a review published in

[75]Moshe Mendelssohn-Frankfurt, *Meziat Ha-Aretz Ha-Chadasha*, Altona 1807.
[76]In his introduction to the book Mendelssohn-Frankfurt quotes Campe's letter to him, in which the author declared himself extremely happy to learn about the coming translation of his book into Hebrew. Mendelssohn-Frankfurt, *Meziat Ha-Aretz*, *op. cit.*, 'Introduction', unpaginated.

Hame'asef,[77] which presented it as a book which would appeal to anyone interested in history and geography. The possibility of presenting the book in terms of non-fiction was of decisive importance for its first translation into Hebrew. The entire Hebrew system was not yet ready to accept fictional narratives, either for children or for adults. The pre-condition for a translation of a text was its value as a non-fictional text, or its potential for becoming such a text.

Even in a case of a writer like Campe, where translations where legitimised by his status among the Enlightenment circles, his books were selected for translation in accordance with their potential contribution to the acquisition of human knowledge and wisdom. The implications of this systemic demand were manifested not only in decisions concerning selection of texts, but also in those determining how texts were to be handled.

3. The handling of a translated text meant in most cases an endeavour to transform the original text into a text of history and geography. Translations replaced the fictional narrative of the source text by historical narrative. While the source text was built on the philanthropist model of a *Rahmenerzählung* (frame-story), the translation totally omitted the *Rahmenerzählung*. In the source text the father promises his children to tell them a fascinating story during the coming week. The frame-story determines the segmentation of the source text which is divided according to the days of the tale. The main character of the source text is actually not Columbus but the children themselves. They are supposed to acquire certain values from the text in the course of its narration, knowledge of the world is only one among them. The narrative situation is used by the narrator to teach the children several matters by means of question and answer.[78] All this is left out in the Hebrew translation: the narrative situation of a *Rahmenerzählung* is replaced by a narrator who relates historical narrative. Hebrew translators, in spite of their wish to transfer both Campe and philanthropist values into Hebrew, have eventually extracted the text from its philanthropist message. In this sense the gap between the explicit intentions of the translation and their realisation became very large. One of the results of this deviation from the source text was that popular understanding of philanthropist ideas, which was communicated via such translations, differed greatly from the original meaning.

The first translation which did preserve the philanthropist narrative structure was Samostz's translation of *Robinson der Jüngere*.[79] However, this is rather an exception, not only because Samostz adhered to the frame-story, but also because he tried, as far as possible, to render a complete translation. In his case an effort to convey ideas of the Jewish Enlightenment movement is much clearer and the gap between his intentions and their realisation is much smaller. Values of productivisation, the importance of studying and understanding the world and love towards mankind govern the text and are presented to the child in the form of a dialogue.

---

[77]'Review of New Books', *Hame'asef*, fifth year, Altona 1831, pp. 97–101 (in Hebrew).

[78]It is interesting to note that the philanthropist system adapted the traditional system of catechism as its most distinguished narrative structure.

[79]David Samostz, *Robinson der Yingere*, Breslau 1824.

4. It was important for a translated text not only to convey Enlightenment values, but also not to contradict Jewish religion. In this sense, Campe, who was in favour of a universal religion, supplied a safe way for accomplishing certain goals of the Jewish Enlightenment movement. The selection of *Die Entdeckung von Amerika* for translation made it even safer because of the informative nature of the text. This enabled the translator to give up relatively easily the fictional dimension of the source text.

5. Translators (and Mendelssohn-Frankfurt was no exception), faced many difficulties because of the linguistic situation of the Hebrew language at that time. This was the case not only because Hebrew lacked many expressions, but mainly because of the lack of linguistic registers, formulas and patterns, that had to be invented, very often as *ad hoc* solutions. Like later translators of Campe, Mendelssohn-Frankfurt had to find equivalents for textual patterns that did not exist in Hebrew. This was true for any textual components, from vocabulary to the structure of paragraphs. However, unlike some later translators (for instance, Samostz), who endeavoured to find a solution for almost every problem, Mendelssohn-Frankfurt, perhaps due to his being the first translator of Campe, had used a different strategy: when a solution was hard to find, the translator simply cut those paragraphs.

Die Entdeckung von Amerika became very popular among writers of the Enlightenment. It was probably due to its potential for becoming a book of history and geography, that Jewish Enlightenment writers outside Germany were impelled to start their career as writers by translating this book, although other editions were already on the market.

This attitude towards Campe, and towards his *Entdeckung* in particular, explains why only three years after the Altona edition had been published, Hermann Bernard (Hirsch Beer Hurwitz), one of the first members of the Enlightenment movement in Russia, published his translation of Campe. His translation was then followed by two other translations: that of Samostz,[80] and a translation made by Günzburg,[81] which was the first complete translation of all three.

Günzburg's translation is of special interest because it explores Campe's importance in the eyes of the Jewish Russian Enlightenment. The entire question of the function of German children's literature in the development of the Hebrew literature in Eastern Europe calls for separate and thorough research. Here I wish only to point to the fact that by translating Campe into Hebrew, Günzburg was hoping to provide a bridge to German culture for the Jewish Russian Enlightenment. This was the case because Günzburg regarded the interplay of relations between Hebrew and German culture as decisive for the development of Hebrew culture in Russia. The German language was regarded by Günzburg as the most important language for the *Maskilim*, even more than Hebrew; by means of translation he hoped to make the German more readily available.

[80]David Samostz, *Meziat Amerika*, Breslau 1824. (Unfortunately I was unable to trace a copy of this book).
[81]Mordechai Aharon Günzburg, *Sefer Galot Eretz Chadasha*, Wilna 1823. In three parts.

For our current discussion of Campe, it is again interesting to note that when a representative of German culture was sought, Campe was most likely to be chosen. He was also among the first German authors, who had a canonised status, to be translated into Yiddish. Campe's *Die Entdeckung von Amerika* was one of the first books to be translated into Yiddish which was not popular literature.[82] According to Meisel it had enjoyed unknown success amongst women readers and replaced books of religious teaching (*Erbauungsliteratur*).[83]

Since Campe became for Hebrew children's literature a symbol of the Enlightenment, he preserved his status throughout the nineteenth century, even after the adaptation of the German texts ceased. Campe continued to function as a model for Hebrew texts late into the nineteenth century, as was the case with *Theophron*.

Campe's *Theophron* served as a model for quite a few children's books which were written as moral texts, for instance, Herz Homberg's *Imre Shefer*,[84] some chapters in Samostz's *Esh Dat*[85] and even the moral *Zeitschrift* for children published in Bavaria in 1817, *Keren Tushia*. It might very well be that moral books for adults such as Mendel Lepin's popular book *Heshbon Nefesh*[86] were also based on *Theophron*.

The persistent reliance on Campe explores some principles of selection of books for translation in the time of the Jewish Enlightenment in Germany. Translations were preferred primarily because it was easier to achieve certain goals of the Enlightenment through them. By translating from the German, translators accomplished at least two goals: (1) They were able to use texts which had already acquired legitimisation and were unquestionably representative of the ideology of the Enlightenment. Hence they could be easily legitimised by the Hebrew system. (2) They managed to adopt the main components of a system considered as ideal for imitation and thus laid the groundwork for the acceptance of a new system.

Just how strong this need to follow the German model was can be discerned in the case of original Hebrew texts.

ORIGINAL TEXTS BASED ON GERMAN MODELS

At the outset, original Hebrew texts for children were few and the distinction between original and translated texts was blurred. Translated texts were so common, that very often the translators did not even cite the name of the original author. This practice makes it, of course, even more difficult to distinguish between original and translation. In the case of poems and fables this distinction becomes impossible, since many translated texts were regarded as original

[82]The book was translated either by Haikel Hurwitz, or by Günzburg himself, as Meisel claims. Josef Meisel, *Haskalah. Geschichte der Aufklärungsbewegung unter den Juden in Russland*, Berlin 1919, p. 187.
[83]*Ibid.*
[84]Naphtali Herz Homberg, *Imre Shefer*, Wien 1808.
[85]David Samostz, *Esh Dat, op. cit.*
[86]Mendel Lepin, *Heshbon-Nefesh*, Lwov 1808.

works, in spite of the fact that they were written "after" [*nach*] certain German poems or fables. Ben Sew's exceptional mentioning of the source text, I have already referred to. He gives a kind of legitimisation for this practice by saying that the ignorance of source texts and writers was already common among German writers and hence it could be justified: "Even the learned Sulzer in his work (*Vorübungen*), a scholarly work, gathered and collected fables of various writers without mentioning their names. Still in order to avoid defamation, I have made this list" [list of original authors].[87]

The dominance of German translated texts over original Hebrew texts, is best demonstrated by the existence of pseudo-translations. I believe that this phenomenon, in spite of being peripheral, is very instructive. I refer here to the writers' tendencies to present an original text as a pseudo-translation (as shown by Toury[88] and Yahalom[89]). As original writing was rare and translations an accepted activity, writers were sometimes reluctant to acknowledge themselves as original authors. Instead, they preferred to present the text either as a translation of contemporary texts or as an adaptation of ancient texts. The last practice became prevalent due to the growing popularity of ancient Greek texts at the time.

Let us take a brief look at the case of Isaak Satanow. In 1789 Satanow published the first part of *Mishle Asaf*.[90] Although the fables were originally written by himself, he preferred to attribute them to Asaph Ben Berachiah (a psalmist mentioned in Chronicles[91]). Satanow was toying with the question of the identity of the original writer. In *Haskamat Geonim*, the Rabbinical Approval, to the book, which was commonly found in many Hebrew children's books of the time, the question of the identity of the writer is discussed. In this Approval, allegedly written by several *Rabbanim*, but actually written by Satanow himself, Satanow hinted at the real authorship of the book:

> "It is not clear to us who had really composed this text. Perhaps this distinguished man himself composed it. This was his way also in his work *Chibore Bina*. For we know this man and his ways."[92]

On a different occasion Satanow responded to the accusations raised against him. His attempt to attribute the text to an ancient Hebrew writer was described as plagiarism. Satanow defended himself by claiming that writers commonly lifted from other writers and never bothered to give credit to true authorship, while he was accused of stealing from himself and attributing it to someone else.[93] The motivation for his reluctance to admit authorship was given in the

---

[87] Ben Sew, *Mesilat Yesharim*, *op. cit.* The list is given in the last page of the book, book unpaginated, my translation.

[88] Gideon Toury, 'Translation, Literary Translation and Pseudotranslation', in E. S. Shaffer (ed.), *Comparative Criticism*, vol. 6, Cambridge 1984, pp. 73–85.

[89] Shelly Yahalom, *Relations entre les littératures française et anglaise au 18e siècle* (Hebrew, with extensive French summary). M.A. thesis, Tel-Aviv University, 1978.

[90] Isaak Satanow, *Mishle Asaf* (in three parts), Berlin 1789–1793.

[91] Chronicles I; 15, 17.

[92] Satanow, *Mishle Asaf*, *op. cit.*, first part, 'Haskamat Geonim', unpaginated, my translation.

[93] Isaak Satanow, 'Haskamat Geonim', unpaginated, in *Kuntras Mi-Sefer Ha-Zohar*, Berlin 1783.

Haskamat Geonim to *Kuntras Mi-Sefer Ha-Zohar*[94] written most likely by Satanow himself. Here he claimed that he had no other choice but to present his original work as ancient or translated if he wished to be taken seriously by his contemporaries, who had no respect for original contemporary works.

It is interesting to note that Satanow's fables were close to the model of German fables for children in the eighteenth century, probably because translations of ancient fables became very popular literature for children in the German system. In their adaptations of these fables or in the writing of new ones, the Germans deliberately imitated the ancient formulas. In such a way, as far as reliance on German models is concerned, Satanow's original writing of fables yielded eventually similar textual formulas for Hebrew translation of German fables.

THE FUNCTION OF YIDDISH LITERATURE IN THE DEVELOPMENT OF HEBREW CHILDREN'S LITERATURE

The most striking similarity between German and Hebrew children's literature is revealed not in the historical model which the Hebrew literature tried consciously to imitate, but surprisingly, the greatest similarity exists in the historical processes which Hebrew literature consciously ignored and rejected, but which nevertheless played an important role in its development. I refer here to the function of chapbooks in the development of Hebrew children's literature.

As is well known, chapbooks, the core of seventeenth-century popular literature, not only served as reading material for children, but had been an important catalyst in the development of children's books.[95] Their historical function can be described by the following:

The new educational system in Western Europe, which was the result of a new concept of childhood, meant an enormous expansion in the size of literate circles and a considerable change in their character. A new, previously unknown public – children – came into being and gradually created a demand for children's books. This demand could not yet be supplied. The lack of sufficient official reading material for children meant that they adopted for their own use whatever already existed: chapbooks. These books, until then read mainly by the poor, were now read by both the poor and by children. At the same time, the literary as well as the religious and educational establishment gradually became aware of the nature of children's reading. Their reactions were identical: each felt an urgent need to compete with and supersede chapbooks by other literature. This competition was a strong motivating force for all the establishments which became involved in the production of books for children, albeit each from a

[94]Satanow, *ibid.*
[95]Zohar Shavit, 'The Function of Yiddish Children's Literature in the Development of Hebrew Children's Literature', *Ha-Sifrut*, vol. 35–36 (1986), pp. 148–153 (in Hebrew); Victor E. Neuberg, *The Penny Histories*, London 1968; *idem, Chapbooks: A Guide to Reference Material*, London 1972.

different point of view: For some the commercial motive dominated, for others the ideological-educational one.

Hence, the non-canonised literature of the eighteenth century had had a decisive function in the development of Western children's literature. In fact, each stage of the development of canonised children's literature can be accounted for not only on the basis of its relation with adult literature and/or the educational system, as is usually the case,[96] but also on the basis of its need to compete with children's reading of chapbooks. The entire process of stratification of the children's system as a distinct system in culture was strongly linked with its emergence from the non-canonised system and consequently the creation of a new systemic antagonism between the adult and the children's systems.

In the case of Hebrew children's literature a similar pattern can be discerned. Yet, due to the special status of Hebrew at the time, the function of the non-canonised system was carried out by Yiddish texts, in the same way that the Yiddish system functioned as the non-canonised system for the entire Hebrew literature.[97] What the German *Volksbücher* were for German children's literature, the Yiddish chapbooks were for Hebrew children's literature.

The ways in which chapbooks functioned in the development of Hebrew children's literature has unfortunately not yet been studied. However, it is impossible to ignore their function totally in a discussion of the development of Hebrew children's literature. Here again I am presenting just some working hypotheses:

(1) As is evident from the description of the inventory of the first official Hebrew books for children, these texts did not have much appeal for Jewish children. This was not only because they were not written in the children's mother tongue, but also because of their didactic and moralistic nature. The Yiddish chapbooks, which were composed of romances, fables, biblical stories, travel tales and sensational stories,[98] were no doubt much more attractive. There is indeed much evidence that they were largely read by children.

(2) Children were used to reading these texts before the emergence of the Enlightenment movement, and continued to do so later.[99] However, before the time of the Enlightenment not much attention was paid to children's reading material. This was the case because in terms of cultural concepts the idea of children reading for their own amusement simply did not exist. Nobody troubled about peripheral texts addressed to women, which were not part of the official reading material for children.[100]

[96]Cf. Townsend, *op. cit.*; Mary F. Thwaite, *From Primer to Pleasure*, London 1972; Harvey Darton, *Children's Books in England*, Cambridge 1958.

[97]Itamar Even-Zohar, 'Aspects of Hebrew-Yiddish Polysystem', *Ha-Sifrut*, vol. 35–36 (1986), pp. 46–54; Chone Schmeruk, *Yiddish Literature: Aspects of its History*, Tel-Aviv 1978.

[98]Arnold Paucker, *The Yiddish Versions of the German Volksbuch*, Diss., Nottingham 1959; *idem*, 'Yiddish Versions of Early German Prose Novels', *Journal of Jewish Studies*, vol. 10 (1959), pp. 151–167; Sara Zfatmann, 'Maasse-bukh. On the Character of the Genre in Old Yiddish Literature', *Ha-Sifrut*, vol. 28 (1979), pp. 126–152 (in Hebrew).

[99]Chone Schmeruk, *The Illustrations in Yiddish Books of the Sixteenth and Seventeenth Centuries*, Jerusalem 1986.

[100]For a similar phenomenon in American children's literature cf. J. S. Bratton, *The Impact of Victorian Children's Fiction*, New York 1981.

(3) Only when Hebrew children's literature started to develop, was there, in social consciousness, a place for the concept of children's reading. People began to be aware of what children read, and "suddenly" realised that their reading material was "wrong" and "harmful" to children from their point of view. As a result they tried to compete with the reading of Yiddish and offer an alternative. The competition was two-fold. The reading of Yiddish texts was prohibited, though it was clear that the effectiveness of the prohibition depended on the ability to offer children alternative reading material. To this end a variety of measures was taken, among them the following:

(a) As was the case with European children's literature some decades earlier, Hebrew children's literature had used elements of the existing inventory of Yiddish chapbooks in order to replenish the Hebrew system. This was done in the following manner: components of Yiddish chapbooks were transferred into Hebrew. Here they either carried new functions or were attributed new legitimisations. Thus, for instance, biblical stories, common in Yiddish chapbooks, were legitimised by Hebrew literature on account of their existence in official German texts. Their transfer into Hebrew involved, of course, a different representation of biblical stories than in Yiddish chapbooks, but at the same time it enabled the Hebrew system to offer replacement for biblical stories in Yiddish.

(b) Yiddish books were translated into Hebrew, but their translation involved a change in their systemic attribution. From being books which officially addressed women and children, they became books for children only.

(c) As already mentioned, the Hebrew books for children were published at first in bi-lingual format: Hebrew and German. This format had served the aims of the Enlightenment movement in regard to the study of both Hebrew and German. However, at least in some cases this format could have created the impression that a non-Hebrew text was Yiddish and not German. I refer here to cases where the German appeared underneath the Hebrew text and was written in Rashi letters and not in the usual Hebrew letters.[101] It seems to me that this format had a real meaning and was not a random measure, because the other option, that of writing texts in parallel columns did exist, as did the option to write German in Latin letters. These two options were technically simpler. The preference for the first format can be explained in terms of an attempt to admit the new Hebrew texts under a disguise of a format that was time-honoured and already familiar.

The scheme of function of Yiddish chapbooks in the development of Hebrew literature manifests the degree of dependence of Hebrew children's literature in Germany on the model of development of German children's literature. Once a certain model was adopted, various elements of it were involved in historical processes, even if ideologically there was no room for them. Although Hebrew writers were ideologically not prepared to recognise the existence of popular Yiddish literature, they were forced to compete with it in order to regain their readers. Yet, their success was marginal. Lacking any genuine readership and

---

[101]See for instance David Samostz, *Tochechot Musar*, Breslau 1819. (Translation of J. H. Campe's *Sittenbüchlein*.)

facing later a stronger tendency towards a merger with German culture, Hebrew children's literature began to decline in Germany. As a matter of fact it totally faded away as a cultural phenomenon and ceased to exist not only in literary life but in historical memory as well.

Whenever the inventory of Hebrew children's literature in Europe is referred to, books published in Germany during the time of the Enlightenment are rarely mentioned. This attitude can perhaps be understood from the normative point of view, because most of the first texts for children did not have later any value as "living texts" for the reading public. However, when dealing with the historical development of Hebrew children's literature and with its main processes, one cannot ignore the German period, not only because it was the formative period of Hebrew children's literature, but also because the historical processes and procedures of the German period determined to a large extent the character of succeeding periods and their historical options. This is most evident in the function German literature continued to carry even after the centre of Hebrew had ceased to exist in Germany and was transferred to the East. In contradistinction to the adult system, where the Russian system began to dominate, German children's literature continued to function for Hebrew children's literature both as a mediating system and as the main source for translations and adaptations. From Campe and the Brothers Grimm to Franz Hoffmann and Wilhelm Hauff, German books were translated into Hebrew. Only later, in Palestine, was the German gradually replaced by the Russian as a mediating system.

Thus it was that the periphery of the literary polysystem preserved contact with the German system long after the adult system had divorced itself from the latter. Hebrew and German children's literatures have known an additional honeymoon at the beginning of the twentieth century, when an attempt was made to rebuild the cultural centre in Germany. This attempt failed, but the children's books published during that period in Germany later became the classics of Hebrew children's literature.

Yiddish Publishing Activities in the
Weimar Republic, 1920–1933

BY LEO AND RENATE FUKS

The evil winds of poverty, persecution, war and revolution had driven a larger number of Eastern fugitives over the borders of the German Empire after 1880. Their German co-religionists were far from happy to receive them for more than one reason. Apart from the financial strain on the German-Jewish welfare institutions there was a general hidden fear among German Jews that the appearance of unassimilated and recognisable Jews who spoke a language of their own would jeopardise their own rather precarious position as German citizens.[1] This fear was expressed in the open disdain and animosity with which the German Jews received their Eastern European brethren. The greater part of the German-Jewish relief and welfare organisations which supported the immigrants aimed at getting them away to the Americas and even further as quickly as possible.[2]

The German Ministry of the Interior also tried to prevent the mass-immigration and transmigration of the Eastern European Jews. In two decrees, of 20th September 1904 and of 26th February 1905, the Minister of the Interior ordered that only those with normal tickets from German shipping companies and a minimum capital of 400 Reichsmark per person and an additional 100 Reichsmark for each child were permitted to pass through German territory and

---

[1]The attitude of German Jewry towards the Jews of Eastern Europe has been described by S. Adler-Rudel in his book *Ostjuden in Deutschland 1880–1940. Zugleich eine Geschichte der Organisationen, die sie betreuten*, Tübingen 1959 (Schriftenreihe wissenschaftlicher Abhandlungen des Leo Baeck Instituts 1); Steven E. Aschheim, *Brothers and Strangers. The Eastern European Jew in German and German Jewish Consciousness, 1800–1923*, Madison 1982; and *idem*, 'Eastern Jews, German Jews and Germany's Ostpolitik in the First World War', in *LBI Year Book XXVIII* (1983); and most recently by Trude Maurer, *Ostjuden in Deutschland 1918–1933*, Hamburg 1986 (Hamburger Beiträge zur Geschichte der deutschen Juden, Band XII); and *idem*, 'Ausländische Juden in Deutschland, 1933–1939', in *Die Juden im Nationalsozialistischen Deutschland/The Jews in Nazi Germany 1933–1943*, herausgegeben von Arnold Paucker mit Sylvia Gilchrist und Barbara Suchy, Tübingen 1986 (Schriftenreihe wissenschaftlicher Abhandlungen des Leo Baeck Instituts 45). In the final section of her book, pp. 741–759, Trude Maurer evaluates the rather negative opinions many historians hold on German-Jewish solidarity with the poor and persecuted Jews of Eastern Europe. She defends the German Jewish community because of the financial assistance it rendered to Eastern Jews. A.o. see also the essays of Jack Wertheimer in *LBI Year Books XXVI, XXVII* and *XXVIII*, and now *idem, Unwelcome Strangers. East European Jews in Imperial Germany*, Oxford 1987.
[2]In 1901 the *Hilfsverein der deutschen Juden* was founded to help the emigrants from the East during their transmigration through Germany.

stay overnight. Russian subjects had also to present a valid passport. Those who did not fulfil these requirements were liable to be arrested and sent back over the German border. The same fate awaited those who managed to stay illegally in the German Empire.[3]

In spite of all these measures more than two million Eastern European Jews left their homes between 1880 and 1914, and most of them took their leave of Europe by way of Germany.[4] Some of the fugitives remained in Germany in spite of all the obstructions which were placed in their path. They managed to get a foothold in one German city or another and a slow process of acculturation started which succeeded when their children were educated at German schools. But the Eastern European Jews who stayed in Germany remained attached to their own Yiddish language and culture. They found a welcome in the Yiddish cultural clubs which were founded by Eastern European Jews who were living legally in Germany. These were mainly students who attended German universities and training colleges. They lived a life of their own and had few contacts with German-Jewish and non-Jewish students.[5] The influx of Eastern European fugitives in their clubs reinforced their cultural connections with Yiddish cultural life and letters.

As were all Jewish aliens in Germany, the Eastern European Jews were compelled to become paying members of the German-Jewish congregations, even if they never made any use of their institutions. By 1912 the number of legal and illegal Eastern European immigrants had increased so much that they started to demand full rights of membership which had hitherto been denied to them. After a fierce struggle which had to be settled by the German authorities, the Eastern European Jews were granted equal rights in the German-Jewish congregations in 1914.[6]

In spite of the generally negative attitude of German Jews towards Eastern European Jews there were groups which had more positive views on the values of Eastern European Jewish culture. From 1901 onwards, the periodical *Ost und West*, with its editor Leo Winz, regularly published translations from Yiddish literary works. The *Jüdischer Verlag*, founded in Berlin by Martin Buber in 1902, pursued the same editorial policy, but with a leaning towards Zionism. Zionist students, especially those organised in the club *Jung Juda*, espoused the cause of the Eastern European Jews in Germany, visited their literary clubs and lectured there.[7]

At the outbreak of the First World War there were about 90,000 Eastern European Jews in the German Empire. Those who were Austro-Hungarian subjects were enlisted in the German army, the Russian subjects were driven into

[3]Adler-Rudel, *op. cit.*, p. 5.
[4]*Ibid.*, pp. 5–6.
[5]The Eastern European Jewish students in Germany numbered about 400 in 1908–1909. Adler-Rudel, *ibid.*, p. 163.
[6]*Ibid.*, p. 28.
[7]Gershom Scholem remembers the veneration the members of his Zionist youth movement had for Yiddish culture. G. Scholem, *Von Berlin nach Jerusalem. Jugenderinnerungen*, Frankfurt a. Main 1977, p. 62.

internment camps. No compensation whatsoever was given to families for the loss of a livelihood which the men had built up with so much trouble. The greater part of the Eastern European Jews in Germany suddenly became completely destitute.[8]

Though the political propaganda of the German and Austrian occupying forces in the East reiterated on all occasions that their armies had come to bring freedom and justice to the Jews and other oppressed national minorities in the Russian Empire, the reality appeared to be quite the contrary. It was the economic policy of the German administration which tried to squeeze out as much wealth as possible, to requisition as many goods as they could lay their hands on from the occupied territories. Complete industries, most of which were Jewish property, were dismantled and sent to Germany, like the textile factories of Lodz. The Polish and Jewish workers lost their jobs without any form of compensation. Jewish workers were requisitioned for forced labour, partly in Germany.[9] But private German firms also enlisted Jewish workers in Poland to replace the Germans who served in the army. About 17,000 Jewish forced labourers were sent from Poland and other occupied territories to Germany and about the same amount came by themselves, enlisted or looking for jobs.[10]

Wherever they came to in Germany, the Jewish workers organised their own societies, mostly in the form of literary clubs, like the *Peretz Verein* in Berlin. Salman Schocken, owner of a chain of department stores in Germany and a noted philanthropist and very active Zionist, tried to alleviate the lot of the inmates of the internment camps and organised the distribution of Yiddish books and periodicals for them.[11] His was the driving force behind many Jewish cultural and social initiatives to help the Eastern European Jews. He also financed the monthly periodical, *Der Jude*, which Martin Buber founded in 1915, and corresponded with Franz Rosenzweig who served in the German army in the East about the possibilities of the new *Akademie für Wissenschaft des Judentums* which Rosenzweig wanted to establish.[12]

During the First World War a change in the attitude towards Eastern European Jews and their culture can be seen amongst part of German Jewry. Many German-Jewish soldiers had become acquainted with the Jewish population in the occupied territories in the East. They had found a warm welcome in Jewish homes, in contrast to that which Eastern European Jews had so often experienced when in Germany. German-Jewish soldiers began to appreciate the interesting and many-faceted Jewish culture which was hidden behind the façade of the typically Eastern European Jewish way of life, that of dress and speech which at first sight had so repelled them. Some scholars such as

[8]Adler-Rudel, *op. cit.*, p. 34.

[9]Zosa Szajkowski, 'East European Jewish Workers in Germany during World War I', *Salo Wittmayer Baron Jubilee Volume*, II, Jerusalem 1974, pp. 895–896. (See also the essays of Szajkowski in *LBI Year Books IX* and *X*.)

[10]Szajkowski, *loc. cit.*, p. 908; Maurer, *op. cit.*, p. 38 gives an estimated total of 30,000.

[11]Volker Dahm, *Das jüdische Buch im Dritten Reich*, II, Frankfurt a. Main 1981, columns 407–408.

[12]Dahm, *op. cit.*, column 409.

Rosenzweig began to understand in the East the need for re-orientation towards Jewish learning for the German Jews.*

In the first part of the war a German victory seemed certain and German-Jewish leaders and the German authorities envisaged with apprehension the consequences of a new political development in the East after a complete defeat of the Russian Empire. They shared a great fear of uncontrollable large-scale Jewish immigration into German territory and held a very negative opinion of Eastern European Jews. The German authorities were influenced by the wave of antisemitism which was prevalent in the country during the war and the Jewish leaders feared even more animosity when the "real" Jews would appear in great numbers. The *Hilfsverein der deutschen Juden*, which distributed American relief funds in German-occupied territories, worked together with the German authorities, sometimes even to the detriment of the Jews in need. A largely Zionist society, the *Komitee für den Osten*, was founded in 1914 and the organisations sharply conflicted in their views on the Jews of the Eastern territories and what should become of them during and after the war.[13]

Towards the end of the war, from April 1918 onwards the German authorities tried to get rid of the Eastern European workers within their territory. The brutal methods they employed mirrored the virulently antisemitic atmosphere in Germany at that time, when the realisation had come that the war was lost.[14] Because of the chaotic situation in Eastern Europe after the outbreak of the Russian Revolution at the end of 1917, the efforts of the German authorities were of no avail. In spite of all official measures the numbers of Eastern European fugitives, Jewish as well as non-Jewish, swelled greatly after the peace-settlement of 1919. In the aftermath of the civil war following the Russian Revolution and with the difficulties for the Jews in the newly created independent Eastern states, new waves of fugitives came to Germany. Among them were quite a few intellectuals, writers, poets and artists who gave new impetus to the intellectual life of the already existing Yiddish cultural clubs. The urgent political problems of the day were hotly discussed also and political organisation among the Eastern European Jews became stronger. The Jewish Socialist Party, the *Bund*, and the Socialist-Zionist Party, *Poale Zion*, were the leading factions, but the clubs had to avoid official political activities as they were distrustfully watched by the German police.[15]

In 1919, the Eastern European Jews in Germany founded a federation of all their organisations called the *Bund ostjüdischer Vereine* which became the *Verband der Ostjuden in Deutschland* after a reorganisation in 1920. From then on the life of the Eastern European Jews in Germany slowly settled down. Primary schools and supplementary Yiddish courses were organised and the cultural life in the clubs began to attract German Jews too and even some interested non-Jews. A Union of Eastern Jewish artists, the *Ostjüdischer Künstlerbund*, founded in 1920,

*See also the contribution by Rivka Horwitz, 'Voices of Opposition to the First World War among Jewish Thinkers', in this volume of the Year Book, esp. pp. 252–253 – (Ed.).
[13]Szajkowski, *loc. cit.*, p. 888.
[14]Szajkowski, *ibid.*, pp. 888 ff.
[15]Maurer, *op. cit.*, pp. 39 ff.

Cover, vignette and tail-piece of the Yiddish Magazine of Art and Letters, 'Milgroym', Berlin 1923
Designed by El Lissitzky

Cover of 'Di jidishe emigratsye', Berlin 1929

Cover of A. M. Stenzel's 'Mendele Moykher-Sforim'
Berlin 1936

Frontispiece and page from P. Markish's 'Der galaganer hon', Berlin 1922
Designed by Joseph Tchaikov

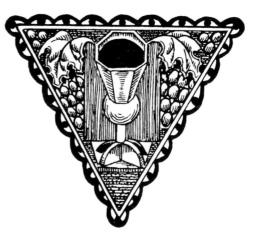

Above and below right:
Title-page and tail-piece of 'Mekhires Yosef'
Edited by M. Weinreich, Berlin 1923
Designed by Joseph Tchaikov

בער בּאלעכאָווערס

זכרונות

אַרויסגענעבּן מיט אַיינפיר
און דערקלערונגען פֿון
ד"ר מ. װישניצער

כּלל-פֿאַרלאַג
בּערלין, 1922-תּרפּ"ג

K L A L - V E R L A G
BERLIN SW 68 ╱ MARKGRAFENSTRASSE 73

Left:
Title-page of Ber Belokhower's 'Zikhroynes'
Berlin 1922

provided studios for artists, organised exhibitions, concerts and theatrical performances. There were many contacts with Russian artists and intellectuals who had fled to Germany for the same reasons as the Jews. In the Berlin *Romanisches Café* and in the Russian cultural club *Heim der Künste* which was situated on the first floor of the *Café Leon*, Russian artists, writers and poets hotly debated new currents in the world of art. Among them were many Jews who were also preoccupied by visions of a new and *avant-garde* Jewish art. They included Lasar (El) Lissitzky, Joseph Tchaikov, Nathan Altmann, Issachar Ber Ryback and Leon Zack, to cite only a few. The Eastern European artists and writers took part in the atmosphere of feverish searching for new forms of intellectual and artistic life which was so typical for life in the Berlin émigré-circles of the time. The apogee of all artistic activities was the first Russian Art Exhibition which was organised in Berlin in 1922 in the Galerie Von Diemen, Unter den Linden. The exhibition was a great success and was the talk of the day in intellectual Berlin.[16]

For a few years, from 1920 until 1925, Berlin became the centre of a short-lived but throbbing Yiddish cultural microcosmos which soon radiated to and influenced most of the Yiddish-speaking world. It did not only draw Yiddish writers, artists and scholars to Berlin, but also exported books and publications, printed in Germany, all over the globe.

Notwithstanding the political and economic difficulties in Eastern Europe caused by civil wars and the instability of the newly created states, the pent-up cultural energy of the Jews burst out in a host of Yiddish writings by young and talented poets and novelists. For the first time the *Bund* and other political parties organised a network of secular schools for girls and boys in Eastern Europe. There was a great demand for Yiddish schoolbooks for primary and secondary schools. These books were difficult to produce in Eastern Europe with its completely destroyed economy. At that time the first Yiddish publishing houses moved from Eastern Europe to Germany. There were Yiddish writers, translators and artists, an eager public waited and longed for Yiddish books and Germany provided excellent possibilities.

We need not elucidate here the causes of the steady inflation of German currency from 1920 onwards. This inflation enabled Yiddish publishing houses, which paid in foreign currency, to make use of the excellent printing facilities in Germany at prices which were lower than anywhere else. Some of the publishing houses already existed in Eastern Europe and moved temporarily to Berlin. Others were set up in Germany to profit from the extraordinary circumstances. There were some publishing houses which also published works of modern Hebrew writers and there were also a few exclusively Hebrew publishing houses. But their history and output deserve a special study.*

One of the first publishing houses which started its work in Berlin in 1921, was

[16]E. Steneberg, *Russische Kunst in Berlin, 1919–1932*, Berlin 1969, pp. 18–19.
*See however an interim contribution to this topic, the essay by Elias Hurwicz, 'Shay Ish Hurwitz and the Berlin He-Athid. When Berlin was a Centre of Hebrew Literature', in *LBI Year Book XII* (1967) – (Ed.).

the *Farlag Yidish*. It came from Kovno (Kaunas) in Lithuania. Its output consisted of several small works and a new series called *Folksbibliotek* of which at least six numbers were published. The translation into Yiddish of Martin Buber's *Reden über das Judentum* testifies to the interest in German-Jewish culture in spite of the many adverse experiences of Eastern Jews in Germany.

The German *Weltverlag* which was founded by Alvin Löwenthal in 1919, specialised in Jewish literature. In 1921, Alexander (Ahron) Eliasberg who was a great lover of Yiddish literature, became its director. In that year too he published four Yiddish books, three of which were translations from the German.

A completely new Yiddish publishing house was *Wostok* (Russian: the East). It started production in Dresden in 1921, but the firm moved to Berlin in the same year. We have not been able to find any data on this new firm, as to whether it was in some way a continuation of an existing firm in Eastern Europe. Neither do we know if the firm was financed by Western European institutions or individuals. Eliah Olshvanger,[17] an experienced and many-sided physician and publicist, was its director. The firm's Berlin address was Spandauer Brücke 2, and its books were printed in Leipzig, at the establishments of W. Drugulin, B. J. Teubner and Spamer. The major part of *Wostok*'s publications consisted of the much-needed Yiddish textbooks for the new Jewish schools in Eastern Europe. Olshvanger and the Yiddish scholar Max Weinreich translated many textbooks of history, geometry, geography, physics and biology from the German. *Wostok* also published Yiddish literary works, among them the collected works (in six volumes) of David Bergelson, one of the most important modern Yiddish writers of the time, two books of Shemarya Gorelik and one work of the young and talented Yiddish poet Moshe Kulbak. Nahum Shtif, historian, literary critic and linguist, is represented with a work on the pogroms in the Ukraine in 1919. *Wostok* also published Max Weinreich's first pioneering work on the history of Old Yiddish literature. All these writers and scholars lived in Berlin at the time their works were published. The *Wostok* books were very well produced and some of them were illustrated by Eastern European Jewish artists who also lived in Berlin by that time, like Joseph Tchaikov, El Lissitzky and Issachar Ber Ryback. *Wostok* introduced a completely new feature in Yiddish book-publishing: the aesthetic element. Hitherto badly printed books on cheap paper had been the general rule, which was understandable because the Yiddish reading public had not the means to buy beautiful and expensive books. But *Wostok*, and the other Yiddish publishing houses in Berlin, too, could profit from the extraordinary circumstances of the inflation in Germany to publish artistically designed books with illustrations by the *avant-garde* of modern artists for very low prices.

---

[17]He was born in Grajev (Poland) and died in New York, 1952. After studying medicine in Würzburg and Berlin at the beginning of the century, he practised as a physician and wrote articles for Russian periodicals. During the First World War he lived in Wilna and founded a Yiddish daily paper, *Di letste nays*, in 1917, when the ban on Yiddish publications in Russia was lifted. In 1919 he fled from the counter-revolution to Berlin and became director of the publishing house, *Wostok*. He was also one of the directors of the organisation for medical care among Russian Jews (OSE) (see below note 22) and translated several popular medical treatises into Yiddish. Adler-Rudel, *op. cit.*, p. 105.

In 1921 another important Yiddish publishing house started its activities in Berlin. It was the *Klal-Farlag*, a continuation of the *Folks-Farlag* of Kiev. Its director, Zeev Wolf Latzki-Bertoldi[18] continued his work in Berlin. He was most probably financed by the important German publishing firm *Ullstein*, but we have not been able to find data about the financial background. *Klal-Farlag*'s Berlin address was Markgrafenstrasse 73 and it had its own printing office. In 1922, the firm published more than fifty numbers of a series of small paperbacks, called *Klal-Bibliotek*, consisting of original Yiddish texts and translations. Another series of historical works for children called *Historishe Yugent Bibliotek* was also started. Original literary works and the much-needed Yiddish school-books were published as well. In 1923, the output of the firm dwindled and in 1924 only one periodical was published.

The *Klal-Farlag* had been of great importance for the export of Yiddish books from Germany. The small, cheap paperbacks must have been a great success with the readers of Yiddish abroad. The firm, like many other Yiddish publishing houses in Germany, advertised their publications in the bibliographical journal *Di Bikhervelt* which made its appearance in Warsaw in 1921.[19] But on the dust-jackets of the books the firm also announced forthcoming publications, as in No. 33 of the *Klal-Bibliotek*: ". . . In the series *Klal-Bikher* we will give larger literary works, original [Yiddish] and translations from the best authors . . .".

Rimon Jewish Art and Literature Publishing Company, Berlin–London, was an international and multi-faceted publishing house. Its Berlin address was Hohenstaufenstrasse 43. The firm was directed by Mark and Rahel Wischnitzer.[20] *Rimon* produced the most beautiful and interesting journal of Jewish art that ever appeared and the like of which had never before been published for Jewish readers. The Hebrew edition of the journal was called *Rimon* and a Yiddish one appeared under the name of *Milgroym*. These journals differed in content in the literary department. While the Yiddish edition was devoted to problems of Yiddish literature, the Hebrew edition was devoted to modern Hebrew literature. But several richly illustrated articles on modern Jewish art appeared in both journals. In *Milgroym* and *Rimon* artists like Marc Chagall and

[18]He was born in Kiev in 1881 and died in Tel-Aviv in 1940. He studied in Berlin from 1901 until 1903 and became an active member of the Eastern Jewish student club. Back in Russia, he was illegally engaged in the Poale-Zionist movement. Apart from his literary work he was also director of *Emigdirekt*, an international Committee for Jewish emigration which was founded in Prague in 1921. Adler-Rudel, *op. cit.*, pp. 105–106.

[19]*Bikhervelt. Kritish bibliografisher zhurnal.* Dershaynt ale tsvey khadoshim in Varshe. Farlag Kultur-Lige. Eight issues of the journal appeared in 1922 and 1923. In 1928 the journal reappeared in a different form in Warsaw.

[20]1882–1955. He was a well-known Jewish historian and communal worker. He originated from Galicia and studied in Vienna and Berlin. In 1919 he lived in London and there probably organised the financial aspects of the *Rimon* publishing house. From 1921 until 1937 he was deeply engaged in all kinds of welfare work for Eastern European Jews. After 1933 he concentrated on the problems of emigration of Jews from Nazi Germany.

His wife Rahel Bernstein was born in Minsk in 1892 and was a well-known historian of Jewish art. After the liquidation of the *Rimon* publishing house Mark and Rahel Wischnitzer worked for the *Encyclopaedia Judaica* in Berlin. They emigrated to Paris in 1938 and went to the United States in 1941.

El Lissitzky expounded their views on Jewish art and illustrated their own and other people's essays. In the literary section of *Milgroym* many interesting *avant-garde* theories on modern Yiddish literature were discussed.[21] Though it was announced that the journal would appear every two months, only six issues were published between 1922 and 1924. The journal can be considered the highlight of Yiddish publication in Germany, combining the talent of the writers and artists with the technical know-how and skill of German printing.

Rimon also published works of Jewish interest in Hebrew, Yiddish, Russian and English. Their only Yiddish publication which did not appear in translation was M. Kleinman's edition of the stories of the *hasidic* rabbi Nahman of Bratslav.

In 1922 and 1923 two smaller publishing houses in Berlin presented interesting and important works. The *Yidisher Kultur Farlag* specialised in translation, mainly from the German. The *Yidisher Literarischer Farlag* published original literary works along with eye-witness accounts of the recent historical events in Russia. Occasional Yiddish publications, periodicals and pamphlets appeared, voicing the opinions of every group and party among the Eastern European Jews in Germany. Among these occasional publications is one Yiddish book published by the *Stybel-Verlag*, financed by a rich Russian leather-merchant who also had books printed in Copenhagen. The *Yalkut Farlag* and the Hebrew publishing house *Moriah* later moved to Palestine.

Several Jewish welfare institutions like the OSE[22] published series of popular medical treatises and pamphlets on child-care and general health between 1922 and at least until 1927. Also, the ORT[23] regularly issued bulletins and pamphlets.

After 1925 the number of Yiddish publications in Germany rapidly diminished. Some periodicals and occasional pamphlets of international Jewish organisations were published, mostly in relation to the problems of emigration and re-emigration of the Eastern European Jews. The German political climate with its growth of National Socialism and organised antisemitism made Eastern European Jews aware that Germany was no longer a safe place. After 1929 they began to look for better places to live in. An exception was the Yiddish writer and poet A. N. Stenzel who managed to remain in Germany until 1938. He was a friend of Else Lasker-Schüler, the well-known German-Jewish poet. She tried to help him with money and goods which she begged from admirers for him and for other destitute authors. Stenzel lived with his German friend, a courageous woman, until he emigrated to London.[24]

---

[21] Arthur Tilo Alt, 'The Berlin *Millgroym* group and Modernism', *Yiddish. A Quarterly Journal devoted to Yiddish and Yiddish Literature*, VI, 1 (1985), p. 33.

[22] OSE (*Obtschestwo Sdrawoochranenija Ewrejew* = *Gesellschaft für den Schutz der Gesundheit der Juden*) was founded in 1912 and did excellent work during the First World War. It became a world-wide international organisation for the protection of the health of the Jewish communities.

[23] ORT (*Obtschestwo remeslennowo i semledeltscheskowo truda sredi jewrejew w Rossii* = *Gesellschaft zur Förderung des Handwerks und der Landwirtschaft unter den Juden*) was founded in Russia in 1880 to provide professional and agricultural training for the impoverished Russian Jews. Like OSE it became after the war, in 1920, an international organisation. The director of the German branch was A. Singalowsky.

[24] Ruth Wolf, *Prins Joessoef van Thebe. Leven en werk van Else Lasker-Schüler*, The Hague 1986, pp. 90 ff.

The feverish cultural life of the Berlin Eastern Jewish centre ended as suddenly as it had begun. The greater part of the Yiddish writers, artists and scholars either went back to Poland and the Soviet Union or found their way to Paris, London and the United States. The fate of those who went back to Eastern Europe is known only too well. They fell victim either to the policy of extermination of the Nazi invaders or the violent repression of Yiddish culture in the Soviet Union after 1938; the writers, their works and their public vanished in the war and the wanton destruction of human beings and their culture.

Nevertheless the influence of the Berlin cultural scene was a lasting one. Its spirit of an international *avant-garde* enriched Yiddish literature in all its centres. Berlin was also the cradle of scholarly study of Yiddish language and literature and the history of the Jews in Eastern Europe. During a conference in Berlin in 1925, the YIVO Institute for Jewish Research was founded. Wilna, which was then part of the Polish Republic, was to be the headquarters of the organisation, with branches in Berlin, Warsaw and New York. An international network of friends would provide the funds for research and publications. The Berlin branch of YIVO was directed by Elijahu Tcherikover, with the cooperation of the famous Jewish historian Simon Dubnow. Jakob Lestschinsky was the head of the department of economics and statistics of the Jewish community in Berlin. The Eastern Jewish Historical Archives in Berlin published material on the persecution of the Jews in the Ukraine and Belorussia during the Revolution and the wars of 1917–1921.

In the years of intense cultural life relations with the German Jews gradually became somewhat less strained. The Zionist movement especially strove to unite German and Eastern European Jews for the common goal. But a full acceptance of the Eastern Jews by the German Jews never took place. We will give here only two instances out of many to illustrate this. When the first issue of the German-Jewish bibliophile journal *Soncino-Blätter* was issued in 1925,[25] an extensive bibliography was published of books which had appeared between 1920 and 1925 on Jewish subjects. There were three divisions: Judaica, Hebraica and Palestine (pp. 115–149). No mention whatsoever is made in this bibliography of the Yiddish publications in Germany. Even the English books of the *Rimon* Publishing House are not listed.

An international press exhibition called *Pressa* was organised in Cologne from May until October 1928. Among the national exhibits the Catholic, Protestant and Jewish religions were also represented, in separate pavilions. In the Jewish pavilion, the *Jüdische Sonderschau der Pressa*, one of the four rooms was reserved for the Yiddish press. Tcherikover, director of the economic and statistical department of the Berlin branch of YIVO, had insisted that among the exhibits of the German-Jewish press the Yiddish periodicals which were then published in Germany were also to be shown. This would have been a token of solidarity amongst all Jews who lived in Germany at a time of growing antisemitism. But the German-Jewish organising committee, with its chairman Max I. Boden-

[25]*Soncino-Blätter, Beiträge zur Kunde des jüdischen Buches.* Published by the *Soncino-Gesellschaft der Freunde des jüdischen Buches,* edited by Hermann Meyer.

heimer, refused Tcherikover's request. In a very critical article on the exhibition of the Jewish press Tcherikover reproached the committee for wilful neglect and contempt.[26]

A Dutch visitor to the exhibition, L. Hirschel, librarian of the *Bibliotheca Rosenthaliana* in Amsterdam, was favourably impressed by the *Jüdische Sonderschau*. He published an enthusiastic account of his visit in the leading Jewish weekly in Holland[27] in which he expressed his amazement at the amount of Yiddish periodicals which were published all over the world. It remains a remarkable fact that neither in the official catalogue of the exhibition nor in the separate brochure which was published for the occasion of the *Jüdische Sonderschau* is there even a mention to be found of the Yiddish press in Germany.[28]

Even the bitter experiences of German persecution and destruction of the European Jews in the Second World War have not put an end to the old prejudices against Yiddish language and literature. It is symptomatic that Margaret T. Edelheim-Muehsam in her first survey on the German-Jewish press written some thirty years ago for the Year Book of the Leo Baeck Institute stated simply that the "number of Yiddish periodicals published in Germany now and then was small and their circulation negligible . . .".[29] The short but very important interlude of Yiddish culture in Germany deserves a better treatment than this, the more so because there are so very few people left to speak up for these vanished Yiddish authors and their public.

[26]E. Tcherikover, 'Di yidishe prese-oysshtelung in keln', *Bikhervelt* I, 4 (July 1928), pp. 39–45.

[27]L. Hirschel, 'De Joodsche pers in de Pressa te Keulen', *De Vrijdagavond, Joodsch Weekblad* V, 14 (6th–13th July 1928), pp. 214–217; 227–230 (with illustrations).

[28]In the library of the *Internationales Zeitungsmuseum der Stadt Aachen* the catalogue of the exhibition, *Katalog der Pressa 1928* is extant. On pp. 249 and 250 there are particulars on the Jewish part of the exhibition. In the brochure *Festschrift zur jüdischen Sonderschau der Pressa 1928*, Cologne 1928, 82 pp., there is no mention whatsoever of Yiddish periodicals.

[29]Margaret T. Edelheim-Muehsam, 'The Jewish Press in Germany', in *LBI Year Book I* (1956), pp. 163–164.

Bibliography

The preparation of a bibliography of Yiddish books and periodicals, published and printed in Germany, presents great difficulties. Students in the field have been seriously hampered by the fact that ". . . Yiddish literature (in its broadest sense comprising all publication activities in the Yiddish language) suffers from an intense case of bibliographical neglect. No national bibliography has devoted itself exclusively to 'Yiddica' . . . The field of Yiddish is, in brief, distinguished more for its *lacunae* than for its concrete achievements . . ." as has been aptly remarked a few years ago.[30]

The tentative list we present here can, therefore, only be considered as a first attempt which we sincerely hope will be supplemented. The list is based on announcements in the Yiddish bibliographical journal *Bikhervelt*. We could only make use of six issues, dating from January 1922 until April 1923. The last two issues were not available, either in Europe or in the United States. Added to these data are bibliographical references in the biographies of Yiddish authors in the *Leksikon fun der nayer yidisher literatur* (New York 1956–1968), advertisements of recent and forthcoming publications on the dust jackets of the Yiddish publications and information gathered from literature and letters of the period.

We have not been able to see the greater part of the listed books and periodicals and, therefore, could not check dates, number of pages and other information. Yiddish books are very scarce in European libraries and when present mostly catalogued together with Hebrew books. Looking for Yiddish publications of our period was a difficult and unrewarding task. We hope that this deficient list will be the start for the collecting of conclusive data on this important period in modern Yiddish literature, before every trace of it has vanished.

The spelling of the names of the authors is according to that of the *Encyclopaedia Judaica* (Jerusalem 1972)). Authors who are not given there and Yiddish texts are rendered according to the transliteration-rules for Yiddish, laid down in Volume I, Index, p. 91.

1919
H. ITZKOWSKI, BERLIN
1. GONZER, M. A., *Der historisher moment*.

1920
2. *UNDZER GEDANK. A Zaml-bukh*. Aroysgegebn funem biuro funem idishn sotsialistishn arbeyter-farband poale-tsion, 112 pp.

VERLAG JUDÄA, BERLIN
3. *Der idisher khurbn in ukrayne*. Materialn un dokumentn redagirt un bearbet fun Leon Chasanowich, ix, 108 pp.

    Financed by the Scandinavian Jewish Relief Committee for the Jewish victims of the pogroms in the Ukraine.

---

[30]Zachary M. Baker, 'Bibliographic Research and Organization of Yiddish Literature. Some Problems and Prospects', *Yiddish. A Quarterly Journal devoted to Yiddish and Yiddish Literature*, IV, 2 (1980), p. 21.

JÜDISCHER VERLAG, BERLIN

4. KAUFMANN, Frits Mordechai, *Die schönsten Lieder der Ostjuden.* 47 ausgewählte Volkslieder. Yidd. texts with German translation.

1921
FARLAG YIDISH, KOVNO-BERLIN

5. BENSON, Joseph, *Frilings-toyt.* A eynakter funem arbeter-lebn, 24 pp. (Folksbibliotek, 6).
6. BUBER, Martin, *Dray redn iber yudntum.* Ibergezetst fun dayths durkh H. Frank, 26 pp.
   Yidd. translation of the three addresses which Buber delivered for the Jewish student organisation Bar Kochba in Prague, 1909–1911.
7. EPELBOYM, B[erish], *In frien harbst.* Dertseylung, 64 pp. (Folksbibliotek, 2).
8. SEGALOWITCH, Zusman, *Osne.* Ertseylung, 56 pp. (Folksbibliotek, 1).
9. SINGMAN, Kalman, *Ven dos harts iz yung.* Lider, 80 pp. (Folksbibliotek, 4).
10. SINGMAN, Kalman, *Ba der ozere.* A eynakter, 26 pp. (Folksbibliotek, 8).
11. VIKTIM, S., *Tsu shpet.* A eynakter, 16 pp.

KLAL-FARLAG, BERLIN

12. KOLODNI, Pesakh, *Gertneray*, 74 pp.
   Another Yidd. work on the same subject by the same author was published in the Yidisher Folks Farlag, Kiev 1919.
13. NOMBERG, Hersh David, *Di mishpokhe*, Drame in 4 aktn, 136 pp.

JÜDISCHER VERLAG

14. FRIEDEMAN, Adolf, *Dos lebn fun Theodor Hertsl*, 128 pp.

WELT FARLAG, BERLIN

15. BROD, Max, *Tikho Brahes veg tsu got.* A roman. Yidish fun S. Birnbaum, 298 pp.
   Brod's historical novel *Tycho Brahes Weg zu Gott* appeared for the first time in 1916.
16. LANDAUER, Gustav, *Oyfruf tsum sotsializm.* Iberzetsung fun daytsh durkh H. Frank un B. Rosenthal. Mit an aynfirung in Gustav Landauers lebn un shafung fun H. Frank, 256 pp.
   Landauer's *Aufruf zum Sozialismus* appeared for the first time in 1911 and was reprinted in Berlin 1920.
17. LEHMANN, Judah, *Eynshteyns relativitetsteorye*, 52 pp.
18. LIEBKNECHT, Karl, *Briv fun front un fun tfise far un nokh dem psak-din.* Iberzetsung un nokhvort fun A. Vilentshuk, 208 pp.

WOSTOK, DRESDEN

19. GORELIK, Shemarya, *Groyse neshomes*, 170 pp.
20. GORELIK, Shemarya, *Yidishe kep*, 132 pp.
21. JUNG, W. and G. H., *Der kleyne geometer.* Ershter kurs fun geometrye. Ibergezetst oyf yidish fun Eliah Olshvanger, 128 pp. with ill.
22. WIPER, R., *Geshikhte fun der nayer tsayt.* Far shuln un aleyn-bildung. Ibergezetst fun Max Weinreich, 198, 4 pp.
23. WIPER, R., *Geshikhte fun mitlalter.* Far shuln un aleynbildung. Ibergezetst fun Max Weinreich, 192, 4 pp.

WOSTOK, BERLIN

24. WIPER, R., *Di uralte eyrope un der mizrekh.* Iberzetsung fun Z. Kalmanovitch, 406 pp.
BERLIN, WITHOUT NAME OF PUBLISHER

25. ARKHIV *funem idishn sotsializm*, I: *Poale-tsion.* Edited by Leon Chazanovitch, 52 pp.

1922
FARLAG POALE TSION, BERLIN

26. MARX, Karl, *Der birgerkrig in frankraykh.* Mit a hakdome fun F. Engels. Yidish fun J. L. Berman, 58 pp.

FARLAG YIDISH, BERLIN

27. AFRIKE. Bearbet un tsuzamengeshtelt fun S. Zirlikh. I, 112 pp. with ill.

FARLAG – YIDISHER KULTUR, BERLIN

28. ANDERSEN, H., *Naye mayselekh.* Iberz. fun Der Nister (pseud. of Pinchas Kaganovitch).
29. BARBUSSE, Henri, *Klorkeyt.* Roman in 2 teyln. Ibergez. fun frantsoysishn R. Seligman, 392 pp.
30. GOETHE, Johann Wolfgang von, *Di yesurim fun dem yungen Werter.* Ibergezetst fun Moshe Luria, 144 pp.
31. GRIMM, Jacob and Wilhelm, *Oysgeklibene mayselekh.* Ibergezetst fun daytsh durkh "Yashar", I: 48 pp.; II: 40 pp., mit bilder fun Ludwig Richter.
32. LITE. *Zamlheft,* redagirt fun A. Katsenelenbogen.
33. LUXEMBURG, Rosa, *Briv fun der tfise (1916–1918).* Ibergez. fun A. Vilentshuk.
34. KWITKO, Leib, *Grin groz,* 206 pp.
35. SHNEURSON, Fishl (Joshua), *Khayim Gravitser, die geshikhte funem gefalenem.* Fun der khabader velt, I, 112 pp.
   Vol. II was published by Yalqut publishing house in Berlin 1926.

KLAL-FARLAG, BERLIN

36. ADUREN. J., *Der shlezisher ger-tsedek, Yosef ben reb Avrohom* (Joseph Streblitski), 32 pp. (Klal-Bibliotek, 12).
37. AKSENFELD, J., *Kabtsn-oyshershpil. Dos shterntikhl.*
38. BAAL-DIMYEN (pseud. of Nohum Shtif), *Humanizm in der elterer yidisher literatur* (Klal-Bibliotek, 19–20).
39. BAAL-MAKHSHOVES (Pseud. of Israel Isidor Elyashev), *Dos dorem yidntum in di yidishe literatur in XIX yorhundert.* A historish-kritishe shtudye, 64 pp. (Klal-Bibliotek, 25–26).
40. BAAL-MAKHSHOVES, *Grobin, Musarnikes,* 64 pp. (Klal-Bibliotek, 41–42).
41. BIALIK, Hayim Nahman, *Shirim un poemen.* Mit an araynfir fun Baal-Makhshoves, 112 pp.
42. BIALIK, Hayim Nahman, *Fun tsar un tsorn. In shekhite-shtot. Dos letste vort* (Klal-Bibliotek, 1).
43. BOLECHOVER, Ber (also called Dov Ber Birkenthal), *Zikhroynes.* Aroysgegebn mit araynfir un derklerungen fun Mark Wischnitzer, 150 pp.
   A Hebrew translation of the original Yiddish text of the memoirs, which are an important source for Polish–Jewish history in the eighteenth century, appeared at the Klal-Farlag at the same time.
44. CHAMISSO, Adalbert von, *Peter Shlemil, der mentsh on a shotn.* Fun daytsh (Klal-Bikher, 5).
45. DIK, Eisik Meir, *Khaytsikl aleyn.*
46. DIK, Eisik Meir, *Lite.*
47. DIK, Eisik Meir, *Shivim-moltsayt.*
48. DINABURG, Benzion, *Oyfn shvel fun mitalter.* Der untergang fun yidishn tsenter in erets-yisroel un der onheyb fun mitlalter (Historishe Yugnt Bibliotek).
49. EICHENDORFF, Joseph, *Zikhroynes fun a shtifer.* Fun daytsh (Klal-Bikher, 4).
50. ETTINGER, S., *Serkele.*
51. FLAUBERT, G., *Herodiade.* Iberz. fun frantsoysish fun R. Seligman, 64 pp. (Klal-Bibliotek, 15–16).
52. FOLKSLIEDER, 2 vols.
53. FRANCE, Anatole, *Der farvalter iber yudea un andere dertseylongen* (Klal-Bikher, 2).
54. GNESIN, Uri Nisan, *Mayse otelo un Samuil Samuilovitsh,* 64 pp. (Klal-Bibliotek, 2–3).
55. GÜDEMANN, M., *Yidishe kulturgeshikhte in mitalter. Yidn in daytshland, dos XIV un XV yorhundert,* Yidish Nohum Shtif, 246 pp.
56. HANOVER, Nathan Note, *Fun tifn zump. Gezeres Chmelnicki.* Ibergez. fun hebreish (Klal-Bibliotek, 47–48).
57. HIRSHKAN, Zvi, *Nit hinter a ployt* (Klal-Bibliotek, 5).
58. HUCH, Ricarda, *Der idisher kever.* Iberz. fun R. Seligman, 40 pp. (Klal-Bibliotek,
59. ISAKS, Aaron, *Avtobiografye.* Yidish Nohum Shtif, 118 pp., with portr. and facs.
60. JUEL, Kurt, *Velt-shtime un velt-oyer* (Klal-Bibliotek, 46).
61. JUEL, Kurt, *Broyt un luft* (Klal-Bibliotek, 43).
62. KALMANOVITCH, Zelig Hirsh, *Di letste kanoim.* Aroysgenumen fun zibetn bukh fun Yosefus Flavius "Yiddishe milkhomes", 22 pp. (Historishe Yugnt Bibliotek).

63. KELLER, Gottfried, *Zibn maysies*. Fun daytsh (Klal-Bikher, 3).
64. KOTIK, Yehezkel, *Mayne zikhroynes*, 2 vols., I: 352 pp.; II: 272 pp.
65. KULBAK, Moshe, *Lider*, 56 pp. (Klal-Bibliotek, 17–18).
66. LATZKI-BERTOLDI, Wolf, *Gezeres denikin*, 64 pp. (Klal-Bibliotek, 37–38).
67. LESTSCHINSKY, Jacob, *Dos yidishe folk in tsifern in der gorer velt*, 396 pp.
68. LEWINSKY, Elhonon Leib, *In hundert fuftsik yor arum* (Klal-Bibliotek, 51–62).
69. LIDER – *Badkhonische*, 2 vols.
70. MARKISH, Perets, *Der galaganer hon*. Tseykhnungen fun Joseph Tchaikov, 30 pp.
71. MARKUS-SZALIT, Rachel, *Mentshelekh un stsenes*. 16 grafishe tseykhnungen tsu Sholem Aleykhems bukh Motl Peyse dem khazns. Baleytvort fun Baal-Makhshoves.
72. MAYSE-BUKH, 2 vols.
73. MAYSIES – *khasidische* (Klal-Bibliotek, 49–50).
74. MÉRIMÉE, Prosper, *Karmen un andere dertseylungen*. Iberz. fun R. Seligman, 124 pp. (Klal-Bikher, 1).
75. MONTAIGNE, M. de, *Umbashtendikeyt un toyt* (Klal-Bibliotek, 39–40).
76. NAHMAN BRATSLAVER, *Di rayze kayn erets-yisroel*.
77. NAHMAN BRATSLAVER, *Sipurey maysies*, (Klal-Bibliotek, 27–32).
78. NOMBERG, Hersh David, *Gezamelte verk*. Ertseylungen. 2 vols., I: 144 pp.; II: 144 pp.
79. NOMBERG, Hersh David, *In a poylisher yeshive*, 32 pp.
80. SATANOVER, M., *Mishley*.
81. SATANOVER, M., *Kohelet*.
82. SHNEUR, Zalman, *Sholem Aleykhems ondenken*, 60 pp. (Klal-Bibliotek, 23–24).
83. SHNEUR, Zalman, *Fun dem zeydns kval*. Mendele Moykher Sforims vertlekh, 64 pp. (Klal-Bibliotek, 21–22).
84. STEINBERG, Jacob, *Bashtanes*, 64 pp. (Klal-Bibliotek, 10).
85. STEINBERG, Jacob, *In a farvorfn vinkl*, 32 pp. (Klal-Bibliotek, 11).
86. WAGNER, W., *Maysies vegn erd*. Iberz. fun Z. Kalmanovitch, 64 pp. (Klal-Bibliotek, 13–14).
87. WAGNER, W., *Maysies vegn fayer un likhtikeyt*. Iberz. fun Z. Kalmanovitch (Klal-Bibliotek, 8–9).
88. WAGNER, W., *Maysies vegn luft*.
89. WISCHNITZER, Mark, *Yidishe baal-melokhe-tsekhn in poyln un lite*, 32 pp. (Klal-Bibliotek, 7).
90. YEIVIN, J. H., *Mantan*.
91. ZEND-AVESTA, *Di lere fun Zoroaster*. Ibergez. fun Judah Elzet (pseud. of Judah Leib Zlotnik).

M. KLEINMAN FARLAG, LEIPZIG
92. STENZEL, Abraham Nahum, *In oyfgeyn*. Tragedye.

MORIAH, BERLIN
93. AGODES [*Di Yidishe*]. Folkstimlekhe ertseylungen, zagn, legendn, mesholim, aforizmen un shprikhverter. Geklibn fun talmud un midroshim nokhn hebreishn "Sefer hoagode". Bearb. un grupirt fun J. H. Ravnitzky un H. N. Bialik, 4 vols., I: 180 pp.; II: 208 pp.; III: 156.; IV: 132 pp.
94. VITSN – *Yidishe*. Bearbet un gezamelt fun J. H., Ravnitzky, 264 pp.

SEKTSYE – YIDISHE – BAYM KOMISARIAT FAR FOLKSBILDUNG, BERLIN
95. KWITKO, Leib, *Ukrainische folksmaysies*. Fun ukrainishe FSSR. Ill. by L. Lissitzky.
86. KWITKO, Leib, *Vaysrusishe folksmaysies*. Fun vaysrusish RSFSR, 104 pp. Ill. by L. Lissitzky.

SHVELN, BERLIN
97. KIPLING, Rudyard, *Elefandl*, 16 pp.
98. KWITKO, Leib, *In vald*. Ill. by Issachar Ber Rybak.

WOSTOK, BERLIN
99. BERNSTEIN, Eduard, *Di daytshe revolutsye. Ir oyfkumen, ir gang un ir oyftu*. Mit a hakdome fun mekhaber tsu der daytsher oysgabe un hakdome fun Aleksander Stein, 348 pp.
Die deutsche Revolution appeared for the first time in 1921.
100. HATSKELES, Helene, *Di natur arum unz*. A lernbukh far folkshuln. Mit a nokhvort tsu di lerer, 118 pp. with ill.
101. HAUPTMANN, Gerhard, *Der koyfer fun soana*. Iberz. fun Eliah Olshvanger, 146 pp.
Der Ketzer von Soana was published for the first time in 1918.

102. MARX, Karl and Friedrich Engels. *Briv.*
103. ONHEYB [DER]. *Zamlbukh far literatur un visnshaft.* Redaktirt fun David Einhorn, Shemarya Gorelik un Max Weinreich, 188 pp.
104. TAGORE, Rabindranath, *Dertseylungen.* Iberz. fun S. Gorelik.
105. BERGELSON, David, *Gezamelte verk,* 6 vols.

WITHOUT NAME OF PUBLISHER
106. EINHORN, David, *Rekviem,* 16 pp.

1923
FARLAG – YIDISHER KULTUR –
107. BIRNBAUM, Nathan, *Gots folk.*
108. DOSTOJEVSKI, F. M., *Di brider Karamasov.* A roman in fir teyln mit an epilog. Ibergez. fun Moshe Luria, 288 pp.
109. GORDON, A. D., *Briv fun erets-yisroel.*
110. TOLLER, Ernst, *Der iberker. Der gerangel fun a mentshn.* Ibergez. fun daytsh mitn heskem fun mekhaber fun Sarah Brenner, 68 pp.
111. TRITSH, D., *Bilder fun erets-yisroel.*
112. YAFE, Leib, *Arbeterzidlungen in erets-yisroel.*

FARLAG – YIDISHER LITERARISHER
113. ALPHERSON, Mordecai, *Draysik yor in Argentine (Memuarn fun a yidishn kolonist).* Mit a hakdome fun H. D. Nomberg.
114. DUBNOW, S., *Algemeyne yidishe geshikhte fun di alte tsaytn biz der hayntiker tsayt.* Ibergez. fun N. Shtif, Z. Kalmanovitch un M. Weinreich, 10 vols.
115. KOIGEN, David, *In shturm fun geshikhte.* Aroysgezukhte bletlekh fun togbukh 1914–1921. Autorisirte iberzetsung fun daytsh fun Z. Kalmanovitch, 248 pp.
116. KWITKO, Leib, *Folkslider fun der pogromtsayt.*
117. MENES, Abraham, *Di sotsiale un virtshaftlekhe farheltenishn bay di yidn in altertum.*
118. NISTER, DER (pseud. of Pinchas Kaganovitch), *Gedakht,* 2 vols., I: 254 pp.; II: 288 pp.
119. OPATOSHU, Joseph, *Farloyrene mentshn.* A roman funem yidishn lebn in amerike, 288 pp.
120. SHNEURSON, Fishl (Joshua), *Di katastrofale tsaytn un di vaksndike doyres,* 244 pp.
121. TCHERIKOWER, Eliah, *Antisemitizm un pogromen in Ukraine, 1917–1918.* Mit a hakdome fun S. Dubnow, I: 332 pp. Part II was edited by Joseph Shechtman and published by the Mizroh-yidisher historischer arkhiv, Berlin 1932.
122. TURGENEW, A., *Di ksovim fun a yeger.* Dertseylungen ibergez. fun B. Slutski.

FUNKEN, BERLIN
123. HOFSTEIN, David, *In tovl fun vent.* Zamlung lider, 64 pp.
124. PINSKI, David, *Naye ertseylungen,* Band I, 216 pp.

KLAL-FARLAG, BERLIN
125. HAMSUN, Knut, *Di brokhe fun der erd.* Ibergez. fun S. Shnayder.
126. HAUSER, O., *Urmentsh un vilder.* Iberz. fun Z. Kalmanovitch, 161 pp.
127. HIRSHKAN, Zvi, *Tsvey veltn,* 155 pp., 3rd edn.
128. LAO-TSE, *Dos bukh funem getlekhn gezets.* Iberz. fun R. Seligman.

PARDES, BERLIN
129. FRANK, H., *Grikhishe khakhomim.* Geshikhtlikhe shilderungen.

RIMON, BERLIN
130. GASTER, Moshe, *Di ksube in ir geshikhtlikher antviklung.* Ibergez. fun english durkh R. Seligman, 54 pp., with ill. *Rimon* also published a Hebrew and a German edition in 1923.
131. KLATZKIN, Jacob, *Herman Kohen.*
132. KULISHER, Alexander, *Lord Bikonsfild, fun 1804 biz 1832.* Ibergez. fun ksav-yad durkh R. Seligman, with portr. and ill. *Rimon* also published a Hebrew edition in 1923.
133. LANDSBERGER, F., *Impresionizm un ekspresionizm.* Ibergez. durkh R. Seligman. Mit 21 bilder, 64 pp.

134. NAHMAN BRATSLAVER, *Sipure maysies*. Fun tekst bearbet durkh Moshe Kleinman.
135. SELIGMAN, Raphael, *Araynfir in der kabole*.
SHVELN, BERLIN
136. KWITKO, Leib, *Foyglen*. Ill. by Issochor Ber Rybak.
137. NISTER, DER (pseud. of Pinchas Kaganovitch), *Mayselekh in ferzn*, 60 pp.
138. RYBAK, Issochor Ber, *Mayn khoreve heym. A gedekhenish*, 31 litografyes.
WOSTOK, BERLIN
139. ABRAMOVITCH, Raphael L. and Abraham Menes, *Dos leyenbukh tsu der geshikhte fun yisroel*, I, 120 pp. with ill.
140. MARTOV, Julius (pseud. of Iulii Osipovich Tsederbaum), *Zikhroynes fun a sotsial-demokrat*, I. Ibergezetst fun rusish, 185 pp. The Russian work also appeared in 1923.
141. WEINREICH, Max, *Mekhiras yosef*. Dos iz aroysgenumen fun sefer "Tam vejoshor" un fun andere sforim, vos in zey shteyn geshribn vunderlikhe maysim.
142. WEINREICH, Max, *Shtaplen*. Fir etiudn tsu der yidisher shprakhwisnshaft un literaturge-shikhte, ii, 260 pp., with ill.
YALKUT, BERLIN
143. SHNEUR, Zalman, *Ahin. Shriftn fun a selbstmerder*, 192 pp.
WITHOUT NAME OF PUBLISHER, BERLIN
144. BERGELSON, David, *Mayse-bikhl*. With ill. by Lasar Segall.

1923–1924
FARLAG – YIDISHER LITERARISHER, BERLIN
145. BRENER, Yosef Hayim, *Arum a pintele*. Ibergez. [fun hebr.] B. Slutski, 204 pp.
146. FAYGENBERG, Rahel, *Untern hamer* (Ukraine – Odeser gegent 1918–1920).
147. HANOVER, Nathan Note, *Yeven metsulo*. Ibergez. fun Wolf Latzki-Bertoldi.
148. KELLERMANN, Bernhard, *Dos gesheenish*. Iberz. [fun daytsh].
149. MAYSE *Gedoyle min uman veukraine*. Bashreybung fun Gontes tsaytn. Mit a hakdome un derklerungen fun S. Dubnow.
150. ZAMLBIKHER, I: *In der tkufe fun der revolutsye*; II: *Pinkes ukrayne*.

1924
FARLAG – YIDISHER LITERARISHER, BERLIN
151. MUKDONI, A. (pseud. of Alexander Kapel), *Der sibirer gehinem*. Zikhroynes un iberlebenishn.
152. REVUTSKI, Abraham, *In di shvere teg oyf ukraine*. Zikhroynes fun a yidishn minister, 318 pp.
KLAL-FARLAG, BERLIN
153. BRIL, Hirsh, *Oyf der shvel*. Dramatishe verk, 100 pp.
MENES FARLAG, LEIPZIG
154. STENZEL, Abraham Nahum, *Lider un gedikhtn*, 8 pp.
  Published in a series of works by young writers and artists.
J. STYBEL, BERLIN
155. BERDITSHEVSKI, Micha Joseph, *Yidishe ksovim fun a vaytn korev*.
WOSTOK, BERLIN
156. HATSKELES, Helene, *Di erd un di velt*, I, 133 pp., with ill.
157. KULBAK, Moshe, *Moshiah ben efrayim*, 132 pp.
YIVO, ECONOMIC-STATISTICAL DEPARTMENT, BERLIN
158. BRUTZKUS, Boris Ber, *Yidishe demografye, statistik un ekonomye*. Tsuzamen mit Jacob Lest-schinsky un Jacob Segal, 4 vols.

1925
FARLAG "DOS FRAYE VORT", BERLIN
159. ROSIN, A. (pseud. Ben-Adir), *In khaos fun lebn un denken*, 190 pp.
RENAISSANCE, BERLIN
160. GUTMAN, Rosa, *Far gor dem noentn*. Lider, 24 pp.

SHEMESH FARLAG, LEIPZIG
161. STENZEL, Abraham Nahum, *Un du bist got*, 92 pp.
WITHOUT NAME OF PUBLISHER
162. EINHORN, David, *Gesamelte lider*.
163. LESTSCHINSKY, Jacob, *Der emes vegn di yidn in rusland*, 64 pp.

1926
ORT, BERLIN
164. BRUTZKUS, Boris Ber, *Di yidishe landvirtshaft in mizrokh-eyrope, ir geshikhtlikhher oyfkum un untergang zint der velt-milkhome*, 116 pp.
EMIGDIREKT, BERLIN
165. LATZKI-BERTOLDI, Wolf, *Di aynvanderung in di yidishe yishuvim in dorem-amerike*, 48 pp.

1927
EMIGDIREKT – HIAS, BERLIN
166. LESTSCHINSKY, Jacob, *Di yidishe vanderungen far di letste 25 yor*, 88 pp.
G. KAHAN, DANZIG
167. KIRSHBAUM, Jacob, *Geshikhte fun di yidn in Dantsig, 1310–1920*, 89 pp.
OSE, BERLIN
This international Jewish welfare organisation published several pamphlets with information on matters of illness and health, especially meant as guidance for emigration to the Americas. We have only been able to trace publications between 1922 and 1927, several of which cannot be given an exact date. The series of pamphlets is called *Folksbibliotek*: the organisation was financed, for the greater part, by the American Jewish Joint Distribution Committee.
168. MELEKH, *Kop-tsoraas* (parkh). Stsenes fun lebn.
169. NEUSTAEDTER, A., *Di trakhome*. Iberarb. in yidish fun D. A. Fridman.
170. OLSHVANGER, Eliah, *Tuberkulos*. Mit a forvort fun profesor Michaelis.
171. OLSHVANGER, Eliah, *Venerishe krankheytn*. Mit bilder.
172. POLIANSKI, A., *A bikhl far yidishe mames*. Mit 15 bilder, 2nd edn.
173. RESE, K., *Gesunte tseyn*. Autorisirte iberzetsung A. Olgravida (?).
174. ROSENTHAL, L., *Ale yedies vos der emigrant darf visn un a bazunder kapitl vegn farhitn dos gezunt*, 220 pp.
175. ROSENTHAL, L., *Klepige krankeytn*.
176. TUGENDREICH, Gustaf, *Dertsiung funem kleynkind*. Autorisirte ibersetsung fun A. Olgravida (?), 54 pp.

1928
EMIGDIREKT, BERLIN
177. LESTSCHINSKY, Jacob, *Di antviklung fun idishn folk far di letste 100 yor*, 325 pp.

1929
EMIGDIREKT, BERLIN
178. LESTSCHINSKY, Jacob, *Di onheybn fun der emigratsye un kolonizatsye bay yidn in 19th yorhundert*, 72 pp.
KAUFMANN, FRANKFURT a. MAIN
179. PAPPENHEIM, Bertha, *Alerley geshikhtn*. Mayse-bukh.

1931–1936
WITHOUT NAME OF PUBLISHER
180. LESTSCHINSKY, Jacob, *Di yidn in poyln*, 152 pp. (1931).
181. STENZEL, Abraham Nahum, *In dorser vald baym yam*, 28 pp. (1933).
182. STENZEL, Abraham Nahum, *Tate-sonetn* (1934).
183. STENZEL, Abraham Nahum, *Mayn fishersdorf*, 31 pp. (1935).

184. STENZEL, Abraham Nahum, *Fundervaytns*, 78 pp. (1935).
185. STENZEL, Abraham Nahum, *Fun der heym*, 78 pp. (1936).
186. STENZEL, Abraham Nahum, *Tsvishn himl un erd*, 80 pp. (1936).
187. STENZEL, Abraham Nahum, *Mendele Moykher Sforim*, 10 pp. (1936).

PERIODICALS

The periodicals presented even more difficulties than the books. Sometimes only single issues are known and it is not possible to determine the date the periodicals were published and the number of issues. There must have been many more periodicals than could be listed here.

1921 BERLIN

188. BAVEGUNG [*Unzer*]. Organ fun di yidishe sotsial demokratishe arbeter organizatsyes in daytshland. Editor: Karl Greger. Published every two weeks. Existed until 1924.
189. MIZRAKH-YUD [*Der*]. Yudishes vokhnblat. Tsentralorgan fun farband fun di mizrakh-yudn in daytshland. Editor: Joseph Lin. Published every week.

1922 BERLIN

190. BIULETIN. [Published by] Tsentral-farvaltung fun farband ORT.
191. ERDARBET. Aroysgegebn fun der tsentral-farvaltung fun farband ORT. Editor: A. Singalowsky. Published every month.
192. FOLKS-GEZUNT. Aroysgegebn fun OSE. Published every month, existed until 1924, or probably longer.
193. KAMF [*Der*]. Monatshrift farn poale-tsionistishn gedank. Editor: Abraham Revutski.
194. TRIBUNE [*Di*]. Social, political and literary monthly, edited by M. Grosman.
195. VEG [*Der*]. Zhurnal far fragn fun yidisher emigratsye un kolonizatsye, aroysgegebn funem yidishn arbeter emigratsye farband.

1923 BERLIN

196. ALBATROS. Zeitschrift für neue Dichtung und Graphik. Schriftleiter Uri Zvi Greenberg. Nrs. 3–4. The first two issues of this important *avant-garde* journal appeared in Warsaw 1922.
197. BLETER *far yidishe demografye, statistik un khronik*. Edited by B. Brutzkus, J. Lestschinsky and J. Segal. Five issues were published, the edition stopped in 1924.
198. VORT [*Dos fraye*]. Organ fun umophengikn sotsialistishn gedank. Editor: Ben-Adir (Pseud. of Abraham Rosin). Published every two weeks.

1924 BERLIN

199. HEYMISH. Klal-Bleter far unterhalt un visn.

1925 LEIPZIG

200. LEBN [*Undzer*].
201. SHABES-OYBS. Zhurnal far literatur un humor.

1926 BERLIN

202. IN SHPAN. Edited by David Bergelson and D. Czarny.

1928–1929 BERLIN

203. VIRTSHAFT *un lebn*. Published by ORT, appeared every two months.

WITHOUT DATE, BERLIN

204. ARKHIV *funem yidishn sotsialist*.

Jewish Thought

Max Brod's Zionist Writings

BY MARK H. GELBER

I

Max Brod (1884–1968), whose centenary in 1984 was marked by ceremonies and lectures in Israel, is chiefly remembered as the devoted friend of Franz Kafka, who saved Kafka's unpublished manuscripts from his well-known imperious destructive impulse, edited the posthumous writings, and wrote the first Kafka biography, thereby establishing the original standards for Kafka scholarship. Nonetheless, Brod's Zionist interpretation of Kafka has been sharply criticised over the years, although in response, this interpretation has also found several staunch defenders, especially among those who knew Kafka or Brod well, for example, Schalom Ben-Chorin. During his lifetime, Brod was celebrated as a major European *homme de lettres*, far more influential and popular than Kafka while the latter lived, and for some time after as well. Whereas Brod's ambitious philosophical-religious treatises, like *Heidentum, Christentum, Judentum* (1921) or *Diesseits und Jenseits* (1947–1948) are largely forgotten, some of his major novels, such as *Tycho Brahes Weg zu Gott* (1915), *Rëubeni, Fürst der Juden* (1925) and *Stefan Rott oder das Jahr der Entscheidung* (1931), are either currently in print, or at any rate available; they continue to reach a diverse readership. Still, Brod has never generated the range or kind of intellectual-critical and scholarly interest accorded writers of the highest rank. Furthermore, despite the limited but respectable scholarly consideration of his life and works, virtually no critical attention has been devoted to his extensive Zionist writings or to his stature as a Zionist thinker. This essay, then, serves to fill this particular literary-historical gap, while illuminating a significant range of cultural tensions, which found expression in Central European Zionism before and after the Holocaust, in Europe and in Israel.

II

Although mentioning Thomas Mann in the context of Max Brod's Zionist writings may seem odd initially, consideration of Mann's largely unknown role in the story, or rather pre-story, of Brod's departure from Czechoslovakia in 1939 provides a novel framework for an analysis of Brod's Zionist works and for a tentative evaluation of his career as a Zionist. In the third section of his memoirs, *Streitbares Leben* (1960) – that is, some twenty years after the events transpired – Brod recounted the developments leading to his precipitous flight from Prague

437

on the eve of the impending Nazi aggression and his arrival in Palestine, marking
the beginning of his new life in the *yishuv*. He made no mention of Mann in this
part of the book. Brod recalled that after the Munich Pact in 1938, he and some
friends made up their minds to emigrate to Palestine, even though they thought
that this time Hitler had been satisfied by the political concessions granted him.
Brod explained that first, this step had always been integral to his life-plan, and
only the precise timing had been left undetermined throughout the years.
Second, the intolerable, new "spiritual climate" in the sham Second Czechoslo-
vakian Republic served as a catalyst. In December 1938, his associate Ludwig
Winder pleaded with cogency the urgency of leaving. By mid-March 1939, Brod
was on his way East, at the same time, as is well-known, Nazi troops were
moving into the rest of the country, sealing the exit routes. In *Streitbares Leben*,
Brod called the land of Israel "the object of our desire and our firm decision for
many years".[1] Despite having been forewarned about the difficult living
conditions in Palestine, especially following the Arab disturbances in 1938, and
the bleak prospects of employment for European intellectuals of his particular
type, Brod claimed that he never regretted his decision, and that never was a
more correct decision made. He reported, in fact, that at this time he declined the
security of an offer to become a professor at an American university – "Wer wagt,
gewinnt",[2] – and he prepared to adjust to the challenging and new social,
economic, and political exigencies in his promised land.

Brod's reference to an offer from an American university in this context forges
the link to Mann. Earlier in *Streitbares Leben*, in the second section of the book,
Brod discussed Mann under the heading: 'Gäste in Prag: Max Reger *et al*'. He
related that in the wake of Hitlerism and the imminent personal threat of
hardship and death, Mann, without Brod approaching him, intervened on his
behalf and arranged a professorship for him at an "American college". Nevertheless, Brod preferred to follow "dem Genius [s]eines Lebens",[3] and emigrate to
Palestine. So we read in Brod's memoirs.

As a matter of fact, though, the true sequence of events and Mann's role in this
story are quite different from the account related in *Streitbares Leben*. There had
been only very limited literary or personal contact between Brod and Mann
before 1938. On occasion Brod had written about Mann or reviewed his books
(e.g. *Der Zauberberg*) in the *Prager Tagblatt*,[4] and he participated in a concerted
international effort to congratulate Mann publicly on the occasion of his fiftieth
birthday in 1925.[5] Typically, Brod valued Mann in terms of Kafka's own
enthusiasm for him. In later years, Brod wrote of his sincere appreciation of
Mann's early appraisal of Kafka's importance for twentieth-century literature.
Also, Brod praised the *Joseph* novels, which he read as a strong defence of Jewry
during the difficult years of the 1930s and 1940s. Mann, for his part, promoted

[1]Max Brod, *Streitbares Leben*, Munich 1960, p. 271.
[2]*Ibid.*, p. 279.
[3]*Ibid.*, pp. 240–241.
[4]See *Prager Tagblatt*, 19th September 1926; 24th August 1930.
[5]See *Berliner Tageblatt*, 6th July 1925.

some of Brod's writings, notably his novel *Stefan Rott*.[6] Yet, when Brod turned to
Mann for help on the 30th November 1938 – which was in fact the true sequence
– he felt compelled to refer to Klaus Mann and Robert Klopstock, who
encouraged him in this move, which Thomas Mann could not have anticipated.
In his letter, Brod made it quite clear that his intention was to come to the
U.S.A.: "Ich bin entschlossen, nach Amerika auszuwandern, so lange es noch
Zeit ist."[7] Furthermore, in order to secure a visa and in lieu of a position, Brod
was willing to place at the disposal of a willing American institution the
manuscripts and books of Franz Kafka, which were in his possession.

The record of Thomas Mann's correspondence from this period provides the
opportunity for documenting what actually took place in Brod's life at this
precarious time, and demonstrates clearly Mann's selfless dedication to fellow
Central European writers endangered by Nazism.[8] On 30th December 1938,
Mann wrote a detailed letter recommending Brod to Alvin Johnson, director of
the New School for Social Research in New York and one of the primary
proponents of its university-in-exile, a graduate faculty of political and social
sciences, which was originally conceived as a refuge and academic repository for
scholars driven from Axis-dominated Europe. The wording of Mann's letter
clearly indicated that Brod himself was actively seeking employment at an
American university. On 10th January 1939, Mann wrote to Monroe Deutsch,
the vice-president of the University of California at Berkeley and a member of the
American Emergency Committee in Aid of Displaced Foreign Scholars, reporting that Brod had just written to him about the parlous situation in Czechoslovakia since the partial occupation of the country, and that Brod felt his life
endangered. In recommending Brod for a position at an American university,
Mann relayed to Deutsch Brod's attractive offer of the Kafka material in
connection with potential placing and terms of employment. Mann soon enlisted
the help of Hendrik Willem van Loon (1882–1944), the Dutch-American
historian and writer, who was also active in the placement of exiled European
scholars, and he subsequently initiated efforts on behalf of Brod, independently
of Mann. On 20th February 1939, Mann wrote to William Bragg of the Royal
Institute in London on Brod's behalf, again mentioning the offer of the Kafka
materials in connection with a possible position for Brod as research librarian or
curator of the collection. Mann also wrote a long letter on 27th February 1939 to
H. M. Lydenberg, the director of the New York Public Library, making a similar
offer.

None of Mann's substantial efforts had yielded positive results, when in early

[6]See letter, Brod to Mann, dated 21st April 1922 (original in Thomas Mann Archive, Zürich).
[7]The complete text of this letter may be found in Peter F. Neumeyer, 'Thomas Mann, Max Brod, and
the New York Public Library', *Modern Language Notes*, vol. 90, No. 3 (1975), p. 420.
[8]Useful synopses of all letters cited below may be found in Hans Bürgin and Hans Otto Mayer (eds.),
Die Briefe Thomas Manns, Regesten und Register, vol. II, Frankfurt a. Main 1980. See also Thomas
Mann, *Tagebücher 1937–39* (ed. Peter de Mendelssohn), Frankfurt a. Main 1980, pp. 339, 373, and
passim. This aspect of Mann's career sheds light on the complicated issue of his relationship to
Zionism, on the one hand, and literary antisemitism in his own work, on the other. See Mark H.
Gelber, 'Thomas Mann and Anti-Semitism', *Patterns of Prejudice*, vol. 17, No. 4 (1983), pp. 31–40;
and *idem*, 'Thomas Mann and Zionism', *German Life and Letters*, vol. 37, No. 1 (1984), pp. 62–68.

March 1939, he received word that Robert P. Goldmann, the President of the Union of American Hebrew Congregations and a member of the Board of Governors of Hebrew Union College in Cincinnati, was to take up the issue of Brod with the staff the following week. In a letter to Goldmann dated 7th March 1939, Mann again recommended Brod strongly, now making tactful reference to his philosophical and religious writings. At the same time, he suggested a personal meeting to discuss the case with Goldmann and Julian Morgenstern, the President of Hebrew Union College, during the following week, when Mann was to be in Cincinnati in conjunction with a lecture tour of the American Mid-West. Mann's letters to Goldmann and Lydenberg in April 1939 indicate that Hebrew Union was prepared to offer Brod a position and that Julian Morgenstern was in touch with Brod, who by this time had already arrived in Palestine. In a letter to Lydenberg dated 17th April 1939 Mann revealed that Brod was trying to come to the United States from Tel-Aviv! It is evident from this letter and others, that the offer from Hebrew Union did not reach Brod in Prague in time. On 4th July 1939, that is, some two months later, Mann wrote again to Morgenstern. This time, Brod had sent him an urgent telegram, announcing his intention of leaving Palestine and seeking immediate clarification concerning the job-offer in Cincinnati. Mann asked Morgenstern to wire Brod and inform him whether or not the position was indeed still open.[9]

This entire episode helps clarify the true sequence of events preceding and following Brod's departure from Czechoslovakia. The striking discrepancy between Brod's literary account and the alternate scenario, which emerges from consideration of Mann's correspondence, has little to do with the faulty memory of the elderly Max Brod or with the issue of recurring, problematical memory structures, characteristic of the genre of literary autobiography. Rather was it the case that Brod wished to present a particular, well-defined image of himself as a committed Zionist in his memoirs, and the related activity of Mann in this context (which Brod had initiated) simply did not conform to the contours of that image. Thus, this aspect could not be integrated easily into *Streitbares Leben*, his ultimate statement of his sense of self.

III

In addition to setting the record straight, this episode provides a contrasting background to an entire series of polemical Zionist writings, which Brod had produced through the years, dating back to his conversion to Zionism, shortly before the First World War. The problematical issue of the possible incongruence between Zionist theory and practice in the history of Zionism or in the personal histories of individual Zionists is thus raised even in this case. Also, this new evidence sheds a certain light on Brod's concept of "humane-universal,

---

[9] I have not been able to locate the original of Brod's telegram, the contents of which are paraphrased in Mann's letter of 4th July 1939. See *Die Briefe Thomas Manns, op. cit.*, p. 323.

humanistically orientated Zionism'', a term he applied to Kafka's Zionism in his late work, *Der Prager Kreis* (1966).[10] Likewise, it is related to the prominence and stature of S. Hugo Bergman (1883–1975) in Brod's memoirs. Bergman, in a way, rivals Kafka as the true hero of *Streitbares Leben*. Not only did he influence Brod decisively on his path to Zionism, but he emigrated to Palestine from Prague in 1920, i.e. well before the cataclysmic events of the 1930s in Central Europe. He contributed early on his prodigious energies and talents in guiding the development of fundamental Zionist institutions in Jerusalem. He served as the first director of the Jewish National Library (1920–1935) and as rector of the Hebrew University (1935–1939), in addition to continuing his own important philosophical work, for example, on Kant and Maimon, in Hebrew.[11] He rejected unequivocally Brod's well-known concept of "Distanzliebe". To put it crudely, Bergman emphasised the irrecoverable "distance" of the Jews from German nationality, whereas Brod emphasised the "love," the total Jewish infatuation with German culture.[12] A valuated, hierarchical dichotomy has been proposed by Gershom Scholem and others between those Central European Zionists who emigrated to Palestine well before the advent of Nazism and those who, although long committed publicly to the Zionist cause, were unable to make the decisive move to Palestine before they were "forced to do so at the last minute".[13] Although this kind of Zionist typology is problematical in its own right, Brod was certainly cognisant of the distinction. Furthermore, this division pertains to the differentiation between the cultural-spiritual orientation to Zionism, on the one hand, and the political Zionist movement on the other. Brod's relationship to these two related spheres, exhibited in his life and writings, was complicated and requires elucidation.

Steps or stages related to the process of Brod's gravitation to Zionism included his response to Leo Hermann's critical review of his early novel, *Ein tschechisches Dienstmädchen* (1909); his gradually developing relationship with Bergman and loose affiliation with the *Bar Kochba* Zionist group; the impact of Martin Buber's famous lectures in Prague, beginning in 1909; the visit of the Yiddish theatre group (1910) and the performances in the Café Savoy; the impressive appearance of the dynamic Zionist ideologue and intellectual, Nathan Birnbaum;* the encounter with East European refugees and teaching at the *Notschule für jüdische Flüchtlinge aus dem Osten* during the First World War. This biographical material

---

[10]Max Brod, *Der Prager Kreis*, Frankfurt a. Main 1979, p. 117.

[11]See B. Shohetman and S. Shumai (eds.), *Writings of Shmuel Hugo Bergman: A Bibliography (1903–1967)*, (Bergman Archive [arc. 1502], 1968). I would like to thank Margot Cohen for her assistance during the period I researched this essay in the Bergman archive and related archives in the Jewish National and University Library, Jerusalem (JNUL).

[12]See letter, Bergman to Brod, 24th July 1935. This letter and other correspondence between Brod and Bergman may be found in the Bergman archive, JNUL.

[13]Gershom Scholem, 'Martin Bubers Auffassung des Judentums', in his *Judaica II*, Frankfurt a. Main 1970, p. 136.

*On Nathan Birnbaum see the essay by Robert S. Wistrich, 'The Clash of Ideologies in Jewish Vienna (1880–1918). The Strange Odyssey of Nathan Birnbaum', in this volume of the Year Book – (Ed.).

is well-known or easily accessible, and there is no need to rehearse it here.[14] Brod's Zionist outlook crystallised as an amalgam of attitudes derived from his eclectic reading, his personal encounters, and individual experiences, tempered by his family background, his personality, and intellectual outlook. In a series of essays and books over the years Brod cultivated an individualised Zionist rhetoric, while delineating his particular Zionist vision. This vision, in turn, informed his political and private relationships and found, concomitantly, a secure niche in his fictive world.

The general outline of Brod's Zionist view can be distilled from his writings on the subject from the First World War through the mid-1920s, including: 'Die dritte Phase des Zionismus' (1917); the several essays published in Buber's *Der Jude* and in *Selbstwehr*, the Prague Zionist organ (edited after 1918 by Felix Weltsch [1884–1964], Brod's close friend and collaborator); the collected essays in *Im Kampf um das Judentum* (1920); *Sozialismus im Zionismus* (1920); and *Zionismus als Weltanschauung* (1925); this last volume compiled together with Weltsch. For Brod, Zionism, as a particular form of Jewish Nationalism, was the chief means of preserving Jewry, by allowing and aiding the Jewish people to determine their own fate in world history. Jewish Nationalism differed from other nationalisms in that it strove actively to redefine the concept and reality of nationhood itself. It endeavoured to give the term new meaning. In effect, Jewish Nationalism was ultimately international, or supranational, and universal in its orientation. For Brod, Zionism, in its true form was pan-humanist. Furthermore, Judaism, as a living source of social justice, determined Zionism's Socialist character. Judaism tended towards the realisation of spirit and spirituality on earth, and Zionism facilitated the process by providing the working laboratory, the political and human possibility for attaining that goal. Brod repeatedly circumscribed the theoretical extent of his Jewish Nationalist-Zionist enthusiasm and commitment by projecting a rather contrived hypothetical collision between "humanistic" and Jewish interests. He invariably pledged his ultimate allegiance to humanity, over and above Jewry. In this way he marked the boundary of his nationalistic leanings.

Two particular problematical aspects which figure in these writings deserve special attention here. The first is a token, but by no means disingenuous, call for the creation of Hebrew culture within Zionism, for example, in 1918 in his essay 'Zionismus'.[15] Simultaneously, however, he affirmed the validity and value of Yiddish and Yiddish culture. He referred to Hebrew and Yiddish simply as "the languages of our people" – the formulation itself is of interest.[16] The second aspect is Brod's singular treatment of the Arab issue in his Zionist writings. The

---

[14]See Brod, 'Judentum als Problem', *Streitbares Leben, op. cit.*, pp. 42f. and pp. 208f; Brod, 'Erfahrungen im ostjüdischen Schulwerk,' in *Der Jude* (1916–1917), pp. 32–36. Cf. Margarita Pazi, *Max Brod*, Bonn 1970, pp. 19–22; and Robert Weltsch, 'Max Brod and his Age', *Leo Baeck Memorial Lecture*, 13, New York, Leo Baeck Institute, 1970. For related insights into Brod's career see Sol Liptzin, *Germany's Stepchildren*, Philadelphia 1944, pp. 270–273; and Lothar Kahn, *Mirrors of the Jewish Mind*, New York – South Brunswick – London 1968, pp. 68–82.

[15]'Zionismus', in *Im Kampf um das Judentum*, Vienna 1920, p. 39 and *passim*.

[16]'Die Krähwinkelei im Zionismus', *ibid.*, p. 123.

existence of an abundant indigenous Arab population in Palestine was, he claimed, a blessing in disguise that posed a challenge, which would determine whether or not the Jewish people had indeed realised a new concept of Nationalism, a Nationalist humanism. The peaceful coexistence of these two nations, that is, the resolution of the "Arab Question", as he called it, would constitute a significant cultural achievement and mark tangible progress for the Jewish mission in the world.

These two aspects, in reality acid tests of Brod's Zionism, are related to his intellectual encounters with Ahad Ha'am and Martin Buber. An imposing figure in the early Zionist panorama, Ahad Ha'am was the major proponent of spiritual-cultural Zionism and an outspoken opponent of Theodor Herzl. Brod's critical appraisal of Ahad Ha'am found expression in the essay 'Die dritte Phase des Zionismus', first published in the respected German journal, *Die Zukunft*. Brod approved of the greater part of Ahad Ha'am's spiritual-cultural ideology, although he levelled certain criticism of his method and person, without ever denigrating Herzl, in fact, while at the same time recognising and lauding Herzl's greater, universalistic achievement. This combination is virtually unique to Brod, and it underscores his consistent tendency to independence, synthesis, mediation, and the accommodation of opposites, as well as a certain degree of political consciousness or acumen. He appreciated Ahad Ha'am's championship of Hebrew culture and the Jewish spirit, but believed that their realisation required a firm political basis – the "Unterbau des Geistigen", as he called it in this essay.[17] He rejected out of hand the elitist tendency in Ahad Ha'am, his underlying Nietzscheanism, favouring the broader social conception of Herzl, who saw Zionism as a true mass movement encompassing all of Jewry.

Brod's sponsorship of Hebrew culture within Zionism was problematical on a personal level in two distinct ways. First, as a writer inextricably bound to the world of German letters, "der jüdische Dichter deutscher Zunge", as he formulated his predicament in 1913,[18] his career as a Zionist was tangibly hampered and he was unduly bothered by his inability to achieve total mastery of Hebrew. He did eventually lecture in Hebrew, and he translated Hebrew poetry (e.g. Rachel, Lea Goldberg, Shin Shalom) into German, but he never really succeeded in writing or reading Hebrew fluently, even later in his career. Brod naturally tended to affirm Buber's clarion call for a modern Jewish cultural renaissance under the aegis of Zionism, but in German – a point of implicit contention between Buber and Ahad Ha'am.[19] The latter rejected resolutely the very possibility of Jewish literature or culture in any language but Hebrew. Secondly, Brod's unwillingness to dismiss Yiddish, as Ahad Ha'am proposed, or to deny its status as a Jewish national language, was certainly rooted in a positive valuation of East European Jewish life, which exerted a strong romantic pull on

[17]'Die dritte Phase des Zionismus', offprint from *Die Zukunft*, 20th January 1917, p. 11.
[18]'Der jüdische Dichter deutscher Zunge', in Hans Kohn (ed.), *Vom Judentum*, Leipzig 1913, pp. 261f.
[19]See Jehuda Reinharz, 'Achad Ha-am und der deutsche Zionismus', in *Bulletin des Leo Baeck Instituts*, Nr. 61 (1982), pp. 3–27. Cf. Mark H. Gelber, 'The jungjüdische Bewegung. An Unexplored Chapter in German-Jewish Literary and Cultural History', in *LBI Year Book XXXI* (1986), pp. 105–119.

Brod and other acculturated or assimilating West and Central European Jewish intellectuals finding their way to new Jewish identities at this time. Unlike other spiritual-cultural Zionists, such as Ahad Ha'am or Martin Buber, who viewed the ghetto existence of East European Jewry as one of the prime causes of Jewish backwardness and cultural degeneracy – the remedy for which was prescribed by their versions of spiritual-cultural expression – Brod was nourished by an idealised view of *shtetl* Jewry, probably because of his own uplifting experience during the war. By demonstrating enthusiasm for East European authenticity and tenacity, or faithfulness to tradition, Brod commensurately weakened the forcefulness and cogency of his Zionist argument.

Brod's initial, utopian understanding of the Arab issue underwent certain changes as the years went by, especially following his first visit to Palestine in 1927, and again following his immigration and his experience of the Arab-Jewish conflict preceding and following the War of Independence. At first, Brod was a vocal supporter of the Left-wing *Hapoel Haza'ir* party, the Palestine Zionist Labour Party, and he was an admirer of the charismatic, intellectual labour leader Chajim Arlosoroff (1899–1933), whose assassination in 1933 on the beach in Tel-Aviv is still a subject of controversy in Israeli political life. As late as the mid-1940s Brod continued to write favourably of Arlosoroff's proposed "Arab-Jewish cultural society".[20] Yet, Brod's correspondence from the 1930s reveals clearly that he had serious misgivings about the bi-national proposal for Palestine, propagated, for example, by Bergman and his *Brith Shalom* group. At a time when he was still resident in Prague, Brod was willing in theory to accept this idea on the condition that some Arab minority group would endorse it publicly first – this according to his letter to Bergman dated 23rd October 1930.[21] Brod persisted, somewhat incredibly, in his view that Arabs in Palestine should sympathise with the difficult Jewish plight in the Diaspora and thus actively assist the Zionist enterprise for that reason, a moral one, in addition to other more expedient economic or social motives.

IV

The incorporation of Zionist material and perspectives in Brod's fiction is a recurrent literary feature deserving a separate analysis. It is instructive to contrast the particular literary functions of the Zionist elements in two early novels, written at the time of his conversion to Zionism, *Jüdinnen* (1911) and *Arnold Beer, Schicksal eines Juden* (1912) with two later novels, in which a significant amount of the narrative designates Palestine/Israel as its setting: *Zauberreich der Liebe* (1928) and *Unambo* (1949). In contradistinction to the first two works, the latter two may certainly be labelled Zionist novels.

In *Jüdinnen*, the issue of Zionism comes to the fore only a few times. Mostly, Zionism is rejected in the direct discourse of unsympathetic or pitiable figures.

[20]'Ibn Roschid=Averroes', *Mitteilungsblatt (MB)*, Tel-Aviv, 28th January 1944, pp. 6–7.
[21]Original in Bergman archive, JNUL.

Irene, the petulant, strong-tempered young woman, who dominates much of the plot with her capricious negativity, remarks at one point: "Man muss gegen den Zionismus sein. Man muss einfach, so wie man gegen die Frauenbewegung sein muss."[22]

On one occasion, an unlikeable, non-discriminating character, Nussbaum, states: "Der Zionismus ist eine reaktionäre Bewegung. Eine reaktionäre Bewegung, die um so gefährlicher ist, als sie sich unter dem Deckmantel des Fortschritts einschleicht."[23] It is significant that Hugo Rosenthal, the good-natured Jewish protagonist in this sentimental *Bildungsroman*, succeeds in maintaining a desirable distance from these unsubstantiated vacuous utterances, much as he eventually manages to steer clear of the sometimes powerfully seductive, but ultimately objectionable, forms of life these characters represent. Another unsympathetic character, Alfred Popper, a fictional devotee of Otto Weininger, and admirer of the Aryan ideal, is painfully aware of his own Jewishness; at one point, Popper explicitly expresses his intention to avoid visiting the Bohemian city Teplitz because of the presence there of so many Zionists.[24] Unlike Popper, Hugo occasionally feels positively about his Jewishness, a characteristic which does not preclude in any way non-particularistic, humane feelings. The patently obvious literary strategy – that is, endowing relatively negative fictional characters with expressions which are invariably rejected by hero and reader alike – informs the limited use of Zionist-related material in this novel. The technique itself is quite transparent and unsophisticated, but at the same time this entire aspect of the text is definitely a minor one.

Similarly, the Zionist-related material in *Arnold Beer* figures in a conventional way. By no means does Arnold's encounter with his aged grandmother, the confrontation with his Jewish roots, make him into a Zionist, as the Kafka-scholar Karl Fingerhut claimed.[25] Rather, Arnold is motivated by this encounter to purposeful activity only in a general sense; his youthful aimlessness, his "indifferentism", is replaced in the end by a resolve to establish a purpose to life. The newly acquired awareness of his heritage provides the real possibility for potential usefulness and industry, in this case, in the field of journalism in Berlin. In fact, the Zionist potential of this novel is never realised in the narrative. However, the limited role of Arnold's friend, the law student and Zionist activist, Krause, prefigures and prepares aesthetically for the later development. He injects Zionist perspectives into Arnold's consciousness well before the climatic meeting with the grandmother. At one point, Arnold ruminates about his condition of depression and loneliness, and in a totally unexpected manner, he refers to Krause. The passage, in Brod's typical "erlebte Rede" reads: "War dies gemeines Menschenlos, oder nur vielleicht typisches Schicksal eines jungen Juden? So weit hatten ihn Krauses Ideen schon beeinflusst, dass er dies in

---

[22] *Jüdinnen*, Munich 1922, p. 105.
[23] *Ibid.*, pp. 105–106.
[24] *Ibid.*, p. 229.
[25] Fingerhut provides an illuminating interpretation of Kafka's *Das Urteil* as an "anti-Arnold Beer". See Hartmut Binder (ed.), *Kafka-Handbuch*, vol. 2, Stuttgart 1979, pp. 278–282. Cf. Ritchie Robertson, *Kafka: Judaism, Politics, and Literature*, Oxford 1985, pp. 29–34.

Erwägung zog."[26] Krause's Zionist notions had penetrated more deeply than Arnold, or the reader, may have suspected. Furthermore, although Arnold had studied the Bible with Krause in the Hebrew original, an activity which he interpreted as being Zionist in nature, it is the Yiddish *cum* Silesian dialect – "Schwall von Jargon und schlesischem Dialekt",[27] – spoken by the grandmother that ultimately makes such a deep and lasting impression on the protagonist – this, despite the trivial, irrational, and often utterly senseless character of her garbled speech.

The later novels, *Zauberreich der Liebe* and *Unambo*, differ from the earlier ones in regard to Zionism, in their polemical nature, first and foremost, and because of their reflection of Zionist endeavours in the land of Israel itself. In *Zauberreich* the non-Jewish protagonist Christof Nowy sails to Palestine in order to retrieve Erich Garta, the Zionist brother of Nowy's dead friend, Richard Garta – the latter is Brod's literary reincarnation of Franz Kafka. The literary strategy dictates that Christof's low opinion of the Jewish race, *qua* race, his mild aversion to Jews, and his initial rejection of Zionism eventually give way to a poignant re-evaluation. This change is effected primarily by his meeting with Erich and the visit to his kibbutz, the true magic kingdom of love, located in the Eastern Galilee. Of course, this section of the text is deeply indebted to Herzl's utopian Zionist novel, *Altneuland* (1902), which employs the same fundamental literary strategy. Synchronic interruptions, which serve to develop the characteristic erotic and sentimental love themes comprising the bulk of the novel, help make the re-evaluation process somewhat more convincing by providing sufficient narrative space and background for the conversion. Still, the unremitting idealisation of the kibbutz tends to detract from the book's possible verisimilitude.

The two issues already isolated above – the language question and the Arab-Jewish conflict – acquire literary form in this novel in ways that are intertwined. First, it is the brother, Erich, who reveals to the friend Richard Garta's (Kafka's) secret enthusiasm for Hebrew, an aspect of his life Christof never knew or suspected, and which now, especially, has a profound impact on him. Whereas at first he dismissed out of hand the "Sprachkampf-Läpperei" he witnessed in Palestine, that is, the renaming in Hebrew of Arabic locations or the Hebraicising of names, he is now persuaded that there is absolutely nothing chauvinistic about these practices. He is told: "Es ist nur die Rückkehr zur Natürlichkeit. Alles Arabische bleibt natürlich arabisch benannt."[28] By distinguishing between this example and the discomfiting Czech-German conflict in his native land, Christof comes to approve whole-heartedly these Zionist tendencies. Concerning the resident Arab population, a kibbutznik claims: "Wir wollen nicht einen einzigen Araber verdrängen . . . das Land ist durch Misswirtschaft unfruchtbar geworden. Es hat bei besserer Bestellung Raum für die Araber wie für viele Hunderttausende einwandernder Juden!"[29]

[26]*Arnold Beer. Schicksal eines Juden*, Berlin/Charlottenburg 1912, p. 48.
[27]*Ibid.*, p. 151.
[28]*Zauberreich der Liebe*, Berlin-Vienna-Leipzig 1928, p. 369.
[29]*Ibid.*, p. 367.

These simplistic economic and geographical arguments correspond to Brod's Zionist writings, and the kibbutzniks, principally, serve as his mouthpiece. For Brod, the kibbutz was the highest expression of Socialist humanism, the true arena for Jewish self-knowledge. Christof Nowy believes in the end that these Jewish pioneers are toiling not just for the sake of the Jews but for mankind as a whole. They take the collective suffering of the entire world upon themselves, for they are, figuratively, a "messianic race".[30] This formulation is strikingly close to one found in Brod's essay, 'Zionismus', mentioned above. There, Zionism was depicted as the second Jewish-initiated, universal, redemption movement. Christianity was the first.

Brod's Zionist *Weltanschauung*, in all of its particulars, surfaces in fictive forms in *Unambo*, but this time Zionism acquires a sense of urgency and a justification missing before, owing to the background of the Holocaust, which overshadows the sentimental love and war motifs. Virtually all of the Jewish freedom fighters in the War of Independence depicted in the novel are Holocaust survivors, whose families were annihilated in Europe. The death-camps are mentioned time and again. As the protagonist Helfin says: "Das kapiert die Welt nicht, fühlt zu wenig, dass in jedem von uns hundert Seelen mitkämpfen, die Hitler in Auschwitz erstickt hat."[31]

Although the novel is written in German, transliterated Hebrew words comprise a significant portion of the text's working vocabulary, and the particular meanings of the Hebrew lexical items are discussed as a rule in lengthy explanations and digressions. The Arab issue in *Unambo* assumes perforce a unique literary shape, but nevertheless, the basic outline of Brod's longstanding view in the main holds here as well. The bloody incident at Deir-Yassin, where Arab women and children were murdered is mentioned by Helfin, indeed lamented by him.[32] It is significant, though, that he attempts, albeit lamely, to rationalise the operation to an extent. He states that the war was forced on the Jews, who only desired peace, and anyway, a few days after Deir-Yassin, Arabs committed the horrible massacre of unarmed physicians, nurses, and university professors driving by convoy to Mount Scopus, after receiving Arab assurances of safe conduct. The difficulty of the Arab predicament is underlined throughout, but the refugee problem, so repeats Helfin, was created by the Arabs themselves. They persuaded their own villagers to flee, in order to return later in jubilant triumph with the victorious Arab armies.

However, in one section of the book, a radically different view of the Arab-Jewish conflict is propounded. A kibbutznik-hero, Dov Popper from Vilna, one of the intrepid defenders at the siege of Zur-Yaakov in the Upper Galilee, echoes some of Brod's standard Zionist views. He insists that the meaning of Zionism in theory is justice, and that the displacement of any Arabs would diminish the justness of the cause. Yet, in Popper's historic view, Zionism, although necessary, is tragic in character, since in practice the movement cannot be

[30]*Ibid.*, p. 403.
[31]*Unambo*, Zürich 1949, p. 57.
[32]*Ibid.*, p. 44.

morally right: "Wir müssen siedeln, und die Araber müssen sich wehren. Sie sind es, nicht wir, die den Verteidigungskampf führen. Ein unauflöslicher Konflikt. Denn wir mögen uns stellen, wie wir wollen; schliesslich verdrängen wir sie doch von ihrem Boden . . ."[33] The utopian answer to the dilemma is articulated by this fictional character as follows: "Wir werden uns in die Araber verlieben müssen. Dann erst werden wir vielleicht anfangen, gegen sie gerecht zu sein. Anders geht es nicht."[34] The literary motif of living two separate lives simultaneously by means of the "Unambo mechanism" is the ultimate, cumulative expression of Brod's life-long struggle and tendency towards synthesis.[35] One narrative strand sees the protagonist Helfin die as a war hero on the "Burma" road to Jerusalem. He had courageously saved the life of his nephew Gad, who would carry on the pioneering work of Israel's founders and define the new Jewish "Menschentypus" in Israel. The other strand sees Helfin, the agonised film-maker, leave the land and meet his end in Brazil from heart failure. It is this type of duality, an inner-outer conflict, which permeated Brod's work and manifested itself in his career as a Zionist as well.

V

Brod strove throughout the years to express a coherent Zionist vision and to remain faithful to his own rhetoric, despite problematical challenges posed by the hard realities of European and Middle Eastern life, on the one hand, and by limitations in his personality and background, on the other. In the end, the evidence adduced from Mann's correspondence cited in this essay does not so much serve to diminish the true accomplishments of Brod as a Zionist; rather, this new material helps illuminate in an alternate way the difficult human process of his Zionist self-identification. As Hugo Bergman wrote in 1964 on the occasion of Brod's 80th birthday, it was "äusserlich und innerlich nicht leicht"[36] for Brod to come to Zionism. Beyond that, Zionism was merely a portal for him to something much larger beyond. As Brod had written in 1917: "One ventures out looking for Zionism, and one finds Judaism, social activism, and the like."[37]

[33] *Ibid.*, p. 231.
[34] *Ibid.*, p. 232.
[35] See Felix Weltsch, 'Aus Zweiheit zur Einheit. Max Brods Weg als Dichter und Denker', in Ernst F. Taussig (ed.), *Ein Kampf um Wahrheit. Max Brod zum 65. Geburtstag*, Tel-Aviv 1949, pp. 8–17.
[36] S. Hugo Bergman, 'Zu Brods 80. Geburtstag', *Israelitisches Wochenblatt für die Schweiz*, 22nd May 1964, pp. 18–19.
[37] 'Die dritte Phase des Zionismus', *loc. cit.*, p. 1. ("Man zieht aus, um den Zionismus zu suchen, und findet das Judentum, den sozialen Aktivismus und Ähnliches.")

Interpreting Hasidism:
The Buber-Scholem Controversy

BY MAURICE FRIEDMAN

In the last twenty years a strange phenomenon has taken place in American intellectual circles in general and Jewish circles in particular. As a result of Gershom Scholem's famous critique of Martin Buber's interpretation of *Hasidism* – that popular communal Jewish mysticism of Eastern European Jewry which Buber did more than anyone to bring to the awareness of the Western world – many intellectuals, scholars, and educated laypersons, Jewish and non-Jewish alike, have leapt to the conclusion that Buber's whole corpus on *Hasidism* has been discredited. A few have gone even further and assumed that Buber as a philosopher of religion and an interpreter of Judaism no longer deserves serious attention. If a quarter of a century ago the intellectual fad among many was to see Buber as "in", now many persons have climbed on the intellectual bandwagon and see Scholem as "in" and Buber as "out". This strange phenomenon has impelled me to set down here the history, the context, and the arguments on both sides of the "Buber-Scholem controversy" – something which has not been done before. Serious and fair-minded readers may perhaps be induced by my essay to take a more balanced view of this controversy or at least to understand its true parameters.

When Gershom Scholem published the English edition of his book *Major Trends in Jewish Mysticism* in 1946, at a time when he had already done a great deal of his research on the *Kabbalah* and Sabbatianism, his final chapter on *Hasidism* not only contained no criticism of Buber's interpretation but agreed with it in almost every important aspect. According to Scholem, *Hasidism* "neutralised" the messianic element in Jewish mysticism without renouncing the popular appeal of later Kabbalism, hence achieving what Buber called "the messianism of the everyday". Its heroic period during the first fifty years after the death of the Baal-Shem (the founder of *Hasidism*, Israel ben Eliezer, 1700–1760) was characterised by a spirit of enthusiasm based on the idea of the immanence of God in all that exists. "Within a geographically small area and also within a surprisingly short period", Scholem declared, "the ghetto gave birth to a whole galaxy of saint-mystics, each of them a startling individuality." This burst of mystical energy did not produce new religious ideas or theories of mystical knowledge. The new element was rather "the spontaneity of feeling generated in sensitive minds by the encounter with the living incarnations of mysticism".

449

Although the continuity of kabbalistic thought was not really interrupted, the *Kabbalah* was used as an instrument of mystical psychology and self-knowledge rather than a penetration of the upper worlds for their own sake. In this "mysticism of the personal life", "almost all the kabbalistic ideas are now placed in relation to values peculiar to the individual life, and those which are not remain empty and ineffective". "The originality of *Hasidism* lies in the fact that mystics who had attained their spiritual aim . . . turned to the people with their mystical knowledge, their 'Kabbalism become Ethos' [this phrase is from Buber's introduction to *The Tales of Rabbi Nachman*]." The existence of the *zaddik* was the actual proof of the possibility of living up to the ideal – "He who . . . is capable of being alone with God is the true centre of the community." The life of the *Hasidim* centres around the personality of the *zaddik*. The opinions of the *zaddik* are less important than his character. "*Personality* takes the place of *doctrine*; what is lost in rationality by this change is gained in efficacy." "A ray of God's essence is present and perceptible everywhere and at every moment." It is the *zaddik* who helps make this palpable for the *Hasid*. The *zaddik* becomes the centre of the new myth, and the *hasidic* tale about the *zaddik* is the religious purveying of that myth.

> "The revival of a new mythology in the world of Hasidism to which attention has been drawn occasionally, especially by Martin Buber, draws not the least part of its strength from its connection between the magical and the mystical faculties of its heroes. When all is said and done it is this myth which represents the greatest creative expression of Hasidism. In the place of the theoretical disquisition, or at least side by side with it, you get the Hasidic tale. Around the lives of the great Zaddikim, the bearers of that irrational something which their mode of life expressed, legends were spun often in their own lifetime . . . To tell a story of the deeds of the saints has become a new religious value, and there is something of the celebration of a religious rite about it. Not a few great Zaddikim . . . have laid down the whole treasure of their ideas in such tales. Their Torah took the form of an inexhaustible fountain of story-telling. Nothing at all has remained theory, everything has become a story."[1]

In 1948, Scholem went to the University of Chicago and spoke to one of Joachim Wach's classes. "He is the sort of historian of religion that I like", Wach said of Scholem, whom he had known as a fellow graduate student in Germany. When Scholem visited Wach in Switzerland, where Wach went every summer to be with his mother, Wach sensed a tension between Scholem and Buber. This tension came out in the open not many years later when Scholem began publicly criticising Buber in his lectures in England and America. Abraham Joshua Heschel was extremely distressed by the nature of these attacks. "You know I do not like some of what Buber has done with *Hasidism*", Heschel said to me, "but whom else do we have like him?"

Both Paul Arthur Schilpp and Fritz Kaufmann wrote to Scholem urging him to contribute an essay on Buber's interpretation of *Hasidism* to *The Philosophy of Martin Buber* volume of *The Library of Living Philosophers* (which I co-edited), and Kaufmann did not give up even after the first attempts met with no success. After Buber had received our list of those we hoped would contribute, he wrote to me

---

[1] Gershom G. Scholem, *Major Trends in Jewish Mysticism*, revised edition, New York 1964, Ninth Lecture – 'Hasidism. The Latest Phase', pp. 329f., 334–344, 348f.

in December 1956, "I am curious what Scholem, whom I appreciate very highly, will do with it. He has a somewhat ambivalent relation to the subject [of Buber's interpretation of *Hasidism*]. My new essay on *Hasidism* is in some regards an answer to his objections."[2] The essay to which Buber was referring was 'Hasidism and Modern Man', which I set at the head of the volume of Buber's *hasidic* interpretations collected under this title. In it Buber looked back over his half century of work in interpreting *Hasidism* and bringing it to the West, distilling from this variegated labour the simple, central message which he more and more came to see as the core of *hasidic* life and teaching: "Man cannot approach the divine by reaching beyond the human; he can approach Him through becoming human. To become human is what he, this individual man, has been created for."

The First World War, which brought Buber to the understanding of dialogue, also brought him to the realisation that the *hasidic* way of life was involved in some mysterious way in the task that had claimed him.

> "I could not become a Hasid. It would have been an unpermissible masquerading had I taken on the Hasidic manner of life – I who had a wholly other relation to Jewish tradition, since I must distinguish in my innermost being between what is commanded me and what is not commanded me. It was necessary, rather, to take into my own existence as much as I actually could of what had been truly exemplified for me in Hasidism, that is to say, of the realization of that dialogue with being whose possibility my thought had shown me."[3]

The form of the "legendary anecdote" that evolved over the years enabled Buber to portray the *hasidic* life in such a way that it became visible as at once reality and teaching. Although Buber saw the kernel of *hasidic* life as given over to decay and destruction, he held in 'Hasidism and Modern Man' that it is still capable of working on the life of men in the present-day West because of its central concern, preserved in personal as well as in communal existence, to overcome the fundamental separation between the sacred and the profane.

Although Kierkegaard and Marx already pointed to the crisis and alienation of modern man a century ago, and the psychoanalysts did the same at the turn of the century, only now can we readily understand this crisis in its true depth and take the injured wholeness of man upon us. Although modern man no longer knows the holy face to face, he knows its heir, the "spiritual", and "recognises" it without allowing it to determine life in any way. One takes culture and ideas with grim seriousness, placing them on golden thrones to which their limbs are chained, but any claim by the spirit on personal existence is warded off through a comprehensive apparatus. "No false piety has ever attained this concentrated degree of inauthenticity." To this behaviour of present-day man, who has got rid of the command of hallowing, "*Hasidism* sets the simple truth that the wretchedness of our world is grounded in its resistance to the entrance of the holy into lived life." "A life that does not seek to realise what the living person, in the ground of his self-awareness, understands or glimpses as the right is not merely

---

[2] Letter from Martin Buber to Maurice Friedman, 7th December 1956.
[3] Martin Buber, *Hasidism and Modern Man*, ed. and trans. with an Introduction by Maurice Friedman, New York 1973, Book I – 'Hasidism and Modern Man', p. 24. See also Buber's *Origin and Meaning of Hasidism*, also ed., trans., and introduced by Maurice Friedman, New York 1973.

unworthy of the spirit; it is also unworthy of life." What underlay this seemingly harsh judgement was Buber's recognition that what was in question was not some separate sphere of the religious or holy, but the quality of life itself, its call to become "humanly holy" in the measure and manner of our personal existence.

Hasidism, Buber claimed, freed the myths which it took over from the *Kabbalah* from their gnostic nature and restored them to their original condition. This mythical essence of *Hasidism* "has entered into the lived life of seven generations, as whose late-born interpreter I function".[4] The impact of this interpretation on the non-Jewish world was such that it was often suggested to Buber that he should liberate *Hasidism* from its "confessional limitations" as part of Judaism and proclaim it as an unfettered teaching of mankind. Buber's response to this demand is one of the finest illustrations of how the life of dialogue meant for him meeting the other and holding one's ground in that meeting:

> "Taking such a 'universal' path would have been for me pure arbitrariness. In order to speak to the world what I have heard, I am not bound to step into the street. I may remain standing in the door of my ancestral house: here too the word that is uttered does not go astray."[5]

As a response to Scholem's objections, this essay was hardly effective, since Scholem had not spelled out these objections and Buber did not in any way refer to them.

In November 1957, in consenting to my plan for the two volumes of his *hasidic* interpretations (*Hasidism and Modern Man* and *The Origin and Meaning of Hasidism*), Buber wrote, "I have in mind to add at some place an explanation of my view about the relation between *Hasidism* and the *Kabbalah*, of course in Vol. II."[6] It is possible that he had Scholem's objections in mind here too, but the explanation was never added. In 1960, when I spent four months in Jerusalem, I visited Scholem and asked him personally whether he would reconsider his decision not to contribute an essay on Buber's interpretation of *Hasidism* to *The Philosophy of Martin Buber*. Scholem was adamant. "Don't you have something already written?" I persisted. "I do, but I wouldn't give it to *you*", he answered. "Besides I don't believe in the principle of *The Library of Living Philosophers*", he asserted. "Why not?" I asked. "Because", replied Scholem, "it gives the philosopher the last word". This reply, as Scholem was later to say of one of Buber's, was unforgettable. He did suggest one of his disciples, Rivka Schatz-Uffenheimer, and she completed a forty-page monograph by that autumn (which was translated from Hebrew into German and English by Fritz Kaufmann's daughter Renate, who had recently moved to Jerusalem, where she works as a librarian at the Hebrew University).

Schatz's essay on 'Man's Relation to God and World in Buber's Rendering of the Hasidic Teaching' begins and ends with a paragraph of praise in between which are forty pages of solid Scholemite criticism. "There is no doubt that Buber has done more than any other scholar to open men's hearts for a profound understanding of *Hasidism*", she wrote. "And even if portions of his teachings

[4]Buber, *Hasidism and Modern Man*, *op. cit.*, p. 41.
[5]*Ibid.*, p. 42.
[6]Letter from Martin Buber to Maurice Friedman, 10th November 1957.

appear to me open to question on essential points, it remains true that these questions grew on the soil which Buber had prepared and sowed." The severity of her criticism was "not meant as a verdict on the final value of Buber's teaching", Schatz added, since that "must be measured by another standard than that of historical criticism". Although Buber insisted in conversation with Schatz that he had no system in his representation of the *hasidic* world, she stressed that his synthetic tapestry was woven of selected strands, and that it was he who determined the hue of the cloth.

Specifically, the affection with which Buber regarded reality as such led him to see *Hasidism* as closing the chasm between God and world, "as though *Hasidism* taught that there is nothing to distinguish this time from the time of the Messiah, the *Zaddik* from the ordinary man, the holy from the profane". Schatz portrayed Buber as full of enthusiasm for the very concrete reality that *Hasidism* saw as problematic, as boundlessly loving that very "world" whose whole ontic existence is set at nought in the eyes of *Hasidism*. "In the eyes of the *Hasidim* the greatness of the *Zaddikim* lay in their knowing how to turn . . . the divine 'being' that has fallen into the world back to its 'nothing', which is the true being." Man's contact with creation is an ideal mission that demanded of man the nullification of creation and of the concrete as such. Life in the world was transformed into life in God because *Hasidism* developed an indifference to the concrete. *Hasidism* held that God speaks to us also in corporeal reality and that we must serve God in that reality by redeeming it. But it did not hold that every action is of equal worth and equally endowed with "sacramental possibility", a view which Schatz sees as originating in Buber's own antinomian relation to the Torah, whose claims set prior limitations on the extension of the holy over the profane.

Schatz did not see Buber as drawing his conclusions out of thin air. "He succumbed to the plenitude of the *hasidic* world of aphorism: this plenitude sharpened to a point, in which you can find everything in the most brilliant and exaggerated form, in which every saying embodies a revolution." But like Scholem, she places *Hasidism* firmly within the context of the *Kabbalah*, and that means of *gnosis* and not of *devotio*:

> "*Hasidism* in fact never for a moment divested itself of the gnostic mode of consciousness and never forgot that our world, in its present state, is the result of 'the breaking of the vessels' of the divinity. It never, even on one page of the thousands on which its teaching is transmitted, forsook its yearning for the restoration of the world to its 'primordial' condition."[7]

Unlike Scholem, Schatz did not entirely deny the validity of Buber's interpretation of *Hasidism*. She said that it was one-sided, which it unquestionably is, and that is another way of saying that it is based much more on the tales than on the teachings, even though Buber was thoroughly familiar with the latter.

The chapter on *Hasidism* is the longest section in Buber's 'Replies to My Critics' in *The Philosophy of Martin Buber*. Buber used it as "a welcome occasion to clarify my thought with definitive precision". In so doing he was replying to

---

[7]Paul A. Schilpp and Maurice Friedman (eds.), *The Philosophy of Martin Buber*, volume of *The Library of Living Philosophers*, LaSalle, Illinois 1967, Rivka Schatz-Uffenheimer, 'Man's Relation to God and World in Buber's Rendering of the Hasidic Teaching', trans. by Renate Kaufmann, p. 407.

Scholem as well as to Rivka Schatz. Agreeing with Schatz's view that his tapestry of *hasidic* interpretation is woven of selective strands, Buber stated that since 1910, when he reached a basic study of the sources, his aim had not been to present a historically comprehensive picture of *Hasidism* but only a selective one. But the principle of selection which ruled here, as in that of his work on Judaism in general, was not a subjective one. "I have dealt with that in the life and teachings of Judaism which, according to my insight, is its proper truth and is decisive for its function in the previous and future history of the human spirit." This involves evaluation from its base up, Buber conceded, but this evaluation had its origin in the immovable central existence of values. "Since I have attained to the maturity of this insight, I have not made use of a filter: I became a filter."

Comparing *Hasidism* with Zen Buddhism, the Sufis, and the Franciscans, Buber pointed out that in all of them there prevailed devotion to the divine and the hallowing of life through this devotion. In *Hasidism* and in *Hasidism* alone, however, it is not the life of monks that is reported but that of spiritual leaders who are married and produce children and who stand at the head of communities composed of families. "In *Hasidism* the hallowing extends fundamentally to the natural and social life. Here alone the whole man, as God has created him, enters into the hallowing." Scholem rightfully designated *devekut*, the "cleaving" of the souls to God, as the central tendency of *hasidic* teaching. But Buber in his reply distinguished between two kinds of *devekut*, as neither Scholem nor Schatz did:

> "Among the zaddikim who sought . . . to elaborate the Kabbalistic doctrine, there predominated the view, already familiar to us from Gnosis, that one must lift oneself out of the 'corporeal' reality of human life into the 'nothing' of pure spirit in order to attain contact with God . . . But opposed to them – without a contest between the two taking place – is the view that this 'constant being with God' . . . is rather reached through man's dedicating to God all that is lived by him."[8]

Devekut as a gnostic spiritualisation of existence is first found in *Hasidism* in its great thinker the Maggid of Mezritch (died 1772). But before that *devekut* as the hallowing of all life originated with his teacher, the Baal-Shem-Tov. Thus the hallowing, not the spiritualisation, is the original teaching of *Hasidism*.

Asked by an author of kabbalistic writings about the secret *kavanot*, or "intentions", that entered into *Hasidism* through the kabbalistic prayer book which it took over, Rabbi Moshe of Kobryn (died 1858) warned:

> "You must keep in mind that the word *Kabbala* is derived from *kabbel*: to accept; and the word *kavana* from *kavven*: to direct. For the final meaning of all the wisdom of the *Kabbala* is to take on oneself the yoke of God's will and the final meaning of all the art of *kavanot* is to direct one's heart to God."

Here, according to Buber, the life of devoted cleaving to God which was meant by the primal faith of Israel opposes the hypertrophy of mystical-magical doctrine.

The Baal-Shem included everything corporeal, without exception, in the

---

[8]*The Philosophy of Martin Buber*, *op. cit.*, Martin Buber, 'Replies to My Critics', trans. by Maurice Friedman, IX, 'On Hasidism', p. 733.

sphere of what can be hallowed through *kavana*, or *intention*, not excluding the coupling of man and wife. "Of a 'nullification' of the concrete there is in *this* line of *Hasidism* – which begins with its beginning – nothing to be found." The beings and things continue to exist undiminished, and when the divine "sparks" are raised from them, this is no annihilation but rather dedication, hallowing, transformation without suspension of concreteness. When the Baal-Shem says, "In the hour when on account of sin you carry out the turning, you raise the sparks that were in it into the upper world", that is no nullification but a bridge-building.

It is not "*Hasidism*" that was faced with the "critical problem" of "life split apart into external action and inner intention", but its spiritual coinage and extension which won the upper hand in the school of the Maggid of Mezritch. But wherever the new mode of life became stronger than the doctrine that grew out of the kabbalistic tradition, the acceptance of the concrete for the sake of its hallowing took place as "decision" and not as "problem". What ultimately concerned Buber was not an act for its own sake, as Schatz imagined, but "the restoration of the immediacy between God and man for the sake of overcoming the eclipse of God".

Therefore, Buber's selection "necessarily directed itself to the unjustly despised 'anecdotes' – stories of lived life – and 'aphorisms' – sayings in which life documents itself". For both expressed with cogent brevity the life of the *zaddikim*. Some *zaddikim* were predominantly teachers of future *zaddikim*; others, like Levi Yitzhak of Berditchev, R. Zusya and R. Moshe Leib of Sasov, are popular figures who helped the broad circle of followers among the *Hasidim*. These latter represent the simply unique in *Hasidism*. The relationship of the master to the disciples has also perhaps taken exemplary shape in the writings of Zen Buddhism, but that of the master to ignorant people is nowhere in the world expressed as it is here.[9]

At another place in the 'Replies' Buber addressed himself to a criticism by Hugo Bergmann, also made by Rivka Schatz and Scholem, that his presentation of the *hasidic* conception of a "Messianism of all times" had weakened the messianic belief. The ever-recurring event of redemption preceding the messianic fulfilment in the ages in no way injures the devotion to the *eschaton*, the final redemption, Buber asserted:

> "Just as I believe not merely in the creative act in the beginning, but also in the creation at all times, in which man has a share as 'God's comrade in the work of creation', and just as I believe not merely in the great acts of revelation in the incomprehensible hours in which one 'sees the voices', but also in the secret and yet revelatory coming into contact of above and below, so I believe in the redeeming act poured forth over the ages, in which man again has a share. These events do not add themselves to one another, but all together they cooperate secretly in preparing the coming redemption of the world."[10]

In *Philosophical Interrogations* Buber explicitly asked that his interpretation of *hasidic* teaching should not be confused with his own thought. "I can by no means

[9]*Ibid.*, pp. 731–739.
[10]*Ibid.*, p. 714.

in my own thinking take responsibility for *hasidic* ideas, although my thinking is indebted to them and bound up with them." For example, he would not say, in representing his own thought, that God wishes to redeem us or that everything desires to become a sacrament; yet the reality meant by these two statements has its place in "my more cautious thought". He also stated at another place that there was much in *Hasidism* that he could by no means make his own, in particular the kabbalistic ideas of the emanations of God and their relationship to one another. "These are essentially Gnostic ideas, and I have always decisively opposed Gnosis, which presumes to know, so to speak, the inner history of God."[11]

In his essay 'Martin Buber and Mysticism' in *The Philosophy of Martin Buber*, Hugo Bergmann challenged the validity of the distinction between *gnosis* and *devotio*, charging that Buber created spurious abstractions for polemical reasons, "tilting against an artificial construction to which he applies the term gnosticism". "Actually both gnosis and devotion are ways to God and it is inadmissible to contrapose the two in this fashion and play them off against one another . . ." "We are always assured by the modern gnostics that without religious devotion no progress can be made in gnosis." Rather than interpreting his own self as the divine self, as Buber thinks, a gnostic such as Sri Aurobindo wishes to extinguish his ego completely and to serve God by the full surrender thereof. At this point, noted Bergmann, Buber's "thought remains enmeshed in a rationalistic prejudice". "He is really paying tribute here to the world view of the nineteenth century." "It is necessary to pierce through these limitations if we are to develop further Buber's own thought in the direction of that 'Great Reality' of which the mystical books of his youth give evidence."

Bergmann quoted Rudolf Steiner's statement that the "investigator of the spirit" practises devotion "towards the truth and the knowledge". "When I have talked of devotion", Buber replied, "I mean by that, exclusively, life as personal service to God." Buber respected completely faithfulness to knowledge, but what mattered to him was whether it proceeded from and is determined by unmediated devotion to God. Not all gnostics, Buber conceded, find the Absolute in the depths of their own soul, though from Simon Magus to modern times there are expressions of this sort. The turning away from one's 'I' postulated by some gnostics, to which Bergmann alluded, Buber could not accept as conclusive evidence against his view, because it is founded upon "precisely the distinction between the surface 'I', as that which is to be stripped away, and the true self, as that in whose depths the Godhead is to be discovered".[12]

In July, 1961, Buber wrote to me that he had read in the journals about a lecture of Scholem's in which he criticised Buber's approach to *Hasidism*.

---

[11]Sydney and Beatrice Rome (eds.), *Philosophical Interrogations*, New York 1970, 'Interrogation of Martin Buber', conducted, edited and Buber's replies trans. by Maurice Friedman, pp. 88–91.

[12]Hugo Bergmann, 'Martin Buber and Mysticism', and Buber, 'Replies to My Critics', in *The Philosophy of Martin Buber, op. cit.*, pp. 306–308, 716f.

"If he publishes it I must answer, and I think to do it in a more general and comprehensive manner than I have done in my answer to Rivka Schatz. I must clarify the difference between a scientific and a religious approach to a great fact in the history of religion. (The 'religious' approach may of course involve some very precise scientific work, philological and historical.) I hope you will translate this essay of mine too."[13]

Scholem did indeed publish, if not this lecture, one like it. Norman Podhoretz, the editor of *Commentary*, some time before this wrote to Michael Wyschogrod asking him to review a number of Buber books in such a way as to help combat "the Buber cult". Wyschogrod replied that if Podhoretz already knew the conclusion, he should review them himself! Podhoretz then heard about Scholem's views on Buber's *Hasidism* and asked him for a critical essay, which Scholem gave him, thus fulfilling his own desire to have the last word rather than let the philosopher have it. This essay was published in the October 1961 issue of *Commentary* and then reproduced in Scholem's *Messianic Idea of Judaism*.

Scholem too began with words of praise. Buber "has that rare combination of a probing spirit and literary elegance which makes for a great writer":

"When an author of such stature and such subtlety set down with untiring seriousness what to him seemed the very soul of Hasidism, it was bound to make a deep impression on our age. In one sense or another we are all his disciples. In fact most of us, when we speak about Hasidism, probably think primarily in terms of the concepts that have become familiar through Buber's philosophical interpretation."[14]

A critical analysis of Buber's interpretation of *Hasidism* is made exceedingly difficult, Scholem added, because "Buber, to whom no one denies possession of an exact knowledge of Hasidic literature, does not write as a scholar who gives clear references to support his contentions". Buber combines facts and quotations in order to present *Hasidism* as a spiritual phenomenon and in so doing does not even consider much material of great significance for the understanding of *Hasidism* as a historical phenomenon, such as the magical element in *Hasidism* and the social character of the *hasidic* community. Since the creative impulse in *Hasidism* was what really mattered to Buber, he felt justified in almost completely ignoring its kabbalistic or "Gnostic" element, which he saw as "a kind of umbilical cord which must be severed as soon as the new spiritual creation exists in its own right".

Of the two types of *hasidic* literature – the teachings which embrace well over a thousand volumes and the legends that have adorned every single leading *hasidic* personality – Buber based his presentation and interpretation almost exclusively on the legends, claiming that they, and not the theoretical literature, are our chief source of knowledge of *Hasidism*. But, said Scholem, the teachings were the first and most authoritative presentation of the meaning of *hasidic* life, whereas the legends were not written down until nearly fifty years later. "The Hasidic authors obviously did not believe they had in any way broken with the gnostic

---

[13]Letter from Martin Buber to Maurice Friedman, 6th July 1961. (See also letters of 11th November 1958; 29th August 1960; 21st January 1962.)

[14]Gershom Scholem, 'Martin Buber's Hasidism. A Critique', *Commentary*, XXXII, No. 4 (October 1961), p. 304. The whole essay is on pp. 304–316.

tradition of the Kabbala and, little as Buber wants to admit it, they wrote clearly and plainly as Gnostics."

At this point the divergence between Scholem as an intellectual historian and Buber as a filter of *hasidic* life and spirit becomes most evident. For Scholem identified the "real doctrines" of Sufism and Catholicism with their dogma, and he put forth the theoretical teachings of *Hasidism* as the primary source for what *hasidic* legends and sayings "really meant". In striking contrast to his statement in *Major Trends*, Scholem now claimed that the Baal-Shem's reinterpretation of individual kabbalistic concepts as key words for the personal life of the pious did not deprive them of their original meaning. Scholem later agreed with Buber that *Hasidism* teaches that man meets God in the concreteness of his dealings with the world and that *Hasidism*'s transformation of simple and insignificant action into vehicles for the sacred was one of the most original aspects of the movement. But like Schatz, he asserted that this contact was for the sake of annihilation.

The undaunted and enthusiastic joy which *Hasidism* demanded of its adherents is not a joy in the here and now, but in what is hidden in the essentially irrelevant garment of the here and now. Letting the hidden light shine forth destroys the here and now instead of realising it in its full concreteness. The concrete meeting of man with reality is a springboard to transcend reality, not to fulfil it. In fact, Buber's existential interpretation to the contrary, the classical literature of *Hasidism* consistently treats the individual and concrete existence of phenomena quite disdainfully and disparagingly. "The concrete in Buber's sense does not even exist in Hasidism."

In contrast to his earlier statements about neutralising Messianism, Scholem now claimed that the mystic's actions were aimed at the messianic reality in which all things have been restored to their proper place in the scheme of creation and thereby deeply transformed and transfigured. Scholem granted that many *Hasidim* regarded the holy sparks not as metaphysical elements of divine being but as subjective feelings of joy and affirmation which are projected into the relation between man and his environment. But this popular or vulgar version, which is reflected in the world of *hasidic* legends and "provides the relative justification for Buber's highly simplified view", does not derive "from the theology of the founders of Hasidism but from the mood of some of its followers".

Buber's approach to *yihud* or "unification" as personal direction rather than magic formula is "very modern, appealing, and suggestive", asserted Scholem, but it is not acceptable. Although Buber's presentation of *hasidic* legends and sayings in the mature form of the anecdote, which dominates his later writings, "will in large measure stand the test of time", the spiritual message he has read into his interpretation of *Hasidism* "is far too closely tied to assumptions that derive from his own philosophy of religious anarchism and existentialism and have no roots in the texts themselves". Scholem's conclusion is an unqualified dismissal of Buber's interpretation of *Hasidism*:

> "Too much is left out in this description of Hasidism, and what is included is overloaded with very personal speculations. Their character may be exalted and they may appeal deeply to the modern mind. But if we would understand the real phenomenon of Hasidism, both in its

grandeur and in its decay (which are in many ways connected), we shall have to start again from the beginning."[15]

Buber was invited by *Commentary* to write a reply to Scholem, but because of repeated illness he could not do so for almost two years. In November 1961, Buber wrote: "The article will not have the form of a rebuttal but only refer as much as necessary to Scholem's opinion."[16] Buber's reply was held up not only by ill health but by Scholem's decision to publish his article in a somewhat changed form in German in the *Neue Zürcher Zeitung*, a form which raised different problems of a technical kind which Buber felt he had to deal with. In February 1962, Buber declared that "a kind of general weakness, together with rather enormous daily obligations, make concentrated mind-work impossible. I have decided to go in the beginning of March for about ten days with my daughter to Tiberias and, putting all other things aside, to do my best in order to finish there the answer to Scholem. There is no other way."[17]

After his eighty-fifth birthday, Buber told me that he had written an answer to Scholem some time before, which completed what he said in the *Responsa* on the matter, and that both would be published in the third, *hasidic* volume of his *Werke*, the latter in somewhat shortened form so that the reader could understand everything without being obliged to read the article by Schatz. He spoke of combining both into one essay for *Commentary* and asked me to translate it.[18] The essay appeared in the September 1963 issue of *Commentary* and began with a long section on the "two different ways in which a great tradition of religious faith can be rescued from the rubble of time and brought back into the light" – that of historical scholarship and that of faithfully and adequately communicating the vitality and power of this faith.

The latter "approach derives from the desire to convey to our own time the force of a former life of faith and to help our age renew its ruptured bond with the Absolute". For this approach first it is necessary to have an adequate knowledge of the tradition in all its spiritual and historical connections, but it is not necessary to present all of them but only a selection of those elements in which its vitalising element was embodied, a selection based not upon objective scholarship but "upon the reliability of the person making the selection in the face of criteria"; "for what may appear to be mere 'subjectivity' to the detached scholar can sooner or later prove to be necessary to the process of renewal". Second, this person "should not be expected to turn away from the traditional reports concerning the life of the pious in order to give primary emphasis to the

[15]Gershom Scholem, *The Messianic Idea in Judaism*, New York 1971, pp. 34f. and 'Martin Buber's Interpretation of Hasidism', pp. 228–250. Although a different translation, this essay is identical with the one in *Commentary* except for the omission of Scholem's statement that "religious anarchist" is not meant to disparage Buber and his confession: "I am an anarchist myself, though not one of Buber's persuasion."
[16]Letter from Martin Buber to Maurice Friedman, 9th November 1961.
[17]Letter from Martin Buber to Maurice Friedman, 10th February 1962.
[18]Letters from Martin Buber to Maurice Friedman, 19th February 1963; 10th March 1963; 15th May 1963; 12th June 1963.

theoretical doctrine to which the founder and his disciples appealed for their authority".

Even in the founding of the great world religions, what was essential was not a comprehensible doctrine but an event which was at once life and word. And when, as in *Hasidism*, religious life reaches back to a much earlier doctrine in order to establish its legitimacy, it is not the old teaching as such which engenders the new life of faith in a later age, but rather the context of personal and community existence in which a far-reaching transformation of the earlier teachings takes place.

In reply to Scholem's objection that his interpretation rested largely upon legendary writings written down fifty years after the theoretical writings, produced in the age "in which Hasidism was actually productive", Buber pointed out that the genre of writing in question, the "legendary anecdote", was fully developed only in the literatures of Sufism, Zen Buddhism, and *Hasidism*, and that in all three it is not theoretical works but legendary tales that stand at the centre of their religious-historical development. This is true not for all kinds of religious mysticism but for the kind whose essential development can be seen most clearly in the mode of lived realisation, in that of the event.

It is not the theological doctrines of Al-Junaid but the stories and sayings handed down about his tenth-century contemporary Al-Hallaj which were decisive for Sufism; for their relationship to God was "so basically an existential one that no theoretical discussion can do it justice, and the only suitable vehicle for expressing this relationship is the anecdote". "When God is well-disposed to His servant, He opens the gates of deeds for him and closes the gates of discussion." This is truer still in Zen in which the disciples experience the "enlightenment" that comes solely from the indescribable mystery of the event, which is narrated just as it happened. In *Hasidism*, the didactic character of the legendary anecdote is developed in incomparably stronger fashion than in Sufism and Zen. In all three movements the legends were transmitted first orally and recorded only much later; whereas their theories were set down by those who originated them or by their immediate disciples.

> "In the history of human faith whenever there is a pressing need to transmit the *factual* character of the spoken teaching to the future generations and to save it from the danger of 'objective' conceptualization, the tendency is to keep the teaching tied to the happening that bore it, to hand it down as part of the personal occurrence from which it is inseparable. Nothing can do this so well as oral transmission which is always assisted by tone and gesture."[19]

In *Hasidism*, this oral transmission was aided by recording, wherever possible, the names of earlier figures who relayed the legends along with the legends themselves. Eventually, to preserve them from too much corruption, the legends were written down and collected. The fact that this took place later, fifty-five years after the death of the Baal-Shem, in no way invalidates their authenticity as

[19]Martin Buber, 'Interpreting Hasidism', ed. and trans. by Maurice Friedman, *Commentary*, XXXVI, No. 3 (September 1963), pp. 218–225.

sources. This is a principle which Buber stated with all explicitness in the Preface to the second edition of *The Kingship of God*.

> "A judgement concerning age or youth of a literary stratum by no means involves one concerning age or youth of the corresponding stratum of religious development, because it still remains to be investigated, for example, whether an early genuine tradition has reached us in a late form or transformation; . . . Without the cooperation of an investigation . . . of the compilations of tradition and of the forms of bias which determine them, the criticism of sources must miscalculate and lead astray."[20]

The fourth part of Buber's *Commentary* essay on 'Interpreting Hasidism' was essentially identical with his reply to Schatz in *The Philosophy of Martin Buber*. Here, as earlier, Buber emphasised that the inner dialectic between transcending earthly life and hallowing it does not belong to a later development of *Hasidism*, but is already apparent in its earliest stages and that the teaching of hallowing the everyday was the original thesis, the doctrine of spiritualisation a later accretion. What was at issue was not a spiritual matter that indirectly affects life but the conduct of life itself. What was most important to Rabbi Shlomo was "whatever he happened to be doing at the moment". The whole of one's life can be actively dedicated to God and become an altar for him. There are no words or actions that are idle in themselves; one makes them so when one talks and acts idly.

In the brief reply to Buber which Scholem appended as a postscript to his essay on Buber's interpretation of *Hasidism*, Scholem does not deal at all with Buber's principal response both to Schatz and himself, namely that there are two streams within *Hasidism* and that the earlier one, originating with the Baal-Shem, emphasises the hallowing of the everyday rather than the nullifying of it. What he does do is to repeat his questioning of the legends as a reliable source for understanding *Hasidism*.

> "There is no basis whatever in the Hasidic tradition for the attempt to construct a possible contradiction between the specifics of this group life and the concepts through which it unfolded . . . The older and more authentic the historical and social framework within which many of these oldest legends move or are enclosed, the less do they stand in real contradiction to the theoretical writings, produced in the same milieu, at the same time or considerably earlier."[21]

Beyond this, Scholem rejected the parallels Buber drew with Zen stories, saying that the latter are not really legends at all but exercises for meditation, a statement which may be true of some of the *koans* proper in Zen but which does not hold for the stories of master-disciple relationship that Zen also gives us.

Scholem closed his postscript with a story about Buber himself. Scholem "once asked Buber why in his writings he had suppressed the significant and unfathomable words regarding the messianic age that were transmitted in the name of Rabbi Israel of Rizhin". One of these was that in the days of the Messiah man will no longer quarrel with his fellow but with himself; another his suggestion that the messianic world will be a world without images "in which the

---

[20]Martin Buber, *The Kingship of God*, third newly enlarged edn., trans. by Richard Scheimann, New York 1963, p. 43.
[21]Scholem, *The Messianic Idea in Judaism*, *op. cit.*, pp. 248f.

image and its object can no longer be related". "I shall always remember his reply", recounts Scholem; Buber said, "Because I do not understand them".[22] To Scholem these sayings were historic evidence of the continuing power of the utopian element of messianic redemption and examples of the kabbalists' attempts to fathom its unfathomable depths. Thus Scholem too did not understand these sayings. What Buber could not understand he would not present as a vital force of *hasidic* faith.

"Both are right", Shmuel Agnon said to me in 1966 concerning the Scholem-Buber controversy. It should be said, rather, that both are right *and* wrong, that is, both are one-sided. Until Scholem and his disciples published what they did, Buber was looked to by the Western world as *the* interpreter of *Hasidism* just as D. T. Suzuki used to be looked to as *the* interpreter of Zen. Because this was so, it was indeed a scholarly lack on Buber's part that he did not indicate more clearly in his essays interpreting *Hasidism* that he was presenting only one of the two major streams of *hasidic* tradition, as he later did say in reply to Scholem and dramatically portrayed in the central conflict of his *hasidic* chronicle-novel *For the Sake of Heaven*. On the other hand, Scholem's failure to recognise the stream stemming from the Baal-Shem and his total rejection of the "hallowing of the everyday" as a valid interpretation of *Hasidism* are even more misleading since now nearly everyone thinks of Scholem as *the* scholarly interpreter, and few recognise his one-sidedness.

Abraham Joshua Heschel was close to Buber in his recognition that there were two streams that came forth from *Hasidism*, and not one as both Gershom Scholem and his disciple Rivka Schatz-Uffenheimer maintain – that of the hallowing of the everyday which began with the Baal-Shem and that of the gnostic nullifying of the particular in favour of the transcendent that began with the Baal-Shem's successor, Dov Baer, the Maggid of Mezritch. This contrast emerges with great clarity in Heschel's essay on the Baal-Shem's friend R. Pinhas of Koretz (or Korzec). In this essay, writes Samuel H. Dresner, Heschel "delineated the ideological conflict which occurred early in the history of the movement, in which each side claimed that it possesses the true meaning of the Besht's legacy":

> "The Maggid of Miedzyrzecz (Mezritch) had stressed the centrality of Kabbalah and established *devekut* as the highest goal. For him, the awareness that all is God would lead man to understand that this world is but so many veils which must be cast aside to enter into the divine embrace. His language is strongly Lurianic, with spiritual ascent beyond time and place the all-consuming goal. For R. Pinhas, on the other hand, the stress is elsewhere. This world is no illusion. It is the place, and now is the time, where man must labor diligently and unremittingly to perfect himself. To escape the world is to violate the Psalmist's admonition that one must first 'turn from evil' and only then 'do good' . . . R. Pinhas emphasized moral virtue and simple faith."[23]

The Maggid introduced the methods of the Lurian *Kabbalah* into the teaching of the Besht – *kavanot* and *yihidum* (special mystical intentions and exercises),

[22]*Ibid.*, p. 250.
[23]Abraham Joshua Heschel, *The Circle of the Baal Shem Tov*, ed. with an introduction, 'Heschel as a Hasidic Scholar', by Samuel H. Dresner, Chicago 1985, p. xlii.

devekut (cleaving to God), and *hitlahavut* (burning enthusiasm, or ecstasy). His disciple, Shneur Zalman, taught that the essence of all things was intellectual contemplation on the greatness of God. Pinhas, in contrast, criticised those who wanted to learn secrets of the Torah and to achieve lofty heights of perception. He preferred unquestioning simplicity, honesty, and humility to *yihudim* and *kavanot*. "The battle between these two forms of Hasidim – the one, scholarly, speculative, and aristocratic; the other, that of the Ukrainian tzaddikim, poetic, moralistic, and popular – continued for generations." The Maggid of Mezritch and many of his followers, such as Levi Yitzhak of Berditchev, believed that true prayer demanded *hitlahavut* and that *hitlahavut* demanded various kinds of special preparation. Pinhas saw every word that one speaks, even one's lying down to sleep, as part of the preparation for prayer.[24]

Both Agnon and Ernst Simon felt that Scholem's essay was on a higher intellectual level than Buber's, but: "The impact which Buber's stories have would never be attained by objective scholarship", Simon said while objecting, as Scholem did not, that the sanctification of the secular attained by *Hasidism* depended to a very large extent on the fulfilment of the Jewish Law. "Buber would not deny that", Simon asserted, "but the stories do not carry enough of the atmosphere of Halakhic life." In a memorial address on Buber, Simon commented that Buber stuck to his original view of *Hasidism* despite Scholem's vigorous criticism:

> "Buber saw in Hasidism the last great religious movement of the Jewish people, and one of our great contributions to the Messianic attempt to approach the Kingdom of God on this earth. Perhaps for this reason he underestimated the weight of the great theoretical writings of the early Hasidic masters, and stressed the anecdotes about their exemplary lives and teachings. He showed them in their daily give-and-take with their disciples, i.e., again in the sphere of dialogue."[25]

The distinguished philosopher and theologian Emil Fackenheim remarked in 1961 in a speech to the Central Conference of American Rabbis that he found most of the criticisms directed against Buber's interpretation of *Hasidism* unimpressive.

> "The most common criticism is that Buber, instead of writing the kind of history which separates sources in painstaking analysis, has given the kind which is a creative synthesis. But the prejudices of positivistic scholarship to the contrary notwithstanding, there is always need for the latter as well as the former type of history, unless one is to be left, not with the spirit of the age or movement one seeks to understand, but merely with its dead bones. Moreover, while Buber's kind of history has great dangers of subjectivity and distortion – which incidentally, Buber himself has been the first to admit – Buber would seem to have coped with these with extraordinary success. His treatment of Hasidism shows him to be capable of practicing the emphatic openness which he preaches."[26]

---

[24] *Ibid.*, pp. 19–30.

[25] Ernst Simon, 'From Dialogue to Peace. Some Consequences of Martin Buber's Philosophy', *Jerusalem Post*, 18th June 1965.

[26] Emil L. Fackenheim, 'Two Types of Reform. Reflections Occasioned by Hasidism', *Central Conferences of American Rabbis*, 72nd Annual Convention, 20th to 24th June 1961, New York, vol. LXXI, ed. by Sidney Regner, New York 1962, p. 216.

According to Fackenheim, it was the fundamental aim of *Hasidism* to reopen the channels clogged by Orthodox authority so that the interrupted life between God and Israel might be resumed. The uniqueness of *Hasidism* lies in the passion with which it sought to storm the heavens, seeking for the God of the here and now, the God of Israel. Fackenheim concluded his talk on 'Two Types of Reform. Reflections Occasioned by Hasidism' with the question of whether such an effort is a concrete possibility of modern life and compatible with modern thought. As an answer, he pointed to Buber's "narrow ridge" upon which we must walk ourselves, not imitating the *Hasidim*, which would be a misunderstanding of *Hasidism* itself, but walking as they walked – not in a world of others but in their own.

> "Man comes to worship feeling instead of God; the symbol, not what it stands for; Jewish genius, not Him whose presence stimulates it. There is, to be sure, an idolatrous emotionalism which, born of impatient need, mistakes projected desires for God. But there is also an idolatry of pseudo-sophistication which, denying man's actual need of the present God, treats the human as if it were divine. Between these two abysses the liberal Jew of today must walk, in sophisticated simplicity, on a narrow ridge . . . Those who walk on the ridge, open to the future, will find strength in the Hasidic examples."[27]

In 1966, at the annual Eranos Conference in Switzerland, Scholem broadened his attack on Buber into a full-scale polemic against Buber's treatment of Judaism. As Ernst Simon remarked in his article 'Buber and Scholem', precisely that which makes Scholem a great scholar is lacking in this critique: the fruitful synthesis between empathy and historical analysis, between spiritual involvement and critical detachment.[28] At the same time passages in this long essay give us insight into layers of the Buber-Scholem controversy that lie deeper than questions of scholarship. The first of these reads, in fact, like a personal confession:

> "No one who has known Buber could escape the strong beams that radiated from him and that made controversy with him doubly passionate. To enter into controversy with Buber meant to be thrown back and forth between admiration and rejection, between the readiness to hear his message and the disappointment over this message and the impossibility of realising it."[29]

Buber sought influence over Jewish youth, wrote Scholem, and it belonged to Buber's bitterest experiences that in the years of the First World War and the years just before and during Hitler's regime this meeting ended in deep estrangement. "One could equally well say that it belonged to the bitterest experiences of these youths that Buber never drew forth the expected consequences of his message."

> "Buber, a highly multifaceted and developed man, had called these youths to go to the land of Israel and undertake out of a creative impulse the formation of the new life that should grow there. They never forgave him that he did not go with them when the hour struck . . . Buber, whose conversations, speeches, and summons centred around the word 'realisation' had

---

[27] *Ibid.*, pp. 222f.
[28] Ernst Simon, 'Scholem und Buber', *Neue Zürcher Zeitung*, 11th June 1967, 'Literatur und Kunst'.
[29] Gershom Scholem, 'Martin Buber's Auffassung des Judentums' in *Schöpfung und Gestaltung. Eranos Jahrbuch*, XXXV (1966), ed. by Adolf Portmann, Zürich 1967, p. 10, my translation.

himself, so it seemed to the disappointed ones, refused it . . . he had made another personal decision, chosen another medium of realisation."[30]

The pathos in this personal statement appears even stronger if we know how hard Scholem himself worked during the years between 1927 and 1938 to help bring Buber to Israel, even if Buber's own eagerness to come during all that time belies what, to the uninformed reader, Scholem might seem to be implying by his statements.

Scholem recognised Buber's creative transformation of Judaism:

"From the hour when as a twenty-year-old he attached himself to the just emerging movement of Zionism to the end of his days he tirelessly sharpened, preserved, and developed the meaning of the creative transformation in the phenomena closest to his heart. The provocation in his conception of Judaism and its history . . . was unmistakable, and Buber, to whom neither self-awareness nor courage can be denied, was ready to pay the price for this . . . new vision."

When Scholem visited Buber in Germany in 1932 he said to him: "Why do you not write finally a presentation of the theology of *Hasidism*?" "I intend to do that" he answered, "but only after you have written a book on the *Kabbalah*." "Is that a promise?" asked Scholem. "Perhaps", Buber replied. "I did not understand at that time he could not have any scientific attitude toward this theme", commented Scholem. In 1943, two years after the appearance of Scholem's book on the *Kabbalah*, he went to Buber to lay before him the fundamental criticisms of Buber's interpretation of *Hasidism* which Scholem had formed during long years of continuous study of the texts. Buber listened with great earnestness and tension.

"When I had finished, he was silent for a long time. Then he said slowly and with emphasis on every word: 'If what you have said be true, dear Scholem, then I have occupied myself with *Hasidism* for forty years wholly in vain, for then it would indeed not at all *interest* me.' It was the last conversation that I had with Buber over the factual problems of *Hasidism*. It closed speech for me. I understood that there was nothing more to say."[31]

That the Buber-Scholem controversy has lost none of its relevance in the intervening years is suggested by the Yale literary critic Harold Bloom's article on my book *Martin Buber's Life and Work. The Early Years – 1878–1923* in a 1982 issue of *The New Republic*. Although the Buber-Scholem controversy itself does not appear until the third volume of my biography, *The Later Years*, Bloom entitles his article 'From Buber to Scholem' and devotes much of the article to Scholem's critique of Buber. "Buber died in 1965, without forgiving Scholem", Bloom adds in comment after quoting one such critique. This statement is pure fiction on Bloom's part. Buber was not even angry with Scholem. In fact, he was proud of him. After one public criticism by Scholem, Buber said privately to Ernst Simon: "He may say of me what he likes. Who else has a former disciple who has founded a whole new field of scholarship!" Scholem was indeed a great scholar of Jewish gnosticism. But he offered no gnostic teaching or philosophy in

[30]*Ibid.*, pp. 10–13, my translation.
[31]*Ibid.*, pp. 47f., my translation. The total essay extends from p. 9 to p. 55. It is published in English translation under the title 'Martin Buber's Conception of Judaism', in Gershom Scholem, *On Jews and Judaism in Crisis*, ed. by Werner J. Dannhauser, New York 1976, pp. 126–171.

his own name, as Bloom seems to imply in his article. After confessing how he and other young people turned from normative Judaism to Buber in the aftermath of the Holocaust, Bloom recounts: "With many others, I made the transition from Buber to Scholem in the early 1960s. Scholem's Jewish Gnosticism is both more securely founded in Jewish spiritual history and more adequate to a post-Holocaust Jewry than Buber's earlier version of a Jewish religious anarchism has proved to be."[32]

Bloom's claim is an interesting and significant statement of his own point of view and doubtless that of others who feel the need of a gnostic and/or apocalyptic reply to Holocaust times. But whether in the long or even the short run this judgement can stand in American, Jewish, and world history is quite another question. It is precisely this question that has led me to present in my three volumes of Martin Buber's life and work not just a synthesis of Buber's intellectual position to set against others but a "dialography" in which I show Buber's thought as growing out of the events and meetings of his own life, including the Holocaust and even his confrontation with Gershom Scholem.

"If Scholem was Joshua, Buber was Moses", Walter Kaufmann remarked concerning the Buber-Scholem controversy in a speech at the 1978 Buber Centennial Conferences in Israel and America.[33] The value of Scholem's scholarly contributions for the generations to come is incontestable. But if anything in this analogy could be regarded by Jew and non-Jew alike as "the promised Land", it would not be Scholem's destruction of the Jericho-walls of all previous scholarship on the *Kabbalah* but Buber's *Tales of the Hasidim, For the Sake of Heaven*, and *The Way of Man*.

A number of years ago, a group of African students met Abraham Joshua Heschel and Heschel's own student of twenty years before, Rabbi Arnold Jacob Wolf, then Hillel Chaplain at Yale University. "How should we begin the study of *Hasidism*?" they asked Heschel. Forgetting the talmudic dictum that one should not speak in the presence of one's teacher, Wolf responded: "We now have Scholem in English. Read him." But Abraham Heschel, the direct descendent of a long line of distinguished *zaddikim* reaching back to the Maggid of Mezritch and a scholar whose knowledge and understanding of the theoretical teachings of *Hasidism* was second to none, said: "No, if you want to know *Hasidism* as it was, begin with Buber."[34]

[32]Harold Bloom, 'From Buber to Scholem. Martin Buber's Life and Work. The Early Years 1878–1923 by Maurice Friedman,' *The New Republic*, 19th and 26th July 1982, pp. 43–45. See my reply, 'Bloom's Buber', *The New Republic*, 11th October 1982, pp. 4, 39.
[33]Walter Kaufmann, 'Buber's Triumphs and Failures', in *Martin Buber. A Centenary Volume* (in Hebrew), ed. by Jochanan Bloch, Haim Gordon, and Menahem Dorman, Tel-Aviv 1981, pp. 37–40; 'Bubers Fehlschläge und sein Triumph', in Jochanan Bloch and Haim Gordon (eds.), *Martin Buber. Bilanz seines Denkens*, Freiburg 1983, pp. 22–39. See also *Martin Buber. A Centenary Volume*, edited by Haim Gordon and Jochanan Bloch, New York 1984, pp. 15f., for the English version of Kaufmann's statement. Cf. Maurice Friedman, 'Walter Kaufmann's Mismeeting with Martin Buber', *Judaism*, XXXI, No. 2 (Spring 1982), pp. 229–239.
[34]Arnold Jacob Wolf, 'The Social Challenge Buber Has Left Us', an address at the conference 'Humanizing Society. A Celebration of the Centennial of the Birth of Martin Buber', sponsored by Fordham University and Hebrew Union College-Jewish Institute of Religion, New York City, 9th February 1978.

The controversy between Scholem and Buber over the interpretation of *Hasidism* exemplifies what Buber has called "the cruel antitheticalness of existence itself": a situation in which – just because each is as he is – different life-stances, instead of contributing to dialogue, are crystallised into fixed opposition. If "every conversation that takes place for the sake of heaven endures", as the *Pirke Avot*, the talmudic "sayings of the fathers", avers, then this controversy, too, will endure in its profound two-sidedness and not, as many people suppose today, with a decision *for* Scholem and *against* Buber.

Post-War Publications on German Jewry

A Selected Bibliography of Books and Articles 1987

Compiled by
IRMGARD FOERG and ANNETTE PRINGLE

Leo Baeck Institute
4 Devonshire Street
London W.1.

CONTENTS

BIBLIOGRAPHY 1987

I. HISTORY

A. General

23866. ADLER, H. G.: *Die Juden in Deutschland; von der Aufklärung bis zum Nationalsozialismus.* München: Piper, 1987. 177 pp. (Serie Piper, Bd. 766.) [First publ. in 1960; for English transl. see No. 7604/YB XV.]

23867. BAUTZ, FRANZ J., ed.: *Geschichte der Juden von der biblischen Zeit bis zur Gegenwart.* Orig.-Ausg., 2., durchgesehene Aufl. München: Beck, 1987. 247 pp., 13 maps. (Beck'sche Reihe, 268.) [Incl.: Der preussisch-deutsche Weg der Judenemanzipation (Walter Grab, 140–164). Antisemitismus, Zionismus und Staat Israel (Hermann Greive, 165–183).]

—— BERING, DIETZ: *Der Name als Stigma; Antisemitismus im deutschen Alltag.* [See No. 24811.]

23868. BIALE, DAVID: *Power and powerlessness in Jewish history.* New York: Schocken, 1987. 256 pp. [Covers also the role of Court Jews, and Jewish responses to absolutism, enlightenment, modern nationalism.]

23869. BREUER, MORDECHAI: *Jüdische Orthodoxie im Deutschen Reich 1871–1918; Sozialgeschichte einer religiösen Minderheit.* Eine Veröffentlichung des Leo Baeck Instituts. Frankfurt am Main: Jüdischer Verlag bei Athenäum, 1986. [For details and contents see No. 22901/YB XXXII.] *Selected reviews*: Zur Geschichte der Neo-Orthodoxie (Yizhak Ahren) [in]: 'Allgemeine', Nr. 42/52–53, Bonn, 25. Dez. 1987/1. Jan. 1988, p. 15. Besprechung (Kurt Gräubig) [in]: deutschland-berichte, Jg. 24, Nr. 3, Bonn, März 1988, pp. 31–32. On the ways of German orthodoxy in the modern period: an examination of Prof. Mordechai Breuer's book [in Hebrew, title transl.] (Yitzchak Brom) [in]: Ha-Ma'yan, Vol. 28, No. 2, Jerusalem, Teveth [= Dec.] 1987, pp. 1–9. Besprechung (T. Rahe) [in]: Judaica, Jg. 43, H. 3, Basel, Sept. 1987, pp. 190–191. Das orthodoxe Judentum im deutschen Kaiserreich (Esriel Hildesheimer) [in]: MB, Jg. 56, No. 32, Tel-Aviv, Jan. 1988, p. 5.

23870. CHAZAN, ROBERT: *European Jewry and the First Crusade.* Berkeley: Univ. of California Press, 1987. IX, 380 pp., bibl. (357–367). [An analysis of how the call to the First Crusade in 1095 resulted in a series of violent assaults on major Jewish communities in the Rhineland.]

23871. COHEN, DANIEL J.: *German Jewry's struggle against expulsion in 1545: R. Joselmann of Rosheim and the appeal of Cardinal [Alessandro] Farnese.* [In Hebrew, with English summary]. [In]: Israel and the nations [see No. 23886]. Jerusalem, 1987. Pp. 43–51.

23872. CRAIG, GORDON A.: *Frederick the Great and Moses Mendelssohn: thoughts on Jewish emancipation.* [In]: LBI Year Book XXXII, London, 1987. Pp. 3–19, footnotes.

23873. *Das Deutsche Judentum und der Liberalismus = German Jewry and Liberalism.* Dokumentation eines internationalen Seminars der Friedrich-Naumann-Stiftung in Zusammenarbeit mit dem Leo Baeck Institute, London. (Bearb.: Beate-Carola Padtberg.) Sankt Augustin: Comdok, 1986. 246 pp., footnotes, index of names (231–239). (Schriften der Friedrich-Naumann-Stiftung: Liberale Texte.) [The first of a series of seminars organised by the Leo Baeck Institute London, together with German foundations and scholars. The papers presented in this volume are in German or English with summaries in the complementary language and each followed by a report on the ensuing discussion. Cont.: Vorwort = Foreword (Ralf Dahrendorf, 7–10). Redaktionelle Anmerkungen = Editor's notes (Beate-Carola Padtberg, 11–14). Einleitung: Deutsches Judentum und Liberalismus = Introduction: German Jewry and Liberalism (Werner E. Mosse, 15–27). Liberalismus und deutsches Bürgertum (Rudolf Vierhaus, 28–43). The historical context of Dohm's treatise on the Jews (Robert Liberles, 44–69). The theologico-political basis of liberal Christian-Jewish relations in modernity (Steven Schwarzschild, 70–95). Das Verhältnis von liberaler Theologie und Judentum um die Jahrhundertwende (Trutz Rendtorff, 96–112). The political and social impact of Liberalism upon Jewish Bürgertum in the 19th century (Henry Wassermann, 113–123, bibl. p. 119). Jews and the crisis of German Liberalism (Peter Pulzer, 124–141). Jüdische Unternehmer zwischen wirtschaftsliberalem Laissez-faire, sozialliberalem Emanzipationsdenken und industriekonservativer Sammlungsbewegung (Hans Dieter Hellige, 142–172).

Deutsche Juden und der Liberalismus: ein Rückblick (George L. Mosse, 173–194; for expanded version in English see No. 23895). Liberale Fragen (Fritz Schatten, 195–210). Podiumsdiskussion (211–220). Plenumsdiskussion (221–227).] [Seminar was held in Königswinter, May 21–23, 1986; for reports see No. 22905/YB XXXII.]

23874. *Deutsche – Polen – Juden: ihre Beziehungen von den Anfängen bis ins 20. Jahrhundert.* Beiträge zu einer Tagung. Hrsg. von Stefi Jersch-Wenzel. Berlin: Colloquium, 1987. XVI, 307 pp., map. footnotes. (Einzelveröffentlichungen der Historischen Kommission zu Berlin, Bd. 58.) [Incl.: Probleme und Aufgaben der Beziehungsgeschichte zwischen Deutschen, Polen und Juden (Wolfgang Wippermann, 1–48). Zum Problem der Juden in der frühen deutschrechtlichen Stadt (Winfried Schich, 65–102). Entstehung, Wachstum und Niedergang der deutschen Siedlungen zwischen Polen und Preussen vom 17.–19. Jahrhundert (Felix Escher, 141–158). See also Nos. 23874, 24308, 24364.]

23875. *Deutsches Judentum in Krieg und Revolution 1916–1923.* Ein Sammelband hrsg. von Werner E. Mosse unter Mitwirkung von Arnold Paucker. Tübingen: Mohr, 1971. [See No. 9225/YB XVII.] *Review*: Besprechung (Wilhelm Schreckenberg) [in]: Geschichte in Wissenschaft und Unterricht, Jg. 37, H. 8, Seelze, Aug. 1986, pp. 513–514.

23876. *Deutsch-jüdische Geschichte; zur Entwicklung der historischen Forschung und Darstellung seit 1945: Ergebnisse, Kritik, Aufgaben.* Symposium auf Schloss Ringberg (Bayern), veranstaltet vom Leo Baeck Institute London und vom Max-Planck-Institut Göttingen vom 25.–28. Nov. 1987. [Papers may be published in the 'Schriftenreihe wissenschaftlicher Abhandlungen des Leo Baeck Instituts' or in the LBI Year Book. For report on this symposium see: Wissenschaft, die nicht 'normal' sein kann: die deutsch-jüdische Geschichtsschreibung – zu einer Tagung mit dem Leo-Baeck-Institut (Barbara Suchy) [in]: Süddeutsche Zeitung, Nr. 300, München, Silvester 1987, p. 38.]

23877. FALK, GERHARD/BULLOUGH, VERN: *Achievement among German Jews born during the years 1785–1885.* [In]: The Mankind Quarterly, Vol. 27, No. 3, Washington, D.C., 1987. Pp. 337–365.

23878. FOSTER, JOHN: *The Jewish entrepreneur and the family.* [In]: Kwiet, Konrad, ed.: From the emancipation to the Holocaust [see No. 23891]. Kensington, Australia, 1987. Pp. 17–26, notes. [Deals mainly with the families Fränkel and Pinkus, linen manufacturers in Neustadt, Upper Silesia.]

23879. GAY, PETER: *Freud, Jews and other Germans; masters and victims in modernist culture.* Oxford; New York: Oxford Univ. Press, 1987. 310 pp., illus. [Paperback edn. of No. 14996/YB XXIV; for German transl. and contents see No. 22009/YB XXXII.] [See also No. 24642.]

23880. *Germania Judaica. Bd. 3: 1350–1519. Teilband 1: Ortschaftsartikel Aach – Lychen.* Hrsg. von Arye Maimon in Zusammenarbeit mit Yacov Guggenheim im Auftrag der Hebr. Univ. in Jerusalem. Tübingen: Mohr, 1987. XXX, 769 pp., bibl. [Historical encyclopaedia of German Jewry; two more parts will complete this third volume which is based also on hitherto unpubl. and unknown source material. For preceding vols. *1: Von den ältesten Zeiten bis 1238* & *2: Von 1238 bis zur Mitte des 14. Jahrhunderts* which appeared as publications of the Leo Baeck Institute, see Nos. 3676/YB IX & 6893/YB XIV. Cf.: Vom Schicksal eines jüdisch-historischen Werkes (E. G. Lowenthal) [in]: 'Allgemeine', Nr. 42/24–25, Bonn, 12./19. Juni 1987, p. 7. Besprechung (Kurt Gräubig) [in]: deutschland-berichte, Jg. 24, Nr. 2, Bonn, Feb. 1988, p. 18. 'Du sprichst von Zeiten, die vergangen sind': Arye Maimon und die 'Germania Judaica' (Eli Rothschild) [in]: MB, Jg. 55, Nr. 30, Tel-Aviv, Nov. 1987, p. 6 (Arye Maimon, orig. Herbert Fischer, born 1903 in Breslau, contributor to 'Germania Judaica' from its first volume onward).]

23881. GRAUS, FRANTIŠEK: *Pest – Geissler – Judenmorde; das 14. Jahrhundert als Krisenzeit.* Göttingen: Vandenhoeck & Ruprecht, 1987. 608 pp. (Veröffentlichungen des Max-Planck-Instituts für Geschichte, 86.) [Incl. section: Die Juden und die Pogromwelle von 1348–1350.]

23882. HALEVI, ILAN: *A history of the Jews, ancient and modern.* Transl. from the French. London: Zed Books, 1987. 272 pp. [Also deals with German Jewry. Cf.: The dream and the holocaust (Michael Ignatieff) [in]: The Observer, London, March 22, 1987.]

23883. HERZIG, ARNO: *Juden und Judentum in der sozialgeschichtlichen Forschung.* [In]: Sozialgeschichte in Deutschland, hrsg. von Wolfgang Schieder und Volker Sellin, Bd. 4: Soziale Gruppen in der Geschichte. Göttingen: Vandenhoeck & Ruprecht, 1987. (Kleine Vandenhoeck-Reihe, Bd. 1531.) Pp. 108–132, notes (126–131), bibl. (131–132). [Refers, a.o., to the Leo Baeck Institute and its relevant publications.]

23884. ILSAR, YEHIEL: *Die Reichspräsidentenwahl 1932.* [In]: Bulletin des LBI, 78, Frankfurt am Main, 1987. Pp. 35–58, notes (56–57). [Study using hitherto unpublished material from the estate of Hermann Badt, July 13, 1887 Breslau – Sept. 1946 Jerusalem, lawyer, Prussian Ministerialdirektor, Zionist, emigrated to Palestine in 1933.]

23885. *Informationen zur modernen Stadtgeschichte, 1987, H.1* [with the issue title]: *Themenschwerpunkt: Juden und Stadt.* Berlin: Deutsches Institut für Urbanistik, 1987. 77 pp., bibl. (56–77). [Mimeog.] [Incl.: Juden als Stadtbewohner (Stefi Jersch-Wenzel, 1–5). Probleme der heutigen Lokal- und Regionalforschung zur Geschichte der deutschen Juden (Monika Richarz, 9–12). [Das Dokumentationszentrum, die Mahn- und Gedenkstätte] Alte Synagoge Essen (Angela Genger, 19–22). Further contributions are listed according to subject.]

23886. *Israel and the nations; essays presented in honor of Shmuel Ettinger.* [In Hebrew, with English summaries; and English section]. Ed. board: Shmuel Almog [et al.]. Jerusalem: The Historical Society of Israel and the Zalman Shazar Center for Jewish History, 1987. 375 (Hebrew), CXLVI (English) pp., footnotes, bibl. Shmuel Ettinger (361–375). [Contributions pertinent to German Jewry are listed according to subject. For complementary jubilee volume see No. 23913.]

23887. JOHNSON, PAUL: *A history of the Jews.* New York: Harper & Row; London: Weidenfeld & Nicolson, 1987. 644 pp., notes. [Covers also German-Jewish history. Cf.: A question of influence (Todd Endelman) [in]: TLS, London, June 26, 1987.]

23888. *Judaism and Christianity under the impact of National Socialism, 1919–1945.* Ed. by Otto Dov Kulka & Paul R. Mendes-Flohr. Jerusalem: The Historical Society of Israel and The Zalman Shazar Center for Jewish History, 1987. 558 pp., footnotes, index (539 ff.). [Cont. the sections: *The historical background* (pp. 25–34; cont.: Christian-Jewish antagonism on the eve of the modern era (Jacob Katz, 27–34). *Secularization of an historical antagonism* (35–96; cont.: The secular roots of modern antisemitism (Shmuel Ettinger, 37–62). Aspects of consecration of politics in the Nazi era (Uriel Tal, 63–96). *Christianity, Judaism and the rise of National Socialism in the Weimar period* (97–179; cont.; Ambivalent dialogue: Jewish-Christian theological encounter in the Weimar Republic (Paul R. Mendes-Flohr, 99–132). The relationship between Protestant theology and Jewish studies during the Weimar Republic (Leonore Siegele-Wenschkewitz, 133–150). German Catholicism's attitude towards the Jews in the Weimar Republic (Rudolf Lill, 151–168). Between Christian anti-Judaism and National Socialist antisemitism: the case of German Catholicism (Hermann Greive, 169–179). *The Churches and the Jews in the Third Reich* (181–268; cont.: Judaism and Christianity in the ideology and politics of National Socialism (Klaus Scholder, 183–196). German Catholicism and the Jews: 1933–1945 (Konrad Repgen, 197–226). German Protestantism and the Jews in the Third Reich (Richard Gutteridge, 227–249). Popular Christian attitudes in the Third Reich to National Socialist policies towards the Jews (Otto Dov Kulka, 251–268). *The Churches and the Jews in Western and Central Europe* (269–378; incl.: Austrian Catholics and the Jews (Erika Weinzierl, 283–304). *The Churches and the Jews in Eastern Europe* (379–432; incl.: The Churches and the 'Final Solution' in Slovakia [and]: The Churches and the 'Final Solution of the Jewish Problem' in Hungary (Livia Rothkirchen, 413–422; 423–431. *The Vatican, the World Council of Churches and the Nazi persecution of the Jews* (433–470; incl.: Catholicism and the Jews during the Nazi period and after (John S. Conway, 435–452). *The Holocaust and contemporary Jewish-Christian encounter* (471–536; incl.: The Holocaust and Christian theology: an interpretation of the problem (Arthur A. Cohen, 473–498). Christian antisemitism and the Holocaust (Franklin H. Littell, 513–530).]

23889. *Die Juden im Nationalsozialistischen Deutschland = The Jews in Nazi Germany 1933–1943.* Hrsg. von Arnold Paucker mit Sylvia Gilchrist und Barbara Suchy. Tübingen: Mohr, 1986. XXIV, 426 pp. (Schriftenreihe wissenschaftlicher Abhandlungen des Leo Baeck Instituts, 45.) [For details and contents see No. 22913/YB XXXII.] *Reviews* (selection, continued): Review (Robert Gellately) [in]: Canadian Journal of History, Vol. 23, No. 1, Saskatoon, Sask., Apr. 1988, pp. 143–145. Von der Emanzipation zum Holocaust: Neuerscheinungen (Heribert Seifert) [in]: Deutsches Allgemeines Sonntagsblatt, Nr. 43, Hamburg, 1. Nov. 1987, p. 14. Besprechung (Kurt Gräubig) [in]: deutschland-berichte, Jg. 23, Nr. 11, Bonn, Nov. 1987, p. 28. Besprechung (ekz-Informationsdienst, 24, Reutlingen, 25. Juli 1987. Das Ende der Emanzipation (Karlheinz Dederke) [in]: Frankfurter Allgemeine Zeitung, 29. Mai 1987, p. 11. Besprechung (Ludger Heid) [in]: Das Historisch-Politische Buch, Jg. 35, H. 1, Göttingen, 1987, pp. 19–20. Besprechung (Dankwart Kluge) [in]: Das Politische Buch, 45/46, Coburg, 1987, pp. 2–3. Die Täuschung des Zugehörigkeitsgefühls (Christine Brink) [in]: Süddeutsche Zeitung, München, 9. Juni 1987. Review [in Spanish] (A. Prieto) [in]: Studia Monastica, 29, No. 1, Barcelona, 1987, pp. 196–197. Wie mit der Entrechtung die Illusionen zerbrachen (Peter Dittmar) [in]: Die Welt, Nr. 252, Hamburg, 29. Okt. 1987, p. 9.

23890. KATZ, JACOB: *Aus dem Ghetto in die bürgerliche Gesellschaft: jüdische Emanzipation 1770–1870.* Frankfurt am Main: Jüdischer Verlag bei Athenäum, 1986. [See No. 22917/YB XXXII.] *Reviews* (selection): Besprechung (Kurt Gräubig) [in]: deutschland-berichte, Jg. 23, Nr. 12, Bonn, Dez. 1987, p. 17. Aus dem Ghetto – aber wohin? (Ingrid Steiger-Schumann) [in]: NZZ, Nr. 202, Zürich, 2. Sept. 1987, p. 30. Jüdische Emanzipation (Alwin Müller-Jerina) [in]: Tribüne, Jg. 26, H. 104, Frankfurt am Main, 1987, p. 214.

23891. KWIET, KONRAD, ed.: *From the emancipation to the Holocaust.* Essays on Jewish literature and history in Central Europe. Kensington, Australia: The Univ. of New South Wales, Faculty of Arts, 1987. [IX], 189 pp., notes. (Kensington studies in humanities and social sciences.) [Cont. (titles condensed, listed fully according to subject): Introduction (Bernd Hüppauf/ Konrad Kwiet, V–IX). Anti-Semitism in Bremen (Dieter K. Buse, 1–16). The Jewish entrepreneur and the family (John Foster, 17–26). Walther Rathenau (Ernst Schulin, 27– 44). The 'Reichskristallnacht' (Martin Broszat, 45–62). Anti-Jewish politics and the implementation of the Holocaust (Hans Mommsen, 63–78). The Eastern Jews and their language (Hans-Peter Bayerdörfer, 81–101). 'I travelled to the Jews': encounters with Eastern Jews (Bernd Hüppauf, 103–126). Jews and Czechs in Prague (Pavel Petr, 127– 135). Theology and history: the example of Benjamin and Scholem (Rolf-Peter Janz, 137– 144). The 'J-Curve': the identity crisis of writers of Jewish descent (John Milfull, 147–154). The German-Jewish emigration and the historian's craft (Kathleen Joy Melhuish, 155– 165). After Auschwitz: the issue of Jewish 'Displaced Persons', 1945–46 (Ian J. Bickerton, 167–179). Vienna 1984 (George Shipp, 181–186).]

23892. LOWENTHAL, ERNST G.: *Die historische Lücke; Betrachtungen zur neueren deutsch-jüdischen Historiographie.* Tübingen: Mohr, 1987. 47 pp., bibl. references. [Protests the tendency of historiography today to neglect the emancipatory development of German-Jewish relations, especially during the period 1880–1930. Revised and enlarged version of a lecture which the author delivered at the Univ. of Tübingen as recipient of the Dr.-Leopold-Lucas-Preis 1986; book incl. also the eulogy on this occasion (pp. 40–44) and chap. 'Der Lucas-Preis' (45–47). Cf.: Besprechung (Boike Jacobs) [in]: 'Allgemeine', Nr. 43/9, Bonn, 4. März 1987, p. 7. Besprechung (Jürgen Wetzel) [in]: Mitteilungen des Vereins für die Geschichte Berlins, Jg. 83, H. 4, Berlin, Okt. 1987, pp. 587–588.]

—— McKALE, DONALD: *From Weimar to Nazism.* [See No. 24325.]

23893. MICHAEL, REUVEN: *Die antijudaistische Tendenz in Christian Wilhelm Dohms Buch Über die bürgerliche Verbesserung der Juden.* [In]: Bulletin des LBI, 77, Frankfurt am Main, 1987. Pp. 11–48, notes (45–48).

23894. *Mittelalter-Rezeption.* Ein Symposion, 1983. Hrsg. von Peter Wapnewski. Stuttgart: Metzler, 1986. 645 pp. [Also on Jews in Germany during the Middle Ages. Cf.: Auf spezieller Spurensuche (Wolfgang Boeckh) [in]: Tribüne, Jg. 26, H. 102, Frankfurt am Main, 1987, pp. 198 & 200.]

23895. MOSSE, GEORGE L.: *German Jews and Liberalism in retrospect.* Introduction to [Leo Baeck Institute] Year Book XXXII. [In]: LBI Year Book XXXII, London, 1987. Pp. XIII– XXV, footnotes, port. [Revised and expanded version of a paper delivered in German at the seminar *Das deutsche Judentum und der Liberalismus* in Königswinter organised jointly by the Leo Baeck Institute London and the Friedrich-Naumann-Stiftung, see pp. 173–194 in No. 23873.]

23896. MOSSE, WERNER E.: *Jews in the German economy; the German-Jewish economic élite 1820–1935.* Oxford: Clarendon Press, 1987. VIII, 420 pp., index (411–420), bibl. (406–409). [Study of German-Jewish bankers, merchants, and industrialists and their activities, assesses the nature of their contribution to the German economic development.]

23897. MÜLLER, ALWIN: *'So lange die Juden nicht frei sind, sind wir selbst nicht frei': die Diskussion um die Judenemanzipation auf den Rheinischen Provinziallandtagen und dem ersten Vereinigten Preussischen Landtag.* [In]: Geschichte in Köln; studentische Zeitschrift am Historischen Seminar, H. 17, Köln, 1985. Pp. 39–74.

23898. *Pardès, 5/1987* [with the issue title]: *Judéité et germanité.* Paris: J.-C. Lattes, 1987. 1 issue. [Cont.: Germanité et judéité (Hermann Cohen, trad. et présenté par Marc B. de Launay). Juifs allemands et Ostjuden (Paul Mendes-Flohr). Un héraut de l'antisémitisme dans l'Allemagne du XIXe siècle (Helmut Berding). Les juifs d'Allemagne à l'époque de l'industrialisation (Avraham Barkai). Réflexions sur les études juives (Gershom Scholem, trad. et présenté par Bernard Dupuy). Les traductions hébraïques du moyen âge (Moritz Steinschneider, présenté par Dominque Bourel). Ludwig Marcus, 1798–1843 (Michel Espagne). Un poème en yiddish ancien (Jean Baumgarten). Judéité et germanité, l'impossible symbiose (D. Azuelos). Fassbinder ou l'ambiguïté (A. Dieckhoff).]

23899. RÖHL, JOHN C. G.: *Kaiser, Hof und Staat: Wilhelm II und die deutsche Politik.* München: Beck, 1987. 262 pp. [Also on the German Emperor's attitude toward Jews and his relations with individual Jews. Cf.: The Kaiser and the Kritik (Gordon A. Craig) [in]: The New York Review of Books, Feb. 18, 1988, pp. 17–18.]

23900. RÜRUP, REINHARD: *Emanzipation und Antisemitismus; Studien zur Judenfrage der bürgerlichen Gesellschaft.* Frankfurt am Main: Fischer, 1987. 268 pp., notes, bibl. (237–262). (Fischer-Taschenbücher, 4385.) [Paperback edn. of No. 12650/YB XXI. Incl.: Die Emanzipation der Juden in Baden.]

23901. RÜRUP, REINHARD: *Emanzipationsgeschichte und Antisemitismusforschung: zur Überwindung antisemitischer Vorurteile.* [In]: Antisemitismus und jüdische Geschichte [see No. 24806]. Berlin, 1987. Pp. 467–478, footnotes.

23902. SCHILLING, DIEBOLD: *Luzerner Chronik des Diebold Schilling 1513.* Faksimile-Ausg. der Handschrift S.23 fol. in der Zentralbibliothek Luzern. Hrsg. von A. Schmid. Luzern: Faksimile Verl., 1981. X, 724 pp., illus. [Incl. descriptions and illustrations of persecutions of Jews in Augsburg, Diessenhofen and Sternberg because of blood libel and charges of desecration of the host.]

23903. SCHOEPS, JULIUS H.: *Über Juden und Deutsche.* Historisch-politische Betrachtung. Stuttgart: Burg-Verl., 1986. 220 pp. [Collection of essays and reviews previously publ. in periodicals and newspapers, covering German-Jewish history in the 19th and 20th centuries; also on the problem of Jewish identity in Germany today.] [See also No. 24768.]

23904. SCHULIN, ERNST: *Walther Rathenau: activities and fate of a German Jew in Wilhelmine times.* [In]: Kwiet, Konrad, ed.: From the emancipation to the Holocaust [see No. 23891]. Kensington, Australia, 1987. Pp. 27–44, notes (42–44).

23905. SORKIN, DAVID: *The genesis of the ideology of emancipation: 1806–1840.* [In]: LBI Year Book XXXII, London, 1987. Pp. 11–40, footnotes.

23906. SORKIN, DAVID: *The transformation of German Jewry, 1780–1840.* Oxford; New York; Oxford Univ. Press, 1987. 255 pp., notes (179–224), bibl. (225–246). (Studies in Jewish history.) [Cont. the two sections: 1. The ideology of emancipation (13 ff.). 2. The subculture (107–178). Cf.: The emancipation transformation (Marc Weiner) [in]: Midstream, Vol. 33, No. 10, New York, Dec. 1987, pp. 54–55.] [Some of the material in this book has previously appeared in a different form [in]: LBI Year Book XXXII (1987), see preceding entry; and [in]: The Jewish response to German culture, see No. 22489/YB XXXI.]

23907. STERN, FRITZ: *Dreams and delusions: the drama of German history.* New York: Knopf, 1987. 323 pp., notes (291–309). [Collection of essays and lectures composed over the past decade and delivered on various occasions. Incl.: Einstein's Germany (25–50). Fritz Haber: the scientist in power and in exile (51–76). The burden of success: reflections on German Jewry (97–114). Germany 1933: fifty years later (119–145). Cf.: After the Reich (Gordon A. Craig) [in]: The New York Review of Books, Oct. 8, 1987, pp. 38–39.]

23908. STERN, FRITZ: *Gold and iron: Bismarck, Bleichröder, and the building of the German Empire.* London; New York: Penguin, 1987. 644 pp. [Orig. publ. New York: Knopf, 1977; for later edns., German translation, and reviews see No. 17888/YB XXVII.]

23909. STERN, FRITZ: *Remembering the uprising.* Transl. from the German by Edna McCown and the author. Introd.: Timothy Garton Ash. [In]: The New York Review of Books, Dec. 3, 1987. Pp. 14–22. [On the 1987 anniversary of the June 17, 1953 uprising in East Germany, Fritz Stern, the Seth Low Professor of History at Columbia University, born in 1926 in Breslau, was invited to deliver the official speech to a ceremonial session of the Bundestag in Bonn.]

23910. STRAUSS, HERBERT A.: *Essays on the history, persecution and emigration of German Jews.* New York; München; London: Saur, 1987. 410 pp., bibl. (Jewish immigrants of the Nazi period in the USA, ed. by Herbert A. Strauss, Vol. 6.)

23911. TOURY, JACOB: *Zur Problematik der jüdischen Führungsschichten im deutschsprachigen Raum 1880–1933.* [In]: Tel Aviver Jahrbuch für deutsche Geschichte, Bd. 16, Gerlingen, 1987. Pp. 251–281, 15 tabs., footnotes.

23912. *Toward modernity: the European Jewish model.* Ed. by Jacob Katz. New Brunswick; Oxford: Transaction Books, 1987. VII, 279 pp., index (271–279), bibl. references. (Publication of the Leo Baeck Institute.) [Papers presented at a symposium organised by the Leo Baeck

Institute in Haifa in 1983. Cont.: Preface and introduction (Jacob Katz, 1–12). Immanent factors and external influences in the development of the Haskalah movement in Russia (Emanuel Etkes, 13–32). 'The heavenly city of Germany' and absolutism à la mode d'Autriche: the rise of the Haskalah in Galicia (Israel Bartal, 33–42). The modernization of Viennese Jewry: the impact of German culture in a multi-ethnic state (Robert S. Wistrich, 43–70). Caution's progress: the modernization of Jewish life in Prague, 1780–1830 (Hillel J. Kieval, 71–106). The historical experience of German Jewry and its impact on the Haskalah and reform in Hungary (Michael Silber, 107–158). The history of an estrangement between two Jewish communities: German and French Jewry during the nineteenth century (Michael Graetz, 159–170). The impact of German-Jewish modernization on Dutch Jewry (Joseph Michman, 171–188). Trieste and Berlin: the Italian role in the cultural politics of the Haskalah (Lois C. Dubin, 189–224). The Englishness of Jewish modernity in England (Todd M. Endelman, 225–246). German-Jewish identity in nineteenth-century America (Michael A. Meyer, 247–268).]

23913. *Transition and change in modern Jewish history; essays presented in honor of Shmuel Ettinger.* [In Hebrew, with English summaries; and English section]. Ed. board: Shmuel Almog [et al.]. Jerusalem: The Historical Society of Israel and the Zalman Shazar Center for Jewish History, 1987. 568 (Hebrew, CXXVII (English) pp., footnotes. [Essays relevant to German Jewry are listed according to subject.] [For complementary jubilee volume see No. 23886.]

23914. Varon, Benno Weiser: *Those formidable German Jews.* [In]: Midstream, Vol. 33, No. 4, New York, Apr. 1987. Pp. 42–46. [Author's impressions on viewing the travelling exhibition 'Jews in Germany under Prussian rule' (see Nos. 20813–20816/YB XXX).]

23915. Volkov, Shulamit: *Soziale Ursachen des Erfolges in der Wissenschaft: Juden im Kaiserreich.* [In]: Historische Zeitschrift, Bd. 245, H. 2, München, Okt. 1987. Pp. 315–342, notes. [Complete German version of a paper of which an abstract in English was publ. earlier, see pp. 179–185 in No. 22914/YB 32.]

23916. Wertheimer, Jack: *Unwelcome strangers: East European Jews in Imperial Germany.* Oxford; New York: Oxford Univ. Press, 1987. XI, 275 pp., statistical tabs. (184–201), notes (202–249), bibl. (250–267). (Studies in Jewish history.) [Cont. the sections: 1: The German State. 2: The East European Jews. 3: The Jewish community.] [Chapters of this book were previously publ. [in]: LBI Year Book XXVI (1981, pp. 23–46) [&]: XXVII (1982, pp. 187–215) [&] XXVIII (1983, pp. 329–349).]

Linguistics/Western Yiddish

——   Baumgarten, Jean: *Un poème en yiddish ancien.* [See in No. 23898.]
——   Bayerdörfer, Hans-Peter: *The Eastern Jews and their language.* [See No. 24530.]
23917. Birnbaum, Salomo A.: *Verleihung der Würde eines Ehrendoktors der Universität Trier an Professor Dr. Salomo A. Birnbaum, 4. Juni 1986.* (Hrsg. vom Dekan des Fachbereichs Sprach- und Literaturwissenschaften [Professor Dr. Walter Röll] im Auftrag des Präsidenten der Universität Trier.) Trier: Univ., [1987]. 26 pp., port. [Incl.: Ansprache und Laudatio (Walter Röll, 9–16). Ansprache (Salomo A. Birnbaum, 17–26). See also the English version of S. A. Birnbaum's 'Ansprache', publ. under the title *Institutum Ascenezicum* [in]: LBI Year Book XVII, London, 1972, pp. 243–249, footnotes.]

23918. Diekhoff, Johannes: *'Das verfrühte Schulenrufen': eine judendeutsche Auricher Posse aus dem Jahre 1902.* [In]: Ostfriesland, H. 3, Leer, 1986. Pp. 18–25, illus., scores, notes (23–25).

23919. Eichenbaum, Edzard/Byl, Jürgen: *Jekutiel Blitz, ein Sohn Wittmunds: er übersetzte als erster die Bibel ins Jiddische.* [In]: Ostfriesland, H. 3, Leer, 1986. Pp. 12–17, illus., notes (16–17). [Jekutiel ben Isaak Blitz, ca. 1634 Wittmund – ca. 1680 Amsterdam[?]; his transl. of the entire Bible into Yiddish appeared in Amsterdam 1676–1678.]

23920. Fuks, Leo: *The romance elements in Old Yiddish.* [In]: Language & Communication, Vol. 7, Supplement, Oxford, 1987. Pp. 23–25, notes.

23921. Katz, Dovid: *Grammar of the Yiddish language.* London: Duckworth, 1987. 290 pp. [Cf.: A double first (Frank Pomeranz) [in]: Jewish Book News & Reviews, Vol. 2, No. 2, London, Nov. 1987, pp. 2–3.]

23922. Klarberg, Manfred: *Aaron ben Samuel and his 'Lovely Prayerbook' revisited.* [In]: Internat. Journal of the Sociology of Languages, 67, Amsterdam 1987. Pp. 27–37, notes (35–36), bibl.

(36–37). [Aaron ben Samuel of Hergershausen, born 1665, author of 'Liblikhe tfile oder kreftige artsnay far gut un neshome', publ. 1709.]

23923. KLUGE, FRIEDRICH: *Rotwelsches Quellenbuch*. Photomechanischer Nachdr. der Ausg. Strassburg, Trübner, 1901, mit einem Nachwort von Helmut Henne und der Rezension von Alfred Götze (1901). Berlin; New York: de Gruyter, 1987. XVI, 519 pp. (Friedrich Kluge: Rotwelsch; Quellen und Wortschatz der Gaunersprache und der verwandten Geheimsprachen, Bd. 1 [orig. no more publ.].) [Hebrew and Yiddish elements were adopted by the German Gaunersprache Rotwelsch which is the root of numerous words and expressions in the German language today.]

23924. [MAITLIS, JACOB]: *Das Ma'assebuch; seine Entstehung und Quellengeschichte*. [Von] Jakob Meitlis. Zugleich Beitrag zur Einführung in die altjiddische Agada. Nachdr. der Ausg. Berlin, Mass, 1933. Mit einem Nachtrag des Verfassers. Hildesheim: Olms, 1987. XIV, 152 pp., illus., bibl. (149–152). [The Yiddish Ma'asse Bukh, first publ. in Basle in 1602.]

23925. *Origins of the Yiddish language*. Papers from the first annual Oxford Winter Symposium in the Yiddish language and literature, 15–17 Dec. 1985. Ed.: Dovid Katz. Oxford: Pergamon Press, 1987. 145 pp. (Winter Studies in Yiddish, Vol. 1.)

23926. STÖRIG, HANS JOACHIM: *Abenteuer Sprache*. Berlin: Langenscheidt, 1987. 398 pp., illus. [Incl. chap.: Jiddisch und Rotwelsch – und ein Blick auf die Zigeunersprache.]

23927. SÜSS, HERMANN: *Eine handschriftliche Abbreviaturenliste aus dem 18. Jahrhundert in der Stadtbibliothek von Bad Windsheim (Mittelfranken)*. [In]: Nachrichten für den jüdischen Bürger Fürths. Isr. Kultusgemeinde Fürth (Blumenstr. 31), Sept. 1987. Pp. 34–43, facsims. [Description of ms. 'Kurzer und gründlicher Unterricht, eine in Juden Teutscher Schreib Art verfasste Schrifft zu lesen und zu verstehen' by Friederich August Constans, a converted Jew, written about 1740.]

23928. THOMMEN, DIETER: *Das Surbtaler Jiddisch; Darstellung auf Grund der Aufnahme des Sprachatlasses der deutschen Schweiz*. Basel, Univ., Lic. Phil., 1987. IV, 76 pp.

23929. TIMM, ERIKA: *Graphische und phonische Struktur des Westjiddischen unter besonderer Berücksichtigung der Zeit um 1600*. Tübingen: Niemeyer, 1987. X, 598 pp. (Hermaea, N. F., Bd. 52.) Zugl.: Trier, Univ., Habil.-Schrift, 1985.

23930. WEXLER, PAUL: *Interdialectal translation as a reflection of lexical obsolescence and dialect distance: the West Yiddish Bible translation of 1679 in the 'Biblia Pentapla' (1711)*. [In]: Internat. Journal of the Sociology of Languages, 67, Amsterdam, 1987. Pp. 7–26, notes (21–23), bibl. (23–26).

23931. *Wunderparlich und seltsame Historien Til Eulen Spiegels*. Hrsg. von John A. Howard. Würzburg: Königshausen & Neumann, 1983. XIV, 246 pp. [An edition of the Yiddish 'Till Eulenspiegel' manuscript on which see also the previous studies: Arnold Paucker: *Yiddish versions of early German prose novels* [in]: The Journal of Jewish Studies, Vol. 10, No. 3–4, London, 1959, pp. 151–167 [&]: Arnold Paucker: *Das deutsche Volksbuch bei den Juden* [in]: Zeitschrift für Deutsche Philologie, Bd. 80, Nr. 3, Berlin, 1961, pp. 302–317. Cf.: Besprechung (Hermann-Josef Müller) [in]: Arbitrium, Jg. 5, München, 1987, pp. 262–267, footnotes (a critical review with corrections of the text and transcription of J. A. Howard).]

B. Communal and Regional History

1. Germany

—— GENERAL. *Germania Judaica. Bd. 3, Teilband 1*. [See No. 23880.]

23932. ALPEN. HUSCHKE, WOLFGANG: *Notizen aus dem Kirchenbuch von Alpen (Kreis Moers)*. (Personenstandsarchiv Brühl A 43 Bl. 158a.) [In]: Genealogie, Jg. 35, H. 9, (Bd. 18), Neustadt/Aisch, Sept. 1986. P. 279. [Entries from a church register, incl. data also for Jewish persons, 1791–1808.]

23933. ANSBACH. ROSENFELD, MOSCHE N.: *Ein Streifzug durch die jüdische Geschichte von Ansbach*. [And]: *Rabbiner Pinchas Kohn, der letzte Ansbacher Rabbiner*. [In]: Nachrichten für den jüdischen Bürger Fürths, Isr. Kultusgemeinde Fürth (Blumenstr. 31), Sept. 1987. Pp. 17–24, illus., facsims., bibl. [&]: 25–27, illus., port., facsims. [Pinchas Kohn, Feb. 27, 1867 Kleinerdlingen – 7. Tamus (= July 2), 1941 Jerusalem, wrote novels under the pseuds. Kopi and Sanon, emigrated in 1939 via Switzerland and England to Palestine.]

23934.   AUFSESS. Wolf, Gerhard Philipp: *Ländliches Judentum in christlichem Umfeld: zur Geschichte der Juden in Aufsess (19. Jahrhundert)*. [In]: Bericht des Historischen Vereins für die Pflege des ehemaligen Fürstbistums Bamberg, 121, Bamberg, 1985. Pp. 117–132. [See also pp. 51–55 in No. 23972.]

——   AUGSBURG. [See also Nos. 23902, 24565–24566.]

——   — Rosenfeld, Mosche N.: *Der jüdische Buchdruck in Augsburg*. [See No. 24483.]

23935.   BADEN. Hahn, Joachim: *Synagogen in Baden-Württemberg*. Mit einem Geleitwort von Dietmar Schlee. (Hrsg. vom Innenministerium des Landes Baden-Württemberg.) Stuttgart: Theiss, 1987. 127 pp., illus., bibl. (120–121). [History of the synagogues, 1300–1938.]

23936.   — Hahn, Joachim: *Zur Geschichte der Juden in Baden-Württemberg*. Bericht über eine Dokumentation. [In]: Informationen zur modernen Stadtgeschichte, H. 1, Berlin, 1987. Pp. 16–19.

——   — *Pinkas Hakehillot . . . Württemberg, Hohenzollern, Baden*. Ed. by Joseph Walk. [In Hebrew]. [See No. 24056.]

23937.   — Riff, Michael Anthony: *The government of Baden against antisemitism: political expediency or principle?* [In]: LBI Year Book XXXII, London, 1987. Pp. 119–134, footnotes. [Deals with the 1880s and 1890s.]

——   — Rürup, Reinhard: *Die Emanzipation der Juden in Baden*. [See in No. 23900.]

——   BAVARIA. [See also Nos. 23973, 24840.]

23938.   — Harris, James F.: *Bavarians and Jews in conflict in 1866: neighbours and enemies*. [In]: LBI Year Book XXXII, London, 1987. Pp. 103–117, footnotes. [Deals with antisemitic excesses in Wiesenfeld and Laudenbach, two small towns in Lower Franconia.]

23939.   — Wiesemann, Falk: *Zum Urbanisierungsprozess der Juden in Bayern*. [In]: Informationen zur modernen Stadtgeschichte, H. 1, Berlin, 1987. Pp. 29–32, bibl.

23940.   BECKUM. Krick, Hugo: *Geschichte und Schicksal der Juden zu Beckum*. Unter Mitarb. von Diethard Aschoff. Warendorf: Archiv des Kreises Warendorf, 1986. 160 pp., illus. (Quellen und Forschungen zur Geschichte des Kreises Warendorf, Bd. 16.) [Also on the Nazi period and post-war Jewish life.]

——   BERLIN. [See also Nos. 24597–24603.]

23941.   — *Berlin, Berlin: die Ausstellung zur Geschichte der Stadt*. Katalog. Hrsg. von Gottfried Korff und Reinhard Rürup. Berlin: Nicolai, 1987. 696 pp., illus., ports., index (666–692). [Exhibition, also on the history of the Jews in Berlin from the beginning to the Nazi period, especially in the sections: Juden, Hugenotten, Böhmen (catalogue pp. 102–112); Aufklärung und Emanzipation (113–125); Anfänge der Diktatur (529–542); 'Volksgemeinschaft' und Terror (543–560); Der 'totale Krieg' (561–584). Catalogue also refers passim to Jewish personalities and incl. essay: Berlin – Umrisse der Stadtgeschichte (Reinhard Rürup, 27–54), a historical survey of Berlin with reference to the contributions of Jews to the development of Berlin from the 18th to the beginning of the 20th century.]

23942.   — Buddensieg, Tilmann/Düwell, Kurt/Sembach, Klaus-Jürgen, eds.: *Wissenschaften in Berlin*. Drei Begleitbände zur Ausstellung 'Der Kongress denkt' vom 14. Juni- 1. Nov. 1987 in der wiedereröffneten Kongresshalle Berlin. Berlin: Mann, 1987. 3 vols. *Bd. 1: Objekte*. 317 pp. [Incl.: Fritz Haber (pp. 228–231). Magnus Hirschfeld (232–233). Exil (234–235).] *Bd. 2: Disziplinen*. 208 pp. [Cont. 33 contributions on the various scientific disciplines in Berlin, incl. also Jewish representative personalities.] *Bd. 3: Gedanken*. 208 pp., illus. [Incl.: Der Fall des Physikers Leo Arons (Stefan Wolff, 76–80). Vom jüdischen Beitrag zur Wissenschaft in Berlin (Ernst G. Lowenthal, 81–84). Albert Einstein (Jakob Szer, 85–89). Carl Einstein: Epochensignatur und Lebenspraxis (Klaus Siebenhaar, 94–97). Benjamins Berlin (Gary Smith, 98–102). 'Eine unparteiische Pflanzstätte jüdischen Wissens': die Hochschule für die Wissenschaft des Judentums, 1872–1942 (Helmuth F. Braun, 120–125). Berliner Wissenschaftler in der Emigration: das Beispiel der Hochschullehrer nach 1933 (Kurt Düwell, 126–134). Die Rolle Berlins in der Geschichte des Technions in Haifa (Zeev W. Sadmon, 135–138). Einstein, Haber, Berlin und Japan: ein Kapitel deutsch-japanischer Wissenschaftsbeziehungen (Eberhard Friese, 139–143). Various other essays deal passim with the Jewish contribution.]

23943.   — Christoffel, Udo, ed.: *Berlin Wilmersdorf: die Juden, Leben und Leiden*. Berlin: Kunstamt Wilmersdorf, 1987. 336 pp., illus., ports., facsims., bibl. (328–336). [Also on the Nazi period and the post-war community; incl. deportation lists and lists referring to confiscation of Jewish property.]

23944.   — Geiger, Ludwig: *Berlin 1688–1840: Geschichte des geistigen Lebens der Preussischen Hauptstadt*.

Bd. 1–2. Neudr. der Ausg. Berlin, Paetel, 1893 & 1895. Aalen: Scientia, 1987. 2 vols. (XVIII, 709; XVI, 651 pp.). [Also on the Jewish contribution to intellectual life in Berlin.]

23945.　— *Jüdische Friedhöfe in Berlin.* [Mit Beiträgen von] Alfred Etzold [et al.]. Berlin/East: Henschel, 1987. 159 pp., illus., plans, bibl. (152–154).

――――　— KAMPE, NORBERT: *The Friedrich-Wilhelms-Universität of Berlin: a case study on the students' 'Jewish Question'.* [See No. 24824.]

23946.　— KLEIN, CHARLOTTE: *A forgotten synagogue* [Kantstrasse 125]. [In]: AJR Information, Vol. 42, No. 6, London, June 1987. P. 8. [Hitherto unpubl. reminiscences by the German-Jewish author (1916 Berlin – 1985 England), who, brought up in an Orthodox family, became a nun yet retained reverence for Judaism and set up a study centre for Christian-Jewish relations.]

23947.　— LOWENTHAL, ERNST G.: *Verdient um Berlin: vom Beitrag jüdischer Bürger.* Ein repräsentativer Querschnitt. [In]: Mitteilungen des Vereins für die Geschichte Berlins, Jg. 83, H. 4, Berlin, Oct. 1987. Pp. 578–582. [Also publ. in]: 'Allgemeine', Nr. 42/10, Bonn, 6. März 1987, pp. 17–18. [on Julius Bab, Hans Goslar, Heinrich Grünfeld, Wilhelm Kleemann, Paul Nathan, Erich Seligmann, Siddy Wronsky.]

23948.　— MATTENKLOTT, GERT: *Ostjuden in Berlin.* [In]: Die Reise nach Berlin. (Hrsg. von der Berliner Festspiele GmbH im Auftrag des Senats von Berlin zur 750-Jahr-Feier Berlins 1987. [Katalog der] Ausstellung im Hamburger Bahnhof, 1. Mai- 1. Nov. 1987.) Berlin: Siedler, 1987. Pp. 210–216.

23949.　— METZGER, KARL-HEINZ: *Kirchen, Moschee und Synagogen in Wilmersdorf.* (Hrsg.: Bezirksamt Wilmersdorf von Berlin.) Berlin: Möller, 1986. 148 pp., illus., bibl. (137–139).

23950.　— RENNERT, JÜRGEN, ed.: *Der Gute Ort in Weissensee.* Bilder vom Jüdischen Friedhof und eine Sammlung jüdischer Stimmen zu Vergehen und Werden, Bleiben und Sein. Aufnahmen von Dietmar Riemann. Berlin/East: Evangelische Verlagsanstalt, 1987. 109 pp., illus. [Obtainable from Luther-Verlag, Bielefeld.]

23951.　— *Von Juden in Steglitz.* Beiträge zur Ortsgeschichte. Hrsg. von der Initiative 'Haus Wolfenstein'. Berlin (41, Handjerystr. 60/61): Initiative 'Haus Wolfenstein' (c/o Christa Langenbeck), 1987. 47 pp., illus.

23952.　— *Wegweiser durch das jüdische Berlin: Geschichte und Gegenwart.* (Nach einer Idee von Nicola Galliner. Mit Beiträgen von Vera Bendt, Nicola Galliner, Stefi Jersch-Wenzel, Thomas Jersch. Dieses Buch basiert zu Teilen auf einem Manuskript von Eike Geisel.) Berlin: Nicolai, 1987. 388 pp., illus., ports., facsims., 1 folded map appended, index of names (380–386), bibl. (373–375). [Cont. the sections: Die jüdische Gemeinde (19–67). Das jüdische Jahr und seine Feiertage (68–91). Synagogen (92–199). Kultur-, Bildungs- und Wohlfahrtseinrichtungen (200–283). Jüdische Friedhöfe (284–359). Zeittafel: von den Anfängen bis nach 1945 (360–369). Berlin-Plan mit Abbildungen jüdischer Einrichtungen und Gebäude von 1936 (map appended). Cf.: Besprechung (Ernst G. Lowenthal) [in]: 'Allgemeine', Nr. 42/30, Bonn, 24. Juli 1987, p. 4.]

――――　— WIECKENBERG, ERNST-PETER: *Juden als Autoren des 'Magazins zur Erfahrungsseelenkunde': ein Beitrag zum Thema 'Juden und Aufklärung in Berlin'.* [See pp. 128–140 in No. 24681.]

23953.　BRANDENBURG. WIEDERANDERS, GERLINDE: *Die Hostienfrevellegende von Kloster Heiligengrabe.* [In]: Kairos, N. F. 29, H. 1–2, Salzburg, 1987. Pp. 99–103, notes. [The monastery Heiligengrabe was founded because of a charge of desecration of the host in 1287; article deals also with the history of the Jews in the Mark Brandenburg in the 13th–16th centuries.]

23954.　BREISACH. HASELIER, GÜNTHER: *Geschichte der Stadt Breisach am Rhein.* Bd. 3: *Der Sturz in den Abgrund 1890–1945.* Mit einem Personen-, Orts- und Sachregister von Julius Kastner. Breisach: Selbstverlag der Stadt, 1985. XV, 717 pp., illus., ports., facsims. [Incl.: Die Breisacher Judengemeinde und ihre Vernichtung (437–462).]

23955.　BREMEN. BUSE, DIETER K.: *Anti-Semitism in mid-nineteenth century Bremen.* [In]: Kwiet, Konrad, ed.: From the emancipation to the Holocaust [see No. 23891]. Kensington, Australia, 1987. Pp. 1–16, notes (14–16).

――――　BRESLAU. Jüdisch-Theologisches Seminar. [See No. 24517.]

23956.　BRUNSWICK. EBELING, HANS-HEINRICH: *Die Juden in Braunschweig: Rechts-, Sozial- und Wirtschaftsgeschichte von den Anfängen der jüdischen Gemeinde bis zur Emanzipation (1282–1848).* Braunschweig: Stadtarchiv und Stadtbibliothek, 1987. XVI, 509 pp., illus., tabs., maps, notes (391–458), index of places and persons (494–509), bibl. (459–490). (Braunschweiger Werkstücke, Reihe A: Veröffentlichungen aus dem Stadtarchiv und der Stadtbibliothek, Bd. 22: der ganzen Reihe Bd. 65.) [Cont. the chaps.: 1: Die ältere jüdische Gemeinde von den Anfängen bis zur Vertreibung, 1282–1546 (pp. 7–110). 2: Die Juden in Melverode, 1578/79–1591 (pp. 111–134). 3: Die jüngere jüdische Gemeinde von der Zeit ihrer Entstehung bis zum Ende des Herzogtums Braunschweig, 1707–1807 (pp. 135–236). 4: Die Braunschweiger Juden im Königreich Westphalen, 1807–1814 (pp. 237–262). 5: Das Zeitalter der Emanzipation – die Juden im Konstitutionellen Staat, 1814–1848 (pp. 263–382). Each chapter covers in detailed subdivisions the legal, economic and social history of the given period and incl. a variety of tables, statistics, maps, and lists of names.] [See also No. 24568.]

——— BUCHAU. [See No. 24197.]

23957. BUTTENHAUSEN. *Juden und ihre Heimat Buttenhausen.* Ein Gedenkbuch zum 200. Jahrestag des Buttenhausener Judenschutzbriefes am 7. Juli 1987. Hrsg. von der Stadt Münsingen. Bearb. von Günter Randecker. Münsingen, Westfalen: Stadtverwaltung, 1987. 120 pp., illus., map.

23958. — SAUER, PAUL: *200 Jahre Judenschutzbrief Buttenhausen.* Eine historische Darstellung. [In]: deutschland-berichte, Jg. 23, H. 10, Bonn, Okt. 1987. Pp. 12–20. [Incl. the Nazi period.]

23959. COLOGNE. BARAM, MEIR: *The Parnas.* [Transl. from the Hebrew by Esther van Handel.] Jerusalem; New York: Feldheim, 1987. 183 pp. [Novel on the persecution of Jews from Cologne during the first Crusade in 1096. Cf.: Kölner Juden im ersten Kreuzzug (Yizhak Ahren) [in]: 'Allgemeine', Nr. 42/31, Bonn, 31. Juli 1987, p. 7.]

——— — CORBACH, IRENE & DIETER: *Sophie Sondhelm und die Kölner Jüdische Kinderheilstätte Bad Kreuznach.* [See No. 24562.]

23960. CRAINSFELD. MÜLLER, FRIEDRICH: *Crainsfeld; aus der Geschichte eines Dorfes im Vogelsbergkreis.* Giessen: Brühlsche Univ. druckerei, 1987. 218 pp., illus. [Chap. 17 deals with the history of the Jews in Crainsfeld from 1626 incl. the Nazi period; also refers to their economic condition.]

23961. DANZIG. DIAMANT, ADOLF: *'Eine Zierde von ganz Danzig': vor 100 Jahren wurde in Danzig die Grosse Synagoge eingeweiht.* [In]: 'Allgemeine', Nr. 42/38, Bonn, 18. Sept. 1987. P. 40.

23962. DORMAGEN. ROHRBACHER, STEFAN: *Die 'Hep-Hep-Krawalle' und der 'Ritualmord' des Jahres 1819 zu Dormagen.* [In]: Antisemitismus und jüdische Geschichte [see No. 24806]. Berlin, 1987. Pp. 135–147, footnotes.

23963. DORTMUND. PFEIFFER, ERNST: *Die Juden in Dortmund.* Das Buch zur Kabelfunk-Serie. Hrsg.: WDR-Kabelfunk Dortmund. Dortmund: HARPA, 1986. 97 pp., illus. [Incl. the Nazi period and post-war Jewish life.]

23964. EDENKOBEN. LURZ, MEINHOLD: *Das Edenkobener Judenbad.* [In]: Pfälzer Heimat, Jg. 37, H. 3, Speyer, Sept. 1986. Pp. 124–127, illus.

23965. ELSDORF. *Juden in Elsdorf.* Arbeitsergebnisse der Projektgruppe der Gemeindehauptschule Elsdorf 'Juden in Elsdorf'. (Projektleiterin: Josi Schlang.) (DDR–4371) Elsdorf: Der Gemeindedirektor, Hauptamt, 1983. 128 pp., illus., facsims. [Incl. the Nazi period.]

23966. ERLANGEN. *Der Israelitische Friedhof in Erlangen.* Hrsg.: Stadt Erlangen, Bürgermeister- und Presseamt. Text: Ilse Sponsel. Erlangen, 1987. 1 folded sheet, illus.

23967. ERMREUTH. WOLF, GERHARD PHILIPP: *Zur Geschichte der Juden in der oberfränkischen Landgemeinde Ermreuth.* [In]: Archiv für Geschichte von Oberfranken, Bd. 66, Bayreuth, 1986. Pp. 419–460.

23968. ESENS. ROKAHR, GERD: *Die Juden in Esens; die Geschichte der jüdischen Gemeinde in Esens von den Anfängen im 17. Jahrhundert bis zu ihrem Ende in nationalsozialistischer Zeit.* Aurich: Ostfriesische Landschaft, 1987. 288 pp., illus., ports., bibl. (245–249). (Abhandlungen und Vorträge zur Geschichte Ostfrieslands, Bd. 65.) [Incl. list: Die jüdischen Einwohner der Stadt Esens, 1933–1940 (233–242).]

——— FRANCONIA. [See also No. 23993.]

23969. — BRANDT, HARM-HINRICH, ed.: *Zwischen Schutzherrschaft und Emanzipation: Studien zur Geschichte der mainfränkischen Juden im 19. Jahrhundert.* Würzburg: Freunde Mainfränkischer Kunst und Geschichte; Schweinfurt: Historischer Verein, 1987. 208 pp., 24 diagrs., map appended, bibl. references. (Mainfränkische Studien, Bd. 39.]

23970. — DIAMANT, ADOLF: *Der 'gottlose Jut' bei Lohr: Aberglaube und Gleichgültigkeit in Franken.* [In]: 'Allgemeine', Nr. 42/10, Bonn, 6. März 1987, p. 19. [Refers to the Maria-Buchen-Wallfahrtskloster founded in 1434 as a result of an anti-Jewish legend. See also: Antisemitismus in Maria Buchen und sein Ende (Fred Rausch) in No. 17013/YB XXVI.]

23971. — GUTH, KLAUS: *Landjudentum in Franken: Lebensformen einer Minderheit im 18. Jahrhundert.* [In]: Archiv für die Geschichte von Oberfranken, 65, Bayreuth, 1985. Pp. 363–378.

—— — HARRIS, JAMES F.: *Bavarians and Jews in conflict in 1866.* [See No. 23938.]

23972. — *Jüdische Landgemeinden in Franken; Beiträge zu Kultur und Geschichte einer Minderheit.* (Hrsg. vom Zweckverband Fränkische-Schweiz-Museum, Tüchersfeld. Red.: Rainer Hofmann.) Bayreuth: Druckerei Lorenz Ellwanger [1987]. 109 pp., diagrs., plans, notes. (Schriften des Fränkische-Schweiz-Museum, Bd. 2.) [Incl.: Möglichkeiten der Quellenforschung am Beispiel Heiligenstadt (Peter Landendorfer, 15–17). Die Juden in Grimms 'Kinder- und Hausmärchen' (Karl Heinz Mistele, 25–27). Zur Frage der Beziehung zwischen Juden und Christen – am Beispiel Aufsess (Gerhard Philipp Wolf, 51–55). Juden in Georgensgmünd (Friedrich Glenk, 57–58). Die jüdische Gemeinde in Gunzenhausen (Wilhelm Lux, 59–60). Die jüdische Gemeinde Mittelweilersbach (Georg Knörlein, 61–68). Die Sonderstellung der jüdischen Gemeinde von Schnaittach im Herzogtum Baiern im 18. Jahrhundert (Walter Tausendpfund, 69–78). Der Konflikt der Rothenberger Juden mit der Metzgerzunft in Schnaittach (Gerhard Renda, 79–86).]

23973. — *Kirche und Kunst, Jg. 63, H. 2/85: [Spuren des Judentums in Bayern].* Erlangen (Kochstr. 6): Verein für Christliche Kunst in der Evangelisch-Lutherischen Kirche in Bayern, 1985. Pp. 36–64, illus., bibl. (62–64). [Incl.: Weiss-Blau – Blau-Weiss: Spuren des Judentums in Bayern (Schalom Ben-Chorin, 39–41). Dorfsynagogen in Franken (Karl H. Mistele, 41–46). Die Synagoge in Binswangen (Karl Öhlschläger, 46–47). Spuren des Judentums in Sulzbürg (Kurt Wappler, 48–49). Die Fischacher Judengemeinde und ihre Synagoge (Michael Piller, 50–52). Das Adolf-Hamburger-Heim in Nürnberg: Synagoge, Gemeindezentrum und Seniorenheim (Ilse Sponsel, 52–55). Der Judenfriedhof in Baiersdorf (Günter Reim, 55–57). Der Leidensweg vier jüdischer Grabsteine aus Nürnberg (Georg Stolz, 57–60). Das Fränkische-Schweiz-Museum im Judenhof zu Tüchersfeld (Rainer Hofmann, 60–62). The articles refer also to the Nazi period.]

23974. — *Das Mittelfränkische Judentum in Geschichte und Gegenwart.* Erlangen (Rathausplatz 1): Staatliches Schulamt in der Stadt Erlangen, 1986. 24 pp., illus., facsims., tabs., map, bibl. (Heimatkundliche Beiträge; Beilage des Amtlichen Schulanzeigers für den Regierungsbezirk Mittelfranken, 1/86.) [Cont.: 'Bewährung liegt noch vor uns – vom Vorurteil zur Partnerschaft' (Ilse Sponsel, 2–3). Geschichte der Juden in Mittelfranken (Alfred Eckert, 4–8; incl. the Nazi period). Geschichtliche Dokumente der mittelfränkischen Judenschaft: Judenfriedhöfe – Synagogen – Schulen und Lehrer am Beispiel Fürth und Mühlhausen (Alfred Eckert, 9–14). Religiöses und häusliches Brauchtum unserer jüdischen Mitbürger einst und heute (Ilse Sponsel, 14–23). Unterrichtshinweise (Hans Kraus).]

23975. — *Reichsstädte in Franken.* Katalog zur Ausstellung. Hrsg. von Rainer A. Müller und Brigitte Buberl unter Mitarbeit von Evamaria Brockhoff. München: Haus der Bayerischen Geschichte, 1987. 295 pp., illus., bibl. (Veröffentlichungen zur Bayerischen Geschichte und Kultur, Nr. 14/87.) [Exhibition on the 5 Franconian Reichsstädte: Dinkelsbühl, Rothenburg, Schweinfurt, Weissenburg, Windsheim; catalogue incl. section: Gemeinde der Juden (74–84).]

23976. — *Reichsstädte in Franken; Aufsätze 2: Wirtschaft, Gesellschaft und Kultur.* Hrsg. von Rainer A. Müller. München: Haus der Bayerischen Geschichte, 1987. 44 pp., illus. (Veröffentlichungen zur Bayerischen Geschichte und Kultur, Nr. 15,2/87.) [Incl.: Die Juden in den kleineren fränkischen Reichsstädten (Ludwig Schnurrer, 84–99).]

23977. — *Zeugnisse jüdischer Geschichte in Unterfranken.* Würzburg: Schöningh, 1987. 83 pp., illus. (Schriften des Stadtarchivs Würzburg, H. 2.) [Cont.: Zum Alter und zur Bedeutung der jüdischen Grabsteine in der Pleich [in Würzburg] (Karlheinz Müller, 9–18). Quellen zu Judenverfolgungen von 1147 bis 1938 (Hans-Peter Baum, 19–58). Die Synagoge in Veitshöchheim – ein Denkmal jüdischen Lebens in einer Randgemeinde Würzburgs (Ludwig Wamser, 59–77). Zur literaturgeschichtlichen Bedeutung der Veitshöchheimer Genisa (Herman Süss, 78–83).]

23978. FRANKFURT am Main. DIAMANT, ADOLF: *'In einer fürchterlichen Tiefe das Baad': historische Reminiszenzen zur Auffindung des Frankfurter Judenbades.* [In]: 'Allgemeine', Nr. 42/28, Bonn, 10. Juli 1987. P. 4.

23979. — FRIEDRICHS, CHRISTOPHER R.: *Politics or pogrom? The Fettmilch uprising in German and Jewish history.* [In]: Central European History, Vol. 19, No. 2, Atlanta, Ga., June 1986. Pp. 186–228, footnotes. [On the anti-Jewish uprising in Frankfurt on Aug. 5, 1614 led by the guild leader Vincenz Fettmilch and on the way it has been depicted by both German and Jewish scholars over the centuries.]

23980. — Schembs, Hans-Otto: *Der Börneplatz in Frankfurt am Main: ein Spiegelbild jüdischer Geschichte.* Hrsg. vom Magistrat der Stadt Frankfurt am Main. Frankfurt: Kramer, 1987. 142 pp., illus., bibl. (139–141). [Remnants of the old Judengasse were discovered during excavations for new buildings on the Börneplatz; for discussion in this connection see: Prüfstein historischen Bewusstseins (Hermann Alter) [in]: 'Allgemeine', Nr. 42/38, Bonn, 18. Sept. 1987, p. 8. Aus der Tiefe des geschichtlichen Raumes: darf man am Frankfurter Börneplatz überhaupt neu bauen?: zum Streit um die Zukunft des wiederentdeckten Judenghettos (Monika Zimmermann) [in]: Frankfurter Allgemeine Zeitung, Nr. 203, 3. Sept. 1987, p. 25. Es geht um Denkmäler jüdischen Lebens in Frankfurt: Tribüne-Gespräch mit dem Oberbürgermeister von Frankfurt, Wolfram Brück [in]: Tribüne, Jg. 26, H. 104, Frankfurt am Main, 1987, pp. 86–102 [&]: Frankfurts 'Offene Wunde': Pressestimmen zu den Auseinandersetzungen um den Börneplatz (Gustav Scherbaum) pp. 103–104 & 106. Das Loch von Frankfurt: ein Fall von Vergangenheitsbewältigung (Walter Boehlich) [in]: Die Zeit, Nr. 29, Hamburg, 10. Juli 1987, pp. 33–34.]

23981. FREIBURG im Breisgau. Fried, Ludwig: *Wechselvolles Schicksal einer jüdischen Gemeinde in Deutschland.* [In]: Isr. Wochenblatt, Jg. 87, Nr. 46, Zürich, 13. Nov. 1987. Pp. 15 & 17. [Short survey of the history of the Jews in Freiburg i.Br. on the occasion of the consecration of a new synagogue in Nov. 1987.]

23982. FÜRTH/Bavaria. *Nachrichten für den jüdischen Bürger Fürths.* Hrsg.: Isr. Kultusgemeinde Fürth. Red.: Ruben J. Rosenfeld. Fürth (Blumenstr. 31), Sept. 1987. 48 pp., illus., ports., facsims. [Incl.: Jacob Ludwig Bencker: ein vergessener 'jüdischer' Dichter aus Franken (Karl H. Mistele, 11–13, notes; J. L. Bencker, born 1790 in Bayreuth, teacher, wrote an anti-Jewish booklet 'Judenkirschen oder komische Gedichte', 1826, in the style of Itzig Feitel Stern). Juden und Freimaurerei in Fürth, II (Werner Heymann, 14–16, bibl.; for pt. I see No. 23010/YB XXXII). Further contributions are listed according to subject.]

——   FULDA. Sonn, Naftali Herbert/Berge, Otto: *Zur Geschichte der jüdischen Schule in Fulda.* [See in No. 24410.]

23983. GELNHAUSEN. *Festschrift ehemalige Synagoge Gelnhausen; Widmung als kulturelle Begegnungsstätte, 25. Sept. 1986.* Hrsg. vom Magistrat der Barbarossastadt Gelnhausen, Bearb. vom Geschichtsverein Gelnhausen. Gelnhausen: Magistrat, 1986. IV, 111 pp., illus., ports., facsims., & 7 pp. appended (Festkonzert Musica Judaica, zur Eröffnung der ehemaligen Synagoge). [Also on the history of the Jews, incl. the Nazi period.]

23984. HAIGERLOCH. Steim, Karl Werner, ed.: *Juden in Haigerloch.* Photos von Paul Weber. Haigerloch: Elser, 1987. 64 pp., illus., ports.

——   HAMBURG. Glückel von Hameln: *Denkwürdigkeiten.* [See No. 24702.]

23985. — Israel, Jonathan I.: *Duarte Nunes da Costa (Jacob Curiel) of Hamburg, Sephardi nobleman and communal leader (1585–1664).* [In]: Studia Rosenthaliana, Vol. 21, No. 1, Assen, The Netherlands, May 1987. Pp. 14–34, footnotes.

23986. — Lorenz, Ina S.: *'Ahasver geht nach Eppendorf' – zur Stadtteilkonzentration der Hamburger Juden im 19. und 20. Jahrhundert.* [In]: Informationen zur modernen Stadtgeschichte, H. 1, Berlin, 1987. Pp. 23–28, bibl.

23987. HANOVER. *'. . . dass die Juden in unsern Landen einen Rabbinen erwehlen . . .'.* Beiträge zum 300. Jahrestag der Errichtung des Landrabbinats Hannover am 10. März 1987. (Hrsg. vom Landesverband der Jüdischen Gemeinden von Niedersachsen, der Jüdischen Gemeinde Hannover und Peter Schulze.) Hannover, 1987. 82 pp., illus., ports., facsims., maps, bibl. (81–82).

23988. — Schulze, Peter: *Die Berliners – eine jüdische Familie in Hannover (1793–1943).* [In]: Hundert Jahre Schallplatte: von Hannover in die Welt. Hamburg: Polygram Deutschland, 1987. Pp. 75–81, ports. [See also in same publication, pp. 41–76]: Die 'Grammophon' in Hannover: 100 Jahre Schallplattengeschichte (Dieter Tasch). [Articles cover, a.o., Emil(e) Berliner, May 20, 1851 Hanover – Aug. 3, 1929 Washington, inventor of, a.o., the record and the microphone, lived in the USA from 1879. His brother Joseph, Hanover Aug. 22, 1858 – May 23, 1938, introduced the telephone to Germany, founder of the Deutsche Grammophon-Gesellschaft. Cora Berliner, social worker, see No. 21332/YB XXX.]

23989. HERNE. *Sie werden nicht vergessen sein: Geschichte der Juden in Herne und Wanne-Eickel.* Eine Dokumentation zur Ausstellung im Stadtarchiv Herne vom 15. März bis zum 10. Apr. 1987. (Bearb.: Kurt Tohermes.) Herne: Oberstadtdirektor, 1987. 77 pp., illus. [Documentation on the history of the Jews incl. the Nazi period and post-war Jewish life (6–60), also on the Jewish cemeteries (61–74).]

23990. HERSFELD. Handtke, D.: *Zur Geschichte der Hersfelder Juden im Mittelalter.* [In]: Hessische Heimat, Jg. 36, Marburg, 1985. Pp. 31–33.

23991. HESSE. Altaras, Thea: *Synagogen in Hessen – was geschah seit 1945?* Königstein: Langewiesche, 1987. 236 pp., 465 illus., plans. (Die Blauen Bücher.) [On architecture, history and fate of 222 Hessian synagogues which could still be traced, in varying condition, after the war.]

23992. — Battenberg, Friedrich, ed.: *Judenverordnungen in Hessen-Darmstadt: das Judenrecht eines Reichsfürstentums bis zum Ende des Alten Reiches.* Eine Dokumentation. Wiesbaden: Kommission für die Geschichte der Juden in Hessen, 1987. IX, 336 pp., illus., 1 map, notes (37–57). (Schriften der Kommission für die Geschichte der Juden in Hessen, 8.)

23993. — Birmann-Dähne, Gerhild: *Haus des ewigen Lebens: Jüdische Friedhöfe in Osthessen und Unterfranken.* (D–8787) Zeitlofs (Heilsbergstr. 1): G. Birmann-Dähne, 1987. 96 pp., 60 illus.

23994. HÖCHST. *Geschichte und Schicksale der Juden zu Höchst.* Hrsg.: Gemeindevorstand Höchst im Odenwald. Höchst, 1985. 223 pp., illus., ports., diagrs., map. [Incl. the Nazi period.]

23995. ICHENHAUSEN. Sharman, Walter: *The Ichenhausen Charter.* Researched and translated. Newcastle upon Tyne (2 Carlton Close): W. Sharman, 1986. 9 pp., 2 facsims., notes (p. 4). [Mimeog.]. [Cont. survey of the history of Jews in Ichenhausen from 1518 and the English transl. of a letter of protection for the Ichenhausen Jews issued in 1717.]

23996. IDSTEIN. *Idstein: Geschichte und Gegenwart.* 2., verbesserte Aufl. Idstein: Magistrat der Stadt, 1987. 1 vol. [Also on the Jews in Idstein.]

23997. KALDENKIRCHEN. Peters, Leo: *Geschichte der Juden in Kaldenkirchen.* [In]: Heimatbuch des Krieses Viersen 1983, Folge 34, Viersen, 1982. Pp. 123–136, illus., facsims., footnotes. [Also on the economic situation; incl. the Nazi period.] [Obtainable from Kulturamt des Kreises, Am Bahnhoff 8, D–4152 Kempen 1.]

23998. KASSEL. Thiele, Helmut: *Die Israelitische Gemeinde zu Kassel im 19. Jahrhundert: Eheschliessungen, Geborene, Verstorbene, 1808–1886.* Kassel, 1986. X, 397 pp., map, plate, bibl. (p. X). [Mimeog., available in the LBI New York.]

23999. KEMPEN. Hermes, Jakob: *Das alte Kempen; eine Stadt im Spiegel der Jahrhunderte.* Krefeld: Lambertz-Tölkes, 1982. 244 pp., illus. [Incl. chap.: Zur Geschichte des Judentums (pp. 45–51, illus., facsims.); covers also the Nazi period and contains list with the names and fate of 67 Jews.]

24000. KIRCHHAIN. Schubert, Kurt: *Juden in Kirchhain: Geschichte der Gemeinde und ihres Friedhofs. Mit einem Beitrag zur Biographie des jüdischen Dichters Henle Kirchhan (1666–1757).* Wiesbaden: Kommission für die Geschichte der Juden in Hessen, 1987. 78 pp., illus., facsims., geneal. tables, plan, bibl. (75–76). (Schriften der Kommission für die Geschichte der Juden in Hessen, 9.)

24001. KOBLENZ. Bar-Jehuda, Benjamin: *Erinnerungen an Koblenz, 1918–1935.* [Von] Benjamin Bar Jehuda = [orig.] Kurt Hermann. Koblenz: Christlich-Jüdische Gesellschaft für Brüderlichkeit, 1986. 77 pp., illus.

24002. — Thill, Hildburg-Helene: *Lebensbilder jüdischer Koblenzer und ihre Schicksale.* Koblenz: Stadtbibliothek, 1987. 386, [143] pp., illus., ports., bibl. (384–386). (Veröffentlichungen der Stadtbibliothek Koblenz, Bd. 21.) [Incl.: Wirtschaftliche und allgemeine Situation der jüdischen Koblenzer 1933–1942 (319–380).]

24003. LANGENZENN. Mahr, Helmut: *Landjudentum in Langenzenn vom 17. bis zum 19. Jahrhundert.* [In]: Nachrichten für den jüdischen Bürger Fürths, Isr. Kultusgemeinde Fürth (Blumenstr. 31), Sept. 1987. Pp. 8–10, facsims., plan of synagogue. [Also on the economic conditions.]

24004. LEIPZIG. Lange, Bernd-Lutz: *Die wechselvolle Geschichte der Leipziger Juden geht bis auf das Jahr 1000 zurück.* [In]: Aufbau, Vol. 53, No. 13, New York, June 19, 1987. Pp. 18–19 & 30. [Shortened and slightly changed version of an article orig. printed in the periodical Leipziger Blätter; incl. the Nazi and post-war periods.]

24005. LIMBURG. Caspary, Eugen: *Die Juden in den Kreisen Limburg und Oberlahn, 1278–1945.* Versuch einer Bestandsaufnahme. [In]: Limburg-Weilburg: Beiträge zur Geschichte des Kreises. Limburg/Lahn: Kreisausschuss des Landkreises Limburg-Weilburg; Kreissparkasse Limburg, 1986. Pp. 126–173, illus., ports., facsims., bibl. references.

24006. LÜNEBURG. Preuss, Werner H.: '. . . widrigen Falls . . . die hiesigen Lande sofort wieder zu verlassen': Aufenthaltsgenehmigung für die Familie Samson Heine – ein bürokratischer Vorgang, Lüneburg 1822.* [In]: Heine Jahrbuch 1987, Jg. 26, Hamburg, 1987. Pp. 116–134, notes (132–134). [Incl. the documentation in connection with the residence permit for Heinrich Heine's father and family (121–132).]

—— MAINFRANKEN. [See No. 23969.]

24007. MANNHEIM. *Jüdisches Gemeindezentrum F 3.* Festschrift zur Einweihung am 13. Sept. 1987, 19. Ellul 5747. Hrsg. vom Oberrat der Israeliten Badens, Karlsruhe [et al.]. Mannheim: Verlagsbüro von Brandt, 1987. 119 pp., 65 illus., ports., diagrs. [Incl. essays on the history of the Mannheim Jewry from the 17th century to the Weimar Republic, the Nazi period and post-war Jewish life.]

24008. —— —— JACOBS, BOIKE: *Gebaut mit gebrochenem Herzen: die Gemeinde Mannheim feierte die Einweihung von Synagoge und Gemeindezentrum.* [In]: 'Allgemeine', Nr. 42/39, Bonn, 25. Sept. 1987. Pp. 3–4, port. [Incl. excerpts from the address by Max Gruenewald, rabbi of Mannheim 1925·1938, who consecrated the new synagogue and the community centre on Sept. 13, 1987.]

24009. —— WATZINGER, KARL OTTO: *Die Emanzipation der Juden in Mannheim von 1807 bis 1862.* [In]: Mannheimer Hefte, H. 2, Mannheim, 1987. Pp. 92–95, notes.

24010. —— WATZINGER, KARL OTTO: *Geschichte der Juden in Mannheim 1650–1945: mit 52 Biographien.* Mit einer Übersicht über die Quellen im Stadtarchiv Mannheim zur Geschichte der Juden von Jörg Schadt und Michael Martin. 2., verbesserte Aufl. Stuttgart: Kohlhammer, 1987. 197 pp., illus., ports., diagrs., bibl. (187–191). (Veröffentlichungen des Stadtarchivs Mannheim, Bd. 12.) [See also No. 24516.]

24011. MARBURG. KOSHAR, RUDY: *Social life, local politics and Nazism: Marburg 1880–1935.* Chapel Hill: Univ. of North Carolina Press, 1986. 395 pp., illus., maps, tabs., notes, bibl. (361–382). [Incl. antisemitism, persecution of Jews, Jews at the university of Marburg.]

24012. MAYEN. HÖRTER, FRIDOLIN: *Quellen zur Geschichte der Juden in Mayen.* [In]: Landeskundliche Vierteljahrsblätter, Jg. 31, H. 4, Trier, 1985. Pp. 131–134.

24013. MICHELSTADT. ROTH, ERNST/HAAS, ALEXANDER: *Landesrabbiner Dr. I. E. Lichtigfeld-Museum – ehemalige Synagoge – in Michelstadt/Odenwald: zur Eröffnung.* Frankfurt am Main: Landesverband der Jüdischen Gemeinden in Hessen, 1978. 50 pp., illus., ports., facsims., tabs. [Also on the history of the Jews in Michelstadt.] [Isaac Emil Lichtigfeld, Jan. 4, 1894 Burstyn, Galicia- Dec. 24, 1967 Frankfurt am Main, lawyer, rabbi, emigrated to England in 1933, returned to Germany in 1954, rabbi of the Jewish community Frankfurt and Landesrabbiner of Hesse.]

24014. MINGOLSHEIM/BADEN. MESSMER, WILLY: *Juden unserer Heimat: die Geschichte der Juden aus den Orten Mingolsheim, Langenbrücken und Malsch.* Bad Schönborn (Beethovenstr. 12): W. Messmer, 1986. 223 pp., illus., ports. [Incl. the Nazi period.]

24015. MÖRFELDEN-WALLDORF. *'Die schlimmste Sache war die Angst, die andauernde Angst . . .': Alltagsgeschichte der jüdischen Familien von Mörfelden und Walldorf (1918–1942).* (Red.: Cornelia Rühlig und Inge Auer.) Mörfelden-Walldorf: Magistrat der Stadt, 1986. 381 pp., illus., ports. (Incl. contribution by Roland Seifert on the fate of 16 families persecuted during the Nazi period, giving personal and professional data.]

24016. MUNICH. EISWALDT, EDITH: *Jüdische Familien in der Landeshauptstadt: ihre Namen gaben München Glanz.* [In]: Münchner Stadtanzeiger, [Beilage der] Süddeutschen Zeitung, München, 11. Dez. 1987. P. 24.

24017. —— SELIG, WOLFRAM: *Hauptsynagoge München 1887–1938.* Eine Gedenkschrift mit einem historischen Rückblick. Hrsg. von Sal Frost. München: Aries Verl., 1987. 160 pp., illus. [Incl.: Die Geschichte der Münchner Synagogen (Wolfram Selig). (Reprints of the following publications): Programm zur Einweihung der Synagoge vom 16. Sept. 1887 [&]: Reden zum Abschied von der alten und zur Einweihung der neuen Synagoge in München, 10. und 16. Sept. 1887 (Joseph Perles). Festgabe 50 Jahre Hauptsynagoge München 1887–1937 [&]: Festpredigt zum 50jährigen Jubiläum der neuen Synagoge in München, 5. Sept. 1937 (Leo Baerwald).]

24018. NAUHEIM. KOLB, STEPHAN: *Die Geschichte der Bad Nauheimer Juden: eine gescheiterte Assimilation.* (Hrsg. vom Magistrat der Stadt Bad Nauheim.) Bad Nauheim: Wetterauer Zeitung, 1987. 324 pp., illus., ports., facsims., bibl. (317–322). [Covers the time 1845–1945; incl.: Liste von jüdischen Bürgern in Bad Nauheim (248–311).]

24019. NEUENSTADT-STEIN. JUNG, NORBERT: *Die Juden von Neuenstadt-Stein am Kocher.* 2., erweiterte Aufl. Hrsg. in Verbindung mit Gottfried Reichert, Verein für Geschichte und Heimatkunde Neuenstadts e.V., von Hans Peter Reckmann. (D–7129) Zaberfeld-Michelbach (Weinstr. 3): N. Jung, 1987. 82 pp., illus. [Incl. the Nazi period.]

24020. NEUNKIRCHEN. PAULUS, OTTMAR: *Die Synagogengemeinde Neunkirchen.* 2., verkürzte Ausg. Neunkirchen: O. Paulus, 1987. 80 pp.

24021. NORDEN. Gödeken, Lina: *Das alte jüdische 'Zentrum' in Norden: die Gebäude der Jüdischen Gemeinde an der Judenlohne und weiterer Besitz*. [In]: Ostfriesland, H. 3, Leer, 1986. Pp. 4–11, illus., plan, bibl. references.

24022. OBERKASSEL. Rey, Manfred van: *Die jüdischen Bürger von Oberkassel*. [In]: Bonner Geschichtsblätter, Bd. 36, Bonn, 1985. Pp. 291–334.

24023. OBERURSEL. Zink, Wolfgang: *Die Friedhöfe der Juden von Oberursel*. (Hrs.: Gesellschaft für Christlich-Jüdische Zusammenarbeit Taunus e.V.) Oberursel: Stadt Oberursel, 1987. 15 pp., illus.

24024. OELDE. Pauls, Albert: *Zur Geschichte der Juden in Oelde*. [In]: Oelde, die Stadt, in der wir leben. Oelde, 1987. pp. 667–700, illus., facsims.

24025. OLDENBURG. Schieckel, Harald: *Getaufte Juden im Gebiet des späteren Landes Oldenburg bis zur Mitte des 19. Jahrhunderts und Übertritte christlicher Ehefrauen von Juden zum Judentum nach der Mitte des 19. Jahrhunderts*. [In]: Genealogie, Jg. 36, H. 12, (Bd. 18), Neustadt/Aisch, Dez. 1987. Pp. 779–785, footnotes.

24026. PADBERG. [Brilling, Bernhard]: *Vom Schutzjuden zum preussischen Staatsbürger: die Chronik der jüdischen Gemeinde Padberg*. Von Norbert Becker [sic]. [In]: 'Allgemeine', Nr. 42/10, Bonn, 6. März 1987. P. 18. [See also ensuing correction of the author's name]: Berichtigung zu 'Padberg' (Die Redaktion) [in]: 'Allgemeine', Nr. 42/12, Bonn, 20. März 1987, p. 7. [This article by Bernhard Brilling first appeared in 1963, see No. 3723/YB IX.]

24027. PADERBORN. Naarmann, Margit: *Die Paderborner Juden 1802–1943: Emanzipation, Integration und Vernichtung*. Paderborn, Phil. Diss., 1986.

—— PALATINATE. [See also No. 24037.]

24028. — Arnold, Hermann: *Juden in der Pfalz: vom Leben pfälzischer Juden*. Landau/Pfalz: Pfälzische Verlagsanstalt, 1987. 232 pp., illus., ports., facsims., maps, bibl. (220–225).

24029. PFUNGSTADT. Wolf, Jürgen Rainer: *Geschichte der Juden in Pfungstadt*. [In]: Archiv für Hessische Geschichte und Altertumskunde, 44, Darmstadt, 1986. Pp. 41–63.

—— PRUSSIA. [See also No. 23897.]

24030. — Baumgart, Peter: *Die jüdische Minorität im friderizianischen Preussen*. [In]: Vorträge und Studien zur preussisch-deutschen Geschichte, hrsg. von Oswald Hauser. Köln: Böhlau, 1983. (Neue Forschungen zur brandenburg-preussischen Geschichte, 2.) Pp. 1–20.

24031. — Brammer, Annegret H.: *Judenpolitik und Judengesetzgebung in Preussen 1812 bis 1847; mit einem Ausblick auf das Gleichberechtigungsgesetz des Norddeutschen Bundes von 1869*. Erstausg. Berlin: Schelzky & Jeep, 1987. 569 pp.

24032. PUDERBACH. Zeiler, Ernst: *Zur Geschichte der Synagoge in Puderbach*. [In]: Heimat-Jahrbuch des Landkreises Neuwied 1988, Neuwied, Neuwieder Verlagsgesellschaft, [1987]. Pp. 97–100, illus., notes. [Also on the history of the Jews in Puderbach, incl. the Nazi period.]

24033. RANDEGG. Moos, Samuel (Semi): *Geschichte der Juden im Hegaudorf Randegg*. Bearb. und ergänzt von Karl Schatz. Mit weiteren Beiträgen von Otto Denzel [et al.]. Hrsg. im Auftrag der Gemeinde Gottmadingen von Karl Schatz und Franz Götz. Gottmadingen: Gemeinde, 1986. 177 pp., 23 illus., ports., map. (Hegau-Bibliothek, Bd. 42.)

24034. REGENSBURG. Matzel, Klaus: *Zum Wortschatz des Regensburger Judenregisters vom Jahre 1476*. [In]: Sprachwissenschaft, Jg. 10, Nr. 3/4, Heidelberg, 1985. Pp. 366–398.

24035. REILINGEN. Bickle, Philipp: *Geschichte der Reilinger Juden*. [In]: 700 Jahre Reilingen: Chronik einer Gemeinde in Nordbaden 1286–1986. Hrsg. von Bernhard Schmehrer. Reilingen: Gemeinde, 1986. Pp. 361–368, illus.

24036. RHEINBERG. Otten, Bärbel: *Die Geschichte der jüdischen Gemeinde in Rheinberg von den Anfängen bis in die Zeit des Nationalsozialismus*. Duisburg, Univ.-Gesamthochschule, Diplomarbeit, 1986. 210 pp., illus., facsims., plans, bibl. (172–174). [Available in the LBI New York.]

—— RHINELAND. [See also No. 23897.]

24037. — *Dokumentation zur Geschichte der jüdischen Bevölkerung in Rheinland-Pfalz und im Saarland von 1800 bis 1945*. Hrsg. von der Landesarchivverwaltung Rheinland-Pfalz in Verbindung mit dem Landesarchiv Saarbrücken. *Bd. 8: Index der Personen- und Ortsnamen sowie judaistischer Sachworte der Bände 1–7*. Bearb. von Eva Schindlmayr. Koblenz: Landesarchivverwaltung Rheinland-Pfalz, 1987. 306 pp. (Veröffentlichungen der Landesarchivverwaltung Rheinland-Pfalz, Bd. 19.) [This *Dokumentation* is now complete. For Vol. 1 see no. 18908/YB XXVIII; Vol. 2 see No. 15923/YB XXV; Vols. 3, 4, 6 & 7 see Nos. 11951–11954/YB XX; Vol. 5 see No. 12690/YB XXI.]

24038.   — Stow, Kenneth R.: *The Jewish family in the Rhineland in the High Middle Ages: form and function.* [In]: The American Historical Review, Vol. 92, No. 5, Washington, Dec. 1987. Pp. 1085–1110, tabs., notes. [Essay based on the poem composed by Eleazar ben Judah of Worms (known as Rokeach) following the murder of his wife and two daughters in Worms in 1197; another source used is the memorial list of Jewish martyrs who perished in Mainz during the massacres of the First Crusade in the spring of 1096.]

24039.   RHÖN. Birmann-Dähne, Gerhild: *Haus des ewigen Lebens: Jüdische Friedhöfe der Rhön und im Lipper Land.* In Fotos und Gedichten [von] Gerhild Birmann-Dähne; Geschichtliches und Dias [von] Heinz-Jürgen Hoppe. Ausstellungskatalog. Fulda: Zeitdruck Verlag K. Masche, 1986. 64 pp., illus.

24040.   RIMBACH. Gebhard, Wolfgang: *Geschichte der Rimbacher Juden.* Rimbach/Odenwald: Gemeinde Rimbach, 1987. 207 pp., illus., ports., facsims., maps, bibl. (181–184). [Also transl. under the title]: *The Jews of Rimbach; a contribution to their history.* Transl. from the German by Cornelia Petermann. St. Louis, Mo.: Westheimer Associates, 1987. XII, 86, 33 pp., illus., bibl. (82–85). [Mimeog., available in the LBI New York.] [Incl. the Nazi period.]

24041.   RONSDORF. Föhse, Ulrich: *'Meine Gedanken sind noch oft in Ronsdorf': ein Beitrag zur kurzen Geschichte der Juden in Ronsdorf.* [In]: Deine Gemeinde, 4/87, Ronsdorf, Evangelisch-Reformierte Gemeinde, 1987. 6 pp., illus., facsims. [See also slightly shortened version]: *Die Geschichte der Juden in Ronsdorf [bei] Wuppertal.* [In]: Aufbau, Vol. 53, No. 26, New York, Dec. 18, 1987. P. 18.

24042.   RUCHHEIM. Barth, Friedrich: *Die Geschichte der Juden in Ruchheim.* Ludwigshafen-Oggersheim (Kerschensteinerstr. 48): F. Barth, [1985]. 24 pp., illus., ports. [Private print of No. 23062/YB XXXII.]

——   SAARLAND. [See also No. 24037.]

24043.   — Jacoby, Fritz: *Zwei Stellungnahmen zur Judenemanzipation aus den Saarstädten: die Petition der Bürger von Saarbrücken, St. Johann und Umgebung von 1843.* [In]: Zeitschrift für die Geschichte der Saargegend, Bd. 33, Saarbrücken, 1985. Pp. 122–147.

24044.   SALZGITTER. Lange, Horst-Günther: *Geschichte der Juden in Salzgitter-Bad von 1800 bis nach dem Ersten Weltkrieg.* [In]: Salzgitter-Jahrbuch, Bd. 7, Salzgitter, 1985. Pp. 29–65.

24045.   SANKT TÖNIS. Peters, Leo: *Geschichte der Juden in St. Tönis.* [In]: Heimatbuch des Kreises Viersen 1982, Folge 33, Viersen, 1981. Pp. 109–126, facsims., footnotes. [Also on the economic situation; incl. the Nazi period.] [Obtainable from Kulturamt des Kreises, Am Bahnhof 8, D-4152 Kempen 1.]

——   SEESEN. [See No. 24053.]

24046.   SILESIA. Jersch-Wenzel, Stefi: *Die Juden als Bestandteil der oberschlesischen Bevölkerung in der ersten Hälfte des 19. Jahrhunderts.* [In]: Deutsche-Polen-Juden [see No. 23874]. Berlin: Colloquium, 1987. Pp. 191–209, tabs., footnotes. [Also on Jewish participation in the Silesian economy.]

24047.   STOMMELN. *Juden in Stommeln: Geschichte einer jüdischen Gemeinde im Kölner Umland.* Teil 2. (Mitarbeiter: Manfred Backhausen [et al.].) Pulheim (Adamistr. 9): Verein für Geschichte und Heimatkunde, 1987. 344 pp., 224 illus., ports., diagrs., map. (Pulheimer Beiträge zur Geschichte und Heimatkunde, Sonderveröffentlichung des Vereins für Geschichte und Heimatkunde, 3.) [Incl. the Nazi period. For pt. 1 see No. 19860/YB XXIX.]

24048.   SULINGEN. Kurth, Eva & Hilmar: *Juden in Sulingen, 1753–1938.* Sulingen: Kreiszeitungs-Verl., 1986. 84 pp., illus., maps.

24049.   URBACH. Ebbinghaus, Gerhard: *Zur Geschichte der Juden des Kirchspiels Urbach.* [In]: Heimat-Jahrbuch des Landkreises Neuwied 1988, Neuwied, Neuwieder Verlagsgesell-schaft, [1987]. Pp. 92–96, port., bibl [Covers the time from 1767 – Nov. 10, 1938 when the last Jews were forced to leave Urbach; incl. also reports on their fate thereafter.]

24050.   VEITSHÖCHHEIM. Wamser, Ludwig: *Archäologie und Zeitgeschichte: Untersuchungen in der ehemaligen Synagoge von Veitshöchheim (Landkreis Würzburg, Unterfranken).* [In]: Nachrichten für den jüdischen Bürger Fürths, Isr. Kultusgemeinde Fürth (Blumenstr. 31), Sept. 1987. Pp. 28–33, illus., plans, map. [Incl. survey of a newly discovered genizah. See also essays by Wamser and Süss in No. 23977.]

24051.   WALDECK. Berbüsse, Volker: *Aus einem 'Zeitalter der Finsterniss und Unduldsamkeit': antijüdische Wuchergesetzgebung im Fürstentum Waldeck.* [In]: Antisemitismus und jüdische Geschichte [see No. 24806]. Berlin, 1987. Pp. 121–134, footnotes.

24052.   WESTPHALIA. Aschoff, Diethard: *Zur Geschichte der Juden in Westfalen: Anmerkungen zum Forschungsstand.* [In]: Westfälische Forschungen, Bd. 36, Münster, 1986. Pp. 136–147.

24053. WOLFENBÜTTEL. Busch, Ralf: *Die jüdischen Reformschulen in Wolfenbüttel und Seesen und ihre Bibliotheken.* [In]: Antisemitismus und jüdische Geschichte [see No. 24806]. Berlin, 1987. Pp. 173–184, footnotes.

24054. — *Samsonschule Wolfenbüttel (1786–1928).* Ausstellung aus Anlass der 200. Wiederkehr des Gründungstages, Wolfenbüttel 1986. (Text: Ralf Busch.) Braunschweig, 1986. 52 pp., illus., ports., plans. (Veröffentlichungen des Braunschweigischen Landesmuseums, 46.) [Land-rabbiner Philipp Samson and his brother Herz Samson, Court Jew of the Duke of Brunswick, founded a school for poor boys in 1786; pupils of the school were, a.o., Samuel Meyer Ehrenberg who later became its director, Isaak Markus Jost, Leopold Zunz; following the post-World-War I inflation, the school was closed in 1928.]

24055. WORMS. Böcher, Otto: *Der alte Judenfriedhof zu Worms.* (Hrsg.: Rheinischer Verein für Denkmalpflege und Landschaftsschutz.) 6. Aufl. Neuss: Neusser Druck u. Verlag, 1987. 11 pp., illus., plan. (Rheinische Kunststätten, H. 148.]

—— — Eidelberg, Shlomo: *Das Minhagbuch von Juspa Schammes.* [See No. 24536.]

—— WÜRTTEMBERG. [See also Nos. 23935–23936.]

24056. — *Pinkas Hakehillot: encyclopaedia of Jewish communities from their foundation till after the Holocaust. Germany, part 2: Württemberg, Hohenzollern, Baden.* Ed. by Joseph Walk. [In Hebrew]. Jerusalem: Yad Vashem, 1986. [12], 549 pp. [Cf.: Gedenket der Juden in Baden und Württemberg! (Esriel Hildesheimer) [in]: MB, Jg. 55, Nr. 28–29, Tel-Aviv, Sept.-Okt. 1987, p. 12.] [Pt. 1: Bavaria, ed. by Baruch Zvi Ophir [et al.], was publ. in 1972 (see No. 10184/YB XVIII); for a German version based on this Hebrew publication see No. 15874/YB XXV.]

24057. — Sauer, Paul: *Zur Geschichte der Juden in Württemberg.* [In]: Ludwigsburger Geschichtsblätter, Bd. 38, Ludwigsburg, 1985. Pp. 89–103.

24058. WÜRZBURG. Flade, Roland: *Die Würzburger Juden: ihre Geschichte vom Mittelalter bis zur Gegenwart.* Mit einem Beitrag von Ursula Gehring-Münzel. Würzburg: Stürtz, 1987. XIV, 434 pp., illus., ports., facsims., bibl. (423–434). [Cont. the sections: Mittelalter und frühe Neuzeit (1–60). Emanzipation (by Ursula Gehring-Münzel, 61–142). Kaiserreich (143–174). Weimarer Republik (175–256). Drittes Reich (257–384). Nachkriegszeit (385–418). Book covers in detail all aspects of Jewish communal, social and economic life during the given periods and deals also with many Jewish personalities active in Jewish or general public affairs. See also the author's *Juden in Würzburg 1918–1933*, No. 21951/YB XXXI.]

—— — Müller, Karlheinz: *Zum Alter und zur Bedeutung der jüdischen Grabsteine in der Pleich.* [See in No. 23977.]

24059. — Roth, Ernst: *Vielseitige Kenntnisse vonnöten: die jüdischen Grabsteine in der Würzburger Pleich.* [In]: 'Allgemeine', Nr. 42/31, Bonn, 31. Juli 1987. P. 7. [Essay gives corrections and additional information in connection with the deciphering of the epitaphs of the newly discovered tombstones. On the discovery see also: Wertvolles Kulturgut geborgen: Grabsteine aus dem mittelalterlichen jüdischen Friedhof in Würzburg [in]: 'Allgemeine', Nr. 42/20, Bonn, 15. Mai 1987, p. 11. Das Hochstift und die Juden: Funde in Würzburg führen zu Konflikt (Andreas Scheppach) [in]: 'Allgemeine', Nr. 42/24–25, Bonn, 12./19. Juni 1987, p. 15. Mehr als 300 Grabsteine bei Abrissarbeiten in Würzburg entdeckt (William Stern) [in]: Aufbau, Vol. 54, No. 1, New York, Jan. 1, 1988, p. 7.]

—— — Schindler, Thomas: *Studentischer Antisemitismus und jüdische Studentenverbindungen in Würzburg 1880–1914.* [See No. 24841.]

1a. Alsace

24060. Burns, Michael: *Emancipation and reaction: the rural exodus of Alsatian Jews, 1791–1848.* [In]: Living with antisemitism, ed. by Jehuda Reinharz [see No. 24835]. Hanover & London, 1987. Pp. 19–41, notes.

—— Glückel von Hameln: *Denkwürdigkeiten.* [On Jewish life in Metz.] [See No. 24702.]

24061. Stauben, Daniel: *Eine Reise zu den Juden auf dem Lande.* Aus dem Franz. von Alain Claude Sulzer. Augsburg: Ölbaum-Verl., 1986. 162 pp. [Transl. of 'Scènes de la vie juive en Alsace' by Daniel Stauben (1825–1875).]

2. Austria

——— BARTAL, ISRAEL: *'The heavenly city of Germany' and absolutism à la mode d'Autriche: the rise of the Haskalah in Galicia.* [See pp. 33–42 in No. 23912.]

24062. BEN-AVNER, YEHUDA: *On the emancipation of the Jews in the Austrian Empire in the period of reaction.* [In Hebrew, title transl.]. [In]: Sefer Aviad, ed. by Yitzchak Raphael [see No. 24519]. Jerusalem: Mossad Harav Kook, 1986. Pp. 92–111.

24063. BURSTYN, RUTH: *Joseph Samuel Bloch (1850–1923): ein Lebensbild; Kämpfer für Wahrheit und Gerechtigkeit.* [In]: Kairos, N.F. 29, H. 1–2, Salzburg, 1987. Pp. 104–115, notes. [J.S.B., Nov. 20, 1850 Dukla, Galicia – Oct. 2, 1923 Vienna, rabbi, publicist, politician, founded 'Dr. Blochs Österreichische Wochenschrift' in 1883 to combat antisemitism.]

24064. GRAETZ, MICHAEL: *From liberalism to nationalism: Adolf Fischhof (1916–1893) and his theory of autonomism.* [In Hebrew, with English summary]. [In]: Translation and change in modern Jewish history [see No. 23913]. Jerusalem, 1987. Pp. 115–134.

24065. HECHT, ALEXANDER: *Der Bund B'nai B'rith und seine Bedeutung für das österreichische Judentum.* Unveränd. Nachdr. der Ausg. Wien, Isr. Humanitätsverein B'nai B'rith, 1914. Bremen: Faksimile-Verl., 1985. 36 pp.

24066. McEWAN, DOROTHEA: *The [Harry] Fischer Family Archive in London: a description of the holdings.* [In]: German History, No. 5, Oxford Univ. Press, Autumn 1987. Pp. 74–81. [Collection of papers on the history of the Jews in the Moravian village Lomnice whence the family descends, covering the time 1710 to the second half of the 19th century when family members settled in Vienna.] [Harry R. Fischer, orig. Heinrich Fischer, Aug. 30, 1903 Vienna – Apr. 12, 1977 London, art-dealer, emigrated in 1938 via Yugoslavia to London, a.o., co-founder of the Marlborough Fine Art Gallery.]

24067. MITTERAUER, MICHAEL, ed.: *'Gelobt sei, der dem Schwachen Kraft verleiht': zehn Generationen einer jüdischen Familie im alten und neuen Österreich.* Vorwort von Rudolf Kirchschläger. Wien: Böhlau, 1987. 319 pp., illus., ports. (Damit es nicht verlorengeht, 14.) [History of the family König based on documents and autobiographical texts from the end of the 17th century to the present day, describes Jewish communal life, persecution during the Nazi period, survival in Theresienstadt. On, a.o., Raphael König, born in 1808, the first Jewish locksmith in Austria; his son Jacob, 1841–1921, founder of the still-functioning iron-trade business in Retz.]

24068. POLLACK, MARTIN: *Des Lebens Lauf: jüdische Familienbilder aus Zwischen-Europa.* Mit 59 Abbildungen. Wien: Brandstätter, 1987. 144 pp., ports. [Biographies of Austrian-Hungarian Jews reflecting emancipation, social and economic rise, assimilation and persecution.]

24069. SCHMIDL, ERWIN A.: *Jews in the Austro-Hungarian armed forces, 1867–1918.* [In]: Studies in Contemporary Jewry, 3, Oxford Univ. Press, 1987. Pp. 127–146.

24070. TOURY, JACOB: *Defense activities of the Österreichisch-Israelitische Union before 1914.* [In]: Living with antisemitism, ed. by Jehuda Reinharz [see No. 24835]. Hanover & London, 1987. Pp. 167–192, notes.

24071. CZERNOWITZ. ERICH, RENATA M.: *Jüdische Spuren in Czernowitz: ehemaliges Bollwerk der Habsburgermonarchie im Osten.* [In]: NZZ, Nr. 229. Zürich, 3./4. Okt. 1987. P. 7, illus. [Report on a visit to the now Soviet-Russian town; also on the history of the Jews.]

24072. GRAZ. SEEWANN, HARALD: *Die Jüdisch-akademische Verbindung Charitas Graz, 1898–1938. Bd. 2: Mit einer Auswahl von Beiträgen zur Geschichte und zur Selbstdarstellung des bis zum Jahre 1938 bestandenen jüdisch-nationalen Waffenstudententums in Österreich.* Graz (Leonhardstr. 27): Steirischer Studentenhistoriker-Verein, 1987. 54 pp., illus., ports., facsims. (Schriftenreihe des Steirischen Studentenhistoriker-Vereines, Folge 13.) [For vol. 1 see No. 23099/YB XXXII.]

24073. HOHENEMS. RAUH, RUDOLF: *Interessante Archivalien und Bestände des Palastarchivs in Hohenems.* [In]: Montfort, Jg. 24, H. 2, Dornbirn, 1972. Pp. 300–337, illus., facsims. [Incl. section on Jews in Hohenems.]

24074. TIROL. BURMEISTER, KARL HEINZ: *Die Personenstandsregister des Rabbinates für Tirol und Vorarlberg (1769–1890).* [In]: Genealogica et Heraldica; 10. Internat. Kongress für genealogische und heraldische Wissenschaften, Wien, 1970. Pp. 43–48.

24075. VIENNA. DVORAK, JOHANN: *Juden in Wien von Lueger bis Hitler.* [In]: Die Neue Gesellschaft/Frankfurter Hefte, Jg. 34, Nr. 10, Bonn, Okt. 1987. Pp. 936–939, notes.

24076. ——— GENÉE, PIERRE: *Wiener Synagogen 1825–1938.* Vorbemerkung von Helmut Zilk und einleitende Worte von Kurt Schubert. Wien: Löcker, 1987. 117 pp., illus., bibl. (112–116).

24077. — *'Heilige Gemeinde Wien': Judentum in Wien*. [Katalog der Ausstellung] Sammlung Max Berger [im] Historischen Museum der Stadt Wien, 12. Nov. 1987 bis 5. Juni 1988. (Red.: Karl Albrecht-Weinberger & Felicitas Heimann-Jelinek.) Wien: Eigenverl. der Museen der Stadt Wien, 1987. 259 pp., illus., bibl. (Historisches Museum der Stadt Wien, Sonderausstellung, 108.) [Exhibition of objets d'art and documents from the Collection Max Berger, illustrating Jewish history and daily life from the beginning of the 18th century to 1938.]

24078. — OXAAL, IVAR/POLLAK, MICHAEL/BOTZ, GERHARD, eds.: *Jews, antisemitism and culture in Vienna*. London; New York: Routledge & Kegan Paul, 1987. XII, 300 pp., notes (241–294), index (295–300). [Cont.: The Jews of young Hitler's Vienna: historical and sociological aspects (Ivar Oxaal, 11–38). Class, culture and the Jews of Vienna, 1900 (Steven Beller, 39–58). Cultural innovation and social identity in fin-de-siècle Vienna (Michael Pollak, 59–74). Viennese culture and the Jewish self-hatred hypothesis: a critique (Allan Janik, 75–88). The contexts and nuances of anti-Jewish language: were all the 'antisemites' antisemites? (Sigurd Paul Scheichl, 89–110). Social democracy, antisemitism and the Jews of Vienna (Robert S. Wistrich, 111–120). The politics of the Viennese Jewish community, 1890–1914 (Walter R. Weitzmann, 121–151). Political antisemitism in interwar Vienna (Bruce F. Pauley, 152–173). Assimilated Jewish youth and Viennese cultural life around 1930 (Richard Thieberger, 174–184). The Jews of Vienna from the 'Anschluss' to the Holocaust (Gerhard Botz, 185–204). Avenues of escape: the Far East (Françoise Kreissler, 205–215). Antisemitism before and after the Holocaust: the Austrian case (Bernd Marin, 216–233). 'Last waltz in Vienna': a postscript (George Clare, 234–240).] [Cf.: The death of Vienna and the birth of psychoanalysis (Norman Stone) [in]: The Sunday Times, London, Feb. 7, 1988.]

24079. — PALMON, ABRAHAM: *The Jewish community of Vienna between the two World Wars, 1918–1938; continuity and change in its internal political life*. [In Hebrew, with English summary]. Jerusalem, Hebrew Univ., Diss., 1985. 360, XXVII pp.

24080. — SPIEL, HILDE: *Vienna's golden autumn 1866–1938*. London: Weidenfeld & Nicolson, 1987. 248 pp., illus. [Also German edn. under the title]: *Glanz und Untergang: Wien 1866–1938*. Autorisierte Übers. aus dem Engl. von Hanna Neves. München: List; Wien: Kremayr & Scheriau, 1987. 240 pp., illus., bibl. (226–230). [Incl. the history of the Jews in Vienna and refers to many Austrian-Jewish personalities. Cf.: Kosher Sachertorte (Richard Grunberger) [in]: History Today, Vol. 37, London, Dec. 1987, p. 58.]

——— — STRICKER, WILLIAM: *Kadimah of Vienna*. [See No. 24544.]

——— — *Theodor Herzl und das Wien des 'Fin de siècle'*. [See No. 24587.]

24081. — TIETZE, HANS: *Die Juden Wiens: Geschichte – Wirtschaft – Kultur*. (Unveränd. Neudr. der 1. Ausg. Wien, E. P. Tal, 1933. Geleitwort: Andreas Tietze. Vorwort: Nikolaus Vielmetti.) Wien (Kärntner Str. 8): Edition Atelier, 1987. VI, 301 pp., illus., ports., chronology (287–291), bibl. (300–302). [H. Tietze, March 1, 1880 Prague – Apr. 11, 1954 New York, art historian, emigrated to the USA in 1938.]

——— — Wistrich, Robert S.: *The modernization of Viennese Jewry: the impact of German culture in a multiethnic state*. [See pp. 43–70 in No. 23912.]

24082. — WISTRICH, ROBERT S.: *Social democracy, the Jews, and antisemitism in fin-de-siècle Vienna*. [In]: Living with antisemitism, ed. by Jehuda Reinharz [see No. 24835]. Hanover & London, 1987. Pp. 193–209, notes. [See also pp. 111–120 in No. 24078.]

24083. — WISTRICH, ROBERT S.: *Vienna in Jewish history*. [In]: Studies in Contemporary Jewry, 3, Oxford Univ. Press, 1987. Pp. 228–236. [Review essay.]

24084. VORARLBERG. BURMEISTER, KARL HEINZ: *Ein jüdischer Türsegen aus Hohenems; zur jüdischen Volkskunde in Vorarlberg*. [In]: Jahrbuch des Vorarlberger Landesmuseumsvereins, 1968/69, Bregenz, 1970. Pp. 261–263, facsims., footnotes. [See also No. 24074.]

3. Czechoslovakia

24085. *The Bulletin of Informations*. Publ. by the Council of the Jewish Religious Communities in the CSR, Prague and by the Central Committee of the Jewish Religious Communities in the SSR, Bratislava, Nr. 1–4 (1985); Nr. 1–2, & 3 (1986); Nr. 4 (1986) – 1 (1987), & 2 (1987). Ed.: Dezider Galský; [form 1987]: Zdenka Meisnereová. Prague: Central Religious Publ. House, 1985–1987. 5 issues. [Formerly, and again Nr. 2 (1987) issued in German under the title: *Informationsbulletin*.] [Issues cont. short essays on the history of former Jewish communities, portrayals of Czech-Jewish personalities, reminiscences by concentration camp survivors, reports on communal life today.]

24086. *Judaica Bohemiae*. Vol. 23, Nos. 1–2. Publication du Musée juif d'Estat, Prague. Réd. en chef: Otakar Petřik. Praha: Státní židovské muzeum v Praze, 1987. 62; 65–123 pp., illus., footnotes. [2 issues.] [*No. 1* incl.: Hebrew literary sources to the Czech history of the first half of the 17th century: end of the Thirty Years' War in the testimonies of contemporaries (Jiřina Šedinová, 38–57). *No. 2*: Stories of the Golem and their relation to the work of Rabbi Löw of Prague (Vladimír Sadek, 85–91). Drei hebräische Drucke gersonidischer Herkunft (Martina Vodsedálková, 92–94; refers to 3 publications by the Prague printer family Gerson 1580 & 1595). Die Auslieferung des synagogalen Silbers im Jahr 1810 (Josef Hráský, 95–100. Nouveau cimetière juif de Prague – monument culturel protégé (František Kafka, 101–113; incl. alphabetical list of persons and families and sites of their burial places, 111–113). See also Nos. 24230, 24376.]

24087. KALESNÁ, JANA: *Übersicht der Matriken in der Slowakei bis zur Verstaatlichung der Matriken-agende [1950]*. [In Czech, title transl.]. Bratislava: Archívna správa ministerstva vnútra SSR, 1982. 525 pp., index of places. [Complete survey of confessional and communal birth-, death-, and marriage-registers which today are kept in archives; incl. registers for Jews from about 1787. Cf.: Besprechung (Vlastimila Hamáčková) [in]: Judaica Bohemiae, Vol. 23, No. 2, Prague, 1987, pp. 115–116.]

24088. KIEVAL, HILLEL J.: *Education and national conflict in Bohemia: Germans, Czechs and Jews*. [In]: Studies in Contemporary Jewry, 3, Oxford Univ. Press, 1987. Pp. 49–71.

24089. KIEVAL, HILLEL J.: *Nationalism and antisemitism: the Czech-Jewish response*. [In]: Living with antisemitism, ed. by Jehuda Reinharz [see No. 24835]. Hanover & London, 1987. Pp. 210–233, notes.

24090. ROTHENBERG, RUTH: *Scrolls with a past: researching into Czech Jewry's legacy*. [In]: AJR Information, Vol. 42, No. 5, London, May 1987. P. 6.

24091. SCHROUBEK, GEORG R.: *Der 'Ritualmord' von Polná [1899]: traditioneller und moderner Wahnglaube*. [In]: Antisemitismus und jüdische Geschichte [see No. 24806]. Berlin, 1987. Pp. 149–172, footnotes.

24092. WLASCHEK, RUDOLF M.: *Zur Geschichte der Juden in Nordostböhmen, unter besonderer Berücksichtigung des südlichen Riesengebirgsvorlandes*. Marburg/Lahn: J. G. Herder-Institut, 1987. XII, 76 pp., illus., facsims., map, tabs., bibl. (70–73). (Historische und landeskundliche Ostmitteleuropa-Studien, 2.) [Incl.: Transporte in den Tod (50–58).]

24093. PRAGUE. LE COMTE, MIA MÜNZER: *I still dream of Prague*. Memoirs. New York: Philosophical Library, 1986. 176 pp. illus., ports. [Author, born in 1909, remembers social life in Prague, the joint lives of Jews and non-Jews; incl. the Nazi period.]

———   — Kieval, Hillel J.: *Caution's progress: the modernization of Jewish life in Prague, 1780–1830*. [See pp. 71–106 in No. 23912.]

24094. — PETR. PAVEL: *Jews and Czechs in Kafka's Prague*. [In]: Kwiet, Konrad, ed.: From the emancipation to the Holocaust [See No. 23891]. Kensington, Australia, 1987. Pp. 127–135, notes.

24095. — WLASCHEK, RUDOLF M.: *Die Prager 'Selbstwehr': Rückblick auf ein Wochenblatt zur 'jüdischen Erneurung'*. [In]: Tribüne, Jg. 26, H. 102, Frankfurt am Main, 1987. Pp. 59–60, 65–66.

4. Hungary

———   SILBER, MICHAEL: *The historical experience of German Jewry and its impact on the Haskalah and reform in Hungary*. [See pp. 107–158 in No. 23912.]

C. German Jews in Various Countries

———   EXILE. [See also Nos. 24138, 24143, 24185, 24826.]

24096. — BERGHAHN, MARION: *Continental Britons: German-Jewish refugees from Nazi Germany*. Oxford: Berg, 1987. 300 pp.

24097. — BONDY, LOUIS WOLFGANG: *Ein Berliner wird Antiquar in London*. [In]: Aus dem Antiquariat,

3, [Beilage zum] Börsenblatt für den Deutschen Buchhandel, Nr. 25, Frankfurt am Main, 27. März 1987. Pp. A 135 – A 139. [L.W.B., born June 19, 1910 in Berlin, journalist in Paris 1932–1933, emigrated via Spain to England in 1936, brought Alfred Wiener's library from Amsterdam to London in 1939, deputy director of the Wiener Library until 1945, from 1947 antiquarian bookseller, also active in local politics.]

24098.   — BOWER, TOM: *The paperclip conspiracy: the hunt for Nazi scientists*. London: Michael Joseph, 1987. 288 pp. [Deals mainly with the recruitment of Nazi scientists by the Western allies, but also with the loss to Germany, and the benefit to the West, of the forced emigration of Jewish talent. Cf.: Picking Hitler's brains (Neal Ascherson) [in]: The Observer, London, Feb. 22, 1987.]

24099.   — BROSER, STEFAN/PAGEL, GERDA, eds.: *Psychoanalyse im Exil; Texte verfolgter Analytiker*. Würzburg: Königshausen & Neumann, 1987. 159 pp., bibl. references.

24100.   — CRAVER, EARLENE: *The emigration of the Austrian economists*. [In]: History of Political Economy, Vol. 18, No. 1, Durham, N.C., 1986. [32 pp.], footnotes.

24101.   — DITTRICH VAN WERINGH, KATHINKA: *Der niederländische Spielfilm der dreissiger Jahre und die deutsche Filmemigration*. Amsterdam: Rodopi, 1987. 136 pp., bibl. (124–127). (Amsterdamer Publikationen zur Sprache und Literatur, Bd. 69.)

———   — DÜWELL, KURT: *Berliner Wissenschaftler in der Emigration: das Beispiel der Hochschullehrer nach 1933*. [See in No. 23942, pp. 126–134 (Bd. 3).]

———   — *Exilforschung. Ein internationales Jahrbuch. Bd. 5: Fluchtpunkte des Exils und andere Themen*. [See No. 24608.]

24102.   — FELDMAN, GERALD D.: *German economic history*. [In]: Central European History, Vol. 19, No. 2, Atlanta, Ga., June 1986. Pp. 174–185, ports. [Refers also to the contributions made by exile economists to the teaching of German economic history at American universities, a.o., by Alexander Gerschenkron, Fritz Redlich, Hans Rosenberg.]

24103.   — FISCHER, KLAUS: *Vom Wissenschaftstransfer zur Kontextanalyse – oder: Wie schreibt man die Geschichte der Wisssenschaftsemigration*. [In]: Antisemitismus und jüdische Geschichte [see No. 24806]. Berlin, 1987. Pp. 267–294, footnotes.

24104.   — FLETCHER, COLIN R.: *Refugee mathematicians: a German crisis and a British response, 1933–1936*. [In]: Historia Mathematica, 13, San Diego, Feb. 1986. Pp. 13–27.

24105.   — HEILBUT, ANTHONY: *Kultur ohne Heimat: deutsche Emigranten in den USA nach 1930*. Aus dem Amerikan. von Jutta Schust. Weinheim: Quadriga, 1987. 388 pp., illus., ports., facsims., bibl. (375–381). [For American orig. see No. 19895/YB XXIX.]

24106.   — HOCH, PAUL K.: *Migration and the generation of new scientific ideas*. [In]: Minerva, Vol. 25, No. 3, London, Autumn 1987. Pp. 209–237, footnotes. [Refers also to German-Jewish émigré scientists in Great Britain and the USA.]

24107.   — HORAK, JAN-CHRISTOPHER: *Fluchtpunkt Hollywood; eine Dokumentation zur Filmemigration nach 1933*. 2., erweiterte u. korrigierte Aufl. unter Mitarb. von Elisabeth Tape. Münster: MAkS-Publ., 1986. 193 pp., illus., bibl. (155– 193). [Augmented and corrected edn. of No. 22000/YB XXXI.]

24108.   — KÖLMEL, RAINER: *Die Anfänge der 'Association of Jewish Refugees' in London*. [In]: Antisemitismus und jüdische Geschichte [see No. 24806]. Berlin, 1987. Pp. 215–230, footnotes.

24109.   — KROHN, CLAUS-DIETER/ZUR MÜHLEN, PATRIK von: *Aktuelle Fragen der Exilforschung*. [In]: Archiv für Sozialgeschichte, Bd. 27, Bonn, 1987. Pp. 680–700. [Review essay.]

24110.   — KROHN, CLAUS-DIETER: *Wissenschaft im Exil: deutsche Sozial- und Wirtschaftswissenschaftler in den USA und die New School for Social Research*. Frankfurt am Main; New York: Campus, 1987. 286 pp., bibl. (270–281). [On the New School see also No. 23146/YB XXXII.]

24111.   — KWIET, KONRAD: *Max Joseph – Lebensweg eines deutsch-jüdischen Emigranten [in Sydney, Australia]*. [In]: Antisemitismus und jüdische Geschichte [see No. 24806]. Berlin, 1987. Pp. 231–242, footnotes. [M. Joseph, Apr. 22, 1894 Schönlanke – Sept. 21, 1974 Sydney, businessman.]

24112.   — LOWENSTEIN, STEVEN M.: *Frankfurt on the Hudson: the German Jewish community of Washington Heights, 1933–1983; its structure and culture*. Detroit: Wayne State Univ. Press, 1987. 403 pp., illus. (Publication of the Leo Baeck Institute.) [The German-Jewish community of Washington Heights in New York City had the largest US settlement of refugees from Nazi Germany.]

24113.   — McCLELLAND, CHARLES E.: *German intellectual history*. [In]: Central European History, Vol. 19, No. 2, Atlanta, Ga., June 1986. Pp. 164–173, notes. [Deals with the major contribution by German-Jewish exile scholars to the teaching of German history at American universities.]

24114. — *Medio siglo de vida Judía en La Paz.* La Paz: Círculo Israelita, 1987. 325 pp. [Also on the refugees from Germany and Austria 1937–1939 and the development of the Comunidad Israelita de Bolivia.]

24115. — MELHUISH, KATHLEEN JOY: *The German-Jewish emigration and the historian's craft.* [In]: Kwiet, Konrad, ed.: From the emancipation to the Holocaust [see No. 23891]. Kensington, Australia, 1987. Pp. 155–165, notes (163–165). [Deals, a.o. with Victor Ehrenberg, Fritz T. Epstein, Felix Gilbert, Hans Kohn, and mainly with Ernest Bramsted, orig. Ernst Kohn-Bramsted, Dec. 16, 1901 Augsburg – Spring 1978 England, historian, emigrated to England in 1933, in Australia from 1952–1969.]

24116. — *Österreicher im Exil: Belgien, 1938–1945.* Eine Dokumentation. Hrsg.: Dokumentations-archiv des Österreichischen Widerstandes. Auswahl und Bearb.: Ulrich Weinzierl. Einleitung: Gundl Herrnstadt-Steinmetz. Wien: Österr. Bundesverl., 1987. 165 pp., illus., ports., facsims., footnotes.

24117. — PETERSON, WALTER F.: *The Berlin liberal press in exile: a history of the Pariser Tageblatt-Pariser Tageszeitung, 1933–1940.* Tübingen: Niemeyer, 1987. XV, 287 pp. (Studien und Texte zur Sozialgeschichte der Literatur, Bd. 18.)

24118. — REGIS, ED.: *Who got Einstein's office: eccentricity and genius at the Institute for Advanced Study.* New York: Addison-Wesley, 1987. 316 pp., appendix, sources. [Deals, a.o., with Einstein's years at the Institute for Advanced Study in Princeton and also with other German-Jewish exile scientists and scholars appointed to the Institute.]

24119. — RIDER, ROBIN E.: *Alarm and opportunity: emigration of mathematicians and physicists to Britain and the United States, 1933–1945.* [In]: Historical Studies in the Physical Sciences, Vol. 15, No. 1, Berkeley, 1984. Pp. 107–176.

24120. — ROMAIN, JONATHAN: *Refugee rabbis' impact on Anglo-Jewry.* [In]: AJR Information, Vol. 42, No. 10, London, Oct. 1987, P. 7.

24121. — ROSENTHAL, BERNARD M.: *Die sanfte Invasion: aus dem kontinentalen Europa emigrierte Buchhändler der 30er und 40er Jahre und ihr Einfluss auf den antiquarischen Buchhandel in den USA.* [In]: Aus dem Antiquariat, 10, [Beilage zum] Börsenblatt für den Deutschen Buchhandel, Nr. 87, Frankfurt am Main, 30. Okt. 1987. Pp. A 389-A 397. [B.M.R., born May 5, 1920 in Munich, antiquarian bookdealer, emigrated via various countries to the USA in 1939 now living in San Francisco.]

24122. — RUBINSTEIN, HILARY L.: *The Jews in Victoria, 1935–1985.* London: Allen & Unwin, 1986. XIV, 284 pp., illus., bibl. [Also on post-World War II immigration of German Jews to Victoria, Australia.]

24123. — SCURLA, HERBERT: *Der Scurla-Bericht: die Tätigkeit deutscher Hochschullehrer in der Türkei 1933–1939.* Hrsg. von Klaus-Detlev Grothusen. Frankfurt am Main: Dagyeli-Verl., 1987. 168 pp. (Schriftenreihe des Zentrums für Türkeistudien, Bd. 3.) [The German official H. Scurla visited Turkey in May 1939 on behalf of the Reichserziehungsministerium; his report on the activities of academic émigrés from Nazi Germany in Ankara and Istanbul is now publ. for the first time with critical annotations by Fritz Neumark, who, as one of the émigrés, publ. in 1980 his own recollections: 'Zuflucht am Bosporus', see No. 17055/YB XXVI.]

24124. — SEYWALD, WILFRIED: *Journalisten im Shanghaier Exil 1939–1949.* Salzburg; Neugebauer, 1987. 375 pp., illus., ports., facsims., bibl. (364–370).

—— — SHARMAN, WALTER: *Saved from the abyss of the shadow of death.* [See No. 24362.]

24125. — SÖLLNER, ALFONS: *Hans J. Morgenthau – ein deutscher Konservativer in Amerika?* Eine Fallstudie zum Wissenstransfer durch Emigration. [In]: Antisemitismus und jüdische Geschichte [see No. 24806]. Berlin, 1987. Pp. 243–266, footnotes.

24126. — SPENCER, GEOFF: *Beloved alien: Walter Fliess, 1901–1985, remembered.* Vancouver; Donhead St. Andrew, Wilts.: Priv. print., 1985. 81 pp., illus., ports. [W. Fliess, Dec. 31, 1901 Grossmühlingen – 1985 England, socialist politician, emigrated in 1933 via Holland to England.]

—— — STADLER, FRIEDRICH, ed.: *Vertriebene Vernunft.* [See No. 24176.]

—— — STERN, FRITZ: *Fritz Haber: the scientist in power and in exile.* [See No. 23907.]

24127. — STERN, FRITZ: *German history in America, 1884–1984.* [In]: Central European History, Vol. 19, No. 2, Atlanta, Ga., June 1986. Pp. 131–163, notes. [Deals also with German-Jewish exile historians and refugee scholars.]

24128. — STIEFEL, ERNST C.: *Die deutsche juristische Emigration in den USA.* [In]: Festschrift für Walter Oppenhoff zum 80. Geburtstag. München: Beck, 1985. Pp. 433–449.

24129. — STRAUSS, HERBERT A./BUDDENSIEG, TILMANN/DÜWELL, KURT, eds.: *Emigration: deutsche Wissenschaftler nach 1933: Entlassung und Vertreibung.* Berlin: Technische Univ., Univ. bibliothek, Abt. Publikationen, 1987. Various pagings, illus., bibl. [Cont.: Vorwort (Herbert A. Strauss, VI-VII). Hilfsorganisationen für deutsche Wissenschaftler im Ausland (Kurt Düwell, VIII-X). '. . . einen Ort zu finden, an dem man aufrecht leben kann': Abschiedsbrief an Wolfgang Köhler, 20. Mai 1933 (Kurt Lewin, XI-XVII). Teil 1: List of displaced German scholars, London, Autumn 1936 (125 pp., index of names). Teil 2: Supplementary list of displaced German scholars, London, Autumn 1937 (16 pp., index of names). Teil 3: The Emergency Committee in Aid of Displaced Foreign Scholars: report, New York, June 1, 1941 (19 pp., with list of grant recipients classified according to disciplines, pp. 5 ff., bibl.). [Publication in connection with the exhibition 'Der Kongress denkt', see No. 23942.]

24130. — STRAUSS, HERBERT A., ed.: *Jewish immigrants of the Nazi period in the USA.* Sponsored by the Research Foundation for Jewish Immigration, New York and Zentrum für Antisemitismusforschung, Technische Univ., Berlin. New York; München; London: Saar, 1979 ff. *Vol. 6:* STRAUSS, HERBERT A.: *Essays on the history, persecution and emigration of German Jews.* 1987. 410 pp. [For previously publ. vols. see No. 23149/YB XXXII.]

24131. — STRAUSS, HERBERT A. [et al.]: *Wissenschaftstransfer durch Emigration nach 1933.* [In]: Forschung Aktuell, Jg. 4, Nr. 16–17, Technische Univ. Berlin, Nov. 1987. Pp. 39–43, ports. [Cont.: Wissenschaftsemigration (Herbert A. Strauss). Die Mediziner (Hans-Peter Kröner). Die Staats- und Politikwissenschaftler (Alfons Söllner). Die Naturwissenschaftler (Klaus Fischer.).]

——— — TAUSIG, FRANZISKA: *Shanghai-Passage: Flucht und Exil einer Wienerin.* [See No. 24177.]

24132. — TRABER, HABAKUK/WEINGARTEN, ELMAR, eds.: *Verdrängte Musik: Berliner Komponisten im Exil.* (Ein Buch der Berliner Festspiel GmbH zum Programmschwerpunkt 'Musik aus dem Exil' der 37. Berliner Festwochen 1987.) Berlin: Argon, 1987. 376 pp., illus., ports. [Incl. (titles condensed): Wege ins Exil (H. Traber, 13–42. Der Komponist Berthold Goldschmidt im Exil (Karoly Csipak, 43–78). Der deutsch-jüdische Beitrag zur Entwicklung des Musiklebens in Israel (Peter Gradenwitz, 79–98). Amerikas Einfluss auf eingewanderte Komponisten (Ernst Krenek, 99–108). Ernst Toch in Amerika (Charlotte E. Erwin, 109–122). Musiker im Exil in Südkalifornien (Leonard Stein, 123–128). Schönberg als Lehrer in Los Angeles (David Raksin, 129–140). Zum Einfluss deutscher Exil-Komponisten auf die Arbeitermusik-Bewegung und das Musikleben in den Vereinigten Staaten der dreissiger Jahre (Albrecht Dümling, 141–164). Komponisten am Berliner Ensemble (Friedrich Dieckmann, 181–194). Notizen zur Filmmusik (H. Traber, 195–204). Biographische Dokumentation (205–360). Programm: Musik aus dem Exil (369–376).]

——— — *Die Vertreibung des Geistigen aus Österreich.* [See No. 24178.]

24133. — WALTHER, PETER TH.: *Emigrierte deutsche Historiker in den Vereinigten Staaten, 1945–1950: Blick oder Sprung über den grossen Teich?* [In]: Cobet, Christoph, ed.: Einführung in Fragen an die Geschichtswissenschaft in Deutschland nach Hitler 1945–1950. Frankfurt am Main: Verlag Cobet, 1986. (Handbuch der Geistesgeschichte in Deutschland nach Hitler 1945–1950, Reihe: Geschichte, Beihefte, 1.) Pp. 41–50, notes (49–50).

24134. — WOLF, HEINZ: *Deutsche Emigrationshistoriker in den USA: Nationalsozialismus aus der Sicht Vertriebener.* [In]: Geschichte, 74, St. Gallen, Jan.-Feb. 1987. Pp. 23–28.

24135. GELIN, JAMES A.: *Starting over: the formation of the Jewish community of Springfield, Massachusetts, 1840–1905.* Lanham, Md.: University Press of America, 1985. X, 161 pp., illus., bibl. [Also on German-Jewish settlers.]

24136. GUGGENHEIM Family. DAVIS, JOHN H.: *The Guggenheims: an American dynasty.* New York: Shapolsky, 1987. 688 pp., illus. [Family of Swiss-Jewish origin, see German edn. No. 21004/YB XXX.]

——— MEYER, MICHAEL A.: *German-Jewish identity in nineteenth-century America.* [See pp. 247–268 in No. 23912.]

24137. NADEL, STANLEY: *Jewish race and German soul in nineteenth-century America.* [In]: American Jewish History, Vol. 77, No. 1, Waltham, Ma., Sept. 1987. Pp. 6–26. [On the influence of both German and German-Jewish immigrants on American life.]

24138. RAFAEL, RUTH KELSON: *Western Jewish History Center: guide to archival and oral history collections.* Berkeley, Ca.: Western Jewish History Center [at the] Judah L. Magnes Memorial

Museum, 1987. XVIII, 208 pp., illus. [Incl. items concerning German-Jewish immigration before 1933 and Jewish refugees from Nazi Germany.]

24139.   ROCHLIN, HARRIET & FRED: *Pioneer Jews: a new life in the Far West.* Boston: Houghton Mifflin, 1984. XII, 243 pp., illus., bibl. [An illus. social history, also on Jewish immigrants from Germany.]

24140.   ROCKAWAY, ROBERT A.: *The Jews of Detroit: from the beginning, 1762–1914.* Detroit: Wayne State Univ. Press, 1986. XI, 162 pp., illus., bibl. [Incl. the 19th-century immigration of German Jews.]

24141.   SAPIR, EDWARD. SISKIN, EDGAR E.: *The life and times of Edward Sapir.* [In]: Jewish Social Studies, Vol. 48, Nos. 3–4, New York, Summer-Fall, 1986. Pp. 283–292, notes. [E.S., Jan. 26, 1884 Lauenburg – Feb. 4, 1939 New Haven, Conn., anthropologist and linguist, from 1889 in the USA.]

24142.   SCHECHTER, MATHILDE ROTH. SCULT, MEL: *The Beale Boste reconsidered: the life of Mathilde Roth Schechter (M.R.S.).* [In]: Modern Judaism, Vol. 7, No. 1, Baltimore, Feb. 1987. Pp. 1–27, notes. [M.R.S., born 1857 in Guttentag, Silesia, grew up in Breslau, married to Salomon Schechter, translator of Heine into English, went in 1902 to New York where she established the National Women's League in 1918.]

24143.   TRAHTEMBERG SIEDERER, LEON: *La immigración judía al Peru 1848–1948.* Una historia documentada de la immigración de los judíos de habla alemana. Lima, Peru (Av. Sucre 1200 Pueblo Libre): Sesator, 1987. 322 pp., illus., ports., notes. [Incl. list of names of the German-speaking immigrants 1850–1947 (pp. 189–322); for refugees from Nazi Germany information on native town, age and profession is added (pp. 307–319).]

———   VEGHAZI, STEFAN: *Juden in Lateinamerika.* [See pp. 89–99 in No. 24809.]

24144.   VICKY. DAVIES, RUSSELL/OTTAWAY, LIZ: *Vicky.* London: Secker & Warburg, 1987. 192 pp., illus., cartoons. [Cf.: Veni vidi, Vicky (John Gross) [in]: The Observer, London, Nov. 22, 1987. See also article on the occasion of an exhibition of Vicky's work at the National Portrait Gallery in London: Vicky: master of the pungent cartoon (Barry Fealdman) [in]: Jewish Chronicle, London, Dec. 18, 1987, p. 10.] [Vicky, orig. Victor Weisz, Apr. 25, 1913 Berlin – Feb. 23, 1966 London (suicide), political cartoonist, graphic artist, emigrated in 1935 to Hungary and Czechoslovakia, from 1936 in England, became one of Great Britain's leading cartoonists.]

24145.   WARBURG, Sir SIEGMUND. ATTALI, JACQUES: *A man of influence: the extraordinary career of S. G. Warburg.* Transl. from the French by Barbara Ellis. Bethesda, Md.: Adler & Adler, 1987. 380 pp., bibl. [Also edn. for England under the title]: *A man of influence: Sir Siegmund Warburg 1902–1982.* London: Weidenfeld & Nicolson, 1986. 368 pp., [And German edn. under the title]: *Siegmund G. Warburg: das Leben eines grossen Bankiers.* Aus dem Franz. von Hermann Kusterer. Düsseldorf: Econ, 1986. 504 pp., bibl. (485–491). [For French orig. see No. 22029/YB XXXI. Cf.: Left bank account (A. J. Sherman) [in]: TLS, London, May 23, 1986 (a critical review debunking the book and correcting some of the many errors).] [Sir S.G., data see No. 18961/YB XXVIII.]

II. RESEARCH AND BIBLIOGRAPHY

A. Libraries and Institutes

24146.   DEUTSCHES LITERATURARCHIV, Marbach am Neckar, *Jahrbuch der Deutschen Schillergesellschaft.* Jg. 31. Im Auftrag des Vorstands hrsg. von Fritz Martini [et al.]. Stuttgart: Kröner, 1987. VII, 582 pp., illus., footnotes. [Incl. literary essays on A. Döblin (Barbara Belhalfaoui-Köhn), Kafka (Malcolm Pasley), Tucholsky (Eberhard Lämmert). See also Nos. 24621, 24863.]

24147.   GERMANIA JUDAICA, Köln. RICHARZ, MONIKA: *Die Bibliothek Germania Judaica in Köln.* [In]: Informationen zur modernen Stadtgeschichte, H. 1, Berlin, 1987. Pp. 33–34.

24148.   INSTITUT FÜR DEUTSCHE GESCHICHTE, Universität Tel-Aviv. *Tel Aviver Jahrbuch für deutsche Geschichte.* Hrsg. vom Institut für Deutsche Geschichte. Bd. 16, 1987. (Red.: Shulamit Volkov, Frank Stern.) Gerlingen: Bleicher, 1987. XII, 447 pp., illus., facsim., tabs., footnotes. [Continuation of: Jahrbuch des Instituts für Deutsche Geschichte, Universität Tel-Aviv.] [Incl.: Umgang mit Minderheiten: vergleichende Reflexionen zu einem Verhaltensproblem in den politischen Kulturen Deutschlands und Frankreichs (Rudolf von Thadden, 239–248; refers also to the Jewish minority). Fritz Naphtali und Viktor Agartz: Wirtschaftsdemokratie und Wirtschaftsneuordnung; zwei Beiträge zur Diskussion (Hans Willi Weinzen/Jehuda Riemer, 423–430; 431–437; for preceding article see No. 22670/YB XXXI.) In memoriam Charles Jehuda Bloch (Shlomo Na'aman, 438–439; Ch.J.B., May 19, 1921 Berlin – 1987 Israel, historian). Further articles are listed according to subject.]

24149. INSTITUT FÜR DIE ERFORSCHUNG DER GESCHICHTE DER JUDEN IN ÖSTERREICH, St. Pölten. HAUER, NADINE: *An den Wurzeln des Antisemitismus: ein wissenschaftliches Zentrum in St. Pölten.*[In]: Morgen, Jg. 11, Nr. 55, Wien, Okt 1987. Pp. 222–223, illus. [Report on the work of the institute and its new domicile in the renovated former synagogue in St. Pölten.]

24150. INSTITUTE OF CONTEMPORARY JEWRY, The Hebrew University of Jerusalem: *Studies in Contemporary Jewry.* An annual. 3. Eds.: Jonathan Frankel [et al.]. New York; Oxford: Oxford Univ. Press, 1987. 345 pp., notes. [Cont. the sections: Symposium: Jews and other ethnic groups in a multi-ethnic world, ed. by Ezra Mendelsohn (3–124). Essays (127–212). Review essays (215–236). Books in review (237–345; incl.: Partial list of recently completed doctoral dissertations, pp. 339–345). Articles referring to German-Jewish history are listed according to subject.]

24151. LEO BAECK INSTITUTE. *Bulletin des Leo Baeck Instituts.* Nr. 76–78. Hrsg. von Joseph Walk, Sarah Fraiman und Itta Shedletzky. Frankfurt am Main: Jüdischer Verlag bei Athenäum, 1987. 78; 95; 122 pp., notes. [3 issues.] [*Nr. 76* incl.: Namensregister 1986: Bulletin Nr. 73–75 (pp. 74–78). *Nr. 78*: Dreissig Jahre Bulletin (Joseph Walk, 3–5). Individual contributions are listed according to subject.] [Cf.: Neues LBI-Bulletin: Nr. 77 (E. G. Lowenthal) [in]: MB, Jg. 56, Nr. 33, Tel-Aviv, Feb. 1988, p. 6.]

24152. — *Leo Baeck Institute Year Book XXXII.* Nineteenth-century antisemitism and Nazi rule. Ed.: Arnold Paucker. London: Secker & Warburg, 1987. XXV, 582 pp., illus., ports., facsims., tabs., diagrs., footnotes, bibl. (455–554). [Cont.: Preface (Arnold Paucker, VII–XI; incl. a note referring to the recent 'historians' debate' (p. XI). German Jews and Liberalism in retrospect: introduction to Year Book XXXII (George L. Mosse, XIII–XXV). Individual contributions are listed according to subject.] [Cf.: German Jewry's twilight: reflected in LBI Year Book XXXII (Ronald Stent) [in]: AJR Information, Vol. 43, No. 3, London, March 1988, p. 4. Leo-Baeck-Institut legt 32. Jahrbuch vor [in]: Aufbau, Vol. 53, No. 25, New York, Dec. 4, 1987, p. 20. Besprechung LBI Year Book XXXII (Kurt Gräubig) [in]: deutschland-berichte, Jg. 24, Nr. 4, Bonn, Apr. 1988, p. 35. Review LBI YB XXXI, 1986 (James F. Harris) [in]: Shofar, West Lafayette, Ind., Purdue Univ., Fall 1987, pp. 50–51.]

24153. — LBI New York. *Library and Archives News.* Ed.: Gabrielle Bamberger. Nos. 25–26. New York: Leo Baeck Institute, Winter & Summer 1987. 8; 8 pp. [2 issues.]

24154. — — *LBI News.* Ed.: Gabrielle Bamberger. Nos. 53–54. New York: Leo Baeck Institute, Winter & Summer-Fall, 1987. 16; 16 pp., front illus., illus., ports., facsims. [2 issues.] [*No. 53* incl.: German-speaking Jews and Zionism (1–9). Major exhibit on Jews in Germany to open at New York Public Library (10–11; refers to the travelling pictorial exhibition 'Jews in Germany under Prussian rule', produced in cooperation with the LBI New York, catalogue see No. 20813/YB XXX). Reports on LBI New York events. *No. 54*: Music material at the LBI (1–6). 'Jews in Germany under Prussian rule': impressions of an exhibition (Kenneth A. Bamberger, 8–11). Reports on LBI New York events. Tribute: Eva Reichmann-Jungmann: a 90th birthday tribute (Max Gruenewald, 13). Obituaries: In memoriam Alexander Altmann, 1906–1987 (Max Gruenewald, 12). In memoriam Ilse Blumenthal-Weiss, 1899–1987. In memoriam Martin G. Goldner, 1902–1987.]

24155. — GORAL, ARIE: *Leo Baeck und das Leo-Baeck-Institut.* Perspektiven eines Vortrags von Ernst Cramer im Hamburger Gemeindehaus. [In]: 'Allgemeine', Nr. 42/21, Bonn, 22. Mai 1987. P. 11.

——— — HERZIG, ARNO: *Juden und Judentum in der sozialgeschichtlichen Forschung.* [See No. 23883.]

24156. — MECKLENBURG, FRANK: *Die Sammlung des Leo Baeck Institutes New York zur Geschichte des deutschsprachigen Judentums.* [In]: Informationen zur modernen Stadtgeschichte, H. 1, Berlin, 1987. Pp. 13–16.

24157. — PAUCKER, ARNOLD: *The Leo Baeck Institute.* Interview by Eckhard Berkenbusch with Arnold Paucker, Director of the Leo Baeck Institute London. Broadcast by the German Language Service of the BBC. Transmission June 14, 1987. [Available on cassette in the LBI London and New York.]

24158. — UDE, KARL: *Der Kulturbeitrag des deutschen Judentums am Beispiel einer Sammlung: im Münchner*

Stadtmuseum gastiert die Wanderausstellung 'Jettchen Geberts Kinder'. [In]: Süddeutsche Zeitung, Nr. 159, München, 15. Juli 1987, p. 12. [For catalogue and further reviews of this travelling exhibition see No. 22912/YB XXXII.]

24159. — WALTER-MECKAUER-KREIS, ed.: *Verleihung der Walter-Meckauer-Plakette 1987 und Eröffnung der Ausstellung 'Die Jüdische Emigration aus Deutschland 1933–1941, die Geschichte einer Austreibung' im Historischen Archiv der Stadt Köln.* Eine Dokumentation. Köln: Walter-Meckauer-Kreis, 1988. 32 pp., illus. [Documentation on the bestowal of the Walter-Meckauer-Plakette 1987 on the Leo Baeck Institute in appreciation of its library and archives; reports were publ. under various headings in many newspapers, a.o., [in]: 'Allgemeine', Nr. 42/44, Bonn, 30. Okt. 1987, p. 6 [& in]: Aufbau, Vol. 53, No. 23, New York, Nov. 6, 1987, p. 4 [& in]: deutschland-berichte, Jg. 23, Nr. 12, Bonn, Dez. 1987, p. 19 [& in]: Tribüne, Jg. 26, H. 103 (p. 49) [& in]: H. 104 (p. 55), Frankfurt am Main, 1987. For catalogue and details of the travelling exhibition 'Die Jüdische Emigration aus Deutschland 1933–1941' see Nos. 22103/ YB XXXI & 23253–23254/YB XXXII.]

—— SCHOCHOW, WERNER: *Jüdische Bibliothekare aus dem deutschen Sprachraum.* [See No. 24560.]

24160. WIENER LIBRARY, London. *The Wiener Library Newsletter.* Ed.: A. J. Wells. Vol. 2, Nos. 3 & 4 (May & Sept. 1987). London, 1987. 2 issues (4 pp. each), illus. [*No. 3* incl.: The Wiener Library and the riddle of our times (Peter Pulzer, p. 1).]

24161. YAD VASHEM, Martyrs' and Heroes' Remembrance Authority. *Yad Vashem Studies.* 17 & 18. Ed. by Aharon Weiss. Jerusalem: Yad Vashem, 1986 & 1987. 2 vols. [Contributions relevant to German Jewry are listed according to subject.]

B. Bibliographies and Catalogues

24162. COHEN, SUSAN SARAH, ed.: *Antisemitism; an annotated bibliography.* Vol. 1. [Publ. by] The Vidal Sassoon International Center for the Study of Antisemitism [of] the Hebrew University of Jerusalem. New York; London: Garland, 1987. 392 pp., author & subject indexes (340–355; 356–392). [Cont. 1255 entries of works about antisemitism publ. in 1984–1985; does not cover antisemitic publications with the exception of a list of antisemitic periodicals (appendix I, pp. 316–325); also incl. listings of bibliographies on antisemitism publ. before 1984 (appendix II, pp. 326–339).]

24163. *Index of articles on Jewish studies.* Nos. 26 & 27: 1985 (with additions from previous years). Comp. and ed. by the editorial board of 'Kiryat Sefer'. (These vols. were ed. by Bitya Ben-Shammai (editor), Susie Cohen [et al.].) Jerusalem: The Jewish National and Univ. Library Press, 1986 & 1987. 2 vols. (XXXVI, 372, [VIII]; XXXIX, 366, [VIII] pp.).

24164. *Jüdisches Lexikon.* Ein enzyklopädisches Handbuch des jüdischen Wissens in 5 Bänden. Begründet von Georg Herlitz und Bruno Kirschner. Unveränderter Nachdr. der Erstausg., Berlin, Jüdischer Verlag, 1927–1930. 2. Aufl. des Nachdrucks. Frankfurt am Main: Jüdischer Verlag bei Athenäum, 1987. 5 vols., illus. [For detailed entry see first edn. of reprint, No. 18980/YB XXVIII.]

24165. MENDELSSOHN-ARCHIV. *Depositum Mendelssohn-Gesellschaft im Mendelssohn-Archiv der Staatsbibliothek Preussischer Kulturbesitz Berlin: Bestandverzeichnis.* (Einführung: Cécile Lowenthal-Hensel.) Berlin, Sept. 1987. [14] pp., index of names.

—— PERSONAL BIBLIOGRAPHIES. [See Nos. 24648 (Heinrich Heine). 24465 (Esriel Hildesheimer). 24669 (Gustav Mahler). 24366 (Ernst Simon). 24607 (Guy Stern). 24806 (Herbert A. Strauss). 24511 (Aron Tänzer). 24512 (Eugen Täubler).

24166. *Post-war publications on German Jewry; a selected bibliography of books and articles 1986.* Compiled by Irmgard Foerg and Annette Pringle. [In]: LBI Year Book XXXII, London, 1987. Pp. 455–554.

24167. RIFF, MICHAEL, ed.: *Dictionary of modern ideologies.* Manchester: Manchester Univ. Press, 1987. XIV, 226 pp. [The entries Antisemitism (17–24), Fascism (89–107), Zionism (222–226) deal also with German-Jewish issues.]

—— RÖSNER-ENGELFRIED, SUSANNE B.: *Bibliographie der jüdischen Kinder- und Jugendliteratur des 20. Jahrhunderts bis 1938.* [See in No. 24558.]

24168. SABLE, MARTIN H.: *Holocaust studies: a directory and bibliography of bibliographies.* Greenwood, Fla.: Penkevill, 1987. IX, 115 pp. [Bibliography covers books in English, Hebrew and

Yiddish; the directory gives information on, a.o., archives, libraries, organisations, Holocaust events and memorials.]

24169. SALAMANDER, RACHEL, ed.: *Literatur zum Judentum.* München: Literaturhandlung, 1987. 220 pp.

24170. TUTOROW, NORMAN E., comp.: *War crimes, war criminals and war crimes trials; an annotated bibliography and source book.* Westport, Conn.; London: Greenwood Press, 1986. XX, 548 pp.

III. THE NAZI PERIOD

A. General

24171. AUSCHWITZ. NAOR, SIMHA: *Krankenschwester in Auschwitz; Aufzeichnungen des Häftlings Nr. 80574.* Vorwort: Tisa von der Schulenburg. Freiburg i.Br.: Herder, 1986. 141 pp., illus., port., facsims. (Herderbücherei, 1350.) [S.N., orig. Stella Breit-Bogner, born 1899 in Vienna.]

24172. — UNGER, MICHAL: *The prisoner's first encounter with Auschwitz.* [In]: Holocaust and Genocide Studies, Vol. 1, No. 2, Oxford, 1986. Pp. 279–296.

—— AUSTRIA. [See also Nos. 24067–24068, 24076, 24078, 24100, 24116, 24230.]

24173. — *Das Jüdische Echo.* Vol. 36, Nr. 1. Hrsg.: Vereinigung Jüdischer Hochschüler Österreichs und Jüdischer Akademiker Österreichs. Wien (Gonzagagasse 22), Okt. 1987. 256 pp., illus., ports., facsims. [deals mainly with the events of the year 1938. Incl. the sections: *Der März 1938 in Österreich* (23–99; incl.: Der Anschluss und die Tragödie des österreichischen Judentums (Herbert Rosenkranz, 29–34); Otto Bauer, Karl Renner und der 'Anschluss' (Anton Pelinka, 35 & 37); Der Anfang des Schlachtens (Jonny Moser, 44–46); 'Auch Mödling mag die Juden nicht . . .': alltäglicher Faschismus in einer österreichischen Kleinstadt 1938 (Peter Malina, 67–74); Der Anschluss in Tirol (Elimelech Rimalt, 75–78); Die Vertreibung der burgenländischen Juden (Jonny Moser, 78–80); Kirche und Juden in Österreich nach dem 11. März 1938 (Erika Weinzierl, 83–91); Kirche und Juden 1938–1945 (Paul Schulmeister, 91–98). *Der November 1938* (99–110; cont.: Von der Annektion zur Reichskristallnacht (Herbert Steiner, 99–105); Die Kristallnacht in Wien: ein Zeugenbericht (Albert Massiczek, 107–110). *Die Kristallnacht* (111–138; incl.: Eine dokumentarische Sammlung (111–116); Österreich 1938: Erinnerungen und Eindrücke (Jehudith Hübner, 116–118). *Aus dem Archiv des Ungeists* (139–192; incl.: Es war keine Überraschung: die Katastrophe der Juden 1938 in Graz (Elfriede Schmidt, 149–153); Leopoldstadt revisited (Georg Eisler, 162–163). Wien anno 1938 (Ari Rath, 173–174). Die Familie März im Zeichen des März 1938 (Eveline März, 178–181). *Literatur, Kunst, Wissenschaft* (193–248; incl.: Österreich 1937/38: literarische Chronik (Sylvia M. Patsch, 212–216); Wiens Synagogen (Pierre Genée, 217–220); Die Universität Wien und der Nationalsozialismus (Brigitte Lichtenberger-Fenz, 235–239); Jüdische Ärzte im Jahre 1938 (Karl Sablik, 240–243). *Israel heute* (cont.: 40 Jahre Israel – 50 Jahre Anschluss (Mosche Meisels, 249–252; on the contribution of Austrian refugees to political life and science in Israel).]

24174. — KURIJ, ROBERT: *Nationalsozialismus und Widerstand im Waldviertel: die politische Situation von 1938–1945.* (A–3580) Horn (Postfach 100): Waldviertler Heimatbund, 1987. 247 pp., illus., bibl. (236–246). (Schriftenreihe des Waldviertler Heimatbundes, Bd. 28.) [Incl. chap. on the situation of the Jewish population.]

24175. — MITTERER, FELIX: *Kein schöner Land; ein Theaterstück und sein historischer Hintergrund.* Innsbruck: Haymon Verl., 1987. 176 pp., illus., ports. [Cont.: Das Stück (Felix Mitterer, 7–91). Der Anlass zum Stück: Das Schicksal des Rudolf Gomperz (Hans Thöny, 93–117). Die Juden in Tirol (Gretl Köfler, 119–134). Dokumente (135–174; incl.: Die Juden, pp. 137–145).] [A play and documents on the life of Rudolf Gomperz (son of the philosopher and classical philologist Theodor Gomperz), born March 11, 1878 in Vienna, engineer, pioneered skiing and winter sports, director of the St. Anton am Arlberg tourist bureau, dismissed in 1938, deported from Vienna after May 1942 to Eastern Europe, presumed to have been shot in the Minsk ghetto.]

24176. — STADLER, FRIEDRICH, ed.: *Vertriebene Vernunft. 1: Emigration und Exil österreichischer Wissenschaft 1930–1940.* Wien: Jugend & Volk, 1987. 584 pp., illus., tabs., bibl. (Veröffentlichungen des Ludwig-Boltzmann-Instituts, Sonderband 2.)

24177. — TAUSIG, FRANZISKA: *Shanghai-Passage: Flucht und Exil einer Wienerin.* Hrsg. vom Verein Kritische Sozialwissenschaft und Politische Bildung. Wien: Verlag für Gesellschaftskritik, 1987. XII, 154 pp. (Biographische Texte, Bd. 5.) [On persecution of the Jews in Vienna, and on exile in Shanghai.]

——— — *Totenbuch Theresienstadt.* [See No. 24377.]

24178. — *Die Vertreibung des Geistigen aus Österreich: zur Kulturpolitik des Nationalsozialismus.* [Ausstellung] Jänner/Feb. 1985. [Hrsg.]: Zentralsparkasse und Kommerzialbank, Wien, in Zusammenarbeit mit der Hochschule für Angewandte Kunst in Wien. (Katalog: Gabriele Koller, Gloria Withalm.) 2., verbesserte und erweiterte Aufl. Wien, 1986. 400 pp., bibl. (375), 'Ergänzungen' (377–400). [Covers a galaxy of Jewish actors, artists, musicians, scholars and writers forced into exile from Austria.]

24179. — WALZL, AUGUST: *Die Juden in Kärnten und das Dritte Reich.* Klagenfurt: Univ.-Verl. Carinthia, 1987. 375 pp., bibl. (357–361).

——— — WEINZIERL, ERIKA: *Austrian Catholics and the Jews.* [See pp. 283 ff. in No. 23888.]

24180. — WEINZIERL, ULRICH, ed.: *Österreichs Fall: Schriftsteller berichten vom 'Anschluss'.* Wien: Verlag Jugend und Volk, 1987. 190 pp. [Anthology of texts taken from contemporary publications, newspapers and periodicals; incl. also hitherto unpubl. texts by Robert Breuer (i.e. Lucien Friedlaender) and Hilde Spiel.]

24181. BAD SODEN. . . . *als wenn nichts gewesen wäre; Fragen an Zeitzeugen zu ihrem Leben im Faschismus.* Dokumente aus Bad Soden, Schwalbach und Hofheim. 2., erweiterte Aufl. Schwalbach: Bund Deutscher Pfadfinder Main-Taunus, 1987. 103 pp., illus. [Also on persecution of Jews in Bad Soden; augmented edn. of No. 19941/YB XXIX.]

——— BAECK LEO. NEIMARK, ANNE E.: *One man's valor: Leo Baeck and the Holocaust.* [See No. 24433.]

24182. BANKIER, DAVID. *The German Communist Party and Nazi antisemitism, 1933–1938.* [In]: LBI Year Book XXXII, London, 1987. Pp. 325–340, footnotes.

24183. BERGEN-BELSEN. *From Bergen Belsen to freedom; the story of the exchange of Jewish inmates of Bergen Belsen with German Templars from Palestine.* A symposium in memory of Haim Pazner [1899–1981]. Jerusalem: Yad Vashem, 1986. 61 pp., ports.

——— BERLIN. [See also Nos. 23941, 23943, 23952, 24097, 24117, 24132, 24208.]

24184. — BEHNKE, KRISTINA: *Juden im Grunewald – wer sich nicht erinnern will . . . ist gezwungen, die Geschichte noch einmal zu erleben.* [Dokumentation zur gleichnamigen] Ausstellung im Evangelischen Gemeindehaus, Berlin-Grunewald, Furtwänglerstr. 5, Okt. bis Dez. 1987. Berlin (33, Trabener Str. 28): K. Behnke, 1987. 430 pp., bibl. (428–430). [Photocopies.] [Incl.: Deportationslisten (198–120). Widerstand (138–147). Todesurteile gegen jüdische Kommunisten (245–249). Eine Arbeit zum Thema 'Emigration' – angeregt durch die Ausstellung – von Schülern der Fichtenberg-Oberschule und der Paulsen-Oberschule (Christina Schulze/Robert Heiduck, 386–397).]

24185. — FRIEDLÄNDER, SOPHIE: *Am meisten habe ich von meinen Schülern gelernt: Lebensgeschichte einer jüdischen Lehrerin in Berlin und im Exil.* Hrsg. von Monika Römer-Jacobs und Bruno Schonig. Berlin: Gewerkschaft Erziehung und Wissenschaft Berlin, 1987. 175, 3 pp., illus. (Lehrer-, Lehrerinnen-Lebensgeschichten, 8.)

24186. — HEIMS, STEVE J., ed.: *Passages from Berlin: recollections of former students and staff of the Goldschmidt Schule (1935–1939).* [N.p.], 1987. IX, 213 pp., illus., ports., facsims. [Obtainable from Marianne Phiebig, 25 Grandview Avenue, White Plains, N.Y. 10605.] [Leonore Goldschmidt (died 1983) together with her husband Ernst (died 1950) founded a school for Jewish pupils in Berlin in 1935 which continued after emigration in Folkestone, England, from 1939–1940.

24187. — KRÜGER, MAREN/NEISS, MARION/VOIGT, MARTINA/WAGENER, BIRGIT/WANDREY, IRINA: *Alltag im Berliner Untergrund 1943 bis 1945.* [In]: Antisemitismus und jüdische Geschichte [see No. 24806]. Berlin, 1987. Pp. 295–312.

24188. — LEIMKUGEL, FRANK/MÜLLER-JAHNCKE, WOLF-DIETER: *Zur Emigration jüdischer Apotheker aus Berlin.* [In]: Pharmazeutische Zeitung, Jg. 132, Nr. 41, Frankfurt am Main, 8. Okt. 1987. Pp. 2561–2568. [Incl. also data and fate of 35 pharmacists who died in the Holocaust.]

24189. — LEVINSON, N. PETER: *Kann das Grab uns trennen? Erinnerungen an Berlin.* [In]: 'Allgemeine', Nr. 42/38, Bonn, 18. Sept. 1987. P. 39.

24190. — RÜRUP, REINHARD, ed.: *Topographie des Terrors: Gestapo, SS und Reichssicherheitshauptamt auf dem 'Prinz-Albrecht-Gelände'.* Eine Dokumentation. (Die Dokumentation ist Teil der Ausstellung 'Berlin, Berlin – die Ausstellung zur Geschichte der Stadt' im Martin-Gropius-Bau,

15. Aug.-22. Nov. 1987.) 2., verbesserte Aufl. Berlin: Arenhövel, 1987. 222 pp., illus., bibl. [Incl.: Das Schicksal der deutschen Juden 1933–1938 & 1939–1945 (pp. 107–113 & 114–119), and deals also with Jewish resistance.]

24191. — SCHOLEM, BETTY: *November. Die Kennkarte. Schmuck und Silber: eine Dokument zur 'Kristallnacht' 1938 in Berlin.* (Kommentiert von Itta Shedletzky.) [In]: Bulletin des LBI, 77, Frankfurt am Main, 1987. Pp. 3–9, notes (9).

24192. — *'Schon damals fingen viele an zu schweigen . . .'.* Quellensammlung zur Geschichte Charlottenburgs von 1933–1945. (Beschaffung und Sichtung des Quellenmaterials von Hans Wienicke, Erläuterungen und Textgestaltung: Uwe Otto und Anne Jörg.) Berlin-Charlottenburg: Bezirksverordnetenversammlung von Charlottenburg, 1986. 256 pp., illus., ports., facsims. [Also on persecutions of the Jews.]

24193. — TUCHEL, JOHANNES/SCHATTENFROH, REINOLD: *Zentrale des Terrors: Prinz-Albrecht-Str. 8: des Hauptquartier der Gestapo.* Berlin: Siedler, 1987. 316 pp., illus., diagrs. [On the headquarters and prison of the Geheime Staatspolizei in Berlin; incl. also accounts on and by Jewish prisoners.]

24194. BESSEL, RICHARD, ed: *Life in the Third Reich.* Oxford: New York: Oxford Univ. Press, 1987. 124 pp., illus. [Incl.: Nazi policy against the Jews (William Carr, 69–82).]

24195. BIELEFELD. MEYNERT, JOACHIM/SCHÄFFER, FRIEDHELM: *Judenverfolgung in Bielefeld.* [In]: Provinz unterm Hakenkreuz: Diktatur und Widerstand in Ostwestfalen-Lippe. Hrsg.: Wolfgang Emer [et al.]. Bielefeld: AJZ Verl., 1984. Pp. 165–190.

24196. BRAACH, EMILIE: *Wenn meine Briefe Dich erreichen könnten; Aufzeichnungen aus den Jahren 1939–1945.* Hrsg. und ausgewählt von Bergit Forchhammer. Orig.-Ausg. Frankfurt am Main: Fischer, 1987. 244 pp., illus., ports., facsims., notes. (Fischer-Taschenbücher, 5658.) [Bergit, child of Emilie Braach, née Hirschfeld, and a Gentile father, was sent to England in August 1939; the letters tell of life in Frankfurt am Main during the war and the fate of Emilie's Jewish and partly Jewish family members.]

24197. BUCHAU. MOHN, JOSEPH: *Der Leidensweg unter dem Hakenkreuz: aus der Geschichte von Stadt und Stift Buchau am Federsee.* Hrsg. von der Stadt Bad Buchau. Buchau: Stadtverwaltung, 1987. 200 pp. [Incl. also historical survey on the history of the Jews in Buchau from 1382 and in Kappel from 1793; cont. data on and fate of 200 Jews living in Buchau in the 1930s.]

24198. CHAMBERLIN, BREWSTER/FELDMAN, MARCIA, eds.: *The liberation of the Nazi concentration camps 1945.* Eyewitness accounts of the liberators. With an introd. by Robert H. Abzug. Washington, D.C.: United States Holocaust Memorial Council. 1987. IX, 214 pp., ports.

24199. CHOLAVSKY, SHALOM: *The German Jews in the Minsk ghetto.* [In]: Yad Vashem Studies, Vol. 17, Jerusalem, 1986. Pp. 219–245.

——— CHURCH. ARING, PAUL GERHARD: *Christen und Juden heute.* [See No. 24784.]

24200. — BARANOWSKI, SHELLEY: *The Confessing Church, conservative elites, and the Nazi state.* Lewiston, N.Y.: Edwin Mellen, 1986. 184 pp. (Texts & studies in religion, vol. 28.) [Also on the Confessing Church's attitude towards the Jews.]

24201. — BUSCH, EBERHARD: *Kirche und Judentum im Dritten Reich.* [In]: Schriftenreihe des Vereins für Rheinische Kirchengeschichte, 84, Bonn, 1985. Pp. 157–177.

24202. — CARGAS, HARRY JAMES. *Hochhuth's 'The Deputy': one generation after.* [In]: Shofar, Vol. 5, No. 1, West Lafayette, Ind., Purdue Univ., Fall 1986. Pp. 30–42, notes (38–42).

——— — *The Churches' response to the Holocaust.* [See No. 24313.]

24203. — CONWAY, JOHN S.: *Rethinking the German church struggle.* [In]: Simon Wiesenthal Center Annual, Vol. 4, White Plains, N.Y., 1987. Pp. 407–414. [Review essay.]

24204. — GERLACH, WOLFGANG: *Als die Zeugen schwiegen . . . : Bekennende Kirche und die Juden.* Vorwort von Eberhard Bethge. Berlin (Leuchtenburgstr. 39): Selbstverlag Institut Kirche und Judentum, 1987. 1 vol. (Studien zu jüdischem Volk und christlicher Gemeinde, Bd. 10.)

24205. — GRAHAM, ROBERT: *The Vatican and the Jewish refugees in Italy during the war.* [In]: La Civiltà Cattolica, Rome, 1987. [Article publ. in the Jesuit journal on the occasion of the 50th anniversary of the encyclical 'Mit brennender Sorge' (March 14, 1987). Cf.: Review [in]: AJR Information, Vol. 42, No. 5, London, May 1987, p. 2.

——— — JONCA, Karol: *Judenverfolgung und Kirche in Schlesien.* [See No. 24364.]

——— — *Judaism and Christianity under the impact of National Socialism.* [See No. 23888.]

24206. — KLAPPERT, BERTOLD: *Barmen V nach dem Holocaust: das Versagen der Bekennenden Kirche gegenüber dem Judentum.* [In]: Schriftenreihe des Vereins für Kirchengeschichte, 84, Bonn, 1985. Pp. 132–150.

——— — MICCOLI, GIOVANNI: *La Santa Sede e le deportazioni.* [See in No. 24369.]

24207.   — MICHAEL, ROBERT: *Theological myth, German antisemitism and the Holocaust: the case of Martin Niemoeller.* [In]: Holocaust and Genocide Studies, Vol. 2, No. 1, Oxford, 1987. Pp. 105–122.

24208.   — MINKNER, DETLEF: *Christuskreuz und Hakenkreuz: Kirche im Wedding 1933–1945.* Berlin (Leuchtenburgstr. 39): Institut Kirche und Judentum, 1986. 205 pp. (Studien zu jüdischem Volk und christlicher Gemeinde, Reihe 2, Bd. 9.) [Deals with the attitude and help extended towards Jews and baptised Jews. Cf.: Besprechung (Franz von Hammerstein) [in]: Judaica, Jg. 44, H. 1, Basel, März 1988, pp. 63–64.]

24209.   — PIUS XI, Pope: *Pius XI und Mussolini, Hitler, Stalin: seine Weltrundschreiben gegen Faschismus, Nationalsozialismus, Kommunismus.* Hrsg.: Alfons Fitzek. Eichstätt: Franz-Sales-Verl., 1987. 232 pp., bibl.

24210.   — PROLINGHEUER, HANS: *Wir sind in die Irre gegangen: die Schuld der Kirche unterm Hakenkreuz, nach dem Bekenntnis des 'Darmstädter Wortes' von 1947.* Köln: Pahl-Rugenstein, 1987. 301 pp., illus., bibl. (283–292). (Kleine Bibliothek, 451.) [Also on the attitude towards Jews and Judaism, a.o. on the foundation of the 'Institut zur Erforschung und Beseitigung des jüdischen Einflusses auf das kirchliche Leben' 1939 in Eisenach.]

———   — Weinzierl, Erika: *Kirche und Juden in Österreich nach dem 11. März 1938.* [And]: SCHULMEISTER, PAUL: *Kirche und Juden 1938–1945.* [See in No. 24173.]

———   COMMUNAL HISTORIES referring to the Nazi period and fully listed in other sections: Baden (Nos. 23935, 24056). Beckum (No. 23940). Breisach (No. 23954). Buttenhausen (Nos. 23957–23958). Crainsfeld (No. 23960). Dortmund (No. 23963). Elsdorf (No. 23965). Esens (No. 23968). Franconia (Nos. 23973–23974, 23977). Fulda (No. 24410). Gelnhausen (No. 23983). Herne (No. 23989). Hesse (No. 23991). Höchst (No. 23994). Kaldenkirchen (No. 23997). Kempen (No. 23999). Koblenz (Nos. 24001–24002). Leipzig (No. 24004). Limburg (No. 24005). Marburg (Nos. 24011, 24475). Mingolsheim (No. 24014). Mörfelden-Walldorf (No. 24015). Nauheim (No. 24018). Neuenstadt-Stein (No. 24019). Paderborn (No. 24027). Palatinate (No. 24037). Puderbach (No. 24032). Rheinberg (No. 24036). Rimbach (No. 24040). Ronsdorf (No. 24041). Saarland (No. 24037). Sankt Tönis (No. 24045). Stommeln (No. 24047). Sulingen (No. 24048). Urbach (No. 24049). Württemberg (Nos. 23935, 24056). Würzburg (No. 24058).

———   CORBACH, IRENE & DIETER: *Sophie Sondhelm und die Kölner Jüdische Kinderheilstätte Bad Kreuznach.* [See No. 24562].

———   CZECHOSLOVAKIA. [See also Nos. 24085, 24092–24093.]

24211.   — NOVAČEK, SILVESTR: *Nazistische Endlösung der jüdischen Frage in Ivančice=Eibenschütz.* [In Czech, with Russian and German summaries]. [In]: Jižní Morava, 20, Prague 1984. Pp. 13–72.

———   — ROTHKIRCHEN, LIVIA: *The Churches and the 'Final Solution' in Slovakia.* [See pp. 413 ff. in No. 23888.]

24212.   CZERNIAKÓW, ADAM: *Im Warschauer Ghetto; das Tagebuch des Adam Czerniaków 1939–1942.* Mit einem Vorwort von Israel Gutman. (Aus dem Poln. übertragen von Silke Lent.) München: Beck, 1986. 302 pp., illus. [Refers also to German Jews deported in 1942 from Berlin, Gelsenkirchen, Hanover and Magdeburg to the Warsaw Ghetto.] [A. Czerniaków, 1880–1942 (suicide), engineer, from 1939 president of the Warsaw Jewish Community Council and first head of the Warsaw Judenrat.]

24213.   DACHAU. *Dachauer Hefte. H. 3: Frauen – Verfolgung und Widerstand.* Red.: Wolfgang Benz und Barbara Distel. Dachau: Verlag Dachauer Hefte, 1987. 1 issue.

24214.   — STEINBACH, PETER: *Modell Dachau: das Konzentrationslager und die Stadt Dachau in der Zeit des Nationalsozialismus und ihre Bedeutung für die Gegenwart.* Passau: Andreas-Haller-Verl., 1987. 55 pp.

24215.   DIAMANT, ADOLF: *Getto Litzmannstadt: Bilanz eines nationalsozialistischen Verbrechens; mit Deportations- und Totenlisten der aus dem Altreich stammenden Juden.* Hrsg.: Zentralrat der Juden in Deutschland. Frankfurt am Main: Selbstverlag, 1986. 1 vol.

24216.   DÜSSELDORF. *1933–1945: Einzelschicksale und Erlebnisse von Bürgern, die im Bereich des heutigen Stadtbezirks 3 wohnten.* Hrsg.: Landeshauptstadt Düsseldorf, Der Oberstadtdirektor, Bezirksverwaltungsstelle 3. (Bearb.: Klaus Bartnik und Egbert Casten.) Düsseldorf (Brinckmannstr. 5), 1983. 142 pp., illus., ports., facsims. [Incl. reports by and on Jewish persons.]

24217.   — *1933–1945: Einzelschicksale und Erlebnisse. Bd. 2: Moritz Sommer.* Hrsg.: Landeshauptstadt Düsseldorf, Der Oberstadtdirektor, Bezirksverwaltungsstelle 3. (Bearb.: Klaus Bartnik und Egbert Casten.) Düsseldorf (Brinckmannstr. 5), 1986. 85 pp., illus., ports., facsims., bibl. (83–84). [Moritz Sommer, June 19, 1872 Leutholt – Apr. 15, 1945 Düsseldorf, artisan, lived illegally in Düsseldorf with German help until a few days before the end of the war when he was hanged in public by a military patrol.]

24218. EICHMANN, ADOLF. *Schuldig: das Urteil gegen Adolf Eichmann.* Hrsg. von Avner W. Less. Mit einem Nachwort von Jochen von Lang. Frankfurt am Main: Athenäum, 1987. VI, 335 pp. [Sentence on Eichmann, never publ. before in any language.]

24219. — YAHIL, LENI: *'Memoirs' of Adolf Eichmann.* [In]: Yad Vashem Studies, Vol. 18, Jerusalem, 1987. Pp. 133–162. [Discusses the book: 'Ich Adolf Eichmann; ein historischer Zeugenbericht', ed. by Rudolf Aschenauer, Leoni am Starnberger See: Druffel, 1980 (see No. 18085/ YB XXVII).]

—— EMIGRATION. [See also Nos. 24096–24134, 24159, 24188.]

24220. — FISCHER, ALFRED JOACHIM: *Das Recht der Unglücklichen: Emigrant im Jahre 1923 und ab 1933.* Erinnerungen. [In]: 'Allgemeine', Nr. 42/38, Bonn, 18. Sept. 1987. P. 35. [Emigration from Wreschen, province of Poznań, to Berlin in 1923, and from Berlin via various countries to England, 1933–1939.]

24221. — FRIED, L.: *Von Berlin nach Kapstadt im Oktober 1936: die letzte Reise der 'Stuttgart'* [In]: 'Allgemeine', Nr. 42/52–53, Bonn, 25. Dez. 1987/1. Jan. 1988. P. 14.

24222. — GROSSBERG, MIMI: *The road to America [by] Mimi Grossberg: her times and her emigration. A bilingual report.* New York: The Austrian Institute, 1986. 103 pp., illus., ports., notes (100–102). *[M.G., née Buchwald, born Apr. 23, 1905 in Vienna, author.]*

—— — KAPLAN, MARION: *Jüdische Emigranten und Nachkriegs-Deutschland.* [See No. 24405.]

24223. — KRALOVITZ, ROLF & BRIGITTE: *Ich darf gar nicht an eine Trennung denken: die Geschichte einer Austreibung.* Köln: Walter-Meckauer-Kreis, 1987. 31 pp.

24224. — LEHMANN, HANS GEORG/HEPP, MICHAEL: *Die individuelle Ausbürgerung deutscher Emigranten 1933–1945.* [In]: Geschichte in Wissenschaft und Unterricht, Jg. 38, H. 3, Seelze, März 1987. Pp. 163–172, notes (171–172).

—— — SCHULZE, CHRISTINA/HEIDUCK, ROBERT: *Eine Arbeit zum Thema 'Emigration'.* [See pp. 386–397 in No. 24184.]

24225. — SPIERO, CLAUDE: *Und wir hielten sie für Menschen; jüdisches Schicksal während der Emigration.* Tatsachenbericht. Frankfurt am Main: Haag & Herchen, 1987. 211 pp. [On Jewish refugees in Western Europe, 1937–1943.]

24226. — ZARIZ, RUTH: *Officially approved emigration from Germany after 1941.* A case study. [In]: Yad Vashem Studies, Vol. 18, Jerusalem, 1987. Pp. 275–291.

—— EXILE. [See Nos. 24096–24134, 24220–24226, 24341–24355, 24606–24612.]

—— FINAL SOLUTION. [See also Nos. 24304–24309.]

24227. — DÖSCHER, HANS-JÜRGEN: *Das Auswärtige Amt im Dritten Reich: Diplomatie im Schatten der 'Endlösung'.* Berlin: Siedler, 1987. 333 pp., illus., ports., facsims., bibl. (318–328). [Also on the involvement of the German Foreign Office in the planning and execution of the Final Solution.]

24228. — GRODE, WALTER: *Die 'Sonderbehandlung 14f13' in den Konzentationslagern des Dritten Reiches.* Ein Beitrag zur Dynamik faschistischer Vernichtungspolitik. Frankfurt am Main: Lang, 1987. 306 pp. (Europäische Hochschulschriften: Reihe 31, Bd. 100.) [Incl. chap.: Die 'Organisation T4' und die 'Endlösung der Judenfrage'.]

24229. — HILBERG, RAUL: *A note on the genesis of the Final Solution.* [In]: Simon Wiesenthal Center Annual, Vol. 4, White Plains, N.Y., 1987. Pp. 337–340. [Review essay.]

24230. — KARNY, MIROSLAV: *Nisko in der Geschichte der 'Endlösung'.* [In]: Judaica Bohemiae, Vol. 23, No. 2, Prague, 1987. Pp. 69–84, illus., footnotes. [On the deportations of Jews from Mährisch-Ostrau and Vienna to Nisko am San in Oct. 1939.]

24231. — REITLINGER, GERALD: *The Final Solution: the attempt to exterminate the Jews of Europe 1939– 1945.* Foreword to new edn. By Michael Bernbaum. Northvale, N.J.; London: Jason Aronson, 1987. XIV, 622 pp., tabs., notes, bibl. (531–541). [First publ. 1968 in London.]

24232. — *Sozialpolitik und Judenvernichtung: gibt es eine Ökonomie der Endlösung?* Autoren: Götz Aly [et al.]. Berlin: Rotbuch-Verl., 1987. 188 pp., illus., facsims., diagrs., tabs., map. footnotes, notes. (Beiträge zur nationalsozialistischen Gesundheits- und Sozialpolitik, 5.) [Cont.: Die Ökonomie der 'Endlösung': Menschenvernichtung und wirtschaftliche Neuordnung (Susanne Heim/Götz Aly, 11–90). Die Zwangsarbeit der Juden in Schlesien im Rahmen der 'Organisation Schmelt' (Alfred Konieczny, 91–110). Die Stellung der Juden in der deutschen Rentenversicherung (Petra Kirchberger, 111–132). 'Vernichtung durch Arbeit': Sterblichkeit in den NS-Konszentrationslagern (Miroslav Kárný, 133–158).]

24233. — *Die Wannsee-Konferenz.* An 85-minute TV-film directed by Manfred Korytowski, script by

Paul Mommertz. [TV-film, based on the original minutes of the Conference, orig. produced for the Bayerischer Rundfunk in 1984, shown in the USA in 1987. See also: Gespräch mit M. Korytowski: Erfolg seines Films in den USA überrascht den Produzenten [in]: Aufbau, Vol. 53, No. 26, New York, Dec. 18, 1987 p. 10 [& in same No., p. 15]: Wannsee-Konferenz, Leserbrief (Robert Kempner). For published Wannsee-Conference minutes see in No. 24319.] [M. Korytowski, born in Königsberg, emigrated with parents to Brazil, lived in Israel, from 1960 in Germany.]

24234. FRANK, ANNE. DONESON, JUDITH E.: *The American history of Anne Frank's diary.* [In]: Holocaust and Genocide Studies, Vol. 2, No. 1, Oxford, 1987. Pp. 149–160.

24235. — GIES, MIEP/with GOLD, ALISON LESLIE: *Anne Frank remembered.* The story of Miep Gies, who helped to hide the Frank Family. New York: Simon & Schuster; London: Bantam Press, 1987. 217 pp., illus. [Also German edn. under the title: *Meine Zeit mit Anne Frank.* (Deutsch von Liselotte Julius.) Bern: Scherz, 1987. 254 pp., illus.

24236. FREEDEN, HERBERT: *Die jüdische Presse im Dritten Reich.* Eine Veröffentlichung des Leo-Baeck-Instituts. Frankfurt am Main: Jüdischer Verl. bei Athenäum, 1987. 203 pp., bibl. (189–192), index of names (199–203). [Cont. the chaps.: 1: Humanismus unter der Zensur. 2: Struktur und Statistik. 3: Grundzüge der Entwicklung. 4: Bleiben oder gehen? 5: Kultur-Kontroverse. 6: Die Gemeinde spricht. 7: Religion und Politik. 8: Der jüdische Staat. 9: 'Der Morgen'. 10: Das Frauenbild in der Presse. 11: Die letzte Station. Cf.: Presse im Ausnahmezustand (Ernst Gottfried i.e.: E. G. Lowenthal) [in]: 'Allgemeine', Nr. 43/9, Bonn, 4. März 1988, p. 27. Besprechung (Kurt Gräubig [in]: deutschland-berichte, Jg. 24, Nr. 4, Bonn, Apr. 1988, pp. 35–36. Besprechung (E. G. Lowenthal) [in]: Isr. Wochenblatt, Jg. 88, Nr. 9, Zürich, 4. März 1988, p. 27. Requiem für die jüdische Presse im Nazi-Reich [in]: MB, Vol. 55, Nr. 31, Tel-Aviv, Dez. 1987, p. 5. Jüdische Zeitungen auf verlorenem Posten (Hannah Vogt) [in]: Das Parlament, Nr. 42, Bonn, 17. Okt. 1987, p. 13. Presse im Ausnahmezustand (Reuven Assor) [in]: Tribüne, Jg. 27, H. 105, Frankfurt am Main, 1988, pp. 195–199.]

24237. GIESSEN. KNAUSS, ERWIN: *Die jüdische Bevölkerung Giessens, 1933–1945.* Eine Dokumentation. 4., wesentlich ergänzte Aufl. Wiesbaden (Mainzer Str. 80): Kommission für die Geschichte der Juden in Hessen, 1987. 294 pp., illus., ports., facsims., list of victims and survivors. (Schriften der Kommission für die Geschichte der Juden in Hessen, 3.)

24238. GOEBBELS, JOSEPH: *Die Tagebücher; sämtliche Fragmente.* Hrsg. von Elke Fröhlich im Auftrag des Instituts für Zeitgeschichte und in Verbindung mit dem Bundesarchiv. Bd. 1 ff. München; London [et al.]: Saur, 1987 ff. *Bde. 1–4: Teil 1, Aufzeichnungen 1924–1941.* [&]: *Interimsregister: Teil 1, Aufzeichnungen 1924–1941.* 1987. 5 vols. (CVIII, 654; V, 764; V, 682; V, 731 [&]: 351 pp. [The complete edn. of J.G.'s diaries is planned to comprise eleven vols. Cf.: 'Wir haben sowieso so viel auf dem Kerbholz . . .': mit den Goebbels-Tagebüchern liegt eine erstrangige Quelle über das NS-Regime und seine Führungs-Clique vor (Jost Dülffer) [in]: Die Zeit, Nr. 42, Hamburg, 9. Okt. 1987, pp. 21–22, port.]

24239. — BÄRSCH, CLAUS-EKKEHARD: *Erlösung und Vernichtung: Dr. phil. Joseph Goebbels.* Zur Psyche und Ideologie eines jungen Nationalsozialisten, 1923–1927. München: Boer, 1987. 431 pp., illus., bibl. (411–425). [Refers also to antisemitism in G.'s ideology.]

24240. GÖRING, HERMANN. IRVING, DAVID: *Göring.* Deutsch von Richard Giese. München: Knaus, 1987. 836 pp., illus., ports., bibl. (781–784). [Minimises Göring's role in the Wannsee-Conference.]

24241. — KUBE, ALFRED: *Pour le mérite und Hakenkreuz: Hermann Göring im Dritten Reich.* 2. Aufl. München: Oldenbourg, 1987 (c1986). 389 pp., bibl. (368–385). (Quellen und Darstellungen zur Zeitgeschichte, Bd. 24.) [Also on Göring's part in the Wannsee-Conference.]

24242. GÖTTINGEN. BECKER, HEINRICH/DAHMS, HANS-JOACHIM/WEGELER, CORNELIA, eds.: *Die Universität Göttingen unter dem Nationalsozialismus: das verdrängte Kapitel ihrer 250jährigen Geschichte.* München; London [et al.]: Saur, 1987. 523 pp., illus., bibl. [Incl. the attitude towards Jewish professors and students during the Nazi period and, after 1945, towards émigrés; also on the re-appointment of former Nazi sympathisers.]

24243. GROSS-GERAU. KAUFMAN, MENAHEM: *Kristallnacht in Gross-Gerau.* [In]: Midstream, Vol. 33, No. 1, New York, Jan. 1987. Pp. 30–32. [Publ. previously, see No. 23282/YB XXXII.]

—— GRUENEWALD, MAX: *Die Unmöglichkeit der Anpassung: Dr. Max Gruenewald und die Reichsvertretung der Juden in Deutschland.* [See No. 24556.]

24244. HANOVER. BUCHHOLZ, MARLIS: *Die Hannoverschen Judenhäuser: zur Situation der Juden in der Zeit der Ghettoisierung und Verfolgung 1941 bis 1945.* Hildesheim: Lax, 1987. VIII, 294 pp., illus., diagrs., map, bibl. (246–252). (Quellen und Darstellungen zur Geschichte Niedersachsens, Bd. 101.)

24245. HATTINGEN. Szigen, Christoph: *Juden in Hattingen.* [In]: Alltag in Hattingen, 1933–1945: eine Kleinstadt im Nationalsozialismus. Hrsg.: Volkshochschule Hattingen. Essen: Klartext-Verl., 1986. Pp. 208–219, illus., bibl.

24246. Heinemann, Joseph: *My ordeal (Mein Erleben) 1936–1946.* Dedicated to my children and children's children in the 80th year of my life. (Forewords by Mark C. Levy and Henry H. Straus. Transl. by Henry Kahn.) Illinois, 1986. 68 pp., illus., facsims., plan. [Priv. print., available in the LBI New York.] [J.H., 1866 Düsseldorf – 1951 Northwood near London, merchant.]

24247. HEYDRICH, REINHARD. Deschner, Günther: *Reinhard Heydrich: Statthalter der totalen Macht.* Frankfurt am Main: Ullstein, 1987. 368 pp., illus. (Ullstein-Buch, Nr. 27559.) [Engl. transl. see No. 19027/YB XXVIII.]

—— HIRSCH, OTTO. Sauer, Paul: *Otto Hirsch: director of the Reichsvertretung.* [See No. 24540.]

24248. HISTORIOGRAPHY. Bartov, Omer: *Historians on the Eastern front: Andreas Hillgruber and Germany's tragedy.* [In]: Tel Aviver Jahrbuch für deutsche Geschichte, Bd. 16, Gerlingen, 1987. Pp. 325–345, footnotes.

24249. — Berghahn, Volker: *Geschichtswissenschaft und grosse Politik.* [In]: Aus Politik und Zeitgeschichte; Beilage zur Wochenzeitung Das Parlament, B 11, Bonn, 14. März 1987. Pp. 25–37, footnotes.

24250. — Bracher, Karl Dietrich: *Zeitgeschichtliche Erfahrungen als aktuelles Problem* [In]: Aus Politik und Zeitgeschichte, Beilage zur Wochenzeitung Das Parlament, B 11, Bonn, 14. März 1987. Pp. 3–14.

24251. — Craig, Gordon A.: *The war of the German historians.* [In]: The New York Review of Books, Vol. 33, No. 21–22, New York, Jan. 15, 1987. Pp. 16–19. [Review article.]

24252. — Diner, Dan, ed.: *Ist der Nationalsozialismus Geschichte? Zu Historisierung und Historikerstreit.* Mit Beiträgen von Wolfgang Benz [et al.]. Übers. von Nele Löw Beer und Rainer Spiss. Orig.-Ausg. Frankfurt am Main: Fischer, 1987. 309 p., bibl. (307–309). (Fischer-Taschenbücher, 4391.)

24253. — Diner, Dan: *Zwischen Aporie und Apologie: über Grenzen der Historisierbarkeit der Massenvernichtung.* [In]: Babylon, H. 2, Frankfurt am Main, Juli 1987. Pp. 23–33, notes.

24254. — Faulenbach, Bernd: *NS-Interpretationen und Zeitklima: zum Wandel in der Aufarbeitung der jüngsten Vergangenheit.* [In]: Aus Politik und Zeitgeschichte; Beilage zur Wochenzeitung Das Parlament, B 22, Bonn, 30. Mai 1987. Pp. 19–30, footnotes.

24255. — Faulenbach, Bernd: *Eine Variante europäischer Normalität? Zur neuesten Diskussion über den 'deutschen Weg' im 19. und 20. Jahrhundert.* [In]: Tel Aviver Jahrbuch für deutsche Geschichte, Bd. 16, Gerlingen, 1987. Pp. 285–309, footnotes.

24256. — Feuerstein (Nicosia), Joachim: *Immer noch 'ruhelose Deutsche'? Der 'Historikerstreit' aus der Sicht eines ausländischen Beobachters.* [In]: Tribüne, Jg. 26, H. 103, Frankfurt am Main, 1987. Pp. 101–106.

24257. — Freeden, Herbert: *Deutscher Historikerstreit aus israelischer Sicht.* [In]: MB, Jg. 55, Nr. 28/29, Tel-Aviv, Sept.-Okt. 1987. P. 6.

24258. — Freeden, Herbert: *Um die Singularität von Auschwitz: die Exkulpierungsversuche deutscher Historiker.* [In]: Tribüne, Jg. 26, H. 102, Frankfurt am Main, 1987. Pp. 119–124.

24259. — Friedländer, Saul: *National identity and the Nazi past: recent historiographical debates in West Germany.* [In]: Israel and the nations [See No. 23886]. Jerusalem, 1987. Pp. CXI–CXXVII, footnotes.

24260. — Friedländer, Saul: *'A Past that refuses to go away': on recent historiographical debates in the Federal Republic of Germany about National-Socialism and the Final Solution.* [In]: Zeitschrift für Religions- und Geistesgeschichte, Jg. 39, H. 2, Köln, 1987. Pp. 97–110, footnotes. [Orig. publ. in Hebrew in Haaretz on Oct. 3, 1986; for German version see in No. 24274.]

24261. — Friedländer, Saul: *Réflexions sur l'historisation du national-socialisme.* [In]: Vingtième Siècle, No. 16, Paris, Oct.-Déc. 1987. Pp. 43–54, footnotes.

24262. — Friedländer, Saul: *Some reflections on the historisation of National Socialism.* [In]: Tel Aviver Jahrbuch für deutsche Geschichte, Bd. 16, Gerlingen, 1987. Pp. 310–324, footnotes. [Also in Hebrew, with English summary, in]: Yalkut Moreshet, No. 43/44, Tel-Aviv, Aug. 1987, pp. 129–142.

24263. — Friedländer, Saul: *West Germany and the burden of the past: the ongoing debate.* [In]: The Jerusalem Quarterly, No. 42, Jerusalem, Spring, 1987. Pp. 3–18.

24264. — *Geschichtswende? Entsorgungsversuche zur deutschen Geschichte.* [Von] Gernot Erler [et al.]. Mit einem Vorwort von Walter Dirks. Freiburg i.Br.: Dreisam, 1987. 172 pp., illus., bibl. (148–166).

24265. — HABERMAS, JÜRGEN: *Eine Art Schadensabwicklung; kleine politische Schriften, 6.* Frankfurt am Main: Suhrkamp, 1987. 178 pp. (Edition Suhrkamp, 1453.)

24266. — HAUG, WOLFGANG FRITZ: *Die Faschisierung des bürgerlichen Subjekts: die Ideologie der gesunden Normalität und der Ausrottungspolitiken im deutschen Faschismus.* Materialanalysen. Berlin: Argument-Verl., 1986. 218 pp. (Das Argument: Argument-Sonderband, AS 80.)

24267. — HAUG, WOLFGANG FRITZ: *Vom hilflosen Antifaschismus zur Gnade der späten Geburt.* Hamburg: Argument-Verl., 1987. 336 pp., bibl. (315–329). [The first part of the book is a slightly modified version of the author's 'Der hilflose Antifaschismus' publ. 20 years ago while the second part, 'Historikerstreit', deals with the new debate.]

24268. — HERDE, GEORG: *Revision des Geschichtsbildes? Anlässlich des sogenannten Historikerstreites.* Dokumentation über das jahrzehntelange Bemühen, den deutschen Faschismus von Kriegsschuld und Verbrechen reinzuwaschen und das alte Feindbild zu erneuern. Frankfurt am Main: VVN, Bund der Antifaschisten, Präsidium, 1987. 11 pp.

24269. — HILLGRUBER, ANDREAS: *The extermination of the European Jews in its historical context; a recapitulation.* [In]: Yad Vashem Studies, Vol. 17, Jerusalem, 1986. Pp. 1–15.

24270. — *'Historikerstreit': die Dokumentation der Kontroverse um die Einzigartigkeit der nationalsozialistischen Judenvernichtung.* Texte von Rudolf Augstein [et al.]. Orig.-Ausg. München: Piper, 1987. 397 pp. (Serie Piper, Bd. 816.) [See also: Völker ohne Vaterland: ein persönlicher Beitrag zum Historikerstreit (Gerd Bucerius) [in]: Die Zeit, Nr. 9, Hamburg, 26. Feb. 1988, pp. 37–38.]

24271. — HOFFMANN, HILMAR, ED.: *Gegen den Versuch, Vergangenheit zu verbiegen.* Eine Diskussion um politische Kultur in der Bundesrepublik aus Anlass der Frankfurter Römerberggespräche 1986. Mit Beiträgen von Rudolf Augstein [et al.]. Frankfurt am Main: Athenäum, 1987. 180 pp. [Incl. essays by, a.o., Martin Broszat, Hans Mommsen, Wolfgang J. Mommsen.]

24272. — HOMANN, URSULA: *Ein Ende ist noch nicht abzusehen: Historikerstreit: Chronologie, Fragen und Probleme.* [In]: Tribune, Jg. 26, H. 102, Frankfurt am Main, 1987. Pp. 103–118.

24273. — KAMPE, NORBERT: *Normalizing the Holocaust? The recent historians' debate in the Federal Republic of Germany.* [In]: Holocaust and Genocide Studies, Vol. 2, No. 1, Oxford, 1987. Pp. 61–80, notes (75–80).

24274. — *Der Kampf um die Erinnerung; Reaktionen in Israel auf den 'Historikerstreit'.* Hrsg.: Deutsch-Israelischer Arbeitskreis für Frieden im Nahen Osten e.V. (Die Übers. besorgten Matthias Morgenstern u. Christian Sterzing.) Frankfurt am Main: Haag & Herechen, 1987. 50 pp. (Israel & Palästina, Sonderheft, 13.) [Incl.: Über den öffentlichen Gebrauch der Historie in Deutschland und in Israel (Matthias Morgenstern, 3–10). 'Ich bin kein Antisemit!': ein Gespräch mit Ernst Nolte (Daniel Dagan, 11–26; first publ. in Haaretz, Apr. 17, 1987). Achtung, Deutschland! (Schewach Weiss, 27–32). Historisierung der Vergangenheit: zur Historikerdebatte in der Bundesrepublik Deutschland über Nationalsozialismus und Endlösung (Saul Friedländer, 36–51; first publ. in Haaretz, Oct. 3, 1986, for English version see No. 24260.]

24275. — KOSIEK, ROLF: *Historikerstreit und Geschichtsrevision.* Tübingen: Grabert, 1987. 239 pp. (Beihefte zu Deutschland in Geschichte und Gegenwart, 15.)

24276. — KÜHNL, REINHARD, ed.: *Streit ums Geschichtsbild: die 'Historiker-Debatte'.* Darstellung, Dokumentation, Kritik. Köln: Pahl-Rugenstein, 1987. 330 pp (Kleine Bibliothek, 481.) [First appeared, also 1987, under the title: 'Vergangenheit, die nicht vergeht' the use of which was banned for further edns.]

——— — LOWENTHAL, ERNST G.: *Die historische Lücke; Betrachtungen zur neueren deutsch-jüdischen Historiographie.* [See No. 23892.]

24277. — MARIENFELD, WOLFGANG: *Der Historikerstreit.* Hannover: Niedersächsische Landeszentrale für Politische Bildung, 1987. 58 pp., bibl. (53–58).

24278. —MARRUS, MICHAEL R.: *The Holocaust in history.* Hanover, N. H.; London: Univ. Press of New England; Toronto: Lester & Orpen Dennys, 1987. 264 pp., bibl. (The Tauber Institute for the Study of European Jewry Series, 7.) [Analysis of the various attempts to integrate Holocaust history into the general stream of historical consciousness. Cont. the sections: *The Holocaust in perspective* (incl.: Hitler's antisemitism; The uniqueness of the Holocaust). *The Final Solution* (incl.: Intentionalists; Functionalists; Functionaries of the Final Solution). *Germany's allies, vanquished states, and collaborationist governments* (incl.: Eastern Europe;

Western and Central Europe; The German administration; Local authorities and the machinery of destruction; German satellites). *Public opinion in Nazi Europe* (cont.: Germans; East Europeans; West Europeans; Support for Jews). *The victims* (cont.: East European ghettos; Central and West European Jewry; The camps). *Jewish resistance* (incl.: Dilemmas and objectives of Jewish resistance; Slovakia and Hungary: rescue as resistance). *Bystanders* (incl.: What was known; Unwanted refugees; The Catholic Church). *The end of the Holocaust* (cont.: Ransom negotiations; Other rescue options; Death marches and liberation).]

24279. — MEIER, CHRISTIAN: *Vierzig Jahre nach Auschwitz: deutsche Geschichtserinnerung heute.* München: Deutscher Kunstverl., 1987. 95 pp., notes (90–96), bibl. [96]). [Incl.: Zur Singularität des Holocausts (24–30).]

24280. — MELNIK, STEFAN: *Annotierte ausgewählte Bibliographie zur Historikerdebatte.* [In]: Liberal, Jg. 29, H. 2, Sankt Augustin, Mai 1987. Pp. 85–95, footnotes.

24281. — MERL, STEFAN: *'Ausrottung' der Bourgeoisie und der Kulaken in Sowjetrussland? Anmerkungen zu einem fragwürdigen Vergleich mit Hitlers Judenvernichtung.* [In]: Geschichte und Gesellschaft, Jg. 13, H. 3, Göttingen, 1987. Pp. 368–381, footnotes. [Refers to Ernst Nolte's publications, see Nos. 23306–23307 & in No. 23298/YB XXXII.]

24282. — MOMMSEN, HANS: *Auf der Suche nach historischer Normalität; Beiträge zum Geschichtsbildstreit in der Bundesrepublik.* Mit einem Vorwort von Hermann Haarmann. Berlin: Argon-Verl., 1987. 63 pp. (Argon-Rotation, 4.)

24283. — NOLTE, ERNST: *Der europäische Bürgerkrieg 1917–1945: Nationalsozialismus und Bolschewismus.* Berlin: Propyläen, 1987. 616 pp. [Cf.: Fantasies of a revisionist historian [in]: AJR Information, Vol. 42, No. 12, London, Dec. 1987, p. 9. Ernst Nolte nimmt kein Wort zurück: zwei Buchveröffentlichungen liefern neuen Zündstoff für den Historikerstreit [in]: 'Allgemeine', Nr. 42/43, Bonn, 23. Okt. 1987, p. 2. Geschichte im Meinungskampf: Anmerkungen zu E. Noltes neuem Buch (Peter Steinbach) [in]: 'Allgemeine', Nr. 43/8, Bonn, 26. Feb. 1988, pp. 1–2 & 4. Wechselseitiges Schreck- und Vorbild (Eckhard Jesse) [in]: Süddeutsche Zeitung, Nr. 230, München, 7. Okt. 1987, p. XXIII. Das 'Zeitgerechte' am Nationalsozialismus: E. Noltes Entlastungsoffensive geht weiter (Heinrich August Winkler) [in]: Die Zeit, Nr. 50, Hamburg, 4. Dez. 1987, pp. 16–17.

24284. — — SCHOEPS, JULIUS H.: *Treitschke redivivus? Ernst Nolte und die Juden.* [In]: Der Tagesspiegel, Berlin, 10. Jan. 1988.

24285. — NOLTE, ERNST: *Das Vergehen der Vergangenheit; Antwort an meine Kritiker im sogenannten Historikerstreit.* Berlin: Ullstein, 1987. 190 pp.

24286. — PAUCKER, ARNOLD: *Preface to LBI Year Books XXXII and XXXIII.* [For comments on the recent 'historians' debate' see p. XI (London, 1987) and pp. XI–XII (London, 1988).]

24287. — PUHLE, HANS-JÜRGEN: *Die neue Ruhelosigkeit: Michael Stürmers nationalpolitischer Revisionismus.* [In]: Geschichte und Gesellschaft, Jg. 13, H. 3, Göttingen, 1987. Pp. 382–399, footnotes.

24288. — PULZER, PETER: *Erasing the past: German historians debate the Holocaust.* [In]: Patterns of Prejudice, Vol. 21, No. 3, London, Autumn 1987. Pp. 3–14, notes. [See also ensuing]: Letter to the Editor: Uniqueness of the Shoah: a complex problem (Leon Poliakov) [in]: Patterns of Prejudice, Vol. 21, No. 4, Winter 1987, p. 58.

24289. — PULZER, PETER: *Germany: whose history?* [In]: The Times Literary Supplement, London, Oct. 2–8, 1987. Pp. 1076 & 1088.

24290. — PULZER, PETER: *The Nazi legacy – Germany searches for a less traumatic past.* [In]: The Listener, London, 25 June 1987. Pp. 16–18.

24291. — *Der 'Revisionismusstreit' oder die 'Entsorgung' der Vergangenheit.* (Hrsg.): Wilfried Busemann [et al.]. Bonn: W. Busemann, [1987?]. 59 pp. (Juso-Geschichtswerkstatt.)

—— — SCHEFFLER, WOLFGANG: *Probleme der Holocaustforschung.* [See No. 24308.]

24292. — SCHNEIDER, MICHAEL: *Die Vergangenheit, die nicht vergehen will.* [And]: BAUCH, HERBERT/ ECKHARDT, DIETER: *Wer von der Vergangenheit nicht reden will, der soll von der Zukunft schweigen: Anmerkungen zu einer unsäglichen Debatte.* [In]: Die Neue Gesellschaft/Frankfurter Hefte, Jg. 34, Nr. 6, Bonn, Juni 1987. Pp. 484–495; 496–502.

24293. — SCHNEIDER, PETER: *Im Todeskreis der Schuld; kritischer Rückblick auf die 'Historikerdebatte'.* [In]: Die Zeit, Nr. 14, Hamburg, 27. März 1987. Pp. 65–66.

24294. — SCHWARTZ, PAUL: *Recent public trends in Western Germany.* [In]: Partisan Review, Vol. 54, No. 2, Boston, 1987. Pp. 235–246.

24295. — STEIN, RICHARD A.: *Against relativism: a comment on the debate on the uniqueness of the Shoah.* [In]: Patterns of Prejudice, Vol. 21, No. 3, London, Autumn 1987. Pp. 27–33, notes.

24296. — Stürmer, Michael: *Weder verdrängen noch bewältigen: Geschichte und Gegenwartsbewusstsein der Deutschen.* [In]: Schweizer Monatshefte, Jg. 66, Zürich, 1986. Pp. 689–694.

24297. — Thalmann, Rita: *La normalisation du passé? La République Fédérale d'Allemagne et le problème juif.* [In]: Vingtième Siècle, No. 16, Paris, Oct.-Déc. 1987. Pp. 55–65, footnotes.

24298. — Türcke, Christoph: *Darüber schweigen sie alle; Tabu und Antinomie in der neuen Debatte über das Dritte Reich.* [In]: Merkur, Jg. 41, H. 9/10 (463/464), Stuttgart, Sept./Okt. 1987. Pp. 762–772, footnotes.

24299. — Ueberschär, Gerd R.: *'Historikerstreit' und 'Präventivkriegsthese'.* Zu den Rechtfertigungs-versuchen des deutschen Überfalls auf die Sowjetunion 1941. [In]: Tribüne, Jg. 26, H. 103, Frankfurt am Main, 1987. Pp. 108–116, footnotes.

24300. — Wippermann, Wolfgang: *Faschismus – nur ein Schlagwort? Die Faschismusforschung zwischen Kritik und kritischer Kritik.* [In]: Tel Aviver Jahrbuch für deutsche Geschichte, Bd. 16, Gerlingen, 1987. Pp. 346–366, footnotes.

24301. HITLER, ADOLF. Broszat, Martin: *Hitler and the collapse of Weimar Germany.* Transl. and with a foreword by Volker R. Berghahn. Oxford: Berg, 1987. 170 pp., bibl.

24302. — — Burrin, Philippe: *Hitler dans le IIIᵉ Reich: maître ou serviteur? Martin Broszat et l'interprétation fonctionnaliste du régime nazi.* [In]: Vingtième Siècle, No. 16, Paris, Oct.–Déc. 1987. Pp. 31–42, footnotes.

24303. — Kershaw, Ian: *The 'Hitler myth': image and reality in the Third Reich.* Oxford: Clarendon Press, 1987. 279 pp., map, tabs., bibl. [Orig. publ. 1983 in German, revised and augmented English version; incl. an evaluation of Hitler's Jewish policy. Cf.: Crisis and charisma (Jeremy D. Noakes) [in]: TLS, London, Jan. 8–14, 1988.]

—— HOLOCAUST. [See also Nos. 24168, 24227–24233, 24269, 24818.]

24304. — Beer, Mathias: *Die Entwicklung der Gaswagen beim Mord an den Juden.* [In]: Vierteljahrs-hefte für Zeitgeschichte, Jg. 35, H. 3, München, Juli 1987. Pp. 403–417, footnotes.

24305. — Marrus, Michael R.: *The history of the Holocaust: a survey of recent literature.* [In]: The Journal of Modern History, Vol. 59, No. 1, Chicago, March 1987. Pp. 114–160.

—— Marrus, Michael R.: *The Holocaust in history.* [See No. 24278.]

24306. — Milton, Sybil: *Images of the Holocaust.* Part 2. [In]: Holocaust and Genocide Studies, Vol. 1, No. 2, Oxford, 1986. Pp. 193–216. [For pt. 1 see No. 23316/YB XXXII.]

24307. — Mommsen, Hans: *Anti-Jewish politics and the implementation of the Holocaust.* [In]: Kwiet, Konrad, ed.: From the emancipation to the Holocaust [see No. 23891]. Kensington, Australia, 1987. Pp. 63–78, notes (77–78).

24308. — Scheffler, Wolfgang: *Probleme der Holocaustforschung.* [In]: Deutsche–Polen–Juden [see No. 23874]. Berlin: Colloquium, 1987. Pp. 259–282, footnotes.

24309. — Steiner, George: *The long life of metaphor: an approach to 'the Shoah'.* [In]: Encounter Magazine, London, Feb. 1987. Pp. 55–61. [Also German version under the title]: *Das lange Leben der Metaphorik: ein Versuch über die 'Shoah'.* [In]: Akzente, Jg. 34, H. 3, München, Juni 1987. Pp. 194–212.

24310. HOLOCAUST ART. Kantor, Alfred: *The book of Alfred Kantor: an artist's journal of the Holocaust.* Preface by John Wykert. New York: Schocken; London: Piatkus, 1987. 224 pp., 160 illus. [Also German edn.]: *Das Buch des Alfred Kantor.* Mit einem Vorwort von Friedrich Heer. Frankfurt am Main: Jüdischer Verlag bei Athenäum, 1987. 22, 127 pp., chiefly illus. [New facsimile edns. of No. 10306/YB XVIII. The album was composed by the Czech A.K. at the age of 22 at a displaced persons' camp in 1945; the 160 drawings are reconstructions of originals he drew and mostly destroyed during his years at Terezin, Auschwitz and Schwarzheide, Dec. 1941–May 1945.]

24311. HOLOCAUST REACTION. Cohen, Richard I.: *The burden of conscience: French Jewish leadership during the Holocaust.* Bloomington: Indiana Univ. Press, 1987. 237 pp., illus. [Also on German/Jewish exiles in France. Cf.: The Jews, the French and the Nazis (Bernard Wasserstein) [in]: New York Times Book Review, New York, May 24, 1987, p. 7.]

24312. — Finger, Seymour Maxwell: *Their brothers' keepers: American Jewry and the Holocaust.* New York: Holmes & Meier, 1987. 300 pp. [For earlier version see No. 21115/YB XXX.]

24313. — *Holocaust Studies Annual. Vol. 2, 1985: The Churches' response to the Holocaust.* Eds.: Jack Fischel and Sanford Pinsker. Greenwood, Fl.: Penkevill, 1986. 187 pp.

24314. — Kulka, Erich: *Attempts by Jewish escapees to stop mass extermination.* [In]: Jewish Social Studies, Vol. 47, New York, Summer-Fall 1985. Pp. 295–306.

24315. — Kwiet, Konrad: *Responses of Australian Jewry's leadership to the Holocaust.* Transl. by Jane

Sydenham-Kwiet. [In]: Jews in the Sixth Continent, ed. by W. D. Rubinstein. Sydney, Australia: Allen & Unwin, 1987. Pp. 201–215, notes (213–215).

24316. — PAUCKER, ARNOLD: *La reazione dell' Inghilterra e degli Stati Uniti alla deportazione degli ebrei.* [In]: Spostamenti di popolazione e deportazioni in Europa, 1939–1945 [see No. 24369]. Bologna: Cappelli, 1987. Pp. 224–235, notes (234–235).

24317. — THALMANN, RITA: *L'Antisémitisme en Europe occidentale et les réactions face aux persécutions nazies des juifs pendant les années trente.* [In]: L'Allemagne nazie et le Génocide juif. Paris: Gallimard, 1985. (Colloque de l'Ecole des Hautes Etudes en Sciences Sociales.]

——— HUNGARY. Rothkirchen, Livia: *The Churches and the 'Final Solution of the Jewish Problem' in Hungary.* [See pp. 423 ff in No. 23888,]

24318. KASSEL. HEITHER, DIETRICH [et al.], eds.: *Als jüdische Schülerin entlassen.* Erinnerungen und Dokumente zur Geschichte der Heinrich-Schütz-Schule in Kassel. 2., erweiterte u. korrigierte Aufl. Kassel: Gesamthochschul-Bibliothek, 1987. 200 pp., illus., bibl. (198–200). (Nationalsozialismus in Nordhessen, H. 5.] [Augmented edn. of No. 22162/YB XXXI.]

24319. KEMPNER, ROBERT M. W.: *SS im Kreuzverhör: die Elite, die Europa in Scherben schlug.* Erweiterte Neuaufl. Nördlingen: Greno, 1987. 380 pp., illus. (Schriften der Hamburger Stiftung für Sozialgeschichte des 20. Jahrhunderts, Bd. 4.) [New edn. of No. 17163/YB XXVI, augmented by hitherto unpubl. material, incl. the complete minutes of the Wannsee-Conference.]

24320. KERPEN. ENGELS, EKKEHARD: *Spuren jüdischer Mitbürger in Kerpen, Sindorf und Türnich.* Arbeit der Schüler der 9. Klassen der Realschule Kerpen im Fach evangelische Religionslehre im Schuljahr 1980/81. Von Ekkehard Engels für die Veröffentlichung überarbeitet. [In]: Kerpener Heimatblätter, Jg. 23, Bd. 4, H. 2–3, Kerpen, 1985. Pp. 334–408, illus., facsims., tabs. [On the Nazi period.]

24321. KÖNIG, STEFAN: *Vom Dienst am Recht: Rechtsanwälte als Strafverteidiger im Nationalsozialismus.* Mit einem Geleitwort von Gerhard Jungfer. Berlin; New York: de Gruyter, 1987. XXVI, 260 pp. [Covers also trials against National Socialists conducted by Jewish lawyers, the exclusion of Jewish lawyers, the attitude of German lawyers towards their Jewish colleagues.]

24322. KÖNIGSBERG. PROPP, ARTHUR: *November 1938 in Königsberg.* (Ed. and transl. from the German by Christopher R. Friedrichs.) [In]: Midstream, Vol. 33, No. 2, New York, Feb. 1987. Pp. 49–54. [Author's experiences during the Kristallnacht.] [A.P., 1890–1965, timber merchant, emigrated via Czechoslovakia to Canada.]

24323. KOONZ, CLAUDIA: *Mothers to the fatherland: women, the family, and Nazi politics.* New York: St. Martin's Press, 1987. XXXV, 556 pp., illus., ports., bibl. (515–541). [Also on the exclusion of Jewish women from professions and from secular and religious women's organisations; also examines German women's part in the persecution of the Jews.]

——— KULKA, OTTO DOV: *The reactions of German Jewry to the National Socialist regime.* [See No. 24557.]

24324. McKALE, DONALD M.: *Curt Prüfer: German diplomat from Kaiser to Hitler.* Kent, Ohio: Kent State Univ. Press, 1987. 270 pp., illus. [Also on German Foreign Office attitudes to the persecution of the Jews.]

24325. McKALE, DONALD M.: *From Weimar to Nazism: Abteilung III of the German Foreign Office and the support of antisemitism, 1931–1935.* [In]: LBI Year Book XXXII, London, 1987. Pp. 297–307, footnotes.

——— MANNHEIM. [See also Nos. 24007–24008, 24010.]

24326. — KELLER, VOLKER: *Symbol für jüdischen Lebenswillen: rituelles Tauchbad in Mannheim entdeckt.* [In]: 'Allgemeine', Nr. 42/24–25, Bonn, 12./19. Juni 1987. P. 24. [On a ritual bath installed in 1938.]

24327. MOSSE, GEORGE L.: *Masses and man: nationalist and fascist perceptions of reality.* Detroit: Wayne State Univ. Press, 1987. 362 pp., notes. [Collection of essays, also on German-Jewish history. Paperback edn. of No. 17169/YB XXVI.]

24328. MÜLLER, INGO: *Furchtbare Juristen: die unbewältigte Vergangenheit unserer Justiz.* Mit einem Vorwort von Martin Hirsch. München: Kindler, 1987. 318 pp., notes (300–316). [Also on the exclusion of Jewish jurists and on trials against Jews.]

24329. MUNICH. *Verdunkeltes München.* Geschichtswettbewerb 1985/86: Die nationalsozialistische Gewaltherrschaft, ihr Ende und ihre Folgen. Hrsg. von der Landeshauptstadt München. (Red.: Marita Krauss.) Buchendorf: Buchendorfer Verl., 1987. 244 pp., illus., bibl. (244).

[Incl. section: Verfolgt, vertrieben, geächtet: jüdische Schicksale in München 1933–1945 (14–66; reports by Jewish and non-Jewish persons on persecution and deportation of Jews in Munich.]

24330. NATHORFF, HERTHA: *Das Tagebuch der Hertha Nathorff, Berlin – New York*. Aufzeichnungen 1933 bis 1945. Hrsg. und eingeleitet von Wolfgang Benz. München: Oldenbourg, 1987. 212 pp. (Schriftenreihe der Vierteljahrshefte für Zeitgeschichte, Bd. 54.) [H.N. née Einstein, born June 5, 1895 in Laupheim, physician, emigrated in 1939 via England to New York.]

24331. NOVEMBER POGROM. BROSZAT, MARTIN: *The 'Reichskristallnacht': a turning point on the road to the Holocaust*. [In]: Kwiet, Konrad, ed.: From the emancipation to the Holocaust [see No. 23891]. Kensington, Australia, 1987. Pp. 45–62, notes (61–62).

24332. — HANSEN, NIELS: *Partnership in a historical dimension: the lessons of November 9, 1938*. [In]: Federal Republic of Germany; statements and speeches, Vol. 10, No. 1, Stuttgart, 1986. [10 pp.]. [On the question whether Hitler's policy toward the Jews prior to World War II was popular with the Germans.]

24333. — JONCA, KAROL: *The case of Herschel Grynszpan: reflections on the premises and consequences of the 'Kristallnacht' in the Third Reich*. [In Polish, title transl., with summaries in German and French]. [In]: Studia nad Faszyzmem i Zbrodniami Hitlerowskimi, 10 (Acta Universitatis Wratislaviensis, Nr. 765), Wroclaw, 1987. Pp. 65–111, footnotes.

24334. — LOEWENBERG, PETER: *The Kristallnacht as a public degradation ritual*. [In]: LBI Year Book XXXII, London, 1987. Pp. 309–323, footnotes.

24335. — MAIRGÜNTHER, WILFRED: *Reichskristallnacht*. Kiel: Neuer Malik-Verl., 1987. 212 pp., bibl. (195–202). [Pogrom in Marburg see Lingelbach essay in No. 24475.]

24336. — MEYER, KARL-HEINZ: *Dokumentation: Reichskristallnacht 1938 – die Juden in der Niedergrafschaft*. Neuenhaus: Kooperative Gesamtschule, Fachbereich Gesellschaft, Aufgabenfeld B, 1980. 284 pp., illus., diagrs., map, bibl. (278–283).

24337. — THALMANN, RITA/FEINERMANN, EMMANUEL: *Die Kristallnacht*. Deutsche Erstausg. Frankfurt am Main: Jüdischer Verlag bei Athenäum, 1987. 235 pp. [Incl. hitherto unpubl. material.]

24338. OBERLAENDER, FRANKLIN AHARON: *Identitätskonflikt sogenannter katholischer 'Nichtarier'*. Eine sozial-psychologische empirische Forschungsarbeit. Frankfurt am Main, Univ., Diplomarbeit, 1986. 219 pp., tabs., bibl. (214–218). [Typescript, available in the LBI New York.]

24339. PEUKERT, DETLEV J. K.: *Inside Nazi Germany: conformity, opposition, and racism in everyday life*. Transl. from the German by Richard Deveson. New Haven, Conn.: Yale Univ. Press; London: Batsford, 1987. 288 pp. [Orig. title: 'Volksgenossen und Gemeindschaftsfeinde', Köln, Bund-Verlag, 1982. Incl. the Germans' reaction to the persecution of the Jews in Germany especially to the November Pogrom 1938.]

24340. PROBSTEIN, HORST: *Die Ausweisung polnischer Juden im Oktober 1938*. Für die Dokumentationswerkstätte Auschwitz (DOWEA). Frankfurt am Main (Gärtnerweg 14): H. Probstein, 1986. 13 pp.

—— PUVOGEL, ULRIKE: *Gedenkstätten für die Opfer des Nationalsozialismus*. [See No. 24406.]

—— REFUGEE POLICY. [See also Nos. 24220–24226.]

24341. — ALDERMAN, GEOFFREY: *Anglo-Jewry and Jewish refugees*. [In]: AJR Information, Vol. 42, No. 6, London, June 1987. P. 3. [See also ensuing Letters to the Editor [in]: No. 8, Aug. 1987, p. 3 [& in]: No. 11, Nov. 1987, p. 15 [& in]: No. 12, Dec. 1987, p. 13.]

24342. — BREITMAN, RICHARD/KRAUT, ALAN M.: *American refugee policy and European Jewry, 1933–1945*. Bloomington: Indiana Univ. Press, 1987. 310 pp., notes.

24343. — EDWARDS, RUTH DUDLEY: *Victor Gollancz*. A biography. London: Gollancz, 1987. 738 pp., illus. [Also on Gollancz's work on behalf of German-Jewish refugees in Britain.]

24344. — *Les Exilés allemands en France (1933–1945)* = *Die deutschen Emigranten in Frankreich*. Colloque bilatéral franco-allemand . . . 23–25 janvier 1986. Textes réunis et publiés par Michel Grunewald et Jean-Marie Valentin. [In]: Revue d'Allemagne, T. 18, No. 2, Strasbourg, Avril-Juin 1986. Pp. 167–382, footnotes. [Incl.: La France découverte par les émigrés (Gilbert Badia, 171–184). La situation administrative des exilés allemands en France, 1933–1945: accueil – repression – internement – déportation (Barbara Vormeier, 185–194). Aspect de la recherche sur l'exil allemand et autrichien dans le sud-est de la France (Jacques Grandjouc, 195–205). Les premières réactions aux autodafés de livres dans l'opinion publicque française (Hélène Roussel, 206–220). 'Das Neue Tage-Buch' et la France (Michel Grunewald, 221–236). Alfred Döblin und Frankreich (Klaus Müller-Salget, 323–336). Feuchtwanger et la France: Mai 1940 ou la rencontre avec le 'diable du je-m'en-foutisme' (Claude Villard, 337–352). Kunst und Politik in Lion Feuchtwangers Roman 'Exil' (Lutz Winckler, 353–366).]

24345.   — FIGES, EVA: *Little Eden: a child at war*. New York: Persea Books, 1987. 140 pp. [The author remembers her experiences in coming to a small Engish country town in 1939 as a seven-year-old refugee from Nazi Germany.]

24346.   — FOSTER, JOHN, ed.: *Community of fate; memoirs of German Jews in Melbourne*. Sydney; London; Boston: Allen & Unwin, 1986. XVII, 174 pp., illus., ports.

24347.   — GRYNBERG, A.: *Le ghetto du bout du monde: les réfugiés juifs de Shanghai 1938–1945*. [In]: Les Nouveaux Cahiers, 87, Paris, 1986–87. Pp. 26–32.

24348.   — KLARSFELD, SERGE/STEINBERG, MAXIME, eds.: *Die Endlösung der Judenfrage in Belgien*. New York; Paris: The Beate Klarsfeld Foundation, [1987?]. 181 pp. [Also on German- and Austrian-Jewish refugees in Belgium; incl. documents in German.]

24349.   — KOHNO, TETSU: *The Jewish question in Japan*. [In]: The Jewish Journal of Sociology, Vol. 29, No. 1, London, June 1987. Pp. 37–54, notes. [Deals also with the Jewish refugees in Shanghai during World War II and the Nazi effort to influence Japanese policy towards those Jews.]

24350.   — MOORE, BOB: *Refugees from Nazi Germany in the Netherlands, 1933–1940*. Dordrecht; Boston; Lancaster: Nijhoff, 1986. XIV, 231 pp., bibl. (221–233). (International Institute for Social History: Studies in social history, 9.) [See also the author's article [in]: LBI Year Book XXIX, London, 1984, pp. 73–101, tabs., footnotes.]

24351.   — RUTLAND, SUZANNE D.: *'Waiting room Shanghai': Australian reactions to the plight of the Jews in Shanghai after the Second World War*. [In]: LBI Year Book XXXII, London, 1987. Pp. 407–433, footnotes.

24352.   — SEIDLER, HARRY: *Internment; the diaries of Harry Seidler, May 1940 to October 1941*. Ed. by Janis Wilton. Sydney, 1986. 146 pp., illus. [On internment on the Isle of Man and in Canada.] [H.S., born 1923 [?] in Vienna, architect, emigrated to England, from 1948 in Australia.]

24353.   — STEINBERG, MAXIME: *L'étoile et le fusil. [3]: La traque des juifs 1942–1944*. Vol. 1–2. Bruxelles: Vie Ouvrière, 1986. 2 vols. (269; 301 pp.), notes, bibl. (vol. 2, pp. 265–282). [Also on the fate of German- and Austrian-Jewish refugees in Belgium. For pts, 1–2 see No. 21155/YB XXX.]

24354.   — WOLFF, MARGO: *The boys of Mon Repos; the rescue operation 'Sesame' from Vichy France*. Transl. by Gertrude Hirschler. Spring Valley, N.Y.: The Town House Press, 1986. 68 pp.

24355.   — ZUCCOTTI, SUSAN: *The Italians and the Holocaust: persecution, rescue and survival*. London: Peter Halban; New York: Basic Books, 1987. 336 pp. [Also on the help extended by the great majority of the Italian people to the rescue of German- and Austrian-Jewish refugees. Cf.: La forza del destino (Adrian Lyttelton ([in]: The New York Review of Books, March 31, 1988, pp. 3 & 6–8. The returning agony (Hugh Denman) [in]: TLS, London, Oct. 2–8, 1987, pp. 1081–1082.]

————   REINHARZ, JEHUDA: *Hashomer Hazair in Germany (II): 1933–1938*. [See No. 24538.]

————   RHINELAND-PALATINATE. [See also No. 24037.]

24356.   — FAUST, ANSELM, ed.: *Die 'Kristallnacht' im Rheinland: Dokumente zum Judenpogrom im November 1938*. Eingeleitet und bearbeitet. Düsseldorf: Schwann, 1987. 224 pp., illus., ports., facsims., bibl. (218–224). (Veröffentlichungen der Staatlichen Archive des Landes Nordrhein-Westfalen: Reihe C, Quellen und Forschungen, Bd. 24.)

24357.   — HESS, ROBERT: *Gedenkstättenführer Rheinland-Pfalz, 1933–1945: Opfer des Nationalsozialismus*. Mainz: Landeszentrale für Politische Bildung Rheinland-Pfalz, 1987. 96 pp., illus., map, bibl. (79–86). (Informationen der Landeszentrale für Politische Bildung Rheinland-Pfalz.)

24358.   SALOMON, ALICE. WIELER, JOACHIM: *Er-Innerung eines zerstörten Lebensabends: Alice Salomon während der NS-Zeit (1933–1937) und im Exil (1937–1948)*. (Darmstadt): Lingbach, 1987. [9], 520, [62] pp., illus., ports., facsims., maps, bibl. (491–514). [A.S., social worker and educationalist, data see No. 18584/YB XXVII.]

————   SCHATZKER, CHAIM: *The Jewish youth movement in Germany in the Holocaust period*. [See No. 24559.]

24359.   SCHEER, REGINA: *Jüdische Blinde im 'Dritten Reich'*. [In]: Die Brücke, Jahrbuch des Blinden- und Sehschwachenverbandes der DDR, Jg. 1986. [Berlin/East?], 1986.

24360.   SCHLESWIG-HOLSTEIN. BEER, UDO: *Das vermögensrechtliche Ende der kleineren jüdischen Gemeinden in Schleswig-Holstein während des Dritten Reiches*. [In]: Zeitschrift der Gesellschaft für Schleswig-Holsteinische Geschichte, Bd. 112, Neumünster, 1987. Pp. 235–243, footnotes.

24361. SCHWABEN. RÖMER, GERNOT: *Die Ausweisung der Juden aus Schwaben.* Schicksale nach 1933
in Berichten, Dokumenten, Zahlen und Bildern. Augsburg: Press-Druck u. Verlags-GmbH,
1987. 256 pp., illus.

24362. SHARMAN, WALTER: *Saved from the abyss of the shadow of death (Psalm 23,4).* Experiences.
Newcastle upon Tyne/England (2 Carlton Close): W. Sharman, 1987. 28, [8] pp. [Mimeog.]
[On 'aryanisation' of the family's knitwear manufacturing business in Munich, emigration
to England in 1938, building up a new factory in Newcastle.] [W.Sh., orig. Schartenberg,
born in July 1913 in Zierenberg/Hesse, businessman, writer.]

24363. SILESIA. JONCA, KAROL: *Holocaust – la tragédie des juifs en Silésie.* [In]: Studia nad
Faszyzmem i Zbrodniami Hitlerowskimi, 12 (Acta Universitatis Wratislaviensis, No. 923),
Wroclaw, 1987. Pp. 285–294, footnotes.

24364. — JONCA, KAROL: *Judenverfolgung und Kirche in Schlesien (1933–1945).* [In]: Deutsche–Polen–
Juden [see No. 23874]. Berlin: Colloquium, 1987. Pp. 211–228, footnotes.

24365. — JONCA, KAROL: *Successive stages of racial policy in the Third Reich (with special regard to Silesia).*
[In Polish, with English summary]. [In]: Dzieje Najnowsze, Rocznik, Vol. 18, no. 3–4,
1986. Pp. 165–193, footnotes.

——— — KONIECZNY, ALFRED: *Die Zwangsarbeit der Juden in Schlesien im Rahmen der 'Organisation
Schmelt'.* [See in No. 24232.]

24366. SIMON, ERNST: *Chapters in my life. Building-up in the time of destruction.* By Akiba Ernst Simon [In
Hebrew]. Tel-Aviv: Sifriat Poalim; Jerusalem: Leo Baeck Institute, 1986. 248 pp. [Cont. (in
Hebrew): Chapters in my life (Ernst Simon, 11–80; publ. for the first time). Building-up in
the time of destruction (Ernst Simon, 81–180; orig. publ. in German under the title *Aufbau
im Untergang: jüdische Erwachsenenbildung im nationalsozialistischen Deutschland als geistiger
Widerstand*, Tübingen: Mohr, 1959 (Schriftenreihe Wissenschaftlicher Abhandlungen des
Leo Baeck Instituts, 2) [see No. 1646/YB V]). Afterword (Aryeh Simon, 181–229).
Bibliography of A. E. Simon's works (231–241).]

24367. *Simon Wiesenthal Center Annual.* Vol. 4. Eds.: Henry Friedlander and Sybil Milton. White
Plains, N.Y.: Kraus Internat. Publ., 1987. 429 pp., footnotes. [Incl.: *Review essays*: German
reactions to Nazi persecution of the Jews (Donald L. Niewyk, 357–369). A brief for
humanity (Wolfgang Scheffler, 383–388). Further essays are listed according to subject.]

24368. SPIEGEL, MARGA: *Retter in der Nacht: wie eine jüdische Familie überlebte.* Mit einer Chronik der
faschistischen Judenverfolgung. 2., verbesserte Aufl. Köln: Röderberg im Pahl-Rugenstein-
Verl., 1987 (c1969). 96 pp., illus., ports., facsims. [On persecution during the Nazi period
and survival with the help of Germans.]

24369. *Spostamenti di popolazione e deportazioni in Europa, 1939–1945.* (Atti del convegno organizzato a
Carpi, Mo., il 4–5 ottobre 1985 dalla Regione Emilia-Romagna. Red.: Rinaldo Falcioni.)
Bologna: Cappelli, 1987. XIV, 506 pp., illus., ports., facsims., diagrs., tabs., notes, index of
names (489–503). (NUC-Studio.) [Incl.: Grande Germania e gerarchia di popoli nel
progetto nazista di nuovo ordine Europeo: incidenze politiche, nazionali e sociali (Enzo
Collotti, 7–42). Le deportazioni degli ebrei dall' Europa occidentale (Wolfgang Scheffler,
69–83). La reazione dell' Inghilterra e degli Stati Uniti alla deportazione degli ebrei (Arnold
Paucker, 224–235). La Santa Sede e le deportazioni (Giovanni Miccoli, 236–249).
Letteratura e memoria della deportazione (Pietro Albonetti, 275–294). La deportazione
dall' Italia: Bolzano (Leopold Steurer, 407–444).]

24370. STEINBERG, WERNER: *Freunde hatte man nicht mehr: als 'Halbjude' im Dritten Reich.* Aufzeichnungen eines Betroffenen, zu einem Bericht zusammengestellt von Viola Roggenkamp. [In]:
Die Zeit, Nr. 26, Hamburg, 19. Juni 1987. P. 58, ports. [W.St., born 1913 in Hamburg,
offspring of a mixed marriage, survived the Nazi period in Hamburg and Lübeck.]

——— STRAUSS, HERBERT A.: *Essays on the history, persecution and emigration of German Jews.* [See No.
23910.]

24371. SWITZERLAND. BACHMANN, DIETER/SCHNEIDER, ROLF, eds.: *Das verschonte Haus: das
Zürcher Schauspielhaus im Zweiten Weltkrieg.* Zürich: Ammann, 1987. 263 pp. [Many Jewish
refugees had a chance to continue their careers at the Zürcher Schauspielhaus.]

24372. — DAHINDEN, MARTIN: *Das Schweizerbuch im Zeitalter von Nationalsozialismus und geistiger
Landesverteidigung.* Bern: Lang, 1987. 219 pp. [Refers also to the attitudes of the Schweize-
rischer Buchhändlerverein (SBV) towards refugee publishers, a.o., Emil Oprecht and
Gottfried Bermann-Fischer.]

——— — *Fünfzig Jahre Haschomer Hazair in der Schweiz.* [See No. 24537.]

24373. — SCHWEIZERISCHER SCHRIFTSTELLER-VERBAND SSV, ed.: *Literatur geht nach Brot: die*

Geschichte des Schweizerischen Schriftsteller-Verbandes. Red.: Otto Böni [et al.]. Aarau: Sauer-länder, 1987. 216 pp., illus. [Also on the attitude of the SSV towards refugees and émigrés 1933–1945.]

24374. — SELIGER, KURT: *Basel – Badischer Bahnhof: in der Schweizer Emigration 1938–1945.* Wien: Österr. Bundesverl., 1987. 211 pp., illus., bibl.

24375. THAMER, HANS-ULRICH: *Verführung und Gewalt: Deutschland 1933–1945.* Berlin: Siedler, 1987. 837 pp., illus., ports., facsims., maps, bibl. (813–821). (Die Deutschen und ihre Nation, Bd. 5.) [Also on the situation of German Jewry during the Nazi period. Cf.: Was so viele fasziniert hat: H.-U. Thamer legt ein Standardwerk über die NZ-Zeit vor (Julius H. Schoeps) [in]: Die Zeit, Nr. 50, Hamburg, 5. Dez. 1986, p. 20.

24376. THERESIENSTADT. FRANKOVÁ, ANITA: *Deportationen aus dem Theresienstädter Ghetto.* Methoden der Abfertigung von Transporten und deren Rückwirkung auf das Leben der Häftlinge im Licht einiger Quellen. [And]: ŠKOCHOVÁ, JARMILA: *Literarische Tätigkeit jugendlicher Häftlinge im Konzentrationslager Theresienstadt.* (Die Möglichkeit, die literarische Tätigkeit der Jugendlichen als historische Quelle zu nutzen). [In]: Judaica Bohemiae, Vol. 23, No. 1, Prague, 1987. Pp. 3–28, illus., footnotes; 29–37, footnotes.

24377. — *Totenbuch Theresienstadt: damit sie nicht vergessen werden.* Hrsg.: Mary Steinhauser und Dokumentationsarchiv des Österr. Widerstandes. Erweiterte Aufl. Wien: Junius-Verl., 1987. 60, 159, 20 pp., illus., ports., facsims., 1 diagr., bibl. (pt. 3, pp. 19–20). [Orig. publ. in 1971, expanded version; dedicated to deportees from Austria, contains the names, dates of birth and death, and transport numbers of 10,000 Austrian Jews.]

24378. TROISDORF. FLÖRKEN, NORBERT: *Troisdorf unter dem Hakenkreuz.* Eine rheinische Klein-stadt und die Nationalsozialisten. Aachen: Alano Verl., 1986. 270 pp., illus., ports., facsims., notes, bibl. (179–193). [Incl. data on about 75 Troisdorf Jews from 1866 onwards (pp. 64–119).]

24379. TWISTRINGEN. FUNKE-WESTERMANN, LYDIA/KRATZSCH, FRIEDRICH: *Geachtet und geächtet: Twistringen und seine Juden 1933–1943.* Harpstedt: Lampe, 1985. 62 pp., illus., ports., map. (Veröffentlichungen des Stadtarchivs Twistringen, Nr. 2.)

24380. VIERSEN. HANGEBRUCH, DIETER: *In der Gewalt der Gestapo: das Schicksal der Juden des Kreises (1933–1945).* Teil 1–2. [In]: Heimatbuch des Kreises Viersen 1978 & 1979, Folge 29 & 30, Viersen, 1977 & 1978. Pp. 152–170, illus.; 239–260, port., facsims. [Part 2 consists of an alphabetical list of 346 Jews living in the region of Viersen during the 1930s with personal data, profession, and their fate during the Nazi period: most of them were deported to Theresienstadt and Riga where they met their deaths.] [Obtainable from: Kulturamt des Kreises, Am Bahnhof 8, D-4152 Kempen 1.]

24381. VILSMEIER, GERHARD: *Deutscher Antisemitismus im Spiegel der österreichischen Presse und ausge-wählter Zeitungen in der Tschechoslowakei, Ungarn, Rumänien und Jugoslawien der Jahre 1933–1938.* Frankfurt am Main: Lang, 1987. 317 pp. (Europäische Hochschulschriften: Reihe 3, Bd. 334.)

—— VOELKER, KARIN: *The B'nai B'rith Order in the Third Reich.* [See No. 24532.] [See also No. 24531.]

24382. VORMEIER, BARBARA: *Le discours juridique dans la pratique de l'exclusion nazie en 1933.* [In]: Sexe et race: la différence dans le discours d'exclusion (1870–1933). Séminaires 1985–1986. Centre d'Etudes et de Recherche Germaniques, Université Paris VII. Paris (2, place Jussieu, bureau 206), n.d. [1987]. Pp. 114–132, notes (129), appendixes (130–132).

24383. WALDNIEL. *Geachtet und geächtet: das Schicksal der Waldnieler Familien Cahn und Levy im Dritten Reich.* Von Klasse 10 B der Gemeinschaftshauptschule Schwalmtal. [In]: Heimatbuch des Kreises Viersen 1984, Folge 35, Viersen, 1983. Pp. 113–120, ports. [Also generally on the persecution of the Jews in Waldniel.] [Obtainable from Kulturamt des Kreises, Am Bahnhof 8, D-4152 Kempen 1.]

24384. WESTPHALIA. MEYNERT, JOACHIM/KLÖNNE, ARNO, eds.: *Verdrängte Geschichte: Verfolgung und Vernichtung in Ostwestfalen 1933–1945.* Bielefeld: AJZ-Verl., 1986. 375 pp. [Incl.: 'Es waren ja keine Gütersloher dabei' oder: Eine Lüge kann weder Trauer noch Scham begründen: Gütersloh im Zeichen des Antisemitismus (Joachim Meynert, 77–94). Die Verfolgung und Vernichtung jüdischer Bürger am Beispiel der protestantischen Kleinstadt Herford (Christine & Lutz Brade, 95–120). 'Man schämt sich': Judenverfolgung in Paderborn (Antonius Rübbelke, 121–146). Zwangsarbeit und Ghettoisierung: zur Existenz sogenannter jüdischer 'Umschulungslager' 1939–1943 am Beispiel des Lagers Bielefeld-Schlosshofstrasse (Joachim Meynert, 147–166). Das 'Arbeitserziehungslager' Lahde 1943–

1945 (Friedrich Brinkmann, 167–198; incl. Jewish inmates). 'Vernichtung durch Arbeit'?
KZ-Häftlinge in Rüstungsbetrieben an der Porta Westfalica (Rainer Fröbe, 221–297; incl.
Jewish prisoners).]

24385. WORMS. Schlösser, Annelore & Karl: *Keiner blieb verschont: die Judenverfolgung 1933–45 in
Worms.* Worms: Verlag Stadtarchiv, 1987. 164 pp., map, bibl. (146–148). (Der Wormsgau,
Beiheft 31.) [Incl.: Die Wormser Todesopfer des Holocaust (113–132).]

24386. WUPPERTAL. Föhse, Ulrich: *Juden in Wuppertal – eine tragische Episode.* [In]: Wirkung des
Schöpferischen; Kurt Herberts zum 85. Geburtstag. Hrsg. von Lothar Bossle. Würzburg:
Creator-Verl., 1986. Pp. 654–659.

24387. ZIONISM. Allen, Jim: *Perdition: a play in two acts.* London; Atlantic Highlands: Ithaca
Press, 1987. VIII, 152 pp. (Jerusalem Studies Series, 13.) [Incl.: Zionism & rescue – a note
(Lenni Brenner, 75–83). Perdition & the Press (111–152).] ['Perdition' which had a play-
reading at the Edinburgh Festival on August 17, 1987, alleges collaboration of, i.a., the
German Zionists and the German-Jewish leadership with the Nazi regime and takes
material out of context thus distorting Jewish history in Germany; a much watered-down
version was finally performed by the DAC Theatre Company, Doncaster, in the Conway
Hall, London, in May 1988. For details on this contentious piece and on the continuing
controversy surrounding it, the reader is referred to entry 23408 in LBI Year Book XXXII
which lists the journals concerned and the London archives where the material is available.]

24388. —— Wistrich, Robert S.: *Perdition: a 'tawdry political pamphlet'.* [In]: Patterns of Prejudice,
Vol. 21, No. 4, London, Winter 1987. Pp. 48–51.

24389. — Bauer, Yehuda: *Negotiations between Jews and Nazis during the Second World War.* [In
Hebrew, with English summary]. [In]: Israel and the nations [see No. 23886]. Jerusalem,
1987. Pp. 335–346, footnotes.

24390. — Blumberg, Arnold: *Nazi Germany's consuls in Jerusalem, 1933–1939.* [In]: Simon Wiesenthal Center Annual, Vol. 4, White Plains, N.Y., 1987. Pp. 125–138.

24391. — Hilton, Michael: *Dealing with the Nazis: the ambiguities of survival.* [In]: European
Judaism, Vol. 20, No. 2, London, Winter 1986. Pp. 30–40.

24392. — Michaelis-Stern, Eva: *Das Haavara-Abkommen.* [In]: MB, Jg. 55, Nr. 30, Tel-Aviv, Nov.
1987. P. 5. [Critical review of 'The transfer agreement' by Edwin Black, see No. 21042/YB
XXX. See also: Antwort auf die Haavara-Fragen von Edwin Black (Mosche Livni, orig.:
Robert Weiss) [in]: MB, Jg. 56, Nr. 32, Tel-Aviv, Jan. 1988, p. 4.]

——   — Nicosia, Francis R.: *Revisionist Zionism in Germany (II).* [See No. 24591.]

24393. — Reguer, Sara: *Palestine and Nazi Germany.* [In]: Simon Wiesenthal Center Annual, Vol.
4, White Plains, N.Y., 1987. Pp. 401–406. [Review essay.]

24394. — Shapira, Anita: *Did the Zionist leadership foresee the Holocaust?* [In]: Living with
antisemitism, ed. by Jehuda Reinharz [see No. 24835]. Hanover & London, 1987. Pp. 397–
412, notes.

24395. Zweig, Zacharias: *'Mein Vater, was machst du hier . . . ? Zwischen Buchenwald und Auschwitz.*
Der Bericht des Zacharias Zweig. Frankfurt am Main: dipa-Verl., 1987. 122 pp., illus.
[Report by Z.Z. on how he and his son survived in Buchenwald.]

B. Jewish Resistance

——   Behnke, Kristina: *Juden im Grunewald.* [See No. 24184.]

24396. Brothers, Eric: *On the anti-fascist resistance of German Jews.* [In]: LBI Year Book XXXII,
London, 1987. Pp. 369–382, footnotes. [On Herbert Baum and members of his resistance
group in Berlin, also on other groups operating in liaison with H. Baum.] [H. Baum, data
see No. 21211/YB XXX.]

24397. Brothers, Eric: *Profile of a German-Jewish resistance fighter: Marianne Prager-Joachim.* [In]: The
Jewish Quarterly, Vol. 34, No. 1, London, 1987. Pp. 31–36, illus., ports., notes (36). [M.
Prager-Joachim, member of the Herbert Baum resistance group, executed by the Nazis at
the age of 21 on March 4, 1943 in Berlin.]

24398. Dertinger, Antje: *Weisse Möwe, gelber Stern: das kurze Leben der Helga Beyer.* Ein Bericht.
Bonn: Dietz Nachfolger, 1987. 205 pp., illus. (Dietz-Taschenbuch, 20.) [Helga Beyer, 1920
Breslau- 1942 concentration camp Ravensbrück, member of the Deutsch-Jüdischer
Wanderbund 'Kameraden', active in resistance, imprisoned from 1938.]

24399. Sandoz, Gérard: *Vom Kreuzberg zum Montparnasse: Kindheit, Widerstand, Exil.* [In]: Die Neue Gesellschaft/Frankfurter Hefte, Jg. 34, Nr. 7, Bonn, Juli 1987. Pp. 594–605. [G.S., orig. Gustav Stern, born 1914 in Poland, publicist, lived in Berlin from 1914, joined the Communist Youth group, active in illegal propaganda work against the Nazis, imprisoned 1935–1937, from then on in exile in France and Switzerland.]

IV. POST WAR

A. General

——— AUSTRIA. [See also Nos. 24078, 24807–24808.]

24400. Albrich, Thomas: *Exodus durch Österreich: die jüdischen Flüchtlinge 1945–1948.* Innsbruck: Haymon, 1987. 265 pp., illus., bibl. (246–250). (Innsbrucker Forschungen zur Zeitgeschichte, Bd. 1.) [Study based on hitherto unpubl. material, also on immigration to Palestine.]

24401. ——— Haslinger, Josef: *Politik der Gefühle; ein Essay über Österreich.* Darmstadt: Luchterhand, 1987. 100 pp. (Sammlung Luchterhand, 692.) [On post-war Austria, incl. report on the life of the Jewish emigrant Ilse M. Aschner and her experiences when she returned to Austria after the war.]

24402. ——— Shipp, George: *Vienna, 1984, and the 'Jewish problem': some impressions.* [In]: Kwiet, Konrad, ed.: From the emancipation to the Holocaust [see No. 23891]. Kensington, Australia, 1987. Pp. 181–186. [On antisemitism as a deeply-ingrained characteristic of Austrian society and its persistence into the 1980s.]

24403. Bickerton, Ian J.: *After Auschwitz: the issue of Jewish 'Displaced Persons', 1945–46.* [In]: Kwiet, Konrad, ed.: From the emancipation to the Holocaust [see No. 23891]. Kensington, Australia, 1987. Pp. 167–179, notes (178–179). [Examination of the role of the United States Army and various Jewish organisations in solving the problem of Holocaust survivors, mostly from eastern countries, assembled in camps in the American zone in Germany.]

——— FEDERAL GERMAN REPUBLIC. Berbüsse, Volker: *Die 'eigentliche Wahrheit' als kulturelle Form: zum latenten Antisemitismus in einem ländlichen Raum der Bundesrepublik Deutschland.* [See No. 24810.]

24404. ——— Friedlander, Evelyn: *Among ghosts and ruins: remnants of Jewish life in rural Germany.* [In]: AJR Information, vol. 42, No. 5, London, May 1987. P. 4. [See also ensuing]: Letter to the Editor [in]: No. 6, June 1987, p. 13.

24405. ——— Kaplan, Marion: *Jüdische Emigranten und Nachkriegs-Deutschland.* [In]: Zeitschrift für Kulturaustausch, Jg. 37, Nr. 2, Stuttgart, 1987. Pp. 266–269.

——— Levinson, Nathan Peter: *Ein Rabbiner in Deutschland; Aufzeichnungen zu Religion und Politik.* [See No. 24473.]

24406. ——— Puvogel, Ulrike: *Gedenkstätten für die Opfer des Nationalsozialismus.* Eine Dokumentation. Bonn: Bundeszentrale für Politische Bildung, 1987. 831 pp., illus., indexes of places (807–817), of persons and subjects (819–827), bibl., 1 map appended. (Schriftenreihe der Bundeszentrale für Politische Bildung, Bd. 245.) [Incl.: Gedenkstätten für Opfer des Nationalsozialismus in der DDR (Peter Sonnet, 769–805, illus., footnotes).]

24407. ——— Sachser, Friedo: *Report on Jewish communities in Central Europe: Federal Republic of Germany [&] German Democratic Republic.* [In]: American Jewish Year Book, 1987, Vol. 87, New York, 1987. Pp. 241–260; 261–262.]

——— Communal Histories. [See also Nos. 23940 (Beckum). 23963 (Dortmund). 23983 (Gelnhausen). 23989 (Herne & Wanne-Eickel). 24007–24008 (Mannheim). 24475 (Marburg). 24058 (Würzburg).

24408. ——— Berlin. Pomerantz, Marsha: *Soul-searchers: Jews living in West Berlin feel comfortable – and feel guilty about feeling comfortable.* [In]: The Jerusalem Post Magazine, Jan 30, 1987. Pp. 4–5, illus. [See also Nos. 23943, 23952.]

24409. ——— Frankfurt am Main. Wachten, Johannes: *Zu Geschichte und Konzeption des Jüdischen Museums Frankfurt am Main.* [In]: Informationen zur modernen Stadtgeschichte, H. 1, Berlin, 1987. Pp. 38–39. [The Jewish Museum Frankfurt will be established in the Rothschildpalais, Untermainkai 15, in 1988.]

24410. — — Fulda. *Jüdisches Leben in Fulda.* Begegnung mit Fuldas ehemaligen jüdischen Mitbürgern vom 25.–30. Mai 1987. (Red.: Klaus Krolopp.) Fulda (Postfach 1020): Der Magistrat der Stadt, 1987. 82 pp., illus. (Reihe 'Dokumentationen zur Stadtgeschichte', Nr. 11.) [At head of title]: Fulda informiert. [Cont.: Zur Geschichte der jüdischen Schule in Fulda (Naftali Herbert Sonn/Otto Berge, 3–38, illus., ports., facsims., notes; incl. the Nazi period). Begegnung mit Fuldas ehemaligen jüdischen Mitbürgern (39–81).]

———— — — Hesse. ALTARAS, THEA: *Synagogen in Hessen – was geschah seit 1945?* [See No. 23991.]

24411. — — Moers. *Besuch jüdischer Gäste in ihrer ehemaligen Heimatstadt Moers, vom 28. Juni- 5. Juli 1987.* Moers: Stadtverwaltung, 1987. 88 pp., illus., ports., facsims.

24412. — — Munich. WETZEL, JULIANE: *Jüdisches Leben in München 1945–1951: Durchgangsstation oder Wiederaufbau?* München (Amalienstr. 83): UNI-Druck, 1987. XXI, 377, [35] pp., illus., ports., facsims., map, plans, tabs., bibl. (361–377). (Miscellanea Bavarica Monacensia, Bd. 135.)

———— GERMAN DEMOCRATIC REPUBLIC. [See also No. 24407 & pp. 769–805 in No. 24406.]

24413. — *Jews in East Germany.* By a correspondent who recently visited them. [In]: AJR Information, Vol. 42, No. 1, London, Jan. 1987. P. 6.

24414. — MERTENS, LOTHAR: *Juden in der DDR: eine schwindende Minderheit.* [In]: Deutschland Archiv, Jg. 19, Köln, Nov. 1986. Pp. 1192–1203, notes (1200–1203).

24415. — *Nachrichtenblatt des Verbandes der Jüdischen Gemeinden in der Deutschen Demokratischen Republik.* Red.: Helmut Aris, Peter Kirchner. Dresden, März, Juni, Sept., Dez. 1987. 4 issues, illus. [*März* incl.: Neues aus der Jüdischen Abteilung des Berlin Museums [in West Berlin] (Hermann Simon, 7–8). *Juni*: Der Friedhof an der Schönhauser Allee in Berlin (Alfred Etzold, 12–13). Further contributions are listed according to subject.]

24416. — Berlin. OSTOW, ROBIN: *The Jews of East Berlin.* [In]: Jewish Spectator, Vol. 52, No. 1, Santa Monica, Ca., Spring 1987. Pp. 52–56. [Interview with Peter Kirchner, member of East Berlin's Jewish community.] [See also No. 23952.]

24417. — Breslau. SCHWIERZ, ISRAEL: *Ein Bild des Niederganges: das 'jüdische' Breslau (Wroclaw) im Jahre 1987.* [In]: 'Allgemeine', Nr. 42/38, Bonn, 18. Sept. 1987. P. 20. [Also publ. under the title]: *Jüdisches Leben in Ruinen: ein Breslau mit wenigen Lichtblicken.* [In]: Aufbau, Vol. 53, No. 11, New York, May 22, 1987. P. 20. [See also ensuing]: Leserbriefe [in]: Aufbau, No. 15, July 17, 1987, p. 9 [& in]: No. 17, Aug. 14, 1987, p. 9 [&]: Jüdische Friedhöfe in Wroclaw (F. D. Lucas) [in]: No. 26, Dec. 18, 1987, p. 15, illus.

———— — Leipzig. [See No. 24004.]

24418. HOLOCAUST TRAUMA. EPSTEIN, HELEN: *Die Kinder des Holocaust; Gespräche mit Söhnen und Töchtern von Überlebenden.* Deutsch von Christian Spiel. München: Beck, 1987. 334 pp. [For American orig. see No. 16186/YB XXV.]

24419. PROSECUTION OF NAZI CRIMES. FRIEDRICH, JÖRG/WOLLENBERG, JÖRG, eds.: *Licht in den Schatten der Vergangenheit: zur Enttabuisierung der Nürnberger Kriegsverbrecherprozesse.* Orig.-Ausg. Frankfurt am Main: Ullstein, 1987. 176 pp. (Ullstein-Buch, Nr. 33088.)

24420. — SCHOEPS, JULIUS H./HILLERMANN, HORST, eds.: *Justiz und Nationalsozialismus: bewältigt – verdrängt – vergessen.* Stuttgart: Burg-Verl., 1987. 204 pp., index of persons (201–204), bibl. (197–200). (Studien zur Geistesgeschichte, Bd. 8.) [Incl.: Bewältigung oder nur Verdrängung? Deutsche Auseinandersetzungen mit der Vergangenheit (Saul Friedländer, 14–31). Der Beitrag der DDR zur Ahndung der Nazi-Justizverbrechen Günther Wieland, 32–54). Viele Chancen wurden vertan: zur Geschichte der NS-Prozesse in der Bundesrepublik Deutschland (Heiner Lichtenstein, 55–70). Die Rechtsprechung des Bundesgerichtshofes in NZ-Prozessen (Ulrich Klug, 92–117). Justiz zwischen Anpassung und Konflikt (Diemut Majer, 118–137). Die traumatische Neurose: Zur forensisch-psychiatrischen Begutachtung von Opfern der Nazi-Verfolgung (Hans Keilson, 138–155). Justiz und politische Kultur in der Bundesrepublik Deutschland (Rudolf Wassermann, 156–177).]

———— — TUTOROW, NORMAN E., comp.: *War crimes, war criminals and war crimes trials.* [See No. 24170.]

B. Restitution

24421. BLÄNSDORF, AGNES: *Zur Konfrontation mit der NS-Vergangenheit in der Bundesrepublik, der DDR und in Österreich: Entnazifizierung und Wiedergutmachungsleistungen.* [In]: Aus Politik und

Zeitgeschichte; Beilage zur Wochenzeitung Das Parlament, B 16, Bonn, 18. Apr. 1987. Pp. 3–18, footnotes.

24422. HUDEMANN, RAINER: *Anfänge der Wiedergutmachung: französische Besatzungszone 1945–1950.* [In]: Geschichte und Gesellschaft, Jg. 13, H. 2, Göttingen, 1987. Pp. 181–216, footnotes.

24423. *Die Wiedergutmachung nationalsozialistischen Unrechts durch die Bundesrepublik Deutschland.* Hrsg. vom Bundesminister der Finanzen in Zusammenarbeit mit Walter Schwarz. Bd. 1 ff. München: Beck, 1974 ff. *Bd. 6:* FINKE, HUGO/GNIRS, OTTO/KRAUS, GERHARD/PENTZ, ADOLF: *Entschädigungsverfahren und sondergesetzliche Entschädigungsregelungen.* 1987. XVII, 405 pp., 28 pp., appended. [For previously publ. vols. and appendix see Nos. 22287–22288/YB XXXI.]

24424. WOLFFSOHN, MICHAEL: *Die Wiedergutmachung und der Westen – Tatsachen und Legenden.* [In]: Aus Politik und Zeitgeschichte; Beilage zur Wochenzeitung Das Parlament, B 16, Bonn, 18. Apr. 1987. Pp. 19–29, footnotes.

C. Antisemitism, Judaism, Nazism in Education and Teaching

24425. ADUNKA, EVELYN: *Teaching of contemporary history in Austrian schools.* [In]: AJR Information, Vol. 42, No. 5, London, May 1987. P. 3. [Incl. the teaching of Jewish history.]

24426. *Antisemitismus heute.* Schwalbach/Ts.: Wochenschau-Verl., 1986. Pp. 245–282, illus., 1 map. (Wochenschau für politische Erziehung, Sozial- und Gemeinschaftskunde: Ausg. Sek. II, Jg. 37, Nr. 6.)

24427. *Das Dritte Reich – bewältigte Vergangenheit?* Ein Planspiel. Hrsg.: Arbeitsgemeinschaft Christlicher Schüler. Hannover ACS, [1986?]. 37 pp.

—— *Das mittelfränkische Judentum in Geschichte und Gegenwart.* [See No. 23974.]

24428. RENN, WALTER/FIRER, RUTH/PATE, GLENN S.: *The treatment of the Holocaust in textbooks: the Federal Republic of Germany, Israel, the United States.* New York: Columbia Univ. Press, 1987. 288 pp. (Holocaust studies series.)

V. JUDAISM

A. Jewish Learning and Scholars

24429. ALTENKUNSTADT, JAKOB KOPPEL. MOTSCHMANN, JOSEF: *Rabbi Altenkunstadt; Skizzen zur Biographie eines bedeutenden Rabbiners.* [In]: Vom Main zum Jura (Postfach 41, D–8628 Weismain), H. 4, Lichtenfels, 1987. Pp. 131–138, ports., notes (138). [J.K.A., 1765 Altenkunstadt – Dec. 12, 1835 Verbó, Slovakia, rabbi, writer, pupil of Ezechiel Landau in Prague.]

24430. ALTMANN, ALEXANDER: *The God of religion, the God of metaphysics and Wittgenstein's 'language-games'.* [In]: Zeitschrift für Religions- und Geistesgeschichte, Jg. 39, H. 4, Köln, 1987. Pp. 289–306, footnotes.

24431. — ALTMANN, ALEXANDER: *Von der mittelalterlichen zur modernen Aufklärung; Studien zur jüdischen Geistesgeschichte.* Tübingen: Mohr, 1986. 336 pp. (Texts and studies in medieval and early modern Judaism, 2.) [Cont. 10 essays, incl.: Lurianic Kabbala in a Platonic key: Abraham Cohen Herrera's 'Puerta del cielo'. Moses Mendelssohn's concept of Judaism re-examined. Zur Frühgeschichte der jüdischen Predigt in Deutschland: Leopold Zunz als Prediger. Hermann Cohens Begriff der Korrelation. Cf.: Der Sinn, der sich verlagert: Alexander Altmann, 1906–1987 (Iso Camartin) [in]: NZZ, Nr. 229, Zürich, 3./4. Okt. 1987, p. 70. Besprechung (Friedrich Niewöhner) [in]: Zeitschrift für Religions- und Geistesgeschichte, Jg. 39, H. 4, Köln, 1987, pp. 352–353.]

24432. — GRUENEWALD, MAX: *In memoriam Alexander Altmann, 1906–1987.* [In]: LBI News, No. 54, New York, Summer-Fall 1987. P. 12. [See also]: Obituary [in]: AJR Information, Vol. 42, No. 8, London, Aug. 1987, p. 13. Rabbi Alexander Altmann gestorben [in]: 'Allgemeine', Nr. 42/26, Bonn, 26. Juni 1987, p. 8. Nachtrag zum Tode von Professor Alexander Altmann

(Ernst G. Lowenthal) [in]: 'Allgemeine', Nr. 42/29, Bonn, 17. Juli 1987, p. 6. Alexander Altmann – the spiritual profile of a German rabbi [in Hebrew, title transl.] (Shoshanna Goldwasser) [in]: Hadoar, Vol. 66, No. 30, New York, July 10, 1987, pp. 14–16. Obituary (Arnold Paucker) [in]: LBI Year Book XXXIII, London, 1988, pp. XII–XIII. Professor Altmann zum Gedenken (Ernst G. Lowenstein [sic, i.e.: Lowenthal] [in]: MB, Jg. 55, Nr. 28/29, Tel-Aviv, Sept.-Okt. 1987, p. 13. [A.A., Apr. 16, 1906 Kassa, Hungary – June 6, 1987 Newton, Mass., 1931–1938 rabbi in Berlin, emigrated to England, rabbi in Manchester and founder of the Institute of Jewish Studies, 1959–1976 professor at Brandeis University, board member of the LBI New York.]

—— BAECK, LEO. FRIEDLANDER, ALBERT H.: *Baeck and Rosenzweig.* [See pp. 9–15 in No. 24489.]

24433. — NEIMARK, ANNE E.: *One man's valor: Leo Baeck and the Holocaust.* New York: Dutton, 1986. 113 pp., illus., ports., bibl. (103). (Jewish biography series.)

24434. BERGMAN, SCHMUEL HUGO. KLUBACK, WILLIAM: *The listening philosopher.* [In]: Midstream, Vol. 33, No. 9, New York, Nov. 1987. Pp. 57–58. [Review essay on 'Tagebücher und Briefe 1901–1975' by Schmuel Hugo Bergman, see No. 22300/YB XXXI. Further reviews (selection): Besprechung (Kurt Gräubig) [in]: deutschland-berichte, Jg. 22, Nr. 10, Bonn, Okt. 1986, p. 39. Franz Kafkas jüdisches Prag (Hartmut Binder) [in]: Frankfurter Allgemeine Zeitung, Nr. 48, Frankfurt am Main, 26. Feb. 1986, p. 26. Besprechung (Uri Robert Kaufmann) [in]: Judaica, Jg. 43, H. 2, Basel, Juni 1987, p. 103. Hugo Bergman – ein reiches Leben (Schalom Ben-Chorin) [in]: MB, Jg. 55, Nr. 23/24, Tel-Aviv, Apr.-Mai 1987, p. 7.]

24435. BOUREL, DOMINIQUE: *Nostalgie et 'Wissenschaft': note sur l'étude du judaïsme allemand.* [In]: Pardès, 5/1987, Paris, 1987. Pp. 187–194, notes (192–193), bibl. (193–194). [Refers also to the Leo Baeck Institute.]

—— BRAUN, HELMUTH F.: *'Eine unparteiische Pflanzstätte jüdischen Wissens': die Hochschule für die Wissenschaft des Judentums, 1872–1942.* [See in No. 23942, Vol. 3, pp. 120–125.]

24436. BREUER, ISAAC. EMANUEL, YONAH: *'The people of the Torah' in the thought of Dr. Isaac Breuer.* [In Hebrew, title transl.]. [In]: Ha-Ma'yan, Vol. 27, No. 2, Jerusalem, Teveth 5747 [= Jan. 1987]. Pp. 13–24. [I.B., data see No. 17248/YB XXVI.]

24437. BREUER, MORDECHAI: *On the manner of halakhic judgments by German rabbis in the age of emancipation.* [In Hebrew, title transl.]. [In]: Sinai, Vol. 100, Pt. 1, Jerusalem, 1987. Pp. 166–186. [See also No. 23869.]

24438. — BREUER, MORDECHAI: *The reactions of German Orthodoxy to antisemitism.* [In]: Israel and the nations [see No. 23886]. Jerusalem, 1987. Pp. 185–213, footnotes. [Refers to the 19th century.]

24439. BRILLING, BERNHARD. LOWENTHAL, ERNST G.: *Historiker, Genealoge und Rabbiner: zum Tode von Professor Bernhard Brilling.* [In]: 'Allgemeine', Nr. 42/29, Bonn, 17. Juli 1987. P. 5. [See also]: Obituary [in]: AJR Information, Vol. 42, No. 9, London, Sept. 1987, p. 16. Bernhard Brilling s.A. (Ernst G. Lowenthal) [in]: MB, Jg. 55, Nr. 30, Tel-Aviv, Nov. 1987, p. 7. (B.B., June 3, 1906 Tremessen, Posen – July 7, 1987 Münster i.W., rabbi, archivist and scholar; one of his last works was to contribute numerous articles on Jewish settlements in Silesia to Vol. 3, pt. 1 of 'Germania Judaica' (see No. 23880).]

24440. BUBER, MARTIN. AMIR, YEHOSHUA: *Faith and revelation in Buber.* [In Hebrew]. [In]: Bar-Ilan; Annual of Bar-Ilan Univ., Vol. 22/23, Ramat-Gan, 1987. Pp. 287–302.

24441. — BANK, RICHARD D.: *Freud and Buber: a 'dialogue' on God.* [In]: Midstream, Vol. 33, No. 3, New York, March 1987. Pp. 31–33.

24442. — BIALIK, ILANA: *'An experiment that didn't fail': Martin Buber and the Kibbutz movement.* [In Hebrew, title transl.]. [In]: Hadoar, Vol. 66, No. 18, New York, May 20, 1987. Pp. 16–17.

24443. — ERLENWEIN, PETER: *Individuation und Bewegung: Überlegungen zum Verhältnis von Tiefenpsychologie und Religion an Hand der Werke C. G. Jungs und Martin Bubers.* [In]: Zeitschrift für Religions- und Geistesgeschichte, Jg. 39, H. 1, Köln, 1987. Pp. 69–83.

24444. — GORDON, HAIM: *Learning to see: a manner of realising Martin Buber's thought.* [In]: Journal of Jewish Studies, Vol. 38, No. 2, Oxford, Autumn, 1987. Pp. 212–220.

24445. — KEPNES, STEVEN D.: *A hermeneutic approach to the Buber-Scholem controversy.* [In]: Journal of Jewish Studies, Vol. 38, No. 1, Oxford, Spring, 1987. Pp. 81–98, notes.

24446. — MENDES-FLOHR, PAUL: *Martin Buber and the metaphysicians of contempt.* [In]: Living with antisemitism, ed. by Jehuda Reinharz [see No. 24835]. Hanover & London, 1987. Pp. 133–164, notes.

24447.   — REBELL, W.: *Mystik und personale Begegnung bei Buber.* [In]: Zeitschrift für Religions- und Geistesgeschichte, Jg. 38, H. 3, Köln, 1986. Pp. 345–358.

24448.   — PORAT, DINA: *Martin Buber in Eretz-Israel during the Holocaust years, 1942–1944.* [In]: Yad Vashem Studies, Vol. 17, Jerusalem, 1986. Pp. 93–143.

24449.   — VIERHEILIG, JUTTA: *Dialogik als Erziehungsprinzip; Martin Buber: Anachronismus oder neue Chance für die Pädagogik?* Frankfurt am Main (Oberer Kirchwiesenweg 7): J. Vierheilig, 1987. 90 pp., bibl. (85–90).

24450.   — WEINRICH, MICHAEL: *Grenzgänger: Martin Bubers Anstösse zum Weitergehen.* München: Kaiser, 1987. 240 pp. (Abhandlungen zum christlich-jüdischen Dialog, Bd. 17.)

24451.   BUDAPEST, Rabbinical Seminary. CARMILLY-WEINBERGER, MOSHE, ed.: *The Rabbinical Seminary of Budapest 1877–1977.* A centennial volume. New York: Sepher-Hermon Press, 1986. XIII, 334, 54[Hebrew] pp., illus., ports., bibl. references. [Incl.: Lists of faculty, graduates, publications (301–332).]

24452.   COHEN, ARTHUR A./MENDES-FLOHR, PAUL, eds.: *Contemporary Jewish religious thought.* Original essays on critical concepts, movements, and beliefs. New York: Scribners, 1987. 1163 pp., notes. [Deals also with the German-Jewish religious thinkers.]

——   COHEN, HERMANN: *Germanité et judéité.* [See in No. 23898.]

——   — ALTMANN, ALEXANDER: *Hermann Cohens Begriff der Korrelation.* [See in No. 24431.]

24453.   — DIETRICH, WENDELL S.: *Cohen and Troeltsch: ethical monotheistic religion and the theory of culture.* Roanoke, Va.: Scholars Press, 1986. XI, 99 pp., bibl. (Brown Judaic studies, No. 120.)

24454.   — HAYOUN, MAURICE-RUBEN: *Le philosophe et l'historien: comment Hermann Cohen voyait son ancien maître Heinrich Graetz.* [In]: Communauté Nouvelle, No. 30, Paris, Mars-Avr. 1987. Pp. 154–157, ports.

24455.   — KLUBACK, WILLIAM: *The idea of humanity: Hermann Cohen's legacy to philosophy and theology.* Lanham, Md.: Univ. Press of America, 1987. VIII, 304 pp., notes, bibl. (Studies in Judaism.) [Cf.: Cohen studies (David Novak) [in]: Midstream, Vol. 33, No. 6, New York, June/July 1987, pp. 60–61.]

24456.   EHRENTREU, HEINRICH. EMANUEL, YONA: *Rabbi Heinrich Ehrentreu – sixty years after his death.* [In Hebrew, title transl.]. [In]: Ha-Ma'yan, Vol. 27, No. 3, Jerusalem, Nissan 5747 [= Apr. 1987]. Pp. 58–68. [H.E., 1854 Alt-Ofen, Hungary – 1927 Munich, rabbi of the Orthodox Ohel Jakob Synagogue in Munich 1887–1927, scholar.]

24457.   EINHORN, DAVID. FRIEDLAND, E. L.: *David Einhorn's four special sabbaths.* [In]: Journal of Reform Judaism, Vol. 34, New York, Summer 1987. Pp. 43–52. [D.E., Nov. 10, 1809 Dispeck, Franconia – Nov. 2, 1879 New York, early Reform rabbi, worked, a.o., in Mecklenburg-Schwerin, Budapest, and from 1866 in New York.]

24458.   FACKENHEIM, EMIL: *Jewish philosophy in the Academy.* [In]: Midstream, Vol. 33, No. 7, New York, Aug./Sept. 1987. Pp. 19–22.

24459.   — FACKENHEIM, EMIL L.: *What is Judaism? An interpretation for the present age.* New York: Summit Books, 1987. 320 pp., bibl. (293–307).

——   — *Vier joodse denkers in de twintigste eeuw.* [See No. 24499.]

24460.   FREUDENTHAL, MAX: *Zum zweihundertjährigen Geburtstag Moses Mendelssohns.* Vier Abhandlungen. [Nachdr. der Ausg.] Berlin, Philo-Verl., 1929. München (Westendstr. 174): H. Freudenthal, 1985. 50 pp. [M.F., June 12, 1868 Neuhaus, Bavaria – July 10, 1937 Munich, rabbi in Dessau, Danzig and Nürnberg, co-editor of the 'Zeitschrift für die Geschichte der Juden in Deutschland'.]

24461.   GOLDZIHER, IGNAZ: *Ignaz Goldziher and his Oriental diary.* A translation and psychological portrait [by] Raphael Patai. Detroit: Wayne State Univ. Press, 1987. 165 pp., port. [Transl. from an unpublished German manuscript.] [I.G., June 22, 1850 Stuhlweissenburg – Nov. 13, 1921 Budapest, one of the founders of modern Islamic scholarship, professor at the Budapest Rabbinical Seminary.]

——   GRAETZ, HEINRICH. [See Nos. 24454, 24481–24482.]

24462.   HAMBURGER, BINYAMIN S.: *The Ashkenazic tradition.* [In Hebrew, title transl.]. [In]: Ha-Ma'yan, Vol. 27, No. 3, Jerusalem, Nissan 5747 [= Apr. 1987]. Pp. 1–10. [Discusses ritual traditions in Germany from the Middle Ages to the 19th century.]

24463.   HESCHEL, ABRAHAM J. HESCHEL, SUSANNAH: *Abraham Joshua Heschel: Tiefentheologie und Politik,* Eine biographische Skizze. [In]: Judaica, Jg. 43, H. 4, Basel, Dez. 1987. Pp. 193–206, bibl. [A.J.H., data see No. 21268/YB XXX.]

24464.   — HESCHEL, SUSANNAH: *My father: Abraham Joshua Heschel.* [In]: Present Tense, Vol. 14, No. 3, New York, 1987. Pp. 48–51.

24465. HILDESHEIMER, ESRIEL. Hildesheimer, Esriel, ed.: *Rabbi Esriel Hildesheimer; a bibliography.* [In Hebrew]. [In]: Alei Sefer, No. 14, Ramat-Gan, 1987. Pp. 143–162. [A bibliographical list of Rabbi Hildesheimer's works, in Hebrew and German, arranged chronologically, ed. by Rabbi H.'s grandson.] [E.H., May 20, 1820 Halberstadt – July 12, 1899 Berlin, rabbi, scholar, educator, and leader of Orthodox Jewry.]

24466. HIRSCH, SAMSON RAPHAEL: *Die Neunzehn Briefe über das Judentum.* Erweiterte Ausg. Zürich: Verlag Morascha, 1987. 120 pp. [Orig. publ. in 1836; new edn. with introductions by Salomon Ehrmann (1920), Isaac Breuer (1936), and Mordechai Breuer. Cf.: Wegweisende Briefe: steigendes Interesse für S.R. Hirsch (Yizhak Ahren) [in]: 'Allgemeine', Nr. 42/29, Bonn, 17. Juli 1987, p. 10.]

24467. — Hirsch, Samson Raphaël: *Dix-neuf épîtres sur le judaïsme.* Traduit de l'allemand [et introd.] par Maurice-Ruben Hayoun. Préface de Josy Eisenberg. Paris: Editions du Cerf, 1987. 213 pp., indexes (205–212), bibl. (197–202).

—— HOLOCAUST. Cohen, Arthur A.: *The Holocaust and Christian theology.* [And]: Littell, Franklin H.: *Christian antisemitism and the Holocaust.* [See pp. 473–498 & 513–530 in No. 23888.]

24468. — Fackenheim, Emil L.: *The Holocaust and philosophy.* [In]: The Journal of philosophy, 82, Lancaster, Pa., 1985. Pp. 505–513.

24469. JAKOBOVITS, IMMANUEL. *Tradition and transition; essays presented to Chief Rabbi Sir Immanuel Jakobovits to celebrate twenty years in office.* Ed. by Jonathan Sacks. London: Jews College Publications, 1986. 324 pp.

24470. *Judaistik in Deutschland.* Hrsg. vom Verband der Judaisten in der Bundesrepublik Deutschland e.V., Frankfurt am Main. Frankfurt am Main, 1987. 35 pp.

24471. KISCH, GUIDO. Thieme, Hans: *Guido Kisch; Nachruf.* [In]: Almanach der Österreichischen Akademie der Wissenschaften, Jg. 136 (1986), Wien, 1987. Pp. 413–420, port. [G.K., historian, data see No. 22347/YB XXXI.]

24472. KOHEN, RAPHAEL. Katz, Jacob: *Rabbi Raphael Kohen – Moses Mendelssohn's opponent.* [In Hebrew, with English summary]. [In]: Tarbiz, Vol. 56. No. 2, Jerusalem, Jan.–March 1987. Pp. 243–264. [R.K., 1722 Livonia – 1803 Hamburg [?], rabbi of Altona-Hamburg-Wandsbek.]

24473. LEVINSON, NATHAN PETER: *Ein Rabbiner in Deutschland; Aufzeichnungen zu Religion und Politik.* Gerlingen: Bleicher, 1987. 200 pp. [N.P.L., born 1921 in Berlin, pupil of Leo Baeck, emigrated in 1941 to the USA, from 1950 rabbi in Germany.]

24474. LEVY, Ze'ev: *Between Yafeth and Shem: on the relationship between Jewish and general philosophy.* New York; Berne: Lang, 1987. X, 253 pp. (American University Studies: Ser. 5, Vol. 21.)

24475. LUCAS, LEOPOLD. Dettmering, Erhart, ed.: *Rabbiner Dr. Leopold Lucas, Marburg 1872–1943 Theresienstadt; Versuch einer Würdigung.* Marburg: Magistrat der Stadt, 1987. 64 pp., illus., ports., facsims., notes. (Marburger Stadtschriften zur Geschichte und Kultur, 21.) [Incl.: Predigten (Leopold Lucas, 27–34). Rede anlässlich der Umbenennung der Schwangasse in Leopold-Lucas-Strasse am 5. März 1986 (Hanno Drechsler). Das organisierte 'Pogrom' vom 9., 10. Nov. 1938 als Herausforderung für drei Generationen Marburger Bürger (Karl Christoph Lingelbach).] [L.L., rabbi and historian, data see No. 20172/YB XXIX.]

—— MENDELSSOHN, MOSES. Altmann, Alexander: *Moses Mendelssohn's concept of Judaism re-examined,* [See in No. 24431.]

—— — Craig, Gordon A.: *Frederick the Great and Moses Mendelssohn.* [See No. 23872.]

—— — Freudenthal, Max: *Zum 200jährigen Geburtstag Moses Mendelssohns.* [See No. 24460.]

24476. — Herzfeld, Erika: *Moses Mendelssohn als Seidenmanufakturunternehmer.* [In]: Nachrichtenblatt des Verbandes der Jüdischen Gemeinden in der DDR, Dresden, März 1987. Pp. 11–13.

—— — Katz, Jacob: *Rabbi Raphael Kohen – Moses Mendelssohn's opponent.* [See No. 24472.]

24477. — Mendes-Flohr, Paul: *Mendelssohn and Rosenzweig.* [In]: Journal of Jewish Studies, Vol. 38, No. 2, Oxford, Autumn 1987. Pp. 203–211, notes. [See also in No. 24489.]

24478. — Meschkowski, Herbert: *Jeder nach seiner Façon: Berliner Geistesleben, 1700–1810.* München: Piper, 1986. 303 pp., illus. [Incl.: Moses Mendelssohn (pp. 156–183).]

24479. — Schweid, Eliezer: *Tolerance between religions in the teachings of Mendelssohn and Rosenzweig.* [In Hebrew]. [In]: Gesher, No. 116, Jerusalem, Summer 1987. Pp. 79–88.

24480. — Strohschneider-Kohrs, Ingrid: *Lessing und Mendelssohn im Dialog des letzten Lebensjahrzehnts 1770–1781.* [In]: Deutsche Vierteljahrsschrift für Literaturwissenschaft und Geistesgeschichte, Jg. 61, H. 3, Stuttgart, Sept. 1987. Pp. 419–440, footnotes.

24481. MEYER, MICHAEL A., ed.: *Ideas of Jewish history*. Ed. with introduction and notes. Detroit: Wayne State Univ. Press, 1987. 374 pp. [Incl. texts by, a.o., Simon Dubnow, Abraham Geiger, Heinrich Graetz.]

24482. MICHAEL, REUVEN: *Jost, Graetz and Dubnow on the singularity of Jewish history*. [In Hebrew, with English summary]. [In]: Transition and change in modern Jewish history [see No. 23913]. Jerusalem, 1987. Pp. 501–526.

—— ROMAIN, JONATHAN: *Refugee rabbis' impact on Anglo-Jewry*. [See No. 24120.]

24483. ROSENFELD, MOSCHE N.: *Der jüdische Buchdruck in Augsburg in der ersten Hälfte des 16. Jahrhunderts = Jewish printing in Augsburg during the first half of the 16th century*. London (N16 6EB, 83 Darenth Road): Selbstverlag des Verfassers, 1985. 64 pp., facsims., bibl. (62–64). [Incl. descriptive bibliography of all Judaica printed in Augsburg 1509–1544 (pp. 19–42).]

24484. ROSENZWEIG, FRANZ: *On Jewish learning*. Ed. and with an introd. by Nahum N. Glatzer. New York: Schocken, 1987. 128 pp. [First publ. in 1965.]

24485. — ROSENZWEIG, FRANZ: *Sprachdenken; Arbeitspapiere zur Verdeutschung der Schrift*. Hrsg. von Rachel Bat-Adam. Haag: Nijhoff, 1984. 361 pp. (Franz Rosenzweig: Der Mensch und sein Werk; Gesammelte Schriften, Bd. 4.) [Papers in connection with F.R.'s and Buber's joint translation of the bible, printed for the first time.]

24486. — ROSENZWEIG, FRANZ: *Zweistromland. Kleinere Schriften zu Glauben und Denken*. Hrsg. von Reinhold und Annemarie Mayer. Haag: Nijhoff, 1984. XXII, 884 pp. (Franz Rosenzweig: Der Mensch und sein Werk; Gesammelte Schriften, Bd. 3.) [Cont. 'Zweistromland', first publ. in 1926, augmented by about 30 essays. For vols. 1–2 of F.R.'s 'Gesammelte Schriften' see No. 16277/YB XXV.]

24487. —FACKENHEIM, EMIL L.: *Return to Kassel: an unscientific postscript to a conference on Franz Rosenzweig*. [In]: Midstream, Vol. 33, No. 4, New York, Apr. 1987. Pp. 30–33. [On the author's ambivalent feelings during his visit to Kassel in 1986; for Conference documentation see Nos. 23033 & 23538/YB XXXII.]

24488. — *Franz Rosenzweig*. [Hrsg.]: Gesamthochschule Kassel, Universität. (Red.: Bernt Armbruster.) Kassel: Gesamthochschule-Bibliothek, 1987. 43 pp. (Kasseler Universitätsreden, 2.)

24489. — *The Franz Rosenzweig Centenary*. [In]: European Judaism, Vol. 20, No. 2, London, Winter 1986. Pp. 2–22, notes. [Cover title]. [Cont.: Editor's column (Albert H. Friedlander, 2–3). Franz-Margrit-Eugen (Hans Rosenstock-Huessy, 3–4; refers to the exchange of letters between Rosenzweig and Eugen Rosenstock-Huessy and his wife Margrit). Mendelssohn and Rosenzweig (Paul Mendes-Flohr, 4–9). Baeck and Rosenzweig (Albert H. Friedlander, 9–15). New York: a letter (Hayim G. Perelmuter, 15–17). A letter: memories of Rosenzweig in London (Charles Wallach, 17–18). Franz Rosenzweig: the path of return (Jonathan Sacks, 18–22; reprinted from: European Judaism, Vol. 8, No. 1, 1973–74).]

24490. — *Franz Rosenzweig zum 25. Dezember 1926: Glückwünsche zum 40. Geburtstag = Congratulations to Franz Rosenzweig on his 40. birthday, 25 December 1926*. [Festschrift] published on the centenary of Franz Rosenzweig's birth. (Transcriptions and translations, edited and with an introduction by Martin Goldner.) New York: Leo Baeck Institute, 1987. 60 pp. & facsimiles (46 leaves) in portfolio. [Limited facsimile edn. – 300 numbered copies – of the portfolio presented to Rosenzweig on his 40th birthday in 1926 by his friends; cont. 46 hand-written contributions, a.o., by Leo Baeck, Martin Buber, Victor Ehrenberg, Nahum Glatzer, Martin Goldner, Friedrich Meinecke, Gershom Scholem, Karl Wolfskehl.] [See also: In memoriam Martin G. Goldner, 1902–1987 [in]: LBI News, No. 54, New York, Summer-Fall 1987, p. 12; M.G. Goldner, July 1, 1902 Breslau – Apr. 1987 California, physician, active in the Jewish youth movement, secretary of and lecturer at Franz Rosenzweig's Freies Jüdisches Lehrhaus in Frankfurt am Main, emigrated to New York in 1938, board member of the LBI New York.]

24491. — *Das Freie Jüdische Lehrhaus – eine andere Frankfurter Schule*. [Kongress der Katholischen Akademie Freiburg i.Br.] Hrsg.: Raimund Sesterhenn. Mit Beiträgen von Michael Bühler [et al.]. München: Schnell & Steiner, 1987. 130 pp. (Schriftenreihe der Katholischen Akademie der Erzdiözese Freiburg.) [Founded by Franz Rosenzweig in 1919.]

24492. — FRIEDMANN, FRIEDRICH GEORG: *System und Offenbarung: zur Philosophie Franz Rosenzweigs*. [In]: Internationale Katholische Zeitschrift 'Communio', Jg. 16, H. 5, Köln, Sept. 1987. Pp. 470–479, footnotes.

24493. — FUCHS, GOTTHARD/HENRIX, HANS HERMANN, eds.: *Zeitgewinn; messianisches Denken nach Franz Rosenzweig*. Frankfurt am Main: Knecht, 1987. 190 pp.

24494. — GREEN, KENNETH HART: *The notion of truth in Franz Rosenzweig's 'The Star of Redemption':* a *philosophical enquiry.* [In]: Modern Judaism, Vol. 7, No. 3, Baltimore, Oct. 1987. Pp. 297–323, notes.

24495. — HENRIX, HANS HERMANN: *'Hauptsache, dass noch Bewährung vor uns liegt': zum 100. Geburtstag von Franz Rosenzweig.* [In]: Stimmen der Zeit, 204, Freiburg i.Br., 1986. Pp. 803–814.

24496. —MOSÈS, STÉPHANE: *Franz Rosenzweig und die dialogische Struktur der biblischen Erzählung.* [In]: Zeitschrift für Religions- und Geistesgeschichte, Jg. 39, H. 1, Köln, 1987. Pp. 84–87.

24497. — OPPENHEIM, MICHAEL D.: *The relevance of Rosenzweig in the eyes of his Israeli critics.* [In]: Modern Judaism, Vol. 7, No. 2, Baltimore, May 1987. Pp. 193–206, notes (204–206).

24498. — PINES, SHLOMO: *Islam according to the 'Star of Redemption': a study of the intentions and sources of Franz Rosenzweig.* [In Hebrew, sub-title transl.]. [In]: Bar-Ilan; Annual of Bar-Ilan University, Vol. 22/23, Ramat-Gan, 1987. Pp. 303–314.

———   — SCHWEID, ELIEZER: *Tolerance between religions in the teachings of Mendelssohn and Rosenzweig.* [See No. 24479.]

24499. — *Vier joodse denkers in de twintigste eeuw: Rosenzweig – Benjamin – Levinas – Fackenheim.* [Door] H. J. Heering [et al.]. Kampen: Kok Agora, 1987. 135 pp. [Cont. essays in Dutch on Franz Rosenzweig (H. J. Heering); Walter Benjamin (Hent de Vries); Emil Fackenheim (Reinier Munk); Emmanuel Levinas (Bas Baanders); also essay on the characteristics of Jewish thinkers, incl., a.o., Hannah Arendt, Martin Buber, Hermann Cohen, Ludwig Wittgenstein (H. J. Heering). Cf.: Review [in Dutch] (R. A. Veen) [in]: Studia Rosenthaliana, Vol. 21, No. 2, Assen, Nov. 1987, pp. 205–208.]

24500. — ŽAK, ADAM: *Vom reinen Denken zur Sprachvernunft: über die Grundmotive der Offenbarungsphilosophie Franz Rosenzweigs.* Stuttgart: Kohlhammer, 1987. 224 pp., bibl. (218–223). (Münchener philosophische Studien, N.F., Bd. 1.)

24501. SAMET, MOSHE: *Orthodoxy.* [In Hebrew]. [In]: Kivunim, No. 36, Jerusalem, Aug. 1987. Pp. 99–114. [On Jewish Orthodoxy in Germany and in Hungary in the 19th century.]

24502. SCHOLEM, GERSHOM: *Origins of the Kabbalah.* Ed. by R. J. Zwi Werblowsky. Transl. from the German by Allan Arkush. Princeton; Guildford Surrey: Princeton Univ. Press; Philadelphia: Jewish Publication Society, 1987. 487 pp. [First English translation.]

———   — Scholem, Gershom: *Réflexions sur les études juives.* [See in No. 23898.]

24503. — FAIERSTEIN, MORRIS M.: *Gershom Scholem and Hasidism.* [In]: Journal of Jewish Studies, Vol. 38, No. 2, Oxford, Autum, 1987. Pp. 221–233.

24504. — JANZ, ROLF-PETER: *Theology and history: the example of Benjamin and Scholem.* [In]: Kwiet, Konrad, ed.: From the emancipation to the Holocaust [see No. 23891]. Kensington, Australia, 1987. Pp. 137–144, notes (143–144).

———   — KEPNES, STEVEN D.: *A hermeneutic approach to the Buber-Scholem controversy.* [See No. 24445.]

24505. — SCHWEID, ELIEZER: *Judaism and mysticism according to Gershom Scholem; a critical analysis and programmatic discussion.* Transl. from the Hebrew, with an introd. by David Avraham Weiner. Atlanta: Scholars Press, 1985. 178 pp., footnotes. [Transl. of No. 20201/YB XXIX.]

24506. SCHWARZ, WERNER: *Schriften zur Bibelübersetzung und mittelalterlichen Übersetzungstheorie.* Unter Mitwirkung von Rainhild D. Wells und Jochen Bepler übers. und bearb. von Heimo Reinitzer. London: Institute of Germanic Studies; Hamburg: Wittig, 1986. 144 pp. (Publication of the Institute of Germanic Studies, Vol. 39.) [Incl. biographical essay on Werner Schwarz by Leonard Forster.] [W.Sch., Feb. 22, 1905 Guttstadt – 1982 London, Germanist, specialised in classical studies and humanism, biblical translation, medieval German literature and Yiddish, emigrated to Palestine in 1933, to England in 1936.

24507. STAROBINSKI-SAFRAN, ESTHER: *Für eine jüdische Annäherung an die Philosophie.* [In]: Judaica, Jg. 43, H. 4, Basel, Dez. 1987. Pp. 221–237, notes (234–237). [Refers, a.o., to Hermann Cohen, Moses Mendelssohn, Franz Rosenzweig.]

24508. STEINHEIM, SALOMON LUDWIG. SHE'AR-YASHUV, AHARON: *The concept of evil according to Salomon Ludwig Steinheim.* [In Hebrew]. [In]: Daat, No. 19, Ramat-Gan, Summer, 1987. Pp. 137–144. [S.L.St., data see No. 21314/YB XXX.]

24509. STEINSCHNEIDER, MORITZ: *Les traductions hébraïques du Moyen Age.* Un texte de Moritz Steinschneider, présenté par Dominique Bourel. [In]: Pardès, 5/1987, Paris, 1987. Pp. 117–128, notes (121–122; 128).

24510. STERN-TÄUBLER, SELMA. ZUBERER, THOMAS: *Verzeichnis des Nachlasses Selma Stern Täubler (Universitätsbibliothek, Basel).* Bern, Vereinigung Schweizerischer Bibliothekare, Diplomarbeit, [1987?]. [See abstract (Th. Zuberer) [in]: Arbido-B, Jg. 2, No. 4, Bern, 1987.] [S.St.-T., historian of German Jewry, data see No. 18270/YB XXVII.]

24511. TÄNZER, ARON. BURMEISTER, KARL HEINZ, ed.: *Rabbiner Dr. Aron Tänzer, Gelehrter und Menschenfreund, 1871–1937*. Bregenz: Fink's Verl., 1987. 112 pp., illus., ports., facsims., English summary (110–111), bibl. (Schriften des Vorarlberg Landesarchivs, 3.) [Incl.: Versuch einer ersten Bibliographie Aron Tänzers (Wolfgang Prechtel, 84–97).]

24512. TÄUBLER, EUGEN: *Ausgewählte Schriften zur Alten Geschichte*. Stuttgart: Steiner, 1987. 343 pp., port., bibl. Eugen Täubler (Johannes Hahn, 326–332). Heidelberger althistorische Beiträge und epigraphische Studien, Bd. 3.) [E. T., scholar, data see 16338/YB XXV.]

24513. TA-SHMA, ISRAEL M.: *Law, custom, and tradition in early Jewish Germany (11th–12th centuries); tentative reflections*. [In Hebrew]. [In]: Sidra, No. 3, Ramat-Gan, 1987. Pp. 85–161.

—— *Towards modernity: the European Jewish model*. Ed. by Jacob Katz. [See No. 23912.]

24514. TREVES, NAFTALI HIRZ. ROTH, ERNST: *Wann starb Naftali Hirz Treves? Über den bedeutendsten Chasan Frankfurts*. [In]: 'Allgemeine', Nr. 42/52–53, Bonn, 25. Dez. 1987/1. Jan. 1988. P. 16. [N.H.T., ca. 1460 – ca. 1542, cantor in Frankfurt am Main, renowned as 'the great kabbalist'.]

24515. TSAMRIYON, TSEMAH: *The educational disposition of the 'Me'assef'*. [In Hebrew]. [In]: Sheviley ha-Hinnukh, Vol. 46, No. 1, New York, Autumn 1987. Pp. 59–64.

24516. UNNA, ISAK. KELLER, VOLKER: *Zum Leben und Werk von Dr. Isak Unna, Rabbiner an der Klaussynagoge in Mannheim 1898–1935*. [In]: Mannheimer Hefte, H. 2, Mannheim, 1987. Pp. 96–115, illus., ports., notes (110), bibl. [Incl.: Bibliographie der Schriften von Rabbiner Dr. Isak Unna, 1890–1975 (pp. 111–115).] [I.U., March 28, 1872 Würzburg – May 19, 1948 Jerusalem, rabbi, classical philologist, emigrated in 1935 to Palestine.]

24517. WECZERKA, HUGO: *Die Herkunft der Studierenden des Jüdisch-Theologischen Seminars zu Breslau 1854–1938*. [In]: Zeitschrift für Ostforschung, Jg. 35, H. 1/2, Marburg/Lahn, 1986. Pp. 88–139, diagrs., tabs., maps, footnotes, English summary (p. 139).

24518. WEISS, ISAAC HIRSCH. KABAKOFF, JACOBS: *Isaac Hirsch Weiss and Solomon Schechter: a correspondence*. [In Hebrew]. [In]: Bitzaron, No. 35/36, New York, Sept. 1987. Pp. 70–81. [I.H.W., 1815 Gross-Meseritz, Moravia – 1905 Vienna, scholar, writer on the history of the Oral Law.]

24519. WOLFSBERG-AVIAD, YESHAYAHU. *Sefer Aviad; a collection of articles and studies in memory of Dr. Yeshayahu Wolfsberg-Aviad*. [In Hebrew, title transl.]. Ed. by Yitzchak Raphael. Jerusalem: Mossad Harav Kook, 1986. [3], 405 pp. [Incl. (in Hebrew, titles transl.): His life (Yitzchak Goldschlag, 1–3). Wolfsberg-Aviad (Joseph Burg, 4–6). A profile (Geula Bat-Yehuda, 7–10). Some words about myself (Yeshayahu Wolfsberg-Aviad, 11–65; written in 1948). 'Zion': organ of the Mizrahi in Germany (Moshe Unna, 66–76). Different attitudes toward Torah with Derekh Eretz (Mordechai Eliav, 77–84).Rabbi Salman Baruch Rabinkow (Avraham Bick, 89–91). The relationship between Rabbi Yitzchak Dov Halevi Bamberger and the Alliance Israélite Universelle (Naftali Bar-Giora-Bamberger, 158–161). Rabbi Zvi Hirsch Kalischer and Rabbi Samson Raphael Hirsch (Meir Hildesheimer, 195–214). The rabbis of Halberstadt and her wise men (Esriel Hildesheimer, 215–262). See also Nos. 24062 & 24554.] [Y. Wolfsberg-Aviad, orig. Oscar Wolfsberg, Sept. 26, 1893 Hamburg – Aug. 1 [or 2?], 1957 Bern, physician, leader of religious Zionism, author, emigrated to Palestine in 1933, from 1948 Israeli ambassador in various countries, 1956–1957 in Switzerland.]

24520. ZIMMER, ERIC: *A book of customs of the school of the Maharil*. [In Hebrew]. [In]: Alei Sefer, No. 14, Ramat-Gan, 1987. Pp. 59–87. [Contends that the book discussed was written by Samuel of Ulma (Ulm?) from the school of Jacob ben Moses Moellin, called Maharil (? 1360 Mainz–1427 Worms).]

—— ZUNZ, LEOPOLD. ALTMANN, ALEXANDER: *Zur Frühgeschichte der jüdischen Predigt in Deutschland: Leopold Zunz als Prediger*. [See in No. 24431.]

B. The Jewish Problem

—— AZUELOS, D: *Judéité et germanité, l'impossible symbiose*. [See in No. 23898.]

24521. BUNZL, JOHN: *Der lange Arm der Erinnerung: jüdisches Bewusstsein heute*. Wien: Böhlau, 1987. 141 pp., bibl. (129–141).

24522. FEIN, HELEN: *Insiders, outsiders, and border-crossers: conceptions of modern Jewry in Marx, Durkheim, Simmel and Weber*. [In]: Antisemitismus und jüdische Geschichte [see No. 24806]. Berlin, 1987. Pp. 479–494, footnotes.

24523. LE RIDER, JACQUES: *L'antisémitisme juif d'Otto Weininger*. Un essai d'étiologie culturelle. [In]: L'Infini, No. 13, Paris, 1986. Pp. 62–83, footnotes.

24524. MILFULL, JOHN: *The 'J-Curve': the identity crisis of German and Austrian writers of Jewish descent.* [In]: Kwiet, Konrad, ed.: From the emancipation to the Holocaust [see No. 23891]. Kensington, Australia, 1987. Pp. 147–154, notes (154).

24525. RATHENAU, WALTHER: *Shema' Israël, écoute Israël.* Trad. de l'allemand [pour la première fois] par Maurice-Ruben Hayoun. [Preceded by]: HAYOUN, MAURICE-RUBEN: *Walther Rathenau ou la question juive vécue.* [In]: Communauté Nouvelle, No. 31, Paris, Mai-Juin 1987. Pp. 118–123; 116–117, illus., port. ['Höre Israel' appeared 1897 in Harden's periodical 'Zukunft' and is incl. in Rathenau's book 'Impressionen', 2. Aufl., Leipzig 1902.]

24526. SCHLUNK, JÜRGEN E.: *Auschwitz and it's function in Peter Weiss' search for identity.* [In]: German Studies Review, Vol. 10, No. 1, Tempe, Ariz., Feb. 1987. Pp. 11–29, notes.

24527. SCHNEIDER, RICHARD CHAIM: *Suche nach der verlorenen Heimat.* [In]: Die Zeit, Nr. 9, Hamburg, 20. Feb. 1987. P. 84. [R. CH. Schneider, born after the war in Munich to parents who survived the Holocaust, in search of identity.]

——— SCHOEPS, JULIUS H.: *Über Juden und Deutsche.* [See No. 23903.]

24528. SCHOTTLAENDER, RUDOLF: *Judesein – Rassismus – Zionismus.* [In]: Die Zeichen der Zeit, H. 4, Berlin/East, 1986. Pp. 98–102.

——— WAGNER, NIKE: *Incognito ergo sum – zur jüdischen Frage bei Karl Kraus.* [See No. 24666.]

C. Jewish Life and Organisations

24529. ADLER, HANS GÜNTHER. HUBMANN, HEINRICH/LANZ, ALFRED O., eds.: *Zu Hause im Exil: zu Werk und Person H. G. Adlers.* Stuttgart: Steiner, 1987. IX, 205 pp., bibl. (202–203). [H.G.A., born July 2, 1910 in Prague, historian and writer, survived Theresienstadt and Auschwitz, emigrated to London in 1947.]

24530. BAYERDÖRFER, HANS-PETER: *The Eastern Jews and their language: a challenge to German literature, 1848–1918.* [In]: Kwiet, Konrad, ed.: From the emancipation to the Holocaust [see No. 23891]. Kensington, Australia, 1987. Pp. 81–101, notes (100–102).

——— B'NAI B'RITH ORDER. HECHT, ALEXANDER: *Der Bund B'nai B'rith und seine Bedeutung für das österreichische Judentum.* [See No. 24065.]

24531. — JAHN, GERHARD: *Die Söhne des Bundes; zur Erinnerung an die Auflösung des jüdischen Ordens B'nai B'rith vor 50 Jahren.* [In]: Die Neue Gesellschaft/Frankfurter Hefte, Jg. 34, Nr. 6, Bonn, Juni 1987. Pp. 555–556.

24532. — VOELKER, KARIN: *The B'nai B'rith Order (U.O.B.B.) in the Third Reich (1933–1937).* [In]: LBI Year Book XXXII, London, 1987. Pp. 269–295, facsim. footnotes.

24533. BRESLAUER, BERNHARD. KAMPE, NORBERT: *Jüdische Professoren im Deutschen Kaiserreich: zu einer vergessenen Enquete Bernhard Breslauers.* [In]: Antisemitismus und jüdische Geschichte [see No. 24806]. Berlin, 1987. Pp. 185–214, footnotes. [B.B., 1851 Posen – 1928 Berlin, lawyer, member of the board of the Berlin Jewish Community, deputy chairman of the Verband der Deutschen Juden, co-founder and first president of the Vereinigung für das Liberale Judentum in Deutschland. The Verband der Deutschen Juden compiled and publicised brochures on discrimination, a.o., in universities for the purpose of defence of equality.]

——— BURMEISTER, KARL HEINZ: *Ein jüdischer Türsegen aus Hohenems; zur jüdischen Volkskunde in Vorarlberg.* [See No. 24084.]

24534. CENTRALVEREIN (C.V.). REINHARZ, JEHUDA: *The response of the 'Centralverein deutscher Staatsbürger jüdischen Glaubens' to antisemitism during the Weimar Republic.* [In]: Israel and the nations [see No. 23886]. Jerusalem, 1987. Pp. LXXXV–CX, footnotes.

——— CHARITAS. Graz. [See No. 24072.]

24535. DAVIDOVITCH, DAVID: *Breaking a glass on the wedding stone; Jewish matrimonial customs which have disappeared in recent generations.* [In Hebrew, with English summary]. [In]: Israel – People and Land; Eretz Israel Museum Yearbook, Vol. 4, Tel-Aviv, 1987. Pp. 253–268. [Discusses a custom prevalent in Southern Germany.]

24536. EIDELBERG, SHLOMO: *Das Minhagbuch von Juspa Schammes.* [In]: Der Wormsgau, Bd. 14 (1982/86), Worms, Stadtbibliothek, 1986. Pp. 20–30, footnotes. [On Jewish rites and ceremonies, also on the history of the Jews in Worms.]

—— FOSTER, JOHN: *The Jewish entrepreneur and the family.* [See No. 23878.]

24537. HASHOMER HAZAIR. *50 Jahre Haschomer Hazair in der Schweiz.* (Red.: Uri R. Kaufmann, Doron Shmerling.) Winterthur: abc-Setzerei, [1984]. 32 pp., illus., ports. [Incl.: 'Chasak we'emaz!' Erinnerungen an den Haschomer Hazair 1959/64 (Jochi Weil, 24–31).]

24538. —— REINHARZ, JEHUDA: *Hashomer Hazair in Germany (II): Under the shadow of the Swastika, 1933–1938.* [In]: LBI Year Book XXXII, London, 1987. Pp. 183–229, illus., ports., footnotes. [Pt. I: '1928–1933' was publ. [in]: LBI Year Book XXXI, London, 1986, pp. 173–208. See also the author's 'Hashomer Hazair in Nazi Germany' [in]: Die Juden im Nationalsozialistischen Deutschland, Tübingen: Mohr, 1986, pp. 317–350 (see Nos. 23606–23607/YB XXXII).]

24539. HIRSCH, BARON MAURICE DE. SWITZER-RAKOS, KENNEE: *Baron de Hirsch, the Jewish Colonization Association and Canada.* [In]: LBI Year Book XXXII, London, 1987. Pp. 385–406, tab., footnotes. [Covers the time before the First World War.] [M.H., data see No. 19212/YB XXVIII.]

24540. HIRSCH, OTTO. SAUER, PAUL: *Otto Hirsch (1885–1941): director of the Reichsvertretung.* [In]: LBI Year Book XXXII, London, 1987. Pp. 341–368, port., footnotes. [O.H., data see No. 22388/YB XXXI.]

24541. HÜPPAUF, BERND: *'I travelled to the Jews': encounters of German writers with Eastern Jews.* [In]: Kwiet, Konrad, ed.: From the emancipation to the Holocaust [see No. 23891]. Kensington, Australia, 1987. Pp. 103–126, notes (124–126).

24542. JEWISH SPORT. BERNETT, HAJO: *Vom Olympiasieger zum 'Reichsfeind': Alfred Flatow und die Deutsche Turnerschaft.* [In]: 'Allgemeine', Nr. 42/38, Bonn, 18. Sept. 1987. P. 37. [A.F., Oct. 8, 1869 Danzig – deported to Theresienstadt on Apr. 10, 1942, won medals at the first Olympic Games in Athens in 1896.]

24543. *Jüdinnen in Deutschland – Parvenue oder Paria?* Kassel: Bibliothek und Studienzentrum der Ersten Deutschen Frauenbewegung, 1987. 29, [12] pp., illus., ports., facsims. [On Henriette Herz, Dorothea Schlegel and Rahel Varnhagen; incl. also 12 pp. 'Dokumententeil' with 3 texts on the Jüdischer Frauenbund.]

24544. KADIMAH. STRICKER, WILLIAM: *Kadimah of Vienna.* [In]: Midstream, Vol. 32, No. 5, New York, May 1986. Pp. 41–44.

24545. KAPLAN, MARION: *Priestess and Hausfrau: women and tradition in the German-Jewish family.* [In]: The Jewish family: myths and realities. Ed. by Steven Cohen and Paula Hyman. New York: Holmes & Meier, 1986. Pp. 62–81.

24546. KOONZ, CLAUDIA: *Reading the writing on the wall.* [In]: Lilith, No. 17, New York, Fall 1987. Pp. 12–14, ports. [On Jewish women in Germany.]

24547. KURZWEIL, ZWI ERICH: *Hauptströmungen jüdischer Pädagogik in Deutschland von der Aufklärung bis zum Nationalsozialismus.* Frankfurt am Main: Diesterweg, 1987. VI, 138 pp., bibl. (123–127).

24548. LEWIN, ERICH. THIEME, HANS: *Nachruf auf Erich Lewin (1902–1986).* [In]: Schlesien, H. 2, Nürnberg, 1987. Pp. 125–126. [E.L., 1902 Rosenberg, Upper Silesia – Dec. 1986 Ramat-Gan, Israel, formerly cantor, from 1939 in Palestine.]

24549. NETER, EUGEN. MARCUS, SHLOMO: *Dr. Eugen-Yizchak Neter (1876 Gernsbach/Murg – 1966 Degania A, Israel).* Jerusalem, 1986. 17 pp., bibl. references. [Typescript, available in the LBI New York. Publ. in Hebrew in]: Koroth, Vol. 9, No. 5/6, Jerusalem, Spring 1987, pp. 148–162. [E.N., Oct. 29, 1876 – Oct. 8, 1966, pediatrician, president of the Jewish Community Mannheim 1938–1940, deported to Gurs, emigrated to Palestine in 1946.]

—— ÖSTERREICHISCH-ISRAELITISCHE UNION. TOURY, JACOB: *Defense activities of the Österreichisch-Israelitische Union before 1914.* [See No. 24070.]

24550. OLLENDORFF, FRANZ. LAPPE, RUDOLF: *Zum Gedächtnis an Professor Franz Ollendorff.* [In]: Nachrichtenblatt des Verbandes der Jüdischen Gemeinden in der DDR, Dresden, März 1987. Pp. 4–6, bibl. [F.O., March 15, 1900 Berlin – Dec. 9, 1981 Israel, engineer, from 1933 teacher at Jewish schools in Berlin, emigrated with pupils and teachers to Palestine in 1934, returned to Germany to organise transfer of Jewish children to Palestine through Youth Aliyah, from 1937 professor at the Technion in Haifa.]

24551. PAUCKER, ARNOLD: *The Jewish defense against antisemitism in Germany, 1893–1933.* [In]: Living with antisemitism, ed. by Jehuda Reinharz [see No. 24835]. Hanover & London, 1987. Pp. 104–132, notes.

24552. PETUCHOWSKI, JAKOB J.: *Feiertage des Herrn: die Welt der jüdischen Feste und Bräuche.* Freiburg i.Br.: Herder, 1987. 142 pp.

24553.	PHILO VERLAG. Braun, Helmuth F.: *Der Philo Verlag (1919–1938): ein Berliner Verlag für jüdische Abwehr- und Aufklärungsliteratur.* [In]: Berlinische Notizen; Zeitschrift des Vereins der Freunde und Förderer des Berlin Museums, 4/87, Berlin, 1987. Pp. 90–103, illus., port., facsims.

24554.	Rappel, D.: *Jewish education in 19th-century Germany in the light of the textbooks.* [In Hebrew, title transl.]. [In]: Sefer Aviad, ed. by Yitzchak Raphael [see No. 24519]. Jerusalem: Mossad Harav Kook, 1986. Pp. 305–316.

24555.	REICHMANN, EVA G. Gruenewald, Max: *Eva Reichmann-Jungmann – a 90th birthday tribute.* [In]: LBI News, No. 54, New York, Summer-Fall, 1987. P. 13. [Further tributes under various headings: [C. C. Aronsfeld/Werner Rosenstock] [in]: AJR Information, Vol. 42, No. 1, London, Jan. 1987, pp. 3–4 [&]: (Dora Segall) [in]: No. 2, Feb. 1987, p. 12. (Ernst G. Lowenthal) [in]: 'Allgemeine', Nr. 42/3, Bonn, 16. Jan. 1987, p. 5 [& in]: Aufbau, Vol. 53, No. 2, New York, Jan. 16, 1987, p. 27.] [E.G.R., historian, sociologist, data see No. 19654/YB XXVIII.]

24556.	REICHSVERTRETUNG DER JUDEN IN DEUTSCHLAND. Gruenewald, Max: *Die Unmöglichkeit der Anpassung: Dr. Max Gruenewald und die Reichsvertretung der Juden in Deutschland. Ein Gespräch mit Lawrence S. Leshnik.* [In]: 'Allgemeine', Nr. 42/52–53, Bonn, 25. Dez. 1987/1. Jan. 1988. P. 12, ports. [See also: Lebenslanger selbstloser Einsatz: zum 88. Geburtstag von Dr. Max Gruenewald (L. S. Leshnik) [in]: 'Allgemeine', Nr. 42/50, Bonn, 14. Dez. 1987, p. 6.]

———	— Sauer, Paul: *Otto Hirsch: director of the Reichsvertretung.* [See No. 24540.]

24557.	REICHSVEREINIGUNG DER JUDEN IN DEUTSCHLAND. Kulka, Otto Dov: *The reactions of German Jewry to the National Socialist regime: new light on the attitudes and activities of the Reichsvereinigung der Juden in Deutschland from 1938–39 to 1943.* [In]: Living with antisemitism, ed. by Jehuda Reinharz [see No. 24835]. Hanover & London, 1987. Pp. 367–379, notes. [For version previously publ. [in]: Die Juden im Nationalsozialistischen Deutschland, 1986, see No. 23620/YB XXXII.]

24558.	Rösner-Engelfried, Susanne B.: *Das Selbst- und Gesellschaftsbild im jüdischen Kinderbuch der 20er und 30er Jahre.* Heidelberg, Hochschule für Jüdische Studien, M.A. Thesis, 1987. [X], 212 pp., illus., facsims., bibl. (204–212). [Incl.: Bibliographie der jüdischen Kinder- und Jugendliteratur des 20. Jahrhunderts, bis 1938 (pp. 171–192).]

———	*Samsonschule Wolfenbüttel (1786–1928).* [See Nos. 24053–24054.]

24559.	Schatzker, Chaim: *The Jewish youth movement in Germany in the Holocaust period (I): Youth in confrontation with a new reality.* [In]: LBI Year Book XXXII, London, 1987. Pp. 157–181, footnotes.

———	Schindler, Thomas: *Studentischer Antisemitismus und jüdische Studentenverbindungen in Deutschland mit besonderer Berücksichtigung Bayerns von 1880 bis 1914.* [See No. 24840.]

———	Schindler, Thomas: *Studentischer Antisemitismus und jüdische Studentenverbindungen in Würzburg 1880–1914.* [See No. 24841.]

24560.	Schochow, Werner: *Jüdische Bibliothekare aus dem deutschen Sprachraum. Eine erste Bestandsaufnahme.* [In]: Antisemitismus und jüdische Geschichte [see No. 24806]. Berlin, 1987. Pp. 515–544.

———	SIMON, ERNST: *Building-up in the time of destruction.* [By] Akiba Ernst Simon. [In Hebrew]. [See pp. 81–180 in No. 24366.]

24561.	— Cohen, Adir: *The privilege and the obligation to educate: issues in the educational thought of Akiva Ernst Simon.* [In Hebrew, with English summary]. [In]: Iyyunim be-Chinukh (Studies in Education), No. 43/44, Haifa, March 1986. Pp. 5–41.

24562.	SONDHELM, SOPHIE. Corbach, Irene & Dieter: *Sophie Sondhelm und die Kölner Jüdische Kinderheilstätte Bad Kreuznach.* Köln: Scriba-Verl., 1987. 70 pp., illus., ports., facsims. (Spurensuche jüdischen Wirkens, 1.) [S.S., March 18, 1887 Kleinlangheim near Kitzingen – Oct. 9, 1944 transported from Theresienstadt to Auschwitz, date of death unknown, trained nurse, head of various Jewish social institutions.]

———	STAATSZIONISTISCHE ORGANISATION. Nicosia, Francis R.: *Revisionist Zionism.* [See No. 24591.]

———	Stow, Kenneth, R.: *The Jewish family in the Rhineland in the High Middle Ages.* [See No. 24038.]

———	Toury, Jacob: *Zur Problematik der jüdischen Führungsschichten, 1880–1933.* [See No. 23911.]

24563.	Unna, Mosche: *die Anfänge der religiösen Kibbuzbewegung in Deutschland.* [In]: Bulletin des LBI, 78, Frankfurt am Main, 1987. Pp. 71–122, notes (155–121). [On Zionist youth movement in Germany and the establishment of training farms with a view to Aliyah, about 1920–1929.] [See also Hebrew essay in No. 24577.]

24564. ZENTRALWOHLFAHRTSSTELLE DER JUDEN IN DEUTSCHLAND. SCHELLER, BERTOLD: *Die Zentralwohlfahrtsstelle: der jüdische Wohlfahrtsverband in Deutschland.* Eine Selbstdarstellung. Frankfurt am Main (Hebelstr. 6): Zentralwohlfahrtsstelle der Juden in Deutschland, 1987. 112 pp., illus., ports., facsims., diagrs., chronology (103–104), bibl. (112). [Covers the time Sept. 9, 1917–1939 and from Aug. 20, 1951 to the present; refers, a.o., to Leo Baeck and Bertha Pappenheim.]

D. Jewish Art and Music

—— ALTARAS, THEA: *Synagogen in Hessen – was geschah seit 1945?* [See No. 23991.]

24565. AUGSBURG. Jüdisches Kulturmuseum. ANSBACHER, B. M.: *Zeugnisse jüdischer Geschichte und Kultur: Jüdisches Kulturmuseum Augsburg.* Augsburg (Halderstr. 8): Jüdisches Kulturmuseum, 1985. 173 pp., illus., bibl. (145–146). [Catalogue on the occasion of the inauguration of the Jüdisches Kulturmuseum on Sept. 1, 1985, depicting and describing art objects related to every event in the Jewish calendar.]

24566. —— RUMP, HANS-UWE: *Jüdisches Kulturmuseum Augsburg.* München: Schnell & Steiner, 1987. 48 pp., illus., ports., notes, bibl. (48). (Bayerische Museen, Bd. 6.) [Incl. survey on the history of the Jews in Augsburg (6–8) and essay on art history of the synagogue (9–21).]

—— BERGER, MAX: *'Heilige Gemeinde Wien': Judentum in Wien.* [Ausstellung der] Sammlung Max Berger. [See No. 24077.]

24567. BENDT, VERONIKA: *Juden in Berlin: Dokumente, Bilder und Kunstwerke aus den Sammlungen des Berlin-Museums.* [In]: Informationen zur modernen Stadtgeschichte, H. 1, Berlin, 1987. Pp. 35–38.

24568. *Braunschweigisches Landesmuseum, Abteilung Jüdisches Museum.* (Texte: Wilfried Knauer. Hrsg.: Gerd Biegel.) Braunschweig, 1987. 20 pp., illus., 1 map. [Also on the wooden synagogue of Hornburg dated 1766 which was saved from destruction during the Nazi period.]

24569. DENEKE, BERNWARD: *Zum Modell einer Laubhütte aus Breslau.* [In]: Schlesien, Jg. 32, H. 3, Nürnberg, 1987. Pp. 129–133, illus., notes (132–133).

—— GENÉE, PIERRE: *Wiener Synagogen 1825–1938.* [See No. 24076.]

—— HOLOCAUST ART. [See No. 24310.]

24570. *Jüdische Künstler, jüdische Themen.* Werke verfolgter jüdischer Künstler und Arbeiten deutscher Künstler mit jüdischen Themen aus dem Besitz des Schleswig-Holsteinischen Landesmuseums. Katalog der Ausstellung im Dr. Bamberger-Haus Rendesburg, bearb. von Thomas Gädeke, 7. Dez. 1986 bis 18. Jan. 1987. Rendsburg: Schlewsig-Holsteinisches Landesmuseum, 1986. 80 pp., illus. (25–67).

24571. MANDELL, ERIC, Collection. VICTOR, WARNER S.: *Rare books from the Eric Mandell Collection [in the] Bertha & Monte H. Tyson Music Department, Gratz College.* Pts. 4 & 5. Philadelphia: Gratz College, [1987]. [Pt. 4]: 32 pp., biogr.–bibl. (11–30), bibl. (31–32); [pt. 5]: 5 pp. [Pt. 4 continues the annotated catalogue of books on Jewish music with the Nos. 73–103 and incl. biogr.-bibl. notes concerning the authors. Pt. 5 is a list of antisemitic literature going back to Richard Wagner (28 numbers). For pts. 1–3 see No. 21355/YB XXX.]

24572. MASER, PETER: *Vor dem Vergessen bewahrt: die Sammlung Ulrich Gerhardts im Berlin-Museum.* [In]: Tribüne, Jg. 26, H. 102, Frankfurt am Main, 1987. Pp. 50–52. [Refers to an exhibition of post cards depicting Jews and Jewish scenes from the collection of U. Gerhardt, part of which was publ. in 1982, see No. 19218/YB XXVIII.]

24573. *The Rosenthaliana Leipnik Haggadah.* Facsimile edition. Tel-Aviv: Turnowsky, 1987. [Haggadah, written and illustrated by Josef ben David from Leipnik in Moravia, 1738. Cf.: Review [in Dutch] (L. Fuks) [in]: Studia Rosenthaliana, Vol. 21, No. 2, Assen, Nov. 1987, pp. 204–205.]

—— SCHIFF, DAVID: *Jewish and musical tradition in the music of Mahler and Schoenberg.* [See in No. 24675.]

—— WAMSER, LUDWIG: *Archäologie und Zeitgeschichte: Untersuchungen in der ehemaligen Synagoge von Veitshöchheim.* [See No. 24050.]

VI. ZIONISM AND ISRAEL

24574. BACH, GABRIEL: *Von Berlin nach Jerusalem.* Der Richter am Obersten Gerichtshof in Israel, Gabriel Bach, berichtet in einem Gespräch [mit Guido Knopp] aus seinem Leben. [In]: deutschland-berichte, Jg. 23, Nr. 1, Bonn, Jan. 1987. Pp. 26–31. [G.B., born March 13, 1927 in Halberstadt, lawyer, emigrated to Palestine in 1940.]

24575. BIRAM, ARTHUR. GOLDSTEIN, H. W.: *Arthur Biram, Nestor des hebräischen Schulwesens.* [In]: MB, Jg. 55, Nr. 25, Tel-Aviv, Juni 1987. P. 4. [A.B., Aug. 1878 Bischofswerde – June 5, 1967 Israel, classical philologist, settled in Haifa in 1914, director of the 'Institut für technische Erziehung', a foundation of the Hilfsverein der Deutschen Juden, which developed into the Haifa Technion.]

24576. BODENHEIMER, MAX. BODENHEIMER, HENRIETTE HANNAH: *Max Bodenheimer; ein zionistisches Lebensbild nach seinen Schriften und Briefen.* Köln: Interpress Publications, 1986. 96 pp., port. [M.B., data see No. 23641/YB XXXII.]

24577. ELIAV, MORDECHAI, ed.: *In the paths of renewal; studies in religious Zionism.* Vol. 2. [In Hebrew]. Ramat-Gan: Bar-Ilan Univ., 1987. 199 pp. [Incl. (in Hebrew): The Mizrachi in Germany and the crisis of 1911 in the world movement: background and consequences (Yaakov Tsur, 17–48). The project of agricultural training farms of the religious Zionists in Germany in its early years (Moshe Unna, 49–64).]

24578. ELONI, YEHUDA: *Zionismus in Deutschland von den Anfängen bis 1914.* Gerlingen: Bleicher, 1987. 570 pp., illus., 1 map, bibl. (538–560). (Schriftenreihe des Instituts für Deutsche Geschichte, Universität Tel-Aviv, 10.)

——— EVENARI, MICHAEL: *Und die Wüste trage Frucht.* [See No. 24694.]

24579. GELBER, JOAV: *Deutsche Juden im politischen Leben des jüdischen Palästina 1933–1948.* Siegfried Moses-Gedenkrede, Jerusalem, 4. Mai 1986. [In]: Bulletin des LBI, 76, Frankfurt am Main, 1987. Pp. 51–72, notes (70–72).

24580. GOLDMANN, NAHUM. BERLIN, ISAIAH: *Nahum Goldmann: personal impressions.* [In Hebrew]. [In]: Gesher, No. 116, Jerusalem, Summer 1987. Pp. 73–78.

——— GRADENWITZ, PETER: *Der deutsch-jüdische Beitrage zur Entwicklung des Musiklebens in Israel.* [See pp. 79–98 in No. 24132.]

24581. GROSS, NACHUM: *The absorption of university-educated immigrants in the 1920s and hydrological research.* [In Hebrew, with English summary]. [In]: Zionism, Vol. 12, Tel-Aviv, 1987. Pp. 127–140. [On three pioneers of hydrological research in Israel who emigrated from Germany between 1923–1925: Martin J. Goldschmidt, Leo Picard, and Stefan Loewengart.]

24582. HEENEN-WOLFF, SUSANN: *Erez Palästina: Juden und Palästinenser im Konflikt um ein Land.* Orig.-Ausg. Frankfurt am Main: Sendler, 1987. 236 pp., illus., bibl. (234–236).

24583. HERZL, THEODOR: *The bell on the left.* Transl. and presented by Harry Zohn. [Preceded by]: ZOHN, HARRY: *The other Herzl.* [In]: Midstream, Vol. 33, No. 5, New York, May 1987. Pp. 13–15; 12–13. [Prose piece from 1901.]

24584. — HERZL, THEODOR: *Ein echter Wiener; Feuilletons.* Kommentiert von André Heller. Wien: Jugend & Volk, Edition Wien, [1987]. 174 pp.

24585. — HERZL, THEODOR: *Old new land: a tale from Vienna.* With an introduction by Jacques Kornberg. New York: Marcus Wiener, 1987. 220 pp., illus. [New edn. of 'Altneuland' with photos of old Vienna and its Jewish population.]

24586. — LAHAD, EZRA: *Herzl as playwright.* [In Hebrew, title transl.]. [In]: Eit-mol, Vol. 13, No. 1 (75), Tel-Aviv, Oct. 1987. Pp. 20–21.

24587. — *Theodor Herzl und das Wien des 'Fin de siècle'.* (Das gleichnamige Symposium fand in Wien vom 1.–3. Mai 1985 statt.) Hrsg. von Norbert Leser. Wien: Böhlau, 1987. 199 pp., bibl. (Schriftenreihe des Ludwig-Boltzmann-Instituts für Neuere Österr. Geistesgeschichte, 5.)

24588. — WACHTEN, JOHANNES: *Theodor Herzl als Literat.* [In]: Illustrierte Neue Welt, Nr. 5, Wien, Mai 1987. Pp. 12–13, illus., port, facsims.

——— LAOR, ERAN: *Wolkensäule – Feuersäule: Rückkehr ins Gelobte Land.* [See No. 24712.]

24589. LAVSKI, HAGIT: *The German inflation and the crises in its wake (1922–1926) from a Zionist perspective.* [In Hebrew, with English summary]. [In]: Zionism, Vol. 12, Tel-Aviv, 1987. Pp. 165–181.

——— NAZISM AND ZIONISM. [See Nos. 24387–24394.]

24590. NEUSTADT, AMNON: *Israels zweite Generation: Auschwitz als Vermächtnis.* Bonn: Dietz Nachf., 1987. 176 pp., bibl. (172–175).

24591. NICOSIA, FRANCIS R.: *Revisionist Zionism in Germany (II): Georg Kareski and the Staatszionistische Organisation, 1933–1938.* [In]: LBI Year Book XXXII, London, 1987. Pp. 231–267, illus., ports., facsim., footnotes. [Pt. I: 'Richard Lichtheim and the Landesverband der Zionisten-Revisionisten in Deutschland, 1926–1933' was publ. [in]: LBI Year Book XXXI, London, 1986, pp. 209–240.]

24592. PENKOWER, MONTY NOAM: *The emergence of Zionist thought.* New York: Associated Faculty Press, 1986. VIII, 159 pp., bibl. [Incl. major Zionist thinkers, a.o., Moses Hess, Theodor Herzl, Leo Pinsker.]

24593. ROSEN, PINCHAS. GROSS, WALTER: *Erzieher im Zionismus: Moses und Rosen.* [And]: ROSENTHAL, JAMES YAAKOV: *Pinchas Rosen – Jurist und Staatsmann.* [In]: MB, Jg. 55, Nr. 23/ 24, Tel-Aviv, Apr.-Mai 1987. P. 10 [&]: 11–12. [In same issue, pp. 13–14, also reprints of]: Verfassung als Staatsbürgerschutz, 1972 (Pinchas Rosen) [&]: Die Aufgaben der Staatskontrolle, 1958 (Siegfried Moses). [[Pinchas Rosen, orig. Felix Rosenblüth, May 1, 1887 Berlin – May 3, 1978 Jerusalem, Zionist leader, Israel's minister of justice 1948–1961.] [Siegfried Moses, May 3, 1887 Lautenburg – Jan 15, 1974 Tel-Aviv, lawyer, Israel's state comptroller 1949–1961.]

—— SADMON, ZEEV W.: *Die Rolle Berlins in der Geschichte des Technions in Haifa.* [See in No. 23942, Vol. 3, pp. 135–138.]

24594. SCHNEIDER, KARLHEINZ/SIMON, NIKOLAUS, eds.: *Der Zionismus und seine europäischen Wurzeln.* Dokumentation einer Arbeitstagung in der Evang. Akademie Arnoldshain, Nov 1986. Mit Beiträgen von John Bunzl [et al.]. Edenkoben (Bahnhofstr. 148): DIAK (c/o C. Sterzing), 1987. 120 pp. (Deutsch-Israelischer Arbeitskreis für Frieden im Nahen Osten, Schriftenband 15.)

—— SEEWAN, HARALD: *Die Jüdisch-akademische Verbindung Charitas Graz.* [See No. 24072.]

—— UNNA, MOSCHE: *Die Anfänge der religiösen Kibbuzbewegung in Deutschland.* [See No. 24563.]

24595. WASSERMANN, EMIL. SAMBURSKY, MIRIAM: *Emil Wassermann: Meine Orientreise.* [In]: Bulletin des LBI, 78, Frankfurt am Main, 1987. Pp. 7–16, notes (16). [Incl. the parts of Wassermann's lecture (1899) on his travels to the Near East that deal with Palestine (pp. 8–15).] E.W., 1842 Wallerstein – 1911 Bamberg, banker.]

—— WOLFSBERG-AVIAD, YESHAYAHU: *Sefer Aviad.* [In Hebrew]. [See No. 24519.]

24596. ZIMMERMANN, MOSHE: *Zionism as a diversionary activity: German Jews and East European immigrants.* [In Hebrew, with English summary]. [In]: Zionism, Vol. 12, Tel-Aviv, 1987. Pp. 73–83. [On the influx of Ostjuden to Germany in the 1890s, and the development of Zionism in Germany in order to channel them out of the country.]

VII. **PARTICIPATION IN CULTURAL AND PUBLIC LIFE**

Section VII had again to be drastically curtailed due to the excess of material stemming from the expansion of German-Jewish studies. Some of the entries now omitted will appear in next year's bibliography – (Ed.).

A. **General**

—— BERLIN. [See also Nos. 23942, 23947, 24132.]

24597. — . . . *Film . . . Stadt . . . Kino . . . Berlin . . .* [Katalog zur gleichnamigen Ausstellung der Stiftung Deutsche Kinemathek, Esplanade, 23. Mai – 30. Juni 1987.] Hrsg. von Uta Berg-Ganschow und Wolfgang Jacobsen. Berlin: Argon, 1987. 207 pp., illus., ports., facsims. [Incl. texts by Rudolf Arnheim, Béla Balázs, Leo Hirsch, Laszlo Moholy-Nagy, Alfred Polgar, Joseph Roth, Kurt Tucholsky.]

24598. — HILDEBRANDT, IRMA: *Zwischen Suppenküche und Salon: 18 Berlinerinnen.* Köln: Diederichs, 1987. 143 pp., illus., ports., bibl. (142–[144]). [Incl. Lina Morgenstern, Alice Salomon, Rahel Varnhagen.]

24599. — LEMHOEFER, DIETER: *Leben, Leistung und Schicksal: jüdische Buchkünstler und Graphiker in Berlin von der Jahrhundertwende bis zum Jahre 1933.* [In]: Aus dem Antiquariat, [Beilage zum]

Börsenblatt für den Deutschen Buchhandel, Nr. 25, Frankfurt am Main, 27. März 1987. Pp. A87 – A96, illus.

24600.   — NOLL, HANS: *Berliner Scharade.* Hamburg: Hoffmann & Campe, 1987. 383 pp. [Refers, a.o., to Elias Canetti, John Heartfield, Wieland Herzfeld, Else Lasker-Schüler.]

24601.   — RODENBERG, JULIUS: *Bilder aus dem Berliner Leben.* (Hrsg. von Gisela Lüttig.) Berlin/East: Rütten & Loening, 1987. 394 pp., illus. [Selection from J.R.'s 'Berliner Erkundungen', 3 vols., 1885–1888, covers especially the social and cultural life in Berlin 1880–1887.] [J.R., orig. Levy, publicist, data see No. 18578/YB XXVII.]

24602.   — ROMPE, ROBERT/TREDER, HANS-JÜRGEN/EBELING, WERNER: *Zur grossen Berliner Physik.* Leipzig: Teubner, 1987. 88 pp. [Refers, a.o., to Max Born, Albert Einstein, Gustav Hertz, Lise Meitner.]

24603.   — SCHRADER, BÄRBEL/SCHEBERA, JÜRGEN, eds.: *Kunstmetropole Berlin 1918–1933.* Dokumente und Selbstzeugnisse. Berlin/East: Aufbau-Verl., 1987. 376 pp., 142 illus., index of names. [Covers theatre life, literature and the press with documentation on and by Jewish representatives from these fields.]

24604.   CORINO, KARL, ed.: *Genie und Geld: vom Auskommen deutscher Schriftsteller.* Nördlingen: Greno, 1987. 487 pp., ports., bibl. [Incl. essays on Sigmund Freud (Paul Kruntorad), Heine (Stephan Reinhardt), Kafka (Hartmut Binder), Else Lasker-Schüler (Judith Kuckart/Jörg Aufenanger), Ludwig Wittgenstein (Paul Kruntorad).]

24605.   *Deutschsprachige Literatur Prags und Böhmens von 1900 bis 1925.* [Hrsg. von der] (Forschungsstelle für Prager deutsche Literatur, Bergische Universität-Gesamthochschule Wuppertal) [unter der Leitung von Jürgen Born]. (D–5000) Wuppertal (1, Postfach 100 127): Forschungsstelle für Prager deutsche Literatur, Bergische Univ., 1987. 155 pp. [Incl.: Selbständig erschienene Veröffentlichungen deutschsprachiger Autoren Prags und Böhmens (1900–1925) im Kontext zeitgeschichtlicher und kultureller Ereignisse (5–58); incl. many Jewish authors.]

24606.   EXILE LITERATURE. *Exil.* Forschung, Erkenntnisse, Ergebnisse. Jg. 7, Nr. 1. Hrsg. von Edita Koch. Maintal (Goethestr. 122): E. Koch, 1987. 107 pp., illus., notes, bibl. [Incl.: 'Charterflug in die Vergangenheit': Hans Sahl erinnert sich an seine Heimatstadt Berlin (Sigrid Kellenter, 5–13). Arnold Zweig im palästinensischen Exil: Erwartungen und Wirklichkeit (Geoffrey V. Davis, 14–33). Paul Walter Jacob am Rio de la Plata (Fritz Pohle, 34–52; P.W.J., stage director, writer, data see No. 22603/YB XXXI). Carl Weiselbergers Dichterkameen: ein Exil-Dokument aus Kanada (Walter Riedel, 61–64; C.W., data see No. 21677/YB XXX). Der Maler Leo Maillet (Max Kühn, 65–71; L.M., orig. Leo Mayer, born 1902 in Frankfurt am Main, emigrated in 1933 to various European countries, lives in Switzerland). Index und Inhalt des Jahrgangs 6/1986 (Gerhard Müller, 98–106).]

24607.   — *Exile and enlightenment; studies in German and comparative literature in honor of Guy Stern.* Ed. by Uwe Faulhaber [et al.]. Detroit: Wayne State Univ. Press, 1987. XX, 282 pp., port., bibl. Guy Stern (Alfred L. Cobbs, 279–282), notes. [Incl.: Peter Weiss: exile, resistance, aesthetics (Ludo Abicht, 123–130). Albert Ehrenstein, 1886–1950: profile of an eternal exile (Alfred Beigel, 153–162). Paul Zech's anti-fascist drama 'Nur ein Judenweib' (Donald R. Daviau, 171–180). 'Zettelwirtschaft': Hermann Broch's 'Massenwahntheorie' and the nature of writing in the letters to Gertrude Lederer (Sander L. Gilman, 181–190). Thomas Theodor Heine's exile 'Märchen' (Donald P. Haase, 207–216). Feuchtwangers Briefwechsel mit Brecht und Thomas Mann (Harold von Hofe/Sigrid Washburn, 217–224). Alfred Neumann's and Erwin Piscator's dramatization of Tolstoy's 'War and peace' and the role of theatre as a contribution to America's war efforts (Gerhard F. Probst, 265–272). Nach dem Exil – Remigration oder endgültiger Abschied? Zum Problem der Heimkehr in der deutschsprachigen Lyrik der Verfolgten des Dritten Reiches (Karin Reinfrank-Clark, 273–278).] [Guy Stern, born Jan. 14, 1922 in Hildesheim, professor of German literature, emigrated to the USA in 1937.]

———   — *Les Exilés allemands en France (1933–1945).* [See No. 24344.]

24608.   — *Exilforschung.* Ein internationales Jahrbuch. Bd. 5: *Fluchtpunkte des Exils und andere Themen.* Hrsg. von Thomas Koebner [et al.]. München: Edition Text + Kritik, 1987. 260 pp. [Incl.: Eine spröde Geliebte: New York aus der Sicht deutscher und österreichischer Exilanten (Helmut F. Pfanner, 40–54). Jüdische und deutsche Identität von Lateinamerika-Emigranten (Patrik von Zur Mühlen, 55–67). Deutschsprachige Literatur in Palästina und Israel (Jürgen Nieraad, 90–110). 'Die Emigranten kämpfen mit Shanghai wie Jacob mit dem Engel' (Mulan Ahlers, 111–122). Siegfried Kracauer im Exil (Karsten Witte, 135–149). Schattenseiten einer erfolgreichen Emigration: Karl Mannheim im englischen Exil (David

Kettler/Volker Meja/Nico Stehr, 170–195). 'Das Kleidungsstück der europäischen Geistigkeit ist einem besudelt worden . . .': Georg Hermann – Jettchen Geberts Vater – im Exil (Laureen Nussbaum, 224–240).]

24609. — *The Germanic Review, Vol. 62, No. 3* [with the issue title]: *Women in exile.* Ed. by Shelley Frisch. New York, Summer 1987. 1 issue, ports., notes. [Cont. essays on: Hilde Domin (Guy Stern). Lotte Jacobi, photographer (Helmut Pfanner/Gary Samson). Else Lasker-Schüler (Sonia M. Hedgepeth). Lili Körber (Viktoria Hertling). Anna Seghers (Alexander Stephan).]

24610. — HUSS-MICHEL, ANGELA: *Literarische und politische Zeitschriften des Exils 1933–1945.* Stuttgart: Metzler, 1987. VII, 225 pp., bibl. (Sammlung Metzler, Bd. 238.)

24611. — *Realismuskonzeptionen der Exilliteratur zwischen 1935 und 1940–41.* Tagung der Hamburger Arbeitsstelle für deutsche Exilliteratur (1986). Hrsg.: Edita Koch. Maintal (Goethestr. 122): E. Koch, 1987. 225 pp. (Exil; Forschung, Erkenntnisse, Ergebnisse, Sonderband 1.) [On the effect of political events on exile writers, a.o., Broch, Döblin, Feuchtwanger, Lukács, Joseph Roth, Arnold Zweig. Incl.: Die Nürnberger Rassengesetze im Spiegel der Exilliteratur (Guy Stern, 184–202).]

24612. — WÜRZNER, HANS, ed.: *Österreichische Exilliteratur in den Niederlanden 1934–1940.* Amsterdam: Rodopi, 1986. 197 pp., illus., bibl. (189–197). Amsterdamer Publikationen zur Sprache und Literatur, Bd. 70.)

24613. THE FRANKFURT SCHOOL. KENNEDY, ELLEN: *Carl Schmitt und die 'Frankfurter Schule': deutsche Liberalismuskritik im 20. Jahrhundert.* [In]: Geschichte und Gesellschaft, Jg. 12, H. 3, Göttingen, 1986. Pp. 380–419, footnotes.

24614. — — JAY, MARTIN: *Les extrêmes ne se touchent pas; eine Erwiderung auf Ellen Kennedy: Carl Schmitt und die Frankfurter Schule.* [In]: Geschichte und Gesellschaft, Jg. 13, H. 4, Göttingen, 1987. Pp. 542–558, footnotes.

24615. — — PREUSS, ULRICH K.: *Carl Schmitt und die Frankfurter Schule: Anmerkungen zu dem Aufsatz von Ellen Kennedy.* [In]: Geschichte und Gesellschaft, Jg. 13, H. 3, Göttingen, 1987. Pp. 400–418, footnotes.

24616. — — SÖLLNER, ALFONS: *Jenseits von Carl Schmitt; wissenschaftsgeschichtliche Richtigstellungen zur politischen Theorie im Umkreis der 'Frankfurter Schule'.* [In]: Geschichte und Gesellschaft, Jg. 12, H. 4, Göttingen, 1986. Pp. 502–529, footnotes.

——— LOWENTHAL, LEO: *An unmastered past.* [See No. 24718.]

24617. GIDAL, NACHUM T.: *Jews in photography.* [In]: LBI Year Book XXXII, London, 1987. Pp. 437–453, illus., ports., facsims. [Cf.: Jewish camera (David Brauner) [in]: The Jerusalem Post, 12. Feb. 1988.]

24618. HERMAND, JOST, ed.: *Geschichten aus dem Ghetto.* Frankfurt am Main: Jüdischer Verlag bei Athenäum, 1987. 315 pp., illus., bibl. (313–314). [Incl. stories by Hermann Blumenthal, Wilhelm Feldmann, Karl Emil Franzos, Max Grünfeld, Heine, Leo Herzberg-Fraenkel, Leopold Kompert, Eduard Kulke, Alfred Meissner, Nathan Samucly, Hermann Schiff.]

24619. JHERING, HERBERT: *Theater in Aktion: Kritiken aus drei Jahrzehnten 1913–1933.* Hrsg. von Edith Krull und Hugo Fetting. Berlin: Argon, 1987. 636 pp. [Incl. critiques on many German- and Austrian-Jewish playwrights. See also No. 24664.]

24620. *Jüdisches Lesebuch, 1933–1938.* Ausgewählt von Henryk M. Broder und Hilde Recher. Nördlingen: Greno, 1987. 266 pp. (Greno 10,20, Bd. 26: Kleine jüdische Bibliothek.) [Collection of texts orig. publ. in 'Jüdischer Almanach', ed. by Friedrich Theiberger and Felix Weltsch, and publ. annually by the Zionist weekly 'Selbstwehr' in Prague.]

24621. KESSLER, HARRY GRAF: *Aus unbekannten Tagebüchern Harry Graf Kesslers.* [Eingeleitet und hrsg. von] Bernhard Zeller. [In]: Jahrbuch der Deutschen Schillergesellschaft, Jg. 31, Stuttgart, 1987. Pp. 3–34, footnotes. [Excerpts from newly discovered diaries 1884–1909, refer also to Jewish personalities.]

24622. KÖNIG, RENÉ: *Soziologie in Deutschland: Begründer, Verfechter, Verächter.* München: Hanser, 1987. 503 pp. [Incl. essays: Die Situation der emigrierten deutschen Soziologen in Europa (pp. 298 ff.). Die Juden und die Soziologie (pp. 329 ff). Also refers passim to German-Jewish sociologists.]

24623. LYMAN, DARRYL: *Great Jews in music.* Middle Village, N.Y.: Jonathan David, 1986. 326 pp., illus., ports. [Incl. biographical articles on Ernst Bloch, Otto Klemperer, Erich Leinsdorf, Gustav Mahler, Felix Mendelssohn, Giacomo Meyerbeer, Jacques Offenbach, Artur Schnabel, Arnold Schoenberg, Rudolf Serkin, Bruno Walter, Kurt Weill; also many short sketches of German-Jewish musicians and composers.]

24624. LYMAN, DARRYL: *Great Jews on stage and screen*. Middle Village, N.Y.: Jonathan David, 1987. 279 pp., illus., ports. [Incl. biographical articles on Herbert Lom, Peter Lorre, Lilli Palmer, Joseph Schildkraut, Erich von Stroheim); also many short sketches of German-Jewish actors.]

24625. MATTENKLOTT, GERT: *Jüdische Frauen im Briefwechsel um 1800: Gedanken zu 'Geschichtlichkeit und Erbe der Romantik'.* [In]: Zeitschrift für Germanistik, 8, Leipzig, 1987. Pp. 39–49. [Mainly on Henriette Herz and Rahel Varnhagen.]

24626. MOSÈS, STÉPHANE: *Spuren der 'Schrift': von Goethe bis Celan.* (Von Eva Moldenhauer aus dem Franz. übertragen). Frankfurt am Main: Jüdischer Verlag bei Athenäum, 1987. 151 pp. [On the Jewish-biblical background in German literary works, incl. Benjamin, Celan, Rosenzweig.]

—— MOSSE, WERNER E.: *Jews in the German economy.* [See No. 23896.]

24627. *Schlesische Lebensbilder.* Bd. 1–4. Namens der Historischen Kommission hrsg. von Friedrich Andreae [et al.]. 2. Aufl. Sigmaringen: Thorbecke, 1985. 4 vols. [Unchanged new print, orig. publ. Breslau, Korn, 1922–1931. Incl. biogr. essays on Jewish Silesians, a.o., Paul Ehrlich, Fritz von Friedlaender-Fuld, Ferdinand Lassalle, Lina Morgenstern; also essays written by Jewish authors and scholars.]

24628. SCHRADER, BÄRBEL/SCHEBERA, JÜRGEN: *Die 'goldenen' zwanziger Jahre: Kunst und Kultur der Weimarer Republik.* Leipzig: Edition Leipzig; Wien: Böhlau, 1987. 279 pp., illus., bibl. (266–270). [Refers to many Jewish personalities.]

24629. SCHWARZ, EGON: *Literatur aus vier Kulturen.* Essays und Besprechungen. Göttingen: Vandenhoeck & Ruprecht, 1987. 134 pp., bibl. (132–134). [Deals with Austrian, German, and US literature and with Jewish literary themes.]

24630. SERKE, JÜRGEN: *Böhmische Dörfer: Wanderungen durch eine verlassene literarische Landschaft.* Wien: Zsolnay, 1987. 480 pp., illus., ports., facsims., bibl. (460–472). [Cont. essays on 47 chiefly Jewish writers.]

24631. SHAKED, GERSHON: *The shadows within: essays on the modern Jewish writer.* Philadelphia: The Jewish Publication Society, 1987. 216 pp. [Incl., a.o., Agnon, Appelfeld, Kafka.]

B. Individual

24632. ASCH, BRUNO. REBENTISCH, DIETER: *Bruno Asch – Weggefährte Ludwig Landmanns: ein preussischer Jude und sozialistischer Stadtkämmerer.* [In]: Frankfurter Rundschau, 4. Sept. 1987. [B. Asch, 1890 Wollstein, Posen–1940 Amsterdam, politician. L. Landmann, May 18, 1868 Mannheim – March 5, 1945 Holland, Lord Mayor of Frankfurt am Main 1924–1933.]

24633. AUSLÄNDER, ROSE: *Der Traum hat offene Augen.* Unveröffentlichte Gedichte 1965–1978. Mit einem Nachwort von Helmut Braun. Orig.–Ausg. Frankfurt am Main: Fischer, 1987. 134 pp. (Fischer-Taschenbücher, 9172.) [See also: Versöhnung war ihr Lebensmotiv: zum Tode der Lyrikerin Rose Ausländer (Hermann Lewy) [in]: 'Allgemeine', Nr. 43/2, Bonn, 15. Jan. 1988, p. 7.] [R.A., née Rosalie Scherzer, May 11, 1907 Czernowitz – Jan. 3, 1988 Düsseldorf, survived the Nazi period in hiding, emigrated to New York in 1946, lived in Düsseldorf from 1965.]

24634. BLUMENTHAL-WEISS, ILSE. LOWENTHAL, ERNST G.: *Abschied von Ilse Blumenthal-Weiss.* [In]: 'Allgemeine', Nr. 42/37, Bonn, 11. Sept. 1987. P. 6. [See also obituaries: (Gert Niers) [in]: Aufbau, Vol. 53, No. 18, New York, Aug. 28, 1987, p. 10. [In]: LBI News, No. 54, New York, Summer-Fall 1987, p. 12.] [I.B.-W., Oct. 14, 1899 Berlin – Aug. 10, 1987 Greenwich, Conn., poetess, writer, emigrated to Holland in 1937, imprisoned at Westerbork and Theresienstadt 1943–1945, emigrated to the USA in 1947, board member of the LBI New York.]

24635. BÖRNE, LUDWIG. *Ludwig Börne und Frankfurt am Main.* Vorträge zur 200. Wiederkehr seines Geburtstages am 6. Mai 1986. Frankfurt am Main: Klostermann, 1987. 158 pp. (Frankfurter Bibliotheksschriften, Bd. 1.)

24636. BROD, MAX: *Max Brod – Franz Kafka: eine Freundschaft. 1: Reiseaufzeichnungen.* Hrsg. unter Mitarbeit von Hannelore Rodlauer von Malcolm Pasley. Frankfurt am Main: S. Fischer, 1987. 323 pp., 42 illus., ports., facsims. [Cont. diaries, letter, and other texts 1909–1912.]

24637. — PAZI, MARGARITA, ed.: *Max Brod, 1884–1984; Untersuchungen zu Max Brods literarischen und philosophischen Schriften.* New York; Berne: Lang, 1987. 268 pp. (New Yorker Studien zur neueren deutschen Literaturgeschichte, Bd. 8.) [Incl. contribution by Julius H. Schoeps on relations between Brod and his father Hans-Joachim Schoeps who jointly edited Kafka's 'Beim Bau der Chinesischen Mauer' in 1931.]

24638. CELAN, PAUL. *Psalm und Hawdalah: zum Werk Paul Celans.* Akten des Internationalen Paul-Celan-Kolloquiums New York 1985. Hrsg. von Joseph P. Strelka. Bern: Lang, 1987. 202 pp. (Jahrbuch für Internationale Germanistik: Reihe A: Kongressberichte, Bd. 20.)

24639. EHRENSTEIN, ALBERT. Laugwitz, Uwe: *Albert Ehrenstein; Studien zu Leben, Werk und Wirkung eines deutsch-jüdischen Schriftstellers.* Frankfurt am Main: Lang, 1987. XI, 347 pp. (Hamburger Beiträge zur Germanistik, Bd. 5.) [See also Beigel essay in No. 24607.]

24640. EINSTEIN, ALBERT: *The collected papers of Albert Einstein. Vol. 1: The early years: 1879–1902.* Ed.: John Stachel. Princeton, N.J.: Princeton Univ. Press, 1987. 440 pp., illus., ports., facsims., tabs., maps, bibl. (391–408). [Vol. 1 cont. 142 documents in the original language, most of them previously unpublished, incl. over 50 letters to Mileva Marić, Einstein's classmate in Zürich and his future wife. The 'Collected papers' will comprise about 40 vols.] [See also Nos. 23907, 24118.]

24641. FREUD, SIGMUND. Arlow, Jacob A.: *Ahad-Ha'am, Freud and the wellsprings of psychoanalysis.* [In]: Hebrew University Studies in Literature and the Arts, Vol. 14, Jerusalem, Autumn 1986. Pp. 189–204.

—— — Bank, Richard D.: *Freud and Buber: a 'dialogue' on God.* [See No. 24441.]

24642. — Gay, Peter: *A godless Jew: Freud, atheism and the making of psychoanalysis.* New Haven: Yale Univ. Press; Cincinnati: Hebrew Union College Press, 1987. XVII, 182 pp., bibl. (157–177). [See also No. 23879.]

24643. — Heenen-Wolff, Susann: *'Wenn ich Oberhuber hiesse . . .': die Freudsche Psychoanalyse zwischen Assimilation und Antisemitismus.* Orig.-Ausg. Frankfurt am Main: Nexus, 1987. 149 pp., illus., bibl. (145–149).

24644. — Roith, Estelle: *The riddle of Freud: Jewish influences on his theory of female sexuality.* London; New York: Tavistock, 1987. 250 pp.

24645. — Wistrich, Robert S.: *The Jewish identity of Sigmund Freud.* [In]: The Jewish Quarterly, Vol. 34, No. 3, London, 1987. Pp. 47–55, illus.

24646. HEINE, HEINRICH: *The Jewish stories and Hebrew songs of Heinrich Heine.* Introd. by Elizabeth Petuchowski. Illus. with 20 lithographs by Max Liebermann, New York: Marcus Wiener, 1987. 180 pp.

24647. — *Heine-Jahrbuch 1987.* Jg. 26. Hrsg. von Joseph A. Kruse, Heinrich-Heine-Institut der Landeshauptstadt Düsseldorf. Hamburg: Hoffmann & Campe, 1987. 310 pp., illus., notes, bibl. [Incl.: Moses Hess und Heinrich Heine: Soldaten im Befreiungskrieg der Menschheit (Helmut Hirsch, 78–91). Zur Biographie Maximilian Heines (Waltraud und Heinz Müller-Dietz, 135–168). Heines Verlagsvertrag mit Michel Lévy Frères vom 23. Sept. 1854 (Michael Werner, 219–222). Heine-Literatur 1985/86 mit Nachträgen (Heike von Berkholz, 273–286). See also No. 24006.]

24648. — Seifert, Siegfried/Volgina, Albina A., comps.: *Heine-Bibliographie 1965–1982.* Berlin/East: Aufbau-Verl., 1986. XIV, 426 pp. [Sequel to No. 7273/YB XIV. Cont. more than 3,100 entries.]

24649. — Shmueli, Efraim: *Heine's gods; pantheism, Spinoza, and the problem of Judaism.* [In Hebrew, title transl.]. [In]: Moznaim, Vol. 60, No. 7, Tel-Aviv, Jan. 1987. Pp. 33–36.

24650. — Tengler, H. F.: *The role of Judaism in Heine's life and work: continuity and change.* [In]: Acta Germanica, Bd. 17 (1984); Jahrbuch des Südafrikanischen Germanistenverbandes, hrsg. von Dieter Welz. Frankfurt am Main: Lang, 1985. Pp. 53–68, footnotes, bibl.

24651. HERMANN, GEORG. Horch, Hans Otto: *Über Georg Hermann: Plädoyer zur Wiedererweckung eines bedeutenden deutsch-jüdischen Schriftstellers.* [In]: Bulletin des LBI, 77, Frankfurt am Main, 1987. Pp. 73–94, notes (92–94). [See also No. 24697.]

24652. — Nussbaum, Laureen. *'Und es kam, wie es kommen musste': das Schicksal Georg Hermanns und seiner Spätwerke im niederländischen Exil.* [In]: Neophilologicus, 71, Groningen, Wolters-Noordhoff, 1987. Pp. 252–265, 402–412, notes. [See also pp. 224–240 in No. 24608.]

24653. HESS, MOSES. Fishman, Aryei: *Moses Hess on Judaism and its aptness for a socialist civilization.* [In Hebrew]. [In]: Bar-Ilan; Annual of Bar-Ilan University, Vol. 22/23, Ramat-Gan, 1987. Pp. 315–327.

24654. — Hirsch, Helmut: *Moses Hess und Heinrich Heine: Soldaten im Befreiungskrieg der Menschheit.* [In]: Heine-Jahrbuch 1987, Jg. 26, Hamburg, 1987. Pp. 78–91, notes (90–91). [Incl. chap.: Die jüdische Wurzel von Moses Hess.] [See also No. 24670.]

24655. JACOB, MATHILDE. Knobloch, Heinz: *'Meine liebste Mathilde': das unauffällige Leben der*

Mathilde Jacob. Vom Autor überarb. Ausg. Berlin: Das Arsenal, 1986. 243 pp., illus. [Biography of M.J., secretary to Rosa Luxemburg, born March 8, 1873 in Berlin, deported to Theresienstadt on July 27, 1942, date and place of death not known. See also No. 24719.]

24656. JONAS, HANS: *The concept of God after Auschwitz: a Jewish voice.* [Transl. from the German by the author.] [In]: The Journal of Religion, Vol. 67, No. 1, Chicago, Jan. 1987. Pp. 1–13, footnotes.

24657. — JONAS, HANS: *Der Gottesbegriff nach Auschwitz: eine jüdische Stimme.* Frankfurt am Main: Suhrkamp, 1987. 48 pp. (Suhrkamp-Taschenbuch, 1516.)

24658. — *Friedenspreis des deutschen Buchhandels, 1987: Hans Jonas.* Ansprachen aus Anlass der Verleihung [durch den] Börsenverein des Deutschen Buchhandels. Frankfurt am Main: Verlag der Buchhändler-Vereinigung, 1987. 58 pp., bibl. (49–54). [Incl. the address by Hans Jonas: Technik, Freiheit und Pflicht.]

—— KAFKA, FRANZ: *Max Brod – Franz Kafka: eine Freundschaft.* [See No. 24636.]

24659. — *Franz Kafka und das Judentum.* Hrsg. von Karl Erich Grözinger, Stéphane Mosès, Hans Dieter Zimmermann. Frankfurt am Main: Jüdischer Verlag bei Athenäum, 1987. 260 pp. [Papers from an international colloquium held in Frankfurt am Main in 1986.]

24660. — GLATZER, NAHUM N.: *Frauen in Kafkas Leben.* Aus dem Amerikan. von Otto Bayer. Zürich: Diogenes, 1987. 131 pp., illus.

24661. — JOFEN, JEAN: *The Jewish mystic in Kafka.* New York; Berne: Lang, 1987. XVII, 249 pp., illus., ports., notes (227–2388). (American University Studies, Ser. 1, Vol. 41. Cf.: The mystery of Kafka's Mysticism unresolved (Ritchie Robertson) [in]: Jewish Chronicle, London, July 3, 1987, p. 31.]

24662. — SCHIRRMACHER, FRANK, ed.: *Verteidigung der Schrift: Kafkas 'Prozess'.* Frankfurt am Main: Suhrkamp, 1987. 220 pp. (Edition Suhrkamp, 1386.) [Cf.: Wende zum Judentum: neue Deutungsversuche (Hartmut Binder) [in]: NZZ, Nr. 48, Zürich, 27./28. Feb. 1988, p. 29.]

24663. — WILK, MELVIN: *Jewish presence in T. S. Eliot and Franz Kafka.* Atlanta, Scholars Press, 1986. 217 pp. (Brown Judaic studies, No. 82.)

24664. KERR, ALFRED. SCHÖNE, LOTHAR: *Der Kritiker – Gegenschöpfer oder Faxenmacher? Der Kampf um das Theater zwischen Ihering und Kerr in der Weimarer Republik.* [In]: NZZ, Nr. 49, Zürich, 28. Feb./1. März 1987. Pp. 65–66, port. [See also No. 24619.]

24665. KLEIN, FELIX. ROWE, DAVID E.: *'Jewish mathematics' at Göttingen in the era of Felix Klein.* [In]: Isis, 77, Brussels, Sept. 1986. Pp. 422–449. [F.K., Apr. 25, 1849 Düsseldorf–June 22, 1925 Göttingen, mathematician.]

24666. KRAUS, KARL. WAGNER, NIKE: *Incognito ergo sum – zur jüdischen Frage bei Karl Kraus.* [In]: Literatur und Kritik, H. 219/220, Wien, Nov./Dez. 1987. Pp. 387–399, notes.

24667. LESSING, THEODOR. MARWEDEL, RAINER: *Theodor Lessing 1872–1933.* Eine Biographie. Darmstadt: Luchterhand, 1987. 446 pp., illus., ports., bibl. (422–439). [Cf.: Provocation beyond his powers (George Steiner) [in]: TLS, London, June 26, 1987, p. 683.]

24668. LIEBERMANN, MAX. BUSCH, GÜNTER: *Max Liebermann: Maler, Zeichner, Graphiker.* Frankfurt am Main: S. Fischer, 1986. 280 pp., illus., bibl. (264–266). [Cf.: Bürger, Preusse, Jude: G. Buschs meisterhaftes Buch über M. Liebermann (Walter Jens) [in]: Die Zeit, Nr. 27, Hamburg, 26. Juni 1987, p. 51.]

24669. MAHLER, GUSTAV. NAMENWIRTH, SIMON MICHAEL: *Gustav Mahler; a critical bibliography.* 1–3. Wiesbaden: Harrassowitz, 1987. 3 vols. (XV, 597; 533; 595 pp.). [See also No. 24675.]

24670. MARX, KARL. ROKITJANSKI, JAKOW: *Zur Geschichte der Beziehungen von Karl Marx und Friedrich Engels zu Moses Hess in Brüssel 1845–1846.* [In]: Marx-Engels-Jahrbuch, 9, Berlin/East, 1986. Pp. 223–267, ports., facsims., notes (257–267). [See also No. 24522.]

24671. OPPENHEIM, SIMON. TREUE, WILHELM: *Die Bankiers Simon und Abraham Oppenheim 1828–1880: der private Hintergrund ihrer beruflichen Tätigkeit, ihre Rolle in der Politik und ihre Nobilitierung.* [In]: Zeitschrift für Unternehmensgeschichte, Jg. 31, Nr. 1, Wiesbaden, 1986. Pp. 31–72.

24672. RIESSER, GABRIEL. BARSCHEL, UWE: *Gabriel Riesser als Abgeordneter des Herzogtums Lauenburg in der Frankfurter Paulskirche 1848, 49.* Neumünster: Wachholtz, 1987. 262 pp. (Schriftenreihe der Stiftung Herzogtum Lauenburg, Bd. 11.) [Cf.: Emanzipation und Einheit Deutschlands (Arie Goral) [in]: 'Allgemeine', Nr. 42/34, Bonn, 21. Aug. 1987, p. 5.]

24673. ROTH, JOSEPH. FRAIMAN, SARAH: *Joseph Roth: Dichter des Offenen.* [In]: Bulletin des LBI, 76, Frankfurt am Main, 1987. Pp. 35–50, notes (48–50). [Incl.: Ironie und Judentum.]

24674. SCHNITZLER, ARTHUR. SPIELMANN, DIANE R.: *Ambivalence in the work of Arthur Schnitzler portrayed through dilletantism and through the Jewish situation.* New York, City Univ., Ph.D. Thesis, 1987. IX, 250 pp., bibl. (242–250).

24675. SCHÖNBERG, ARNOLD. *Journal of the Arnold Schoenberg Institute.* Vol. 9, Nos. 1 & 2. Los Angeles, Ca., Arnold Schoenberg Institute at the Univ. of Southern California, 1986. 2 issues. [*No. 1* incl.: Tagebücher (see No. 24731). *No. 2*: Schoenberg's representation of the divine in 'Moses und Aron' (Michael Cherlin). Jewish and musical tradition in the music of Mahler and Schoenberg (David Schiff).]

24676. — ZELINSKY, HARTMUT: *Arnold Schönberg – der Wagner Gottes; Anmerkungen zum Lebensweg eines deutschen Juden aus Wien.* [In]: Neue Zeitschrift für Musik, Mainz, Apr. 1986. Pp. 7–19, illus., port., notes (17–19). [See also Raksin essay in No. 24132.]

24677. STERN, GERSON. SCHÜTZ, HANS J.: *Eine jüdischer Bestseller – mitten in Nazi-Deutschland.* [In]: Börsenblatt für den deutschen Buchhandel, Jg. 43, Nr. 91, Frankfurt am Main, 13. Nov. 1987. Pp. 3174–3176, ports. [Refers to Gerson Stern and his novel 'Weg ohne Ende', Berlin, Erich Reiss Verl., 1934, which went through 10 editions by 1938.] [G.St., July 7, 1874 Holzminden – Jan. 15, 1956 Jerusalem, emigrated to Palestine in 1939.]

24678. STROUSBERG, BETHEL HENRY. OHLSEN, MANFRED: *Der Eisenbahnkönig Bethel Henry Strousberg; eine preussische Gründerkarriere.* Berlin/East: Verlag der Nation, 1987. 350 pp., illus. [B.H.St., data see No. 21655/YB XXX.]

24679. — WOLTER, HEINZ: *Bethel Henry Strousberg: Aufstieg und Fall des preussischen 'Eisenbahnkönigs'.* [In]: Gestalten der Bismarckzeit, Bd. 2. Berlin/East: Akademie-Verl., 1986. Pp. 91–117, port., notes (115–117).

24680. SZONDI, PETER. SPARR, THOMAS: *Peter Szondi.* [In]: Bulletin des LBI, 78, Frankfurt am Main, 1987. Pp. 59–69, notes (69). [P.Sz., May 27, 1929 Budapest – Oct. 1971 Berlin, literary historian.]

24681. VARNHAGEN, RAHEL. HAHN, BARBARA/ISSELSTEIN, URSULA, eds.: *Rahel Levin Varnhagen: die Wiederentdeckung einer Schriftstellerin.* Göttingen: Vandenhoeck & Ruprecht, 1987. 207 pp. (Zeitschrift für Literaturwissenschaft und Linguistik, Beiheft 14.) [Cont. 16 papers presented at a colloquium in Turin in Apr. 1986. Incl.: 'Mein lieber Schwester-Freund': Rahel und Ludwig Robert in ihren Briefen (Consolina Vigliero, 44–55). Juden als Autoren des 'Magazins zur Erfahrungsseelenkunde': ein Beitrag zum Thema 'Juden und Aufklärung in Berlin' (Ernst-Peter Wieckenberg, 128–140). Rahel-Philologie im Zeichen der antisemitischen Gefahr (Konrad Feilchenfeldt, 187–195).]

24682. WERFEL, FRANZ. JUNGK, PETER STEPHAN: *Franz Werfel: eine Lebensgeschichte.* Frankfurt am Main: S. Fischer, 1987. 452 pp., illus., ports., facsims., notes (352–433).

24683. ZWEIG, ARNOLD. FUCHS, KONRAD: *Ein deutsch-jüdisches Schicksal: zum 100. Geburtstag des Schriftstellers Arnold Zweig.* [In]: Tribüne, Jg. 26, H. 104, Frankfurt am Main, 1987. Pp. 56, 58–60. [See also: Einmal Zionist, immer Zionist (Schalom Ben-Chorin) [in]: MB, Jg. 55, Nr. 30, Tel-Aviv, Nov. 1987, pp. 4 & 6. Das Exil in der Heimat (Doris Maurer) [in]: Die Zeit, Nr. 46, Hamburg, 6. Nov. 1987, p. 76.]

24684. ZWEIG, STEFAN: *The Jewish legends.* With an introd. by Leon Botstein. New York: Marcus Wiener, 1987. 238 pp.

24685. — GELBER, MARK H., ed.: *Stefan Zweig – heute.* New York; Berne: Lang, 1987. 226 pp. (New Yorker Studien zur neueren deutschen Literaturgeschichte, Bd. 7.) [Incl.: Der zeitgeschichtliche Hintergrund des Werkes von St. Zweig (Norbert Leser, 10–24). Die Gnade der Vernunft und die des Unglücks: Zweig und Roth – ein Briefwechsel (Gershon Shaked, 141–159). Stefan Zweig und die Judenfrage von heute (Mark H. Gelber, 160–180). Der Tod des Entdeckers des Paradieses (Alberto Dines, 181–200).]

VIII. AUTOBIOGRAPHY, MEMOIRS, LETTERS, GENEALOGY

24686. BAUM, VICKI: *Es war alles ganz anders.* Erinnerungen. Köln: Kiepenheuer & Witsch, 1987. 472 pp., illus., ports. [New edn. of memoirs first publ. posthumously in 1962.] [V.B., Jan. 24, 1888 Vienna – Aug. 29, 1960 Hollywood, harpist, writer of novels and filmscripts, emigrated to the USA in 1932.]

24687. BEHREND, ITZIG: *The family chronicle of Itzig Behrend.* (Selection by William Bonwitt.) [In]: Midstream, Vol. 33, No. 8, New York, Oct. 1987. Pp. 35–30. [For complete edn. of I. Behrend's chronicle, transl. into English by William Bonwitt, and for details on earlier German publications, see No. 17729/YB XXVI.] [I.B., 1765–1845, Jewish trader in Grove.]

24688. BENJAMIN, WALTER: *Briefe an Siegfried Kracauer.* Mit vier Briefen von Siegfried Kracauer an

Walter Benjamin. Hrsg. vom Theodor W. Adorno Archiv. (Red.: Rolf Tiedemann und Henri Lonitz.) Marbach am Neckar: Deutsches Literaturarchiv, 1987. 126 pp., illus., ports., facsims., notes. (Marbacher Schriften, 27.) [Cont. 54 letters and cards by Benjamin, 1924–1940, publ. for the first time.]

24689. — BENJAMIN, WALTER: *Moscow diary*. Transl. by Richard Sieburth. Foreword by Gershom Scholem. Ed. by Gary Smith. Cambridge, Mass.: Harvard Univ. Press, 1986. 160 pp., illus.

—— BERLINER FAMILY, Hanover. [See No. 23988.]

24690. BLOCH, ERNST/METZGER, ARNOLD: *'Wir arbeiten im gleichen Bergwerk': Briefwechsel 1942–1972.* Hrsg. von Karola Bloch, Ilse Metzger und Eberhard Braun. Frankfurt am Main: Suhrkamp, 1987. 200 pp. [Arnold Metzger, philosopher, data see No. 16656/YB XXV.]

—— BROD, MAX: *Max Brod – Franz Kafka: eine Freundschaft*. [See No. 24636.]

24691. CASPARIUS, HANS: *In my view; a pictorial memoir*. With an introd. by Silvia Beamish. Leamington Spa: Berg Publ., 1987. 160 pp., illus., ports. (An Oswald Wolff Book.) [H.C., 1900 Berlin – 1986 London, actor, photographer, film-maker, emigrated from Vienna to London in 1936.]

24692. EHRENSTEIN, ALBERT: *'Wo ich leben werde, wissen die Götter': Briefe aus der Zeit des Exils*. Mit einem Nachwort hrsg. von Peter Engel. Siegen: Universität-Gesamthochschule, 1987. 25 pp. (Vergessene Autoren der Moderne, 26.) (A.E., data see No. 20381/YB XXIX.]

—— EINSTEIN, ALBERT: *The collected papers of Albert Einstein*. [See No. 24640.]

24693. — EINSTEIN, ALBERT: *Zur Notwendigkeit jüdischer Bildung*. Ein unbekannter Brief von Albert Einstein, eingeleitet von Yizhak Ahren. [In]: 'Allgemeine', Nr. 42/50, Bonn, 11. Dez. 1987. P. 10. [Letter to Rabbi Lazar Schonfeld, Apr. 16, 1936.]

24694. EVENARI, MICHAEL: *Und die Wüste trage Frucht*. Ein Lebensbericht. Gerlingen: Bleicher, 1987. 343 pp. [M.E., orig. Walter Schwarz, born Oct. 9, 1904 in Metz, botanist, emigrated to Palestine in 1933, specialist in ecology and physiology of desert plants.]

24695. FECHENBACH, FELIX: *Mein Herz schlägt weiter; Briefe aus der Schutzhaft*. Mit einem Vorwort von Heinrich Mann. Erweiterte Neuauflage der 1. Ausg. St. Gallen, Kultur-Verlag, 1936. Nachwort von Peter Steinbach. Passau (Milchgasse 2): Andreas-Haller-Verl., 1987. 64 pp. [F.F., socialist journalist, was imprisoned by the Nazis in March 1933 and murdered on Aug. 7, 1933; data see No. 21464/YB XXX.]

24696. FISCHER, BRIGITTE B.: *My European heritage; life among great men of letters*. Transl. from the German by Harry Zohn. Boston: Branden, 1986. 275, [38] pp., illus., ports., facsims. [Transl. of No. 15725/YB XXIV.] [B.B.F., born 1905 in Berlin, daughter of the publisher Samuel Fischer.]

24697. FREUD, SIGMUND: '. . . dass wir nicht auch gestorben sind': unveröffentlichte Briefe Sigmund Freuds an Georg Hermann. [Mitgeteilt, kommentiert und eingeleitet von] Gert Mattenklott. [In]: Neue Rundschau, Jg. 98, H. 3, Frankfurt am Main, 1987. pp. 5–21, notes, facsims. [Freud's letters, Vienna Feb. 1, 1936 – March 14, 1936 (pp. 7–20) are from the Georg-Hermann-Archive in the Leo Baeck Institute New York and publ. for the first time.]

24698. — FREUD, SIGMUND: *The letters of Sigmund Freud and Arnold Zweig*. Ed. by Ernst L. Freud. Transl. by Elaine and William Robson-Scott. New York: New York Univ. Press, 1987. IX, 190 pp. [American edn. of No. 9111/YB XVI; for German paperback edn. see No. 21702/YB XXX.]

24699. — HES, JOZEF PHILIP: *A note on an as yet unpublished letter by Sigmund Freud*. [In]: Jewish Social Studies, Vol. 48, Nos. 3–4, New York, Summer-Fall, 1986. Pp. 321–324, notes. [Letter to Dr. Feuchtwang, May 6, 1931.]

24700. FÜRNBERG, LOUIS: *Briefe, 1932–1957*. Auswahl in 2 Bänden. (Hrsg. im Auftrag der Akademie der Künste der DDR von Lotte Fürnberg und Rosemarie Poschmann.) Berlin/East: Aufbau-Verl., 1986. 2 vols. (814; 692 pp.), illus., ports. [L.F., May 24, 1909 Iglau, Moravia – June 23, 1957 Weimar, writer, emigrated in 1939 via Italy to Palestine, returned to Prague in 1946, lived in the GDR from 1954.]

24701. FÜRST, JACOB: *Chronicle of the families Leonhard Fuerst and Viktor Israel from recollections of Jacob Fuerst, Krefeld*. Transl. by Justin J. Mueller. Manchester, Vt., 1987. [61], [27], [2] pp., facsims. [Transl. of: Chronik der Familien Leonhard Fürst und Victor Israel. Photocopy of typescript, available in the LBI New York.]

24702. GLÜCKEL VON HAMELN: *Denkwürdigkeiten der Glückel von Hameln*. Aus dem Jüdisch-Deutschen übers., mit Erläuterungen versehen und hrsg. von Alfred Feilchenfeld. Nachdr. der 4. Aufl. Berlin, Jüdischer Verlag, 1923. Frankfurt am Main: Athenäum, 1987. 333 pp., illus. (Die kleine weisse Reihe, Bd. 99.) [Autobiography, incl. accounts of Jewish life in Hamburg,

Altona and Metz. For English edn. see No. 15332/YB XXIV.] [G.v.H., 1645 Hamburg – 1724 Metz.]

24703. GRAYEFF, FELIX: *Migrant scholar*. An autobiography. Ed. by Eleonore Engelhardt and Albert Raffelt. Freiburg i.Br.: Universitätsbibliothek, 1986. VII, 92 pp., port., facsim., bibl. F. Grayeff (89–92). [F.G., 1906 Königsberg – 1981 England, philologist, philosopher, historian, emigrated to Australia, New Zealand and England.]

24704. HALBRICH, OTTO: *Reise nach Jerusalem*. Ebenhausen bei München: Langewiesche Brandt, 1987. 254 pp. [Memoirs.] [O.H., born May 12, 1904 in Worms, lived in a kibbutz in Palestine 1924–1926, emigrated from Germany via Canada and the USA to Chile where he became a teacher, from 1942 living in Argentina.]

24705. HAMBURGER, MICHAEL: *Verlorener Einsatz*. Erinnerungen. (Übers. von Susan Nurmi-Schomers und Christian Schomers.) Stuttgart: Flugasche-Verl., 1987. 299 pp., illus., ports., index of names (296–299). [Transl. of 'A mug's game – intermittent memoirs, 1924–1954', see No. 14059/YB XXII.] [M.H., born March 22, 1924 in Berlin, literary historian, poet, translator, emigrated with family to England in 1933.]

24706. HENSEL, FANNY: *The letters of Fanny Hensel to Felix Mendelssohn*. Collected, ed. and transl. with introductory essays and notes by Marcia J. Citron. New York: Pendragon Press, 1987. 1 vol., illus., scores. [Collection of the letters which Fanny Hensel, née Mendelssohn, wrote to her brother Felix from 1821 to 1847, presented in the orig. German and in English translation; incl. essay by M. J. Citron: The relationship between Fanny and Felix.]

—— KAFKA, FRANZ: *Max Brod – Franz Kafka: eine Freundschaft*. [See No. 24636.]

24707. KALÉKO, MASCHA: *Aus den sechs Leben der Mascha Kaléko*. Biographische Skizzen, ein Tagebuch [1938–1945] und Briefe. [Bearb. von] Gisela Zoch-Westphal. (Mit 62 Fotos und Zeichnungen, sowie 19 Dokumenten.) Berlin: arani, 1987. 226 pp., illus., ports., facsims., bibl. (212–215). [M.K., June 7, 1912 Schidlow – Jan. 21, 1975 Zürich, poet, grew up in Berlin, emigrated in 1938 to the USA.]

—— König Family, Austria. [See No. 24067.]

24708. LACHS, MINNA: *Warum schaust du zurück: Erinnerungen 1907–1941*. Wien: Europaverl., 1986. 269 pp. [M.L., née Schiffmann, born 1908 in Trembowla, Galicia, educationalist, from 1914 in Vienna, active in Jewish youth movement, emigrated in 1938 via Switzerland and Spain to the USA, returned to Vienna in 1947, vice president of the Austrian Unesco commission in 1956.]

24709. LACKNER, STEPHAN: *Auf dem Weg zu mir selbst*. [In]: Neue Deutsche Hefte, 193, Jg. 34, H. 1, Berlin, 1987. Pp. 45–56. [Reminiscences about childhood in Bad Homburg, about his Jewish father and Gentile mother, encounter with antisemitism.] [St.L., orig. Morgenroth, author, art-historian, data see No. 18529/YB XXVII.]

24710. LANDAU, LOLA: *Vor dem Vergessen: meine drei Leben*. Frankfurt am Main: Ullstein, 1987. 391 pp. [L.L., born Dec. 3, 1892 in Berlin, writer, married to the German expressionist writer and pacifist Armin T. Wegner, emigrated without husband to Palestine in 1936, lives in Jerusalem.]

24711. LANDAUER, GUSTAV: *Ein Brief Gustav Landauers*. [Veröffentlicht und erläutert von] Walter Tornin. [In]: Internationale wissenschaftliche Korrespondenz zur Geschichte der deutschen Arbeiterbewegung, Jg. 23, H. 3, Berlin, Sept. 1987. Pp. 376–394, notes. [Hitherto unpubl. letter by G.L. to Helmut Tornin, presented and with explanatory essay by the latter's son, Walter Tornin.]

24712. LAOR, ERAN: *Wolkensäule – Feuersäule: Rückkehr ins Gelobte Land*. Wien: Böhlau, 1987. 300 pp. [Third part of the author's autobiography covering the time 1946 to 1974; for previous vols. see Nos. 10233/YB XVIII & 17754/YB XXVI.] [E.L., orig. Erik Landstein, born June 1, 1900 in Cifer, Slovakia, lived in Vienna, Istanbul and, from Nov. 1934, in Palestine, active in Jewish refugee relief in Europe 1946–1947, worked for the Jewish Agency in Geneva after the establishment of the State of Israel, lives in Jerusalem.]

24713. LASKER-SCHÜLER, ELSE: *Franz Marc – Else Lasker-Schüler: 'Der Blaue Reiter präsentiert Eurer Hoheit sein blaues Pferd'*. Karten und Briefe. Hrsg. und kommentiert von Peter-Klaus Schuster. (Katalog zur [gleichnamigen] Ausstellung in der Staatsgalerie moderner Kunst, München, 20. Nov. 1987 – 31. Jan. 1988.) München: Prestel, 1987. 167 pp., illus., facsims. [Catalogue for an exhibition of the illustrated correspondence between Franz Marc and E. L.-Sch. See also the address, delivered at the opening of the exhibition: Grüsse an den Prinzen Jussuf: über Taten und Träume der Else Lasker-Schüler (Friedhelm Kemp) [in]: Süddeutsche Zeitung, Nr. 286, München, 12./13. Dez. 1987, p. 143.]

24714. LEWALD, FANNY: *Freiheit des Herzens; Lebensgeschichte – Briefe – Erinnerungen.* Hrsg. und mit einem Nachwort von Gerhard Wolf. Berlin/East: Buchverlag Der Morgen, 1987. 369 pp., port. (Märkischer Dichtergarten.) [F.L., March 24, 1811 Königsberg – Aug. 5, 1889 Dresden, novelist and champion of women's rights.]

24715. LINKSZ, ARTHUR: *Fighting the third death.* Transl. from Hungarian by John J. Alpar. New York (N.Y. 10028, 35 East 84th Street): A. Linksz, 1986. 340 pp. [Memoirs up to 1918 by A.L., born 1900 in Hungary: on adolescence at the end of the Austro-Hungarian Empire, and on his ancestors many of whom were rabbis.]

24716. LÖWENTHAL, GERHARD: *Ich bin geblieben.* Erinnerungen. München: Herbig, 1987. 397 pp., illus. [G.L., born on Dec. 8, 1922 in Berlin, TV presenter of 'ZDF-Magazin' from 1969 till his retirement on Dec. 23, 1987.]

24717. LOWENTHAL, ERNST G.: *Eine Barmizwa in Köln vor 70 Jahren: aus Jugenderinnerungen.* [In]: 'Allgemeine', Nr. 42/52–53, Bonn, 25. Dez. 1987/1. Jan. 1988. P. 13, notes.

24718. LOWENTHAL, LEO: *An unmastered past; the autobiographical reflections of Leo Lowenthal.* Ed., with an introduction by Martin Jay. Preface by Jürgen Habermas. Berkeley: Univ. of California Press, 1987. 240 pp., illus. [Provides insights into Lowenthal's personal odyssey and into his intellectual contributions especially as a founding member and last surviving figure of the Frankfurt School.] [L.L., sociologist, data see No. 19485/YB XXVIII; his publications appear in Germany under his orig. name: Löwenthal.]

24719. LUXEMBURG, ROSA: *Rosa Luxemburg im Gefängnis; Briefe und Dokumente aus den Jahren 1915– 1918.* Hrsg. u. eingeleitet von Charlotte Beradt. Frankfurt am Main: Fischer, 1987. 153 pp. (Fischer-Taschenbücher, 5659.) [New edn. of a collection of R.L.'s letters to her secretary Mathilde Jacob, orig. publ. in 1973. See also No. 24655.]

24720. — QUACK, SYBILLE: *Rosa Luxemburg an Paul Levi: ein Nachtrag.* [In]: Internationale wissenschaftliche Korrespondenz zur Geschichte der deutschen Arbeiterbewegung, Jg. 23, H. 2, Berlin, Juni 1987. Pp. 207–212, notes. [Seven hitherto unpubl. letters by R.L. to Paul Levi written in 1914, a supplement to No. 20523/YB XXIX.]

24721. MAHLER, GUSTAV: *Mahler's unknown letters.* Ed.: Herta Blaukopf. Transl. by Richard Stokes. London: Gollancz; Hanover, N.H.: Univ. Press of New England, 1987. 240 pp., illus., notes. [More than 150 previously unpubl. letters to critics, colleagues, family members and admirers. Cf.: On bicycle and podium (Donald Mitchell) [In]: TLS, London, June 19, 1987, pp. 657–658. For German edn. see No. 20697/YB XXIX.]

24722. MENDELSSOHN, ROBERT von: *Erinnerungen des Robert von Mendelssohn.* Aufgezeichnet von Kristina Behnke. [In]: Grunewald Gemeinde, Berlin, Dez. 1986. Pp. 13–22, illus., ports. [Obtainable from Gemeindehaus, Furtwänglerstr. 5, D-1000 Berlin 33.] [R.v.M., born 1902 in Berlin, son of the banker Franz von Mendelssohn, survived the Nazi period in Germany.]

24723. MENDELSSOHN BARTHOLDY, FELIX: *Felix Mendelssohn: a life in letters.* Ed. by Rudolf Elvers. Transl. from the German by Craig Tomlinson. New York: Fromm, 1986. XV, 334 pp., illus., ports., facsims. [Transl. of No. 21716/YB XXX.]

——— METZGER, ARNOLD. [See No. 24690.]

24724. NELKI, WOLFGANG: *The story of my family: the German-Jewish family of Hermann Nelki.* London, [1987]. 118 pp. [Mimeog., available in the LBI New York.] [W.N., born June 11, 1911 in Berlin, emigrated in 1933 via Belgium to England.]

24725. OLDEN, RUDOLF/OLDEN, PETER: *Briefe aus den Jahren 1935–1936.* Hrsg. von Charmian Brinson und Marian Malet. Berlin: Verlag Europäische Ideen, 1987. 56 pp., notes (48–56). (europäische ideen, H. 64.) [Rudolf O., Jan. 14, 1885 Stettin – Sept. 17, 1940 drowned on the 'City of Benares', lawyer, writer, emigrated in 1933 via various countries to England. Peter O., born in 1905, half-brother of Rudolf.]

24726. ORFALI, STEPHANIE: *A Jewish girl in the Weimer Republic.* Berkeley, Ca.: Ronin Publ., 1987. XII, 240 pp., illus., ports. [Autobiography: girlhood in an assimilated Jewish family, encounter with antisemitism.] [St.O., née Braun, born 1911 in Nürnberg, emigrated to Palestine in 1934.]

24727. RIESS, CURT: *Das war ein Leben!* Erinnerungen. Erweiterte, neu durchgesehene Ausg. München: Langen Müller, 1986. 431 pp. [Augmented edn. of No. 14908/YB XXIII.] [C.R., born June 21, 1902 in Würzburg, publicist, emigrated in 1933 via various countries to the USA.]

24728. — RIESS, CURT: *Meine berühmten Freunde.* Erinnerungen. Orig.-Ausg. Freiburg i.Br.: Herder, 1987. 252 pp. (Herder-Taschenbuch, 1503.) [Incl. chaps. on Vicki Baum, Elisabeth Bergner, Fritz Lang, Ernst Lubitsch, Fritzi Massary, Max Reinhardt, Billy Wilder.]

—— ROTH, JOSEPH. [See pp. 141–159 in No. 24685.]

24729. SALTEN, FELIX: *Leiden, Streiche, Kumpaneien; aus den unveröffentlichten Erinnerungen.* [In]: Morgen, Jg. 11, Nr. 53, Wien, Juni 1987. Pp. 144–148, ports., facsim. [F.S., writer, data see No. 23660/YB XXXII.]

24730. SCHOENBERG, ARNOLD: *Letters.* Selected and ed. by Erwin Stein. Transl. by Eithne Wilkins and Ernst Kaiser. Berkeley, Ca.: Univ. of California Press, 1987. 310 pp. [Paperback edn. of No. 4875/YB X; for German orig. see No. 1872/YB V.]

24731. —— SCHÖNBERG, ARNOLD: *Tagebücher* = *Diaries.* Los Angeles, Ca.: Arnold Schoenberg Institute at the Univ. of Southern California, 1986. 1 vol. (Journal of the Arnold Schoenberg Institute, Vol. 9, No. 1.) [Cont. diaries of the years 1912, 1913, and 1923 in the orig. German language and in English translation, edited, introduced and with commentary by Jerry McBride [et al.]. The 1923 diary is printed for the first time.]

24732. SCHREKER FAMILY, Austria. SCHÖNY, HEINZ: *Nochmals Franz Schreker.* [In]: Genealogie, Jg. 36, H. 8 (Bd. 18), Neustadt/Aisch, Aug. 1987. Pp. 625–635, facsim., footnotes. [Addition to No. 18694/YB XXVII. Refers also to the Jewish ancestors of Franz Schreker.]

24733. SEGAL, LILLI: *Vom Widerspruch zum Widerstand; Erinnerungen einer Tochter aus gutem Hause.* Berlin/East: Aufbau-Verl., 1986. 252 pp. [L.S., née Schlesinger, born 1913 in Berlin, emigrated in 1933 to France, joined the French resistance, was captured and transported to Auschwitz whence she escaped to Switzerland in 1944, returned to the GDR after the war, reunited with husband and son who had survived by living underground in France.]

—— SIMON, ERNST: *Chapters in my life.* [By] Akiba Ernst Simon. [In Hebrew]. [See in No. 24366.]

24734. SOMARY, FELIX: *The raven of Zürich.* The memoirs of Felix Somary. Transl. by A. J. Sherman. London: Hurst, 1986. XXIV, 303 pp., illus. [For orig. German edn. see No. 4225/YB IX.] [F.S., Nov. 20, 1881 Vienna – July 11, 1956 Zürich, political economist, banker in Zürich from 1919, adviser to politicians.]

24735. SPIELREIN, SABINA: *Tagebuch einer heimlichen Symmetrie; Sabina Spielrein zwischen Jung und Freud.* Hrsg.: Aldo Carotenuto. Vorwort: Johannes Cremerius. Freiburg i.Br.: Kore-Verl., 1986. 372 pp., illus. (Sabina Spielrein, Bd. 1.) [For Engl. transl. and reviews see No. 19386/YB XXVIII. S. Spielrein's diaries and her correspondence with Jung and Freud are here publ. for the first time in the original German language and include, also for the first time, the letters by Jung. See also No. 24855.]

24736. STARER, ROBERT: *Continuo: a life in music.* New York: Random House, 1987. XIII, 206 pp., illus. [R.St., composer, data see No. 23745/YB XXXII.]

—— STEIN, EDITH. [See Nos. 24793–24794.]

24737. TORBERG, FRIEDRICH: *Liebste Freundin und Alma: Briefwechsel mit Alma Mahler-Werfel.* Nebst einigen Briefen an Franz Werfel, ergänzt durch zwei Aufsätze Friedrich Torbergs im Anhang und einem Vorwort von David Axmann. (Hrsg. von David Axmann und Marietta Torberg.) München: Langen Müller, 1987. 288 pp., ports.

24738. VARNHAGEN, RAHEL: *Briefe und Aufzeichnungen.* (Hrsg. von Dieter Bähtz.) Frankfurt am Main: Insel, 1986. 424 pp., illus. [Edn. for West Germany of No. 23747/YB XXXII.]

24739. —— VARNHAGEN, RAHEL/WIESEL, PAULINE: *Ein jeder machte seine Frau aus mir wie er sie liebte und verlangte.* Ein Briefwechsel. Hrsg. und mit einem Nachwort versehen von Marlis Gerhardt. Orig.-Ausg. Darmstadt: Luchterhand, 1987. 121 pp. (Sammlung Luchterhand, Bd. 708.)

24740. —— VIGLIERO, CONSOLINA: *'Verlassen Sie sich nicht selbst!': zu einem ungedruckten Brief von Rahel Levin.* [In]: Bulletin des LBI, 77, Frankfurt am Main, 1987. Pp. 49–71, notes (66–71). [Incl. a hitherto unpubl. letter by Rahel – not then married – to Alexander von der Marwitz, May 24, 1810 (pp. 49–52).]

24741. WASSERMANN, JAKOB: *Tagebuch aus dem Winkel.* Mit einem Nachwort von Dierk Rodewald. München: Langen Müller, 1987. 205 pp. [First publ. posthumously Amsterdam, Querido, 1935, now re-issued for the first time; the title was provided by Wassermann for 4 short stories which here are combined with prose-pieces of personal sentiment.]

24742. WEIL, HEINZ: *Am Rande des Strudels; Erinnerungen 1913–1983.* Vorwort von Peter Scholl-Latour. Stuttgart: Kohlhammer, 1986. 177 pp., illus., ports. (Lebendige Vergangenheit, Bd. 10.) [H.W., born 1913 in Württemberg, jurist, joined the French Foreign Legion from 1938 to 1945, returned to Germany and became Landgerichtspräsident of Württemberg.]

24743. WESTHEIMER, RUTH, K.: *All in a lifetime.* An autobiography by Dr. Ruth K. Westheimer with Ben Yagoda. New York: Warner Books, 1987. XII, 225 pp., illus., ports., facsims. [R.K.W., née Karola Siegel, born June 4, 1928 in Wiesenfeld near Lohr, sex therapist, radio and television personality, emigrated to Switzerland in 1939, lived after the war in Palestine where she served in the Haganah, studied in France and went to the USA in 1956.]

24744.   WIESEL, ELIE: *Gesang der Toten: Erinnerungen und Zeugnis. Mit den Nobelpreisreden von Oslo.* (Aus dem Französ. von Christian Sturm. Aus dem Engl. von Rudolf Walter.) Freiburg i.Br.: Herder, 1987. 191 pp. [Autobiography. Cf.: Fühlt sich schuldig, überlebt zu haben: und wo war Gott in Auschwitz (Richard Chaim Schneider) [in]: Die Zeit, Nr. 26, Hamburg, 19. Juni 1987, p. 18.]

24745.   WOLFSKEHL, KARL: *Briefwechsel zwischen Annemarie Meiner und Karl Wolfskehl.* [Hrsg. von] Herbert G. Göpfert. [In]: Buchhandelsgeschichte 1986/4, [Beilage zum] Börsenblatt für den Deutschen Buchhandel, Nr. 94, Frankfurt am Main, 25. Nov. 1966. Pp. B 131–142, notes. [See also ensuing]: Von der Schwierigkeit mit Wolfskehls Handschrift (Herbert G. Göpfert) [in]: Buchhandelsgeschichte 1987/3, 25. Sept. 1987, pp. B 127–128.

———   ZWEIG, ARNOLD. [See No. 24698.]

24746.   ZWEIG, MAX: *Lebenserinnerungen.* Vorwort von Hans Mayer. Gerlingen: Bleicher, 1987. 263 pp., illus., ports. [M.Z., born June 22, 1892 in Prossnitz, Moravia, writer, emigrated in 1934 from Berlin via Czechoslovakia to Palestine.]

24747.   ZWEIG, STEFAN: *Rainer Maria Rilke und Stefan Zweig in Briefen und Dokumenten.* Hrsg. von Donald A. Prater. Frankfurt am Main: Insel, 1987. 179 pp.

24748.   — ZWEIG, STEFAN: *Stefan Zweig's unpublished letters of 1938 to Ben Huebsch.* [Introduced and annotated by] Jeffrey B. Berlin. [In]: Deutsche Vierteljahrsschrift für Literaturwissenschaft und Geistesgeschichte, Jg. 61, H. 2, Stuttgart, Juni 1987. Pp. 325–328, footnotes. [St. Z.'s letters to his American publisher.]

24749.   — ZWEIG, STEFAN: *The world of yesterday.* An autobiography. Transl. by Cedar and Eden Paul. London: Cassell, 1987. 344 pp. (Cassell biographies.) [Paperback reprint of the orig. edn., publ. in 1943; the orig. German edn. appeared one year later in Sweden.]

———   — SHAKED, GERSHON: *Die Gnade der Vernunft und die des Unglücks: Zweig und Roth – ein Briefwechsel.* [See pp. 141–159 in No. 24685.]

IX. GERMAN-JEWISH RELATIONS

A. General

24750.   AUSTRIA. BOTZ, GERHARD: *Die versäumte 'Trauerarbeit': Kurt Waldheim und die verdrängte Nazi-Vergangenheit der Österreicher.* [In]: Tribüne, Jg. 26, H. 102, Frankfurt am Main, 1987. Pp. 140–145, footnotes. [Refers also to Austrian-Jewish relations and the participation in the persecution of the Jews.]

24751.   — FRIED, ERICH: *Nicht verdrängen, nicht gewöhnen; Texte zum Thema Österreich.* Hrsg. von Michael Lewin. Wien: Europaverl., 1987. 265 pp., port., bibl.

24752.   — PELINKA, ANTON/WEINZIERL, ERIKA, eds.: *Das grosse Tabu: Österreichs Umgang mit seiner Vergangenheit.* (Mit Beiträgen von Ernst Hanisch [et al.]). Wien: Edition S, Österr. Staatsdruckerei, 1987. 197 pp., bibl. [On how Austria is coming to terms today with its Nazi past.]

24753.   — RIEDL, JOACHIM: *Mit Waldheim leben.* [In]: Die Zeit, Nr. 29, Hamburg, 10. Juli 1987. Pp. 9–11. [Also on antisemitic attitudes in Austria today.]

24754.   *Babylon.* Beiträge zur jüdischen Gegenwart. H. 2. Hrsg.: Dan Diner [et al.]. Frankfurt am Main: Verlag Neue Kritik, Juli 1987. 140 pp. [Incl.: 'Daraus muss man ja Folgerungen ziehen . . .': ein Gespräch mit Hans Mayer (Ruth Fühner, 34–39; touches also on the question of knowledge of the Holocaust). See also Nos. 24253, 24777.]

24755.   BÖLL, HEINRICH. REID, J. H.: *Heinrich Böll: a German for his time.* Oxford: Berg Publ., 1987. 256 pp., bibl. [Also on Böll's engagement in German-Jewish relations.]

24756.   GAREIS, SVEN/VULTEJUS, MALTE von: *Lernort Dachau? Eine empirische Einstellungsuntersuchung bei Besuchern der KZ-Gedenkstätte Dachau.* Berlin: Janssen, 1987. [12], 229, 52 pp., diagrs., bibl. [230–233].

24757.   GIORDANO, RALPH: *Die zweite Schuld oder Von der Last Deutscher zu sein.* Hamburg: Rasch & Röhring, 1987. 368 pp. [Cf.: Der Deutschen Last und Selbstbewusstsein (Peter Steinbach) [in]: 'Allgemeine', Nr. 43/46, Bonn, 13. Nov. 1987, pp. 3–4. Deutsche Identitätssuche (Fred Luchsinger) [in]: NZZ, Nr. 24, Zürich, 30./31. Jan. 1988, p. 95. Verdrängung statt

Bewältigung? (Dieter Tiemann) [in]: Das Parlament, Nr. 1, Bonn, 1. Jan. 1988, p. 12. Die Lebenslüge der Deutschen (Fritz J. Raddatz) [in]: Die Zeit, Nr. 46, Hamburg, 6. Nov. 1987, p. 17.]

24758. GLASER, HERMANN: *Totschweigen, entlasten, umschulden: die 'Bewältigung der Vergangenheit' im Nachkriegsdeutschland.* [And]: HÜBSCH, MONIKA: *'Die Schuldkonten sind ausgeglichen': 'Vergangenheitsbewältigung' im Spiegel von Leserbriefen zu 'Bitburg'.* [In]: Tribüne, Jg. 26, H. 103, Frankfurt am Main, 1987. Pp. 117–124; 125–136.

24759. HIRSCH, HELMUT: *Emigranten fordern die Rettung der Deutschen: zur Entstehung und Verkürzung eines Dokuments.* [In]: Siegener Hochschulblätter, Jg. 9, Siegen, Okt. 1986. Pp. 33–44, notes (42–44).

——— HISTORIANS' DEBATE. [See Nos. 24248–24300.]

24760. HOMANN, URSULA: *Wahrlich kein Ruhmesblatt: die Geschichte unserer 'Vergangenheitsbewältigung'.* [In]: Tribüne, Jg. 26, H. 104, Frankfurt am Main, 1987. Pp. 120–137, bibl.

24761. LEVKOV, ILYA I., ed.: *Bitburg and beyond; encounters in American, German and Jewish history.* New York: Shapolsky, 1987. 734 pp., illus., ports., facsims., tabs.

24762. MORRIS, RODDLER F.: *Philosemitism on the German right: the case of the novelist Walter Bloem.* [In]: Simon Wiesenthal Center Annual, Vol. 4, White Plains, N.Y., 1987. Pp. 203–260. [Walter Bloem, 1868–1951, nationalist writer, leading member of the Reichsschrifttumskammer after 1933.]

24763. MOSSE, GEORGE L.: *Germans and Jews: the right, the left, and the search for a 'third force' in pre-Nazi Germany.* Detroit: Wayne State Univ. Press, 1987. 260 pp., notes. [Paperback edn. of No. 9143/YB XVI.]

24764. NA'AMAN, SHLOMO: *Jews in the 'Deutscher Nationalverein', 1859–1867.* [In Hebrew, with English summary]. [In]: Israel and the nations [see No. 23886]. Jerusalem, 1987. Pp. 113–127, footnotes. [For English article on same subject see No. 22931/YB XXXII.]

24765. PRAWER, SIEGBERT S.: *Distanzliebe zur deutschen Literatur und Kultur.* Dankrede. [In]: Deutsche Akademie für Sprache und Dichtung, Jahrbuch 1986, Darmstadt, 1987. Pp. 47–51. [Address by S. S. Prawer, recipient of the Friedrich-Gundolf-Preis 1986 conferred by the Deutsche Akademie für Sprache und Dichtung; eulogy was delivered by Michael Hamburger.]

24766. SCHMIDT, JOHANN N.: *'Those unfortunate years': Nazism in the public debate of post-war Germany.* [Lecture delivered at Indiana Univ. on Oct. 15, 1986.] Bloomington: Jewish Studies Program, Indiana Univ., 1987. 13 pp., notes. (The Dorit and Gerald Paul program for the study of Germans and Jews.)

24767. SCHOEPS, JULIUS. *Oberstabsarzt-Dr.-Julius-Schoeps-Kaserne in Hildesheim eingeweiht.* [In]: deutschland-berichte, Jg. 23, Nr. 5, Bonn, Mai 1987. Pp. 32–38. [Julius Schoeps (father of Hans-Joachim Schoeps), Jan. 5, 1864 Neuenburg, West-Prussia – Dec. 27, 1942 Theresienstadt, physician in Berlin, 1913–1920 army physician, deported to Theresienstadt in June 1942 where he died shortly before his 79th birthday; his wife Käthe was deported from Theresienstadt to Auschwitz-Birkenau in May 1944, exact date of death unknown.]

24768. ——— SCHOEPS, JULIUS H.: *Die missglückte Emanzipation: zur Geschichte des deutsch-jüdischen Verhältnisses.* [In]: Frankfurter Allgemeine Zeitung, Nr. 81, 6. Apr. 1987. Pp. 14–15, port. [Address delivered in Hildesheim on the occasion of the naming of a Bundeswehr barracks after the author's grandfather.]

24769. WALTER, RUDOLF, ed.: *Das Judentum lebt – ich bin ihm begegnet.* Freiburg i.Br.: Herder, 1985. 167 pp. [Contributions by 21 Germans about their encounters with Jews and Judaism, a.o., by Albrecht Goes, Hans Küng, Gertrud Luckner; refers also to the Nazi period.]

——— THE JEW IN LITERATURE. [See also Nos. 24857, 24860–24862.]

——— ——— BREUER, DIETER: *Antisemitismus und Toleranz in der frühen Neuzeit: Grimmelshausens Darstellung der Vorurteile gegenüber den Juden.* [See No. 24812.]

——— ——— DAVIAU, DONALD R.: *Paul Zech's anti-fascist drama 'Nur ein Judenweib'.* [See pp. 171–180 in No. 24607.]

——— ——— FISCHER, JENS MALTE: *Literarischer Antisemitismus im 20. Jahrhundert.* [See No. 24819.]

24770. ——— FRANK, MARGIT: *Das Bild des Juden in der deutschen Literatur im Wandel der Zeitgeschichte.* Studien zu jüdischen Gestalten und Namen in deutschsprachigen Romanen und Erzählungen 1918–1945. Freiburg i.Br.: Burg-Verl., 1987. 303 pp., bibl. (277–299). (Reihe Hochschulproduktionen Germanistik . . . , Bd. 9.) [Deals mainly with Jewish authors but also with Hans Fallada, Ernst Glaeser, Heinrich and Thomas Mann; incl. chapter on German-Jewish symbiosis.]

24771. — GRIMM, JACOB & WILHELM: Kinder- und Haus-Märchen. BOTTIGHEIMER, RUTH B.: *Grimms' bad girls and bold boys: the moral and social vision of the tales.* New Haven, Conn.: Yale Univ. Press, 1987. 224 pp. [Also on the relation of antisemitism to the economics of work and money in the plots of fairy tales.]

—— —— MISTELE; KARL HEINZ: *Die Juden in Grimms 'Kinder- und Hausmärchen'.* [See pp. 25–27 in No. 23972.]

24772. — LARSEN, EGON: *Justice for Shylock: Shakespeare, Heine and [the actor] Antony Sher.* [In]: AJR Information, Vol. 42, No. 6, London, June 1987. P. 9.

—— — MISTELE, KARL H.: *Jacob Ludwig Bencker: ein vergessener 'jüdischer' Dichter aus Franken.* [See pp. 11–13 in No. 23982.]

24773. — NEUBAUER, HANS-JOACHIM: *'Auf Begehr: Unser Verkehr': über eine judenfeindliche Theaterposse im Jahre 1815.* [In]: Antisemitismus und jüdische Geschichte [see No. 24806]. Berlin, 1987. Pp. 313–328, footnotes.

—— — ORLAND, BEATE: *The literary stereotype as humus for anti-Semitism: the Jew and Jewry in trivial literature 1815–1848.* [See No. 24829.]

—— — RÖSNER-ENGELFRIED, SUSANNE B.: *Das Selbst- und Gesellschaftsbild im jüdischen Kinderbuch der 20er und 30er Jahr.* [See No. 24558.]

24774. — SAAR, FERDINAND von: *Seligmann Hirsch.* Kritisch hrsg. und gedeutet von Detlef Haberland. Tübingen: Niemeyer, 1987. 252 pp. (Ferdinand von Saar, Kritische Texte und Deutungen, Bd. 3.)

—— — Wenzel, Edith: *Synagoga und Ecclesia: zum Antijudaismus im deutschsprachigen Spiel des späten Mittelalters.* [See No. 24804.]

B. German-Israeli Relations

24775. BRODER, HENRYK M.: *Ich liebe Karstadt und andere Lobreden.* Augsburg: Ölbaum-Verl., 1987. 203 pp.

24776. *deutschland-berichte.* Hrsg.: Rolf Vogel. Jg. 23, Nr. 1–12. Bonn, 1987. 11 issues & Themenregister (18 pp.). [Contributions are listed according to subject.]

—— FREEDEN, HERBERT: *Deutscher Historikerstreit aus israelischer Sicht.* [See No. 24257.]

24777. FRIEDLÄNDER, SAUL: *Die Shoah als Element in der Konstruktion israelischer Erinnerung.* [In]: Babylon, H. 2, Frankfurt am Main, Juli 1987. Pp. 10–22, notes.

24778. *'Geduld, sage ich, eine Abkürzung gibt es nicht'; Gespräche während einer Israel-Reise.* Hrsg.: Gerhild Frasch [et al.]. Frankfurt am Main: Haag & Herchen, 1987. 191 pp. (Arnoldshainer Texte, Bd. 45.)

—— *Der Kampf um die Erinnerung: Reaktionen in Israel auf den 'Historikerstreit'.* [See No. 24274.]

24779. LICHARZ, WERNER: *Dieses Jahr in Jerusalem: Begegnungen in Israel – Profile aus den Quellen des Judentums.* Frankfurt am Main: Haag & Herchen, 1987. 353 pp. [Incl. chaps. on Martin Buber and Franz Rosenzweig.]

24780. MEROZ, YOHANAN: *Israel's centrality in the restoration of relations between Germans and Jews.* [In Hebrew, with English summary]. [In]: Gesher, No. 115, Jerusalem, Winter 1986/87. Pp. 7–15.

24781. MEROZ, YOHANAN: *Zwang zur Erinnerung.* [In]: Evangelische Kommentare, Jg. 20, Nr. 5, Stuttgart, Mai 1987. Pp. 277–279.

24782. SPROLL, HEINZ/STEPHAN, GERHARD, eds.: *Begegnung und Dialog; Ludwigsburger Beiträge zum israelisch-deutschen und christlich-jüdischen Gespräch.* Ludwigsburg: Pädagogische Hochschule, 1987. 189 pp., bibl. (Ludwigsburger Hochschulschriften, 6.)

24783. *Tribüne.* Zeitschrift zum Verständnis des Judentums. Jg. 26, H. 101–104. Hrsg. von Elisabeth Reisch. Frankfurt am Main: Tribüne-Verl., 1987. 4 issues, footnotes. [*H. 101* incl.: 'Partnerschaften und Liebesehen': Streiflichter von der 10. Deutsch-Israelischen Konferenz (Erich Rotter, 25 & 28–29). Die Zeitschrift Tribüne und die Vergangenheitsbewältigung: zur angemessenen Auseinandersetzung mit der Geschichte (Peter Steinbach, 58–73). *H. 102:* Konturen eines 'besonderen Verhältnisses': die Zeitschrift Tribüne und die deutsch-israelischen Beziehungen (Peter Steinbach, 86–102). *H. 103:* Konfliktreiche Verständigung: Schulbuchempfehlungen zum deutsch-israelischen Verhältnis (Ursula Homann, 26–34). *H. 104:* Schuld vererbt sich nicht: Betrachtungen über die 'neue Linke' und Israel

(Michael Marek/Michael Türk, 138–147). Further contributions are listed according to subject.]

C. **Church and Synagogue**

—— *Antisemitismus und jüdische Geschichte*. [See No. 24806.]

24784. ARING, PAUL GERHARD: *Christen und Juden heute – und die 'Judenmission'?* Geschichte und Theologie protestantischer Judenmission in Deutschland, dargestellt und untersucht am Beispiel des Protestantismus im mittleren Deutschland. Frankfurt am Main: Haag & Herchen, 1987. X, 426 pp. [Covers the period 1700–1941.]

24785. BRAHAM, RANDOLPH L., ed.: *The origins of the Holocaust: Christian antisemitism*. New York: Columbia Univ. Press, 1986: London: Orbis Books, 1987. 85 pp.

24786. *Christian Jewish Relations*. Vol. 20, Nos. 1–4. Ed.: Norman Solomon. London: Institute of Jewish Affairs in association with the World Jewish Congress, 1987. 4 issues. [*No. 2* incl.: Reaction to Waldheim's papal audience (25–27).]

24787. *Freiburger Rundbrief*. Beiträge zur christlich-jüdischen Begegnung. Jg. 37/38 (1985/86). Schriftleitung: Gertrud Luckner, Clemens Thoma. Freiburg i.Br.: Freiburger Rundbrief, Sommer 1987. 212 pp., footnotes, 'Literaturhinweise' (99–136), 'Immanuel' (149–166). [1 issue.] [Incl.: Festakademie aus Anlass des 85. Geburtstages von Dr. Gertrud Luckner am 22. Sept. 1985 (34–48; various addresses and reply by G. Luckner refer to the help she extended to the persecuted during the Nazi period). Akten deutscher Bischöfe über die Lage der Kirche 1933–1945, bearb. von Ludwig Volk: Buchbericht (Friedhelm Jürgensmeier, 52–54; review essay with regard to the German Catholic bishops' attitude towards Jews during the Nazi period as documented in the two vols. 'Akten', publ. Mainz, 1983 & 1985). Auf dem 21. Deutschen Evangelischen Kirchentag: Ansprache beim Eröffnungsgottesdienst, Düsseldorf, 5. Juni 1985 (Albert H. Friedlander, 68–69). Edith Stein – Teresia Benedicta a Cruce OCD [&]: Zum Karmeliterinnenkonvent in Auschwitz [&]: Zur Seligsprechung von Edith Stein (Ernst Ludwig Ehrlich, 77–80). *Immanuel*; Dokumente des heutigen religiösen Denkens und Forschens in Israel; Hebräische Veröffentlichungen aus Israel in deutscher Übersetzung. Jg. 13/14: 1985/86 (149–166 = pp. IM 1 – IM 18). *Registerband*: Nachtrag zu den Jahrgängen 31–35/36: 1979–1984 [&] zu Immanuel, Jg. 8–11/12: 1979–1983/84 (167–209; 210–212).]

24788. HOMMEL, GISELA: *Anti-semitic tendencies in Christian feminist theology in Germany*. [In]: European Judaism, Vol. 21, No. 1, London, Summer, 1987. Pp. 43–48.

—— *Judaism and Christianity under the impact of National Socialism*. [See No. 23888.]

24789. *Die Katholische Kirche und das Judentum: Dokumente von 1945–1986*. Magdeburg: Alma-Morawska-Seminar, 1986. [Available in the library of the Jüdische Gemeinde, Oranienburger Str. 28, DDR–1040 Berlin.]

24790. LOTTER, FRIEDRICH: *Zur Ausbildung eines kirchlichen Judenrechts bei Burchard von Worms und Ivo von Chartres*. [In]: Antisemitismus und jüdische Geschichte [see No. 24806]. Berlin, 1987. Pp. 69–98, footnotes.

24791. LUTHER, MARTIN. ROYNESDAL, OLAF: *Martin Luther and the Jews*. Milwaukee, Wisc., Marquette Univ., Ph.D. Thesis, 1986. 418 pp.

24792. — VOLK, ERNST: *Martin Luther und die Juden*. [In]: Schriftenreihe des Vereins für Rheinische Kirchengeschichte, 81, Bonn, 1985. Pp. 55–81.

24793. STEIN, EDITH: *Aus meinem Leben*. Mit einer Weiterführung über die zweite Lebenshälfte von Maria Amata Neyer. Sonderausg. Freiburg i.Br.: Herder, 1987. 407 pp. [E. Stein's memoirs, covering the time from her birth in 1891 till 1916, orig. appeared under the title: 'Aus dem Leben einer jüdischen Familie: Kindheit und Jugend' (1965), new edn. Freiburg, Herder, 1985. See also following entry.] [E.St., Oct. 12, 1891 Breslau – Aug. 2, 1942 deported to Auschwitz, date and place of death not known, philosopher, converted in 1922 and became a Carmelite nun, beatified by Pope John Paul II on May 1, 1987.]

24794. — STEIN, EDITH: *Life in a Jewish family*. Transl. from German by Josephine Koeppel. Washington, D.C. (20002, 2131 Lincoln Road N.E.): ICS Publications, 1987. VIII, 548 pp., illus. [Cf.: Why did the Pope beatify Edith Stein? (Benjamin Goodnick) [in]: Midstream, Vol. 33, No. 9, New York, Nov. 1987, pp. 35–36.]

24795. — BATZDORFF, SUSANNE M.: *Remembering my aunt Edith Stein*. [In]: Jewish Spectator, Vol. 52,

No. 1, Santa Monica, Ca., Spring 1987. Pp. 14–17. [See also: Erinnerungen an Edith Stein (Susanne M. Batzdorff) [in]: Aufbau, Vol. 53, No. 10, New York, May 8, 1987, pp. 2–3, ports.]

24796. — BEJAS, ANDRÉS: *Edith Stein – von der Phänomenologie zur Mystik*. Eine Biographie der Gnade. Frankfurt am Main: Lang, 1987. 207 pp., port., bibl. (168–207). (Disputationes theologicae, Bd. 17.)

24797. — ENDRES, ELISABETH: *Edith Stein: christliche Philosophin und jüdische Märtyrerin*. München: Piper, 1987. 301 pp., illus., ports., bibl. (295–297). [Cf.: Jüdische Konvertiten und die Phänomenologie (Daniel Krochmalnik) [in]: 'Allgemeine', Nr. 42/38, Bonn, 18. Sept. 1987, p. 27.]

24798. — FELDMANN, CHRISTIAN: *Liebe, die das Leben kostet: Edith Stein – Jüdin, Philosophin, Ordensfrau*. Freiburg i.Br.: Herder, 1987. 142 pp., bibl. (140–142).

24799. — HERBSTRITH, WALTRAUD: *Edith Stein: Versöhnerin zwischen Juden und Christen*. Leutesdorf: Johannes-Verl., 1987. 78 pp.

24800. — HOLBÖCK, FERDINAND: *'Wir haben den Messias gefunden!' Die selige Edith Stein und andere jüdische Konvertiten vor und nach ihr*. Stein am Rhein: Christiana-Verl., 1987. 160 pp., illus., ports.

24801. — JOHN PAUL II, Pope: *Rede bei der Feier der Seligsprechung der Karmelitin Edith Stein am 1. Mai 1987 im Kölner Stadion Müngersdorf*. [In]: deutschland-berichte, Jg. 23, Nr. 6, Bonn, Juni 1987. Pp. 4–7. [See also: Gefühle der Juden wurden berücksichtigt (Ernst Ludwig Ehrlich) [in]: 'Allgemeine', Nr. 42/19, Bonn, 8. Mai 1987, p. 3. Papst-Besuch in der Bundesrepublik; Schatten der Vergangenheit: die Seligsprechung Edith Steins erinnert an Versäumnisse der Amtskirche (Hansjakob Stehle) [in]: Die Zeit, Nr. 17, Hamburg, 17. Apr. 1987, p. 11.]

24802. — MOOSSEN, INGE: *Das unselige Leben der 'seligen' Edith Stein; eine dokumentarische Biographie*. Mit einem Nachwort von Paul Gerhard Aring. Frankfurt am Main: Haag & Herchen, 1987. 275 pp.

24803. — STALLMACH, JOSEF: *Das Werk Edith Steins im Spannungsfeld von Wissen und Glauben*. [In]: Internationale Katholische Zeitschrift 'Communio', Jg. 16, H. 2, Köln, März 1987. Pp. 149–158, footnotes. [On E. St.'s process from Judaism to Catholicism.]

24804. WENZEL, EDITH: *Synagoga und Ecclesia: zum Antijudaismus im deutschsprachigen Spiel des späten Mittelalters*. [In]: Internationales Archiv für Sozialgeschichte der deutschen Literatur, Bd. 12, Tübingen, 1987. Pp. 57–81, footnotes.

24805. WIRTH, WOLFGANG: *Solidarität der Kirche mit Israel; die theologische Neubestimmung des Verhältnisses der Kirche zum Judentum nach 1945 anhand der offiziellen Verlautbarungen*. Frankfurt am Main: Lang, 1987. 232 pp. (Europäische Hochschulschriften: Reihe 23, Bd. 312.)

D. Antisemitism

24806. *Antisemitismus und jüdische Geschichte; Studien zu Ehren von Herbert A. Strauss*. Hrsg. von Rainer Erb und Michael Schmidt. Grusswort von Shepard Stone. Berlin: Wissenschaftlicher Autorenverlag, 1987. 557 pp., illus., footnotes, bibl. H. A. Strauss (545–552). [Cont. the sections: *Antike und Mittelalter* (15–98; incl.: Zur Ausbildung eines kirchlichen Judenrechts bei Burchard von Worms und Ivo von Chartres (Friedrich Lotter, 69–98). *Emanzipation und Judenfeindschaft* (99–214; incl.: Aus einem 'Zeitalter der Finsterniss und Unduldsamkeit': antijüdische Wuchergesetzgebung im Fürstentum Waldeck (Volker Berbüsse, 121–134). Die 'Hep-Hep-Krawalle' und der 'Ritualmord' des Jahres 1819 zu Dormagen (Stefan Rohrbacher, 135–148). Der 'Ritualmord' von Polná: traditioneller und moderner Wahnglaube (Georg R. Schroubek, 149–172). Jüdische Professoren im Deutschen Kaiserreich: zu einer vergessenen Enquete Bernhard Breslauers (Norbert Kampe, 185–214). *Emigration und Untergrund* (215–312). *Kunst und Literatur* (313–408; incl.: 'Auf Begehr: Unser Verkehr': über eine judenfeindliche Theaterposse im Jahre 1815 (Hans-Joachim Neubauer, 313–328). Christliche Restauration und Antijudaismus: Aspekte der Kunst der deutschen Romantik (Peter Dittmar, 329–364). Marginalität als Modus der ästhetischen Reflexion: Juden und 'unehrliche Leute' im Werk Wilhelm Raabes (Michael Schmidt, 381–408). *Religionsgeschichte* (409–466; cont.: Monotheismus und Antisemitismus – auf immer unerklärbar? Das Erfinden und Wiederabschaffen der Opfer und der Götter (Gunnar Heinsohn, 409–448). 'Ahasverus redivivus' oder: Wir glauben, dass der Antichrist ein Jude sei (Reinhard

Scheerer, 449–466). *Bestandsaufnahmen* (467–544; incl.: Emanzipationsgeschichte und Antisemitismusforschung: zur Überwindung antisemitischer Vorurteile (Reinhard Rürup, 467–478). Insiders, outsiders, and border-crossers: conceptions of modern Jewry in Marx, Durkheim, Simmel and Weber (Helen Fein, 479–494). *Anhang* (545–557; incl.: Bibliographie Herbert A. Strauss, 545–552). Further essays are listed according to subject.] [Cf.: Besprechung (Ludger Heid) [in]: Das Historisch-Politische Buch, Jg. 35, H. 11, Göttingen, 1987, p. 353.]

—— AUSTRIA. [See also Nos. 24078, 24830, 24835.]

24807. — BIHAL, P. TH.: *Abwehr des Judenhasses, Aktionen gegen den Antisemitismus in Österreich.* [And]: STIEGNITZ, PETER: *Die Wurzeln des Bösen: Sozialanalyse des historischen Antisemitismus in Österreich.* [In]: Tribüne, Jg. 26, H. 101, Frankfurt am Main, 1987. Pp. 40–46; 83–91, footnotes.

24808. — WEISS, HILDE: *Antisemitische Vorurteile in Österreich: theoretische und empirische Analysen.* 2. Aufl., mit einem Nachwort bezugnehmend auf den österreichischen Präsidentschaftswahlkampf. Wien: Braumüller, 1987. 167 p., diagrs. (Sociologica, 1.) [On Austrian antisemitism today and its historical and social roots.]

—— BANKIER, DAVID: *The German Communist Party and Nazi antisemitism, 1933–1938.* [See No. 24182.]

24809. *Begegnungen: Judentum und Antisemitismus in Zeit und Geist.* München: Kurt Schobert Verl., 1986. 164 pp., illus., facsims., notes. [Obtainable from Thomas Schindler, Am Happach 46/407, D–8708 Gerbrunn.] [Cont.: Von der mittelalterlichen Judenfeindschaft zum modernen Antisemitismus: Juden und Nichtjuden in Deutschland vom Mittelalter bis zur Neuzeit (Peter Herde, 7–55, notes [44–55]). Juden in Lateinamerika (Stefan Veghazi, 89–99; also on German-Jewish immigration). Fragen an das Judentum: religionssoziologische Randbemerkungen (Kurt Schobert, 101–162, notes [148–157], bibl. [157–162]). See also No. 24841.]

24810. BERBÜSSE, VOLKER: *Die 'eigentliche Wahrheit' als kulturelle Form: zum latenten Antisemitismus in einem ländlichen Raum der Bundesrepublik Deutschland.* [In]: Bulletin des LBI, 78, Frankfurt am Main, 1987. Pp. 17–34, notes (33–34).

—— BERĐING, HELMUT: *Un héraut de l'antisémitisme dans l'Allemagne du XIXe siècle.* [See in No. 23898.]

24811. BERING, DIETZ: *Der Name als Stigma; Antisemitismus im deutschen Alltag 1812–1933.* Stuttgart: Klett-Cotta, 1987. 567 pp., chronology (537–541), notes (397–506), index (543–567), bibl. (507–536). [Cont.: *1. Einleitung* (13–40). *2. Historischer Teil* (41–202; incl.: Durchführung der Namensannahme nach dem Emanzipationsedikt vom 11. März 1812; Letzte Namensannahmen 1845/46; Judenfeindliche Sonderbestimmungen für Namenswechsel bis 1907; Überblick über die Weimarer Zeit – Ausblick auf das Dritte Reich). *3. Systematischer Teil* (203–396; incl.: Name und Berufsstruktur; Wirtschaftsantisemitismus; Jüdische Namen im Zentralbereich preussischer Identität, u.a., im Agrarbereich, beim Militär).] [Cf.: Antisemitismus: Armutszeugnis des menschlichen Geistes oder Ist der antisemitische Bazillus unausrottbar? (Ursula Homann) [in]: Das Parlament, Nr. 1, Bonn, 1. Jan. 1988, p. 12. 'Hab'n Sie nicht den kleinen Cohn geseh'n?' (Julius H. Schoeps) [in]: Die Zeit, Nr. 6, Hamburg, 5. Feb. 1988, p. 19.]

24812. BREUER, DIETER: *Antisemitismus und Toleranz in der frühen Neuzeit: Grimmelshausens Darstellung der Vorurteile gegenüber den Juden.* [In]: Simpliciana 9, Schriften der Grimmelshausen-Gesellschaft, Wetzikon, Schweiz, 1987. Pp. 27–47.

—— BREUER, MORDECHAI: *The reaction of German Orthodoxy to antisemitism.* [In Hebrew]. [See No. 24438.]

—— BUSE, DIETER K.: *Anti-Semitism in mid-nineteenth century Bremen.* [See No. 23955.]

24813. CLAUSSEN, DETLEV: *Grenzen der Aufklärung: zur gesellschaftlichen Geschichte des modernen Antisemitismus.* Orig.-Ausg. Frankfurt am Main: Fischer, 1987. 232 pp., notes (190–227), bibl. (228–[233]). (Fischer-Taschenbücher, 6634.)

24814. CLAUSSEN, DETLEV: *Vom Judenhass zum Antisemitismus: Materialien einer verleugneten Geschichte.* Orig.-Ausg. Darmstadt: Luchterhand, 1987. 269 pp., bibl. references. (Sammlung Luchterhand, Bd. 677.) [Documents, covering antisemitism 1781–1985.]

—— COHEN, SUSAN SARAH, ed.: *Antisemitism; an annotated bibliography.* Vol. 1. [See No. 24162.]

24815. *Current research on antisemitism.* Ed. by Herbert A. Strauss and Werner Bergmann. Vol. 1 ff. Berlin; New York: de Gruyter, 1987 ff. *Vol. 1: The persisting question.* Ed. by Helen Fein, 1987. XIV, 430 pp. [See No. 24818.] [The series is planned to comprise 5 vols.]

24816.	ERB, RAINER: *'Warum ist der Jude zum Ackerbürger nicht tauglich?':* zur Geschichte eines antisemitischen Stereotyps. [In]: Antisemitismus und jüdische Geschichte [see No. 24806]. Berlin, 1987. Pp. 99–120, footnotes.

24817.	*Fanatismus und Massenwahn; Quellen der Verfolgung von Ketzern, Hexen, Juden und Aussenseitern.* Hrsg. von Anton Grabner-Haider [et al.]. Graz: Leykam, 1987. 160 pp.

24818.	FEIN, HELEN, ed.: *The persisting question: sociological perspectives and social contexts of modern antisemitism.* Berlin; New York: de Gruyter, 1987. XIV, 430 pp., diagrs. (Current research on antisemitism, vol. 1.) [Cont. the parts: *1: Explanations* (3–64; incl.: Antisemitism through the ages (Jacob Katz, 46–57). *2: Dimensions/effects* (67–208; incl.: Christian sources of antisemitism (Harold E. Quinley/Charles Y. Glock, 190–208). *3: Comparative contexts* (211–276). *4: Impacts on the Holocaust* (cont.: The impact of antisemitism on the enactment and success of 'The Final Solution of the Jewish Question' (Helen Fein, 279–287). Dimensions of Nazi prejudice (Peter Merkl, 288–316). The persecution of the Jews and German popular opinion in the Third Reich (Ian Kershaw, 317–352; first publ. [in]: LBI Year Book XXVI, London, 1981). *5: The question today* (355–428; incl.: Are we entering a new era of antisemitism? (Eric J. Hobsbawm, 374–379). Other articles impinge on Central European antisemitism and German Jewry as well.]

24819.	FISCHER, JENS MALTE: *Literarischer Antisemitismus im zwanzigsten Jahrhundert: zu seinen Stereotypen und seiner Pathologie.* [In]: Erkundungen; Beiträge zu einem erweiterten Literaturbegriff: Helmut Kreuzer zum 60. Geburtstag. Hrsg. von Jens Malte Fischer [et al.]. Göttingen: Vandenhoeck & Ruprecht, 1987. Pp. 117–138, footnotes, bibl.

24820.	FREY, WINFRIED: *Ritualmordlüge und Judenhass in der Volkskultur des Spätmittelalters.* [In]: Volkskultur des europäischen Spätmittelalters. Hrsg. von Peter Dinzelbacher und Hans-Dieter Mück. Stuttgart: Kröner, 1987. (Böblinger Forum, Bd. 1.) Pp. 177–197.

24821.	GILES, GEOFFREY J.: *Students and National Socialism in Germany.* Princeton; London: Princeton Univ. Press, 1985. XV, 360 pp., bibl. [Refers also to antisemitism of students' fraternities such as the Kyffhäuser-Verband der Vereine Deutscher Studenten. Cf.: The Nazis' problems with students (Jill Stephenson) [in]: Patterns of Prejudice, Vol. 21, No. 4, London, Winter 1987, pp. 56–57.]

——	HARRIS, JAMES F.: *Bavarians and Jews in conflict in 1866.* [See No. 23938.]

24822.	HARTMANN, FRANK: *Von der Praxis der Philosophie zum 'praktischen Antisemitismus'.* Antirationalistischer Affekt und antitheoretischer Gestus als Grundlage nationalsozialistischen Philosophierens. [In]: Widerspruch; Münchner Zeitschrift für Philosophie, 13, München (Tengstr. 14), 1987. Pp. 50–55.

——	HEENEN-WOLF, SUSANN: *'Wenn ich Oberhuber hiesse . . .': die Freudsche Psychoanalyse zwischen Assimilation und Antisemitismus.* [See No. 24643.]

24823.	HOFFMANN, CHRISTHARD: *Antiker Völkerhass und moderner Rassenhass: Heinemann an Wilamowitz.* [In]: Quaderni di Storia, 25, Bari, Gennaio/Giugno 1987. Pp. 145–157, notes (152–157). [Incl. 2 letters of 1895 by Isaak Heinemann to his teacher Ulrich von Wilamowitz-Moellendorff.] [I. Heinemann, June 5, 1876 Frankfurt am Main – July 29, 1957 Jerusalem, Judaist, classical philologist, emigrated in 1939 to Palestine.]

——	*Judaism and Christianity under the impact of National Socialism.* [See No. 23888.]

24824.	KAMPE, NORBERT: *Jews and antisemites at universities in Imperial Germany (II): The Friedrich-Wilhelms-Universität of Berlin: a case study on the students' 'Jewish Question'.* [In]: LBI Year Book XXXII, London, 1987. Pp. 43–101, tabs., diagrs., footnotes. [Pt. I: 'Jewish students: social history and social conflict' was publ. [in]: LBI Year Book XXX, London, 1985, pp. 357–394.]

24825.	KLINGEMANN, CARSTEN, ed.: *Rassenmythos und Sozialwissenschaften in Deutschland: ein verdrängtes Kapitel sozialwissenschaftlicher Wirkungsgeschichte.* Opladen: Westdeutscher Verl., 1987. 395 pp., bibl. (Beiträge zur sozialwissenschaftlichen Forschung, Bd. 85.) [Incl. section on Jews and sociology in a racial context, also on the academics' attitude towards racism.]

24826.	LEUSCHEN-SEPPEL, ROSE-MARIE: *Refugees from Nazi Germany and the scientific study of antisemitism.* [In]: Simon Wiesenthal Center Annual, Vol. 4, White Plains, N.Y., 1987. Pp. 139–174.

24827.	LEWIS, BERNARD: *'Treibt sie ins Meer!': die Geschichte des Antisemitismus.* (Ins Deutsche übertr. von Erwin Duncker.) Frankfurt am Main: Ullstein, 1987. 342 pp. [Transl. of No. 23820/YB XXXII.]

——	MCKALE, DONALD M.: *From Weimar to Nazism: Abteilung III of the German Foreign Office and the support of antisemitism, 1931–1935.* [See No. 24325.]

24828. MOMIGLIANO, ARNALDO: *Tra storiae storicismo*. Pisa: Nistri-Lischi, 1987. 264 pp. [Incl.: German academic antisemitism; German-Jewish scholars and writers. Cf.: History and understanding (George Steiner) [in]: TLS, London, May 1, 1987.]

24829. ORLAND, BEATE: *The literary stereotype as humus for anti-Semitism: the Jew and Jewry in trivial literature 1815–1848*. [In]: Reports of the DFG [Deutsche Forschungs-Gemeinschaft], 2/87; German research, Bonn, 1987. Pp. 4–6 & 22, illus.

24830. *Patterns of Prejudice*. Vol. 21, Nos. 1–4. Ed.: Antony Lerman. London: Institute of Jewish Affairs in association with the World Jewish Congress, 1987. 4 issues. [*No. 1, Spring 1987* incl.: Austrian identity and antisemitism (John Bunzl, 3–8, notes). Waldheim in the press: a selected survey (Richard Grunberger, 9–13, notes). *No. 4, Winter 1987*: Fear of the father figure: Judaeophobic tendencies in the new social movements in West Germany (Micha Brumlik, 19–37, notes; transl. of an edited version of the author's article in no. 23824/YB XXXII). Further contributions are listed according to subject.]

24831. PEAL, DAVID: *Antisemitism by other means? The rural cooperative movement in late nineteenth-century Germany*. [In]: LBI Year Book XXXII, London, 1987. Pp. 135–153, footnotes.

24832. PEAL, DAVID: *Jewish responses to German antisemitism: the case of the Böckel movement, 1887–1894*. [In]: Jewish Social Studies, Vol. 48, No. 3–4, New York, Summer–Fall, 1986. Pp. 269–282, notes.

24833. PFAHL, ARMIN: *Ein 'Ahne' des Nationalsozialismus: Otto Böckel, der erste Antisemit im Deutschen Reichstag*. [In]: Tribüne, Jg, 26, H. 101, Frankfurt am Main, 1987. Pp. 108–118, footnotes.

24834. POLIAKOV, LÉON: *Geschichte des Antisemitismus. Bd. 6: Emanzipation und Rassenwahn.* (Die deutsche Übers. besorgte Rudolf Pfisterer.) Worms: Heintz, 1987. 361 pp.

24835. REINHARZ, JEHUDA, ed.: *Living with antisemitism; modern Jewish responses*. Hanover, N.H.; London: Univ. Press of New England, 1987. X, 498 pp., notes. (The Tauber Institute for the Study of European Jewry series, 6.) [Incl.: Preface (Jehuda Reinharz, IX–X). Reactions to antisemitism in modern Jewish history (Ben Halpern, 3–18). Emancipation and reaction: the rural exodus of Alsatian Jews, 1791–1848 (Michael Burns, 19–41). Crisis as a factor in modern Jewish politics, 1840 and 1881–82 (Jonathan Frankel, 42–58). Conversion as a response to antisemitism in modern Jewish history (Todd M. Endelman, 59–83). The Jewish defense against antisemitism in Germany, 1893–1933 (Arnold Paucker, 104–132). Martin Buber and the metaphysicians of contempt (Paul Mendes-Flohr, 133–164). Defense activities of the Österreichisch-Israelitische Union before 1914 (Jacob Toury, 167–192). Social democracy, the Jews, and antisemitism in Fin-de-siècle Vienna (Robert S. Wistrich, 193–209). Nationalism and antisemitism: the Czech-Jewish response (Hillel J. Kieval, 210–233). The reactions of German Jewry to the National Socialist regime: new light on the attitudes and activities of the Reichsvereinigung der Juden in Deutschland from 1938–39 to 1943 (Otto Dov Kulka, 367–379; for version previously publ. [in]: Die Juden im Nationalsozialistischen Deutschland, 1986, see No. 23620/YB XXXII). Did the Zionist leadership foresee the Holocaust? (Anita Shapira, 397–412).]

—— REINHARZ, JEHUDA: *The response of the 'Centralverein deutscher Staatsbürger jüdischen Glaubens' to antisemitism during the Weimar Republic*. [See No. 24534.]

—— RIFF, MICHAEL ANTHONY: *The government of Baden against antisemitism: political expediency or principle?* [See no. 23937.]

24836. ROOS-SCHUMACHER, HEDWIG: *Der Kyffhäuserverband der Vereine Deutscher Studenten 1880–1914/18. Ein Beitrag zum nationalen Vereinswesen und zum politischen Denken im Kaiserreich*. (D–3170) Gifthorn: Selbstverlag, 1986. 519 pp. (Deutsche Akademische Schriften, N.F., Bd. 17.) [On the most significant antisemitic students' corporation of Imperial Germany. Cf.: Der Kyffhäuserverband im Kaiserreich (Norbert Kampe) [in]: Neue Politische Literatur, Jg. 31, H. 3, Stuttgart, 1986, pp. 493–494 (review essay, provides additional information on the overtly antisemitic attitude of the corporation). See also No. 24824.]

—— RÜRUP, REINHARD: *Emanzipation und Antisemitismus*. [See No. 23900.]

24837. SACKETT, ROBERT EBEN: *Images of the Jew: popular joketelling in Munich on the eve of World War I*. [In]: Theory and Society, Vol. 16, No. 4, Dordrecht, July 1987. Pp. 527–563, notes (556–563).

24838. SARID, A.: *Richard Wagner and Wilhelm Marr – the forerunners of modern antisemitism*. [In Hebrew, title transl.]. [In]: Yalkut Moreshet, No. 41, Tel-Aviv, June 1986. Pp. 97–118.

24839. SCHINDLER, THOMAS: *Die Judenfeindschaft christlicher Theologieprofessoren und Studentenverbindungen im 19. Jahrhundert*. [In]: Beiträge zur österreichischen Studentengeschichte, Bd. 13, Wien (Tuersgasse 21), Österr. Verein für Studentengeschichte, 1986. Pp. 33–50.

24840. SCHINDLER, THOMAS: *Studentischer Antisemitismus und jüdische Studentenverbindungen in Deutschland mit besonderer Berücksichtigung Bayerns von 1880 bis 1914.* Würzburg, Univ., M.A. Thesis, 1987. 127 pp., illus., notes (88–118), bibl. (119–127). [Obtainable from the author, Am Happach 46/407, D–8708 Gerbrunn.]

24841. SCHINDLER, THOMAS: *Studentischer Antisemitismus und jüdische Studentenverbindungen in Würzburg 1880–1914.* [In]: Begegnungen [see No. 24809]. München, 1986. Pp. 57–88, facsims., notes (74–80).

24842. SCHINDLER, THOMAS: *Wirceburgia 1885–1914; der spätere Burschenbund im B.D. vor dem Ersten Weltkrieg.* [In]: Wiener Corps-Briefe, Jg. 7, Nr. 3, Wien (Wiener Senioren Convent, Berggasse 8), Okt. 1987. Pp. 21–24. [Also on antisemitic attitudes.]

24843. SHOHAM, S. GIORA: *German socialism and anti-semitism: social character and the disruption of the symbiosis between Germans and Jews.* [In]: Clio, Vol. 15, No. 3, Fort Wayne, Indiana Univ., Spring 1986. Pp. 303–320, notes (318–320).

24844. STRAUSS, HERBERT A.: *Antisemitismus und Holocaust als Epochenproblem.* [In]: Aus Politik und Zeitgeschichte; Beilage zur Wochenzeitung Das Parlament, B 11, Bonn, 14. März 1987. Pp. 15–23.

24845. STRAUSS, HERBERT A./KAMPE, NORBERT, eds.: *Antisemitismus; von der Judenfeindschaft zum Holocaust.* Bonn, 1985. 288 pp. (Schriftenreihe der Bundeszentrale für politische Bildung, Bd. 213.) [For contents see No. 22865/YB XXXI.] *Reviews* (continuation of No. 23887/YB XXXII): Besprechung (Peter Fiedler) [in]: Freiburger Rundbrief, Jg. 37/38 (1985/86), Freiburg i.Br., Sommer 1987, p. 132. Continuity and uniqueness in National Socialism and antisemitism [in Hebrew] [Nachum Orland] [in]: Gesher, No. 116, Jerusalem, Summer 1987, pp. 124–126 (also on other publications). Besprechung (Bernd Estel) [in]: Kölner Zeitschrift für Soziologie und Sozialpsychologie, Jg. 39, H. 1, Wiesbaden, 1987, pp. 197–200. Besprechung (Y. Michal Bodemann) [in]: Soziologische Revue, Jg. 10, München, 1987, pp. 179–181.

—— STRAUSS, HERBERT A.: *Antisemitismus und jüdische Geschichte; Studien zu Ehren von Herbert A. Strauss.* [See No. 24806.]

—— THALMANN, RITA: *L'Antisémitisme en Europe occidentale* . . . [See No. 24317.]

24846. TOURY, JACOB: *From duel to self-defence: Jews of Central Europe defend their honour and their lives.* [In Hebrew, title transl.]. [In]: Eit-Mol, Vol. 12, No. 4 (72), Tel-Aviv, Apr. 1987. Pp. 3–5. [On cases in Germany and in Austria, 1880–1920.]

—— VILSMEIER, GERHARD: *Deutscher Antisemitismus . . . 1933–1939.* [See No. 24381.]

24847. WISTRICH, ROBERT: *Der antisemitische Wahn: von Hitler bis zum Heiligen Krieg gegen Israel.* Aus dem Engl. von Karl Heinz Siber. Ismaning bei München: Verlag Hueber; München: Nymphenburger, 1987. 526 pp., bibl. (497–510). [Transl. of No. 22869/YB XXXI. Cf.: Kontinuität des Antisemitismus: R. Wistrichs faszinierende Studie (Nachum Orland) [in]: Frankfurter Allgemeine Zeitung, Nr. 198, 28. Aug. 1987, p. 8. Unbequeme Erinnerungen (Julius H. Schoeps) [in]: Die Zeit, Nr. 42, Hamburg, 9. Okt. 1987, p. 23.]

24848. WISTRICH, ROBERT S.: *Ideological anti-Semitism in the 20th century.* [In]: Midstream, Vol. 33, No. 4, New York, Apr. 1987. P. 17–22.

24849. WISTRICH, ROBERT: *'Paranoia can sometimes be justified': Jews and the Nazi legacy.* Robert Wistrich interviewed by Tony Lerman. [In]: The Jewish Quarterly, Vol. 34, No. 1, London, 1987. Pp. 10–13.

24850. WISTRICH, ROBERT S.: *Radical antisemitism in France and Germany.* [In Hebrew, with English summary]. [In]: Israel and the nations [see No. 23886]. Jerusalem, 1987. Pp. 157–184, footnotes. [Covers the 19th century.]

24851. ZENTRUM FÜR ANTISEMITISMUSFORSCHUNG, Technische Universität Berlin. STRAUSS, HERBERT A./BERGMANN, WERNER, eds.: *Lerntag über Vorurteilsforschung heute* – gemeinsam mit der Research Foundation for Jewish Immigration New York – am 9. Nov. 1986. Berlin: Univ. bibliothek der Technischen Univ., Abt. Publikationen, 1987. 92 pp., notes, bibl. (Lerntage des Zentrums für Antisemitismusforschung, 4.)

E. Noted Germans and Jews

24852. FONTANE, THEODOR: *Briefe an Moritz Lazarus.* Folge 1–2, Hrsg. und kommentiert von Joachim Krueger. [In]: Fontane Blätter, Bd. 5, H. 5 (H. 37), pp. 412–417 [&]: Bd. 6, H. 4

(H. 42), pp. 369–383. Potsdam, GDR, 1984 & 1986. [Hitherto unpublished letters, 1874–1895, from the Lazarus Archives at the University Library of the Humboldt-Univ. in East Berlin.]

24853. — SCHULZE, CHRISTA: *Theodor Fontanes und Wilhelm Wolfsohns Begegnungen 1848/49 in Berlin. (Mit Briefen Fontanes aus der Frühzeit ihrer Freundschaft)*. [In]: Fontane Blätter, Bd. 6, H. 5 (H. 43), Potsdam, GDR, 1987. Pp. 481–503, footnotes. [Wilhelm Wolfsohn, Oct. 20, 1820 Odessa – Aug. 13, 1865 Dresden, poet and translator.]

24854. HUMBOLDT, ALEXANDER von. HONIGMANN, PETER: *Alexander von Humboldts Verhältnis zu Juden*. [In]: Bulletin des LBI, 76, Frankfurt am Main, 1987. Pp. 3–34, notes (31–43).

24855. JUNG, CARL GUSTAV. MACLEAN, GEORGE: *Jung the 'protector'*. [In]: Midstream, Vol. 33, No. 4, New York, Apr. 1987. Pp. 39–41. [On C. G. Jung's collaboration with the Nazis, and on his relationship with Sabina Spielrein (see No. 24735).]

24856. KELLER, GOTTFRIED: *Ein Brief Gottfried Kellers an einen Unbekannten [i.e. Ludwig Bernays]*. [In]: Zürcher Taschenbuch auf das Jahr 1987. Zürich: Buchdruckerei an der Sihl, 1986. Pp. 102–115, port., facsim.

24857. LESSING, G. E. GROSSE, WILHELM: *Stundenblätter Lessings 'Nathan' und die Literatur der Aufklärung*. Stuttgart: Klett, 1987. 122 pp., 32 pp. appended.

——— — STROHSCHNEIDER-KOHRS, INGRID: *Lessing und Mendelssohn*. [See No. 24480.]

24858. — WALKER, COLIN: *The young Lessing and the Jews*. [In]: Hermathena, No. 140, Trinity College, Univ. of Dublin, Summer 1986. Pp. 32–54, notes (51–54). [Revised and augmented version of a lecture delivered at Trinity College on Nov. 10, 1983 to commemorate the 25th anniversary of the death of Ernst Scheyer, émigré lecturer of German at the college for 12 years.]

24859. NIETZSCHE, FRIEDRICH. BROWN, MALCOLM B.: *Friedrich Nietzsche und sein Verleger Ernst Schmeitzner; eine Darstellung ihrer Beziehung*. Sonderdruck. Frankfurt am Main: Buchhändler-Vereinigung, 1987. [76] pp., illus. From: Archiv für Geschichte des Buchwesens, Bd. 28, 1987. [Discusses also antisemitism. Pubication of dissertation, see No. 23848/YB XXXII.]

24860. RAABE, WILHELM. DENKLER, HORST: *Das 'wirkliche Juda' und der 'Renegat': Moses Freudenstein als Kronzeuge für Wilhelm Raabes Verhältnis zu Juden und Judentum*. [In]: The German Quarterly, Vol. 60, No. 1, Cherry Hill, N.J., Winter 1987. Pp. 5–18, notes.

24861. — SCHMIDT, MICHAEL: *Marginalität als Modus der ästhetischen Reflexion: Juden und 'unehrliche Leute' im Werk Wilhelm Raabes*. [In]: Antisemitismus und jüdische Geschichte [see No. 24806]. Berlin, 1987. Pp. 381–408, footnotes.

24862. — THUNECKE, JÖRG: *'Such a firm earth and such an ethereal sky': die Thematisierung assimilatorischer und zionistischer Tendenzen in Wilhelm Raabes 'Hungerpastor' und George Eliots 'Daniel Deronda'*. [In]: Jahrbuch der Raabe-Gesellschaft 1987, Braunschweig, 1987. Pp. 156–178, footnotes.

24863. RILKE, RAINER MARIA. POELCHAU, MARIA: *Rilkes Briefe an Resi Hardy (1917–1920)*. [In]: Jahrbuch der Deutschen Schillergesellschaft, Jg. 31, Stuttgart, 1987. Pp. 35–52, port., facsim., footnotes. [Incl. 5 letters by Rilke to Resi Hardy, orig. Therese H., Hamburg 1890 – Oct. 28, 1969, daughter of Rudolf Hardy, the founder and owner of the Hamburg banking house Hardy & Hinrichsen, who because of her Gentile husband, Hans Ulrich Poelchau, survived the Nazi period in Germany.]

24864. WEBER, MAX. CAMIC, CHARLES: *Weber and the Judaic economic ethic: a comment on Fahey*. [And]: FAHEY, TONY: *Text and context in interpreting a text: reply to Camic*. [In]: American Journal of Sociology, Vol. 89, No. 6, Chicago, 1984. Pp. 1410–1416, footnotes, bibl.; [&]: 1417–1420. [Refers to the article: 'Max Weber's ancient Judaism' by Tony Fahey [in]: American Journal of Sociology, Vol. 88, Chicago, July 1982, pp. 62–87.]

——— — FEIN, HELEN: *Insiders, outsiders, and border-crossers: conceptions of modern Jewry in Marx, Durkheim, Simmel and Weber*. [See No. 24522.]

X. FICTION, POETRY AND HUMOUR

24865. ASCHER, CAROL: *The flood*. Freedom, Ca.: Crossing Press, 1987. 191 pp. [Novel about a German-Jewish family which in 1951 finds a new home in Kansas as part of a small community of European exiles.]

24866. DEMBICKI, LEO: *Das dunkle Licht*. Roman einer Epoche 1924–1944. Böblingen: Tykve, 1987. 460 pp. [The love story of a Jewess and a German in Prague during crucial years.]

24867. ERRELL, RICHARD: *Das Nizzani-Fragment*. Roman. Mannheim: Persona-Verl., 1987. 371 pp. [While Christian anti-Judaism is uncovered as the root of antisemitism throughout the ages, the author pleads for tolerance and humanism as a means to overcome prejudice.] [R.E., born Feb. 7, 1899 in Krefeld, painter, graphic artist, writer, emigrated in 1933 to Prague, in 1937 to Palestine, living in Switzerland from 1960.]

24868. FAERBER, MEIR M.: *Israel in Tanka-Versen*. Göttingen: Graphikum, 1987. 32 pp. [M.M.F., data see No. 22884/YB XXXI.]

24869. FREUNDLICH, ELISABETH: *Der Seelenvogel*. Roman. Wien: Zsolnay, 1986. 348 pp. [Story of the social and economic rise of an Austrian-Jewish family of artisans, 1870–1930.]

24870. HERZ, HERMANN: *Der Rabbi von Seldwyla*. Erzählungen. Mit einem Nachwort von Hermann Josef Perrar. Königstein/Ts.: Jüdischer Verl. bei Athenäum, 1986. 88 pp. [H.H., 1927–1984.]

24871. HIRSCH, KARL JAKOB: *Hochzeitsmarsch in Moll*. Roman. Mit einem Nachwort von Hans J. Schütz. Bad Homburg: Oberon, 1986. 190 pp. [Novel on the problems arising for a German Jew during the first years of the Nazi period. First publ. in instalments in 'Isr. Familienblatt', Berlin, 1936, while author already lived in exile in Switzerland. Data see No. 18490/YB XXVII.]

24872. KATZ, HENRY W.: *Schlossgasse 21 in einer kleinen deutschen Stadt*. Roman. Orig.-Ausg. Frankfurt am Main: Fischer, 1986. 446 pp. (Fischer-Taschenbücher, 5106: Verboten und verbrannt, Exil.) [The story of an Eastern Jewish family, sequel to No. 22889/YB XXXI; first edn. in English, New York 1940, now publ. for the first time in German.]

24873. KEILSON, HANS: *Sprachwurzellos*. Gedichte. Giesson: Edition Literarischer Salon, 1986. 47 pp. [Collection of poems from 1933 to the present on Jewish themes, persecution, emigration, and exile.] [H.K., data see No. 21544/YB XXX.]

24874. KÖNIGSDORF, HELGA: *Respektloser Umgang*. Erzählung. Darmstadt: Luchterhand, 1986. 115 pp. [A German Jewess, born during the Nazi period and now mortally ill, experiences a hallucinatory rencontre with Lise Meitner.] [H.K., born 1938 in Gera, mathematician, living in the GDR.]

24875. LOTAR, PETER: *Das Land, das ich dir zeige*. Roman. Wuppertal: Brockhaus, 1987. 287 pp. (Brockhaus-Taschenbücher, Bd. 815.) [Autobiographical novel on life in exile in Switzerland; sequel to 'Eine Krähe war mit mir', Stuttgart, Deutsche Verlags-Anstalt, 1978, in which the author gives fictional account of his youth in Czechoslovakia and the problems of Czech, Jewish and German side-by-side life up to 1939.] [P.L., orig. Lothar Chitz, Feb. 12, 1910 Prague – July 12 [or 13?], 1986 Ennetbaden, Switzerland, writer, stage-director, actor, emigrated in 1939 to Switzerland.]

24876. MORTON, FREDERIC: *Ewigkeitsgasse*. Roman. (Aus dem Amerikan. von Hermann Stiehl.) München: Bertelsmann, 1986. 477 pp. [Orig. title: 'The Forever Street'. Story of a Jewish family in Vienna from the turn of the century to the Holocaust.] F.M., orig. Fritz Mandelbaum, born Oct. 5, 1924 in Vienna, writer, emigrated in 1938 via London to the USA.]

24877. NATONEK, HANS: *Kinder einer Stadt*. Roman. Wien: Zsolnay, 1987. 343 pp. (Bücher der böhmischen Dörfer.) [Orig. publ. in 1932.] [H.N., data see No. 19513/YB XXVIII.]

24878. PETIŠKA, EDUARD, ed.: *Der Golem; jüdische Sagen und Märchen aus dem alten Prag*. (Aus dem Tschechischen übers. von Alexandra Baumrucker.) München: Kovar, 1987. 167 pp., illus. [New transl. of No. 14989/YB XXIII.]

24879. PRYCE-JONES, DAVID: *The afternoon sun*. London: Weidenfeld and Nicolson, 1987. 214 pp. [Novel on four generations of a Viennese Jewish family: rise to wealth and respectability, persecution and death, search for Jewish identity in Israel. Cf.: A family fortune (Gabriele Annan) [in]: The New York Review of Books, June 11, 1987, pp. 28–29.]

24880. REWALD, RUTH: *Vier spanische Jungen*. Hrsg. und mit einem Nachwort von Dirk Krüger. Köln: Röderberg, 1987. 191 pp., illus. [Novel, written in 1937, now publ. for the first time.] [R.R., 1906 Berlin – 1942 Auschwitz, writer of children's books, emigrated to France in 1933, arrested by the Gestapo in July 1942.]

24881. ROSS, CARLO: *. . . aber Steine reden nicht*. Recklinghausen: Edition Bitter, 1987. 208 pp. [Fictionalised experiences during the Nazi period in Hagen in Westphalia where the author, born in 1928, lived with his mother until their deportation in Jan. 1942; a book for young people.]

24882. SCHULZ, BRUNO: *Die Mannequins und andere Erzählungen*. Hrsg. von Jerzy Jarzebski. Aus dem Poln. von Josef Hahn. (Mit Zeichnungen des Autors.) Frankfurt am Main: Suhrkamp,

1987. 331 pp., illus., bibl. [B.Sch., born in Drohobycz, Galicia – 1942 shot by the SS, writer, graphic artist.]

24883. SEIDE, ADAM: *Rebecca oder Ein Haus für Jungfrauen jüdischen Glaubens besserer Stände in Frankfurt am Main*. Roman. Frankfurt am Main: Athenäum, 1987. 226 pp.

24884. SOMMER, ERNST: *Botschaft aus Granada*. Roman. Wien: Zsolnay, 1987. 422 pp. (Bücher der böhmischen Dörfer.) [First edn. Mährisch-Ostrau, 1938. On the persecution of the Jews in Spain , 1492.] [E.S., 1888 Iglau – 1955 England, lawyer in Karlsbad, writer, emigrated in 1938.]

24885. SPIES, GERTY: *Im Staub gefunden*. Gedichte; eine Auswahl. (Vorwort von Rachel Salamander.) München: Kaiser, 1987. 94 pp. (Kaiser-Traktate, N.F., 1.) [G.Sp., born 1897 in Munich, survivor of Theresienstadt, see No. 21187/YB XXX.]

24886. SPITZER, LEONIE: *Die familie Höchst*. Hrsg. von Helene Adolf. Bad Soden: Woywod, 1986. 124 pp., port. [Novel on an Austrian Jewish family at the time of the First World War. Incl. biogr. essay on the author.] [L.Sp., 1891 Vienna – 1940 Oxford, teacher in Vienna, writer, emigrated via Italy in 1939 to Oxford.]

24887. WEIGEL, HANS: *Man derf schon; Kaleidoskop jüdischer und anderer Witze*. Graz: Styria, 1987. 125 pp.

24888. WEIL, GRETE: *Tramhalte Beethovenstraat*. Roman. Neuausg. Frankfurt am Main: Fischer, 1986. 143 pp. (Fischer-Taschenbücher, 5301.) [Novel on life in exile, first publ. in 1963.] [G.W., data see No. 17703/YB XXVI.]

24889. WELT, ELLY: *Berliner Labyrinth*. Roman. Aus dem Amerikan. von Guy Montag. Zürich: Benziger, 1987. 441 p. [On a partly Jewish boy who survives the Nazi period in hiding while his Jewish family is killed. Transl. of No. 23865/YB XXXII.]

Index to Bibliography

List of Contributors

BEER, Udo, Dr. jur., b. 1954 in Altenholz (Germany). Taking bar examinations. Author of *Die Juden, das Recht und die Republik. Verbandswesen und Rechtsschutz 1919–1933* (1986); 'Juden in der Schleswig-Holsteinischen Armee', in *Zeitschrift der Gesellschaft für Schleswig-Holsteinische Geschichte*, 111 (1986); 'Das vermögensrechtliche Ende der kleineren jüdischen Gemeinden in Schleswig-Holstein während des Dritten Reiches', in *Zeitschrift der Gesellschaft für Schleswig-Holsteinische Geschichte*, 112 (1987); and of other essays.

CARLEBACH, Julius, D.Phil.(Sussex), b. 1922 in Hamburg. Reader in Sociology, University of Sussex. Author of i.a. *The Jews of Nairobi* (1962); *Caring for Children in Trouble* (1970); *Karl Marx and the Radical Critique of Judaism* (1978); 'Deutsche Juden und der Säkularisierungsprozess in der Erziehung. Kritische Bemerkungen zu einem Problemkreis der jüdischen Emanzipation', in *Das Judentum in der Deutschen Umwelt 1800–1850* (1977); 'Family Structure and the Position of Jewish Women', in *Revolution and Evolution. 1848 in German-Jewish History* (1981); 'Orthodox Jewry in Germany: The Final Stages', in *Die Juden im Nationalsozialistischen Deutschland/The Jews in Nazi Germany, 1933–1943* (1986). Member of the Executive Committee of the LBI, London. (Contributor to Year Books XVIII and XXIV.)

COHN, Werner, Ph.D., b. 1926 in Berlin. Professor emeritus of Sociology, University of British Columbia. Author of *The Gypsies* (1973); and scholarly articles on sociology.

FRIEDMAN, Maurice Stanley, Ph.D., b. 1921. Professor of Religious Studies, Philosophy and Comparative Literature, San Diego State University. Author of i.a. *Martin Buber: The Life of Dialogue* (1955); *Martin Buber's Life and Work*, 3 vols. (1981, 1983); and numerous books on psychology as well as innumerable articles. Editor and translator of Martin Buber, *Hasidism and Modern Man* (1973); co-editor, with Paul A. Schilpp, of *The Philosophy of Martin Buber*, vol. of *The Library of Living Philosophers* (1967); and translator of many works of Martin Buber.

FRIESEL, Evyatar, Ph.D., b. 1930 in Germany. Associate Professor, Department of Jewish History, The Hebrew University, Jerusalem. Author of *Zionist Policy after the Balfour Declaration* (1977, in Hebrew); and *Atlas of Modern Jewish History* (1983, in Hebrew). (Contributor to Year Book XXXI.)

FUKS, Lajb (Leo), Ph.D., b. 1908 in Kalisz (Poland). Formerly Librarian and Lecturer in Hebrew and Yiddish Language and Literature, University of Amsterdam. Author of several publications in the field of Old Yiddish literature and Hebrew bibliography.

FUKS-MANSFELD, Renate Gertrud, Ph.D., b. 1930 in Berlin. Lecturer in Jewish History and Yiddish Language and Literature, University of Amsterdam.

573

Author of various publications on the history of the Jews in the Netherlands and Hebrew bibliography.

GELBER, Mark H., Ph.D., b. 1951 in New York. Senior Lecturer, Department of Foreign Literatures and Linguistics, Ben-Gurion-University, Beersheva. Editor of *Stefan Zweig – heute* (1986); *Identity and Ethos. A Festschrift for Sol Liptzin on the Occasion of his 85th Birthday* (1986). Author of 'What is Literary Anti-Semitism?', in *Jewish Social Studies*, XLVII, No. 1 (1985); 'Pedagogical Guidelines for Literary Anti-Semitism', in *Patterns of Prejudice*, 20, No. 1 (1986); 'Das Judendeutsch in der deutschen Litcratur', in Stéphane Moses and Albrecht Schöne (eds.), *Juden in der deutschen Literatur* (1986); and of essays on Martin Buber, Stefan Zweig, Karl Emil Franzos, Thomas Mann, Nelly Sachs and Gustav Freytag. (Contributor to Year Book XXXI.)

HORWITZ, Rivka, Ph.D., b. 1926 in Bad Homburg (Germany). Professor of Jewish Thought, Ben-Gurion-University, Beersheva. Author of *Buber's Way to "I and Thou"* (1978). Editor of an Anthology of Rosenzweig (1987); and a collection of essays on Isaac Breuer (forthcoming 1988, in Hebrew).

LAMBERTI, Marjorie, Ph.D., b. 1937 in Connecticut. Professor of History, Middlebury College, Vermont. Author of *Jewish Activism in Imperial Germany. The Struggle for Civil Equality* (1978); *State, Society and the Elementary School in Imperial Germany* (forthcoming in 1989); 'The Attempt to Form a Jewish Bloc: Jewish Notables and Politics in Wilhelmian Germany', in *Central European History* (1970); 'State, Church and the Politics of School Reform during the Kulturkampf', in *Central European History* (1986). (Contributor to Year Books XVII, XXIII, XXV and XXVII.)

LIBERLES, Robert, Ph.D., b. 1944 in Lynn, Mass. Senior Lecturer and Chairman of Jewish History, Ben-Gurion-University, Beersheva. Author of *Religious Conflict in Social Context. The Resurgence of Orthodox Judaism in Frankfurt am Main* (1985); and of articles for *Modern Judaism* and *AJS Review*. Member of the Jerusalem Board of the LBI. (Contributor to Year Books XXVII and XXXI.)

MARGALIOT, Abraham, Ph.D., b. 1920 in Chemnitz, d. 1987 in Jerusalem. Formerly Lecturer, Institute of Contemporary Jewry, Hebrew University, Jerusalem. Author of *Die Reaktion der jüdischen Organisationen in Deutschland auf die nationalsozialistischen Anfeindungen* (1971, in Hebrew); 'Emigration – Planung und Wirklichkeit', in *Die Juden im Nationalsozialistischen Deutschland/The Jews in Nazi Germany. 1933–1943* (1986); and of various articles on German Jewry, Zionism and the Holocaust. Co-editor of *Documents on the Holocaust* (1981); Editor of *Deutsches Judentum unter dem NS-Regime* (forthcoming, in series Comprehensive History of the Holocaust, Yad Vashem, Jerusalem). Formerly Member of the Jerusalem Board of the LBI.

MATTHÄUS, Jürgen, M.A., b. 1959 in Dortmund. Currently working on Ph.D. on Australian history. Author of *Das Verhältnis zwischen dem "Centralverein deutscher Staatsbürger jüdischen Glaubens" (CV) und der "Zionistischen Vereinigung für Deutschland" (ZVfD) im Ersten Weltkrieg* (unpubl. diss., 1986).

Mosse, Werner E., Ph.D., Fellow of the Royal Historical Society, b. 1918 in Berlin. Professor emeritus, University of East Anglia, Norwich. Author of i.a. *Liberal Europe – The Age of Bourgeois Realism 1848–1875* (1974); *Jews in the German Economy. The German-Jewish Economic Elite 1820–1935* (1987); *The German-Jewish Economic Elite 1820–1935. A Social History* (forthcoming); 'German Jews: Citizens of the Republic', in *Die Juden im Nationalsozialistischen Deutschland/The Jews in Nazi Germany. 1933–1943* (1986). Editor (in collaboration with Arnold Paucker) of *Entscheidungsjahr 1932. Zur Judenfrage in der Endphase der Weimarer Republik* (1965, 1966); *Deutsches Judentum in Krieg und Revolution 1916–1923* (1971); *Juden im Wilhelminischen Deutschland 1890–1914* (1976); with Arnold Paucker and Reinhard Rürup of *Revolution and Evolution. 1848 in German-Jewish History* (1981). Chairman of the London Board of the LBI. (Contributor to Year Books IV, XV, XXIV and XXVIII.)

Nicosia, Francis R. J., Ph.D., b. 1944 in Philadelphia. Associate Professor of History, St. Michael's College, Vermont. Author of *The Third Reich and the Palestine Question* (1985); and of articles in scholarly journals and collections of essays on German Middle East policy during the inter-war period and on aspects of Zionism in Germany. Editor of *Records of the Central Zionist Archives*, in Sybil Milton and Henry Friedlander (eds.), *Documents on the Holocaust: An International Series* (1989). (Contributor to Year Books XXIV, XXXI and XXXII.)

Niederland, Doron, Ph.D., b. 1954 in Rehovot (Israel). Author of 'Deutsche Ärzte-Emigration und gesundheitspolitische Entwicklungen in "Erez-Israel" (1933–1948)', in *Medizinhistorisches Journal*, 20 (1985).

Reinharz, Jehuda, Ph.D., b. 1944 in Haifa. Richard Koret Professor of Modern Jewish History and Director, Tauber Institute for the Study of European Jewry, Brandeis University. Author of *Fatherland or Promised Land: The Dilemma of the German Jew, 1893–1914* (1975); *Chaim Weizmann. The Making of a Zionist Leader* (1985); and of numerous essays. Editor of Volume IX of *The Letters and Papers of Chaim Weizmann* (1977); editor of i.a. *Dokumente zur Geschichte des deutschen Zionismus 1882–1933* (1981); co-editor of (and contributor to) *Mystics, Philosophers and Politicians. Essays in Jewish Intellectual History in Honor of Alexander Altmann* (1982); co-editor of (and contributor to) *The Jewish Response to German Culture from the Enlightenment to the Second World War* (1985); editor of *Living with Antisemitism. Modern Jewish Responses* (1987). Fellow of the New York LBI. (Contributor to Year Books XXII, XXIV, XXX, XXXI and XXXII.)

Schatzker, Chaim, Ph.D., b. 1928 in Lwow. Professor of Jewish History (Strochlitz Professor of Holocaust Studies), Haifa University. Author of i.a. *Die jüdische Jugendbewegung in Deutschland* (1974); *Das Deutschlandbild in israelischen Geschichtslehrbüchern* (1979); *Die Juden in den deutschen Geschichtsbüchern* (1981); *Jüdische Jugend im zweiten Kaiserreich. Sozialisations- und Erziehungsprozesse der jüdischen Jugend in Deutschland, 1870–1917* (1988); and various essays on historical and educational topics concerning the Holocaust. Member of the Jerusalem Board of the LBI. (Contributor to Year Books XXIII and XXXII.)

SCHMELZER, Menahem, D.H.L., b. 1934 in Kecel (Hungary). Professor in Medieval Hebrew Literature and Jewish Bibliography, The Jewish Theological Seminary of America, New York. Editor of Aron Freiman, *Union Catalog of Hebrew Manuscripts and their Location* (1973); Alexander Marx, *Bibliographical Studies and Notes on Rare Books and Manuscripts in the Library of the Jewish Theological Seminary of America* (1977); Isaac ben Abraham ibn Ezra, *Poems* (1980); author of articles and reviews on medieval Hebrew poetry and Jewish bibliography.

SCHORSCH, Ismar, Ph.D., b. 1935 in Hannover. Chancellor and Professor of Jewish History, The Jewish Theological Seminary of America, New York. Author of *Jewish Reactions to German Anti-Semitism 1870–1914* (1972); 'Emancipation and the Crisis of Religious Activity', in *Revolution and Evolution. 1848 in German-Jewish History* (1981); 'German Judaism: From Confession to Culture', in *Die Juden im Nationalsozialistischen Deutschland/The Jews in Nazi Germany. 1933–1943* (1986). Editor of Heinrich Graetz, *The Structure of Jewish History and Other Essays* (1975). Fellow of the American Academy for Jewish Research. Member of the Executive Committee of the LBI, New York. (Contributor to Year Books XI, XIX, XXII, XXV, XXVIII and XXXI.)

SHAVIT, Zohar, Ph.D., b. 1951 in Petach-Tikva (Israel). Senior Lecturer in Poetics and Comparative Literature, Tel-Aviv University. Author of *The Literary Life in Eretz-Israel 1910–1933* (1982, in Hebrew); *Poetics of Children's Literature* (1986); and numerous articles on the history of Hebrew and children's literature.

TOURY, Jacob, Ph.D., b. 1945 in Beuthen. Professor emeritus of Jewish History, Tel-Aviv University. Author of i.a. *Die politischen Orientierungen der Juden in Deutschland. Von Jena bis Weimar* (1966); *Turmoil and Confusion in the Revolution of 1848* (1968, in Hebrew); 'Der Eintritt der Juden ins deutsche Bürgertum', and 'Die Revolution von 1848 als innerjüdischer Wendepunkt', in *Das Judentum in der Deutschen Umwelt 1800–1850* (1977); *Soziale und politische Geschichte der Juden in Deutschland* (1977); *Die Jüdische Presse im Österreichischen Kaiserreich 1802–1918* (1982); *Jüdische Textilunternehmer in Baden-Württemberg 1683–1938* (1984); and of numerous contributions to learned periodicals etc. in English, German and Hebrew. (Contributor to Year Books XI, XIII, XVI, XXII, XXVI and XXX.)

WISTRICH, Robert Solomon, Ph.D., b. 1945 in Lenger, U.S.S.R. Professor of Modern European and Jewish History, Hebrew University, Jerusalem. Author of *Revolutionary Jews from Marx to Trotsky* (1976); *The Left against Zion* (1979); *Socialism and the Jews: the Dialectic of Emancipation in Germany and Austria-Hungary* (1982); *Who's Who in Nazi Germany* (1982); *Hitler's Apocalypse* (1985); *The Jews of Vienna in the Age of Franz Joseph* (1988); and of numerous articles in historical and literary journals. Member of the Jerusalem Board of the LBI. (Contributor to Year Books XXI, XXII and XXVI.)

Abstracts of articles in this Year Book are included in *Historical Abstracts* and *America: History and Life*.

General Index to Year Book XXXIII
of the Leo Baeck Institute